Street by Street

C000097579

BIRMINGHAM
WOLVERHAMPTON
DUDLEY, SOLIHULL, STOURBRIDGE,
WALSALL, WEST BROMWICH
Aldridge, Brownhills, Codsall, Coleshill, Dorridge, Halesowen, Knowle, Pelsall, Sutton Coldfield, Wombourne

2nd edition November 2003
© Automobile Association Developments Limited 2003

Original edition printed May 2001

Ordnance Survey® This product includes map data licensed from Ordnance Survey ® with the permission of the Controller of Her Majesty's Stationery Office. © Crown copyright 2003. All rights reserved. Licence number 399221.

Published by AA Publishing (a trading name of Automobile Association Developments Limited, whose registered office is Millstream, Maidenhead Road, Windsor, Berkshire SL4 5GD. Registered number 1878835).

Mapping produced by the Cartography Department of The Automobile Association. (A01723)

A CIP Catalogue record for this book is available from the British Library.

Printed by GRAFIASA S.A., Porto, Portugal

The contents of this atlas are believed to be correct at the time of the latest revision. However, the publishers cannot be held responsible for loss occasioned to any person acting or refraining from action as a result of any material in this atlas, nor for any errors, omissions or changes in such material. This does not affect your statutory rights. The publishers would welcome information to correct any errors or omissions and to keep this atlas up to date. Please write to Publishing, The Automobile Association, Fanum House (FH17), Basing View, Basingstoke, Hampshire, RG21 4EA.

ML033z

Key to map pages	ii-iii
Key to map symbols	iv-1
Enlarged map pages	2-7
Main map pages	8-199
Index – towns & villages	200
Index – streets	201-243
Index – featured places	243-252
Acknowledgements	252

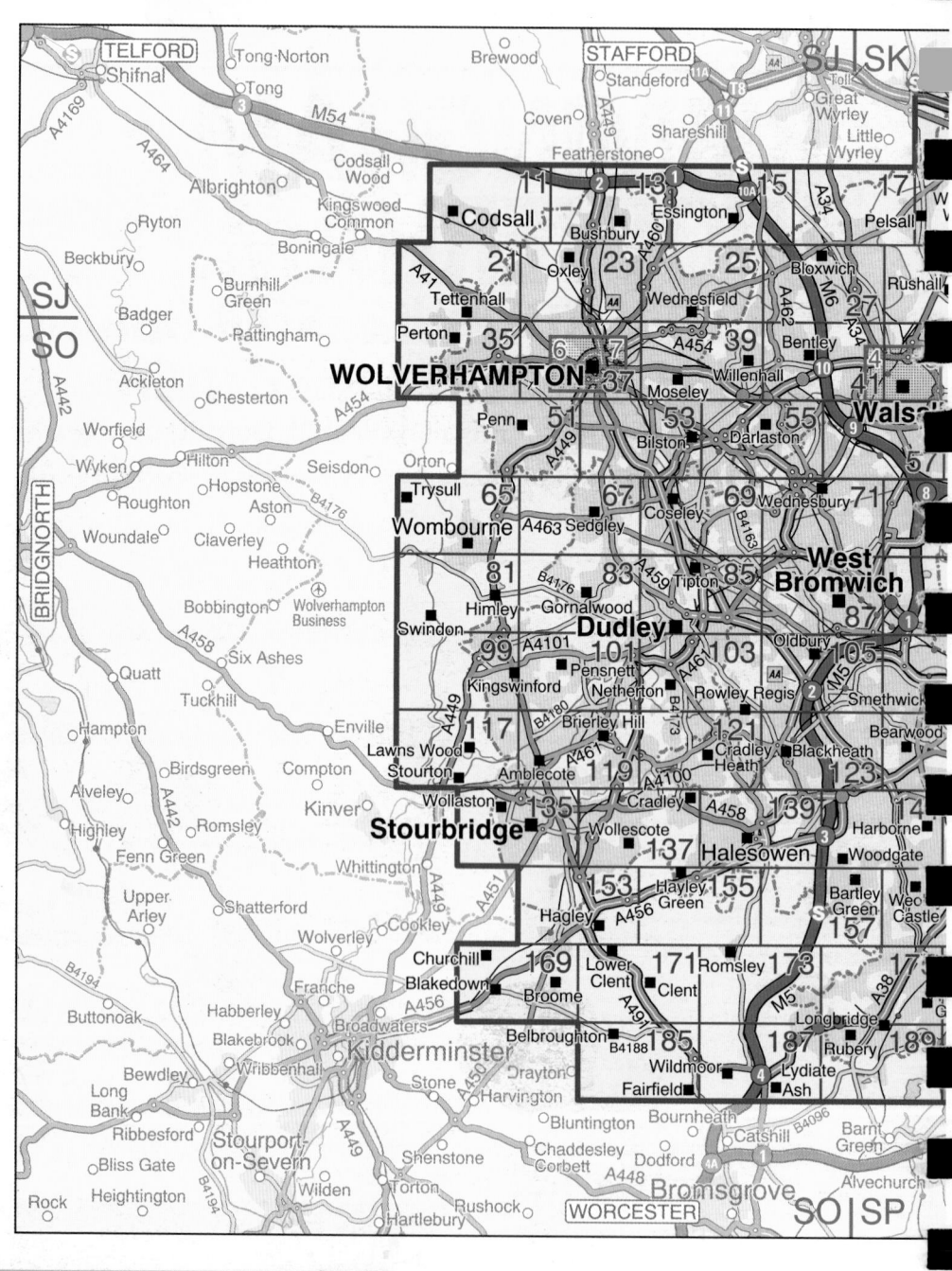

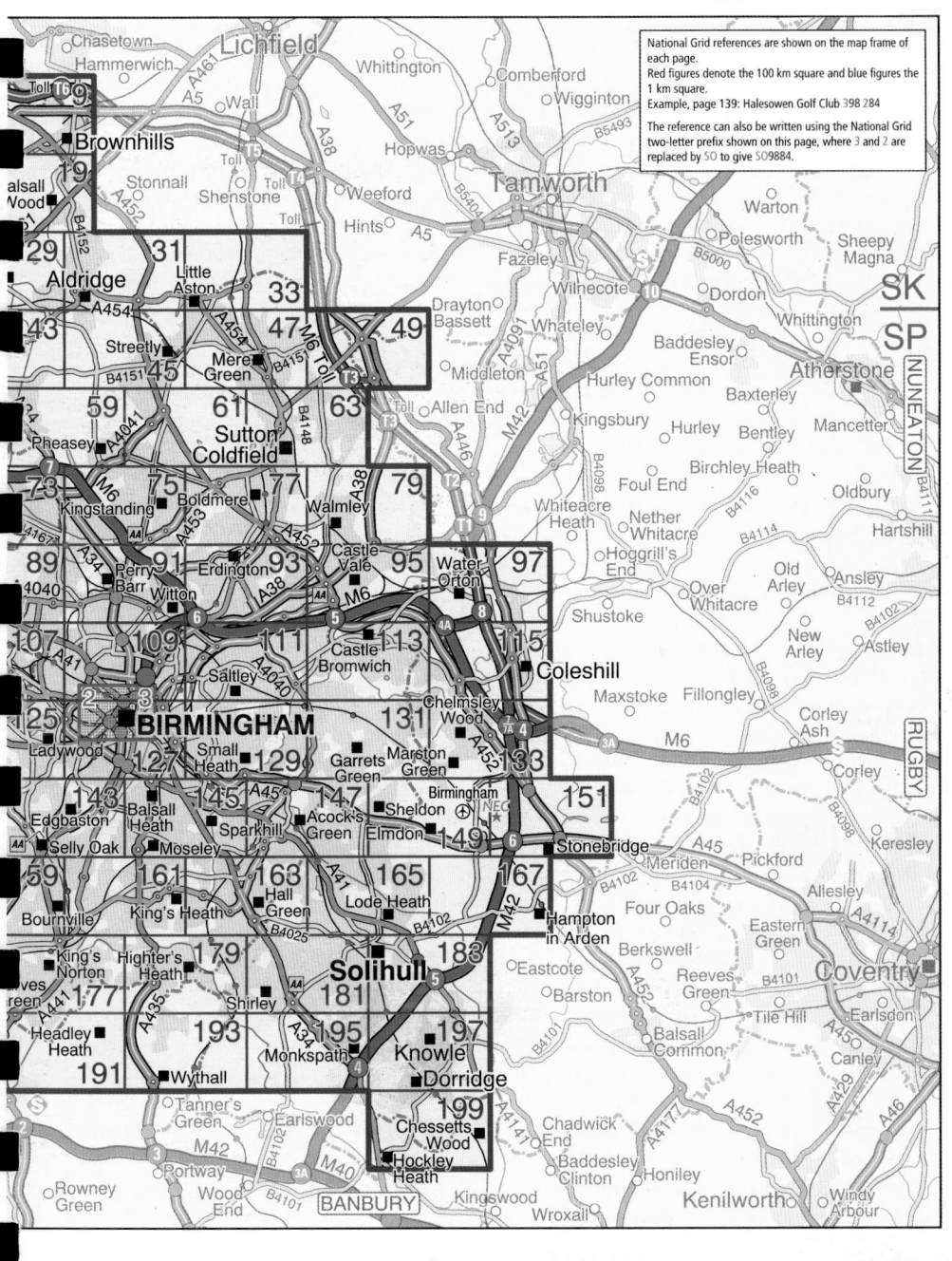

National Grid references are shown on the map frame of each page.
Red figures denote the 100 km square and blue figures the 1 km square.
Example, page 139: Halesowen Golf Club 398 284

The reference can also be written using the National Grid two-letter prefix shown on this page, where 3 and 2 are replaced by SO to give SO9884.

4.2 inches to I mile **Scale of main map pages** **1:15,000**

| 0 | 1/4 | miles | 1/2 | | 3/4 | | 1 |
| 0 | 1/4 | 1/2 | kilometres 3/4 | I | I 1/4 | I 1/2 |

	Motorway/Toll Motorway
Junction 9	Motorway junction
Services	Motorway service area
	Primary road single/dual carriageway
Services	Primary road service area
	A road single/dual carriageway
	B road single/dual carriageway
	Other road single/dual carriageway
	Minor/private road, access may be restricted
	One-way street
	Pedestrian area
	Track or footpath
	Road under construction
	Road tunnel
AA	AA Service Centre
P	Parking
P+	Park & Ride
	Bus/coach station
	Railway & main railway station
	Railway & minor railway station

	Underground station
	Light railway & station
	Preserved private railway
LC	Level crossing
	Tramway
	Ferry route
	Airport runway
	County, administrative boundary
	Mounds
17	Page continuation 1:15,000
3	Page continuation to enlarged scale 1:10,000
	River/canal, lake, pier
	Aqueduct, lock, weir
465 Winter Hill	Peak (with height in metres)
	Beach
	Woodland
	Park
	Cemetery
	Built-up area

Symbol	Description	Symbol	Description
	Featured building		Abbey, cathedral or priory
JUUUUUL	City wall		Castle
A&E	Hospital with 24-hour A&E department		Historic house or building
PO	Post Office	Wakehurst Place NT	National Trust property
	Public library	M	Museum or art gallery
i	Tourist Information Centre		Roman antiquity
i	Seasonal Tourist Information Centre		Ancient site, battlefield or monument
	Petrol station, 24-hour Major suppliers only		Industrial interest
†	Church/chapel		Garden
	Public toilets		Garden Centre Garden Centre Association Member
	Toilet with disabled facilities		Garden Centre Wyevale Garden Centre
PH	Public house AA recommended		Farm or animal centre
	Restaurant AA inspected		Zoological or wildlife collection
Madeira Hotel	Hotel AA inspected		Bird collection
	Theatre or performing arts centre		Nature reserve
	Cinema		Aquarium
	Golf course	V	Visitor or heritage centre
▲	Camping AA inspected		Country park
	Caravan site AA inspected		Cave
	Camping & caravan site AA inspected		Windmill
	Theme park		Distillery, brewery or vineyard

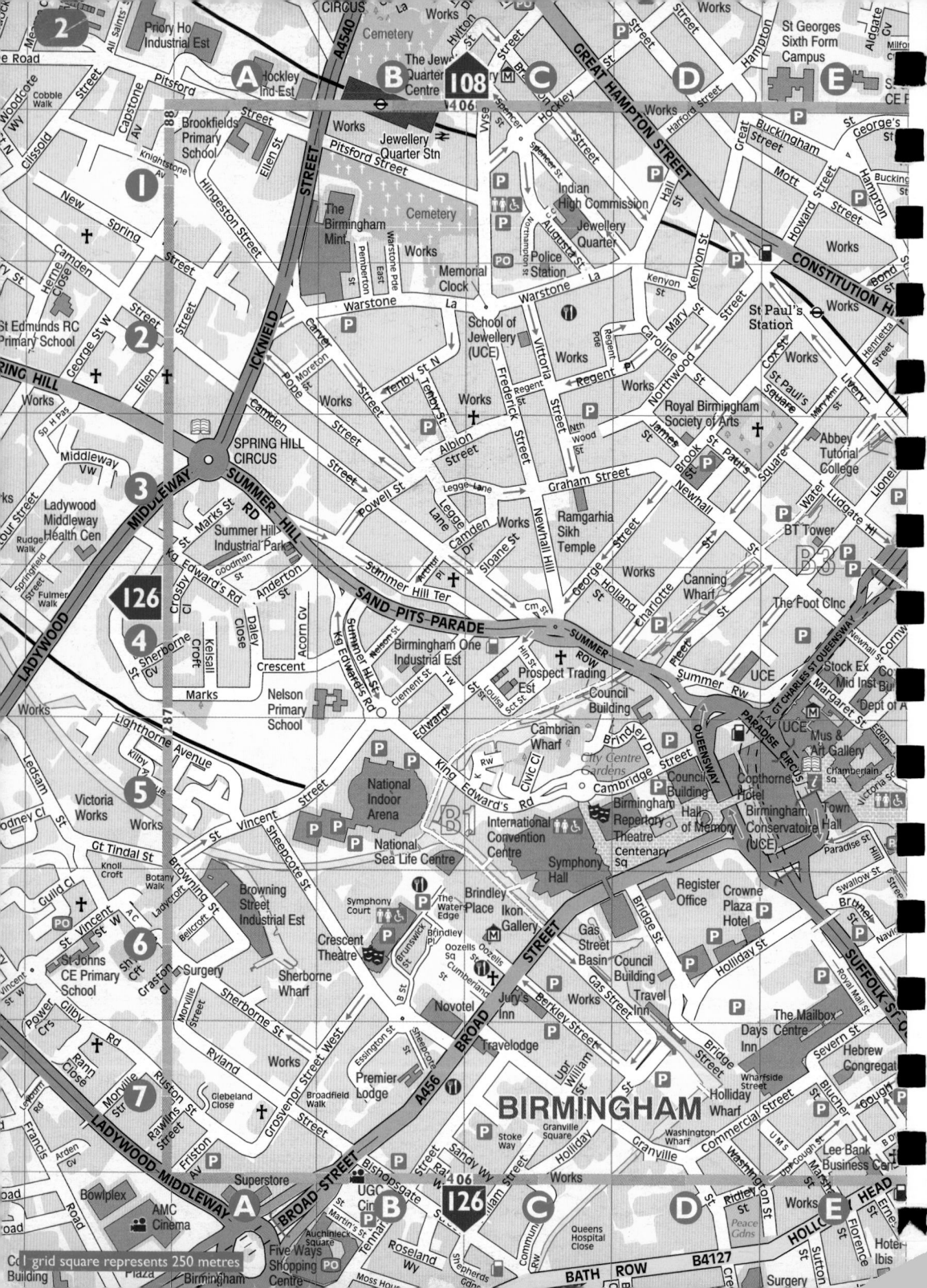

2
Priory Ho Industrial Est
CIRCUS
Cemetery
Works
Hylton St
108
St Georges Sixth Form Campus
Aldgate Gv
A
B
C
D
E
Hockley Ind Est
The Jewellery Quarter Centre
GREAT HAMPTON STREET
Hampton St
A4540
A406
Cobble Walk
Woodcote Wy
Street
Capstone Av
Pitsford
Brookfields Primary School
Street
Ellen St
Works
Jewellery Quarter Stn
Pitsford Street
Vyse St
Spencer St
Hockley St
Harford Street
Great Hampton Row
Buckingham Street
George's St
Mott Street
Howard Street
Hampton St
Clissold
Knightstone Av
Hingeston Street
New Spring Street
The Birmingham Mint
Cemetery
Pemberton St
Warstone Pde East
Works
Indian High Commission
Jewellery Quarter
Augusta St
Northampton St
Police Station
Memorial Clock
Hall St
Kenyon St
CONSTITUTION HILL
Bond St
Works
Camden Street
Herne Close
St Edmunds RC Primary School
George St W
Warstone La
School of Jewellery (UCE)
Vittoria Street
Frederick Street
Regent Pde
Regent Pl
Caroline St
Mary St
Northwood St
St Paul's Station
Cox St
Works
Henrietta Street
SPRING HILL
Ellen St
ICKNIELD STREET
Carver Street
Pope Street
Moreton St
Tenby St N
Tenby St
Works
Regent St
Works
Royal Birmingham Society of Arts
St Paul's Square
Mary Ann St
Livery St
Sp H Pas
Middleway Vw
Camden Street
Works
Albion Street
Nth Wood St
James St
Brook St
St Paul's Square
Abbey Tutorial College
SPRING HILL CIRCUS
Powell St
Legge Lane
Graham Street
Ladywood Middleway Health Cen
MIDDLEWAY
SUMMER HILL RD
Marks St
Summer Hill Industrial Park
Legge Lane
Camden Dr
Works
Sloane St
Newhall Hill
Ramgarhia Sikh Temple
George Street
Newhall St
Water St
Ludgate Hill
BT Tower
B3
Rudge Walk
Springfield Street
Fulmer Walk
Kg Edward's Rd
Goodman St
Anderton St
Summer Hill Ter
Arthur Pl
Holland St
Charlotte St
Canning Wharf
The Foot Clnc
126
LADYWOOD
Crosby Cl
4
Sherborne Gv
Croft
Kelsall
Daley Close
Acorn Gv
SAND PITS PARADE
Cm St
SUMMER ROW
Birmingham One Industrial Est
Hln St
Prospect Trading Est
Fleet St
Summer Rw
UCE
Stock Ex
Mid Inst
Margaret St
Dept of A
Crescent
Marks
Nelson Primary School
Summer Hill St
Kg Edward's Rd
Nelson St
Clement St
Edward St
Loulsa St
Council Building
Works
Lighthorne Avenue
Kilby Av
National Indoor Arena
King Edward's Rd
Cambrian Wharf
Brindley Dr
Civic Cl
City Centre Gardens
Cambridge Street
QUEENSWAY
PARADISE CIRCUS
GT CHARLES ST QUEENSWAY
Mus & Art Gallery
Chamberlain Sq
Council Building
Copthorne Hotel
Ledsam St
5
Victoria Works
Works
Vincent Street
Street
B1
International Convention Centre
Birmingham Repertory Theatre
Hall of Memory
Birmingham Conservatoire (UCE)
Town Hall
Victoria Sq
Rodney Cl
Gt Tindal St
Knoll Croft
Botany Walk
Browning St
Sheepcote St
National Sea Life Centre
Symphony Hall
Centenary Sq
Paradise St
Hill St
Swallow St
Guild Cl
Ladycroft
Browning Street Industrial Est
Symphony Court
The Waters Edge
Brindley Place
Ikon Gallery
Register Office
Crowne Plaza Hotel
Bruneil St
St Vincent St W
Bellcroft
Crescent Theatre
Brunswick St
Brindley Pl
Oozells Sq
Oozells St
Gas Street Basin
Council Building
Bridge St
Holliday St
SUFFOLK ST QUEENSWAY
6
St Johns CE Primary School
Shy Cft
Graston Cl
Surgery
Sherborne Wharf
Cumberland St
Jury's Inn
Gas Street
Works
Travel Inn
Royal Mail St
Power Crs
Gilby Rd
Morville Street
Sherborne St
Ryland
Novotel
BROAD STREET
Berkley Street
The Mailbox Centre
Days Inn
Severn St
Hebrew Congregat
Rann Close
Works
Grosvenor Street West
Essington St
Sheepcote St
Travelodge
Upr William St
Bridge Street
7
Morville Str
Ruston St
Rawlins Street
Glebeland Close
Broadfield Walk
Premier Lodge
A456
BIRMINGHAM
Holliday Wharf
Wharfside Street
Commercial Street
Blucher St
Gough St
LADYWOOD MIDDLEWAY
Francis Rd
Arden Gv
Friston Av
Street
Stoke Way
Granville Square
Holliday St
Granville
Washington Wharf
Washington St
Upr Gough St
Lee Bank Business Cen
Superstore
BROAD STREET
Bishopsgate
Sandy Wy
Works
Ridley St
Bowlplex
AMC Cinema
UGC Cin
126
A406
Peace Gdns
Works
HOLLOWAY HEAD
Florence St
Auchinleck Square
Martin's St
Tennant St
Roseland Wy
Queens Hospital Close
Commercial St
Five Ways Shopping Centre
BATH ROW
B4127
Sutton St
Surgery
Hotel Ibis
Each grid square represents 250 metres
Birmingham
Moss House
Shepherds Gdns

Works
St Chads Industrial Estate
Brearley Close
New Town Row
Manchester Street
Blews St
Aston Expressway Industrial
Street
109
Lower Tower St
Works
Ward St
Brewery St
Grand Union Canal Wk
F
G
H
J
K
Premier Trading Est
Dartmouth Middleway
Great Lister Street
Bullock St
Kellett Rd
Kellett Road
Rupert St
New Summer St
Hospital St
Summer Lane
Cecil Street
Bagot
Staniforth Street
Moland St
Legge
Corporation Street
Aston Rd
Enterprise Wy
Love La
Aston Science Park
Oxygen St
Holt
Venture Way
Adams St
Windsor St
Heneage Street
Parkway Industrial Centre
William St
Hanley Street
Cliveland Street
Henrietta St
Lower Loveday St
Princip Street
Lancaster St
Works
Aston University (Institute of Art & Design)
Lister Street
Lawson St
Council Building
Grand Union Canal Walk
Price St
Vesey St
Loveday
Bath St
Gdwy Ct
Shadwell St
Salvation Army
W B La
Lench St
Aston University
Woodcock St
Heneage St West
Aston Science Park
Ashted Circus
Windsor St
Gt Brook St
Moorcroft Place
Heneage Place
Overton Place
Old Snow Hl
St Chads Queensway
Lancaster Circus Queensway
Fire Stn
Aston Street
Woodcock Sports Centre
Woodcock St
Jennens Road
Lawley Middleway
Forster St
South
St Chad's RC Cath
St Mary's Rw
Dental Hospital
Diana Princess of Wales Hospital (for Children)
St Chad's Circus Queensway
Whittall St
James Watt Queensway
B4
Ab Rw
Belmont Rw
Howe St
Cardigan Street
JFK Mem
Snow Hill Queensway
Weaman St
Printing Ho
Steelhouse Lane
Police Stn
Police Headquarters
Magistrates Court (Victoria Law Courts)
Corporation St
Central Hall
Coleshill Street
B4114
Snow Hill Station
Colmore Circ
Newton St
Birmingham Crown Court
Stafford St
Prince's St
Nova Scotia St
Gopsal St
Penn St
Curzon Circus
BCC
Church Street
Queensway
Chapel St
Jennens Road
Millennium Point
127
St Hotel Du Vin
Colmore Rw
CAB
Old Sq
Dalton Street
Queen Elizabeth Law Courts
Fox Street
Grosvenor Street
IMAX Cinema
Thinktank Museum
Curzon
Great Western Arcade
The Minories
The Priory
Dale End
Queensway
Edmund St
Barwick St
Row
St Philips Pl
Priory Courts
Priory Walk
Queensway Trading Estate
Bartholomew Rw
Albert Street
Colmore
T R W
St Philips Cathedral
Temple Row
North Western Arcade
Dalton Way
Bull St
Open Market
Bartholomew St
Banbury St
Council Building
Cherry St
Corporation St
Martineau Square
Priory Sq
Dl End
Albert St
Moor St Queensway
Park Street
Fazeley St
Andover St
Works
Waterloo St
City Plaza Shopping Centre
Ticket Shop
Cannon St
Temple Pas
Temple St
Fore St
Warwick Pas
Union Street
Carrs La
Freeman Street
New Bartholomew St
New Canal Street
Benacre Dr
Fazeley
Fazeley Industrial Estate
B2
New St
Ethel St
Piccadilly Ar
Lwr
Hotel
Council Building
High Street
Pavilions Shopping Centre
Wks
Bordesley
Stephenson
New St
Odeon Cinema
A4400
Moor Street Station
Shaw's Pas
Street
Council Building
Pickford Street
Barn St
Works
Halcyon Gallery
Pallasades Shopping Centre
New St Stn (lower level)
Rotunda
Bullring Shopping Centre
A41
Park St
Allison St
Cov St
Meriden Street
Trent St
Ltl Ann St
Works
Liverpool
Lane
Queens Dr
Bus Stn
The Mayfair Centre
Well La
Orwell Pas
Coventry St
Rea Ter
Street
Works
Alexandra Theatre
Station St
Cinema
Old Rep Thtr
Dudley
Edgbaston Street
PR St
Digbeth
Moat Lane
Digbeth
Police Stn
Allcock Street
Bromley St
Hack St
Heath Mill
Chinese Quarter
Pershore St
Indoor Mkt
Gloster St
St Martins Mkt
Open Mkt
Upper Dean Street
Council Building
Oxford
Trading Estate
Works
Milk St
Floodgate
Works
Gibb St
Lower Trinity St
Posthouse Hotel
Smallbrook Queensway
Hurst St
A441
Bradford St
Mill La
Digbeth Coach Station
High St Deritend
B4100
Adderley
Holloway Circus Queensway
Ladywell Wk
Hotel Ibis
Arcadian Shopping Centre
Planet Ice Arena
Wholesale Markets
Dean St
Works
Bull Ring Trading Estate
High St Bordesley
Hippodrome Theatre
Thorp St
Inge St
UGC Cinema
Windmill St
Bow St
Essex Street
Street
Claybrook St
Pershore Street
Works
Bradford
Green St
Birchall Street
Rea St
Works
Warwick St
Works

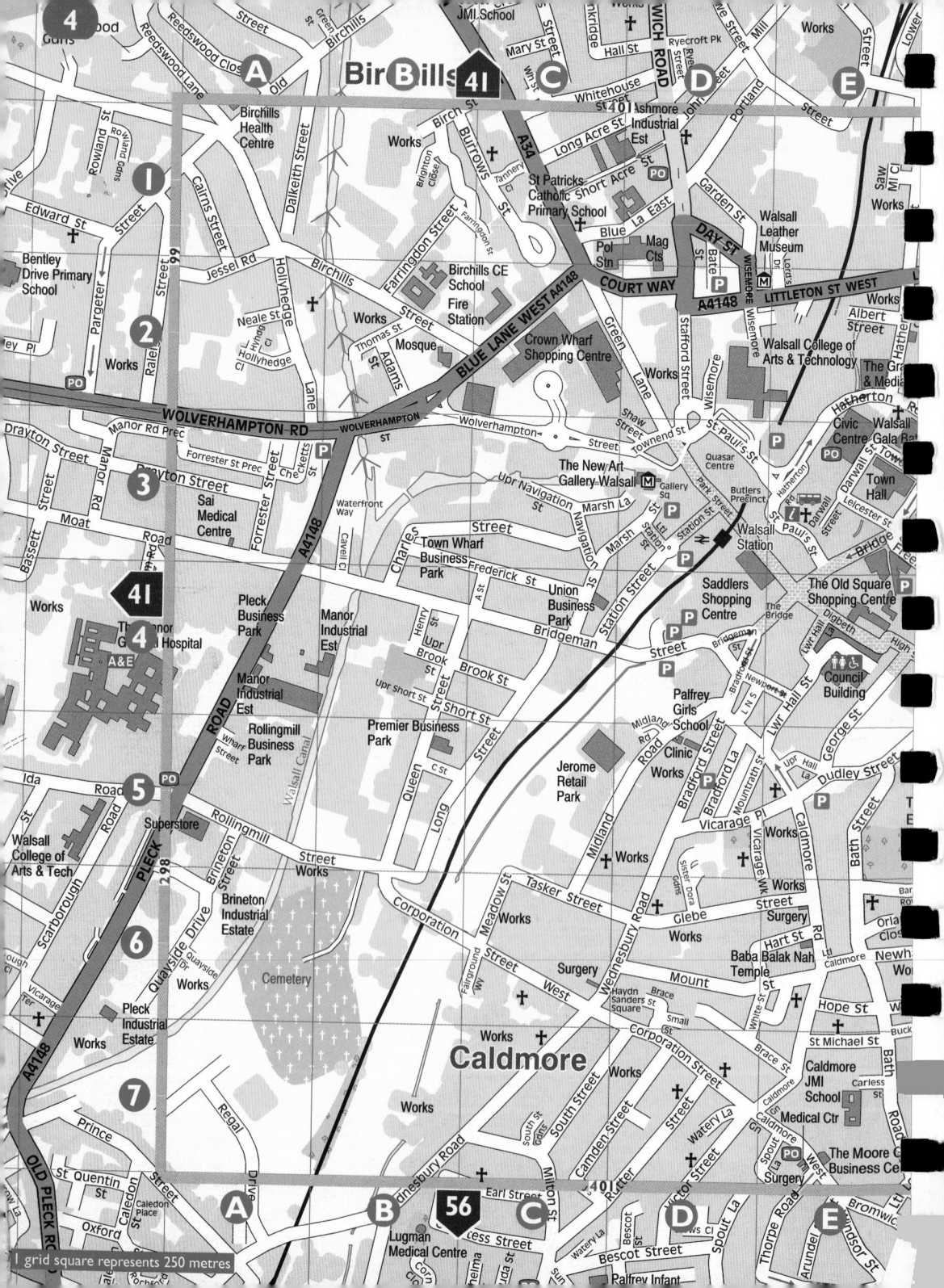
4
Birchills
41
Birchills Health Centre
Bentley Drive Primary School
St Patricks Catholic Primary School
Birchills CE School
Fire Station
Mosque
Crown Wharf Shopping Centre
Pol Stn
Mag Cts
Walsall Leather Museum
Walsall College of Arts & Technology
Civic Centre
Town Hall
Quasar Centre
The New Art Gallery Walsall
Butlers Precinct
Walsall Station
Saddlers Shopping Centre
The Old Square Shopping Centre
Council Building
Town Wharf Business Park
Union Business Park
Sai Medical Centre
The Manor General Hospital
A&E
Pleck Business Park
Manor Industrial Est
Rollingmill Business Park
Premier Business Park
Palfrey Girls School
Clinic
Jerome Retail Park
Superstore
Walsall College of Arts & Tech
Brineton Industrial Estate
Cemetery
Pleck Industrial Estate
Caldmore
Baba Balak Nah Temple
Caldmore JMI School
Medical Ctr
Surgery
The Moore Business Ce
Lugman Medical Centre
Palfrey Infant
WOLVERHAMPTON RD
BLUE LANE WEST A4148
COURT WAY
LITTLETON ST WEST
A4148
A34
PLECK ROAD
OLD PLECK ROAD
Walsall Canal
56
1 grid square represents 250 metres

A454
MELLISH
Moss Close
Buchanan Cl
Victoria Ms
Victoria Ter
Works
Community Centre
Cecil St
William St
Butts
Butts JMI School
Road
The Butts
Butts St
A461
LICHFIELD STREET
F
G
H
J
K
42
02
Rushwood Cl
View
Road
WS4
Cameron
Surgery
Buchanan Road
Argyle
Argyle Cl
Road
Fernleigh Road
A454
1
2
3
4
5
6
7
99
98
Teddesley Street
The Cloisters
Warwick St
Forster St
Upper
Queen Marys High School
LITTLETON ST E
Lower Forster St
Surgery
Arboretum Road
Arboretum
Hydesville Tower School
Chamber of Commerce
Ward Street
Walhouse Rd
Street
Surgery
Superstore
Persehouse Street
Rushall Street
Dog Kennel La
Walhouse Cl
Walhouse Road
Rowley Street
Charlotte Street
Sovereign Walk
Calder Avenue
BROADWAY
NORTH
Lichfield
Whittimere St
Intown Row
Works
Walsall Mus
Intown
CAB
County Court
Eyland Gv
Lower
Holtshill Lane
Balls Hl
Paddock Lane
Tantarra St
Works
Lincoln Road
The Limes
Crabtree Rd
Nutmeg Gv
Prince's Avenue
Street
Works
Warewell Cl
Warewell St
Wedge St
Balls St
Union Street
Chuckery Primary School
Old Masters Cl
The Chuckery
Tong Street
Goodall Street
Upper Rushall St
Ablewell St
Paddock La
The Ditch
Tantarra St
Bott
Bank St
Lane
Works
Lime Street
Selborne St
Chuckery
Road
Beacon
Willows
Lincoln Rd
A4148
The Grange Playhouse
Peal St
Church Hl
Church St
Bullock's Row
Hill St
Pool Street
Box St
Eldon St
Works
Walsingham Street
Moncrieffe Street
Florence Street
Lumley Road
Road
St Matthew's Cl
New St
Blue Coat CE Comprehensive School
Birmingham St
Surgery
Springhill Road
Blue Coat CE Junior School
Richmond St
Burleigh St
Works
Kinnerley Street
Council Building
Street
Grove Ter
Hatch Pl
Langford Close
Bernard St
Dove Close
The Crescent
Beaconsfield Court
PO
The Crescent
Dandy's Walk
Blue Coat CE Infant School
Works
Sutton Road
Prince's Av
Orwell Road
Boscobel Road
Lysways Street
Emery St
Birmingham Road
Mayfield Preparatory School
Beech Court
B4151
The Pines
Emery Close
Jesson Road
Queen Marys Grammar School
Sutton Road
Broadway N
Sandwell Street
Drayman Cl
Sandy Mt Road
Mandeville Gdns
St Marys the Mount RC School
Sycamore House Medical Centre
Gloucester
Doveridge Place
Works
Highgate
Belvidere Road
Highgate Av
Birmingham Road
Parklands Gardens
Beacon Dr
Gillity Cl
Edinburgh Road
WALSALL
WS1
Sandwell Walk
Road
Fairfield Mt
Jesson Road
Spring Ct
Jesson Cl
BROADWAY NORTH
Gillity Ave
Road
Little Gorway
57
Follyhouse Lane
Avion Close
Highgate Cl
Gorway Gdns
Gorway
A4148
Sikh Temple
Sandwell St
Elizabeth Rd

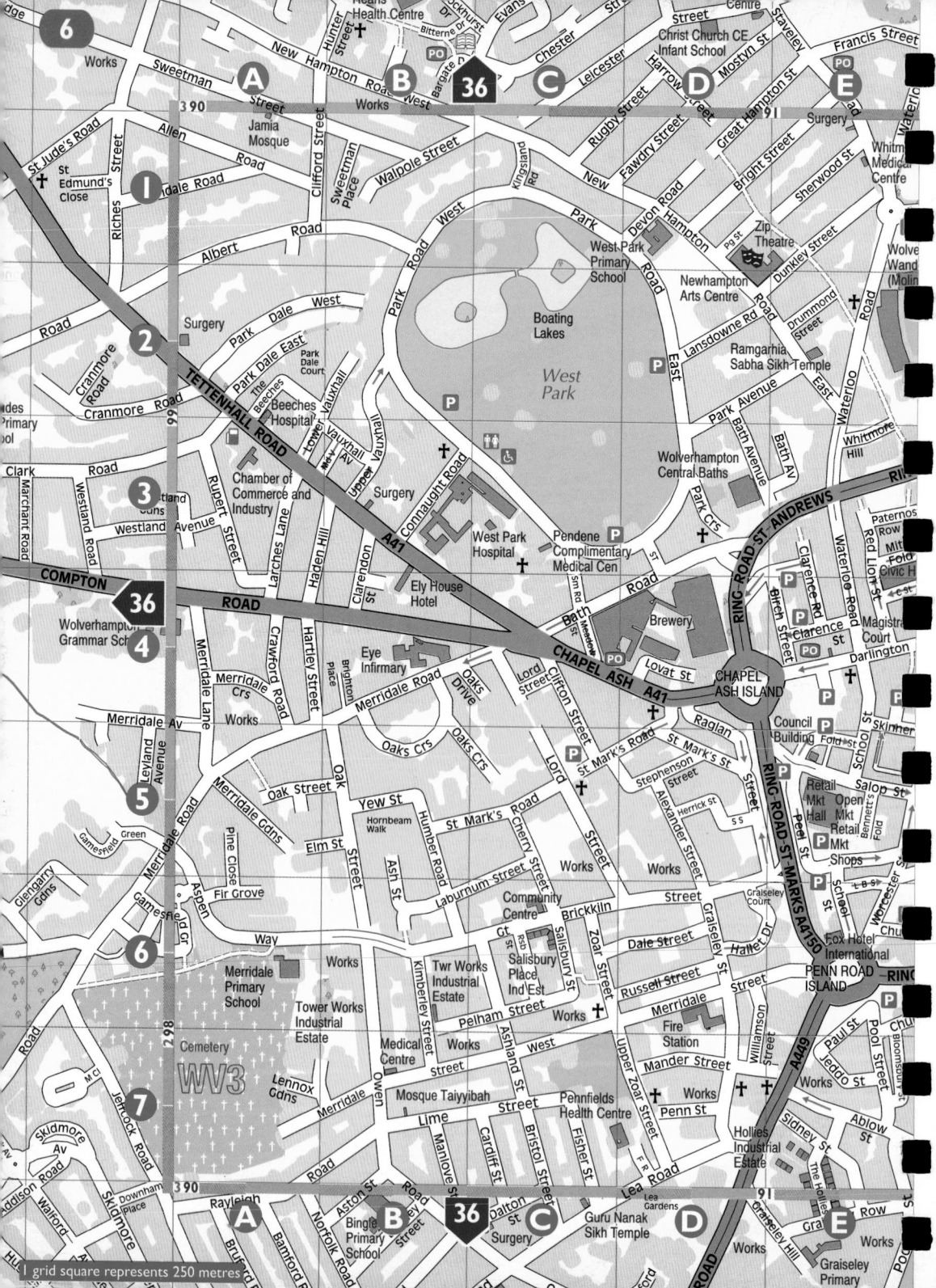
6
Works
Sweetman
Street
New Hampton Road West
Health Centre
Hunter Street
Bitterne Dr
Bargate Dr
Evans
PO
36
Chester
Leicester
Christ Church CE Infant School
Street
Mostyn St
Staveley
Francis Street
Harrow Street
Rugby Street
Fawdry Street
Great Hampton St
Surgery
Bright Street
Sherwood St
Whitmore Medical Centre
A
B
C
D
E
390
91
Jamia Mosque
Allen Road
St Jude's Road
St Edmund's Close
Riches Street
Clifford Street
Sweetman Place
Walpole Street
Kingsland Rd
New Hampton Road
Devon Road
Pg St
Zip Theatre
Dunkley Street
1
Albert Road
West Park Road
Park Road West
West Park Primary School
Boating Lakes
Newhampton Arts Centre
Park Road East
Lansdowne Rd
Drummond Street
Ramgarhia Sabha Sikh Temple
Waterloo Road
West Park
P
2
Surgery
Park Dale West
Park Dale East
Park Dale Court
Cranmore Road
The Beeches
Beeches Hospital
Lower Vauxhall
Vauxhall Av
Upper Vauxhall
TETTENHALL ROAD
Primary
Clark Road
Park Avenue
Bath Avenue
Bath Av
Whitmore Hill
Wolverhampton Central Baths
3
Westland Gdns
Westland Road
Marchant Road
Westland Avenue
Rupert Street
Chamber of Commerce and Industry
Larches Lane
Haden Hill
Surgery
Connaught Road
West Park Hospital
Pendene Complimentary Medical Cen
Park Crs
RING ROAD ST ANDREWS
Paternos
Red Lion St
Clarence Rd
Birch Street
COMPTON ROAD
36
Clarendon St
A41
Ely House Hotel
Bath Road
Sm Rd
Meadow St
Brewery
Clarence St
Magistrates Court
Darlington
Wolverhampton Grammar School
4
Merridale Lane
Crawford Road
Hartley Street
Brighton Place
Eye Infirmary
Oaks Drive
Lord Street
Clifton Street
CHAPEL ASH A41
Lovat St
CHAPEL ASH ISLAND
Merridale Crs
Works
Merridale Road
Merridale Av
Leyland Avenue
Raglan
Council Building
Fold St
Skinner
School St
Oaks Crs
Oak Street
Oak
Lord Street
St Mark's Road
St Mark's St
Stephenson Street
Alexander Street
Herrick St
Street
RING ROAD ST MARKS A4150
Retail Mkt Hall
Open Mkt
Retail Mkt Shops
Bennett's Fold
Salop St
Peel St
5
Merridale Gdns
Yew St
Hornbeam Walk
Humber Road
St Mark's Road
Cherry Street
Gamesfield Green
Pine Close
Elm St
Ash St
Laburnum Street
Works
Works
Worcester St
School St
Glengarry Gdns
Merridale Road
Fir Grove
Aspen Way
Gamesfield Gr
Community Centre
Brickkiln Street
Graiseley Court
Graiseley St
6
Gt Rsb St
Salisbury St
Zoar Street
Dale Street
Hallet Dr
Fox Hotel International
Merridale Primary School
Works
Kimberley Street
Twr Works Industrial Estate
Salisbury Place Ind Est
Russell Street
PENN ROAD ISLAND
RING
Tower Works Industrial Estate
Pelham Street
Works
Merridale Street
Fire Station
Williamson Street
A449
Paul St
Pool Street
Bloomsbury St
298
Cemetery
WV3
Road
Medical Centre
Works
Ashland St
West
Mander Street
Works
Jeddo St
M Cl
Street
Lennox Gdns
7
Jeffcock Road
Merridale
Mosque Taiyyibah
Lime Street
Penn St
Pennfields Health Centre
Upper Zoar Street
Ablow St
Sidney St
Skidmore Av
Owen Road
Manlove St
Cardiff St
Bristol Street
Fisher St
F R
Hollies Industrial Estate
The Hollies
Addison Road
Downham Place
Walford
Skidmore
Lea Road
Rayleigh
Aston St
Bingley Street
36
Dalton St
Lea Gardens
Graiseley Hill
Graiseley Row
Bingley Primary School
Surgery
Guru Nanak Sikh Temple
Works
Works
Graiseley Primary
Bamford
Norfolk Road
Bruford
ROAD
1 grid square represents 250 metres

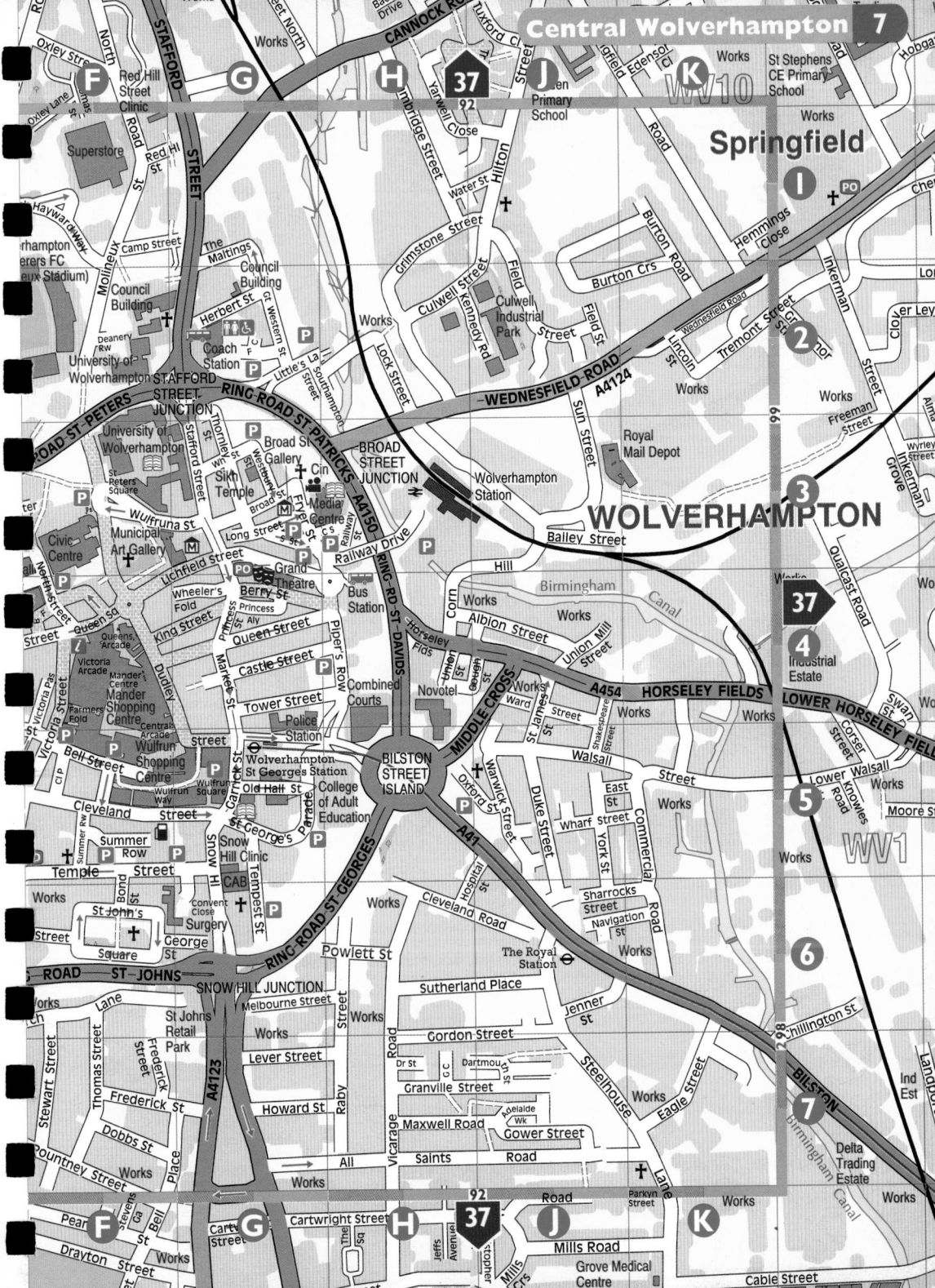
Springfield
WOLVERHAMPTON
WV10
WV1
Cannock Road
Stafford Street
Ring Road St Peters
Ring Road St Patricks
Ring Rd St Davids
Ring Road St Georges
Ring Road St Johns
Wednesfield Road
A4124
A4150
A454
Horseley Fields
Lower Horseley Fields
Middle Cross
A41
A4123
Bilston
Stafford Street Junction
Broad Street Junction
Bilston Street Island
Snow Hill Junction
Wolverhampton Station
Wolverhampton St Georges Station
The Royal Station
Bus Station
Coach Station
University of Wolverhampton
Civic Centre
Municipal Art Gallery
Grand Theatre
Mander Shopping Centre
Wulfrun Shopping Centre
Victoria Arcade
Queens Arcade
Central Arcade
Farmers Fold
Combined Courts
Police Station
College of Adult Education
Novotel
Snow Hill Clinic
Surgery
Red Hill Street Clinic
Superstore
Council Building
Sikh Temple
Gallery
Cin
Media Centre
Culwell Industrial Park
Royal Mail Depot
Primary School
St Stephens CE Primary School
Industrial Estate
Ind Est
Delta Trading Estate
St Johns Retail Park
Grove Medical Centre
Birmingham Canal
Works
37
92
99
298
F
G
H
J
K
1
2
3
4
5
6
7

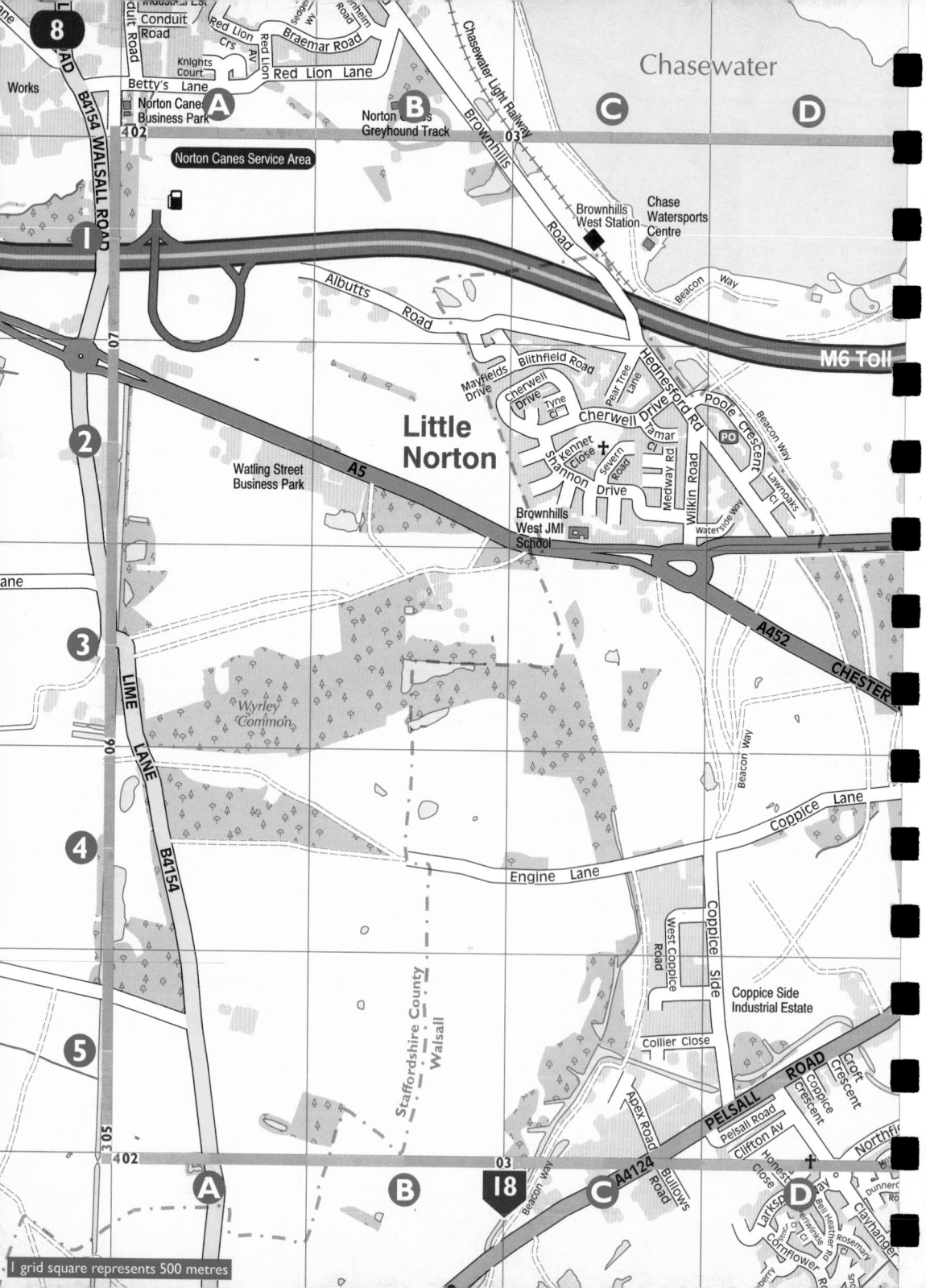

8

B4154 WALSALL ROAD

Works

Conduit Road

Industrial Est

Knights Court

Betty's Lane

Norton Canes Business Park

Sedge Way

Red Lion Crs

Red Lion Av

Braemar Road

Red Lion Lane

Norton Canes Greyhound Track

Chasewater Light Railway

Brownhills Road

Chasewater

A · **B** · **C** · **D**

402

I

Norton Canes Service Area

Brownhills West Station

Chase Watersports Centre

Beacon Way

M6 Toll

Albutts Road

Mayfields Drive

Blithfield Road

Cherwell Drive

Pear Tree Lane

Hednesford Rd

Poole Crescent

Beacon Way

PO

2

L07

A5

Watling Street Business Park

Little Norton

Tyne Cl

Cherwell

Tamar Cl

Kennet Close

Shannon

Severn Road

Medway Rd

Wilkin Road

Lawnoaks Cl

Waterside Way

Drive

Brownhills West JMI School

A452 CHESTER

3

90

Wyrley Common

4

LIME LANE

B4154

Engine Lane

Coppice Lane

Beacon Way

Coppice Side

West Coppice Road

Coppice Side Industrial Estate

5

505

Staffordshire County Walsall

Collier Close

Apex Road

PELSALL ROAD

Pelsall Road

Clifton Av

Croft Crescent

Coppice Crescent

Northfi

402

A · **B** · **18** · **C** A4124 · **D**

Beacon Way

Bullows Road

Honeysuckle Close

Larkspur

Bell Heather Cl

Twinnie Cl

Rosemary

Cornflower Rd

Clayhanger

Dunnerd

03

1 grid square represents 500 metres

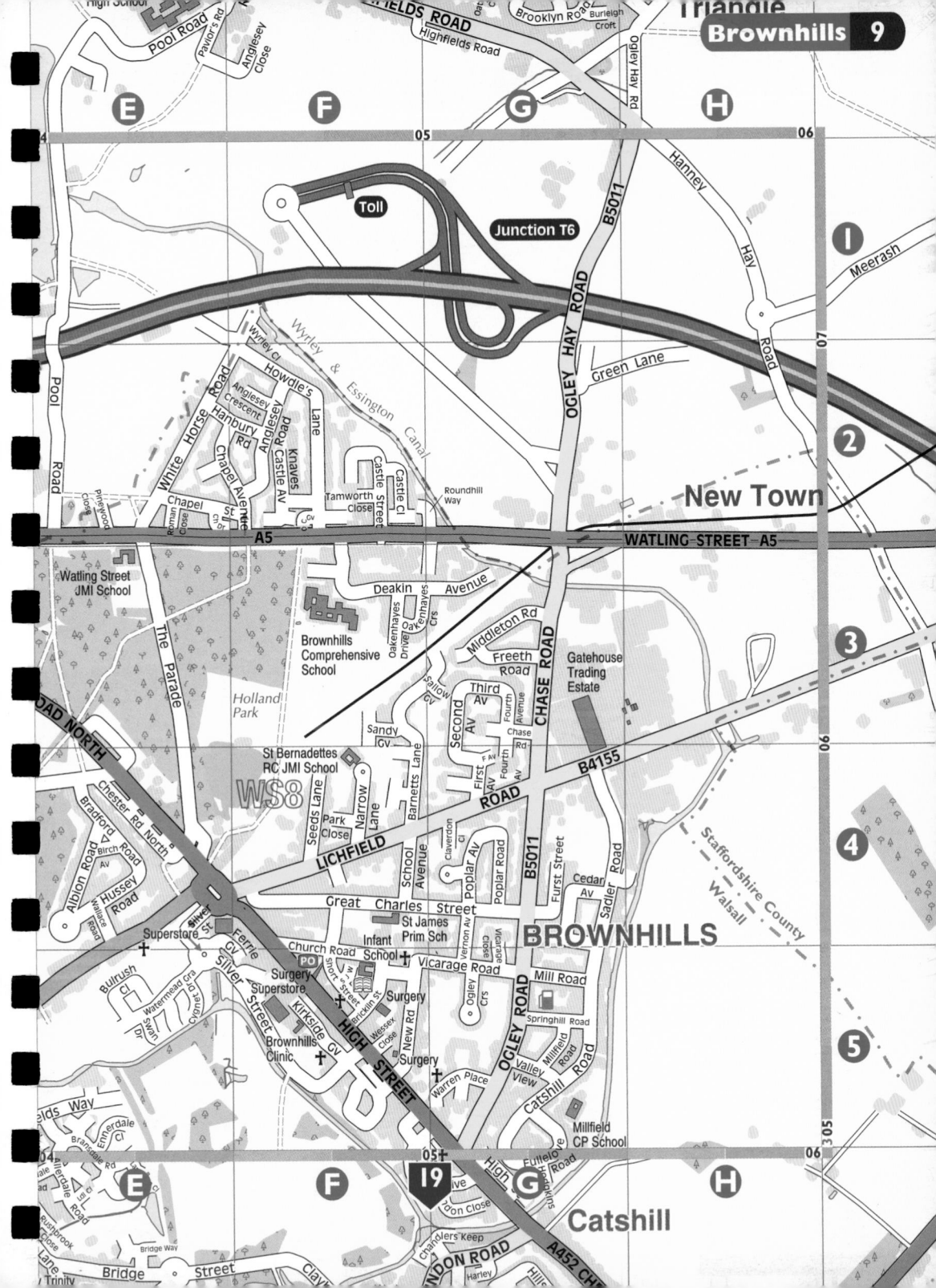

Toll
Junction T6
New Town
WATLING STREET A5
A5
B5011
OGLEY HAY ROAD
CHASE ROAD
Hanney Hay Road
Meerash
Green Lane
Wyrley & Essington Canal
Pool Road
White Horse Road
Howdle's Lane
Anglesey Crescent
Anglesey Road
Hanbury Rd
Chapel Avenue
Castle Av
Knaves
Castle Street
Castle Cl
Tamworth Close
Roundhill Way
Chapel St
Pinewood Close
Roman Close
Watling Street JMI School
The Parade
Deakin Avenue
Oakenhayes Drive
Oakenhayes Crs
Brownhills Comprehensive School
Middleton Rd
Freeth Road
Third Av
Second Av
Fourth Avenue
Chase Rd
First Av
Fourth Av
Gatehouse Trading Estate
Holland Park
Sallow Gv
Sandy Gv
Barnetts Lane
St Bernadettes RC JMI School
WS8
Seeds Lane
Narrow Lane
Park Close
LICHFIELD ROAD
B4155
Chester Rd North
Bradford Road
Birch Av
Albion Road
Hussey Road
Wallace Road
School Avenue
Claverdon Cl
Poplar Av
Poplar Road
Furst Street
Cedar Av
Sadler Road
Great Charles Street
St James Prim Sch
Infant School
Vernon Av
Vicarage Close
BROWNHILLS
Superstore
Silver St
Ferrie Gv
Church Road
PO
Vicarage Road
Mill Road
Short Street
Surgery
Superstore
Bricklin St
Ogley Crs
Bulrush Cl
Watermead Gra
Cygnet Dr
Swan Dr
Silver Street
Kirkside Gv
HIGH STREET
Wessex Close
New Rd
Springhill Road
Millfield Road
Brownhills Clinic
Valley View
Catshill Road
Warren Place
Millfield CP School
Staffordshire County
Walsall
Ennerdale Cl
Bransdale Rd
Allerdale Road
Rushbrook Close
Bridge Way
Bridge Street
Fullelove Road
Hopkins
High
Chandlers Keep
A452
Catshill
Highfields Road
Brooklyn Road
Burleigh Croft
Ogley Hay Rd
Pool Road
Paviors Rd
Anglesey Close
E F G H
1 2 3 4 5
05 06 07
19

10
M54
White House
Gunstone
Moors Farm
Whitehouse Lane
Port Lane
Chillington Lane
River Penk
Staffordshire Way
Mill Lane
Cemetery
Church Hl
Gunstone La
Watery Lane
Wood Lane
Sandy Lane
Meadows Grove
Old Farm Dr
Bilbrook Road
Millennium Wy
Church Road
Drury Lane
St Nicholas CE VC First School
Bakers Wy
CODSALL
Moat Brook Av
Fairfield Drive
Station Road
Canford Crs
Wilkes Road
Wheel Av
Arps Road
Wolverhampton Road
Elliotts Lane
Codsall Clinic
Codsall Station
Codsall Middle School
Codsall High School
St Christophers RC Primary School
Bilbrook Middle School
Lane Green First Sch
Lime Tree Road
Orchard Lane
Bilbrook Medical Centre
Springfield House
Oaken Drive
Oaken Lanes
Chapel Lane
Broadway
Windsor Gdns
Queens Gdns
Hill
Histons Dr
Princes Drive
Princes Gdns
Lansdowne Av
Duck Lane
Brookfield Rd
Ringhills Road
Wesley Green
Oak Road
Bilbrook Station
Hollybush Lane
Manor Fold
Suckling Green Lane
Oaken Park
Park Road
Birches Park Road
Madeira Av
Parkes Av
Kynaston Crs
Birches
Meadow Vale
Charters Av
Birches First School
Keepers Lane
Stafford Lane
Greenhills
Wergs
Hawthorne La
Beech Gdns
20
1 grid square represents 500 metres

M54
Lower Pendeford Farm
Lawn Lane
Upper Hattons
Pendeford Hall Lane
Monarch's Way
Pendeford Mill Nature Reserve
Bilbrook
Wobaston Road
Joeys Lane
Mill Gv
Pendeford Mill Lane
Wobaston Rd
Lane Green
Alexander Rd
Florence
Clifton Gdns
Downie Rd
Barnhurst Lane
Balliol Business Park
Pendeford Business Park
Overstrand
Shropshire Union Canal
Lane Green Road
Pendeford
Pendeford La
Armstead Rd
The Droveway
Sonning Dr
Leybourne Crs
Weyhill Cl
Camellia Gdns
Fuchsia Dr
Ivy Cft
Clematis Dr
Lavender
Whitburn Cl
Pendeford Health Cen
Howland Cl
Eldridge Cl
Halesworth Rd
Emsworth Cl
Ashwells Grove
Alverstoke Close
Highbrook Cl
Portswood Close
Blaydon
Middlefield
Fallowfield
Torfield
Cornfield
Ryefield
Smallwood Cl
The Covert
Barnwood Rd
Barnhurst Lane
Aldersley
Duffield
Gainford Close
Sholing Cl
Lane Green Avenue
Birches Avenue
Palmers Cl
South View Close
Penshaw Cl
Daisy Wk
Rathlin Close
Welney Gdns
Jasmine
Newcott Cl
Tebworth
Tiffany
Pagnam Cl
Wobaston
12
22
89
90
05
04
03
88

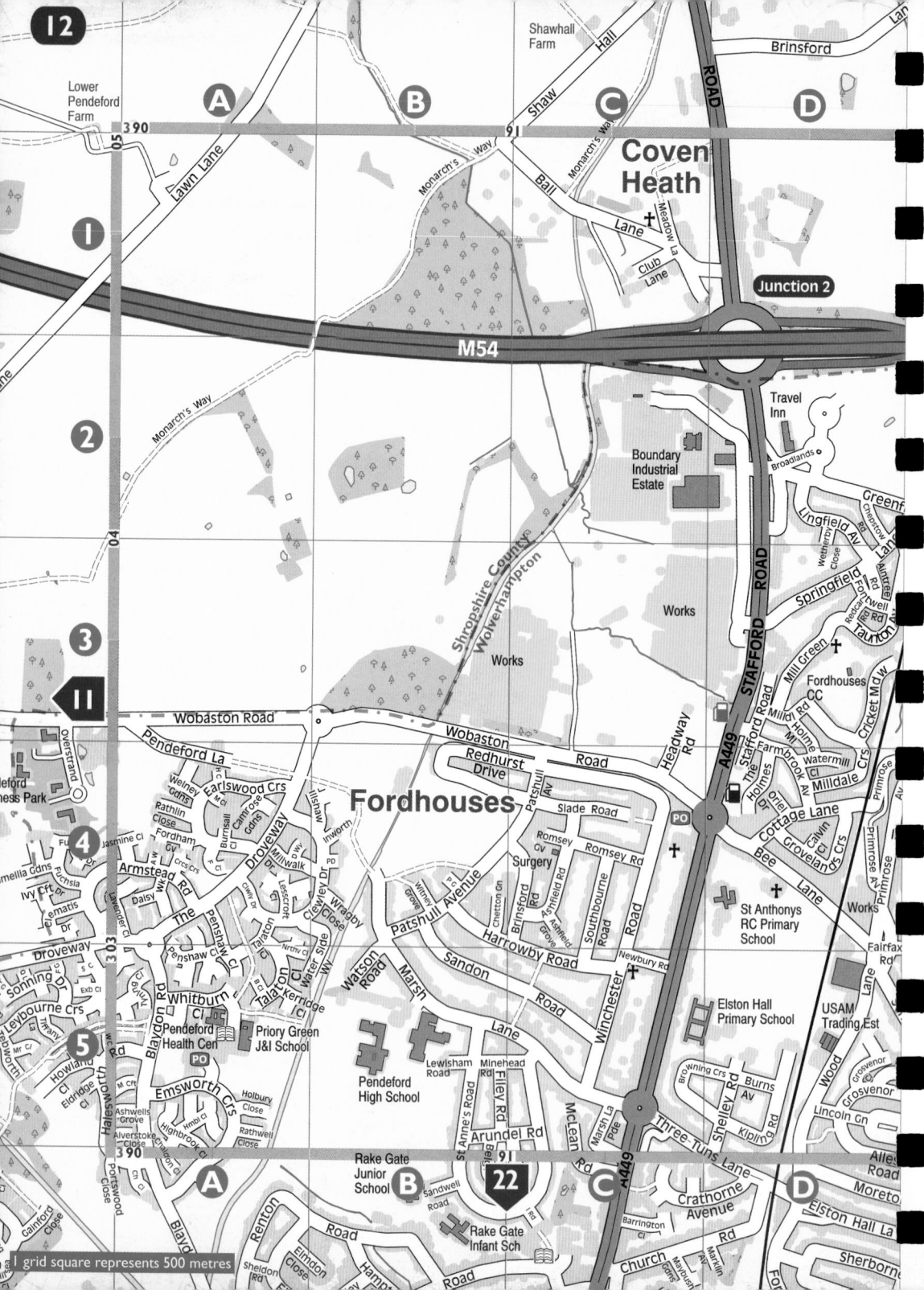

12

Lower Pendeford Farm

390

05

A

Lawn Lane

Shawhall Farm

Shaw Hall

Brinsford

B

91

Monarch's Way

C

Monarch's Way

Meadow La

Club Lane

Coven Heath

ROAD

D

Junction 2

1

04

M54

2

Monarch's Way

Travel Inn

Boundary Industrial Estate

Broadlands

Greenf

Lingfield Av

Chestnut Cl

Wetherfield Rd

Springfield

Portwell Rd

Redcar

TAUNTON

Mill Green

Fordhouses CC

3

II

Shropshire County Wolverhampton

Works

Wobaston Road

Headway Rd

STAFFORD ROAD

A449

Cricket Mdw

Milldale

Watermill Cl

Primrose

Works

03

390

deford ness Park

Overstrand

Pendeford La

Wobaston Redhurst Drive

Road

Farmbrook Av

Holme

The

Holmes Milldl Rd

Cottage Lane

4

Weiney Gdns

Earlswood Crs

Camrose Gdns

Rathlin Close

Burnsall

Fordham Gv

Crcs Crs

Milwalk

Droveway

Tillshaw

Pendeford La

Inworth

Fordhouses

Patshull

Slade Road

Romsey GV

Romsey Rd

Surgery

Bee

Lane

Orrell Cl

Grovelands Crs

Calvin

St Anthonys RC Primary School

Works

Fairfax Rd

Lane

Camella Gdns

Ivy Cft

Clematis Dr

Fensia

Jasmine Cl

Armstead Rd

The Penshaw Cl

Daisy

Lavender Cl

Bewley Dr

Lessorte

Wragby Close

Water Side

Patshull Avenue

Chetton Gn

Brinsford Rd

Ashfield Rd

Ashfield Grove

Southbourne Road

Winchester Road

Newbury Rd

Elston Hall Primary School

Browning Crs

USAM Trading Est

Grosvenor

Grosvenor

Wood

Lincoln Gn

Alles Road

Moreto

5

Sonning Dr

Leybourne Crs

Howland Cl

Eldridge Cl

Droveway

Blaydon Rd

Whitburn Cl

Pendeford Health Cen

PO

Priory Green J&I School

Penshaw Cl

Talaton

Kerridge Cl

Nrth Cl

Watson Road

Marsh Lane

Sandon Road

Harrowby Road

Lewisham Road

Minehead Road

Filey Rd

McLean Rd

Three-Tuns Lane

Shelley Rd

Kipling Rd

Burns Av

Lincoln Gn

Halesworth Rd

Ashwells Grove

Alverstoke Close

Highbrook Cl

Hmbl Cl

Emsworth Crs

Holbury Close

Rathwell Close

Pendeford High School

St Anne's Road

Arundel Rd

Marsh La Pde

Crathorne Avenue

Barrington Rd

Elston Hall La

Sherborne

390

Gainford Close

Portswood Close

A

Blaydo

Renton Road

Elfndon Close

Hampt

Rake Gate Junior School

B

Sandwell Road

91

22

Rake Gate Infant Sch

C

A449

Church

Fol

D

Moreto

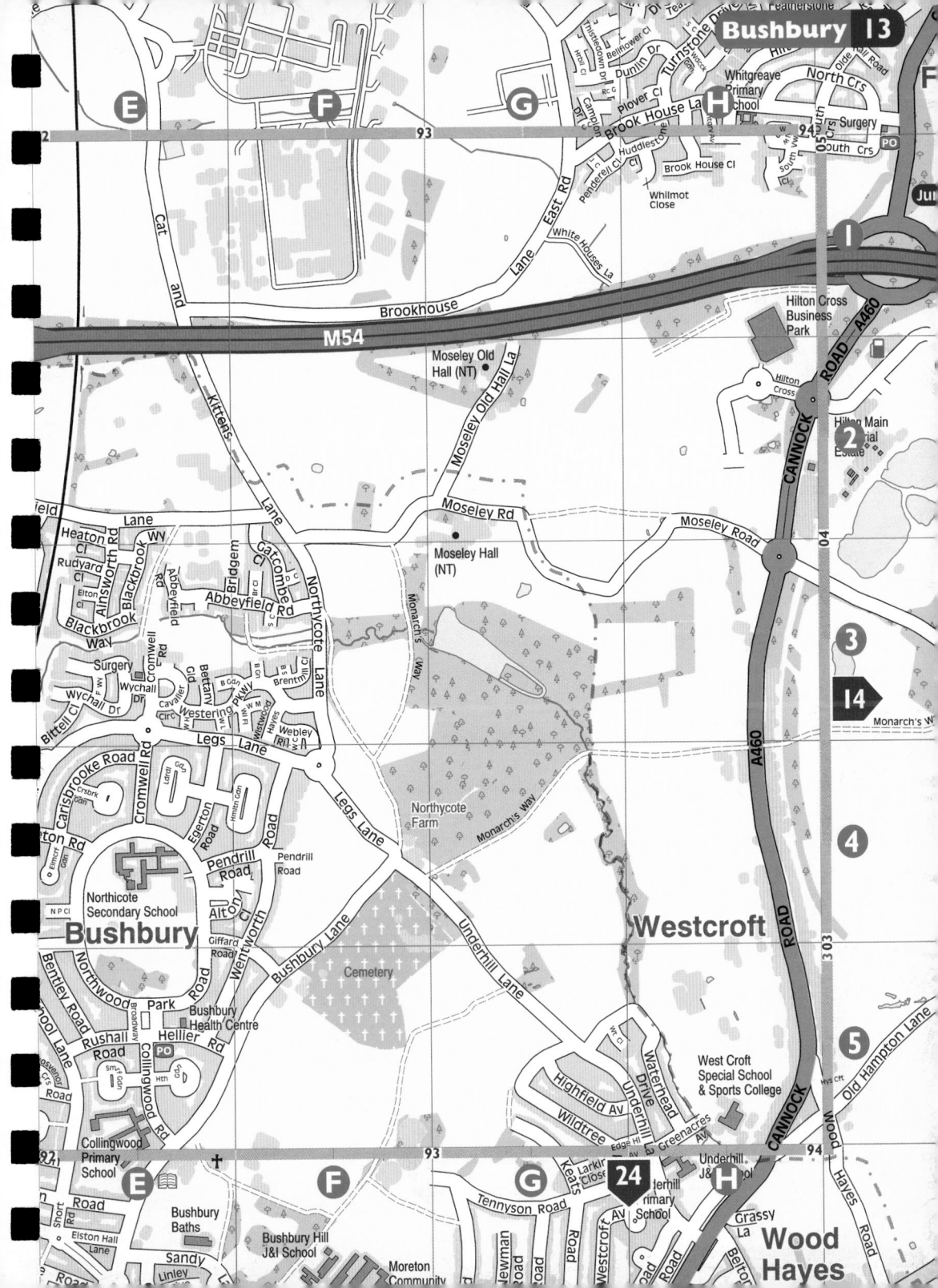
M54
Brookhouse Lane
East Rd
Cat and Kittens Lane
Moseley Old Hall (NT)
Moseley Old Hall La
Hilton Cross Business Park
Hilton Cross
CANNOCK ROAD A460
Hilton Main Industrial Estate
Moseley Rd
Moseley Road
Moseley Hall (NT)
Monarch's Way
Northycote Lane
Northycote Farm
Legs Lane
Abbeyfield Rd
Blackbrook Way
Wychall Dr
Westering Pkwy
Cromwell Rd
Carisbrooke Road
Egerton Road
Pendrill Road
Northicote Secondary School
Bushbury
Bushbury Lane
Cemetery
Underhill Lane
Westcroft
Northwood Park Road
Bushbury Health Centre
Rushall Road
Hellier Rd
Collingwood Rd
Collingwood Primary School
Highfield Av
Waterhead Drive
Wildtree Av
Greenacres Av
West Croft Special School & Sports College
Old Hampton Lane
Wood Hayes Road
Underhill J&I School
Tennyson Road
Keats Road
Bushbury Baths
Bushbury Hill J&I School
Wood Hayes
Whitgreave Primary School
Brook House La
Brook House Cl
North Crs
South Crs
Surgery
Turnstone Drive
Dunlin Dr
Plover Cl
White Houses La
Whilmot Close
14
24
93
94

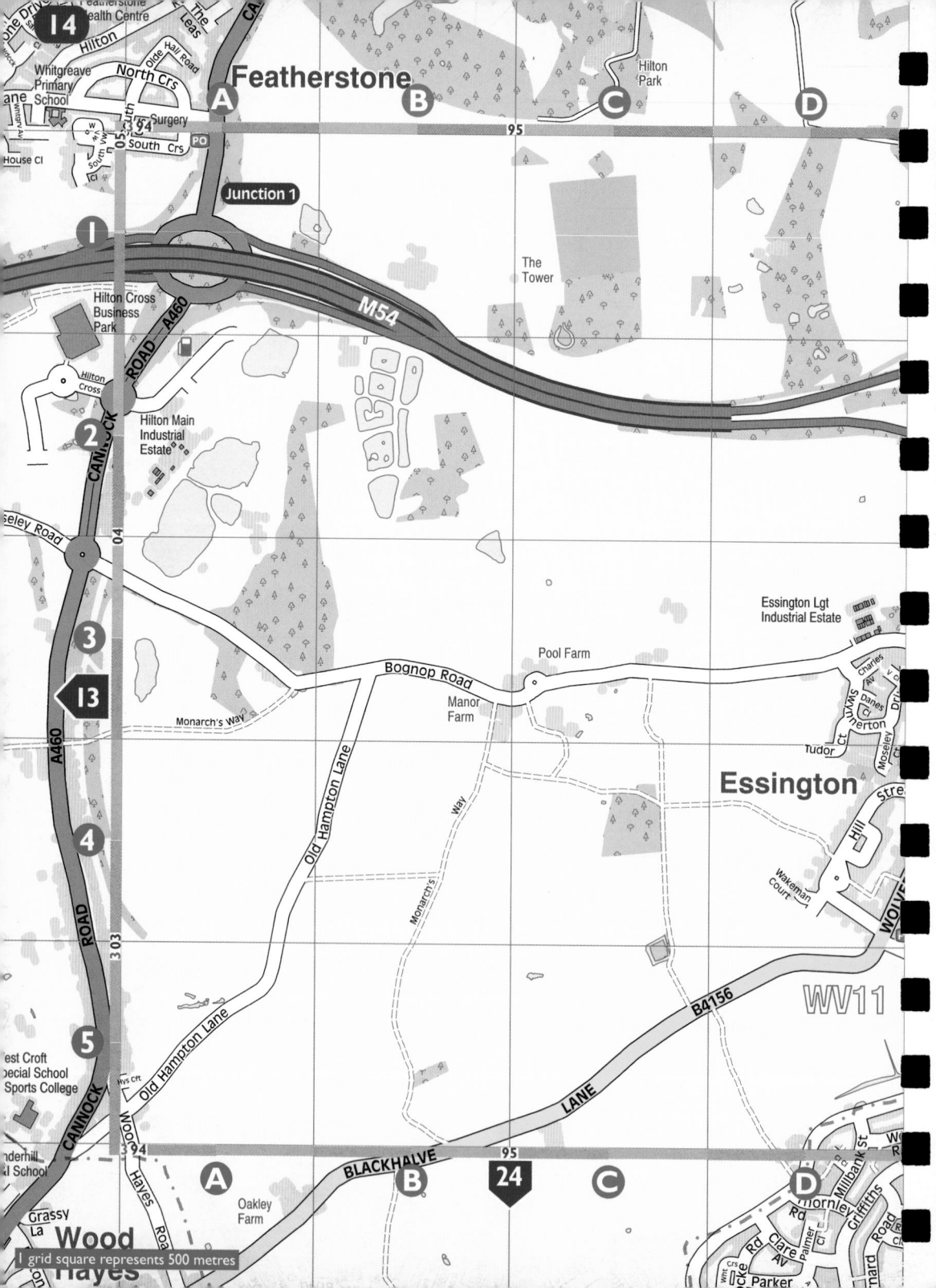
14
Featherstone Health Centre
The Leas
Hilton
Olde Hall Road
Whitgreave Primary School
North Crs
Featherstone
Hilton Park
Surgery
South Crs
PO
House Cl
Junction 1
The Tower
M54
Hilton Cross Business Park
A460
CANNOCK ROAD
Hilton Cross
Hilton Main Industrial Estate
Moseley Road
Essington Lgt Industrial Estate
Pool Farm
Bognop Road
Manor Farm
Monarch's Way
13
Old Hampton Lane
Essington
Tudor
Wakeman Court
WV11
B4156
LANE
BLACKHALVE
Oakley Farm
Wood Hayes
Grassy La
Woodhayes Road
Millbank St
Thornley Rd
Griffiths
Clare Av
Palmer Cl
Parker
24
A
B
C
D
1
2
3
4
5
1 grid square represents 500 metres

Travelodge
Hilton Park Service Area
Landywood
Old
New Landywood Lane
Wyrley
The Ride
Holly Bank
Long Lane
Springhill
BROAD LANE
B4210
Junction 10a
M6
B4156
A462
HOBNOCK ROAD
BURSNIPS ROAD
St Johns CE Primary School
BROWNSHORE LANE
Forrest Av
Kingsway
Hawthorne Rd
Parkes Crs
Works
Elmwood Av
Ferndale Rd
Rowan Dr
Hollybank Av
Mitre Close
Brownshore Lane
Larchmere Drive
St Johns Rd
Surgery
Willow Gv
Rosewood Gdns
New Street
Buttermere Drive
Thirlmere Drive
High Hill
Red Lane
Sneyd Farm
Holly Bank House
Kitchen Lane
Upper Sneyd Rd
Appleby Gdns
Sneyd Lane
Sneyd Community School
Abbey CP Sch
Vernon
Sneyd Reservoir
Rogers Cl
Drmm Cl
Fane Rd
Simmons Rd
Snape Road
Ferguson St
Drive
Coppice Cl
Hill Pl
Acorn Rd
Higgs Rd
Brindley Av
Danesmore Park Primary
Perks Rd
Maree Gv
Coppice Fm Wy
Lochalsh Gv
Hebden Gv
Kewstoke Close
Druid Pk Rd
Withywood Cl
Kewstoke Road
Waldale Cl
Sherringham Dr
Albany Gv
Astoria Cl
Astoria Close
Radstock Rd
Cedar Pk
Reedly Rd
Allens
ESSINGTON
16
26
96
97
98
05
04
03
2
3
4
5
E
F
G
H
I

16
Springhill
Newtown
Wallington Heath
BLOXWICH
Long Lane
Hobble End Lane
New Landywood Lane
Wyrley and Essington Canal
STAFFORD ROAD
A34
BROAD LANE
B4210
Staffordshire County
Walsall
15
26
Bloxwich Golf Club
Abbey CP School
Bloxwich North Station
Bloxwich Station
Sneyd Community School
Sneyd Reservoir
Mossley Primary School
Stafford Road Sports Club
Works
St Peters C JMI School
BELL LANE
SNEYD LANE A4124
Wetherby
Turton Cl
Saddleworth Rd
Redbourn Road
Nairn Road
Ferndown Cl
Elgin Rd
Ralston Cl
Werneth Grove
Canton Road
Alnwick Rd
Turnberry
Hoylake Cl
Astbury Rd
Burslem Cl
Gleneagles Rd
Selsdon Road
Colliery Drive
Walton Heath
Sunningdale Way
Muirfield
Staunton
Enville Cl
Formby Way
Turnberry Close
Carnoustie Close
Birkdale Rd
Troon Cl
Enderley Drive
Sanstone Rd
Baslow Rd
Lydford
Thurlstone Rd
William Wiggin Avenue
Muxloe Cl
Haverhill Cl
Belfry Cl
Woodbridge Cl
Churston Cl
Evesham Crs
Cleeve Rd
Cleeve Wy
Whitby Cl
Pershore Rd
Pershore Cl
Tintern Way
Tintern Crs
Kirkstall Crs
Byland Way
Tewkesbury Road
Glastonbury Crescent
Fountains Rd
Waverley Rd
Cresswell Crs
Abingdon Rd
Abingdon Way
Fisher Road
Fisher Rd
Broad La Gardens
Baytree Cl
Bealeys Lane
Baytree Road
Abbey Square
Netley Rd
Netley Way
Neath Rd
Neath Way
Margam Wy
Easby Wy
Buildwas Cl
Vernon Way
Roche Rd
Mossley La
Sneyd La
Parker St
SAND BANK
Sand Bank
Wolverhampton Road
Clarendon St
New St
Marlborough St
Samuel St
Park Rd
Park Road
Cemetery Wy
Croxdene Av
The Oaks
Mulberry Rd
Mossley Clnc
Hall Rd
Close
The Gn
1 grid square represents 500 metres

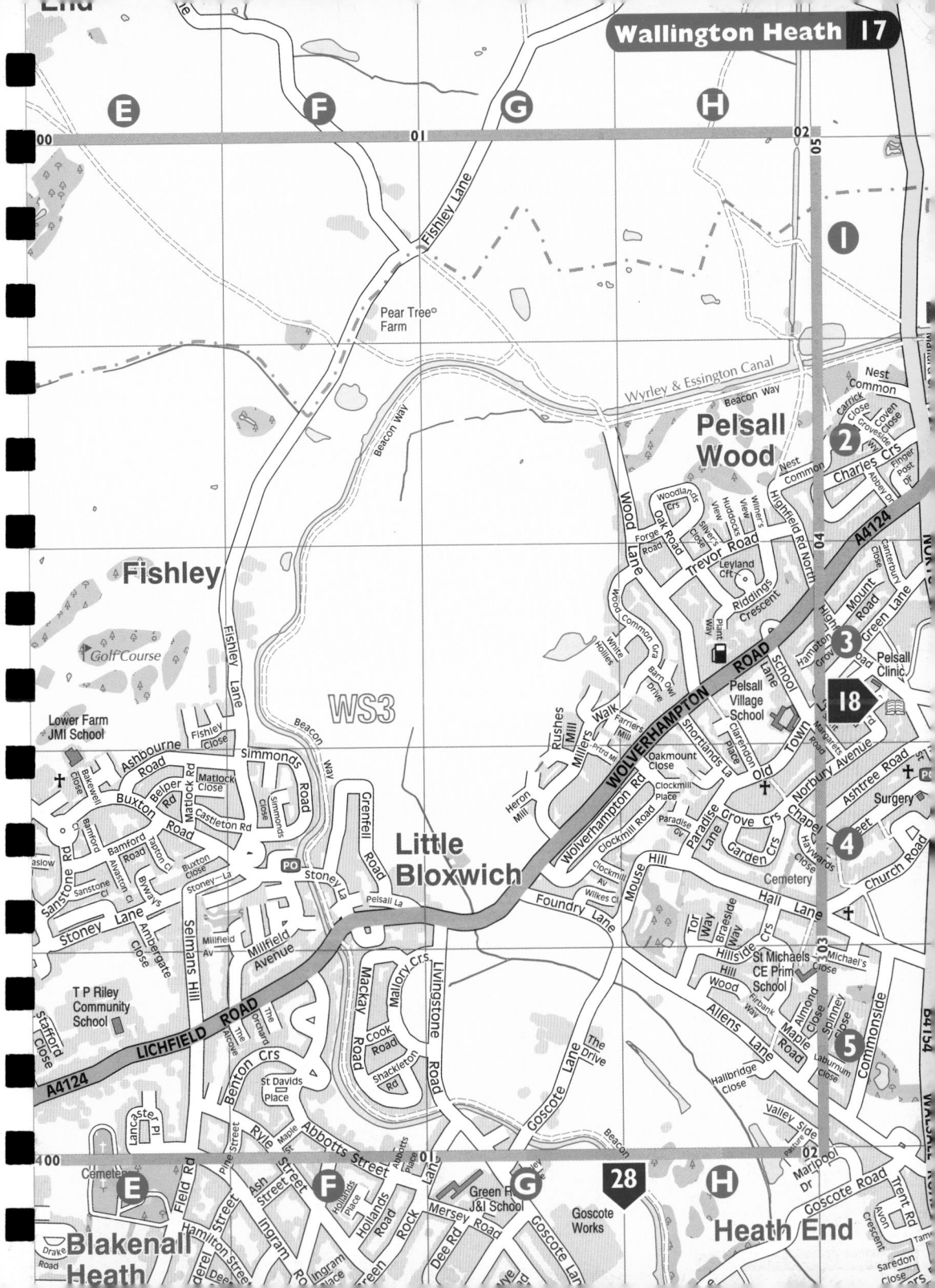

E F G H

00   01   05

I

Fishley Lane

Pear Tree Farm

Wyrley & Essington Canal

Beacon Way

Pelsall Wood

Nest Common

Carrick Close

Cowen Close

Grove Close

2

Charles Crs

Abbey Dr

Finger Post Dr

Woodlands Crs

Oak Road

Viewer's View

Hudlocks View

Silver's End

Winner's View

A4124

Forge Road

Trevor Road

Highfield Rd North

Wood Lane

Leyland Cft

Riddings Crescent

Mount Road

Green Lane

Canterbury Grove

3

Wood Common Cres

White Hollies

Plant Way

High Road

Hampton Grove

School Lane

Pelsall Clinic

Fishley

Beacon Way

Barn Owl Drive

WS3

Pitra Mill

Pelsall Village School

Clarendon Place

Margaret's Road

Old Town Road

18

Lower Farm JMI School

Fishley Close

Simmonds

Matlock Close

Castleton Rd

Simmonds

Rushes Mill

Millers Mill

Farriers Mill

Rushes Walk

White Hollies

Heron Mill

Oakmount Close

Clockmill Place

Paradise Grove

Norbury Avenue

Ashtree Road

Surgery

4

Ashbourne Road

Belper Rd

Bakewell Close

Bamford Road

Buxton Road

Tapton Cl

Matlock Rd

Avaston Cl

Castleton Rd

Simmonds

Stoney La

Buxton Close

Byways

Grenfell Road

Beacon Way

PO

Stoney La

Pelsall La

Little Bloxwich

WOLVERHAMPTON ROAD

Wolverhampton Rd

Clockmill Road

Clockmill Av

Wilkes Cl

Paradise Lane

Grove Crs

Garden Crs

Hanyards

Cemetery

Chapel St

Church Road

Shortlands La

Mouse Hill

Foundry Lane

Tor Way

Braeside Crs

Hall Lane

5

Bamford Road

Santstone Rd

Santstone Cl

Stoney Lane

Ambergate Close

Selmans Hill

Millfield Av

Millfield Avenue

Mackay Road

Cook Road

Shackleton Rd

Mallory Crs

Livingstone Road

Goscote Lane

The Drive

Hills de

St Michaels CE Prim School

Michael's Close

Hill Wood

Allens Lane

Firbank Way

Almond Close

Maple Road

Spinney Close

Laburnum Road

Commonside

T P Riley Community School

Stafford Close

A4124

LICHFIELD ROAD

The Orchard

The Arrow

Benton Crs

St Davids Place

Lancaster Pl

Field Rd

Pine Street

Ryle St

Maple St

Abbotts Street

Abbotts Place

Hallbridge Close

Valley Side

Marpool Dr

Goscote Road

Pasture La

B4154

B4210

Cemetery

E F G H

00   02

Blakenall Heath

Drake Road

Hamilton Street

Ingram Road

Ash Street

Rock Street

Holland Place

Hollands Road

Dee Rd

Mersey Road

Green R J&I School

Goscote La

28

Goscote Works

Heath End

Trent Rd

Avon Crescent

Saredon Close

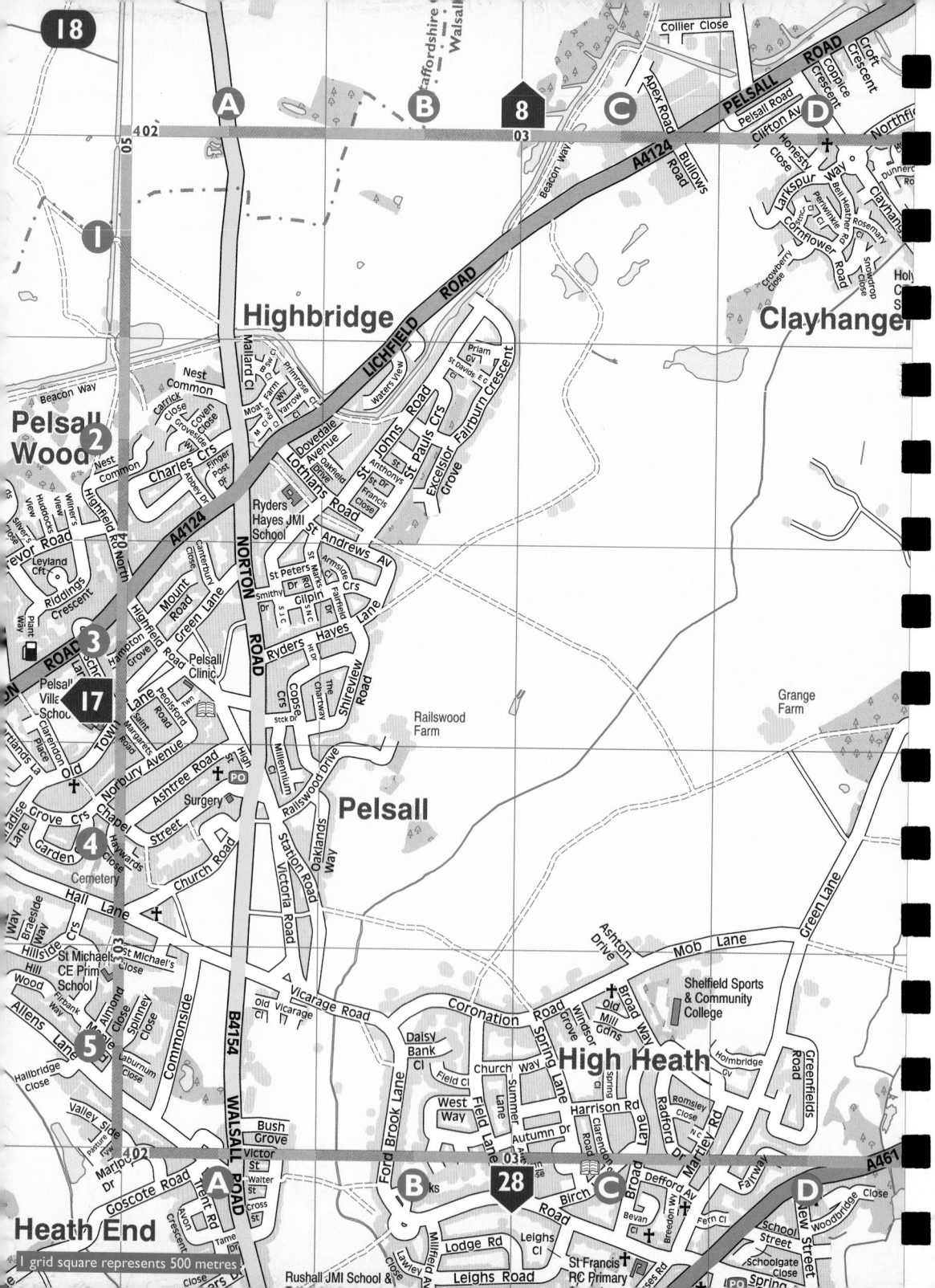

Highbridge
Pelsall Wood
Clayhanger
Pelsall
High Heath
Heath End
Railswood Farm
Grange Farm
LICHFIELD ROAD
A4124
PELSALL ROAD
NORTON ROAD
WALSALL ROAD
B4154
Mob Lane
Coronation Road
Vicarage Road
Green Lane
Hall Lane
Church Road
Station Road
Ryders Hayes Lane
Ryders Hayes JMI School
Pelsall Village School
Pelsall Clinic
Surgery
Cemetery
St Michaels CE Prim School
Shelfield Sports & Community College
St Francis RC Primary
Rushall JMI School &
Staffordshire
Walsall
Collier Close
Apex Road
Bullows Road
Beacon Way
Croft Crescent
Coppice Crescent
Pelsall Road
Clifton Av
Honesty Close
Larkspur Way
Cornflower Road
Clayhanger
Nest Common
Charles Crs
Highfield Rd North
Riddings Crescent
Leyland Cft
Dovedale Avenue
Lothians Road
St Johns Road
St Pauls Crs
Excelsior Grove
Fairburn Crescent
St Andrews Av
Gilpin Crs
Mount Road
Highfield Road
Norbury Avenue
Ashtree Road
Chapel Street
Grove Crs
Old Town Lane
Copse Crs
Shireview Road
Railswood Drive
Millennium Cl
Oaklands Way
Victoria Road
Commonside
Hillside Crs
Allens Lane
Valley Side
Goscote Road
Ford Brook Lane
Field Lane
Spring Lane
Harrison Rd
Autumn Dr
Broad Lane
Radford Dr
Martley Rd
Defford Av
Birch Road
Lodge Rd
Leighs Road
Greenfields Road
Fairway
School Street
New Street
Woodbridge Close
Daisy Bank Cl
Church Way
West Way
Bush Grove
Victor St
Walter St
Cross St
Trent Rd
Ashton Drive
Broad Way
A461
A
B
C
D
1
2
3
4
5
8
17
28
402
03
04
05
1 grid square represents 500 metres

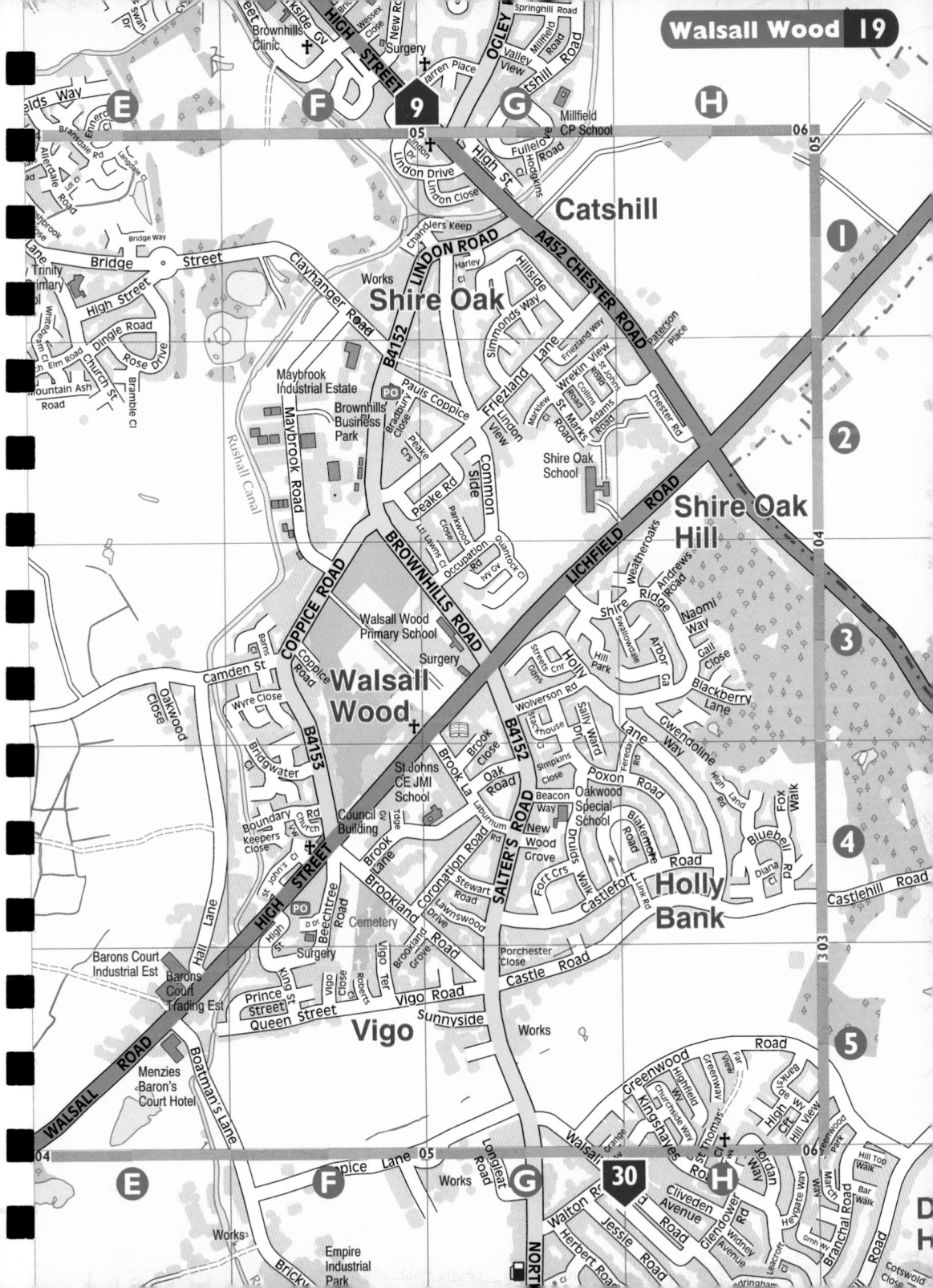
Catshill
Shire Oak
Shire Oak Hill
Walsall Wood
Holly Bank
Vigo
A452 CHESTER ROAD
LICHFIELD ROAD
WALSALL ROAD
HIGH STREET
COPPICE ROAD
BROWNHILLS ROAD
SALTER'S ROAD
LINDON ROAD
B4152
B4153
Maybrook Industrial Estate
Brownhills Business Park
Walsall Wood Primary School
Shire Oak School
Millfield CP School
St.Johns CE JMI School
Oakwood Special School
Council Building
Barons Court Industrial Est
Barons Court Trading Est
Menzies Baron's Court Hotel
Empire Industrial Park
Brownhills Clinic
Rushall Canal
Cemetery
Surgery
Works
Castlehill Road
Castle Road
Vigo Road
Queen Street
Sunnyside
Greenwood
Kingshayes
Lichfield Road
Bridge Street
Clayhanger Road
Maybrook Road
Camden St
Hall Lane
Boatman's Lane
Lindon Drive
Lindon Close
Chandlers Keep
Friezland Lane
Common Side
Peake Rd
Pauls Coppice
Blackberry Lane
Gwendoline Way
Poxon Road
Castlefort Road
Brookland Road
Coronation Road
Lawnswood Drive
Beechtree Road
Porchester Close
Jessie Road
Cliveden Avenue
Branchal Road
Walton Rd
Herbert Road
Coppice Lane
Longleat Road
9
30
E F G H
1 2 3 4 5
05 06 04
303

A
B
C
D
1
2
3
4
5
385
86
01
02
300
10
34
Middle Lane
Manor Fold
Hollybush Lane
Oaken Lanes
Shop Lane
Stafford Lane
Pine Walk
Farway Gdns
Wayside Acres
Poplars
Drive
Hawthorne La
Beech Gdns
A41
HOLYHEAD ROAD
Greenhills
Heath House Lane
Heath House
Wergs Hall Road
Wrottesley Hall
Monarch's Way
Wrottesley Park Road
Westcroft Road
Wergs
Wrottesley
Cranmoor
Cranmoor Lodge Farm
The Parkway
Bowen-Cooke Av
Fowler Cl
Dean Ct
Stephenson Dr
Collier Rd
Webb Av
Edward Rd
Mere Oak Rd
Mercia Cl
Cocton
Idonia Road
Turnberry Gv
Hawkstone Ct
St Andrews Drive
Hoylake Rd
Moor Pk
Gleneagles Rd
Troon Ct
Franklyn Cl
Shawbury Gv
Shackleton Dr
Manston Dr
Parkway
Egelwin Cl
Offa's Dr
Harald Cl
Drive
Athelstan Gv
Gaydon Cl
Livingstone Av
Perton First Sch
Penda Gv
Levington Close
Reynolds
Piper Cl
Gainsborough Dr
Perton Clnc
Lakeside Medical Cen
Milton Ct
Coleridge Drive
Auden Ct
Darwin
Epsom Cl
Sandown Dr
Church Rd
Spenser Av
Sandown First School
Elgin Ct
Perton
PO
Meon
Lytham Rd
Cloverdale
Portrush
Formby Av
Stanley
Wrds Ct
Browning Cl
Lingfield
1 grid square represents 500 metres

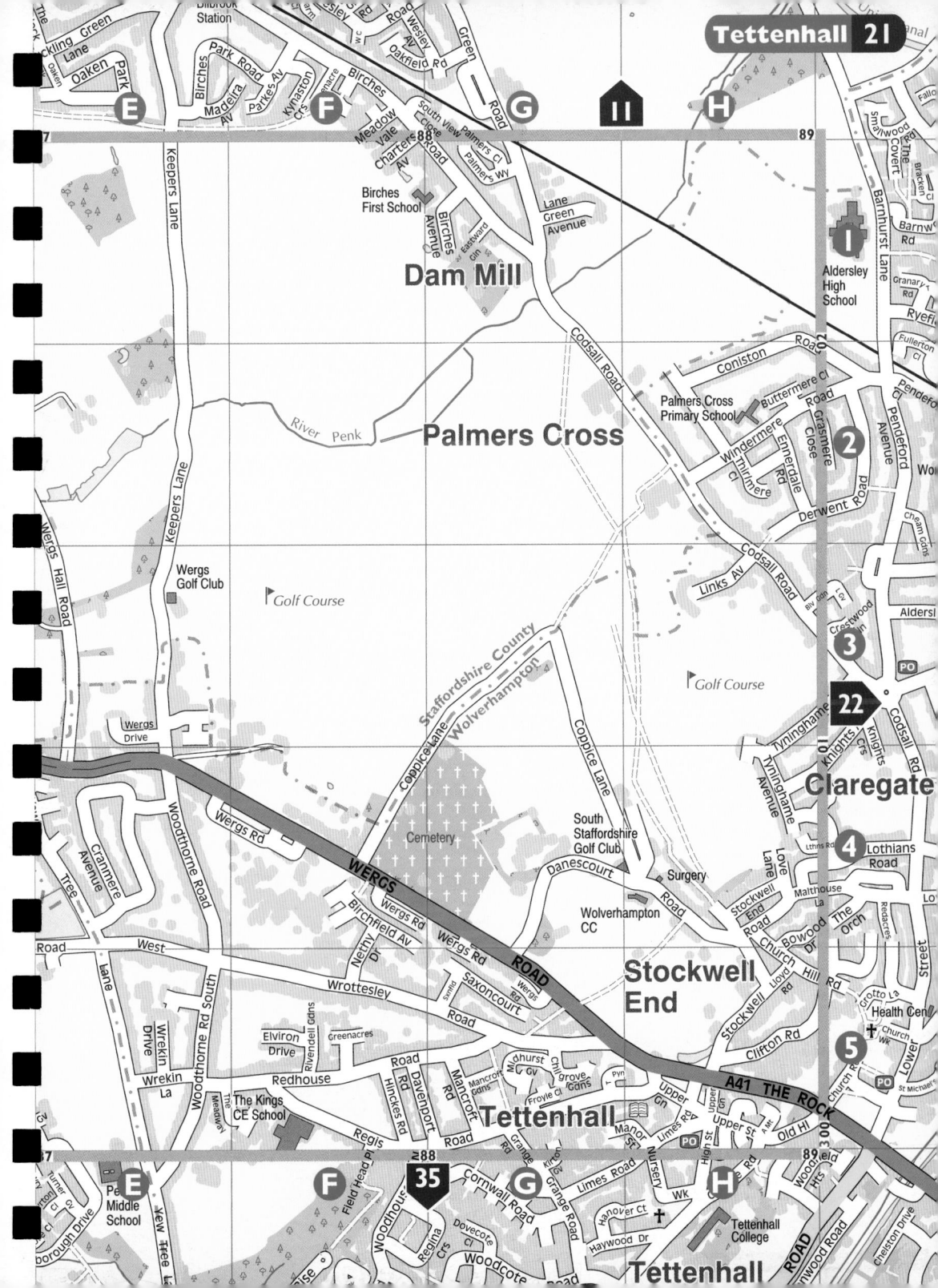

Dilbrook Station

Oaken
Oaken Lane
Ckling Green Lane
Park

Birches
Park Road
Madeira Av
Parkes Av
Kynaston Crs

E

Wesley Av
Oakfield
Wesley Rd

Green

F

Meadow Vale
South View Close
Palmers Cl
Charters Road
Av

G

Palmers Cl
Palmers Wy

Palmers Road

II

H

Fallo
Smallwood Covert
The
Bracken
Barnhurst Lane
Barnw Rd

Keepers Lane

Birches First School

Birches Avenue

Eastward Gdns

Lane Green Avenue

Dam Mill

Codsall Road

I
Aldersley High School

Granary Rd
Ryefi
Fullerton Cl

Coniston Road

Palmers Cross Primary School

Buttermere Cl
Grasmere Road

Pendefo
Pendeford Avenue
Wo

River Penk

Palmers Cross

Windermere Cl
Emerdale Rd
Close

Thirlmere Cl

2
Derwent Road

Cheam Cl

Keepers Lane

Wergs Hall Road

Wergs Golf Club

Golf Course

Links Av
Codsall Road
Blv Gdn

Crestwood
Aldersl

3

PO

Wergs Drive

Staffordshire County
Coppice Lane
Wolverhampton

Golf Course

Tyninghame Road
Knights
Knights Crs
Codsall Rd

22

Tyninghame Avenue

Claregate

Cranmere Avenue
Tree
Road

Woodthorne Road

Wergs Rd
Wergs Rd

Cemetery

Coppice Lane

South Staffordshire Golf Club

Danescourt Road

Surgery
Wolverhampton CC

Stockwell End Road

Love Lane

Malthouse La

4
Lothians Road

Church Hill Rd
Bowood Dr
The Orch
Redacres

Lthns Rd

West Lane

Wergs Rd
Birchfield Av
Nethy Dr

Saxoncourt Road
Wergs Rd

Wergs

WERGS ROAD

Bowood Dr

Stockwell Rd
Lloyd Rd

Grotto La
Health Cen
Church WK
St Michaels
Church

Wrottesley

Wrekin Drive
Wrekin La

Elviron Drive
Rivendell Gdns
Greenacres

Road

Redhouse Road
Davenport Rd
Hinckes Rd
Mancroft
Gdns

Midhurst Gv
Chilgrove Gdns
Froyle Cl
Pyn
Upper Gn

Clifton Rd

5
PO

Church Rd
Old HI
Woodfield Hts 100

West Lane

The Kings CE School
The Meadow

Regis Road

Manor Road

Upper St
Upper St

High St

Tettenhall

Grange Road
Kirton Cl
Grange Road

Limes Road
Nursery

PO

Manor Rd

Wk
St Michaels

E
Pe
Middle School

Turner Cl
Cl 2

borough Drive

F

Field Head Pl

35

Woodhouse

Cornwall Road
Regina Crs

Dovecote Cl
Woodcote Road

G

Hanover Ct
Haywood Dr

Limes Road

Wk

H

Tettenhall College

Cheston Road

Tettenhall

ROAD
Inwood Road

Stockwell End

A41 THE ROCK

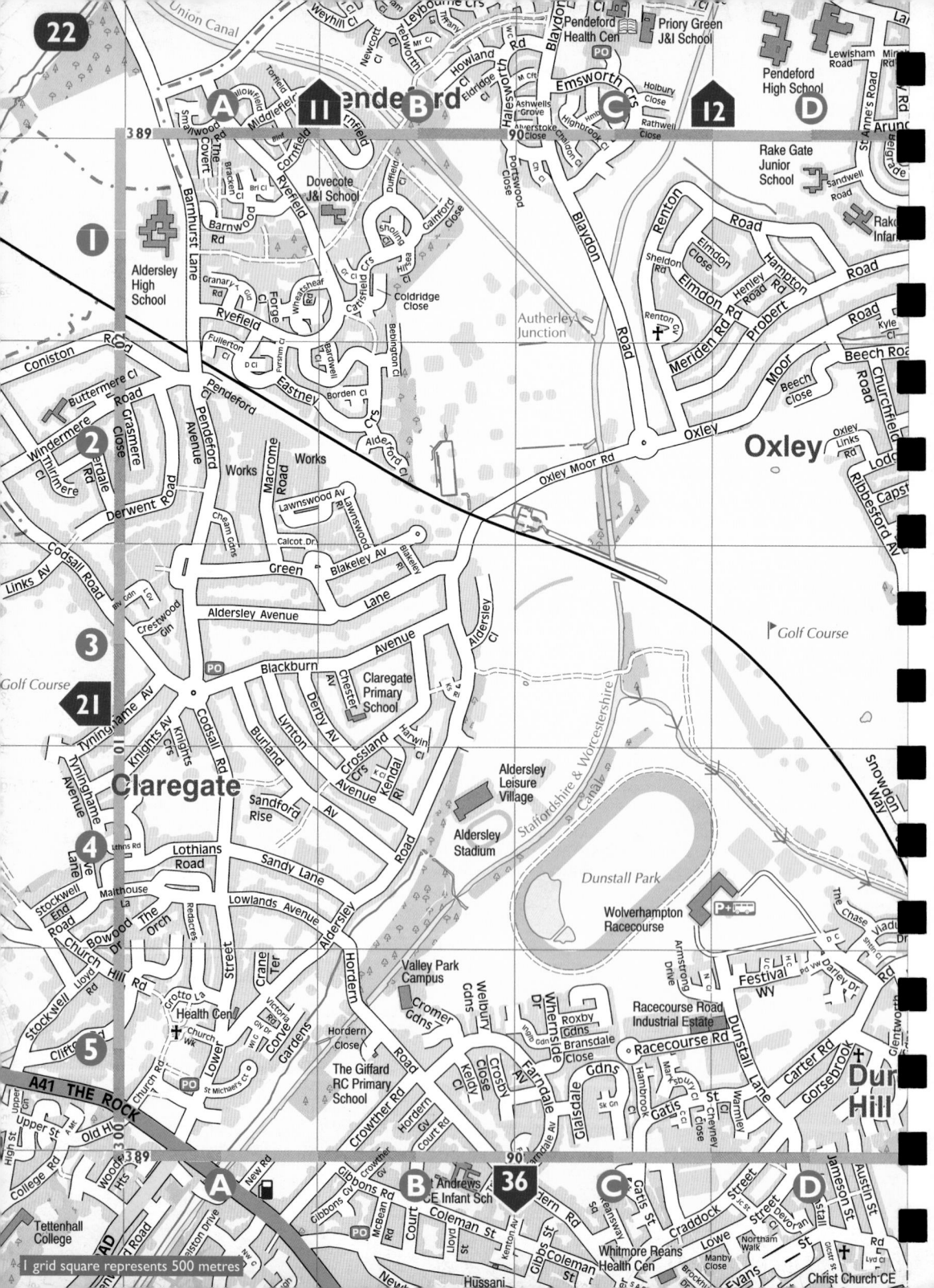
Pendeford
Oxley
Claregate
Dunstall Hill
Union Canal
Pendeford Health Cen
Priory Green J&I School
Pendeford High School
Rake Gate Junior School
Dovecote J&I School
Aldersley High School
Autherley Junction
Golf Course
Claregate Primary School
Aldersley Leisure Village
Aldersley Stadium
Staffordshire & Worcestershire Canal
Dunstall Park
Wolverhampton Racecourse
Valley Park Campus
The Giffard RC Primary School
Racecourse Road Industrial Estate
Tettenhall College
Whitmore Reans Health Cen
St Andrews CE Infant Sch
Christ Church CE
Health Cen
A41 THE ROCK
Barnhurst Lane
Pendeford Avenue
Oxley Moor Rd
Blaydon Road
Codsall Road
Blackburn Avenue
Aldersley Avenue
Green Lane
Aldersley Road
Lowlands Avenue
Sandy Lane
Lothians Road
Hordern Road
Crowther Rd
Dunstall Lane
Carter Rd
Festival Wy
Probert Road
Moor Road
Renton Road
Hampton Rd
Snowdon Way
Ribbesford Av
Coniston Road
Windermere Road
Derwent Road
Church Hill Rd
Stockwell Road
Coleman St
Craddock Street
Evans St
Jameson St
Austin St
Gatis St
Racecourse Rd
1 grid square represents 500 metres
11
12
21
36
389
90
300

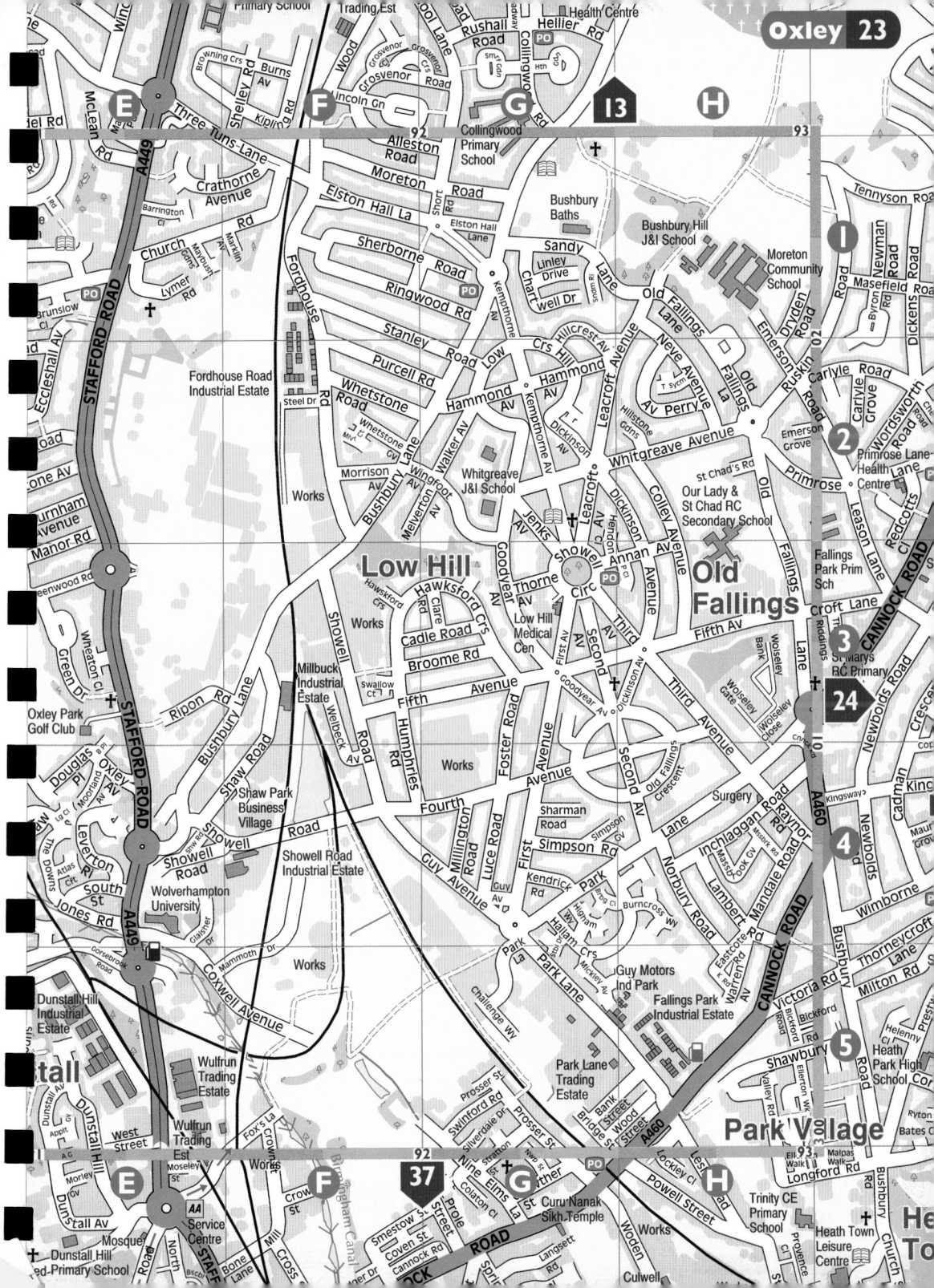

Primary School
Trading Est
Health Centre
Rushall Road
Hellier Rd
Browning Crs
Burns Av
Shelley Rd
Kipling Rd
Grosvenor Road
Lincoln Gn
Collingwood Rd
Collingwood Primary School
E
F
G
13
H
92
93
McLean Rd
Three Tuns Lane
Alleston Road
Moreton Road
Elston Hall La
Short Rd
Elston Hall Lane
Crathorne Avenue
Barrington Cl
Church Rd
Markin Av
Lymer Rd
Brunslow Cl
Eccleshall Av
STAFFORD ROAD
A449
Fordhouse Rd
Sherborne Road
Ringwood Rd
Stanley Road
Purcell Rd
Whetstone Road
Whetstone Gv
Steel Dr
Fordhouse Road Industrial Estate
Bushbury Baths
Sandy Lane
Linley Drive
Chartwell Dr
Kempthorne Av
Bushbury Hill J&I School
Moreton Community School
Tennyson Road
Newman Road
Masefield Road
Dickens Road
Byron Rd
Emerson Road
Dryden Road
Ruskin Road
Old Fallings Lane
Hillcrest Av
Low Hill Crs
Hammond Av
Leacroft Avenue
Neve Avenue
Perry Av
Old Fallings La
Carlyle Road
Carlyle Grove
Wordsworth Road
Emerson Grove
Primrose Lane
Primrose Lane Health Centre
Hillstone Gdns
Dickinson Av
Whitgreave Avenue
St Chad's Rd
Our Lady & St Chad RC Secondary School
Walker Av
Wingfoot Av
Melverton Av
Bushbury Lane
Morrison Av
Whitgreave J&I School
Works
Jenks Av
Leacroft Av
Hendon Cl
Dickinson Avenue
Colley Avenue
Leason Lane
Redcotts Cl
CANNOCK ROAD
Fallings Park Prim Sch
Low Hill
Old Fallings
Showell Circ
Annan Av
Goodyear Av
Thorne Av
Hawksford Crs
Clare Rd
Cadle Road
Broome Rd
Low Hill Medical Cen
First Av
Second Av
Third Av
Fifth Av
Fifth Avenue
Croft Lane
Riddings
Wolseley Bank
Wolseley Gate
Wolseley Close
St Marys RC Primary
24
Newbolds Road
Millbuck Industrial Estate
Swallow Ct
Showell Road
Welbeck Av
Humphries Rd
Foster Road
Dickinson Av
Third Avenue
Oxley Park Golf Club
Ripon Rd
Green Dr
Wheaton Cl
Douglas Pl
Oxley Av
Moorland Rd
Shaw Road
Shaw Park Business Village
Fourth Avenue
Old Fallings Crescent
Surgery
Inchlaggan Road
Raynor Rd
A460
Kingsway
Cadman
Leverton Ri
The Downs
Atlas Cft
South St
Jones Rd
Showell Road
Showell Road Industrial Estate
Guy Avenue
Millington Road
Luce Road
Sharman Road
Simpson Rd
Simpson Gv
Kendrick Rd
Park Lane
Burncross Wy
Hallam Crs
Norbury Road
Lambert Rd
Mandale Road
Wimborne
Wolverhampton University
Glaisher Dr
Mammoth Dr
Gorsebrook Road
Coxwell Avenue
Park La
Park Lane
Challenge Wy
Guy Motors Ind Park
Mickley Av
Fallings Park Industrial Estate
Eastcote Rd
Warren Av
Bushbury Lane
Thorneycroft Lane
Milton Rd
Victoria Rd
Bickford Road
Helenny Cl
Heath Park High School
Dunstall Hill Industrial Estate
Dunstall
Wulfrun Trading Estate
Park Lane Trading Estate
Shawbury Road
Ellerton Wk
Valley Rd
Park Village
Dunstall Av
Dunstall Hill
West Street
Wulfrun Trading Est
Moseley St
Fox's La
Crown St
Works
Prosser St
Swinford Rd
Silverdale Dr
Bank Street
Wood Street
Bridge St
Lockley Cl
Longford Rd
Malpas Walk
Morley Gv
37
Nine Elms La
Colaton Cl
Stratton St
Powell Street
Guru Nanak Sikh Temple
Trinity CE Primary School
Heath Town Leisure Centre
Dunstall Av
AA Service Centre
Mosque
Dunstall Hill Primary School
North Road
Bone Mill Lane
Cross
Birmingham Canal
Smestow St
Coven St
Cannock Rd
Prole Street
Langsett Rd
Woden
Culwell
Works
Provence Cl
Church

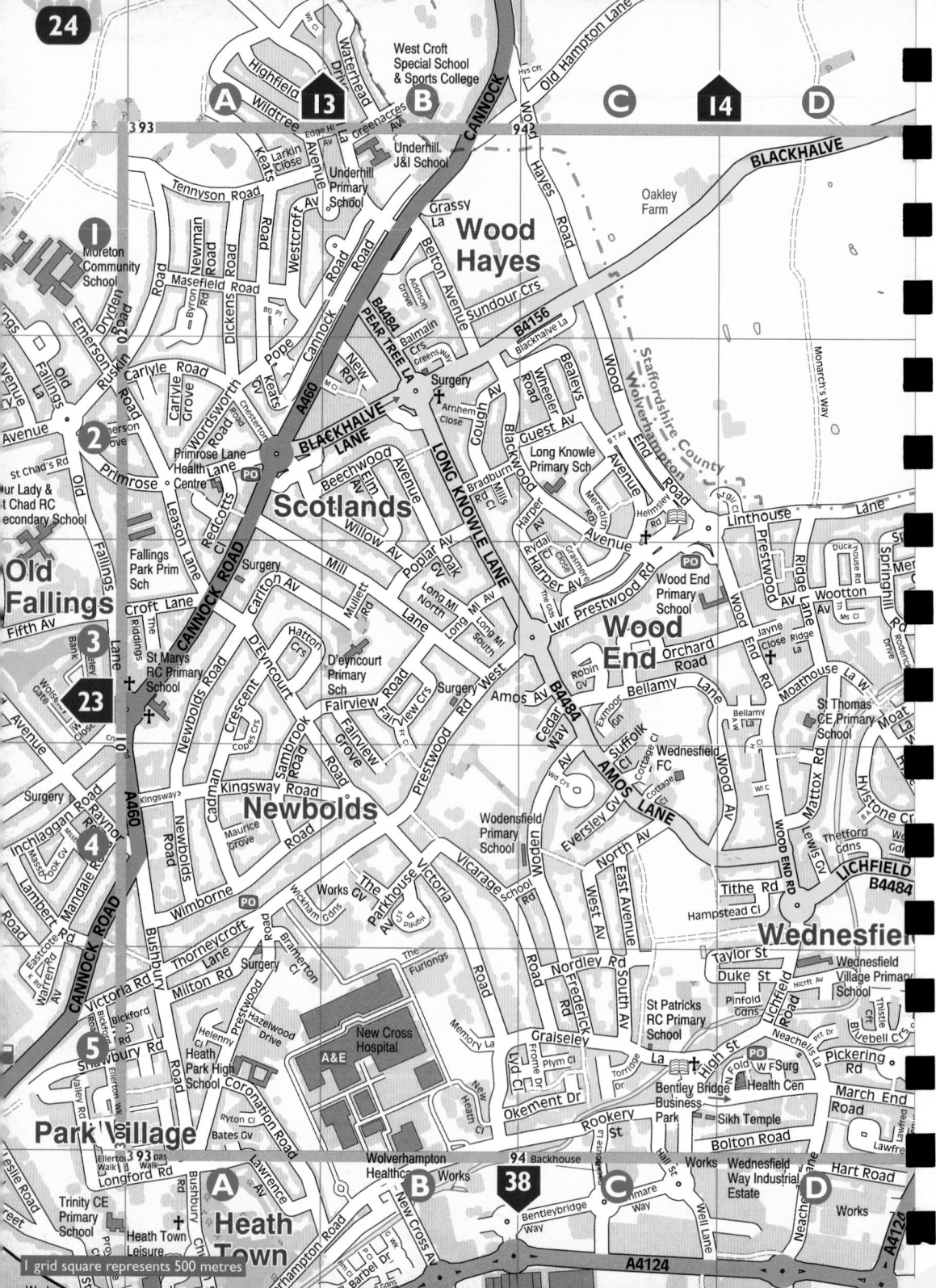
Wood Hayes
Scotlands
Old Fallings
Wood End
Newbolds
Wednesfield
Park Village
Heath Town
Oakley Farm
New Cross Hospital
CANNOCK ROAD
BLACKHALVE LANE
LONG KNOWLE LANE
AMOS LANE
LICHFIELD
A460
A4124
B4484
B4156
13
14
23
38
1 grid square represents 500 metres

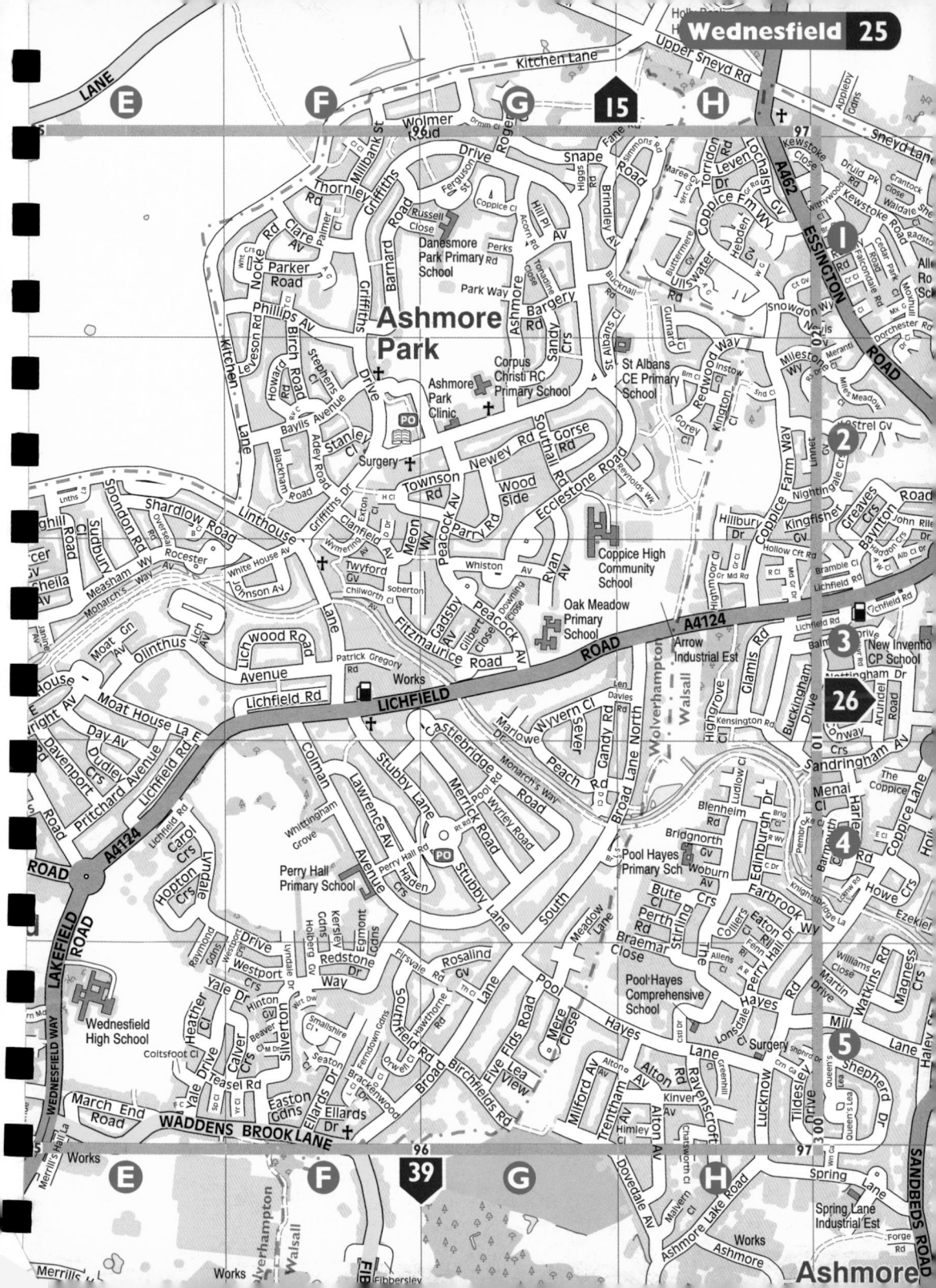

Ashmore Park
Ashmore
Kitchen Lane
Upper Sneyd Rd
Sneyd Lane
Wolmer Road
Snape Road
Essington Road
A462
Lichfield Road
A4124
Lakefield Road
Wednesfield Way
Waddens Brook Lane
March End Road
Linthouse Lane
Griffiths Drive
Broad Lane North
Broad Lane South
Stubby Lane
Castlebridge Road
Fitzmaurice Road
Peacock Av
Ecclestone Road
Coppice Farm Way
Hayes Lane
Pool Hayes Lane
Spring Lane
Sandbeds Road
Ashmore Lake Road
Moat House La E
Danesmore Park Primary School
Corpus Christi RC Primary School
Ashmore Park Clinic
St Albans CE Primary School
Coppice High Community School
Oak Meadow Primary School
Arrow Industrial Est
New Invention CP School
Perry Hall Primary School
Pool Hayes Primary Sch
Pool Hayes Comprehensive School
Wednesfield High School
Spring Lane Industrial Est
Surgery
Works
Wolverhampton
Walsall

15
26
39

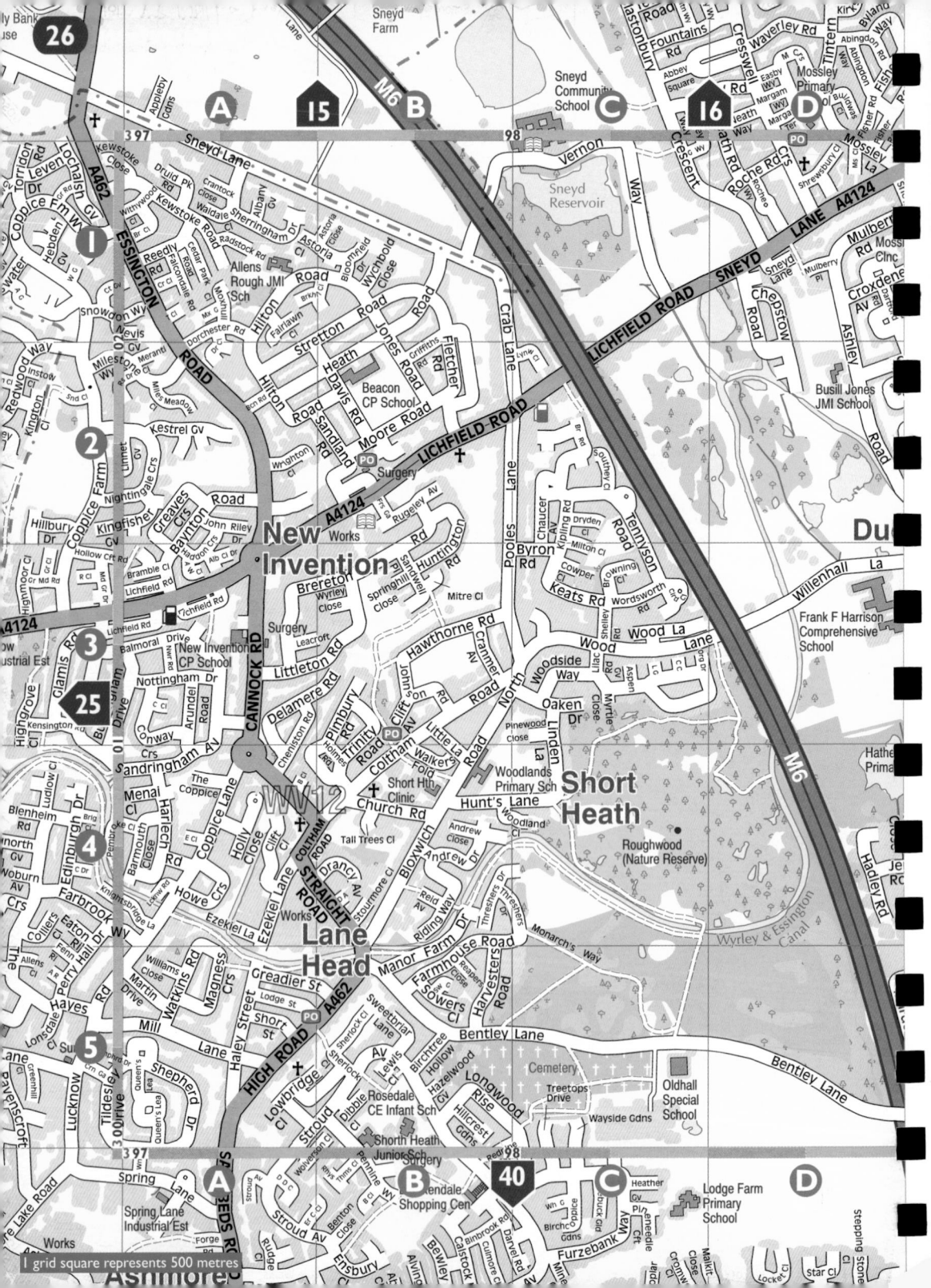

26
15
16
25
40
A
B
C
D
1
2
3
4
5
397
98
Sneyd Farm
Sneyd Community School
Mossley Primary School
Sneyd Lane
Sneyd Reservoir
Vernon Way
Waverley Rd
Fountains Rd
Cresswell Crescent
Roche Rd
Mossley La
Shrewsbury Cl
A4124
Sneyd Lane
Lichfield Road
M6
A462
Essington Road
Cannock Rd
Coppice Farm Way
Kewstoke Road
Allens Rough JMI Sch
Hilton Road
Stretton Road
Jones Road
Heath Davis Rd
Fletcher Rd
Wychbold Close
Beacon CP School
Moore Road
Sandland Rd
Surgery
Works
Crab Lane
Poolees Lane
Chepstow Road
Ashley Road
Busill Jones JMI School
Croxdene Av
Mulberry Pl
New Invention
Huntington Rd
Rugeley Av
Brereton Rd
Springhill Close
Mitre Cl
Tennyson Road
Byron Rd
Keats Rd
Wordsworth Rd
Willenhall La
Wood La
Wood Lane
Frank F Harrison Comprehensive School
Hawthorne Rd
Cranmer Av
New Invention CP School
Nottingham Dr
Balmoral Drive
Littleton Rd
Delamere Rd
Arundel Road
Conway Crs
Sandringham Av
Woodside Way
Oaken Dr
Linden La
North Road
Short Heath
Roughwood (Nature Reserve)
Woodlands Primary Sch
Hunt's Lane
Short Hth Clinic
Church Rd
Coltham Av
WV12
Tall Trees Cl
Bloxwich Road
Andrew Dr
Coltham Road
Straight Road
Lane Head
Ezekiel Lane
Farbrook Wy
Harlech Rd
Howe Crs
Menai Cl
Blenheim Rd
Edinburgh Dr
Wyrley & Essington Canal
Monarch's Way
Manor Farm Dr
Farmhouse Road
Harvesters Road
Sowers Cl
Greadier St
Lodge St
Short St
Haley Street
Magness Crs
Watkins Rd
Martin Drive
Mill Lane
Hayes Rd
Perry Hall Dr
High Road
Bentley Lane
Cemetery
Treetops Drive
Longwood Rise
Hillcrest Gdns
Hazelwood Gv
Oldhall Special School
Wayside Gdns
Rosedale CE Infant Sch
Short Heath Junior Sch
Sweetbriar Lane
Lowbridge Cl
Stroud Av
Shepherd Dr
Tildesley Drive
Lucknow
Ravenscroft
Spring Lane
Spring Lane Industrial Est
Works
Ashmore
Lodge Farm Primary School
Rendale Shopping Cen
Furzebank Way
Surgery
Hadley Rd
Ensbury
Bewley
Stepping Stone
1 grid square represents 500 metres

Stafford Road Sports Club
LICHFIELD
A4124
St Davids Place
St Peters C JMI School
Works
BELL LANE
Cemetery
Bloxwich Station
BLOXWICH
Bloxwich CE Primary Sch
Blakenall Heath
Green Rock J&I School
ELMORE GREEN ROAD
HIGH STREET
Elmore Green JMI School
Old Hall Ind Est
Field Rd Ind Est
Bloxwich Hospital
Pinfold Industrial Estate
Blakenall Heath Junior School
Willenhall Lane Industrial Estate
Crossings Industrial Est
B4210
SOMERFIELD ROAD
Bloxwich Leisure Centre
Sunshine Infant School
Leamore Primary School
Leamore Industrial Estate
Blakenall FC
Harden Primary School
Surgery
Bloxwich Business Park
Infant School
Castle Special School
Christ Church CE Primary School
Vulcan Industrial Est
GREEN LANE
Leamore Ind Est
Deeleys Ind Estate
Leamore
College of Continuing Education
Works
BLOXWICH ROAD
A34
Beechdale CP School
Works
Reedswood Retail Park
Superstore
UPPER GN LANE
Crown Whf Shop Park
North Walsall Primary Sch
17
28
41

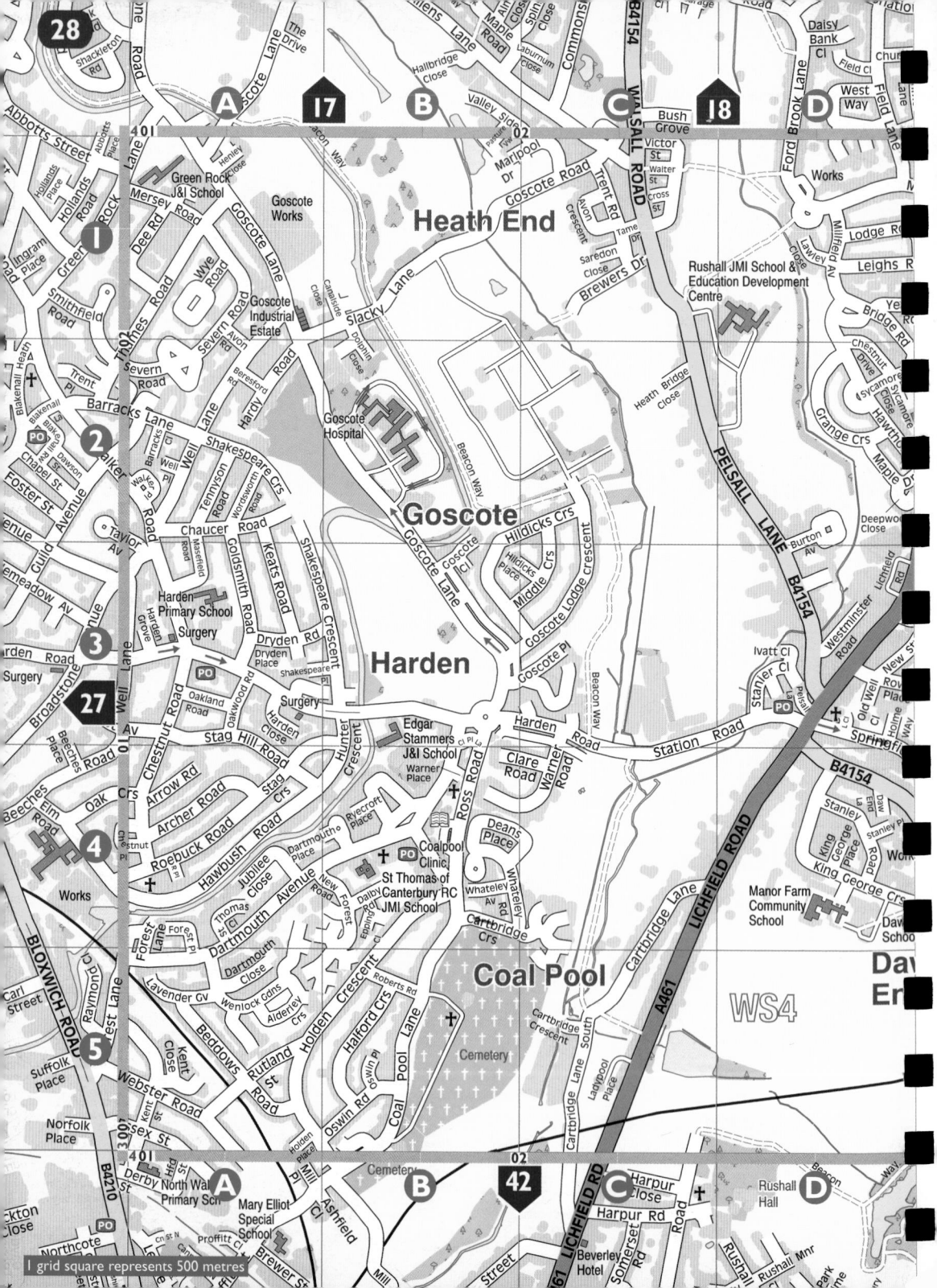

Heath End
Goscote
Harden
Coal Pool
WS4
Goscote Works
Green Rock J&I School
Goscote Industrial Estate
Goscote Hospital
Harden Primary School
Surgery
Edgar Stammers J&I School
Coalpool Clinic
St Thomas of Canterbury RC JMI School
Rushall JMI School & Education Development Centre
Manor Farm Community School
Cemetery
Works
North Walsall Primary Sch
Mary Elliot Special School
Rushall Hall
Beverley Hotel
Goscote Lane
Slacky Lane
Goscote Road
Walsall Road
Pelsall Lane
Lichfield Road
Station Road
Harden Road
Barracks Lane
Green Rock Lane
Blakenall Heath
Bloxwich Road
Coal Pool Lane
Holden Crescent
Cartbridge Lane
Beacon Way
B4154
A461
B4210
17
18
27
42
A
B
C
D
1
2
3
4
5
401
02
300
01

1 grid square represents 500 metres

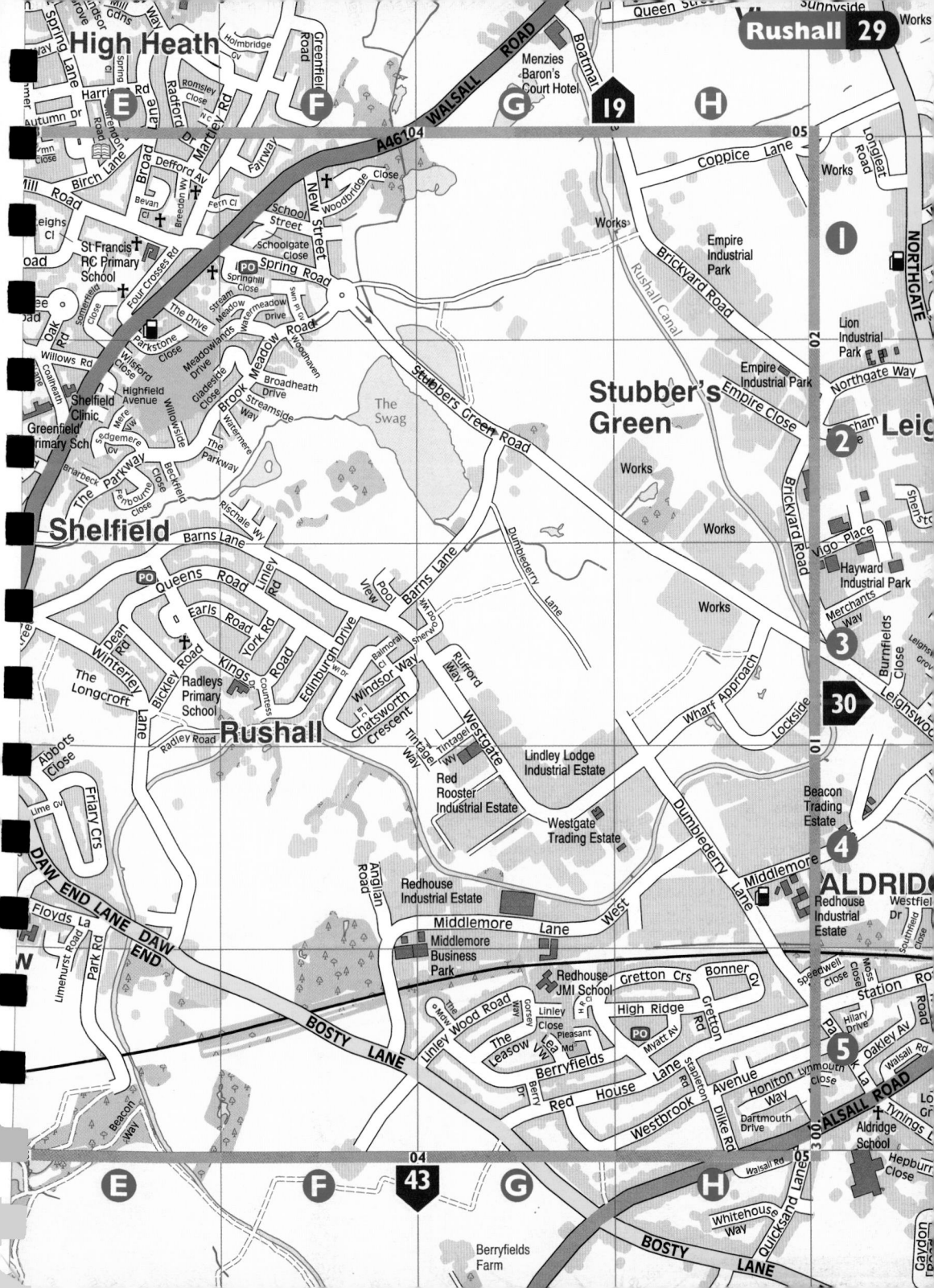

Rushall 29
High Heath
Shelfield
Rushall
Stubber's Green
Leig
ALDRIDG
E
F
G
H
I
2
3
4
5
19
30
43
04
05
02
01
00
A4610
WALSALL ROAD
Menzies Baron's Court Hotel
Boatman
Queen Street
Sunnyside
Works
Holmbridge Gv
Greenfield Road
Spring Lane
Spring Cl
Harrison Rd
Autumn Dr
Clarendon Road
Radford Dr
Romsley Close
Martley Rd
Fairway
Birch Lane
Broad Lane
Defford Av
Breedon Wy
Bevan Cl
Fern Cl
Mill Road
Leighs Cl
New Street
Woodbridge Close
School Street
Schoolgate Close
Spring Road
Springhill Close
St Francis RC Primary School
Four Crosses Rd
Somerfield Close
Oak Rd
Willows Rd
Coalheath Lane
Parkstone Close
The Drive
Stream Meadow
Watermeadow Drive
Meadow Road
Meadowlands Drive
Woodhaven
Wisford Close
Highfield Avenue
Gladeside Close
Brook Meadow Road
Broadheath Drive
Streamside Way
Shelfield Clinic
Greenfield Primary Sch
Sedgemere Gv
Willowside
Watermere
The Parkway
Beckfield Close
Briarbeck
Fenbourne Close
The Swag
Stubbers Green Road
Coppice Lane
Longleat Road
Empire Industrial Park
Rushall Canal
Brickyard Road
NORTHGATE
Lion Industrial Park
Northgate Way
Empire Close
Vigo Place
Hayward Industrial Park
Merchants Way
Burnfields Close
Leighs Grov
Leighswood
Barns Lane
Rischale Wy
Dumblederry Lane
Queens Road
Linley Rd
Earls Road
York Rd
Dean Rd
Winterley Lane
The Longcroft
Bickley Road
Kings Rd
Radleys Primary School
Countess
Edinburgh Drive
Windsor Way
Balmoral Cl
Chatsworth Crescent
Pool View
Sherwood Wk
Rufford Way
Westgate
Tintagel Wy
Tintagel Way
Radley Road
Red Rooster Industrial Estate
Lindley Lodge Industrial Estate
Westgate Trading Estate
Wharf Approach
Lockside
Beacon Trading Estate
Abbots Close
Friary Crs
Lime Gv
DAW END LANE
DAW END
Floyds La
Limehurst Road
Park Rd
Anglian Road
Redhouse Industrial Estate
Middlemore Lane West
Middlemore Lane
Middlemore Business Park
Westfield Dr
Southfield Close
Speedwell Close
Moss Close
Station Road
BOSTY LANE
The Mdw
Linley Wood Road
Gorsey Way
Linley Close
The Leasow
Lea Vw
Pleasant Md
Redhouse JMI School
Gretton Crs
Bonner Gv
High Ridge
Gretton Rd
Myatt Av
Hilary Drive
Park La
Oakley Av
Walsall Rd
Berryfields
Berry Dr
Red House Lane
Stapleton
Westbrook Avenue
Dike Rd
Honiton Way
Lynmouth Close
Dartmouth Drive
WALSALL ROAD
Tynings La
Aldridge School
Beacon Way
Walsall Rd
Hepburn Close
Whitehouse Way
Quicksand Lane
Berryfields Farm
Gaydon

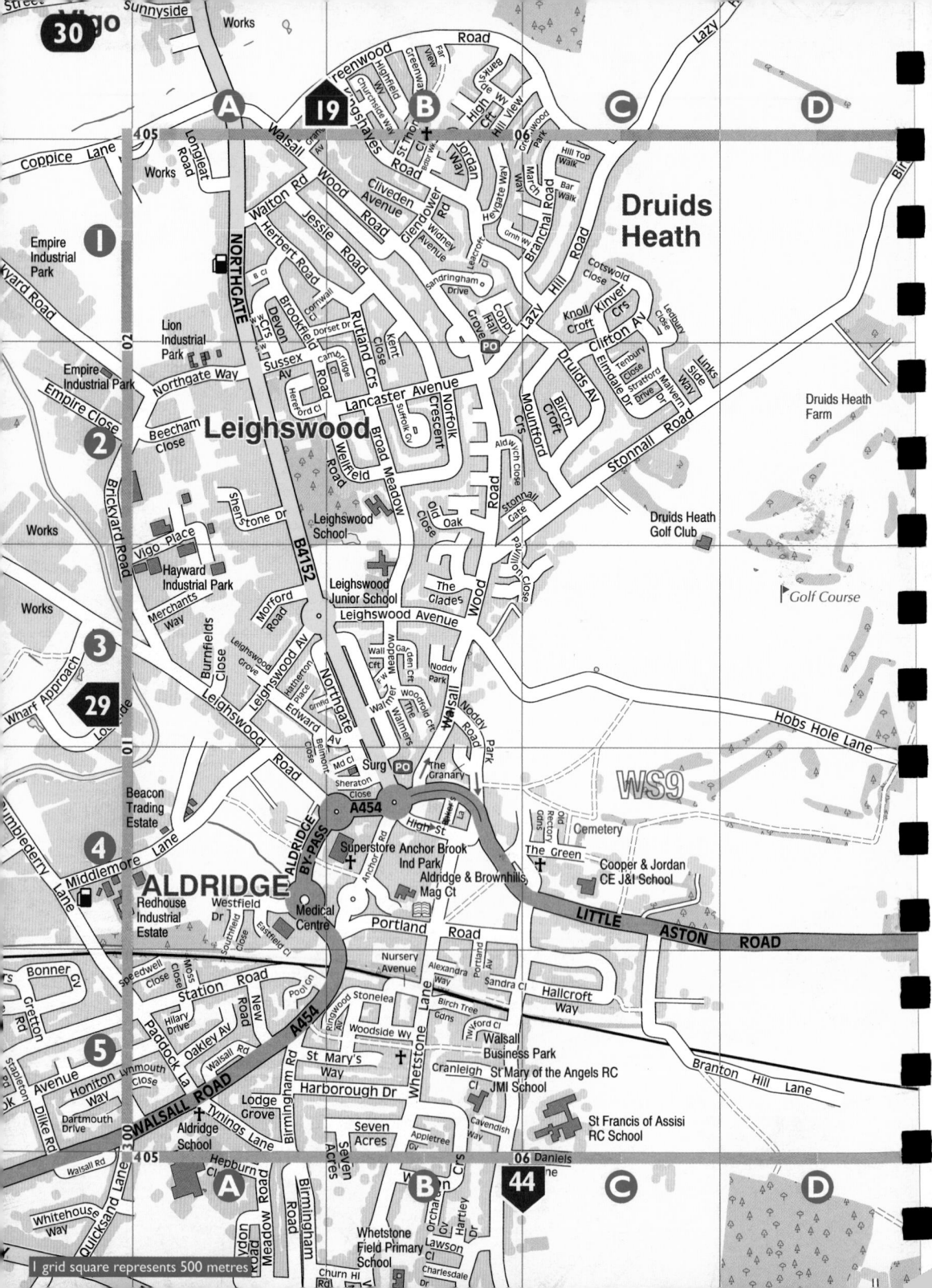

30
19
29
44
A
B
C
D
1
2
3
4
5
Druids Heath
Leighswood
ALDRIDGE
Empire Industrial Park
Lion Industrial Park
Hayward Industrial Park
Beacon Trading Estate
Redhouse Industrial Estate
Anchor Brook Ind Park
Walsall Business Park
Leighswood School
Leighswood Junior School
Cooper & Jordan CE J&I School
St Mary of the Angels RC JMI School
St Francis of Assisi RC School
Aldridge School
Whetstone Field Primary School
Druids Heath Farm
Druids Heath Golf Club
Golf Course
Cemetery
Superstore
Medical Centre
Aldridge & Brownhills Mag Ct
WS9
NORTHGATE
B4152
A454
ALDRIDGE BY-PASS
WALSALL ROAD
LITTLE ASTON ROAD
Stonnall Road
Hobs Hole Lane
Branton Hill Lane
Lazy Hill Road
Coppice Lane
Walsall Wood Road
1 grid square represents 500 metres

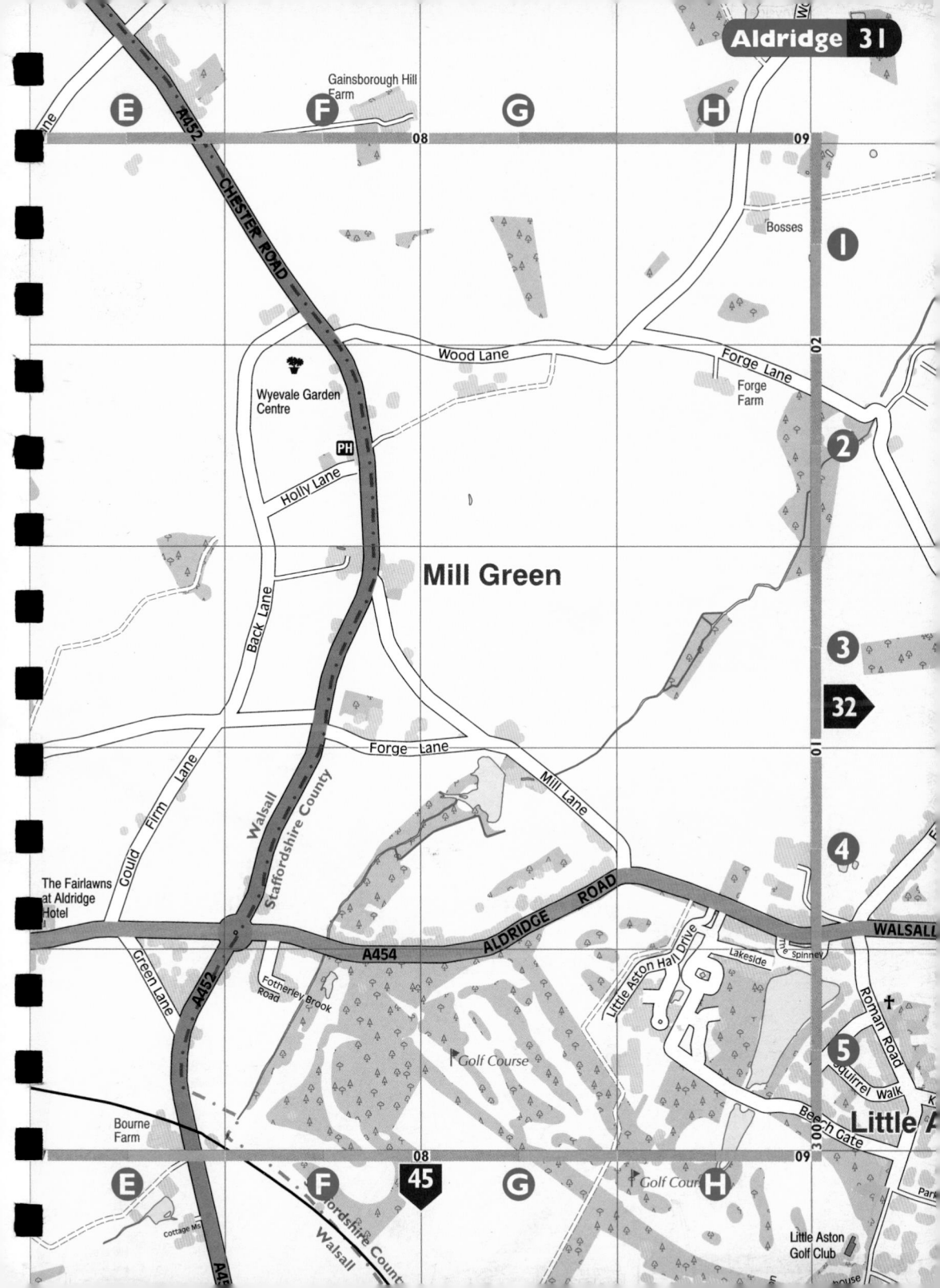

E

R d52

CHESTER ROAD

Gainsborough Hill
Farm

F

G

H

08

09

Bosses

I

02

Wood Lane

Forge Lane

Forge
Farm

Wyevale Garden
Centre

2

PH

Holly Lane

Mill Green

3

Back Lane

32

Forge Lane

Mill Lane

10

4

Gould Firm Lane

Walsall Staffordshire County

The Fairlawns
at Aldridge
Hotel

WALSALL

ALDRIDGE ROAD

A454

Little Aston Hall Drive

Lakeside

Spinney

Green Lane

A452

Fotherley Brook
Road

Roman Road

5

Squirrel Walk

Golf Course

Little A

Beech Gate

3300

Bourne
Farm

E

F

G

H

08

45

09

Golf Course

Little

Fordshire County
Walsall

Cottage Ms

Little Aston
Golf Club

A4

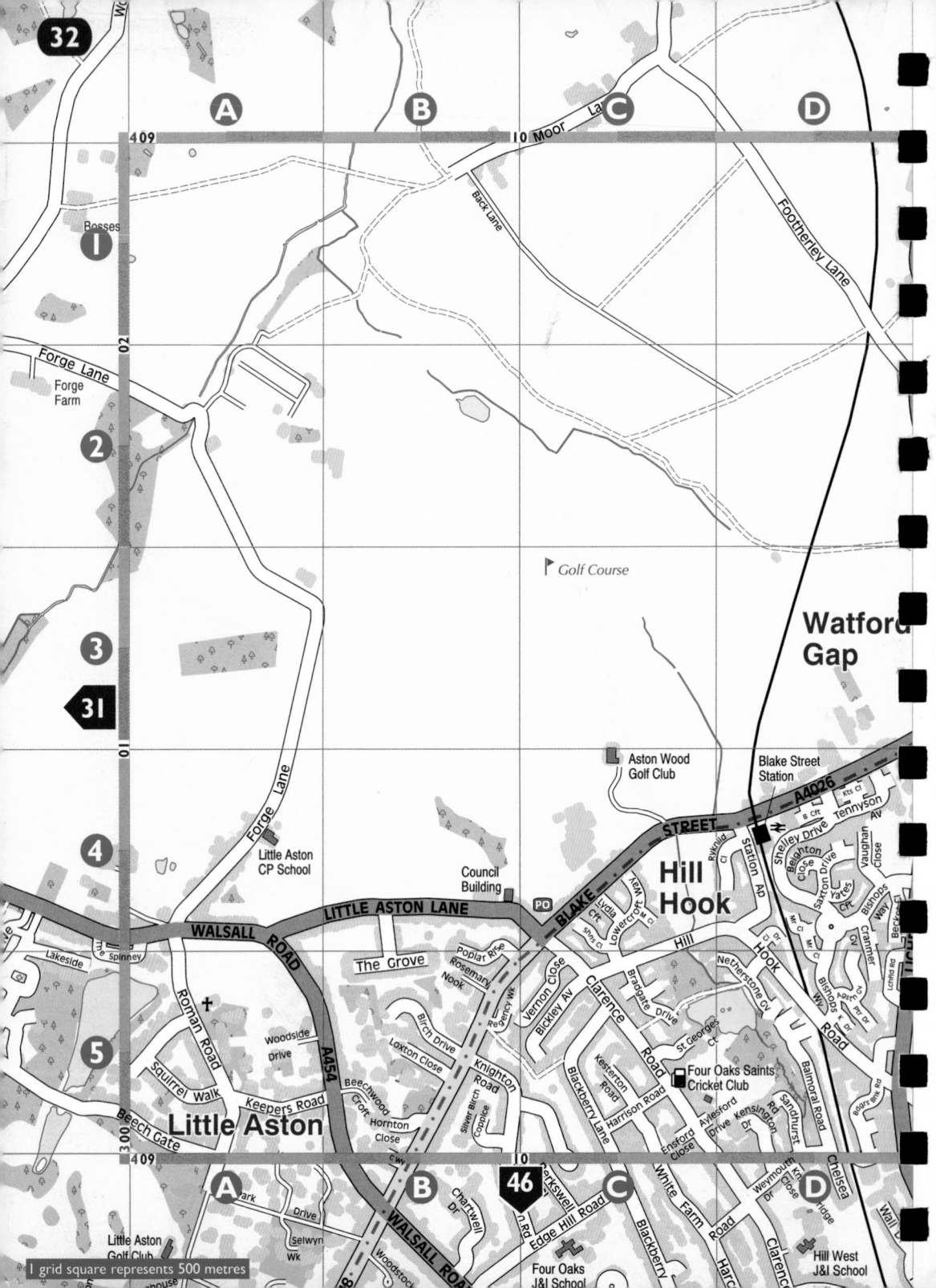

32

409 10 Moor La

A   B   C   D

Rosses

Forge Lane
Forge
Farm

1

2

Golf Course

Watford
Gap

3

31

Aston Wood
Golf Club

Blake Street
Station

A4026   Kts Ct

B Cft   Tennyson
STREET   Shelley Drive   AV
Beighton   Vaughan
Little Aston   Council   Close   Close
CP School   Building   Hill   Hook   Saxton Drive   Yates   Bishops
PO   BLAKE   Station Ap   Yares Cft   Way
LITTLE ASTON LANE   Lydia   RWknld   Hill   Mr Ct   Cranmer   Beckett
Hook
WALSALL   ROAD   Lowercroft   Vernon Close   Netherstone Cv   CV   Bishops Rd
The Grove   Poplar Rise   Cft   Hook   Bldgs gate Rd
Lakeside   The Spinney   Rosemary   Bickley Av   Road   Bradgate Drive   St Georges   Road
Nook   Regency Wk   Clarence   Ct   Balmoral Road
Woodside   Birch Drive   Kesterton   Four Oaks Saints
Roman Road   Drive   Loxton Close   Silver Birch   Road   Cricket Club
Knighton   Coppice   Blackberry Lane   Aylesford   Sandhurst
4   Squirrel Walk   Road   Harrison Road   Drive   Kensington   Chelsea
Keepers Road   Beechwood   Ensford   Dr   Rd
5   Croft   Close   Weymouth   Chelsea
Little Aston   A454   Hornton Close   White Farm   Road   Wall
Beech Gate   Close

A   B   46   C   D
Park Drive   Chartwell   Edge Hill Road   White Farm   Clarence
Little Aston   Dr   Parkswell   Blackberry   Road   Hill West
Golf Club   Selwyn   Rd   Harc   J&I School
Wk   WALSALL ROA   Four Oaks   Woodstock
J&I School

1 grid square represents 500 metres

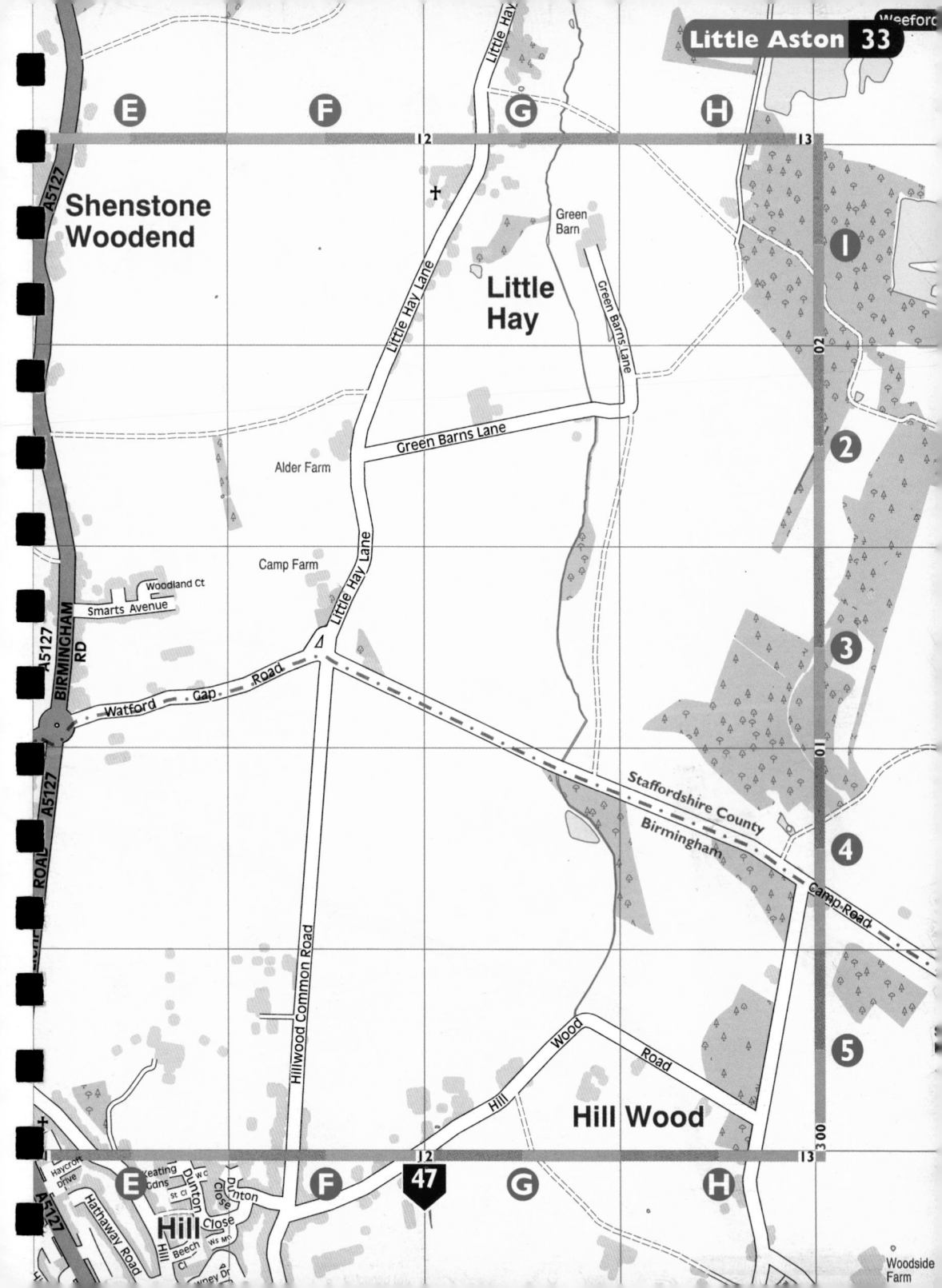

Weeford

E   F   G   H

12   13

A5127

Shenstone
Woodend

Little Hay Lane

✝

Green
Barn

Little
Hay

Green Barns Lane

02

I

Green Barns Lane

Alder Farm

2

Camp Farm

Little Hay Lane

3

Woodland Ct

Smarts Avenue

BIRMINGHAM RD

Watford   Gap   Road

01

A5127

Staffordshire County

4

Birmingham

Camp Road

A5127 ROAD

Hillwood Common Road

5

Wood   Road

Hill

Hill Wood

3 00

✝

E   F   47   G   H

12   13

Haycroft Drive

Keating Gdns
St Cl

Dunton Close

Dunton Close

Hill   Close

Hatthaway Road

Beech Cl

Ws Mr

wney Dr

Woodside
Farm

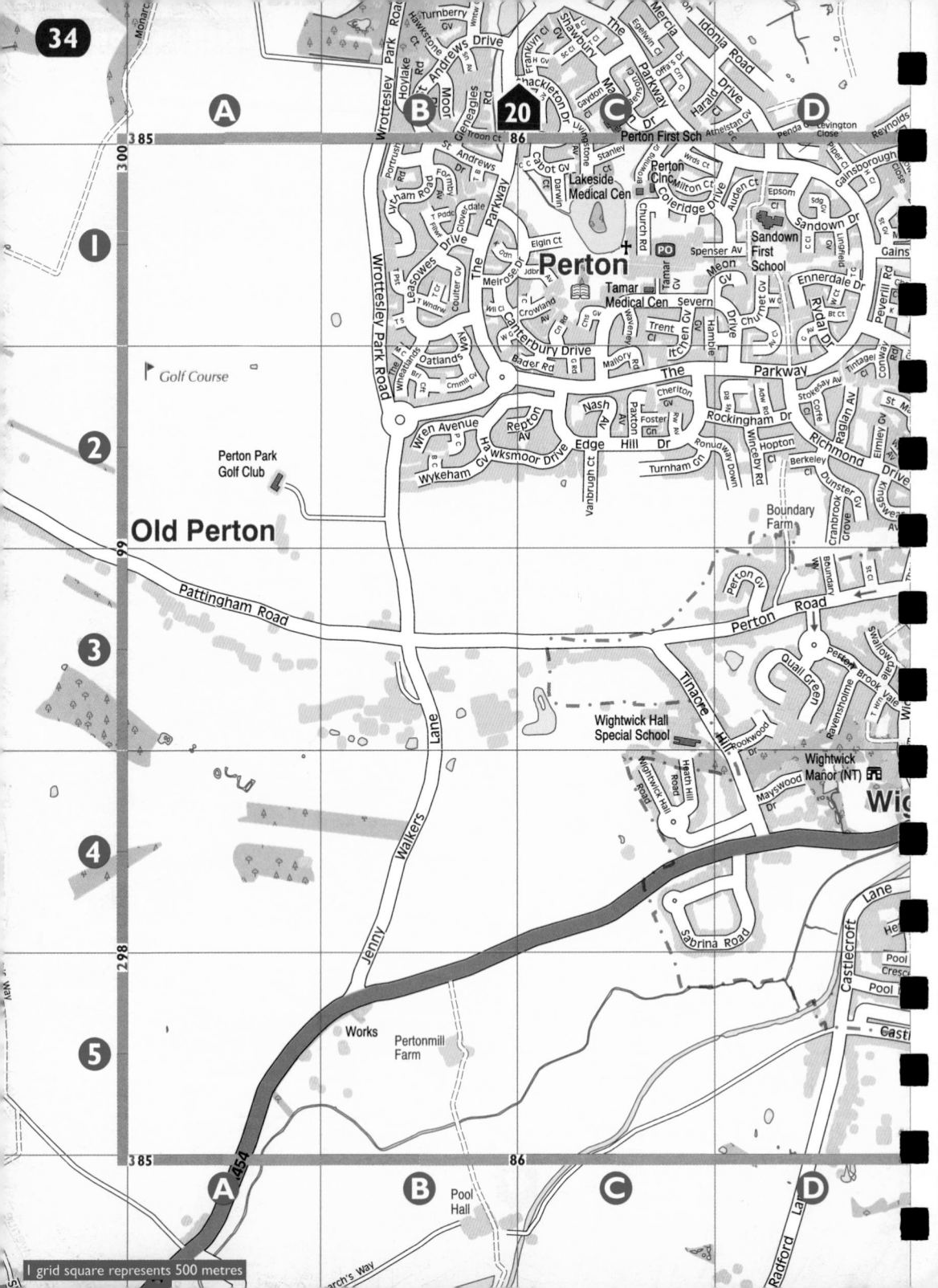

A
B
20
C
D

Turnberry Gv
Wrottesley Park Road
Hoylake
St Andrews Drive
Moor
Gleneagles
Troon Gv
Shackleton Dr
Livingstone
Shawbury
The
Parkway
Mercia
Idonia Road
Harald Drive
Reynolds

385
300
86

Perton First Sch
Penda
Levington
Close

St Andrews Dr
Portrust
Vyham Road
Darwin
Lakeside
Medical Cen
Perton
Clinic
Auden Ct
Epsom
Gainsborough
Sandown
Dr

1

Leasowes
Drive
Meon
Perton
Sandown
First
School
Ennerdale Dr
Peverill Rd
Gains

The Parkway
Melrose Gr
Elgin Ct
Perton
Tamar
Medical Cen
Spenser Av
Rydal D
Gv

Crowland
Av
Catterbury Drive
Trent
Cl
Itchen
Severn
Hamble
Churnet Gv
Richmond
Drive

Oatlands
Bader Rd
Mallory Rd
The
Parkway

2

Wren Avenue
Repton
Av
Nash
Av
Cheriton
Gv
Rockingham Dr
Raglan Av
St M

Wykeham
wksmoor Drive
Edge Hill Dr
Paxton
Foster
Gn
Winceby Rd
Hopton
Corfe
Kings

Vanbrugh Ct
Turnham
Ronudway Down
Berkeley
Cl
Dunster
Cl
Cranbrook
Grove

Boundary
Farm

Old Perton

Perton Park
Golf Club

Perton Gv
Perton
Road

Golf Course

99

385

Pattingham Road

3

Perton Road
Quail Green
Perton Brook Vale
Swallowdale
Ravensholme
Wig

Tinacre
Lane
Wightwick Hall
Special School
Rookwood
Dr

4

Walkers
Lane
Wightwick Hall
Heath Hill Road
Wightwick
Manor (NT)
Mayswood
Dr

Sabrina Road
Castlecroft
Lane
He

298

Jenny
Lane
Works
Pertonmill
Farm
Pool
Cresc
Pool

5

385
A454
86

A
B
Pool
Hall
C
D

Radford La

Castlecroft

arch's Way

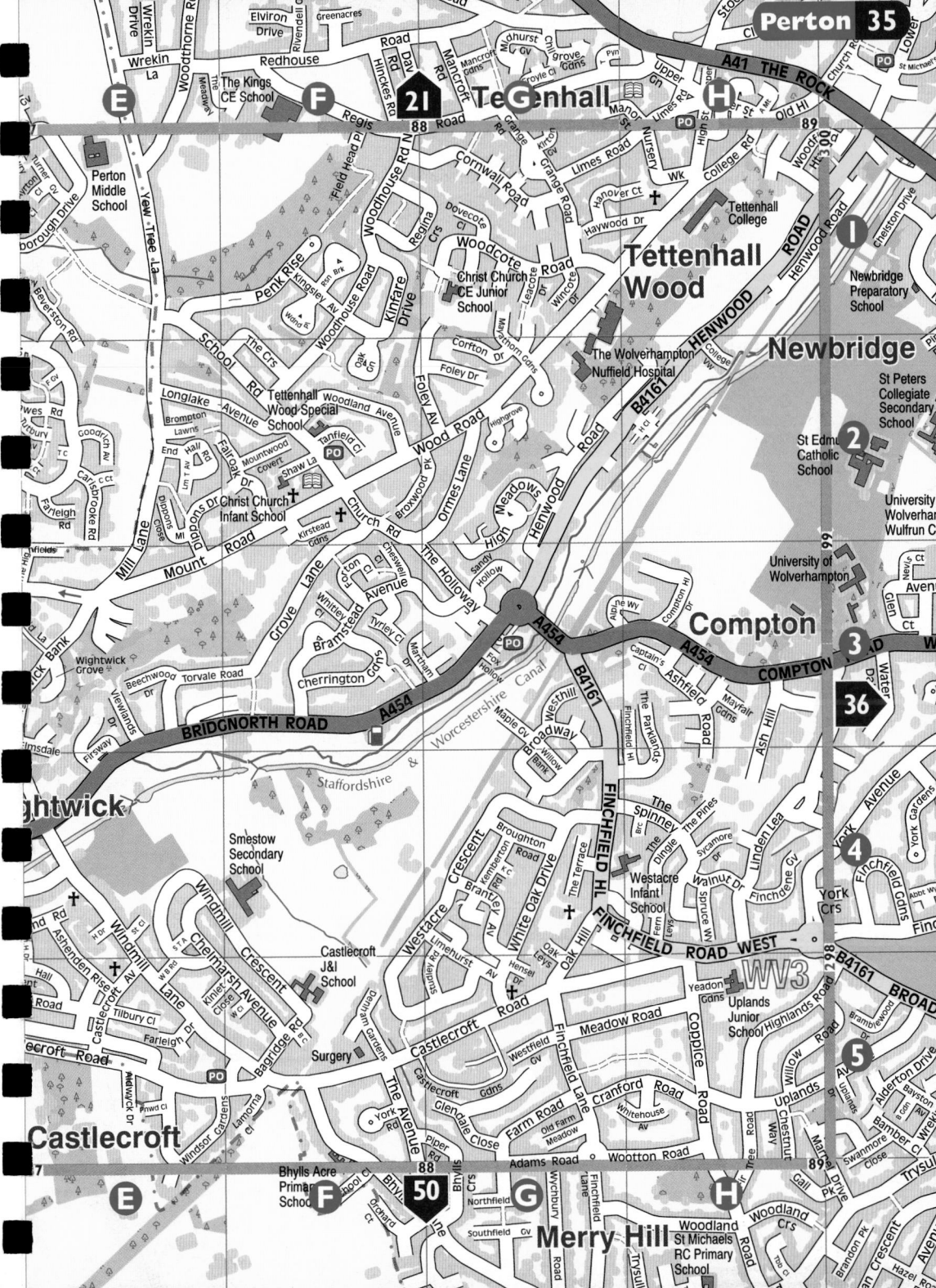
Tettenhall
Tettenhall Wood
Newbridge
Compton
Wightwick
Castlecroft
Merry Hill
WV3
A41 THE ROCK
HENWOOD ROAD
B4161
A454
BRIDGNORTH ROAD
COMPTON ROAD
FINCHFIELD HL
FINCHFIELD ROAD WEST
B4161 BROAD
Staffordshire & Worcestershire Canal
The Kings CE School
Perton Middle School
Tettenhall College
Christ Church CE Junior School
The Wolverhampton Nuffield Hospital
Newbridge Preparatory School
St Peters Collegiate Secondary School
St Edmu Catholic School
University of Wolverhampton
Tettenhall Wood Special School
Christ Church Infant School
Smestow Secondary School
Westacre Infant School
Castlecroft J&I School
Uplands Junior School
Surgery
Bhylls Acre Primary School
St Michaels RC Primary School
Wrekin Drive
Wrekin La
Woodthorne Rd
Elviron Drive
Greenacres
Redhouse Road
Regis Road
Mancroft Rd
Mancroft Gdns
Hinckes Rd
Davy Rd
Midhurst Gv
Chilgrove Gdns
Croyle Cl
Upper Gn
Manor St
Limes Rd
Old Hl
Yew Tree La
Field Head Pl
Woodhouse Rd N
Woodhouse Road
Cornwall Road
Grange Road
Limes Road
Nursery Wk
College Rd
Hanover Ct
Haywood Dr
Henwood Road
Chelston Drive
Penk Rise
Kingsley Av
Regina Crs
Dovecote Cl
Woodcote Road
Kinfare Drive
Leacote Dr
Wincote Dr
Beverston Rd
School Rd
The Crs
Corfton Dr
Mayhorn Gdns
Foley Dr
Foley Av
College Vw
Longlake Avenue
Woodland Avenue
Brompton Lawns
Tanfield Cl
Wood Road
Highgrove
Fairoak Dr
Mountwood Covert
Shaw La
Goodrich Av
Carisbrooke Rd
Farleigh Rd
Broxwood Pk
Ormes Lane
High Meadows
Henwood Road
Dippons Dr
Dippons Close
Mill Lane
Mount Road
Church Rd
Kirstead Gdns
Grove Lane
Forton Cl
Cheswell Cl
The Holloway
Sandy Hollow
Bramstead Avenue
Whitley Cl
Tyrley Cl
Martham Dr
Cherrington Gdns
Fox Hollow
Alpine Wy
Compton Hl
Nevis Ct
Glen Ct
Wightwick Grove
Wightwick Bank
Beechwood Dr
Torvale Road
Viewlands Dr
Firsway
Elmsdale
Captain's Cl
Ashfield Road
Mayfair Gdns
Ash Hill
Water Dr
Westhill
Maple Gv
Broadway
Willow Bank
The Parklands
Finchfield Hl
York Avenue
York Gardens
The Spinney
The Pines
The Dingle
Sycamore Dr
Linden Lea
Broughton Road
Westacre Crescent
Kemberton Rd
Brantley Av
White Oak Drive
The Terrace
Walnut Dr
Spruce Wy
Fern Leys
Finchdene Gv
Finchfield Gdns
York Crs
Abbot Wy
Windmill Crescent
Chelmarsh Avenue
Windmill Lane
Castlecroft Av
Ashenden Rise
Tilbury Cl
Farleigh Dr
Kinlet Close
Bagridge Rd
Limehurst Av
Studley Rd
Hensel Dr
Oak Leys
Oak Hill
Denham Gardens
Castlecroft Road
Meadow Road
Westfield Gv
Finchfield Lane
Coppice Road
Yeadon Gdns
Highlands Road
Willow Road
Bramblewood Dr
Alderton Drive
Bayston Av
Uplands Av
Castlecroft Gdns
The Avenue
York Rd
Glendale Close
Farm Road
Old Farm Meadow
Cranford Road
Whitehouse Av
Chestnut Way
Marnel Drive
Swanmore Close
Bamber Cl
Wrekin
Trysull
Aldwick Dr
Windsor Gardens
Lamorna Cl
Piper Rd
Adams Road
Wootton Road
Bhylls Crs
Northfield Gv
Southfield Gv
Wychbury Road
Woodland Road
Woodland Crs
Gail Pk
Brandon Pk
Hazel Road
88
89
298
299
300
21
36
50

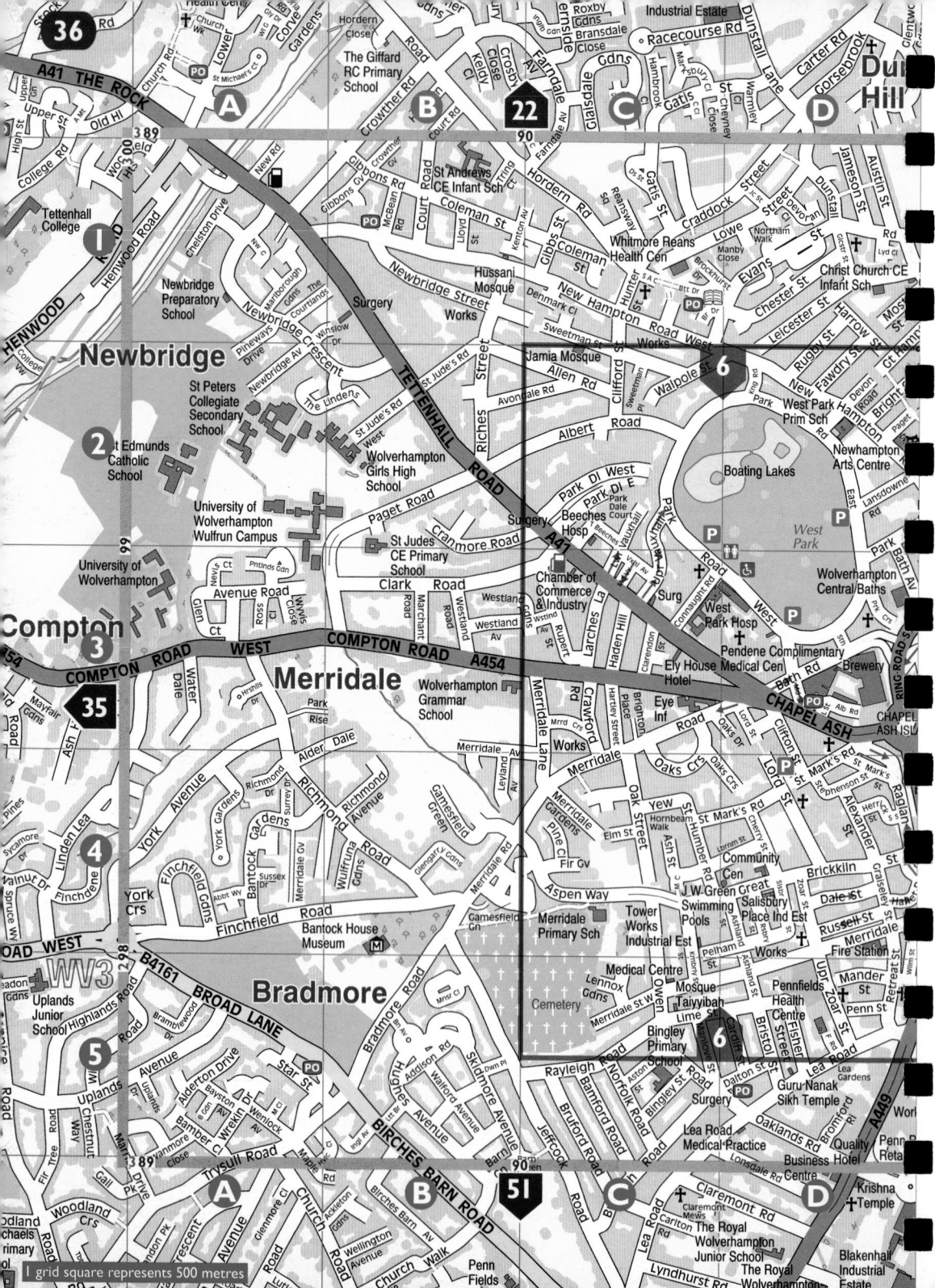

I grid square represents 500 metres

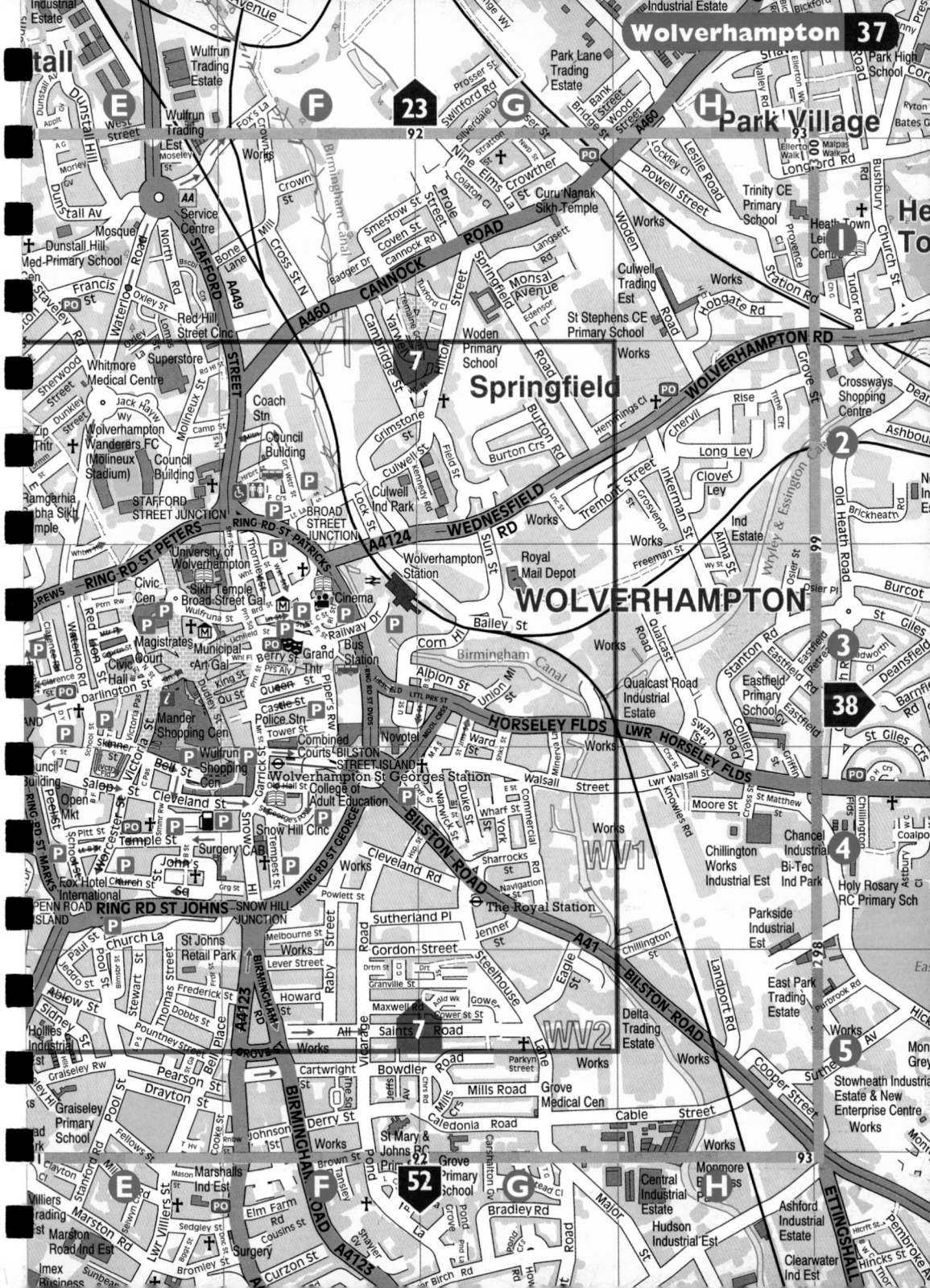

Park Village
Springfield
WOLVERHAMPTON
WV1
WV2
Wolverhampton Station
Wolverhampton St Georges Station
The Royal Station
Wolverhampton Wanderers FC (Molineux Stadium)
University of Wolverhampton
Mander Shopping Cen
Wulfrun Shopping Cen
Bus Station
Birmingham Canal
Wyrley & Essington Canal
CANNOCK ROAD
A460
STAFFORD STREET
A449
WOLVERHAMPTON RD
WEDNESFIELD RD
A4124
HORSELEY FLDS
LWR HORSELEY FLDS
BILSTON ROAD
A41
BIRMINGHAM ROAD
A4123
RING RD ST PETERS
RING RD ST PATRICKS
RING RD ST GEORGE
RING RD ST JOHNS
RING RD ST MARKS
STAFFORD STREET JUNCTION
BROAD STREET JUNCTION
BILSTON STREET ISLAND
SNOW HILL JUNCTION
PENN ROAD ISLAND
ETTINGSHALL

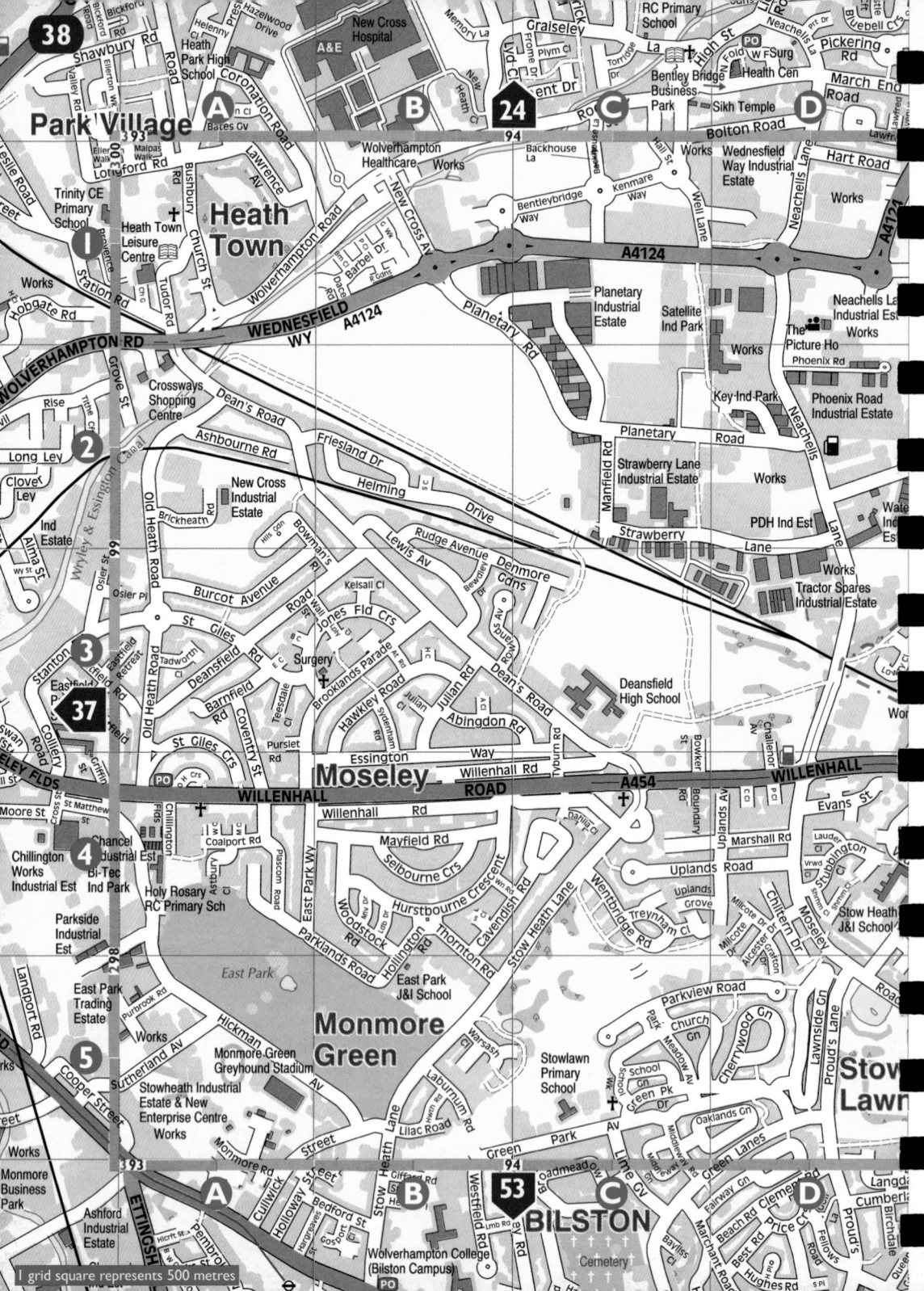
38
Park Village
Shawbury Rd
Heath Park High School
Coronation Road
New Cross Hospital
A&E
Graiseley
RC Primary School
High St
Bentley Bridge Business Park
Health Cen
Sikh Temple
March End Road
Pickering Rd
Bolton Road
24
A
B
C
D
393
94
Longford Rd
Lawrence Av
Bushbury Rd
Wolverhampton Healthcare
Works
Backhouse La
Wednesfield Way Industrial Estate
Hart Road
Trinity CE Primary School
Heath Town
Heath Town Leisure Centre
Church St
Wolverhampton Road
New Cross Av
Bentleybridge Way
Kenmare Way
Well Lane
Neachells Lane
A4124
Station Rd
Hobgate Rd
Tudor Rd
Barbel Dr
WEDNESFIELD WY
Planetary Industrial Estate
Planetary Rd
Satellite Ind Park
Neachells La Industrial Est
The Picture Ho
Phoenix Rd
WOLVERHAMPTON RD
Grove St
Crossways Shopping Centre
Dean's Road
Key Ind Park
Phoenix Road Industrial Estate
Rise
Long Ley
Clover Ley
Ashbourne Rd
Friesland Dr
Planetary Road
Helming Drive
Manfield Rd
Strawberry Lane Industrial Estate
Wyrley & Essington Canal
New Cross Industrial Estate
Brickheath Rd
Old Heath Road
Ind Estate
Alma St
Bowman's Rd
Lewis Av
Rudge Avenue
Denmore Gdns
Strawberry Lane
PDH Ind Est
Tractor Spares Industrial Estate
Osier St
Osier Pl
Burcot Avenue
Kelsall Cl
Jones Fld Crs
St Giles Rd
Tadworth Cl
Deansfield Rd
Stanton Rd
Eastfield Retreat
Surgery
Brooklands Parade
Hawkley Road
Julian Rd
Abingdon Rd
Deansfield High School
37
Barnfield Rd
Coventry St
Teesdale Cl
Colliery Road
St Giles Crs
Purslet Rd
Essington Way
Willenhall Rd
Tyburn Rd
Bowker St
Challenor Av
Moseley
A454
WILLENHALL ROAD
Moore St
St Matthew St
Chillington Flds
Coalport Rd
Mayfield Rd
Selbourne Crs
Hurstbourne Crescent
Cavendish Rd
Boundary Rd
Uplands Av
Evans St
Marshall Rd
Uplands Road
Uplands Grove
Stubbington Cl
Chancel Industrial Est
Chillington Works Industrial Est
Bi-Tec Ind Park
Holy Rosary RC Primary Sch
Astbury Cl
Plascom Road
East Park Wy
Woodstock Rd
Hollington Rd
Thornton Rd
Stow Heath Lane
Wentbridge Rd
Treynham Cl
Milcote Dr
Alcester Dr
Grafton Dr
Chiltern Dr
Moseley Rd
Stow Heath J&I School
Parkside Industrial Est
298
Parklands Road
East Park
East Park J&I School
Landport Rd
East Park Trading Estate
Purbrook Rd
Works
Hickman Av
Monmore Green
Parkview Road
Park Church Gn
Meadow Av
Cherrywood Gn
Lawnside Gn
Proud's Lane
Stow Lawn
Cooper Street
Sutherland Av
Monmore Green Greyhound Stadium
Warsash Cl
Laburnum Rd
Stowlawn Primary School
School Gn
Green Pk Dr
Stowheath Industrial Estate & New Enterprise Centre
Lilac Road
Oaklands Gn
Green Park Av
Green Lanes
Lime Gv
Middleway Rd
Street
Monmore Business Park
Monmore Rd
Broadmeadow
53
BILSTON
Cullwick
Holloway Street
Bedford St
Stow Heath Lane
Giffard Rd
Westfield Rd
Ashford Industrial Estate
ETTINGSH
Wolverhampton College (Bilston Campus)
Cemetery
Bayliss Cl
Marchant Road
Fairway Gn
Beach Rd
Best Rd
Price Cres
Clement Rd
Hughes Rd
Fellows Road
Proud's
Cumberland
Birchdale
1 grid square represents 500 metres

Wednesfield High School
WEDNESFIELD WAY
WADDENS BROOK LANE
Merrills Hall
Wolverhampton
Walsall
FIBBERSLEY B4484
Fibbersley
Willenhall Town FC
Noose Lane
Watery Lane
Lakeside JMI Sch
WV13
Reflex Ind Park
WEDNESFIELD RD
WELLINGTON PL
Thorne Road
Clothier St Prim School
Clothier Street
Bloxwich Rd S
Victoria Street
Temple Road
TEMPLE BAR
Cemetery Road
Villiers St
Monmer La
Ashmore Lake Road
Ashmore Lake
WILLENHALL
Spring Lane Industrial Est
SANDBEDS ROAD
Morgan Cl
Lake Way
Monmer Close Ind Est
St Annes Industrial Estate
Elm Street Infant School
Chancel Industrial Estate
Albion Rd Jun Sch
New Hall St
Moat St
Cem
Wood St
FIELD ST
Park Road
Pinson Rd
PINSON RD B4484
Portobello
Middleton Trading Estate
Shri Guru Ravidass Temple
Croft Foundry Industrial Est
Wolverhampton St
Surgery
SOMERFORD PL
B4464 NEW ROAD
The Lock Mus
Police Stn
Town Hall
Willenhall Leisure Centre
WALSALL ST
St Giles CE Prim Sch
Birmingham St
BILSTON LANE
Willenhall Trading Estate
BILSTON ST
ROSE HL
B4484
Longacre
Longacres
A454 THE KEYWAY
BILSTON LANE B4590
Owen Road Trading Est
Neptune Ind Est
ARMSTRONG WY
A463
A462
Keyway Retail Park
St Thomas More Catholic School
Vinculum Wy
BILSTON ROAD
Moseley Park School & Technology College
Waite Road
Five Oaks Road
Dilloways Lane
Hawksswell Drive
Beccles Drive
Rockland Gdns
Hunters Close
Darlaston Lane
Romney House Industrial Estate
Ames Road
Surgery
25
40
54
96
97
95
E F G H I
1 2 3 4 5

40
26
39
55
A
B
C
D
1
2
3
4
5
397
398
300
298
High Road
Sandbeds Road
Clarkes La
Crescent Rd
A462
Bentley Lane
Cemetery
Treetops Drive
Oldhall Special School
Rosedale CE Inf Sch
Shorth Heath Junior Sch
Surgery
Brackendale Shopping Cen
Lodge Farm Primary School
Spring Lane Industrial Est
Ashmore Lake
Ashmore Lake Road
WILLENHALL
Bentley
Furzebank Way
Poplar Avenue
Stroud Av
Wing Cl
Star Cl
Rowlands Avenue
Monmouth Rd
Attlee Road
Lilac Gv
Lime Av
Edinburgh Avenue
Churchill Road
Bentley West Primary School
Jane L Special School
Quality Hotel
Wilkes Avenue
Cunningham Rd
King Charles Primary School
Mountbatten Rd
Wolverhampton Rd West
Wolverhampton Rd W
Pugh Crs
King Charles Avenue
Anson Road
B4464
Bentley Mill Industrial Est
Black Country Route
Willenhall Ind Est
St Annes Industrial Estate
Monmer Close Ind Est
Elm Street Infant School
Albion Rd Jun Sch
Slater St
Durham Av
Walsall Road
Sikh Temple
Coronation Avenue
Somerset Rd
Riverbank Road
Devon Road
County Bridge Primary School
Bure Grove
St Giles Prim Sch
Birmingham St
Shepwell Gn
Bilston Lane
Owen Road Industrial Estate
Owen Road Trading Est
Owen Rd
Downs Road
Wellman's Rd
A454
Neptune Ind Est
Neptune Industrial Est
Keyway Retail Park
Vinculum Wy
A463
Lane B4590
Midland Road
Crescent Works Industrial Park
Holland Ind Park
Monarch's Way
Willenhall Rd
Bentley Rd South
Marshland Wy
Travel Inn
Axcess 10 Business Park
Wrexham Avenue
Bentley Mill Way
Millers Close
Cemetery Road
Phoenix Works Industrial Estate
Heath Works
Works
Darlaston Green
Kendricks Rd
Tramway Cl
Richards St
Wesson Rd
Yardley St
Garrington St
Addenbrooke St
Horton St
Bush St
Owen St
Ames Road
Hall St East
St Josephs Catholic Prim Sch
Romney House Ind Estate
Salisbury Primary
1 grid square represents 500 metres

Priestley Road
Davy Rd
Cavendish **E**
Crompton Cl
Edison
Surgery
Lister Road **F**
Harvey Cl

27 400
Beechdale School
Stephenson Avenue **G**
Cable Dr

H Norfolk Place

Webster Road
Suffolk Place
Essex St
North Walsall Primary Sch
Darby Hfd

Reedswood Way
Norfolk Rd
Reedswood Retail Park
Superstore
Reedswood Retail Park

UPPER GN LANE
A34 GREEN LANE
Works
Crown Whf Shop Park
Stockton Close

Northcote St
Gladstone Street
Alma St

I
Surgery
Cannon St N
Proffitt St
Portland
Marlowe Road
North

Victory La
Birchover Road
Parkview-Crs
Basalt Cl
Bentley Dr
Armstrong Dr
Red River
Bentley
Burgh Wy
Pike Rd
Balmoral Wy

Croft Street
Hospital St
Croft JMI Sch
Croft St
Penkridge

WS2
Bentley Lane Ind Park
Pouk Hill
Wayside Walk
Westville Rd
Dalton Road

Miner Street
Reedswood Lane
Reedswood
Old Birchills

Birchills
Mary St
Lewis St
Hall St
Whitehouse St
Ashmore Ind Est
Short Acre St
Prim Sch
2

Bentley Lane
Bentley New
Bentley Dr
Kent Av
Edward St
Rowland Street
Pargeter Street
Raleigh Street
Cairns Street
Jessel Road
Hollyhedge La
Hollyhedge Cl
Neale St
Thomas Adams St
Birchills Health Cen
Dalkeith Street
Birchills Street
Farringdon Street
4
Birchills CE Sch Fire Stn
Mosque

Maple Leaf Industrial Est
Bloxwich Lane Industrial Est
Bentley Lane
Bentley Drive Prim Sch
Friezeland Rd
Deemore
Laneside Gdns
Bentley Place
PO
Works
BLUE LA W
Crown-Wharf Shopping Centre
3
Stafford St
P
Walsall Leath Muse
Mag Cts
Littleton

M6
Bloxwich Lane
Wolverhampton Rd
WOLVERHAMPTON ROAD A454
WOLVERHAMPTON RD A454
P
42
The New Art Gallery Walsall
Upr Navigation Steet
Station St
Walsall Shop Cen
P
P
Coll

Junction 10
Primley Infant School
York Av
Blay Av
Ripon Rd
Drayton St
Drayton Street
Sai Medical Centre
Moat Road
Forrester St
Forrester St Prec
P
Town Wharf Business Park
Charles St
Marsh La
Frederick St
Union
Bridgeman Street
Premier Business Park
P
Clinic

Alumwell Junior School
Alum Well Avenue
Chester Pl
Norwich Av
Exeter Pl
Jerome
Primley Pl
Dorothy Pattison Hospital
A&E The Manor General Hospital
Pleck Business Park
Rollingmill Business Park
Manor Industrial Est
Upper Brook St
Upr Short St
Short St
Brook St
Business Park
Jerome Retail Park
4
Palfrey Girls Sch
Bradford St
Vicarage Pl

Alumwell Community School
Ely Rd
Southbourne
Durham Rd
Durham Road
Walsall College of Arts & Tech
Ida Rd
PO
Superstore
Rollingmill St
Brineton Industrial Estate
Cemetery
Clement St
Queen Street
Long Street
Corporation St West
Meadow St
Tasker St
Surgery
Mount St
Glebe St
Baba Balak Nah Temple
Brace St

Primley Av
Reservoir Pl
Reservoir St St Johns Rd
Flaxhall Street
Scarborough Rd
Brinton St
PLECK ROAD
Pleck Industrial Estate
Regal Dr
Fairground Way
Wednesbury Road
5
Caldmore
South Street
Camden St
Station St
Victoria St

Works
Reservoir Rd
Nahak Sar Sikh Temple
Prince St
Quentin St
Old Caledon
4
Luqman Medical Cntess
H
Earl St
Palfrey Infant School
Spout La

DARLASTON ROAD A4038
E
Hough Road
Hucker Road
Berkeley Street
Kingsley St
Dora Street
Sheridan St
F
56 400
Oxford Street
G
PO Wednesbury Rd
Ford St
Hillary Primary
Crescent
Whitmore St
Rosamond Rd
Palfrey Junior
Whitehall Rd
Dale St

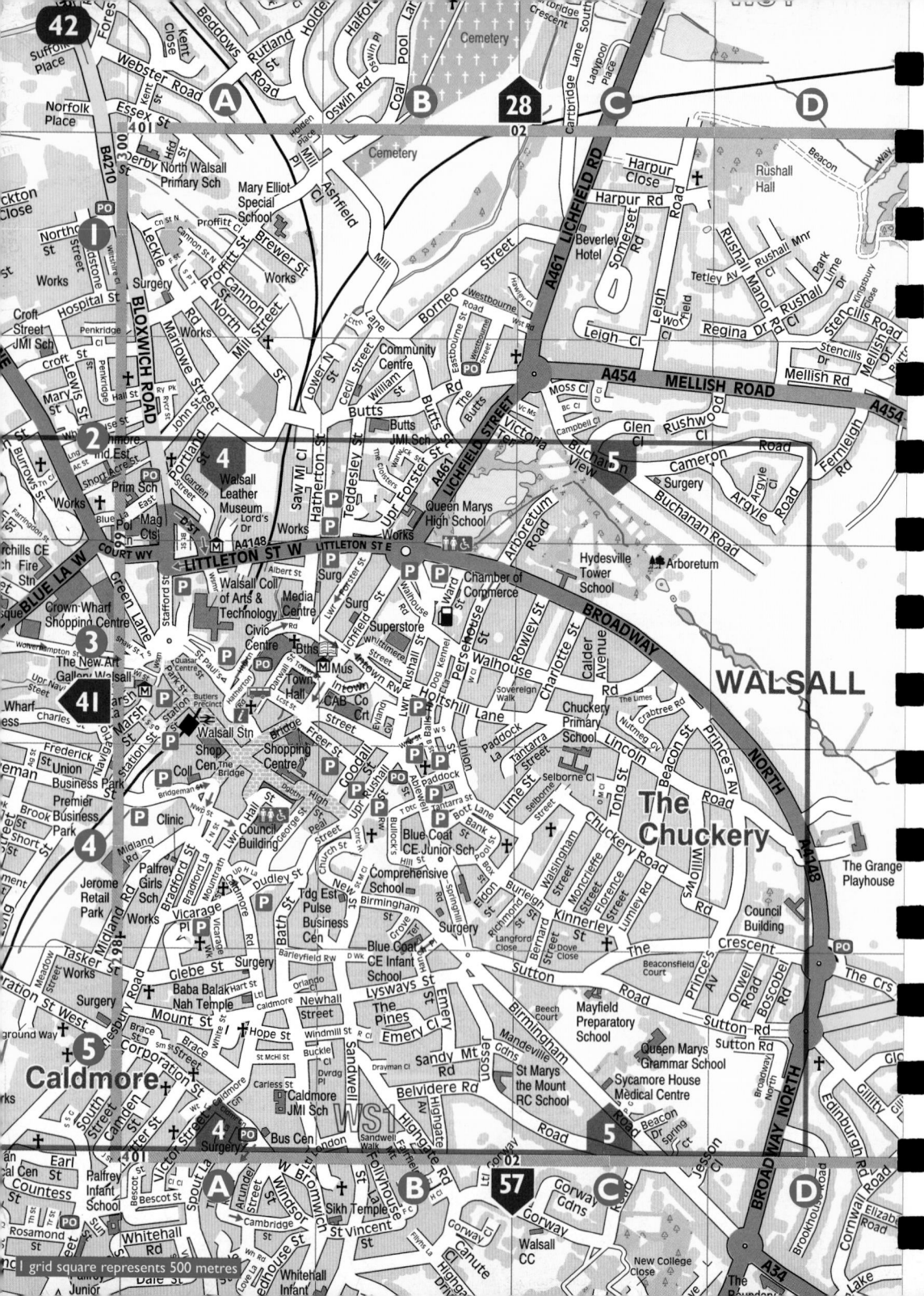

42
28
41
57
A
B
C
D
1
2
3
4
5
Suffolk Place
Norfolk Place
Kent Close
Webster Road
Beddows Road
Rutland St
Essex St
Oswin Rd
Coal Pool Lane
Cemetery
Cartbridge Crescent
Cartbridge Lane South
Ladypool Place
Derby St
North Walsall Primary Sch
Mary Elliot Special School
Proffitt St
Brewer St
Cannon St North
Mill Street
Ashfield Cl
Harpur Close
Harpur Rd
Somerset Rd
Leigh Rd
Leigh Cl
Beverley Hotel
Rushall Hall
Beacon Way
Rushall Manor Rd
Rushall Mnr Cl
Park Lime Dr
Tetley Av
Regina Dr
Kingsbury Close
Stencills Road
Stencills Dr
Mellish Rd
A461 LICHFIELD RD
A454 MELLISH ROAD
A454
B4210
Hospital St
Croft Street JMI Sch
Penkridge Cl
Croft St
Lewis St
Mary St
Works
Surgery
BLOXWICH ROAD
Marlowe Street
John St
Borneo Street
Westbourne Road
Eastbourne St
Westbourne Street
Community Centre
Cecil Street
William St
Lower N St
Butts Rd
The Butts
Butts St
Butts JMI Sch
Moss Cl
Glen Cl
Rushwood Cl
Campbell Cl
Victoria Ter
Buchanan View
Buchanan Road
Cameron Road
Argyle Cl
Argyle Road
Fernleigh Rd
Burrows St
Short Acre St
Prim Sch
Blue La E
Pol Stn
Mag Cts
Portland St
Garden Street
Walsall Leather Museum
Lord's Dr
Saw Mi Cl
Hatherton St
Teddesley St
Upr Forster St
Queen Marys High School
Arboretum Road
Arboretum
Hydesville Tower School
A148
LITTLETON ST W
LITTLETON ST E
COURT WY
BLUE LA W
Green Lane
Stafford St
Walsall Coll of Arts & Technology
Media Centre
Albert St
Surg
Chamber of Commerce
Ward St
Persehouse St
Rowley St
Charlotte St
Calder Avenue
BROADWAY
Crown Wharf Shopping Centre
Wolverhampton St
The New Art Gallery Walsall
Civic Centre
Bths
Mus
Town Hall
Intown Rw
Whittimere Street
Superstore
Lichfield St
Rushall St
Walhouse Rd
Holtshill Lane
Sovereign Walk
WALSALL
The Limes
Crabtree Rd
Nutmeg Gv
Chuckery Primary School
Lincoln Rd
Beacon St
Prince's Av
Paddock La
Tantarra Street
Selborne Cl
Tong St
Charles St
Marsh St
Station St
Walsall Stn
Shop Cen
The Bridge
Bridge Street
Freer St
Shopping Centre
CAB Co Crt
Frederick St
Union Business Park
Premier Business Park
Navigation St
Bridgeman St
Coll
Clinic
Council Building
Goodall St
Upr Rushall St
Ablewell St
Paddock La
High St
Peal Street
George St
Lwr Hall La
Lime St
Selborne Street
Chuckery Road
Walsingham Street
Moncrieffe Street
Florence Street
Lumley Rd
Willows Rd
The Chuckery
NORTH
A4148
The Grange Playhouse
Brook St
Short St
Midland Rd
Jerome Retail Park
Palfrey Girls Sch
Bradford St
Bradford La
Mountrath St
Caldmore Rd
Dudley St
Vicarage Pl
Vicarage Wk
Church St
New St
Blue Coat CE Junior Sch
Bank St
Pool St
Bullock's Row
Bott Lane
Comprehensive School
Tdg Est Pulse Business Cen
Birmingham St
Grove Ter
Springhill Rd
Eldon St
Burleigh St
Richmond St
Kinnerley St
Langford Close
Bernard Street
Dove Close
The Crescent
Council Building
Beaconsfield Court
Tasker St
Meadow Street
Glebe St
Surgery
Barleyfield Rw
Blue Coat CE Infant School
Sutton Road
Prince's Av
Orwell Road
Boscobel Rd
The Crs
Corporation St West
Chesbury Road
Baba Balak Nah Temple
Hart St
Mount St
Caldmore
Newhall Street
Lysways St
The Pines
Emery St
Emery Cl
Birmingham Road
Mayfield Preparatory School
Beech Court
Sutton Rd
Hope St
Windmill St
White St
Brace Street
Sandwell St
Sandy Mt Rd
Jesson Rd
Mandeville Gdns
St Marys the Mount RC School
Queen Marys Grammar School
Sycamore House Medical Centre
Caldmore
Corporation St
South Street
Camden St
Carless St
Caldmore JMI Sch
Belvidere Rd
Highgate Av
WS1
Victor Street
Surgery
Bus Cen
Sandwell Walk
Fairfield Rd
Highgate Rd
Beacon Dr
Spring Ct
Jesson Cl
BROADWAY NORTH
Broadway North
Edinburgh Rd
Gillity
Earl St
Countess St
Palfrey Infant School
Bescot St
Spout La
Arundel Street
Windsor St
W Bromwich St
Follyhouse La
Sikh Temple
St Vincent St
Gorway Gdns
Gorway Cl
Gorway Road
Walsall CC
Canute
Cambridge St
Rosamond St
Whitehall Rd
Whitehall Infant
Dale St
New College Close
A34
Brookhouse Road
Cornwall Road
Elizabeth Road
1 grid square represents 500 metres

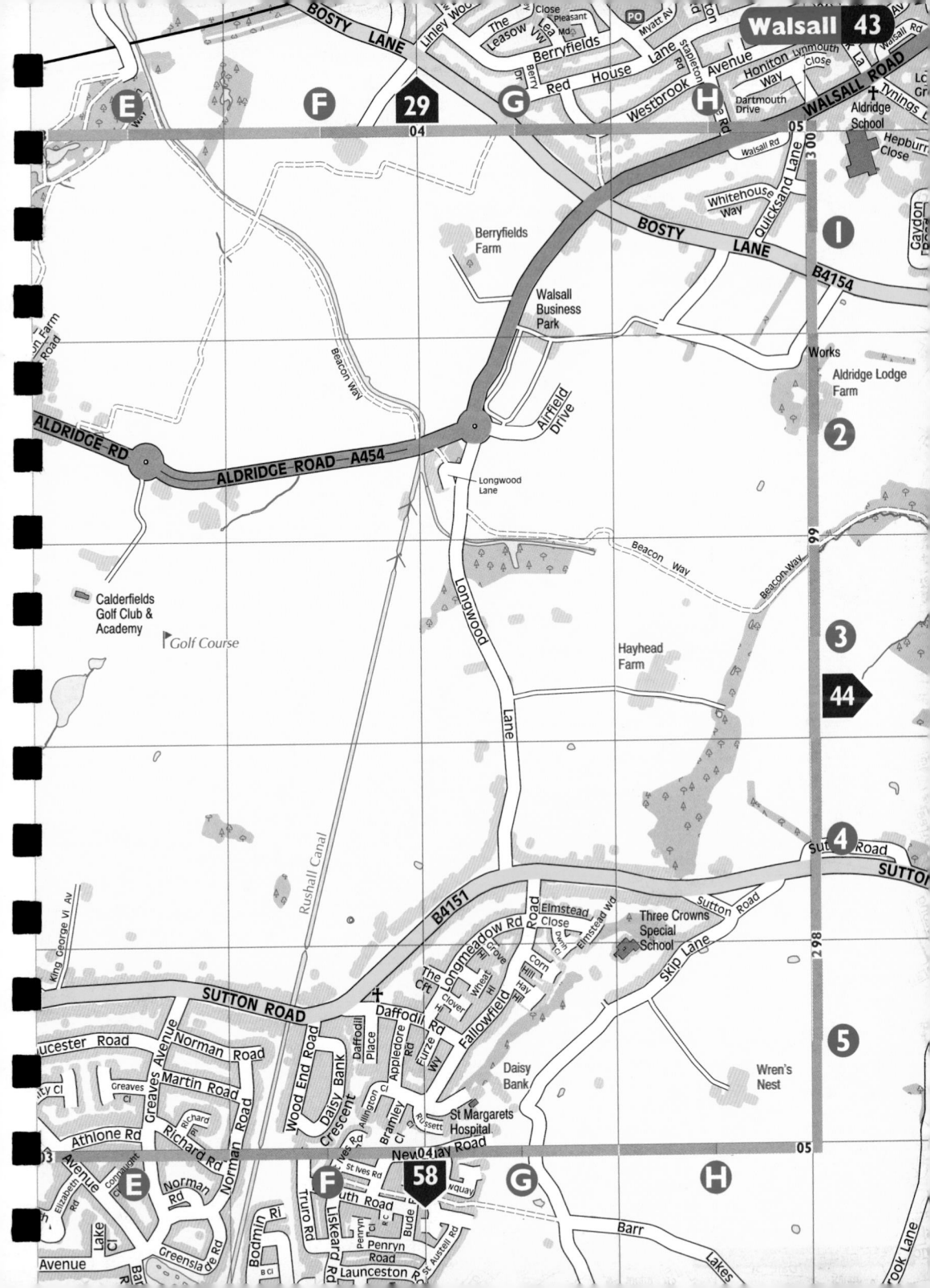
BOSTY LANE
Berryfields
Red House Lane
Westbrook Avenue
Honiton Way
Dartmouth Drive
WALSALL ROAD
Aldridge School
Hepburn Close
29
04
05
Walsall Rd
Whitehouse Way
Quicksand Lane
BOSTY LANE
B4154
Berryfields Farm
Walsall Business Park
Works
Aldridge Lodge Farm
Beacon Way
Airfield Drive
ALDRIDGE RD
ALDRIDGE ROAD A454
Longwood Lane
Beacon Way
Longwood Lane
Calderfields Golf Club & Academy
Golf Course
Hayhead Farm
44
Rushall Canal
B4151
SUTTON ROAD
Sutton Road
Elmstead Close
Longmeadow Rd
Three Crowns Special School
Skip Lane
Daffodil Rd
Daffodil Place
Fallowfield Road
Norman Road
Martin Road
Greaves Avenue
Wood End Road
Daisy Bank Crescent
Daisy Bank
Wren's Nest
St Margarets Hospital
Athlone Rd
Richard Rd
Newquay Road
58
Barr
Penryn Road
Launceston Rd
Liskeard Rd
Truro Rd
Bodmin Ri
Greensla de Rd
Avenue
Lake Cl
King George VI Av

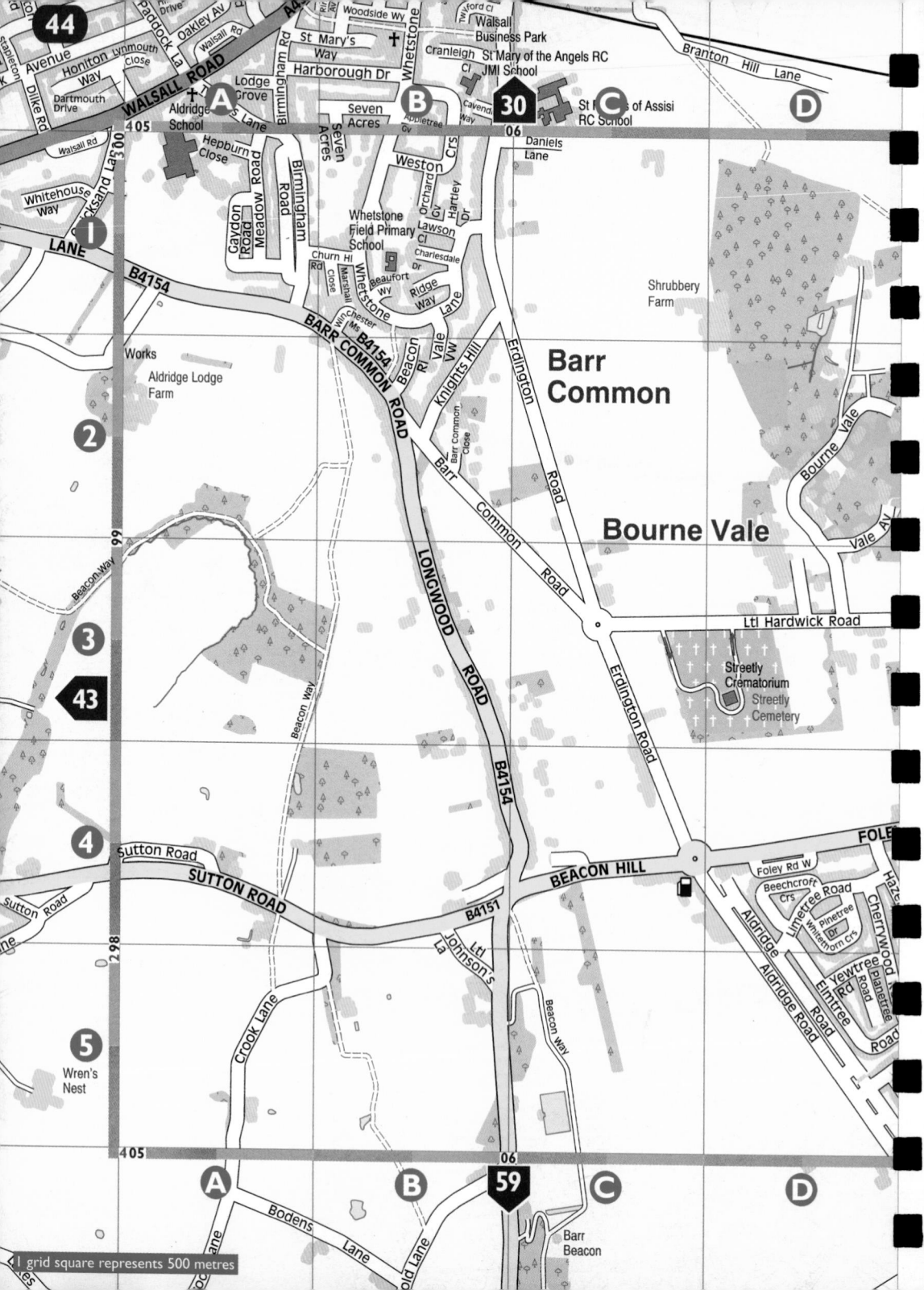

44
30
43
59
A
B
C
D
1
2
3
4
5
405
06
300
99
298
WALSALL ROAD
Walsall Rd
Oakley Av
Paddock La
Avenue
Honiton Way
Lynmouth Close
Dartmouth Drive
Dike Rd
Aldridge School
Lodge Grove
Birmingham Rd
St Mary's Way
Harborough Dr
Woodside Wy
Whetstone
Walsall Business Park
Cranleigh Cl
St Mary of the Angels RC JMI School
Seven Acres
Appletree Gv
Cavendish Way
St Francis of Assisi RC School
Branton Hill Lane
Daniels Lane
Hepburn Close
Gaydon Road
Meadow Road
Birmingham Road
Weston Crs
Orchard Gv
Hartley Dr
Whetstone Field Primary School
Lawson Cl
Charlesdale Dr
Churn Hl Rd
Close
Marshall
Whetstone
Beaufort Wy
Ridge Way
Lane
Whitehouse Way
Sandlands La
LANE
B4154
BARR COMMON ROAD
Winchester Ms
Beacon Rl
Vale Vw
Knights Hill
Erdington Road
Barr Common
Shrubbery Farm
Works
Aldridge Lodge Farm
Barr Common Close
Barr Common Road
Bourne Vale
Vale Av
Beacon Way
LONGWOOD ROAD
Ltl Hardwick Road
Streetly Crematorium
Streetly Cemetery
Erdington Road
Sutton Road
SUTTON ROAD
B4151
BEACON HILL
FOLE
Foley Rd W
Beechcroft Crs
Limetree Road
Pinetree Dr
Whitethorn Crs
Cherrywood
Aldridge Road
Elmtree Road
Yewtree Rd
Planetree Road
Road
Ltl Johnson's La
Crook Lane
Beacon Way
Wren's Nest
Bodens Lane
Old Lane
Barr Beacon
1 grid square represents 500 metres

Golf Course
Squirrel Walk
Beech Gate
Little A
Farm
08
09
300
Golf Course
Staffordshire County
Walsall
Cottage Ms
Little Aston Golf Club
Stonehouse Dr
Roman Pk
Roman
Claverdon Dr
Claverdon
Road
Barns Cft
Drive
Lane
Alderhithe Gv
Rosemary Drive
Royston Cha
Vercourt
Fallow Field
Roman Lane
Roman
The Headlands
Wayside Drive
Raglan Close
Windermere Dr
Chester Road
Lindrosa Road
Coniston Road
Leacliffe Wy
Newick Av
Little Aston Park Rd
Talbot Avenue
Talbot Av
Talbot Avenue
Leafy Gld
Chestnut Cl
Derwent Close
Grasmere Av
ROSEMARY
St Margaret's
Hardwick
Keswick Gv
Rydal
Chesterwood
Lester Gv
PO
Hardwick Road
Hardwick Road
Ltl Hardwick Rd
Leslie Rd
Burnett Road
Streetly Methodist Recreation Centre
Marwood Cft
Featherston Road
Streetly Wood
Sunnybank Close
The Downs
Carlton Cft
Horsley Rd
B4138
Bushey Cl
Ollison Dr
Redwood Cl
Carlton Av
Church Cl
Foley
Eastmoor Cl
46
Plainview Close
Greenacres Cl
Lane
Inglewood Grove
Chester Rd
Meadow Cl
Wood
FOLEY ROAD EAST
B4151
B74
The Old
ROAD WEST
B4151
ROAD
Highgate
Middleton Road
Redlands Way
Astor Rd
Streetly
Schoolacre Rl
Foley Wd Cl
Blackwood Road
Silver Birch Road
Grosvenor Avenue
Chester Road
Thorney Road
Chester Road
Manor Primary School
Fairgreen Way
Links Vw
ROAD
Sutton Coldfield Golf Club
Amberley Wy
Cedar Drive
Blackwood School
Egerton Rd
Langham Gn
Briar Av
Hawthorn Road
Icknield Close
Streetly Hockey & CC
Road
Streetly Clinic
Bracken Wy
Crest Vw
Mayfield Road
Daneways Cl
Pr Wy
Road
St Anne's RC JMI School
Broomlea Cl
Conifer Rd
Lrchw Crs
Manor
Avenue
Thornhill Park
Lowlands
Ferndale Road
PO
CHESTER ROAD
A452
THORNHILL
Frankburn Rd
Blackwood Drive
Nicholas Rd
Oakwood Dr
Alder Wy
Ashwood
Lilac Av
Northside Drive
Chstr Rd
Qns
Thornhill Park Dr
Whitley Dr
Tudor Gv
Millcroft Road
Maxholm Road
Laurel Dr
Bridle Lane
Bridlewood
Francis Cl
Kingscroft Rd
Kingscroft Close
07
08
09
Grove Wy
Banks
Valley Road
60
Lilac Av
Cowthorn Close
Golf Course
Hundred Acre
Hillsd Dr
Nighwood Dr
Crescent
Laneside Av
Chester Road
Works
Old Lindens Cl
Forest Close
Matchl Close
Aldridge Road
forth Dr
Oakmount Rd
A4138
Kims
A452
31
E
F
G
H
1
2
3
4
5

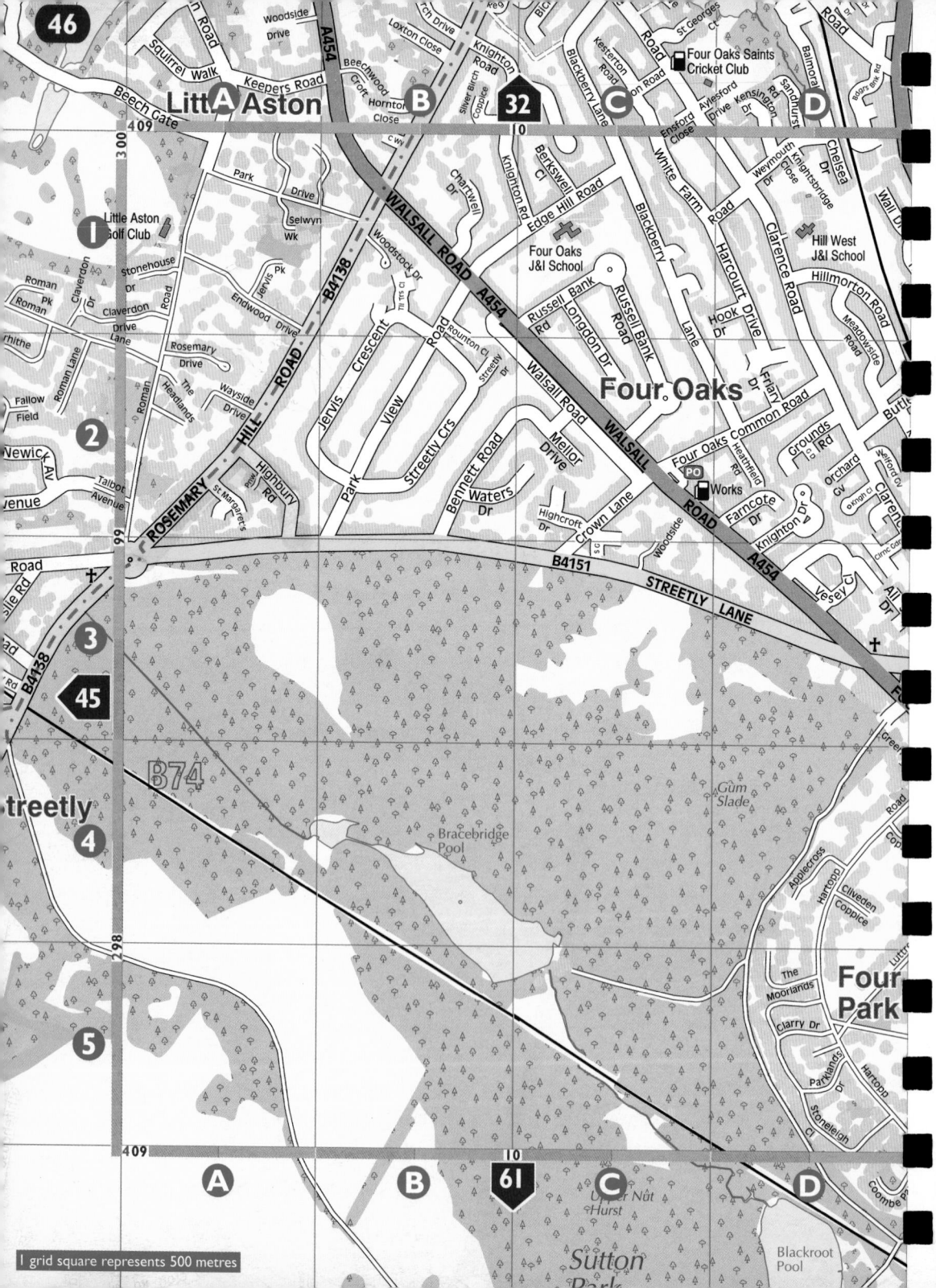

Little Aston
Four Oaks
Four Oaks Saints Cricket Club
Little Aston Golf Club
Four Oaks J&I School
Hill West J&I School
WALSALL ROAD
A454
B4138
ROSEMARY HILL ROAD
B4151
STREETLY LANE
Bracebridge Pool
Gum Slade
Upper Nut Hurst
Sutton Park
Blackroot Pool
Four Park
treetly
B74
Keepers Road
Squirrel Walk
Beech Gate
Park Drive
Selwyn Wk
Stonehouse Dr
Claverdon Drive
Roman Pk
Roman Lane
Rosemary Drive
The Headlands
Wayside Drive
Fallow Field
Newick Av
Talbot Avenue
Highbury Rd
St Margarets
Jervis Crescent
Park View Road
Streetly Crs
Woodstock Dr
Endwood Drive
Chartwell Dr
Knighton Rd
Knighton Road
Berkswell Cl
Edge Hill Road
Blackberry Lane
Kesterton Road
White Farm Road
Harcourt Drive
Clarence Road
Hillmorton Road
Meadowside Road
Russell Bank Rd
Russell Bank Road
Longdon Dr
Walsall Road
Mellor Drive
Bennett Road
Waters Dr
Highcroft Dr
Crown Lane
Woodside
Four Oaks Common Road
Heathfield Rd
Friary Dr
Hook Dr
Grounds Rd
Orchard Gv
Farncote Dr
Knighton Dr
Vesey Cl
Works
PO
Beechwood Croft
Hornton Close
Loxton Close
Silver Birch Coppice
Woodside Drive
Aylesford Drive
Ensford Close
Kensington Rd
Sandhurst
Balmoral
Weymouth Close
Knightsbridge
Chelsea Dr
Applecross
Hartopp
Cliveden Coppice
The Moorlands
Clarry Dr
Parklands Dr
Stoneleigh Cl
A
B
C
D
1
2
3
4
5
409
300
299
298
10
32
45
61

I grid square represents 500 metres

Hill Wood
33
48
62
Hill
Mere Green
Roughley
Ley Hill
Oaks
Moor Hall
Doe Bank
LICHFIELD ROAD
A5127
A454
A453
B4151
BELWELL LANE
LITTLE SUTTON ROAD
MERE GN RD
TAMWORTH RD
Butlers Lane Stn
Arthur Terry School
Mere Green Combined School
Works
Four Oaks Medical Centre
Surgery
Moor Hall Primary School
Little Sutton Primary School
Woodside Farm
Moor Hall Hotel
Moor Hall Golf Club
Golf Course
Coppice Primary School
Four Oaks Station
Highclare St Paul's School
St Josephs Catholic
Hathaway Road
Hillside Road
Gresley Cl
Village Road
Sara Close
Beaton Rd
Belwell Dr
Irnham Road
Tower Road
Gibbons
Dugdale Crs
Bodington Rd
Brentnall Dr
Grange La
Mayall Dr
Homestead Dr
Randle Dr
Cartwright Rd
Rednall Dr
Clarendon Road
Worcester Cl
Willmott Road
Lane
Roughley Dr
Harvey Dr
Homer Rd
Rowallan Rd
Holte Drive
Sharrat Field
Mere Pool
Weeford Road
Cremorne Road
Jordan Road
Dower Road
Devereux Rd
Trinity Road
Ley Hill Road
Little Sutton Lane
Streather Road
Essex Road
Heath Rd
Grosvenor Cl
Lockhart Dr
Croft
Moor Hall Drive
Brockhurst Rd
Ferrers Cl
Little Sutton Road
Aulton Rd
Blaydon Av
Dutton's
Cressington Drive
The Fordrough
Hawkesford Cl
Pine Leigh
Laureates Walk
The Orchards
Ladywood Road
Bracebridge Road
Wentworth Gdns
Ravenswood
Station Dr
Bowlas Av
Oaklands Rd
Rocklands Dr
Kenilworth Close
Cedar Bridge Cft
Knowles Drive
Blackroot Rd
Beaconsfield Road
Halloughton Road
Barker Road
Carnoustie Cl
Troon Cl
Gleneagles Drive
Andrews
Carlton Close
Honeyborne Road
Moor Meadow Rd
Birch Croft Rd
Ashfurlong Crs
Whitehouse
300
298
99

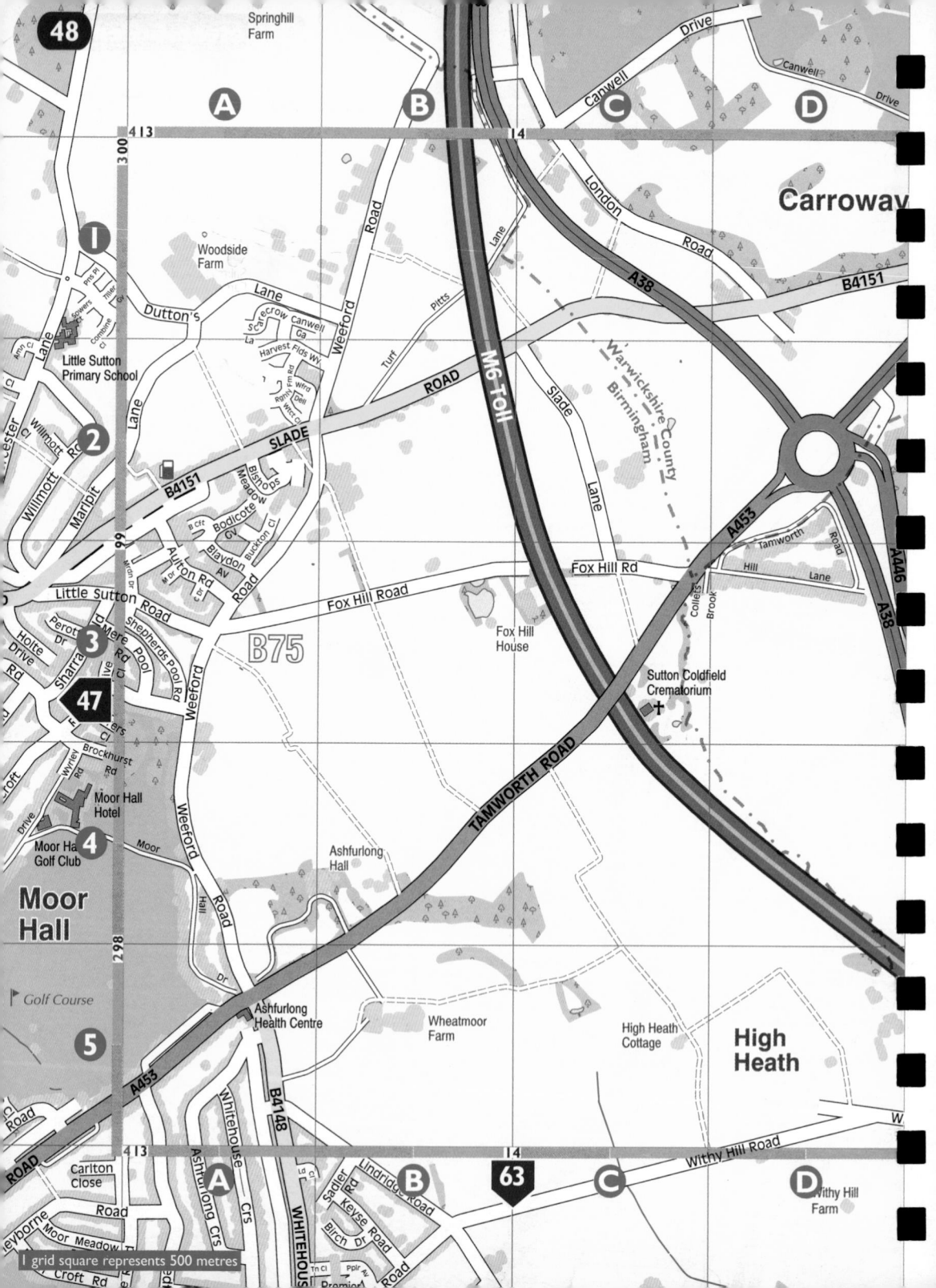

48

A B C D

Springhill
Farm

Drive

Canwell

Canwell

Carroway

London

Road

A38

B4151

I

Woodside
Farm

Lane

Dutton's

Weeford

Pitts

Turf

Warwickshire County
Birmingham

Little Sutton
Primary School

Scarecrow

Canwell
Ga

Harvest Flds Wy.

ROAD

M6 Toll

Slade

Lane

2

SLADE

B4151

Bishp Cps

Bodicote

Buckton Cl

Blaydon
Av

Ashton Rd

Road

Weeford

Fox Hill Road

Fox Hill Rd

Colls's

Brook

Hill

Tamworth

Lane

Road

A453

A38

A446

Willmott Rd

Maripit

Little Sutton
Road

B75

Fox Hill
House

Road

3

Mere Rd

Shepherds Pool Rd

Perott Dr

Holte
Drive

Sharral

47

Brocknurst
Rd

Wyrley
Rd

Sutton Coldfield
Crematorium

TAMWORTH ROAD

Moor Hall
Hotel

4

Moor Hall
Golf Club

Weeford

Moor

Road

Ashfurlong
Hall

Moor
Hall

Road

Hill

298

Golf Course

Dr

5

Ashfurlong
Health Centre

A453

Wheatmoor
Farm

High Heath
Cottage

High
Heath

B4148

Whitehouse

Withy Hill Road

Withy Hill Road

W

A B C D

63

Carlton
Close

WHITEHOUSE

Sadler

Lindridge Road

Keyse Road

Birch Dr

Withy Hill
Farm

Ashfurlong Crs

Road

Cheyporne

Moor Meadow

Croft Rd

Road

Road

413

ROAD

I grid square represents 500 metres

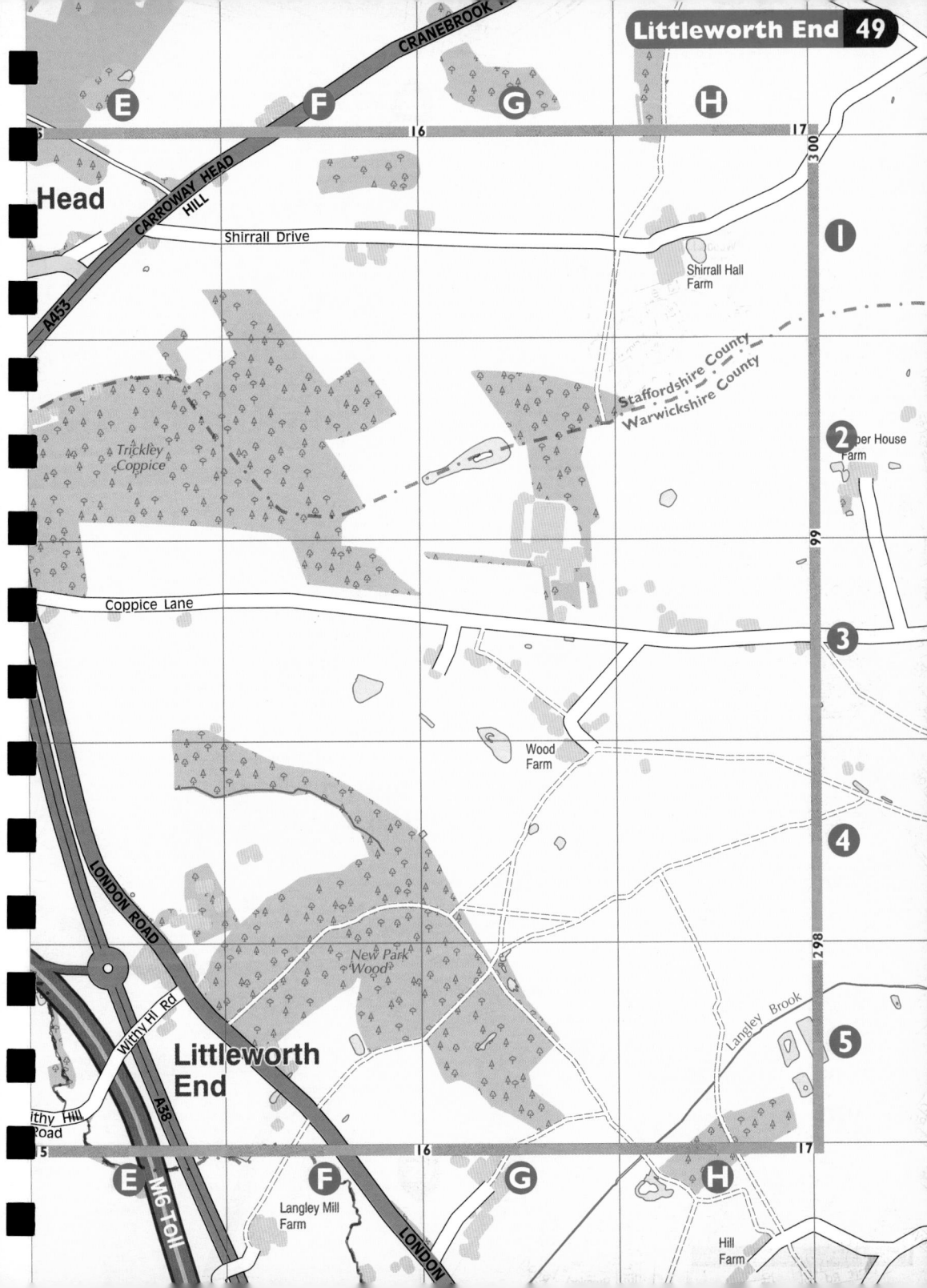

CRANEBROOK

E   F   G   H

16   17   300

Head

CARROWAY HEAD HILL

A453

Shirrall Drive

Shirrall Hall
Farm

I

Staffordshire County
Warwickshire County

2   per House
Farm

Trickley
Coppice

99

Coppice Lane

3

Wood
Farm

4

298

LONDON ROAD

New Park
Wood

Langley Brook

5

Withy Hl Rd

Littleworth
End

ithy Hill
Road

A38

M6 Toll

16   17

E   F   G   H

Langley Mill
Farm

LONDON

Hill
Farm

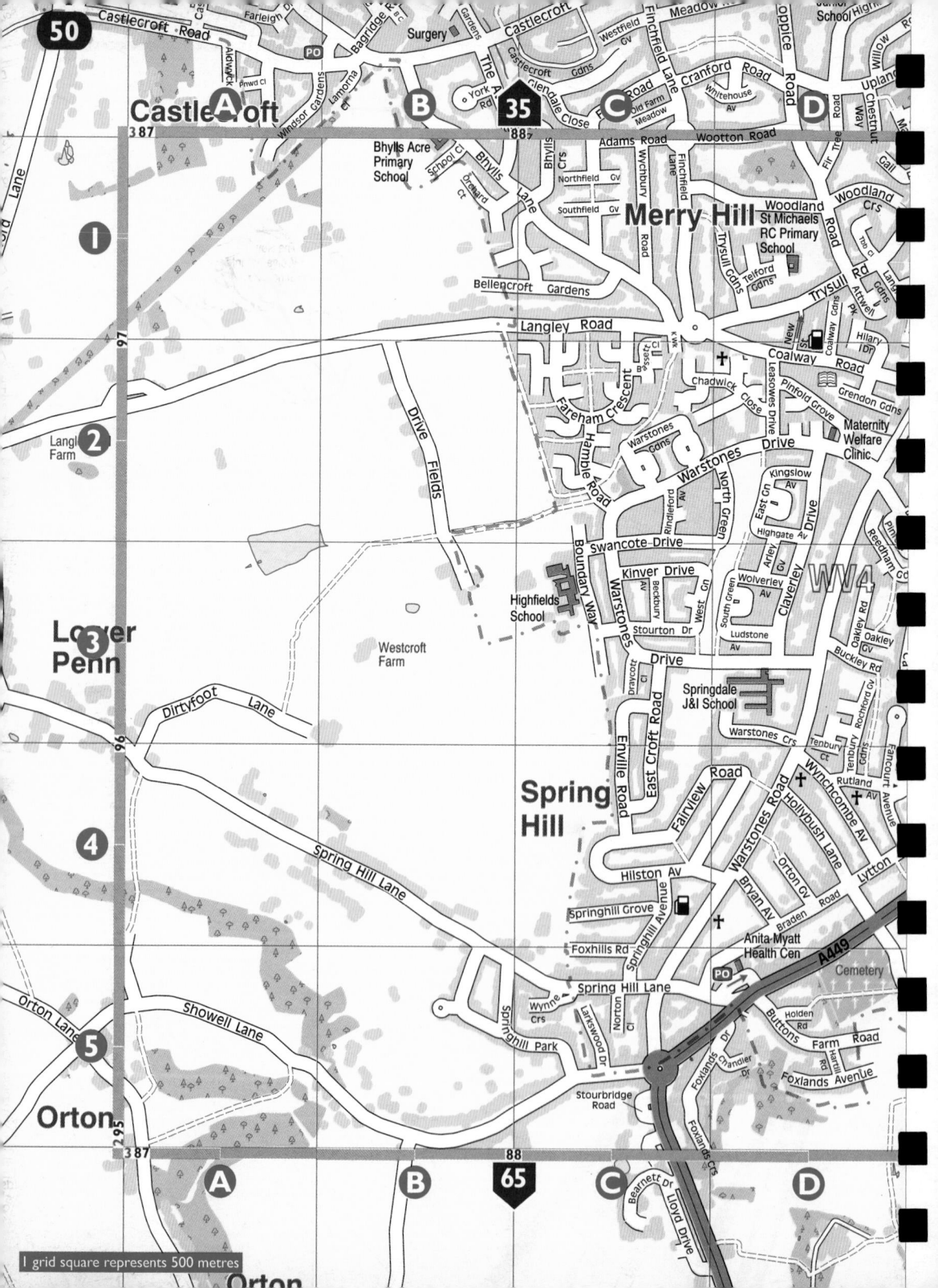

50
Castlecroft Road
Farleigh
Aldwyck
Pnwd Cl
PO
Bagridge Rd
Surgery
Gardens
Castlecroft
Westfield Gv
Finchfield Lane
Meadow
Coppice Road
Junior School
Windsor Gardens
Lamorna Cl
The A
York Rd
Castlecroft Gdns
Glendale Close
Old Farm
Meadow
Cranford Road
Whitehouse Av
Willow
Upland
Chestnut Way
Fir Tree Road
Castlecroft
35
A
B
C
D
387
88
Adams Road
Wootton Road
Bhylls Acre Primary School
School Cl
Bhylls Lane
Bhylls Crs
Orchard Ct
Northfield Gv
Southfield Gv
Wychbury Road
Finchfield Lane
Merry Hill
Woodland Road
Woodland Crs
St Michaels RC Primary School
Trysull Gdns
Telford Gdns
Trysull Rd
Attwell Pk
Bellencroft Gardens
Langley Road
Bassett Cl
New St
Coalway Gdns
Hilary Dr
Coalway Road
Chadwick Close
Leasowes Drive
Pinfold Grove
Grendon Gdns
Maternity Welfare Clinic
Fareham Crescent
Hamble Road
Warstones Gdns
Warstones Drive
North Green
Rindleford Av
Kingslow Av
East Gn
Drive
Highgate Av
Drive Fields
Langley Farm
1
2
3
4
5
97
96
295
Swancote Drive
Boundary Way
Kinver Drive
Beckbury Av
West Gn
Arley Gv
Wolverley Av
Claverley
WV4
Reedham
Highfields School
Warstones
South Green
Stourton Dr
Ludstone Av
Oakley Rd
Oakley Gv
Buckley Rd
Lower Penn
Westcroft Farm
Drive
Draycott Cl
Springdale J&I School
Warstones Crs
Tenbury Ct
Tenbury Gdns
Rochford Gv
Fancourt Avenue
Dirtyfoot Lane
East Croft Road
Enville Road
Fairview Road
Spring Hill
Warstones Road
Wynchcombe Av
Hollybush Lane
Rutland Av
Orton Gv
Lytton
Hilston Av
Bryan Av
Braden Road
Spring Hill Lane
Springhill Grove
Springhill Avenue
Anita Myatt Health Cen
Foxhills Rd
A449
Cemetery
PO
Spring Hill Lane
Wynne Crs
Larkswood Dr
Norton Cl
Springhill Park
Holden Rd
Buttons Farm Road
Hartill Rd
Foxlands Dr
Chandler Dr
Foxlands Avenue
Orton Lane
Showell Lane
Stourbridge Road
Foxlands Crs
Orton
387
88
65
Bearnett Dr
Lloyd Drive
1 grid square represents 500 metres
Orton

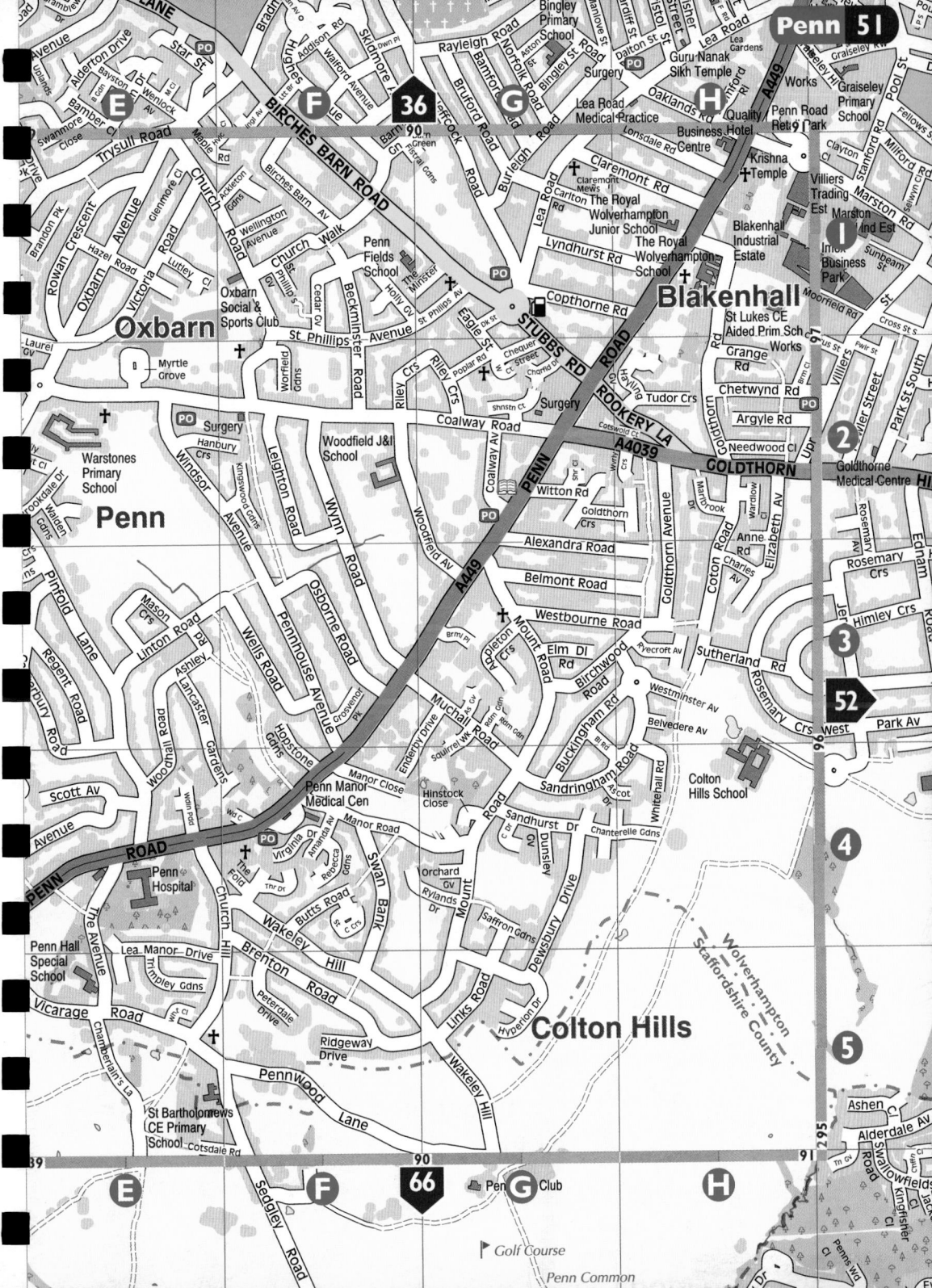
36
Bingley Primary School
Rayleigh Road
Lea Road
Lea Gardens
Guru Nanak Sikh Temple
Surgery
Works
Graiseley Primary School
Pool St
Penn Road Retail Park
Quality Hotel
Lea Road Medical Practice
Business Centre
Oaklands Rd
Lonsdale Rd
Alderton Drive
Star St
Addison Rd
Walford Avenue
Skidmore
Hughes
Bamford
Norfolk Road
Bingley St
Dalton St
Brufford Road
Burleigh Road
Swanmore Close
Trysull Road
Bamber Cl
Wenlock Av
Birches Barn Road
Birches Barn Av
Claremont Rd
Claremont Mews
Carlton Rd
The Royal Wolverhampton Junior School
The Royal Wolverhampton School
Krishna Temple
Villiers Trading Est
Marston Rd
Marston Ind Est
Blakenhall Industrial Estate
Imex Business Park
Brandon Pk
Rowan Crescent
Hazel Road
Oxbarn Avenue
Victoria Road
Glenmore Cl
Church Road
Wellington Avenue
Church Walk
Penn Fields School
The Minster
Lutley Cl
Lyndhurst Rd
Blakenhall
Moorfield Rd
Copthorne Rd
St Lukes CE Aided Prim Sch
Oxbarn Social & Sports Club
Oxbarn
St Phillips Avenue
Cedar Gv
Beckminster Road
Eagle St
Stubbs Rd
Chequer Street
Poplar Rd
Riley Crs
Grange Rd
Goldthorn Rd
Chetwynd Rd
Argyle Rd
Needwood Cl
Myrtle Grove
Laurel Gv
Worfield Gdns
Surgery
Tudor Crs
Rookery La
Hayling Gv
Coalway Road
A4039
Goldthorn
Goldthorne Medical Centre
Warstones Primary School
Hanbury Crs
Windsor Avenue
Woodfield J&I School
Leighton Road
Kingswood Gdns
Coalway Av
Penn Road
A449
Witton Rd
Goldthorn Crs
Marlbrook Dr
Wardlow Cl
Elizabeth Av
Rosemary Av
Ednam
Penn
Walden Gdns
Wynn Road
Woodfield Av
Alexandra Road
Belmont Road
Goldthorn Avenue
Coton Road
Anne Rd
Charles Av
Rosemary Crs
Pinfold Lane
Mason Crs
Linton Road
Wells Road
Pennhouse Avenue
Osborne Road
Westbourne Road
Appleton Crs
Mount Road
Elm Dl Rd
Birchwood Road
Pyecroft Av
Sutherland Rd
Himley Crs
Regent Road
Ashley Rd
Lancaster Gardens
Grosvenor Pk
Muchall Road
Westminster Av
Belvedere Av
West Park Av
52
Woodhall Road
Hopstone Gdns
Enderby Drive
Squirrel Wk
Buckingham Rd
Whitehall Rd
Sandringham Road
Ascot Dr
Colton Hills School
Scott Av
Manor Close
Penn Manor Medical Cen
Hinstock Close
Sandhurst Dr
Chanterelle Gdns
Dunsley Gv
Manor Road
Virginia Dr
Amanda Av
Rebecca Gdns
Swan Bank
Orchard Gv
Rylands Dr
Penn Hospital
The Fold
Church Hill
Butts Road
Mount Road
Dewsbury Drive
Wakeley Hill
Saffron Gdns
Penn Hall Special School
The Avenue
Lea Manor Drive
Trimpley Gdns
Brenton Road
Peterdale Drive
Links Road
Hyperion Dr
Wolverhampton
Staffordshire County
Vicarage Road
Colton Hills
Chamberlain's La
Ridgeway Drive
Pennwood Lane
St Bartholomews CE Primary School
Cotsdale Rd
Ashen Cl
Alderdale Av
Swallowfields
Sedgley Road
66
Penn Golf Club
Golf Course
Penn Common
Kingfisher Cl
E
F
G
H
I
2
3
4
5
89
90
91
95
96

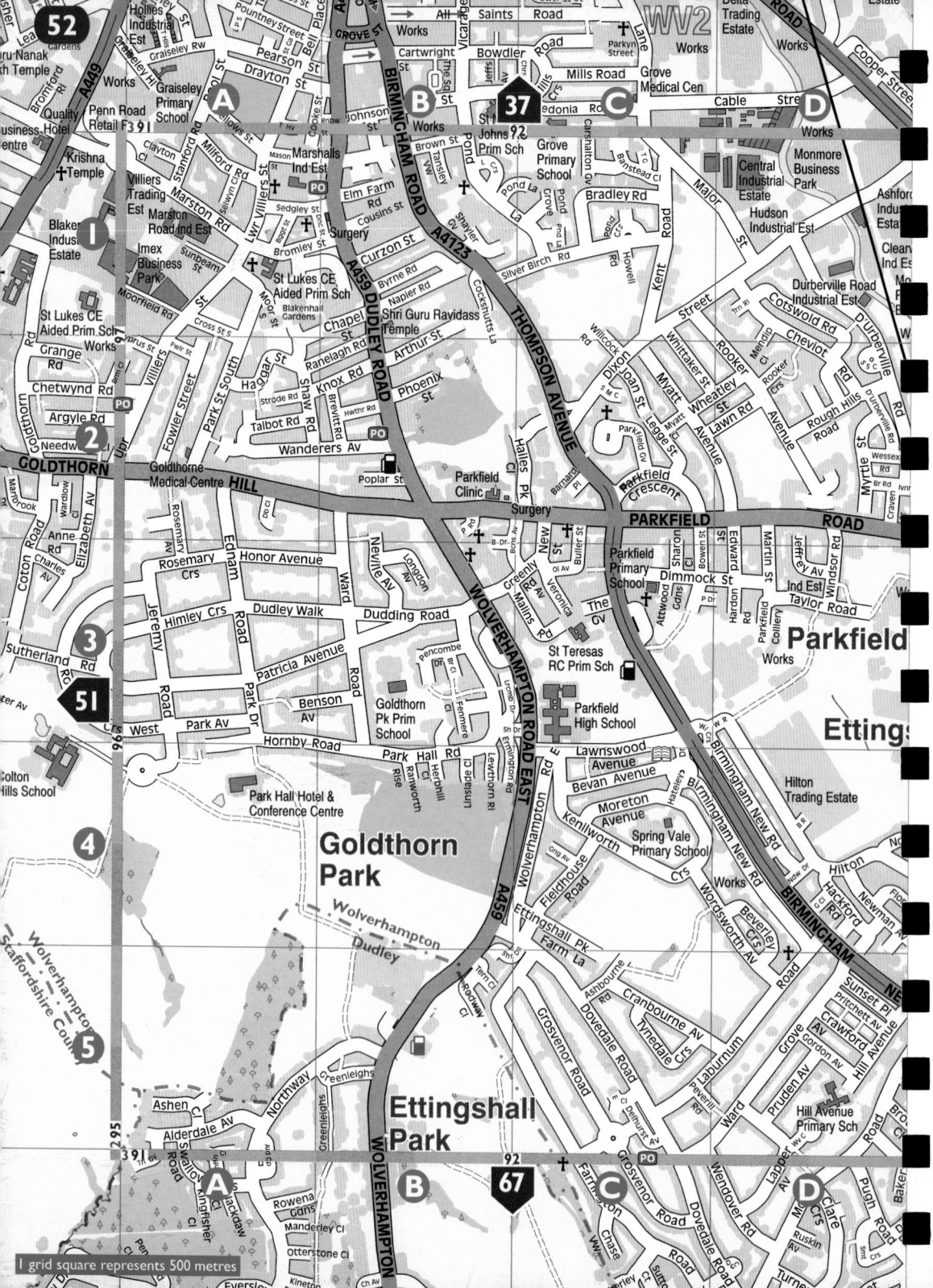

52
37
51
67
WV2
A
B
C
D
1
2
3
4
5
391
92
295
96
97
All Saints Road
Delta Trading Estate
Works
Hollies Industrial Est
Pountney Street
Graiseley Rw
Pearson St
Drayton St
Bell Place
Grove St
Cartwright St
Bowdler Road
Parkyn Street
Mills Road
Grove Medical Cen
Cooper Street
Guru Nanak Temple
Bromford Rl
A449
Graiseley Primary School
Penn Road Retail Park
Quality Hotel
Business Centre
Krishna Temple
Johnson St
Brown St
St Johns Prim Sch
Grove Primary School
Carshalton Gv
Banstead Cl
Cable Street
Monmore Business Park
Central Industrial Estate
Hudson Industrial Est
Ashford Industrial Estate
Clayton Cl
Stanford Rd
Milford Rd
Marshalls Ind Est
Elm Farm Rd
Cousins St
Pond La
Bradley Rd
Major St
Kent Road
Villiers Trading Est
Marston Rd
Marston Road Ind Est
Blakenhall Industrial Estate
Imex Business Park
Sunbeam St
Lwr Villiers St
Sedgley St
Bromley St
Surgery
Curzon St
Byrne Rd
Napier Rd
Silver Birch Rd
Howell Rd
Durberville Road Industrial Est
Cotswold Rd
Cheviot Rd
St Lukes CE Aided Prim Sch
Moorfield Rd
Moor St
Cross St S
Blakenhall Gardens
Shri Guru Ravidass Temple
Chapel St
Cockshutts La
Thompson Avenue
A4123
Birmingham Road
A459 Dudley Road
Willcock Rd
Dixon Street
Whittaker St
Rooker Avenue
Mendip Cl
Rooker Crs
D'Urberville Rd
Grange Rd
Cyprus St
Villiers
Fowler Street
Park St South
Haggar St
Ranelagh Rd
Arthur St
Knox Rd
Phoenix St
Joan St
Myatt Avenue
Wheatley St
Lawn Rd
Rough Hills Road
Chetwynd Rd
Argyle Rd
Needwood Cl
Goldthorn Rd
Strode Rd
Shaw Rd
Brevitt Rd
Talbot Rd
Wanderers Av
Parkfield Gv
Legge St
Myrtle St
Wessex Rd
Goldthorn Hill
Goldthorne Medical Centre
Poplar St
Parkfield Clinic
Hallies Pk Cl
Barnard Pl
Parkfield Crescent
Parkfield Road
Marlbrook
Wardlow Cl
Elizabeth Av
Coton Road
Anne Rd
Charles Av
Rosemary Av
Rosemary Crs
Ednam Road
Honor Avenue
Ward
Nevile Av
Longdon Av
New St
Buller St
Parkfield Primary School
Sharon Cl
Bowen St
Edward
Martin St
Jeffrey Av
Windsor Rd
Dimmock St
Ind Est
Taylor Road
Jeremy
Himley Crs
Dudley Walk
Dudding Road
Greenly Rd
Mallins Rd
Veronica Av
The Gv
Attwood Gdns
Hardon Rd
Parkfield Colliery
Parkfield
Sutherland Rd
Patricia Avenue
Pencombe Dr
Wolverhampton Road East
St Teresas RC Prim Sch
Works
Park Dr
Benson Av
Goldthorn Pk Prim School
Fenmore
Parkfield High School
Ettingshall
West
Park Av
Hornby Road
Park Hall Rd
Lawnswood Avenue
Birmingham New Rd
Colton Hills School
Park Hall Hotel & Conference Centre
Rise
Ranworth
Herbhill Cl
Linstade Cl
Lewthorn Rl
Ermington Rd
Bevan Avenue
Moreton Avenue
Hateley Dr
Hilton Trading Estate
Kenilworth Crs
Spring Vale Primary School
Goldthorn Park
Wolverhampton Rd E
Fieldhouse Road
Gng Av
Wordsworth Av
Hilton
Hackford Rd
Newman Av
A459
Wolverhampton
Dudley
Ettingshall Pk Farm La
Beverley Crs
Birmingham New Rd
Wolverhampton
Staffordshire County
Rodway Cl
Tern Cl
Ashbourne Rd
Cranbourne Av
Tynedale Crs
Grosvenor Road
Dovedale Road
Laburnum Road
Sunset Pl
Pritchett Av
Crawford Av
Hill Avenue
Grove
Gordon Av
Pruden Av
Northway
Greenleighs
Peverill Rd
Ward
Hill Avenue Primary Sch
Ashen Cl
Alderdale Av
Ettingshall Park
Delhurst Av
Swallow Cl
Kingfisher Cl
Jackdaw
Rowena Gdns
Manderley Cl
Otterstone Cl
Kineton
Eversley
Wolverhampton
Farrington
Chase
Grosvenor Road
Dovedale Road
Wendover Rd
Lapper Av
Clare Crs
Pugh Road
Ruskin Av
Turner
Baker
Ch Av
I grid square represents 500 metres

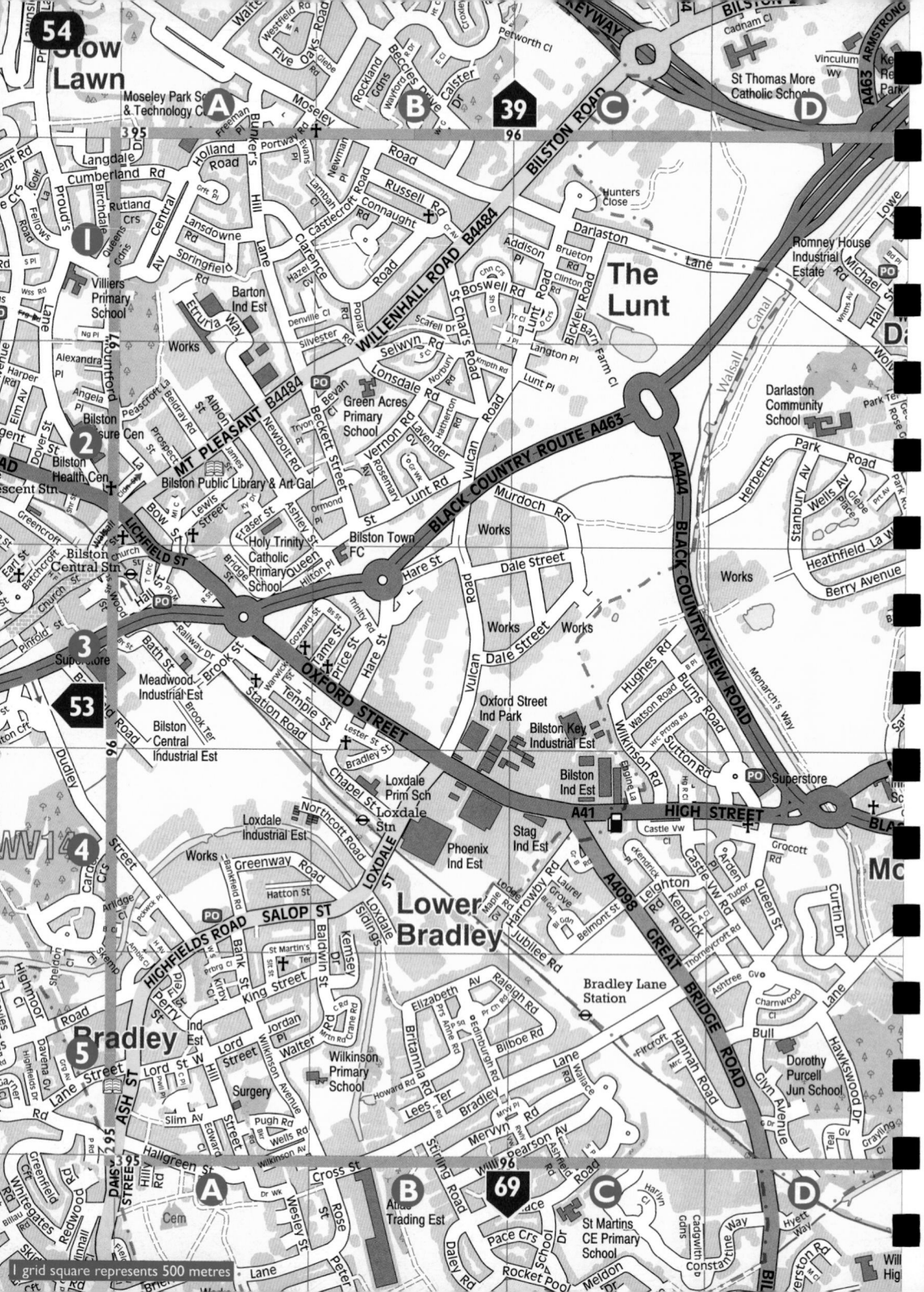
54
Stow Lawn
Moseley Park School & Technology College
A
B
C
D
39
53
69
395
96
1
2
3
4
5
Westfield Rd
Five Oaks Rd
Glebe Rd
Beccles Drive
Rockland Gdns
Caister Dr
Petworth Cl
Moseley Road
Freeman Pl
Bunker's Hill Lane
Portway Rd
Evans St
Newman Pl
Holland Road
Langdale Dr
Cumberland Rd
Proud's Lane
Golf La
Fellows Road
Birchdale
Rutland Crs
Queens Gdns
Central Av
Lansdowne Rd
Springfield Rd
Clarence Road
Castlecroft Road
Lambah Cl
Connaught Rd
Russell Rd
Hazel Gv
Denville Cl
Silvester Rd
Poplar Rd
WILLENHALL ROAD B4484
BILSTON ROAD
Hunters Close
Darlaston Lane
Addison Pl
Brueton Rd
Clinton Rd
Boswell Rd
St Chad's Road
Lunt Road
Bickley Road
Barn Farm Cl
The Lunt
Langton Pl
Lunt Pl
Scafell Dr
Selwyn Rd
Lonsdale Rd
Norbury Rd
Kmpth Rd
Villiers Primary School
Barton Ind Est
Etruria Way
Works
Alexandra Pl
Harper Rd
Elm Av
Angela Pl
Mountford La
Bilston Leisure Cen
Peascroft La
Beldray Rd
Albion St
Prospect St
MT PLEASANT B4484
Newbolt Rd
Bevan Cl
Green Acres Primary School
Tryon Pl
Beckett Street
Vernon Rd
Lavender Gv
Hatherton Rd
Vulcan Road
Rosemary Av
Lunt Rd
BLACK COUNTRY ROUTE A463
Bilston Library & Art Gal
Bilston Health Cen
Dover St
Bow St
Lewis Street
Fraser St
Ashley St
Ormond Pl
Bilston Town FC
Holy Trinity Catholic Primary School
Queen St
Hilton Pl
Hare St
Murdoch Rd
Works
Dale Street
Greencroft
Earl St
Batchcroft
Bilston Central Stn
Church St
LICHFIELD ST
Bridge St
Hall St
Pinfold St
Superstore
Bath St
Railway Dr
Brook St
Meadwood Industrial Est
Bilston Central Industrial Est
Brook Ter
Station Road
Warwick St
Temple St
Gozzard St
Tame St
Price St
Trinity Rd
OXFORD STREET
Lester St
Bradley St
Chapel St
Oxford Street Ind Park
Bilston Key Industrial Est
Bilston Ind Est
Engine La
Dudley Street
Romney House Industrial Estate
Michael Rd
Hall St
Walsall Canal
Darlaston Community School
Park Road
Herberts Park Road
Stanbury Av
Wells Av
Glebe Place
Heathfield La
Berry Avenue
A4444 BLACK COUNTRY NEW ROAD
Monarch's Way
Hughes Rd
Burns Road
Watson Road
Wilkinson Rd
Sutton Rd
Superstore
St Thomas More Catholic School
Cadnam Cl
Vinculum Wy
A463
ARMSTRONG
A41 HIGH STREET
Castle Vw Cl
Grocott Rd
Loxdale Prim Sch
Loxdale Stn
Phoenix Ind Est
Stag Ind Est
Northcott Road
Loxdale Industrial Est
WV14
Greenway Road
Hatton St
LOXDALE ST
Loxdale Sidings
Lower Bradley
A4098 GREAT BRIDGE ROAD
Harrowby Rd
Laurel Grove
Belmont St
Jubilee Rd
Kendrick Rd
Leighton Rd
Castle Vw Rd
Arden Pl
Tudor Rd
Queen St
Curtin Dr
Thorneycroft Rd
Ashtree Gv
Charnwood Cl
Bull Lane
Hawkswood Dr
Dorothy Purcell Jun School
Glyn Avenue
Teal Gv
Grayling Cl
HIGHFIELDS ROAD
SALOP ST
Bank St
Baldwin St
Kemsey Dr
St Martin's Ter
King Street
Perry St
Field St
Kirby Cl
Ind Est
Jordan Pl
Walter St
Crane Rd
Wilkinson Avenue
Wilkinson Primary School
Elizabeth Av
Raleigh Rd
Britannia Rd
Edinburgh Rd
Bilboe Rd
Bradley Lane Station
Fircroft
Hannah Road
Howard Rd
Lees Ter
Bradley Lane
Wallace Rd
Mervyn Rd
Pearson Av
Ashfield Rd
Bradley
Lane Street
Lord St W
Lord Street
Hill Street
Surgery
Slim Av
Edward Street
Pugh Rd
Wells Rd
ASH ST
Hallgreen St
Highmoor Cl
Road
Davies
Sheldon Cl
Skemp
Arlidge Cl
Cardiff Crs
Davena Gv
Highfields Dr
Greenfield Cft
Whitegates Rd
Redwood Rd
DAISY STREET
Cem
Wesley St
Rose St
Peter
Cross St
Atlas Trading Est
Stirling Road
Daley Rd
Pace Crs
School Dr
Rocket Pool
St Martins CE Primary School
Harlyn Cl
Cadgwith Gdns
Constantine Way
Hyett Way
Meldon
Lane
1 grid square represents 500 metres

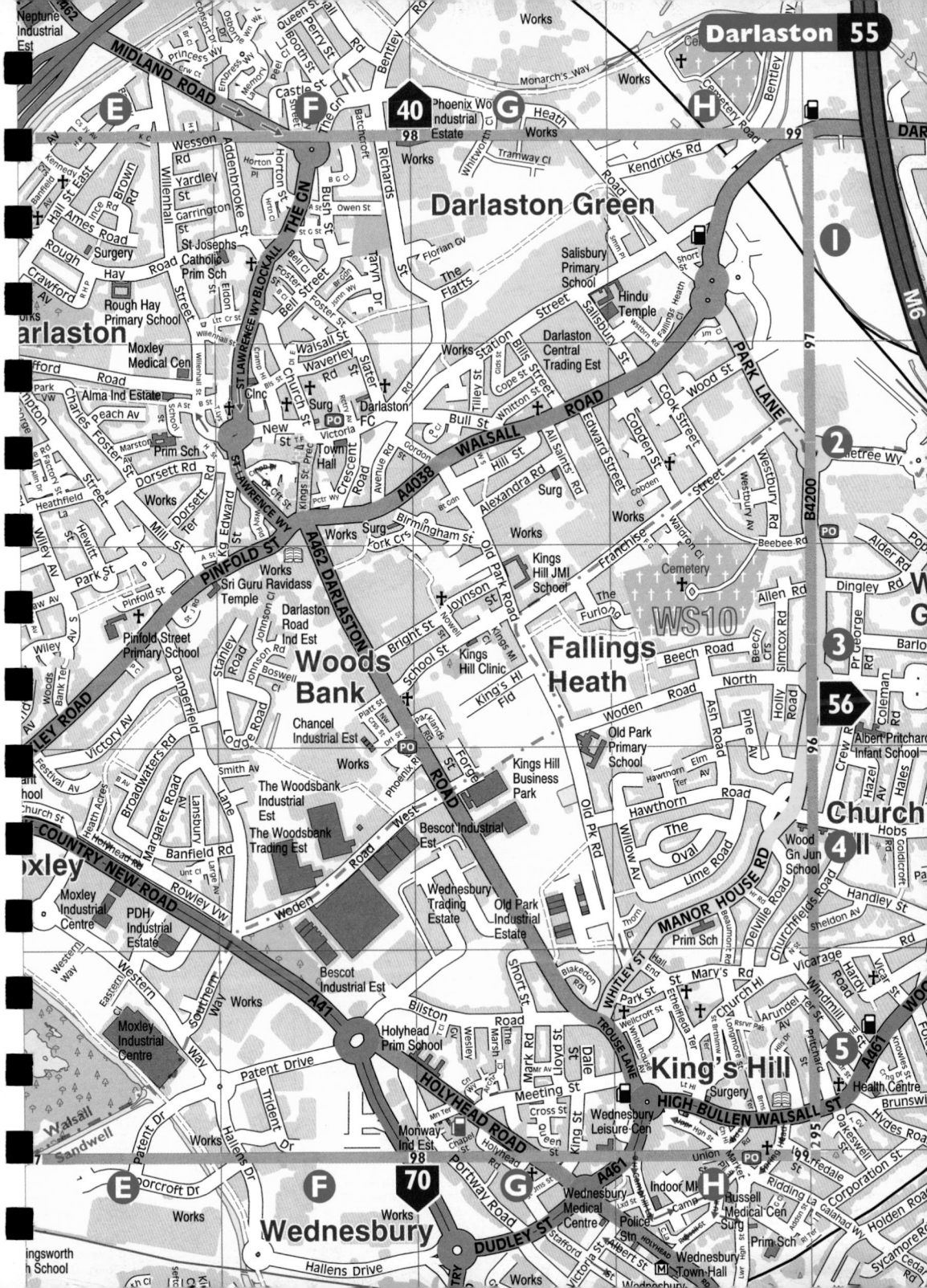
Neptune Industrial Est
MIDLAND ROAD
Princess Wy
Castle St
Bentley Rd
Works
Monarch's Way
Cemetery Road
E
F
G
H
40
98
99
Phoenix Works Industrial Estate
Heath Works
Tramway Cl
Kendricks Rd
Wesson Rd
Yardley St
Garrington St
Addenbrooke St
Horton St
THE GN
Bush St
Owen St
Richards St
Darlaston Green
Brown Rd
Ames Road
Rough Hay Road
Surgery
Crawford Av
Rough Hay Primary School
St Josephs Catholic Prim Sch
ST LAWRENCE WY BLOCKALL
Florian Gv
The Flatts
Salisbury Primary School
Hindu Temple
Darlaston
Moxley Medical Cen
Walsall St
Waverley Rd
Station Street
Darlaston Central Trading Est
Salisbury St
PARK LANE
I
M6
Alma Ind Estate
Charles Foster St
Peach Av
Clnc
Surg
PO
Darlaston FC
Victoria
Town Hall
Bull St
Tilley St
WALSALL ROAD
Wood St
Cook Street
Cobden St
2
Prim Sch
Dorsett Rd
Works
Crescent Road
Avenue Rd
A4038
Hill St
Alexandra Rd
All Saints' Rd
Edward Street
Westbury Rd
Heathfield La
Wiley Av
Hewitt St
Park St
Mill St
Kg Edward St
ST LAWRENCE WY
Birmingham St
York Crs
A462 DARLASTON ROAD
Works
Kings Hill JMI School
Franchise St
Cemetery
B4200
97
PINFOLD ST
Sri Guru Ravidass Temple
Pinfold St
Pinfold Street Primary School
Darlaston Road Ind Est
Johnson Rd
Stanley Road
Bright St
Joynson St
Old Park Road
The Furlong
WS10
Allen Rd
Dingley Rd
3
Barlow
Woods Bank
Kings Hill Clinic
King's Hl Fld
Fallings Heath
Beech Road
North Woden Road
Ash Road
Pine Av
Holly Road
56
Coleman Rd
Albert Pritchard Infant School
Victory Av
Broadwaters Rd
Lodge Road
Chancel Industrial Est
Forge St
Parklands Rd
Old Park Primary School
Festival Av
Smith Av
The Woodsbank Industrial Est
Works
Kings Hill Business Park
Hawthorn Road
The Oval
Church
Hobs Rd
Margaret Road
Lansbury Av
Banfield Rd
The Woodsbank Trading Est
West Road
Bescot Industrial Est
Willow Av
Lime Road
Wood Gn Jun School
4
COUNTRY NEW ROAD
Holyhead Rd
Moxley
Rowley Vw
Moxley Industrial Centre
PDH Industrial Estate
Woden Road
Wednesbury Trading Estate
Old Park Industrial Estate
Old Pk Rd
MANOR HOUSE RD
Prim Sch
Delville Road
Churchfields Road
Handley St
Sheldon Av
Western Way
Southern Way
Works
Bescot Industrial Est
A41
Short St
WHITLEY ST
St Mary's Rd
Park St
Church Hl
Vicarage Road
Windmill
Moxley Industrial Centre
Holyhead Prim School
Bilston Road
Wesley
The Marsh
Mark Rd
Lloyd St
Dale St
TROUSE LANE
King's Hill
Pritchard
A461
5
Patent Drive
Trident Dr
HOLYHEAD ROAD
Meeting St
Cross St
Queen St
King St
Wednesbury Leisure Cen
HIGH BULLEN WALSALL ST
Surgery
Health Centre
Walsall
Sandwell
Patent Dr
Works
Hallens Dr
Monway Ind Est
98
295
99
Moorcroft Dr
Works
70
Portway Road
Wednesbury Medical Centre
Indoor Mkt
Russell Medical Cen
Surg
Corporation St
Holden Rd
Wednesbury
DUDLEY ST
Police Stn
Albert St
Wednesbury Town Hall
Prim Sch
Hallens Drive
Works
Hydes Road

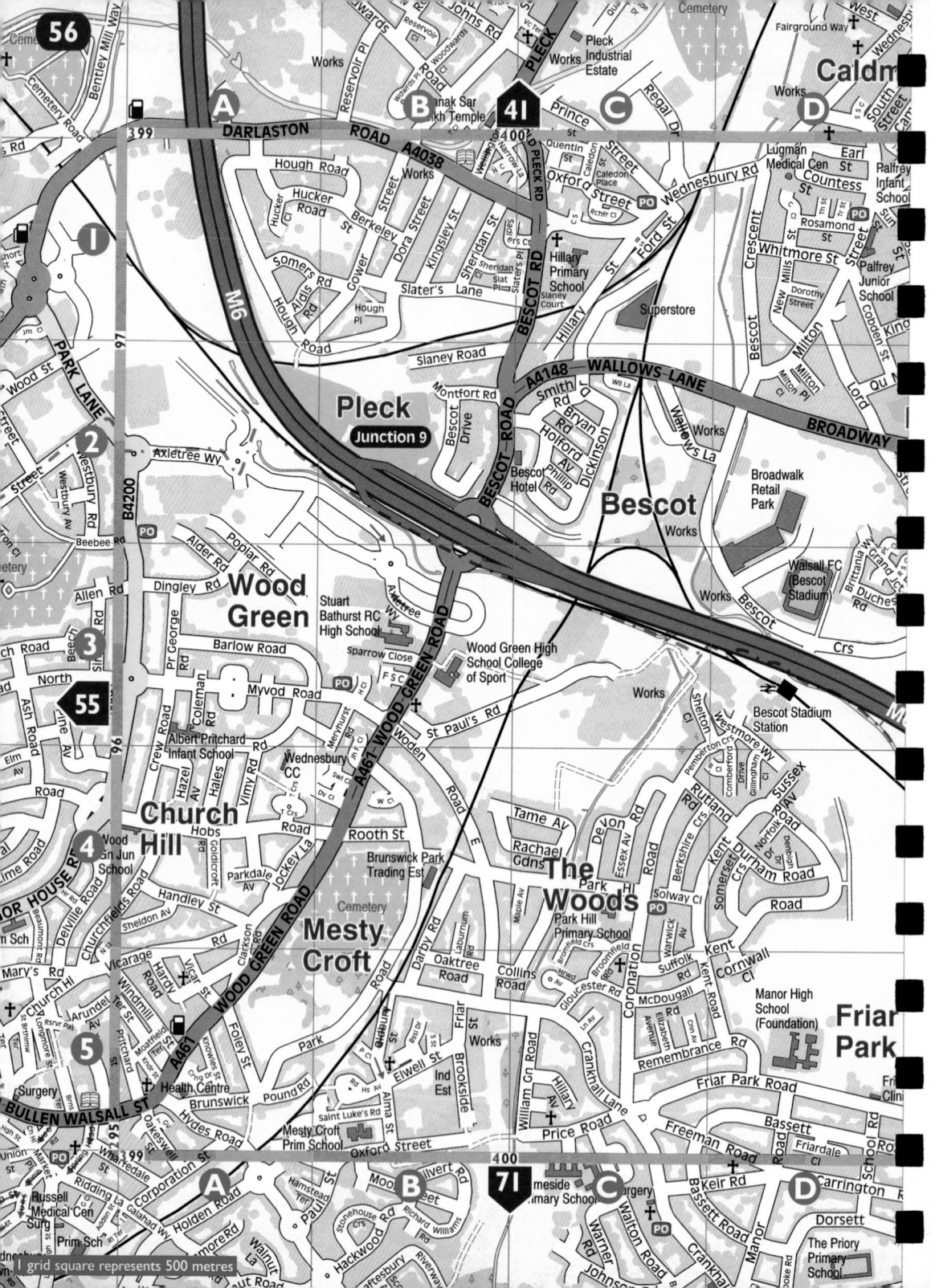

56
55
41
71
A
B
C
D
1
2
3
4
5
399
400
97
96
95
Cemetery
Bentley Mill Way
Cemetery Road
Works
Reservoir Pl
Reservoir Cl
Johns Rd
Woodwards Road
Woodwards Cl
Nanak Sar Sikh Temple
PLECK
Pleck Industrial Estate
Fairground Way
West
Wednesbury
Caldm
Prince St
Regal Dr
DARLASTON ROAD
A4038
Hough Road
Hucker Road
Hucker Cl
Berkeley St
Cower Street
Dora Street
Kingsley St
Sheridan St
Sheridan Cl
Wellington
Narrow La
PLECK RD
Quentin St
Caledon St
Caledon Place
Oxford Street
Street
Wednesbury Rd
Rchfr Cl
Ford St
Lugman Medical Cen
Earl St
Countess St
Palfrey Infant School
Rosamond St
Whitmore St
Crescent
Street
Palfrey Junior School
Somers Rd
Aldis Rd
Hough Pl
Slater's Lane
Slat Pl
Slaters Pl
Slaney Court
Hillary Primary School
Hillary St
Superstore
New Mills St
Dorothy Street
Cobden St
Milton St
Milton Pl
Bescot
M6
BESCOT RD
Slaney Road
Road
A4148
WALLOWS LANE
Wll La
Montfort Rd
Smith Rd
Bryan Rd
Holford Av
Dickinson
Phillip Rd
Bescot Drive
Bescot Hotel
BESCOT ROAD
Pleck
Junction 9
Wallows La
Works
Broadwalk Retail Park
BROADWAY
Lord
King
Qu
PARK LANE
Wood St
Westbury Rd
Westbury Av
Street
Axletree Wy
B4200
PO
Beebee Rd
Alder Rd
Poplar Rd
Dingley Rd
Wood Green
Allen Rd
Stuart Bathurst RC High School
Axletree Wy
Bescot
Works
Walsall FC (Bescot Stadium)
Britannia Wy
Grand Jct
Duches Rd
Bescot Crs
Beech
Pr George Rd
Barlow Road
Sparrow Close
Wood Green High School College of Sport
North
Ash Road
Coleman Rd
Myvod Road
FSC
H Cl
WOOD GREEN ROAD
A461
St Paul's Rd
Works
Bescot Stadium Station
Shelton Cl
Westmore Wy
Pemberton Crs
Comberford Drive
Gillingham Cl
Sussex Av
Crew Road
Albert Pritchard Infant School
Merryhurst Rd
Wednesbury CC
Woden Road
Elm Av
Hazel Av
Hales
Vimy Rd
Road
Rutland Rd
Berkshire Crs
Norfolk Dr
Denbigh Dr
Church Hill
Hobs Road
Rooth St
Tame Av
Devon Rd
Essex Av
Rachael Gdns
Kent Crs
Durham Road
Wood Gn Jun School
Goldicroft
Parkdale Av
Jockey La
Brunswick Park Trading Est
The Woods
Park Hl
Solway Cl
Somerset Road
Delville Road
Churchfields Road
Handley St
Sheldon Av
Cemetery
Mesty Croft
Maple Av
Park Hill Primary School
Warwick Av
Road
Beaumont Rd
Clarkson Rd
Darby Rd
Laburnum Rd
Oaktree Road
Collins Road
Broomfield Crs
Broomfield Rd
Coronation Road
Suffolk Rd
Kent Rd
Cornwall Cl
Mary's Rd
Vicarage Road
Hardy Rd
Vicar St
Church Hl
Arundel Av
Windmill Ter
Foley St
Friar St
Gloucester Rd
McDougall Rd
Elizabeth Avenue
Kent Road
Manor High School (Foundation)
Friar Park
Moatfield Ter
Pritchard St
Knowles St
Park
Oldbury Rd
Works
William Gn Road
Crankhall Lane
Remembrance Rd
Surgery
Health Centre
Brunswick
Pound Rd
Elwell St
Ind Est
Brookside
Hillary Av
Friar Park Road
BULLEN WALSALL ST
Hydes Road
Saint Luke's Rd
Alma St
Price Road
Freeman Road
Bassett Cl
Friardale Cl
School Rd
Oakeswell St
Mesty Croft Prim School
Oxford Street
Wharfedale
Corporation St
Ridding La
Galahad Wy
Holden Road
Hamstead Ter
Paul St
Moor Street
Silvert Rd
Richard Williams Rd
Stonehouse Crs
Hackwood Rd
Walnut La
Meside Primary School
Surgery
Walton Road
Warner Rd
Bassett Road
Keir Rd
Manor Road
Carrington
Dorsett
The Priory Primary School
Russell Medical Cen
Surg
Prim Sch
Union St
Market
1 grid square represents 500 metres

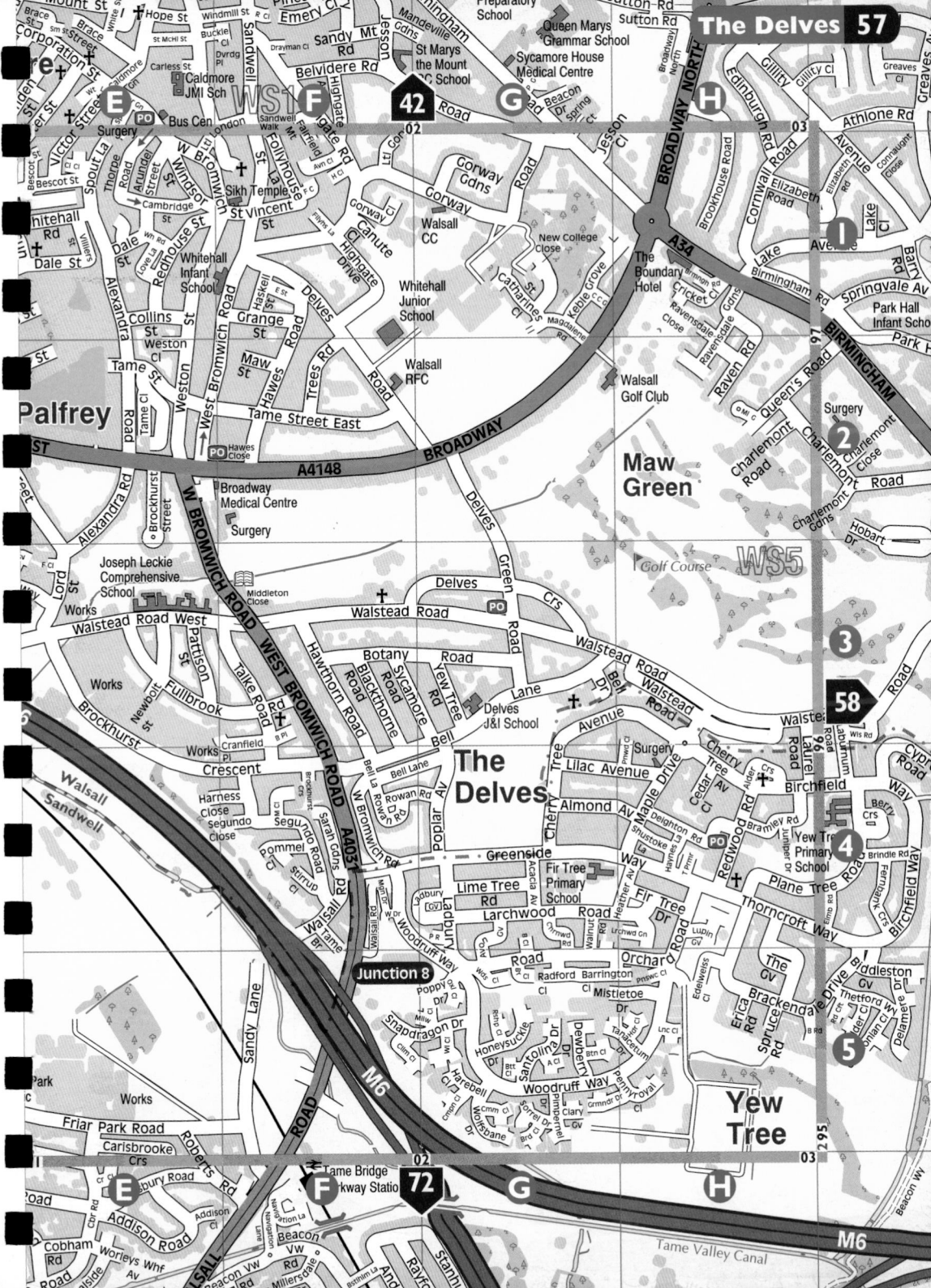

Palfrey
Maw Green
The Delves
Yew Tree
WS1
WS5
BROADWAY
A4148
BROADWAY NORTH
A34
BIRMINGHAM
W BROMWICH ROAD
WEST BROMWICH ROAD
A4031
M6
Junction 8
Walsall Sandwell
Tame Valley Canal
Golf Course
Walsall Golf Club
The Boundary Hotel
Whitehall Junior School
Walsall RFC
Walsall CC
Queen Marys Grammar School
Sycamore House Medical Centre
St Marys the Mount RC School
Caldmore JMI Sch
Sikh Temple
Whitehall Infant School
Broadway Medical Centre
Surgery
Joseph Leckie Comprehensive School
Delves J&I School
Fir Tree Primary School
Yew Tree Primary School
Park Hall Infant School
Tame Bridge Parkway Station
Walstead Road
Walstead Road West
Delves Green Road
Delves Road
Greenside Way
Bell Lane
Crescent
Works
42
58
72

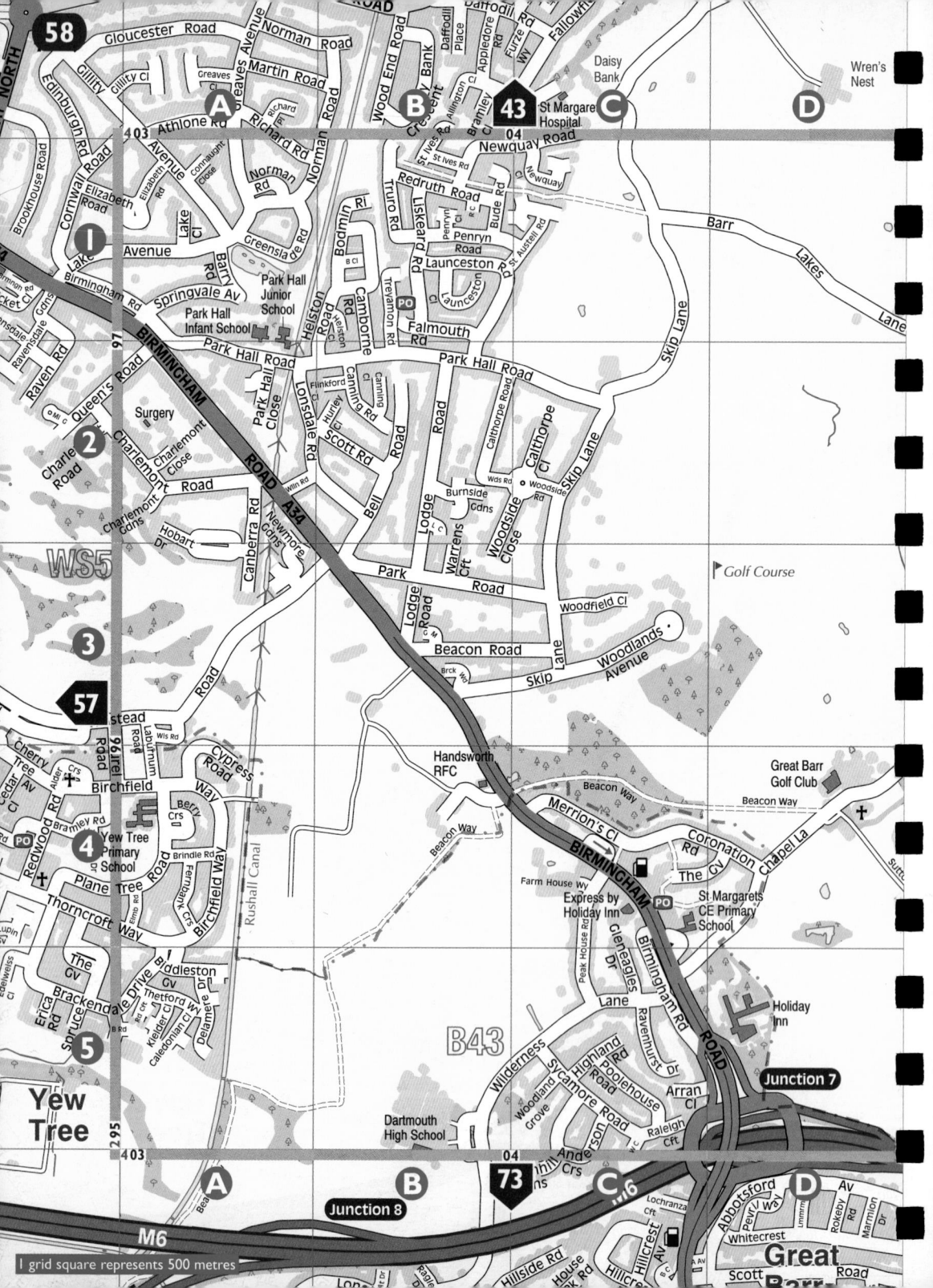
58
43
57
73
Gloucester Road
Norman Road
Martin Road
Greaves Avenue
Wood End Road
Daisy Bank
St Margarets Hospital
Wren's Nest
Athlone Rd
Richard Rd
Newquay Road
Redruth Road
Barr Lakes Lane
Skip Lane
Edinburgh Rd
Cornwall Road
Brookhouse Road
Lake Avenue
Birmingham Rd
Springvale Av
Park Hall Junior School
Park Hall Infant School
Park Hall Road
Falmouth Rd
Penryn Road
Launceston Rd
Queen's Road
Surgery
Charlemont Road
Charlemont Close
Charlemont Gdns
BIRMINGHAM ROAD A34
Park Hall Close
Lonsdale Rd
Scott Rd
Bell Road
Lodge Road
Calthorpe Cl
Woodside Close
Burnside Gdns
Warrens Cft
Hobart Dr
Canberra Rd
Newmore Gdns
WS5
Park Road
Golf Course
Woodfield Cl
Beacon Road
Woodlands Avenue
Handsworth RFC
Great Barr Golf Club
Beacon Way
Merrion's Cl
Coronation Rd
Chapel La
The Gv
Farm House Wy
Express by Holiday Inn
St Margarets CE Primary School
Birchfield Way
Cypress Road
Yew Tree Primary School
Plane Tree Road
Thorncroft Way
Brackendale Drive
Biddleston Gv
Rushall Canal
Holiday Inn
Gleneagles Dr
Birmingham Rd
Peak House Rd
Lane
B43
Wilderness
Highland Rd
Poolehouse Road
Sycamore Road
Woodland Grove
Ravenhurst Dr
Arran Cl
Junction 7
Dartmouth High School
Raleigh Cft
Anderson Crs
Yew Tree
Junction 8
M6
Abbotsford
Whitecrest
Great Barr
Scott Road
Hillside Rd
Hillcrest Av
1 grid square represents 500 metres

Pheasey
Barr Beacon
Beacon Farm
Crook House
Old Hall
The Barr Beacon School
Doe Bank Wood
Meadow View JMI School
Pheasey Park Farm Primary School
Sundridge Primary S
Kings Business Park
Century Industrial Estate
Winster Grove Industrial Est
Winster Grove Industrial Cen
Whitecrest Primary
BEACON ROAD
B4154
BEACON RD
QUESLETT ROAD
A4041
Crook Lane
Bodens Lane
Pinfold Lane
Chapel Lane
Old Hall La
Bridle Lane
Doe Bank Lane
Aldridge Road
Maxholm Road
Laurel Dr
Wimperis Way
Raeburn Road
Collingwood Dr
Chantrey Way
Gainsborough Crescent
Tyndale Crescent
Hillingford Av
Queslett Road
Waverley Av
Garnet Av
Comsey Rd
Park Farm Road
Stonehurst Road
Ivanhoe Rd
Foxwood Av
Handsworth Drive
Brackenfield Road
Ringinglow Road
Shady Lane
Horns Crs
Surgery
Pheasey Clnc
Super Store
Works
44
60
74
E
F
G
H
1
2
3
4
5
06
07
96
97
295

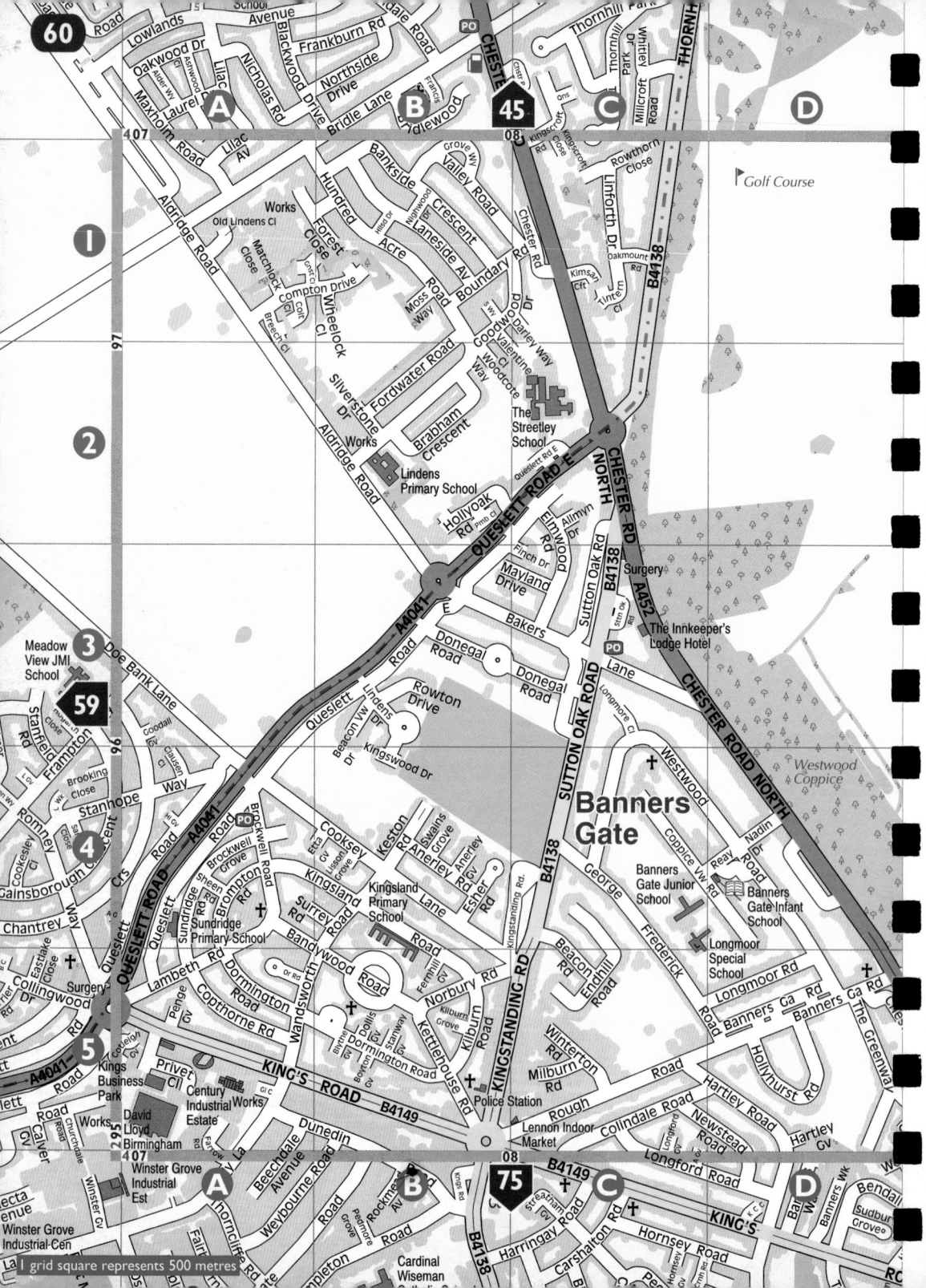

45
59
75
A
B
C
D
1
2
3
4
5
407
08
97
96
295
Lowlands
Avenue
Blackwood
Frankburn Rd
Oakwood Dr
Lilac
Nicholas Rd
Northside Drive
Bridle Lane
Maxholm Road
Laurel Dr
Thornhill Park
Whitley Dr
Millcroft Road
THORNHILL
Kingscroft Rd
Kingscroft Close
Rowthorn Close
Linforth Dr
Golf Course
Lilac Av
Grove Wy
Valley Road
Bankside
Hundred Acre
Nighwood Dr
Crescent
Laneside Av
Boundary Rd
Chester Rd
Works
Old Lindens Cl
Aldridge Road
Matchlock Close
Forest Close
Compton Drive
Colt Cl
Breech Cl
Wheelock Cl
Moss Way
Road
Goodwood Dr
Darley Way
Valentine Cl
Woodcote Way
Oakmount Rd
Kimsan Cft
Tintern Cl
B4138
Fordwater Road
Silverstone Dr
Brabham Crescent
The Streetley School
Lindens Primary School
Queslett Rd E
QUESLETT ROAD E
CHESTER RD NORTH
Hollyoak Rd
Pmb Cl
Elmwood Rd
Allmyn Dr
Finch Dr
Mayland Drive
Sutton Oak Rd
Surgery
A452
A4041
Bakers Lane
The Innkeeper's Lodge Hotel
PO
Donegal Road
Rowton Drive
Lindens Dr
Beacon Vw Dr
Kingswood Dr
Queslett Road
SUTTON OAK ROAD
Longmore Cl
Westwood
CHESTER ROAD NORTH
Westwood Coppice
Banners Gate
Meadow View JMI School
Doe Bank Lane
Stanfield Rd
Frampton
Goodall Gv
Clausen Cl
Way
Brooking Close
Stanhope
Romney
Crescent
Cookesley Cl
Gainsborough Crs
Chantrey Way
Eastlake Close
Collingwood Dr
QUESLETT ROAD
Brockwell Road
Brockwell Grove
Cooksey Lane
Keston Rd
Swains Grove
Anerley Rd
Anerley Gv
Esher Rd
Kingsland Primary School
Kingsland Road
Surrey Road
Brompton Rd
Sundridge Primary School
Sundridge Rd
Lambeth Rd
Bandywood Road
Fernhill Gv
Norbury Rd
Kilburn Road
Kilburn Grove
Dormington Road
Copthorne Rd
Penge Gv
Wandsworth Road
Blythe Gv
Dollis Gv
Stanway Gv
Boyton Gv
Kettlehouse Rd
Kingstanding Rd.
KINGSTANDING RD
B4138
Beacon Rd
Endhill Road
George Frederick Road
Coppice Vw Rd
Reay Road
Nadin Dr
Banners Gate Junior School
Banners Gate Infant School
Longmoor Special School
Longmoor Rd
Banners Ga Rd
The Greenway
Winterton Rd
Milburn Rd
Rough Road
Hollyhurst Rd
Hartley Road
Hartley Gv
Colindale Road
Newstead Road
Longford Road
Lennon Indoor Market
Police Station
KING'S ROAD
B4149
Privet Cl
Century Industrial Estate
Works
Kings Business Park
David Lloyd Birmingham
Dunedin
Beechdale Avenue
Weybourne Road
Rockmead Av
Pedmore Grove
Road
Thorncliffe Rd
Winster Grove Industrial Est
Winster Gv
Churchdale Road
Calver Gv
Winster Grove Industrial Cen
Streatham Gv
Harringay Road
Carshalton Rd
Hornsey Road
KING'S
Banners Wk
Bendall
Sudbury Grove
Cardinal Wiseman
Surgery
A4041

1 grid square represents 500 metres

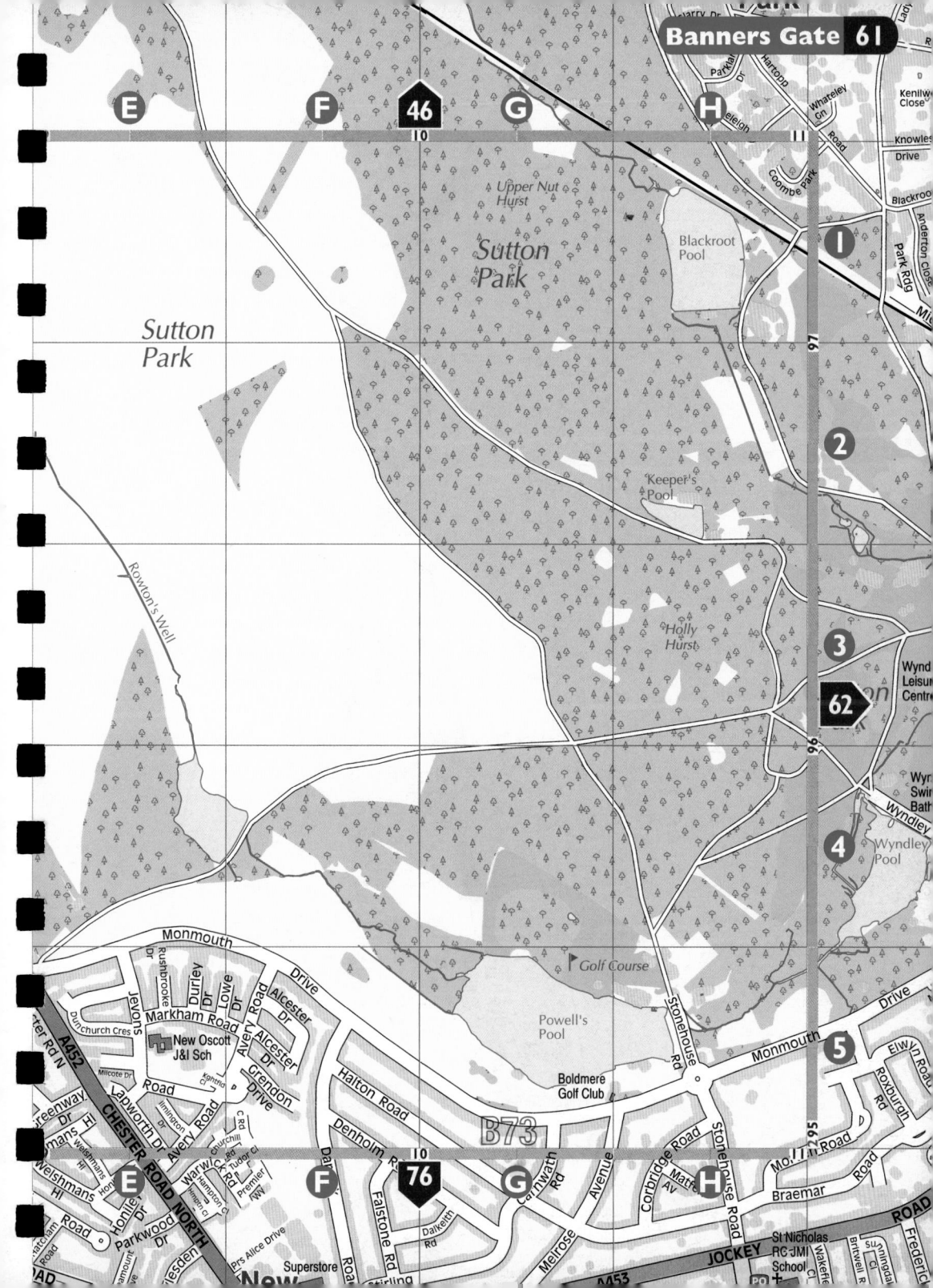

E   F   **46**   G   H

Park
Parkhall Dr
Hartopp
Kenilw
Close
Wheteley Grn
Heleigh
Coombe Park
Kn
Knowles
Drive
Blackroo
Anderton Close
Park Rd
Park Rd

Upper Nut
Hurst

Sutton
Park

Blackroot
Pool

I

Sutton
Park

2

Keeper's
Pool

Rowton's Well

3

Holly
Hurst

Wynd
Leisure
Centre

62

Wyr
Swir
Bath
Wyndley

4

Wyndley
Pool

Monmouth
Drive

Golf Course

Monmouth
Drive

5

Rushbrooke Dr
Durley Dr
Lowe Dr
Alcester Dr
Markham Road
Jevons
Dunchurch Cres
Avery Road
Alcester Dr
Grendon Drive
Milcote Dr
New Oscott
J&I Sch
Road
Ilmington Dr
Kentro
Avery Road
Churchill
Tudor Cl
Premier
C Rd

Powell's
Pool

Boldmere
Golf Club

Stonehouse Rd

Elwyn Road
Roxburgh
Mol
Road

A452

Greenway Dr
Ilmans Hi
Weldmans
Welshmans
Hi
Honile
Dr
Parkwood Dr
Iiesden
Road

CHESTER ROAD NORTH

Warwic Cl
Hampton Cl

E   F   **76**   G   H

Halton Road

Denholm Road

Dart
Falstone Rd
Dalkeith Rd
Carnwath Rd

B73

Melrose Avenue

Corbridge Road
Stonehouse Road
Matl
Av

Braemar Road
Frederi
ROAD

Mrs Alice Drive

Superstore
Stirling Road

New

St Nicholas
RC JMI
School
Symingdal
Wakefie
Britwell R
Cl
PO

JOCKEY

A453

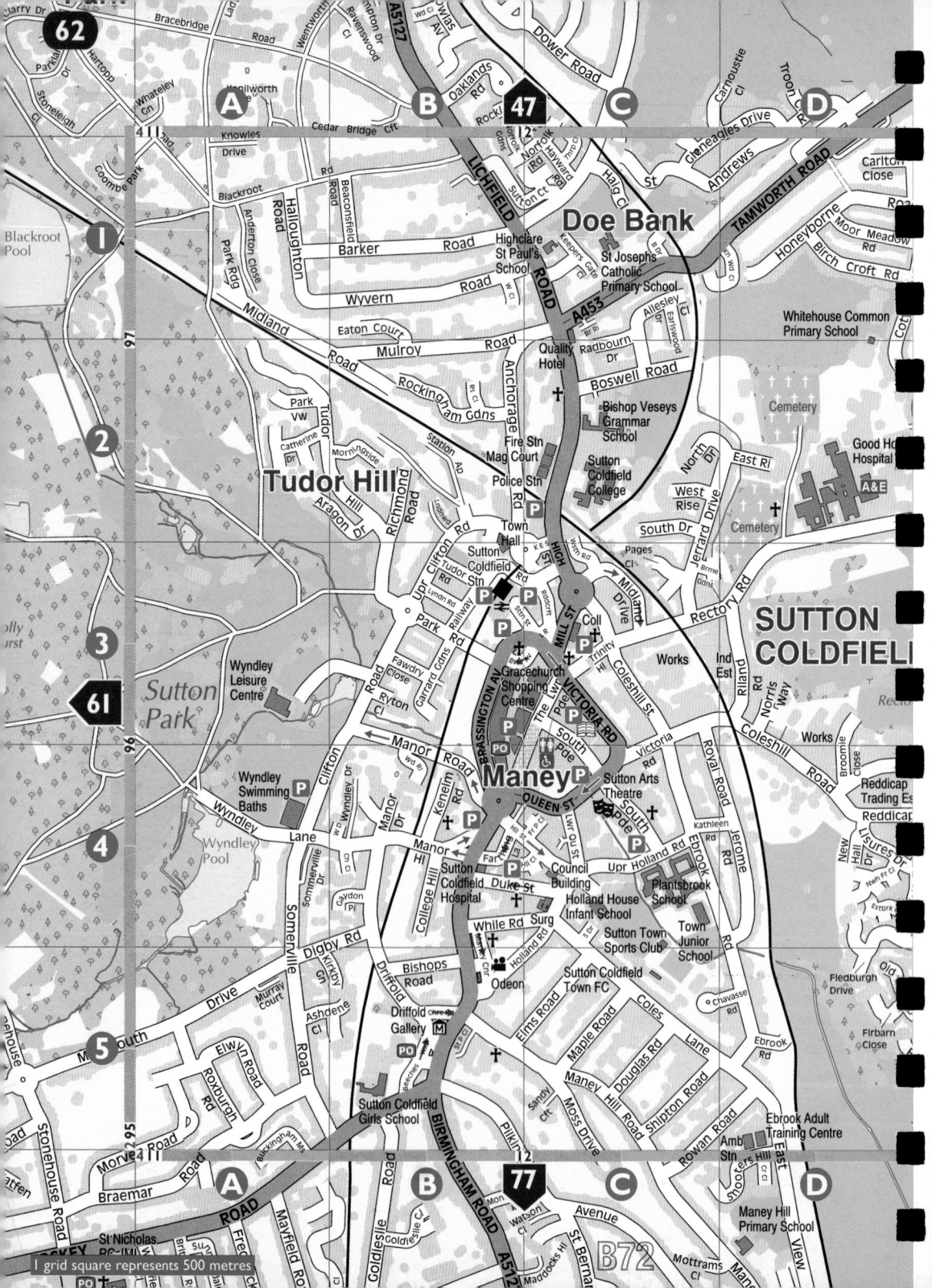

62
47
61
77
A
B
C
D
1
2
3
4
5
Doe Bank
Tudor Hill
Maney
SUTTON COLDFIELD
Sutton Park
Blackroot Pool
Wyndley Pool
Bracebridge Road
Kenilworth
Oaklands Rd
Dower Road
Carnoustie Cl
Troon Cl
Gleneagles Drive
St Andrews
Carlton Close
TAMWORTH ROAD
A5127
LICHFIELD ROAD
A453
Knowles Drive
Cedar Bridge Cft
Coombe Park
Blackroot Rd
Halloughton Road
Beaconsfield Road
Anderton Close
Park Rdg
Barker Road
Wyvern Road
Highclare St Paul's School
St Josephs Catholic Primary School
Keepers Gate
Haig Cl
Sutton Ct
Norfolk Rd
Hayward Rd
Honeyborne
Moor Meadow Rd
Birch Croft Rd
Whitehouse Common Primary School
Midland Road
Eaton Court
Mulroy Road
Quality Hotel
Radbourn Dr
Allesley Cl
Earlswood
Boswell Road
Rockingham Gdns
Anchorage Rd
Park Vw
Tudor Hill
Catherine Dr
Morningside
Station Ap
Bishop Veseys Grammar School
Fire Stn
Mag Court
Police Stn
Sutton Coldfield College
Cemetery
North Dr
East Ri
West Rise
Good Hope Hospital
A&E
South Dr
Jerrard Drive
Aragon Dr
Richmond Road
Town Hall
HIGH ST
Sutton Coldfield Tudor Stn
Upr Clifton Rd
Tudor Rd
Lyndn Rd
Railway
Park Rd
Pages Cl
Midland Drive
Rectory Rd
MILL ST
Coll
Trinity Hl
Coleshill St
Works
Ind Est
Riland Rd
Norris Way
Wyndley Leisure Centre
Fawdry Close
Garrard Gdns
Ryton Cl
Clifton Road
Gracechurch Shopping Centre
BRASSINGTON AV
The Lwr Pde
VICTORIA RD
South Pde
Victoria Rd
Royal Road
Coleshill Road
Broomie Close
Reddicap Trading Es
Manor Road
Wyndley Swimming Baths
Wyndley Dr
Manor Dr
Kenelm Rd
QUEEN ST
Sutton Arts Theatre
South Pde
Kathleen Rd
Jerome Rd
Ebrook Rd
New Hall Dr
Lisures Dr
Wyndley Lane
Manor Hl
Farthing La
Hill St
Lwr Qu St
Upr Holland Rd
Plantsbrook School
Sommerville Dr
Sutton Coldfield Hospital
Duke St
Council Building
Holland House Infant School
College Hill
Gaydon Pl
While Rd
Surg
Holland Rd
Sutton Town Sports Club
Town Junior School
Digby Rd
Kirkby Gn
Somerville Road
Bishops Road
Driffold
Odeon
Sutton Coldfield Town FC
Elms Road
Maple Road
Coles Lane
Chavasse Rd
Fledburgh Drive
Murray Court
Ashdene Cl
Driffold Gallery
Douglas Rd
Firbarn Close
Ebrook Rd
Monmouth Drive
Elwyn Road
Roxburgh Rd
Sutton Coldfield Girls School
Maney Hill Road
Shipton Road
Moss Drive
Sandy Cft
Rowan Road
Ebrook Adult Training Centre
Amb Stn
Shooters Hill
East View
Stonehouse Road
Morven Road
Braemar Road
BIRMINGHAM ROAD
Goldieslie Road
Mayfield Road
Watson Cl
Avenue
St Bernard
Maddocks Hl
Mottrams Cl
Maney Hill Primary School
St Nicholas RC (JMI)
B72
1 grid square represents 500 metres

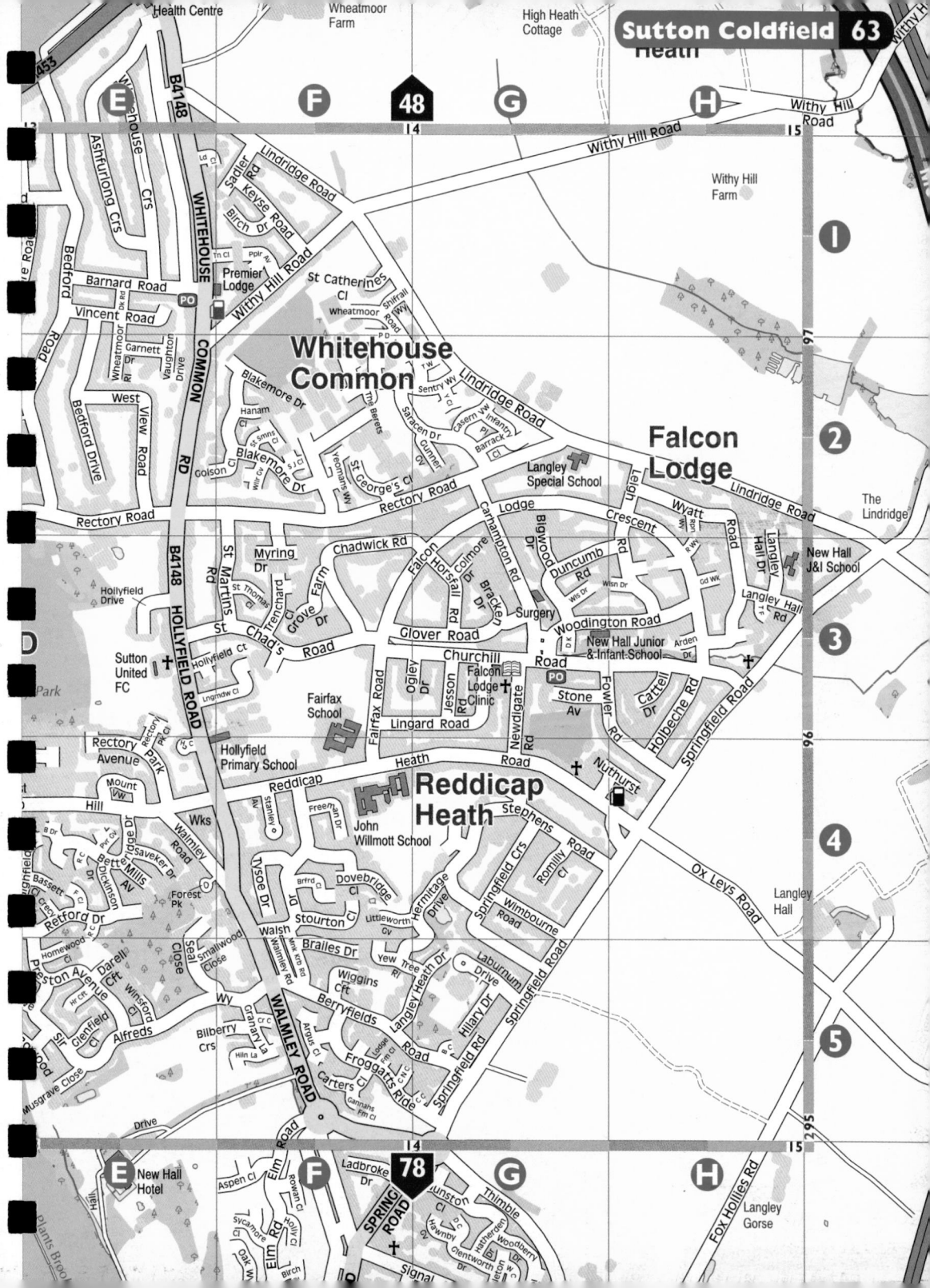
Whitehouse Common
Falcon Lodge
Reddicap Heath
Withy Hill Road
Lindridge Road
Rectory Road
Springfield Road
Ox Leys Road
WALMLEY ROAD
HOLLYFIELD ROAD
WHITEHOUSE COMMON RD
Langley Special School
New Hall Junior & Infant School
John Willmott School
Fairfax School
Hollyfield Primary School
Sutton United FC
New Hall J&I School
Withy Hill Farm
The Lindridge
Langley Hall
Langley Gorse
New Hall Hotel
Premier Lodge
Falcon Lodge Clinic
Surgery

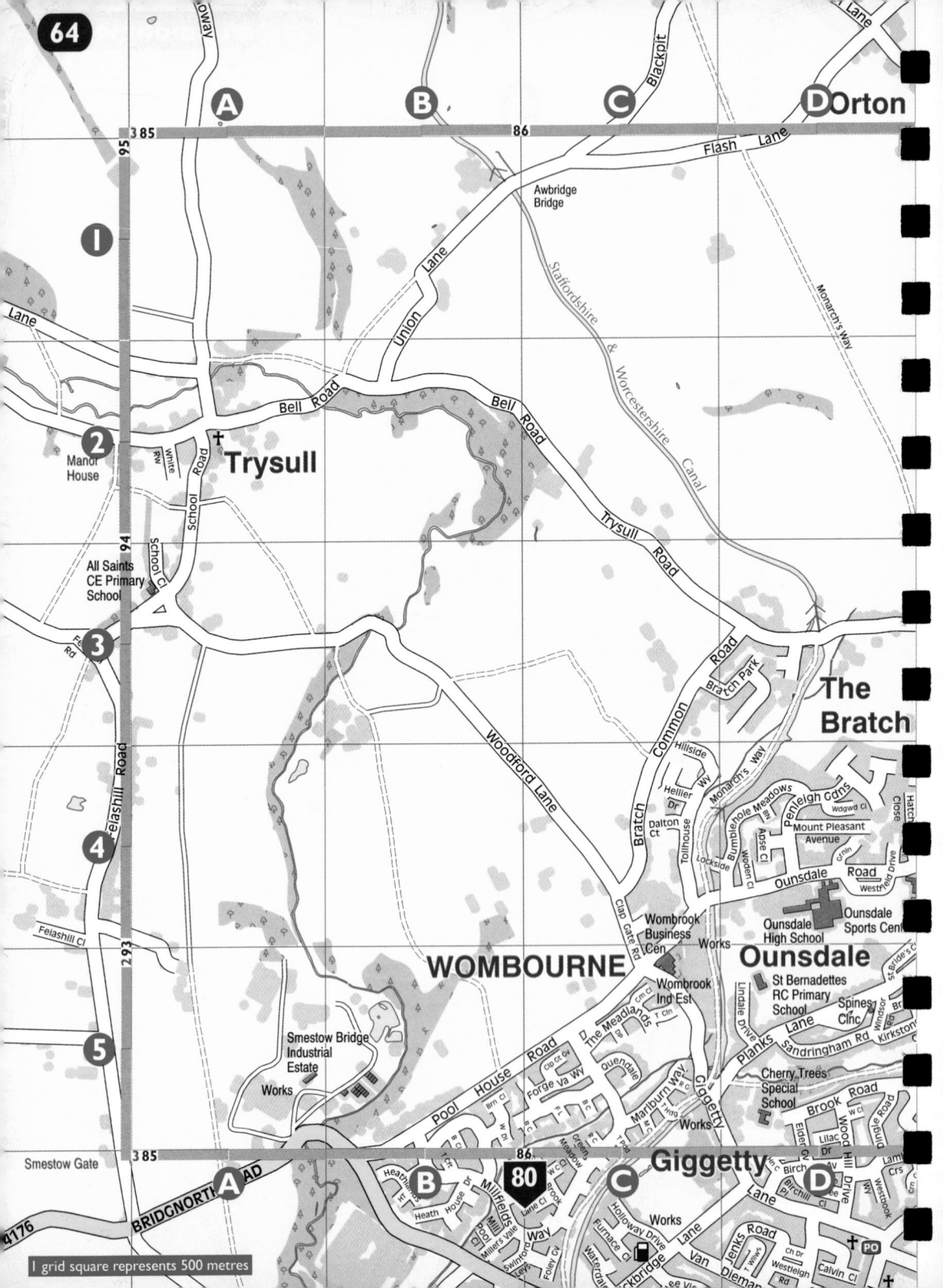

Orton
Flash Lane
Awbridge Bridge
Union Lane
Staffordshire & Worcestershire Canal
Monarch's Way
Bell Road
Trysull
Manor House
School Road
All Saints CE Primary School
School Cl
Trysull Road
Common Road
Bratch Park
The Bratch
Woodford Lane
Feiashill Road
Feiashill Cl
Hillside
Hellier Dr
Dalton Ct
Tollhouse Wy
Bumblehole Meadows
Penleigh Gdns
Mount Pleasant Avenue
Ounsdale Road
Ounsdale High School
Ounsdale Sports Cen
Ounsdale
Wombrook Business Cen
Works
WOMBOURNE
Clap Gate Rd
Wombrook Ind Est
St Bernadettes RC Primary School
Lindale Drive
Spines Clnc
Planks Lane
Sandringham Rd
Smestow Bridge Industrial Estate
Pool House Road
The Meadlands
Quendale
Marlburn Way
Giggetty
Cherry Trees Special School
Brook Road
Wood Hill Drive
Smestow Gate
BRIDGNORTH ROAD
Heath House Dr
Millfields Way
Giggetty Lane
Holloway Drive
Jenks Road
Calvin Cl
80
1 grid square represents 500 metres

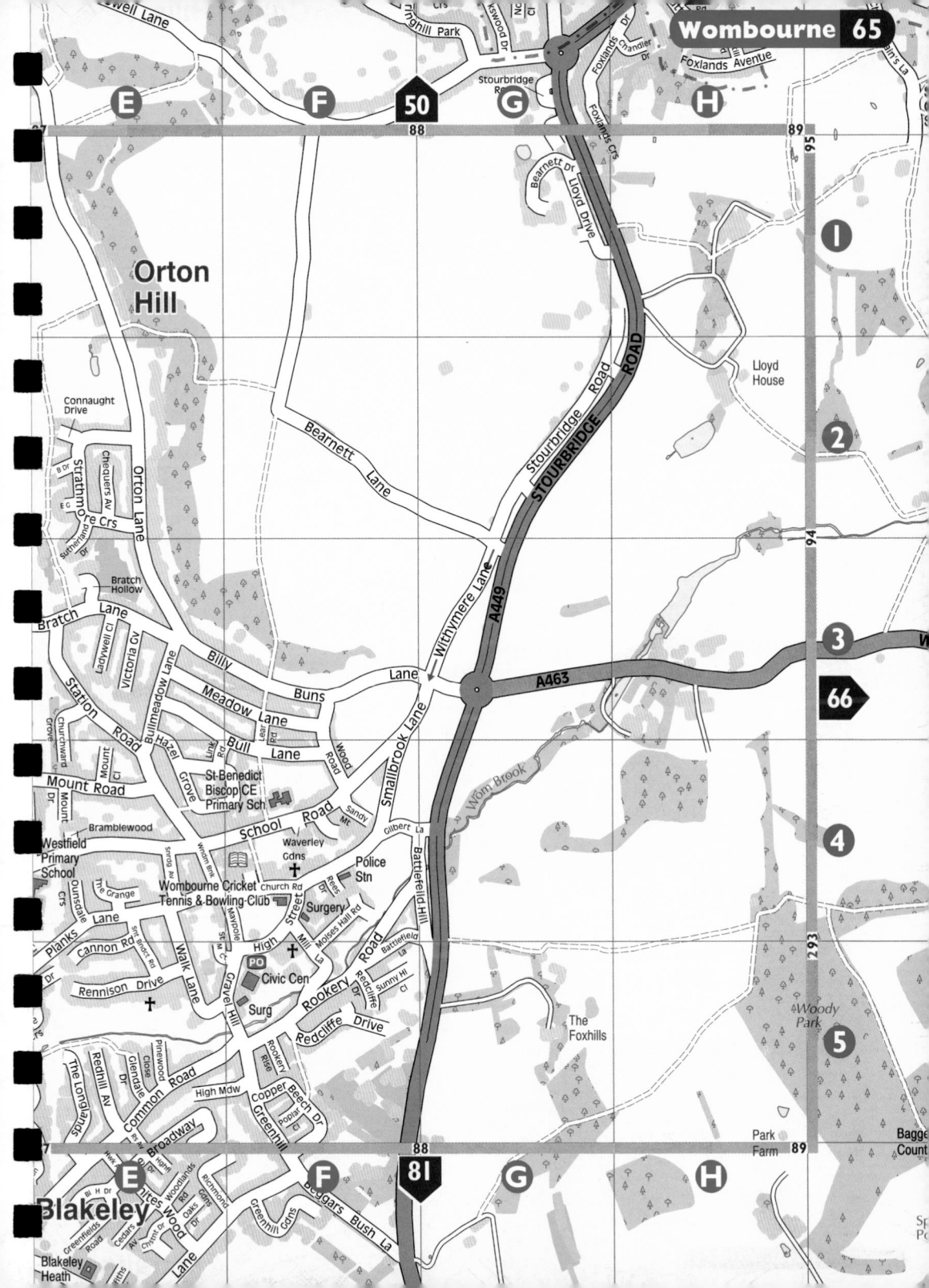

E   F   **50**   G   H

88

89

95

I

Stourbridge
Rd

Foxlands Avenue

Bearnett Dr   Lloyd Drive

Foxlands Crs

Foxlands Chandler Dr

Lloyd
House

2

94

Orton
Hill

Connaught
Drive

Bearnett   Lane

Stourbridge   Road

STOURBRIDGE   ROAD

B Dr
E G   Chequers Av
Strathmore Crs
Sutherland Dr

Orton   Lane

Bratch
Hollow

Bratch   Lane

Ladywell Cl
Victoria Gv

Bullmeadow Lane

Billy

Meadow Lane

Buns

Bull   Lane

Withymere Lane

A449

Lane

Smallbrook Lane

Wood   Road

A463

3

66

W

Wom Brook

Station
Road

Churchward
Grove

Mount
Cl   Mount   Dr

Mount Road

Hazel   Grove

Link   Rd

St Benedict
Biscop CE
Primary Sch

School   Road

Sandy
Mt

Gilbert   La

4

293

Westfield
Primary
School

Ounsdale
Crs

The Grange

Bramblewood

Smestow Rd

Wom Brook

Waverley
Gdns

Church Rd

Police
Stn

Rees

Battlefield Hill

Planks
Lane

Cannon Rd

Walk   Lane

Gravel Hill

High   Street

Mill   St

Marpole

Surgery

Mill   Road

Rookery   Road

Battlefield
La

Molses Hall Rd

Sunny Hl
Cl

The
Foxhills

Woody
Park

5

Rennison   Drive

PO
Civic Cen

Surg

Redcliffe   Drive

Redcliffe   Rd

Copper Beech Dr

The Longlands
Redhill Av
Glendale Close
Pinewood Rd

Common   Road

High Mdw

Rookery Rd

Poplar Cl

Greenhill   Road

Park
Farm

Bagge
Count

7

Blakeley

E   F   **81**   G   H

Broadway

Bl H Dr

Whites Wood   Lane

Woodlands
Rd
Richmond
Oaks

Beggars   Bush   La

Greenhill Gdns

Sp
Po

88   89

Greenfields
Road

The Cedars Av

Pitts

Blakeley
Heath

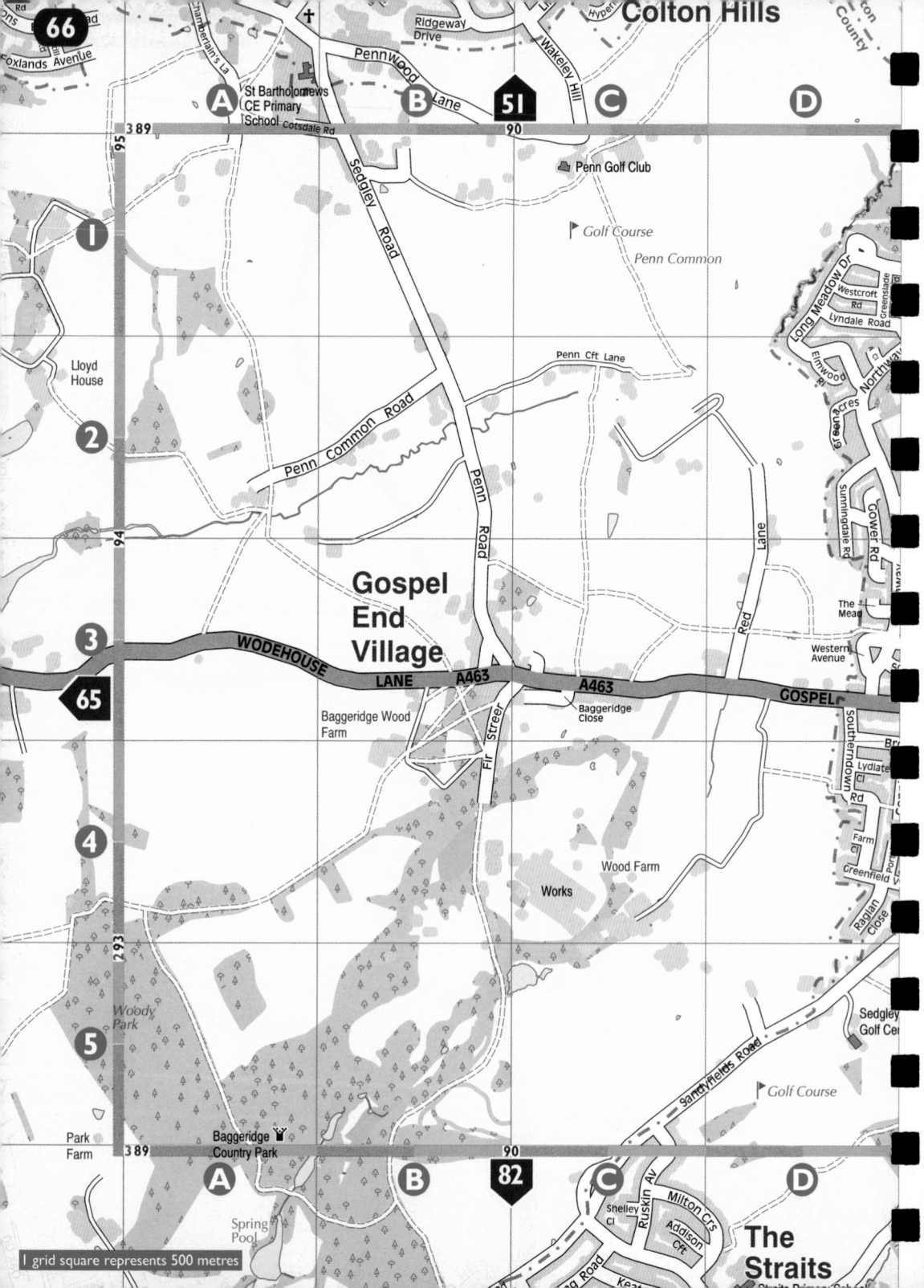

Colton Hills
Foxlands Avenue
Chamberlain's La
Ridgeway Drive
Pennwood Lane
Wakeley Hill
St Bartholomews CE Primary School
Cotsdale Rd
51
A
B
C
D
389
90
95
Penn Golf Club
Golf Course
Penn Common
Sedgley Road
Lloyd House
Long Meadow Dr
Westcroft Rd
Greenslade
Lyndale Road
Elmwood Rl
Northway
Penn Cft Lane
Penn Common Road
Greenacres
Penn Road
Red Lane
Sunningdale Rd
Gower Rd
94
Gospel End Village
The Mead
Western Avenue
WODEHOUSE LANE A463
A463
GOSPEL
65
Baggeridge Wood Farm
Fir Street
Baggeridge Close
Southerndown Rd
Lydiate Cl
Farm Cl
Greenfield
Wood Farm
Works
Raglan Close
293
Woody Park
Sedgley Golf Ce
Sandyfields Road
Golf Course
Park Farm
Baggeridge Country Park
82
Shelley Cl
Ruskin Av
Milton Crs
Addison Cft
Spring Pool
The Straits
1 grid square represents 500 metres

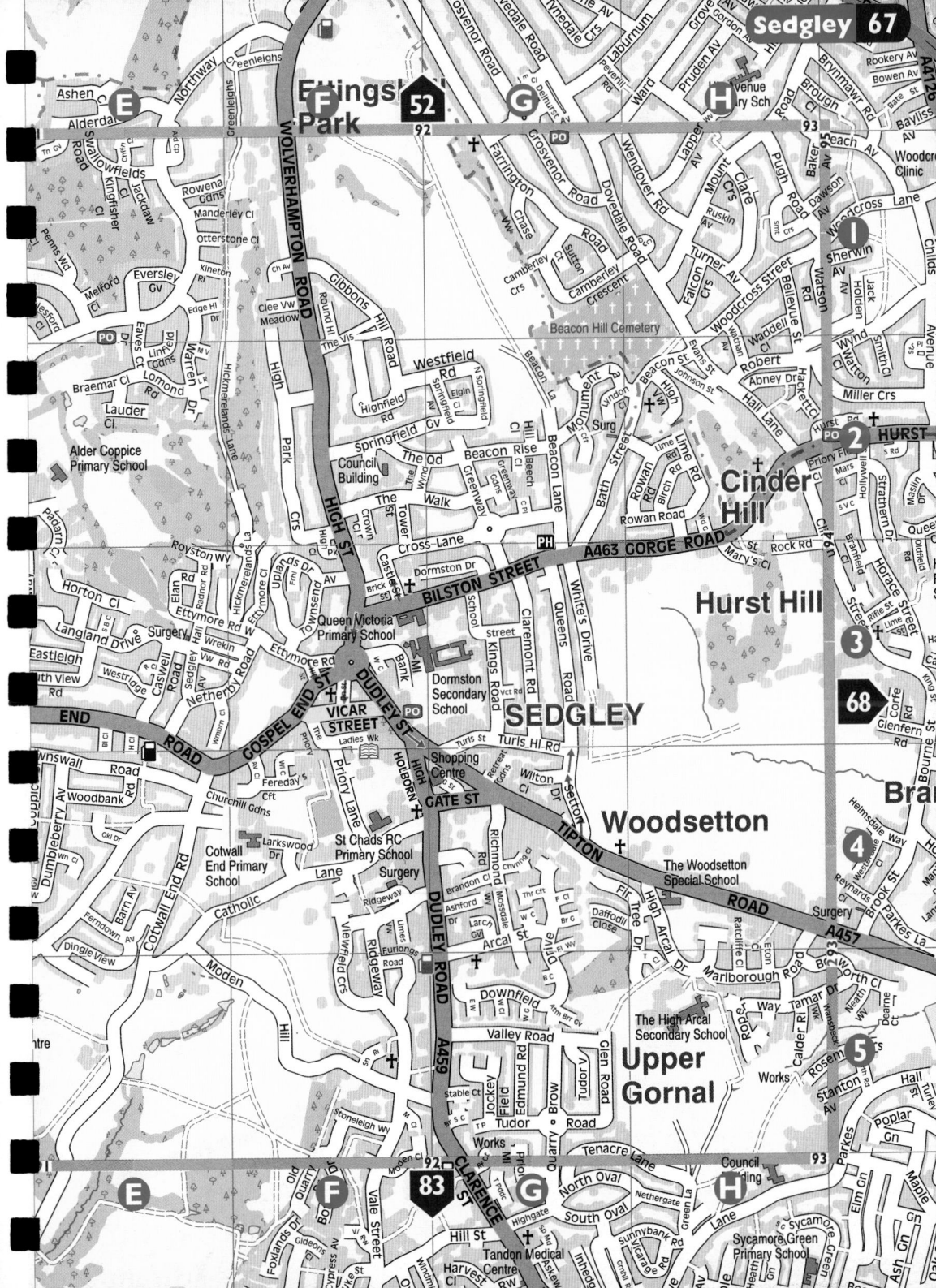

Ettingshall Park
Sedgley
Cinder Hill
Hurst Hill
Woodsetton
Upper Gornal
Beacon Hill Cemetery
Alder Coppice Primary School
Queen Victoria Primary School
Dormston Secondary School
Cotwall End Primary School
St Chads RC Primary School
The Woodsetton Special School
The High Arcal Secondary School
Sycamore Green Primary School
Tandon Medical Centre
Woodcross Clinic
Council Building
WOLVERHAMPTON ROAD
HIGH ST
A463 GORGE ROAD
BILSTON STREET
GOSPEL END ST
DUDLEY ST
VICAR STREET
DUDLEY ROAD
A459
TIPTON ROAD
A457
CLARENCE ST
52
68
83

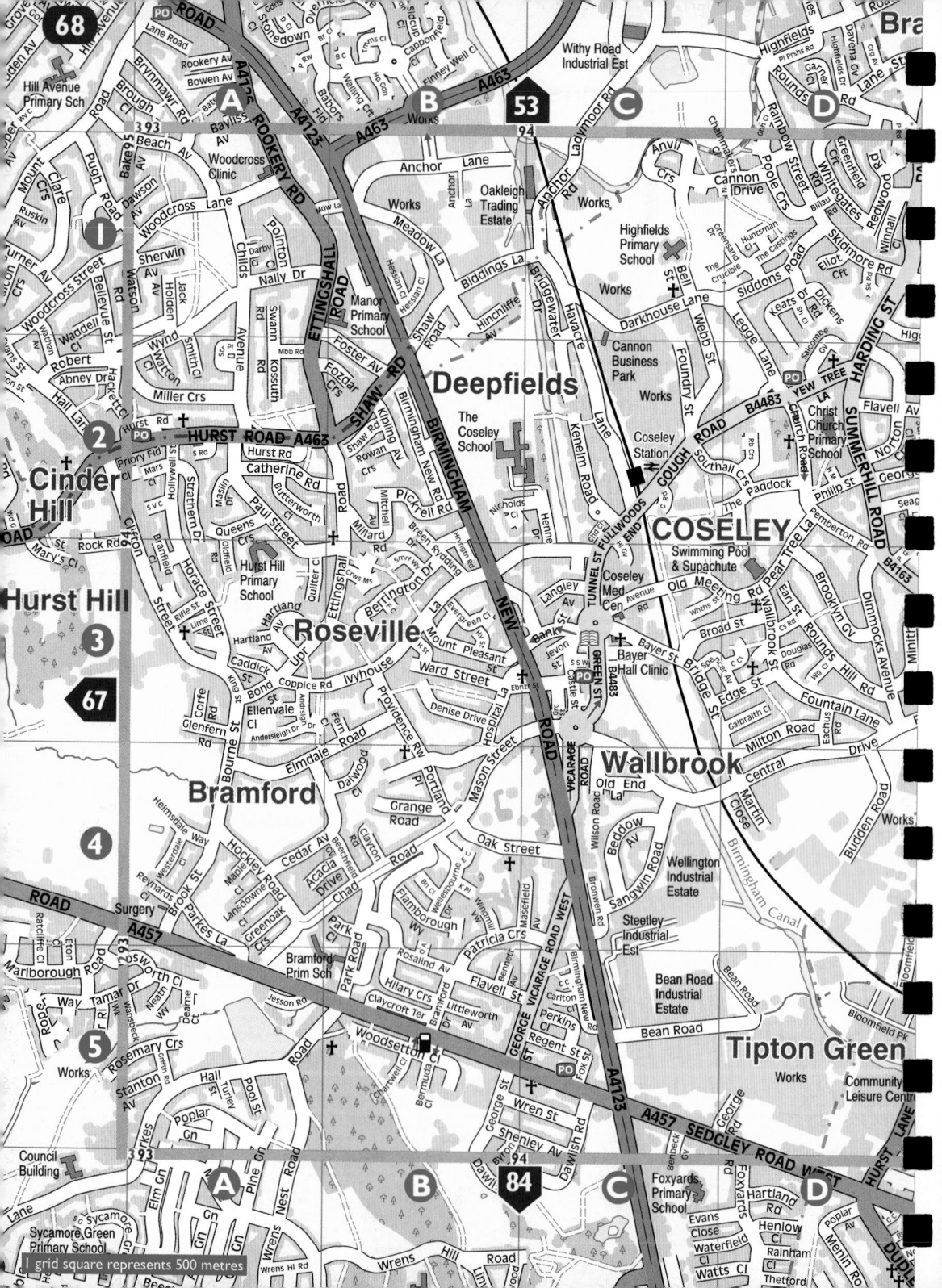
68
53
67
84
Deepfields
COSELEY
Roseville
Wallbrook
Bramford
Tipton Green
Cinder Hill
Hurst Hill
The Coseley School
Coseley Station
Highfields Primary School
Manor Primary School
Hurst Hill Primary School
Bramford Prim Sch
Foxyards Primary School
Sycamore Green Primary School
Christ Church Primary School
Hill Avenue Primary Sch
Woodcross Clinic
Oakleigh Trading Estate
Withy Road Industrial Est
Cannon Business Park
Wellington Industrial Estate
Steetley Industrial Est
Bean Road Industrial Estate
Coseley Swimming Pool & Supachute
Bayer Hall Clinic
Coseley Med Cen
Community Leisure Centre
Council Building
Birmingham Canal
BIRMINGHAM NEW ROAD A4123
ROOKERY RD A4123
ETTINGSHALL ROAD
HURST ROAD A463
SEDGLEY ROAD WEST A457
GEORGE VICARAGE ROAD WEST
SUMMERHILL ROAD
HARDING ST
GOUGH ROAD B4483
1 grid square represents 500 metres

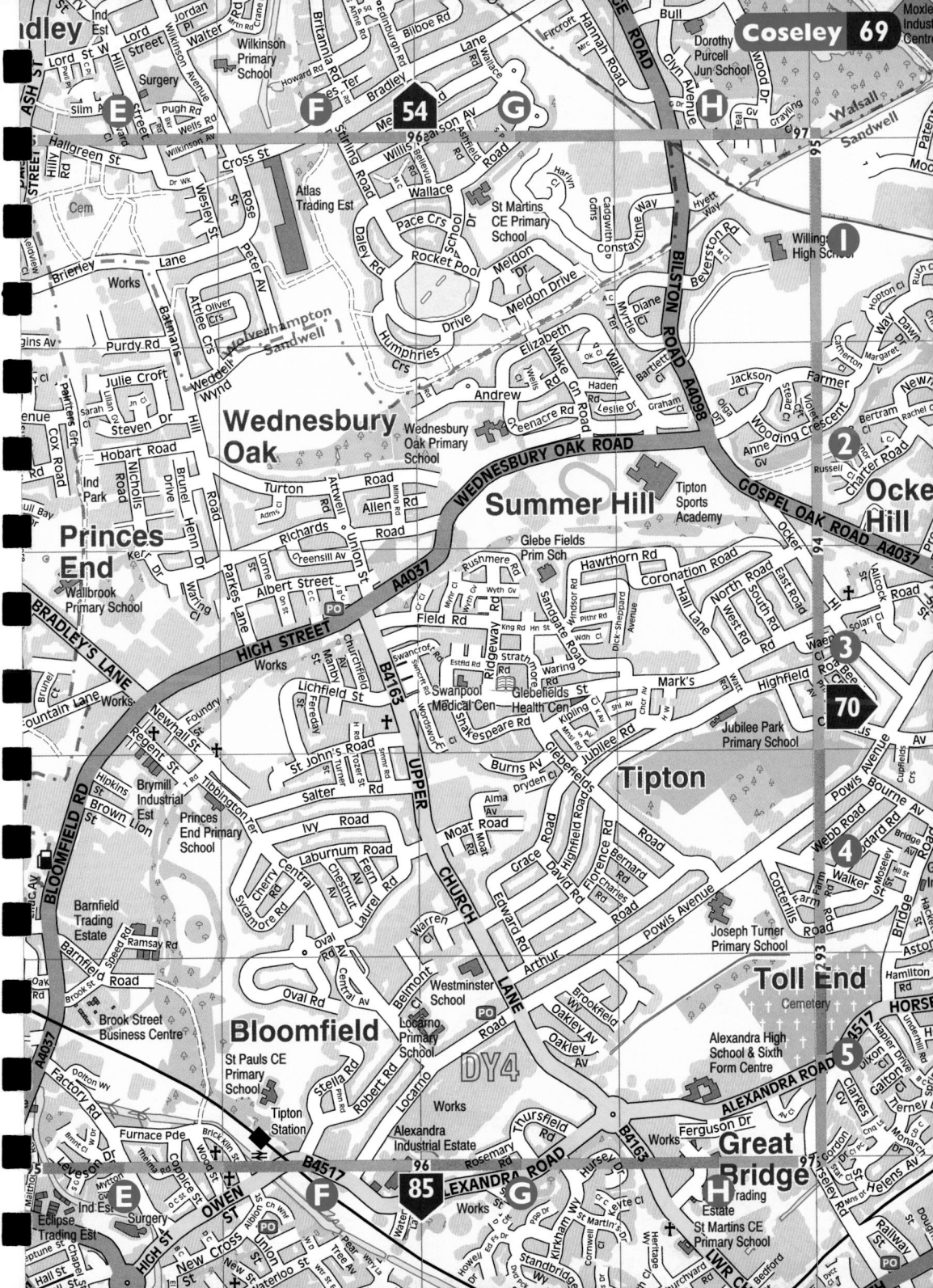

Coseley 69
Wednesbury Oak
Summer Hill
Princes End
Tipton
Toll End
Bloomfield
Great Bridge
Ocker Hill
DY4
54
70
85
Atlas Trading Est
Wilkinson Primary School
St Martins CE Primary School
Dorothy Purcell Jun School
Wednesbury Oak Primary School
Tipton Sports Academy
Glebe Fields Prim Sch
Wallbrook Primary School
Swanpool Medical Cen
Glebefields Health Cen
Jubilee Park Primary School
Brymill Industrial Est
Princes End Primary School
Barnfield Trading Estate
Brook Street Business Centre
Westminster School
Locarno Primary School
St Pauls CE Primary School
Tipton Station
Alexandra Industrial Estate
Joseph Turner Primary School
Alexandra High School & Sixth Form Centre
Cemetery
Eclipse Trading Est
St Martins CE Primary School
WEDNESBURY OAK ROAD
GOSPEL OAK ROAD A4037
BILSTON ROAD A4098
HIGH STREET
A4037
BRADLEY'S LANE
BLOOMFIELD RD
UPPER CHURCH LANE
B4163
ALEXANDRA ROAD
B4517
Wolverhampton
Sandwell
Walsall

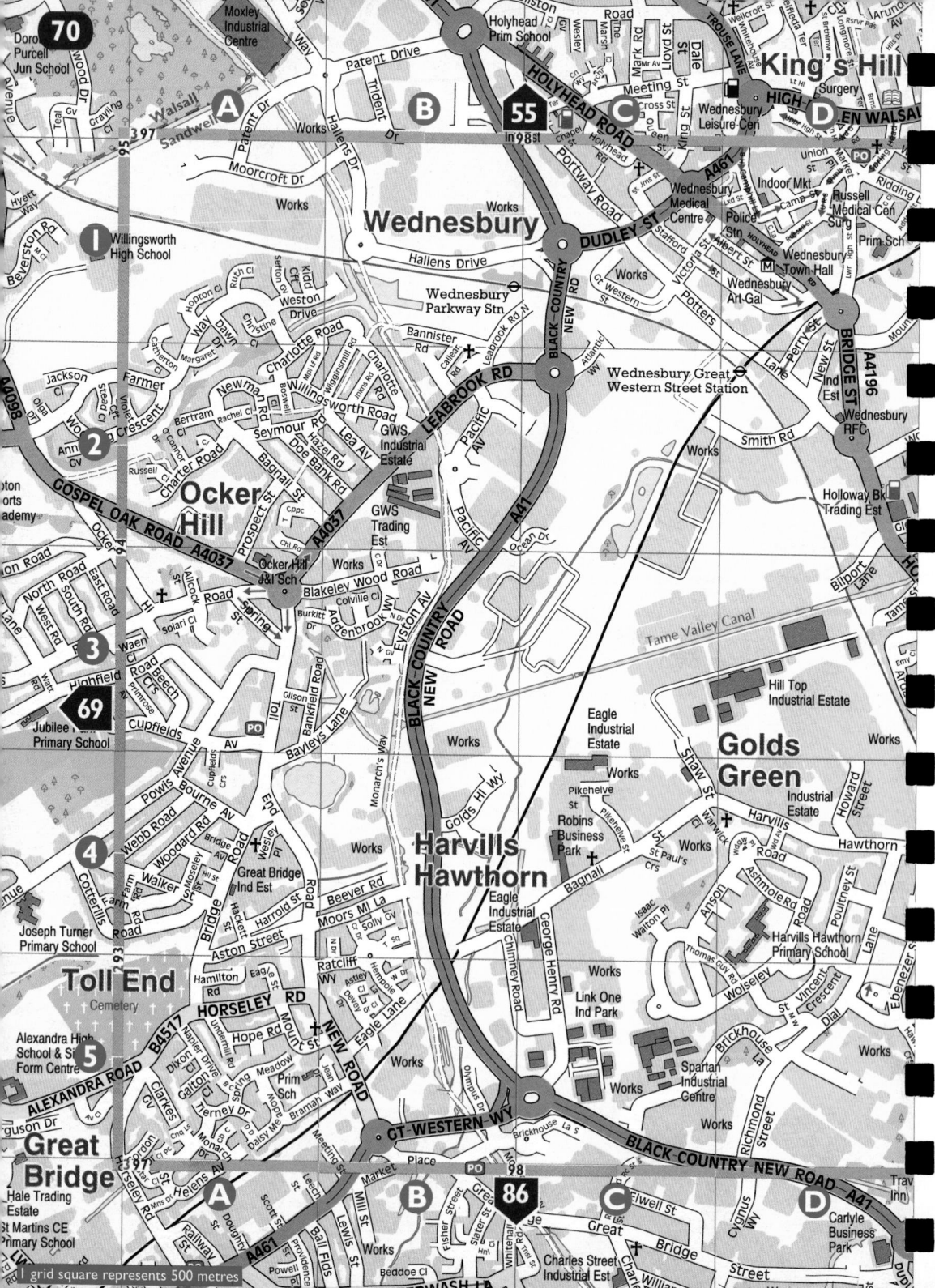
70
Moxley Industrial Centre
Holyhead Prim School
King's Hill
Surgery
Wednesbury Leisure Cen
Patent Drive
Trident
Hallens Dr
Moorcroft Dr
Walsall
Sandwell
55
HOLYHEAD ROAD
Meeting St
Cross St
Mark Rd
Lloyd St
Dale St
King St
Wesley
Marsh
TROUSE LANE
HIGH
WALSALL
Union St
Market Pl
PO
Indoor Mkt
Ridding La
Camp St
Russell Medical Cen
Wednesbury Medical Centre
Police Stn
Portway Road
DUDLEY ST
A461
Works
Wednesbury
Hallens Drive
Willingsworth High School
Beverston Rd
Hyett Way
Weston Drive
Kidd Cft
Hopton Cl
Ruth Cl
Christine
Dawn Dr
Margaret
Way
Charlotte Road
Wednesbury Parkway Stn
Bannister Rd
Leabrook Rd N
BLACK-COUNTRY NEW RD
Stafford
Victoria St
Albert St
Gt Western St
Potters Lane
Wednesbury Town Hall
Wednesbury Art Gal
Prim Sch
BRIDGE ST
A4196
Perry St
New St
Ind Est
Wednesbury RFC
Wednesbury Great Western Street Station
Atlantic Wy
LEABROOK RD
Willingsworth Road
Wigginsmill Rd
Charlotte Rd
Newman Rd
Farmer
Jackson Cl
Carterton
Crescent
Olga Dr
A4098
Bertram Cl
Rachel Cl
Seymour Rd
Hazel Rd
Lea Av
Doe Bank Rd
GWS Industrial Estate
A4037
Pacific Av
Smith Rd
Charter Road
O'Connor Dr
Russell
Ocker Hill
Bagnall St
Prospect St
GWS Trading Est
Holloway Bk Trading Est
GOSPEL OAK ROAD A4037
Ocker Hill J&I Sch
Blakeley Wood Road
Colville Cl
Addenbrook Wy
Eyston Av
Ocean Dr
A41
Billport Lane
North Road
South Rd
East Road
West Rd
Allcock Road
Spring St
Solari Cl
Waen Cl
Highfield Road
Beech Crs
Primrose Av
Watt Rd
69
Jubilee Park Primary School
Cupfields Av
Burkitt Dr
Gilson St
Toll End
Bankfield Road
Bayleys Lane
BLACK-COUNTRY NEW ROAD
Tame Valley Canal
Hill Top Industrial Estate
Eagle Industrial Estate
Golds Green
Industrial Estate
Shaw St
Howard Street
Powis Avenue
Bourne Av
Webb Road
Woodard Rd
Bridge Av
Bridge Road
Wesley Pl
Monarch's Way
Golds Hl Wy
Harvills Hawthorn
Pikehelve St
Robins Business Park
Bagnall St
St Paul's Crs
Warwick Cl
Harvills Road
Hawthorn
Ashmole Rd
Poultney St
Walker St
Moseley St
Hill St
Cotterills Road
Farm Rd
Joseph Turner Primary School
Great Bridge Ind Est
Hackett St
Harrold St
Beever Rd
Moors Ml La
Solly Gv
Aston Street
Eagle Industrial Estate
George Henry Rd
Chimney Road
Isaac Walton Pl
Anson
Thomas Guy Rd
Harvills Hawthorn Primary School
Wolseley
St Vincent Crescent
Dial
Ebenezer St
Lane
Toll End
Cemetery
Hamilton Rd
Eagle St
HORSELEY RD
Ratcliff Wy
Astley Cl
Hempole La
Eagle Lane
Link One Ind Park
Brickhouse La
Hope Rd
Mount St
NEW ROAD
Alexandra High School & Sixth Form Centre
B4517
ALEXANDRA ROAD
Dixon Cl
Napier Drive
Galton Cl
Spring Meadow
Prim Sch
Tierney Dr
Bramah Way
Olympus Dr
Spartan Industrial Centre
Richmond Street
Cygnus Wy
Ferguson Dr
Great Bridge
Clarkes Gv
Monarch
Daisy Me
GT-WESTERN WY
BLACK-COUNTRY NEW ROAD - A41
Brickhouse La S
Meeting St
Market Place
86
Horseley Rd
Helens Av
Scott St
Leech St
Mill St
Lewis St
Fisher Street
Slater St
Elwell St
Great Bridge
Street
Trav Inn
Carlyle Business Park
Hale Trading Estate
St Martins CE Primary School
Railway St
Doughty St
A461
Ball Flds
Providence
Powell
Beddoe Cl
Charles Street Industrial Est
Works
1 grid square represents 500 metres

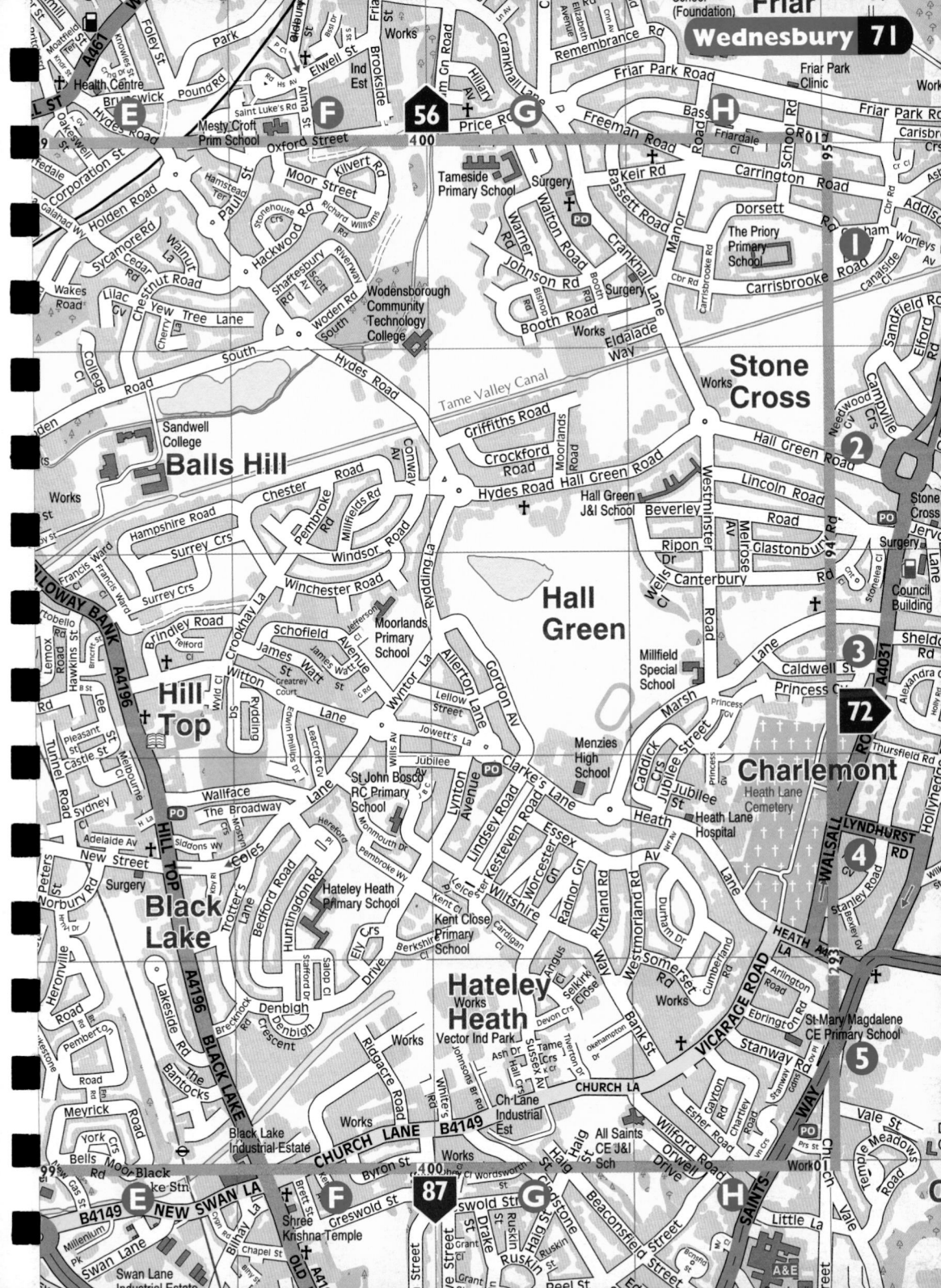
Friar
Wednesbury
71
56
72
87
Stone Cross
Balls Hill
Hall Green
Hill Top
Black Lake
Hateley Heath
Charlemont
Tame Valley Canal
Sandwell College
Wodensborough Community Technology College
Tameside Primary School
The Priory Primary School
Hall Green J&I School
Millfield Special School
Menzies High Sch
Moorlands Primary School
St John Bosco RC Primary School
Hateley Heath Primary School
Kent Close Primary School
Mesty Croft Prim School
St Mary Magdalene CE Primary School
All Saints CE J&I Sch
Heath Lane Hospital
Heath Lane Cemetery
Council Building
Friar Park Clinic
Health Centre
Black Lake Industrial Estate
Ch Lane Industrial Est
Vector Ind Park
Swan Lane Industrial Estate
Shree Krishna Temple
Black Lake Stn
Friar Park Road
Freeman Road
Carrington Road
Crankhall Lane
Bassett Road
Hydes Road
Hall Green Road
Lincoln Road
Westminster Road
Clarke's Lane
Heath Lane
Church Lane
Vicarage Road
Walsall Road
Black Lake
Hill Top
Holloway Bank
Oxford Street
Chestnut Road
South Road
New Swan La
A461
A4196
A4031
B4149
A41

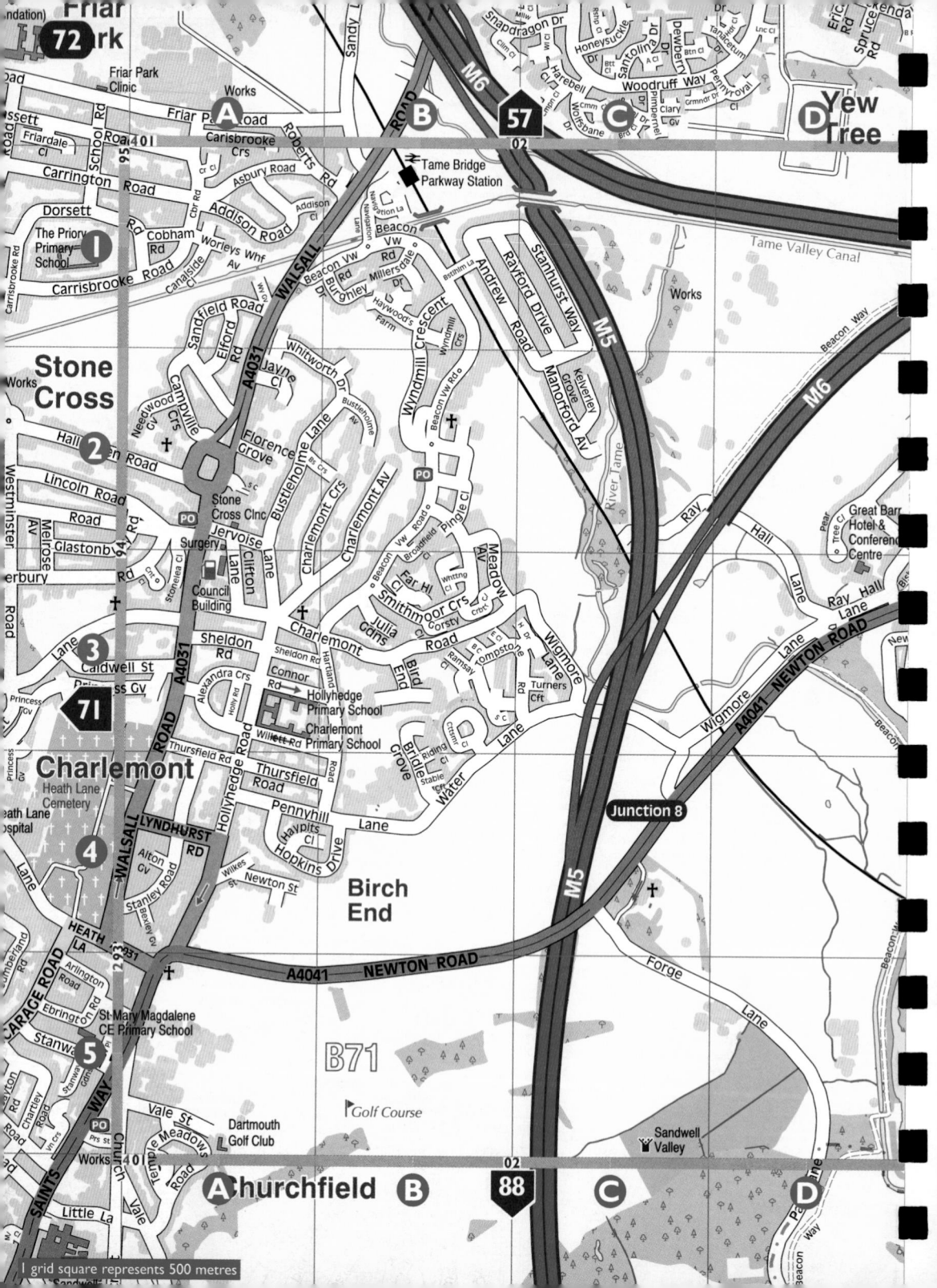

Friar Park
72
Friar Park Clinic
Works
Friar Park Road
Carisbrooke Crs
Roberts Rd
Friardale Cl
School Rd
Carrington Road
Asbury Road
Addison Road
Addison Cl
Dorsett Rd
The Priory Primary School
Cobham Rd
Worleys Whf Av
Canalside Cl
Carrisbrooke Road
Carrisbrooke Rd
Sandy La
WALSALL ROAD
M6
57
Snapdragon Dr
Honeysuckle Dr
Santolina Dr
Dewberry Dr
Tanacetum
Harebell Cl
Woodruff Way
Pennyroyal Cl
Wolfsbane Dr
Pimpernel
Clary Gv
Yew Tree
Tame Bridge Parkway Station
Navigation La
Beacon Vw
Beacon Vw Rd
Burghley Dr
Millersdale Dr
Haywood's Farm
Tame Valley Canal
Stanhurst Way
Rayford Drive
Andrew Road
Manorford Av
Kelverley Grove
M5
Works
Beacon Way
Sandfield Road
Elford Rd
A4031
Whitworth Dr
Jayne Cl
Wyndmill Crescent
Wyndmill Crs
Stone Cross
Works
Needwood Gv
Campville Crs
Bustleholme Lane
Bustleholme Av
Florence Grove
Hall Green Road
Lincoln Road
Westminster Road
PO
Stone Cross Clnc
Charlemont Crs
Charlemont Av
Pingle Cl
River Tame
Ray Hall Lane
Great Barr Hotel & Conference Centre
Pear Tree Cl
Melrose Av
Glastonbury Rd
Jervoise Lane
Surgery
Clifton Lane
Council Building
Stonelea Cl
Broadfield Cl
Meadow Av
Far Hl Cl
Smithmoor Crs
Julia Gdns
Corsty Cl
Charlemont Road
Sheldon Rd
Wigmore Lane
Tompstone Rd
Ramsay Cl
Turners Cft
Bird End
Caldwell St
Princess Gv
71
Alexandra Crs
Holly Rd
Connor Rd
Hartland Road
Hollyhedge Primary School
Charlemont Primary School
Willett Rd
Bridle Grove
Riding Cl
Stable Cft
Water Lane
Cttsmr Cl
Wigmore Lane
A4041 NEWTON ROAD
Charlemont
Heath Lane Cemetery
Heath Lane Hospital
Thursfield Rd
Thursfield Road
Hollyhedge Road
Pennyhill Lane
Haypits Cl
Hopkins Drive
Junction 8
LYNDHURST RD
Alton Gv
Stanley Road
Bexley Gv
Wilkes St
Newton St
Birch End
HEATH LA
A4031
A4041 NEWTON ROAD
Forge Lane
CARAGE ROAD
Arlington Road
Ebrington Rd
St Mary Magdalene CE Primary School
Stanway Rd
B71
Golf Course
Chartley Road
Vale St
Temple Meadows Road
Dartmouth Golf Club
Sandwell Valley
Beacon Way
Park Lane
SAINTS WAY
Church Vale
Little La
Churchfield
88
1 grid square represents 500 metres

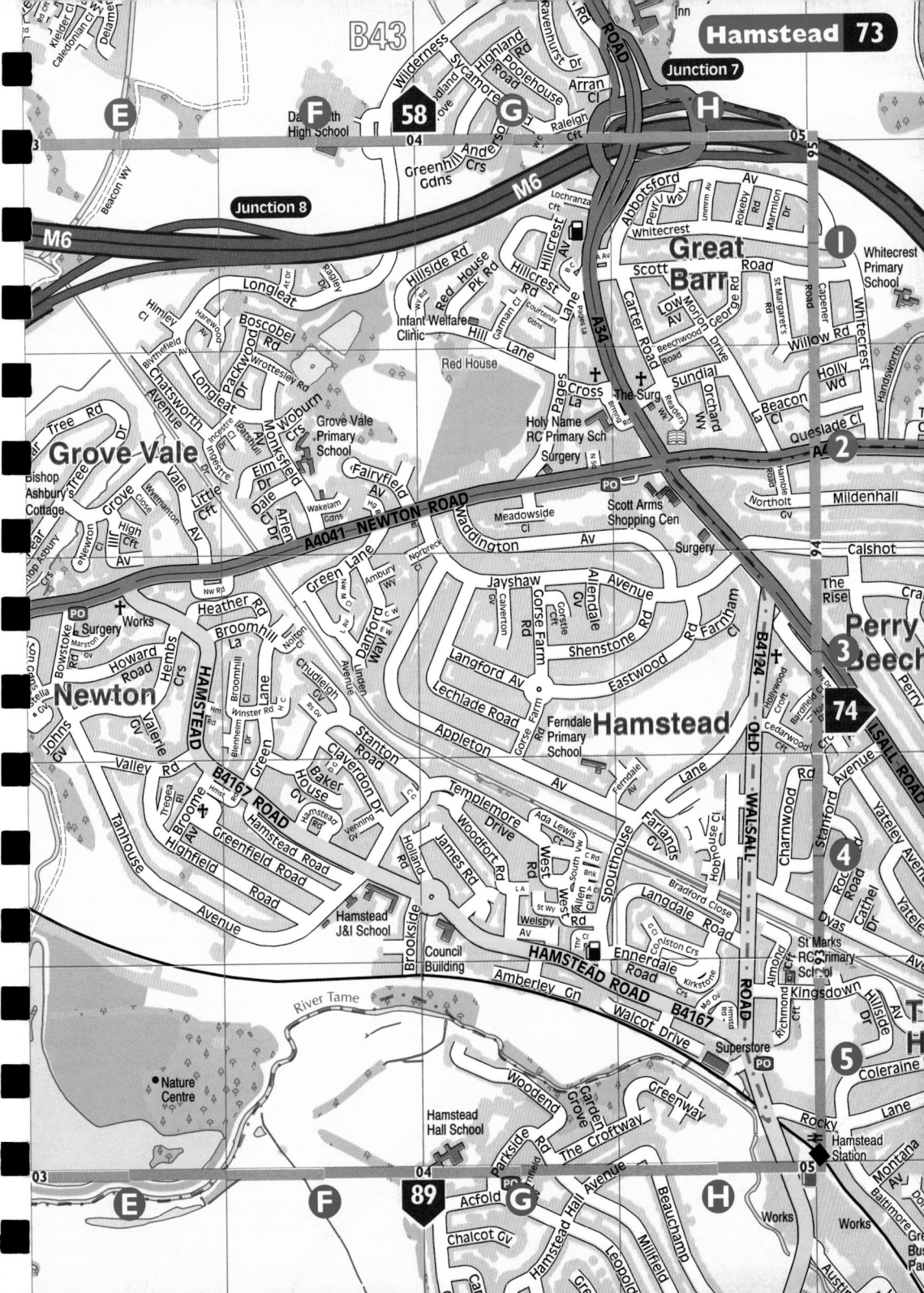

B43
Junction 7
Junction 8
M6
A34
A4041 NEWTON ROAD
HAMSTEAD ROAD
B4167 ROAD
OLD WALSALL ROAD
B4124
Great Barr
Grove Vale
Newton
Hamstead
Perry Beeches
Red House
River Tame
Nature Centre
Hamstead Hall School
Hamstead J&I School
Council Building
Ferndale Primary School
Whitecrest Primary School
Grove Vale Primary School
Holy Name RC Primary Sch
St Marks RC Primary School
Scott Arms Shopping Cen
Infant Welfare Clinic
Bishop Ashbury's Cottage
Hamstead Station
Superstore
Surgery
Works
58
74
89

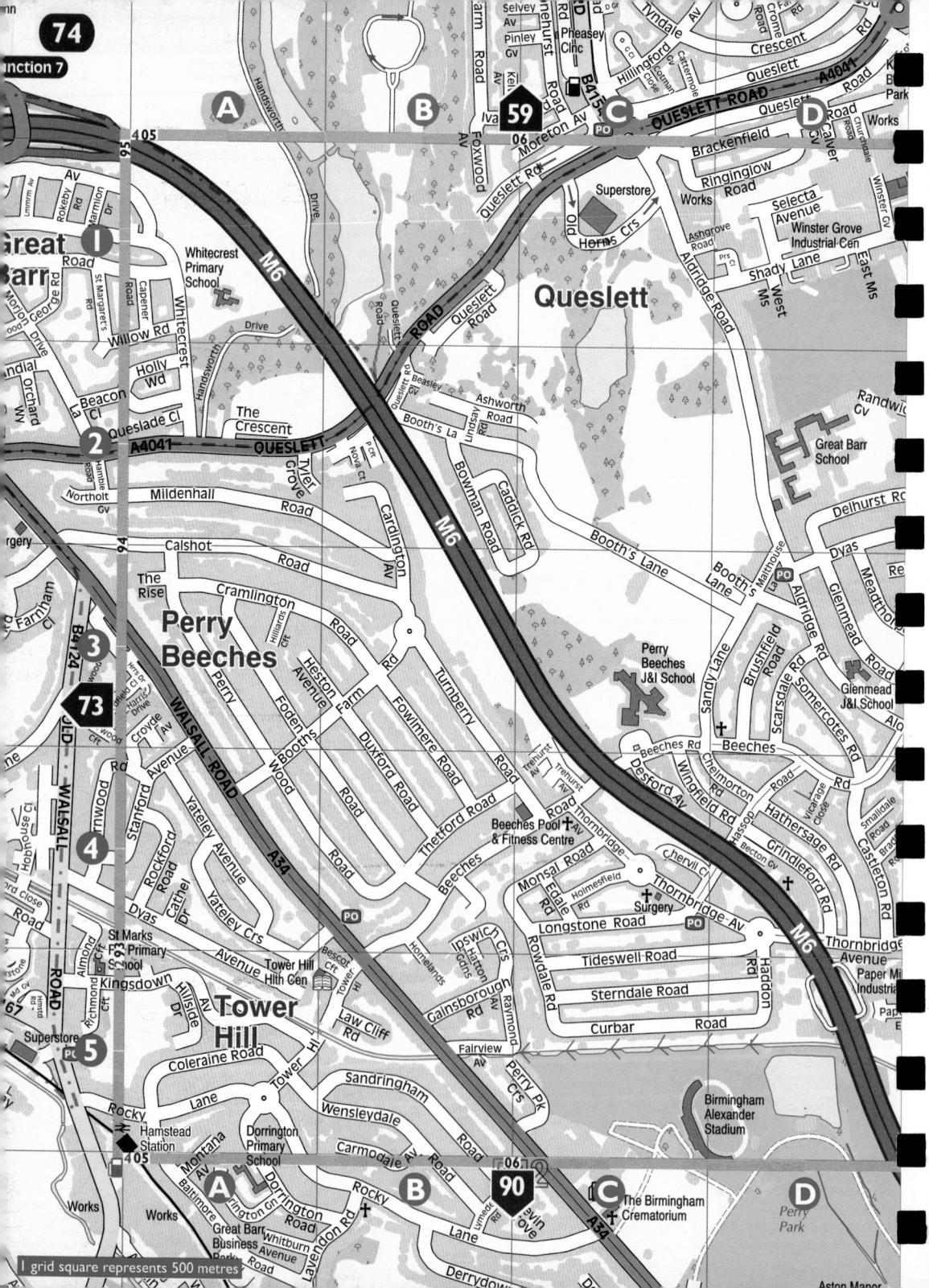
74
Junction 7
59
73
90
A
B
C
D
405
95
94
93
06
1
2
3
4
5
Great Barr
Queslett
Perry Beeches
Tower Hill
M6
A4041
QUESLETT ROAD
QUESLETT
A34
WALSALL ROAD
OLD WALSALL ROAD
B4124
B4157
Whitecrest Primary School
Superstore
Works
Winster Grove Industrial Cen
Great Barr School
Perry Beeches J&I School
Glenmead J&I School
Beeches Pool & Fitness Centre
Surgery
St Marks RC Primary School
Tower Hill Hlth Cen
Hamstead Station
Dorrington Primary School
Birmingham Alexander Stadium
The Birmingham Crematorium
Great Barr Business Park
Perry Park
Paper Mill Industrial
Aston Manor
Pheasey Clinc
PO
Handsworth Drive
Whitecrest
Willow Rd
Holly Wd
Beacon Cl
Queslade Cl
The Crescent
Tyler Grove
Mildenhall Road
Northolt Gv
Calshot Road
Cardington Av
Cramlington Road
The Rise
Farnham Cl
Perry Wood Road
Foden Road
Heston Avenue
Booths Farm Rd
Duxford Road
Fowlmere Road
Turnberry Road
Thetford Road
Beeches Road
Bowman Road
Caddick Rd
Booth's Lane
Booth's La
Ashworth Road
Lindsay Rd
Beasley Gv
Queslett Rd
Queslett Road
Old Horns Crs
Aldridge Road
Brackenfield
Ringinglow Road
Selecta Avenue
Ashgrove Road
Shady Lane
West Ms
East Ms
Winster Gv
Calver Gv
Churchdale
Moreton Av
Foxwood Av
Hillingford
Tyndale Crescent
Crome Road
Randwick Gv
Delhurst Rd
Dyas
Glenmead Road
Meadthorpe
Sandy Lane
Brushfield Road
Scarsdale Rd
Somercotes Rd
Beeches Rd
Chelmorton Rd
Wingfield Rd
Desford Av
Hassop Road
Hathersage Rd
Grindleford Rd
Castleton Rd
Becton Gv
Vicarage Close
Trehurst Av
Thornbridge Av
Thornbridge Avenue
Chervil Cl
Monsal Road
Edale Rd
Holmesfield Rd
Longstone Road
Tideswell Road
Sterndale Road
Curbar Road
Haddon Rd
Rowdale Rd
Ipswich Crs
Hatton Gdns
Gainsborough Rd
Raymond Av
Fairview Av
Perry Pk Crs
Homelands
Bescot Cft
Tower Hl
Law Cliff Rd
Yateley Avenue
Yateley Crs
Stanford Avenue
Rockford Road
Cathel Dr
Croyde Av
Dyas Avenue
Kingsdown Av
Hillside Dr
Almond Cft
Richmond Cft
Coleraine Road
Rocky Lane
Sandringham
Wensleydale Road
Carmodale Av
Montana Av
Dorrington Road
Lavendon Rd
Whitburn Avenue
Baltimore Road
Lymede Rd
Derrydown
Hobhouse Cl
Orchard Wy
George Rd
St Margaret's Rd
Capener Road
Rokeby Rd
Marmion Dr
Hamble Road
1 grid square represents 500 metres

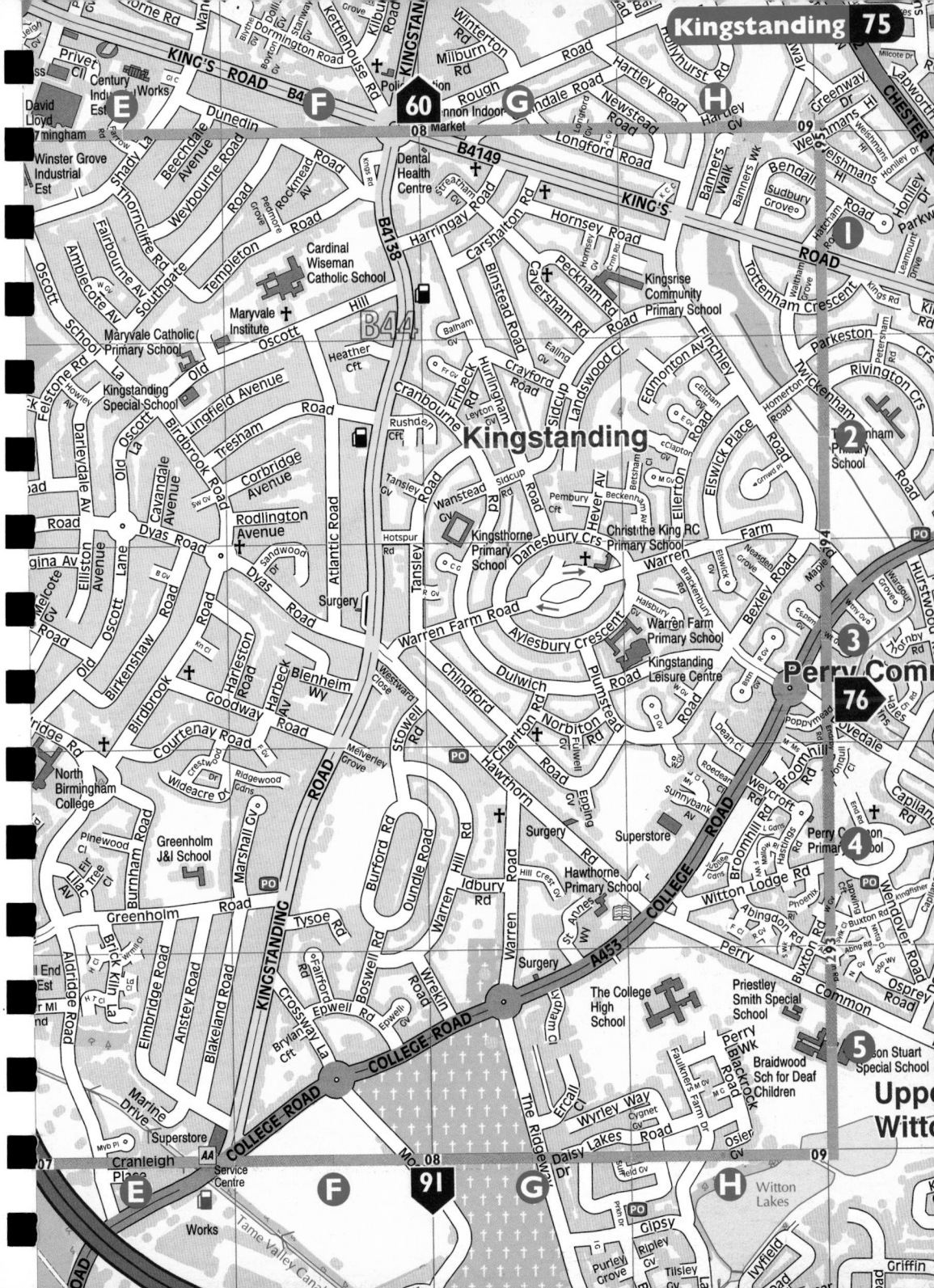
Kingstanding
King's Road
B4149
B4138
B44
Kingstanding Road
College Road
A453
Perry Common
Cardinal Wiseman Catholic School
Maryvale Institute
Maryvale Catholic Primary School
Kingstanding Special School
Kingsrise Community Primary School
Kingsthorne Primary School
Christ the King RC Primary School
Warren Farm Primary School
Kingstanding Leisure Centre
North Birmingham College
Greenholm J&I School
Hawthorne Primary School
The College High School
Priestley Smith Special School
Braidwood Sch for Deaf Children
Perry Common Primary School
Winster Grove Industrial Est
Century Industrial Est
Dental Health Centre
Superstore
Surgery
Service Centre
Works
Tame Valley Canal
Witton Lakes
Upper Witton
60
76
91

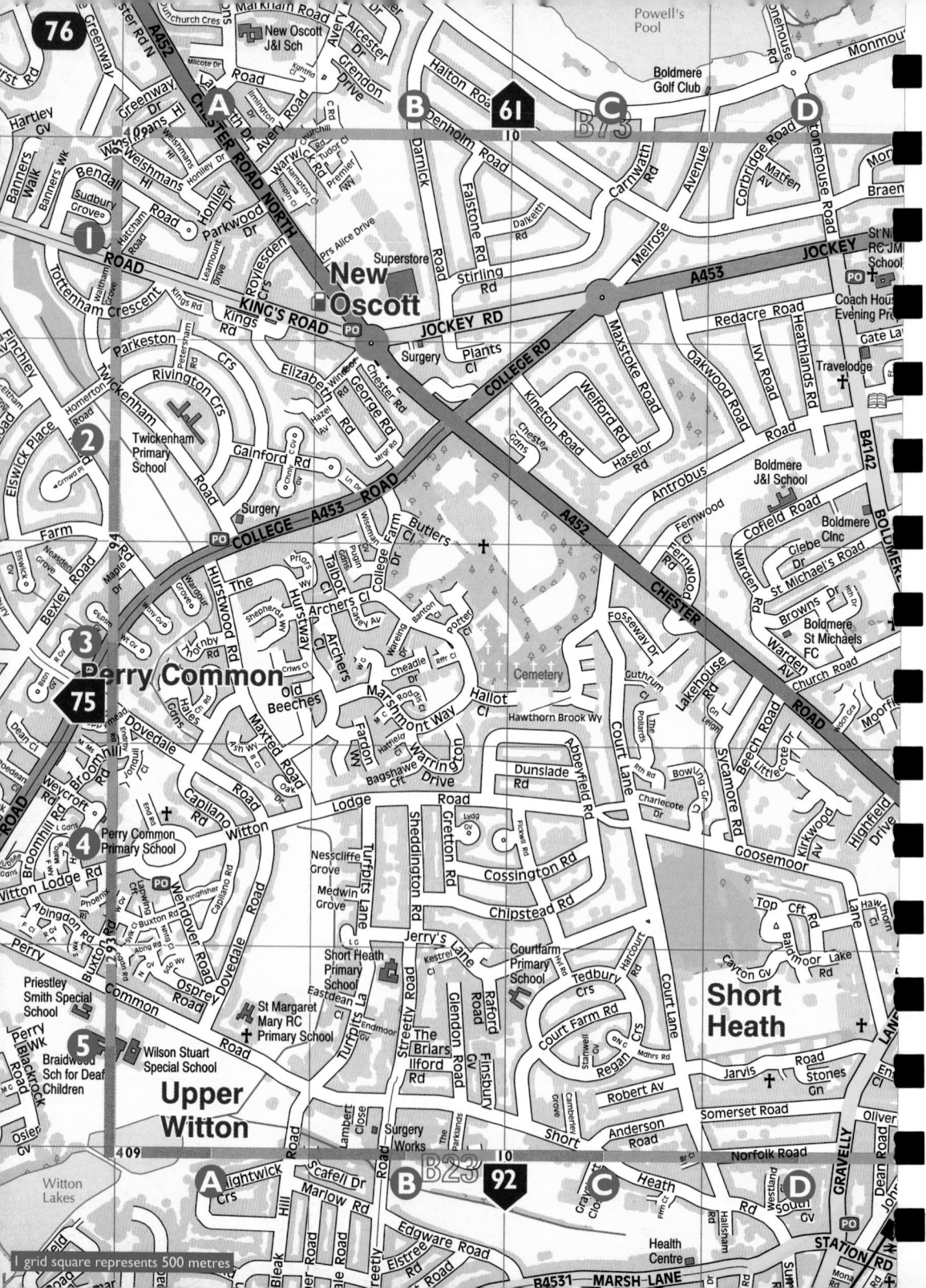

76
61
75
92
New Oscott
Perry Common
Short Heath
Upper Witton
Powell's Pool
Boldmere Golf Club
New Oscott J&I Sch
Superstore
Surgery
Twickenham Primary School
Perry Common Primary School
Priestley Smith Special School
Braidwood Sch for Deaf Children
Wilson Stuart Special School
St Margaret Mary RC Primary School
Short Heath Primary School
Courtfarm Primary School
Boldmere J&I School
Boldmere Clnc
Boldmere St Michaels FC
Coach House Evening Prep
Travelodge
Cemetery
Health Centre
Works
Witton Lakes
CHESTER ROAD NORTH
CHESTER ROAD
KING'S ROAD
JOCKEY RD
COLLEGE ROAD
COLLEGE RD
A452
A453
B4142
B73
B23
B4531
MARSH LANE
STATION RD
GRAVELLY LANE
Witton Lodge Road
Perry Common Road
Goosemoor Lane
Court Lane
Short Heath Road
1 grid square represents 500 metres

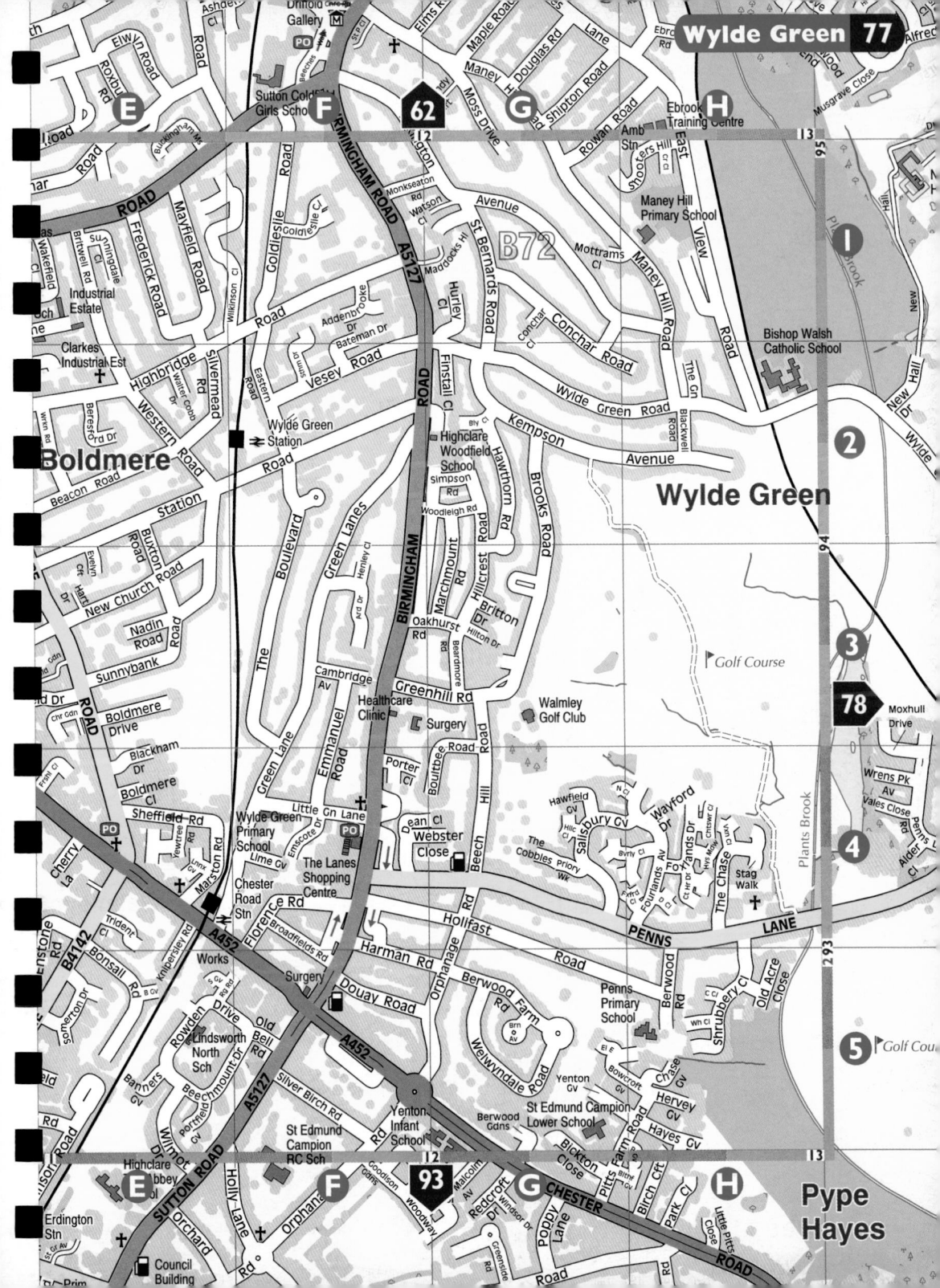
Boldmere
Wylde Green
Pype Hayes
B72
BIRMINGHAM ROAD
A5127
A452
CHESTER ROAD
SUTTON ROAD
PENNS LANE
Wylde Green Station
Chester Road Stn
Erdington Stn
Maney Hill Primary School
Bishop Walsh Catholic School
Highclare Woodfield School
Walmley Golf Club
Golf Course
Wylde Green Primary School
The Lanes Shopping Centre
Penns Primary School
St Edmund Campion Lower School
St Edmund Campion RC Sch
Yenton Infant School
Lindsworth North Sch
Clarkes Industrial Est
Ebrook Training Centre
Sutton Coldfield Girls School
Driffold Gallery
Council Building
Healthcare Clinic
Surgery
Plants Brook
62
78
93
95
94
293
12
13

78
77
63
94
A
B
C
D
1
2
3
4
5
413
14
95
94
293
Thimble End
Walmley
Walmley Ash
Pype Hayes
New Hall Hotel
Bishop Walsh Catholic School
New Shipton Farm
Deanery CE Primary School
Surgery
The Shrubbery School
Walmley CC
Walmley Junior School
Pype Hayes Golf Club
Golf Course
Langley Gorse
Fox Hollies
Minworth Ind Park
Castle Vale Industrial Estate
Castle Vale Ind Estate
Metalloys Industrial Est
Nature Park
Works
Plants Brook
Springfield Road
Walmley Road
B4148
Fox Hollies Rd
Fox Hollies Road
Webster Way
Thimble End Road
Signal Hayes Road
Signal Hayes Rd
Wylde Green Road
New Hall Dr
Walmley Ash Road
Eastleigh Cft
Hemlingford Rd
Ashurst Rd
Orton Avenue
Windyridge Road
Rosslyn Road
Parkhill Rd
Plants Brook Rd
Westlands Rd
Faircroft Av
Overdale Av
Brook Lane
Bonner Dr
Pentridge Close
Ashford Dr
Blakesley Close
Maybrook Road
Forge Lane
Fulford Dr
A38
Newmarsh Rd
Oversley Rd
Hadleigh Cft
Winton Grove
Marfield Cl
Lyneham Gdns
Delmore Way
Stapleton Cl
Coleville Rd
Cheswood Dr
Wilford Gv
Forge Cft
Harbury Cl
Lytham Cl
Anton Dr
Tamar Dr
Moat Cft
Dovey Dr
Welland Wy
Fowey Cl
Tudman Cl
Penns Wd Drive
Ashfern Dr
Trident Cl
Hawnchwood Dr
Eldon Drive
Penns Lake Rd
Alder Cl
Vales Close
Wrens Pk Av
Moxhull Drive
Crawford Rd
Coldstream Road
Allendale Road
Baxterley Gn
The Av
Warren House Wk
Water Ml Crs
Cater Dr
Terry Drive
Squires Cft
Ladbroke Dr
Braunston Cl
Hatherden Dr
Woodberry Dr
Clentworth Dr
Littleton Cl
Squirrel Hollow
Weaver Av
Arun Way
Swale Road
Chater Dr
Warrington Rd
Shottery Gv
Guys Cliffe Av
Monkspath
Harvington Wy
Hidcote Av
Ledbury Way
Meadow Foxes Rd
Greenacres
Lawnswood
Farm Rd
Kinver Croft
Malvern Dr
Foldyard Cl
Brookhus Farm Rd
Turchill Drive
The Riddings
Oakland Cft
Sherratt Cl
Townsend Dr
Patterton Dr
Lane Cft
Pytman Dr
Calder Dr
Juniper Dr
Oak Farm Cl
Ledbury Wy
Falstaff Cl
Elm Rd
Aspen Cl
Rowan Cl
Sycamore Cl
Holly Cl
Oak Wy
Birch Cl
Alfreds
Glenfield Cl
Bowood End
Musgrave Close
Bilberry Crs
Granary La
Argus Cl
Froggatts
Carters Cl
Hilary
Langley
Berryfields
Springfield Rd
Drive
Lane
Shrubbery Cl
Old Acre Close
The Chase
Stag Walk
Little Pitts Close
View Road
New Hall
1 grid square represents 500 metres
Pype Hayes

Grove

E

F

Ox Leys
Farm

G x Leys Road

H

**Grove
End**

95

Bull's Lane

A38

Fairview
Farm

16

Grove Lane

Church Lane

I

2 **B76**
Over Green

Bull's Lane

Curdworth Lane

94

Golf Course

Wishaw Lane

Wiggins Hill Road

3

Warwickshire County
Birmingham

Peddimore
Hall

4

Peddimore

Lane

Wishaw Lane

Wiggins Hill
Farm

93

A38

5

Peddimore
Lane

Hurst Green
Farm

KI

Superstore

Farvale Rd

Redmoor Way

Oxsall Close

Cottage Lane

Hurst Gn Rd

Summer La

Lawrence
Drive

W Dr

Longley AV

Birmingham & Fazeley Canal

the Greaves

Stockton Cl

Lindridge Dr

Gt Thornley

KINGSBURY ROAD

Kingsbury Close

95
4097

Works

Kingsbury
Business Park

5
**Minworth
Industrial
Park**

E

Oakenhayes
Crs

F

16

G

H

17

Old   Kingsbury   Road

PO
Minworth

Minworth

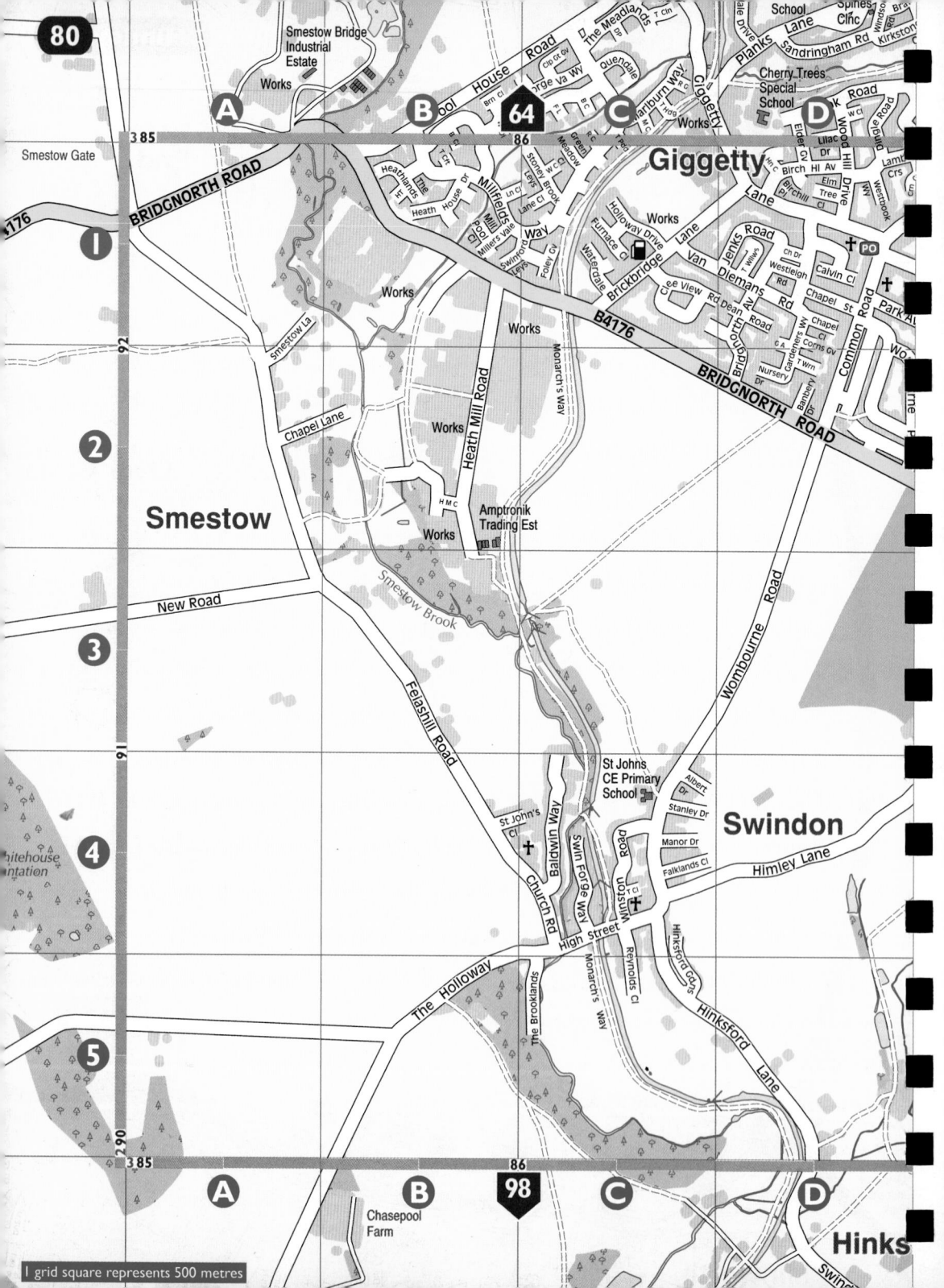
64
98
A
B
C
D
1
2
3
4
5
385
86
92
91
290
Smestow Bridge Industrial Estate
Works
Smestow Gate
BRIDGNORTH ROAD
B4176
Giggetty
Smestow
Swindon
Hinks
Amptronik Trading Est
St Johns CE Primary School
Cherry Trees Special School
School
Spines Clinic
Planks Lane
Sandringham Rd
Kirkstone
The Meadlands
Quendale
House Road
Marlburn Way
Giggetty Lane
Heathlands
Heath House Dr
Millfields Way
Mill Pool
Millers Vale
Swinford Leys
Stoney Brook Leys
Green Meadow
Lane Cl
Foley Gv
Waterdale
Furnace Cl
Holloway Drive
Brickbridge Lane
Van Diemans Rd
Jenks Road
Westleigh Rd
Calvin Cl
Chapel St
Common Road
Park Av
Clee View Rd
Dean Road
Bridgnorth Av
Gardeners Way
Chapel Cl
Corns Gv
Nursery Dr
Banbery Dr
Elder Gv
Lilac Dr
Wood Hill Drive
Birch Hl Av
Birchill Pl
Elm Tree Cl
Westbook Wy
Lamb Crs
Smestow La
Chapel Lane
Heath Mill Road
Monarch's Way
Smestow Brook
New Road
Felashill Road
Wombourne Road
Albert Dr
Stanley Dr
Manor Dr
Falklands Cl
Himley Lane
St John's Cl
Baldwin Way
Church Rd
Swin Forge Way
Winston Road
High Street
The Holloway
The Brooklands
Reynolds Cl
Hinksford Gdns
Hinksford Lane
Whitehouse Plantation
Chasepool Farm
PO
1 grid square represents 500 metres

Woody
The Foxhills
Surg
Redcliffe Drive
Rookery Rise
Copper Beech
Poplar Cl
Pinewood Close
Glendale Dr
Redhill Av
The Longlands
High Mdw
Greenhill
E
F
G
H
65
88
89
Park Farm
Bagge
Count
The Broadway
Woodlands
Richmond Gdns
Oaks Dr
Whites Wood
Blakeley
Greenfields Road
Cedars Av
Greenhill Gdns
Beggars Bush La
Sytch Lane
Blakeley Heath Primary Sch
Griffiths Dr
Neachless Av
Dickinson Rd
Gate Cl
Greenhill Farm
I
92
Rock Pool
2
Golf Cour
Himley Hall Golf Centre
Himley Hall & Park
Himley Hall
STOURBRIDGE ROAD
Plantation Lane
Nature Reserve
Himley Plantation
Bridgnorth Road
Cherry Lane
Churns Hill Lane
Himley Country Hotel
Great Pool
School Road
Himley La
Himley House Hotel
3
DUDLEY ROAD
82
Himley
A449
B4176
Works
91
Home Farm
WOLVERHAMPTON ROAD
4
Staffordshire County
Dudley
Holbeache Lane
Maidensbridge Primary School
Beachcroft Road
Claydon Road
Holcroft Road
Beachwood Av
Brook Street
Victoria St
Maidensbridge Rd
Collindale Ct
Monteagle Drive
Camden Way
Copper Beech Dr
Hedgerow Dr
Rokewood Cl
Keyes Drive
Hewell Cl
Charterfield Dr
5
Oakdale Trading Estate
Lane
90
Cancel Industrial Est
Oakdale Trading Est
87
Albert St
Albion St
99
Cross Street
Forge Lane
Blaze Hill Road
Blaze Park
Lyndon Grove
Richmond Park
Grove Park
Dawley Road
WOLVERHAMPTON
Ambrose Crescent
Charterfield Drive
Catesby Dr
Digby Rd
Redruth Cl
Charterfield Shopping Cen
Avondale Road
Courtland Rd
B4175
Midland House
Dovedale Rd
ford
Wall
Enville Rd
PO
STREET
DUDLEY

Woody Park
A
B
66
C
D
Sedgley Golf Cen
Golf Course
Park Farm
Baggeridge Country Park
90
Sandyfields Road
Spring Pool
Island Pool
The Straits
Straits Primary School
Ruskin Av
Milton Crs
Shelley Cl
Addison Cft
Kipling Road
Keats Close
Meredith Rd
Chaucer Av
Tennyson Road
Kingsley Gv
Longfellow Rd
Wordsworth Rd
Sandyfields Rd
St Michaels Road
Himley Gdns
Byron Cft
Browning Cl
Irving Rd
Masefield Rd
Shakespeare Rd
Burns Gv
Rhodes Cl
Spencer Cl
Coleridge Ri
Cotwall End Road
PO
Surgery
High Arcal Road
DY3
Rock Pool
Golf Course
Himley Hall Golf Centre
Himley Hall Park
Himley Hall
Higharcal Wood
Wallows Wd
The Straits
Straits Gn
St Andrew's Cl
Staffordshire County
Dudley
Grafton Gdns
Acton Dr
The Aly
Musk La
St Chad's Cl
Ladbrook Gv
Straits
Orchard Gv
Musk La W
HIMLEY ROAD B4176
ROAD
81
Eaton Crs
Manor Dr
Road
Hopyard La
Brick Kiln Lane
Louise
Himley Wood
Hopyard Lane
Summit Pl
HIMLEY
Oakland Dr
Home Farm
PH
Elm Cl
Guy's La
Maple Dr
Brookbank Rd
Flaven La
Staffordshire County
Dudley
Brookbank Gdns
Sandfield Gv
Windsor Ct
B4175 CINDER RO
Works
Works
Works
Lane
Oak Lane
Collindale Ct
Monteagle Drive
Camden Way
The Oak Industrial Park
Ham Lane
The Pensnett Trading Estate
Oakdale Trading Estate
Rokewood Cl
Keyes Drive
Central Trading Estate
STALLINGS LANE
STALLINGS LANE B4175
Hedgerow Dr
Charterfield Dr
Chancel Industrial Est
Works
Catesby Dr
Jay Road
Hawkeswell
Oakdale Trading Est
Chancel Industrial Est
90
Works
100
Tansey Trading Estate
Tansey Green
Smithy Lane
Digby Rd
Charterfield Shopping Cen
Avondale Cl
Hinsford Close
Redruth Cl
Pensnett Trading Estate
First
The Pensnett Trading Estate
Works
1 grid square represents 500 metres

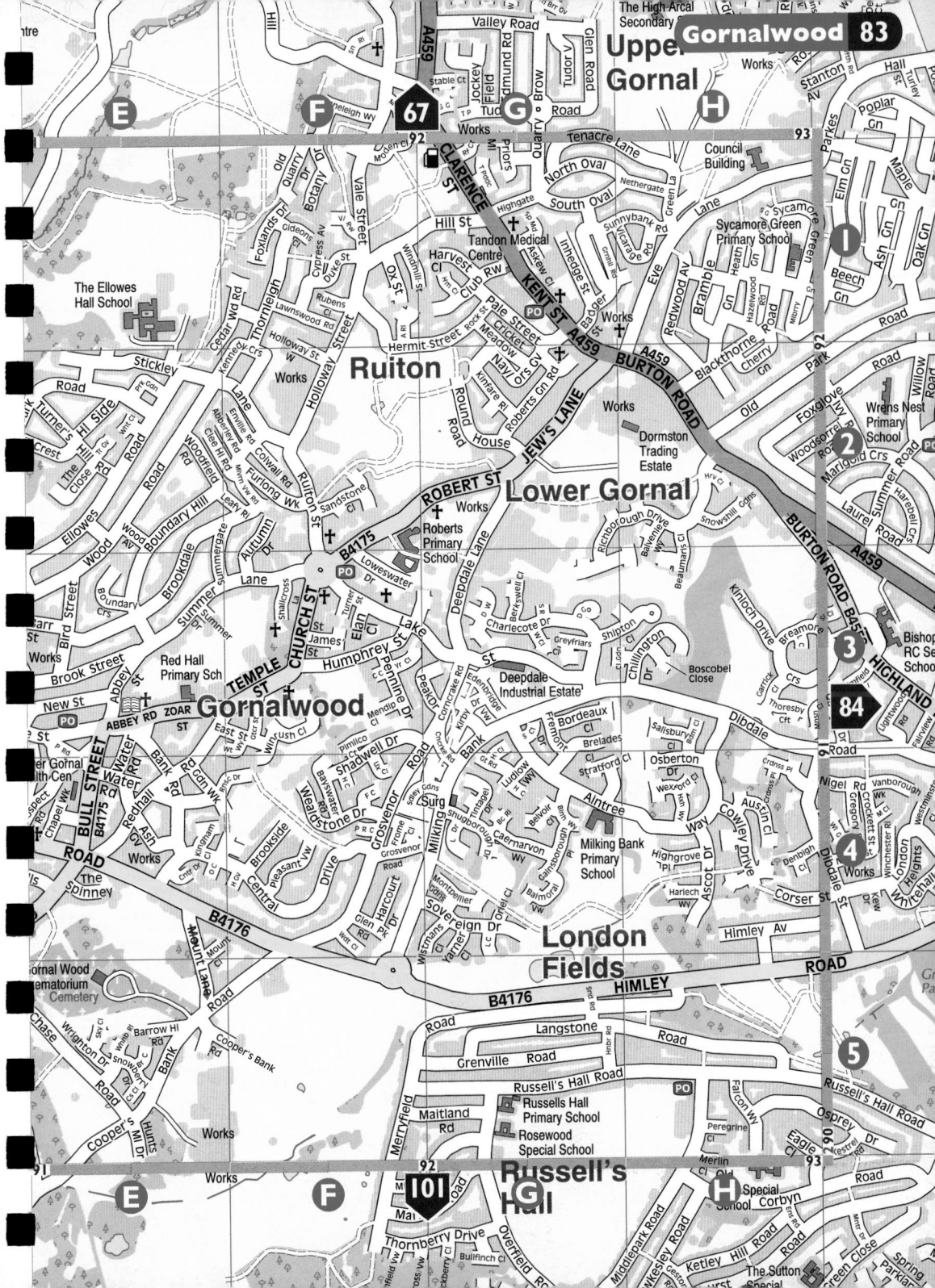

Upper Gornal
Ruiton
Lower Gornal
Gornalwood
London Fields
Russell's Hall
E
F
G
H
I
2
3
4
5
67
84
101
92
93
91
90
A459
CLARENCE ST
KENT ST
BURTON ROAD
JEW'S LANE
ROBERT ST
B4175
CHURCH ST
TEMPLE ST
ABBEY RD
ZOAR ST
BULL STREET
B4176
HIMLEY ROAD
HIGHLAND
BURTON ROAD B4555
Valley Road
Glen Road
Tenacre Lane
North Oval
South Oval
Hill St
Vale Street
Holloway Street
Hermit Street
Pale Street
Cricket Meadow
Round House Road
Stickley Lane
Ruiton St
Summer Lane
Brook Street
New St
Humphrey St
Lake St
Deepdale Lane
Dibdale Road
Aintree Way
Milking Bank
Grosvenor Road
Central Drive
Sovereign Dr
Himley Av
Langstone Road
Grenville Road
Russell's Hall Road
Merryfield Rd
Maitland Rd
Thornberry Drive
Overfield Road
Middlepark Road
Ketley Hill Road
Mount Lane
Cooper's Bank Road
Park Road
Old Park Road
Corser St
Dibdale St
The Ellowes Hall School
Tandon Medical Centre
Sycamore Green Primary School
Council Building
Wrens Nest Primary School
Dormston Trading Estate
Roberts Primary School
Red Hall Primary Sch
Deepdale Industrial Estate
Milking Bank Primary School
Russells Hall Primary School
Rosewood Special School
Boscobel Close
Works
PO

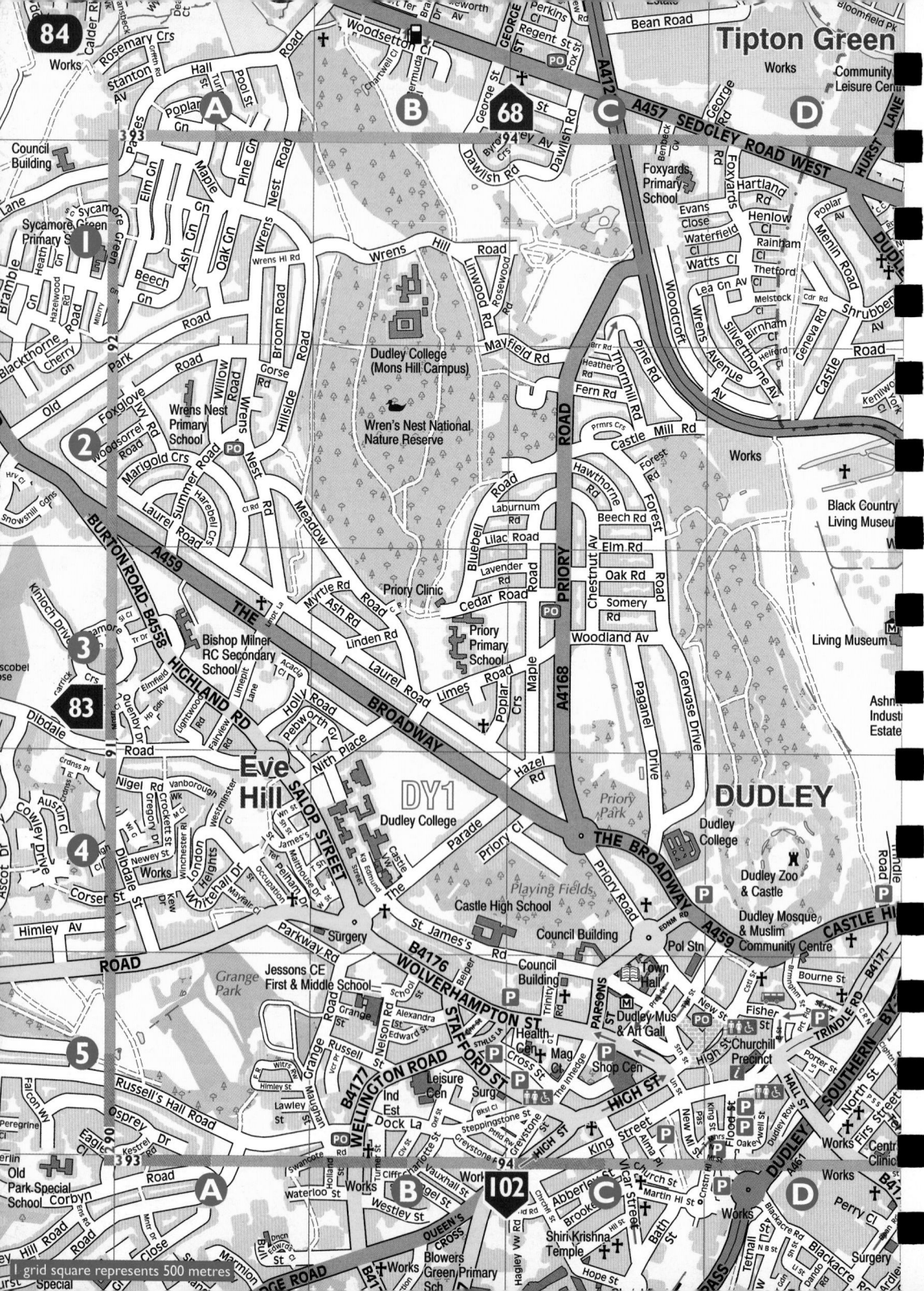

84
68
83
102
Tipton Green
Works
Community Leisure Centre
Bean Road
A457 SEDGLEY ROAD WEST
A4123
Foxyards Primary School
Council Building
Sycamore Green Primary School
Wrens Hill Road
Dudley College (Mons Hill Campus)
Wren's Nest National Nature Reserve
Wrens Nest Primary School
Mayfield Rd
Castle Mill Rd
Black Country Living Museum
Living Museum
BURTON ROAD B4558
A459 THE BROADWAY
Bishop Milner RC Secondary School
HIGHLAND RD
Priory Clinic
Priory Primary School
PRIORY ROAD A4168
Eve Hill
SALOP STREET
DY1
Dudley College
DUDLEY
Priory Park
Dudley Zoo & Castle
Dudley Mosque & Muslim Community Centre
CASTLE HILL
Playing Fields
Castle High School
Council Building
Pol Stn
Town Hall
Dudley Mus & Art Gall
Churchill Precinct
Shop Cen
Leisure Cen
Grange Park
Jessons CE First & Middle School
B4176 WOLVERHAMPTON ST
STAFFORD ST
B4177 WELLINGTON ROAD
HIGH ST
King Street
Vicar Street
Surgery
Russell's Hall Road
Old Park Special School
QUEEN'S CROSS
Blowers Green Primary Sch
Shiri Krishna Temple
SOUTHERN BY-PASS
1 grid square represents 500 metres

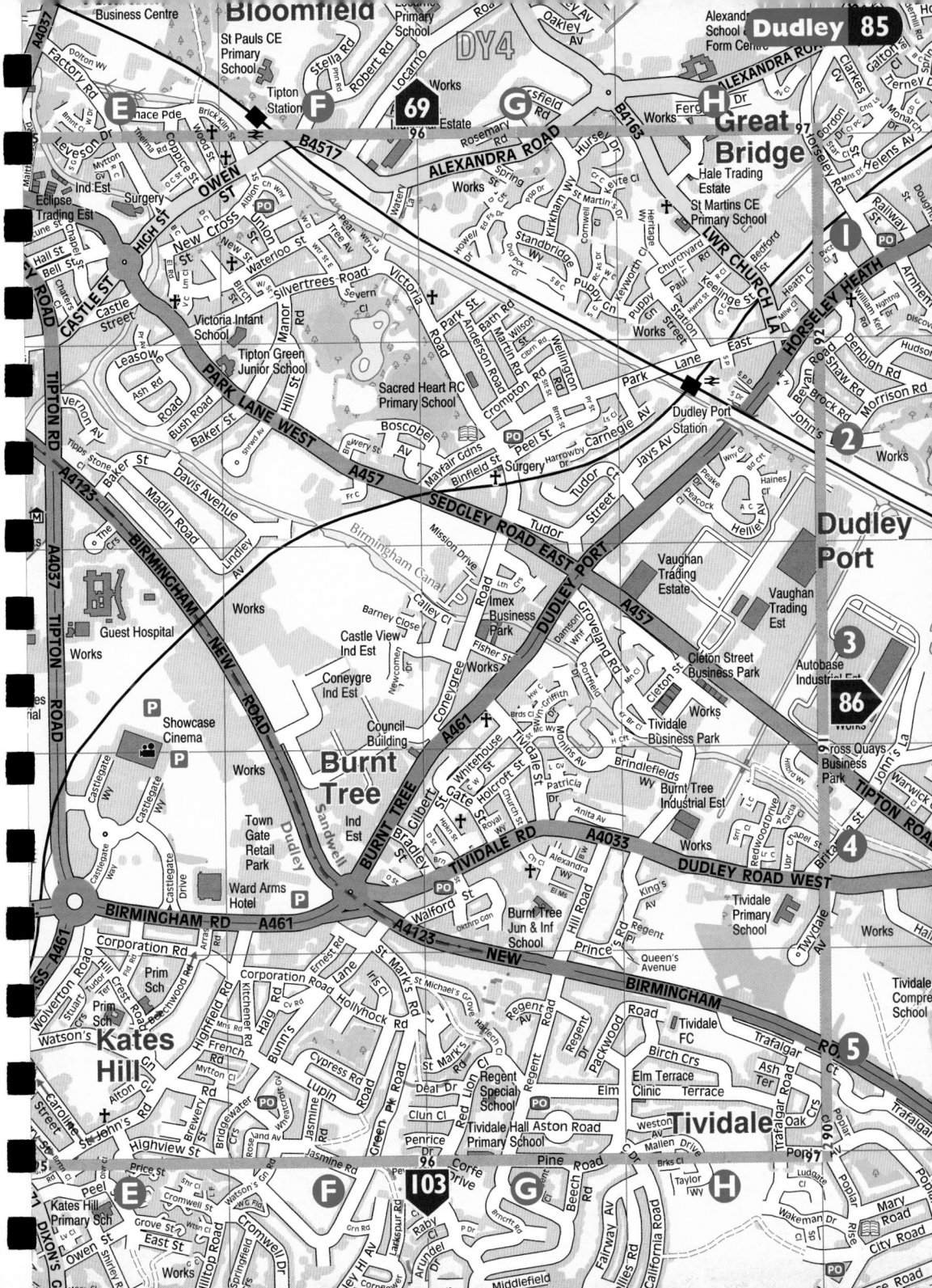
Bloomfield
Business Centre
St Pauls CE Primary School
Tipton Station
DY4
Great Bridge
Hale Trading Estate
St Martins CE Primary School
ALEXANDRA ROAD
OWEN ST
HIGH ST
Eclipse Trading Est
Victoria Infant School
Tipton Green Junior School
Sacred Heart RC Primary School
PARK LANE WEST
HORSELEY HEATH
LWR CHURCH LA
Dudley Port Station
SEDGLEY ROAD EAST
DUDLEY PORT
Dudley Port
Vaughan Trading Estate
Vaughan Trading Est
Imex Business Park
Castle View Ind Est
Coneygre Ind Est
Birmingham Canal
Guest Hospital
Showcase Cinema
Cleton Street Business Park
Autobase Industrial Est
Tividale Business Park
Cross Quays Business Park
Burnt Tree
Burnt Tree Industrial Est
Town Gate Retail Park
Ward Arms Hotel
BIRMINGHAM NEW ROAD
TIPTON ROAD
TIVIDALE RD
DUDLEY ROAD WEST
BIRMINGHAM RD
Burnt Tree Jun & Inf School
Tividale Primary School
Tividale Compre School
Kates Hill
Tividale FC
Regent Special School
Tividale Hall Primary School
Elm Terrace Clinic
Tividale
Kates Hill Primary Sch
69
86
103

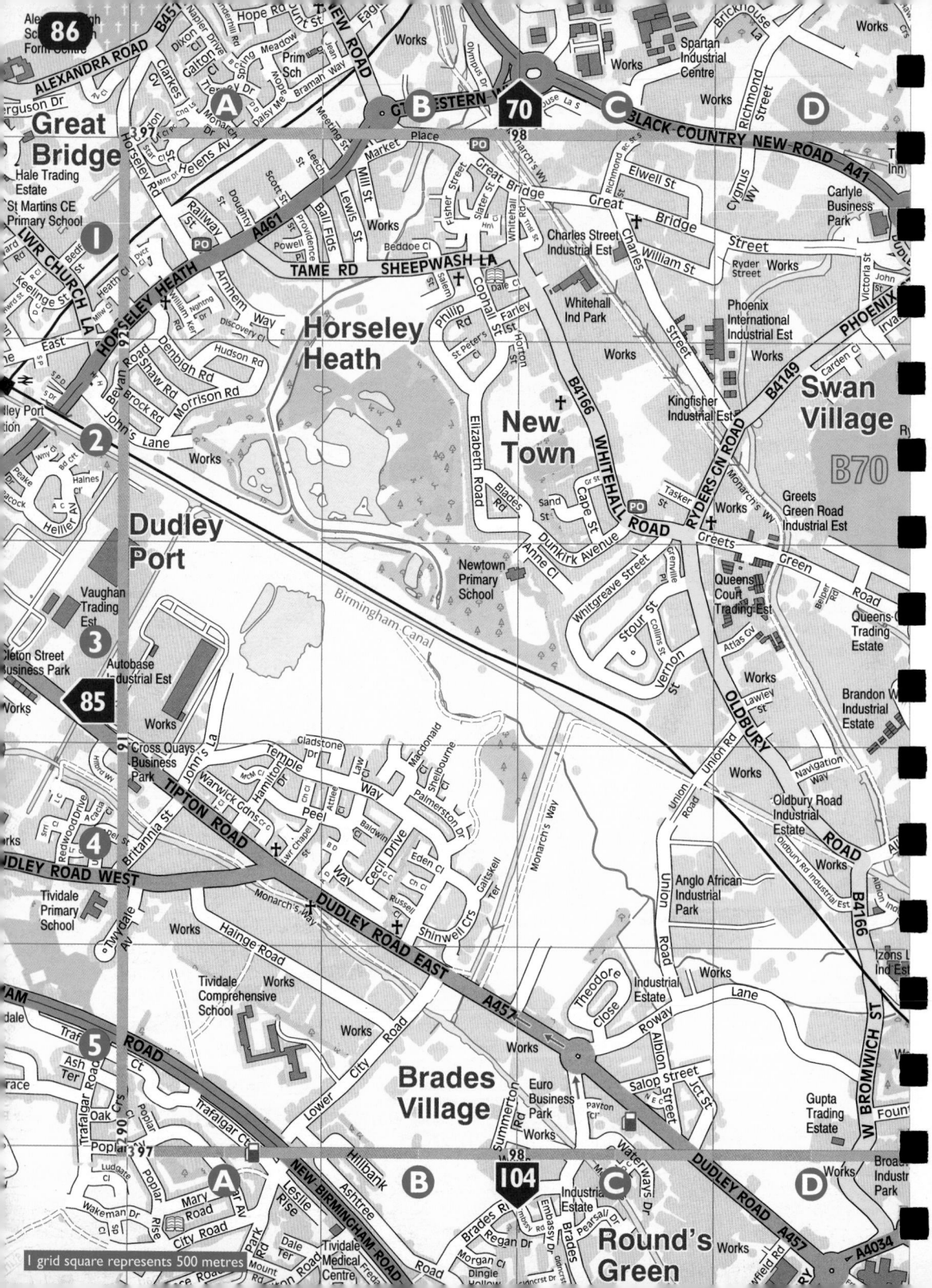
86
70
85
104
Great Bridge
Horseley Heath
Dudley Port
New Town
Swan Village
Brades Village
Round's Green
B70
ALEXANDRA ROAD
BLACK COUNTRY NEW ROAD A41
GT WESTERN WAY
Great Bridge Street
HORSELEY HEATH A461
TAME RD
SHEEPWASH LA
LWR CHURCH LA
WHITEHALL ROAD B4166
RYDERS GN ROAD B4149
PHOENIX
OLDBURY ROAD
TIPTON ROAD
DUDLEY ROAD WEST
DUDLEY ROAD EAST A457
DUDLEY ROAD A457
W BROMWICH ST B4166
NEW BIRMINGHAM ROAD
Birmingham Canal
Monarch's Way
Hale Trading Estate
St Martins CE Primary School
Vaughan Trading Est
Autobase Industrial Est
Cross Quays Business Park
Tividale Primary School
Tividale Comprehensive School
Tividale Medical Centre
Spartan Industrial Centre
Charles Street Industrial Est
Whitehall Ind Park
Phoenix International Industrial Est
Kingfisher Industrial Est
Carlyle Business Park
Greets Green Road Industrial Est
Queens Court Trading Est
Queens Trading Estate
Brandon Industrial Estate
Oldbury Road Industrial Estate
Anglo African Industrial Park
Industrial Estate
Euro Business Park
Gupta Trading Estate
Newtown Primary School
Works
Elizabeth Road
Dunkirk Avenue
Whitgreave Street
Union Road
Lower City Road
Hainge Road
Trafalgar Road
Summerton Rd
Roway Lane
Albion Street
Salop Street
Theodore Close
Temple Way
Cecil Drive
Shinwell Crs
Palmerston Dr
Britannia St
John's Lane
Denbigh Rd
Morrison Rd
Hudson Rd
Arnhem Way
Railway St
Great Bridge
Market Place
Mill St
Lewis St
Ball Flds
Richmond Street
Brickhouse La
Elwell St
William St
Cygnus Way
Greets Green Road
Navigation Way
Mary Road
City Road
Wakeman Dr
Hillbank
Ashtree
Leslie Rise
Brades Rd
Regan Dr
Embassy Dr
Waterways Dr
1 grid square represents 500 metres

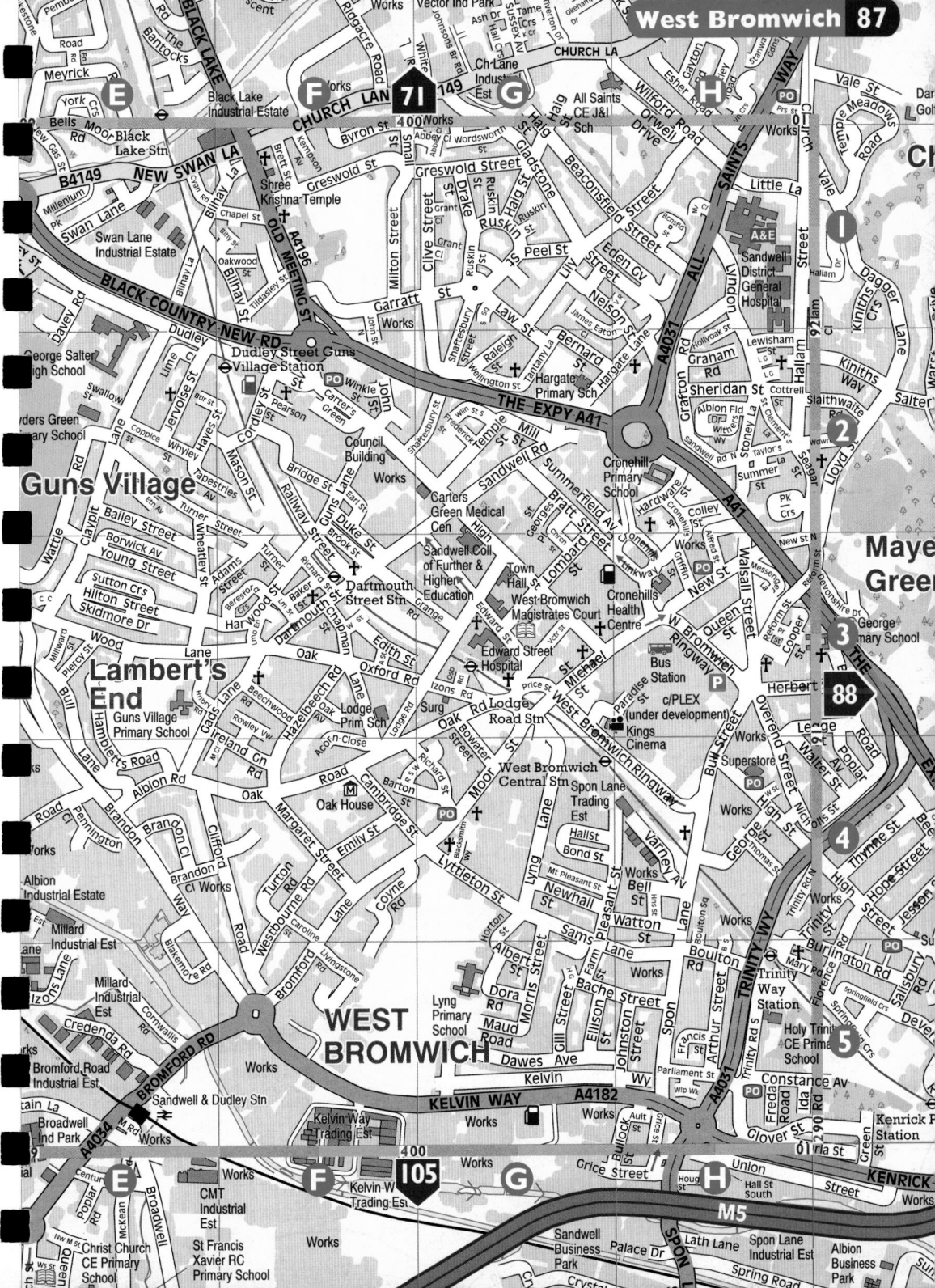
West Bromwich
87
71
105
88
E
F
G
H
I
2
3
4
5
400
01
92
91
90
Guns Village
Lambert's End
WEST BROMWICH
Mayers Green
BLACK LAKE
Black Lake Industrial Estate
Black Lake Stn
CHURCH LA
CHURCH LANE
Ch Lane Industrial Est
All Saints CE J&I Sch
Vector Ind Park
Works
B4149
NEW SWAN LA
Swan Lane
Swan Lane Industrial Estate
Millenium Pk
Shree Krishna Temple
Greswold St
Greswold Street
OLD MEETING ST
A4196
BLACK COUNTRY NEW RD
Dudley Street Guns Village Station
George Salter High School
Dudley St
Bilhay La
Bilhay St
Oakwood St
Tildasley St
Chapel St
Milton Street
Clive Street
Drake St
Ruskin St
Haig St
Gladstone St
Beaconsfield Street
Peel St
Eden Gv
Lily Street
Nelson St
Garratt St
Law St
Raleigh St
Shaftesbury Street
Bernard St
Hargate Lane
Hargate Primary Sch
THE EXPY A41
ALL SAINTS WAY
A4031
Sandwell District General Hospital
A&E
Lyndon
London Street
Hallam Street
Vale St
Temple Meadows Road
Little La
Dagger Lane
Kiniths Crs
Kiniths Way
Lewisham St
Graham Rd
Sheridan St
Grafton Rd
Cottrell St
Slaithwaite Rd
Salter's
Albion Fld Dr
Stoney La
Taylor's La
Sandwell Rd N
Summer St
Seagar St
Lloyd St
Pk Crs
Cronehill Primary School
Hardware St
Cronehills St
Colley St
Linkway
Walsall Street
New St
Queen St
Reform St
Devonshire Dr
Cooper St
St George Primary School
Herbert St
THE
Jervoise St
Hayes St
Whyley St
Mason St
Cordley St
Pearson St
Winkle St
John St
Carter's Green
Council Building
Bridge St
Guns Lane
Duke St
Carters Green Medical Cen
High St
Sandwell Rd
Summerfield Av
Bratt Street
Lombard St
Sandwell Coll of Further & Higher Education
Town Hall
West Bromwich Magistrates Court
Cronehills Health Centre
W Bromwich Ringway
Bus Station
Paradise St
c/PLEX (under development)
Kings Cinema
Tapestries Av
Turner Street
Bailey Street
Borwick Av
Young Street
Wheatley St
Adams Street
Sutton Crs
Hilton Street
Skidmore Dr
Wattle Rd
Claypit Lane
Railway Street
Dartmouth Street Stn
Dartmouth St
Chapman St
Baker St
Harwood St
Grange Rd
Edward St
Edward Street Hospital
Michael St
Oak Lane
Edith St
Oxford Rd
Izons Rd
Lodge Road Stn
Lodge Rd
Lodge Prim Sch
Surg
Guns Village Primary School
Hambletts Road
Beechwood Rd
Hazelbeech Rd
Ireland Gn Rd
Rowley Vw
Acorn Close
Oak Road
Bowater Street
Moor St
West Bromwich Central Stn
West Bromwich Ringway
Spon Lane Trading Est
Bull Street
Overend Street
Walter St
Superstore
Lodge Road
Poplar Av
High St
George St
Albion Rd
Brandon Cl
Brandon Way
Clifford Road
Pennington
Cambridge St
Barton St
Richard St
Oak House
Margaret Street
Emily St
Blacksmith Wy
Lyttleton St
Lyng Lane
Hall St
Bond St
Newhall St
Pleasant St
Bell St
Varney Av
Watton St
Sams Lane
Boulton Rd
TRINITY WY
Trinity Way Station
Burlington Rd
Thynne St
Hope Street
Trinity St
Salisbury
Springfield Crs
Holy Trinity CE Primary School
Albion Industrial Estate
Millard Industrial Est
Millard Industrial Est
Credenda Rd
Cornwallis Rd
Izons Lane
Turton Rd
Westbourne Rd
Caroline St
Coyne Rd
Bromford Lane
Livingstone Rd
Blakemore Rd
Albert St
Dora Rd
Maud Road
Morris Street
Lyng Primary School
Gill Street
Ellison St
Bache Street
Johnston Street
Spon Lane
Arthur Street
Francis St
Trinity Rd S
Constance Av
Freda Road
Ida Rd
Dawes Ave
Kelvin Wy
KELVIN WAY
A4182
Parliament St
Bromford Road Industrial Est
BROMFORD RD
A4034
Sandwell & Dudley Stn
Broadwell Ind Park
Kelvin Way Trading Est
Bullock St
Grice Street
Union St
Hall St South
Clover St
KENRICK
Kenrick Park Station
M5
CMT Industrial Est
Poplar Rd
McKean Rd
Broadwell
Christ Church CE Primary School
St Francis Xavier RC Primary School
Sandwell Business Park
Palace Dr
Lath Lane
Spon Lane Industrial Est
Albion Business Park
Spring Road
SPON

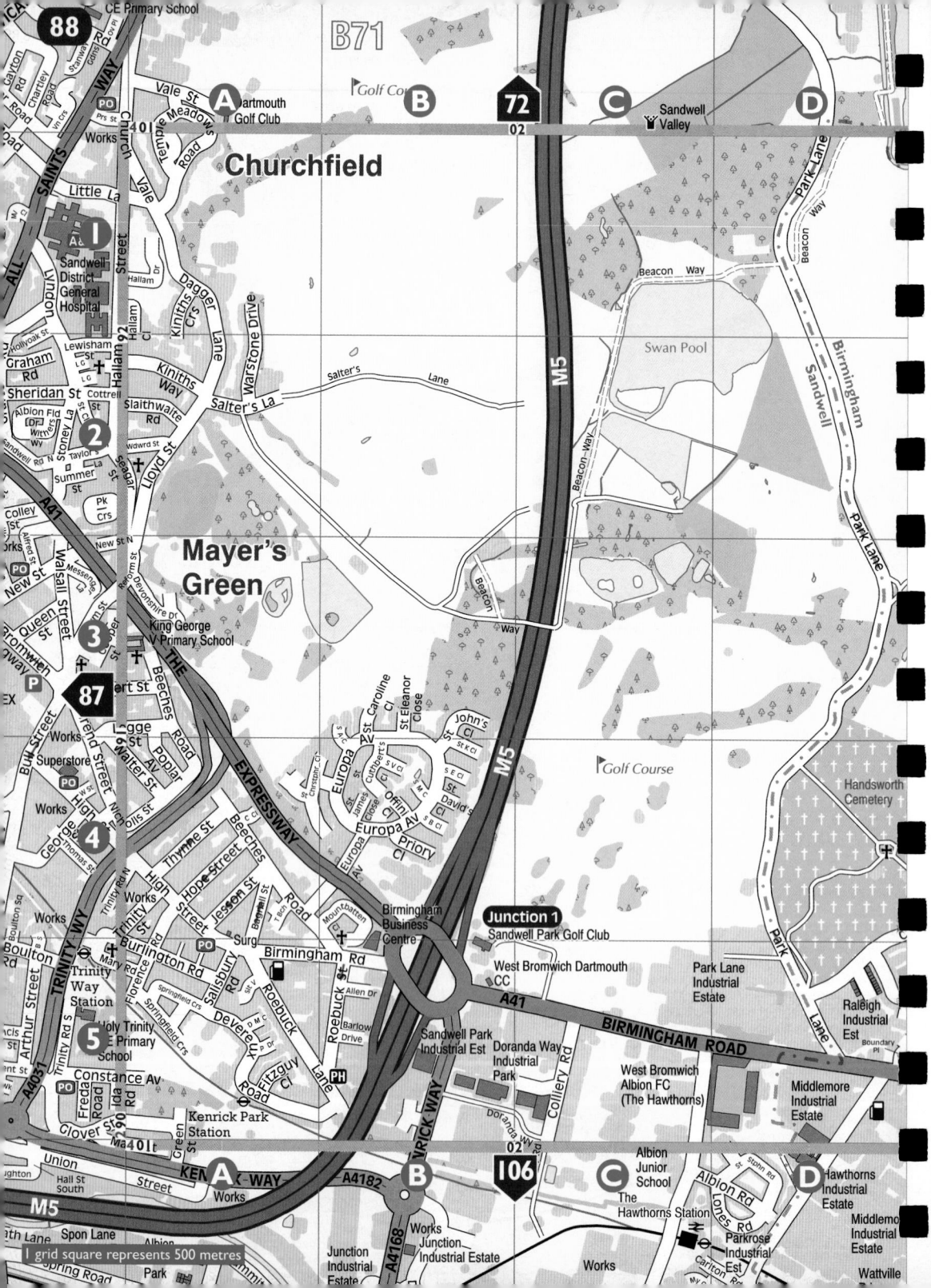

88
B71
72
Churchfield
Dartmouth Golf Club
Sandwell Valley
Golf Course
Sandwell District General Hospital
Swan Pool
Salter's Lane
Beacon Way
Park Lane
Birmingham Road
Sandwell
M5
Mayer's Green
King George V Primary School
87
THE EXPRESSWAY
Golf Course
Handsworth Cemetery
Junction 1
Sandwell Park Golf Club
Birmingham Business Centre
West Bromwich Dartmouth CC
Park Lane Industrial Estate
Raleigh Industrial Est
A41
BIRMINGHAM ROAD
Sandwell Park Industrial Est
Doranda Way Industrial Park
West Bromwich Albion FC (The Hawthorns)
Middlemore Industrial Estate
Trinity Way Station
Holy Trinity CE Primary School
Kenrick Park Station
106
Albion Junior School
The Hawthorns Station
Hawthorns Industrial Estate
Parkrose Industrial Est
Junction Industrial Estate
Works
M5
A4182
A4168
A4031
1 grid square represents 500 metres

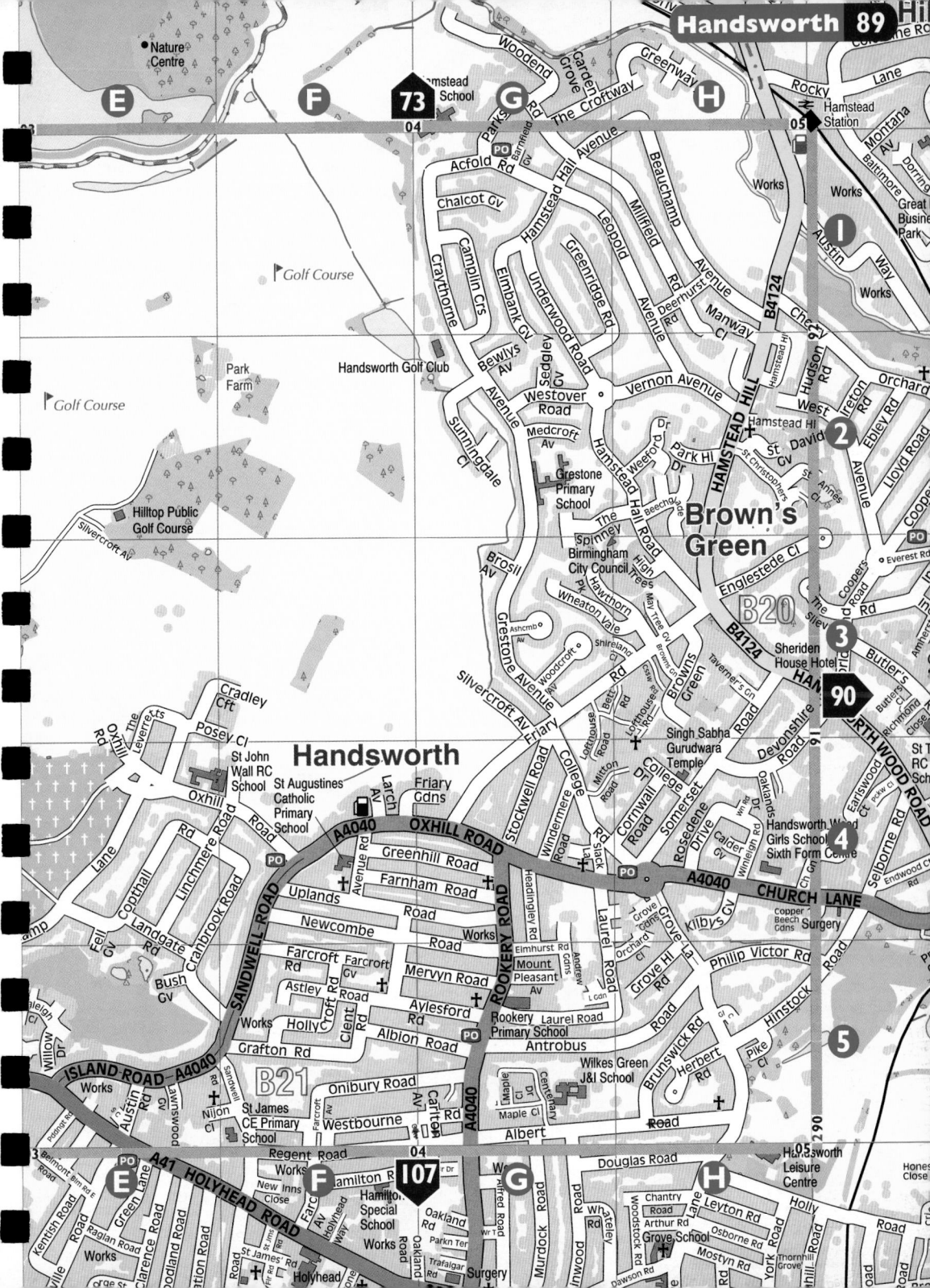

Nature Centre
Hamstead School
Golf Course
Handsworth Golf Club
Park Farm
Hilltop Public Golf Course
Hamstead Station
Works
Great Business Park
Grestone Primary School
Brown's Green
Birmingham City Council
Sheriden House Hotel
Handsworth
St John Wall RC School
St Augustines Catholic Primary School
Singh Sabha Gurudwara Temple
Handsworth Wood Girls School Sixth Form Centre
Rookery Primary School
Wilkes Green J&I School
St James CE Primary School
Hamilton Special School
Handsworth Leisure Centre
Grove School
Surgery
Holyhead
B20
B21
B4124
A4040
A41
HAMSTEAD HILL
OXHILL ROAD
CHURCH LANE
SANDWELL ROAD
ROOKERY ROAD
ISLAND ROAD
HOLYHEAD ROAD
HANDSWORTH WOOD ROAD
Hamstead Hall Avenue
Hamstead Hall Road
Vernon Avenue
Westover Road
Friary Road
Oxhill Road
Farnham Road
Greenhill Road
Newcombe Road
Mervyn Road
Aylesford Rd
Albion Road
Antrobus Road
Albert Road
Regent Road
Douglas Road
73
90
107

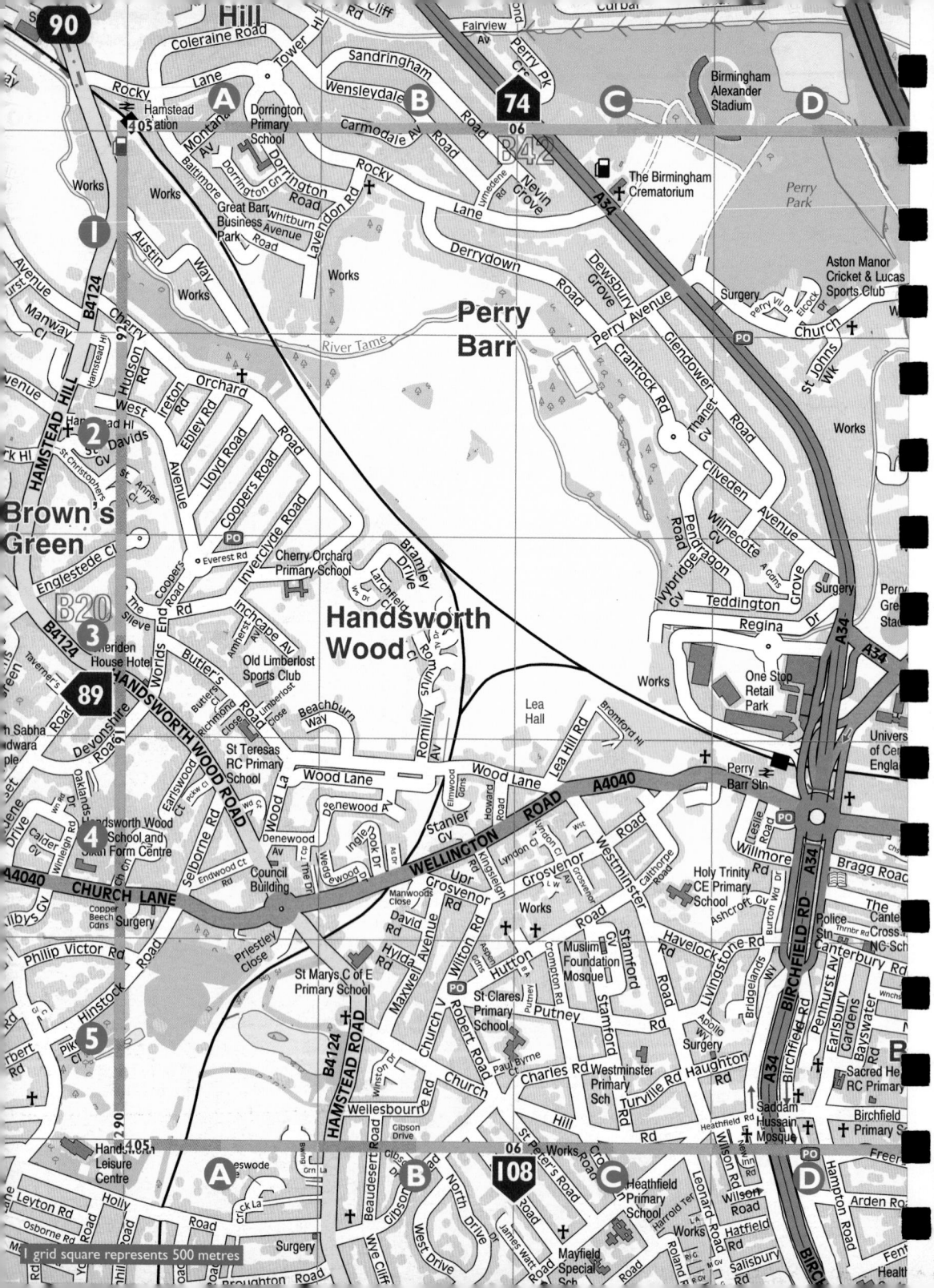
90
74
89
108
A
B
C
D
1
2
3
4
5
405
06
92
91
290
Hill
Coleraine Road
Tower Hl
Sandringham
Wensleydale
Fairview Av
Perry Pk Cres
Rocky Lane
Hamstead Station
Montana Av
Dorrington Primary School
Carmodale Av
Road
B42
Birmingham Alexander Stadium
Baltimore Rd
Dorrington Gn
Dorrington Road
Lavendon Rd
Lymedene Rd
Nevin Grove
The Birmingham Crematorium
A34
Perry Park
Works
Great Barr Business Park
Whitburn Avenue
Derrydown Road
Austin Way
Dewsbury Grove
Aston Manor Cricket & Lucas Sports Club
Surgery
Perry Vil Dr
Elcock Dr
Church
Perry Barr
Perry Avenue
Cherry
Manway Cl
B4124
Hamstead Hl
River Tame
Crantock Rd
Glendower Road
St Johns Wk
Hudson Rd
Orchard
West
Ireton Rd
Ebley Rd
Thanet Gv
Hamstead Hl
HAMSTEAD HILL
St Davids Gv
St Christophers
St Annes Cl
Lloyd Road
Coopers Road
Avenue
Cliveden Avenue
Brown's Green
Inverclyde Road
PO
Everest Rd
Cherry Orchard Primary School
Bramley Drive
Larchfield Cl
Wilnecote Gv
Ivybridge Road
Pendragon
Englestede Cl
Coopers End Rd
Teddington Grove
B20
The Slieve
Inchcape Av
Amherst Av
Handsworth Wood
Romulus Cl
Regina Dr
B4124
Sheriden House Hotel
Butler's Road
Old Limberlost Sports Club
One Stop Retail Park
Worlds
HANDSWORTH WOOD ROAD
Butlers Cl
Richmond Close
Limberlost Close
Beachburn Way
Lea Hall
Lea Hill Rd
Bromford Hl
Devonshire Road
St Teresas RC Primary School
Romilly Av
Wood Lane
Perry Barr Stn
Earlswood Ct
Wood La
Elmwood Gdns
Howard Road
A4040
Oaklands Dr
Handsworth Wood Girls School and Sixth Form Centre
Selborne Rd
Denewood Av
Stanier Gv
WELLINGTON ROAD
Westminster Road
Leslie Road
Calder Gv
Winleigh Rd
Endwood Ct
Council Building
Ingleb...ook Dr
Wedgewood
Kingsleigh
Lyndon Cl
Grosvenor
Willmore Rd
A34
Bragg Road
CHURCH LANE
Copper Beech Gdns
Surgery
Manwoods Close
Upr Grosvenor Rd
Calthorpe Road
Holy Trinity CE Primary School
Ashcroft Gv
Burton Wd Dr
BIRCHFIELD RD
Police Stn
The Canter Cross
Philip Victor Rd
Priestley Close
David Rd
Hylda Rd
Maxwell Avenue
Wilton Rd
Muslim Foundation Mosque
Stamford Road
Havelock Rd
Livingstone Rd
Bridgelands Wy
Canterbury Rd
Hinstock Road
St Marys C of E Primary School
Hutton
St Clares Primary School
Putney
Crompton Rd
Apollo Wy
Surgery
Birchfield Rd
Penhurst Av
Earlsbury Gardens
Bayswater Rd
Church V
Robert Road
Paul Byrne Ct
Charles Rd
Westminster Primary Sch
Turville Rd
Haughton Rd
Sacred Heart RC Primary
HAMSTEAD ROAD
Winston Dr
West Rd
Church
Hill
Saddam Hussain Mosque
Wellesbourne Road
Gibson Drive
Heathfield Rd
Birchfield Primary S
Handsworth Leisure Centre
Beaudesert Road
St Peter's Road
Works
Croft
Wilson Rd
New Inn Rd
Freer
Heathfield Primary School
Hampton Road
Leyton Rd
Holly Road
Crick La
Gibson Road
North Drive
Harrold Ter
Leonard Road
Wilson Road
Arden Road
Osborne Rd
Surgery
West Drive
James Watt
Mayfield Special Sch
Hatfield Rd
Salisbury Rd
Roland Rd
Broughton Road
Wye Cliff
1 grid square represents 500 metres

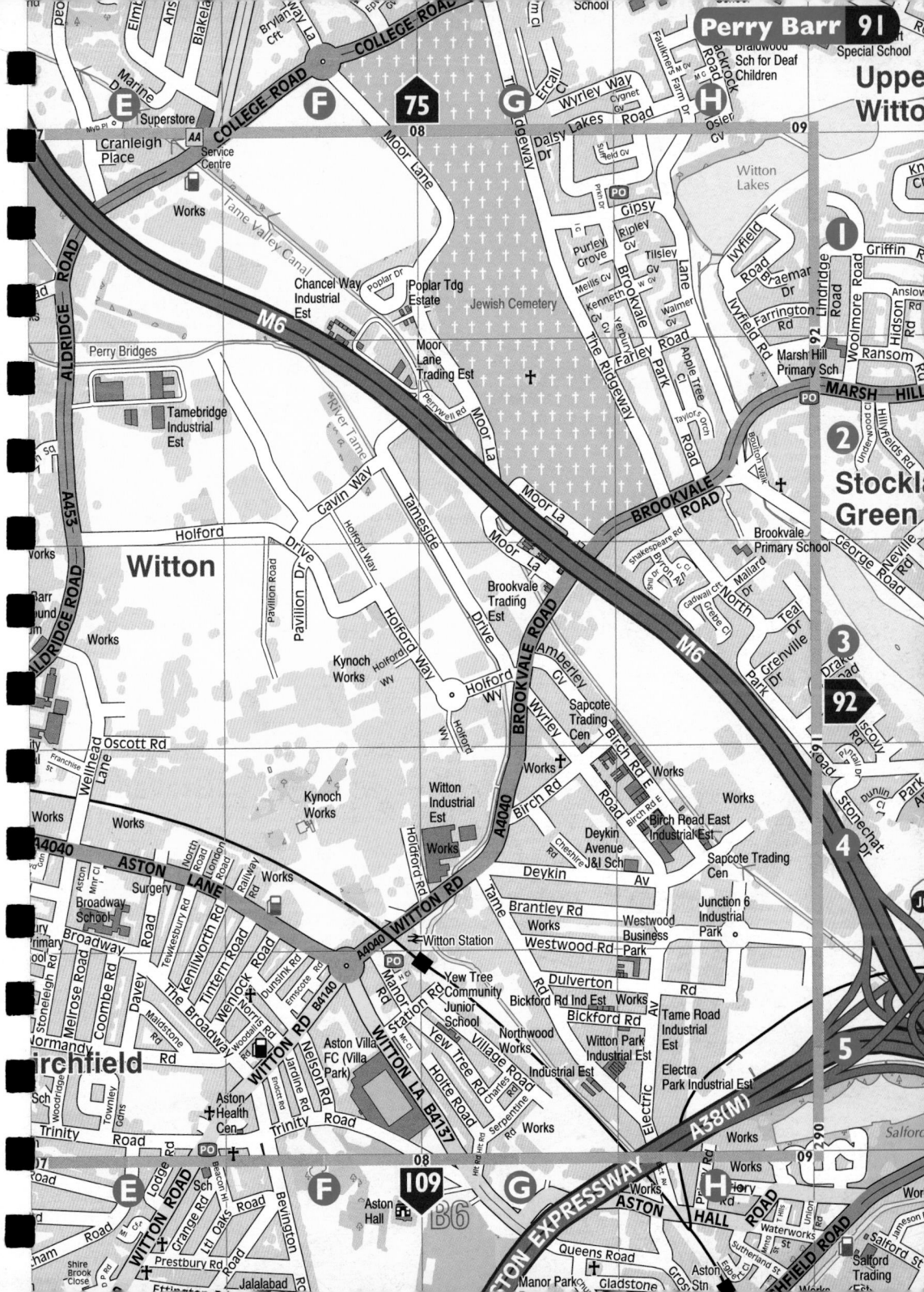
Witton
Upper Witton
Stockland Green
Birchfield
M6
A38(M)
Aston Expressway
College Road
Aldridge Road
A453
Brookvale Road
A4040
Aston Lane
Witton Rd
Witton La B4137
Jewish Cemetery
Witton Lakes
Tame Valley Canal
River Tame
Perry Bridges
Tamebridge Industrial Est
Chancel Way Industrial Est
Poplar Tdg Estate
Moor Lane Trading Est
Brookvale Trading Est
Kynoch Works
Witton Industrial Est
Sapcote Trading Cen
Birch Road East Industrial Est
Deykin Avenue J&I Sch
Junction 6 Industrial Park
Westwood Business Park
Bickford Rd Ind Est
Tame Road Industrial Est
Witton Park Industrial Est
Electra Park Industrial Est
Aston Villa FC (Villa Park)
Witton Station
Yew Tree Community Junior School
Northwood Works
Aston Health Cen
Broadway School
Brookvale Primary School
Marsh Hill Primary Sch
Braidwood Sch for Deaf Children
Aston Hall
Aston Hall Road
Salford Trading Est
Superstore
Service Centre
75
92
109

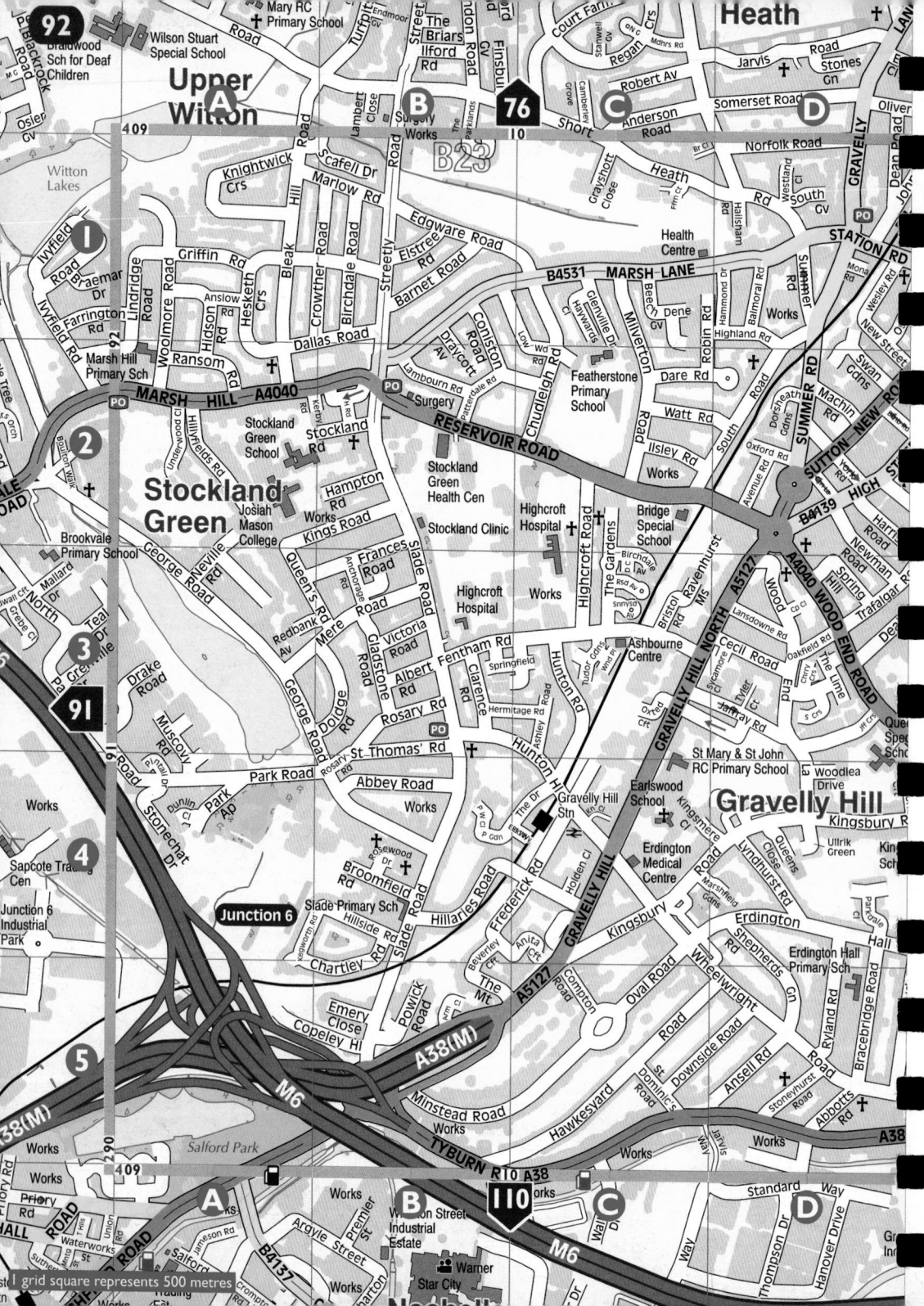

92
76
91
110
A
B
C
D
409
410
290
Upper Witton
Heath
Stockland Green
Gravelly Hill
B23
Witton Lakes
Salford Park
Junction 6
1
2
3
4
5
Braidwood Sch for Deaf Children
Wilson Stuart Special School
Mary RC Primary School
The Briars
Ilford Rd
Surgery Works
Health Centre
Works
Marsh Hill Primary Sch
Stockland Green School
Josiah Mason College
Surgery
Stockland Green Health Cen
Stockland Clinic
Highcroft Hospital
Featherstone Primary School
Bridge Special School
Brookvale Primary School
Ashbourne Centre
St Mary & St John RC Primary School
Earlswood School
Gravelly Hill Stn
Erdington Medical Centre
Erdington Hall Primary Sch
Slade Primary Sch
Sapcote Trading Cen
Junction 6 Industrial Park
Witton Street Industrial Estate
Warner Star City
MARSH HILL A4040
RESERVOIR ROAD
B4531 MARSH LANE
STATION RD
SUTTON NEW ROAD
B4139 HIGH ST
A4040 WOOD END ROAD
GRAVELLY HILL NORTH
A5127
GRAVELLY HILL
GRAVELLY
SUMMER RD
A38(M)
M6
TYBURN RD A38
A38
B4137
George Road
Slade Road
Gladstone Road
Kings Road
Park Road
Abbey Road
Fentham Rd
Hunton Hl
Hunton Rd
Highcroft Road
Chudleigh Rd
Milverton Road
Robin Rd
Dare Rd
Watt Rd
Ilsley Rd
Dallas Road
Griffin Rd
Lindridge Road
Woolmore Road
Hidson Rd
Ransom Rd
Hesketh Crs
Bleak Hill Road
Crowther Road
Birchdale Road
Streetly Road
Marlow Rd
Scafell Dr
Knightwick Crs
Edgware Road
Elstree Rd
Barnet Road
Coniston Road
Draycott Av
Lambourn Rd
Ivyfield Road
Braemar Dr
Farrington Rd
Ivyfield Rd
Heath Rd
Norfolk Road
Somerset Road
Robert Av
Anderson Road
Short Heath Road
Regan Crs
Jarvis Road
Stones Gn
Grayshott Close
Westland Cl
South Gv
Kingsbury Road
Erdington Hall Road
Oval Road
Wheelwright Road
Shepherds Gn
Lyndhurst Rd
Ansell Rd
Downside Road
Hawkesyard Road
Minstead Road
Copeley Hl
Emery Close
Powick Road
Chartley Rd
Hillside Rd
Broomfield Rd
Hillaries Road
Frederick Rd
Holden Cl
Rosary Rd
St Thomas' Rd
Dodge Rd
Albert Rd
Victoria Road
Mere Road
Frances Road
Queen's Rd
Redbank Av
Hampton Rd
Stockland Rd
Neville Rd
George Road
Drake Road
Muscovy Rd
Stonechat Dr
Park Ap
Dunlin Cl
North Teal Dr
Mallard Dr
Grenville
Boulton Walk
Underwood Cl
Hillyfields Rd
Cecil Road
Jaffray Rd
Tyler Ct
Wood End
Lansdowne Rd
Oakfield Rd
The Lime
Newman Road
Harris Road
Spring Hill
Trafalgar Rd
Woodlea Drive
Kingsbury Rd
Ullrik Green
Queens Close
Kingsmere Cl
Marshfield Gdns
Parkvale Cl
Ryland Rd
Bracebridge Road
Abbotts Rd
Stoneyhurst Road
Dominic's Road
St
Compton Road
Beverley Cft
Anita Cft
The Mt
Jarvis Way
Standard Way
Thompson Dr
Hanover Drive
Argyle Street
Premier St
Jameson Rd
Waterworks St
Priory Rd
HALL ROAD
Dorsheath Gdns
Machin Rd
Swan Gdns
New Street
Wesley Rd
Mona Rd
Balmoral Rd
Hammond Dr
Highland Rd
Beech Dene Gv
Glenville Dr
Haywards Cl
Low Wd Rd
Avenue Rd
Oxford Rd
Ravenhurst Ms
Bristol Rd
The Gardens
Clarence Rd
Ashley Road
Hermitage Rd
Springfield
Oxted Cft
Tudor Gdns
Wardens
1 grid square represents 500 metres

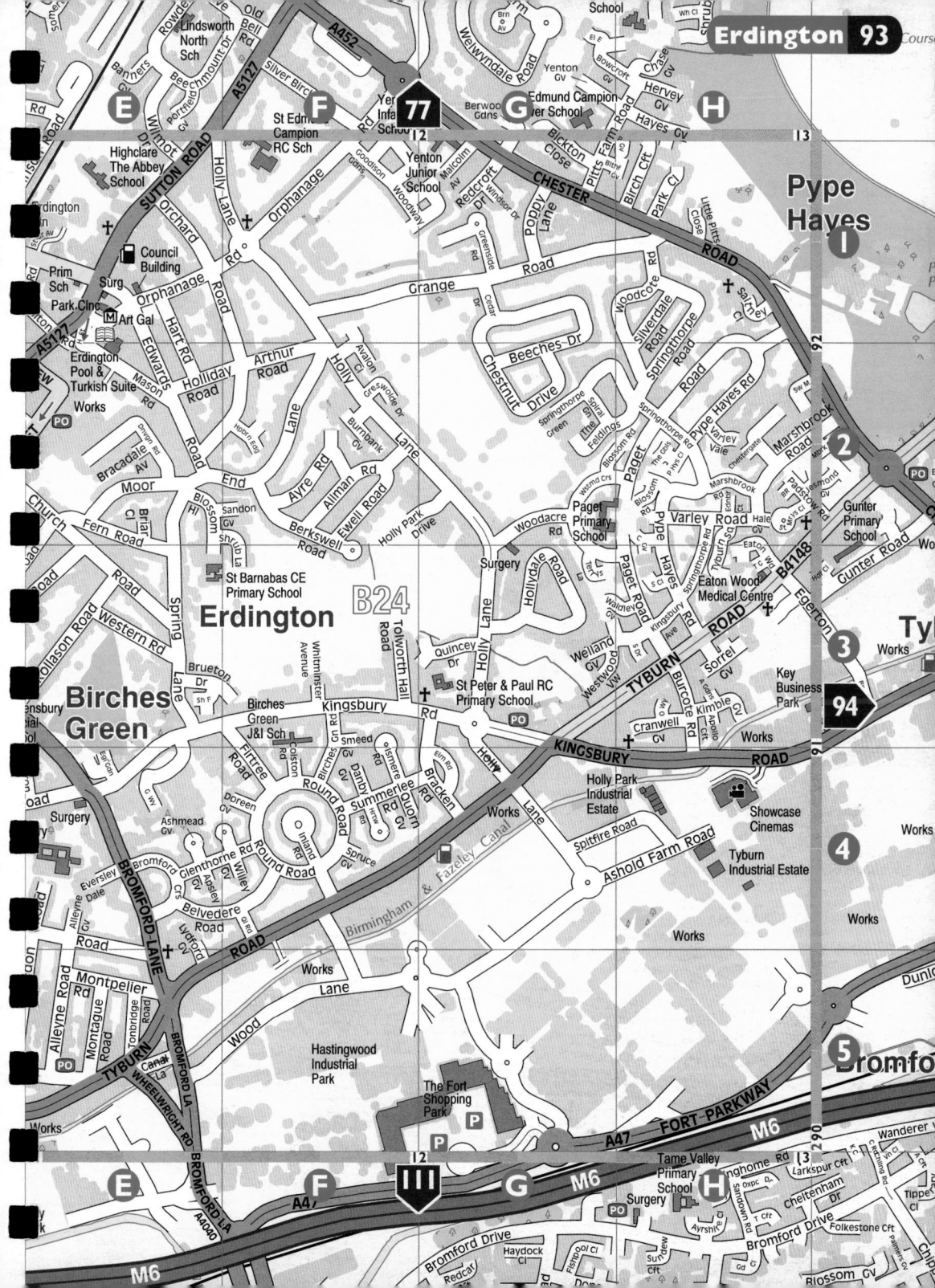
Erdington
Birches Green
Pype Hayes
B24
77
94
111
E
F
G
H
1
2
3
4
5
12
13
92
91
290
A452
A5127
A47
A4040
B4148
M6
SUTTON ROAD
CHESTER ROAD
TYBURN ROAD
KINGSBURY ROAD
FORT PARKWAY
BROMFORD LANE
BROMFORD LA
WHEELWRIGHT RD
Grange Road
Orphanage Road
Holly Lane
Moor End
Church Road
Fern Road
Western Rd
Rollason Road
Spring Lane
Holliday Road
Arthur Road
Edwards Road
Hart Rd
Mason Rd
Bracadale Av
Berkswell Road
Ewell Road
Allman Rd
Ayre Rd
Holly Park Drive
Woodacre Rd
Chestnut Drive
Beeches Dr
Silverdale Road
Springthorpe Road
Pype Hayes Rd
Marshbrook Road
Varley Road
Gunter Road
Paget Road
Hollydale Road
Tolworth Hall Road
Whitminster Avenue
Quincey Dr
Brueton Dr
Firtree Road
Round Road
Summerlee Rd
Bracken Rd
Glenthorne Rd
Belvedere Road
Montpelier Rd
Alleyne Road
Montague Road
Tonbridge Road
Wood Lane
Spitfire Road
Ashold Farm Road
Sorrel Gv
Burcote Rd
Cranwell Gv
Kimble Gv
Westwood Vw
Welland Gv
Birmingham & Fazeley Canal
Bromford Drive
Cheltenham Dr
Haydock Cl
Redcar
Larkspur Cft
Folkestone Cft
Blossom Gv
Wanderer
Council Building
Art Gal
Erdington Pool & Turkish Suite
Highclare The Abbey School
St Edmund Campion RC Sch
Yenton Junior School
Edmund Campion
Paget Primary School
St Barnabas CE Primary School
St Peter & Paul RC Primary School
Birches Green J&I Sch
Gunter Primary School
Eaton Wood Medical Centre
Key Business Park
Holly Park Industrial Estate
Showcase Cinemas
Tyburn Industrial Estate
Hastingwood Industrial Park
The Fort Shopping Park
Tame Valley Primary School
Surgery
Works
PO

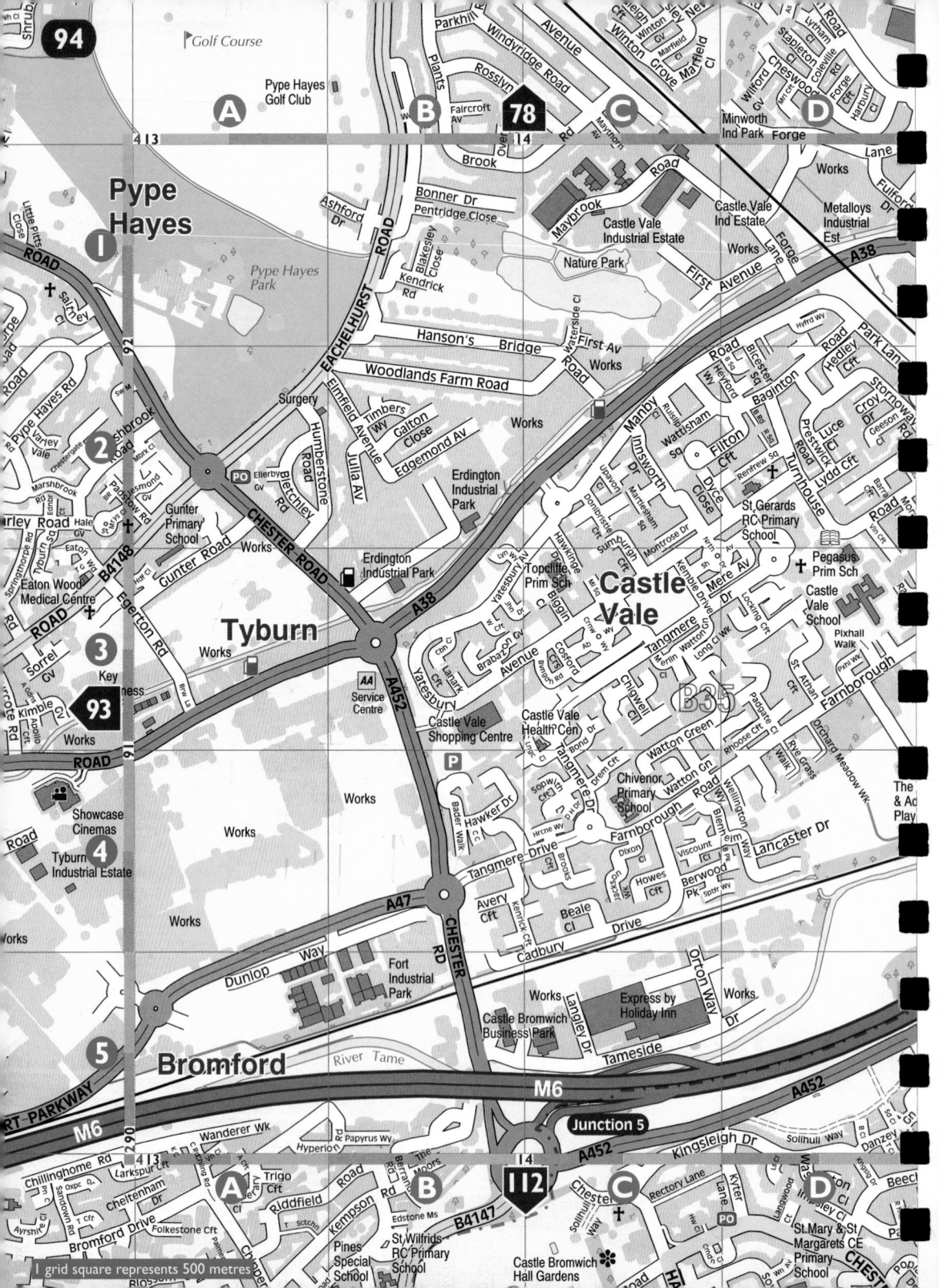
94
Golf Course
Pype Hayes Golf Club
A
B
C
D
78
Pype Hayes
Pype Hayes Park
1
2
3
4
5
Windyridge Road
Rosslyn
Plants
Faircroft Av
Brook
Bonner Dr
Pentridge Close
Ashford Dr
Eachelhurst Road
Blakesley Close
Kendrick Rd
Maybrook Road
Castle Vale Industrial Estate
Castle Vale Ind Estate
Nature Park
First Avenue
Forge Lane
Minworth Ind Park
Works
Metalloys Industrial Est
A38
Hanson's Bridge
Woodlands Farm Road
Waterside Cl
First Av
Surgery
Elmfield Avenue
Humberstone Road
Timbers Wy
Galton Close
Edgemond Av
Julia Av
Bletchley Rd
Erdington Industrial Park
Chester Road
Gunter Primary School
Gunter Road
Egerton Rd
B4148
Eaton Wood Medical Centre
Tyburn
Key
Sorrel Gv
Kimble Cl
93
Showcase Cinemas
Tyburn Industrial Estate
Service Centre
A452
Castle Vale
Castle Vale Shopping Centre
Castle Vale Health Cen
Topcliffe Prim Sch
St Gerards RC Primary School
Pegasus Prim Sch
Castle Vale School
Pixhall Walk
Farnborough Road
Tangmere Drive
Chivenor Primary School
Watton Green
Lancaster Dr
Yatesbury Avenue
Hawker Dr
Bader Walk
Cadbury Drive
Beale Cl
Avery Cft
A47
Dunlop Way
Fort Industrial Park
Castle Bromwich Business Park
Express by Holiday Inn
Orton Way
Langley Dr
Tameside Dr
River Tame
Bromford
M6
Junction 5
Kingsleigh Dr
Solihull Way
Wanderer Wk
Hyperion Rd
Papyrus Wy
112
B4147
Chillinghome Rd
Bromford Drive
Riddfield Road
Kempson Rd
Pines Special School
St Wilfrids RC Primary School
Castle Bromwich Hall Gardens
Rectory Lane
St Mary & St Margarets CE Primary School
1 grid square represents 500 metres

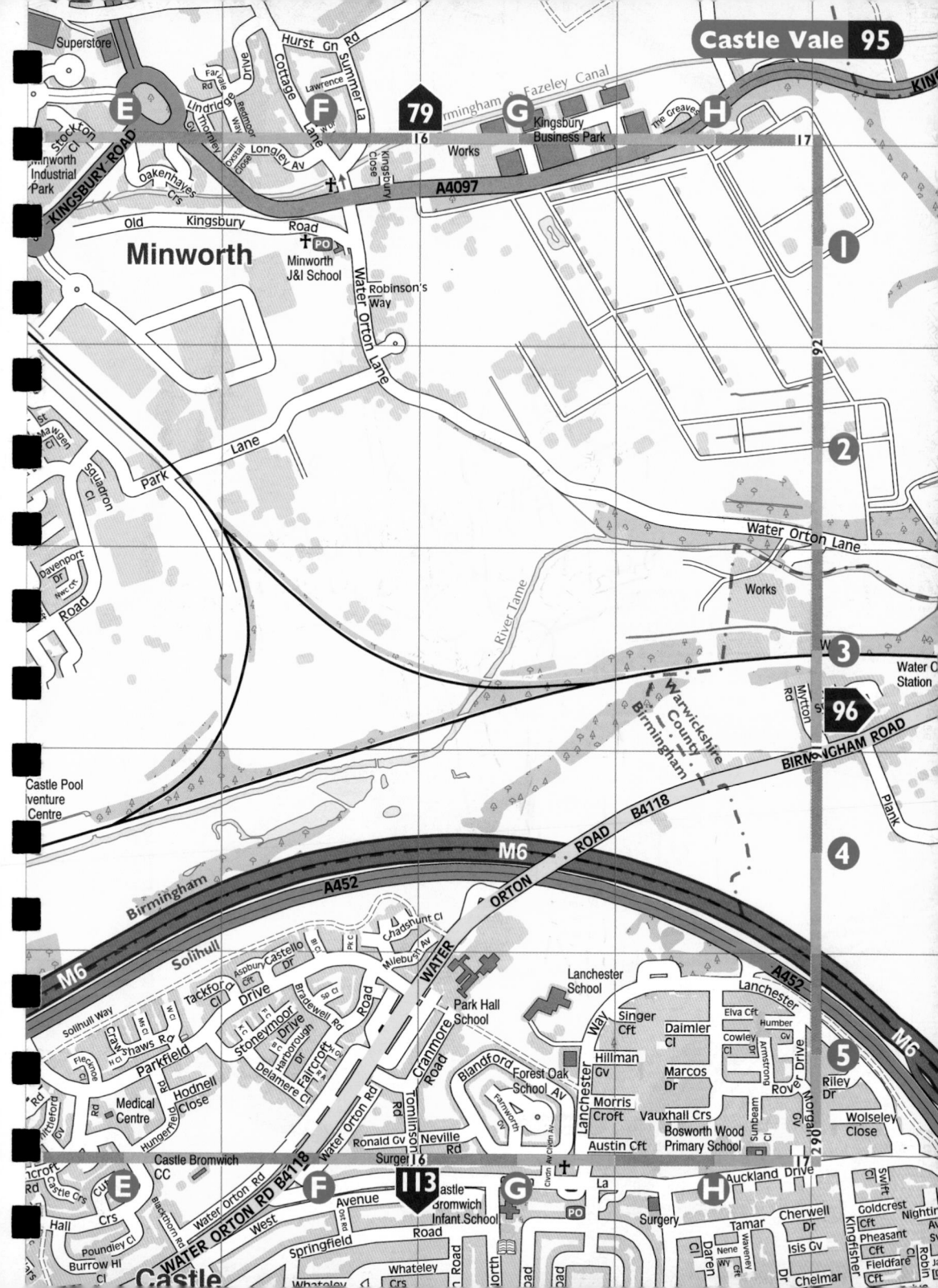
Superstore
Hurst Gn Rd
Summer La
Cottage Lane
Lawrence
Drive
Far Vale Rd
Redmoor Way
Lindridge
Thornley Gv
Oxstall Close
Longley Av
Stockton Cl
Minworth Industrial Park
KINGSBURY ROAD
Oakenhayes Crs
Kingsbury Close
Birmingham & Fazeley Canal
Kingsbury Business Park
The Greaves
Works
A4097
Old Kingsbury Road
Minworth
PO
Minworth J&I School
Water Orton Lane
Robinson's Way
Park Lane
Mawgen Cl
Squadron Cl
Davenport Dr
Road
Water Orton Lane
Works
River Tame
Water Orton Station
Mytton Rd
Warwickshire County
Birmingham
BIRMINGHAM ROAD
B4118
WATER ORTON ROAD
Plank
Castle Pool Adventure Centre
M6
A452
Birmingham
Solihull
Chadshunt Cl
Castello Dr
Aspbury Cft
Milebush Av
Tackford Cl
Drive
Bradewell Rd
Road
Park Hall School
Lanchester School
Lanchester Way
Singer Cft
Daimler Cl
Elva Cft
Humber Gv
Cowley Cl
Armstrong Dr
Solihull Way
Crawshaws Rd
Stoneymoor Drive
Harborough Dr
Faircroft
Parkfield
Fleckno Cl
Medical Centre
Hodnell Close
Hungerfield Rd
Delamere Cl
Cranmore Road
Blandford
Forest Oak School
Av
Farnworth Gv
Hillman Gv
Marcos Dr
Morris Croft
Vauxhall Crs
Rover Drive
Riley Dr
Morgan
Wolseley Close
Bosworth Wood Primary School
Sunbeam Cl
Austin Cft
Water Orton Rd
Tomlinson Rd
Ronald Gv
Neville Rd
Castle Bromwich CC
Surgery
Castle Crs
Hall Crs
Poundley Cl
Burrow Hl Cl
Blackthorn Rd
Water Orton Rd
WATER ORTON RD B4118
West Avenue
Castle Bromwich Infant School
PO
Springfield Road
Whateley Crs
Surgery
Auckland Drive
Tamar
Cherwell Dr
Isis Gv
Nene Wy
Waveney
Daren Cl
Chelmar
Kingfisher
Goldcrest Cft
Pheasant Cft
Fieldfare Cft
Swift Cl
Castle
79
96
113
92
90
16
17
E
F
G
H
1
2
3
4
5

96
KINGSBURY
Church La
Coleshill Rd
Breeden Dr
Curdworth Primary School
The Mount
A
B
C
D
417
18
Oaklands
Coleshill Road
Marsh Lane
Coleshill Road
M6 (Toll)
A446
Coleshill Road
LICHFIELD ROAD
River Tame
Works
Water Orton Lane
MARSH LANE
B4118
Water Orton
Old Church Road
Minworth Rd
Manor House La
Mercer Av
Marsh La
Works
Works
Water Orton Station
MNWRT RD
PO
Hargrave Close
NEW ROAD
B4117
Salisbury Dr
George Road
Maud Rd
Overton Drive
Edward Rd
Turnpike Dr
Park Gv
Industrial Estate
Jack o'Watton Business Park
95
Mytton
Smiths Wy
Orton Cl
Addison Pl
Water Orton CC
Mickle Meadow
BIRMINGHAM ROAD
Plank
Lane
Coleshill
Road
COLESHILL ROAD
WATTON LANE
Gypsy Lane
Coleshill Road
Welland Cl
Vesey Cl
Peter's St
St Av
Blaise
Openfield
Jaques Cl
Woodlands
Lane
Vicarage
Water Orton Primary School
B4117
Attleborough Lane
Attleboro Farm
Junction 8
Junction 4a
A452
Lanchester Way
Elva Cft
Humber
Cowley Cl
Armstrong Dr
Rover Drive
Riley Dr
Wolseley Close
Morgan Gv
Sunbeam Cl
M6
1
2
3
4
5
92
290
114
Auckland Drive
Cherwell Dr
Tamar
Goldcrest Cft
Nightingale Av
Pheasant Cft
Swallow Av
Isis Gv
Jackdaw Dr
1 grid square represents 500 metres

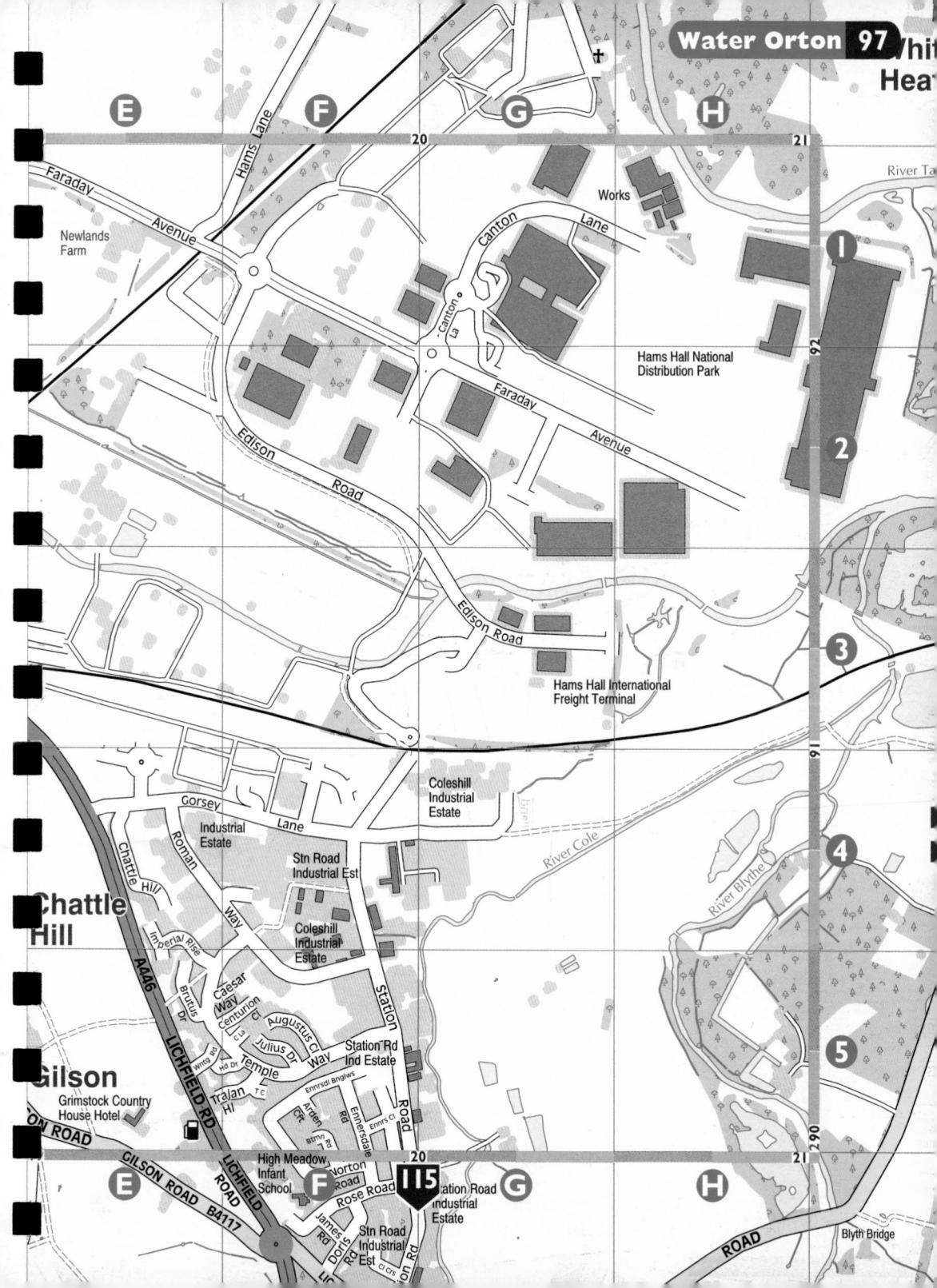

Whit
Hea

E F G H I

River Ta

20 21

Faraday
Avenue

Newlands
Farm

Works

Canton Lane

Canton

Canton La

92

Hams Hall National
Distribution Park

Edison

Road

Faraday Avenue

2

Edison Road

3

Hams Hall International
Freight Terminal

River Cole

bye

91

Coleshill
Industrial
Estate

River Cole

River Blythe

4

Gorsey Lane

Industrial
Estate

Roman

Chattle Hill

Stn Road
Industrial Est

Coleshill
Industrial
Estate

Way

**Chattle
Hill**

Imperial Rise

Brutus Dr

Caesar
Way

Centurion

Augustus Cl

Station

5

A446

Cl 3

Julius Dr

Way

Station Rd
Ind Estate

290

Gilson

Temple
Hl

LICHFIELD RD

Trajan
Hl

Wntg Rd

Hd Dr

T Cl

Arden
Crt

Berrn

Ennersdale
Rd

Ennrsdl Bnglws

Ennrs Cl

Station
Road

Grimstock Country
House Hotel

High Meadow
Infant School

Norton
Road

115

Station Road
Industrial Estate

ON ROAD

GILSON ROAD B4117

LICHFIELD ROAD

E F G H

Rose Road

20 21

James
Rd

Dors
Rd

Stn Road
Industrial Est

Cl Crs

on Rd

ROAD

Blyth Bridge

98

A   **B**   **80**   **C**   **D**

3 85
90   86

1

Chasepool
Farm

Chasepool Road

Camp
Farm

2

89

3

Greensforge

Staffordshire & Worcestershire Canal

Monarch's Way

Mile Flat

Swindon Road

Hink

Ashwood

4

Smestow Brook

Doctors Lane

2 88

Great Checkhill Road

5

Checkhill
Farm

Little Checkhill Lane

Greensforge Lane

3 85
86

A   **B**   **116**   **C**   **D**

I grid square represents 500 metres

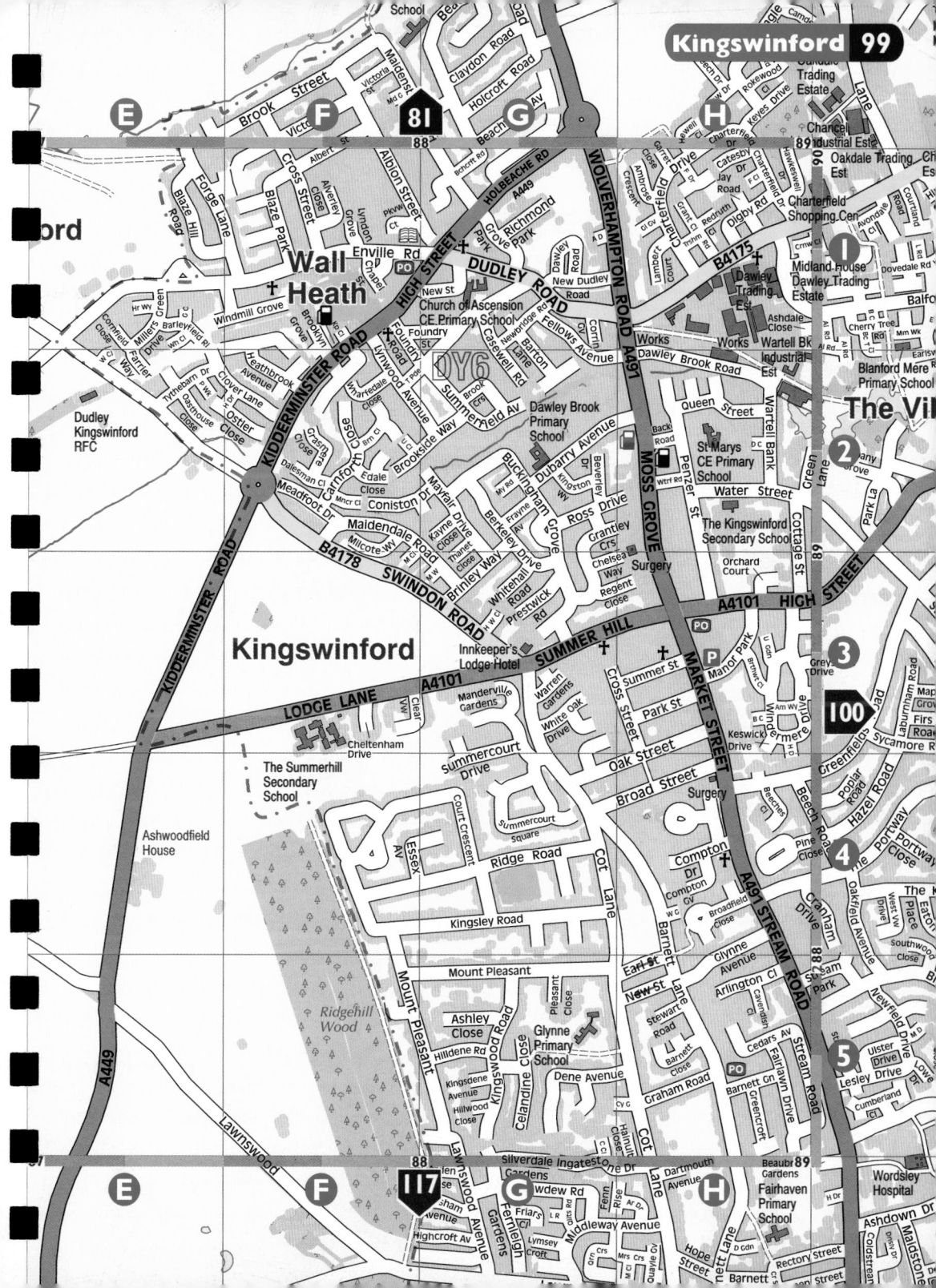
Wall Heath
Kingswinford
DY6
Dudley Kingswinford RFC
Dawley Brook Primary School
Church of Ascension CE Primary School
St Marys CE Primary School
The Kingswinford Secondary School
The Summerhill Secondary School
Glynne Primary School
Fairhaven Primary School
Blanford Mere Primary School
Innkeeper's Lodge Hotel
Wordsley Hospital
Ashwoodfield House
Ridgehill Wood
Charterfield Shopping Cen
Oakdale Trading Est
Chancel Industrial Est
Dawley Trading Est
Midland House Dawley Trading Estate
Wartell Bk Industrial Est
KIDDERMINSTER ROAD
WOLVERHAMPTON ROAD A491
MOSS GROVE
MARKET STREET
A491 STREAM ROAD
SWINDON ROAD B4178
DUDLEY ROAD
HIGH STREET
HOLBEACHE RD
A4101 HIGH STREET
SUMMER HILL
LODGE LANE A4101
A449
B4175
81
100
117
E
F
G
H
I
2
3
4
5
88
89
90

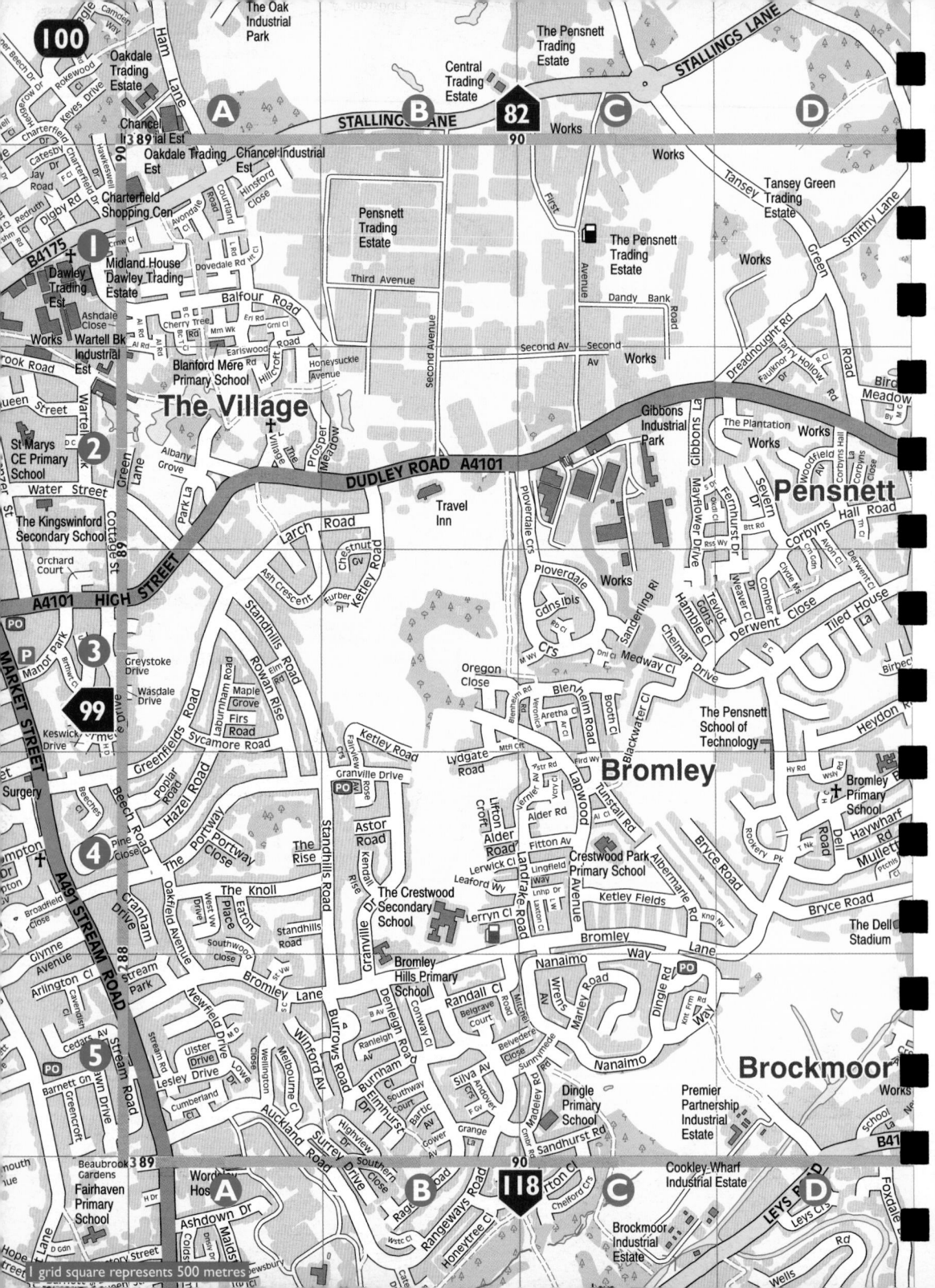
The Oak Industrial Park
The Pensnett Trading Estate
Central Trading Estate
STALLINGS LANE
82
Oakdale Trading Estate
Chancel Ind Est
Oakdale Trading Est
Chancel Industrial Est
Charterfield Shopping Cen
Midland House
Dawley Trading Estate
Dawley Trading Est
B4175
Pensnett Trading Estate
Third Avenue
Second Avenue
Works
Tansey Green Trading Estate
Smithy Lane
Dandy Bank Road
Balfour Road
Blanford Mere Primary School
The Village
Gibbons Industrial Park
The Plantation
Pensnett
DUDLEY ROAD A4101
St Marys CE Primary School
Water Street
The Kingswinford Secondary School
Travel Inn
A4101 HIGH STREET
MARKET STREET
99
The Pensnett School of Technology
Bromley
Bromley Primary School
Crestwood Park Primary School
The Crestwood Secondary School
Bromley Hills Primary School
The Dell Stadium
A491 STREAM ROAD
Bromley Lane
Brockmoor
Dingle Primary School
Premier Partnership Industrial Estate
Cookley Wharf Industrial Estate
Brockmoor Industrial Estate
Fairhaven Primary School
118
LEYS ROAD
1 grid square represents 500 metres

Russell's Hall
Russells Hall Hospital
A&E
Woodside
Hart's Hill
Round Oak
HIGH STREET
A4101
KINGSWINFORD ROAD
STOURBRIDGE ROAD
A461
HIGHGATE ROAD
PEDMORE ROAD
A4036
DUDLEY ROAD
PENSNETT ROAD
B4179
COMMONSIDE
JOHN STREET
BANK STREET
83
102
119
Russell's Hall Road
Grenville Road
Marston Road
Thornberry Drive
Overfield Road
Middlepark Road
Hawkesley Road
Ketley Hill Road
Ashenhurst
Quentin Dr
Abbotsford Dr
Vicarage Lane
Elgar Crs
St Marks CE Primary School
Holly Hall (GM) School
Old Park Special School
The Sutton Special School
Russells Hall Primary School
Holly Hall Clinic
Council Building
Highgate Primary School
The Wallows Industrial Estate
Paddys Wide Water Industrial Estate
Woodside Industrial Estate
Pedmore Road Industrial Est
Hurst Business Park
Waterfront Business Park
Dudley County Court
Copthorne Hotel
Travelodge
Waterfront Way
Canal St
Brockmoor Primary School
The Brierley Hill Health Centre
The Brier Special School
Old Bush Trading Estate
Enterprise Trading Estate
Merry Hill
Lodge Farm
Navigation
Pennsnett Industrial Park
Works

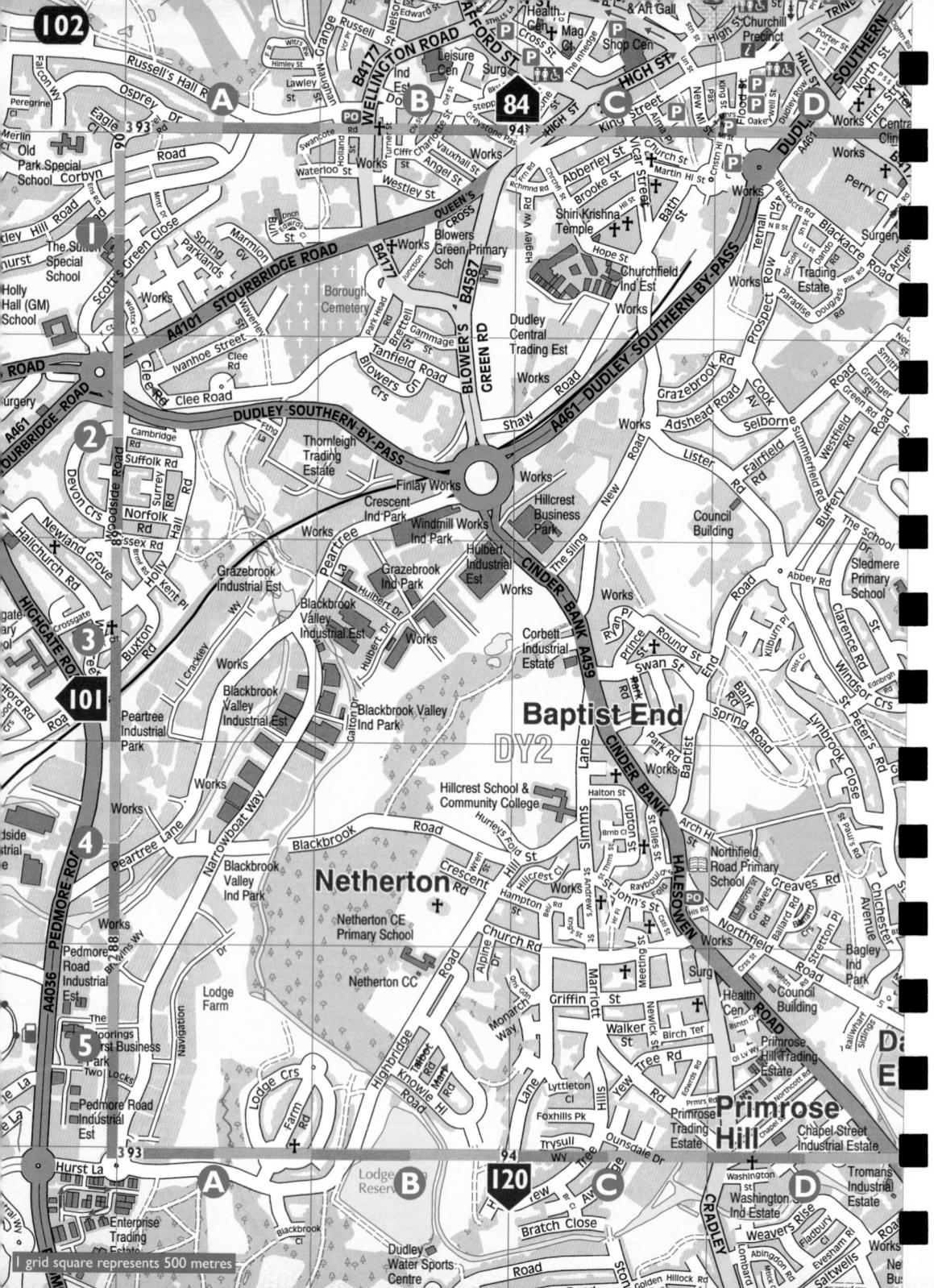

102
84
101
120
A
B
C
D
1
2
3
4
5
393
394
90
89
88
DY2
Baptist End
Netherton
Primrose Hill
Wellington Road
B4177
High St
King Street
Russell's Hall Rd
Osprey Dr
Eagle Cl
Falcon Wy
Peregrine Cl
Merlin Cl
Old Park Special School
Corbyn Road
The Sutton Special School
Holly Hall (GM) School
Scott's Green Close
Spring Parklands
Marmion Gv
A4101 Stourbridge Road
Queen's Cross
Borough Cemetery
Ivanhoe Street
Clee Rd
Clee Road
Waverley St
Dudley Southern-By-Pass
A461 Dudley Southern-By-Pass
Blowers Green Primary Sch
Blower's Green Rd
B4587
Tanfield Road
Gammage St
Brettell St
Blowers Crs
Dudley Central Trading Est
Shaw Road
Works
Churchfield Ind Est
Shiri Krishna Temple
Hope St
Abberley St
Brooke St
Vicar Street
Bath St
Church St
Martin Hl St
Westley St
Angel St
Vauxhall St
Waterloo St
Lawley St
Leisure Cen
Ind Est
Surg
Shop Cen
Churchill Precinct
Health Cen
Mag Ct
Cross St
Stepp
Greystone Pas
Russell St
Grange
Maughan
Himley St
Tetnall St
Blackacre Rd
Blackacre Road
Blackacre Trading Estate
Prospect Row
Paradise
Dougass Rd
Perry Cl
Surgery
Southern
Grazebrook Rd
Grazebrook Road
Adshead Road
Cook Av
Selborne
Lister Rd
Fairfield Rd
Summerfield Rd
Westfield Rd
Green Rd
Council Building
Buffery
The School Dr
Sledmere Primary School
Abbey Rd
Clarence Rd
Windsor Crs
St Peter's Rd
Lynbrook Close
Kilburn Pl
New Road
The Sling
Hillcrest Business Park
Thornleigh Trading Estate
Finlay Works
Crescent Ind Park
Windmill Works Ind Park
Peartree La
Grazebrook Ind Park
Hulbert Industrial Est
Hulbert Dr
Grazebrook Industrial Est
Blackbrook Valley Industrial Est
Blackbrook Valley Ind Park
Corbett Industrial Estate
Cinder Bank
A459
Ryan Pl
Prince St
Round St
Swan St
Park Rd
Baptist End Rd
Bank Rd
Spring Road
Hillcrest School & Community College
Halton St
Upton St
Simms Lane
St Giles St
Arch Hl St
Halesowen Road
Northfield Road Primary School
Greaves Rd
Chichester Avenue
Northfield Road
Bagley Ind Park
Council Building
Primrose Hill Trading Estate
Primrose Trading Estate
Chapel Street Industrial Estate
Tromans Industrial Estate
Washington St
Washington Ind Estate
Cradley
Weavers Rise
Evesham Rd
Saltwells
Cambridge Rd
Suffolk Rd
Surrey Rd
Norfolk Rd
Devon Crs
Woodside Road
Hall Rd
Newland Grove
Halichurch Rd
Holly
Kent Pl
Buxton Rd
Crossgate
Highgate Road
Peartree Industrial Park
Crackley
Narrowboat Way
Peartree Lane
Blackbrook Road
Blackbrook St
Hillcrest Cl
Hampton St
St John's St
Church Rd
Netherton CE Primary School
Netherton CC
Alpine Dr
Marriott
Griffin St
Meeting St
Walker St
Birch Ter
Yew Tree Rd
Monarch Way
Highbridge Road
Knowle Hl
Lyttleton Cl
Foxhills Pk
Trysull Wy
Ounsdale Dr
Bratch Close
Lodge Farm
Lodge Crs
Farm Rd
Navigation
A4036 Pedmore Road
Pedmore Road Industrial Est
The Moorings
Hurst Business Park
Two Locks
Hurst La
Enterprise Trading Estate
Dudley Water Sports Centre
Golden Hillock Rd
Lodge Reservoir
1 grid square represents 500 metres

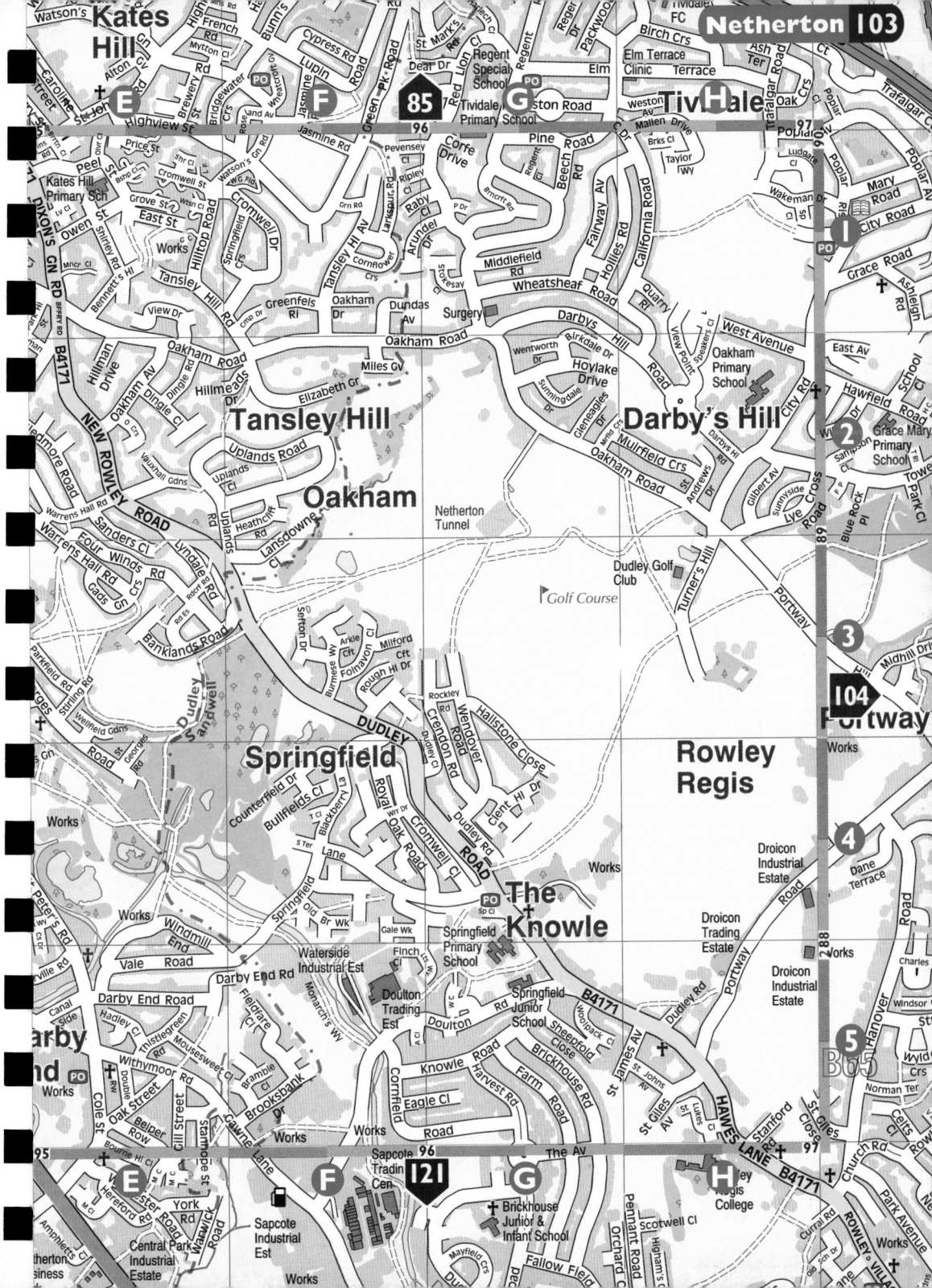
Kates Hill
Tividale
Tansley Hill
Darby's Hill
Oakham
Netherton Tunnel
Dudley Golf Club
Golf Course
Springfield
Rowley Regis
The Knowle
Portway
Waterside Industrial Est
Doulton Trading Est
Springfield Primary School
Springfield Junior School
Droicon Industrial Estate
Droicon Trading Estate
Sapcote Industrial Est
Central Park Industrial Estate
Brickhouse Junior & Infant School
Oakham Primary School
Grace Mary Primary School
Kates Hill Primary Sch
Tividale Primary School
Regent Special School
Elm Terrace Clinic
New Rowley Road
Dudley Road
Oakham Road
Hawes Lane
B4171
85
104
121

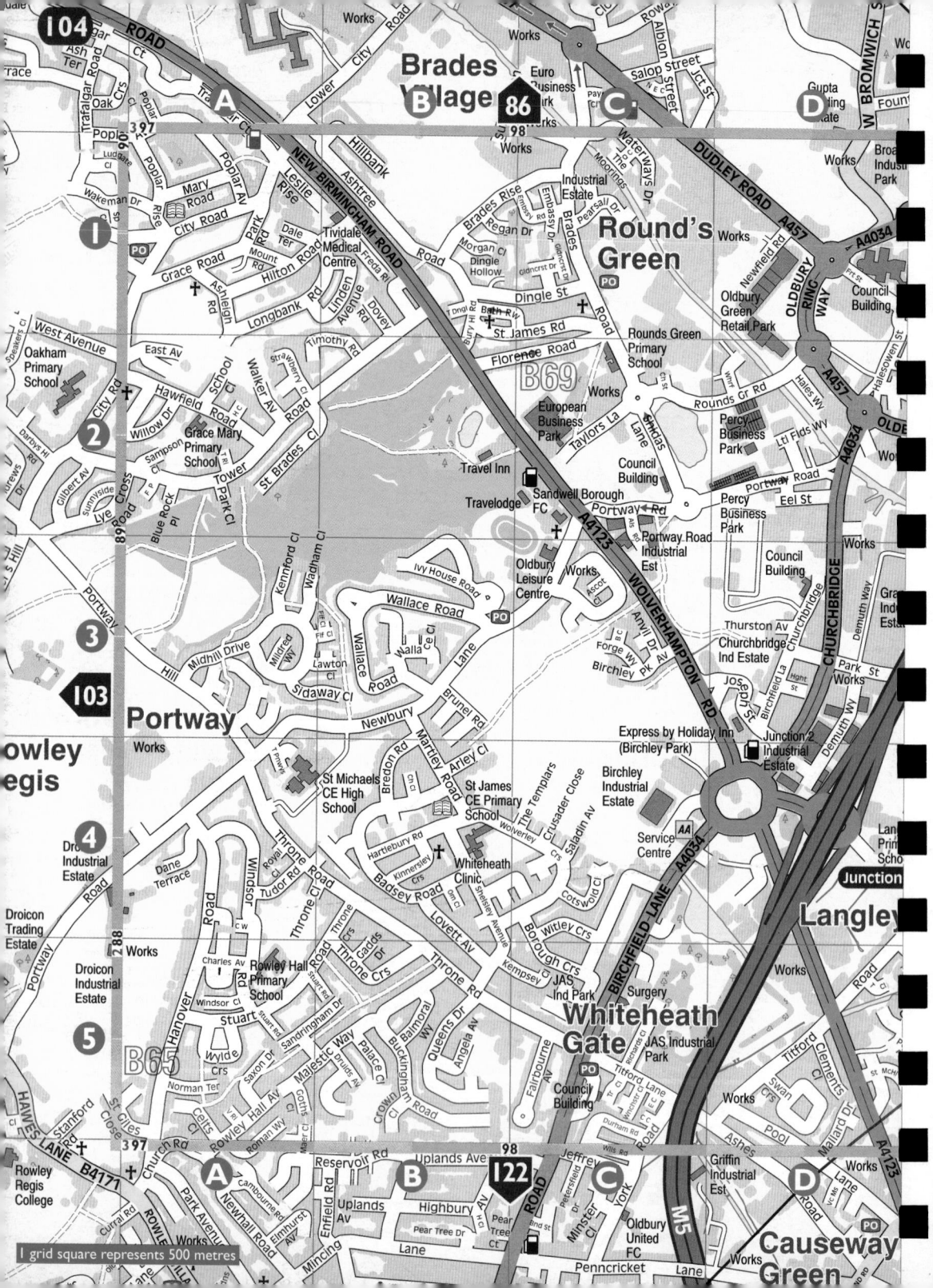

104
86
103
122
A
B
C
D
1
2
3
4
5
397
98
Brades Village
Round's Green
Portway
Whiteheath Gate
Langley
Causeway Green
Rowley Regis
B69
B65
NEW BIRMINGHAM ROAD
WOLVERHAMPTON RD
A4123
DUDLEY ROAD
A457
A4034
OLDBURY RING WAY
CHURCHBRIDGE
BIRCHFIELD LANE
M5
HAWES LANE
B4171
Works
Euro Business Park
Salop Street
Albion Street
Jct St
Gupta Trading Estate
Broadwell Industrial Park
Industrial Estate
Brades Rise
Regan Dr
Embassy Dr
Pearsall Dr
Waterways Dr
The Moorings
Tividale Medical Centre
Hillbank
Ashtree
Leslie Rise
Poplar Av
Poplar Rise
Mary Road
City Road
Wakeman Dr
Trafalgar Road
Oak Crs
Ash Ter
Lower City Road
Grace Road
Hilton Road
Mount Rd
Dale Ter
Park Rd
Longbank Rd
Linden Avenue
Dovey Rd
Freda Rd
Ashleigh Rd
Dingle St
Dingle Hollow
Morgan Cl
St James Rd
Bath Rw
Bury Hl Rd
Florence Road
Timothy Rd
West Avenue
East Av
Oakham Primary School
City Rd
Hawfield Road
Willow Dr
School Cl
Walker Av
Strawberry Cl
Grace Mary Primary School
Sampson Cl
Tower Road
St Brades Cl
Park Cl
Blue Rock Pl
Lye Cross Road
Gilbert Av
Sunnyside
Rounds Green Primary School
Rounds Gr Rd
Oldbury Green Retail Park
Newfield Rd
Council Building
European Business Park
Taylors La
Shidas Lane
Percy Business Park
Ltl Flds Wy
Hales Wy
Travel Inn
Travelodge
Sandwell Borough FC
Portway Rd
Portway Road
Eel St
Portway Road Industrial Est
Oldbury Leisure Centre
Ascot Cl
Ivy House Road
Wallace Road
Kennford Cl
Wadham Cl
Midhill Drive
Mildred Wy
Lawton Cl
Sidaway Cl
Lane
Forge Wy
Anvil Dr
Birchley Pk Av
Thurston Av
Churchbridge Ind Estate
Park St
Demuth Way
Joseph St
Birchfield La
Express by Holiday Inn (Birchley Park)
Junction 2 Industrial Estate
Birchley Industrial Estate
Service Centre
Newbury
Brunel Rd
Martley Road
Arley Cl
Bredon Rd
St Michaels CE High School
St James CE Primary School
The Templars
Crusader Close
Saladin Av
Wolverley Crs
Hartlebury Rd
Kinnersley Crs
Whiteheath Clinic
Badsey Road
Lovett Av
Shelsley Avenue
Cotswold Cl
Witley Crs
Borough Crs
Kempsey Cl
JAS Ind Park
Surgery
JAS Industrial Park
Dane Terrace
Windsor Road
Royal Cl
Tudor Rd
Throne Road
Throne Cl
Throne Crs
Gadds Dr
Throne Rd
Droicon Industrial Estate
Droicon Trading Estate
Portway
Hanover Road
Charles Av
Rowley Hall Primary School
Windsor Cl
Stuart Rd
Sandringham Dr
Majestic Way
Balmoral Wy
Queens Dr
Angela Av
Palace Cl
Buckingham Road
Crown Cl
Wylde Crs
Norman Ter
Saxon Dr
Rowley Hall Av
Celts
Roman Wy
St Giles Close
Stanford Rd
Church Rd
Reservoir Rd
Uplands Ave
Uplands Av
Highbury Av
Pear Tree Dr
Pear Tree Ct
Lane
Enfield Rd
Cambourne Rd
Newhall Road
Elmhurst Av
Park Avenue
Curral Rd
Rowley Regis College
Fairbourne Av
Council Building
Titford Lane
Durham Rd
Wlls Rd
Jeffrey Road
Petersfield Dr
Minster Cl
York Road
Oldbury United FC
Penncricket Lane
Griffin Industrial Est
Ashes Pool
Swan Crs
Titford Cl
Clements Rd
Mallard Dr
Causeway Green
Junction
Mincing Lane
1 grid square represents 500 metres

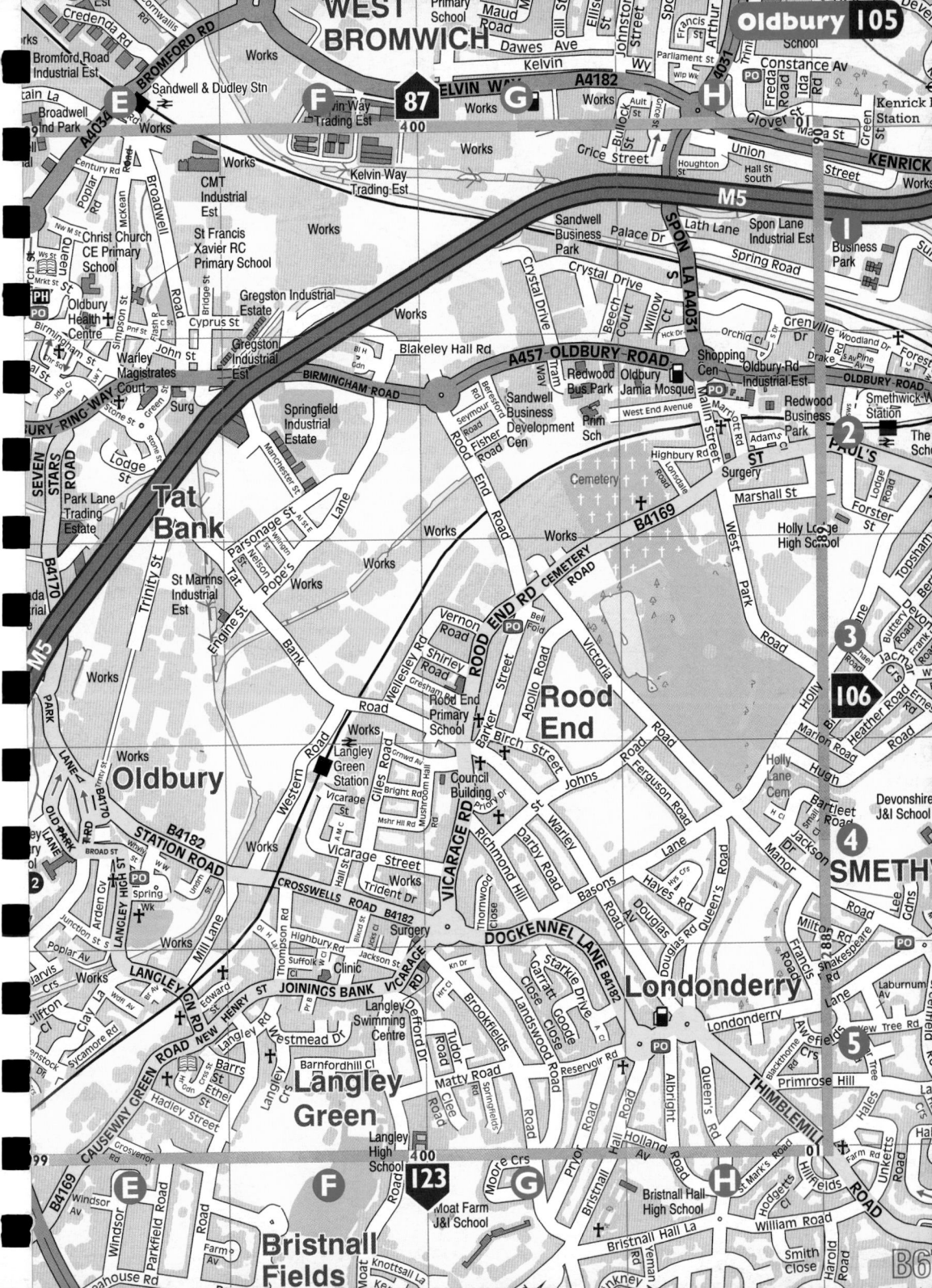

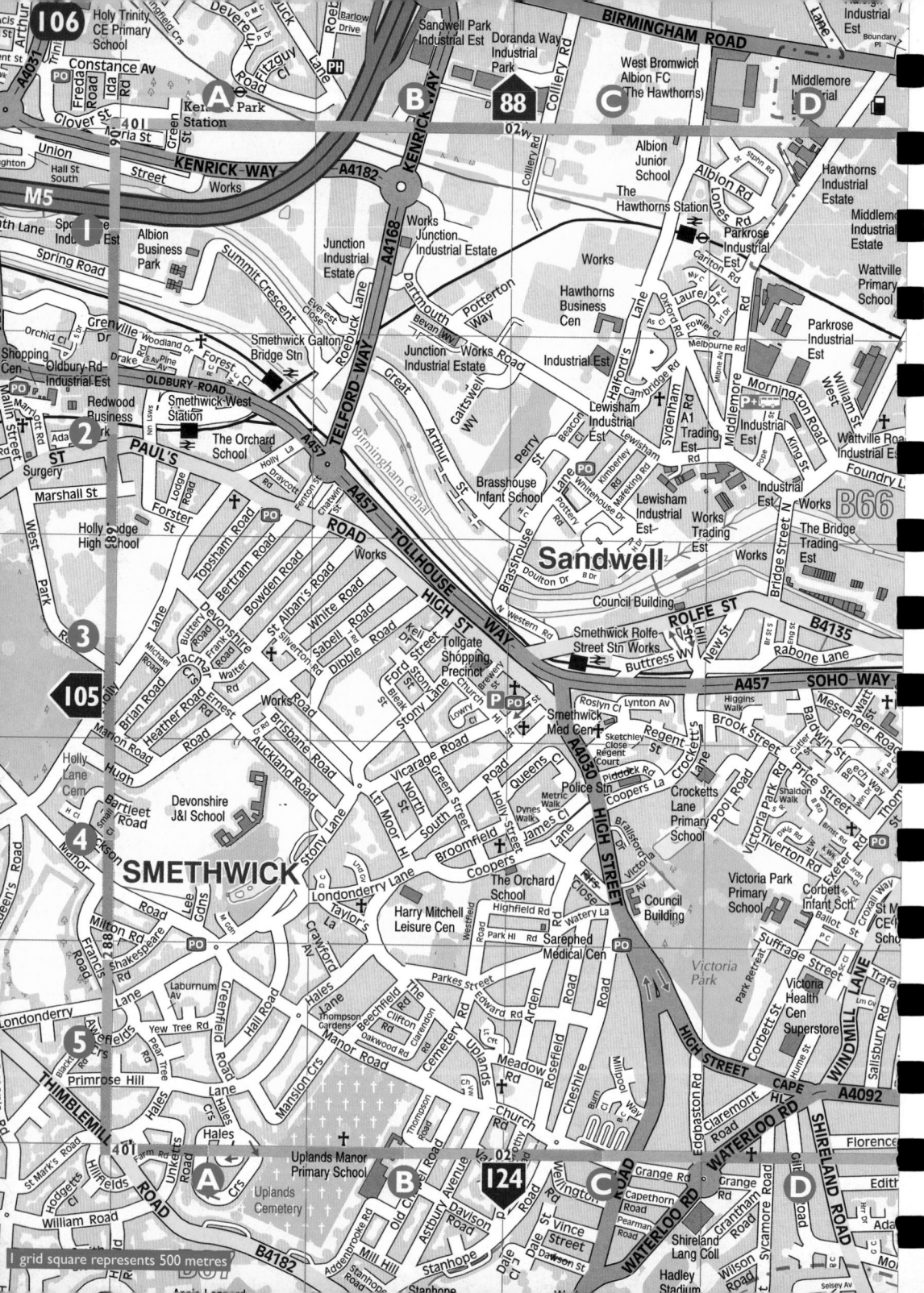

106
Holy Trinity CE Primary School
Constance Av
Freda Road
Ida Rd
Glover St
Kenrick Park Station
Union Street
Hall St South
KENRICK WAY
A4182
M5
Sandwell Park Industrial Est
Doranda Way Industrial Park
88
Colliery Rd
BIRMINGHAM ROAD
West Bromwich Albion FC (The Hawthorns)
Albion Junior School
Albion Rd
Lones Rd
The Hawthorns Station
Parkrose Industrial Est
Hawthorns Industrial Estate
Middlemore Industrial Est
Middlemore Industrial Estate
Wattville Primary School
Spring Road
Albion Business Park
Summit Crescent
Junction Industrial Estate
Works Junction Industrial Estate
A4168
TELFORD WAY
Roebuck Lane
Dartmouth
Potterton Way
Works Road
Hawthorns Business Cen
Industrial Est
Halford's Lane
Oxford Rd
Laurel Dr
Melbourne Rd
Parkrose Industrial Est
Grenville Dr
Orchid Cl
Woodland Dr
Forest Cl
Shopping Cen
Oldbury Rd Industrial Est
Smethwick Galton Bridge Stn
OLDBURY ROAD
Smethwick West Station
Redwood Business Park
Marriott Rd
The Orchard School
A457
Great Arthur St
Caitswell Wy
Birmingham Canal
Lewisham Industrial Est
Cambridge Rd
Sydenham Rd
A1 Trading Est
Middlemore Rd
Mornington Road
Industrial Est
William St West
Wattville Road Industrial Est
Foundry La
PAUL'S ST
Surgery
Marshall St
West Park Rd
Holly Lodge High School
Forster St
Lodge Road
Fenton St
Chatwin St
TOLLHOUSE WAY
Brasshouse Infant School
Perry St
Kimberley Rd
Mafeking Rd
Whitehouse Dr
Lewisham Industrial Est
Works Trading Est
Industrial Est
Works
B66
Bridge Street N
The Bridge Trading Est
Sandwell
Brasshouse Lane
Doulton Dr
Topsham Road
Bertram Road
Bowden Road
St Alban's Road
White Road
Sabell Rd
Dibble Road
Works
HIGH ST
ROAD
Council Building
ROLFE ST
Western Rd
Smethwick Rolfe Street Stn Works
Buttress Wy
New St
B4135
Rabone Lane
A457
SOHO WAY
Devonshire Road
Jacmar Crs
Frank Road
Walter Rd
Silverton Rd
Tollgate Shopping Precinct
Brewery St
Stony Lane
Church Hl
105
Holly Lane
Brian Road
Heather Road
Ernest Rd
Marion Road
Auckland Road
Brisbane Road
Vicarage Road
Smethwick Med Cen
Roslyn Cl
Lynton Av
Regent St
Sketchley Close
Regent Court
Piddock Rd
Police Stn
Coopers La
Crockett's Lane
Higgins Walk
Brook Street
Baldwin St
Messenger Road
Price Street
Beech Way
Holly Lane Cem
Hugh Road
Bartleet Road
Devonshire J&I School
Lti Moor Hl
North St
South Rd
Green Street
Queens Cl
Holly Street
James Cl
Broomfield
Coopers Lane
A4030 HIGH STREET
Brallsford Dr
Victoria Av
Crocketts Lane Primary School
Pool Road
Victoria Park Rd
Tiverton Rd
Exeter Rd
Manor
SMETHWICK
Londonderry Lane
Taylor's La
The Orchard School
Harry Mitchell Leisure Cen
Highfield Rd
Watery La
Park Hl Rd
Sarephed Medical Cen
Council Building
Victoria Park Primary School
Corbett Infant Sch
Ballot St
Croxall Way
Milton Rd
Shakespeare Rd
Francis Road
Crawford Av
Westfield Road
Victoria Park
Park Retreat
Suffrage Street
Victoria Health Cen
Superstore
WINDMILL LANE
Salisbury Rd
Londonderry Lane
Awefields Crs
Laburnum Av
Greenfield Road
Hall Road
Hales Lane
Thompson Gardens
Beechfield Rd
Clifton Rd
Oakwood Rd
Parkes Street
Edward Rd
Arden Road
Yew Tree Rd
Pear Tree Rd
Primrose Hill
Manor Road
Mansion Crs
Cemetery Rd
Uplands
Meadow Rd
Rosefield Road
Cheshire Road
Millpool Way
HIGH STREET
CAPE HL
A4092
Corbett St
Hume St
THIMBLEMILL ROAD
Hales Lane
Hales Crs
Church Rd
Claremont Road
WATERLOO RD
SHIRELAND ROAD
Florence
St Mark's Road
Hillfields
Hodgetts Cl
Farm Rd
Unketts Road
Uplands Manor Primary School
Uplands Cemetery
Old Chapel Road
Astbury Avenue
Davison Road
124
Wellington
Grange Rd
Capethorn Road
Pearman Road
Grantham Road
Sycamore Road
Edgbaston Rd
Edith
William Road
B4182
Addenbrooke Rd
Mill Hill
Stanhope Road
Dale Cl
Dale St
Vince Street
Dawson St
WATERLOO RD
Shireland Lang Coll
Hadley Stadium
Wilson Road
Selsey Av
1 grid square represents 500 metres

Soho
Winson Green
Rotton Park
ISLAND ROAD A4040
A41 HOLYHEAD ROAD
SOHO ROAD A41
BOOTH STREET
B4136
RABONE LANE
BOULTON RD
HANDSWORTH NEW RD
A4040
WINSON GN RD
CRANFORD STREET
HEATH STREET
GROVE LANE
A457
DUDLEY ROAD
CAPE HILL
ROTTON PARK ROAD
ICKNIELD
Handsworth Booth Street Stn
Winson Green Stn
Soho Benson Road Stn
James Watt Industrial Park
HM Prison
Summerfield Hospital
City Hospital
Summerfield Park
Handsworth Leisure Centre
Handsworth Boys Grammar School
Handsworth Mosque & Islamic Cen
Matthew Boulton Community Primary Sch
Birmingham Canal
Birmingham Sandwell
B21
89
108
125
E
F
G
H
1
2
3
4
5
04
05
03

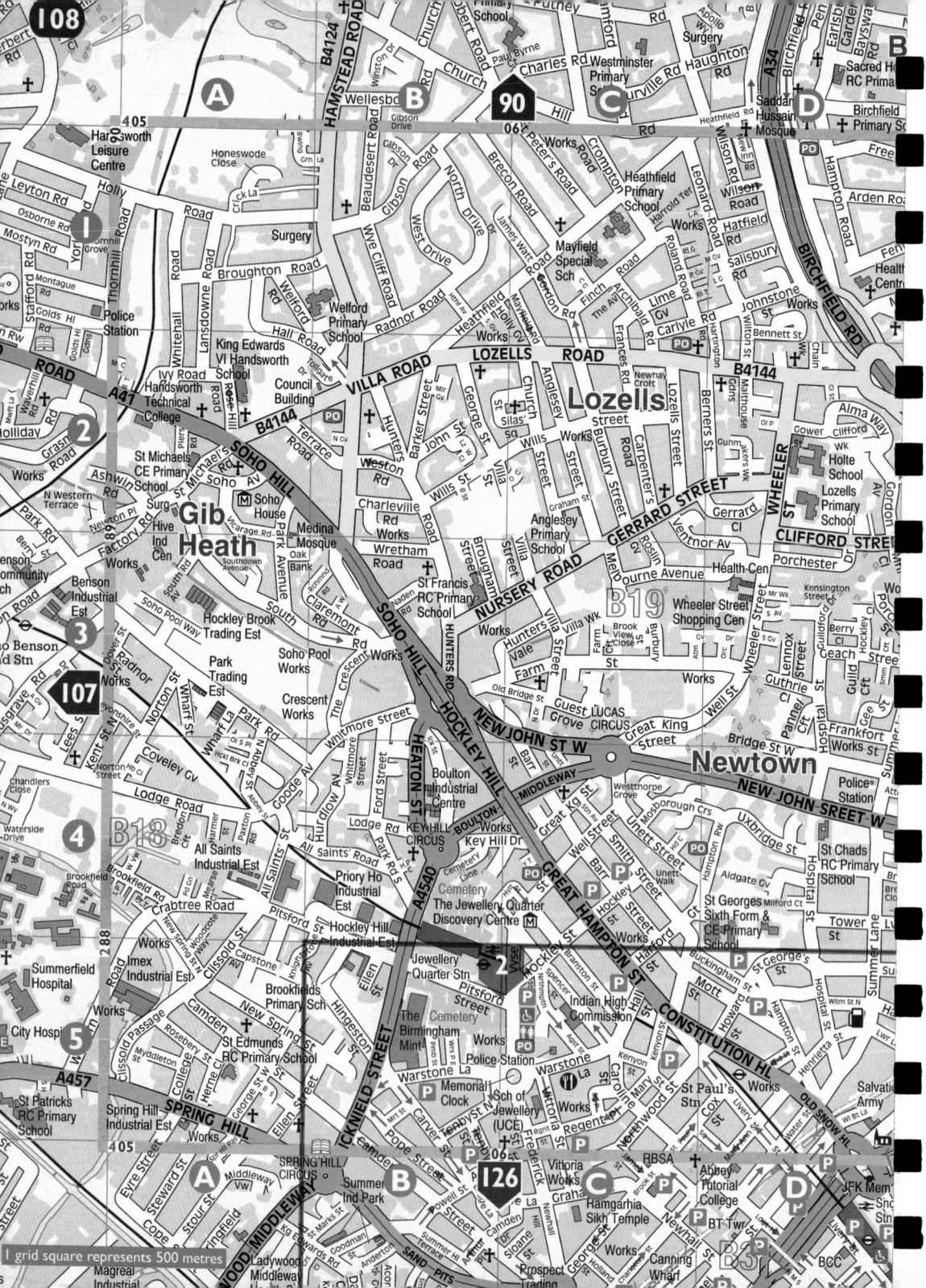

108
90
107
126
A
B
C
D
1
2
3
4
5
405
06
89
288
Handsworth Leisure Centre
Honeswode Close
HAMSTEAD ROAD
B4124
Wellesbourne
Gibson Drive
Beaudesert Road
Gibson Road
North Drive
West Drive
Wye Cliff Road
Church Hill
Charles Rd
Westminster Primary School
Curville Rd
Haughton Rd
Surgery
Saddam Hussain Mosque
Heathfield Rd
Birchfield Primary School
A34
BIRCHFIELD RD
St Peter's Road
Brecon Road
Crompton Road
Heathfield Primary School
Leonard Road
Wilson Rd
Hampton Road
Arden Road
Hatfield Rd
Salisbury Rd
Mayfield Special Sch
James Watt Dr
Gordon Rd
Finch Road
Archibald Rd
Roland Road
Lime Gv
Johnstone St
Carlyle Rd
Bennett St
Leyton Rd
Osborne Rd
Mostyn Rd
York Rd
Thornhill Road
Stafford Rd
Montague Rd
Golds Hl
Police Station
Broughton Road
Whitehall Road
Lansdowne Road
Welford Rd
Welford Primary School
Radnor Road
Hall Road
King Edwards VI Handsworth School
Ivy Road
Handsworth Technical College
Council Building
VILLA ROAD
B4144
LOZELLS ROAD
Frances Rd
Lozells
Lozells Street
Berners St
Malthouse Gdns
Alma Way
Gower
Clifford
Holte School
Lozells Primary School
WHEELER ST
A41
ROAD
Holliday Rd
Grasmere Road
St Michaels CE Primary School
Soho Av
Soho House
SOHO HILL
Ashwin Rd
N Western Terrace
Park Rd
Newton Pl
Factory Rd
Hive Ind Cen
Gib Heath
Vicarage Rd
Park Avenue
Medina Mosque
Southdown Avenue
Benson Community Sch
Benson Industrial Est
Terrace Road
Hunters Rd
Barker Street
George St
John St
Weston Rd
Charleville Rd
Wills St
Villa St
Church St
Silas' Sq
Anglesey Street
Wills Street
Burbury Street
Carpenter's Road
Wretham Road
Oak Bank
St Francis RC Primary School
Brougham Street
Anglesey Primary School
Villa Street
NURSERY ROAD
GERRARD STREET
Gerrard Cl
Ventnor Av
CLIFFORD STREET
Porchester Dr
Melbourne Avenue
Health Cen
B19
Wheeler Street Shopping Cen
Kensington Street
Soho Pool Way
Hockley Brook Trading Est
South Road
Claremont Rd
Soho Pool Works
The Crescent
Crescent Works
Hunters Vale
Villa Wk
Brook View Close
Farm St
Old Bridge St
Guest Grove
LUCAS CIRCUS
Great King Street
Well St
Wheeler Street
Lennox Street
Guthrie Cl
Hospital St
Frankfort Works St
Bridge St W
Newtown
NEW JOHN ST W
NEW JOHN SREET W
Police Station
Radnor St
Park Trading Est
Norton St
Wharf St
Wharf La
Park Rd
Devonshire St
Lees St
Kent St N
Coveley Gv
Whitmore Street
HEATON ST
HOCKLEY HILL
Boulton Industrial Centre
MIDDLEWAY
BOULTON
Chandlers Close
Lodge Road
Waterside Drive
B18
All Saints Industrial Est
All Saints' St
All Saints' Road
Hurdlow Av
Ford Street
Lodge Rd
KEY HILL CIRCUS
Key Hill Dr
Westthorpe Grove
Mosborough Crs
Unett Street
Uxbridge St
St Chads RC Primary School
Great King St
Well Street
Smith Street
Hockley Street
Brookfield Rd
Crabtree Road
Priory Ho Industrial Est
A4540
Cemetery Lane
Cemetery
The Jewellery Quarter Discovery Centre
GREAT HAMPTON ST
Hampton Rw
Aldgate Gv
St Georges Sixth Form & CE Primary School
Tower St
Summer Lane
Pitsford St
Hockley Hill Industrial Est
Clissold St
Capstone Av
Imex Industrial Est
Summerfield Hospital
Jewellery Quarter Stn
Ellen St
Hingeston St
Brookfields Primary Sch
New Spring St
Camden St
Pitsford Street
The Birmingham Mint
Indian High Commission
Buckingham St
St George's St
Mott St
Howard St
Hampton St
CONSTITUTION HL
City Hospital
Clissold Passage
Rosebery St
St Edmunds RC Primary School
Warstone La
Memorial Clock
Police Station
Warstone La
Caroline St
Mary St
Northwood St
St Paul's Stn
Cox St
Livery St
OLD SNOW HL
Salvation Army
A457
St Patricks RC Primary School
Spring Hill Industrial Est
SPRING HILL
George St
ICKNIELD STREET
Carver St
Pope Street
Sch of Jewellery (UCE)
Frederick St
Vittoria St
Regent Pl
Vittoria Works
RBSA
Abbey Tutorial College
JFK Mem
SPRING HILL CIRCUS
Summer Ind Park
Middleway Vw
Eyre Street
Steward St
Stour St
Cope St
LADYWOOD MIDDLEWAY
Powell St
Camden Dr
Sloane St
Newhall St
Hamgarhia Sikh Temple
BT Twr
B3
Canning Wharf
Prospect Trading
Summer Hill Terrace
SAND PITS
Ladywood Middleway
Magreal Industrial
BCC
Snow Hill Stn
1 grid square represents 500 metres

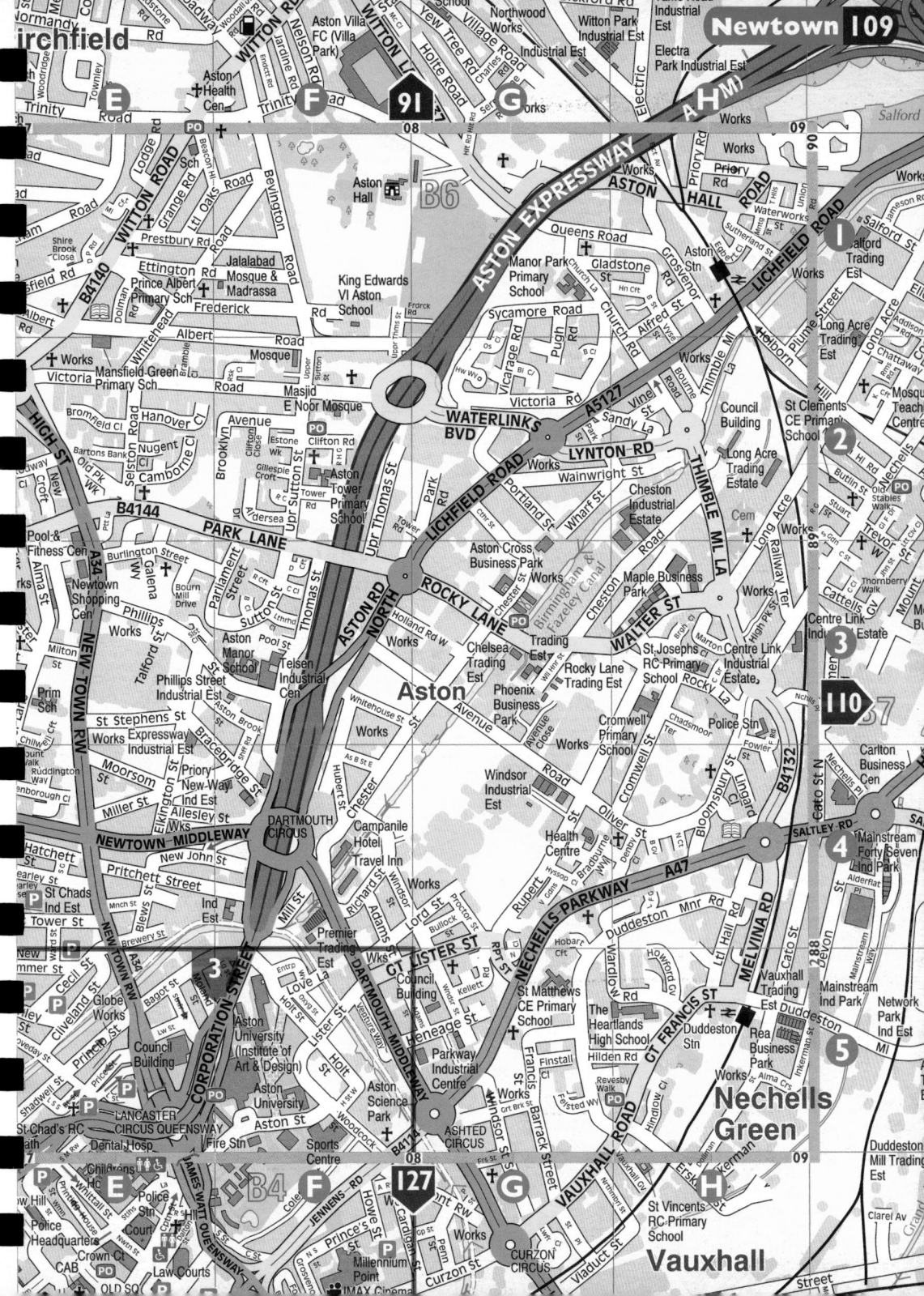

Newtown 109
Birchfield
Aston Villa FC (Villa Park)
Witton Park Industrial Est
Electra Park Industrial Est
Northwood Works
Industrial Est
Aston Health Cen
Witton Road
Trinity Road
Aston Expressway
Aston Hall
B6
Aston Hall Road
Priory Rd
Queens Road
Manor Park Primary School
Gladstone St
Aston Stn
Lichfield Road
Salford Trading Est
King Edwards VI Aston School
Jalalabad Mosque & Madrassa
Prince Albert Primary Sch
Frederick Rd
Albert Road
Sycamore Road
Vicarage Rd
Pugh Rd
Victoria Rd
Church Rd
Alfred St
Long Acre Trading Est
Mosque Teaching Centre
St Clements CE Primary School
Mansfield Green Primary Sch
Victoria Road
Masjid E Noor Mosque
Waterlinks Bvd
A5127
Lynton Rd
Wainwright St
Thimble Ml La
Council Building
Long Acre Trading Estate
Cheston Industrial Estate
High St
Selston Road
Hanover Cl
Camborne Cl
Aston Tower Primary School
Park Lane
B4144
Pool & Fitness Cen
Newtown Shopping Cen
A34
New Town Rw
Aston Cross Business Park
Birmingham & Fazeley Canal
Maple Business Park
Walter St
Rocky Lane
Aston Rd North
Phillips Street Industrial Est
Aston Manor School
Telsen Industrial Cen
Chelsea Trading Est
Rocky Lane Trading Est
St Josephs RC Primary School
Centre Link Industrial Estate
Aston
Phoenix Business Park
Police Stn
110
B7
Expressway Industrial Est
Cromwell Primary School
Windsor Industrial Est
Carlton Business Cen
Dartmouth Circus
Newtown Middleway
Campanile Hotel
Travel Inn
Health Centre
Oliver St
Saltley Rd
Mainstream Forty Seven Ind Park
Nechells Parkway
A47
Melvina Rd
B4132
St Chads Ind Est
Premier Trading Est
Gt Lister St
Council Building
St Matthews CE Primary School
The Heartlands High School
Gt Francis St
Duddeston Stn
Vauxhall Trading Est
Duddeston
Mainstream Ind Park
Network Park Ind Est
Corporation Street
Aston University (Institute of Art & Design)
Aston University
Aston Science Park
Parkway Industrial Centre
Dartmouth Middleway
Rea Business Park
Nechells Green
Lancaster Circus Queensway
Fire Stn
Sports Centre
Ashted Circus
Vauxhall Road
Duddeston Mill Trading Est
B4
127
Jennens Rd
Police Stn
Police Headquarters
Law Courts
James Watt Queensway
Millennium Point
IMAX Cinema
Curzon Circus
St Vincents RC Primary School
Vauxhall

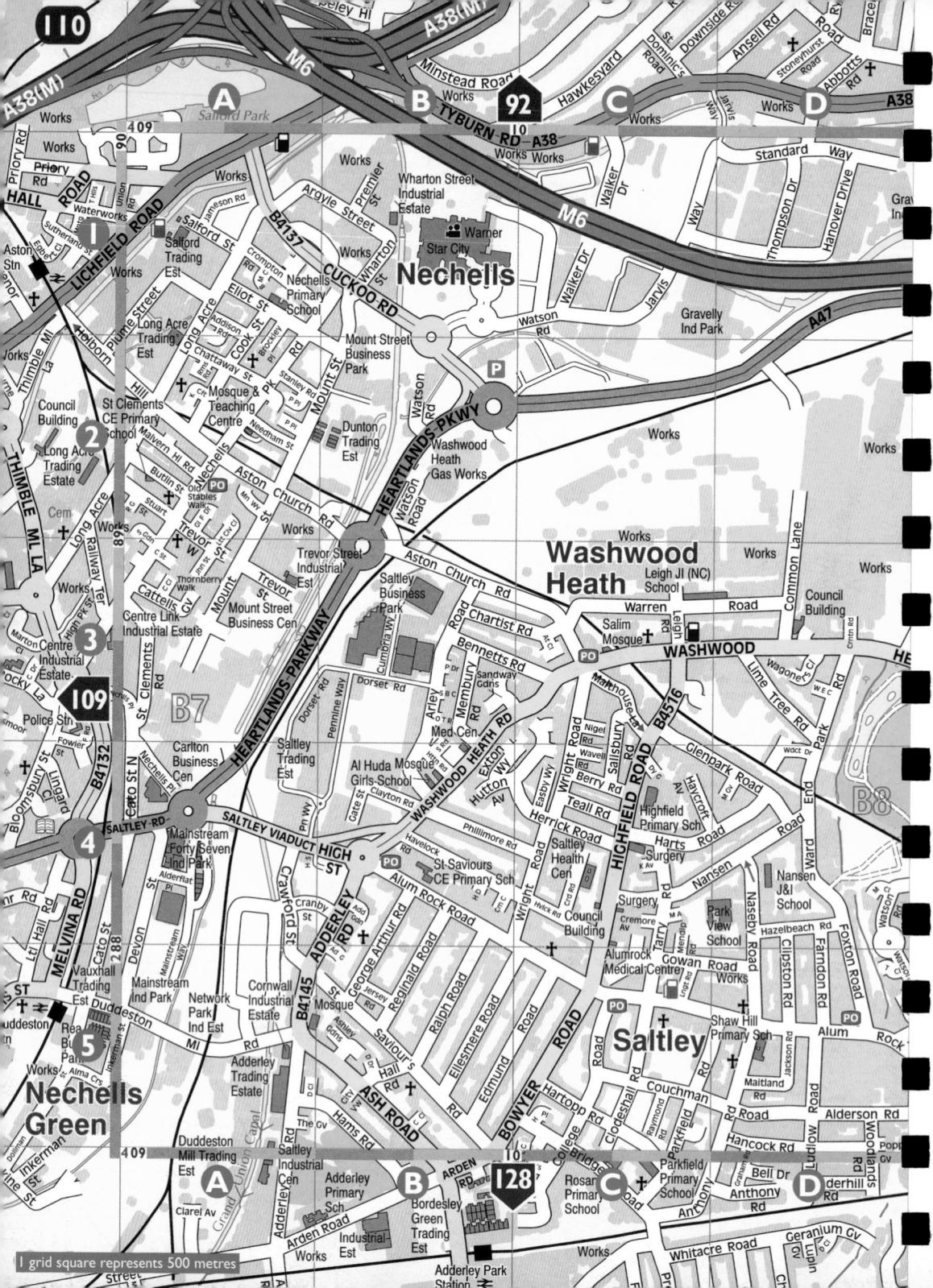

110
92
109
128
A
B
C
D
1
2
3
4
5
409
10
90
89
288
M6
A38(M)
A38
A47
TYBURN RD
Minstead Road
Hawkesyard
Standard Way
Walker Dr
Thompson Dr
Hanover Drive
Abbotts Rd
Ansell Rd
Downside Rd
Dominic's Road
Salford Park
Works
Priory Rd
HALL ROAD
LICHFIELD ROAD
Waterworks
Sutherland St
Aston Stn
Salford Trading Est
Salford St
Jameson Rd
Argyle Street
Premier St
B4137
Wharton Street Industrial Estate
Warner Star City
Nechells
CUCKOO RD
Nechells Primary School
Eliot St
Cook St
Long Acre
Long Acre Trading Est
Plume Street
Holborn Hill
Thimble Ml La
THIMBLE ML LA
Council Building
St Clements CE Primary School
Long Acre Trading Estate
Mount Street Business Park
Mount St
Watson Rd
Gravelly Ind Park
Chattaway St
Mosque & Teaching Centre
Needham St
Dunton Trading Est
Washwood Heath Gas Works
HEARTLANDS PKWY
Malvern Hl Rd
Butlin St
Nechells Pk Rd
Aston Church Rd
Old Stables Walk
Stuart St
Trevor St
Trevor St W
Watson Road
Cem
Railway Ter
Works
Thornberry Walk
Cattells Gv
Mount St
Trevor Street Industrial Est
Mount Street Business Cen
Saltley Business Park
Aston Church Rd
Washwood Heath
Leigh JI (NC) School
Common Lane
Council Building
Warren Road
Salim Mosque
Leigh Rd
Chartist Rd
Bennetts Rd
WASHWOOD HEATH RD
Centre Link Industrial Estate
High Pk St
Marton Cl
Centre Industrial Estate
St Clements Rd
B7
HEARTLANDS PARKWAY
Cumbria Wy
Dorset Rd
Pennine Way
Membury Rd
Arley Rd
Sandway Gdns
Malthouse La
B4516
Lime Tree Rd
Wagoners Cl
Glenpark Road
Park Rd
Police Stn
Fowler St
Bloomsbury St
Lingard Cl
B4132
Cato St N
Nechells Pl
Carlton Business Cen
Saltley Trading Est
Al Huda Girls School
Mosque
Med Cen
Exton Wy
Hutton Av
Easby Wy
Wright Road
Nigel Rd
Wavell Rd
Berry Rd
Salisbury Rd
HIGHFIELD ROAD
Havcroft Av
Teall Rd
Herrick Road
Highfield Primary Sch
Harts Road
End Road
Ward End
B8
SALTLEY RD
SALTLEY VIADUCT
HIGH ST
Clayton Rd
Gate St
Phillimore Rd
Mainstream Forty Seven Ind Park
Havelock Rd
St Saviours CE Primary Sch
Alum Rock Road
Saltley Health Cen
Surgery
Nansen Road
Nansen J&I School
Watson Rd
Melvina Rd
MELVINA RD
Ltl Hall Rd
Cato St
Devon St
Alderflat Pl
Crawford St
Cranby St
ADDERLEY RD
George Arthur Rd
Reginald Road
Wright Road
Council Building
Cremore Av
Tarry Rd
Park View School
Naseby Road
Hazelbeach Rd
Clipston Rd
Farndon Rd
Foxton Road
Vauxhall Trading Est
Mainstream Ind Park
Mainstream Way
Network Park Ind Est
Cornwall Industrial Estate
B4145
Mosque
Jersey Rd
Ralph Road
Ellesmere Road
Edmund Road
BOWYER ROAD
Alumrock Medical Centre
Gowan Road
Works
Shaw Hill Primary Sch
Saltley
Alum Rock Rd
Duddeston Mill Rd
Duddeston
Inkerman St
Alma Crs
Nechells Green
Adderley Trading Estate
Saviour's Rd
Ashley Gdns
Hall Rd
City Vw
ASH ROAD
Hams Rd
Hartopp Rd
Clodeshall Rd
Raymond Rd
Parkfield Rd
Couchman Rd
Maitland Rd
Jackson Rd
Ludlow Road
Alderson Rd
Woodlands Rd
Hancock Rd
Bell Dr
Anthony Rd
Dollman St
Inkerman St
Vine St
Duddeston Mill Trading Est
The Gv
Saltley Industrial Cen
Adderley Primary Sch
Arden Road
ARDEN RD
Bordesley Green Trading Est
Industrial Est
College Rd
Bridge Road
Rosary Primary School
Parkfield Primary School
Anthony Rd
Whitacre Road
Geranium Gv
Lupin Gv
Clarel Av
Grand Union Canal
Adderley Rd
Works
Adderley Park Station
1 grid square represents 500 metres

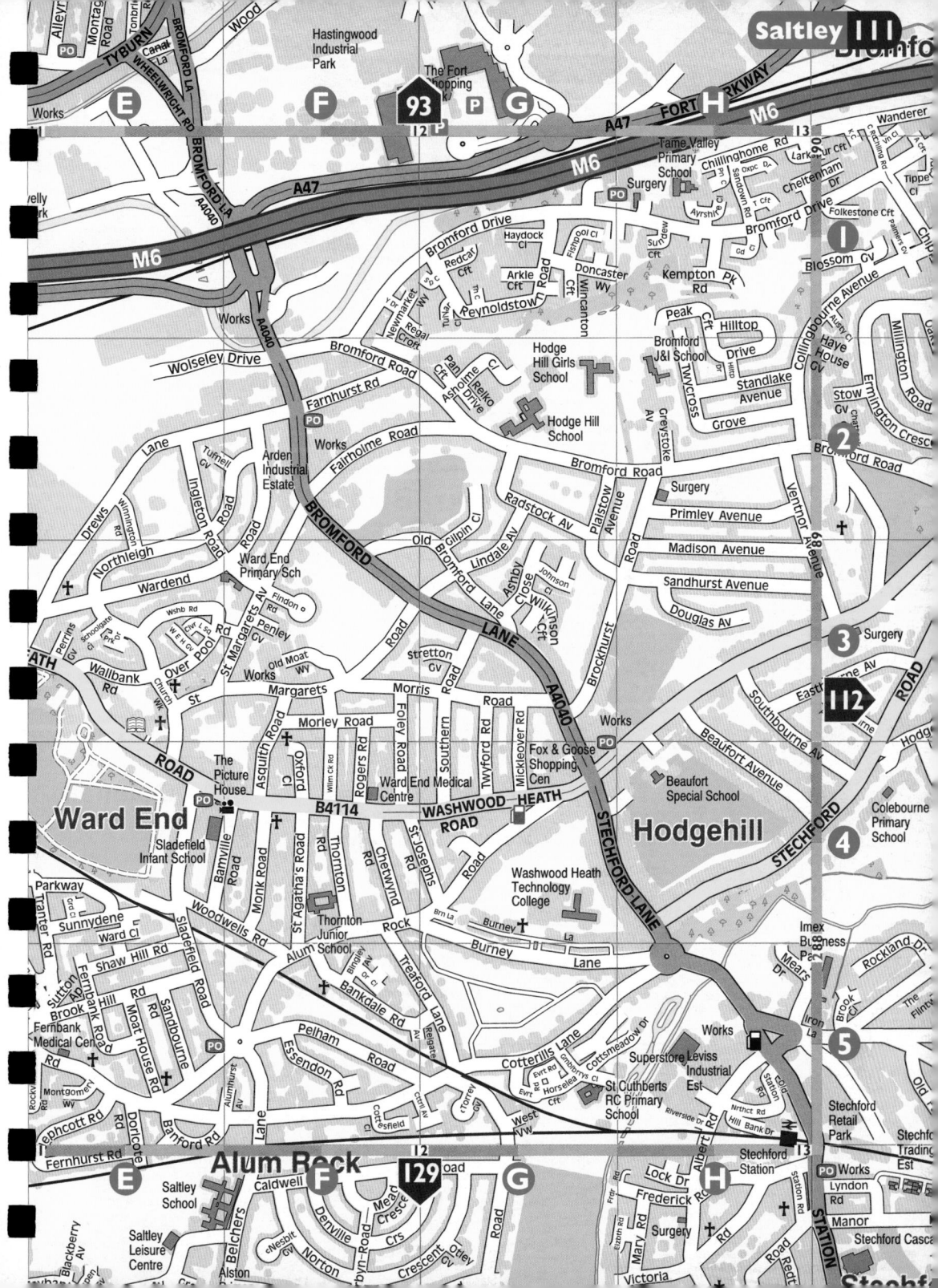

Saltley 111
Hastingwood Industrial Park
The Fort Shopping Park
93
E
F
G
H
M6
A47
FORT PARKWAY
TYBURN
BROMFORD LA
WHEELWRIGHT RD
A4040
Tame Valley Primary School
Chillinghome Rd
Sandown Rd
Cheltenham Dr
Surgery
Bromford Drive
Haydock Cl
Redcar Cft
Arkle Cft
Doncaster Wy
Kempton Pk Rd
Reynoldstown Road
Wincanton Cft
Newmarket Wy
Regal Croft
Works
Wolseley Drive
Bromford Road
Farnhurst Rd
Asholme Cl
Relko Drive
Hodge Hill Girls School
Hodge Hill School
Bromford J&I School
Peak Cft
Hilltop Drive
Twycross Grove
Standlake Avenue
Greystoke Av
Collingbourne Avenue
Haye House Gv
Millington Road
Stow Gv
Ermington Crescent
Blossom Gv
Folkestone Cft
Wanderer
Fairholme Road
Arden Industrial Estate
BROMFORD LANE
Radstock Av
Plaistow Avenue
Primley Avenue
Madison Avenue
Sandhurst Avenue
Douglas Av
Ventnor Avenue
Surgery
Lindale Av
Gilpin Cl
Ashby Close
Johnson Cl
Wilkinson Cft
Brockhurst Road
Drews Lane
Ingleton Road
Northleigh Road
Wardend
Ward End Primary Sch
Findon Rd
Penley Gv
St Margarets Av
Over Pool Rd
Wallbank Rd
Old Moat Wy
Stretton Gv
Morris Road
St Margarets Road
Morley Road
Asquith Road
Oxford Cl
Rogers Rd
Foley Road
Southern Road
Twyford Rd
Mickleover Rd
Fox & Goose Shopping Cen
Eastbourne Av
Southbourne Av
Beaufort Avenue
Beaufort Special School
112
The Picture House
Ward End Medical Centre
B4114
WASHWOOD HEATH ROAD
Ward End
Sladefield Infant School
Hodgehill
STECHFORD LANE
STECHFORD ROAD
Colebourne Primary School
Washwood Heath Technology College
Bamville Road
Monk Road
St Agatha's Road
Thornton Rd
Chetwynd Rd
St Josephs Rd
Thornton Junior School
Rock
Burney Lane
Burney La
Parkway
Tranter Rd
Sunnydene
Ward Cl
Shaw Hill Rd
Woodwells Rd
Sladefield Road
Alum Rock
Fernbank Road
Brook Hill Rd
Moat House Rd
Sandbourne
Fernbank Medical Cen
Bankdale Rd
Treaford Lane
Pelham Road
Essendon Rd
Cotterills Lane
Cottsmeadow Dr
Horselea Cft
St Cuthberts RC Primary School
Superstore
Leviss Industrial Est
Works
Imex Business Park
Rockland Dr
Mears Dr
Iron La
Station Rd
Riverside Dr
Hill Bank Dr
Stechford Retail Park
Stechford Trading Est
Montgomery Wy
Tephcott Rd
Dorlcote Rd
Banford Rd
Alumhurst Av
West Vw
Fernhurst Rd
Alum Rock
129
Caldwell
Saltley School
Saltley Leisure Centre
Belchers
Denville
Norton
Crescent
Mead Crescent
Otley Gv
Blackberry Av
Alston
Lock Dr
Frederick Rd
Mary Rd
Surgery
Albert Rd
Stechford Station
Works
Lyndon Rd
Manor
STATION
Stechford Cascade
Victoria
1
2
3
4
5
12
13

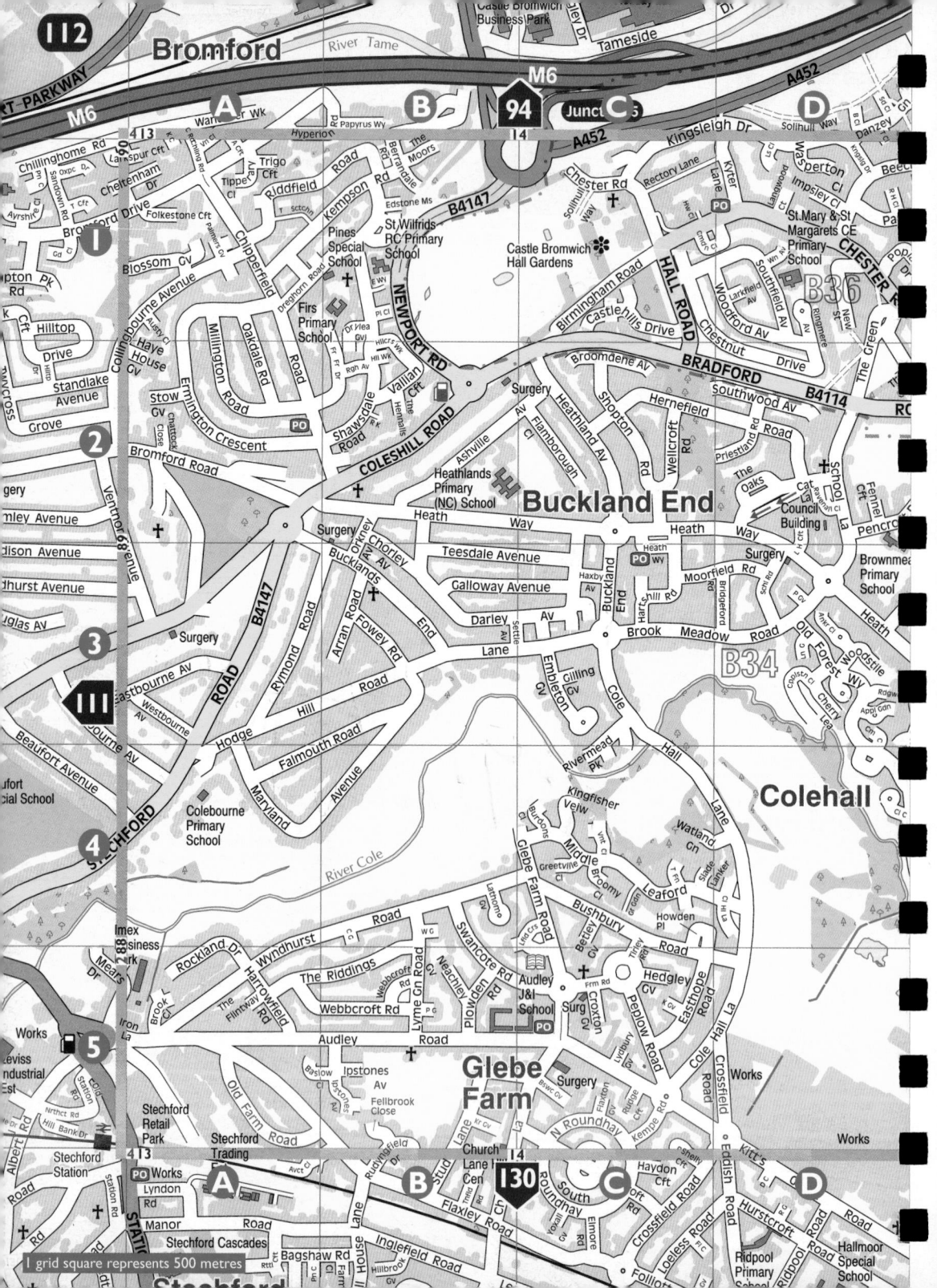
112
Bromford
River Tame
M6
A452
94
Junction 5
Castle Bromwich Business Park
Tameside
A
B
C
D
1
2
3
4
5
Chillinghome Rd
Larkspur Cft
Cheltenham Dr
Bromford Drive
Folkestone Cft
Blossom Gv
Chipperfield
Riddfield Road
Trigo Cft
Kempson Rd
Berrandale Rd
The Moors
Hyperion Rd
Papyrus Wy
Edstone Ms
B4147
St Wilfrids RC Primary School
Pines Special School
Firs Primary School
Dreghorn Road
NEWPORT RD
Castle Bromwich Hall Gardens
Chester Rd
Rectory Lane
Kingsleigh Dr
Solihull Way
Birmingham Road
Castlehills Drive
HALL ROAD
Chestnut Drive
Woodford Av
Southfield Av
St.Mary & St Margarets CE Primary School
CHESTER RD
B36
Wasperton Cl
Impsley Cl
Danzey Gn
Hilltop Drive
Collingbourne Avenue
Haye House Gv
Standlake Avenue
Grove
Millington Road
Oakdale Rd
Road
Stow Gv
Ermington Road
Ermington Crescent
Chattock Close
Shawsdale Road
Vallian Cft
COLESHILL ROAD
Bromford Road
Venthor Avenue
Surgery
Ashville Av
Flamborough Cl
Heathland Av
Shopton Rd
Wellcroft Rd
Hernefield Road
Southwood Av
Broomdene Av
BRADFORD
B4114
Priestland Rd
The Oaks
Council Building
School La
Fennel Cft
Heathlands Primary (NC) School
Buckland End
Heath Way
Orkney Av
Chorley Av
Bucklands End
Teesdale Avenue
Galloway Avenue
Darley Av
Buckland End
Hartshill Rd
Moorfield Rd
Brownmead Primary School
Brook Meadow Road
Old Forest Wy
Woodstile
Lane
B34
Arran Road
Fowey Rd
Rymond Road
B4147
ROAD
Eastbourne Av
Westbourne Av
Beaufort Avenue
111
Hill Road
Hodge
Falmouth Road
Maryland Avenue
Embleton Gv
Gilling Gv
Cole Hall Lane
Rivermead Pk
Kingfisher Veiw
Watland Gn
Colehall
Colebourne Primary School
STECHFORD
River Cole
Middle Broomy Cl
Leaford
Glebe Farm Road
Bushbury Road
Howden Pl
Wyndhurst Road
Rockland Dr
Harrowfield Rd
The Riddings
Webbcroft Rd
Lyme Gn Road
Swancote Rd
Plowden Rd
Neachley Gv
Audley J&I School
Betley Gv
Hedgley Gv
Easthope Road
Peplow Road
Croxton Gv
Imex Business Park
Mears Dr
Brook Cl
Iron La
Works
Audley Road
Ipstones Av
Fellbrook Close
Glebe Farm
Surgery
Cole Hall La
Crossfield Road
Kempe Rd
N Roundhay
Old Farm Road
Stechford Retail Park
Stechford Trading Est
Stechford Station
Church Lane Ind Cen
130
Eddish Road
Kitt's
Haydon Cft
South Roundhay
Flaxley Road
Crossfield Road
Loeless Road
Hurstcroft Road
Ridpool Primary School
Hallmoor Special School
Lyndon Rd
Manor Road
Stechford Cascades
Bagshaw Rd
Inglefield Road
House Lane
Rudyngfield Dr
Station Rd
Albert Rd
Old Station Rd
Hill Bank Dr
1 grid square represents 500 metres
Stechford

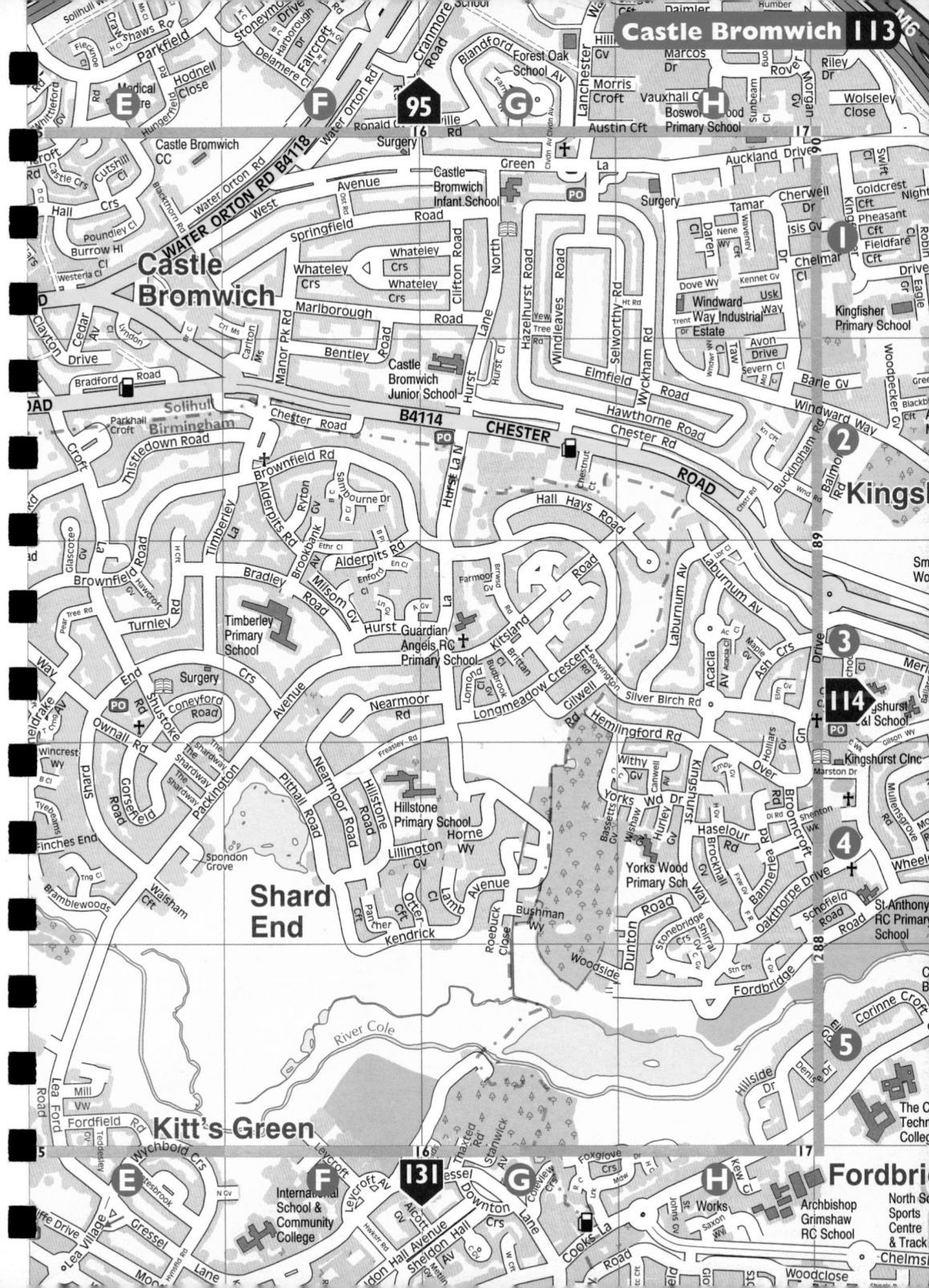
Castle Bromwich
Shard End
Kitt's Green
Kingshurst
Fordbridge
Water Orton Rd B4118
B4114 Chester Road
River Cole
Castle Bromwich CC
Castle Bromwich Infant School
Castle Bromwich Junior School
Kingfisher Primary School
Windward Way Industrial Estate
Timberley Primary School
Guardian Angels RC Primary School
Hillstone Primary School
Yorks Wood Primary Sch
St Anthonys RC Primary School
International School & Community College
Archbishop Grimshaw RC School
North Solihull Sports Centre & Track
Forest Oak School
Boswor[th] Wood Primary School
Kingshurst Clnc
Solihull
Birmingham
95
114
131

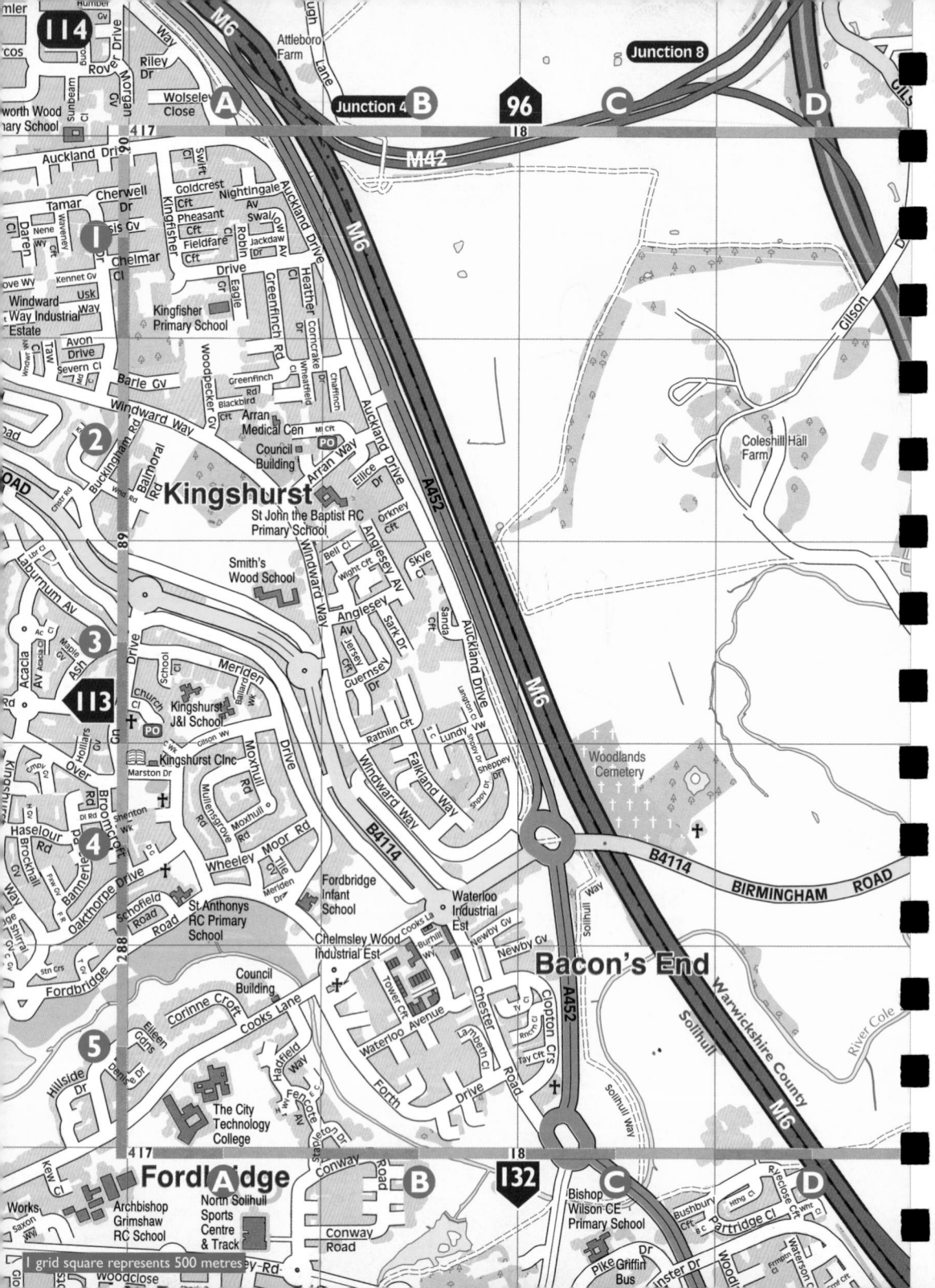

114

Junction 4   **96**   Junction 8

M42

M6

M6

A452

Auckland Drive

Gilson

Coleshill Hall Farm

Attleboro Farm

Kingsfisher Primary School

Windward Way Industrial Estate

Kingshurst

Arran Medical Cen

Council Building

St John the Baptist RC Primary School

Smith's Wood School

Windward Way

Anglesey Av

Anglesey Av

113

Kingshurst J&I School

Kingshurst Clnc

Moxhull Rd

Moxhull Rd

Wheeley Rd

Moor Rd

Windward Way

Falkland Way

B4114

Woodlands Cemetery

BIRMINGHAM ROAD

B4114

Fordbridge Infant School

Waterloo Industrial Est

Chelmsley Wood Industrial Est

Bacon's End

A452

Clopton Crs

Solihull

Warwickshire County

River Cole

St Anthonys RC Primary School

Council Building

Corinne Croft

Cooks Lane

Waterloo Avenue

Chester Road

The City Technology College

Hillside Dr

Fordbridge

132

Archbishop Grimshaw RC School

North Solihull Sports Centre & Track

Conway Road

Conway Road

Bishop Wilson CE Primary School

Griffin Bus

1 grid square represents 500 metres

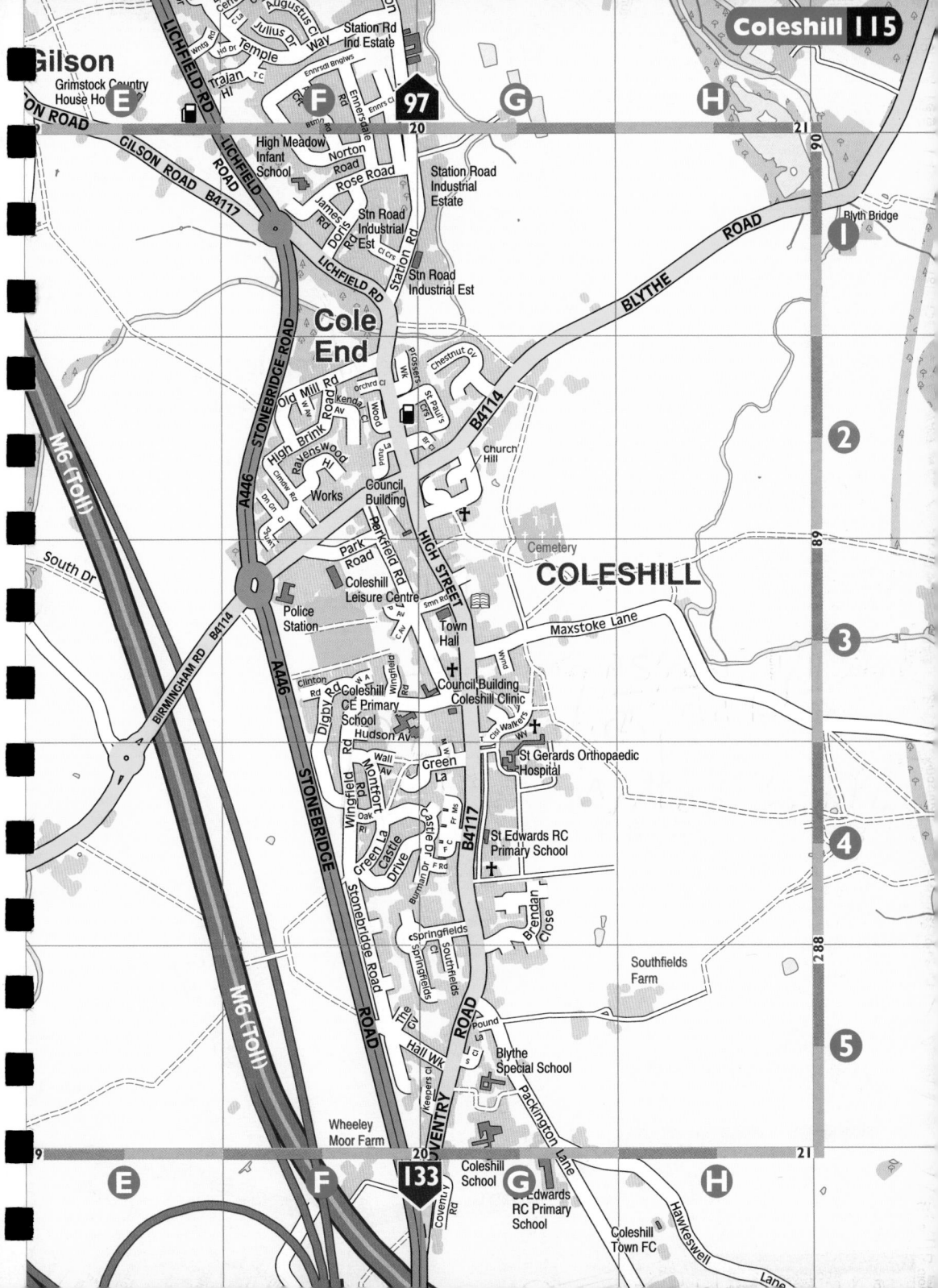
Gilson
Grimstock Country House Ho
Station Rd Ind Estate
97
High Meadow Infant School
Station Road Industrial Estate
Stn Road Industrial Est
Stn Road Industrial Est
Blyth Bridge
BLYTHE ROAD
GILSON ROAD B4117
LICHFIELD RD
Cole End
STONEBRIDGE ROAD A446
M6 (Toll)
Church Hill
Council Building
Works
Cemetery
COLESHILL
Coleshill Leisure Centre
Police Station
Town Hall
Maxstoke Lane
BIRMINGHAM RD B4114
Council Building
Coleshill Clinic
Coleshill CE Primary School
St Gerards Orthopaedic Hospital
St Edwards RC Primary School
HIGH STREET
B4117
Southfields Farm
COVENTRY ROAD
Blythe Special School
Packington Lane
Wheeley Moor Farm
133
Coleshill School
St Edwards RC Primary School
Coleshill Town FC
Hawkeswell Lane

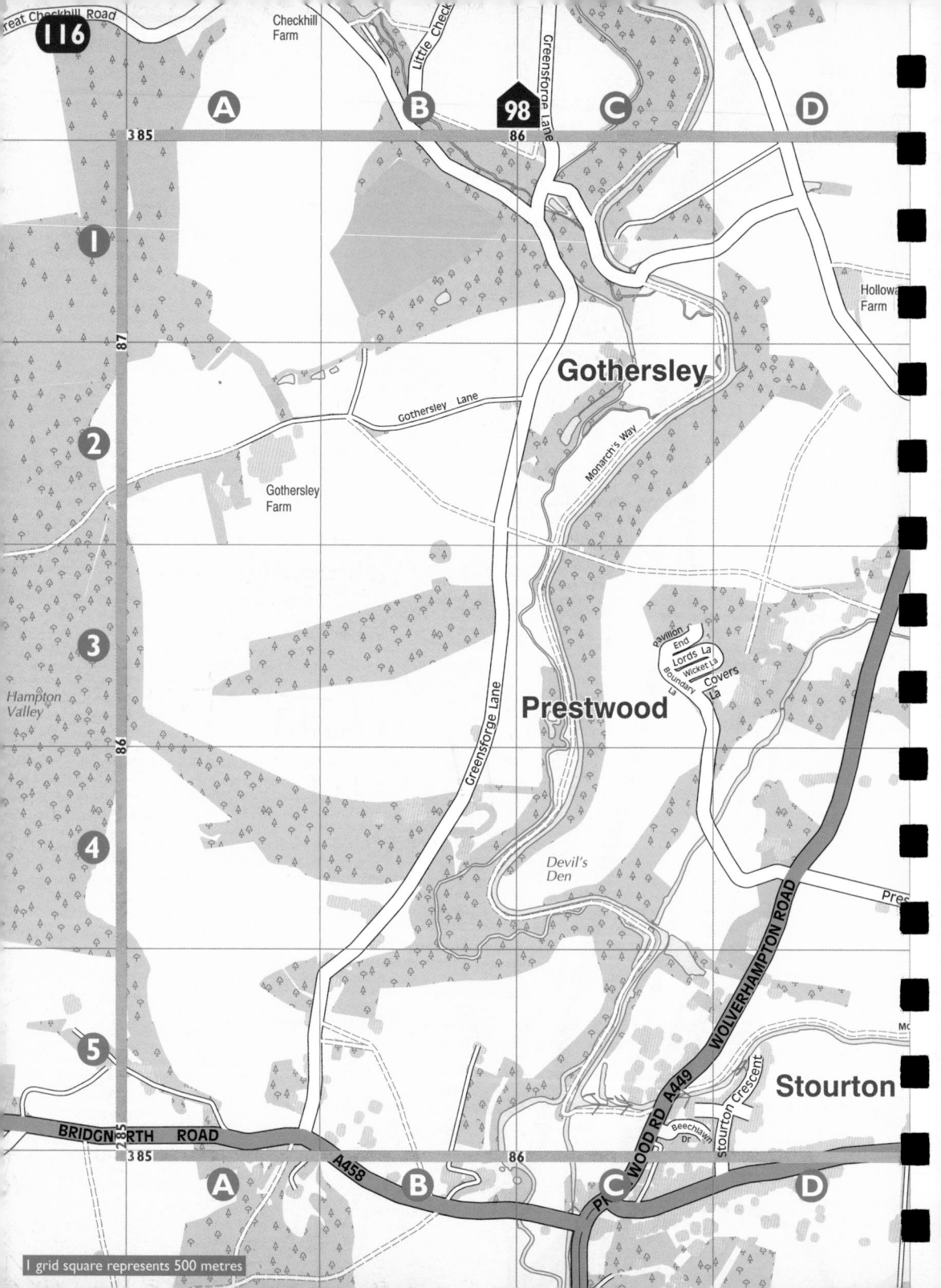

116

A   B   C   D

98
86

385

87

Checkhill Farm
Little Check
Greensforge Lane
Holloway Farm

1

Gothersley

Gothersley Lane
Monarch's Way

2

Gothersley Farm

3

Hampton Valley

Pavilion
End
Lords La
Wicket La
Boundary La
Covers
La

Prestwood

86

4

Devil's Den

WOLVERHAMPTON ROAD
Pre

5

Stourton

BRIDGNORTH ROAD
385
A458
86
PK. WOOD RD A449
Stourton Crescent
Beechlawn Dr
MO

A   B   C   D

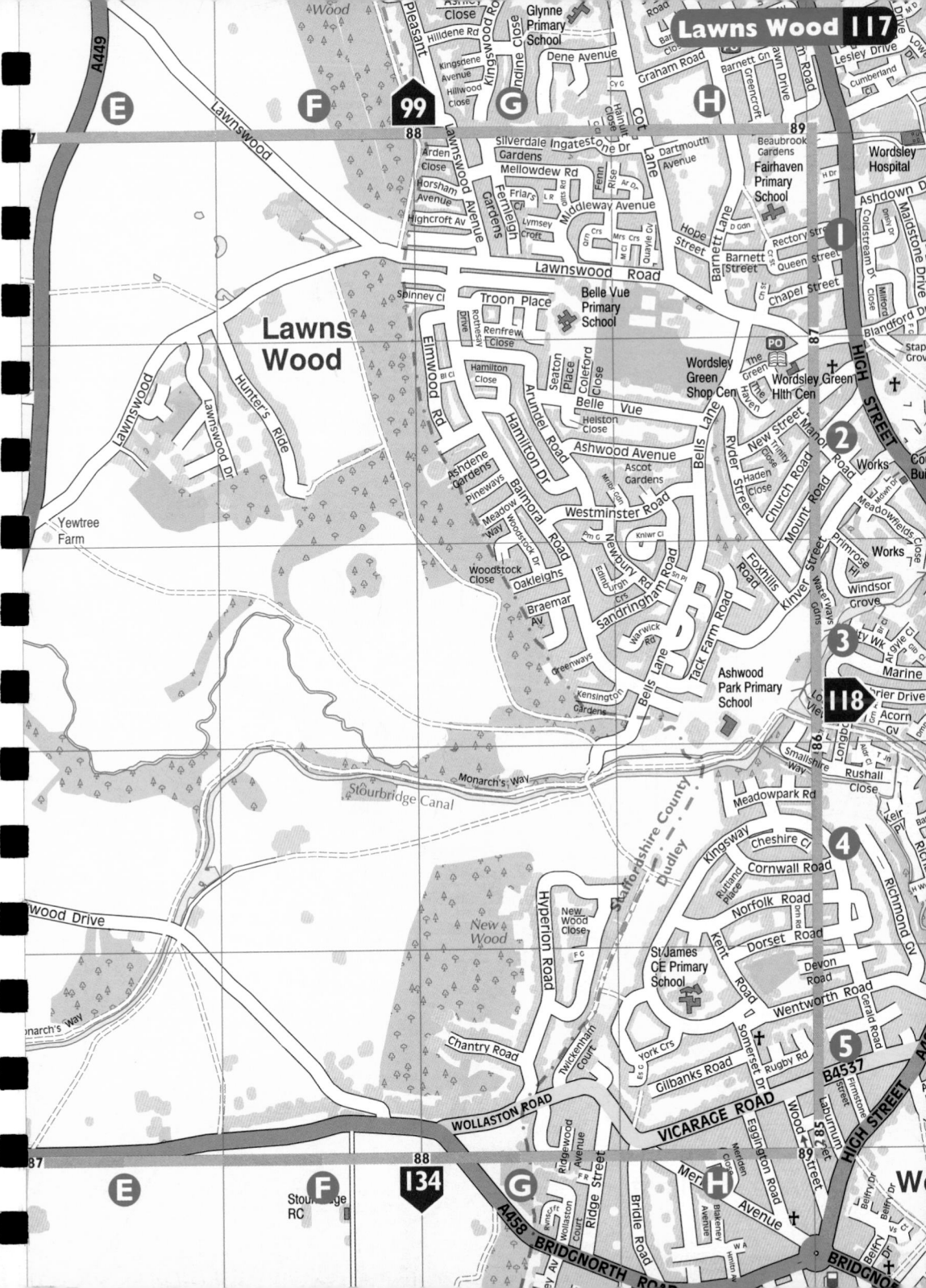
Lawns Wood
Lawnswood
Lawnswood Road
Lawnswood Avenue
Hunter's Ride
Lawnswood Dr
Yewtree Farm
Elmwood Rd
Spinney Cl
Troon Place
Belle Vue Primary School
Renfrew Close
Hamilton Close
Hamilton Dr
Arundel Road
Seaton Place
Coleford Close
Belle Vue
Helston Close
Ashwood Avenue
Ascot Gardens
Westminster Road
Balmoral Road
Ashdene Gardens
Pineways
Meadow Way
Woodstock Dr
Woodstock Close
Oakleighs
Braemar Av
Newbury Rd
Sandringham Road
Greenways
Kensington Gardens
Bells Lane
Tack Farm Road
Warwick Rd
Foxhills Road
Kinver Street
Ryder Street
Haden Close
Church Road
Mount Road
Manor Road
New Street
Trinity Close
Wordsley Green Shop Cen
Wordsley Green Hlth Cen
The Green
The Haven
Wordsley Green
Ashwood Park Primary School
Smallshire Way
Rushall Close
Meadowpark Rd
Monarch's Way
Stourbridge Canal
Staffordshire County Dudley
Kingsway
Cheshire Cl
Cornwall Road
Rutland Place
Norfolk Road
Dorset Road
Kent Road
Devon Road
Wentworth Road
Gerald Road
Richmond Gv
St James CE Primary School
York Crs
Somerset Dr
Rugby Rd
Gilbanks Road
Hyperion Road
New Wood Close
New Wood
Chantry Road
Twickenham Court
Wollaston Road
Vicarage Road
B4537
Eggington Road
Wood Street
Laburnum Street
Firmstone Street
High Street
Ridgewood Avenue
Ridge Street
Bridle Road
Meriden Close
Meriden Avenue
Blakeney Avenue
Wollaston Court
A458 Bridgnorth Road
A449
Stourbridge RC
Pleasant
Hilldene Rd
Kingsdene Avenue
Hillwood Close
Kingswood Road
Glynne Primary School
Dene Avenue
Graham Road
Barnett Gn
Greencroft
Arden Close
Horsham Avenue
Highcroft Av
Silverdale Gardens
Ingatestone Dr
Mellowdew Rd
Fernleigh Gardens
Friars Cl
Lymsey Croft
Middleway Avenue
Cot Lane
Dartmouth Avenue
Hainult Close
Fenn Rise
Beaubrook Gardens
Fairhaven Primary School
Hope Street
Barnett Lane
Barnett Street
Rectory Street
Queen Street
Chapel Street
Wordsley Hospital
Ashdown Dr
Coldstream Dr
Maidstone Drive
Milford Close
Blandford Dr
Lesley Drive
Cumberland Cl
Meadowfields Close
Primrose Hl
Windsor Grove
Waterways Gdns
Works
Argyle Cl
Marine
Acorn Gv
Keir Pl
Wollaston Drive
Wordsley
Ridge Street
Belfry Dr
99
118
134
88
89
87
86
85
E
F
G
H
1
2
3
4
5

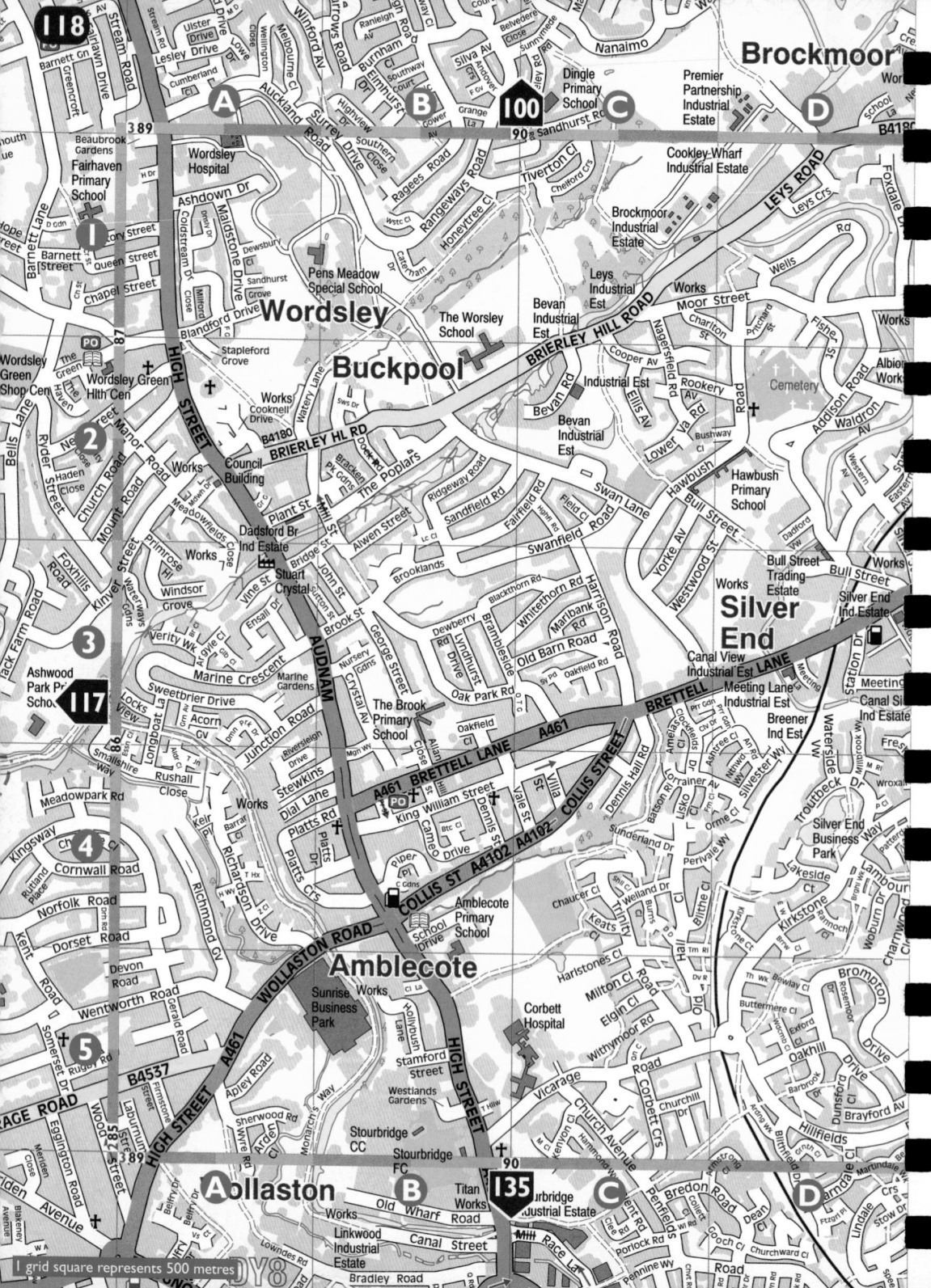
118
100
117
135
Brockmoor
Wordsley
Buckpool
Silver End
Amblecote
Wollaston
A
B
C
D
1
2
3
4
5
389
390
287
286
285
B4180
B4180
A461
A4102
B4537
Stream Road
Fairlawn Drive
Barnett Gn
Greencroft
Ulster Drive
Lesley Drive
Lowe Dr
Wellington Close
Cumberland Cl
Melbourne Cl
Winford Av
Auckland Road
Surrey Drive
Highview Dr
Burnham Cl
Elmhurst Dr
Southway Court
Ranleigh Av
Silva Av
Andover Crs
Belvedere Close
Sunnymede
Gower Av
Grange La
Sandhurst Rd
Nanaimo
Dingle Primary School
Premier Partnership Industrial Estate
Beaubrook Gardens
Fairhaven Primary School
Wordsley Hospital
Southern Close
Ragees Road
Rangeways Road
Tiverton Cl
Chelford Crs
Cookley Wharf Industrial Estate
Leys Road
Leys Crs
Foxdale Dr
Ashdown Dr
Coldstream Dr
Maidstone Drive
Dewsbury Cl
Sandhurst Grove
Milford Close
Pens Meadow Special School
Honeytree Cl
Caterham Dr
Brockmoor Industrial Estate
Leys Industrial Est
Bevan Industrial Est
Wells Rd
Barnett Lane
Barnett Street
Queen Street
Chapel Street
Blandford Drive
Stapleford Grove
The Worsley School
Brierley Hill Road
Moor Street
Charlton St
Pritchard St
Fisher St
Works
Wordsley Green Shop Cen
The Green
Wordsley Green Hlth Cen
The Haven
High Street
Watery Lane
Cooknell Drive
Cooper Av
Nagersfield Rd
Bevan Rd
Industrial Est
Ellis Av
Rookery Av
Road
Cemetery
Addison Road
Albion Works
Waldron Av
Bells Lane
Ryder Street
Haden Close
Church Road
Manor Road
Mount Road
Brierley Hl Rd
Council Building
Bracken Pk Gdns
Dock Rd
The Poplars
Ridgeway Road
Lower Va Rd
Bushway Cl
Bevan Industrial Est
Hawbush
Hawbush Primary School
Western Av
Eastern Av
Meadowfields Close
Plant St
Mill St
Alwen Street
Sandfield Rd
Fairfield Rd
Field Cl
Swan Lane
Bull Street
Dadford Vw
Foxhills Road
Kinver Street
Primrose Hl
Dadsford Br Ind Estate
Bridge St
Stuart Crystal
John St
Brooklands
Swanfield Road
Yorke Av
Westwood St
Bull Street Trading Estate
Works
Bull Street
Windsor Grove
Waterways Gdns
Vine St
Ensall Dr
Sutton St
Brook St
Blackthorn Rd
Whitethorn Rd
Harrison Road
Marlbank Rd
Silver End Ind Estate
Black Farm Road
Verity Wk
Argyle Cl
Marine Crescent
Marine Gardens
Audnam
Nursery Gdns
George Street
Dewberry Rd
Lyndhurst Drive
Brambleside
Old Barn Road
Oakfield Rd
Canal View Industrial Est
Brettell Lane
Meeting Lane Industrial Est
Station Dr
Meeting
Canal Side Ind Estate
Ashwood Park Primary School
Locks View
Sweetbrier Drive
Acorn Gv
Junction Road
Crystal Av
Oak Park Rd
The Brook Primary School
Allan Close
Oakfield Cl
Breener Ind Est
Longboat La
Riversleigh Drive
Stewkins
Dial Lane
Amelas Cl
Clockfields Dr
Ashtree Cl
Silvester Wy
Waterside Vw
Troutbeck Dr
Millbrook Wy
Smallshire Way
Rushall Close
Meadowpark Rd
Works
King William Street
Dennis St
Vale St
Villa St
Collis Street
Dennis Hall Rd
Lorrainer Av
Lisko Cl
Orme Cl
Kingsway
Cornwall Road
Rutland Place
Keir Pl
Barrat Cl
Richardson Drive
Richmond Gv
Platts Rd
Platts Dr
Platts Crs
Cameo Drive
Piper Pl
Collis St
Sunderland Dr
Batson Rl
Perivale Wy
Silver End Business Park
Lakeside Ct
Lambourn
Norfolk Road
Dorset Road
Kent Road
Devon Road
Wollaston Road
Amblecote Primary School
School Drive
Chaucer Cl
Keats Cl
Trinity
Welland Dr
Burns Cl
Blithe Cl
Hall
Kirkstone Ct
Kirkstone
Woburn Dr
Charnwood Cl
Wentworth Road
Gerald Road
Somerset Dr
Rugby Rd
Sunrise Business Park
Hollybush Lane
Harlstones Cl
Milton Cl
Road
Old
Bewlay Cl
Brompton
Buttermere Cl
Rosemoor Dr
Corbett Hospital
Elgin Cl
Withymoor Rd
Exford Cl
Oakhill
Drive
Apley Road
Stamford Street
Westlands Gardens
Vicarage Road
Church Avenue
Corbett Crs
Churchill Dr
Dunsford Cl
Brayford Av
Hillfields
Vicarage Road
Wood Street
Eggington Road
Laburnum Street
Firmstone Street
High Street
Sherwood Rd
Wyre Rd
Arden Cl
Monarch's Way
Stourbridge CC
Stourbridge FC
Kenyon Cl
Hammond Wy
Armstrong Cl
Blithfield Dr
Martindale
Meriden Close
Meriden Avenue
Blakeney Avenue
Belfry Dr
Titan Works
Stourbridge Industrial Estate
Bredon Road
Penfields
Collett
Dean Cl
Lindale Crs
Stow Dr
Old Wharf Road
Works
Linkwood Industrial Estate
Canal Street
Mill Race La
Porlock Rd
Gooch Cl
Churchward Cl
Pennine Wy
Road
Lowndes Rd
Bradley Road
DY8
1 grid square represents 500 metres

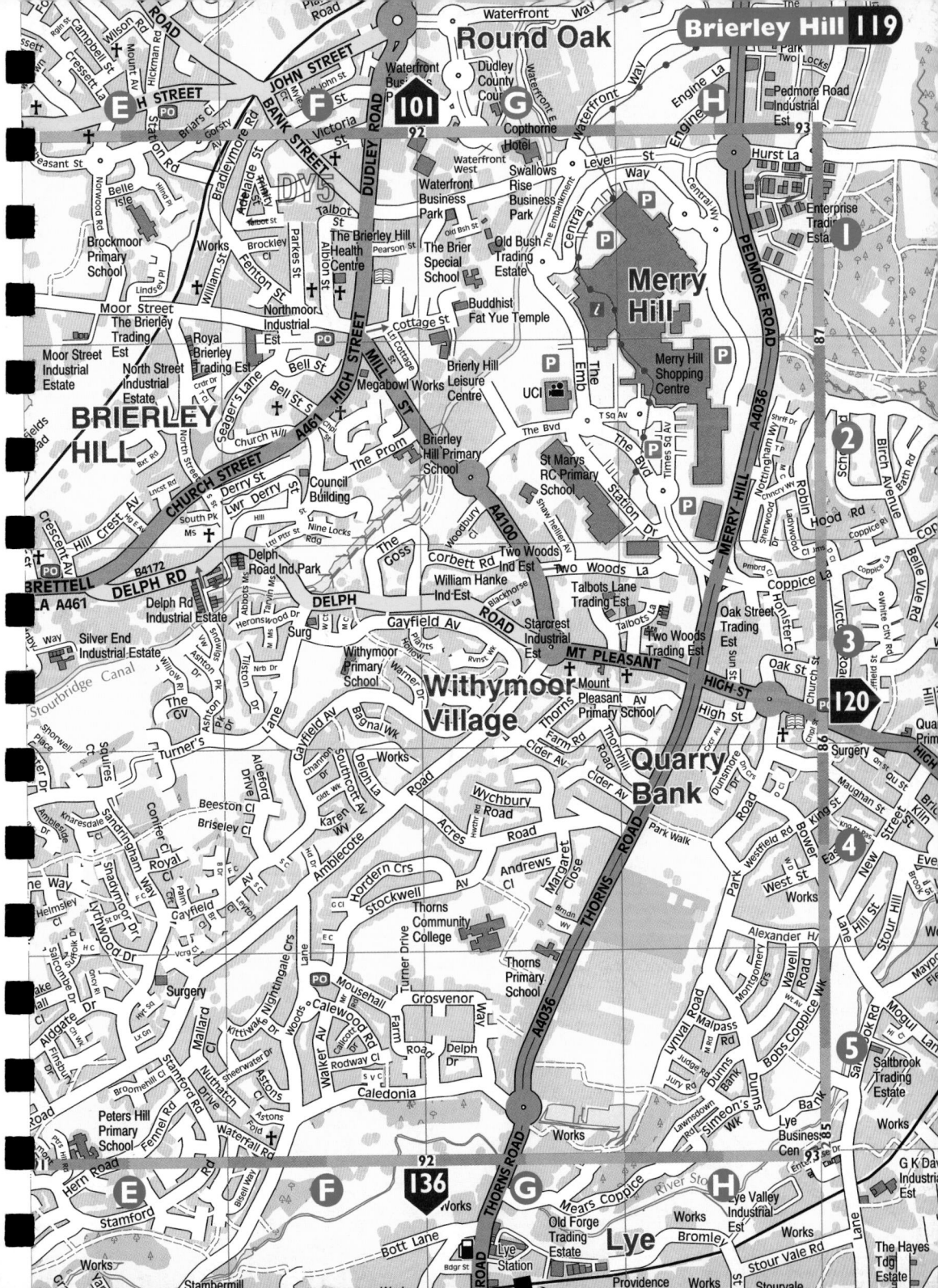

Brierley Hill 119
Round Oak
Waterfront Way
Waterfront Business Park
Dudley County Court
Copthorne Hotel
Waterfront West
Swallows Rise Business Park
Level St
Pedmore Road Industrial Est
Two Locks
Hurst La
Enterprise Trading Estate
Engine La
JOHN STREET
BANK STREET
DUDLEY ROAD
H STREET
Station Rd
Briars Cl
Bradleymore Rd
Adelaide St
Trinity St
Victoria St
DY5
Talbot St
Belle Isle
Norwood Rd
Brockmoor Primary School
Works
Brockley Cl
Fenton St
Parkes St
Albion St
William St
The Brierley Hill Health Centre
Pearson St
The Brier Special School
Old Bush Trading Estate
Old Bsh St
Buddhist Fat Yue Temple
Merry Hill
Merry Hill Shopping Centre
Central Way
The Embankment
PEDMORE ROAD
A4036
Moor Street
The Brierley Trading Est
Moor Street Industrial Estate
Northmoor Industrial Est
Royal Brierley Trading Est
North Street Industrial Estate
Cottage St
Lt Cottage St
Bell St
HIGH STREET
MILL ST
Megabowl Works
Brierly Hill Leisure Centre
UCI
The Emb
The Bvd
T Sq Av
Times Sq Av
BRIERLEY HILL
Seager's Lane
Church Hill
A461
CHURCH STREET
North Street
The Prom
Brierley Hill Primary School
St Marys RC Primary School
Station Dr
MERRY HILL
Nottingham Wy
Robin Hood Rd
Birch Avenue
Bath Rd
Coppice Rl
Belle Vue Rd
Crescent Av
Hill Crest Av
South Pk
Derry St
Lwr Derry St
Council Building
Nine Locks Rdg
The Goss
Woodbury Cl
A4100
Shaw Hellier Av
Corbett Rd
Two Woods Ind Est
Two Woods La
William Hanke Ind Est
Talbots Lane Trading Est
Coppice La
Honister Cl
Oak Street Trading Est
Victoria Road
White City Rd
BRETTELL LA A461
B4172
DELPH RD
Delph Road Ind Park
Delph Rd Industrial Estate
DELPH ROAD
Blackhorse La
Starcrest Industrial Est
Two Woods Trading Est
Talbots La
Silver End Industrial Estate
Heronswood Dr
Gayfield Av
Surg
Withymoor Primary School
Plants Hollow
Warner Dr
MT PLEASANT
HIGH ST
Oak St
Church St
120
Stourbridge Canal
Withymoor Village
Mount Pleasant Primary School
Thorns Farm Rd
Cider Av
Thornhill Road
High St
Surgery
Quarry Bank
Dunsmore Dr
Ashton Dr
Tilston Dr
The Gv
Turner's Lane
Shorwell Place
Squires Ct
Alderford Drive
Channon Dr
Southcott Av
Delph La
Bagnal Wk
Works
Wychbury Road
Acres Road
Maughan St
King St
New Street
Beeston Cl
Briseley Cl
Karen Wy
Conifer Cl
Sandringham Way
Amblecote Road
Hordern Crs
Stockwell Av
Andrews Cl
Margaret Close
THORNS ROAD
Park Walk
Westfield Rd
Bower Lane
West St
Royal Cl
Gayfield
Shadymoor Dr
Lythwood Dr
Helmsley Cl
Thorns Community College
Alexander H
Hill St
Stour Hill
Thorns Primary School
Montgomery Crs
Wavell Road
Bobs Coppice Wk
Salcombe Dr
Surgery
Nightingale Crs
Lane
Turner Drive
Mousehall Farm Road
Grosvenor Way
Calewood Rd
Delph Dr
Lynval Road
Malpass Rd
Aldgate Dr
Mallard Cl
Kittiwake Dr
Walker Av
Rodway Cl
Caledonia
Judge Rd
Dunns Bank
Saltbrook Trading Estate
Stamford Rd
Nuthatch Drive
Sheerwater Dr
Astons Fold
Broomehill Cl
Fennel Rd
Peters Hill Primary School
Waterfall Rd
Simeon's Wk
Lye Business Cen
Works
Hern Road
92
93
136
Works
THORNS ROAD
Mears Coppice
River Stour
Lye Valley Industrial Est
G K Davies Industrial Est
Stamford
Bisell Way
Old Forge Trading Estate
Lye
Bromley
Bott Lane
Lye Station
Stour Vale Rd
The Hayes Tdg Estate
Works
Stambermill
Providence
Stourvale

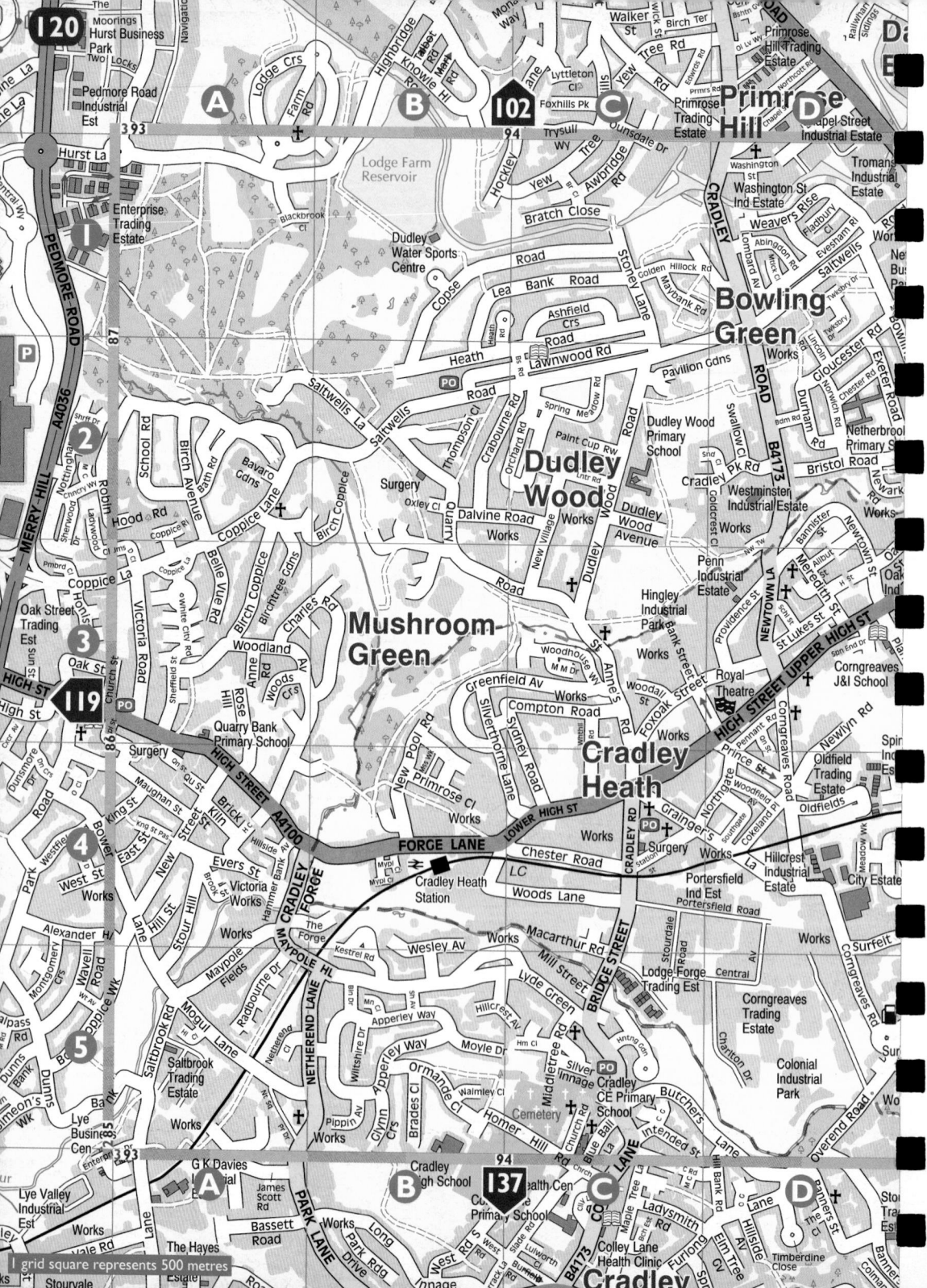
120
102
119
137
A
B
C
D
1
2
3
4
5
393
94
87
86
85
Hurst Business Park
Pedmore Road Industrial Est
Enterprise Trading Estate
PEDMORE ROAD
A4036
MERRY HILL
Primrose Hill
Primrose Trading Estate
Primrose Hill Trading Estate
Chapel Street Industrial Estate
Tromans Industrial Estate
Washington St Ind Estate
Lodge Farm Reservoir
Dudley Water Sports Centre
Bowling Green
Dudley Wood
Dudley Wood Primary School
Westminster Industrial Estate
Penn Industrial Estate
Hingley Industrial Park
Mushroom Green
Cradley Heath
Royal Theatre
Corngreaves J&I School
Oldfield Trading Estate
Hillcrest Industrial Estate
City Estate
Portersfield Ind Est
Lodge Forge Trading Est
Corngreaves Trading Estate
Colonial Industrial Park
Cradley Heath Station
Quarry Bank Primary School
Oak Street Trading Est
Victoria Works
Saltbrook Trading Estate
Lye Business Cen
Lye Valley Industrial Est
Cradley CE Primary School
Cemetery
Cradley High School
Colley Lane Health Clinic
Cradley
HIGH STREET
A4100
FORGE LANE
LOWER HIGH ST
HIGH STREET UPPER HIGH ST
CRADLEY FORGE
MAYPOLE HL
NETHEREND LANE
PARK LANE
BRIDGE STREET
CRADLEY RD
NEWTOWN LA
B4173
CRADLEY ROAD
Saltwells Road
Lawnwood Rd
Lea Bank Road
Stoney Lane
Dudley Wood Road
Chester Road
Woods Lane
Macarthur Rd
Mill Street
Overend Road
Corngreaves Road
Coppice Lane
Victoria Road
Bratch Close
1 grid square represents 500 metres

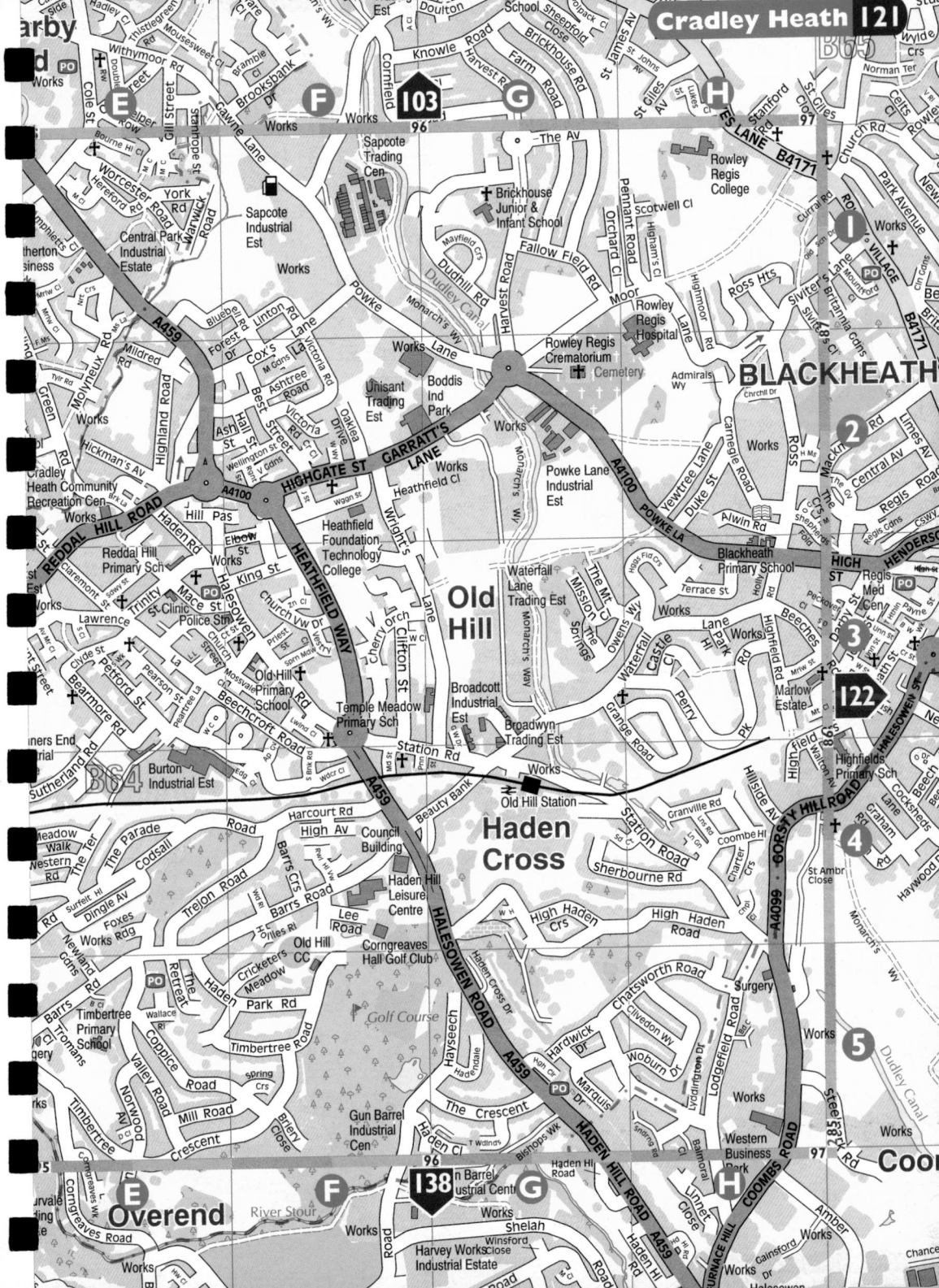
103
138
122
96
97
E
F
G
H
1
2
3
4
5
BLACKHEATH
Old Hill
Haden Cross
Overend
Sapcote Trading Cen
Sapcote Industrial Est
Central Park Industrial Estate
Brickhouse Junior & Infant School
Rowley Regis College
Rowley Regis Hospital
Rowley Regis Crematorium
Cemetery
Unisant Trading Est
Boddis Ind Park
Powke Lane Industrial Est
Heathfield Foundation Technology College
Waterfall Lane Trading Est
Cradley Heath Community Recreation Cen
Reddal Hill Primary Sch
Old Hill Primary School
Temple Meadow Primary Sch
Broadcott Industrial Est
Broadwyn Trading Est
Blackheath Primary School
Regis Med Cen
Marlow Estate
Highfields Primary Sch
Burton Industrial Est
Old Hill Station
Council Building
Haden Hill Leisure Centre
Corngreaves Hall Golf Club
Golf Course
Old Hill CC
Timbertree Primary School
Gun Barrel Industrial Cen
Harvey Works Industrial Estate
Western Business Park
Surgery
Police Stn
Clinic
Works
A459
A4100
A4099
B4171
B64
B65
REDDAL HILL ROAD
HIGHCATE ST
GARRATT'S LANE
HEATHFIELD WAY
POWKE LA
HALESOWEN ROAD
HADEN HILL ROAD
CORSTY HILL ROAD
COOMBS ROAD
HIGH ST
Station Rd
Station Road
Dudley Canal
Monarch's Way
River Stour
Sheepfold Close
Brickhouse Rd
Farm Road
Knowle Road
Harvest Rd
Cornfield
Doulton
Withymoor Rd
Mousesweet Cl
Brookspank Dr
Cawne Lane
Gill Street
Stanhope St
Worcester Road
Hereford Rd
York Rd
Warwick Road
The Av
Pennant Road
Orchard Cl
Scotwell Cl
Higham's Cl
Fallow Field Rd
Mayfield Crs
Dudhill Rd
Harvest Road
Moor Lane
Highmoor Rd
Ross Hts
Siviter's Lane
Park Avenue
Church Rd
Stanford Rd
St Giles Av
St James Av
Powke Lane
Linton Rd
Bluebell Rd
Forest Dr
Cox's Lane
Victoria Rd
Ashtree Road
Best Street
Oaklea Drive
Mildred Rd
Molyneux Rd
Highland Road
Hickman's Av
Hill Pas
Haden Rd
Elbow St
King St
Mace St
Trinity St
Church Street
Lawrence St
Claremont St
Clyde St
Petford St
Bearmore Rd
Pearson St
Beechcroft Road
Sutherland Rd
Heathfield Cl
Wright's Lane
Clifton St
Cherry Orch
Church Vw Dr
Priest St
Admirals Wy
Carnegie Road
Yewtree Lane
Duke St
Alwin Rd
Ross
Central Av
Regis Road
Limes Av
Terrace St
The Mt
Mission Cl
The Springs
Owens Wy
Waterfall Castle Cl
Lane Park Rd
Perry Pk
Grange Road
Highfield Rd
Beeches Rd
Darby St
Payne St
Halesowen St
Beauty Bank
Harcourt Rd
High Av
Barrs Crs
Barrs Road
Trejon Road
Codsall Road
The Parade
Meadow Walk
The Ter
Western Rd
Dingle Av
Foxes Rdg
Lee Road
Cricketers Meadow
Haden Park Rd
The Retreat
Timbertree Road
Coppice Road
Valley Road
Norwood Av
Mill Road
Crescent
Briery Close
Spring Crs
Tromans
Newland Gdns
Corngreaves Road
Timbertree
Granville Rd
Coombe Hl
Sherbourne Rd
Charter Crs
High Haden Crs
High Haden Road
Chatsworth Road
Clivedon Wy
Woburn Dr
Hardwick Dr
Marquis Dr
Lodgefield Road
Lyddington Dr
Haden Cross Dr
Hayseech
The Crescent
Haden Cl
Bishops Wk
Linnet Close
Balmoral
Furnace Hill
Amber
Steelpark Rd
St Ambr Close
Haywood Dr
Cocksheds Lane
Graham Rd
Beech
Hillside Av
Walton Av
Shelah
Winsford Close
Haden Hl
Gainsford
Chance
Henderson
Wylde Crs
Norman Ter
Celts
Rowley
Britannia Gdns
Mountford
Village

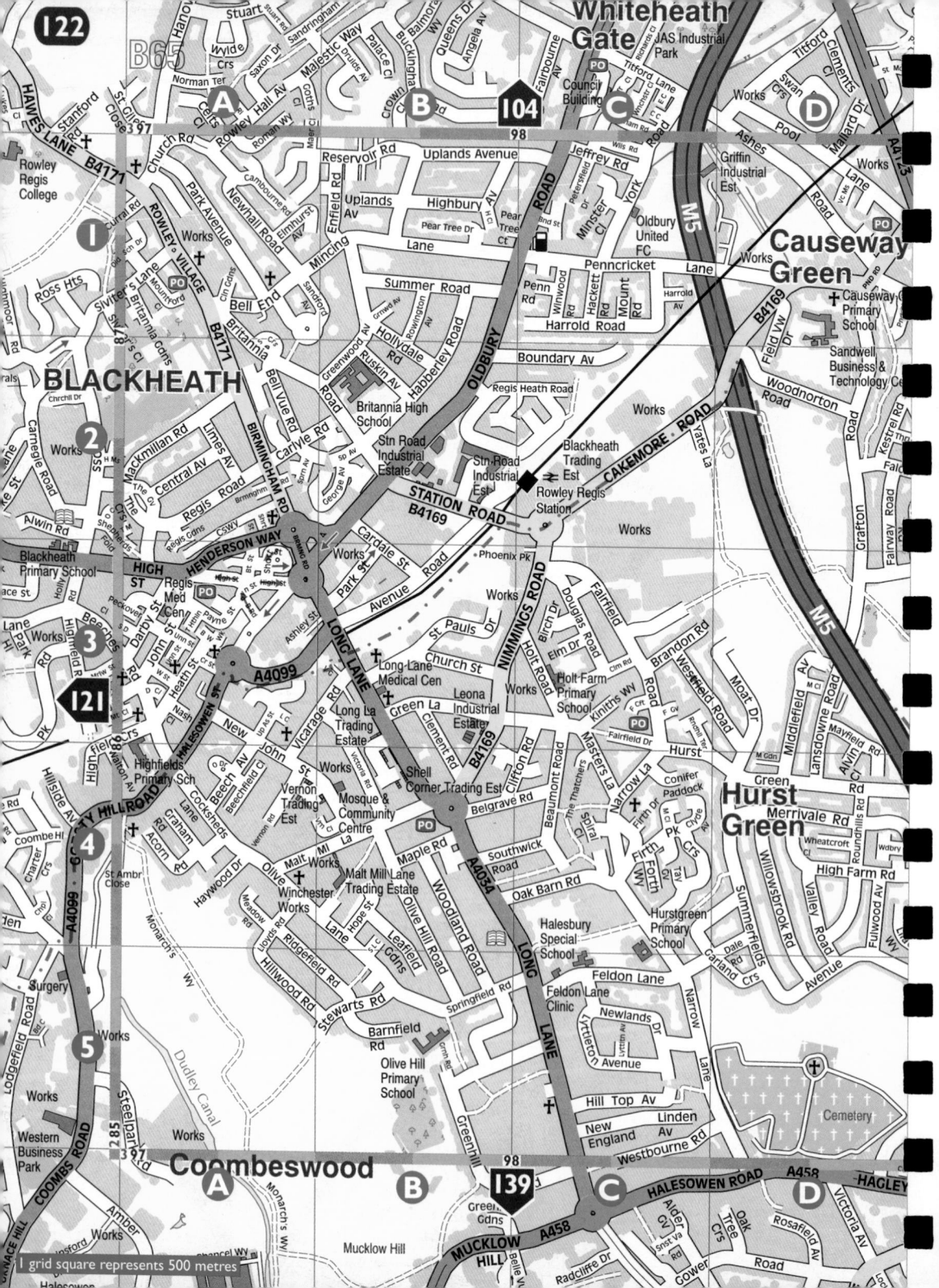

122
B65
Whiteheath Gate
JAS Industrial Park
104
121
139
BLACKHEATH
Causeway Green
Hurst Green
Coombeswood
Rowley Regis College
Rowley Regis Station
Blackheath Trading Est
Britannia High School
Stn Road Industrial Estate
Blackheath Primary School
Highfields Primary Sch
Long Lane Medical Cen
Leona Industrial Estate
Long La Trading Estate
Shell Corner Trading Est
Vernon Trading Est
Mosque & Community Centre
Malt Mill Lane Trading Estate
Holt Farm Primary School
Hurstgreen Primary School
Halesbury Special School
Feldon Lane Clinic
Olive Hill Primary School
Oldbury United FC
Griffin Industrial Est
Causeway Green Primary School
Sandwell Business & Technology Ce
Western Business Park
Cemetery
Dudley Canal
Mucklow Hill
HAWES LANE
ROWLEY VILLAGE
B4171
OLDBURY ROAD
STATION ROAD
B4169
CAKEMORE ROAD
NIMMINGS ROAD
LONG LANE
A4034
A4099
HALESOWEN ST
HIGH ST
HENDERSON WAY
BIRMINGHAM RD
HALESOWEN ROAD
A458
MUCKLOW HILL
COOMBS ROAD
M5
A4123
Penncricket Lane
Harrold Road
Boundary Av
Summer Road
Uplands Avenue
Reservoir Rd
Highbury Av
Woodnorton Road
Brandon Rd
Westfield Road
Moat Dr
Merrivale Rd
High Farm Rd
Feldon Lane
Westbourne Rd
Hill Top Av
New England
Linden Av
Newlands Dr
Lyttleton Avenue
Narrow Lane
Southwick Road
Oak Barn Rd
Belgrave Rd
Maple Rd
Woodland Road
Olive Hill Road
Hillwood Rd
Ridgefield Rd
Stewarts Rd
Springfield Rd
Barnfield Rd
Greenhill
Steelpark Rd
Lodgefield Road
Carnegie Road
Mackmillan Rd
Central Av
Regis Road
Park Avenue
Newhall Road
Mincing Lane
Bell End
Britannia Rd
Habberley Road
Hollydale Rd
Carlyle Rd
Cardale St
Park St
Avenue Road
St Pauls Dr
Church St
Green La
Clement Rd
Vicarage Rd
John St
New John St
Beech Av
Cocksheds Lane
Graham Rd
Acorn Rd
Haywood Dr
Olive Lane
Coombe Hl
Hillside Av
Douglas Road
Holt Road
Fairfield Dr
Clifton Rd
Beaumont Road
Masters La
Hurst Green Rd
Summerfields Avenue
Willowsbrook Rd
Valley Road
Carland Crs
Middlefield Av
Lansdowne Road
Mayfield Rd
Grafton Road
Fairway Road
Titford Lane
Jeffrey Rd
York Road
Minster Cl
Pool Road
Ashes Road
Victoria Av
Rosafield Av
Radcliffe Dr
Gower Road
1 grid square represents 500 metres

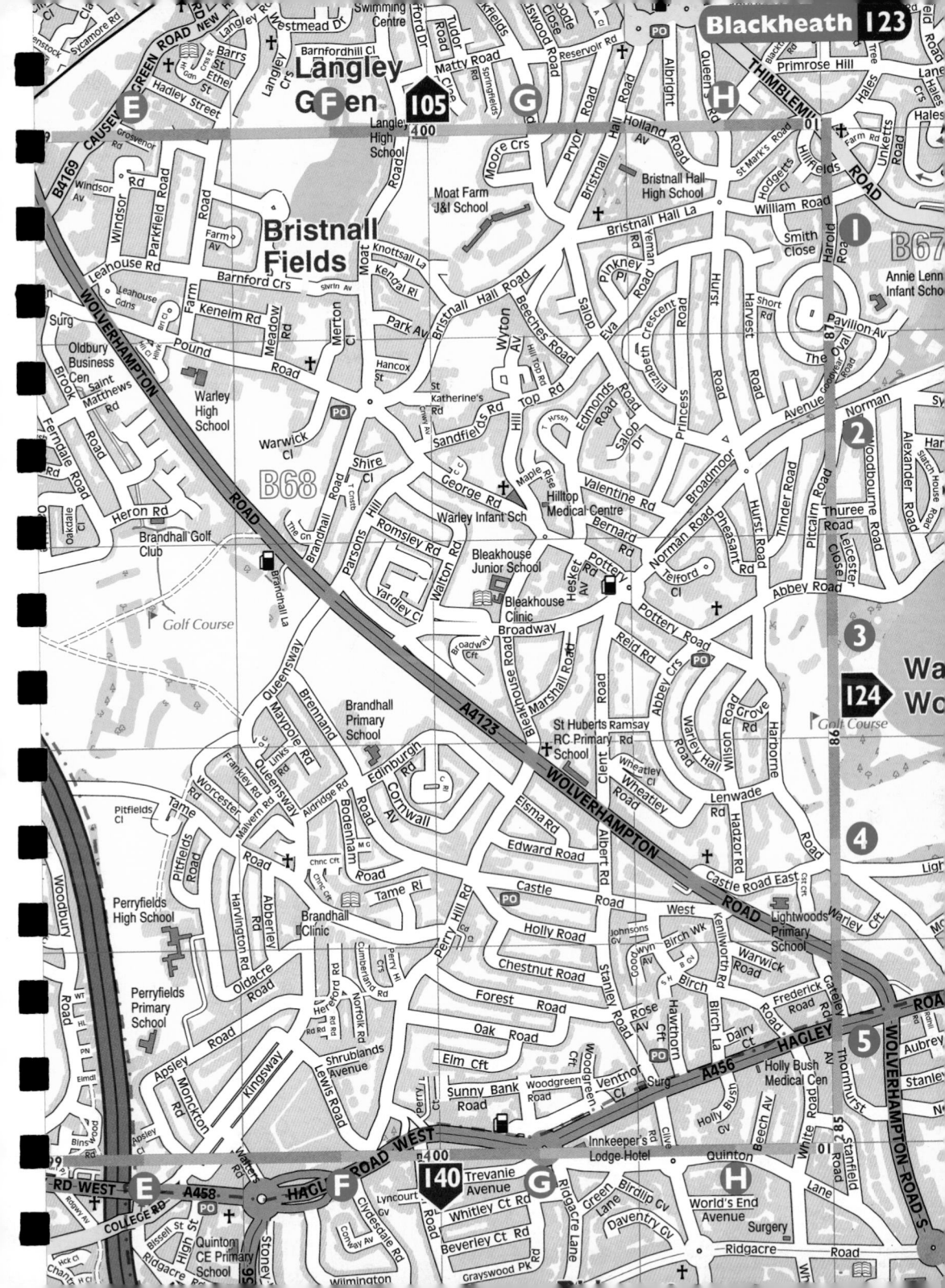
Langley Green
Bristnall Fields
105
124
140
B68
B67
Langley High School
Moat Farm J&I School
Bristnall Hall High School
Warley High School
Oldbury Business Cen
Brandhall Golf Club
Golf Course
Warley Infant Sch
Bleakhouse Junior School
Bleakhouse Clinic
Hilltop Medical Centre
Brandhall Primary School
St Huberts RC Primary School
Perryfields High School
Perryfields Primary School
Brandhall Clinic
Lightwoods Primary School
Holly Bush Medical Cen
Innkeeper's Lodge Hotel
Quinton CE Primary School
Annie Lennard Infant School
World's End Avenue
Surgery
WOLVERHAMPTON ROAD
A4123
HAGLEY ROAD WEST
A456
A458
B4169
THIMBLEMILL ROAD
COLLEGE RD
Broadway
Castle Road
Castle Road East
Queensway
Pottery Road
Abbey Road
Norman Avenue
Bristnall Hall Road
Bristnall Hall La
Hill Top Rd
George Rd
Edward Road
Holly Road
Chestnut Road
Forest Road
Oak Road
Elm Cft
Sunny Bank Road
Ridgacre Road
Ridgacre Lane
Quinton
E
F
G
H
1
2
3
4
5

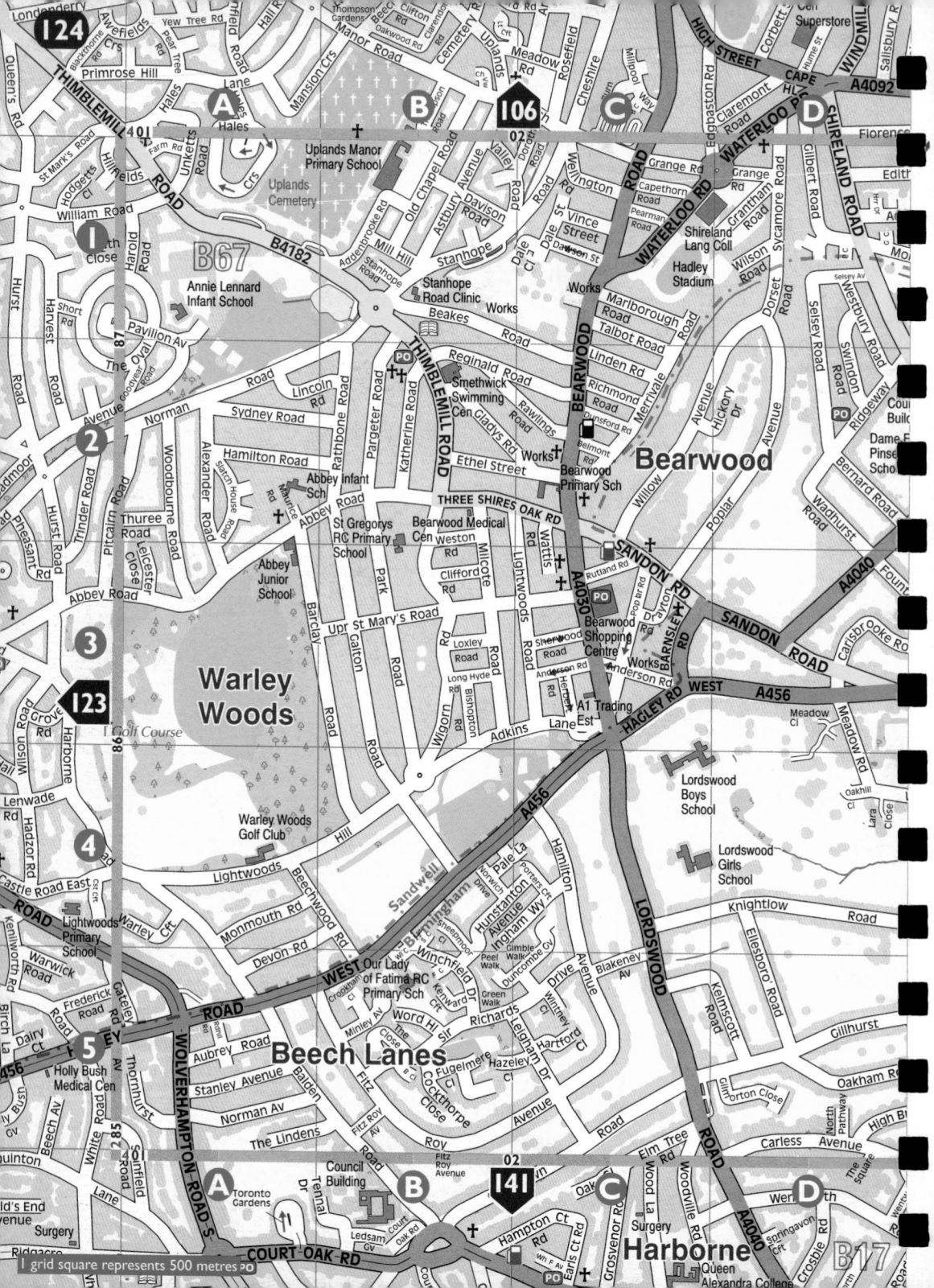
124
106
123
141
A
B
C
D
1
2
3
4
5
401
02
87
285
B67
B17
Londonderry
Awefields Crs
Yew Tree Rd
Blackthorne Rd
Pear Tree Rd
Primrose Hill
Queen's Rd
THIMBLEMILL ROAD
Hales Lane
Hales Crs
St Mark's Road
Hillfields
Hodgetts Cl
Unketts Road
Farm Rd
William Road
Manor Road
Mansion Crs
Thompson Gardens
Clifton Rd
Oakwood Rd
Cemetery Road
Uplands
Meadow Rd
Rosefield
Cheshire
Uplands Manor Primary School
Uplands Cemetery
Old Chapel Road
Astbury Avenue
Valley Road
Davison Road
Addenbrooke Rd
Mill Hill
Stanhope Road
Stanhope
Wellington Road
Dale Cl
Dale St
Vince Street
Dawson St
B4182
Annie Lennard Infant School
Stanhope Road Clinic
Works
Beakes Road
Short Rd
Harvest Road
Hurst Road
Harold Road
Pavilion Av
The Oval
Goodyear Road
Norman Avenue
Sydney Road
Lincoln Rd
Rathbone Road
Pargeter Road
Katherine Road
THIMBLEMILL ROAD
PO
Reginald Road
Smethwick Swimming Cen
Gladys Rd
Rawlings Road
Hamilton Road
Woodbourne Road
Alexander Road
Slatch House Road
Trinder Road
Pitcairn Road
Pheasant Rd
Hurst Road
Thuree Road
Leicester Close
Maurice Rd
Abbey Infant Sch
Abbey Road
Ethel Street
Abbey Road
Abbey Junior School
St Gregorys RC Primary School
Bearwood Medical Cen
Weston Rd
Clifford Rd
Milcote
Park
Lightwoods Road
Wattis Rd
Barclay Road
Galton Road
Upr St Mary's Road
Loxley Road
Long Hyde Rd
Bishopton
Wigorn Rd
Adkins Lane
Warley Woods
Golf Course
Warley Woods Golf Club
Hill
Wilson Road
Grove Rd
Harborne
Lenwade Rd
Hadzor Rd
Castle Road East
Lightwoods
Beechwood Rd
Monmouth Rd
Devon Rd
Lightwoods Primary School
Warley Cft
Kenilworth Rd
Warwick Road
Frederick Road
Dairy Ct
Birch La
HAGLEY ROAD
A456
Holly Bush Medical Cen
Gateley Rd
Thornhurst Av
WOLVERHAMPTON ROAD S
Aubrey Road
Stanley Avenue
Balden
Norman Av
The Lindens
Beech Av
White Road
Quinton
Stanfield Road
Lane
Surgery
Ridgacre
Toronto Gardens
Council Building
Tennal Dr
Ledsam Gv
Court Oak Rd
COURT OAK RD
Hampton Ct
Earls Ct Rd
Grosvenor Rd
Harborne
Queen Alexandra College
Beech Lanes
Sandwell
Birmingham
WEST
ROAD
Our Lady of Fatima RC Primary Sch
Crookham Cl
Minley Av
Word Hl
The Close
Kenward Cft
Winchfield Dr
Sheepmoor
Peel Walk
Green Walk
Gimble Walk
Duncombe Gv
Ingham Wy
Hunstanton Avenue
Norwich Drive
Pale La
Porters Cft
Hamilton Avenue
Sir Richards Drive
Leigham Dr
Wintney Cl
Hartford Cl
Hazeley Cl
Fugelmere Cl
Cockthorpe Close
Fitz Roy Av
Fitz Roy Avenue
Roy
Avenue
Road
Blakeney Av
Elm Tree Rd
Wood La
Woodville Rd
A4040
Springavon Cft
Crosbie Rd
Wentworth
High Street
Corbetts
Superstore
Hume St
WINDMILL
Salisbury R
CAPE HL
A4092
Edgbaston Rd
Claremont Road
WATERLOO RD
SHIRELAND ROAD
Florence
Edith
Grange Rd
Capethorn Road
Pearman Road
Shireland Lang Coll
Hadley Stadium
Wilson Road
Grantham Road
Sycamore Road
Gilbert Road
Dorset Road
Selsey Av
Selsey Road
Westbury Road
Swindon Road
Ridgeway
Marlborough Road
Talbot Road
Linden Rd
Richmond Road
Dunsford Rd
Merrivale
Belmont Rd
BEARWOOD ROAD
Bearwood
Bearwood Primary Sch
THREE SHIRES OAK RD
Willow Avenue
Hickory Dr
Poplar Avenue
Dame E Pinsent Schoo
Bernard Road
Wadhurst Road
A4040
SANDON RD
SANDON ROAD
Rutland Rd
Pop Br Rd
Dayton Dr
BARNSLEY RD
A4030
Bearwood Shopping Centre
Sherwood Road
Anderson Rd
Herbert Rd
A1 Trading Est
HAGLEY RD WEST
A456
Carisbrooke Ro
Meadow Cl
Meadow Rd
Oakhill Cl
Lara Close
Lordswood Boys School
Lordswood Girls School
Knightlow Road
Ellesboro' Road
LORDSWOOD ROAD
Kelmscott Road
Gillhurst
Oakham Rd
Glim Orton Close
North Pathway
Carless Avenue
High Br
The Square
1 grid square represents 500 metres

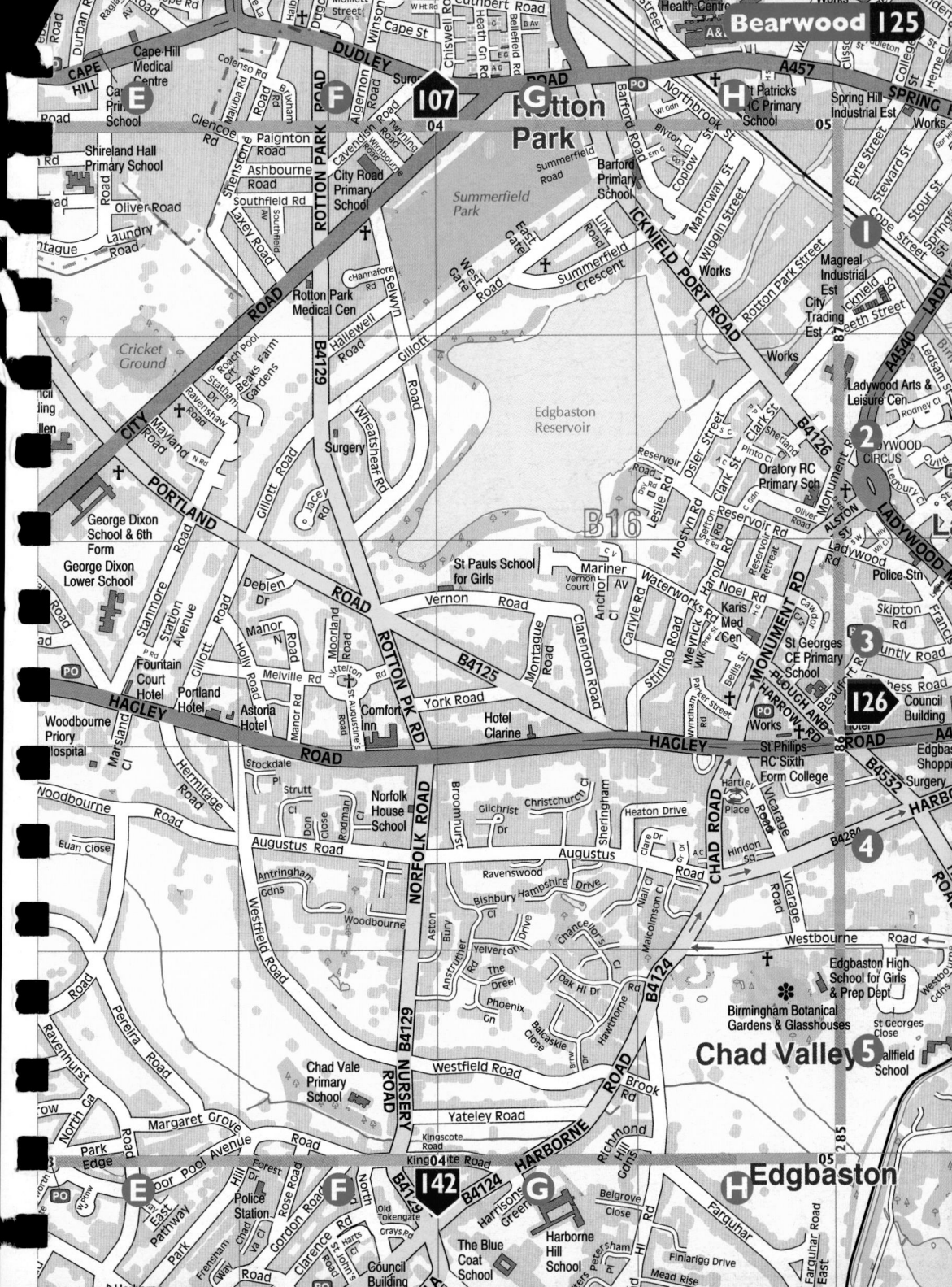
Rotton Park
Summerfield Park
Edgbaston Reservoir
Cricket Ground
Chad Valley
Edgbaston
Birmingham Botanical Gardens & Glasshouses
HAGLEY ROAD
CITY ROAD
PORTLAND ROAD
DUDLEY ROAD
ROTTON PARK ROAD
ICKNIELD PORT ROAD
MONUMENT RD
HARBORNE ROAD
NORFOLK ROAD
Augustus Road
Westfield Road
Westbourne Road
Vernon Road
107
126
142
B16

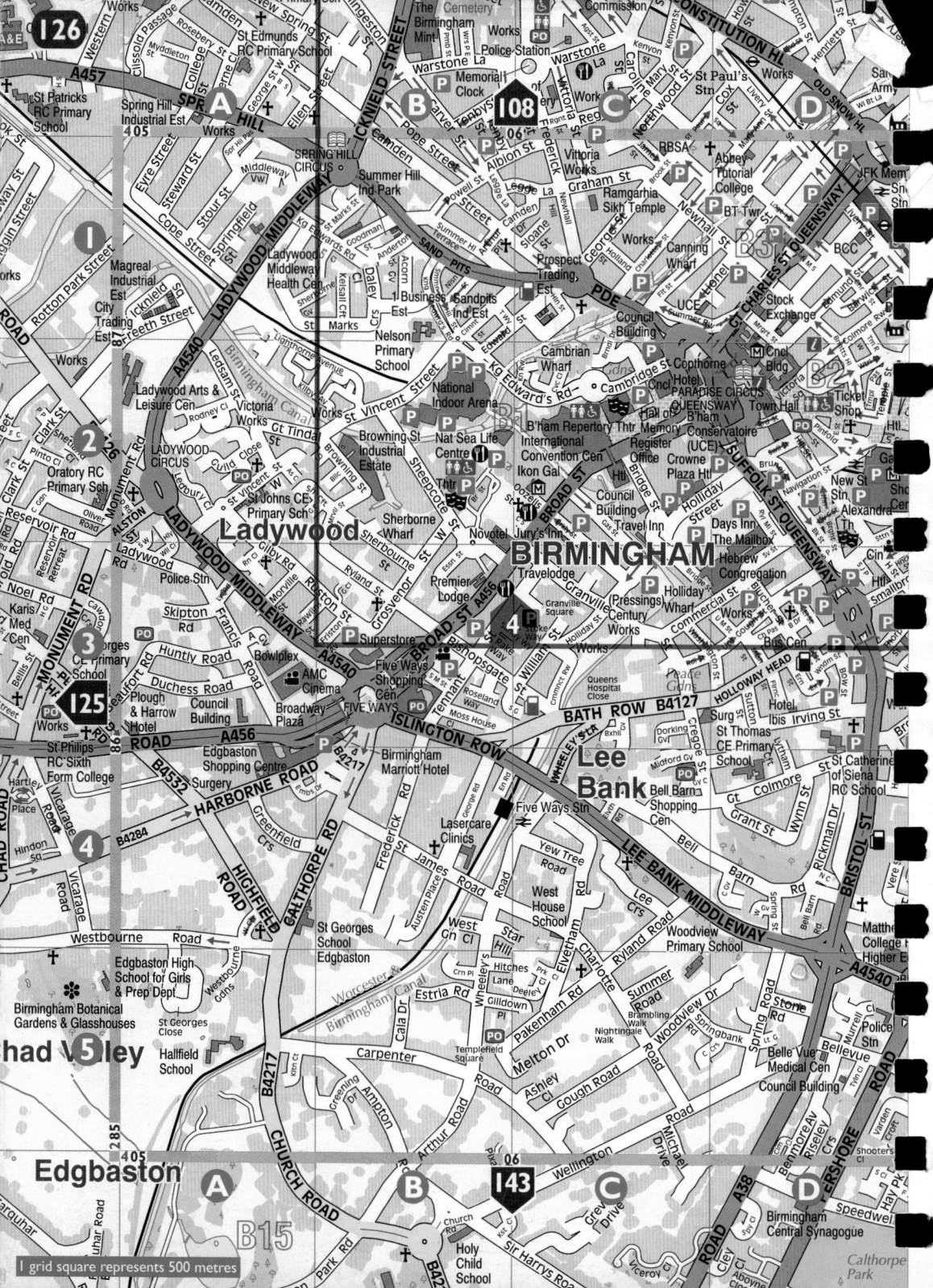

126
108
125
143
A
B
C
D
1
2
3
4
5
405
06
285
Spring Hill
Spring Hill Industrial Est
St Patricks RC Primary School
St Edmunds RC Primary School
The Birmingham Mint
Cemetery
Works Police Station
Warstone La
Memorial Clock
Constitution Hl
Old Snow Hl
St Paul's Stn
Icknield Street
Spring Hill Circus
Summer Hill Ind Park
Ladywood Middleway
Ladywood Middleway Health Cen
Sand Pits
Sandpits Ind Est
Prospect Trading Est
Ramgarhia Sikh Temple
Canning Wharf
Vittoria Works
RBSA
Abbey Tutorial College
BT Twr
JFK Meml
Snow Hill Stn
Gt Charles St Queensway
Stock Exchange
BCC
B3
Magreal Industrial Est
City Trading Est
Rotton Park Street
Icknield Sq
Freeth Street
Cope Street
Stour St
Steward St
Eyre Street
Springfield St
Nelson Primary School
Lighthorne Avenue
Kg Edward's Rd
Cambrian Wharf
Cambridge St
Copthorne Hotel
Paradise Circus Queensway
Cncl Bldg
Town Hall
Ticket Shop
B2
National Indoor Arena
Council Building
UCE
Ladywood Arts & Leisure Cen
Victoria Works
Birmingham Canal
Ladywood Circus
Oratory RC Primary Sch
St Johns CE Primary Sch
Browning St Industrial Estate
Nat Sea Life Centre
B1
B'ham Repertory Thtr
Hall of Memory
International Convention Cen
Register Office
B'ham Conservatoire (UCE)
Crowne Plaza Htl
Ikon Gal
Council Building
Travel Inn
Holliday Street
Days Inn
The Mailbox
Hebrew Congregation
Suffolk St Queensway
Navigation St
New St Stn
Alexandra
Ladywood
Sherborne Wharf
Novotel
Jury's Inn
BIRMINGHAM
Broad St
Travelodge
Premier Lodge
Granville Square
Pressings Century Works
Holliday Wharf
Commercial St
Bus Cen
Monument Rd
Reservoir Rd
Noel Rd
Karis Med Cen
St Georges CE Primary School
Police Stn
Skipton Rd
Huntly Road
Duchess Road
Bowlplex
AMC Cinema
Superstore
Broad St A456
Five Ways Shopping Cen
Bishopsgate St
Queens Hospital Close
Peace Gdns
Holloway Head
Bath Row B4127
Hotel Ibis
Irving St
Plough & Harrow Hotel
Council Building
Broadway Plaza
Five Ways
Islington Row
A4540
A456
St Philips RC Sixth Form College
Edgbaston Shopping Centre
Surgery
Harborne Road
B4532
B4217
Birmingham Marriott Hotel
Lee Bank
Bell Barn Shopping Cen
St Thomas CE Primary School
St Catherine of Siena RC School
Gt Colmore St
Five Ways Stn
Lasercare Clinics
Yew Tree Road
Hartley Place
Vicarage Road
Hindon Sq
B4284
Greenfield Crs
Highfield Road
Calthorpe Rd
Frederick Rd
St James Road
West House School
Lee Bank Middleway
Bristol St
Bell Barn Rd
Rickman Dr
Woodview Primary School
Westbourne Road
St Georges School Edgbaston
Edgbaston High School for Girls & Prep Dept
Birmingham Botanical Gardens & Glasshouses
St Georges Close
Hallfield School
Chad Valley
Worcester & Birmingham Canal
Estria Rd
Gilldown Pl
Templefield Square
Ryland Road
Charlotte Rd
Pakenham Rd
Melton Dr
Summer Road
Brambling Walk
Nightingale Walk
Woodview Dr
Springbank
Spring Road
Stone Rd
Belle Vue Medical Cen
Bellevue
Police Stn
Council Building
Carpenter Road
Ampton
Arthur Road
Ashley Cl
Gough Road
Michael Drive
Wellington Road
A38
Pershore Road
Edgbaston
B15
Church Road
Grey Drive
Holy Child School
Sir Harrys Road
Birmingham Central Synagogue
Speedwell
Calthorpe Park
1 grid square represents 500 metres

Nechells Green
Vauxhall
Bordesley
Digbeth
Highgate
Sparkbrook
109
128
144
B4
B5
B12
E
F
G
H
I
2
3
4
5
08
09
Council Building
Aston University
Aston Science Park
Parkway Industrial Centre
ASHTED CIRCUS
CURZON CIRCUS
GARRISON CIRCUS
BORDESLEY CIRCUS
CAMP-HILL CIRCUS
HADEN CIRCUS
Dental Hosp
Fire Stn
Sports Centre
Childrens Hospital
Police Headquarters
Law Courts
Millennium Point
IMAX Cinema
Thinktank Museum
Trading Estate
Open Mkt
Pavilions Shop Centre
Moor Street Stn
Odeon Cinema
Rotunda
Bullring Shopping Centre
Bus Stn
The Mayfair Centre
Indoor Mkt
Hotel Ibis
Planet Ice Arena
Wholesale Mkts
Digbeth Coach Stn
Bull Ring Trading Est
Fazeley Industrial Estate
Fazeley Ind Est
St Vincents RC Primary School
Duddeston Mill Trading Est
Birmingham Adventure Park
St Andrews Industrial Est
Birmingham City FC (St Andrews Stadium)
Kingston Local Park
Industrial Kingston Estate
Trident Retail Park
Bordesley Stn
St Annes RC Primary School
The Harper Bell School
Calthorpe Special Sch
Highgate Tdg Est
Highgate Retail Park
Chandos Prim Sch
St Albans CE Sch
Middleway Industrial Estate
Birmingham Central Mosque
Highgate Medical Cen
Percy Shurmer Primary School
Joseph Chamberlain Sixth Form College
Business Centre
Ladypool Primary School
Christ Church CE Primary School
Regents Park Primary School
Health Centre
Council Building
CORPORATION ST
JAMES WATT QUEENSWAY
MOOR ST QUEENSWAY
PARK ST
VAUXHALL ROAD
LAWLEY MIDDLEWAY
WATERY LA MIDDLEWAY
A4540
HIGH ST DERITEND
HIGH ST BORDESLEY
COVENTRY ROAD
COVENTRY RD
A45
SMALL HEATH HWY
SMALL HEATH HIGHWAY
BRADFORD ST
BARFORD ST
A441 SHERLOCK STREET
GOOCH STREET
BELGRAVE MIDDLEWAY
HIGHGATE MIDDLEWAY
NEW MOSELEY RD
CAMP HILL
B4100
B4730
A41
STRATFORD
A4167
HIGHGATE
HADEN
Landor Street
Garrison Street
Curzon St
Jennens Rd
Belmont Rw
Coleshill St
Albert St
Moseley St
Cheapside
Warwick St
Kingston Rd
Dart Street
Henley Street
Kyotts Lake Rd
Braithwaite Rd
Priestley Road
Main Street
Long Street
Montgomery St
Grand Union Canal
River Rea

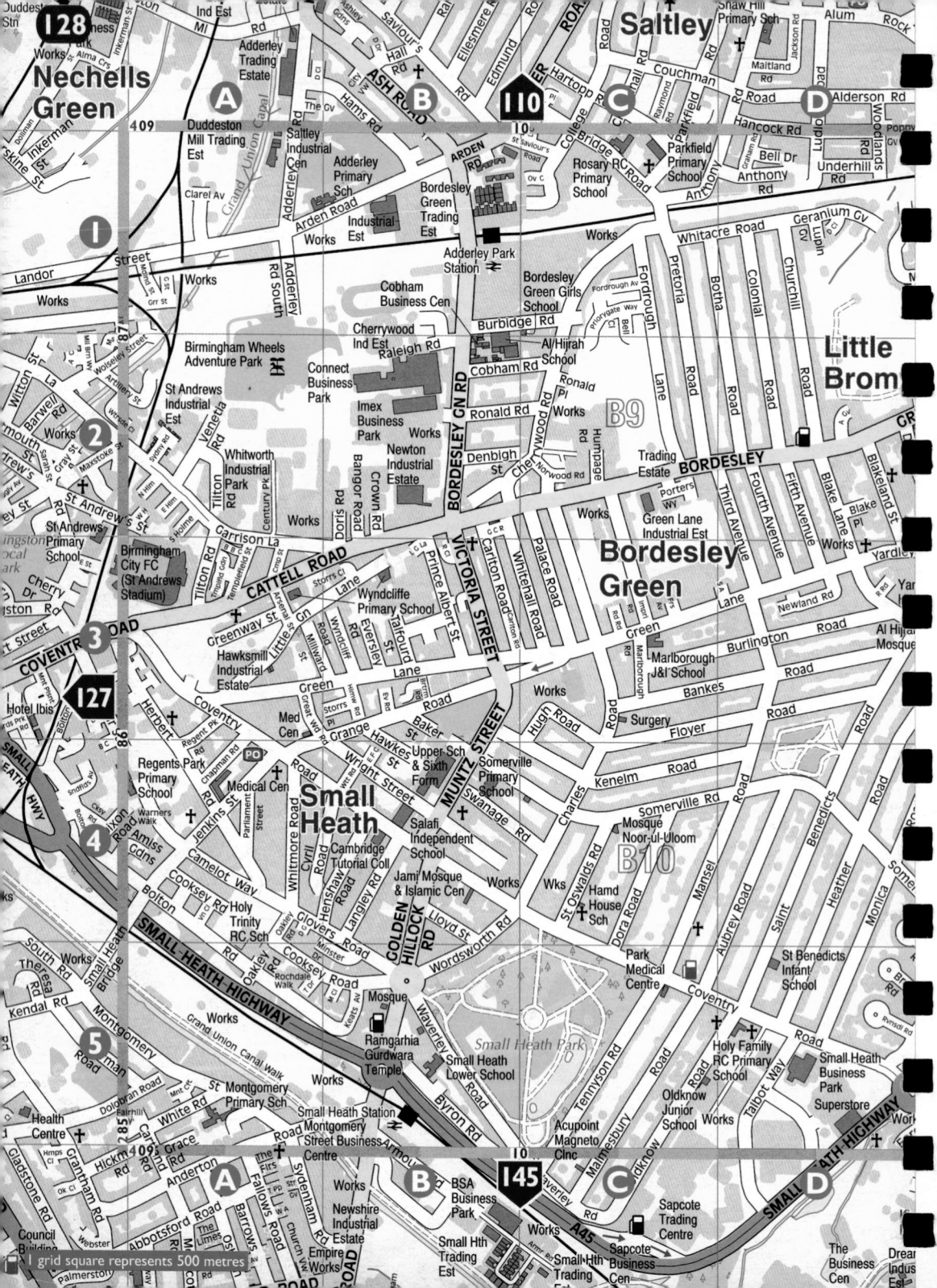
128
Nechells
Green
Saltley
Little
Brom
Bordesley
Green
Small
Heath
B9
B10
110
127
145
A
B
C
D
1
2
3
4
5
Duddeston Mill Trading Est
Adderley Trading Estate
Saltley Industrial Cen
Adderley Primary Sch
Bordesley Green Trading Est
Industrial Est
Adderley Park Station
Cobham Business Cen
Bordesley Green Girls School
Al Hijrah School
Cherrywood Ind Est
Birmingham Wheels Adventure Park
Connect Business Park
Imex Business Park
Newton Industrial Estate
St Andrews Industrial Est
Whitworth Industrial Park
St Andrews Primary School
Birmingham City FC (St Andrews Stadium)
Wyndcliffe Primary School
Hawksmill Industrial Estate
Hotel Ibis
Regents Park Primary School
Medical Cen
Med Cen
Upper Sch & Sixth Form
Somerville Primary School
Salafi Independent School
Cambridge Tutorial Coll
Jami Mosque & Islamic Cen
Holy Trinity RC Sch
Mosque Noor-ul-Uloom
Hamd House Sch
Park Medical Centre
St Benedicts Infant School
Holy Family RC Primary School
Small Heath Business Park
Superstore
Oldknow Junior School
Acupoint Magneto Clnc
Small Heath Park
Small Heath Lower School
Ramgarhia Gurdwara Temple
Small Heath Station
Montgomery Primary Sch
Montgomery Street Business Centre
Health Centre
Council Building
BSA Business Park
Newshire Industrial Estate
Empire Works
Small Hth Trading Est
Small Hth Trading
Sapcote Trading Centre
Sapcote Business Cen
The Business Cen
Trading Estate
Green Lane Industrial Est
Marlborough J&I School
Surgery
Al Hijrah Mosque
Rosary RC Primary School
Parkfield Primary School
Shaw Hill Primary Sch
Landor Street
Cattell Road
Coventry Road
Bordesley Green Rd
Victoria Street
Muntz Street
Golden Hillock Rd
Small Heath Highway
Grand Union Canal
Grand Union Canal Walk
Small Heath Bridge
A45
1 grid square represents 500 metres

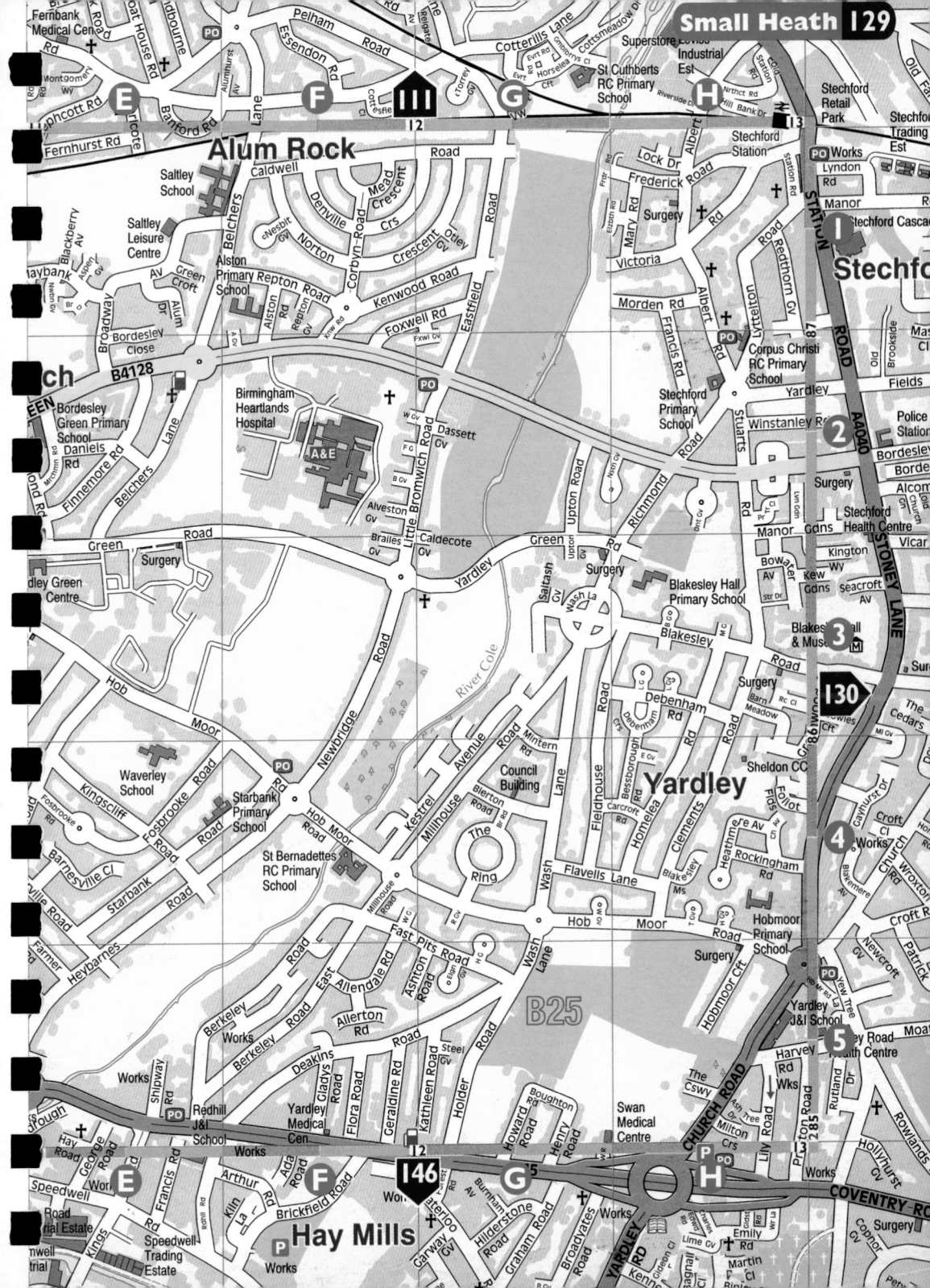
Alum Rock
Stechford
Yardley
Hay Mills
Birmingham Heartlands Hospital
A&E
Saltley School
Saltley Leisure Centre
Alston Primary School
Bordesley Green Primary School
Waverley School
Starbank Primary School
St Bernadettes RC Primary School
Stechford Primary School
Corpus Christi RC Primary School
Blakesley Hall Primary School
Hobmoor Primary School
Yardley J&I School
Redhill J&I School
St Cuthberts RC Primary School
Council Building
Sheldon CC
Stechford Retail Park
Stechford Trading Est
Stechford Station
Stechford Health Centre
Police Station
Swan Medical Centre
Yardley Medical Cen
Speedwell Trading Estate
Superstore
Industrial Est
River Cole
B4128
A4040
B25
STONEY LANE
STATION ROAD
CHURCH ROAD
COVENTRY ROAD
YARDLEY RD
Speedwell Rd
Hob Moor Road
Yardley Green Road
Little Bromwich Road
Newbridge Road
Wash Lane
Flavells Lane
Blakesley Road
Richmond Road
Station Rd
111
130
146

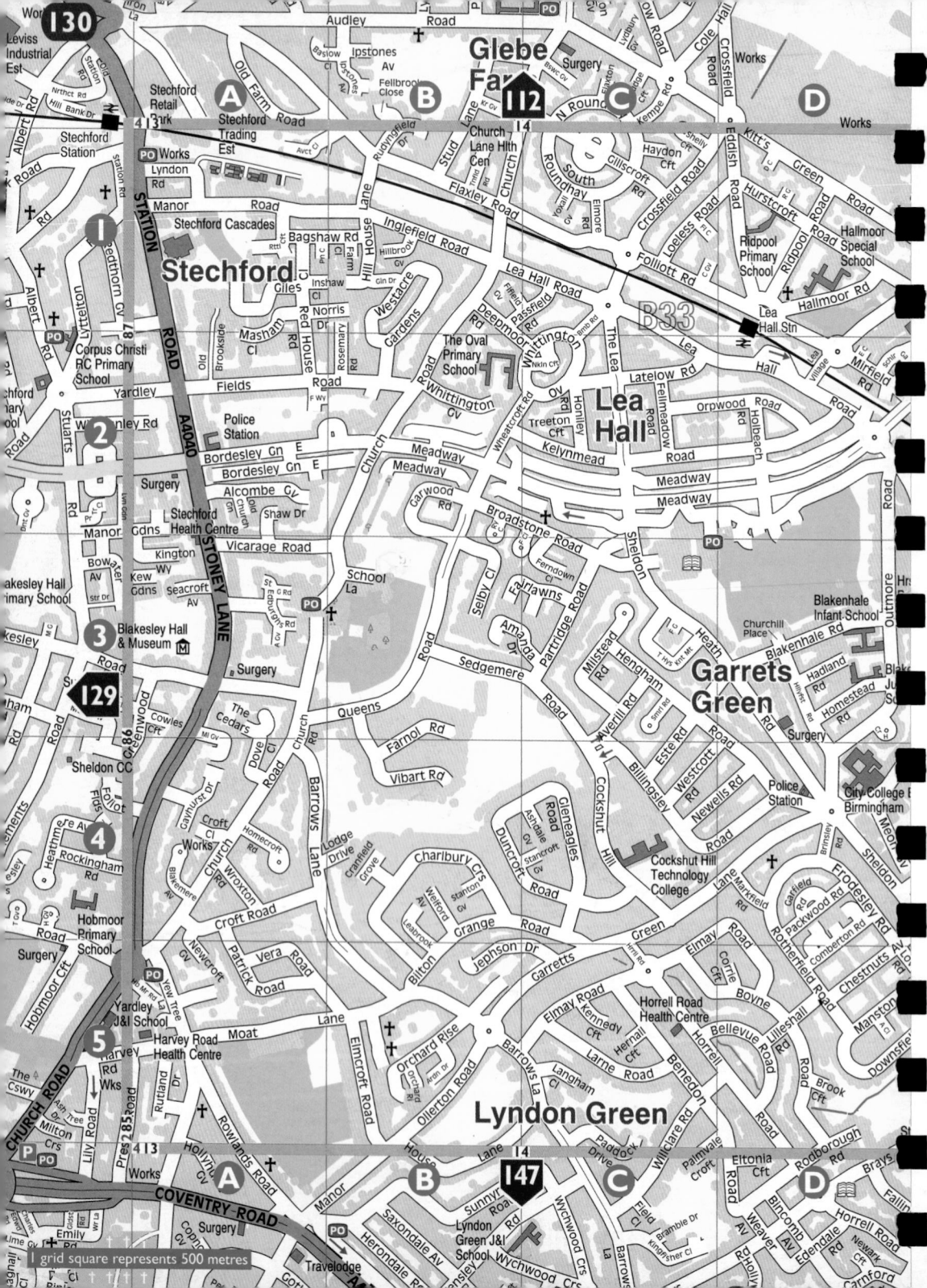

130
129
112
147
Glebe Farm
Stechford
Lea Hall
Garrets Green
Lyndon Green
Stechford Retail Park
Stechford Trading Est
Stechford Station
Stechford Cascades
Leviss Industrial Est
Corpus Christi RC Primary School
Police Station
Stechford Health Centre
Blakesley Hall & Museum
Sheldon CC
Hobmoor Primary School
Yardley J&I School
Harvey Road Health Centre
The Oval Primary School
Church Lane Hlth Cen
Ridpool Primary School
Hallmoor Special School
Lea Hall Stn
Blakenhale Infant School
City College Birmingham
Cockshut Hill Technology College
Horrell Road Health Centre
Lyndon Green J&I School
Travelodge
STATION ROAD
STONEY LANE
A4040
COVENTRY ROAD
CHURCH ROAD
B33
Audley Road
Old Farm Road
Flaxley Road
Inglefield Road
Lea Hall Road
Folliott Rd
Meadway
Broadstone Road
Sedgemere Road
Yardley Fields Road
Vicarage Road
Church Road
Barrows Lane
Garretts Green Lane
Moat Lane
Grange Road
Croft Road
Cockshut Hill
Sheldon Heath Road
Kitt's Green Road
Hallmoor Rd
Manor Road
Lyndon Rd
Works
Surgery
1 grid square represents 500 metres

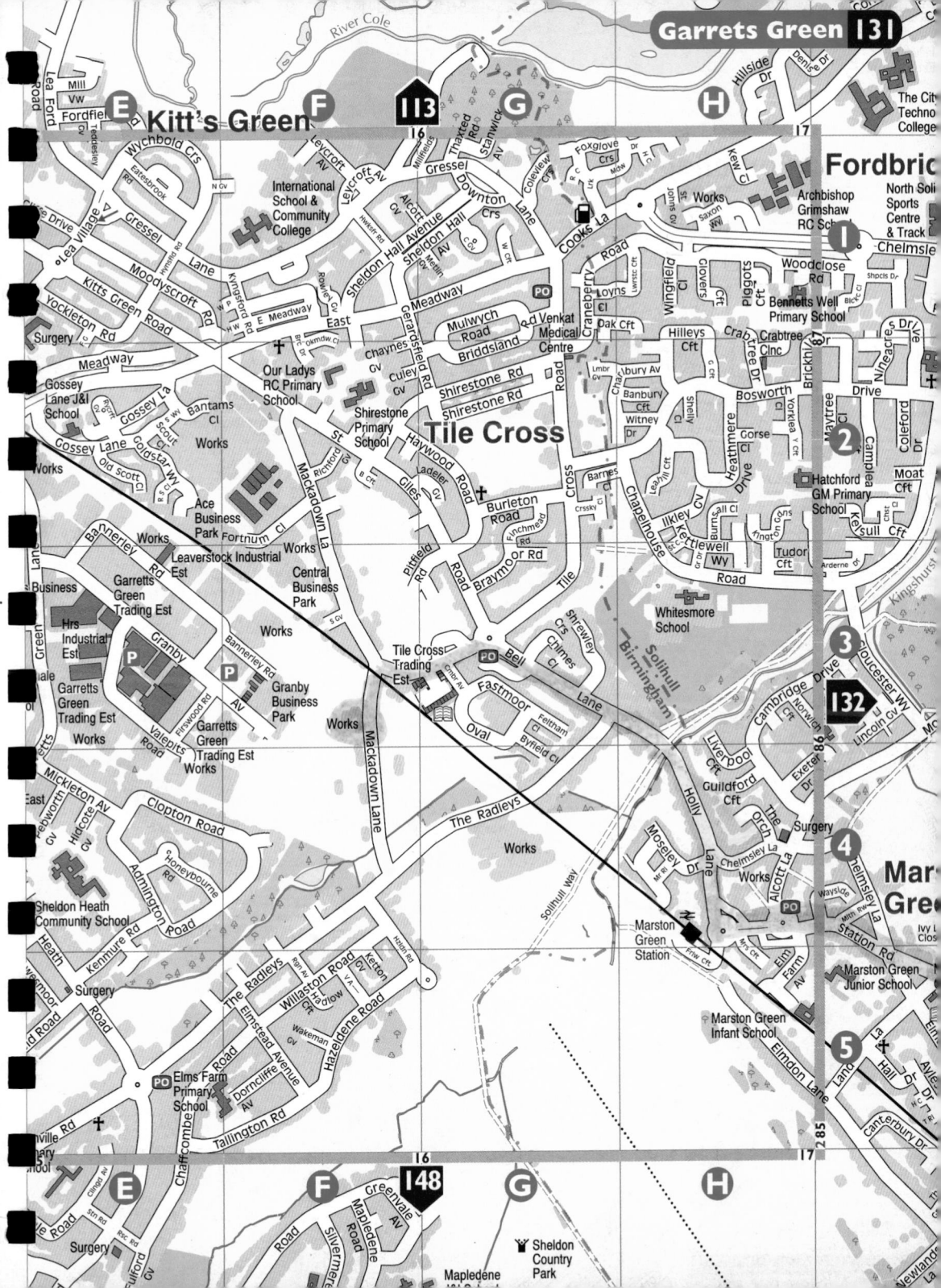

Garrets Green 131
River Cole
113
Kitt's Green
Fordbridge
Tile Cross
132
148
16
17
E
F
G
H
1
2
3
4
5
Mill Vw
Fordfield Rd
Lea Ford Road
Wychbold Crs
Leycroft Av
Millfields
Thaxted Rd
Stanwick Av
Coleview Crs
Foxglove Crs
Kew Cl
Hillside Dr
Denise Dr
The City Technology College
International School & Community College
Gressel Lane
Downton Crs
Sheldon Hall Avenue
Alcott Gv
Lea Village
Moodyscroft Rd
Kitts Green Road
Yockleton Rd
Kyngsford Rd
E Meadway
Meadway
East Meadway
Cooks La
Craneberry Road
Wingfield Cl
Glovers Cft
Piggots Cft
Works
Saxon Wy
Archbishop Grimshaw RC School
North Solihull Sports Centre & Track
Chelmsley
Woodclose Rd
Bennetts Well Primary School
Mulwych Road
Briddsland
Venkat Medical Centre
Loyns Cl
Oak Cft
Hilleys Cft
Crabtree Dr
Crabtree Clnc
Brickhill Dr
Nineacres Drive
Surgery
Gosssey Lane J&I School
Gossey La
Gossey Lane
Bantams Cl
Our Ladys RC Primary School
Chaynes Gv
Culey Gv
Gerardsfield Rd
Shirestone Rd
Shirestone Primary School
Charlbury Av
Banbury Cft
Witney Dr
Bosworth Cl
Heathmere Drive
Gorse Cl
Maytree Cl
Camplea Cft
Coleford Dr
Moat Cft
Hatchford GM Primary School
Kelsull Cft
Old Scott Cl
Coldstar Wy
Ace Business Park
Richford Gv
Mackadown La
St Giles Road
Haywood Road
Ladeler Gv
Burleton Road
Finchmead Rd
Braymoor Rd
Barnes Cl
Tile Cross Road
Chapelhouse Road
Ilkley Gv
Kettlewell Wy
Tudor Cft
Bannerley Rd
Fortnum Cl
Leaverstock Industrial Est
Central Business Park
Pitfield Rd
Business
Garretts Green Trading Est
Hrs Industrial Est
Granby Av
Bannerley Rd
Granby Business Park
Whitesmore School
Shrewley Crs
Chimes Cl
Solihull Birmingham
Tile Cross Trading Est
Bell Lane
Fastmoor Oval
Feltham Cl
Byfield Cl
Cambridge Drive
Gloucester Wy
Lincoln Gv
Norwich Cft
Liverpool Cft
Exeter Dr
Guildford Cft
The Orch
Firswood Rd
Valepits Road
Mackadown Lane
Mickleton Av
Pebworth Gv
Hidcote Gv
Clopton Road
The Radleys
Holly Lane
Moseley Dr
Chelmsley La
Alcott La
Wayside
Chelmsley La
Marston Green
Honeybourne Rd
Admington Road
Sheldon Heath Community School
Kenmure Rd
Solihull Way
Marston Green Station
Elm Farm Av
Station Rd
Marston Green Junior School
Marston Green Infant School
Elmdon Lane
Hall Dr
Canterbury Dr
Heath Road
Surgery
Ketton Gv
Willaston Road
Hadlow Cft
Elmstead Avenue
Hazeldene Road
Wakeman Gv
Elms Farm Primary School
Dorncliffe Av
Tallington Rd
Chaffcombe Road
Greenvale Av
Mapledene Road
Silvermere
Sheldon Country Park
Mapledene
Fulford Gv
Newlands
285

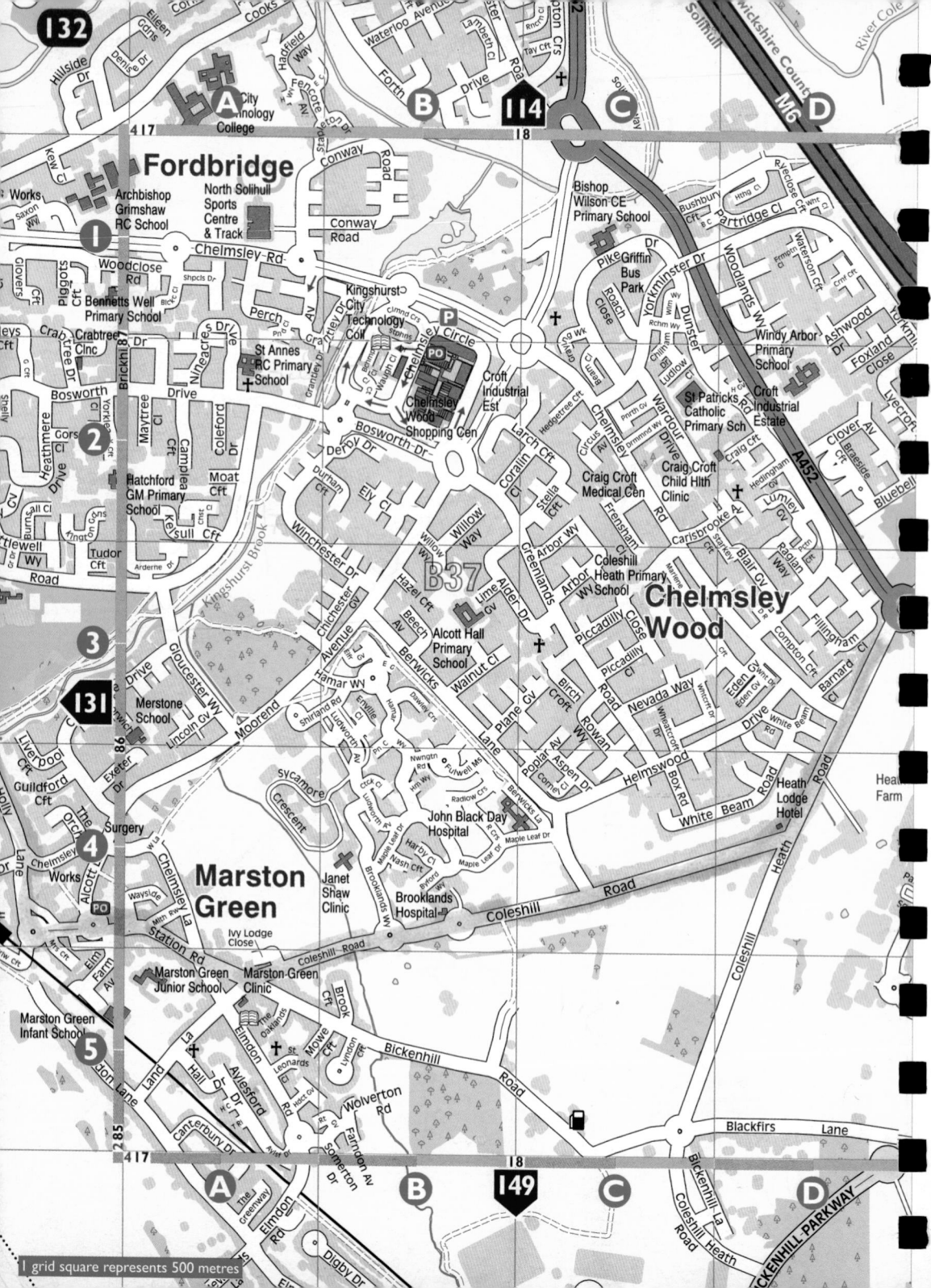

132
114
131
149
A
B
C
D
1
2
3
4
5
417
18
285
86
Fordbridge
Chelmsley Wood
Marston Green
B37
M6
A452
City Technology College
Archbishop Grimshaw RC School
North Solihull Sports Centre & Track
Bennetts Well Primary School
Crabtree Clnc
St Annes RC Primary School
Kingshurst City Technology Coll
Chelmsley Wood Shopping Cen
Croft Industrial Est
Bishop Wilson CE Primary School
Griffin Bus Park
Windy Arbor Primary School
Croft Industrial Estate
St Patricks Catholic Primary Sch
Craig Croft Medical Cen
Craig Croft Child Hlth Clinic
Coleshill Heath Primary School
Alcott Hall Primary School
Hatchford GM Primary School
Merstone School
Surgery
Works
John Black Day Hospital
Janet Shaw Clinic
Brooklands Hospital
Marston Green Junior School
Marston Green Clinic
Marston Green Infant School
Heath Lodge Hotel
Heath Farm
Kingshurst Brook
River Cole
Chelmsley Rd
Chelmsley Circle
Bosworth Dr
Bosworth Drive
Conway Road
Coleshill Road
Coleshill Heath Road
Bickenhill Road
Bickenhill La
Blackfirs Lane
Station Rd
Moorend Avenue
Berwicks Lane
Yorkminster Dr
Partridge Cl
Woodlands Wy
Dunster
Wardour Drive
Frensham Cl
Carisbrooke Av
Blair Gv
Raglan Way
Piccadilly Close
Nevada Way
Helmswood
White Beam Road
Rowan Road
Greenlands
Arbor Wy
Alder Dr
Larch Cft
Coralin Cl
Willow Way
Winchester Dr
Chichester Gv
Hazel Cft
Beech Av
Walnut Cl
Plane Gv
Birch Croft
Poplar Av
Aspen Dr
Hamar Wy
Sycamore Crescent
Maple Leaf Dr
Brooklands Wy
Elmdon Rd
Aylesford Dr
Hall Dr
Canterbury Dr
Wolverton Rd
Somerton Dr
Farndon Av
Gloucester Wy
Lincoln Gv
Exeter Dr
Liverpool Cft
Guildford Cft
Chelmsley La
Heathmere Drive
Maytree Cl
Camplea Cft
Coleford Dr
Ninacres Drive
Kelsull Cft
Tudor Cft
Ely Cl
Durham Cft
Fillingham Cl
Compton Cft
Barnard Cl
Clover Av
Foxland Close
Ashwood Dr
Lyecroft
Bluebell
Woodclose Rd
Perch Av
Grantley Dr
Brickhill Dr
Waterloo Avenue
Forth Drive
Hillside Dr
Denise Dr
Hadfield Way
Fencote Av
Kew Cl
Saxon Wy
BICKENHILL PARKWAY
1 grid square represents 500 metres

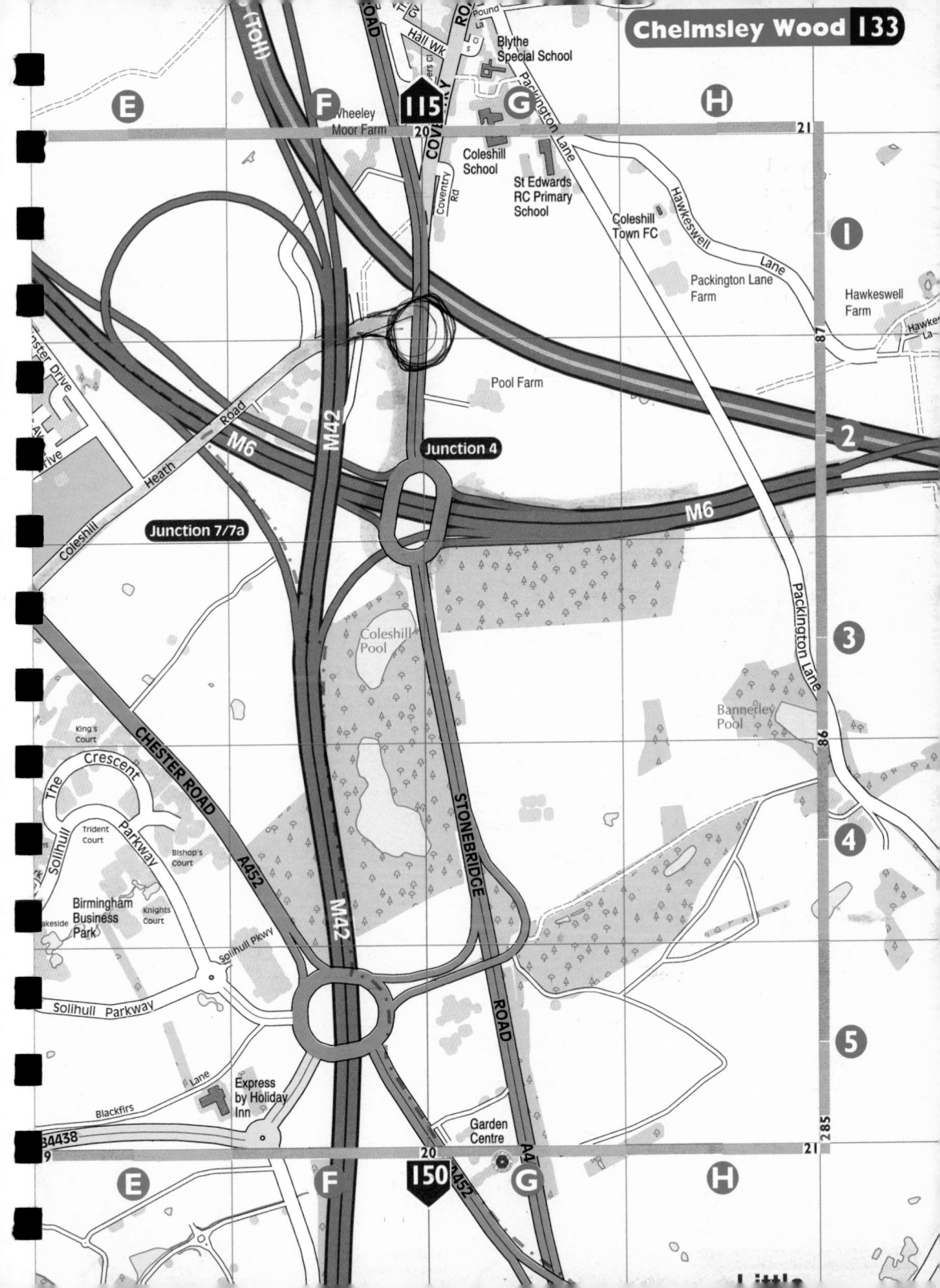

E F 115 G H
20

Coventry Road (Toll)
Hall Wk
Pound La
Blythe Special School
Wheeley Moor Farm
Packington Lane
Coleshill School
Coventry Rd
St Edwards RC Primary School
Coleshill Town FC
Hawkeswell Lane
I

Packington Lane Farm
Hawkeswell Farm
Hawke La
87

Pool Farm
2

Chester Drive
Road
M6
Heath
Junction 4
M6
Packington Lane

Junction 7/7a
Coleshill
3

Coleshill Pool
Bannerley Pool
86

King's Court
The Crescent
CHESTER ROAD
Solihull Parkway
Trident Court
Bishop's Court
A452
STONEBRIDGE ROAD
4

Birmingham Business Park
Lakeside
Knights Court
M42
5

Solihull Parkway
Solihull Pkwy
Lane
Blackfirs
Express by Holiday Inn
Garden Centre
A4
285

B4438
9
E F 150 G H
20 A452 21

Little

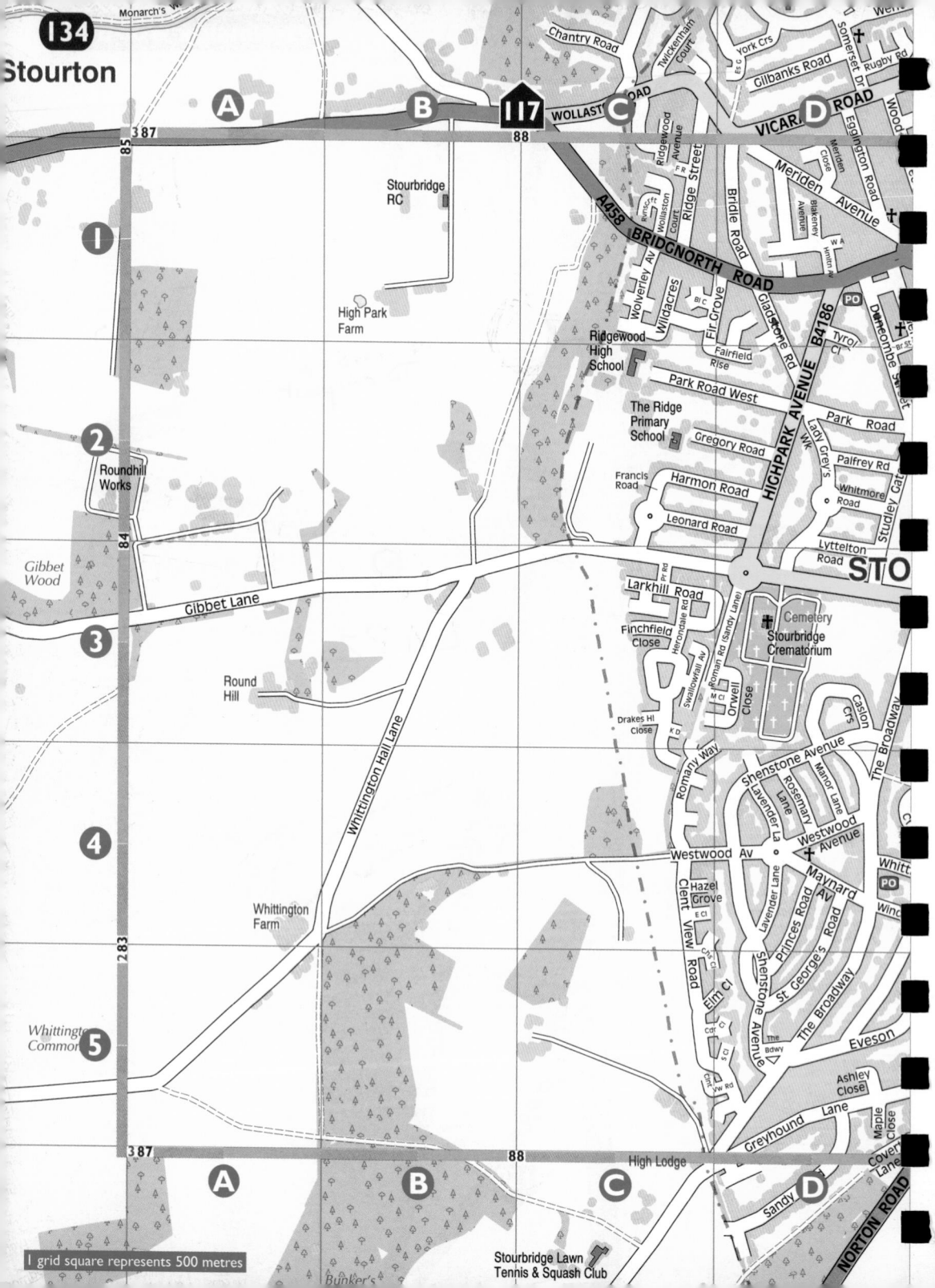

117 WOLLAST ROAD

A458 BRIDGNORTH ROAD

Stourbridge RC

High Park Farm

Ridgewood High School

The Ridge Primary School

Roundhill Works

Gibbet Wood

Gibbet Lane

Round Hill

Whittington Hall Lane

Whittington Farm

Whittington Common

VICAR ROAD

Chantry Road
Twickenham Court
York Crs
Gilbanks Road
Somerset Dr
Rugby Road

Meriden Avenue
Meriden Close
Eglington Road
Wood
Blakeney Avenue
Whitmal Rd

Ridgewood Avenue
Ridge Street
Bridle Road
Gladstone Rd
B4186
PO
Tyrol Cl
Deneombe St

Wolverley Av
Wildacres
Fir Grove
Fairfield Rise
Park Road West
Park Road
HIGHPARK AVENUE
Lady Grey's Wk
Park Road
Palfrey Rd
Whitmore Road
Studley Gate
STO

Gregory Road
Francis Road
Harmon Road
Leonard Road
Lyttelton Road

Larkhill Road
Finchfield Close
Herondale Rd
Roman Rd (Sandy Lane)
Cemetery
Stourbridge Crematorium

Swallowtail Av
Orwell Close
M Cl
K D

Drakes Hl Close

Romany Way
Shenstone Avenue
Rosemary Lane
Lavender La
Manor Lane
Westwood Avenue
Caslon Crs
The Broadway

Westwood Av
Hazel Grove
Client View Road
Lavender Lane
Princes Road
St George's Road
Maynard Av
PO
Whitt
Wind

Elm Cl
Shenstone Avenue
The Broadway
Eveson

Ashley Close
Greyhound Lane
Maple Close
Cover Lane
Sandy
NORTON ROAD

High Lodge

Stourbridge Lawn Tennis & Squash Club

Wollaston
Stourbridge Industrial Estate
Linkwood Industrial Estate
DY8
Beauty Bank Primary School
Sovereign Trading Est
Town Hall
Council Building
Crystal Leisure Centre
Stourbridge Town
Magistrates Court
Parkfield Redhill Secondary School
Gainsborough Trading Estate
Stamber
URBRIDGE
Greenfield Primary School
The Picture House
Old Swinford Hospital Sch
Stourbridge Coll of Technology & Art
Stevens Dental Health Centre
Council Building
Gig Mill Primary School
Old Swinford
Stourbridge Junction Station
Oldswinford CE Primary Sch
Norton
St Josephs Catholic Primary School
Ham Dingle Primary School
Stourbridge Golf Club
Golf Course
Racecourse Farm
Pedmore CE Primary
Peters Hill Primary School
HIGH STREET
BRIDGNORTH ROAD
ENVILLE STREET
BIRMINGHAM STREET
ST JOHN'S ROAD
BATH ROAD
NEW RD
WORCESTER ST
SOUTH ROAD
HEATH LANE
GLASSHOUSE HL
BROOK RD
HAGLEY ROAD
NORTON ROAD
HAM LANE
GRANGE R
Racecourse Lane
118
136
152

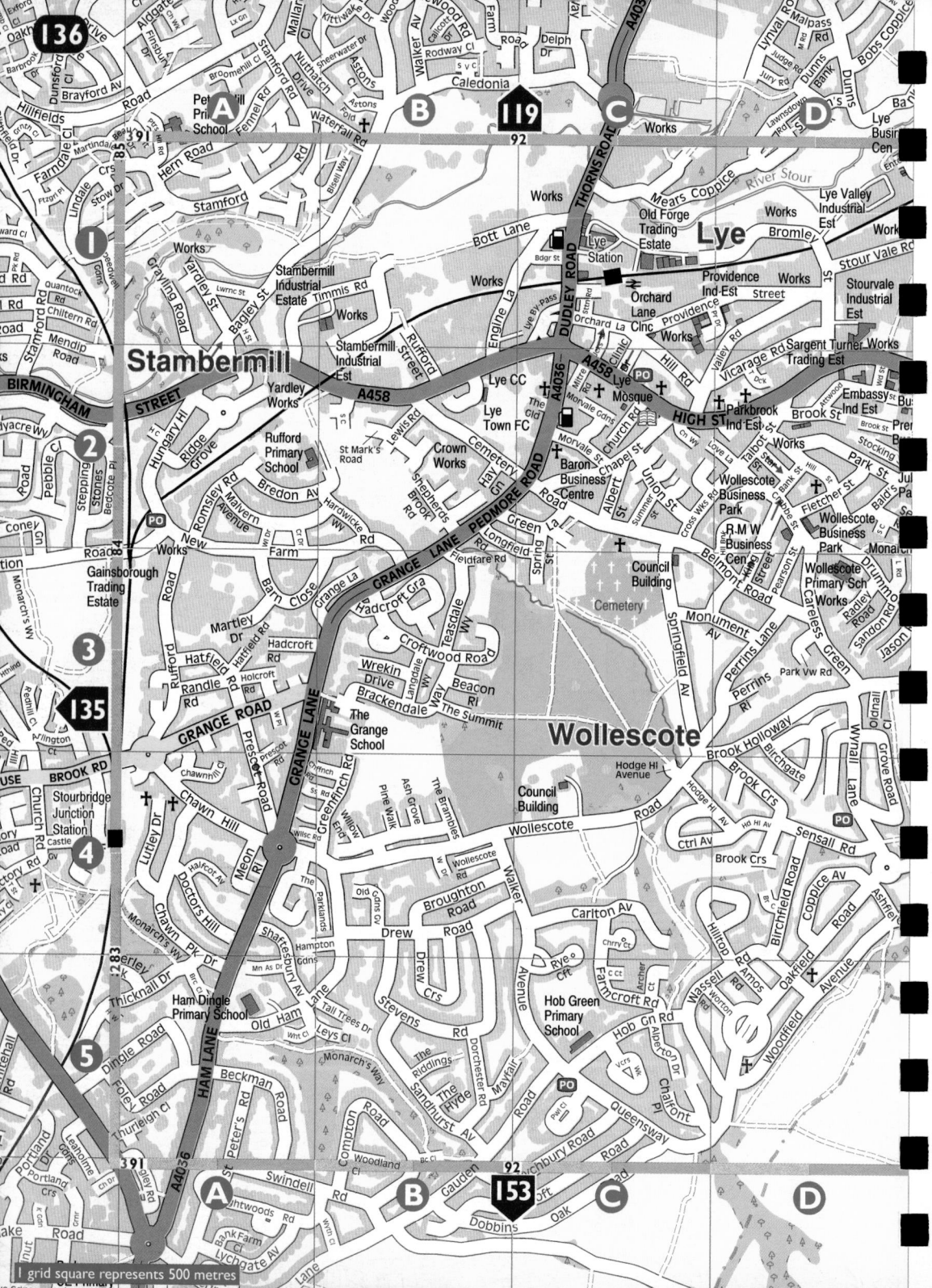
136
119
135
153
Stambermill
Lye
Wollescote
1 grid square represents 500 metres

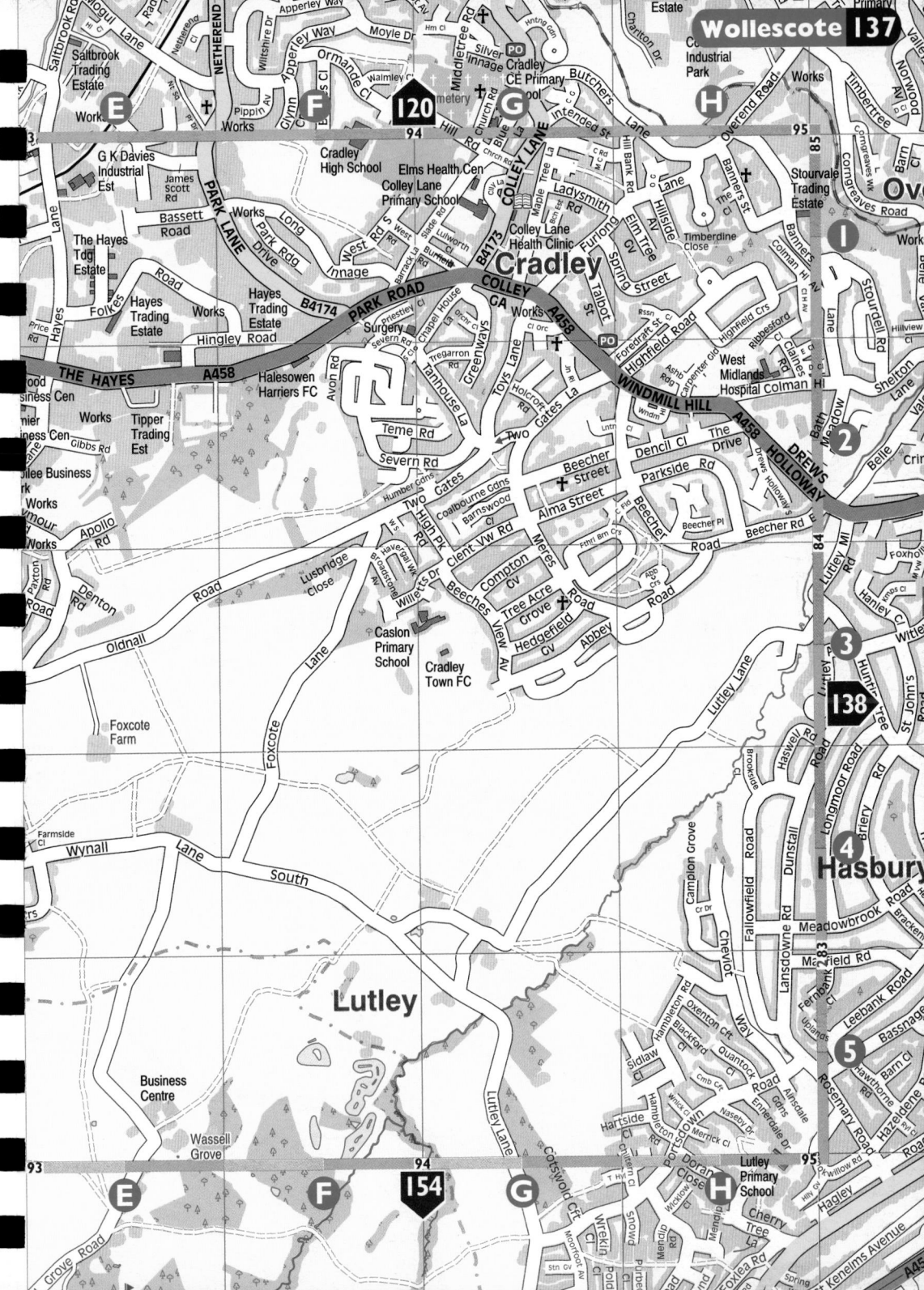
Cradley
Lutley
Hasbury
Cradley High School
Colley Lane Primary School
Elms Health Cen
Colley Lane Health Clinic
Caslon Primary School
Cradley Town FC
Halesowen Harriers FC
West Midlands Hospital
Lutley Primary School
Saltbrook Trading Estate
G K Davies Industrial Est
The Hayes Tdg Estate
Hayes Trading Estate
Tipper Trading Est
Stourvale Trading Estate
Foxcote Farm
Business Centre
Wassell Grove
THE HAYES
A458
PARK ROAD
B4174
COLLEY LANE
B4173
WINDMILL HILL
DREWS HOLLOWAY
PARK LANE
NETHEREND
Hingley Road
Oldnall Road
Foxcote Lane
Wynall Lane South
Lutley Lane
Lutley Mill Road
Longmoor Road
Meadowbrook Road
Cheviot Way
Fallowfield Road
Beecher Road
Alma Street
Two Gates Lane
120
138
154

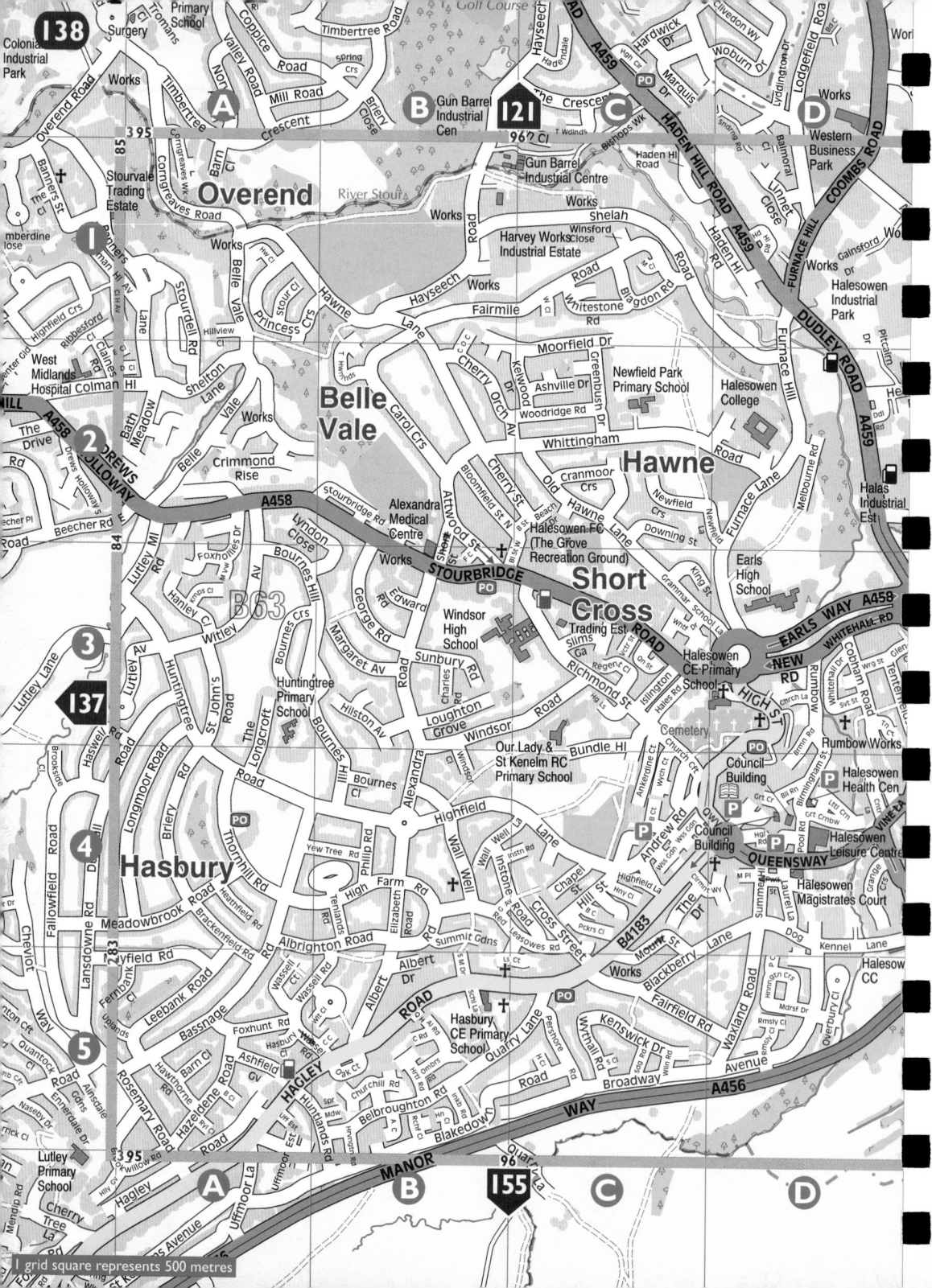

138
121
137
155
A
B
C
D
1
2
3
4
5
395
85
84
283
96
Colonial Industrial Park
Surgery
Primary School
Tromans
Golf Course
Coppice Road
Valley Road
Timbertree Road
Timbertree Crescent
Spring Crs
Mill Road
Briery Close
Gun Barrel Industrial Cen
Gun Barrel Industrial Centre
Hayseech
The Crescent
Bishops Wk
Hardwick Dr
Clivedon Wy
Woburn Dr
Marquis Dr
Lodgefield Road
Lyddington Dr
Works
Western Business Park
Balmoral
Linnet Close
Haden Hill Road
Haden Hl Road
A459
Haden Hill Road
Coombs Road
Furnace Hill
Overend Road
Banners St
The Cl
Stourvale Trading Estate
Corngreaves Road
Corngreaves Wk
Barn Cl
Overend
River Stour
Shelah Road
Harvey Works Industrial Estate
Winsford Close
Gainsford Dr
Halesowen Industrial Park
Dudley Road
Belle Vale
Stourdell Rd
Hawne Lane
Hayseech Road
Princess Crs
Stour Cl
Fairmile
Whitestone Rd
Blagdon Rd
Highfield Crs
Ribbesford
Claines Rd
West Midlands Hospital
Colman Hl
Hillview Cl
Shelton Lane
Moorfield Dr
Cherry Orch Av
Kelwood Dr
Greenbush Dr
Ashville Dr
Woodridge Rd
Newfield Park Primary School
Halesowen College
Pitcairn Dr
Bath Meadow
Carol Crs
Whittingham Road
Hawne
Melbourne Rd
Furnace Lane
The Drive
A458
Drews Holloway
Crimmond Rise
Bloomfield St N
Cherry St
Cranmoor Crs
Old Hawne Lane
Newfield Crs
Halas Industrial Est
Beecher Rd E
Stourbridge Rd
Alexandra Medical Centre
Attwood St
Halesowen FC (The Grove Recreation Ground)
Downing St
King St
Earls High School
Lutley Ml Rd
Foxhollies Dr
Lyndon Close
Bournes Hill
Short St
Stourbridge Road
Short Cross
Grammar School La
Earls Way
Whitehall Rd
Hanley Cl
Witley Av
B63
Bournes Crs
George Rd
Edward Rd
Windsor High School
Trading Est.
Cross
Halesowen CE Primary School
New Rd
Cobham Road
Rumbow
Lutley Lane
Lutley Av
Huntingtree Road
St John's Road
Margaret Av
Sunbury Rd
Richmond St
Islington
Hales Rd
High St
Huntingtree Primary School
Hilston Av
Charles Rd
Loughton Grove
Windsor Road
Bundle Hl
Cemetery
Haswell Rd
The Longcroft
Our Lady & St Kenelm RC Primary School
Church Cft
Ankerdine Ct
Rumbow Works
Brookside
Longmoor Road
Bournes Cl
Council Building
Birmingham St
Halesowen Health Cen
Briery Rd
Alexandra Road
Highfield Lane
Andrew Rd
Pool Rd
Vine La
Fallowfield Road
Thornhill Rd
Yew Tree Rd
Philip Rd
Wall Well
Wall Well La
Queensway
Halesowen Leisure Centre
Hasbury
High Farm Rd
Instone Road
Chapel St
Hill St
Highfield La
Halesowen Magistrates Court
Grange Rd
Cheviot
Lansdowne Rd
Meadowbrook Road
Heathfield Rd
Tenlands Rd
Elizabeth Road
Cross Street
The Dr
Summer Hill
Laurel La
Brackenfield Rd
Albrighton Road
Summit Gdns
Red Leasowes Rd
B4183
Mount St
Blackberry Lane
Dog Kennel Lane
Mayfield Rd
Albert Dr
Works
Halesow CC
Fernbank Cl
Leebank Road
Wassell Ct
Wassell Rd
Albert Rd
Hagley Road
Hasbury CE Primary School
Quarry Lane
Pershore Rd
Kenswick Dr
Fairfield Rd
Waxland Road
Overbury Cl
Way
Quantock Cl
Bassnage Road
Foxhunt Rd
Ashfield Gv
Wythall Rd
Mdrsf Dr
Rosemary Road
Hawthorne Rd
Barn Cl
Hazeldene Road
Hagley
Churchill Rd
Belbroughton Rd
Broadway
Avenue
A456
Manor Way
Ainsdale Gdns
Ennerdale Dr
Naseby Dr
Huntlands Rd
Blakedown
Lutley Primary School
Willow Rd
Uffmoor Est
Uffmoor La
Quarry La
Mendip Rd
Cherry Tree La
Hagley Road
Avenue
1 grid square represents 500 metres

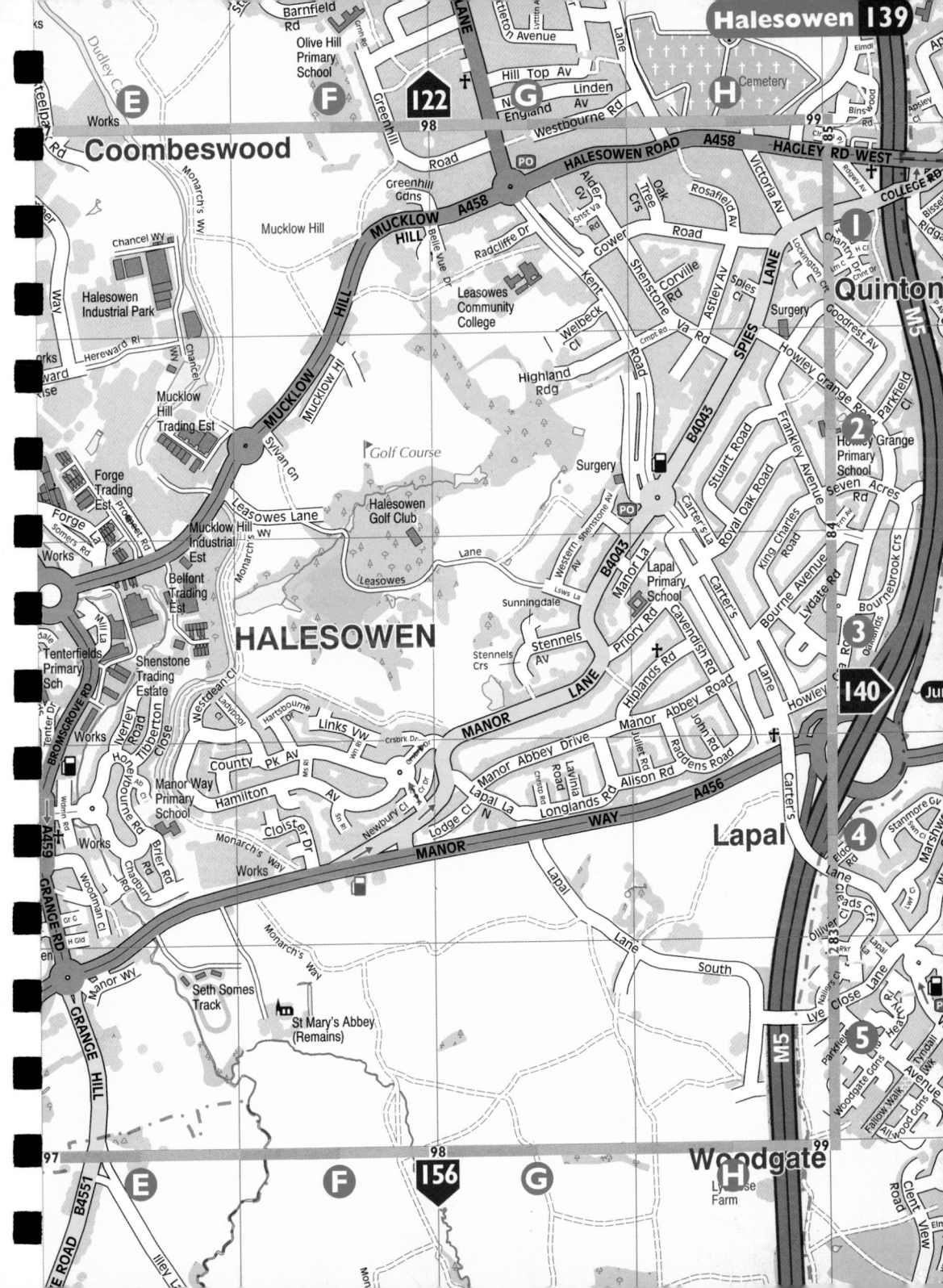

Coombeswood
Mucklow Hill
Halesowen Industrial Park
Mucklow Hill Trading Est
Forge Trading Est
Mucklow Hill Industrial Est
Belfont Trading Est
Shenstone Trading Estate
Tenterfields Primary Sch
Manor Way Primary School
HALESOWEN
Golf Course
Halesowen Golf Club
Leasowes Community College
Olive Hill Primary School
Cemetery
Quinton
Howley Grange Primary School
Lapal Primary School
Lapal
Woodgate
Seth Somes Track
St Mary's Abbey (Remains)
HALESOWEN ROAD
HAGLEY RD WEST
MUCKLOW HILL
MANOR WAY
MANOR LANE
GRANGE HILL
BROMSGROVE RD
SPIES LANE
M5
A458
A456
A459
B4043
B4551
122
156
140
98
99
E
F
G
H
1
2
3
4
5

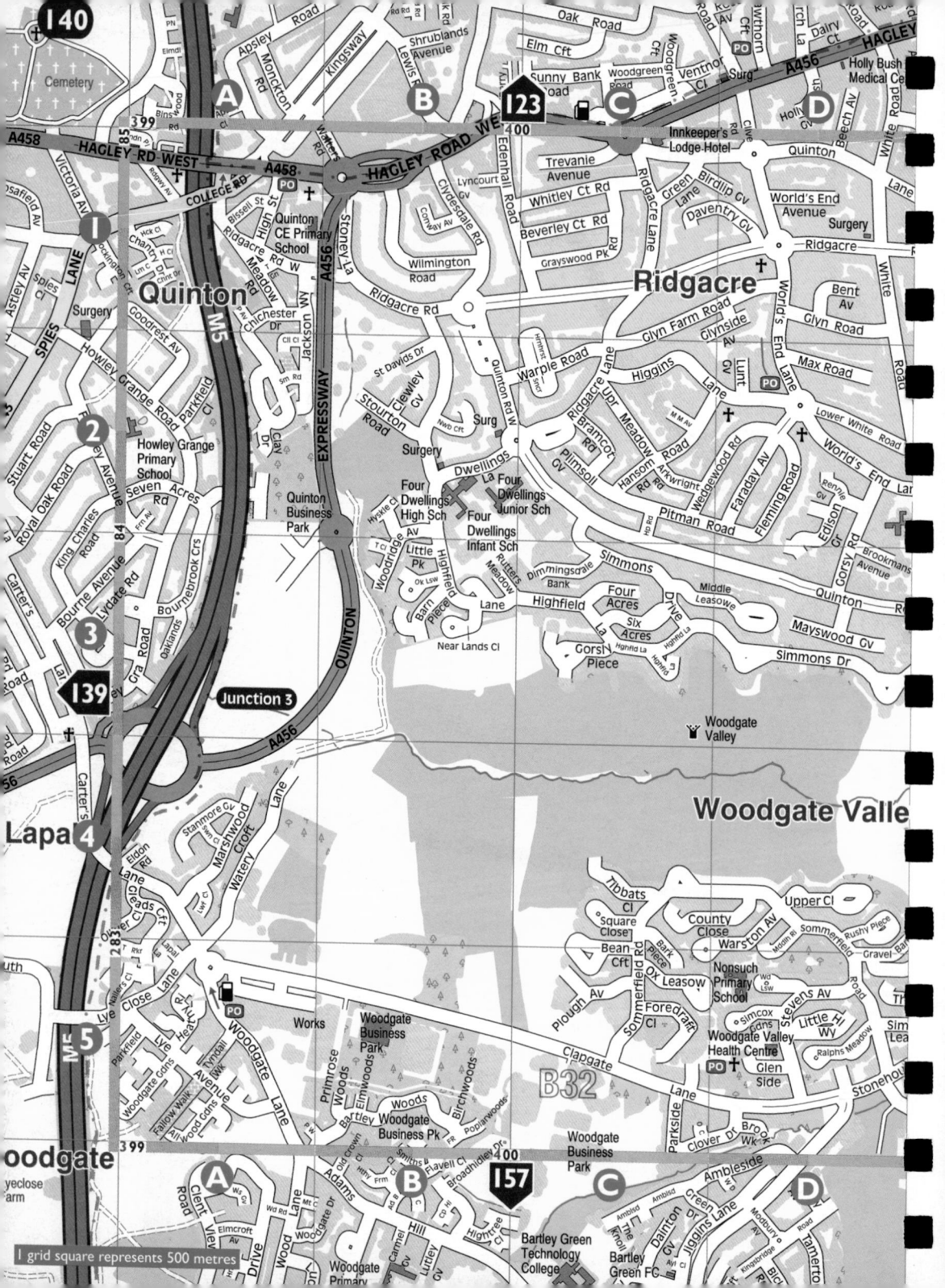

140
Cemetery
Apsley Road
Monckton Rd
Kingsway
Shrublands Avenue
Lewis Rd
Oak Road
Elm Cft
Sunny Bank Road
Woodgreen Road
Woodgreen Cft
Ventnor Cl
Surg
A456
HAGLEY
Holly Bush Medical Ce
Binswood
A
B
C
D
123
399
400
Innkeeper's Lodge Hotel
A458
HAGLEY RD WEST
HAGLEY ROAD WEST
COLLEGE RD
PO
Victoria Av
Edenhall Road
Trevanie Avenue
Whitley Ct Rd
Beverley Ct Rd
Grayswood Pk Rd
Lyncourt Gv
Clydesdale Rd
Ridgacre Lane
Green Lane
Birdlip Gv
Daventry Gv
Quinton Lane
World's End Avenue
Surgery
Beech Av
White Road
1
SPIES LANE
Spies Cl
Astley Av
Bissell St
High St
Quinton CE Primary School
Stoney La
Ridgacre Rd W
Meadow Rd
Wilmington Road
Ridgacre Rd
Ridgacre
Quinton
Chichester Dr
Jackson Wy
A456
Bent Av
Glyn Farm Road
Glynside Av
Glyn Road
Surgery
Goodrest Av
Howley Grange Road
Parkfield Cl
M5
St Davids Dr
Clewley Gv
Stourton Road
Warple Road
Quinton Rd W
Higgins Lane
Lunt Gv
Max Road
World's End Lane
Upr Meadow
Lower White Road
EXPRESSWAY
2
Stuart Road
Howley Grange Primary School
Seven Acres Rd
Surg
Surgery
Dwellings La
Bramcot Rd
Plimsoll Gv
Hansom Road
Arkwright Rd
Wedgewood Rd
Faraday Av
Fleming Road
World's End La
Royal Oak Road
King Charles Road
Quinton Business Park
Four Dwellings High Sch
Four Dwellings Junior Sch
Four Dwellings Infant Sch
Pitman Road
Edison Gr
Gorsy Rd
Brookmans Avenue
Woodridge Av
Little Pk
Highfield
Rutters Meadow
Dimmingsdale Bank
Simmons
Middle Leasowe
Quinton
Bourne Avenue
Lydate Rd
Bournebrook Crs
Carter's
Barn Piece
Lane
Highfield
Four Acres
Six Acres
Drive
Mayswood Gv
QUINTON
3
Cra Road
Oaklands
Near Lands Cl
Gorsly Piece
Simmons Dr
139
Junction 3
Woodgate Valley
A456
Carter's
Lane
Lapal
4
Stanmore Gv
Marshwood Croft
Watery
Eldon Rd
Woodgate Valle
Tibbats Cl
Square Close
County Close
Upper Cl
Warston Av
Sommerfield
Rushy Piece
Gravel Bar
Bean Cft
Sommerfield Rd
Bark Piece
Ox Leasow
Nonsuch Primary School
Stevens Av
Plough Av
Forecraft Cl
Simcox Gdns
Little Hi Wy
Woodgate Valley Health Centre
Ralphs Meadow
Glen Side
Stonehou
Gleads Cft
Lane
283
Lye Close Lane
Heath Rd
Woodgate Lane
Works
Woodgate Business Park
5
M5
Parkfield
Lye Avenue
Tyndall Wk
Woodgate Gdns
Fallow Walk
Allwood Gdns
Primrose Woods
Elmwoods
Bartley Woods
Woodgate Business Pk
Birchwoods
Poplarwoods
Clapgate Lane
B32
Parkside
Clover Dr
Brook Wk
399
400
oodgate
Lyeclose Farm
Woodgate Business Park
Ambleside
157
Smiths
Flavell Cl
Broadhidley Dr
Adams
Old Crown Cl
Clent View Road
Wd Rd
Lane
Woodgate Dr
Hill
Hightree Cl
Elmcroft Av
Drive
Wood
Carmel Gv
Littley Gv
Woodgate Primary
Bartley Green Technology College
The Knoll
Bartley Green FC
Dainton Gv
Green Dr
Jiggins Lane
Modbury Av
Kingsbridge
Road
Tamerto
1 grid square represents 500 metres

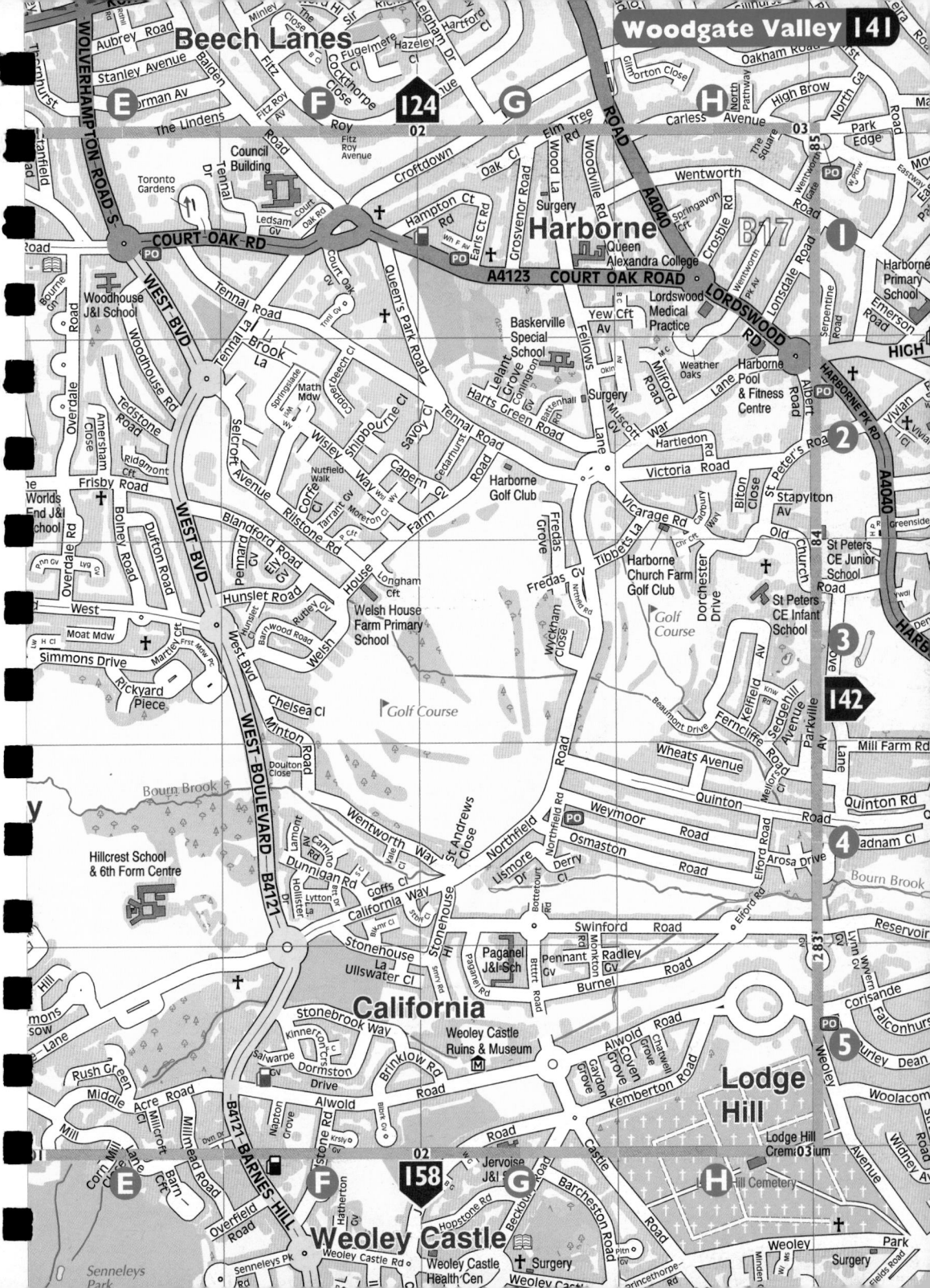
Beech Lanes
Harborne
California
Lodge Hill
Weoley Castle
WOLVERHAMPTON ROAD S
COURT OAK RD
A4123 COURT OAK ROAD
A4040
LORDSWOOD RD
HARBORNE PK RD
WEST BVD
WEST BOULEVARD B4121
B4121 BARNES HILL
Council Building
Toronto Gardens
Queen Alexandra College
Lordswood Medical Practice
Baskerville Special School
Harborne Pool & Fitness Centre
Harborne Primary School
Woodhouse J&I School
Worlds End J&I School
Harborne Golf Club
Harborne Church Farm Golf Club
St Peters CE Junior School
St Peters CE Infant School
Welsh House Farm Primary School
Golf Course
Bourn Brook
Hillcrest School & 6th Form Centre
Paganel J&I Sch
Weoley Castle Ruins & Museum
Lodge Hill Crematorium
Lodge Hill Cemetery
Jervoise J&I S
Weoley Castle Health Cen
Surgery
Senneleys Park
B17
124
142
158
02
03

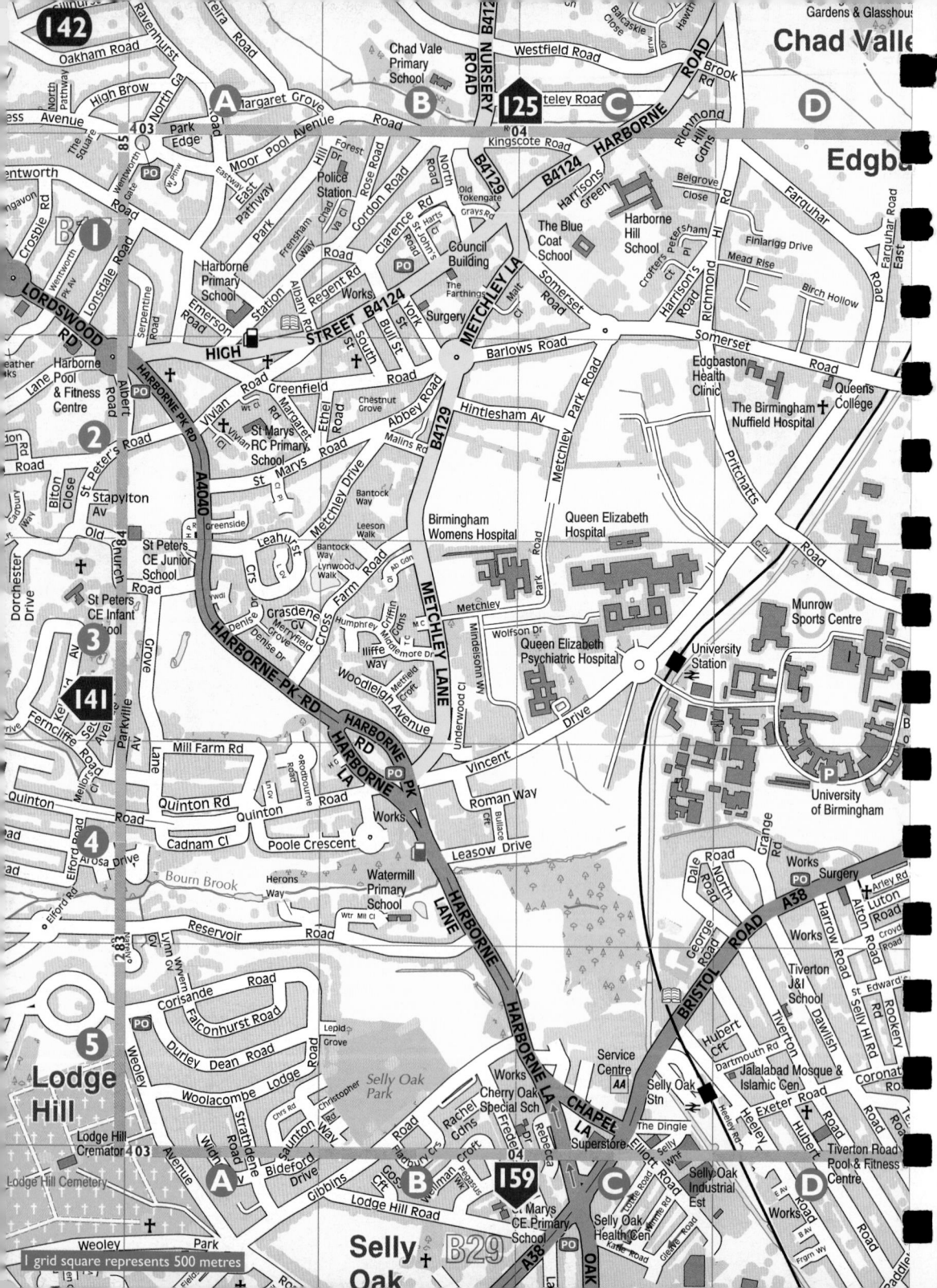

142
125
141
159
Chad Valley
Edgbaston
Lodge Hill
Selly Oak
B29
A
B
C
D
1
2
3
4
5
Oakham Road
High Brow
Margaret Grove
Westfield Road
Chad Vale Primary School
NURSERY ROAD
B4129
Moor Pool Avenue
Park Edge
The Square
Police Station
Gordon Road
Rose Road
Clarence Rd
Old Tokengate
HARBORNE ROAD
B4124
Richmond Hill Cdns
Harrisons Green
Belgrove Close
Farquhar Road
The Blue Coat School
Harborne Hill School
Finlarigg Drive
Mead Rise
Birch Hollow
Council Building
The Farthings
Harborne Primary School
HIGH STREET B4124
LORDSWOOD RD
Lonsdale Road
Crosbie Rd
Harborne Pool & Fitness Centre
Albert Road
HARBORNE PK RD
A4040
Surgery
METCHLEY LA
Somerset Road
Barlows Road
Metchley Park Road
Edgbaston Health Clinic
The Birmingham Nuffield Hospital
Queens College
Greenfield
Chestnut Grove
Abbey Road
Hintlesham Av
Malins Rd
St Marys RC Primary School
St Marys Road
St Peter's Road
Stapylton Av
Biton Close
Metchley Drive
Bantock Way
Leeson Walk
Pritchatts Road
Birmingham Womens Hospital
Queen Elizabeth Hospital
St Peters CE Junior School
Leahurst Crs
Lynwood Walk
Cross Farm Road
METCHLEY LANE
St Peters CE Infant School
Dorchester Drive
Church Road
Grasdene Gv
Merryfield Grove
Denise Dr
Humphrey
Griffin Gdns
Middlemore Dr
Iliffe Way
Woodleigh Avenue
Metfield Croft
Underwood Cl
Mendelssohn Wy
Wolfson Dr
Queen Elizabeth Psychiatric Hospital
Munrow Sports Centre
University Station
University of Birmingham
Vincent Drive
Grove Lane
Parkville Av
Ferncliffe Road
Mill Farm Rd
Quinton Rd
Quinton Road
Rodbourne Road
HARBORNE RD
HARBORNE LA
Roman Way
Bullace Cft
Leasow Drive
Works
Cadnam Cl
Poole Crescent
Arosa Drive
Elford Road
Bourn Brook
Herons Way
Watermill Primary School
HARBORNE LANE
Reservoir Road
Wtr Mll Cl
Dale Road
North Road
Grange Rd
George Road
BRISTOL ROAD A38
Surgery
Arley Rd
Luton Road
Alton Road
Harrow Road
Tiverton J&I School
St Edward's Rd
Selly Hl Rd
Rookery Rd
Dawlish Rd
Corisande Road
Falconhurst Road
Durley Dean Road
Lodge Road
Lepid Grove
Selly Oak Park
Weoley Avenue
Woolacombe Lodge
Strathdene Road
Christopher Way
Saunton Way
Cherry Oak Special Sch
Rachel Gdns
Service Centre
Selly Oak Stn
Hubert Cft
Dartmouth Rd
Jalalabad Mosque & Islamic Cen
Exeter Road
Tiverton Road
Hubert Road
Heeley Rd
CHAPEL LA
The Dingle
Superstore
Elliott Road
Selly Oak Industrial Est
Tiverton Road Pool & Fitness Centre
Lodge Hill Crematorium
Lodge Hill Cemetery
Bideford Drive
Gibbins
Lodge Hill Road
Flaxbury Crs
Wellman Croft
St Marys CE Primary School
Selly Oak Health Cen
Gleave Road
Katie Road
A38
OAK
Weoley Park
1 grid square represents 500 metres

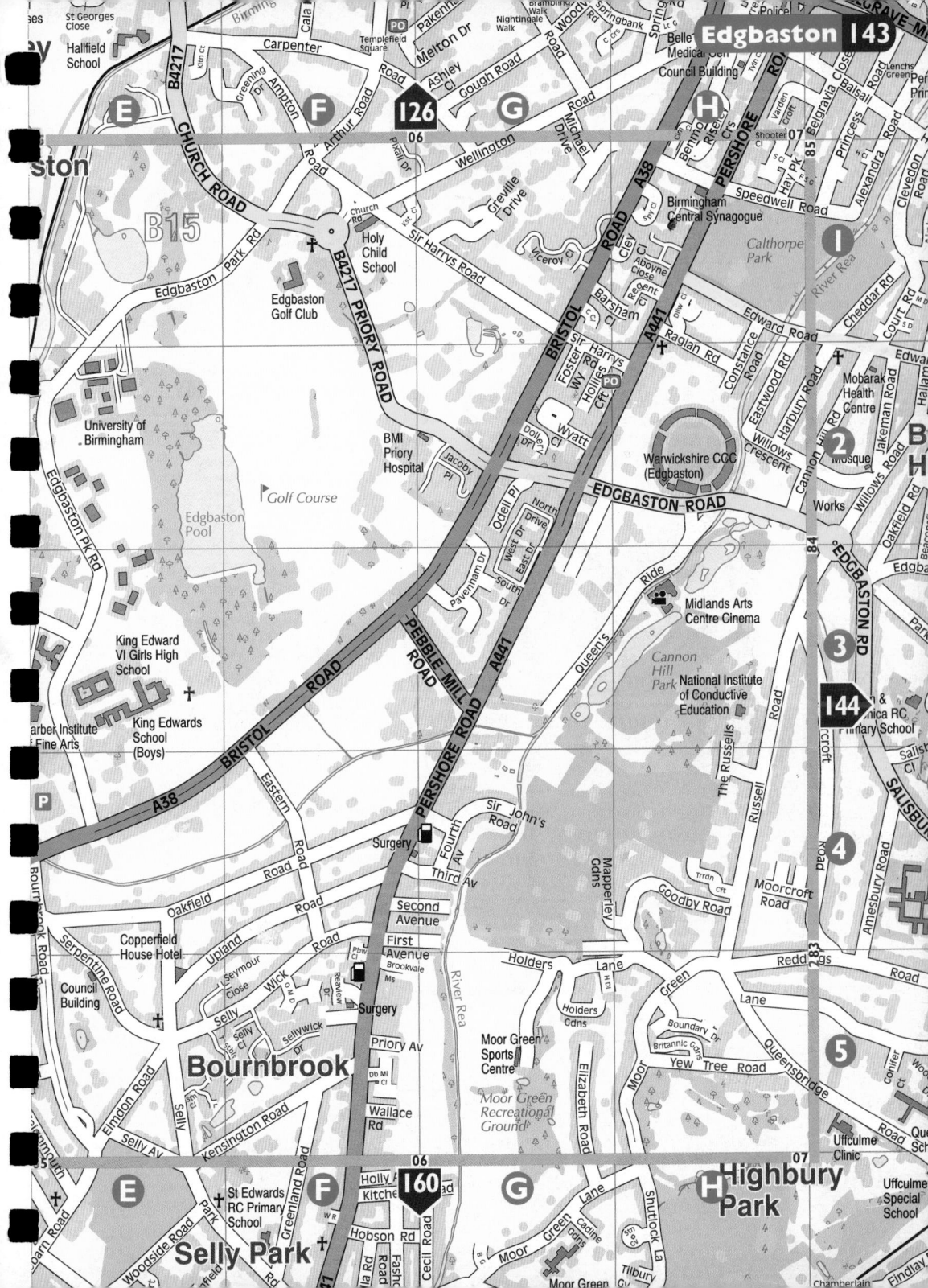
St Georges Close
Hallfield School
Carpenter Road
Templefield Square
Melton Dr
Pakenham
Nightingale Walk
Springbank
Belle Vue Medical Centre
Council Building
Greening Dr
Ampton Road
Arthur Road
Ashley Cl
Gough Road
Michael Drive
B4217
CHURCH ROAD
Wellington Road
Pixall Dr
Benmore
Risely Crs
PERSHORE ROAD
Shooter Cl
Varden Croft
Belgravia Close
Balsall
Princess Road
Alexandra Road
Clevedon Road
Hay Pk
Speedwell Road
Birmingham Central Synagogue
Greville Drive
Church Rd
Holy Child School
Sir Harrys Road
B15
Edgbaston Park Rd
Edgbaston Golf Club
B4217 PRIORY ROAD
Viceroy Cl
Cley Cl
Aboyne Close
Regent Cl
Barsham Cl
Calthorpe Park
River Rea
Cheddar Rd
Court Rd
Edward Road
Raglan Rd
Constance Road
Eastwood Rd
Harbury Road
Sir Harrys Rd
Foster Wy
Hollies Cft
BRISTOL ROAD
A38
A441
Mobarak Health Centre
Jakeman Road
Cannon Hill Rd
Mosque
Willows Road
Willows Crescent
University of Birmingham
BMI Priory Hospital
Wyatt Cl
Dollery Dr
Jacoby Pl
Warwickshire CCC (Edgbaston)
EDGBASTON ROAD
Works
Oakfield Rd
Golf Course
Edgbaston Pool
Edgbaston Pk Rd
Odell Pl
North Drive
West Dr
East Dr
South Dr
Pavenham Dr
EDGBASTON RD
Queen's Ride
Midlands Arts Centre Cinema
King Edward VI Girls High School
King Edwards School (Boys)
Barber Institute of Fine Arts
PEBBLE MILL ROAD
Cannon Hill Park
National Institute of Conductive Education
The Russells
Russell Road
144
SALISBURY
Salisbury Cl
BRISTOL ROAD
A38
Eastern Road
PERSHORE ROAD
Sir John's Road
Fourth Av
Third Av
Surgery
Mapperley Gdns
Moorcroft Road
Goodby Road
Amesbury Road
Oakfield Road
Second Avenue
First Avenue
Upland Road
Copperfield House Hotel
Serpentine Road
Bournbrook Road
Council Building
Seymour Close
Wick
Brookvale Ms
Reaview Dr
Surgery
River Rea
Holders Lane
Holders Gdns
Green Lane
Reddings Road
Boundary Dr
Britannic Gdns
Yew Tree Road
Queensbridge Road
Selly Cl
Sellywick Dr
Priory Av
Moor Green Sports Centre
Elizabeth Road
Moor Green Lane
Bournbrook
Elmdon Road
Selly Road
Kensington Road
Wallace Rd
Moor Green Recreational Ground
Uffculme Clinic
Selly Av
St Edwards RC Primary School
Greenland Road
160
Holly Rd
Kitchener Road
Highbury Park
Shutlock La
Uffculme Special School
Woodside Road
Park Rd
Hobson Rd
Cecil Road
Selly Park
Moor Green Lane
Cadine Gdns
Tilbury Gv
Moor Green
Chamberlain
Findlay Rd
126
06
07

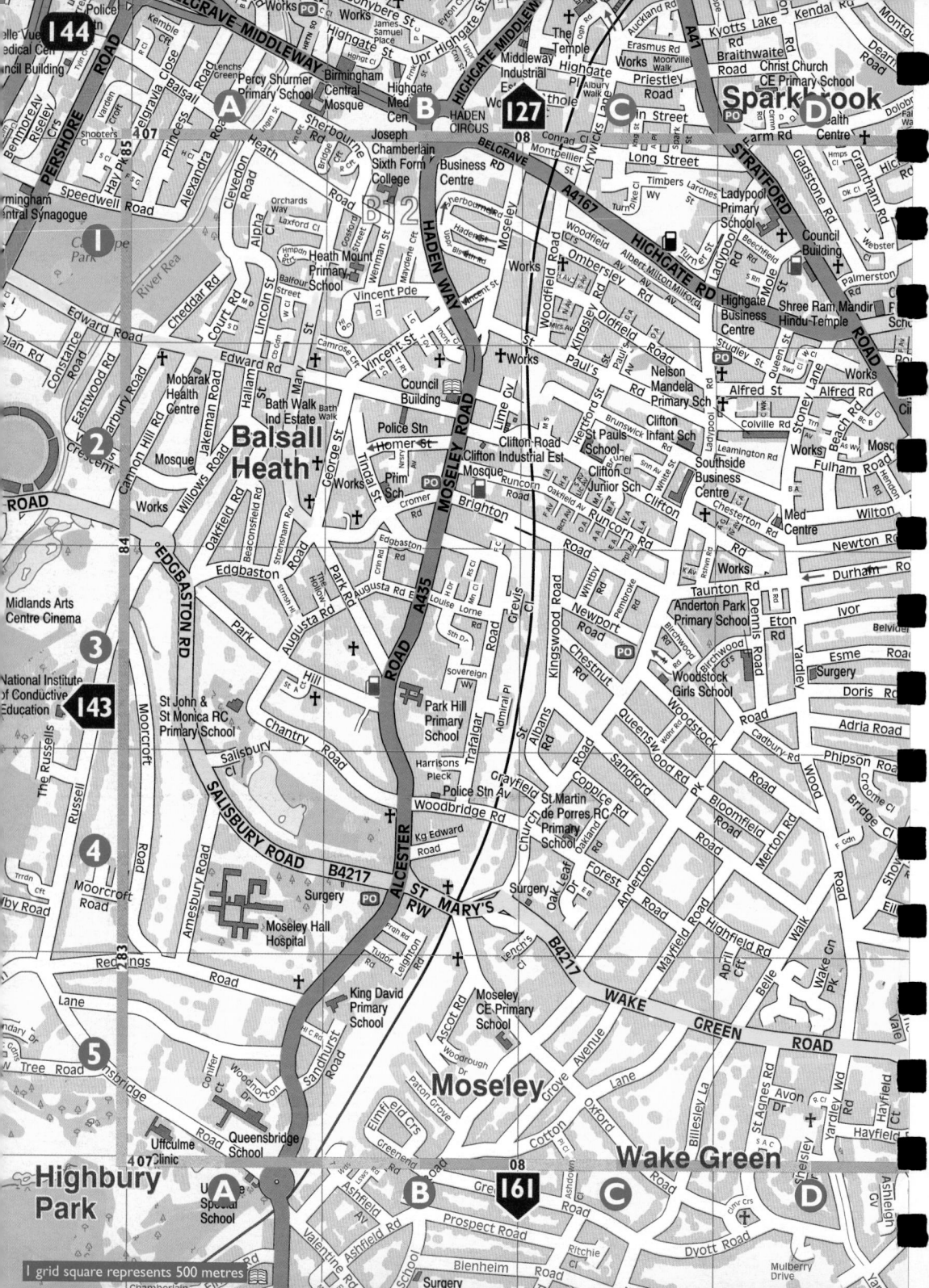
144
127
143
161
Balsall Heath
Sparkbrook
Moseley
Wake Green
Highbury Park
B12
BELGRAVE MIDDLEWAY
HIGHGATE MIDDLEWAY
PERSHORE ROAD
HADEN WAY
MOSELEY ROAD
ALCESTER ROAD
A435
EDGBASTON RD
SALISBURY ROAD
B4217
ST MARY'S RW
WAKE GREEN ROAD
HIGHGATE RD
A4167
STRATFORD ROAD
A41
Birmingham Central Mosque
Percy Shurmer Primary School
Joseph Chamberlain Sixth Form College
Heath Mount Primary School
Mobarak Health Centre
Bath Walk Ind Estate
Council Building
Police Stn
Clifton Industrial Est
Clifton Infant Sch
Clifton Junior Sch
Nelson Mandela Primary Sch
Ladypool Primary School
Christ Church CE Primary School
Shree Ram Mandir Hindu Temple
Anderton Park Primary School
Woodstock Girls School
Park Hill Primary School
St John & St Monica RC Primary School
St Martin de Porres RC Primary School
Moseley Hall Hospital
King David Primary School
Moseley CE Primary School
Queensbridge School
Uffculme Clinic
Midlands Arts Centre Cinema
National Institute of Conductive Education
Birmingham Central Synagogue
Southside Business Centre
Highgate Business Centre
Middleway Industrial Est
1 grid square represents 500 metres

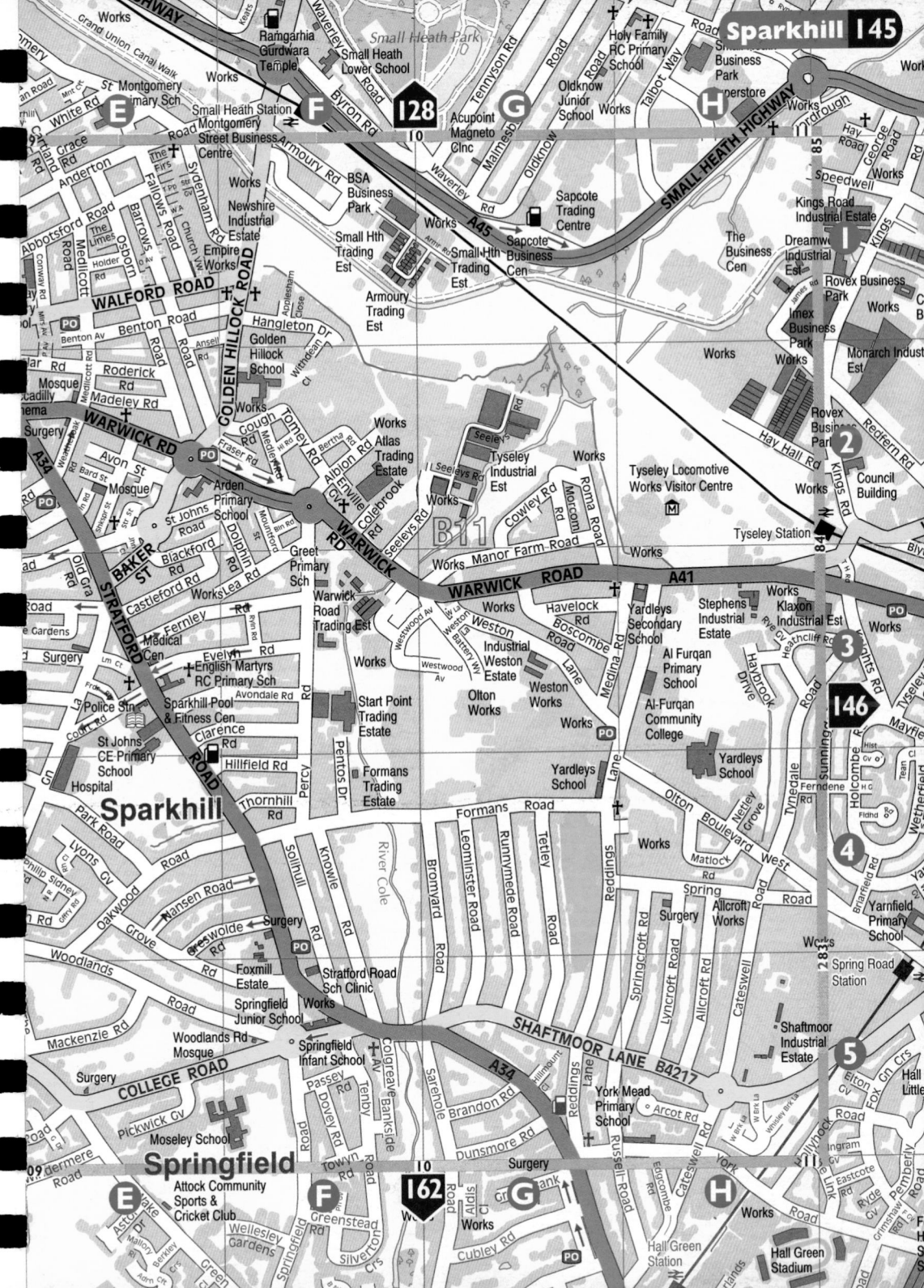
Small Heath Park
Ramgarhia Gurdwara Temple
Small Heath Lower School
Holy Family RC Primary School
Small Heath Business Park
Montgomery Primary Sch
Small Heath Station
Montgomery Street Business Centre
Acupoint Magneto Clnc
Oldknow Junior School
SMALL HEATH HIGHWAY
BSA Business Park
Newshire Industrial Estate
Empire Works
Sapcote Trading Centre
Small Hth Trading Est
Sapcote Business Cen
The Business Cen
Kings Road Industrial Estate
Rovex Business Park
Imex Business Park
Monarch Industrial Est
WALFORD ROAD
GOLDEN HILLOCK ROAD
Golden Hillock School
Armoury Trading Est
WARWICK RD
Atlas Trading Estate
Tyseley Industrial Est
Tyseley Locomotive Works Visitor Centre
Council Building
Tyseley Station
Arden Primary School
Greet Primary Sch
Warwick Road Trading Est
WARWICK ROAD
A41
Yardleys Secondary School
Stephens Industrial Estate
Klaxon Industrial Est
STRATFORD ROAD
Medical Cen
English Martyrs RC Primary Sch
Police Stn
Sparkhill Pool & Fitness Cen
St Johns CE Primary School
Hospital
Industrial Weston Estate
Weston Works
Olton Works
Start Point Trading Estate
Al Furqan Primary School
Al-Furqan Community College
Yardleys School
Formans Trading Estate
Sparkhill
Olton Boulevard West
River Cole
Surgery
Allcroft Works
Yarnfield Primary School
Spring Road Station
Foxmill Estate
Stratford Road Sch Clinic
Springfield Junior School
SHAFTMOOR LANE B4217
Shaftmoor Industrial Estate
Woodlands Rd Mosque
Springfield Infant School
COLLEGE ROAD
Moseley School
York Mead Primary School
Springfield
Attock Community Sports & Cricket Club
Hall Green Station
Hall Green Stadium
128
146
162
B11
A34
A45

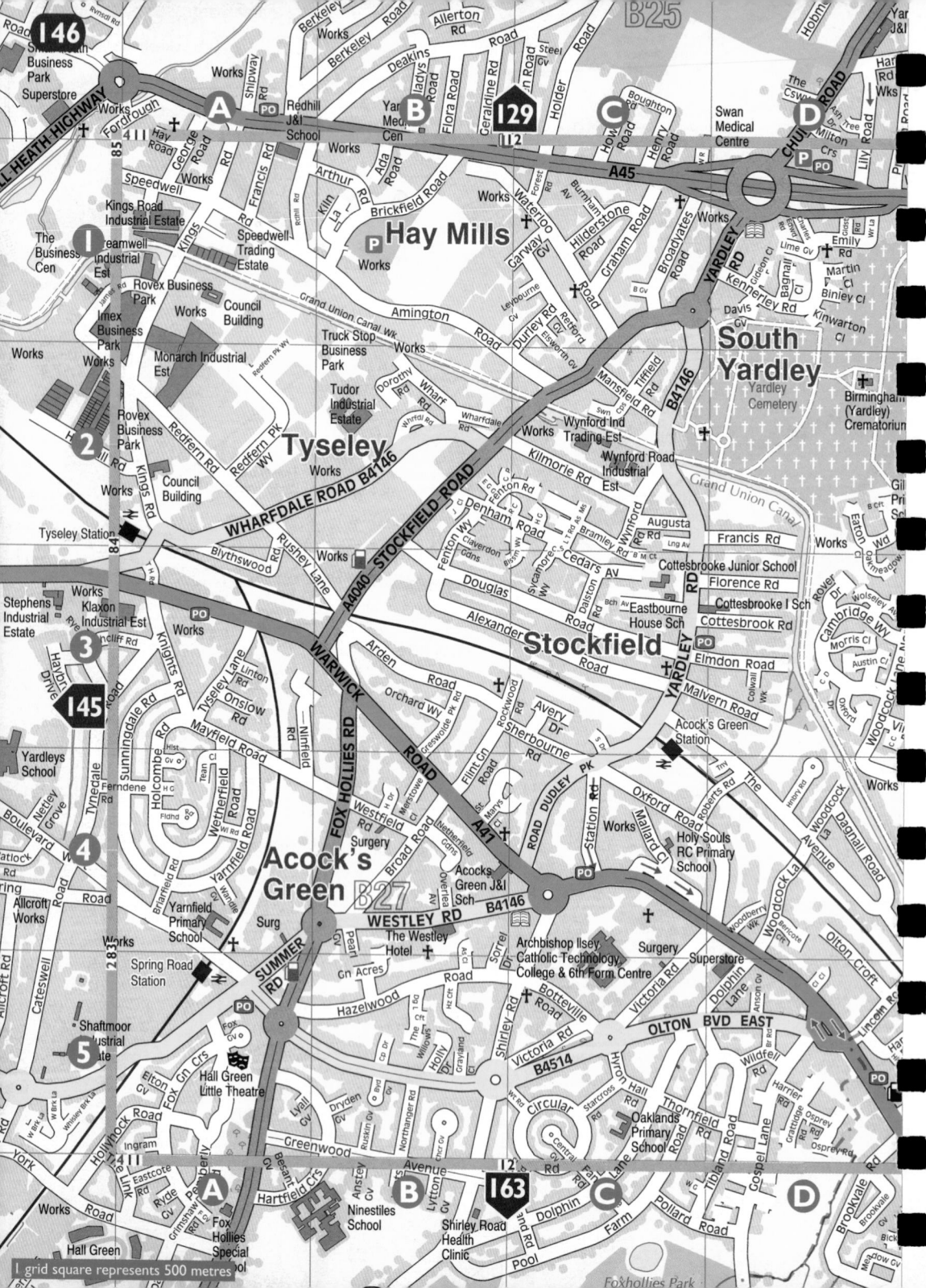
146
129
145
163
B25
B27
A
B
C
D
1
2
3
4
5
85
84
83
411
412
Hay Mills
Tyseley
South Yardley
Stockfield
Acock's Green
Small Heath Business Park
Superstore
Small Heath Highway
Fordrough
Hay Road
George Road
Works
Shipway Rd
Redhill J&I School
Berkeley Road
Allerton Rd
Deakins Road
Gladys Road
Flora Road
Geraldine Rd
Holder Road
Steel Gv
Boughton Rd
Howard Road
Henry Road
Swan Medical Centre
Church Road
Ash Tree Rd
Milton Crs
Lily Rd
A45
Speedwell Rd
Francis Rd
Arthur Rd
Ada Road
Brickfield Road
Kiln La
Kings Road Industrial Estate
Kings Rd
Speedwell Trading Estate
The Business Cen
Creamwell Industrial Est
Rovex Business Park
Imex Business Park
Council Building
Monarch Industrial Est
Grand Union Canal Wk
Amington Road
Truck Stop Business Park
Tudor Industrial Estate
Dorothy Rd
Wharf Rd
Wharfdale Rd
Redfern Pk Wy
Redfern Rd
Waterloo Rd
Garway Gv
Hilderstone Road
Graham Road
Broadyates Road
Burnham Av
Forest Rd
Leybourne Gv
Durley Rd
Retford Gv
Elsworth Gv
Mansfield Rd
Tiffield Rd
Yardley Rd
B4146
Kennerley Rd
Gideon Cl
Bagnall Cl
Davis Gv
Emily Rd
Lime Gv
Martin Cl
Binley Cl
Kinwarton Cl
Yardley Cemetery
Birmingham (Yardley) Crematorium
Wynford Ind Trading Est
Wynford Road Industrial Est
Kilmorie Rd
Grand Union Canal
Wharfdale Road B4146
Stockfield Road
A4040
Tyseley Station
Blythswood Rd
Rushey Lane
Fenton Rd
Denham Road
Fenton Wy
Claverdon Gdns
Sycamore Wy
Bramley Rd
Cedars Av
Wynford Rd
Augusta Rd
Francis Rd
Douglas Road
Dalston Rd
Cottesbrooke Junior School
Florence Rd
Cottesbrooke I Sch
Cottesbrook Rd
Eastbourne House Sch
Alexander Road
Elmdon Road
Malvern Road
Colwall Wk
Cambridge Wy
Morris Cl
Austin Cl
Rover Dr
Wolseley Av
Oakmeadow
Eaton Wd
Stephens Industrial Estate
Klaxon Industrial Est
Ryecliff Rd
Haybridge Drive
Knights Rd
Tyseley Lane
Linton Rd
Onslow Rd
Warwick Road
A41
Arden Road
Orchard Wy
Greswolde Pk Rd
Rockwood Rd
Avery Dr
Sherbourne Rd
Acock's Green Station
Dudley Pk Road
Station Rd
Oxford Road
Roberts Rd
Mallard Cl
Holy Souls RC Primary School
The Avenue
Woodcock La
Dagnall Road
Olton Croft
Woodcock Lane
Yardleys School
Tynedale Rd
Sunningdale Rd
Holcombe Rd
Mayfield Road
Ninfield Rd
Fox Hollies Rd
Flint Gn Road
Wetherfield Road
Yarnfield Road
Briarfield Rd
Netley Grove
Boulevard
Westfield Rd
Merstowe Cl
Broad Road
Netherfield Gdns
St Marys Cl
Surgery
Acocks Green J&I Sch
Overlea Av
Allcroft Works
Road
Yarnfield Primary School
Westley Rd
The Westley Hotel
Archbishop Ilsley Catholic Technology College & 6th Form Centre
Surgery
Superstore
Woodberry Wk
Bericote Cft
Spring Road Station
Summer Rd
Surg
Pearl Gv
Gn Acres
Hazelwood Road
Botteville Road
Victoria Rd
Dolphin Lane
Anson Gv
Olton Bvd East
Lincoln Rd
Cateswell Road
Allcroft Rd
Shaftmoor Industrial Estate
Fox Gn Crs
Fox Gv
Hall Green Little Theatre
Shirley Rd
Victoria Rd
B4514
Hyron Hall Rd
Wildfell Rd
Thornfield Rd
Harrier Rd
Osprey Rd
Elton Gv
Lyall Gv
Dryden Gv
Ruskin Gv
Northanger Rd
Holly Dr
Grayland Cl
Circular Rd
Starcross Rd
Oaklands Primary School
Tilsland Road
Gospel Lane
Hollyhock Road
Ingram
Greenwood Avenue
York Road
The Link
Eastcote Rd
Ryde Gv
Pemberley Rd
Grimshaw Rd
Besant Gv
Hartfield Crs
Anstey Gv
Ninestiles School
Lytton Gv
Shirley Road Health Clinic
Pool Farm Rd
Dolphin Rd
Pollard Road
Brookvale Rd
Works Road
Hall Green
Fox Hollies Special School
Foxhollies Park
1 grid square represents 500 metres

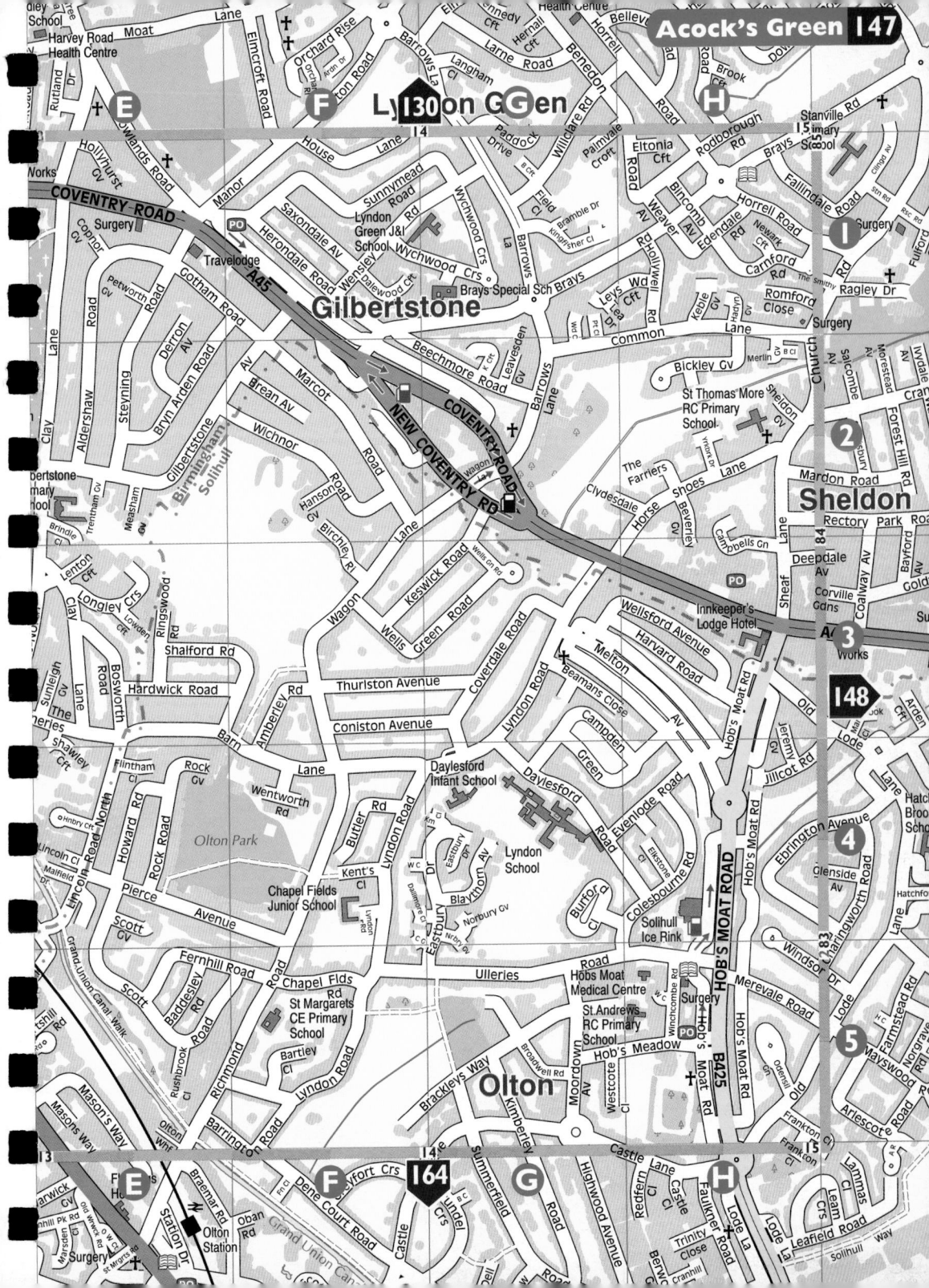
Lyndon Green
Gilbertstone
Sheldon
Olton
COVENTRY ROAD
A45
NEW COVENTRY RD
HOB'S MOAT ROAD
B425
Olton Park
Lyndon School
Chapel Fields Junior School
Daylesford Infant School
Solihull Ice Rink
Hobs Moat Medical Centre
St Andrews RC Primary School
St Margarets CE Primary School
St Thomas More RC Primary School
Lyndon Green J&I School
Brays Special Sch
Innkeeper's Lodge Hotel
Travelodge
Olton Station
Grand Union Canal
Birmingham
Solihull
130
148
164

148
131
147
165
A
B
C
D
1
2
3
4
5
Sheldon
Elms Farm Primary School
Stanville Primary School
Surgery
Council Building
Mapledene J&I School
Sheldon Country Park
Golf Course
Hatchford Brook Golf Club
Marston Green Infant School
Thomas More C Primary School
Innkeeper's Lodge Hotel
Works
Hatchford Brook Primary School
Valley Infant School
Elmdon Park
A45
B26
B425
HOB'S MOAT ROAD
Downsfield Road
Tallington Rd
Chaffcombe Road
Doncliffe Av
Hazeldene
Wakeman Gv
Rodborough Rd
Brays Rd
Fallindale Road
Horrell Road
Edendale Rd
Carnford Rd
The Smithy
Ragley Dr
Romford Close
Fulford Gv
Church Rd
Greenvale Av
Mapledene Road
Silvermere Rd
Parkdale Road
Berryfield Road
Park Road
Cranes Park Road
Whitecroft Road
Salcombe Av
Morestead Av
Ivydale Av
Shaftsbury Rd
Forest Hill Rd
Warmington Rd
Dovercourt Road
Normanton Av
Shepheard Rd
Mardon Road
Olorenshaw Road
Arden Oak Rd
June Cft
Ann Cft
Sheldonfield Road
Rectory Park Road
Deepdale Av
Bayford Av
Trysull Av
Goldthorne Av
Coalway Av
Corville Gdns
Sheaf Lane
Campbells Gn
Coventry Rd
Bantry Cl
The Gld
Wells Rd
Valley Road
Arden Cft
Rangoon Road
Croft Down Rd
Glencroft Rd
Hillside Cft
Victor Rd
Irving Rd
Goodway Rd
Langley Rl
Walford Dr
Eden Road
Streamside Wy
Quinton Cl
Studley Cft
Gaydon Rd
Ventnor Road
Meriden Rl
Springfield Crescent
Mountjoy Crs
Hatchford Brook Rd
Tanford Rd
Hatchford Av
Fallowfield Road
Elmdon Pk Road
Elmdon Cl
Wolverley Rd
Lode Lane
Maribrook Cl
Jeremy Gv
Jillcot Rd
Hob's Moat Rd
Glenside Av
Charingworth Road
Windsor Dr
Merevale Road
Farmstead Rd
Norgrave Rd
Linsey Rd
Tanhouse Farm Road
Cophams Close
Mayswood Road
Arlescote Road
Old Rd
Frankton Cl
Lammas Cl
Leam Crs
Leafield Road
Damson Parkway
Main Rd
Solihull Way
Faulkner Rd
1 grid square represents 500 metres

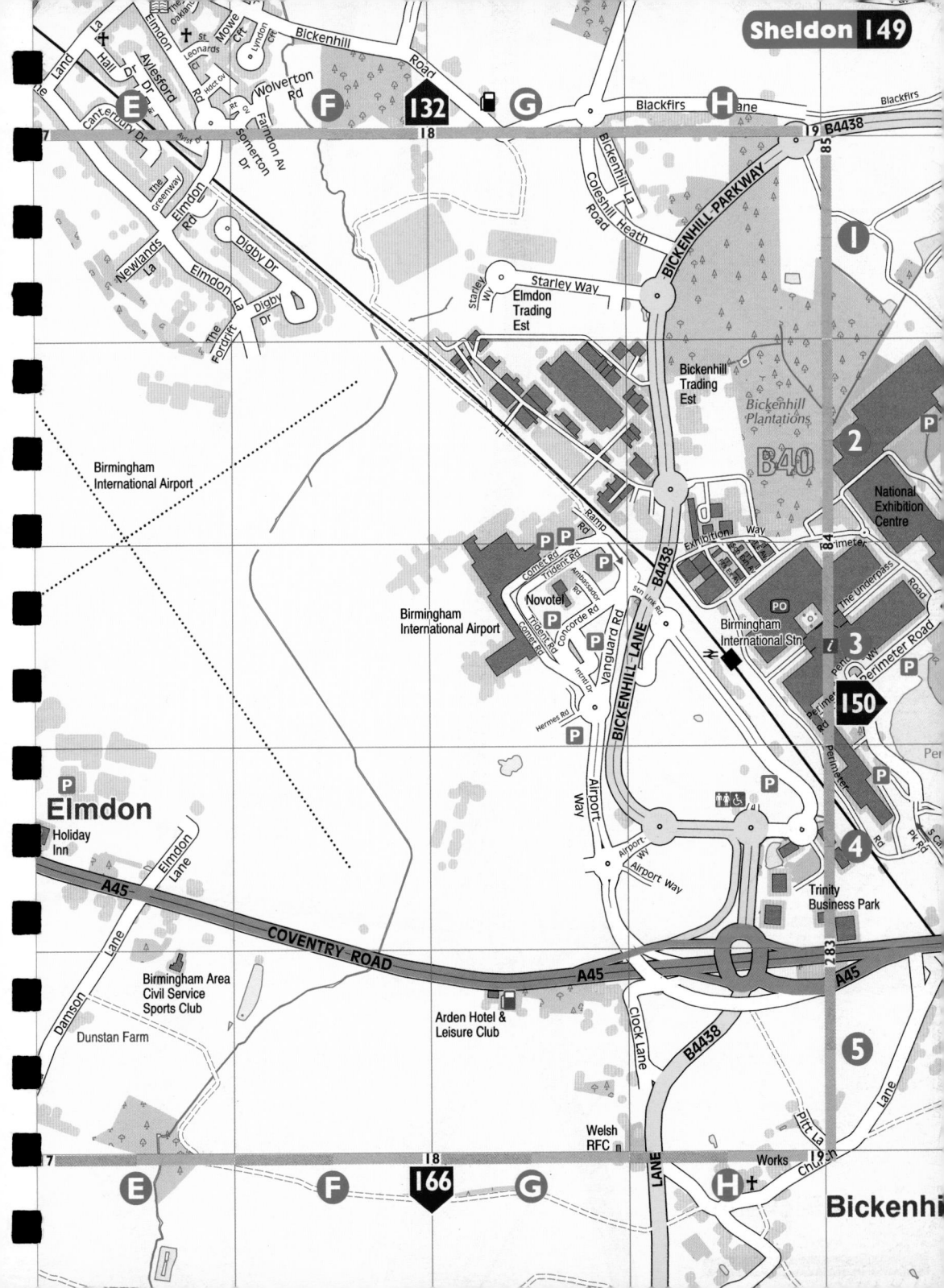
132
150
166
Bickenhill Road
Blackfirs Lane
Wolverton Rd
Aylesford Dr
Hall Dr
Canterbury Dr
Elmdon Rd
Farndon Av
Somerton Dr
The Greenway
Newlands La
Elmdon La
Digby Dr
The Fordrift
Bickenhill La
Coleshill Heath Road
BICKENHILL PARKWAY
B4438
Starley Way
Elmdon Trading Est
Bickenhill Trading Est
Bickenhill Plantations
Birmingham International Airport
Exhibition Way
National Exhibition Centre
Perimeter Road
The Underpass
Ramp Rd
Comet Rd
Trident Rd
Ambassador Rd
Novotel
Concorde Rd
Vanguard Rd
BICKENHILL LANE
Stn Link Rd
Birmingham International Stn
Hermes Rd
Airport Way
Trinity Business Park
Elmdon
Holiday Inn
Elmdon Lane
A45
COVENTRY ROAD
Birmingham Area Civil Service Sports Club
Damson Lane
Dunstan Farm
Arden Hotel & Leisure Club
Clock Lane
Pitt La
Welsh RFC
Works
Church
Bickenhi

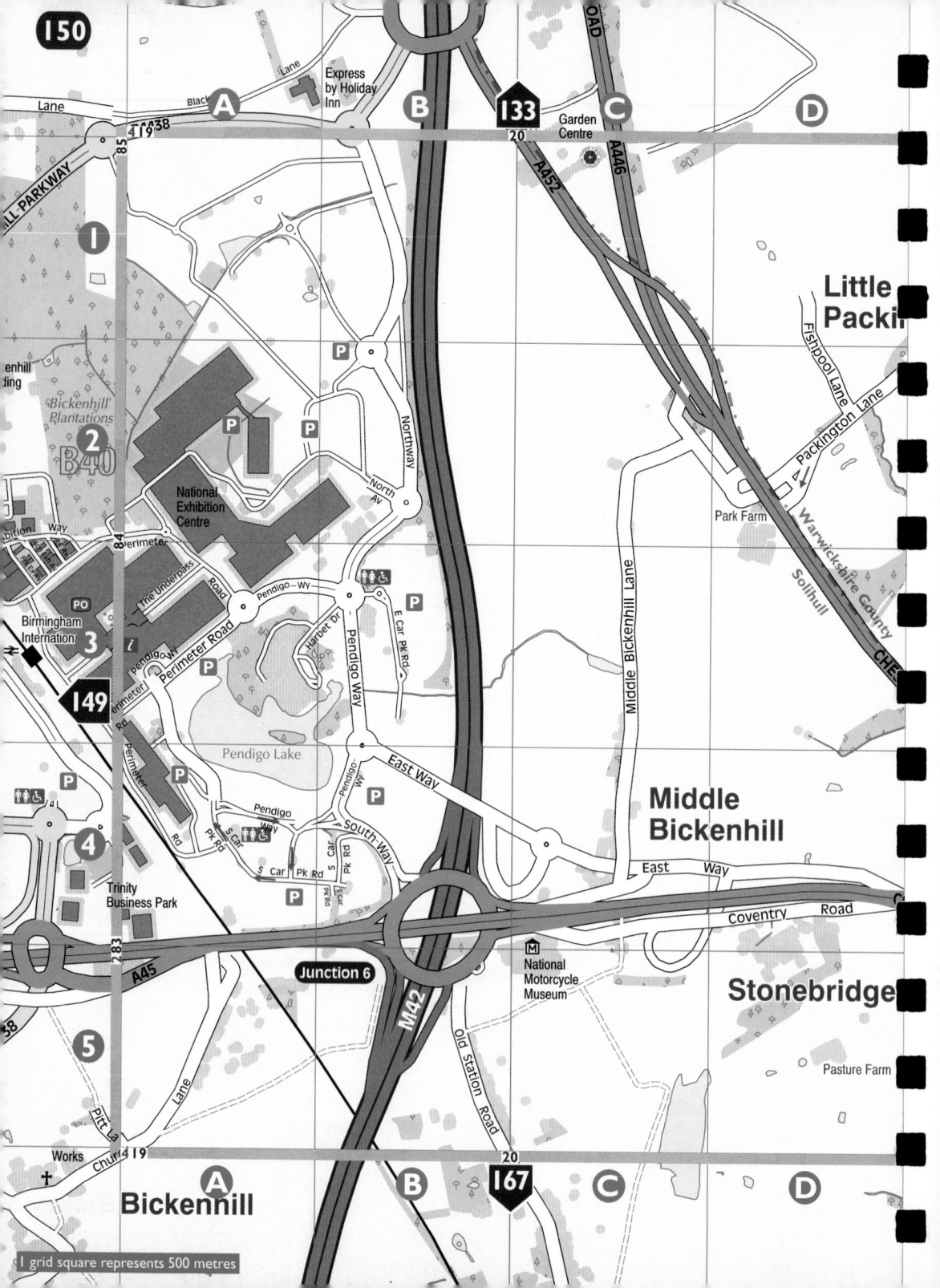

150

A

B

133
20

C

D

Lane

Lane
Black

Express
by Holiday
Inn

OAD

Garden
Centre

Little
Packi

HILL PARKWAY

85
41 938

A452

A446

Fishpool Lane

Packington Lane

I

*Bickenhill
Plantations*

enhill
ding

2
B40

P

P

P

Northway

North
Av

Warwickshire County

Park Farm

Solihull

CHE

National
Exhibition
Centre

bition Way

84

Perimeter

The Underpass

Perimeter Road

Road

Pendigo Wy

Harbet Dr

Pendigo Way

Middle Bickenhill Lane

PO

Birmingham
International

3
i

Pendigow

Perimeter

E Car Pk Rd

P

P

149

Rd

Perimeter
Rd

P

Pendigo Lake

Pendigo
Way

Pendigo
W'y

East Way

P

P

Middle
Bickenhill

4

S Car
Pk Rd

S Car Pk Rd

South Way

S Car Pk Rd

East   Way

Coventry   Road

C

Trinity
Business Park

P

283

A45

Junction 6

M42

National
Motorcycle
Museum

M

Stonebridge

5

58

Pitt La

Chu 419

Lane

Old Station Road

Pasture Farm

Works

✝

A

Bickenhill

B

167
20

C

D

I grid square represents 500 metres

of Arden Hotel
Golf & Country Club
E
F
G
H
21
22
23
85
I
gton
River Blythe
Packington Park
2
84
Packington
Hall
Hall Pool
Great Pool
3
The
Dec
ROAD
The Mill
Farm
4
BIRMINGHAM
ROAD
OVENTRY ROAD
Shepher
283
KENILWORTH
Geary's
Heath
5
BIRMINGHAM
Golf Course
Road
ROAD
Warwickshire County
21
22
23
E
F
G
H
Stonebridge
Golf Club
The Somers
Somers

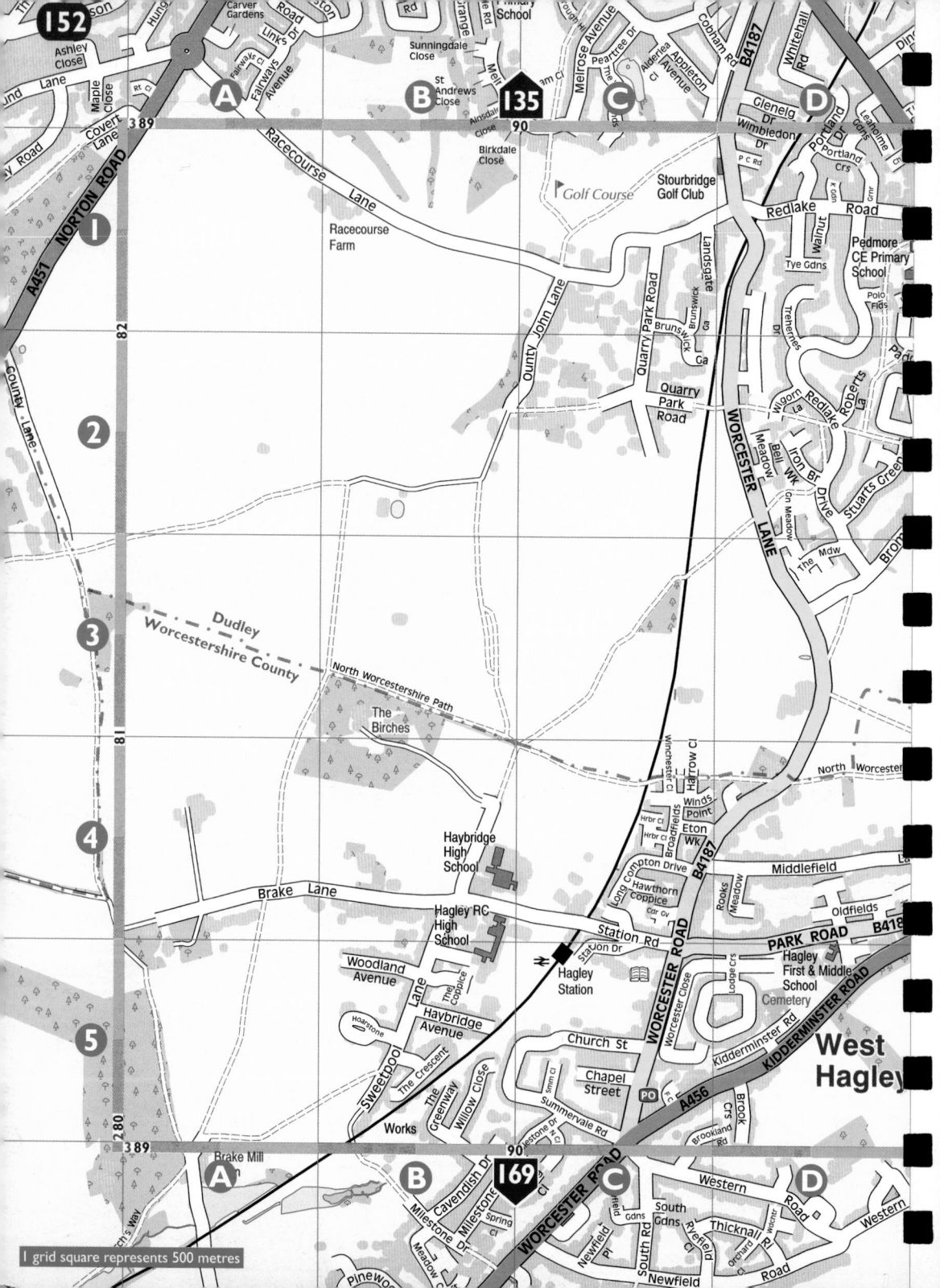

152
135
169
A
B
C
D
1
2
3
4
5
389
90
82
81
280
Ashley Close
Maple Close
Covert Lane
NORTON ROAD
A451
County Lane
Carver Gardens
Links Dr
Fairways Avenue
Sunningdale Close
St Andrews Close
Ainsdale Close
Birkdale Close
Racecourse Lane
Racecourse Farm
Melrose Avenue
Peartree Dr
Alderlea Cl
Appleton Avenue
Cobham Rd
B4187
Whitehall Rd
Glenelg Dr
Wimbledon Dr
Portland Dr
Portland Crs
Leaholme Gdns
Golf Course
Stourbridge Golf Club
Redlake Road
Walnut
Pedmore CE Primary School
Tye Gdns
Polo Flds
Landsgate
Quarry Park Road
Brunswick Ga
County John Lane
Trehernes Dr
Wigorn La
Redlake
Roberts La
Meadow
Bell Wk
Iron Br
Drive
Stuarts Green
Gn Meadow
The Mdw
WORCESTER LANE
Dudley
Worcestershire County
North Worcestershire Path
The Birches
Winchester Cl
Harrow Cl
Winds Point
Broadfields
Eton Wk
Hrbr Cl
Haybridge High School
Long Compton Drive
Hawthorn Coppice
Cdr Gv
Middlefield
Rooks Meadow
Oldfields
Brake Lane
Hagley RC High School
Station Rd
Station Dr
PARK ROAD
Hagley Station
WORCESTER ROAD
Worcester Close
Lodge Crs
Hagley First & Middle School
Cemetery
KIDDERMINSTER ROAD
Kidderminster Rd
West Hagley
Woodland Avenue
Lane
The Coppice
Haybridge Avenue
Hoarstone
Sweetpool
The Crescent
The Greenway
Willow Close
Church St
Chapel Street
Smm Cl
Summervale Rd
PO
A456
Brook Crs
Brookland Rd
Works
Brake Mill
Milestone Dr
Cavendish Dr
Spring Cl
Western Road
South Gdns
South Rd
Newfield
Ryefield Cl
Thicknall Ri
Orchard Cl
Western
Road
Pinewood
Meadow
1 grid square represents 500 metres

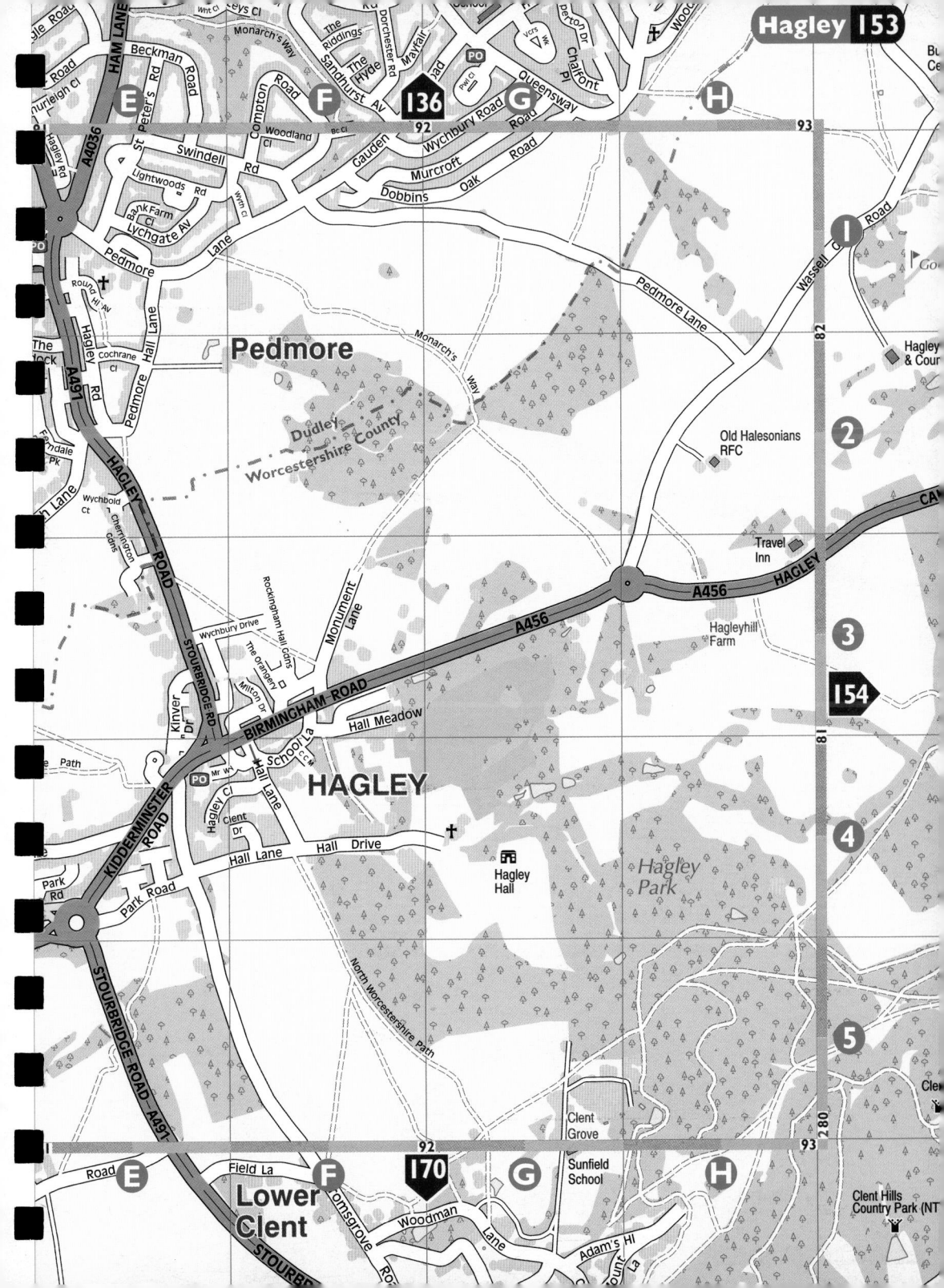
Pedmore
HAGLEY
Lower Clent
Hagley Park
Hagley Hall
Old Halesonians RFC
Travel Inn
Hagleyhill Farm
Clent Grove
Sunfield School
Clent Hills Country Park (NT
Dudley
Worcestershire County
Monarch's Way
North Worcestershire Path
HAM LANE
A4036
A491
HAGLEY ROAD
STOURBRIDGE RD
STOURBRIDGE ROAD
KIDDERMINSTER ROAD
BIRMINGHAM ROAD
A456
HAGLEY
Pedmore Lane
Pedmore Hall Lane
Wassell Road
Dobbins Oak Road
Murcroft
Wychbury Road
Queensway
Gauden Road
Swindell Rd
Lightwoods Rd
Bank Farm Cl
Lychgate Av
Woodland Cl
Compton Road
Sandhurst Av
Beckman Road
St Peter's Rd
Hagley Rd
Cochrane Cl
Round Hl Av
Wychbold Ct
Cherrington Gdns
Wychbury Drive
Rockingham Hall Gdns
The Orangery
Monument Lane
Milton Dr
Kinver Dr
Hall Meadow
School La
Hall Lane
Hall Drive
Hagley Cl
Clent Dr
Park Road
Field La
Woodman Lane
Adam's Hl
The Riddings
The Hyde
Dorchester Rd
Mayfair
Chalfont Pl
PO
E
F
G
H
136
170
154
92
93
82
81
280
2
3
4
5

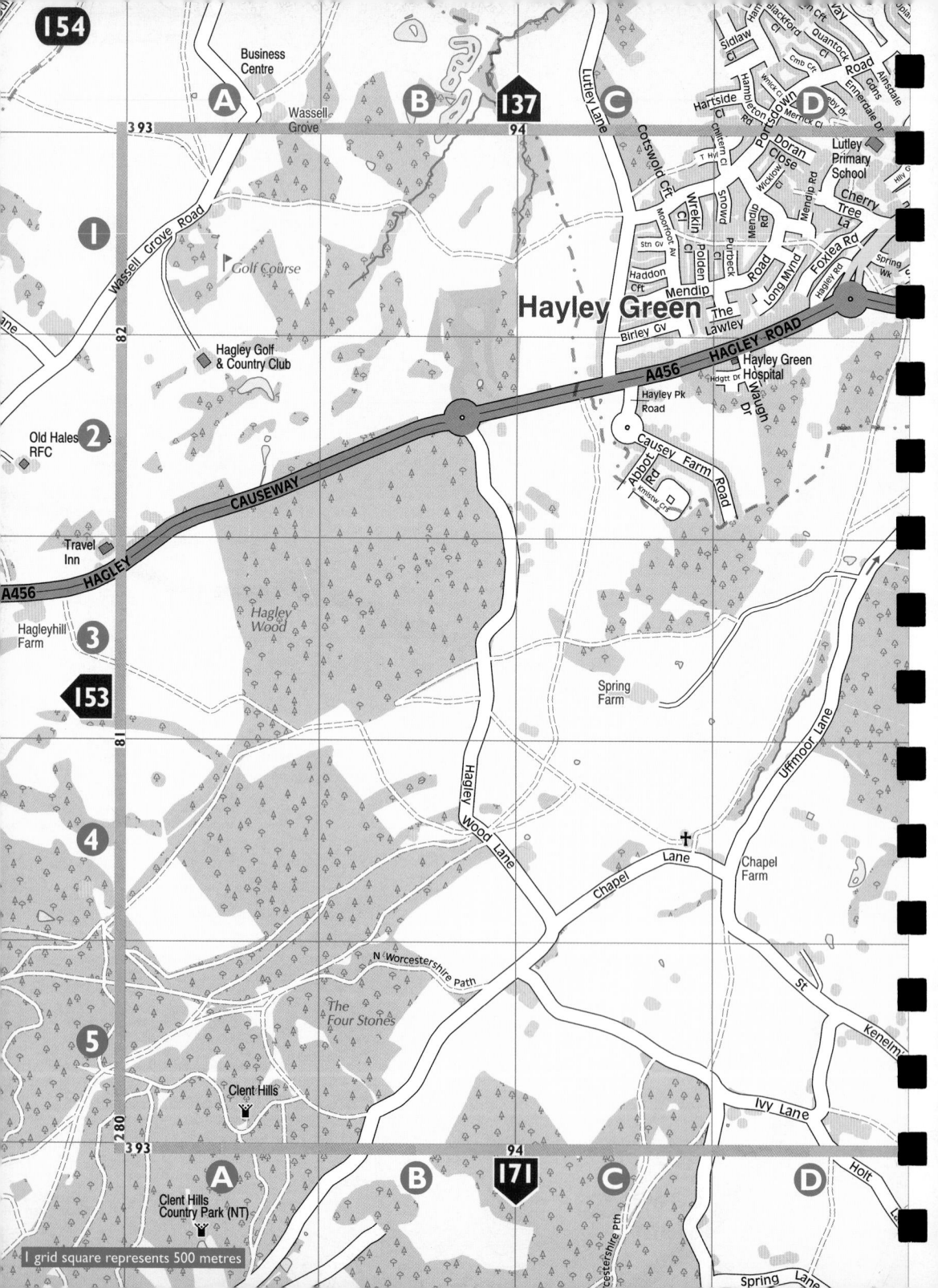

154

A — Business Centre
Wassell Grove

393 82

B

137

C — Lutley Lane / Cotswold Cft

D — Sidlaw Cl / Hartside Cl / Hamberton Rd / Portsdown Rd / Wrekin Cl / Snowd / Wicklow Cl / Mendip Rd / Lutley Primary School / Cherry Tree La / spring Wk

Doran Close

Hayley Rd

Foxlea Rd

Wassell Grove Road

I

Golf Course

Hagley Golf & Country Club

Hayley Green

Stn Gv / Haddon Cft / Mendip / Birley Gv / The Lawley / Long Mynd Road / Mendip Road / Polden / Purbeck / Moorfoot Av

A456 **HAGLEY ROAD**

Hayley Green Hospital

Hayley Pk Road

Waugh Dr

2 — Old Hales RFC

CAUSEWAY

Causey Farm Road

Abbot Rd

Kmirsw Crs

Travel Inn

A456 **HAGLEY**

3 — Hagleyhill Farm

Hagley Wood

153

81

Spring Farm

Uffmoor Lane

4

Hagley Wood Lane

5

The Four Stones

N Worcestershire Path

Chapel Lane

Chapel Farm

St Kenelm

Ivy Lane

Clent Hills

280 393

A — Clent Hills Country Park (NT)

B

171

C

cestershire Pth

D — Holt Rd

Spring Lane

I grid square represents 500 metres

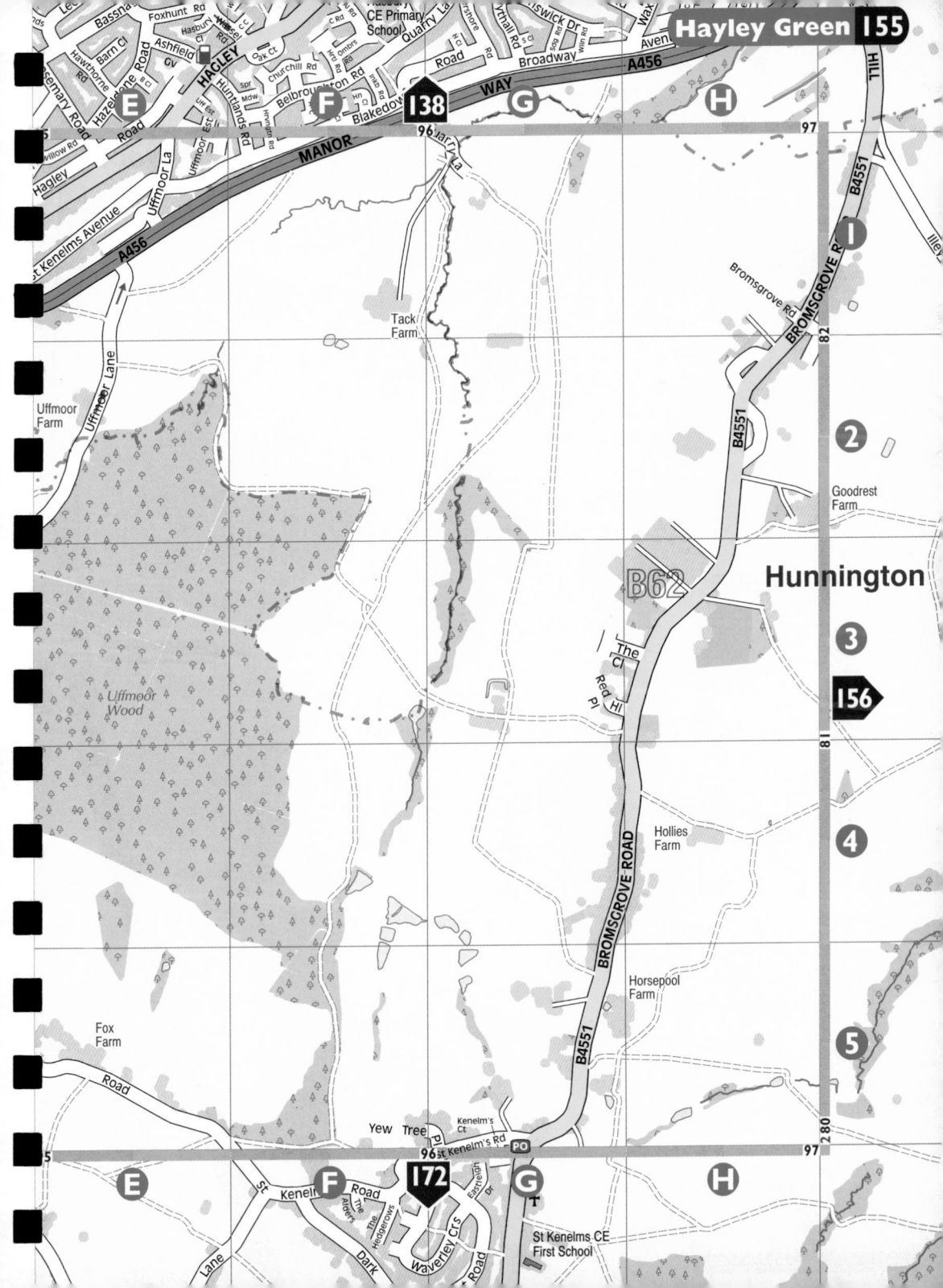

CE Primary School
Foxhunt Rd
Bassnage
Hawthorne Rd
Barn Cl
Ashfield Gv
HAGLEY
Quarry La
Broadway
A456
Churchill Rd
Belbroughton Rd
Blakedown
Huntlands Rd
Uffmoor Est
Hazeldene Road
Road
MANOR WAY
138
Willow Rd
Hagley
Uffmoor La
St Kenelms Avenue
A456
Uffmoor Lane
Uffmoor Farm
Tack Farm
Uffmoor Wood
Bromsgrove Rd
BROMSGROVE RD
B4551
Goodrest Farm
Hunnington
B62
The Cl
Red Hl
Pl
156
Hollies Farm
BROMSGROVE ROAD
Horsepool Farm
B4551
Fox Farm
Road
Yew Tree Pl
Kenelm's Ct
St Kenelm's Rd
PO
172
St Kenelm Road
The Alders
The Hedgerows
Waverley Crs
Eastleigh Dr
Dark Lane
St Kenelms CE First School
E
F
G
H
I
2
3
4
5
96
97
82
81
280

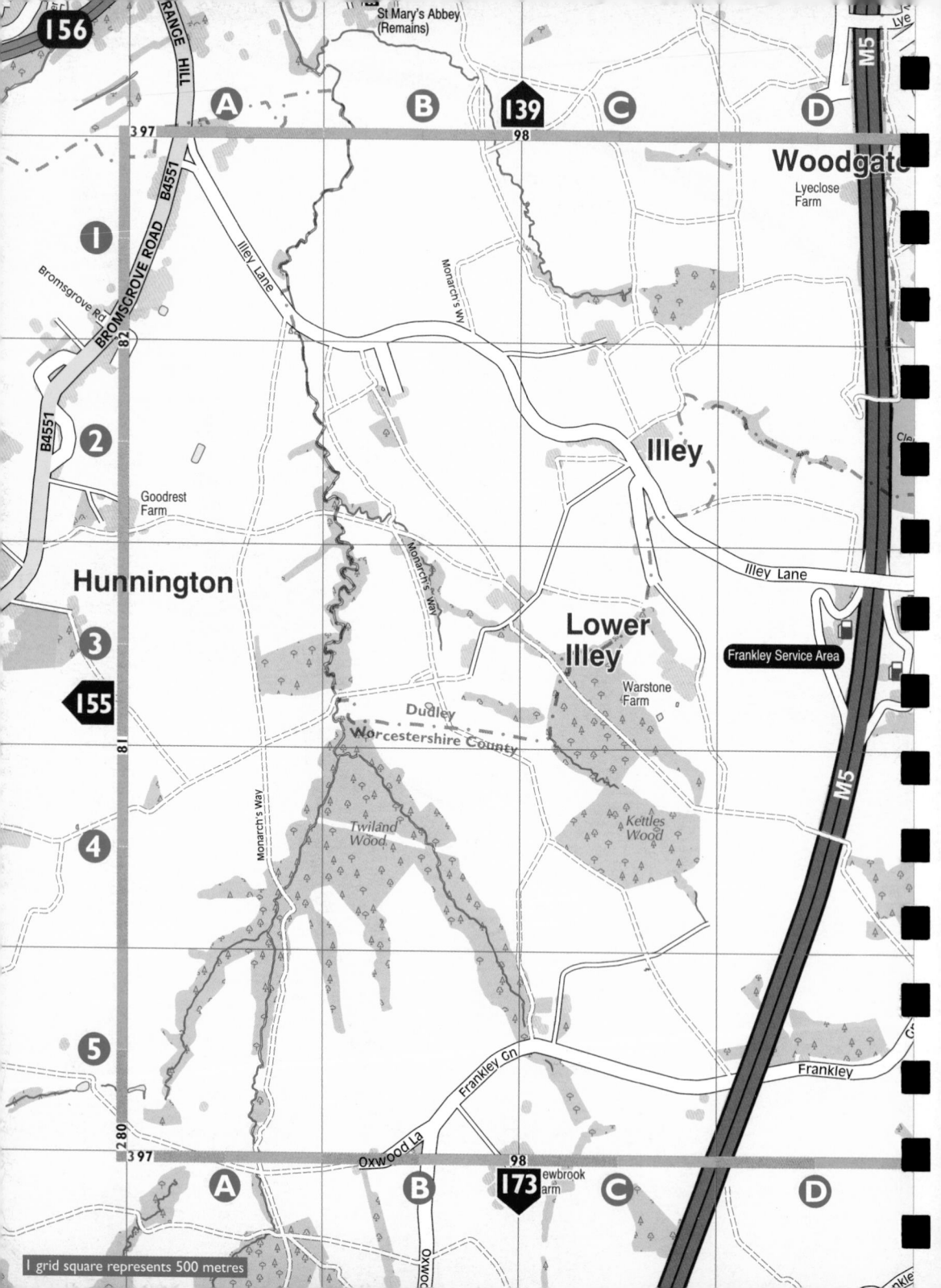

156

A | **B** | **139** | **C** | **D**

3 97 | 98

Woodgate

Lyeclose
Farm

I

Bromsgrove Rd

Illey Lane

Monarch's Wy

82

2

Goodrest
Farm

Illey

Hunnington

Monarchs Way

**Lower
Illey**

Frankley Service Area

3

Warstone
Farm

155

81

Dudley
Worcestershire County

4

Monarch's Way

Twiland
Wood

Kettles
Wood

M5

5

Frankley

Frankley Gn

280

3 97 | 98

A | **B** | **173** | **C** | **D**

Oxwood La

ewbrook
arm

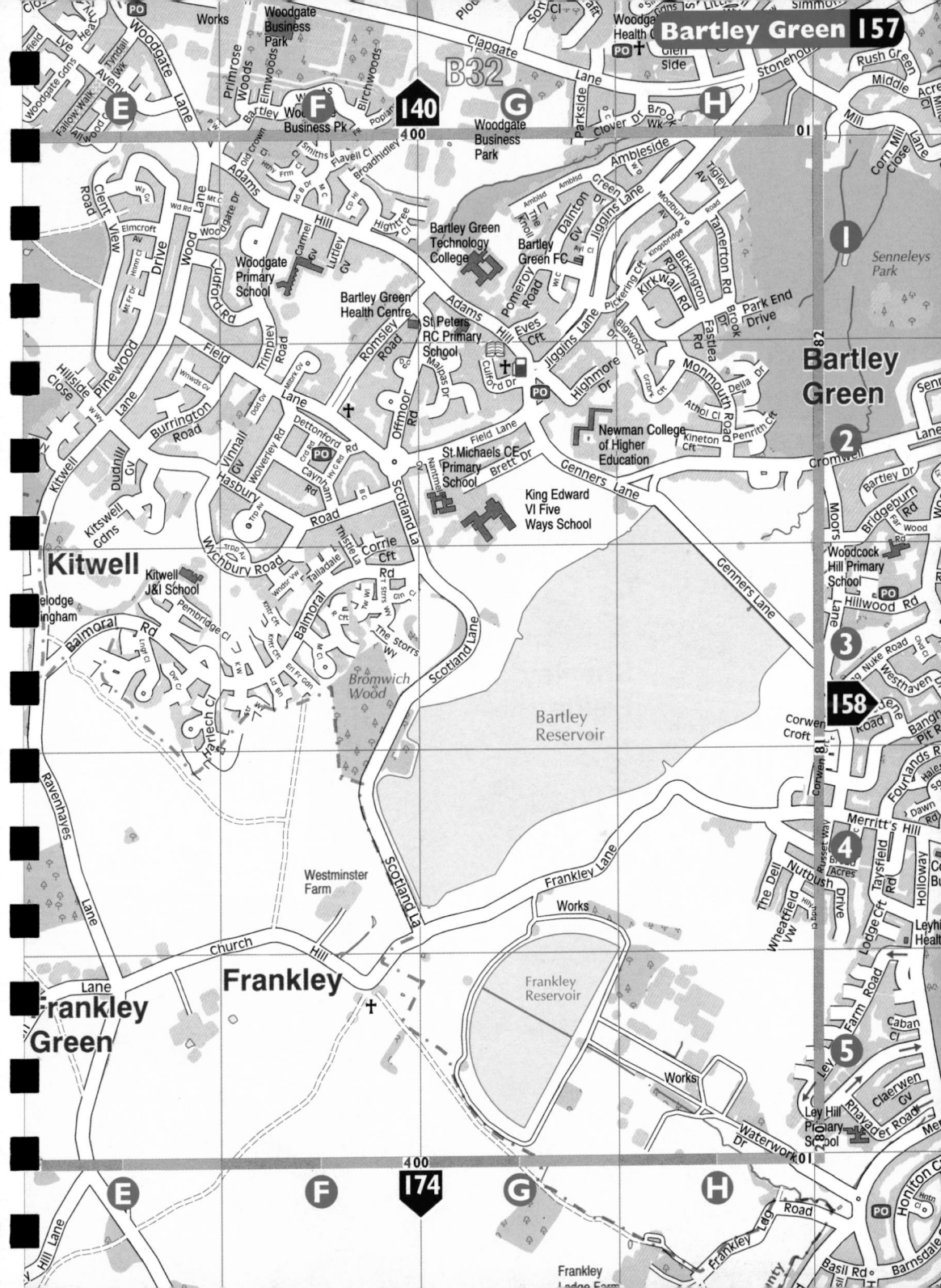
B32
140
158
174
400
Bartley Green
Kitwell
Frankley
Frankley Green
Woodgate Business Park
Woodgate Business Pk
Works
Woodgate Primary School
Bartley Green Technology College
Bartley Green FC
Bartley Green Health Centre
St Peters RC Primary School
St.Michaels CE Primary School
Newman College of Higher Education
King Edward VI Five Ways School
Kitwell J&I School
Woodcock Hill Primary School
Ley Hill Primary School
Senneleys Park
Bromwich Wood
Bartley Reservoir
Frankley Reservoir
Westminster Farm
Frankley Lodge Farm
Clapgate Lane
Adams Hill
Field Lane
Genners Lane
Scotland Lane
Frankley Lane
Church Hill
Ravenhayes Lane
Balmoral Road
Wychbury Road
Hasbury Road
Kitwell Lane
Pinewood Drive
Wood Lane
Woodgate Lane
Woodgate Drive
Clent View Road
Elmcroft Av
Jiggins Lane
Ambleside
Green Dr
Tigley Av
Modbury Av
Tamerton Rd
Bickington Rd
Kirkwall Rd
Pickering Cft
Park End Drive
Brook Dr
Fastlea Rd
Monmouth Road
Highmore Dr
Pomeroy Road
Dalinton Gv
Eves Cft
Romsley Road
Offmoor Rd
Malpas Dr
Culford Dr
Brett Dr
Dettonford Rd
Caynham Rd
Wolverley Rd
Vinnall Gv
Burrington Road
Dudnill Gv
Kitwell Gdns
Hillside Close
Trimpley Road
Udford Rd
Lutley Gv
Carmel Gv
Hightree Cl
Broadhidley Dr
Flavell Cl
Primrose Woods
Elmwoods
Birchwoods
Parkside
Clover Dr
Brook Wk
Stonehouse
Rush Green
Middle Acre
Mill
Corn Mill Close
Cromwell Lane
Bartley Dr
Bridgeburn Rd
Moors Lane
Hillwood Rd
Nuke Road
Westhaven Dr
Corwen Croft
Fourlands Rd
Merritt's Hill
Nutbush Drive
The Dell
Wheatfield Vw
Taysfield Rd
Holloway
Lodge Cft
Ley Hill Farm Road
Caban Cl
Claerwen Gv
Rhayader Road
Waterworks Dr
Honiton Cr
Basil Rd
Barnsdale
Frankley Ldg Road
Hill Lane
Pembridge Cl
Harlech Cl
Talladale
Corrie Cft
Thistle La
The Storrs Wy
Athol Cl
Kineton Cft
Penrith Cft
Della Dr
Bigwood Dr
Fallow Walk
Woodgate Gdns
Tyndall Wk
Lye Avenue
Smiths
Old Crown Cl

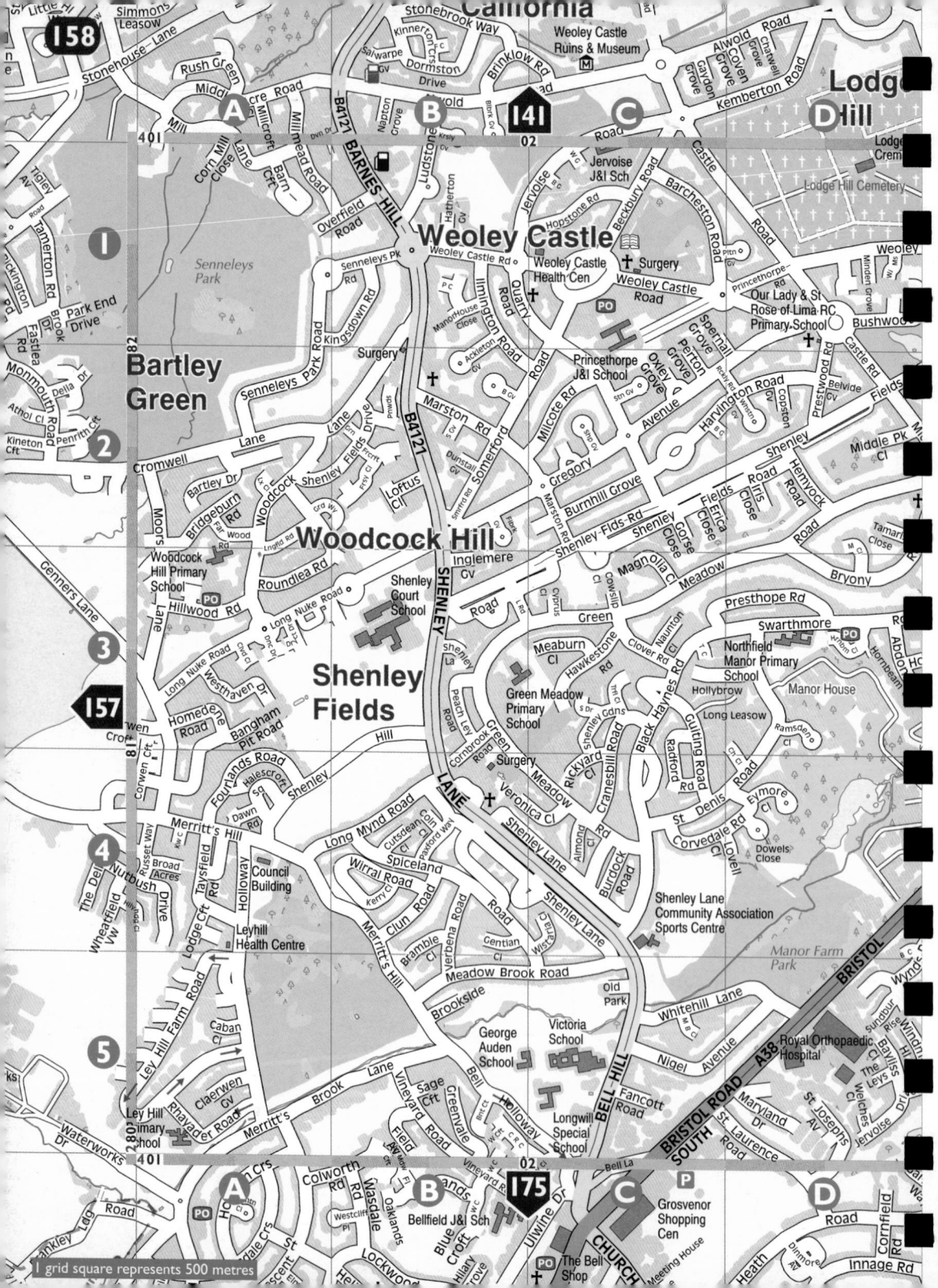

158
141
157
175
A
B
C
D
1
2
3
4
5
401
02
82
81
280
California
Weoley Castle Ruins & Museum
Lodge Hill
Lodge Hill Cemetery
Weoley Castle
Bartley Green
Senneleys Park
Woodcock Hill
Shenley Fields
Shenley Court School
Woodcock Hill Primary School
Princethorpe J&I School
Our Lady & St Rose of Lima RC Primary School
Weoley Castle Health Cen
Jervoise J&I Sch
Green Meadow Primary School
Northfield Manor Primary School
Manor House
Shenley Lane Community Association Sports Centre
Manor Farm Park
Royal Orthopaedic Hospital
Victoria School
George Auden School
Longwill Special School
Council Building
Leyhill Health Centre
Ley Hill Primary School
Bellfield J&I Sch
Grosvenor Shopping Cen
The Bell Shop
Meeting House
Surgery
BARNES HILL
B4121
SHENLEY LANE
BELL HILL
BRISTOL ROAD SOUTH
A38
BRISTOL
CHURCH
Stonehouse Lane
Middle Acre Road
Stonebrook Way
Dormston Drive
Brinklow Rd
Alwold Road
Kemberton Road
Barchester Road
Beckbury Road
Jervoise Road
Weoley Castle Rd
Weoley Castle Road
Senneleys Park Road
Kingsdown Rd
Ilmington Road
Quarry Road
Marston Rd
Somerford Road
Milcote Rd
Gregory Avenue
Harvington Road
Shenley Fields Road
Shenley Fields Drive
Burnhill Grove
Cromwell Lane
Woodcock Lane
Bridgeburn Rd
Roundlea Rd
Long Nuke Road
Hillwood Rd
Moors Lane
Genners Lane
Homedene Road
Bangham Pit Road
Westhaven Dr
Fourlands Road
Shenley Hill
Merritt's Hill
Long Mynd Road
Wirral Road
Clun Road
Spiceland Road
Meadow Brook Road
Brookside
Merritt's Brook Lane
Ley Hill Farm Road
Rhayader Road
Waterworks Dr
Green Meadow Road
Presthope Rd
Black Haynes Rd
Cranesbill Road
Guiting Road
St Denis Road
Corvedale Rd
Whitehill Lane
Nigel Avenue
Fancott Road
Bell Holloway
Vineyard Road
Shenley Lane
Bryony Road
Hemyock Road
1 grid square represents 500 metres

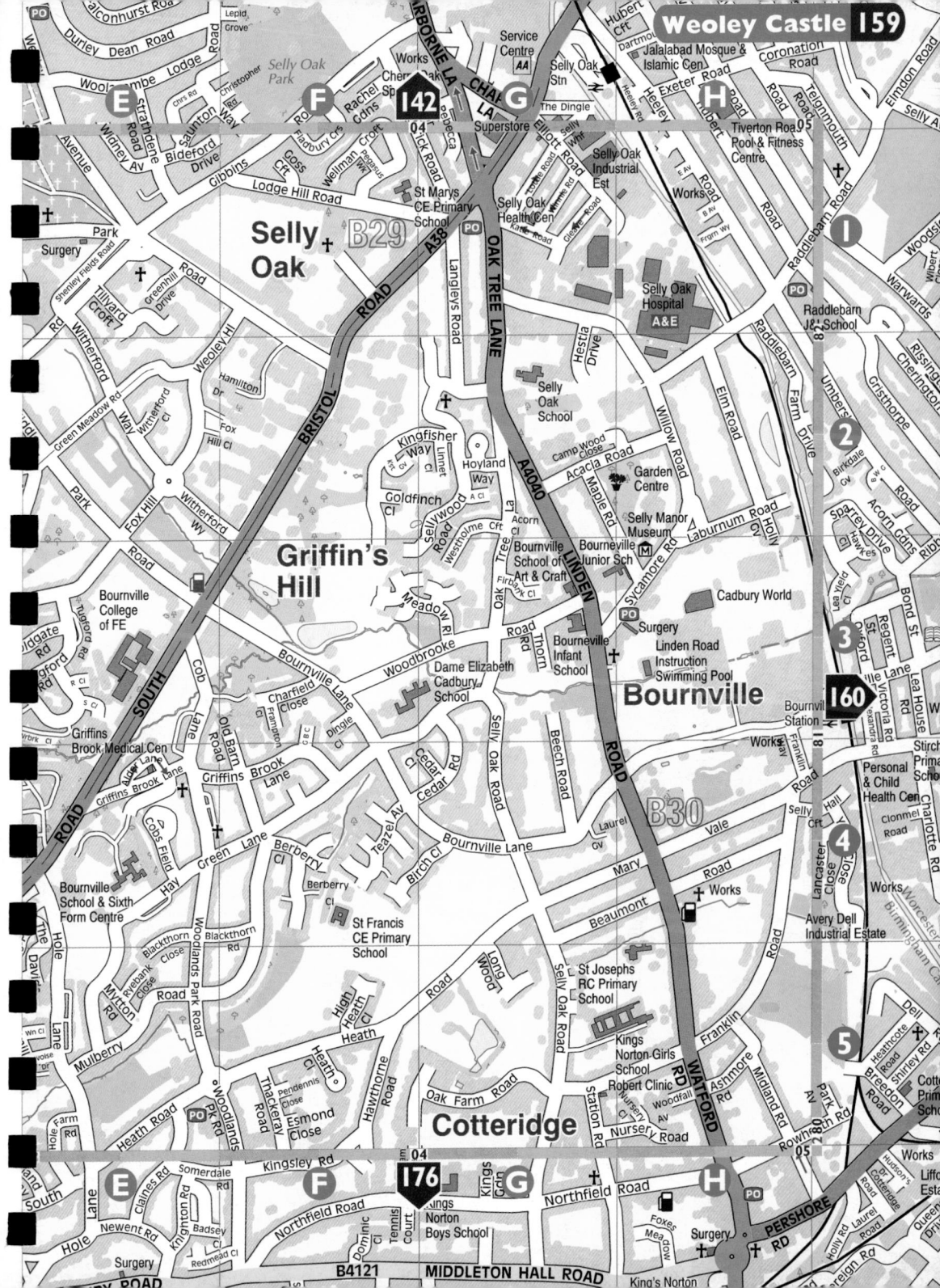
Selly Oak
Griffin's Hill
Bournville
Cotteridge
Selly Oak Park
B29
B30
BRISTOL ROAD SOUTH
A38
OAK TREE LANE
LINDEN ROAD
A4040
WATFORD RD
PERSHORE RD
B4121 MIDDLETON HALL ROAD
142
160
176
Selly Oak Hospital
A&E
Cadbury World
Selly Manor Museum
Bournville College of FE
Selly Oak Stn
Bournville Station
Kings Norton Boys School
Kings Norton Girls School
St Francis CE Primary School
Dame Elizabeth Cadbury School
Selly Oak School
Bourneville Junior Sch
Bourneville Infant School
Bournville School of Art & Craft
Bournville School & Sixth Form Centre
Griffins Brook Medical Cen
St Joseph's RC Primary School
Avery Dell Industrial Estate
Tiverton Road Pool & Fitness Centre
Selly Oak Industrial Est
Selly Oak Health Cen
Jalalabad Mosque & Islamic Cen
Raddlebarn J&I School
Linden Road Instruction Swimming Pool
Personal & Child Health Cen
Garden Centre
Superstore
Service Centre
St Marys CE Primary School
Robert Clinic
Surgery
Works

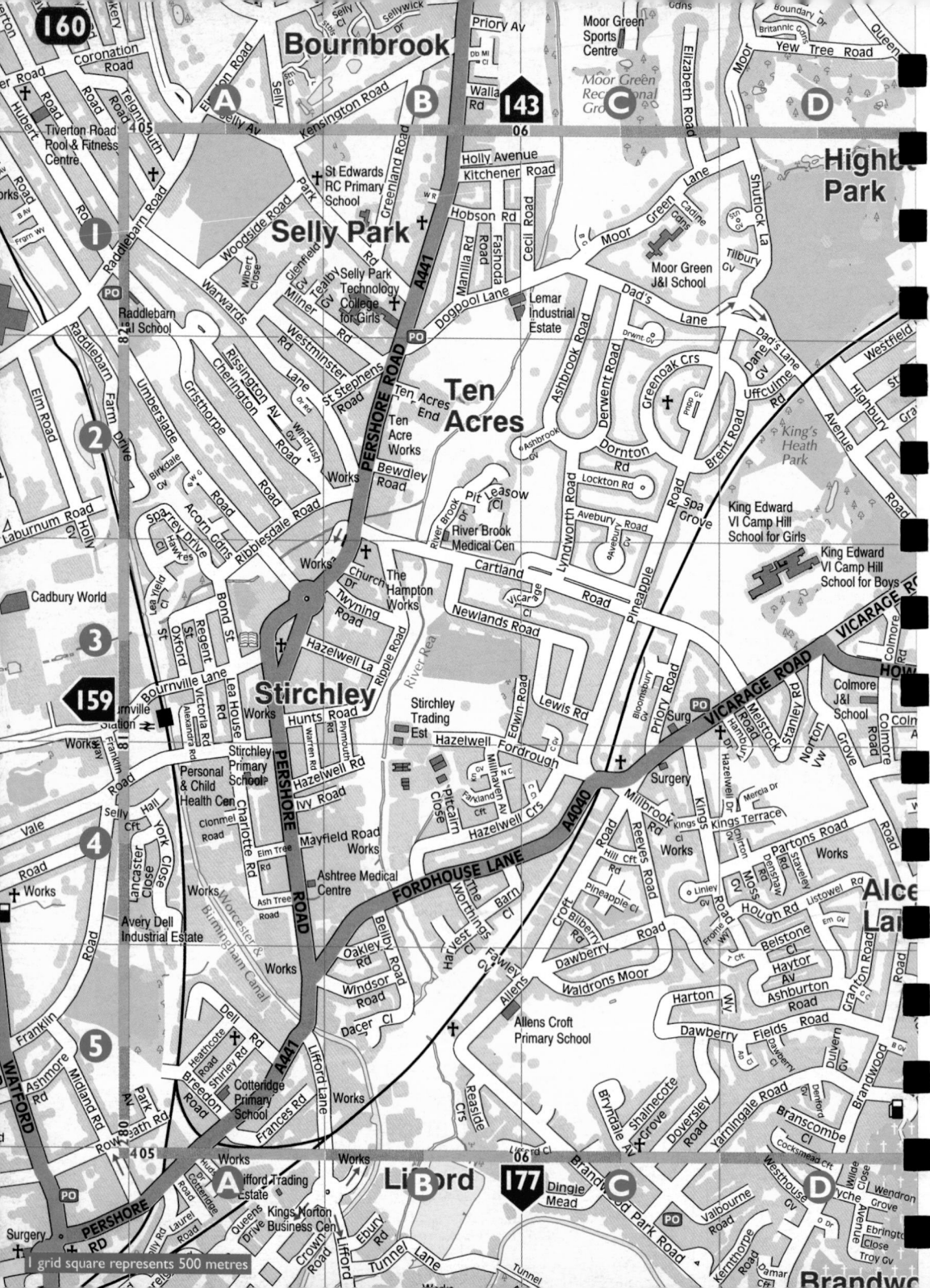
160
143
159
177
Bournbrook
Selly Park
Ten Acres
Stirchley
Highbury Park
Moor Green Sports Centre
Moor Green Recreational Ground
Tiverton Road Pool & Fitness Centre
St Edwards RC Primary School
Selly Park Technology College for Girls
Moor Green J&I School
Lemar Industrial Estate
Raddlebarn J&I School
Ten Acre Works
River Brook Medical Cen
King's Heath Park
King Edward VI Camp Hill School for Girls
King Edward VI Camp Hill School for Boys
Cadbury World
The Hampton Works
Stirchley Trading Est
Stirchley Primary School
Personal & Child Health Cen
Colmore J&I School
Mayfield Road Works
Ashtree Medical Centre
Avery Dell Industrial Estate
Allens Croft Primary School
Cotteridge Primary School
Lifford Trading Estate
Kings Norton Business Cen
PERSHORE ROAD
FORDHOUSE LANE
VICARAGE ROAD
A441
A4040
Worcester & Birmingham Canal
River Rea
1 grid square represents 500 metres

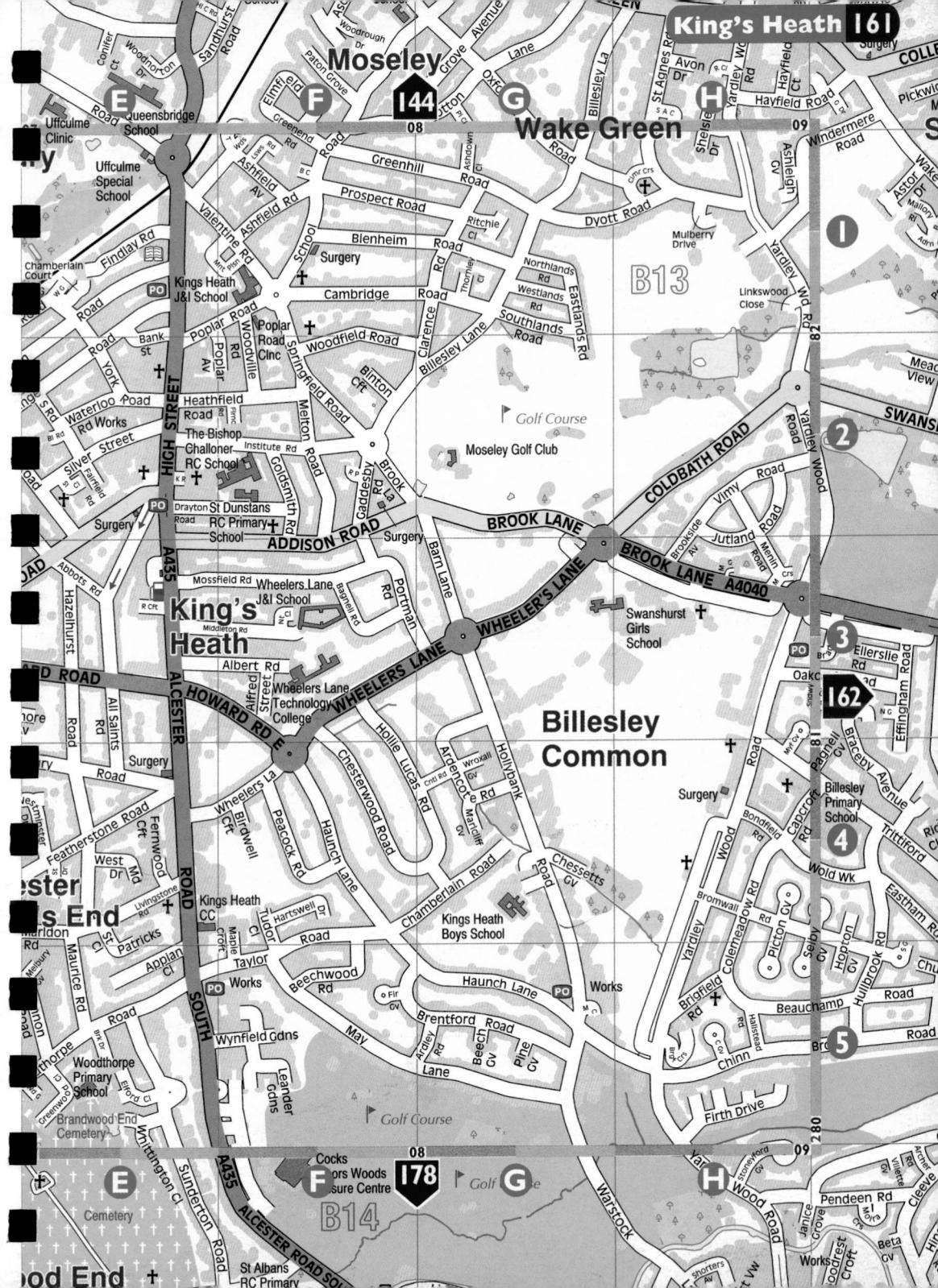
Moseley
Wake Green
King's Heath
Billesley Common
B13
B14
144
162
178
Golf Course
Moseley Golf Club
HIGH STREET
ALCESTER ROAD SOUTH
A435
BROOK LANE
BROOK LANE A4040
WHEELER'S LANE
WHEELERS LANE
COLDBATH ROAD
ADDISON ROAD
HOWARD RD E
Swanshurst Girls School
Kings Heath Boys School
Wheelers Lane Technology College
Wheelers Lane J&I School
Kings Heath J&I School
The Bishop Challoner RC School
St Dunstans RC Primary School
Billesley Primary School
Woodthorpe Primary School
Uffculme Clinic
Uffculme Special School
Queensbridge School
Brandwood End Cemetery
Kings Heath CC
Cocks Moors Woods Leisure Centre
St Albans RC Primary

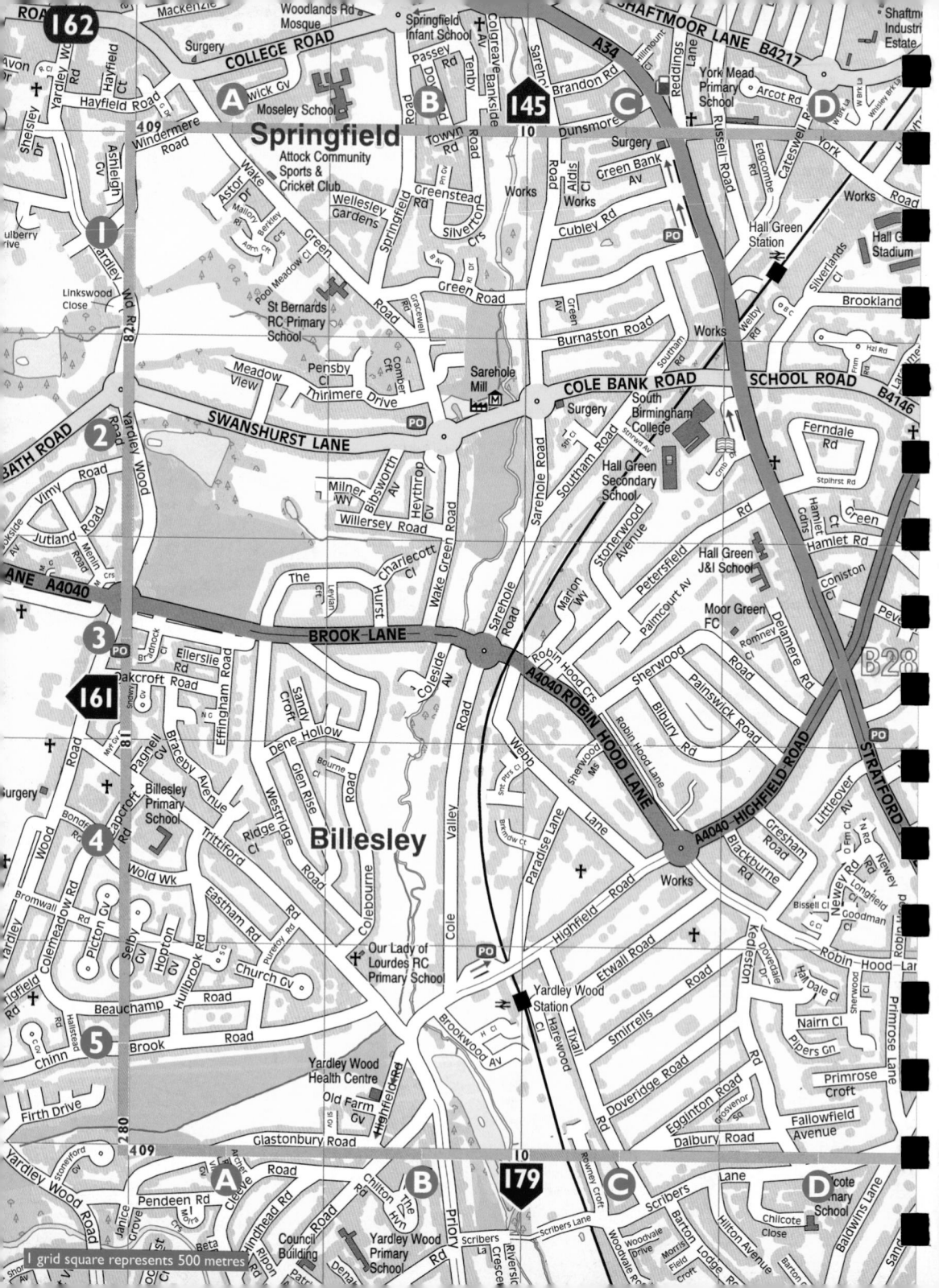
162
145
161
179
Springfield
Billesley
COLLEGE ROAD
SHAFTMOOR LANE B4217
A34
Woodlands Rd Mosque
Springfield Infant School
Surgery
Moseley School
Hayfield Road
Windermere Road
Attock Community Sports & Cricket Club
Wake Green Road
Greenstead Rd
Wellesley Gardens
Silverton Crs
Brandon Rd
Dunsmore Rd
Green Bank Av
Cubley Rd
Works
York Mead Primary School
Arcot Rd
Reddings Lane
Russell Road
Hall Green Station
Hall Green Stadium
St Bernards RC Primary School
Pool Meadow Cl
Green Road
Burnaston Road
Linkswood Close
Yardley Wood Road
Meadow View
Pensby Cl
Thirlmere Drive
Sarehole Mill
COLE BANK ROAD
SCHOOL ROAD
B4146
SWANSHURST LANE
BATH ROAD
South Birmingham College
Hall Green Secondary School
Southam Road
Sarehole Road
Ferndale Rd
Willersey Road
Bibsworth Av
Heythrop Gv
Milner Wy
Vimy Road
Jutland Road
Menin Road
A4040
Charlecott Cl
Stonerwood Avenue
Petersfield Rd
Hall Green J&I School
Moor Green FC
Hamlet Rd
Coniston Cl
BROOK LANE
Ellerslie Rd
Oakcroft Road
Effingham Road
Sandy Croft
Dene Hollow
A4040 ROBIN HOOD LANE
Robin Hood Crs
Sherwood Road
Painswick Road
Delamere Rd
B28
STRATFORD ROAD
A4040 HIGHFIELD ROAD
Billesley Primary School
Braceby Avenue
Westridge Road
Glen Rise
Bourne Road
Colebourne Road
Cole Valley Road
Webb Lane
Paradise Lane
Highfield Road
Gresham Road
Blackburne Rd
Littleover Av
Trittiford Rd
Wold Wk
Eastham Rd
Colemeadow Rd
Picton Gv
Selby Gv
Hopton Gv
Hullbrook Rd
Church Gv
Our Lady of Lourdes RC Primary School
Etwall Road
Kedleston Rd
Robin Hood Lane
Beauchamp Road
Brook Road
Chinn
Yardley Wood Station
Smirrells Road
Harewood Cl
Tixall Rd
Nairn Cl
Pipers Gn
Primrose Lane
Primrose Croft
Yardley Wood Health Centre
Old Farm Gv
Highfield Rd
Brookwood Av
Doveridge Road
Egginton Road
Fallowfield Avenue
Dalbury Road
Firth Drive
Glastonbury Road
Yardley Wood Road
Pendeen Rd
Cleeve Road
Hindhead Rd
Chilton Rd
Council Building
Yardley Wood Primary School
Priory Rd
Scribers Lane
Woodvale Drive
Barton Lodge Rd
Hilton Avenue
Chilcote Close
Baldwins Lane
1 grid square represents 500 metres

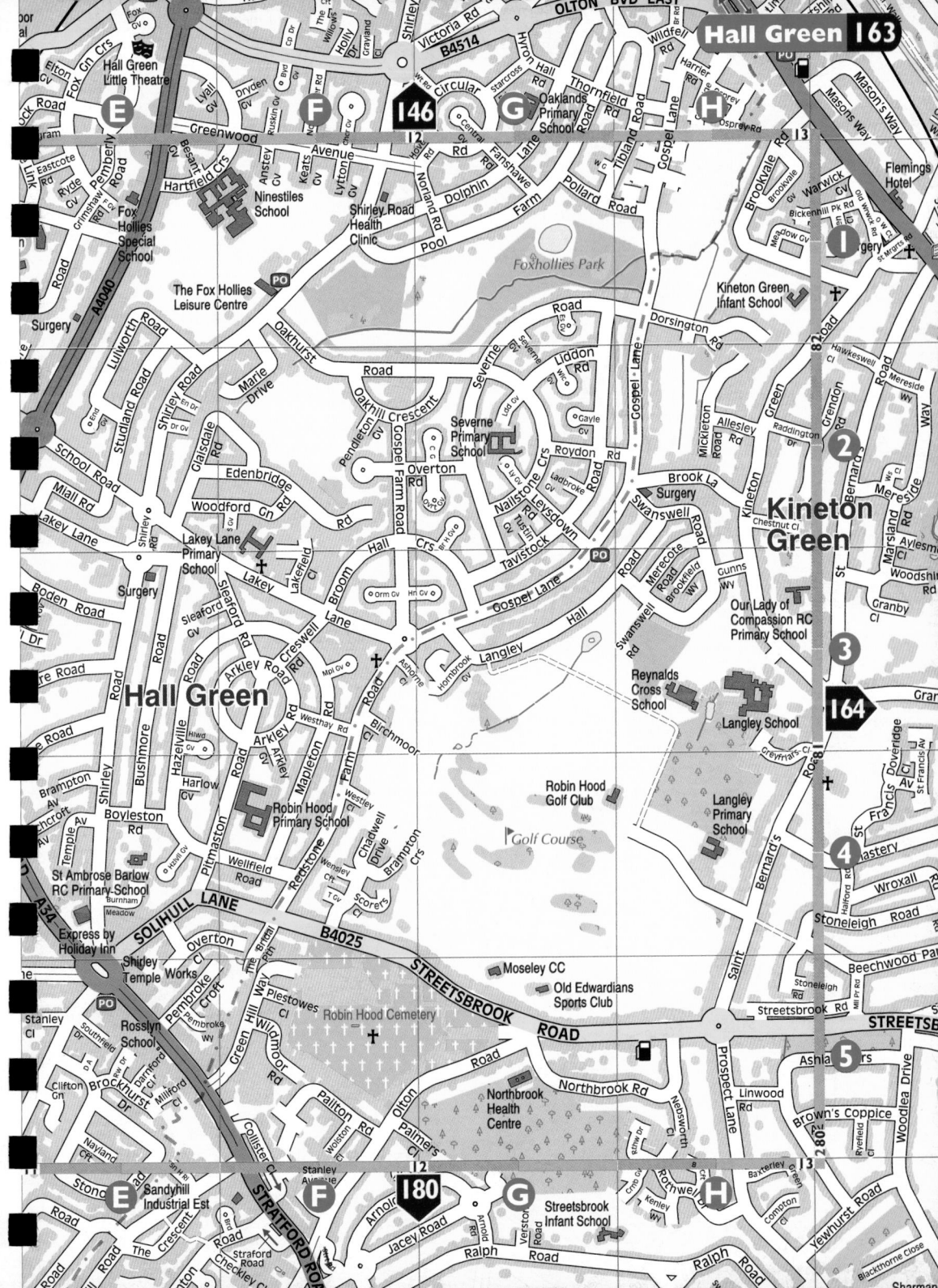
146
164
180
E
F
G
H
1
2
3
4
5
12
13
Hall Green
Kineton Green
OLTON BVD EAST
B4514
Victoria Rd
Circular
Hall Green Little Theatre
Fox Gn Crs
Elton Gv
Greenwood
Avenue
Oaklands Primary School
Hyron Hall Rd
Thornfield Rd
Tibland Road
Gospel Lane
Wildfell Rd
Harrier Rd
Osprey Rd
Mason's Way
Masons Way
Flemings Hotel
Brookvale Rd
Warwick Gv
Bickenhill Pk Rd
Kineton Green Infant School
Ninestiles School
Hartfield Crs
Fox Hollies Special School
Shirley Road Health Clinic
Norland Rd
Dolphin
Fanshawe
Lane
Pollard Road
Farm
Pool
Foxhollies Park
The Fox Hollies Leisure Centre
PO
Surgery
A4040
Lulworth Road
Studland Road
Shirley Road
Oakhurst
Road
Marie Drive
Oakhill Crescent
Pendleton Gv
Gospel Farm Road
Severne Primary School
Severne Gv
Liddon Rd
Gayle Gv
Dorsington Rd
Roydon Rd
Brook La
Overton Rd
Edenbridge Rd
Woodford Gn Rd
Naillstone Crs
Ladbroke Gv
Leysdown
Tustin Gv
Tavistock
Swanswell Road
Merecote Road
Brookfield Wy
Gunns Wy
School Road
Miall Rd
Lakey Lane
Lakey Lane Primary School
Lakefield Cl
Glaisdale Rd
Hall Crs
Broom
Gospel Lane
Langley
Hall
Hornbrook Gv
Ashorne Cl
Mickleton Road
Allesley Rd
Kineton Green
Raddington Dr
Grendon Rd
Bernard's
Mereside Wy
Marsland Rd
Aylesmo
Woodshir Rd
Granby Cl
Chestnut Cl
Our Lady of Compassion RC Primary School
Reynalds Cross School
Langley School
Greyfriars Cl
Doveridge Cl
Francis Av
St Francis Av
Boden Road
Surgery
Sleaford Gv
Sleaford Rd
Creswell Rd
Arkley Road
Arkley Rd
Westhay Rd
Birchmoor
Mapleton Rd
Farm Cl
Bushmore Road
Hazelville Road
Harlow Gv
Pitmaston Road
Robin Hood Primary School
Westley Cl
Chadwell Drive
Brampton Crs
Robin Hood Golf Club
Golf Course
Langley Primary School
Wroxall Rd
Halford Rd
Stoneleigh Road
Brampton Av
Temple Av
Boyleston Rd
Wellfield Road
Redstone
Wensley Cft
Scorers Cl
St Ambrose Barlow RC Primary School
Burnham Meadow
A34
SOLIHULL LANE
B4025
Express by Holiday Inn
Overton Cl
The Bridal Pth
STREETSBROOK ROAD
Moseley CC
Old Edwardians Sports Club
Saint Bernard's Road
Beechwood Par
Stoneleigh
Streetsbrook Rd
STREETSB
Shirley Temple
Works
Pembroke Croft
Pembroke Wy
Plestowes Cl
Green Hill Way
Wildmoor Rd
Robin Hood Cemetery
Stanley Cl
Southfield Dr
Rosslyn School
Darnford Cl
Brockhurst Dr
Millford Cl
Clifton Gn
Nayland Cft
Colliste
Pallton Rd
Olton Road
Palmers
Northbrook Health Centre
Northbrook Rd
Nebsworth Cl
Prospect Lane
Linwood Rd
Brown's Coppice
Ryefield Cl
Woodlea Drive
Baxterley Green
Compton Cl
Yewhurst Road
Blackthorne Close
Sandyhill Industrial Est
Stanley Avenue
Arnold Rd
Jacey Road
Streetsbrook Infant School
Kenley Wy
Ralph Road
The Crescent
Straford Road
Checkley Cl
STRATFORD ROAD

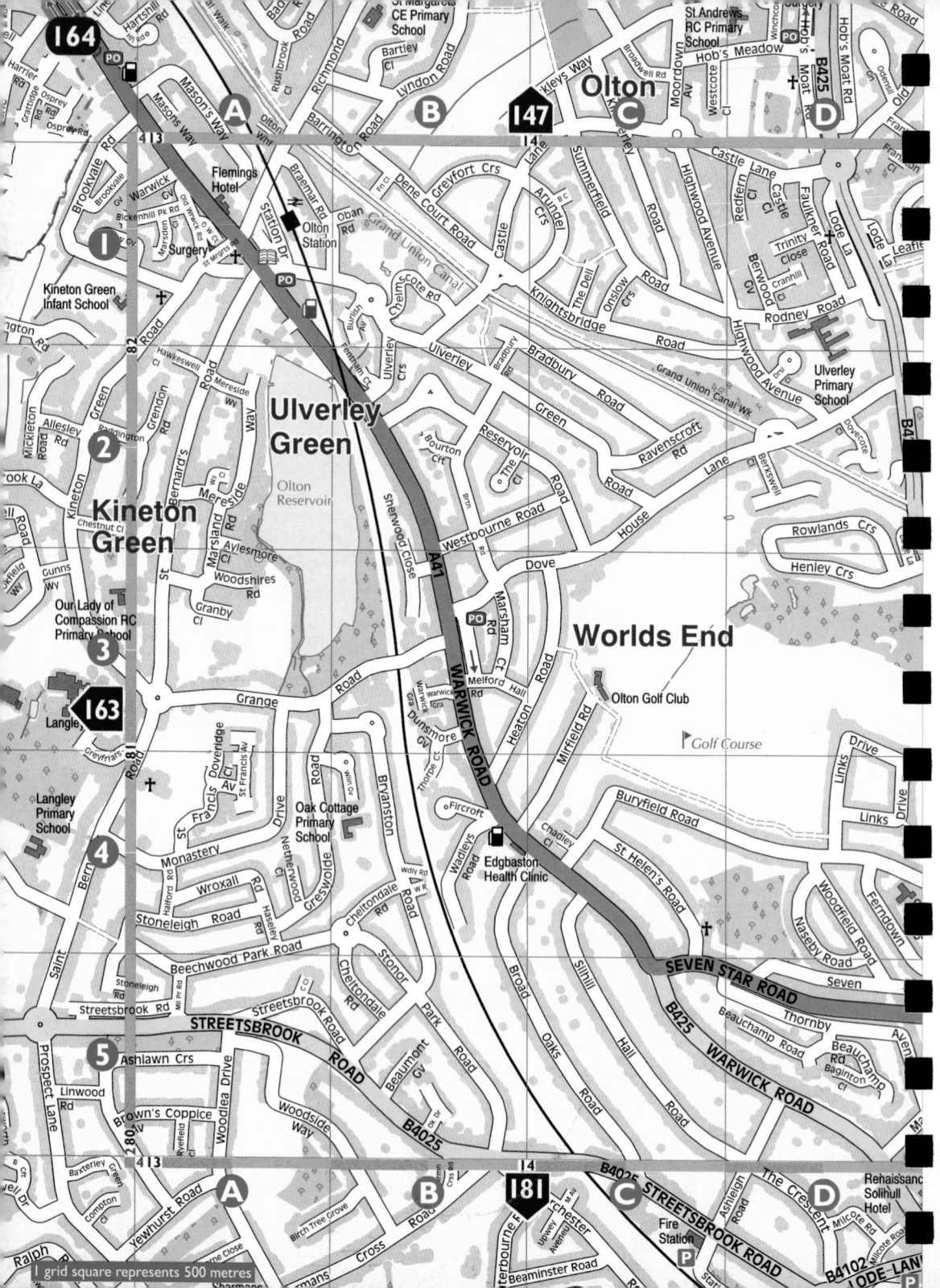
164
147
163
181
A
B
C
D
1
2
3
4
5
413
14
82
81
280
Olton
Ulverley Green
Kineton Green
Worlds End
Olton Reservoir
Grand Union Canal
Grand Union Canal Wk
Olton Station
Flemings Hotel
Surgery
Kineton Green Infant School
Our Lady of Compassion RC Primary School
Langley Primary School
Oak Cottage Primary School
Edgbaston Health Clinic
Olton Golf Club
Golf Course
Ulverley Primary School
St.Andrews RC Primary School
St Margarets CE Primary School
Renaissance Solihull Hotel
Fire Station
A41
WARWICK ROAD
SEVEN STAR ROAD
B425 WARWICK ROAD
STREETSBROOK ROAD
B4025
B4025 STREETSBROOK ROAD
B4102
LODE LANE
B425
Mason's Way
Masons Way
Richmond
Rushbrook Cl
Bartley Cl
Lyndon Road
Barrington Road
Braemar Rd
Station Dr
Oban Rd
Dene Court Road
Greyfort Crs
Castle Lane
Arundel Crs
Summerfield
Highwood Avenue
Castle Lane
Redfern Cl
Castle Cl
Faulkner Road
Lode La
Trinity Close
Berwood Gv
Cranhill Cl
Rodney Road
Hob's Meadow
Hob's Moat Rd
Broadwell Rd
Moordown Av
Westcote Cl
Chelmscote Rd
Burlish Av
Fentham Ct
Ulverley Crs
Ulverley Green Road
Bradbury Road
Bradbury Rd
Knightsbridge Road
The Dell
Onslow Crs
Reservoir Road
Ravenscroft Rd
House Lane
Dove House Lane
Berkswell
Dovecote
Rowlands Crs
Henley Crs
Westbourne Road
Bourton Cft
The Cl
Sherwood Close
Marsham Ct
Marsham Rd
Melford Hall Rd
Heaton Road
Mirfield Rd
Grange Road
Dunsmore Gv
Thorpe Ct
Fircroft
Wadleys Road
Buryfield Road
Links Drive
Chadley Cl
St Helen's Road
Woodfield Road
Ferndown
Naseby Road
Seven
Thornby
Beauchamp Road
Beauchamp Rd
Baginton Cl
Brookvale Rd
Warwick Gv
Bickenhill Pk Rd
Marsden Cl
Old Warwick Rd
Hawkeswell Cl
Mereside Wy
Mereside Way
St Bernard's Road
Grendon Rd
Raddington
Allesley Rd
Mickleton Road
Kineton Green Road
Chestnut Cl
Gunns Wy
Marsland Rd
Aylesmore Cl
Woodshires Rd
Granby Cl
Greyfriars
Doveridge Cl
St Francis Av
St Francis Av
Monastery Drive
Halford Rd
Wroxall Rd
Netherwood Cl
Greswolde Road
Haseley Rd
Stoneleigh Road
Beechwood Park Road
Cheltondale Rd
Cheltondale Road
Stonor Road
Stonor Park Road
Bryanston Road
Streetsbrook Rd
Streetsbrook Road
Stoneleigh
Saint Bernards Road
Prospect Lane
Ashlawn Crs
Linwood Rd
Brown's Coppice Av
Ryefield Cl
Woodlea Drive
Woodside Way
Beaumont Gv
Broad Oaks Road
Silhill Hall Road
Ashleigh Road
The Crescent
Milcote Rd
Baxterley Green
Compton Cl
Yewhurst Road
Birch Tree Grove
Cross Road
Upwey Avenue
Beaminster Road
Ralph
1 grid square represents 500 metres

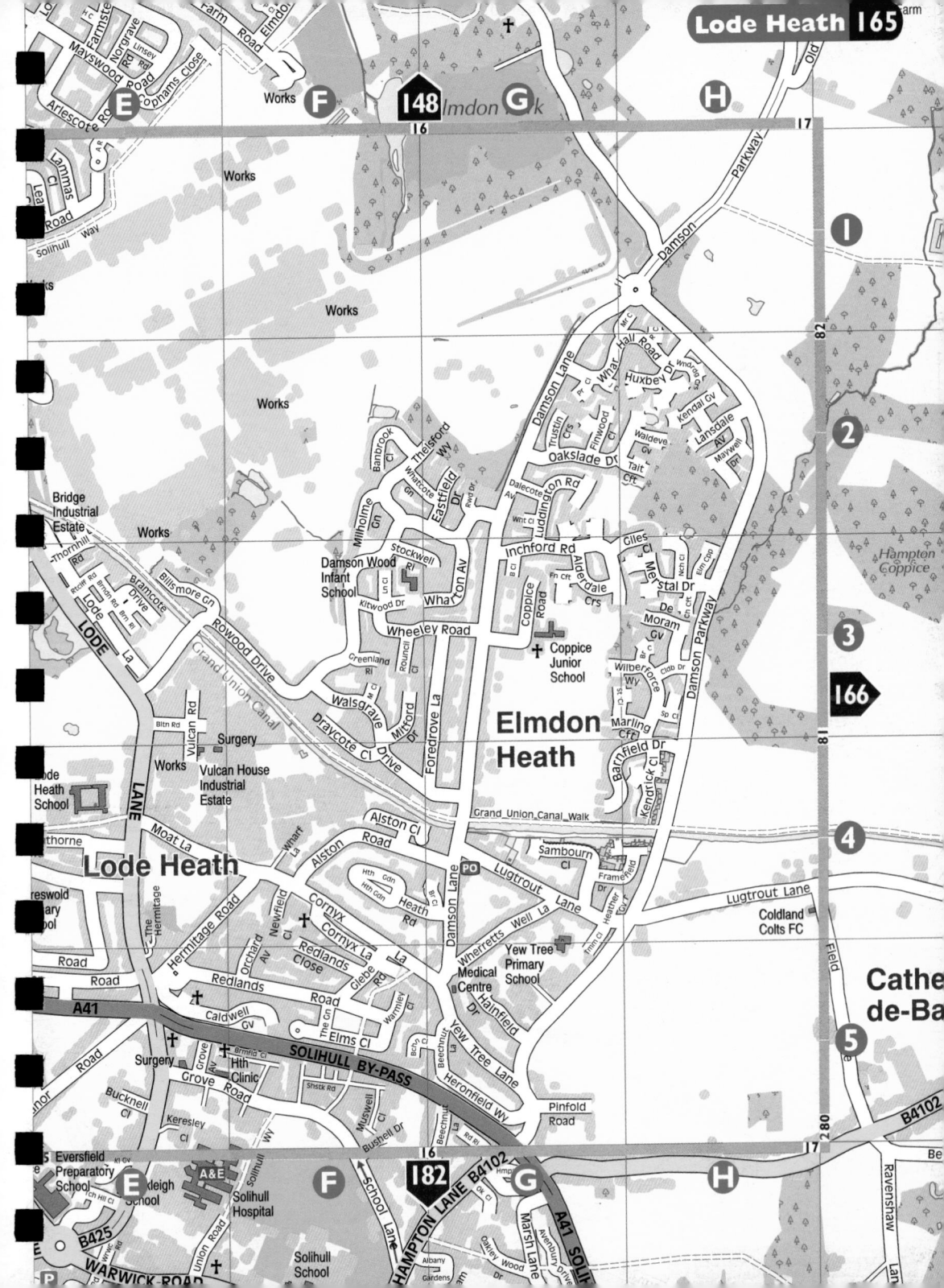

Elmdon Heath
Lode Heath
148
182
166
Works
Bridge Industrial Estate
Damson Wood Infant School
Coppice Junior School
Vulcan House Industrial Estate
Surgery
Lode Heath School
Yew Tree Primary School
Medical Centre
Coldland Colts FC
Hampton Coppice
Eversfield Preparatory School
Solihull Hospital
Solihull School
Hth Clinic
Grand Union Canal
Grand Union Canal Walk
Damson Parkway
Damson Lane
Lode Lane
Solihull By-Pass
Hampton Lane B4102
Warwick Road
Lugtrout Lane
Wheeley Road
Rowood Drive
Moat La
Alston Road
Hermitage Road
Redlands Road
Grove Road
Yew Tree Lane
Pinfold Road
Oakslade Dr
Inchford Rd
Wharton Av
Foredrove La
Coppice Road
Cornyx La

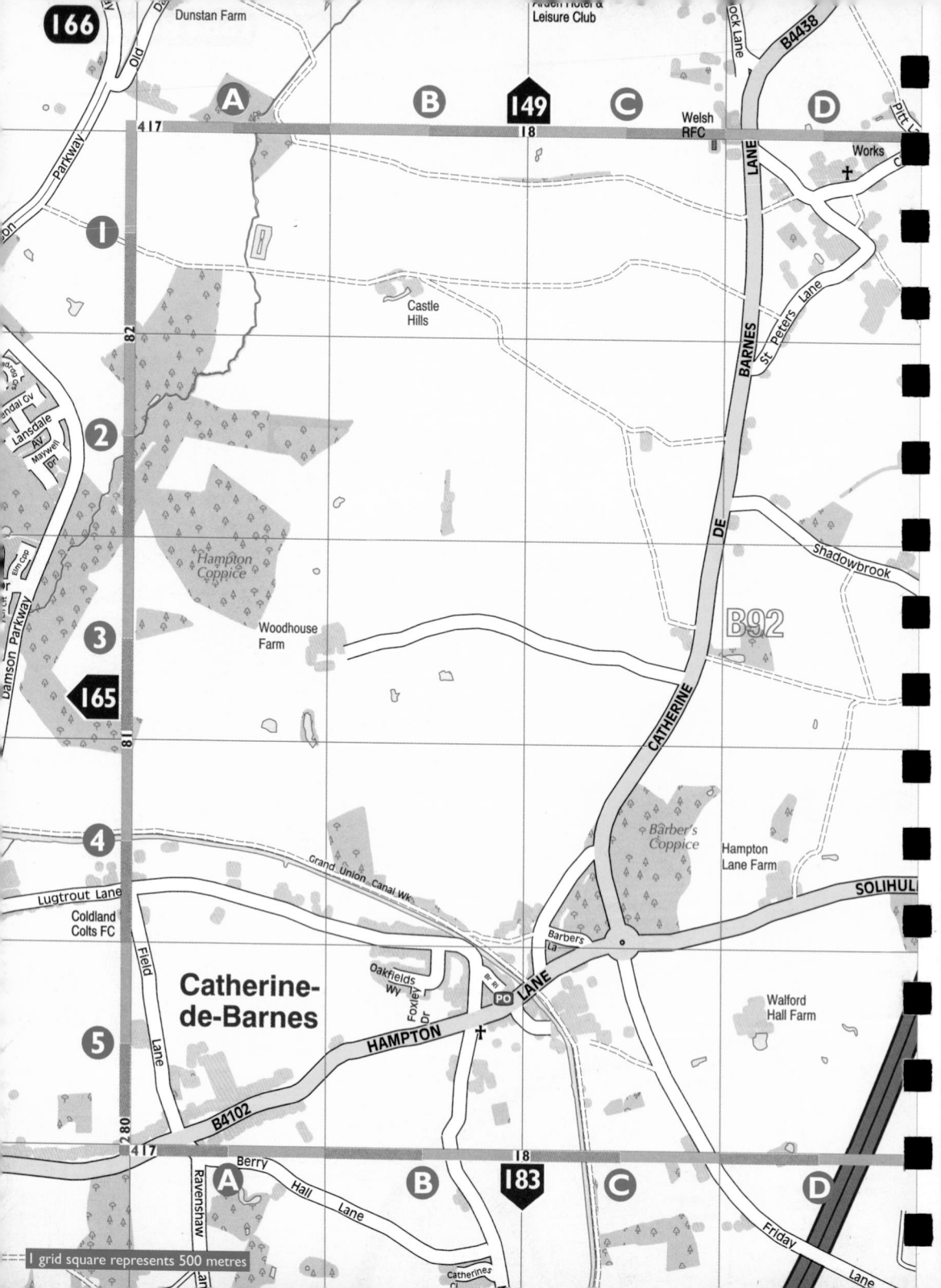

166
Dunstan Farm
Leisure Club
Old
Parkway
Welsh RFC
Works
B4438
A
B
149
C
D
417
18
1
2
3
4
5
82
81
280
Castle Hills
St Peters Lane
BARNES
LANE
DE
CATHERINE
Lansdale Av
Maywell Dr
Hampton Coppice
Woodhouse Farm
Damson Parkway
165
Shadowbrook
B92
Barber's Coppice
Hampton Lane Farm
Grand Union Canal Wk
Lugtrout Lane
Coldland Colts FC
SOLIHULL
Barbers La
Field Lane
Catherine-de-Barnes
Oakfields Wy
Foxley Dr
PO
LANE
HAMPTON
B4102
Walford Hall Farm
Berry Hall Lane
Ravenshaw Lane
183
Friday Lane
Catherines
1 grid square represents 500 metres

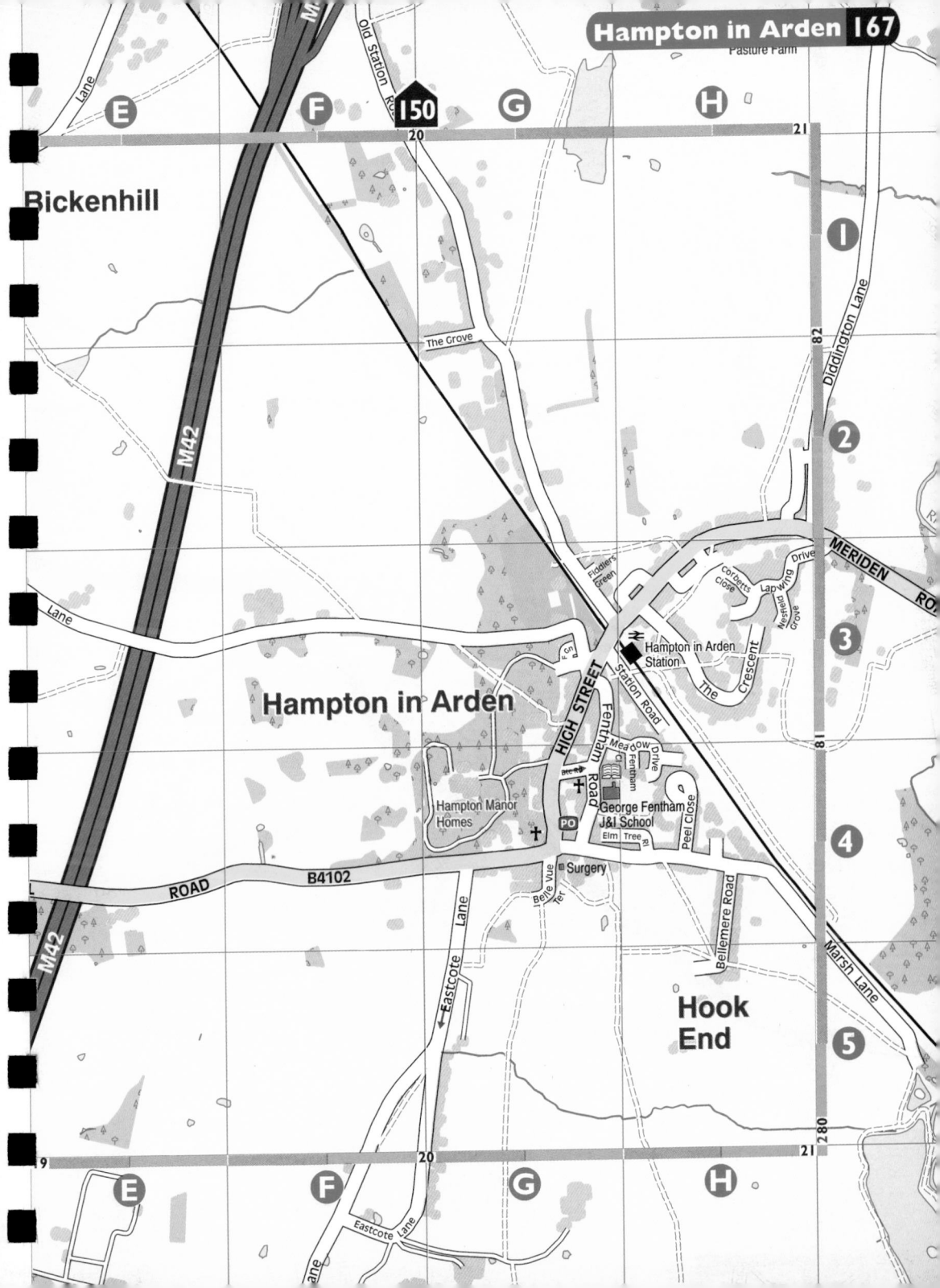

Pasture Farm

E F 150 G H

20

Bickenhill

21

I

82

2

The Grove

MERIDEN RO

M42

Fiddlers Green

3

Lane

Lapwing Grove

Nesfield Road

Drive

corberts Close

Hampton in Arden Station

The Crescent

81

Hampton in Arden

HIGH STREET

Fentham Road

Station Road

Meadow Drive

Fentham

George Fentham J&I School

Peel Close

4

Hampton Manor Homes

PO

Elm Tree

Belle Vue Ter

Surgery

ROAD B4102

Eastcote Lane

Bellemere Road

Marsh Lane

Hook End

5

M42

280

9

20

21

E F G H

Eastcote Lane

Lane

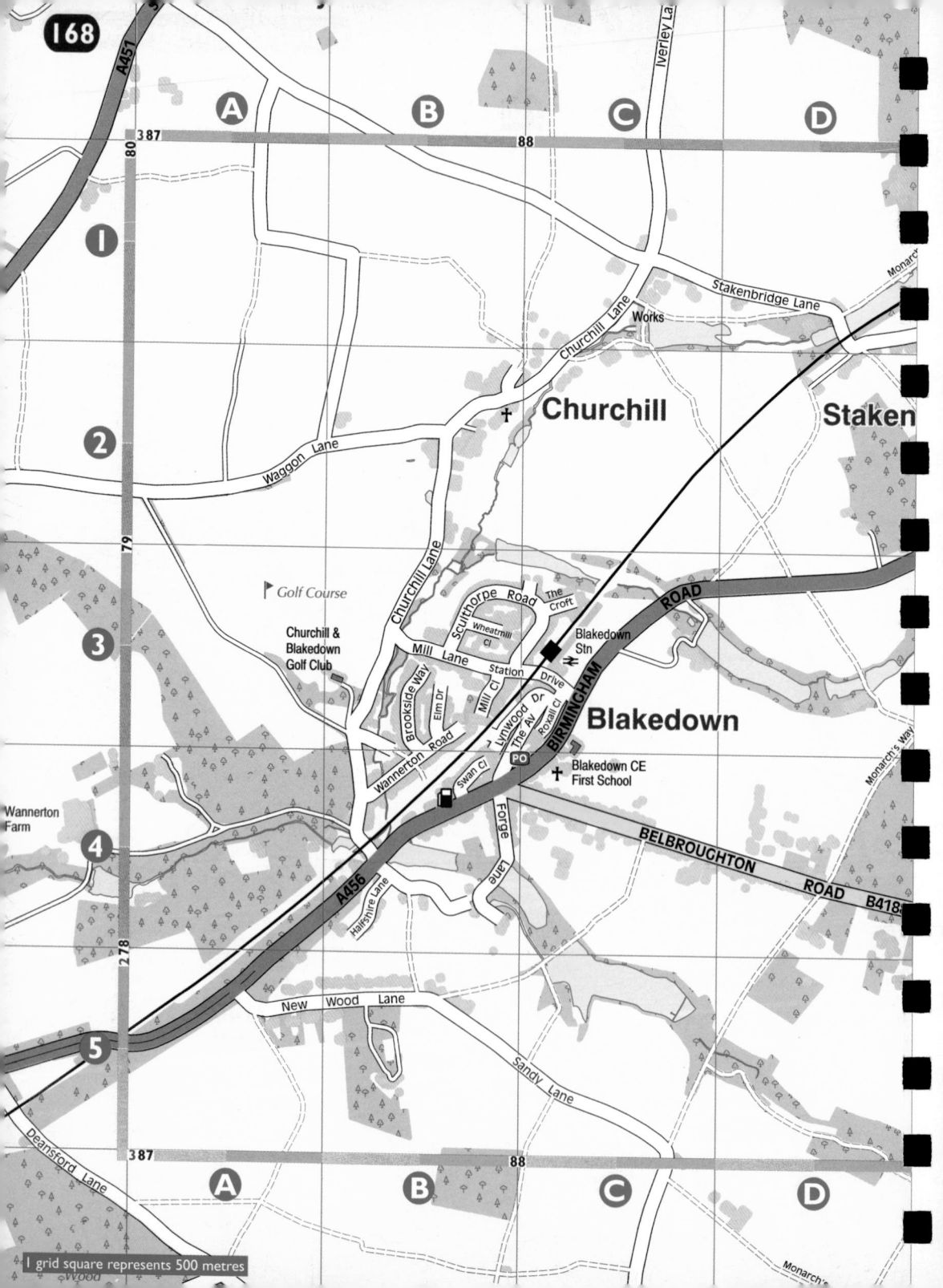

A451

387

80

88

A B C D

1

Iverley La

Monarch

Stakenbridge Lane

Churchill Lane

Works

Staken

2

Churchill

Waggon Lane

79

Golf Course

Churchill Lane

Scutthorpe Road

The Croft

Wheatmill Cl

BIRMINGHAM ROAD

3

Churchill & Blakedown Golf Club

Mill Lane

Station Drive

Blakedown Stn

Blakedown

Brookside Way

Elm Dr

Mill Cl

Lynwood Dr

The Av

Royall Cl

Wannerton Farm

Wannerton Road

Swan Cl

PO

Blakedown CE First School

278

4

A456

Forge Lane

BELBROUGHTON ROAD B418

Halfshire Lane

Monarch's Way

5

New Wood Lane

Sandy Lane

Deansford Lane

387

88

A B C D

Monarch's

1 grid square represents 500 metres

Wood

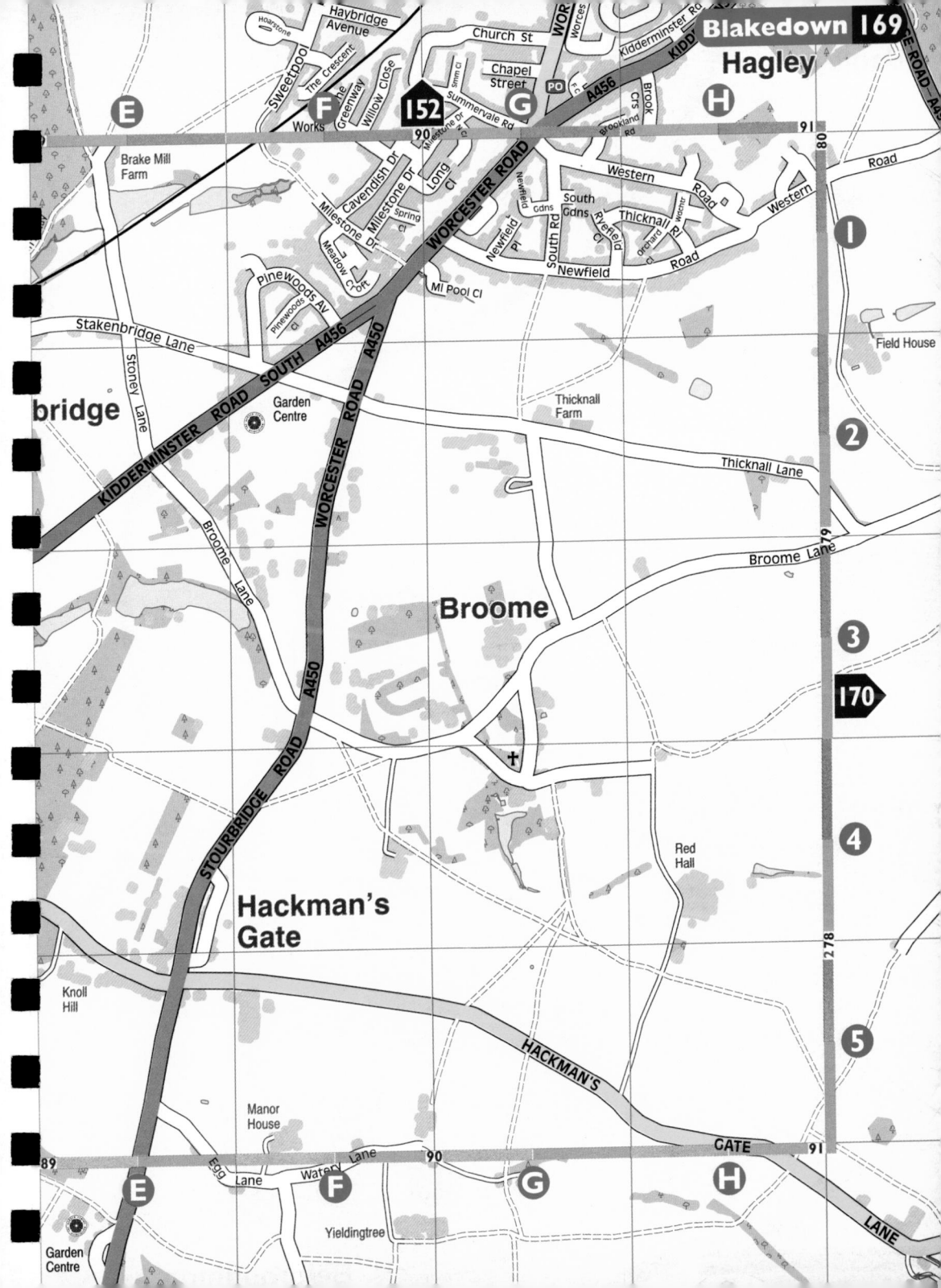

Hagley

Haybridge Avenue

Hoarstone

Sweetpool

The Crescent

Church St

WOR

Worces

Kidderminster Rd

KIDD

E ROAD—A45

E

F

The Greenway

Willow Close

Works

152

90

Chapel Street

Smm Cl

Summervale Rd

PO

F C

G

Milestone Dr

A456

Brook

Brockland Crts

Brockland Rd

H

80

91

Road

Cavendish Dr

Milestone Dr

Long Cl

Spring Cl

WORCESTER ROAD

Newfield Pl

South Gdns

Western

Road

Road

Thicknall

Rd

wchstr

Western

Brake Mill Farm

Milestone Dr

Meadow Ct

South Gdns

Newfield Gdns

South Rd

Ryefield

orchard

Road

1

Pinewoods Av

Pinewoods Cl

Ml Pool Cl

Newfield

Newfield

Field House

Stakenbridge Lane

KIDDERMINSTER ROAD SOUTH A456

A450 WORCESTER ROAD

Garden Centre

Thicknall Farm

Thicknall Lane

2

bridge

Stoney Lane

Broome Lane

79

Broome Lane

Broome

3

A450

170

Hackman's Gate

STOURBRIDGE ROAD A450

†

4

Red Hall

Knoll Hill

278

5

Manor House

Egg Lane

Watery Lane

HACKMAN'S

89

90

E

F

G

GATE

91

H

Garden Centre

Yieldingtree

LANE

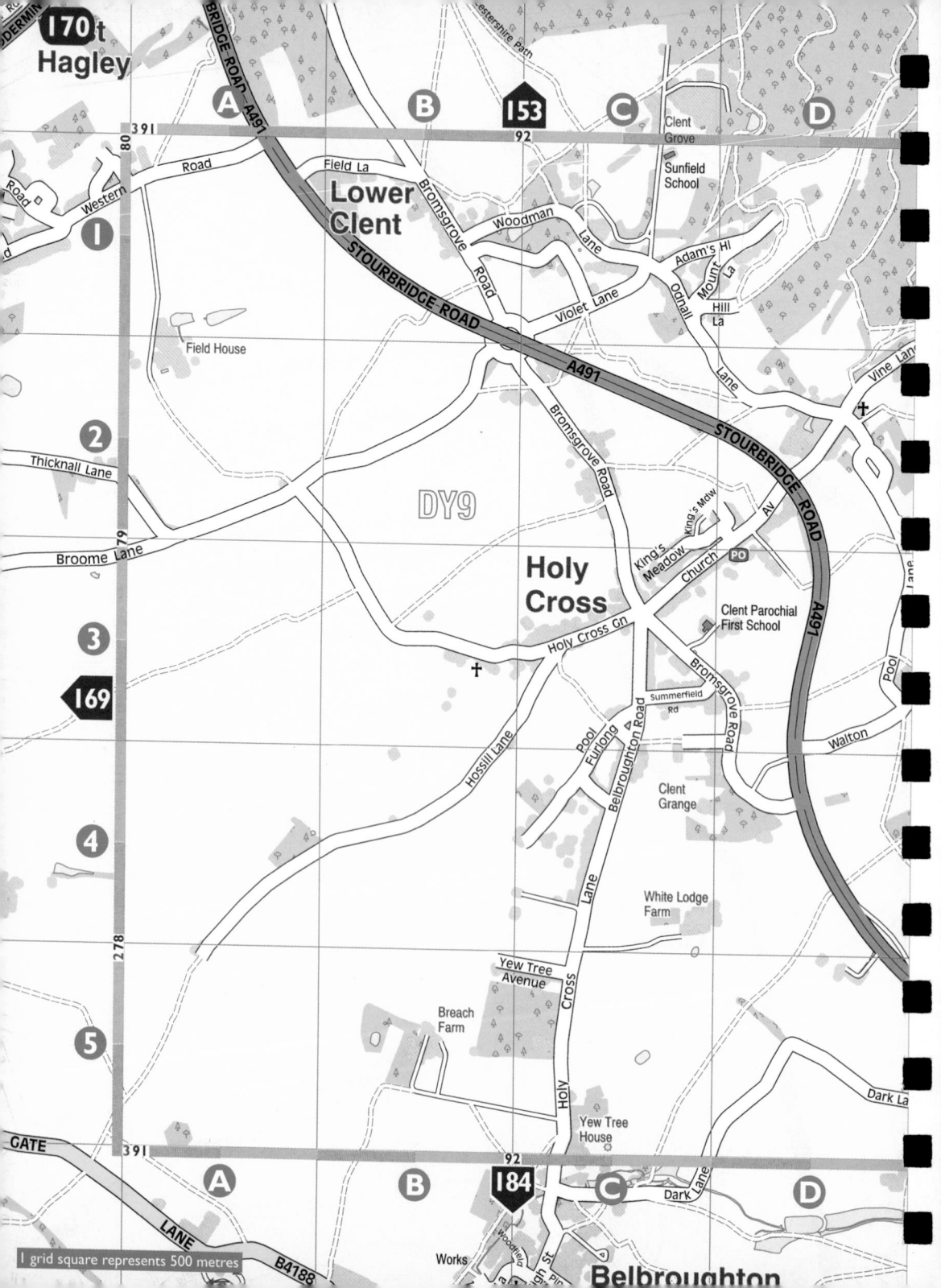
170
Hagley
A
B
153
C
D
391
92
80
Clent Grove
Sunfield School
Field La
Lower Clent
Road
Western
Bromsgrove
Woodman
Lane
Adam's Hl
Mount La
Odnall
Hill La
Road
Violet Lane
STOURBRIDGE ROAD
A491
Field House
Vine Lane
Bromsgrove Road
STOURBRIDGE ROAD
Thicknall Lane
DY9
King's Mdw
King's Meadow
Church Av
PO
79
Broome Lane
Holy Cross
Clent Parochial First School
A491
Holy Cross Gn
Bromsgrove Road
Summerfield Rd
169
Pool Furlong
Belbroughton Road
Walton
Hossill Lane
Clent Grange
Pool
White Lodge Farm
Lane
278
Yew Tree Avenue
Cross
Breach Farm
Holy
Dark La
Yew Tree House
GATE
391
92
A
B
184
C
Dark Lane
D
LANE
B4188
Works
Belbroughton
1 grid square represents 500 metres

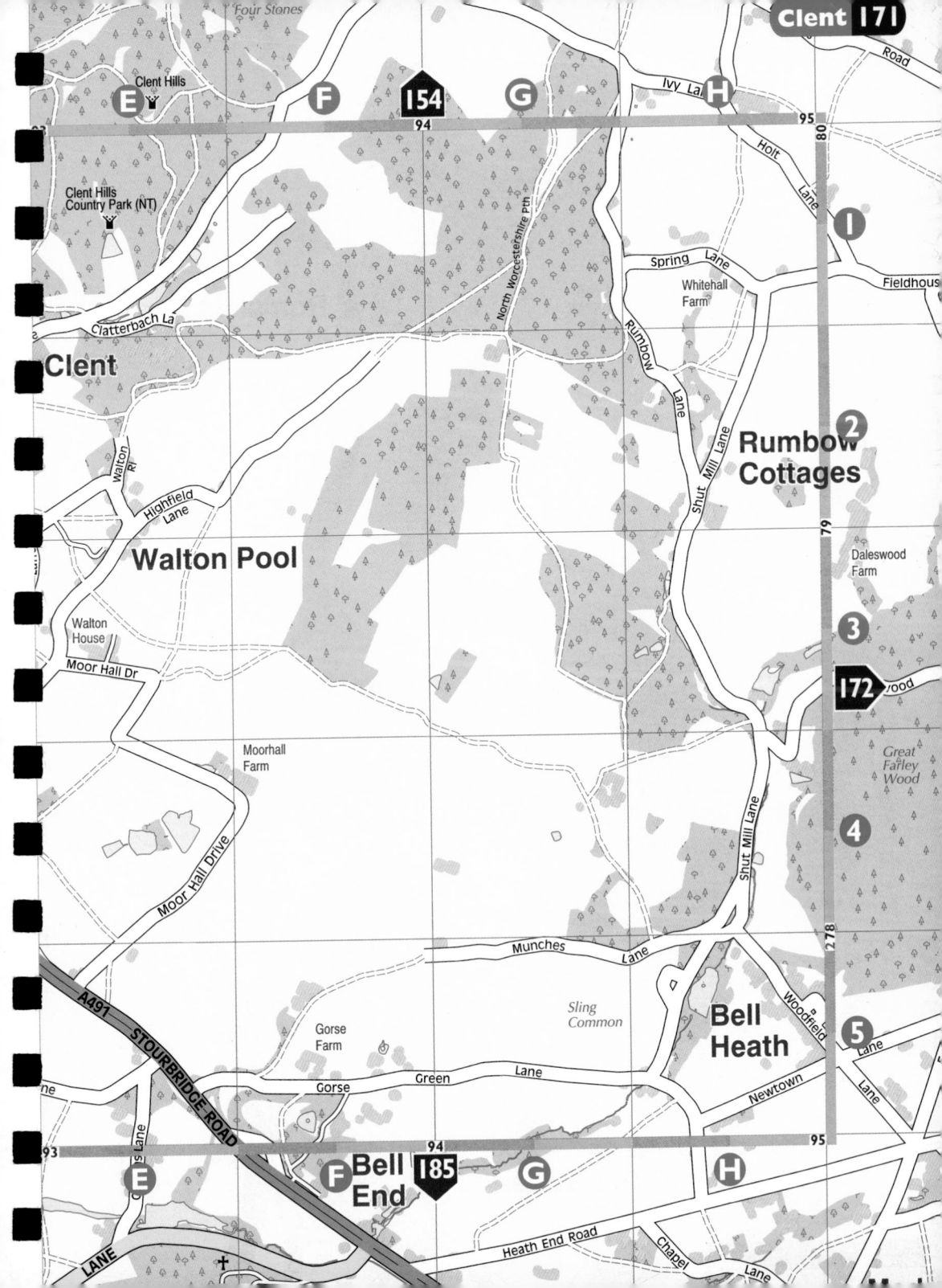

Four Stones
Clent Hills
Clent Hills Country Park (NT)
E
F
154
G
H
Ivy La
Road
94
95
80
Holt
Lane
I
Spring Lane
Whitehall Farm
Fieldhous
North Worcestershire Pth
Clatterbach La
Clent
Rumbow Lane
Shut Mill Lane
2
Rumbow Cottages
Walton Rd
Highfield Lane
Walton Pool
79
Daleswood Farm
Walton House
3
Moor Hall Dr
172
wood
Moorhall Farm
Great Farley Wood
4
Moor Hall Drive
Shut Mill Lane
278
Munches Lane
A491
STOURBRIDGE ROAD
Sling Common
Bell Heath
Woodfield
5
Lane
Gorse Farm
Gorse
Green
Lane
Newtown
Lane
ne
93
94
95
Lane
E
F
Bell End
185
G
H
LANE
Heath End Road
Chapel
Lane

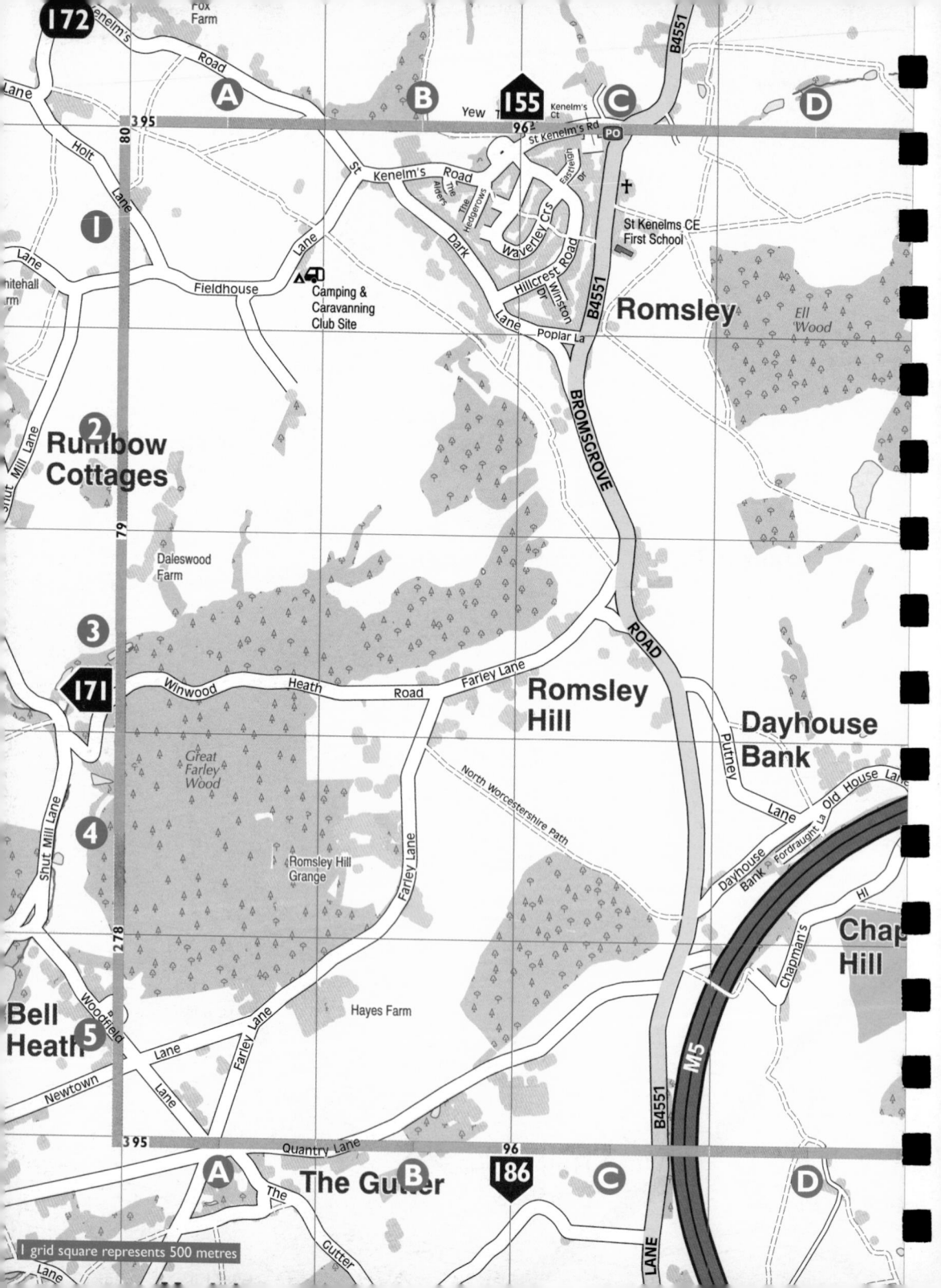

172

Fox Farm

Kenelm's Road

A

B

Yew Tr **155** Kenelm's Ct

St Kenelm's Rd

C

PO

D

80 395

962

St Kenelm's Road

St Kenelm's Lane

The Alders

The Hedgerows

Waverley Crs

Eastfield Dr

Winston Dr

Hillcrest Road

St Kenelms CE First School

Holt Lane

Lane

1

Lane

Whitehall Farm

Fieldhouse

Camping & Caravanning Club Site

Dark Lane

Poplar La

Romsley

Ell Wood

B4551

BROMSGROVE

2 Rumbow Cottages

Shut Mill Lane

79

Daleswood Farm

3

171

Winwood

Heath

Road

Farley Lane

ROAD

Romsley Hill

Dayhouse Bank

Great Farley Wood

North Worcestershire Path

Putney Lane

Dayhouse Bank

Fordraught La

Old House Lane

4

Shut Mill Lane

278

Farley Lane

Romsley Hill Grange

Chapman's

Hl

Chap **Hill**

Bell Heath

5

Woodfield Lane

Hayes Farm

Farley Lane

M5

Newtown Lane

395

Quantry Lane

96

B4551

A

The Gutter

B

186

C

D

LANE

The Gutter

I grid square represents 500 metres

Lane

Romsley 173
Frankley Gn
Frankley
156
Oxwood La
Newbrook Farm
Oxwood Lane
Long Saw Croft
Monarch's Way
Newtown Lane
Yew Tree Lane
Yew Tree Farm
Pound La
Frankley Hill
M5
Newtown Farm
Frankley Hl La
Worcestershire County
Birmingham
Frankley
Qu Elizabeth Rd
Boleyn Rd
Holly Hill Infant School
Frankley Community High School
Frankley Health Centre
174
New St
Lysander Rd
Prospero
Arden Rd
Ringwood Dr
Gannow Green Lane
Newtown Lane
Romany Rd
Boleyn Road
Cornwall Rd
Devon Road
Devon Rd
Fordway
Ormond Rd
Reaside Junior School
Mitten Av
Gannow Mnr Gdns
Rubery Lane
The Pines
Brookdale Close
Cross Farms La
New Inns Lane
man's
Windmill Hill (look out)
North Worcestershire Path
Waseley Hills Country Park
Madley Cl
Clent Road
Grange Crs
Waseley Road
Romsley Cl
Leasowe Rd
Rea Avenue
Windmill Avenue
Cock Hill Lane
The Doweries
Birmingham Great Park
Deelands Rd
Rubery Farm Gv
Dencer Cl
Sandstone Av
Cock Hill
Pinewood Cl
Hillview
Cleves Road
Rubery Clinic
187
Barrington Road
Richmond Rd
Gunner Lane
Gannow Middle School
The Av
Works
Kineton Rd
Rochford Cl
Brook Rd
Heron Wy
Callowbrook Lane
Callowbridge Rd
A38
Bristol Rd
Police Station
Beverley Road
Leach Gn
E
F
G
H
1
2
3
4
5
97
98
99
80
79
78

174
157
173
188
Frankley Hill
Frankley Beeches
Frankley Lodge Farm
Worcestershire County
Birmingham
Egghill Lane
Frankley Hill Lane
Frankley Beeches Road
Frogmill Junior School
The Beeches Infant School
Trescott Primary School
Council Building
North Worcs Golf Club
Golf Course
Frankley Community High School
Frankley Health Centre
Frankley Ind Park
New St
Holly Hill Road
Rubery La
Reaside Clinic
Birmingham Great Park
Premier Lodge
Colmers Farm J&I School
Superstore
Colmers Farm Secondary School
BRISTOL RD SOUTH
A38
BRISTOL ROAD SOUTH
Rubery
Long
St Columbas RC Primary School
Works
Tessall Lane
Frankley Beeches Rd
Hollymoor Way
Long Saw Dr
Roundabout
1 grid square represents 500 metres

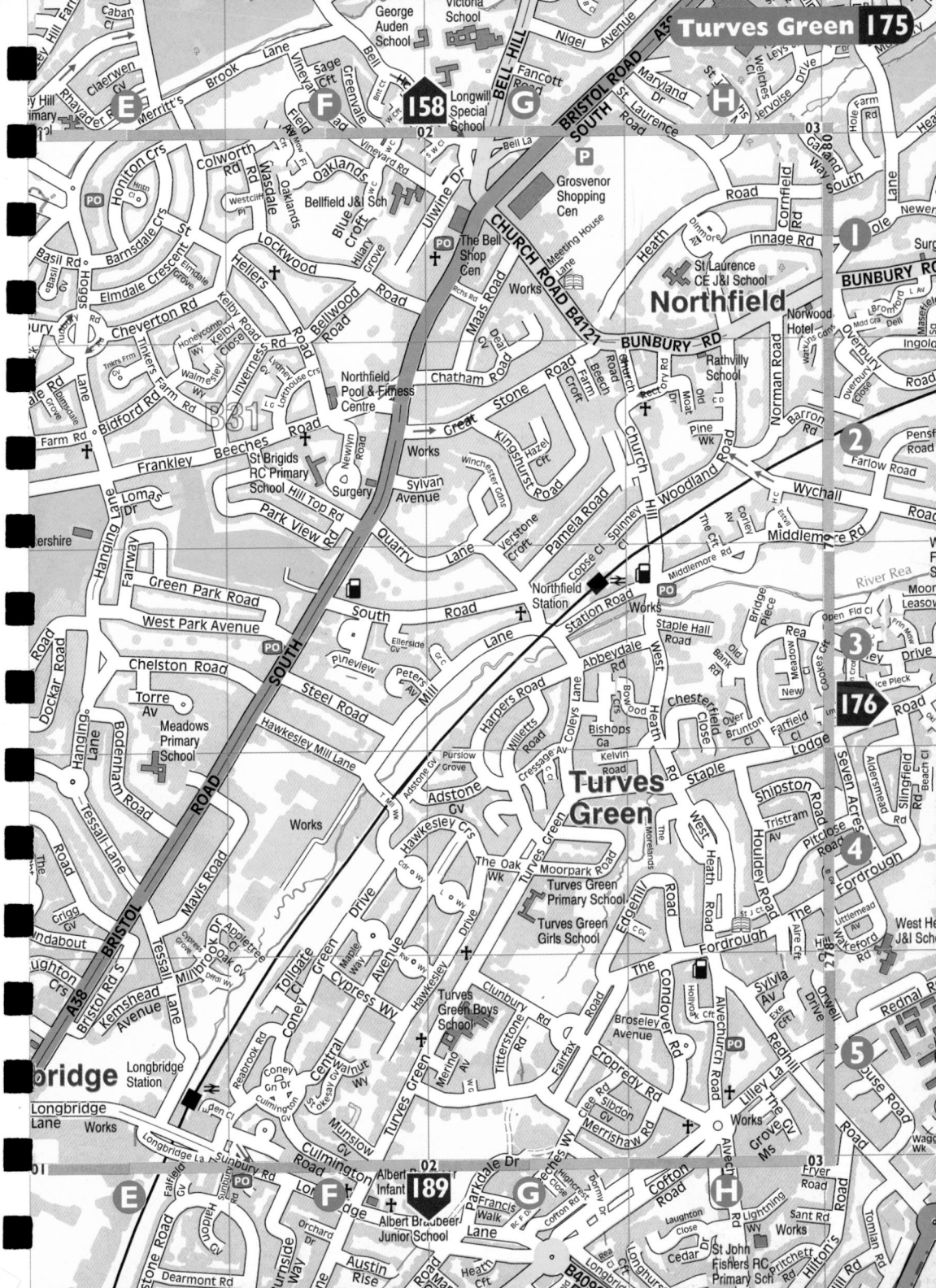
George Auden School
Victoria School
Bell Hill
Nigel Avenue
Bristol Road South
A38
Claerwen Gv
Merritt's Brook Lane
Vineyard
Sage Cft
Greenvale
Field
Bell
158
Longwill Special School
Fancott Road
Maryland Dr
St Laurence Road
Welches Cl
Jervoise Drive
Hole Farm Rd
E
F
G
H
02
03
Colworth Rd
Honiton Crs
Wasdale Rd
Oaklands
Vineyard Rd
Bell La
Grosvenor Shopping Cen
Cornfield Rd
Road
Heath
South
Lane
Newent
Westcliff Pl
Bellfield J&I Sch
Blue Croft
Ulwine Dr
PO
The Bell Shop Cen
Church Road B4121
Meeting House Lane
Dinmore Av
Innage Rd
Hole
I
Barnsdale Crs
St
Lockwood
Hellers
Hilary Grove
St Laurence CE J&I School
Surge
Bunbury Rd
Basil Rd
Basil Gv
Hoggs
Elmdale Crescent
Elmdale Grove
Road
Works
Northfield
Norwood Hotel
Bromford Dell
Maas Road
Deal Gv
Bunbury Rd
Rathvilly School
Norman Road
Overbury
Ingolds
Cheverton Rd
Tinkers Farm Rd
Kelby Road
Kelby Close
Walmesley Wy
Honeycomb Wy
Inverness Rd
Lyaney Gv
Lofthouse Crs
Bellwood Road
Road
Northfield Pool & Fitness Centre
Chatham Road
Road
Farm Croft
Beech Road
Church Rd
Rectory Rd
Moat Dr
Old
Overbury Close
Road
Bidford Rd
Dimsdale Grove
Lane
B31
Great Stone Road
Kingshurst Road
Hazel Cft
Pine Wk
Barron Rd
2
Pensford Road
Farm Rd
Frankley Beeches Road
St Brigids RC Primary School
Newlyn Road
Surgery
Works
Winchester Gdns
Church Hill
Woodland Road
Farlow Road
Wychall Road
Lomas Dr
Hill Top Rd
Sylvan Avenue
Pamela Road
Spinney Cl
The Cft
Corley Av
Middlemore Rd
Park View Rd
Quarry Lane
Verstone Croft
Copse Cl
Middlemore Rd
River Rea
Hanging Lane
Fairway
Green Park Road
Northfield Station
PO
Moor Leasow
South Road
Station Road
Works
Bridge Piece
Open Fld Cl
West Park Avenue
Ellerside Gv
Lane
Staple Hall Road
Rea
Drive
3
Road
Dockar Road
Chelston Road
Pineview
Gr C
Peters Av
Mill
Abbeydale Rd
West Heath Rd
Old Bank Rd
Meadow Cl
Cookes Cft
New Cl
Ice Pleck
176
Road
Torre Av
Meadows Primary School
Steel Road
Harpers Road
Willetts Road
Coleys Lane
Bow Wood Crs
Chesterfield Close
Over Brunton Cl
Farfield Cl
Lodge
Bishops Ga
Kelvin Road
Hawkesley Mill Lane
Purslow Grove
Adstone Gv
Cressage Av
Staple
Hanging Lane
Bodenham Road
Adstone Gv
Turves Green
Shipston Road
Seven Acres Road
Aldersmead Rd
Slingfield Rd
Beach Cl
Tessall Lane
Road
Works
Hawkesley Crs
West Heath Road
The Morelands
Tristram Av
Houldey Road
Pitclose Road
4
Fordrough
The Oak Wk
Moorpark Road
Turves Green Primary School
Edgehill Road
Road
Mavis Road
Drive
Turves Green Girls School
Littlemead Av
West Heath J&I School
Grigg Gv
Roundabout
Bristol
Appletree Cl
Cypress Grove
Oak Gv
Millbrook Dr
Maple Way
Avenue
Green
Tollgate Cl
Drive
Coney Green
Cypress Wy
Hawkesley
The Fordrough
The Condover
The Aire Cft
Wakeford Rd
Kemshead Avenue
Bristol Rd S
A38
Lane
Turves Green Boys School
Clunbury Rd
Road
Hollyoak Cft
Alvechurch Road
Sylvia Av
Drive
Orwell
Rednal Road
Broseley Avenue
Exe Cft
Redhill
PO
5
Reabrook Rd
Coney Gn Dr
Central
Walnut Wy
Merino Av
Titterstone Rd
Fairfax
Cropredy Rd
Condover Rd
Lilley La
The Gv
Grove Ms
Works
House Road
Longbridge Station
Culmington Gv
St Okesay Gv
Turves Green
Clee Rd
Sibdon Gv
Merrishaw Rd
Alvechurch
Longbridge Lane
Works
Eden Cl
Munslow Grove
Waggon Wk
Longbridge La
Sunbury Rd
Culmington Road
Parkdale Dr
Beeches Wy
Highcrest Close
Dormy Dr
Fryer Road
PO
Albert Bradbeer Infant
189
Francis Walk
Cofton Rd
Cofton Road
Lightning Wy
Sant Rd
Laughton Close
Cedar Dr
Works
Haldon Gv
Sunbury Gv
Orchard Dr
Albert Bradbeer Junior School
Lane
St John Fishers RC Primary Sch
Pritchett Rd
Hilton's
Tomlan Rd
Dearmont Rd
Burnside Way
Austin Rise
Heath Cft
Rea Cl
Longbridge
B4096
Longhurst Cft

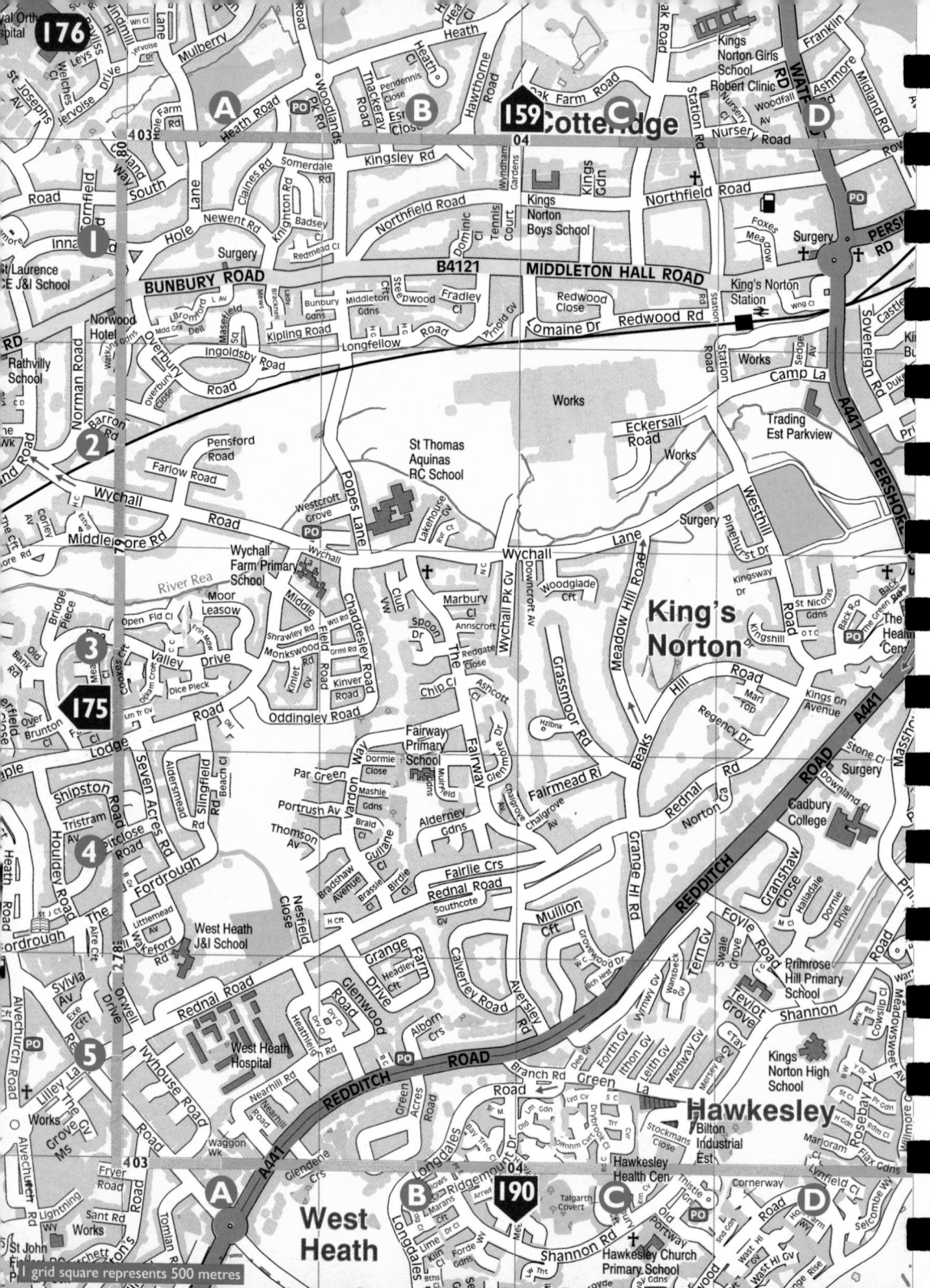
176
159
175
190
A
B
C
D
1
2
3
4
5
403
04
Cotteridge
Kings Norton Girls School
Robert Clinic
Heath Road
Pendennis Close
Woodlands Pk Rd
Thackeray Road
Hawthorne Road
Oak Farm Road
Station Rd
Nursery Road
Franklin
Ashmore Rd
Midland Rd
Woodfall Av
Mulberry
Jervoise Drive
Welches Cl
Leys
St Josephs Av
Hole Farm Rd
Kingsley Rd
Somerdale Rd
Claines Rd
Knighton Rd
Badsey Cl
Redmead Cl
Northfield Road
Wyndham Gardens
Tennis Court
Dominic Cl
Kings Gdn
Kings Norton Boys School
Foxes Meadow
Surgery
PO
Newent Rd
Hole Lane
Bunbury Road
B4121
Middleton Hall Road
Pershore Rd
Kings Norton Station
St Laurence CE J&I School
Norwood Hotel
Rathvilly School
Norman Road
Masefield Sq
Bunbury Gdns
Middleton Gdns
Steepwood
Fradley Cl
Redwood Close
Redwood Rd
Lomaine Dr
Kipling Road
Longfellow Road
Arnold Gv
Ingoldsby Road
Overbury Road
Overbury Close
Works
Camp La
Sedge Av
Sovereign Rd
Station Road
Eckersall Road
Trading Est Parkview
A441
Barron Rd
Pensford Road
Farlow Road
Wychall Road
Middlemore Rd
Corley Av
St Thomas Aquinas RC School
Westcroft Grove
Popes Lane
Lakehouse Gv
Wychall Lane
Westhill
Pinehurst Dr
Wychall Farm Primary School
River Rea
Moor Leasow
Open Fld Cl
Bridge Piece
Valley Drive
Dice Pleck
Middle Field Road
Chaddesley Road
Shrawley Rd
Monkswood Rd
Kinlet Gv
Kinver Road
Oddingley Road
Club Vw
Spoon Dr
Marbury Cl
Annscroft
The Redgate Close
Chip Cl
Ashcott Cl
Wychall Pk Gv
Downcroft Av
Woodglade Cft
Grassmoor Rd
Meadow Hill Road
King's Norton
Kingsway Dr
St Nicolas Gdns
Kingshill Dr
Back Rd
The Green
The Health Cen
Hill Road
Marl Top
Regency Dr
Kings Gn Avenue
Beaks
Stone Cl
Downland Cl
Cadbury College
Masshouse
Lodge Road
Over Brunton Cl
Cookes Cft
Seven Acres Rd
Aldersmead Rd
Slingfield Rd
Beach Cl
Shipston Road
Tristram Av
Pitclose Road
Houldey Road
Fordrough
The Fordrough
Littlemead Av
Wakeford Rd
West Heath J&I School
Fairway Primary School
Dormie Close
Par Green
Vardon Way
Mashie Gdns
Portrush Av
Braid Cl
Thomson Av
Gullane Cl
Bradshaw Avenue
Brassie Cl
Birdie Cl
Alderney Gdns
Fairway
Glenmore Dr
Chalgrove Av
Fairmead Ri
Rednal Rd
Norton Ga
Grange Hl Rd
Fairlie Crs
Rednal Road
Southcote Gv
Nesfield Close
H Cft
Mullion Cft
Grovewood Dr
Redditch Road
Granshaw Close
Halladale
Dormie Drive
Foyle Road
Swale Grove
Tern Gv
Primrose Hill Primary School
Teviot Grove
Shannon
Grange Farm Drive
Headley Cft
Glenwood Road
Calverley Road
Aversley Rd
Albom Crs
Heathfield Rd
West Heath Hospital
Ivyhouse Road
Sylvia Av
Exe Cft
Orwell Drive
Alvechurch Road
Lilley La
The Grove Ms
Nearhill Rd
Nearhill Road
Waggon Wk
Green Acres Road
Branch Rd
Green La
Dee Gv
Forth Gv
Ithon Gv
Leith Gv
Medway Gv
Mersey Gv
Wansbeck Gv
Wyrley Gv
Hawkesley
Bilton Industrial Est
Stockmans Close
Drybrook Cl
Kings Norton High School
Cowslip Cl
Meadowsweet Av
Rosebay Av
Marjoram Cl
Flax Gdns
Lynfield Cl
Cornerway
Willmore
Longdales
Ridgemount Dr
Bay Tree Cl
Hawkesley Health Cen
Talgarth Covert
Thistle Grn
Old Portway
Shannon Rd
Hawkesley Church Primary School
Wast Hl Gv
Selcombe Wy
Glendene Crs
Fryer Road
Lightning Wy
Sant Rd
Works
Tomlan Rd
West Heath
Lime Cft
Kiln Cl
Forde Wy
Marans Cft
St John Fisher RC
1 grid square represents 500 metres

Lifford
Brandwood End
Walker's Heath
Allens Croft Primary School
Cotteridge Primary School
Lifford Trading Estate
Kings Norton Business Cen
Woodthorpe Primary School
Brandwood End Cemetery
Cemetery
Lindsworth School
Monyhull Hospital
Kings Norton Primary School
Broadmeadow J&I School
Bells Farm Primary School
The Oaks Primary Sch
Medical Cen
Hillmeads Health Centre
St Pauls RC Primary School
Moundsley Hall
Moundsley Farm
Worcester & Birmingham Canal
Stratford - upon - Avon Canal
Lifford Lane
Broad Meadow Lane
Monyhull Hall Road
Parson's Hill
Bells Lane
Druids Lane
Walkers Heath Road
Icknield St
Gay Hill
Longdales Road
Primrose Hill
Crabmill Lane
Dark Lane
Brandwood Park Road
Broad Lane
Shelfield Road
Tunnel Lane
Wharf Road
Hillmeads Road
Gildas Avenue
160
178
191

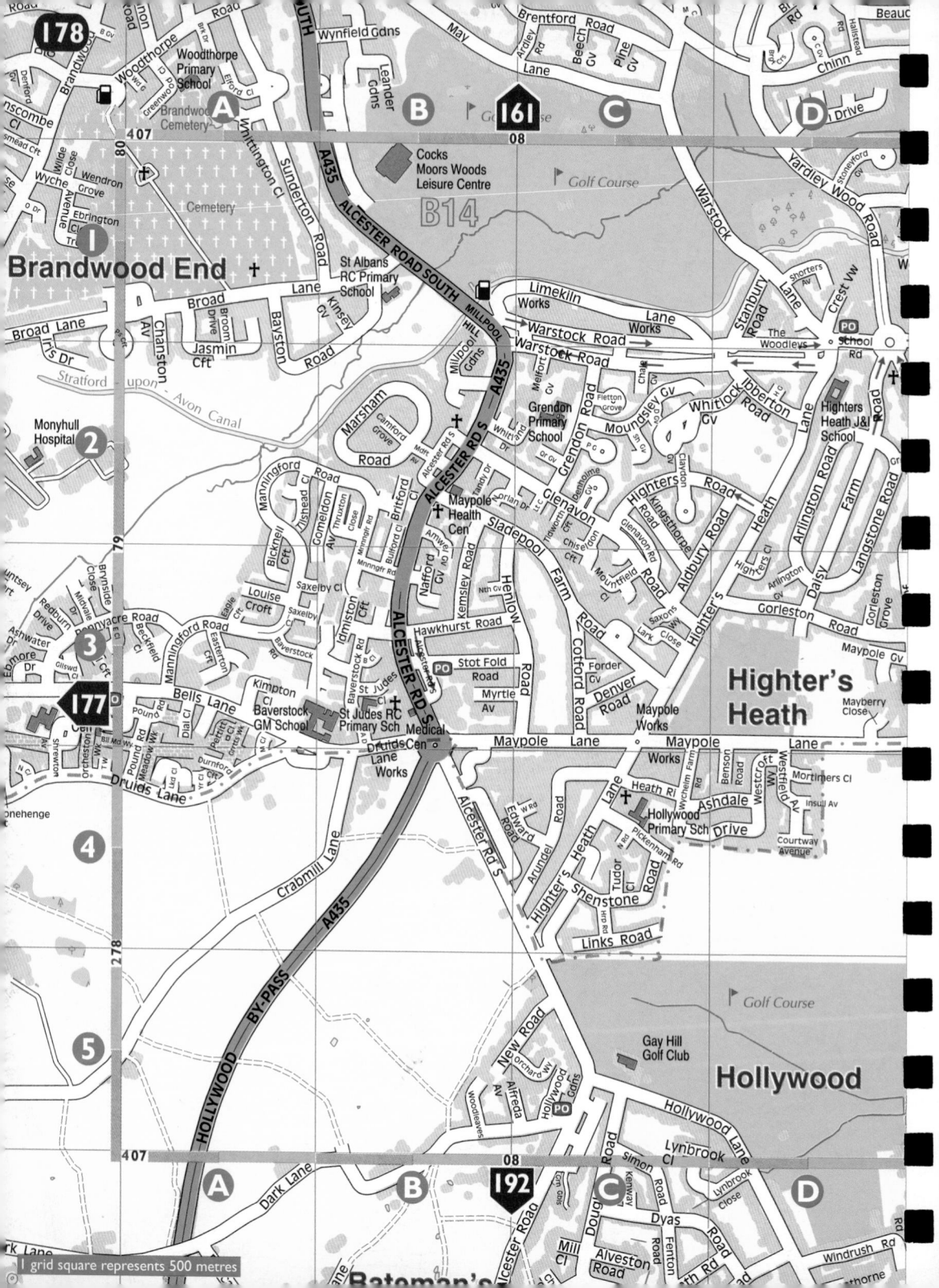
178
161
177
192
A
B
C
D
1
2
3
4
5
407
08
80
79
278
B14
Brandwood End
Brandwood Cemetery
Cemetery
Woodthorpe Primary School
Woodthorpe Road
Whittington Cl
Sunderton Road
Wynfield Gdns
Leander Gdns
Cocks Moors Woods Leisure Centre
Golf Course
A435
ALCESTER ROAD SOUTH
MILLPOOL HILL
ALCESTER RD S
Brentford Road
May Lane
Warstock Lane
Yardley Wood Road
Chinn
Drive
Stoneyford
Shorters Av
Crest Vw
Limekiln Lane
Works
Warstock Road
The Woodleys
School Rd
Stanbury Road
St Albans RC Primary School
Broad Lane
Kinsey Gv
Bayston Road
Jasmin Cft
Broom Drive
Chanston Av
Iris Dr
Stratford - upon - Avon Canal
Monyhull Hospital
Millpool Gdns
Marsham Road
Camford Grove
Melfort Gv
Grendon Primary School
Grendon Road
Fletton Grove
Moundsley Gv
Whitlock Gv
Ibberton Road
Highters Heath J&I School
Highters Heath Lane
Manningford Road
Tilshead Cl
Comeldon Av
Thruxton Close
Britford Cl
Bulford Cl
Maypole Health Cen
Glenavon Road
Sladepool Farm Road
Highters Road
Kingsthorpe Road
Aldbury Road
Arlington Road
Daisy Farm Road
Langstone Road
Bicknell Cft
Saxelby Cl
Louise Croft
Nafford Gv
Kemsley Road
Henlow Road
Mountfield Cl
Gorleston Road
Gorleston Grove
Pennyacre Road
Manningford Road
Beckfield Cl
Baverstock Rd
Idmiston Cft
Hawkhurst Road
Stot Fold Road
Myrtle Av
Cotford Road
Forder Gv
Denver Road
Saxons Wy
Lark Close
Highter's Road
Highter's Heath
Maypole Gv
Mayberry Close
Bells Lane
Kimpton Cl
Baverstock GM School
St Judes RC Primary Sch
St Judes Cl
Medical Cen
Maypole Works
Maypole Lane
Druids Lane
Lane Works
Alcester Rd S
Edward Road
Arundel Road
Heath Rl
Hollywood Primary Sch
Ashdale Drive
Westcroft Wy
Westfield Av
Mortimers Cl
Insull Av
Courtway Avenue
Pickenham Rd
Tudor Cl
Shenstone Road
Links Road
Crabmill Lane
HOLLYWOOD BY-PASS
Gay Hill Golf Club
Hollywood
New Road
Orchard Wy
Alfreda Av
Woodleaves
Hollywood Gdns
Hollywood Lane
Lynbrook Cl
Lynbrook Close
Simon Road
Kenway
Dyas Road
Fenton Road
Alveston Road
Mill Cl
Dark Lane
Windrush Rd
Alcester Road
Bateman's
1 grid square represents 500 metres

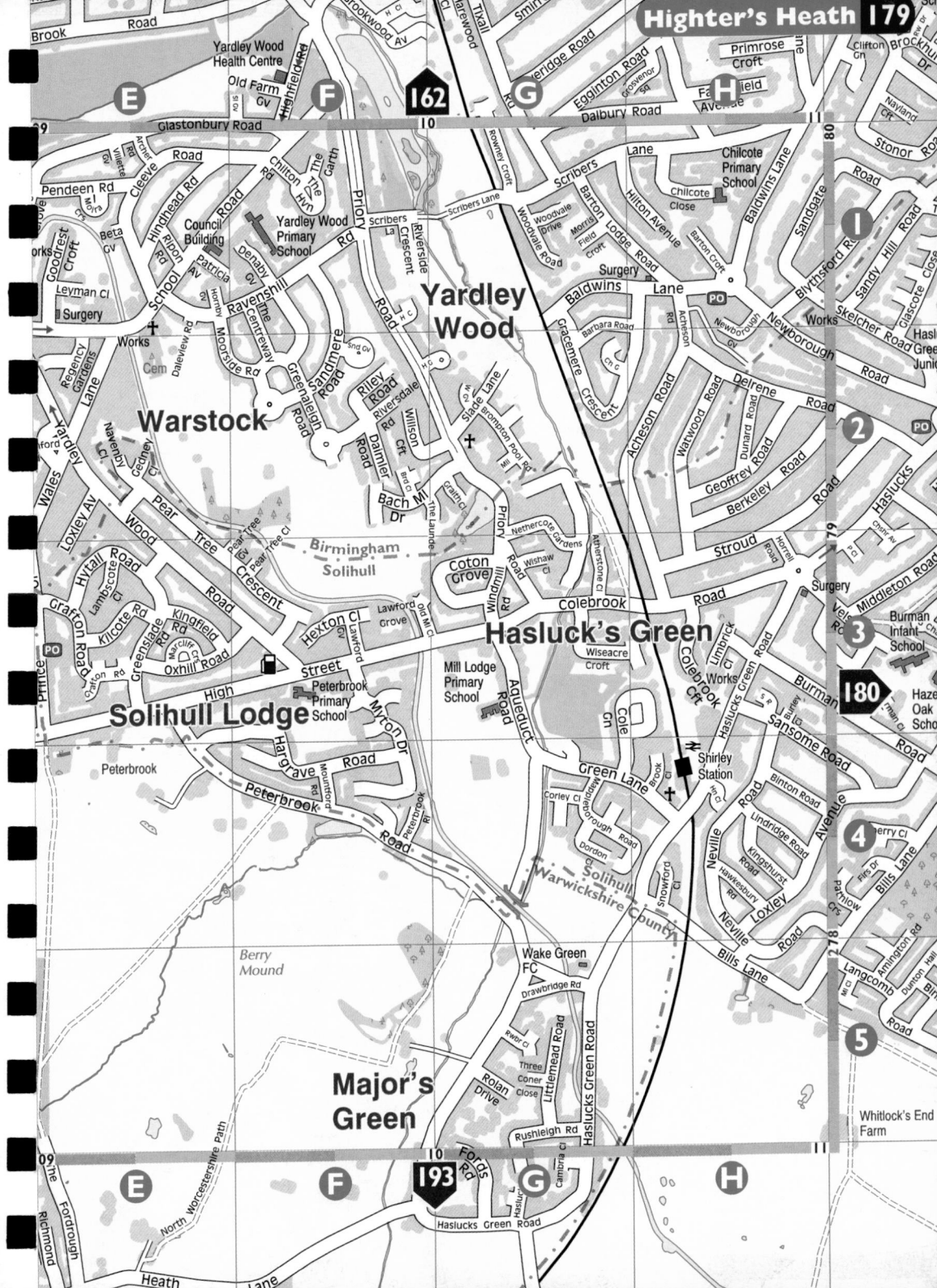
Yardley Wood
Warstock
Hasluck's Green
Solihull Lodge
Major's Green
Birmingham
Solihull
Warwickshire County
162
180
193
Yardley Wood Health Centre
Council Building
Yardley Wood Primary School
Chilcote Primary School
Mill Lodge Primary School
Peterbrook Primary School
Burman Infant School
Shirley Station
Wake Green FC
Berry Mound
Whitlock's End Farm
Peterbrook
Glastonbury Road
Priory Road
Scribers Lane
Baldwins Lane
Newborough Road
Colebrook Road
High Street
Peterbrook Road
Aqueduct Road
Green Lane
Bills Lane
Haslucks Green Road
Burman Road
Sansome Road
Stroud Road
Berkeley Road
Geoffrey Road
Acheson Road
Slade Lane
Windmill Road
Yardley Wood Road
Pear Tree Crescent
School Road
Ravenshill Road
Hargrave Road
Littlemead Road
Rolan Drive
North Worcestershire Path

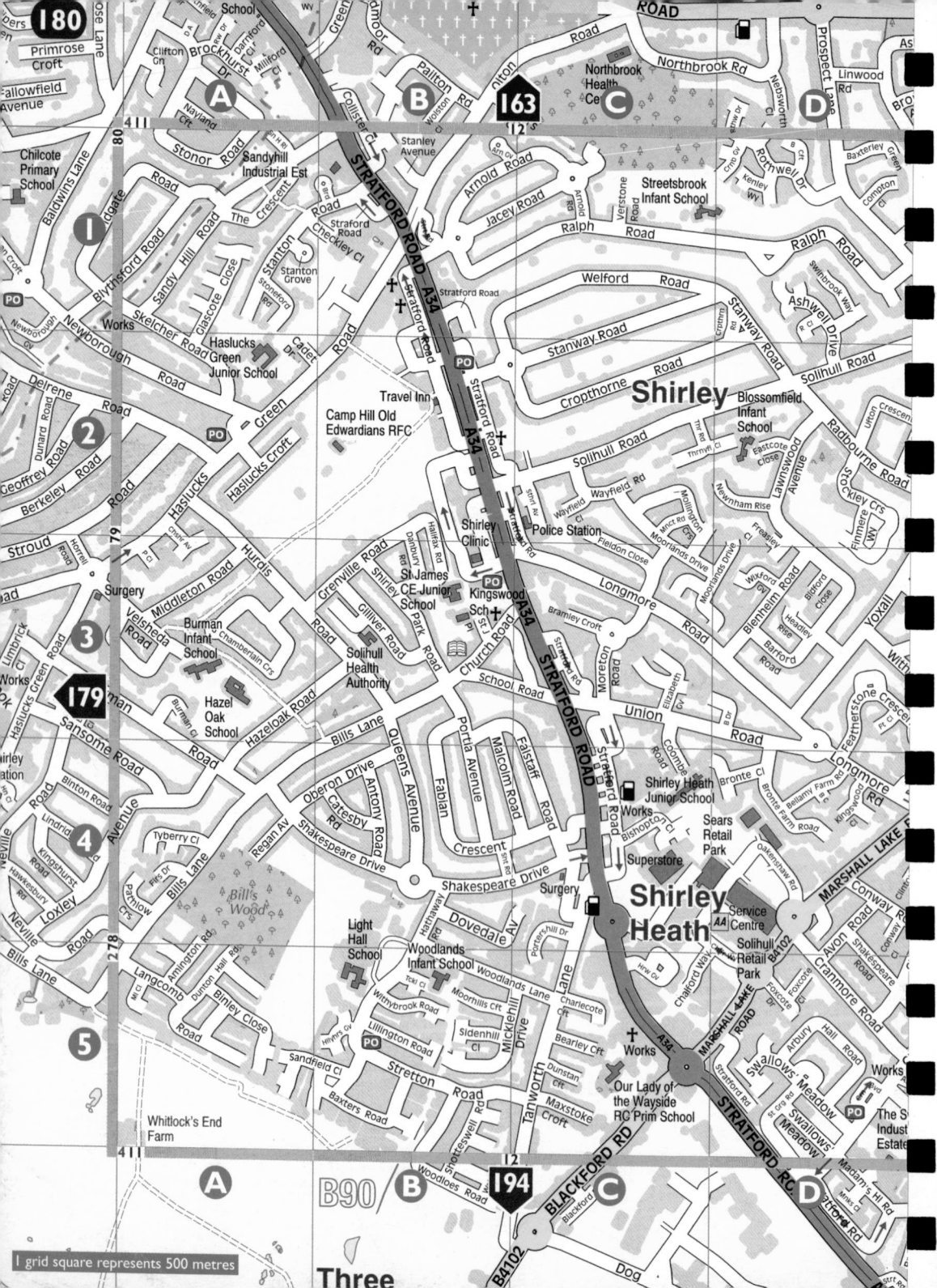

180
163
179
194
Primrose Croft
Fallowfield Avenue
Brockhurst Dr
Stonor Road
Sandyhill Industrial Est
Chilcote Primary School
Baldwins Lane
Blythsford Road
The Crescent
Sandy Hill Road
Glascote Close
Stanton Grove
Skelcher Road
Haslucks Green Junior School
Newborough Road
Delrene Road
Geoffrey Road
Berkeley Road
Haslucks Croft
Green Road
Travel Inn
Camp Hill Old Edwardians RFC
STRATFORD ROAD A34
Stratford Road
Arnold Road
Jacey Road
Ralph Road
Northbrook Health Centre
Northbrook Rd
Prospect Lane
Linwood Rd
Streetsbrook Infant School
Welford Road
Stanway Road
Cropthorne Road
Solihull Road
Shirley
Blossomfield Infant School
Radbourne Road
Wayfield Rd
Newnham Rise
Shirley Clinic
Police Station
Fieldon Close
Moorlands Drive
Longmore Road
Stroud
Surgery
Middleton Road
Hurdis
Velsheda Road
Burman Infant School
Chamberlain Crs
Grenville Road
Shirley Park Road
St James CE Junior School
Kingswood Sch
Gilliver Road
Solihull Health Authority
Church Road
School Road
Hazel Oak School
Hazeloak Road
Sansome Road
Bills Lane
Queens Avenue
Portia Avenue
Malcolm Road
Falstaff Road
Fabian Crescent
Oberon Drive
Antony Road
Catesby Rd
Shakespeare Drive
Union Road
Bronte Cl
Shirley Heath Junior School
Works
Sears Retail Park
Superstore
Shirley Heath
Service Centre
Solihull Retail Park
MARSHALL LAKE ROAD
Bill's Wood
Light Hall School
Woodlands Infant School
Woodlands Lane
Dovedale Av
Withybrook Road
Lillington Road
Stretton Road
Baxters Road
Sandfield Cl
Tanworth Lane
Maxstoke Croft
Our Lady of the Wayside RC Prim School
Whitlock's End Farm
Swallows Meadow
Cranmore Road
Avon Road
BLACKFORD RD
B4102
B90
Woodloes Road
Three
Dog
1 grid square represents 500 metres

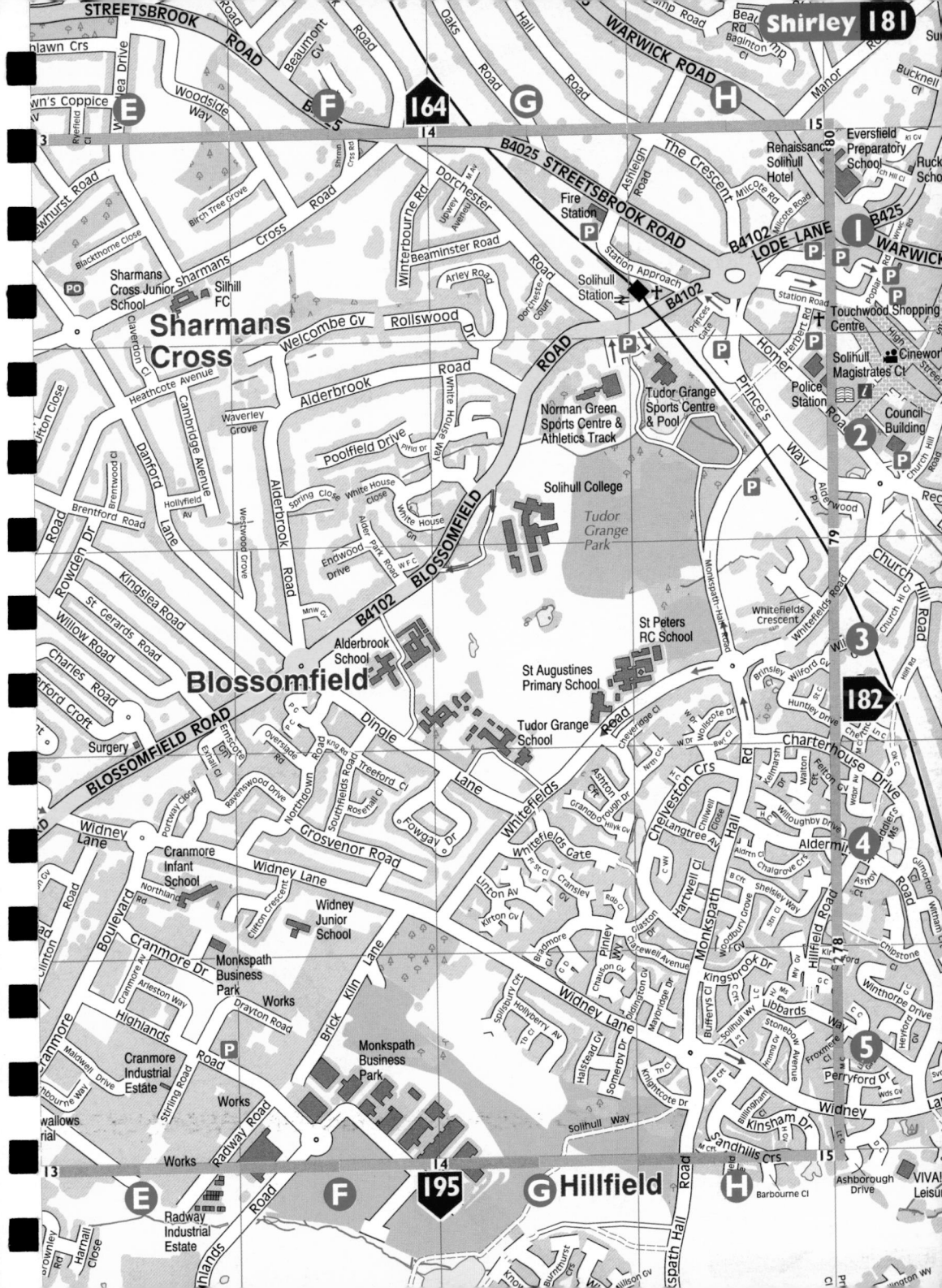

Shirley 181
STREETSBROOK ROAD
WARWICK ROAD
164
182
195
E
F
G
H
I
2
3
4
5
13
14
15
78
79
80
B4025 STREETSBROOK ROAD
B4102
LODE LANE
B425
Woodside Way
Beaumont Gv
Oaks Road
Hall Road
Manor
Bucknell Cl
Baginton Cl
The Crescent
Ashleigh Road
Millcote Rd
Eversfield Preparatory School
Renaissance Solihull Hotel
Fire Station
Station Approach
Solihull Station
Station Road
Touchwood Shopping Centre
Solihull Magistrates Ct
Police Station
Council Building
Homer Road
Princes Gate
Prince's Way
Church Hill Road
Sharmans Cross Road
Sharmans Cross Junior School
Silhill FC
Sharmans Cross
Birch Tree Grove
Blackthorne Close
Winterbourne Rd
Dorchester Road
Beaminster Road
Arley Road
Dorchester Court
Welcombe Gv
Rollswood Dr
Alderbrook Road
Heathcote Avenue
Claverdon Cl
Cambridge Avenue
Danford Lane
Hollyfield Av
Waverley Grove
Westwood Grove
Poolfield Drive
White House Way
Spring Close
White House Close
White House Gn
Alder Park Road
Endwood Drive
BLOSSOMFIELD ROAD
Norman Green Sports Centre & Athletics Track
Tudor Grange Sports Centre & Pool
Solihull College
Tudor Grange Park
Monkspath Hall Road
Whitefields Crescent
Whitefields Road
St Peters RC School
St Augustines Primary School
Tudor Grange School
Alderbrook School
Blossomfield
Brentford Road
Rowden Dr
Kingslea Road
St Gerards Road
Willow Road
Charles Road
Surgery
Emscote Grn
Exhall Cl
Overslade Rd
Northdown Road
Southfields Road
Treeford Cl
Rosehall Cl
Dingle Lane
Fowgay Dr
Grosvenor Road
Ravenswood Drive
Portway Close
Widney Lane
Cranmore Infant School
Northland Rd
Clifton Crescent
Widney Junior School
Boulevard
Cranmore Dr
Monkspath Business Park
Works
Arleston Way
Drayton Road
Highlands Road
Cranmore Industrial Estate
Maidwell Drive
Stirling Road
Radway Road
Brick Kiln Lane
Whitefields Gate
Linton Av
Kirton Gv
Cransley Gv
Pinley Wy
Clarewell Avenue
Bradmore Cl
Chauson Gv
Oldington Gv
Maybridge Dr
Spilsbury Cft
Hollyberry Av
Halstead Gv
Somerby Dr
Knightcote Dr
Solihull Way
Chelveston Crs
Langtree Av
Chilwell Close
Hartwell Cl
Monkspath Hall Rd
Woodbury Grove
Kingsbrook Dr
Bufferys Cl
Libbards Way
Stonebow Avenue
Kinsham Dr
Sandhills Crs
Charterhouse Drive
Kelmarsh Dr
Walton Cl
Felton Gv
Willoughby Drive
Aldermin
Chalgrove Crs
Shelsley Way
Hillfield Road
Chipstone Cl
Winthorpe Drive
Heyford Gv
Froxmere Cl
Perryford Dr
Widney
Wilford Gv
Brinsley Cl
Huntley Drive
Cheveridge Cl
Wollscote Dr
Ashton Cft
Grandborough Dr
Gilmorton Cl
Witham
Ashby Ct
Hillfield
Barbourne Cl
Ashborough Drive
Radway Industrial Estate
Harnall Close
Burnthurst
Monkspath Hall Road

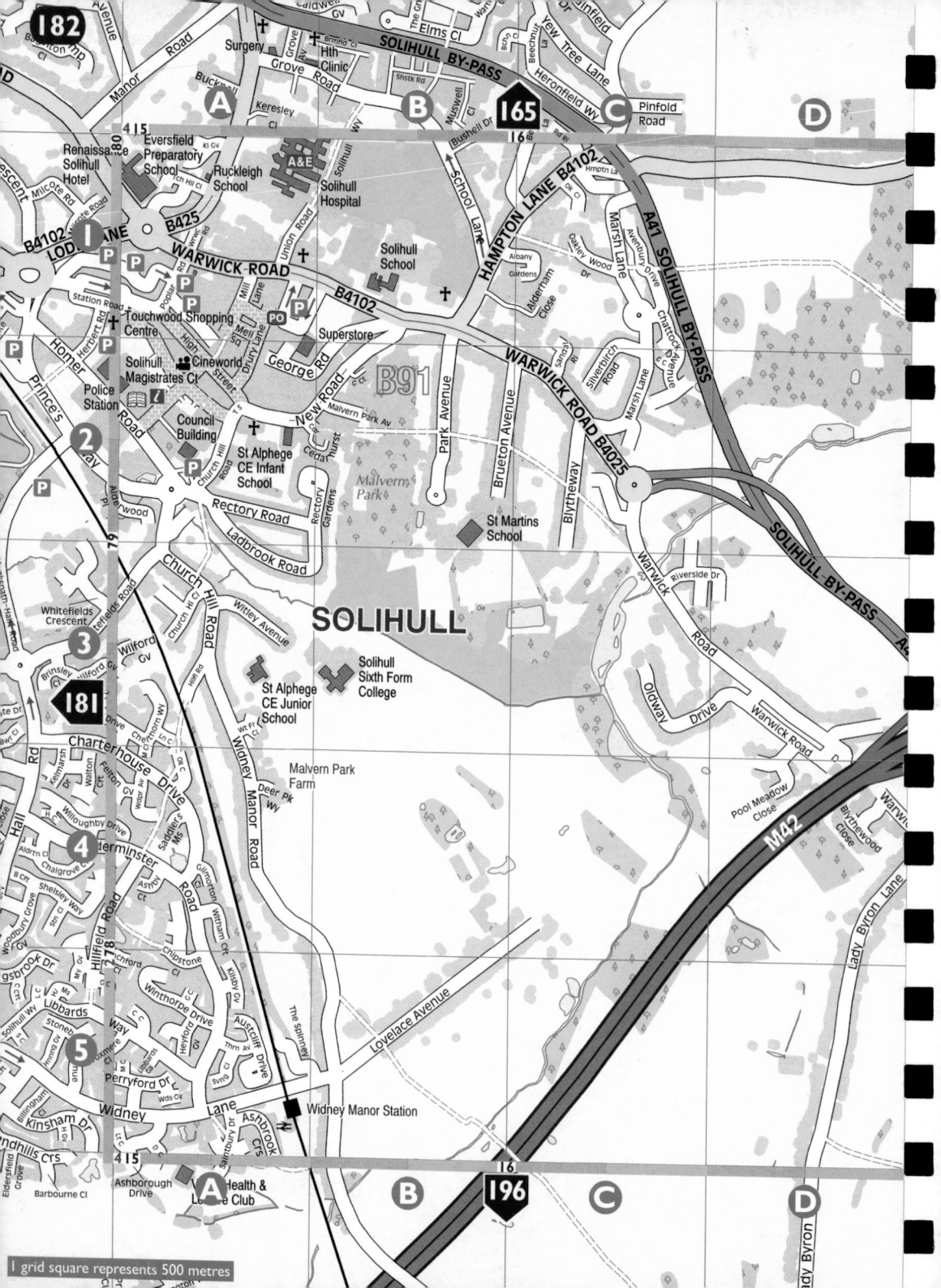
182
165
181
196
A
B
C
D
A
B
C
D
1
2
3
4
5
415
415
16
16
80
79
78
SOLIHULL
B91
SOLIHULL BY-PASS
A41 SOLIHULL BY-PASS
SOLIHULL-BY-PASS
M42
WARWICK ROAD
WARWICK ROAD B4025
B4102
B425
HAMPTON LANE B4102
Manor Road
Grove Road
Elms Cl
Yew Tree Lane
Heronfield Wy
Pinfold Road
Surgery
Hth Clinic
Keresley Cl
Muswell Cl
Bushell Dr
School Lane
Eversfield Preparatory School
Renaissance Solihull Hotel
Ruckleigh School
Solihull Hospital
A&E
Union Road
Solihull School
Milcote Rd
Station Road
Herbert Rd
Homer Road
Poplar Rd
Mill Lane
Touchwood Shopping Centre
Mell Sq
Drury Lane
High Street
George Rd
Superstore
Solihull Magistrates Ct
Cineworld
Police Station
Council Building
Prince's Way
New Road
Malvern Park Av
Church Hill Road
St Alphege CE Infant School
Rectory Road
Rectory Gardens
Ladbrook Road
Malvern Park
Park Avenue
Brueton Avenue
Blytheway
St Martins School
Marsh Lane
Oakley Wood Dr
Avenbury Drive
Alderham Close
Albany Gardens
Chattock Avenue
Silverbirch Road
Sandal Ri
Riverside Dr
Warwick Road
Oldway Drive
Alderwood Pl
Whitefields Crescent
Whitefields Road
Church Hill Cl
Witley Avenue
Wilford Gv
Brinsley Cl
St Alphege CE Junior School
Solihull Sixth Form College
Widney Manor Road
Malvern Park Farm
Deer Pk Wy
Pool Meadow Close
Blythewood Close
Charterhouse Drive
Kelmarsh Dr
Walton Cft
Felton Gv
Willoughby Drive
Saddlers Ms
Chalgrove Cr
Shelsley Way
Woodbury Grove
Hillfield Road
Gilmorton Cl
Witham Cft
Chipstone Cl
Kilsby Gv
Winthorpe Drive
Austcliff Drive
Heyford Gv
Libbards Way
Perryford Dr
Lovelace Avenue
The Spinney
Lady Byron Lane
Widney Lane
Widney Manor Station
Kinsham Dr
Billingham Cl
Ashbrook Crs
Saintbury Dr
Ashborough Drive
Barbourne Cl
Eldersfield Grove
Health & Leisure Club
1 grid square represents 500 metres

de-Barnes
HAMPTON
Lane
B4102
E
F
166
G
H
18
19
80
79
278
17
Berry
Hall
Lane
Ravenshaw
Lane
Catherines Cl
Henwood
Lane
Friday
Lane
I
River Blythe
Grand Union Canal Walk
Barston Lane
M42
2
Eastc
Cow
Hayes
Works
Ravenshaw
Way
3
Knowle
Henwood Hall
Farm
Junction 5
Grove
Farm
4
Copt
Heath
A4141
WARWICK ROAD
Jc La
Jacobean Lane
Queen Eleanors Dr
Minster Cl
Copt Heath
Golf Club
Broadfern Road
Holland Av
Golf Course
Longdon Cft
Lghtwd Cl
Wychwood Avenue
Hampton Road
5
Longdon
Hall
Alveston Grove
197
Barnbrook Rd
Road
Ragley
Close
Whitefield Rd
Hall
Arden
Vale
Road
Hampton Rd
Knowle
FC
Knowle Village
CC
High Trees
Rd
Langfield
Abbots Cl
Road
Warwick
Stourton Cl
Mockley Wd
Kixley
Farm

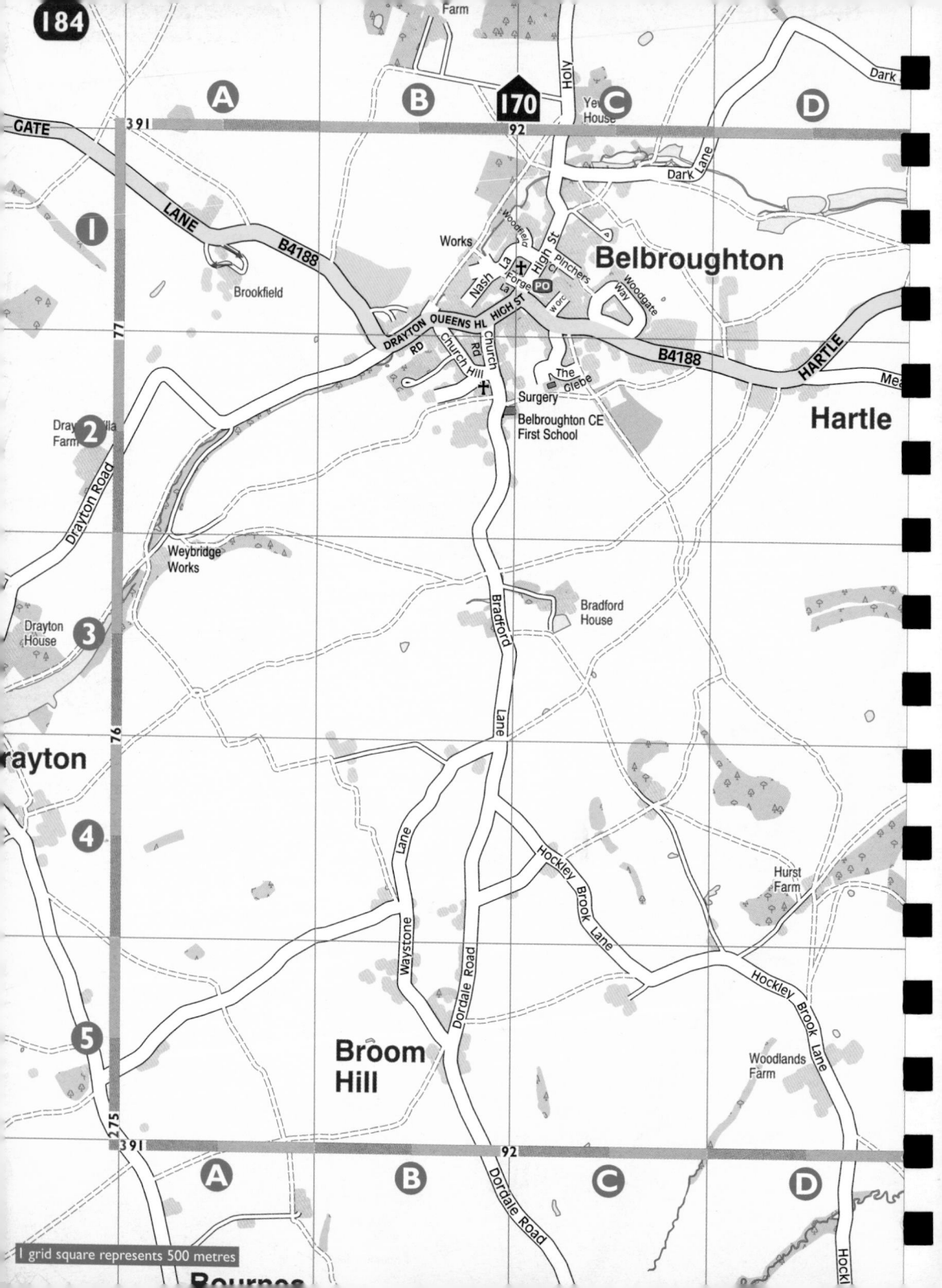

Farm
Holy
170
A
B
C
D
Yew House
GATE
391
92
Dark Lane
Dark
LANE
B4188
Works
Belbroughton
Woodfield
High St
Pinchers
Nash La
Forge La
PO
Woodgate Way
Worc
Brookfield
DRAYTON RD
QUEENS HL
HIGH ST
Church Rd
Church Hill
Church
B4188
HARTLE
The Glebe
Surgery
Belbroughton CE First School
Hartle
Drayton Road
Drayton Villa Farm
77
Weybridge Works
Bradford Lane
Bradford House
Drayton House
76
Drayton
Waystone Lane
Dordale Road
Hockley Brook Lane
Hurst Farm
Broom Hill
Woodlands Farm
275
A
B
C
D
Dordale Road
1 grid square represents 500 metres

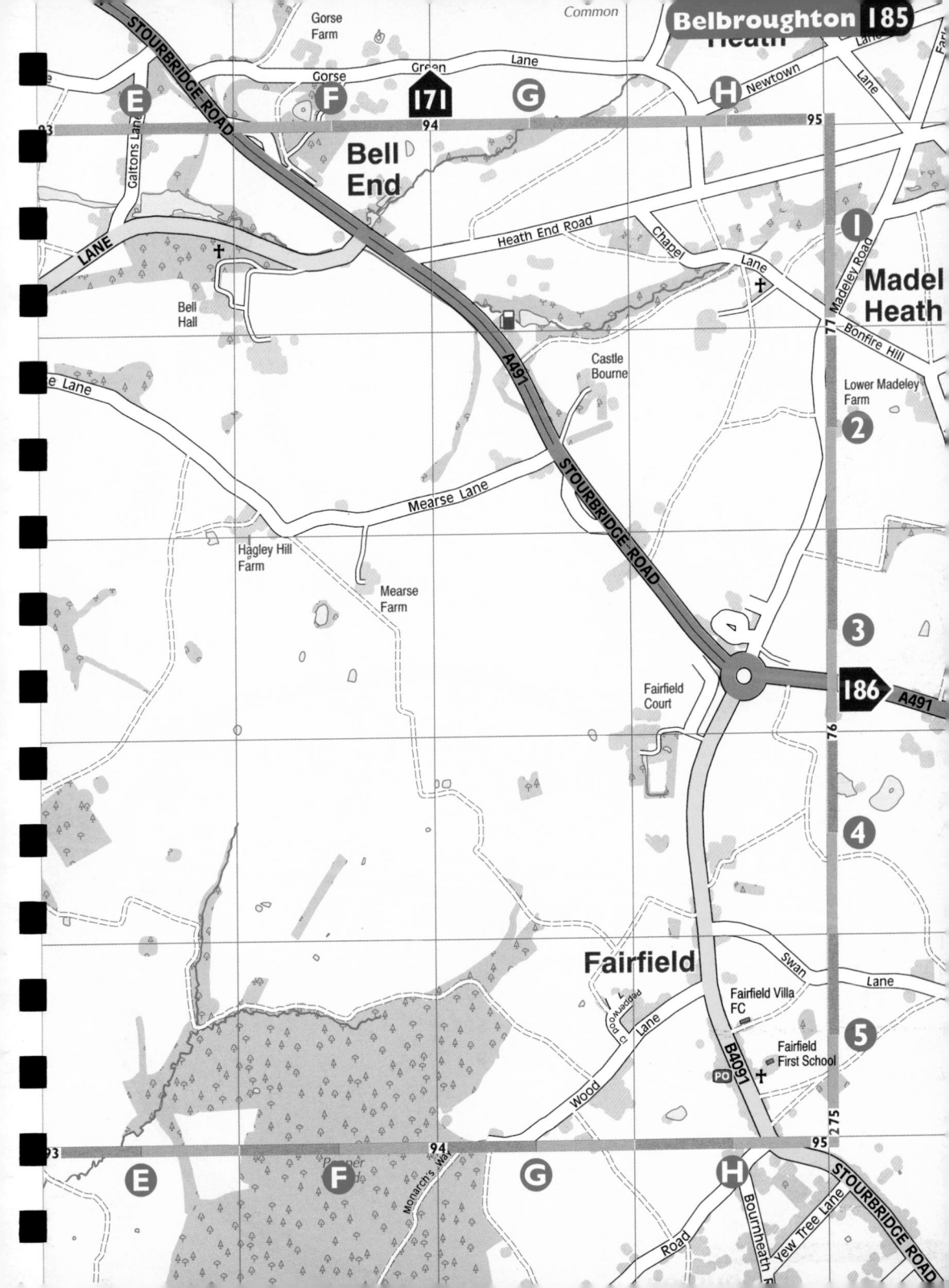

Gorse Farm
Common
Heath
Green Lane
Gorse
171
Newtown
E
F
G
H
Lane
93
94
95
Galtons Lane
STOURBRIDGE ROAD
Bell End
LANE
Heath End Road
Chapel
Lane
Bell Hall
Madeley Road
Madel Heath
77
Bonfire Hill
A491
Castle Bourne
Lower Madeley Farm
2
e Lane
STOURBRIDGE ROAD
Mearse Lane
Hagley Hill Farm
Mearse Farm
3
186
A491
Fairfield Court
76
4
Fairfield
Swan
Lane
Peppewood
Lane
Fairfield Villa FC
5
Fairfield First School
B4091
PO
Wood
275
Monarch's Way
Road
Bournheath
Yew Tree Lane
STOURBRIDGE ROAD

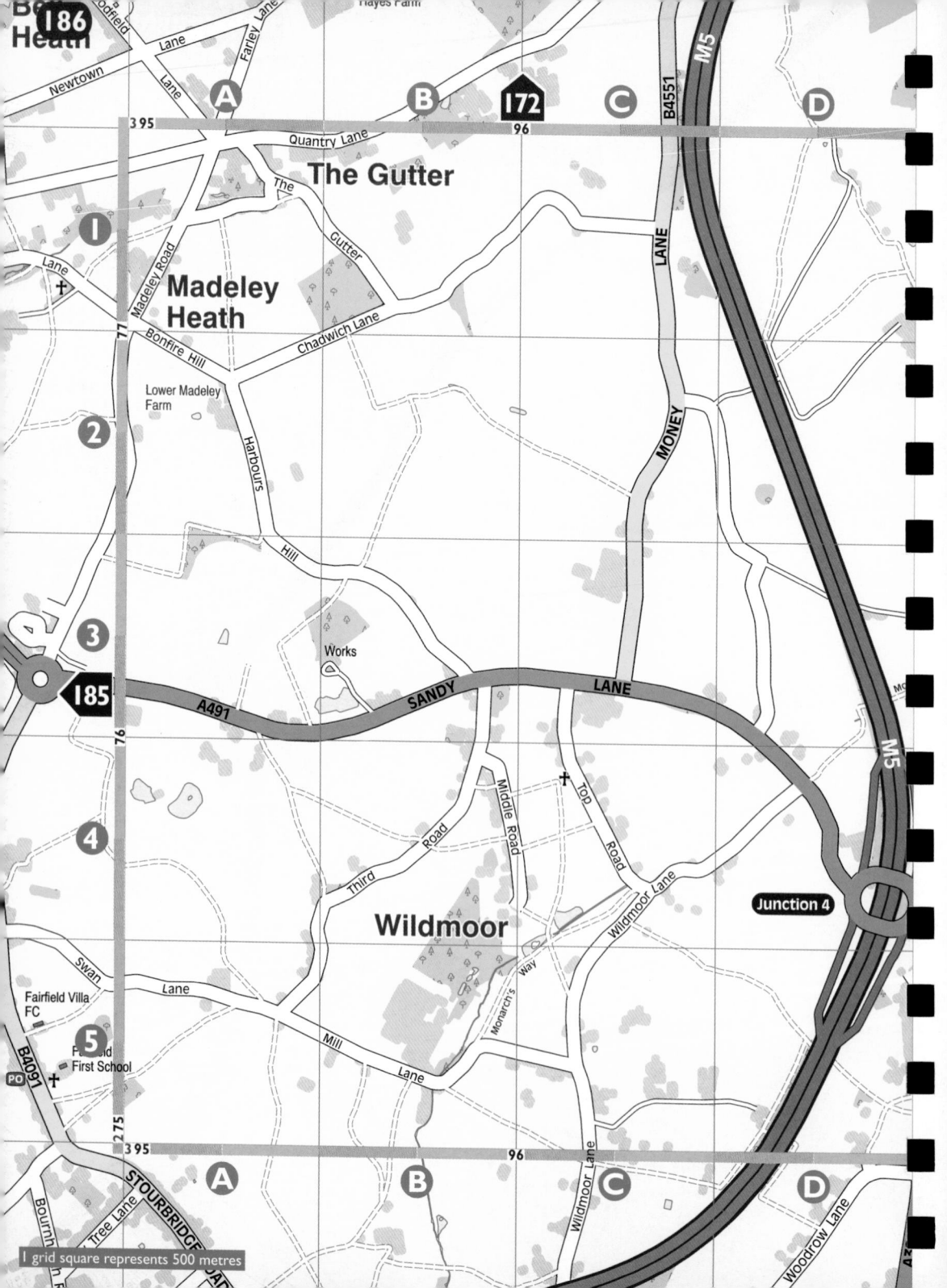
186
172
185
A
B
C
D
1
2
3
4
5
395
96
77
76
275
Newtown
Lane
Farley Lane
Quantry Lane
The Gutter
The Gutter
Madeley Road
Madeley Heath
Bonfire Hill
Chadwich Lane
Lower Madeley Farm
Harbours Hill
MONEY LANE
B4551
M5
Works
A491 SANDY LANE
Middle Road
Top Road
Third Road
Wildmoor
Wildmoor Lane
Monarch's Way
Junction 4
Swan Lane
Mill Lane
Fairfield Villa FC
First School
B4091
PO
STOURBRIDGE
Tree Lane
Woodrow Lane
1 grid square represents 500 metres

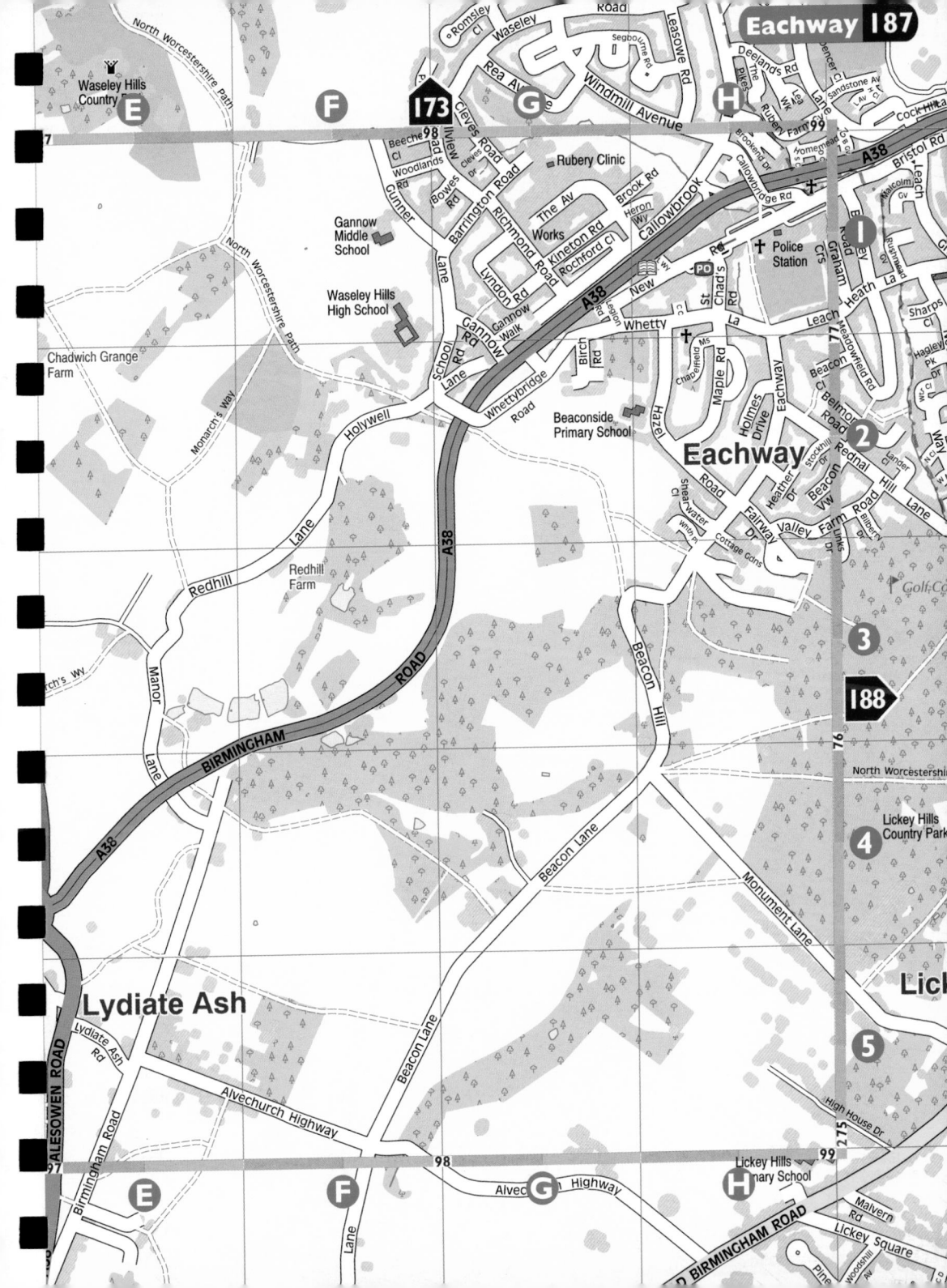

Waseley Hills Country Park
North Worcestershire Path
Chadwich Grange Farm
Monarch's Way
Gannow Middle School
Waseley Hills High School
Rubery Clinic
Works
Police Station
Beaconside Primary School
Eachway
Redhill Farm
Lickey Hills Country Park
Lydiate Ash
Lickey Hills Primary School
Golf Co
173
188
A38
BIRMINGHAM ROAD
Holywell Lane
Redhill Lane
Manor Lane
Beacon Lane
Beacon Hill
Monument Lane
Alvechurch Highway
Birmingham Road
HALESOWEN ROAD
Lydiate Ash Rd
High House Dr
Lickey Square
Malvern Rd
Windmill Avenue
Leasowe Rd
Rea Av
Waseley Rd
Romsley Cl
Cleves Road
Barrington Road
Richmond Road
Lyndon Rd
Kineton Rd
Rochford Cl
The Av
Brook Rd
Heron Wy
Callowbrook La
Gannow Walk
Gannow Rd
School Lane
Gunner Lane
Bowes Rd
Woodlands Rd
Whettybridge Road
Whetty La
New Rd
St Chad's Rd
Graham Crs
Leach Heath La
Bristol Rd
Eachway
Maple Rd
Holmes Drive
Hazel Road
Fairway Dr
Valley Farm Road
Beacon Cl
Belmont Road
Rednal Hill Lane
Meadowfield Rd
Sharps Cl
Hagley Pk Dr
Cottage Gdns
Shearwater Cl
Heather Dr
Beacon Vw
Links Dr
Bilberry Dr
Lander Cl
Deelands Rd
Rubery Farm Gv
Sandstone Av
Cock Hill La
Callowbridge Rd
Brookend Dr
Homemead Gv
Birch Rd
Legion Rd
Chapelfield Ms
Malcolm Gv
Rushmead Gv
Segbourne Rd
E F G H 1 2 3 4 5
97 98 99 275 276 277

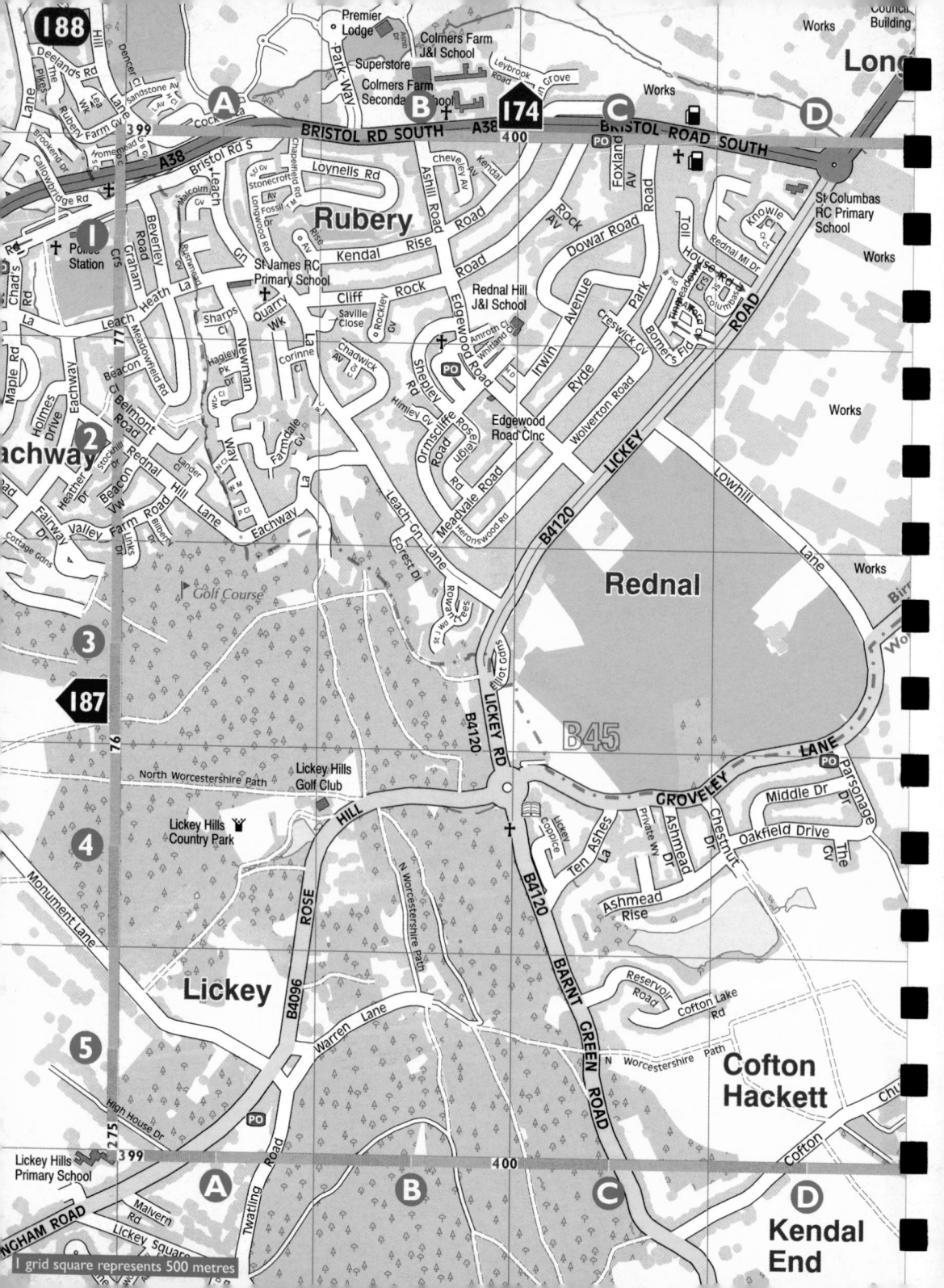

188
174
187
Rubery
Rednal
Lickey
Cofton Hackett
Kendal End
Long
Premier Lodge
Colmers Farm J&I School
Superstore
Colmers Farm Secondary School
Works
Council Building
BRISTOL RD SOUTH
BRISTOL ROAD SOUTH
A38
Bristol Rd S
St Columbas RC Primary School
Police Station
St James RC Primary School
Rednal Hill J&I School
Edgewood Road Clnc
LICKEY ROAD
B4120
LICKEY RD
Golf Course
Lickey Hills Golf Club
Lickey Hills Country Park
North Worcestershire Path
N Worcestershire Path
ROSE HILL
B4096
B45
GROVELEY LANE
BARNT GREEN ROAD
Lowhill Lane
Monument Lane
Warren Lane
Twatling Road
High House Dr
Lickey Hills Primary School
Malvern Rd
Lickey Square
Cofton Lake Rd
Reservoir Road
Ashmead Rise
Oakfield Drive
Parsonage Dr
Middle Dr
Ten Ashes La
Lickey Coppice
Elliot Gdns
Forest Dl
Leach Gn Lane
Meadvale Road
Wolverton Road
Ryde Park Road
Irwin Avenue
Dowar Road
Rock Av
Kendal Rise Road
Cliff Rock Road
Edgewood Road
Shepley Rd
Ormscliffe Road
Loynells Rd
Ashill Road
Eachway
Beacon Hill
Rednal Hill Lane
Valley Farm Road
Holmes Drive
Maple Rd
Beverley Road
Graham Crs
Leach Heath La
Newman Way
Farmdale Gv
Toll House Rd
Foxland Av
1 grid square represents 500 metres

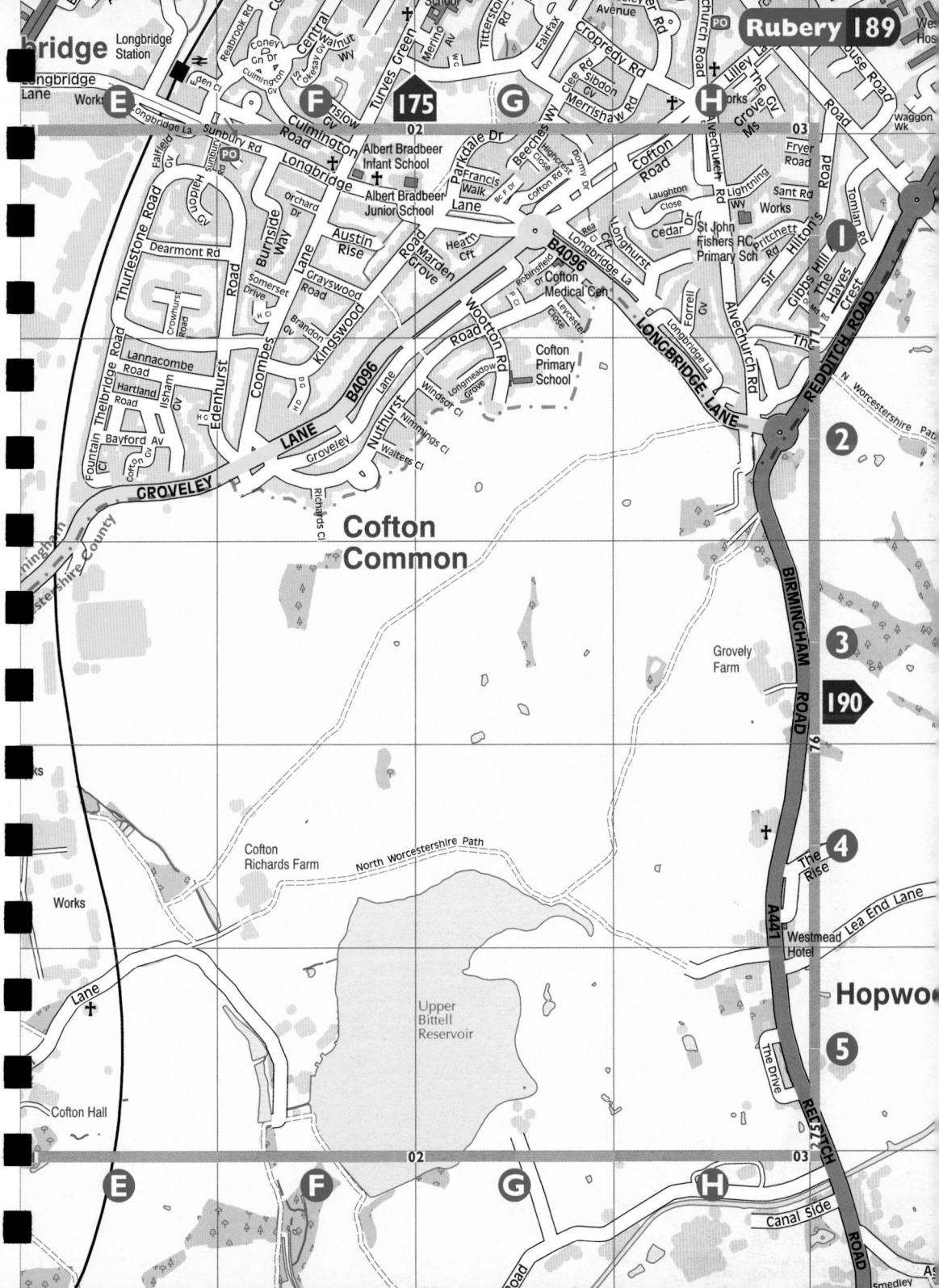
Longbridge
Longbridge Station
Longbridge Lane
Works
175
E
F
G
H
I
2
3
4
5
02
03
190
Culmington Road
Sunbury Rd
Longbridge La
Albert Bradbeer Infant School
Albert Bradbeer Junior School
Longbridge Lane
Parkdale Dr
Francis Walk
Beeches Wy
Highcrest Close
Cofton Rd
Dormy Dr
Cofton Road
Cropredy Rd
Merrishaw Rd
Sibdon Gv
Clee Gv
Fairfax
Titterstone Rd
Merino Av
Turves Green
Central Av
Walnut Wy
Coney Gn Dr
Culmington Gv
Okesay Gv
Reabrook Rd
Lilley La
The Grove
Grove Ms
Alvechurch Rd
Fryer Road
Laughton Close
Lightning Wy
Sant Rd
Works
Cedar Dr
St John Fishers RC Primary Sch
Pritchett Rd
Hilton's Road
Tomlan Rd
Gibbs Hill Rd
The Hayes
The Crest
Sir Hilton's Rd
Forrell Gv
Alvechurch Rd
Longbridge La
LONGBRIDGE LANE
REDDITCH ROAD
N Worcestershire Path
Waggon Wk
Thurlestone Road
Falfield Gv
Haldon Gv
Dearmont Rd
Burnside Way
Orchard Dr
Austin Rise
Heath Cft
Marden Grove
Kingswood Road
Grayswood Road
Somerset Drive
Brandon Gv
Crowhurst Road
Coombes Lane
Edenhurst Road
Lannacombe Road
Hartland Road
Thelbridge Road
Ilsham Gv
Bayford Av
Fountain Cl
Cofton Gv
B4096
GROVELEY LANE
Wootton Road
Wootton Rd
Robinsfield Dr
Cofton Medical Cen
Leycester Close
Cofton Primary School
Longmeadow Grove
Windsor Cl
Nimmings Cl
Nuthurst
Groveley Lane
Walters Cl
Richards Cl
Cofton Common
Worcestershire County
Grovely Farm
BIRMINGHAM ROAD
A441
The Rise
Lea End Lane
Westmead Hotel
Hopwood
The Drive
REDDITCH ROAD
Cofton Richards Farm
North Worcestershire Path
Works
Lane
Upper Bittell Reservoir
Cofton Hall
Canal Side
Smedley

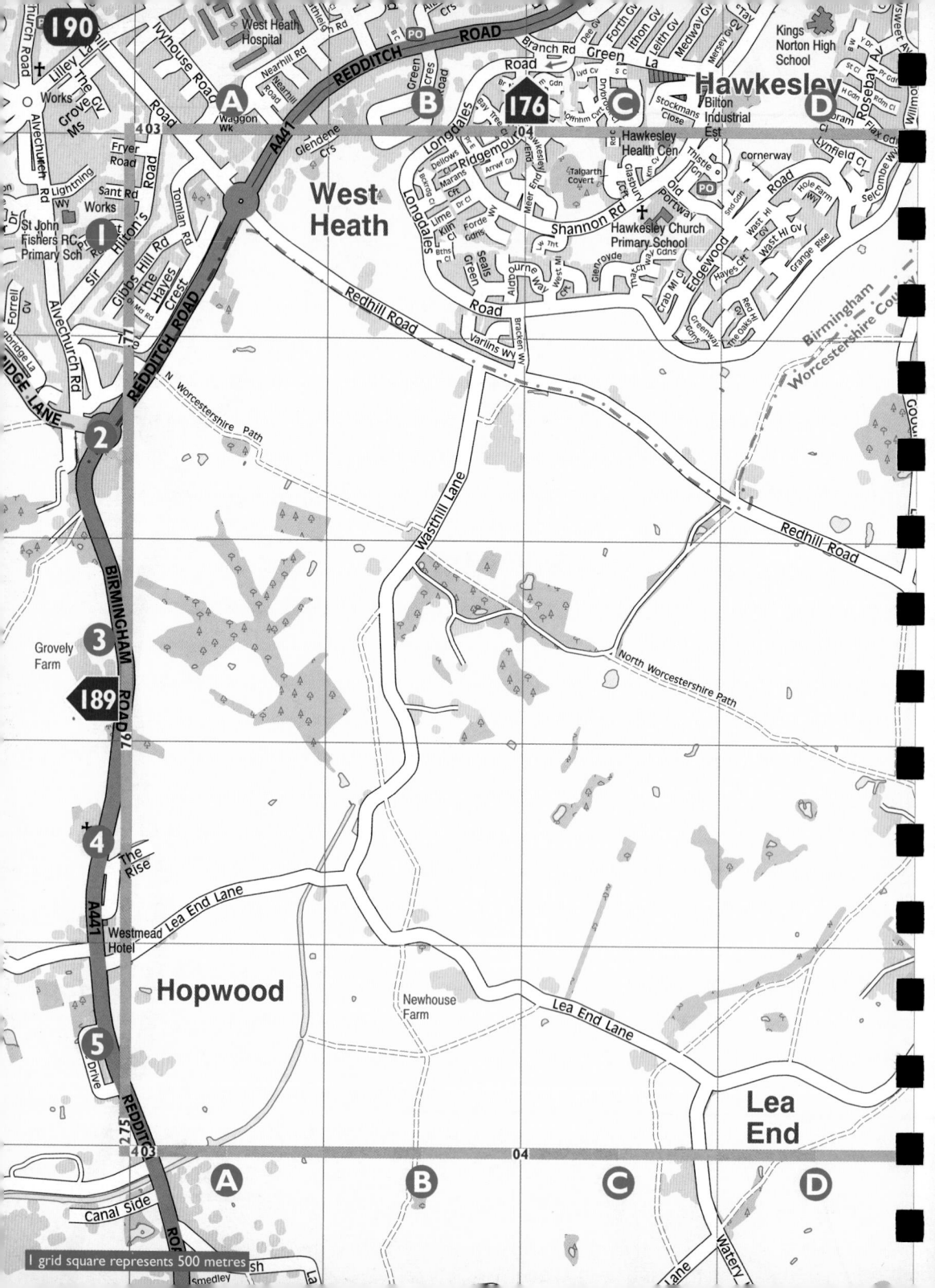
190
West Heath Hospital
Redditch Road
A441
West Heath
Hawkesley
Kings Norton High School
Hawkesley Health Cen
Bilton Industrial Est
Hawkesley Church Primary School
176
Redhill Road
Wasthill Lane
North Worcestershire Path
N Worcestershire Path
Birmingham Road
Grovely Farm
189
Lea End Lane
Westmead Hotel
Hopwood
Newhouse Farm
Lea End
Canal Side
Birmingham
Worcestershire County
St John Fishers RC Primary Sch
1 grid square represents 500 metres

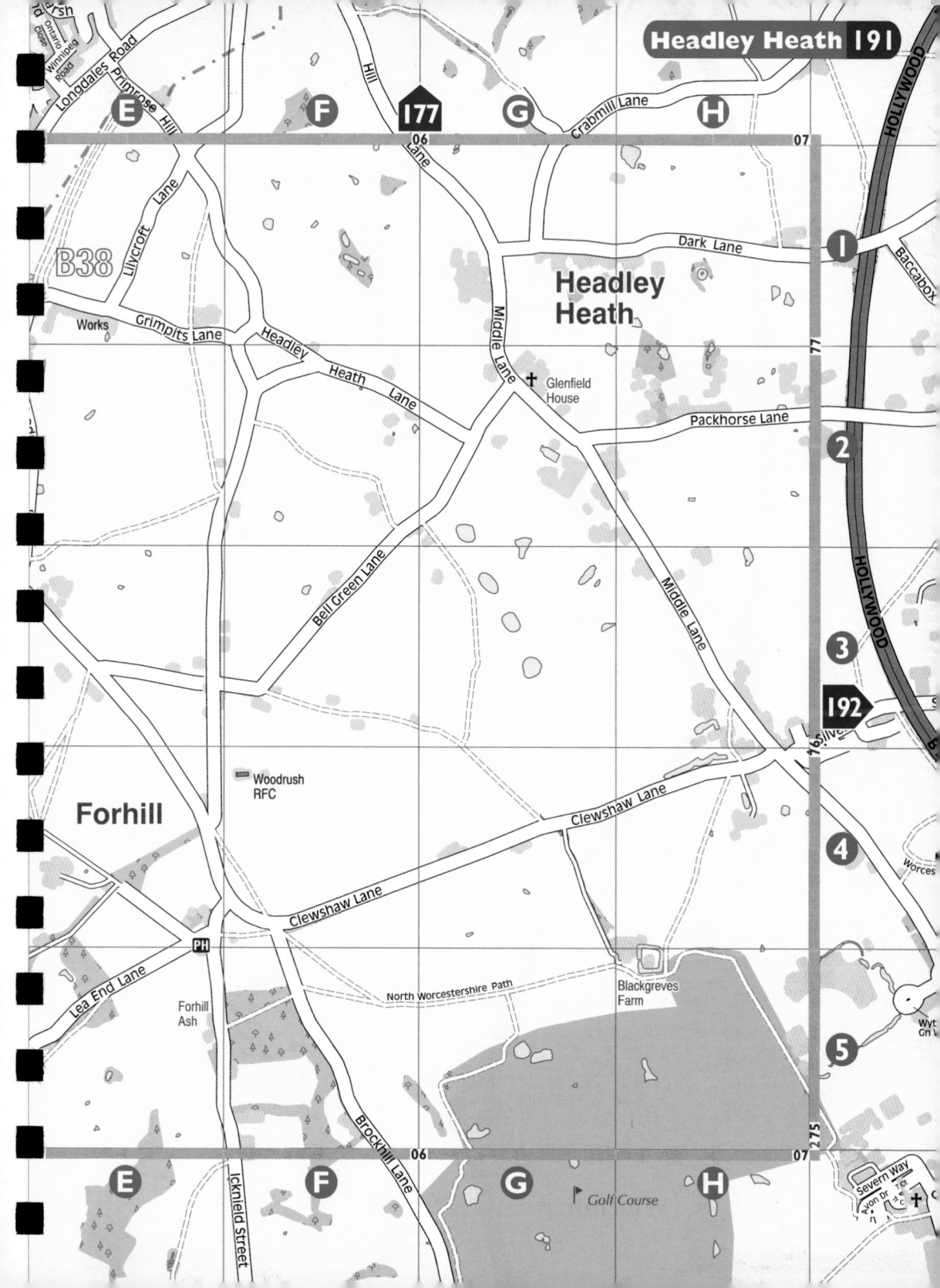

E F **177** G H

07

HOLLYWOOD

Hill Lane

Crabmill Lane

BaCCabox

Dark Lane

1

77

Lonsdales Road

Winnned Road

Primrose Hill

B38

Lilycroft Lane

Headley Heath

Middle Lane

† Glenfield House

Packhorse Lane

2

Works

Grimpits Lane

Headley Heath Lane

HOLLYWOOD

3

Bell Green Lane

Middle Lane

192

Silver

Forhill

Woodrush RFC

Clewshaw Lane

4

Worces

Clewshaw Lane

PH

North Worcestershire Path

Blackgreves Farm

5

Wyt Gn V

Lea End Lane

Forhill Ash

06

07

275

Severn Way

Avon Dr

†

E F **Brockhill Lane** G ▶ *Golf Course* H

Icknield Street

06

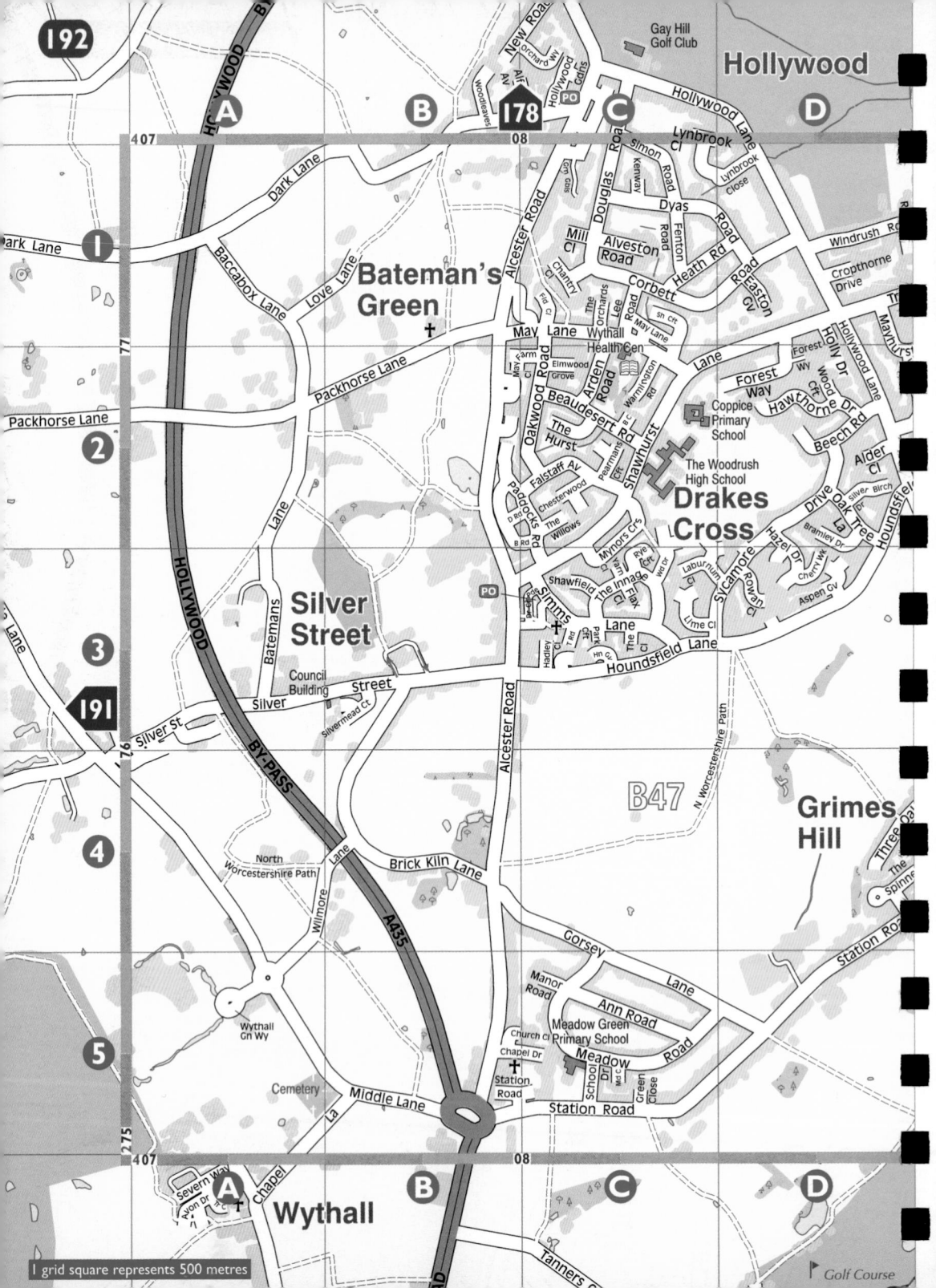
192
178
191
Hollywood
Gay Hill Golf Club
Bateman's Green
Drakes Cross
Silver Street
Grimes Hill
Wythall
B47
HOLLYWOOD BY-PASS
A435
New Road
Orchard Wy
Alf Av
Woodleaves
Hollywood Gdns
Hollywood Lane
Lynbrook Cl
Lynbrook Close
Simon Road
Douglas Road
Kenway
Dyas Road
Fenton Road
Alveston Road
Mill Cl
Heath Rd
Easton Gv
Corbett Road
Windrush Rd
Cropthorne Drive
Alcester Road
Dark Lane
Park Lane
Baccabox Lane
Love Lane
Chantry Cl
The Orchards
Lee Road
Sh Cft
May Lane
Wythall Health Cen
Elmwood Grove
May Farm Cl
Arden Road
Warmington Rd
Oakwood Road
Beaudesert Rd
The Hurst
Pearmans Cft
Shawhurst Lane
Forest Way
Forest Wy
Holly Dr
Hollywood Lane
Wood Cft
Hawthorne Dr
Beech Rd
Alder Cl
Coppice Primary School
The Woodrush High School
Packhorse Lane
Falstaff Av
Paddocks Rd
Chesterwood
The Willows
Mynors Crs
Rye Cft
Yarn Cl
Wd Dr
Laburnum Cl
Sycamore
Hazel Dr
Bramley Dr
Oak Tree La
Silver Birch Dr
Drive
Houndsfield Lane
Rowan Cl
Cherry Wk
Aspen Gv
Lime Cl
Shawfield
The Innage
Flax Cl
Simms Lane
Park Cft
The Cl
Hadley Cl
Hn Cv
PO
Batemans Lane
Council Building
Silver Street
Silver St
Silvermead Ct
N Worcestershire Path
North Worcestershire Path
Brick Kiln Lane
Wilmore Lane
Gorsey Lane
Manor Road
Ann Road
Meadow Green Primary School
Church Cl
Chapel Dr
Station Road
Meadow Road
School Dr
Green Close
Station Rd
Three Oaks
The Spinney
Wythall Gn Wy
Cemetery
Middle Lane
Chapel La
Severn Way
Avon Dr
Tanners
407
08
77
76
275
A
B
C
D
1
2
3
4
5
1 grid square represents 500 metres
Golf Course

Major's Green
179
Rwbr Cl
Three Coner Close
Rolan Drive
Littlemead Road
Haslucks Green Road
Rushleigh Rd
Whitlock's End Farm
E
F
G
H
10
11
Fords Rd
Cambria Cl
Haslucks Cl
Haslucks Green Road
North Worcestershire Path
Fordrough
Heath Lane
I
Whitlock's End Station
Trueman's Heath
Tythebarn Lane
Highgate United FC
Horse Shoe Associated FC
Th Acres
Three Acres La
Tythebarn Lane
2
Dickens Heath Primary School
Houndsfield Lane
Works
Whitlock's End
Meadow Pleck
Round Cl
Dckns Hth Rd
Birchy Close
Fishers Dr
Birchy Leasowes Lane
Old Dickens Heath Road
Packmores
Gorcott La
3
Rumbush Lane
194
River Cole
Tilehouse Lane
Green Lane
Selsdon Close
Dickens Heath Road
Kiln Lane
Wythall Station
Littleshaw Croft
Lowbrook La
Tidbury Green Primary School
4
Tidbury Green
Innisfree House School
Surgery
Norton Lane
Worcestershire County
Solihull
Rumbush Lane
Cleobury Farm
5
River Cole
Rumbush
Fulford Hall
Fulford Hall Road
Cleobury Lane
275
Fulford Heath

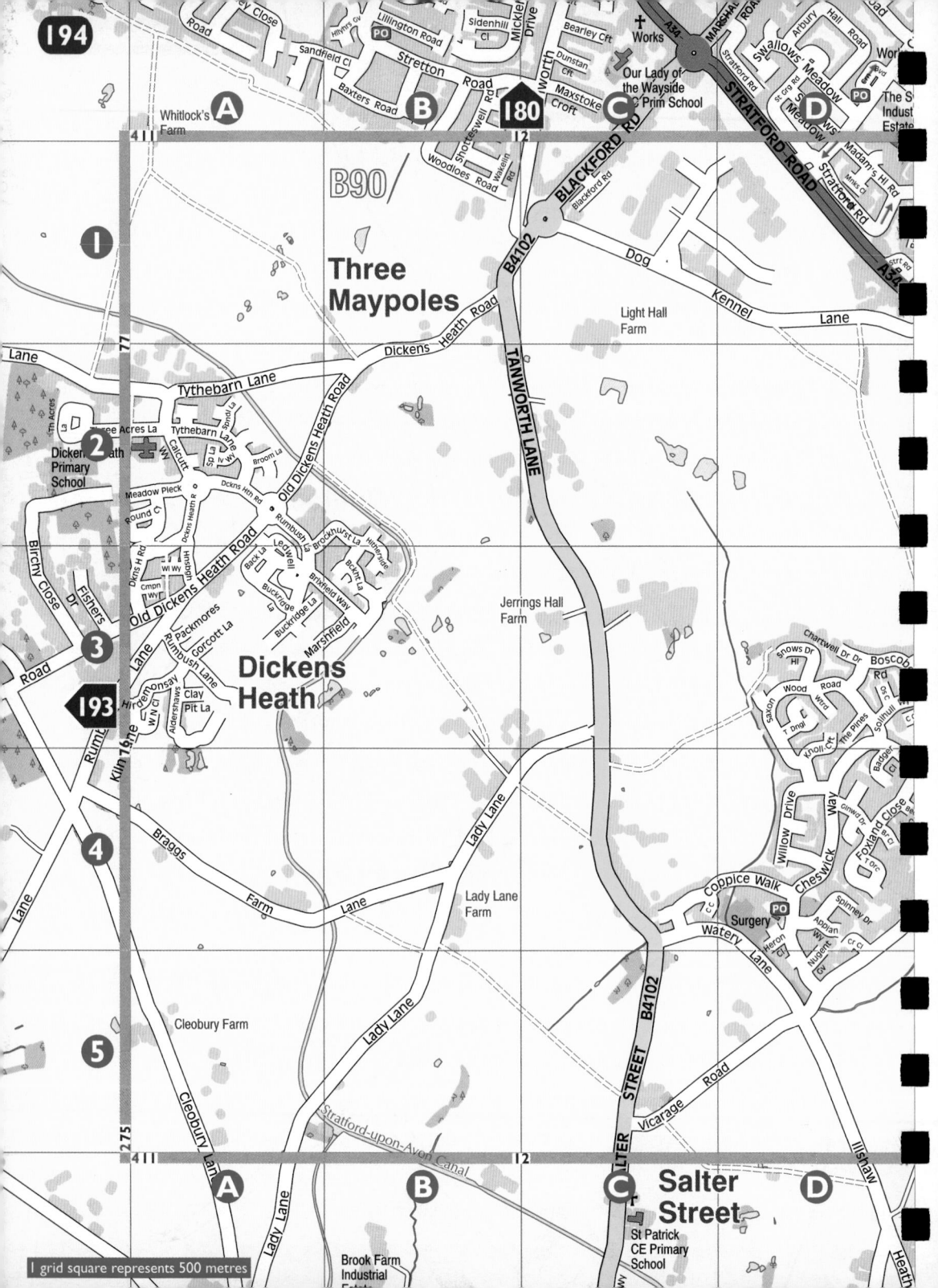
Three Maypoles
Dickens Heath
Salter Street
B90
180
193
A
B
C
D
1
2
3
4
5
411
12
275
77
Stretton Road
Baxters Road
Lillington Road
Sandfield Cl
Sidenhill Cl
Bearley Cft
Dunstan Cft
Maxstoke Croft
Works
Our Lady of the Wayside CE Prim School
STRATFORD ROAD
A34
Stratford Rd
Swallows' Meadow
Arbury Hall Road
The S Indust Estate
Madam's Hl Rd
Whitlock's Farm
Woodloes Road
Shottteswell Rd
BLACKFORD RD
Blackford Rd
B4102
Dog Kennel Lane
Light Hall Farm
Dickens Heath Road
TANWORTH LANE
Tythebarn Lane
Three Acres La
Dickens Heath Primary School
Old Dickens Heath Road
Meadow Pleck
Round Cl
Calcutt Wy
Broom La
Rumbush La
Brockhurst La
Hitherside
Ledwell
Back La
Brixfield Way
Buckridge La
Marshfield
Birchy Close
Fishers Dr
Packmores
Gorcott La
Rumbush Lane
Hirdemonsay
Aldershaws
Clay Pit La
Kiln Lane
Jerrings Hall Farm
Braggs Farm Lane
Lady Lane
Lady Lane Farm
Cleobury Farm
Cleobury Lane
Stratford-upon-Avon Canal
Chartwell Dr
Snows Dr
Wood Road
Saxon
Boscobel Rd
The Pines
Knoll Cft
Badger Cl
Foxland Close
Willow Drive
Cheswick Way
Coppice Walk
Surgery
PO
Spinney Dr
Appian Wy
Heron Cl
Nugent Gv
Watery Lane
SALTER STREET
Vicarage Road
Illshaw Heath
St Patrick CE Primary School
Brook Farm Industrial Estate
Road
Lane

1 grid square represents 500 metres

Cranmore Industrial Estate
Highlands Road
Maidwell Drive
Stirling Road
Works
Radway Road
Monkspath Business Park
181
Solihull Way
Halstead Gv
Somerby Dr
Knightcote Dr
Perryford Dr
Widney Lane
Sandhills Crs
Hillfield
Eldersfield Grove
Barbourne Cl
Ashborough Drive
VIVA! Health & Leisure C
Radway Industrial Estate
Harnall Close
Regency Hotel
UCI
Knowlands Road
Whitemoor Drive
Millison Gv
Gillows Cft
Caldeford Avenue
Rushford Cl
Cryersoak
Lakeside Drive
Monkspath Hall Road
PO
Farmhouse Wy
Abberton Grove
Primsland Cl
Hollington Wy
Whitford Drive
Milford Grove
Health Centre
Burnaston Crs
Kettlebrook Rd
Monkspath Primary School
Harvington Dr
Cotheridge Cl
Hay Lane
Crimscote Cl
Meerhill Av
Rainsbrook Dr
Thornton Road
Palefield Rd
Shilton Cl
Felgate Cl
Hillwood Av
Pensham Cft
Deanbrook Cl
Shelly Lane
Shelly Crs
Charlesworth Av
Pebworth Av
Longstone
Denby Cft
Farnborough Dr
Grey Mill Cl
Rushwick Grove
Frankholmes Drive
Rowthorn Dr
Welham Cft
Elmbridge Dr
Chadstone Cl
Kemerton Wy
Westgrove Av
Tilesford Cl
Elkington Cft
Kerswell Dr
Stapenhall Road
Horton Gv
Talton Cl
Stanbrook Road
Fullbrook Cl
Solihull Way
Creynolds Lane
A34 STRATFORD ROAD
Travel Inn
Monkspath
Superstore
Garden Centre
196
Longleat Dr
Cheswick Green Primary School
Shirley Park Sports Club & Golf Club
Golf Course
Cheswick Green
Junction 4
A3400
River Blythe
Monkspath Hill Farm
Blythe Ga
Blythe Gate
M42
STRATFORD ROAD
Winterton Farm
Blythe Business Park
Boulevard
Sidenhales Farm
Central
Oak Lodge
E F G H
1 2 3 4 5
14 15 76 77 275

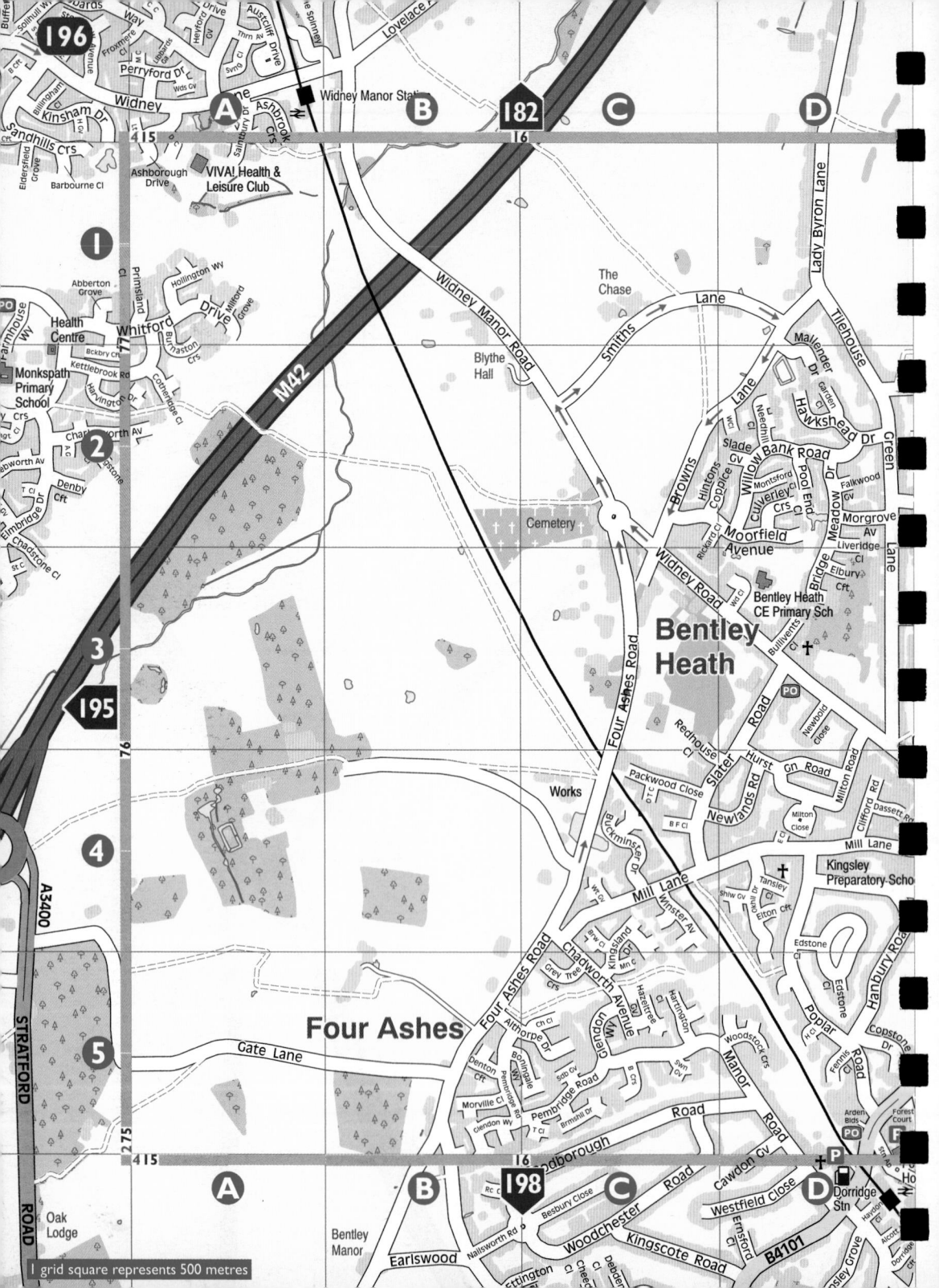

196

182

195

198

Widney

Kinsham Dr

Sandhills Crs

Eldersfield Grove

Barbourne Cl

Ashborough Drive

VIVA! Health &
Leisure Club

Abberton Grove

Hollington Wy

Primsland Drive

Milford Grove

Whitford

Health Centre

Monkspath Primary School

Bckbry Trl

Kettlebrook Rd

Burnaston Crs

Cotteridge Cl

Chadworth Av

Denby Cft

Elmbridge Dr

Chadstone Cl

M42

Blythe Hall

Widney Manor Road

The Chase

Lane

Smiths

Lane

Lady Byron Lane

Tilehouse

Green Lane

Mallender Dr

Garden Cl

Hawkshead Dr

Falkwood Gv

Morgrove Av

Meadow Dr

Liveridge Cl

Elbury Cl

Bridge

Slade Gv

Willow Bank Road

Hintons Coppice

Montsford Cl

Culverley Crs

Pool End Cl

Browns

Moorfield Avenue

Bentley Heath CE Primary Sch

Bullivents Cl

Cemetery

Widney Road

Bentley Heath

PO

Redhouse Cl

Newbold Close

Hurst Gn Road

Road

Slater Rd

Newlands Rd

Milton Road

Clifford Rd

Dassett Rd

Milton Close

Mill Lane

Works

Packwood Close

B F Cl

Buckminster Dr

Kingsley Preparatory Scho

Tansley

Elton Cft

Edstone Cl

Edstone Cl

Hanbury Road

Mill Lane

Winster Av

Chadworth Avenue

Kingsland

Grey Tree Crs

Hazeltree Cft

Hartington

Woodstock Crs

Poplar Road

Fennis Cl

Copstone Dr

Four Ashes

Gate Lane

Four Ashes Road

Althorpe Dr

Denton Cft

Morville Cl

Clendon Wy

Pennridge Dr

Pembridge Road

Borrodale

Manor

Road

Arden Bldgs

Forest Court

PO

Dorridge Stn

STRATFORD

A3400

198

Earlswood

Bentley Manor

Nailsworth Rd

Besbury Close

Godborough

Woodchester Road

Cawdon Gv

Kingscote Road

Westfield Close

B4101

Oak Lodge

ROAD

1 grid square represents 500 metres

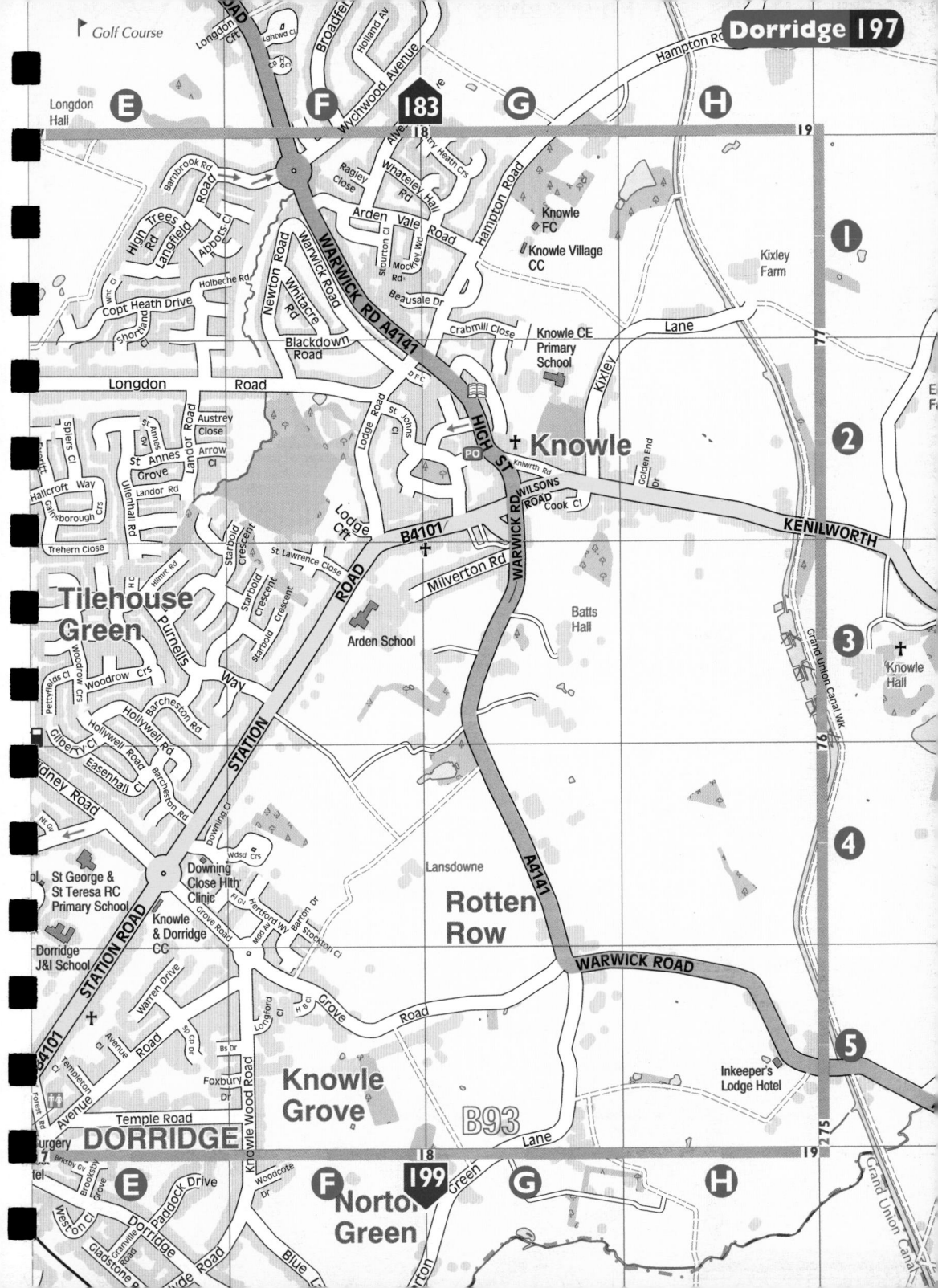
Golf Course
Longdon Hall
Tilehouse Green
Knowle
Knowle FC
Knowle Village CC
Knowle CE Primary School
Kixley Farm
Batts Hall
Arden School
Knowle Hall
Lansdowne
Rotten Row
Knowle Grove
Inkeeper's Lodge Hotel
DORRIDGE
Norton Green
St George & St Teresa RC Primary School
Downing Close Hlth Clinic
Knowle & Dorridge CC
Dorridge J&I School
Surgery
WARWICK RD A4141
WARWICK ROAD
HIGH ST
STATION ROAD
B4101
KENILWORTH
Grand Union Canal
Grand Union Canal Wk
Hampton Road
Longdon Road
Kixley Lane
Grove Road
Knowle Wood Road
Temple Road
Wychwood Avenue
Arden Vale Road
Copt Heath Drive
Milverton Rd
Purnells Way
Station Road
Dorridge Road
Paddock Drive
Blue Lane
183
199
E
F
G
H
1
2
3
4
5
18
19
77
76
275
B93

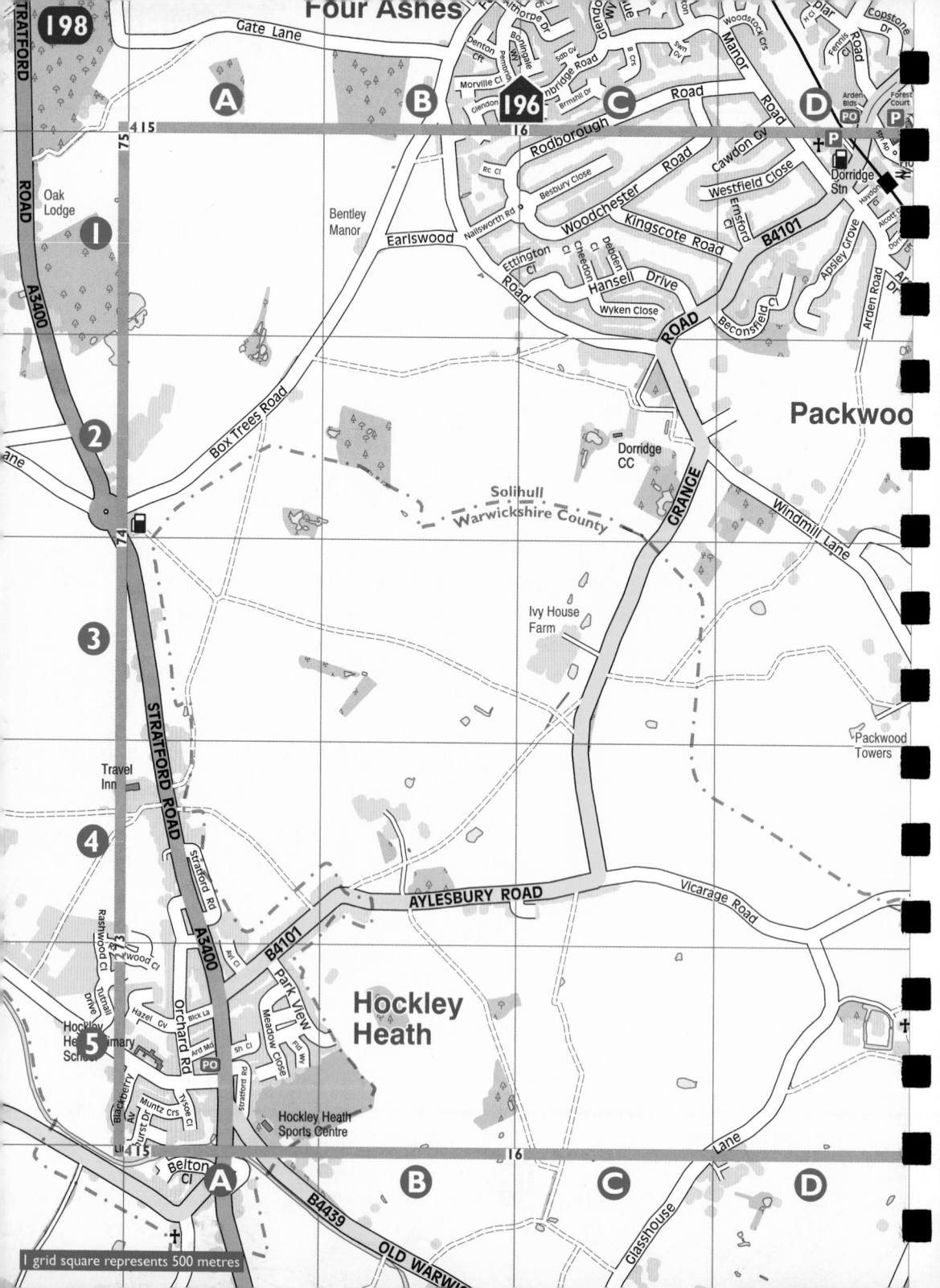

Four Ashes

198

Gate Lane

196

A B C D

Walthorpe
Denton Cft
Bollinghale
Morville Cl Pemberton
Glendon
RC Cl
Besbury Close
Nailsworth Rd
Earlswood
Ettington Cl
Cheedon
Debden
Hansell Drive
Wyken Close
Beconsfield Cl

STRATFORD ROAD
A3400

Oak Lodge

I

2

Box Trees Road

ane

74

3

Travel Inn

4

Stratford Rd

Rashwood Cl
Rashwood Cl

5
Hockley Heath Primary School
PO

Bentley Manor

Earlswood

Rodborough Road
Woodchester Road
Kingscote Road
Cawdon Gv
Westfield Close
Ernsford
Apsley Grove
Arden Road
Arden Dr
B4101
ROAD

Manor Road
Fennis Road
Copstone Dr

Arden Blds
PO

Dorridge Stn

D P

Forest Court

Packwoo

Solihull
Warwickshire County

Dorridge CC

GRANGE ROAD

Ivy House Farm

Windmill Lane

Packwood Towers

AYLESBURY ROAD

Vicarage Road

STRATFORD ROAD A3400
B4101
Hazel Gv
Blck La
Orchard Rd
Ard Md
Tuffnall Drive
Sh Cl
PARK VIEW
Meadow Close
Fld Wy

Hockley Heath

Muntz Crs
Tysoe Cl
Blackberry Av
Hurst Dr
Lii
Stratford Rd

Hockley Heath Sports Centre

415

A Belton Cl

B B4439 OLD WARWI

C Glasshouse Lane

D

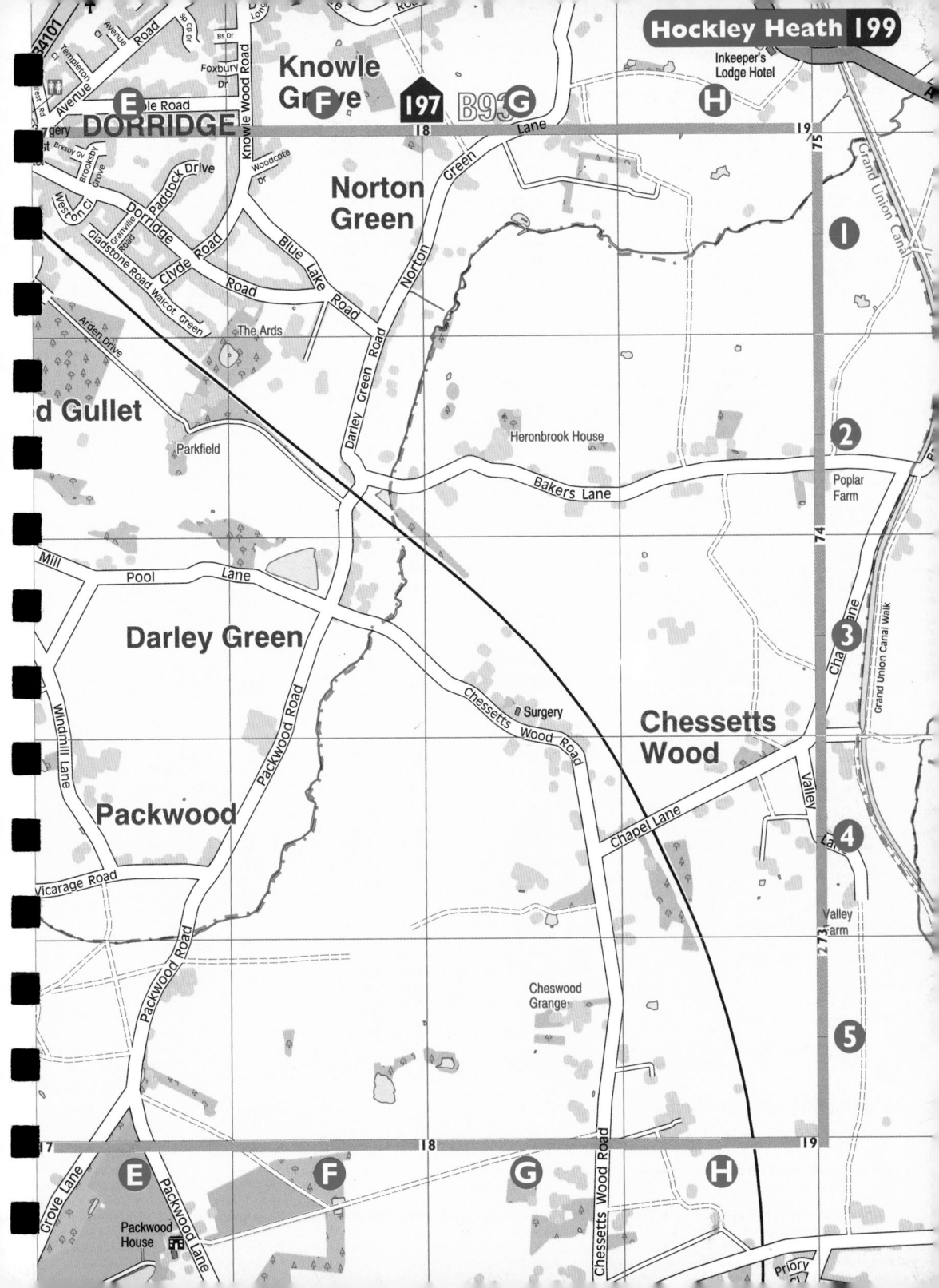

84101

Knowle Grove

197 B93 **G**

DORRIDGE **E** **F**

Inkeeper's
Lodge Hotel **H**

Foxbur

Avenue Road

Templeton

Bs Dr

gery

Brsksby Gv

Brockwell
Grove

Weston Cl

Dorridge Road

Granville
Road

Gladstone Road

Clyde Road

Walcot Green

Paddock Drive

Woodcote
Dr

Knowle Wood Road

Blue Lake Road

**Norton
Green**

Norton Green Lane

75

I

d Gullet

Arden Drive

Parkfield

The Ards

Darley Green Road

Heronbrook House

Bakers Lane

Poplar
Farm

2

74

Mill Pool Lane

Darley Green

Packwood Road

Windmill Lane

Chessetts Wood Road

Surgery

**Chessetts
Wood**

Valley Lane

Ch ne

3

Grand Union Canal Walk

Packwood

Chapel Lane

4

Valley
Farm

273

Vicarage Road

Cheswood
Grange

5

17

18

19

E **F** **G** **H**

Chessetts Wood Road

Grove Lane

Packwood Lane

Packwood
House

Priory

Acock's Green	146	A4
Alcester Lane's End	160	D4
Aldridge	30	A4
Alum Rock	129	E1
Amblecote	118	B5
Ashmore Lake	39	H1
Ashmore Park	25	F1
Ashwood	98	C4
Aston	109	F3
Bacon's End	114	C5
Balls Hill	71	E2
Balsall Heath	144	A2
Banners Gate	60	C4
Baptist End	102	C3
Barr Common	44	C2
Bartley Green	157	H2
Bateman's Green	192	B1
Bearwood	124	C2
Beech Lanes	124	A5
Belbroughton	184	C1
Bell End	185	F1
Belle Vale	138	B2
Bell Heath	171	H5
Bentley	40	B2
Bentley Heath	196	C3
Bescot	56	C2
Bickenhill	166	D1
Bilbrook	11	E3
Billesley	162	A4
Billesley Common	161	G3
Bilston	53	G1
Birch End	72	B4
Birches Green	93	E3
Birchfield	90	D5
Birchills	41	H2
Birmingham	2	C7
Blackheath	121	H2
Black Lake	71	E4
Blakedown	168	C3
Blakeley	81	E1
Blakenall Heath	27	C1
Blakenhall	51	H1
Bloomfield	69	F5
Blossomfield	181	E3
Bloxwich	27	E2
Boldmere	77	E2
Bordesley	127	G2
Bordesley Green	128	C3
Bournbrook	143	E5
Bourne Vale	44	C2
Bournville	159	H3
Bowling Green	120	D1
Brades Village	85	B5
Bradley	53	H5
Bradmore	36	A5
Bramford	68	A4
Brandwood End	177	H1
The Bratch	64	D3
Brierley Hill	119	E2
Bristnall Fields	123	F1
Brockmoor	100	D5
Bromford	94	A5
Bromley	100	C4
Broome	169	H2
Broom Hill	184	B5
Brownhills	9	F4
Brown's Green	89	H2
Buckland End	112	C2
Buckpool	118	B2
Burnt Tree	85	F4
Bushbury	13	E4
Caldmore	4	B7
California	141	E5
Carroway Head	48	D1
Castle Bromwich	113	E1
Castlecroft	35	E5
Castle Vale	94	C3
Catherine-de-Barnes	166	A5
Catshill	19	G1
Causeway Green	122	D1
Chad Valley	125	H5
Chapman's Hill	172	D4
Charlemont	71	H4
Chattle Hill	97	E4
Chelmsley Wood	132	C3
Chessetts Wood	199	H3
Cheswick Green	195	E4
The Chuckery	5	J4
Churchfield	88	A1
Church Hill	56	A2
Churchill	168	C2
Cinder Hill	67	H2
Claregate	21	H4
Clayhanger	18	D1
Clent	171	E2
Coal Pool	28	B5
Codsall	10	B3
Cofton Common	189	F2
Cofton Hackett	188	D5
Cole End	115	F1
Coleshall	112	D4
Coleshill	115	G3
Colton Hills	51	G5
Compton	35	H3
Coombeswood	139	E1
Copt Heath	183	E4
Coseley	68	C2
Cotteridge	159	G5
Coven Heath	12	C1
Cradley	137	G1
Cradley Heath	120	C4
Dam Mill	21	F1
Darby End	102	D5
Darby's Hill	103	H2
Darlaston	55	E1
Darlaston Green	55	G1
Darley Green	199	E3
Daw End	28	D5
Dayhouse Bank	172	D3
Deepfields	68	B2
The Delves	57	G4
Dickens Heath	194	A3
Digbeth	3	J6
Doe Bank	62	C1
Dorridge	197	E5
Drakes Cross	192	C2
Druids Heath	30	C1
Dudley	84	D4
Dudley Port	86	A2
Dudley's Fields	26	C2
Dudley Wood	120	C2
Dunstall Hill	22	D5
Eachway	187	H2
Edgbaston	142	D1
Elmdon	149	E4
Elmdon Heath	165	G3
Erdington	93	E3
Essington	14	D4
Ettingshall	52	D3
Ettingshall Park	52	B5
Eve Hill	84	A4
Fairfield	185	G5
Falcon Lodge	63	H2
Fallings Heath	55	G3
Fishley	17	E3
Fordbridge	132	A1
Fordhouses	12	B4
Forhill	191	E4
Four Ashes	196	A5
Four Oaks	46	C2
Four Oaks Park	46	D5
Frankley	157	F5
Frankley	173	H3
Frankley Green	157	E5
Frankley Hill	173	H2
Friar Park	56	D5
Garrets Green	130	C3
Gib Heath	108	A2
Giggetty	80	C1
Gilbertstone	147	F1
Gilson	97	E5
Glebe Farm	112	B5
Golds Green	70	C2
Goldthorn Park	52	B4
Gornalwood	83	E3
Goscote	28	B2
Gospel End Village	66	B3
Gothersley	116	C2
Gravelly Hill	92	D4
Great Barr	73	H1
Great Bridge	69	H5
Greensforge	98	B3
Griffin's Hill	159	F3
Grimes Hill	192	D4
Grove Vale	73	E2
Gunstone	10	C1
Guns Village	87	E2
The Gutter	186	A1
Hackman's Gate	169	F4
Haden Cross	121	G4
Hagley	153	F4
Halesowen	139	E3
Hall Green	71	G5
Hall Green	163	E3
Hampton in Arden	167	F3
Hamstead	73	C3
Handsworth	89	F4
Handsworth Wood	90	B3
Harborne	141	C1
Harden	28	B3
Hardwick	45	F3
Hartle	184	D2
Hart's Hill	101	G4
Harvills Hawthorn	70	B4
Hasbury	138	A4
Hasluck's Green	179	C3
Hateley Heath	71	H3
Hawkesley	176	C5
Hawne	138	C2
Hayley Green	154	C1
Hay Mills	146	B1
Headley Heath	191	C1
Heath End	28	B1
Heath Town	38	A1
Highbridge	18	A1
Highbury Park	160	D1
Highgate	127	F4
High Heath	18	C5
High Heath	48	D5
Highter's Heath	178	D3
Hill	47	E1
Hillfield	195	G1
Hill Hook	32	C4
Hill Top	71	E3
Hill Wood	33	G5
Himley	81	F3
Hinksford	98	D1
Hockley Heath	198	B5
Hodgehill	111	H4
Holly Bank	19	H4
Hollywood	178	D5
Holy Cross	170	C3
Hook End	167	H5
Hopwood	190	A5
Horseley Heath	86	A1
Hunnington	155	H5
Hurst Green	122	D4
Hurst Hill	67	H3
Illey	156	C2
Kates Hill	85	E5
Kineton Green	163	H2
King's Heath	161	E5
King's Hill	56	A3
Kingshurst	114	A2
King's Norton	176	C3
Kingstanding	75	G2
Kingswinford	99	F3
Kitt's Green	113	H1
Kitwell	157	E5
Knowle	197	G2
Knowle Grove	197	F5
The Knowle	103	G4
Ladywood	126	A2
Lambert's End	87	E3
Lane Green	11	E4
Lane Head	26	A4
Lanesfield	53	E4
Langley	104	D4
Langley Green	105	F5
Lapal	139	H4
Lawns Wood	117	F1
Lea End	190	D5
Lea Hall	130	C2
Leamore	27	E4
Lee Bank	126	C4
Leighswood	30	A2
Ley Hill	47	E4
Lickey	188	A5
Lifford	177	F1
Little Aston	32	A5
Little Bloxwich	17	F4
Little Bromwich	128	D2
Little Hay	33	G1
Little Norton	8	B2
Little Packington	150	D1
Littleworth End	49	E5
Lode Heath	165	G4
Lodge Hill	141	H5
Londonderry	105	G3
London Fields	83	G4
Longbridge	174	D5
Lower Bradley	54	B4
Lower Clent	170	D5
Lower Gornal	83	G2
Lower Illey	156	C3
Low Hill	23	F3
Lozells	108	C2
The Lunt	54	C1
Lutley	137	F5
Lydiate Ash	186	C5
Lye	136	C1
Lyndon Green	130	B5
Madeley Heath	186	A1
Major's Green	179	F5
Maney	62	B4
Marston Green	132	A4
Maw Green	57	H2
Mayer's Green	88	A3
Mere Green	47	E2
Merridale	36	A3
Merry Hill	50	C1
Merry Hill	119	H1
Mesty Croft	56	A4
Middle Bickenhill	150	C4
Mill Green	45	E5
Minworth	95	E1
Monkspath	195	G3
Monmore Green	38	A5
Moor Hall	47	H4
Moseley	38	A4
Moseley	144	B5
Moxley	54	D4
Mushroom Green	120	B3
Nechells	110	B1
Nechells Green	109	H5
Netherton	102	B4
Newbolds	24	A4
Newbridge	35	H2
New Invention	26	A2
New Oscott	76	B1
Newton	73	E3
New Town	9	H2
New Town	86	B2
Newtown	16	C2
Newtown	108	C4
Northfield	175	H1
Norton	135	E5
Norton Green	199	F1
Oakham	103	F2
Ocker Hill	70	A2
Oldbury	105	E4
Old Fallings	23	H5
Old Hill	121	G5
Old Perton	34	A2
Old Swinford	135	G4
Olton	147	G5
Orton Hill	65	E1
Ounsdale	64	D5
Overend	138	A4
Over Green	79	H2
Oxbarn	51	E1
Oxley	22	D2
Packwood	199	E4
Packwood Gullet	198	D2
Palfrey	56	D2
Palmers Cross	21	F2
Parkfield	52	D3
Park Village	23	H5
Pedmore	153	F2
Pelsall	18	B4
Pelsall Wood	17	H2
Pendeford	11	C5
Penn	51	E3
Pensnett	100	D2
Perry Barr	90	B1
Perry Beeches	74	A3
Perry Common	75	H3
Perton	34	C1
Pheasey	59	G4
Pleck	56	B2
Portobello	39	E3
Portway	104	B3
Prestwood	116	C3
Priestfield	53	F2
Primrose Hill	102	D5
Princes End	69	E2
Pype Hayes	93	H1
Quarry Bank	119	H4
Queslett	74	C1
Quinton	140	A1
Reddicap Heath	63	G4
Rednal	188	C3
Ridgacre	140	C1
Romsley	172	C1
Romsley Hill	172	C3
Rood End	105	G3
Roseville	68	A3
Rotten Row	197	G4
Rotton Park	107	G5
Roughley	47	G2
Round Oak	101	G5
Round's Green	104	C1
Rowley Regis	103	H4
Rubery	188	A1
Ruiton	83	F2
Rumbow Cottages	171	H2
Rumbush	195	G5
Rushall	29	E3
Russell's Hall	101	G1
Saltley	110	C5
Sandwell	106	C3
Scotlands	24	A2
Sedgley	67	G3
Selly Oak	159	F1
Selly Park	160	A1
Shard End	113	F4
Sharmans Cross	181	E1
Sheldon	147	H2
Shelfield	29	E2
Shenley Fields	158	A3
Shenstone Woodend	33	E1
Shire Oak	19	F1
Shire Oak Hill	19	F2
Shirley	180	C2
Shirley Heath	180	C4
Short Cross	138	C3
Short Heath	26	C4
Short Heath	76	D5
Silver End	118	D3
Silver Street	192	A3
Small Heath	128	A4
Smestow	80	A2
Smethwick	106	A4
Soho	107	E3
Solihull	182	A3
Solihull Lodge	179	E3
South Yardley	146	D1
Sparkbrook	127	H5
Sparkhill	145	E4
Springfield	7	K1
Springfield	103	F4
Springfield	162	A1
Springhill	15	H2
Spring Hill	50	C4
Stakenbridge	168	D2
Stambermill	136	A2
Stechford	130	A1
Stirchley	159	H4
Stockfield	146	C3
Stockland Green	92	A2
Stockwell End	21	G5
Stonebridge	150	D5
Stone Cross	71	H2
Stourbridge	134	D3
Stourton	116	D5
Stow Lawn	38	D5
The Straits	82	D1
Streetly	45	H4
Stubber's Green	29	G2
Summer Hill	69	G2
Sutton Coldfield	62	D5
Swan Village	86	D2
Swindon	80	D4
Tansley Hill	103	F2
Tat Bank	105	E2
Ten Acres	160	B2
Tettenhall	21	G5
Tettenhall Wood	35	H1
Thimble End	78	D1
Three Maypoles	194	B1
Tidbury Green	193	G4
Tile Cross	131	G2
Tilehouse Green	197	E3
Tipton	69	G4
Tipton Green	68	D5
Tividale	85	E2
Toll End	69	H5
Tower Hill	74	A5
Trueman's Heath	193	E1
Trysull	64	A2
Tudor Hill	62	A2
Turves Green	175	G4
Tyburn	94	A4
Tyseley	146	A2
Ulverley Green	164	A2
Upper Gornal	67	G5
Upper Witton	76	A5
Vauxhall	127	H1
Vigo	19	F5
The Village	100	D4
Wake Green	161	G1
Walker's Heath	177	F4
Wallbrook	68	C4
Wall Heath	99	F1
Wallington Heath	16	C4
Walmley	78	B3
Walmley Ash	78	D4
Walsall	5	F7
Walsall Wood	19	F3
Walton Pool	171	E3
Ward End	111	E4
Warley Woods	124	A3
Warstock	179	E2
Washwood Heath	111	G3
Water Orton	96	B3
Watford Gap	32	D3
Wednesbury	70	B1
Wednesbury Oak	69	F2
Wednesfield	24	D4
Weoley Castle	158	B1
Wergs	20	D4
West Bromwich	87	F5
Westcroft	13	H4
West Hagley	152	D5
West Heath	190	A1
Whiteheath Gate	104	C5
Whitehouse Common	63	F2
Whitlock's End	193	F1
Wightwick	34	D4
Wildmoor	186	B6
Willenhall	39	H2
Winson Green	107	G4
Withymoor Village	119	G3
Witton	91	E5
Wollaston	135	E1
Wollescote	136	C3
Wolverhampton	7	J3
Wombourne	64	B5
Woodcock Hill	158	A2
Wood End	24	C3
Woodgate	156	D1
Woodgate Valley	157	E2
Wood Green	56	A3
Wood Hayes	24	B1
Woods Bank	55	F3
Woodsetton	67	G4
Woodside	101	H3
The Woods	135	E4
Wordsley	118	A1
Worlds End	164	C3
Wylde Green	77	H2
Yardley	129	H4
Yardley Wood	179	G1
Yew Tree	57	H5

USING THE STREET INDEX

Street names are listed alphabetically. Each street name is followed by its postal town or area locality, the Postcode District, the page number, and the reference to the square in which the name is found.

Standard index entries are shown as follows:

Abberley Cl *HALE* B63 ....138 B5

Street names and selected addresses not shown on the map due to scale restrictions are shown in the index with an asterisk:

Aaron Manby Ct *TPTN/OCK* DY4 * 69 F3

GENERAL ABBREVIATIONS

ACC...ACCESS
ALY...ALLEY
AP...APPROACH
AR...ARCADE
ASS...ASSOCIATION
AV...AVENUE
BCH...BEACH
BLDS...BUILDINGS
BND...BEND
BNK...BANK
BR...BRIDGE
BRK...BROOK
BTM...BOTTOM
BUS...BUSINESS
BVD...BOULEVARD
BY...BYPASS
CATH...CATHEDRAL
CEM...CEMETERY
CEN...CENTRE
CFT...CROFT
CH...CHURCH
CHA...CHASE
CHYD...CHURCHYARD
CIR...CIRCLE
CIRC...CIRCUS
CL...CLOSE
CLFS...CLIFFS
CMP...CAMP
CNR...CORNER
CO...COUNTY
COLL...COLLEGE
COM...COMMON
COMM...COMMISSION
CON...CONVENT
COT...COTTAGE
COTS...COTTAGES
CP...CAPE
CPS...COPSE
CR...CREEK
CREM...CREMATORIUM
CRS...CRESCENT
CSWY...CAUSEWAY
CT...COURT
CTRL...CENTRAL
CTS...COURTS
CTYD...COURTYARD
CUTT...CUTTINGS
CV...COVE
CYN...CANYON
DEPT...DEPARTMENT
DL...DALE
DM...DAM
DR...DRIVE
DRO...DROVE
DRY...DRIVEWAY
DWGS...DWELLINGS
E...EAST
EMB...EMBANKMENT
EMBY...EMBASSY
ESP...ESPLANADE
EST...ESTATE
EX...EXCHANGE
EXPY...EXPRESSWAY
EXT...EXTENSION
F/O...FLYOVER
FC...FOOTBALL CLUB
FK...FORK
FLD...FIELD
FLDS...FIELDS
FLS...FALLS
FLS...FLATS
FM...FARM
FT...FORT
FWY...FREEWAY
FY...FERRY
GA...GATE
GAL...GALLERY
GDN...GARDEN
GDNS...GARDENS
GLD...GLADE
GLN...GLEN
GN...GREEN
GND...GROUND
GRA...GRANGE
GRG...GARAGE
GT...GREAT
GTWY...GATEWAY
GV...GROVE
HGR...HIGHER
HL...HILL
HLS...HILLS
HO...HOUSE
HOL...HOLLOW
HOSP...HOSPITAL
HRB...HARBOUR
HTH...HEATH
HTS...HEIGHTS
HVN...HAVEN
HWY...HIGHWAY
IMP...IMPERIAL
IN...INLET
IND EST...INDUSTRIAL ESTATE
INF...INFIRMARY
INFO...INFORMATION
INT...INTERCHANGE
IS...ISLAND
JCT...JUNCTION
JTY...JETTY
KG...KING
KNL...KNOLL
L...LAKE
LA...LANE
LDG...LODGE
LGT...LIGHT
LK...LOCK
LKS...LAKES
LNDG...LANDING
LTL...LITTLE
LWR...LOWER
MAG...MAGISTRATE
MAN...MANSIONS
MD...MEAD
MDW...MEADOWS
MEM...MEMORIAL
MKT...MARKET
MKTS...MARKETS
ML...MALL
ML...MILL
MNR...MANOR
MS...MEWS
MSN...MISSION
MT...MOUNT
MTN...MOUNTAIN
MTS...MOUNTAINS
MUS...MUSEUM
MWY...MOTORWAY
N...NORTH
NE...NORTH EAST
NW...NORTH WEST
O/P...OVERPASS
OFF...OFFICE
ORCH...ORCHARD
OV...OVAL
PAL...PALACE
PAS...PASSAGE
PAV...PAVILION
PDE...PARADE
PH...PUBLIC HOUSE
PK...PARK
PKWY...PARKWAY
PL...PLACE
PLN...PLAIN
PLNS...PLAINS
PLZ...PLAZA
POL...POLICE STATION
PR...PRINCE
PREC...PRECINCT
PREP...PREPARATORY
PRIM...PRIMARY
PROM...PROMENADE
PRS...PRINCESS
PRT...PORT
PT...POINT
PTH...PATH
PZ...PIAZZA
QD...QUADRANT
QU...QUEEN
QY...QUAY
R...RIVER
RBT...ROUNDABOUT
RD...ROAD
RDG...RIDGE
REP...REPUBLIC
RES...RESERVOIR
RFC...RUGBY FOOTBALL CLUB
RI...RISE
RP...RAMP
RW...ROW
S...SOUTH
SCH...SCHOOL
SE...SOUTH EAST
SER...SERVICE AREA
SH...SHORE
SHOP...SHOPPING
SKWY...SKYWAY
SMT...SUMMIT
SOC...SOCIETY
SP...SPUR
SPR...SPRING
SQ...SQUARE
ST...STREET
STN...STATION
STR...STREAM
STRD...STRAND
SW...SOUTH WEST
TDG...TRADING
TER...TERRACE
THWY...THROUGHWAY
TNL...TUNNEL
TOLL...TOLLWAY
TPK...TURNPIKE
TR...TRACK
TRL...TRAIL
TWR...TOWER
U/P...UNDERPASS
UNI...UNIVERSITY
UPR...UPPER
V...VALE
VA...VALLEY
VIAD...VIADUCT
VIL...VILLA
VIS...VISTA
VLG...VILLAGE
VLS...VILLAS
VW...VIEW
W...WEST
WD...WOOD
WHF...WHARF
WK...WALK
WKS...WALKS
WLS...WELLS
WY...WAY
YD...YARD
YHA...YOUTH HOSTEL

POSTCODE TOWNS AND AREA ABBREVIATIONS

ACGN...Acock's Green
ALDR...Aldridge
ALE/KHTH/YWD...Alcester Lane's End/King's Heath/Yardley Wood
ALVE...Alvechurch
AST/WIT...Aston/Witton
BDMR/CCFT...Bradmore/Castlecroft
BFLD/HDSWWD...Birchfield/Handsworth Wood
BHAMNEC...Birmingham N.E.C.
BHTH/HG...Balsall Heath/Highgate
BILS/COS...Bilston/Coseley
BKDE/SHDE...Buckland End/Shard End
BKHL/PFLD...Blakenhall/Priestfield
BLKHTH/ROWR...Blackheath/Rowley Regis
BLOX/PEL...Bloxwich/Pelsall
BNTWD...Burntwood
BORD...Bordesley
BRGRVE...Bromsgrove east
BRGRVW...Bromsgrove west
BRLYHL...Brierley Hill
BRWNH...Brownhills
BVILLE...Bournville
CBHAM...Central Birmingham
CBHAMNE...Central Birmingham northeast
CBHAMNW...Central Birmingham northwest
CBHAMW...Central Birmingham west
CBROM...Castle Bromwich
CDSL...Codsall
CDYHTH...Cradley Heath
CHWD/FDBR/MGN...Chelmsley Wood/Fordbridge/Marston Green
CNCK/NC...Cannock/Norton Canes
COVEN...Coven
CSCFLD/WYGN...Central Sutton Coldfield/Wylde Green
CSHL/WTROR...Coleshill/Water Orton
CVALE...Castle Vale
DARL/WED...Darlaston/Wednesbury
DIG/EDG...Digbeth/Edgbaston
DOR/KN...Dorridge/Knowle
DSYBK/YTR...Daisy Bank/Yew Tree
DUDN...Dudley north
DUDS...Dudley south
DUNHL/THL/PER...Dunstall Hill/Tettenhall/Perton
EDG...Edgbaston
ERDE/BCHGN...Erdington east/Birches Green
ERDW/GRVHL...Erdington west/Gravelly Hill
ETTPK/GDPK/PENN...EttingshallPark/Goldthorn Park/Penn
FOAKS/STRLY...Four Oaks/Streetly
GTB/HAM...Great Barr/Hamstead
GTWY...Great Wyrley
HAG/WOL...Hagley/Wollescote
HALE...Halesowen
HDSW...Handsworth
HHTH/SAND...Hateley Heath/Sandwell
HIA/OLT...Hampton in Arden/Olton
HLGN/YWD...Hall Green/Yardley Wood
HLYWD...Hollywood
HOCK/TIA...Hockley Heath/Tanworth-in-Arden
HRBN...Harborne
HWK/WKHTH...Hawkesley/Walker's Heath
KGSTG...Kingstanding
KGSWFD...Kingswinford
KIDD...Kidderminster
KINVER...Kinver
LDYWD/EDGR...Ladywood/Edgbaston Reservoir
LGLYGN/QTN...Langley Green/Quinton
LGN/SDN/BHAMAIR...Lyndon Green/Sheldon/Birmingham Airport
LICHS...Lichfield south
LOZ/NWT...Lozells/Newtown
MGN/WHC...Mere Green/Whitehouse Common
MOS/BIL...Moseley/Billesley
NFLD/LBR...Northfield/Longbridge
OLDBY...Oldbury
PBAR/PBCH...Perry Bar/Perry Beeches
POL/KGSB/FAZ...Polesworth/Kingsbury/Fazeley
RBRY...Rubery
RCOVN/BALC/EX...Rural Coventry north/Balsall Common/Exhall
RIDG/WDGT...Ridgacre/Woodgate
RMSLY...Romsley
RUSH/SHEL...Rushall/Shelfield
SCFLD/BOLD...Sutton Coldfield/Boldmere
SEDG...Sedgley
SHHTH...Short Heath
SHLY...Shirley
SLYOAK...Selly Oak
SMHTH...Small Heath
SMTHWK...Smethwick
SMTHWKW...Smethwick west
SOLH...Solihull
SPARK...Sparkhill/Sparkbrook
STETCH...Stetchford
STRBR...Stourbridge
TPTN/OCK...Tipton/Ocker Hill
VAUX/NECH...Vauxhall/Nechells
WALM/CURD...Walmley/Curdworth
WASH/WDE...Washwood Heath/Ward End
WBROM...West Bromwich
WLNHL...Willenhall
WMBN...Wombourne
WNSFLD...Wednesfield
WOLV...Wolverhampton
WOLVN...Wolverhampton north
WSL...Walsall
WSLW...Walsall west
WSNGN...Winson Green
YDLY...Yardley

Index - streets

A

Aaron Manby Ct
TPTN/OCK DY4 * ...**69** F3
Abberley Cl *HALE* B63 ...**138** B5
Abberley Rd *LGLYGN/QTN* B68 ...**123** F4
SEDG DY3 ...**83** E2
Abberley St *DUDS* DY2 ...**102** C1
SMTHWK B66 ...**107** F4
Abberton Cl *HALE* B63 ...**139** E4
Abberton Gv *SOLH* B91 ...**195** H1
Abbess Gv *YDLY* B25 ...**130** A3
Abbey Cl *HHTH/SAND* B71 ...**87** G1
Abbey Crs *HALE* B63 ...**137** H3
LGLYGN/QTN B68 ...**123** H3
Abbeydale Rd *NFLD/LBR* B31 ...**175** G3
Abbey Dr *BLOX/PEL* WS3 ...**18** A2
Abbeyfield Rd
ERDW/GRVHL B23 ...**76** C3
WOLVN WV10 ...**13** E3
Abbey Rd *DUDS* DY2 ...**102** D3
ERDW/GRVHL B23 ...**92** B4
HALE B63 ...**137** G3
HRBN B17 ...**142** B2
SEDG DY3 ...**83** E3
SMTHWKW B67 ...**123** H3
Abbey Sq *BLOX/PEL* WS3 ...**16** A5
Abbey St *SEDG* DY3 ...**83** E3
WSNGN B18 ...**108** A4
Abbey St North *WSNGN* B18 ...**108** A4
Abbot Rd *HALE* B63 ...**154** C2
Abbots Cl *DOR/KN* B93 ...**197** E1
RUSH/SHEL WS4 ...**29** E4
Abbotsford Av *GTB/HAM* B43 ...**73** H1
Abbotsford Dr *DUDN* DY1 ...**101** G2
Abbotsford Rd *SPARK* B11 ...**145** E1
Abbots Ms *BRLYHL* DY5 ...**119** F3
Abbots Rd *ALE/KHTH/YWD* B14 ...**161** E3
Abbots Wy *BDMR/CCFT* WV3 ...**36** A4
WSNGN B18 ...**108** B3
Abbotts Pl *BLOX/PEL* WS3 ...**27** H1
Abbotts Rd *ERDE/BCHGN* B24 ...**92** D5
Abbotts St *BLOX/PEL* WS3 ...**17** F5
Abdon Av *SLYOAK* B29 ...**158** D3
Aberdeen St *WSNGN* B18 ...**107** G5
Aberford Cl *SHHTH* WV12 ...**40** B1
Abigails Cl
LGN/SDN/BHAMAIR B26 ...**130** D5
Abingdon Cl *WOLV* WV1 ...**38** B3
Abingdon Rd *BLOX/PEL* WS3 ...**16** B5
DUDS DY2 ...**120** D1
ERDW/GRVHL B23 ...**75** H5
WOLV WV1 ...**38** B3
Abingdon Wy *BLOX/PEL* WS3 ...**16** B5
CVALE B35 ...**94** C3
Ablewell St *WSL* WS1 ...**5** F4
Ablow St *BKHL/PFLD* WV2 ...**6** E7
Abney Dr *BILS/COS* WV14 ...**67** H2
Aboyne Cl *DIG/EDG* B5 ...**143** H1
Ab Rw *CBHAMNE* B4 ...**3** K3
Acacia Av
CHWD/FDBR/MGN B37 ...**113** H3
DSYBK/YTR WS5 ...**57** G4
Acacia Cl
CHWD/FDBR/MGN B37 ...**113** H3
DUDN DY1 ...**84** A3
OLDBY B69 ...**85** H4
Acacia Crs *CDSL* WV8 ...**10** D4
Acacia Dr *BILS/COS* WV14 ...**68** A4
Acacia Rd *BVILLE* B30 ...**159** G2
Acfold Rd
BFLD/HDSWWD B20 ...**89** G1
Acheson Rd *HLGN/YWD* B28 ...**179** H2
Ackleton Gdns
BDMR/CCFT WV3 ...**51** F1
Ackleton Gv *SLYOAK* B29 ...**158** B2
Acorn Cl *ACGN* B27 * ...**146** B2
BVILLE B30 ...**159** G2
WBROM B70 ...**87** F4
Acorn Gdns *SLYOAK* B29 ...**160** A2
Acorn Gv *CBHAMW* B1 ...**2** A4
CDSL WV8 ...**10** A5
STRBR DY8 ...**118** A3
Acorn Rd *RMSLY* B62 ...**122** A4
WNSFLD WV11 ...**25** G1
Acorn St *WLNHL* WV13 ...**40** A3
Acre Ri *SHHTH* WV12 ...**25** H5
Acres Rd *BRLYHL* DY5 ...**119** G4
Acton Dr *SEDG* DY3 ...**82** D3
Acton Gv *BILS/COS* WV14 ...**53** F4
KGSTG B44 ...**75** G1
Ada Lewis Ct *GTB/HAM* B43 ...**73** G4
Adams Brook Dr
RIDG/WDGT B32 ...**157** F1
Adams Cl *SMTHWK* B66 ...**105** H2
TPTN/OCK DY4 ...**69** F2
Adam's Hl *HAG/WOL* DY9 ...**170** C1
RIDG/WDGT B32 ...**157** G1
Adams Rd *BDMR/CCFT* WV3 ...**50** C1
BRWNH WS8 ...**19** G2
Adams St *VAUX/NECH* B7 ...**3** K1
WBROM B70 ...**87** E3
WSLW WS2 ...**4** B2
Ada Rd *SMTHWK* B66 ...**124** D1
YDLY B25 ...**146** B1
Ada Wrighton Cl *SHHTH* WV12 ...**26** A3
Addenbrooke Dr
SCFLD/BOLD B73 ...**77** F1
Addenbrooke Rd
SMTHWKW B67 ...**124** B1
Addenbrooke St *BLOX/PEL* WS3 ...**27** G3
DARL/WED WS10 ...**40** B5
Addenbrook Wy *TPTN/OCK* DY4 ...**70** B3
Adderley Gdns *WASH/WDE* B8 ...**110** B4
Adderley Park Cl
WASH/WDE B8 * ...**110** C5
Adderley Rd *WASH/WDE* B8 ...**128** A1
Adderley Rd South
WASH/WDE B8 ...**128** A1
Adderley St *BORD* B9 ...**127** G3
Addison Cl *DARL/WED* WS10 ...**72** A1
Addison Cft *SEDG* DY3 ...**82** C1
Addison Gv *WNSFLD* WV11 ...**24** B1

Addison Pl BILS/COS WV14....54 B1
CSHL/WTROR B46....96 B3
Addison Rd
ALE/KHTH/YWD B14....161 F3
BDMR/CCFT WV3....36 B5
BRLYHL DY5....118 D2
DARL/WED WS10....72 A1
VAUX/NECH B7....110 A1
Addison St DARL/WED WS10....70 D1
Addison Ter DARL/WED WS10 *....70 D1
Adelaide Av WBROM B70....71 E4
Adelaide St BHTH/HG B12....127 F4
BRLYHL DY5....119 F1
Adelaide Wk BKHL/PFLD WV2....7 J7
Adey Rd WNSFLD WV11....25 F2
Adkins La SMTHWKW B67....124 B3
Admington Rd STETCH B33....131 E4
Admiral Pl MOS/BIL B13....144 B3
Admirals Wy
BLKHTH/ROWR B65....121 H2
Adrian Cft MOS/BIL B13....162 A1
Adria Rd SPARK B11....144 D3
Adshead Rd DUDS DY2....102 C2
Adstone Gv NFLD/LBR B31....175 F4
Adwalton Rd
DUNHL/THL/PER WV6....34 D2
Agenoria Dr STRBR DY8....135 F2
Ainsdale Cl STRBR DY8....135 F5
Ainsdale Gdns HALE B63....137 H5
Ainsworth Rd WOLVN WV10....13 E3
Aintree Gv BKDE/SHDE B34....113 F3
Aintree Rd WOLVN WV10....12 D3
Aintree Wy DUDN DY1....83 G4
Aire Cft NFLD/LBR B31....175 H4
Airfield Dr ALDR WS9....43 G2
Airport Wy HIA/OLT B92....149 H4
Akrill Cl WBROM B70 *....87 F1
Alamein Rd WLNHL WV13....39 E4
Albany Crs BILS/COS WV14....53 G2
Albany Gdns SOLH B91....182 B1
Albany Gv KGSWFD DY6....100 A2
SHHTH WV12....26 A1
Albany Rd HRBN B17....142 A1
Albemarle Rd STRBR DY8....135 F5
Albermarle Rd KGSWFD DY6....100 C4
Albert Av BHTH/HG B12....144 C1
Albert Clarke Dr SHHTH WV12....26 A3
Albert Cl CDSL WV8....10 A3
Albert Dr HALE B63....138 B5
SEDG DY3....80 C4
Albert Rd ALE/KHTH/YWD B14....161 F3
AST/WIT B6....109 E2
ERDW/GRVHL B23....92 B3
HALE B63....138 B5
HDSW B21....89 G5
HRBN B17....141 H2
LGLYGN/QTN B68....123 G4
STETCH B33....129 H1
WOLV WV1....6 A1
Albert St BRLYHL DY5....101 F2
CBHAMNE B4....3 H5
DARL/WED WS10....70 C1
HAG/WOL DY9....136 C2
KGSWFD DY6....99 F1
STRBR DY8....135 F2
TPTN/OCK DY4....69 F3
WBROM B70....87 G5
WSL WS1....4 E2
Albert St East OLDBY B69....105 F2
Albion Av WLNHL WV13....40 A3
Albion Field Dr HHTH/SAND B71....87 H2
Albion Rd BRWNH WS8....9 E4
HDSW B21....89 F5
HHTH/SAND B71....106 C1
SPARK B11....145 F2
WBROM B70....86 D4
Albion St BILS/COS WV14....54 A2
BRLYHL DY5....119 F1
CBHAMW B1....2 B3
KGSWFD DY6....99 F1
OLDBY B69....86 C5
TPTN/OCK DY4....85 F1
WLNHL WV13....39 H3
WOLV WV1....7 H4
Alborn Crs HWK/WKHTH B38....176 B5
Albrighton Rd HALE B63....138 A4
Albright Rd LGLYGN/QTN B68....105 H5
Albury Wk BHTH/HG B12....127 G5
Albutts Rd CNCK/NC WS11....8 B1
Alcester Dr SCFLD/BOLD B73....61 F5
WLNHL WV13....38 D5
Alcester Rd HLYWD B47....192 B4
MOS/BIL B13....144 B4
Alcester Rd South
ALE/KHTH/YWD B14....161 E3
ALE/KHTH/YWD B14....178 B2
Alcester St BHTH/HG B12....127 F4
Alcombe Gv STETCH B33....130 A2
Alcott Cl DOR/KN B93....198 D1
Alcott Gv STETCH B33....131 F1
Alcott La
CHWD/FDBR/MGN B37....131 H4
The Alcove BLOX/PEL WS3....17 F5
Aldbourne Wy
HWK/WKHTH B38....190 B1
Aldbury Rd
ALE/KHTH/YWD B14....178 C3
Aldeburgh Cl BLOX/PEL WS3....16 C4
Aldeford Dr BRLYHL DY5....119 F4
Alderbrook Cl SEDG DY3....66 D2
Alderbrook Rd SOLH B91....181 F2
Alder Cl HLYWD B47....192 D2
WALM/CURD B76....78 A4
Alder Coppice SEDG DY3....52 A5
Alder Crs DSYBK/YTR WS5....57 H4
Alder Dl BDMR/CCFT WV3....36 A4
Alderdale Av SEDG DY3....52 A5
Alderdale Crs HIA/OLT B92....165 G3
Alder Dr CHWD/FDBR/MGN B37....132 B3
Alderflat Pl VAUX/NECH B7....110 A4
Alderford Cl CDSL WV8....22 B2
Alder Gv RMSLY B62....139 G1
Alderham Cl SOLH B91....182 C1
Alderhithe Gv FOAKS/STRLY B74....45 H2
Alder La NFLD/LBR B31....159 E4
Alderlea Cl STRBR DY8....135 G5
Alderley Crs BLOX/PEL WS3....28 A5
Alderminster Rd SOLH B91....181 H4
Aldermore Dr MGN/WHC B75 *....63 F2
Alderney Gdns
HWK/WKHTH B38....176 B4
Alder Park Rd SOLH B91....181 F2
Alderpits Rd BKDE/SHDE B34....113 F3
Alder Rd BHTH/HG B12....144 C3
DARL/WED WS10....56 A2
KGSWFD DY6....100 C4
Aldersea Dr AST/WIT B6....109 F2
Aldershaw Rd
LGN/SDN/BHAMAIR B26....147 E2
Aldershaws SHLY B90....194 A3
Aldersley Av
DUNHL/THL/PER WV6....22 A3
Aldersley Cl
DUNHL/THL/PER WV6....22 B3
Aldersley Rd
DUNHL/THL/PER WV6....22 B5
Aldersmead Rd NFLD/LBR B31....176 A4
Alderson Rd WASH/WDE B8....110 D5
The Alders RMSLY B62....172 B1
Alderton Cl SOLH B91....181 H4
Alderton Dr BDMR/CCFT WV3....36 A5
Alder Wy FOAKS/STRLY B74....45 E5
Alderwood Pl SOLH B91....181 H2
Alderwood Ri SEDG DY3....83 F1
Aldgate Dr BRLYHL DY5....119 E5
Aldgate Gv LOZ/NWT B19....108 D4
Aldis Cl HLGN/YWD B28....162 C1
WSLW WS2 *....56 A1
Aldis Rd WSLW WS2....56 A1
Aldridge By-Pass ALDR WS9....30 A4
Aldridge Cl LGLYGN/QTN B68....105 G5
STRBR DY8....118 A4
Aldridge Rd FOAKS/STRLY B74....31 G5
FOAKS/STRLY B74....44 D5
LGLYGN/QTN B68....123 F4
PBAR/PBCH B42....91 E3
RUSH/SHEL WS4....42 D2
Aldridge St DARL/WED WS10....55 F1
Aldwych Cl ALDR WS9....30 B2
Aldwyck Dr BDMR/CCFT WV3....35 E5
Alexander Gdns
PBAR/PBCH B42....90 D3
Alexander Hl BRLYHL DY5....119 H4
Alexander Rd ACGN B27....146 B3
CDSL WV8....11 E4
SMTHWKW B67....124 A2
WSLW WS2....40 D3
Alexander St BDMR/CCFT WV3....6 D5
Alexander Ter
SMTHWKW B67 *....106 B3
Alexandra Av HDSW B21....107 F2
Alexandra Crs HHTH/SAND B71....72 A3
Alexandra Pl BILS/COS WV14....53 H2
Alexandra Rd BVILLE B30....160 A3
DARL/WED WS10....55 G2
DIG/EDG B5....144 A1
ETTPK/GDPK/PENN WV4....51 G3
HALE B63....138 B4
HDSW B21....107 F2
TPTN/OCK DY4....85 G1
WSL WS1....57 E1
Alexandra St DUDN DY1....84 B5
Alexandra Wy ALDR WS9....30 B5
TPTN/OCK DY4....85 G4
Alford Cl RBRY B45....188 C1
Alfreda Av HLYWD B47....178 B5
Alfred Rd HDSW B21....107 G1
SPARK B11....144 D2
Alfred St ALE/KHTH/YWD B14....161 F3
AST/WIT B6....109 H1
BHTH/HG B12....144 D2
BLOX/PEL WS3....27 F1
DARL/WED WS10....55 E3
SMTHWK B66....106 D2
WBROM B70....87 H2
Algernon Rd
LDYWD/EDGR B16....107 F5
Alice St BILS/COS WV14....53 H2
Alison Cl TPTN/OCK DY4....69 G1
Alison Dr STRBR DY8....135 E5
Alison Rd RMSLY B62....139 G4
Allan Cl STRBR DY8....118 B3
Allbut St CDYHTH B64....120 D3
Allcock St BORD B9....127 G3
TPTN/OCK DY4....70 A3
Allcroft Rd SPARK B11....145 H5
Allenby Cl KGSWFD DY6....100 C4
Allen Cl GTB/HAM B43....73 G4
Allendale Gv GTB/HAM B43....73 G3
Allendale Rd WALM/CURD B76....78 A3
YDLY B25....129 F5
Allen Dr DARL/WED WS10....55 E2
WBROM B70....88 B5
Allen Rd DARL/WED WS10....55 H3
TPTN/OCK DY4....69 F2
DUNHL/THL/PER WV6....36 C2
Allens Av WSNGN B18 *....107 H3
Allens Cl SHHTH WV12....25 H5
Allens Croft Rd
ALE/KHTH/YWD B14....160 B5
Allens Farm Rd NFLD/LBR B31....174 D2
Allens La BLOX/PEL WS3....17 H5
Allens Rd WSNGN B18....107 H3
Allen St WBROM B70....87 F3
Allerdale Rd BRWNH WS8....19 E1
Allerton La HHTH/SAND B71....71 G3
Allerton Rd YDLY B25....129 F5
Allesley Cl MGN/WHC B75....62 C1
Allesley Rd HIA/OLT B92....163 H2
Allesley St AST/WIT B6....109 E4
Alleston Rd WOLVN WV10....23 F1
Alleyne Gv ERDE/BCHGN B24....93 E4
Alleyne Rd ERDE/BCHGN B24....93 E5
The Alley SEDG DY3....82 D3
Allingham Gv GTB/HAM B43....59 H4
Allington Cl DSYBK/YTR WS5....43 F5
Allison St DIG/EDG B5....3 J6
Allman Rd ERDE/BCHGN B24....93 F2
Allmyn Dr FOAKS/STRLY B74....60 C2
All Saints Dr FOAKS/STRLY B74....46 D3
All Saints Rd
ALE/KHTH/YWD B14....161 E3
BKHL/PFLD WV2....7 H7
DARL/WED WS10....55 G2
WSNGN B18....108 A4
All Saints' St WSNGN B18....108 A4
All Saints Wy HHTH/SAND B71....87 H1
Allsops Cl BLKHTH/ROWR B65....103 F5
Allwell Dr ALE/KHTH/YWD B14....178 B3
Allwood Gdns RIDG/WDGT B32....140 A5
Alma Av TPTN/OCK DY4....69 G4
Alma Crs VAUX/NECH B7....109 H5
Alma Pl DUDS DY2....84 C5
Alma St DARL/WED WS10....55 E2
DARL/WED WS10....56 B5
HALE B63....137 G2
LOZ/NWT B19....109 E3
SMTHWK B66....107 E3
WLNHL WV13....39 H3
WOLVN WV10....37 H2
WSLW WS2....41 H1
Alma Wy LOZ/NWT B19....108 D2
Almond Av DSYBK/YTR WS5....57 G4
WSLW WS2....40 C1
Almond Cl BLOX/PEL WS3....17 H5
SLYOAK B29....158 C4
Almond Cft PBAR/PBCH B42....73 H5
Almond Gv
DUNHL/THL/PER WV6....37 E1
Almond Rd KGSWFD DY6....100 A1
Alnwick Rd BLOX/PEL WS3....16 C3
Alperton Dr HAG/WOL DY9....136 C5
Alpha Cl BHTH/HG B12....144 A1
Alpine Dr DUDS DY2....102 B5
Alpine Wy BDMR/CCFT WV3....35 G3
Alport Cft BORD B9....127 H2
Alston Cl FOAKS/STRLY B74....47 E3
SOLH B91....165 F4
Alston Gv BORD B9....129 F1
Alston Rd BORD B9....129 F1
OLDBY B69....104 C2
SOLH B91....165 F4
Alston St LDYWD/EDGR B16....125 H2
Althorpe Dr DOR/KN B93....196 B5
Alton Av SHHTH WV12....25 H5
Alton Cl WOLVN WV10....13 E4
Alton Cottages
ETTPK/GDPK/PENN WV4 *....66 B2
Alton Gv DUDS DY2....85 E5
HHTH/SAND B71....72 A4
Alton Rd SLYOAK B29....142 D4
Alum Dr BORD B9....129 E1
Alumhurst Av WASH/WDE B8....111 F5
Alum Rock Rd WASH/WDE B8....110 B4
Alumwell Cl WSLW WS2 *....41 F4
Alum Well Rd WSLW WS2....41 F4
Alvaston Cl BLOX/PEL WS3....17 E4
Alvechurch Hwy BRGRVE B60....187 E5
Alvechurch Rd HALE B63....138 B5
NFLD/LBR B31....189 H1
Alverley Cl KGSWFD DY6....99 F1
Alverstoke Cl COVEN WV9....11 H5
Alveston Gv BORD B9....129 F2
DOR/KN B93....197 F1
Alveston Rd HLYWD B47....192 C1
Alvin Cl RMSLY B62....122 D4
Alvington Cl SHHTH WV12....40 B1
Alwen St STRBR DY8....118 B3
Alwin Rd BLKHTH/ROWR B65....121 H2
Alwold Rd SLYOAK B29....141 G5
Amanda Av
ETTPK/GDPK/PENN WV4....51 F4
Amanda Dr
LGN/SDN/BHAMAIR B26....130 B3
Ambassador Rd
CHWD/FDBR/MGN B37....149 G3
Amber Dr OLDBY B69 *....105 E4
Ambergate Cl BLOX/PEL WS3....17 E4
Ambergate Dr KGSWFD DY6....99 G1
Amberley Gn GTB/HAM B43....73 G5
Amberley Gv AST/WIT B6....91 G3
Amberley Rd HIA/OLT B92....147 F4
Amberley Wy FOAKS/STRLY B74....45 E4
Amber Wy RMSLY B62....138 D1
Amberwood Cl SHHTH WV12....40 B2
Amblecote Av KGSTG B44....75 E1
Amblecote Rd BRLYHL DY5....119 F4
Ambleside RIDG/WDGT B32....157 G1
Ambleside Cl BILS/COS WV14....54 A4
Ambleside Dr BRLYHL DY5....119 E4
Ambleside Gv SHHTH WV12....25 H1
Ambleside Wy KGSWFD DY6....99 H3
Ambrose Cl WLNHL WV13....39 E3
Ambrose Crs KGSWFD DY6....99 H1
Ambury Wy GTB/HAM B43....73 F3
Amelas Cl STRBR DY8....118 C4
Amersham Cl RIDG/WDGT B32....141 E2
Amesbury Rd MOS/BIL B13....144 A4
Ames Rd DARL/WED WS10....55 E1
Amherst Av BFLD/HDSWWD B20....90 A3
Amington Cl MGN/WHC B75....47 H2
Amington Rd SHLY B90....180 A5
YDLY B25....146 B1
Amiss Gdns SMTHH B10....128 A4
Amity Cl SMTHWK B66 *....106 D4
Amos Av WNSFLD WV11....24 B3
Amos La WNSFLD WV11....24 C4
Amos Rd HAG/WOL DY9....136 D5
Amphlett Cft TPTN/OCK DY4....85 H2
Amphletts Cl DUDS DY2....121 E1
Ampton Rd EDG B15....126 B5
Amroth Cl RBRY B45....188 B1
Amwell Gv
ALE/KHTH/YWD B14....178 B2
Anchorage Rd
ERDW/GRVHL B23....92 B3
FOAKS/STRLY B74....62 B2
Anchor Cl LDYWD/EDGR B16....125 G3
Anchor La BILS/COS WV14....68 B1
Anchor Rd ALDR WS9....30 B4
BILS/COS WV14....68 C1
Andersleigh Dr BILS/COS WV14....68 A3
Anderson Crs GTB/HAM B43....73 G1
Anderson Rd ERDW/GRVHL B23....76 C5
SMTHWK B66....124 C3
TPTN/OCK DY4....85 G1
Anderton Cl FOAKS/STRLY B74....62 A1
Anderton Park Rd
MOS/BIL B13....144 C4
Anderton Rd SPARK B11....145 E1
Anderton St CBHAMW B1....2 A4
Andover Crs KGSWFD DY6....100 B5
Andover St DIG/EDG B5....3 K5
Andrew Cl SHHTH WV12....26 B4
Andrew Dr SHHTH WV12....26 B4
Andrew Gdns HDSW B21....89 G5
Andrew Rd HALE B63....138 C4
HHTH/SAND B71....72 B1
TPTN/OCK DY4....69 G2
Andrews Cl BRLYHL DY5....119 G4
Andrews Rd ALDR WS9....19 H3
Anerley Gv KGSTG B44....60 B4
Anerley Rd KGSTG B44....60 B4
Angela Av BLKHTH/ROWR B65....104 B5
Angela Pl BILS/COS WV14....53 H2
Angelica Cl DSYBK/YTR WS5....57 G5
Angelina St BHTH/HG B12....127 F5
Angel Pas STRBR DY8....135 G2
Angel St DUDN DY1....102 B1
Anglesey Av CBROM B36....114 B3
Anglesey Crs BRWNH WS8....9 F2
Anglesey Rd BRWNH WS8....9 F2
Anglesey St LOZ/NWT B19....108 C2
Anglian Rd ALDR WS9....29 F4
Angus Cl HHTH/SAND B71....71 G5
Anita Av TPTN/OCK DY4....85 G4
Anita Cft ERDW/GRVHL B23....92 C4
Ankadine Rd STRBR DY8....135 H1
Ankerdine Ct HALE B63....138 C4
Ankermoor Cl BKDE/SHDE B34....112 D3
Annan Av WOLVN WV10....23 G3
Ann Cft
LGN/SDN/BHAMAIR B26....148 B3
Anne Cl WBROM B70....86 C3
Anne Gv TPTN/OCK DY4....69 H2
Anne Rd BRLYHL DY5....120 A3
ETTPK/GDPK/PENN WV4....51 H3
SMTHWK B66....107 E2
Ann Rd HLYWD B47....192 C5
Annscroft HWK/WKHTH B38....176 B3
Ann St WLNHL WV13....39 H2
Ansbro Cl WSNGN B18....107 H4
Ansculf Rd STRBR DY8....118 D3
Ansell Rd ERDE/BCHGN B24....92 D5
SPARK B11....145 E1
Anslow Gdns WNSFLD WV11....25 F1
Anslow Rd ERDW/GRVHL B23....92 A1
Anson Cl DUNHL/THL/PER WV6....20 C5
Anson Gv ACGN B27....146 D5
Anson Rd WBROM B70....70 C4
WSLW WS2....40 C3
Anstey Cft
CHWD/FDBR/MGN B37 *....114 A5
Anstey Gv ACGN B27....163 F1
Anstey Rd KGSTG B44....75 E5
Anston Wy WNSFLD WV11....24 D3
Anstruther Rd EDG B15....125 G5
Anthony Rd WASH/WDE B8....128 C1
Anton Dr WALM/CURD B76....78 C5
Antony Rd SHLY B90....180 B4
Antringham Gdns EDG B15....125 F4
Antrobus Rd HDSW B21....89 G5
SCFLD/BOLD B73....76 C2
Anvil Crs BILS/COS WV14....68 C1
Anvil Dr OLDBY B69....104 C3
Apex Rd BRWNH WS8....8 C5
Apley Rd STRBR DY8....118 A5
Apollo Cft ERDE/BCHGN B24....93 H3
Apollo Rd HAG/WOL DY9....137 E2
LGLYGN/QTN B68....105 G3
Apollo Wy BFLD/HDSWWD B20....90 C5
Apperley Wy HALE B63....120 B5
Appian Cl ALE/KHTH/YWD B14....161 E5
Appian Wy SHLY B90....194 D4
Appleby Cl
ALE/KHTH/YWD B14....160 D5
Appleby Gdns WNSFLD WV11....15 G5
Appleby Gv SHLY B90....195 H2
Applecross FOAKS/STRLY B74....46 D4
Appledore Rd DSYBK/YTR WS5....43 F5
Appledorne Gdns
BKDE/SHDE B34....112 D3
Applesham Cl SPARK B11....145 F1
Appleton Av GTB/HAM B43....73 G3
STRBR DY8....135 G5
Appleton Cl BVILLE B30....159 G2
Appleton Crs
ETTPK/GDPK/PENN WV4....51 G3
Apple Tree Cl ERDW/GRVHL B23....91 H2
Appletree Cl NFLD/LBR B31....175 E4
Appletree Gv ALDR WS9....30 B5
DUNHL/THL/PER WV6....23 E5
Applewood Gv CDYHTH B64....121 F4
April Cft MOS/BIL B13....144 D5
Apse Cl WMBN WV5....64 D4
Apsley Cl LGLYGN/QTN B68....123 E5
Apsley Gv DOR/KN B93....198 D1
ERDE/BCHGN B24....93 E4
Apsley Rd LGLYGN/QTN B68....123 E5
Aqueduct Rd SHLY B90....179 G3
Aragon Dr SCFLD/BOLD B73....62 A2
Arboretum Rd WSL WS1....5 G2
Arbor Ga ALDR WS9....19 H3
Arbor Wy
CHWD/FDBR/MGN B37....132 C3
Arbury Dr STRBR DY8....117 H1
Arbury Hall Rd SHLY B90....180 D5
Arcal St SEDG DY3....67 G4
Archer Cl DARL/WED WS10....55 G5
LGLYGN/QTN B68 *....105 F5
Archer Ct HAG/WOL DY9....136 C5
Archer Rd ALE/KHTH/YWD B14....179 E1
BLOX/PEL WS3....28 A4
Archers Cl ERDW/GRVHL B23....76 A3
The Arches SPARK B11 *....127 H4
Arch Hill St DUDS DY2....102 C4
Archibald Rd LOZ/NWT B19....108 C1
Arcot Rd HLGN/YWD B28....145 H5
Ardarth Rd HWK/WKHTH B38....177 E3
Ardav Rd WBROM B70....70 D3
Arden Buildings DOR/KN B93....196 D5
Arden Cl STRBR DY8....117 G1
STRBR DY8....135 E1
Ardencote Rd MOS/BIL B13....161 G4
Arden Ct HIA/OLT B92 *....167 G3
Arden Cft CSHL/WTROR B46....97 F5
HIA/OLT B92....148 A3
Arden Dr DOR/KN B93....198 D1
LGN/SDN/BHAMAIR B26....130 B5
MGN/WHC B75....63 H3
SCFLD/BOLD B73....77 F3
Arden Gv LDYWD/EDGR B16....126 A3
OLDBY B69....105 E4
Arden Meads HOCK/TIA B94....198 A5
Arden Oak Rd
LGN/SDN/BHAMAIR B26....148 B2
Arden Pl DARL/WED WS10....54 D4
Arden Rd ACGN B27....146 B3
AST/WIT B6....108 D1
DOR/KN B93....198 D1
HLYWD B47....192 C2
RBRY B45....174 A4
SMTHWKW B67....106 C5
WASH/WDE B8....128 A1
Arden Vale Rd DOR/KN B93....197 F1
Arderne Dr
CHWD/FDBR/MGN B37....132 A3
Ardingley Wk BRLYHL DY5....118 D5
Ardley Cl DUDS DY2....102 D1
Ardley Rd ALE/KHTH/YWD B14....161 G5
Aretha Cl KGSWFD DY6....100 C3
Argil Cl WNSFLD WV11....24 D2
Argus Cl WALM/CURD B76....63 F5
Argyle Cl RUSH/SHEL WS4....5 K1
STRBR DY8....118 A3
Argyle Rd BKHL/PFLD WV2....51 H2
RUSH/SHEL WS4....5 K1
Argyle St VAUX/NECH B7....110 A1
Arkle Cft BLKHTH/ROWR B65....103 F3
CBROM B36....111 G1
Arkley Gv HLGN/YWD B28....163 F3
Arkley Rd HLGN/YWD B28....163 F3
Arkwright Rd
RIDG/WDGT B32....140 C2
WSLW WS2....27 F5
Arlen Dr GTB/HAM B43....73 F2
Arlescote Cl MGN/WHC B75....47 G3
Arlescote Rd HIA/OLT B92....148 A5
Arleston Wy SHLY B90....181 E5
Arley Cl OLDBY B69....104 B4
Arley Dr STRBR DY8....135 E4
Arley Gv
ETTPK/GDPK/PENN WV4....50 D3
Arley Rd SLYOAK B29....142 D4
SOLH B91....181 G1
WASH/WDE B8....110 B3
Arley Vls WSNGN B18 *....107 F5
Arlidge Cl BILS/COS WV14....53 H4
Arlington Cl KGSWFD DY6....99 H5
Arlington Ct STRBR DY8....135 H3
Arlington Gdns STRBR DY8 *....135 H3
Arlington Gv
ALE/KHTH/YWD B14....178 D3
Arlington Rd
ALE/KHTH/YWD B14....178 D2
HHTH/SAND B71....71 H5
Armada Cl ERDW/GRVHL B23....92 B5
Armoury Rd SPARK B11....128 B5
Armside Cl BLOX/PEL WS3....18 A3
Armstead Rd COVEN WV9....12 A4
Armstrong Cl STRBR DY8....135 H1
Armstrong Dr CBROM B36....95 H5
DUNHL/THL/PER WV6....22 C4
WSLW WS2....41 E1
Armstrong Wy WLNHL WV13....39 H5
Arnhem Cl WNSFLD WV11....24 B2
Arnhem Rd WLNHL WV13....39 E5
Arnhem Wy TPTN/OCK DY4....86 A1
Arnold Cl WSLW WS2....40 D2
Arnold Gv BVILLE B30....176 B1
SHLY B90....180 B1
Arnold Rd SHLY B90....180 C1
Arnwood Cl WSLW WS2....40 D3
Arosa Dr HRBN B17....141 H4
Arps Rd CDSL WV8....10 B4
Arran Cl GTB/HAM B43....58 C5
Arran Rd BKDE/SHDE B34....112 B3
Arran Wy CBROM B36....114 A2
Arras Rd DUDS DY2....85 E4
Arrow Cl DOR/KN B93....197 E2
Arrowfield Gn
HWK/WKHTH B38....190 B1
Arrow Rd BLOX/PEL WS3....28 A4
Arsenal St BORD B9....128 A3
Arthur Gunby Cl
MGN/WHC B75 *....63 F1
Arthur Harris Cl SMTHWK B66....124 D1
Arthur Pl CBHAMW B1....2 B4
Arthur Rd EDG B15....143 F1
ERDE/BCHGN B24....93 F2
HDSW B21....107 H1
TPTN/OCK DY4....69 G5
YDLY B25....146 A1
Arthur St BILS/COS WV14 *....53 H2
BKHL/PFLD WV2....52 B2
SMTHH B10....127 H3
WBROM B70....87 H5
Artillery St BORD B9....127 H2
Arton Cft ERDE/BCHGN B24....92 D4
Arundel Av DARL/WED WS10....55 H5

Arundel Crs HIA/OLT B92 ....164 C1
Arundel Dr OLDBY B69 ....103 F1
Arundel Gv
DUNHL/THL/PER WV6 ....35 E2
Arundel Pl SPARK B11 ....144 C1
Arundel Rd
ALE/KHTH/YWD B14 ....178 C4
SHHTH WV12 ....26 A3
STRBR DY8 ....117 G2
WOLVN WV10 ....12 B5
Arundel St WSL WS1 ....57 E1
Arun Wy WALM/CURD B76 ....78 C2
Asbury Rd DARL/WED WS10 ....72 A1
Ascot Cl LDYWD/EDGR B16 ....125 H2
OLDBY B69 ....104 C3
Ascot Dr DUDN DY1 ....83 H4
ETTPK/GDPK/PENN WV4 ....51 G4
Ascot Gdns STRBR DY8 ....117 H2
Ascot Rd MOS/BIL B13 ....144 B5
Ash Av BHTH/HG B12 ....144 C2
Ashborough Dr SOLH B91 ....196 A1
Ashbourne Gv AST/WIT B6 * 109 E1
Ashbourne Rdg HALE B63 ....137 H2
Ashbourne Rd BLOX/PEL WS3 ....17 E4
ETTPK/GDPK/PENN WV4 ....52 C5
LDYWD/EDGR B16 ....125 F1
WOLV WV1 ....38 A2
Ashbourne Wy SHLY B90 ....180 D5
Ashbrook Crs SOLH B91 ....182 A5
Ashbrook Dr RBRY B45 ....174 B5
Ashbrook Gv BVILLE B30 ....160 C2
Ashbrook Rd BVILLE B30 ....160 C2
Ashburn Gv WLNHL WV13 ....40 A3
Ashburton Rd
ALE/KHTH/YWD B14 ....160 D5
Ashbury Covert BVILLE B30 ....177 G2
Ashby Cl CBROM B36 ....111 G3
Ashby Ct SOLH B91 ....182 A4
Ash Cl CDSL WV8 ....10 C4
Ashcombe Av
BFLD/HDSWWD B20 ....89 G3
Ashcombe Gdns
ERDE/BCHGN B24 ....93 H3
Ashcott Cl HWK/WKHTH B38 ....176 B3
Ash Crs CHWD/FDBR/MGN B37 ....113 H3
KGSWFD DY6 ....100 A3
Ashcroft SMTHWK B66 * 107 E4
TPTN/OCK DY4 * 85 G4
Ashcroft Gv
BFLD/HDSWWD B20 ....90 D4
Ashdale Cl KGSWFD DY6 ....99 H1
Ashdale Dr
ALE/KHTH/YWD B14 ....178 C4
Ashdale Gv
LGN/SDN/BHAMAIR B26 ....130 C4
Ashdene Cl SCFLD/BOLD B73 ....62 A5
Ashdene Gdns STRBR DY8 ....117 G2
Ashdown Cl MOS/BIL B13 ....161 G1
RBRY B45 ....174 A3
Ashdown Dr STRBR DY8 ....118 A1
Ash Dr HHTH/SAND B71 ....71 G5
Ashen Cl
ETTPK/GDPK/PENN WV4 ....52 A5
Ashenden Ri BDMR/CCFT WV3 ....35 E4
Ashenhurst Rd DUDN DY1 ....101 H1
Ashes Rd OLDBY B69 ....104 D5
Ashfern Dr WALM/CURD B76 ....78 B4
Ashfield Av
ALE/KHTH/YWD B14 ....161 F1
Ashfield Cl BLOX/PEL WS3 ....42 A1
Ashfield Crs DUDS DY2 ....120 C1
HAG/WOL DY9 ....136 D4
Ashfield Gv HALE B63 ....138 A5
WOLVN WV10 ....12 C4
Ashfield Rd
ALE/KHTH/YWD B14 ....161 F1
BDMR/CCFT WV3 ....35 H3
BILS/COS WV14 ....54 C5
WOLVN WV10 ....12 C4
Ashford Dr SEDG DY3 ....67 G4
WALM/CURD B76 ....94 A1
Ashfurlong Crs MGN/WHC B75 ....63 E1
Ash Gn DUDN DY1 ....84 A1
Ash Gv BHTH/HG B12 ....144 D2
BORD B9 * 127 H2
HAG/WOL DY9 ....136 B4
SEDG DY3 ....83 E4
Ashgrove Rd KGSTG B44 ....74 C1
Ash Hl BDMR/CCFT WV3 ....35 H4
Ashill Rd RBRY B45 ....188 B1
Ashland St BDMR/CCFT WV3 ....6 C6
Ashlawn Crs SOLH B91 ....163 H5
Ashleigh Dr BFLD/HDSWWD B20 ....90 B4
Ashleigh Gv MOS/BIL B13 ....161 H1
Ashleigh Rd OLDBY B69 ....104 A1
SOLH B91 ....181 H1
Ashley Cl EDG B15 ....126 C5
KGSWFD DY6 ....99 G5
STRBR DY8 ....134 D5
Ashley Gdns CDSL WV8 ....10 B3
WASH/WDE B8 ....110 B5
Ashley Mt DUNHL/THL/PER WV6 ....21 H5
Ashley Rd BLOX/PEL WS3 ....26 D1
ERDW/GRVHL B23 ....92 C3
ETTPK/GDPK/PENN WV4 ....51 E5
Ashley St BILS/COS WV14 ....54 A2
BLKHTH/ROWR B65 ....122 A3
Ashley Ter SLYOAK B29 * 159 G1
Ashmead Dr RBRY B45 ....188 C4
Ashmead Gv ERDE/BCHGN B24 ....93 E4
Ashmead Ri RBRY B45 ....188 C4
Ash Ms ACGN B27 ....146 C2
Ashmole Rd WBROM B70 ....70 D4
Ashmore Av WNSFLD WV11 ....25 G1
Ashmore Lake Rd SHHTH WV12 ....39 H1
Ashmore Lake Wy SHHTH WV12 ....39 H1
Ashmore Rd BVILLE B30 ....159 H5
Ashold Farm Rd
ERDE/BCHGN B24 ....93 G4
Asholme Cl CBROM B36 ....111 G2
Ashorne Cl ACGN B27 ....163 F3
Ashover Gv WSNGN B18 ....107 G5
Ash Rd DARL/WED WS10 ....55 H3
DUDN DY1 ....84 B3
TPTN/OCK DY4 ....85 E2
WASH/WDE B8 ....110 B5
Ashstead Cl WALM/CURD B76 ....78 D5
Ash St BDMR/CCFT WV3 ....6 B5
BILS/COS WV14 ....54 A5
BLOX/PEL WS3 ....27 H1
CDYHTH B64 ....121 E2
Ashted Circ VAUX/NECH B7 ....109 G5
Ash Ter OLDBY B69 ....85 H5
Ashton Cft LDYWD/EDGR B16 ....126 A2
SOLH B91 ....181 G4
Ashton Dr RUSH/SHEL WS4 ....18 C4
Ashton Park Dr BRLYHL DY5 ....119 E3
Ashton Rd YDLY B25 ....129 F5
Ashtree Cl STRBR DY8 ....118 C4
Ash Tree Dr
LGN/SDN/BHAMAIR B26 ....129 H5
Ashtree Gv BILS/COS WV14 ....54 D5
Ash Tree Rd BVILLE B30 ....160 A4
Ashtree Rd BLOX/PEL WS3 ....18 A4
CDYHTH B64 ....121 F2
OLDBY B69 ....104 B1
Ashurst Rd WALM/CURD B76 ....78 B5
Ashville Av BKDE/SHDE B34 ....112 B2
Ashville Dr HALE B63 ....138 C2
Ashwater Dr
ALE/KHTH/YWD B14 ....177 H3
Ash Wy ERDW/GRVHL B23 ....76 A3
SPARK B11 ....144 D2
Ashwell Dr SHLY B90 ....180 D1
Ashwells Gv COVEN WV9 ....11 H5
Ashwin Rd HDSW B21 ....107 H2
Ashwood Av STRBR DY8 ....117 G2
Ashwood Cl FOAKS/STRLY B74 ....45 E5
Ashwood Dr
CHWD/FDBR/MGN B37 ....132 D1
Ashwood Gv
ETTPK/GDPK/PENN WV4 ....51 G3
Ashwood Lower La
KGSWFD DY6 * 98 C4
Ashworth Rd PBAR/PBCH B42 ....74 B2
Askew Bridge Rd SEDG DY3 * 82 D3
Askew Cl SEDG DY3 ....83 G1
Aspbury Cft CBROM B36 ....95 F5
Aspen Cl ACGN B27 ....146 B4
WALM/CURD B76 ....78 B1
Aspen Dr
CHWD/FDBR/MGN B37 ....132 C4
Aspen Gdns
BFLD/HDSWWD B20 ....90 B5
Aspen Gv BORD B9 ....129 E1
HLYWD B47 ....192 D3
SHHTH WV12 ....26 C3
Aspen Wy BDMR/CCFT WV3 ....6 A6
Asquith Dr OLDBY B69 ....86 B4
Asquith Rd WASH/WDE B8 ....111 F4
Asra Cl SMTHWK B66 ....106 C1
Astbury Av SMTHWKW B67 ....124 B1
Astbury Cl BLOX/PEL WS3 ....16 C3
WOLV WV1 ....38 A4
Aster Wk COVEN WV9 ....12 A4
Astley Av RMSLY B62 ....139 H1
Astley Cl TPTN/OCK DY4 ....70 B5
Astley Rd HDSW B21 ....89 F5
Aston Brook Gn AST/WIT B6 * 109 F4
Aston Brook St AST/WIT B6 * 109 E3
Aston Brook St East
AST/WIT B6 ....109 F4
Aston Bury EDG B15 ....125 F4
Aston Church Rd
VAUX/NECH B7 ....110 A2
Aston Cl BILS/COS WV14 ....54 C4
Aston Expressway AST/WIT B6 ....109 G1
Aston Hall Rd AST/WIT B6 ....109 G1
Aston La BFLD/HDSWWD B20 ....91 E4
Aston Manor Cl
BFLD/HDSWWD B20 ....91 E4
Aston Rd AST/WIT B6 ....3 J1
OLDBY B69 ....85 G5
WLNHL WV13 ....39 E3
Aston Rd North AST/WIT B6 ....109 F3
Astons Cl BRLYHL DY5 ....119 F5
Astons Fold BRLYHL DY5 ....119 F5
Aston St BDMR/CCFT WV3 ....36 C5
CBHAMNE B4 ....3 J2
TPTN/OCK DY4 ....70 A5
Astor Dr MOS/BIL B13 ....162 A1
Astoria Cl SHHTH WV12 ....26 B1
Astor Rd FOAKS/STRLY B74 ....45 G4
KGSWFD DY6 ....100 B4
Athelney Ct BLOX/PEL WS3 * 18 A4
Athelstan Gv
DUNHL/THL/PER WV6 ....20 C5
Atherstone Cl SHLY B90 ....179 G3
Atherstone Rd WOLV WV1 ....38 B3
Athlone Rd DSYBK/YTR WS5 ....43 E5
Athol Cl RIDG/WDGT B32 ....157 H2
Athole St BHTH/HG B12 ....127 G5
Atlantic Rd KGSTG B44 ....75 F3
Atlantic Wy DARL/WED WS10 ....70 C2
Atlas Cft WOLVN WV10 ....23 E4
Atlas Est AST/WIT B6 * 91 G4
Atlas Gv WBROM B70 ....86 D3
Attenborough Cl LOZ/NWT B19 ....108 D4
Attingham Dr GTB/HAM B43 ....73 F1
Attleborough La
CSHL/WTROR B46 ....96 A5
Attlee Cl OLDBY B69 ....86 B4
Attlee Crs BILS/COS WV14 ....69 E1
Attlee Rd WSLW WS2 ....40 C2
Attwell Pk BDMR/CCFT WV3 ....50 D1
Attwell Rd TPTN/OCK DY4 ....69 F2
Attwood Cl WASH/WDE B8 ....110 C3
Attwood Gdns
ETTPK/GDPK/PENN WV4 ....52 C3
Attwood St HAG/WOL DY9 ....136 D2
HALE B63 ....138 B2
Aubrey Rd RIDG/WDGT B32 ....124 A5
SMHTH B10 ....128 D5
Auchinleck Sq EDG B15 * 126 B3
Auckland Dr CBROM B36 ....113 H1
Auckland Rd KGSWFD DY6 ....100 A5
SMTHWKW B67 ....106 A4
SPARK B11 ....127 G5
Auden Ct DUNHL/THL/PER WV6 ....34 D1
Audley Rd STETCH B33 ....112 A5
Audnam STRBR DY8 ....118 A3
Augusta Rd ACGN B27 ....146 C2
MOS/BIL B13 ....144 A3
Augusta Rd East MOS/BIL B13 ....144 B3
Augusta St WSNGN B18 ....2 C1
Augustine Gv FOAKS/STRLY B74 ....32 D5
WSNGN B18 ....107 H3
Augustus Cl CSHL/WTROR B46 ....97 F5
Augustus Ct EDG B15 ....125 H4
Augustus Rd EDG B15 ....125 G4
Augustus St WSLW WS2 ....4 C4
Aulton Rd MGN/WHC B75 ....48 A3
Ault St WBROM B70 ....87 H5
Austcliff Dr SOLH B91 ....182 A5
Austen Pl EDG B15 ....126 B4
Austin Cl ACGN B27 ....146 D3
DUDN DY1 ....83 H4
Austin Cft CBROM B36 ....95 G5
Austin Ri NFLD/LBR B31 ....189 F1
Austin Rd HDSW B21 ....89 E5
Austin St DUNHL/THL/PER WV6 ....36 D1
Austin Wy PBAR/PBCH B42 ....90 A1
Austrey Cl DOR/KN B93 ....197 E2
Austrey Gv SLYOAK B29 * 158 C2
Austrey Rd KGSWFD DY6 ....100 C4
Austy Cl CBROM B36 ....112 A1
Autherley Jct COVEN WV9 * 22 C1
Autumn Berry Gv SEDG DY3 ....67 G5
Autumn Cl RUSH/SHEL WS4 ....18 C5
Autumn Dr RUSH/SHEL WS4 ....18 C5
SEDG DY3 ....83 F3
Autumn Gv LOZ/NWT B19 ....108 C3
Avalon Cl ERDE/BCHGN B24 ....93 F2
Avebury Gv BVILLE B30 ....160 C3
Avebury Rd BVILLE B30 ....160 C2
Ave Maria Cl CDYHTH B64 ....121 E3
Avenbury Dr SOLH B91 ....182 C1
Avenue Cl DOR/KN B93 ....197 E5
VAUX/NECH B7 ....109 G4
Avenue Perry WOLVN WV10 ....23 H2
Avenue Rd
ALE/KHTH/YWD B14 ....160 D2
AST/WIT B6 ....109 G3
BDMR/CCFT WV3 ....36 A3
BILS/COS WV14 ....68 C3
BLKHTH/ROWR B65 ....122 B3
DARL/WED WS10 ....55 F2
DOR/KN B93 ....197 E5
DUDS DY2 ....101 G3
ERDW/GRVHL B23 ....92 D2
HDSW B21 ....89 F4
The Avenue ACGN B27 ....146 D4
BDMR/CCFT WV3 ....35 F5
BLKHTH/ROWR B65 ....121 G1
ETTPK/GDPK/PENN WV4 ....51 E4
KIDD DY10 ....168 B3
LOZ/NWT B19 ....108 C1
RBRY B45 ....187 G1
WALM/CURD B76 ....78 A2
Averill Rd
LGN/SDN/BHAMAIR B26 ....130 C4
Avern Cl TPTN/OCK DY4 ....69 H5
Aversley Rd HWK/WKHTH B38 ....176 B5
Avery Cft CVALE B35 ....94 B4
Avery Dell BVILLE B30 * 160 B5
Avery Dr ACGN B27 ....146 C3
Avery Myers Cl
LGLYGN/QTN B68 ....105 F4
Avery Rd SCFLD/BOLD B73 ....76 A1
SMTHWK B66 ....107 F3
Aviemore Crs GTB/HAM B43 ....59 F4
Avington Cl SEDG DY3 ....67 F4
Avion Cl WSL WS1 ....57 F1
Avocet Cl STETCH B33 ....130 A1
Avon Cl BRLYHL DY5 ....100 D2
DUNHL/THL/PER WV6 ....34 D2
Avon Crs BLOX/PEL WS3 ....28 C1
Avondale Cl KGSWFD DY6 ....100 A1
Avondale Rd
DUNHL/THL/PER WV6 ....36 B2
SPARK B11 ....145 F3
Avon Dr CBROM B36 ....113 H2
MOS/BIL B13 ....144 D5
WLNHL WV13 ....40 A3
Avon Gv DSYBK/YTR WS5 ....57 G5
Avon Ms STRBR DY8 * 117 G2
Avon Rd BLOX/PEL WS3 ....28 A1
HALE B63 ....137 F2
SHLY B90 ....180 D5
STRBR DY8 ....135 F4
Avon St SPARK B11 ....145 E2
Awbridge Br WMBN WV5 ....64 C1
Awbridge Rd DUDS DY2 ....120 C1
Awefields Crs SMTHWKW B67 ....105 H5
Awlmakers Gv BLOX/PEL WS3 ....27 G3
Axletree Wy DARL/WED WS10 ....56 B3
Ayala Cft CBROM B36 ....112 A1
Aylesbury Cl HOCK/TIA B94 ....198 A5
Aylesbury Crs KGSTG B44 ....75 G3
Aylesbury Rd HOCK/TIA B94 ....198 B4
Aylesford Cl SEDG DY3 ....66 D1
Aylesford Dr
CHWD/FDBR/MGN B37 ....132 A5
FOAKS/STRLY B74 ....32 C5
Aylesford Rd HDSW B21 ....89 F5
Aylesmore Cl HIA/OLT B92 ....164 A2
RIDG/WDGT B32 ....157 G1
Ayre Rd ERDE/BCHGN B24 ....93 F2
Ayrshire Cl CBROM B36 ....111 H1
Ayrton Cl DUNHL/THL/PER WV6 ....35 E1
Azalea Cl CDSL WV8 ....10 D4
Azalea Gv BORD B9 ....128 D2
Aziz Isaac Cl
LGLYGN/QTN B68 * 105 G3

B

Babington Rd HDSW B21 ....107 G2
Bablake Cft HIA/OLT B92 ....164 C1
Babors Fld BILS/COS WV14 ....53 E5
Babworth Cl COVEN WV9 ....12 A5
Baccabox La HLYWD B47 ....192 A1
Bacchus Rd WSNGN B18 ....107 H3
Bache St WBROM B70 ....87 G5
Bach Mill Dr
ALE/KHTH/YWD B14 ....179 F2
Backhouse La WNSFLD WV11 ....38 C1
Back La ALDR WS9 ....31 F3
LICHS WS14 ....32 B1
SHLY B90 ....194 A3
Back Rd HWK/WKHTH B38 ....176 D3
KGSWFD DY6 ....99 H2
Baddesley Rd HIA/OLT B92 ....147 E5
Bader Rd
DUNHL/THL/PER WV6 ....34 B2
WSLW WS2 ....40 D3
Bader Wk CVALE B35 ....94 B4
Badger Cl SHLY B90 ....194 D4
Badger Dr WOLVN WV10 ....37 F1
Badgers Bank Rd
FOAKS/STRLY B74 ....32 D5
Badgers Cl BLOX/PEL WS3 ....18 A2
Badgers Cft RMSLY B62 ....121 H5
Badger St HAG/WOL DY9 ....136 C1
SEDG DY3 ....83 G1
Badminton Cl DUDN DY1 ....83 H3
Badsey Cl NFLD/LBR B31 ....176 A1
Badsey Rd OLDBY B69 ....104 B4
Baggeridge Cl SEDG DY3 ....66 C3
Baggott St BKHL/PFLD WV2 ....52 A1
Baginton Cl SOLH B91 ....164 D5
Baginton Rd CVALE B35 ....94 D2
Bagley St HAG/WOL DY9 ....136 A1
Bagnall Cl
LGN/SDN/BHAMAIR B26 ....146 D1
Bagnall Rd BILS/COS WV14 ....53 G2
Bagnall St BLOX/PEL WS3 ....27 G3
TPTN/OCK DY4 ....70 A2
WBROM B70 ....88 A4
Bagnall Wk BRLYHL DY5 ....119 F3
Bagnell Rd
ALE/KHTH/YWD B14 ....161 F3
Bagot St CBHAMNE B4 ....3 H1
Bagridge Cl BDMR/CCFT WV3 ....35 F5
Bagridge Rd BDMR/CCFT WV3 ....35 F5
Bagshawe Cft
ERDW/GRVHL B23 ....76 B4
Bagshaw Rd STETCH B33 ....130 A1
Bailey Rd BILS/COS WV14 ....53 F1
Bailey St WBROM B70 ....87 E2
WOLVN WV10 ....7 J3
Baker Av BILS/COS WV14 ....67 H1
Baker House Gv GTB/HAM B43 ....73 F4
Baker Rd BILS/COS WV14 ....54 A5
Bakers Gdns CDSL WV8 ....10 A3
Baker's La ALDR WS9 ....30 B4
DOR/KN B93 ....199 G2
FOAKS/STRLY B74 ....60 B3
Baker St BORD B9 ....128 B3
HDSW B21 ....107 H1
SPARK B11 ....145 E3
TPTN/OCK DY4 ....85 E2
WBROM B70 ....87 F3
Bakers Wy CDSL WV8 ....10 A3
Bakewell Cl BLOX/PEL WS3 ....17 E4
Balaams Dr NFLD/LBR B31 ....174 B4
Balaclava Rd
ALE/KHTH/YWD B14 ....161 E2
Balcaskie Cl EDG B15 ....125 G5
Balden Rd RIDG/WDGT B32 ....124 A5
Baldmoor Lake Rd
ERDW/GRVHL B23 ....76 D4
Bald's La HAG/WOL DY9 ....136 D2
Baldwin Cl OLDBY B69 ....86 B4
Baldwin Rd BVILLE B30 ....177 E2
Baldwins La HLGN/YWD B28 ....179 H1
Baldwin St BILS/COS WV14 ....54 B4
SMTHWK B66 ....106 D3
Baldwin Wy SEDG DY3 ....80 C4
Balfour Dr OLDBY B69 ....86 B4
Balfour Rd KGSWFD DY6 ....100 A1
Balfour St BHTH/HG B12 ....144 A1
Balham Gv KGSTG B44 ....75 G1
Balking Cl BILS/COS WV14 ....53 F5
Ballarat Wk STRBR DY8 ....135 F2
Ballard Crs DUDS DY2 ....102 D4
Ballard Rd DUDS DY2 ....102 D4
Ballard Wk
CHWD/FDBR/MGN B37 ....114 A3
Ball Flds TPTN/OCK DY4 ....86 A1
Ball La COVEN WV9 ....12 C1
Ballot St SMTHWK B66 ....106 D4
Balls Hl WSL WS1 ....5 G3
Balls St WSL WS1 ....5 G3
Balmain Crs WNSFLD WV11 ....24 B2
Balmoral Cl RMSLY B62 ....121 H5
RUSH/SHEL WS4 ....29 F3
Balmoral Dr SHHTH WV12 ....25 H3
WMBN WV5 ....65 E2
Balmoral Rd CBROM B36 ....114 A2
ERDW/GRVHL B23 ....92 D1
ETTPK/GDPK/PENN WV4 ....51 G3
FOAKS/STRLY B74 ....32 D5
RIDG/WDGT B32 ....157 F3
STRBR DY8 ....117 G2
Balmoral Vw DUDN DY1 ....83 G4
Balmoral Wy
BLKHTH/ROWR B65 ....104 B5
WSLW WS2 ....41 E1
Balsall Heath Rd DIG/EDG B5 ....127 E5
Baltimore Rd PBAR/PBCH B42 ....90 A1
Balvenie Wy DUDN DY1 ....83 H3
Bamber Cl BDMR/CCFT WV3 ....36 A5
Bamford Cl BLOX/PEL WS3 ....17 E4
Bamford Rd BDMR/CCFT WV3 ....36 C5
BLOX/PEL WS3 ....17 E4
Bampfylde Pl PBAR/PBCH B42 * 74 C4
Bamville Rd WASH/WDE B8 ....111 E4
Banbery Dr WMBN WV5 ....80 D2
Banbrook Cl HIA/OLT B92 ....165 F2
Banbury Cl SEDG DY3 ....67 G5
Banbury Cft
CHWD/FDBR/MGN B37 ....131 H2
Banbury St DIG/EDG B5 ....3 J4
Bancroft Cl BILS/COS WV14 ....68 B4
Bandywood Rd KGSTG B44 ....60 A4
Banfield Av DARL/WED WS10 ....55 E1
Banfield Rd DARL/WED WS10 ....55 E4
Banford Rd WASH/WDE B8 ....111 E5
Bangham Pit Rd
NFLD/LBR B31 ....158 A3
Bangor Rd BORD B9 ....128 B2
Bangor Vls DARL/WED WS10 * 55 H2
Bankdale Rd WASH/WDE B8 ....111 F5
Bankes Rd SMHTH B10 ....128 C3
Bank Farm Cl HAG/WOL DY9 ....153 E1
Bankfield Rd BILS/COS WV14 ....53 H3
TPTN/OCK DY4 ....70 A3
Banklands Rd DUDS DY2 ....103 E3
Bank Rd DUDS DY2 ....102 D3
SEDG DY3 ....83 E3
Bankside GTB/HAM B43 ....73 G4
MOS/BIL B13 ....145 F5
WMBN WV5 ....64 D4
Bankside Crs FOAKS/STRLY B74 ....60 B1
Bankside Wy ALDR WS9 ....19 H5
Banks St WLNHL WV13 ....39 G3
Bank St ALE/KHTH/YWD B14 ....161 E2
BILS/COS WV14 ....54 A4
BILS/COS WV14 ....68 C3
BRLYHL DY5 ....101 F5
CDYHTH B64 ....120 C3
HAG/WOL DY9 ....136 D2
HHTH/SAND B71 ....71 G5
WOLVN WV10 ....23 G5
WSL WS1 ....5 G4
Bankwell St BRLYHL DY5 ....101 F5
Bannerlea Rd
CHWD/FDBR/MGN B37 ....113 H4
Bannerley Rd STETCH B33 ....131 E2
Banners Ct SCFLD/BOLD B73 * 60 D5
Banners Gate Rd
SCFLD/BOLD B73 ....60 D5
Banners Gv ERDW/GRVHL B23 ....77 E5
Banners La HALE B63 ....137 H1
Banners St HALE B63 ....137 H1
Banners Wk KGSTG B44 ....75 H1
Bannister Rd DARL/WED WS10 ....70 B1
Bannister St CDYHTH B64 ....120 D2
Banstead Cl BKHL/PFLD WV2 ....52 C1
Bantams Cl STETCH B33 ....131 E2
Bantock Av BDMR/CCFT WV3 ....36 B5
Bantock Gdns
BDMR/CCFT WV3 ....36 A4
The Bantocks WBROM B70 ....71 E5
Bantock Wy HRBN B17 ....142 A3
Banton Cl ERDW/GRVHL B23 ....76 B3
Bantry Cl
LGN/SDN/BHAMAIR B26 ....148 A3
Baptist End Rd DUDS DY2 ....102 C4
Barbara Rd HLGN/YWD B28 ....179 G2
Barbel Dr WOLV WV1 ....38 B1
Barbers La HIA/OLT B92 ....166 C4
Barbourne Cl SOLH B91 ....195 H1
Barbrook Dr BRLYHL DY5 ....118 D5
Barcheston Rd DOR/KN B93 ....197 E4
SLYOAK B29 ....158 C1
Barclay Rd SMTHWKW B67 ....124 A3
Barcroft WLNHL WV13 ....39 H2
Bardfield Cl PBAR/PBCH B42 ....73 H3
Bardon Dr SHLY B90 ....180 D3
Bard St SPARK B11 ....145 E2
Bardwell Cl CDSL WV8 ....22 B2
Barford Cl DARL/WED WS10 ....40 A5
WALM/CURD B76 ....63 F4
Barford Crs
ALE/KHTH/YWD B14 ....177 G3
Barford Rd SHLY B90 ....180 D3
WSNGN B18 ....107 G5
Barford St DIG/EDG B5 ....127 F3
Bargate Dr
DUNHL/THL/PER WV6 ....36 C1
Bargery Rd WNSFLD WV11 ....25 G1
Barham Cl SHLY B90 ....195 G3
Barker Rd FOAKS/STRLY B74 ....62 B1
Barker St LGLYGN/QTN B68 ....105 G4
LOZ/NWT B19 ....108 B2
Bark Piece RIDG/WDGT B32 ....140 C4
Barlands Cft BKDE/SHDE B34 ....112 D3
Barle Gv CBROM B36 ....113 H2
Barley Cl ALDR WS9 ....45 E3
CDSL WV8 ....22 A1
SEDG DY3 * 67 H4
Barley Cft
DUNHL/THL/PER WV6 ....34 B2
Barleyfield Ri KGSWFD DY6 ....99 E1
Barleyfield Rw WSL WS1 ....4 E6
Barlow Cl LGLYGN/QTN B68 ....123 E1
RBRY B45 ....173 G3
Barlow Dr WBROM B70 ....88 B5
Barlow Rd DARL/WED WS10 ....56 A3
Barlows Rd EDG B15 ....142 B2
Barmouth Cl SHHTH WV12 ....26 A4
Barnabas Rd ERDW/GRVHL B23 ....92 D2
Barnaby Sq WOLVN WV10 ....13 F3
Barnard Cl
CHWD/FDBR/MGN B37 ....132 D3
Barnard Pl BKHL/PFLD WV2 ....52 C2
Barnard Rd MGN/WHC B75 ....63 E1
WNSFLD WV11 ....25 F1
Barn Av SEDG DY3 ....67 E4
Barnbrook Rd DOR/KN B93 ....197 E1
Barn Cl BVILLE B30 ....160 B4
CDYHTH B64 ....138 A1
HAG/WOL DY9 ....136 A3
HALE B63 ....138 A5

Barn Cft RIDG/WDGT B32 158 A1
Barncroft Rd OLDBY B69 103 G1
Barncroft St WBROM B70 71 E3
Barnes Cl STETCH B33 131 G2
Barnes Hl SLYOAK B29 141 F5
Barnesville Cl SMHTH B10 129 E4
Barnet Rd ERDW/GRVHL B23 92 B1
Barnett Cl BILS/COS WV14 53 H4
  KGSWFD DY6 99 H5
Barnett Gn KGSWFD DY6 99 H5
Barnett La KGSWFD DY6 99 H4
Barnett Rd WLNHL WV13 39 E4
Barnetts La BRWNH WS8 9 F4
Barnett St STRBR DY8 117 H1
  TPTN/OCK DY4 85 G2
Barney Cl TPTN/OCK DY4 85 F3
Barn Farm Cl BILS/COS WV14 54 C1
Barnfield Dr HIA/OLT B92 165 H4
Barnfield Gv
  BFLD/HDSWWD B20 89 G1
Barnfield Rd RMSLY B62 122 B5
  TPTN/OCK DY4 69 E4
  WOLV WV1 38 A3
Barnford Cl SMHTH B10 * 128 A3
Barnford Crs LGLYGN/QTN B68 123 E1
Barnfordhill Cl
  LGLYGN/QTN B68 105 F5
Barn Gn BDMR/CCFT WV3 51 F1
Barnhurst La CDSL WV8 11 F4
Barn La HDSW B21 107 G2
  HIA/OLT B92 147 E3
  MOS/BIL B13 161 G3
Barn Meadow YDLY B25 129 H3
Barnmoor Ri SOLH B91 165 E3
Barn Owl Dr BLOX/PEL WS3 17 H3
Barnpark Covert
  ALE/KHTH/YWD B14 177 G3
Barn Piece RIDG/WDGT B32 140 B3
Barnsbury Av
  CSCFLD/WYGN B72 77 G5
Barns Cl ALDR WS9 19 F3
Barns Cft FOAKS/STRLY B74 45 H2
Barnsdale Crs NFLD/LBR B31 175 E1
Barns La RUSH/SHEL WS4 29 E2
Barnsley Rd HRBN B17 124 C3
Barnstaple Rd SMTHWK B66 106 D4
Barn St DIG/EDG B5 3 K6
Barnswood Cl HALE B63 137 G2
Barnt Green Rd RBRY B45 188 C5
Barnwood Rd CDSL WV8 22 A1
  RIDG/WDGT B32 141 F3
Barons Cl HRBN B17 141 H1
Barrack Cl MGN/WHC B75 63 G2
Barrack La HALE B63 137 F1
Barracks Cl BLOX/PEL WS3 28 A2
Barracks La BLOX/PEL WS3 27 H2
Barrack St VAUX/NECH B7 109 G5
  WBROM B70 71 E3
Barra Cft CVALE B35 94 D2
Barrar Cl STRBR DY8 118 A4
Barratts Cft BRLYHL DY5 83 E5
Barratts Rd HWK/WKHTH B38 177 E5
Barr Common Cl ALDR WS9 44 B2
Barr Common Rd ALDR WS9 44 B2
Barrhill Cl GTB/HAM B43 73 G1
Barrington Cl DSYBK/YTR WS5 57 G5
  WOLVN WV10 23 E1
Barrington Rd HIA/OLT B92 147 E5
  RBRY B45 187 G1
Barr Lakes La DSYBK/YTR WS5 58 C1
Barron Rd NFLD/LBR B31 175 H2
Barrow Hill Rd BRLYHL DY5 83 E5
Barrows La
  LGN/SDN/BHAMAIR B26 130 A4
Barrows Rd SPARK B11 145 E1
Barrow Wk DIG/EDG B5 127 E5
Barrs Crs CDYHTH B64 121 F4
Barrs Rd CDYHTH B64 121 E5
Barrs St LGLYGN/QTN B68 105 E5
Barr St LOZ/NWT B19 108 C4
  SEDG DY3 83 E3
Barry Rd DSYBK/YTR WS5 58 A1
Barsham Cl DIG/EDG B5 143 G1
Barsham Dr BRLYHL DY5 119 E4
Barston La SOLH B91 183 G3
Bartholomew Rw CBHAMNE B4 3 J4
Bartholomew St DIG/EDG B5 3 J5
Bartic Av KGSWFD DY6 100 B5
Bartleet Rd SMTHWKW B67 105 H4
Bartlett Cl TPTN/OCK DY4 69 H2
Bartley Cl HIA/OLT B92 147 F5
Bartley Dr NFLD/LBR B31 158 A2
Bartley Woods
  RIDG/WDGT B32 140 B5
Barton Cft HLGN/YWD B28 179 H1
Barton Dr DOR/KN B93 197 F4
Barton La KGSWFD DY6 99 G1
Barton Lodge Rd
  HLGN/YWD B28 179 G1
Barton Rd
  ETTPK/GDPK/PENN WV4 52 D4
Bartons Bank LOZ/NWT B19 109 E2
Barton St WBROM B70 87 F4
Bar Wk ALDR WS9 30 C1
Barwell Cl DOR/KN B93 196 C4
Barwell Rd BORD B9 127 H2
Barwick St CBHAMNW B3 3 F4
Basalt Cl WSLW WS2 41 E1
Basil Gv NFLD/LBR B31 175 E1
Basil Rd NFLD/LBR B31 175 E1
Baslow Cl BLOX/PEL WS3 16 D4
  STETCH B33 112 A5
Baslow Rd BLOX/PEL WS3 16 D4
Basons La LGLYGN/QTN B68 105 G4
Bassano Rd
  BLKHTH/ROWR B65 122 A3
Bassenthwaite Ct KGSWFD DY6 99 H3
Bassett Cl
  ETTPK/GDPK/PENN WV4 50 C2
  SHHTH WV12 40 B1
  WALM/CURD B76 63 E4
Bassett Cft SMHTH B10 127 H4
Bassett Rd DARL/WED WS10 71 G1
  HALE B63 137 E1
Bassetts Gv
  CHWD/FDBR/MGN B37 113 G4
Bassett St WSLW WS2 41 G3
Bassnage Rd HALE B63 138 A5
Batchcroft BILS/COS WV14 53 H3
  DARL/WED WS10 40 B5
Batchelor Cl STRBR DY8 118 B4
Bateman Dr SCFLD/BOLD B73 77 F2
Bateman Rd CSHL/WTROR B46 97 F5
Batemans La HLYWD B47 192 A3
Bates Cl WALM/CURD B76 78 C4
Bates Gv WNSFLD WV11 24 A5
Bate St ETTPK/GDPK/PENN WV4 53 E5
  WSLW WS2 4 D1
Bath Av WOLV WV1 6 E3
Batheaston Cl
  HWK/WKHTH B38 190 B1
Bath Meadow HALE B63 138 A2
Bath Pas DIG/EDG B5 3 G7
Bath Rd BRLYHL DY5 120 A2
  STRBR DY8 135 F1
  TPTN/OCK DY4 85 G1
  WOLV WV1 6 C4
  WSL WS1 4 E7
Bath Rw EDG B15 126 C3
  OLDBY B69 104 B1
Bath St BILS/COS WV14 54 A3
  CBHAMNE B4 3 G2
  DUDS DY2 102 C1
  SEDG DY3 67 G2
  WLNHL WV13 39 H4
  WOLV WV1 * 7 J5
  WSL WS1 4 E5
Bath Wk BHTH/HG B12 144 A2
Batmans Hill Rd BILS/COS WV14 69 E1
Batson Ri STRBR DY8 118 C4
Battenhall Rd HRBN B17 141 G2
Battery Wy SPARK B11 145 G3
Battlefield Hl WMBN WV5 65 F4
Battlefield La WMBN WV5 65 F5
Bavaro Gdns BRLYHL DY5 120 A2
Baverstock Rd
  ALE/KHTH/YWD B14 178 B3
Baxterley Gn SOLH B91 180 D1
  WALM/CURD B76 78 B2
Baxter Rd BRLYHL DY5 119 E2
Baxters Rd SHLY B90 180 B5
Bayer St BILS/COS WV14 68 C3
Bayford Av
  LGN/SDN/BHAMAIR B26 148 A3
  NFLD/LBR B31 189 E2
Bayley Crs DARL/WED WS10 40 A5
Bayleys La TPTN/OCK DY4 70 A4
Baylie St STRBR DY8 135 F3
Baylis Av WNSFLD WV11 25 F2
Bayliss Av
  ETTPK/GDPK/PENN WV4 68 A1
Bayliss Cl BILS/COS WV14 53 G1
  NFLD/LBR B31 158 D5
Baynton Rd SHHTH WV12 26 A3
Bayston Av BDMR/CCFT WV3 36 A5
Bayston Rd
  ALE/KHTH/YWD B14 178 A1
Bayswater Rd
  BFLD/HDSWWD B20 90 D5
  SEDG DY3 83 F4
Baytree Cl BLOX/PEL WS3 16 C5
Bay Tree Cl HWK/WKHTH B38 176 B5
Baytree Rd BLOX/PEL WS3 16 C5
Baywell Cl SHLY B90 195 G1
Beach Av BHTH/HG B12 144 D2
  ETTPK/GDPK/PENN WV4 68 A1
Beach Brook Cl SPARK B11 144 D2
Beachburn Wy
  BFLD/HDSWWD B20 90 A3
Beach Cl NFLD/LBR B31 176 A4
Beachcroft Rd KGSWFD DY6 81 G5
Beach Dr HALE B63 138 C2
Beach Rd BILS/COS WV14 53 H1
  SPARK B11 144 D2
Beach St HALE B63 138 C2
Beachwood Av KGSWFD DY6 81 G5
Beacon Cl GTB/HAM B43 73 H2
  RBRY B45 187 H2
  SMTHWK B66 106 C2
Beacon Dr WSL WS1 5 J7
Beacon Hl ALDR WS9 44 C4
  AST/WIT B6 109 G1
  RBRY B45 187 G3
Beacon La BRGRVE B60 187 F5
  SEDG DY3 67 G2
Beacon Ri ALDR WS9 44 B2
  HAG/WOL DY9 136 B3
  SEDG DY3 67 G2
Beacon Rd ALDR WS9 59 F1
  DSYBK/YTR WS5 58 B3
  GTB/HAM B43 59 G5
  KGSTG B44 60 C4
  SCFLD/BOLD B73 77 E2
  SHHTH WV12 26 A2
Beaconsfield Av
  ETTPK/GDPK/PENN WV4 52 B3
Beaconsfield Ct WSL WS1 5 K6
Beaconsfield Crs BHTH/HG B12 * 144 A2
Beaconsfield Dr
  ETTPK/GDPK/PENN WV4 52 B3
Beaconsfield Rd BHTH/HG B12 144 A3
  FOAKS/STRLY B74 62 B1
Beaconsfield St
  HHTH/SAND B71 87 H1
Beacon St BILS/COS WV14 67 H2
  WSL WS1 5 J5
Beacon Vw RBRY B45 187 H2
Beacon View Dr KGSTG B44 60 B4
Beacon View Rd
  HHTH/SAND B71 72 B2
Beacon Wy ALDR WS9 19 G4
  RUSH/SHEL WS4 42 D1
Beadborough Wk ALDR WS9 30 B1
Beakes Rd SMTHWKW B67 124 B1
Beaks Farm Gdns
  LDYWD/EDGR B16 125 F2
Beaks Hill Rd
  HWK/WKHTH B38 176 C4
Beak St CBHAMW B1 3 F6
Beale Cl CVALE B35 94 C4
Beales St AST/WIT B6 109 H1
Beale St STRBR DY8 135 F2
Bealeys Av WNSFLD WV11 24 C2
Bealeys La BLOX/PEL WS3 16 C5
Beamans Cl HIA/OLT B92 147 G3
Beaminster Rd SOLH B91 181 F1
Bean Cft RIDG/WDGT B32 140 C5
Bean Rd DUDS DY2 102 D1
  TPTN/OCK DY4 68 D5
Beardmore Rd
  CSCFLD/WYGN B72 77 G3
Bearley Cft SHLY B90 180 C5
Bearmore Rd CDYHTH B64 121 E3
Bearnett Dr
  ETTPK/GDPK/PENN WV4 65 G1
Bearnett La WMBN WV5 65 F2
Bearwood Rd SMTHWK B66 124 C2
Beasley Gv PBAR/PBCH B42 74 B2
Beaton Cl WLNHL WV13 39 E3
Beaton Rd FOAKS/STRLY B74 47 E2
Beatrice St BLOX/PEL WS3 27 G4
Beatrice Wk TPTN/OCK DY4 85 G4
Beaubrook Gdns STRBR DY8 117 H1
Beauchamp Av
  BFLD/HDSWWD B20 89 H1
Beauchamp Cl
  CHWD/FDBR/MGN B37 132 B2
  WALM/CURD B76 78 D4
Beauchamp Rd MOS/BIL B13 161 H5
  SOLH B91 164 C5
Beaudesert Cl HLYWD B47 192 C2
Beaudesert Rd
  BFLD/HDSWWD B20 108 B1
  HLYWD B47 192 C2
Beaufort Av CBROM B36 111 H3
Beaufort Rd LDYWD/EDGR B16 125 H3
Beaufort Wy ALDR WS9 44 B1
Beaulieu Av KGSWFD DY6 100 B5
Beaumaris Cl DUDN DY1 83 H3
Beaumont Cl TPTN/OCK DY4 69 E5
Beaumont Dr BRLYHL DY5 118 D5
  HRBN B17 141 H3
Beaumont Gdns WSNGN B18 107 H3
Beaumont Gv SOLH B91 164 B5
Beaumont Rd BVILLE B30 159 G4
  DARL/WED WS10 55 H4
  RMSLY B62 122 C4
Beausale Dr DOR/KN B93 197 F1
Beauty Bank CDYHTH B64 121 F4
Beauty Bank Crs STRBR DY8 135 E1
Beaver Cl WNSFLD WV11 25 F5
Bebington Cl COVEN WV9 22 B1
Beccles Dr WLNHL WV13 39 F5
Beckbury Av
  ETTPK/GDPK/PENN WV4 50 C3
Beckbury Rd SLYOAK B29 158 C1
Beck Cl SMTHWK B66 106 C5
Beckenham Av KGSTG B44 75 G2
Beckensall Cl DUDN DY1 84 B5
Becket Cl MGN/WHC B75 32 D4
Beckett St BILS/COS WV14 54 A2
Beckfield Cl
  ALE/KHTH/YWD B14 178 A3
  RUSH/SHEL WS4 29 E2
Beckford Cft DOR/KN B93 * 196 D5
Beckman Rd HAG/WOL DY9 136 A5
Beckminster Rd
  BDMR/CCFT WV3 51 F1
Beconsfield Cl DOR/KN B93 198 D1
Becton Gv PBAR/PBCH B42 74 D4
Bedcote Pl STRBR DY8 135 H2
Beddoe Cl TPTN/OCK DY4 86 B1
Beddow Av BILS/COS WV14 68 C4
Beddows Rd BLOX/PEL WS3 28 A5
Bedford Dr MGN/WHC B75 63 E2
Bedford Rd HHTH/SAND B71 71 F4
  MGN/WHC B75 63 E1
  SPARK B11 127 G4
Bedford St TPTN/OCK DY4 85 H1
  WOLV WV1 53 E1
Bedford Ter LOZ/NWT B19 * 108 D1
Bedlam Wood Rd
  NFLD/LBR B31 174 C4
Bedworth Cft TPTN/OCK DY4 85 H2
Bedworth Gv BORD B9 129 F2
Beebee Rd DARL/WED WS10 55 H3
Beecham Cl ALDR WS9 30 A2
Beech Av BHTH/HG B12 144 C2
  CHWD/FDBR/MGN B37 132 B3
  RIDG/WDGT B32 140 D1
  RMSLY B62 122 A4
Beech Cl MGN/WHC B75 47 E1
  SEDG DY3 67 G2
  WOLVN WV10 22 D2
Beech Ct SMTHWK B66 105 G2
  WSL WS1 5 H6
Beech Crs DARL/WED WS10 55 H3
  TPTN/OCK DY4 70 A3
Beechcroft Av HLGN/YWD B28 162 D4
Beechcroft Crs
  FOAKS/STRLY B74 44 D4
Beechcroft Est HALE B63 137 G1
Beechcroft Pl WOLVN WV10 23 E4
Beechcroft Rd CBROM B36 112 D1
  CDYHTH B64 121 E3
Beechdale Av KGSTG B44 75 E1
Beechdale Rd BLOX/PEL WS3 26 D2
Beech Dene Gv
  ERDW/GRVHL B23 92 C1
Beecher Pl HALE B63 137 H2
Beecher Rd HALE B63 137 H2
Beecher Rd East HALE B63 137 H2
Beecher St HALE B63 137 G2
Beeches Av ACGN B27 146 C3
Beeches Cl KGSWFD DY6 99 H4
  RBRY B45 187 F1
Beeches Dr ERDE/BCHGN B24 93 G2
Beeches Farm Dr
  NFLD/LBR B31 189 G1
Beeches Pl BLOX/PEL WS3 27 H3
Beeches Rd
  BLKHTH/ROWR B65 121 H3
  BLOX/PEL WS3 27 H4
  HHTH/SAND B71 88 A3
  LGLYGN/QTN B68 123 G1
  PBAR/PBCH B42 74 C4
The Beeches WBROM B70 88 A4
  WOLV WV1 6 A2
Beeches View Av HALE B63 137 G3
Beeches Wk SCFLD/BOLD B73 62 B5
Beeches Wy NFLD/LBR B31 189 G1
Beechey Cl GTB/HAM B43 59 H3
Beech Farm Cft NFLD/LBR B31 175 G2
Beechfield Cl RMSLY B62 122 A4
Beechfield Gv BILS/COS WV14 68 B4
Beechfield Rd SMTHWKW B67 106 B5
  SPARK B11 144 D1
Beech Gdns CDSL WV8 20 D1
Beech Ga FOAKS/STRLY B74 31 H5
Beechglade
  BFLD/HDSWWD B20 89 H2
Beech Gn DUDN DY1 84 A1
Beech Gv ALE/KHTH/YWD B14 161 G5
Beech Hill Rd
  CSCFLD/WYGN B72 77 G4
Beech Hurst HWK/WKHTH B38 176 C5
Beechlawn Dr KINVER DY7 116 C5
Beechmore Rd
  LGN/SDN/BHAMAIR B26 147 F2
Beechmount Dr
  ERDW/GRVHL B23 77 E5
Beechnut Cl SOLH B91 165 F5
Beechnut La SOLH B91 165 G5
Beech Rd BVILLE B30 159 G3
  DARL/WED WS10 55 H3
  DUDN DY1 84 C2
  ERDW/GRVHL B23 76 D4
  HLYWD B47 192 D2
  KGSWFD DY6 99 H4
  OLDBY B69 103 G1
  STRBR DY8 135 E4
  WLNHL WV13 39 E3
  WOLVN WV10 22 D2
Beech Tree Av WNSFLD WV11 24 C2
Beech Tree Cl KGSWFD DY6 100 A1
Beechtree Rd ALDR WS9 19 F4
Beech Wk HWK/WKHTH B38 176 D5
Beech Wy SMTHWK B66 106 D4
Beechwood Av WNSFLD WV11 24 B2
Beechwood Cl BLOX/PEL WS3 16 D4
  SHLY B90 194 D4
Beechwood Ct
  DUNHL/THL/PER WV6 * 35 G2
Beechwood Cft
  FOAKS/STRLY B74 32 B5
Beechwood Dr
  DUNHL/THL/PER WV6 35 E3
Beechwood Park Rd
  SOLH B91 164 A5
Beechwood Rd
  ALE/KHTH/YWD B14 161 F5
  DUDS DY2 85 E5
  GTB/HAM B43 73 H2
  SMTHWKW B67 124 A4
  WBROM B70 87 F3
Bee La WOLVN WV10 12 D4
Beeston Cl AST/WIT B6 109 G2
  BRLYHL DY5 119 E4
Beeton Rd WSNGN B18 107 G3
Beet St BLKHTH/ROWR B65 122 A3
Beever Rd TPTN/OCK DY4 70 B4
Beggars Bush La WMBN WV5 81 F1
Beighton Cl FOAKS/STRLY B74 32 D4
Beilby Rd BVILLE B30 160 B4
Belbroughton Rd
  HAG/WOL DY9 170 C4
  HALE B63 138 B5
  KIDD DY10 168 C4
  STRBR DY8 135 E4
Belchers La BORD B9 129 E2
Beldray Pk BILS/COS WV14 * 54 A2
Beldray Rd BILS/COS WV14 54 A2
Belfry Cl BLOX/PEL WS3 16 C4
Belfry Dr STRBR DY8 135 E1
The Belfry
  DUNHL/THL/PER WV6 34 B1
Belgrade Rd WOLVN WV10 12 B5
Belgrave Ct KGSWFD DY6 100 B5
Belgrave Int DIG/EDG B5 126 D5
Belgrave Middleway
  DIG/EDG B5 127 E5
Belgrave Rd BHTH/HG B12 144 B1
  RMSLY B62 122 B4
Belgrave Ter HDSW B21 108 A2
Belgrave Wk WSLW WS2 41 F2
Belgravia Cl DIG/EDG B5 127 E5
Belgrove Cl EDG B15 142 C1
Belinda Cl WLNHL WV13 39 F2
Bellamy Cl SHLY B90 180 D4
Bellamy Farm Rd SHLY B90 180 D4
Bellamy La WNSFLD WV11 24 D3
Bell Barn Rd EDG B15 126 D4
Bell Cl BORD B9 128 C1
  CBROM B36 114 B3
  DARL/WED WS10 55 F1
Bellcroft LDYWD/EDGR B16 2 A6
Bell Dr DSYBK/YTR WS5 57 G3
  WASH/WDE B8 128 D1
Bellefield Av WSNGN B18 107 G5
Bellefield Rd WSNGN B18 107 G5
Belle Isle BRLYHL DY5 119 E1
Bellemere Rd HIA/OLT B92 167 H5
Bellencroft Gdns
  BDMR/CCFT WV3 50 B1
Bell End BLKHTH/ROWR B65 122 A1
Belle V HALE B63 138 A2
Bellevue DIG/EDG B5 126 D5
Belle Vue STRBR DY8 117 G2
Bellevue Av
  LDYWD/EDGR B16 * 107 F5
Belle Vue Dr RMSLY B62 139 F1
Belle Vue Gdns
  BLKHTH/ROWR B65 * 122 A1
Belle Vue Rd BRLYHL DY5 120 A3
Bellevue Rd BILS/COS WV14 69 F1
  LGN/SDN/BHAMAIR B26 130 C5
Bellevue St BILS/COS WV14 67 H1
Belle Vue Ter HIA/OLT B92 167 G4
Belle Wk MOS/BIL B13 144 D5
Bellfarm Ms CDYHTH B64 * 121 F2
Bell Fold LGLYGN/QTN B68 105 G3
Bell Green La
  HWK/WKHTH B38 191 F3
Bell Heather Rd BRWNH WS8 18 D1
Bell Hl NFLD/LBR B31 158 C5
Bell Holloway NFLD/LBR B31 158 B5
Bellington Cft SHLY B90 195 G2
Bellis St LDYWD/EDGR B16 125 H3
Bell La BLOX/PEL WS3 27 F1
  DSYBK/YTR WS5 57 G4
  NFLD/LBR B31 175 G1
  STETCH B33 131 G3
Bellman Cl DARL/WED WS10 55 F1
Bell Meadow HAG/WOL DY9 152 D2
Bell Meadow Wy
  ALE/KHTH/YWD B14 177 H3
Bell Pl BKHL/PFLD WV2 37 E5
Bell Rd DSYBK/YTR WS5 58 B2
  DUDS DY2 102 C4
  WMBN WV5 64 A2
Bells Farm Cl
  ALE/KHTH/YWD B14 177 G3
Bells La HWK/WKHTH B38 177 G3
  STRBR DY8 117 H3
Bells Moor Rd WBROM B70 71 E5
Bell St BILS/COS WV14 53 G2
  BRLYHL DY5 101 F2
  BRLYHL DY5 119 F2
  DARL/WED WS10 55 F1
  TPTN/OCK DY4 85 E1
  WBROM B70 87 H4
  WOLV WV1 7 F5
Bell St South BRLYHL DY5 119 F2
Bell Vue Rd
  BLKHTH/ROWR B65 122 A2
Bellwood Rd NFLD/LBR B31 175 F1
Belmont Cl ALDR WS9 30 A3
  TPTN/OCK DY4 69 F5
Belmont Covert NFLD/LBR B31 158 D4
Belmont Gdns BILS/COS WV14 54 C4
Belmont Pas CBHAMNE B4 127 G2
Belmont Rd BRLYHL DY5 101 F3
  ETTPK/GDPK/PENN WV4 51 G3
  HAG/WOL DY9 136 C3
  HDSW B21 107 E1
  RBRY B45 187 H2
  SMTHWK B66 124 C2
Belmont Rd East HDSW B21 107 E1
Belmont Rw CBHAMNE B4 3 K3
Belmont St BILS/COS WV14 54 C4
Belper DUDN DY1 84 B5
Belper Rd BLOX/PEL WS3 17 E4
  WBROM B70 86 D3
Belper Rw DUDS DY2 103 E5
Belstone Cl
  ALE/KHTH/YWD B14 160 D5
Belton Av WNSFLD WV11 24 B1
Belton Gv RBRY B45 174 C5
Belvedere Av
  ETTPK/GDPK/PENN WV4 51 H3
Belvedere Cl KGSWFD DY6 100 B5
Belvedere Gdns
  DUNHL/THL/PER WV6 21 H3
Belvedere Rd ERDE/BCHGN B24 93 E4
Belvide Gdns CDSL WV8 10 B3
Belvide Gv SLYOAK B29 158 D2
Belvidere Gdns SPARK B11 144 D3
Belvidere Rd WSL WS1 5 F7
Belvoir Cl DUDN DY1 83 G4
Belwell Dr FOAKS/STRLY B74 47 E5
Belwell La FOAKS/STRLY B74 47 E3
Bembridge Cl SHHTH WV12 25 H2
Bembridge Rd STETCH B33 130 C2
Benacre Dr DIG/EDG B5 3 K5
Benbeck Gv TPTN/OCK DY4 84 C1
Bendall Rd KGSTG B44 75 H1
Benedon Rd
  LGN/SDN/BHAMAIR B26 130 C5
Benmore Av DIG/EDG B5 143 H1
Bennett Av DUDN DY1 68 B5
Bennett Rd FOAKS/STRLY B74 46 E2
Bennett's Fold BKHL/PFLD WV2 6 E5
Bennett's Hl CBHAMNW B3 3 F5
  DUDS DY2 103 E1
Bennetts Rd WASH/WDE B8 110 B3
Bennett St LOZ/NWT B19 108 D1
Ben Nevis Wy STRBR DY8 135 G1
Benson Av
  ETTPK/GDPK/PENN WV4 52 A3
Benson Cl DUNHL/THL/PER WV6 20 C5
Benson Rd
  ALE/KHTH/YWD B14 178 D4
  WSNGN B18 107 H3
Bent Av RIDG/WDGT B32 140 D1
Bentham Ct NFLD/LBR B31 158 B5
Bentley Bridge Pk
  WLNHL WV13 * 38 B1
Bentleybridge Wy
  WLNHL WV13 38 C1
Bentley Dr CDSL WV8 10 B3
  WSLW WS2 41 F3
Bentley Farm Cl DOR/KN B93 196 C4
Bentley Gv SLYOAK B29 158 B2
Bentley La SHHTH WV12 26 B5
  WSLW WS2 41 E1
Bentley Mill Cl WSLW WS2 40 D4
Bentley Mill La WSLW WS2 40 D4
Bentley Mill Wy WSLW WS2 40 D4
Bentley New Dr WSLW WS2 41 F2
Bentley Pl WSLW WS2 41 G3

Bentley Rd CBROM B36 .....113 F2
WOLVN WV10 .....13 E5
Bentley Rd North WSLW WS2 .....40 C4
Bentley Rd South
DARL/WED WS10 .....40 B5
Bentmead Gv
HWK/WKHTH B38 .....177 E4
Benton Av SPARK B11 .....145 E1
Benton Cl SHHTH WV12 .....40 B1
Benton Crs BLOX/PEL WS3 .....17 F5
Benton Rd SPARK B11 .....145 E1
Bentons Mill Cft
VAUX/NECH B7 .....110 A1
Bent St BRLYHL DY5 .....101 F5
Ben Willetts Wk
BLKHTH/ROWR B65 .....122 A3
Beoley Cl CSCFLD/WYGN B72 .....77 G2
Beoley Gv RBRY B45 .....188 A1
Berberry Cl BVILLE B30 .....159 F4
Beresford Crs WBROM B70 .....87 F3
Beresford Dr SCFLD/BOLD B73 .....77 E2
Beresford Rd BLOX/PEL WS3 .....28 A2
OLDBY B69 .....105 G2
The Berets MGN/WHC B75 .....63 F2
Bericote Cft ACGN B27 .....146 D4
Berkeley Cl
DUNHL/THL/PER WV6 .....34 D2
WSLW WS2 .....40 D2
Berkeley Dr KGSWFD DY6 .....99 G2
Berkeley Rd SHLY B90 .....179 H2
YDLY B25 .....129 E5
Berkeley Rd East YDLY B25 .....129 F5
Berkeley St WSLW WS2 .....56 B1
Berkley Crs MOS/BIL B13 .....162 A1
Berkley St CBHAMW B1 .....2 C6
Berkshire Cl HHTH/SAND B71 .....71 F4
Berkshire Crs DARL/WED WS10 .....56 C4
The Berkshire BLOX/PEL WS3 * 16 C4
Berkswell Cl DUDN DY1 .....83 G3
FOAKS/STRLY B74 .....46 C1
HIA/OLT B92 .....164 D2
Berkswell Rd ERDE/BCHGN B24 .....93 F2
Bermuda Cl DUDN DY1 .....68 B5
Bernard Pl WSNGN B18 * 107 H4
Bernard Rd HRBN B17 .....124 D2
LGLYGN/QTN B68 .....123 G2
TPTN/OCK DY4 .....69 G4
Bernard St HHTH/SAND B71 .....87 G2
WSL WS1 .....5 H6
Berners St LOZ/NWT B19 .....108 C2
Bernhard Dr HDSW B21 .....107 G1
Bernwall Cl STRBR DY8 .....135 F3
Berrandale Rd CBROM B36 .....112 B1
Berrington Dr BILS/COS WV14 .....68 B3
Berrington Wk DIG/EDG B5 .....127 E5
Berrow Dr EDG B15 .....125 G5
Berrowside Rd
BKDE/SHDE B34 .....113 G3
Berry Av DARL/WED WS10 .....54 D3
Berrybush Gdns SEDG DY3 .....67 G4
Berry Cl LOZ/NWT B19 .....108 D3
Berry Crs DSYBK/YTR WS5 .....58 A4
Berry Dr ALDR WS9 .....29 G5
SMTHWK B66 .....106 C3
Berryfield Rd
LGN/SDN/BHAMAIR B26 .....148 B2
Berryfields ALDR WS9 .....29 G5
Berryfields Rd
WALM/CURD B76 .....63 F5
Berry Hall La SOLH B91 .....183 E1
Berry Rd DUDN DY1 .....84 C1
WASH/WDE B8 .....110 C4
Berry St WOLV WV1 .....7 G4
WSNGN B18 .....107 H3
Bertha Rd SPARK B11 .....145 F2
Bertram Cl TPTN/OCK DY4 .....70 A2
Bertram Rd BORD B9 .....128 B3
SMTHWK B67 .....106 A3
Berwick Gv GTB/HAM B43 .....59 F4
NFLD/LBR B31 .....174 D2
Berwicks La
CHWD/FDBR/MGN B37 .....132 B3
Berwood Farm Rd
CSCFLD/WYGN B72 .....77 G5
Berwood Gdns
ERDE/BCHGN B24 .....77 G5
Berwood Gv HIA/OLT B92 .....164 D1
Berwood La ERDE/BCHGN B24 .....94 A3
Berwood Pk CVALE B35 .....94 C4
Berwood Rd WALM/CURD B76 .....77 H5
Besant Gv ACGN B27 .....146 A5
Besbury Cl DOR/KN B93 .....198 C1
Bescot Crs WSL WS1 .....56 D3
Bescot Cft PBAR/PBCH B42 .....74 B4
Bescot Dr WSLW WS2 .....56 B2
Bescot Rd WSLW WS2 .....56 C1
Bescot St WSL WS1 .....57 E1
Besford Gv NFLD/LBR B31 .....174 D2
SHLY B90 .....195 H2
Bessborough Rd YDLY B25 .....129 H4
Best Rd BILS/COS WV14 .....53 H1
Best St CDYHTH B64 .....121 F2
Beswick Gv STETCH B33 .....112 C5
Beta Gv ALE/KHTH/YWD B14 .....179 E1
Betjeman Pl WOLVN WV10 .....24 A1
Betley Gv STETCH B33 .....112 C5
Betony Cl DSYBK/YTR WS5 .....57 G5
Betsham Cl KGSTG B44 .....75 H2
Bettany Gld WOLVN WV10 .....13 E3
Betteridge Dr
WALM/CURD B76 .....63 E4
Bett Rd BFLD/HDSWWD B20 .....89 G3
Bevan Av
ETTPK/GDPK/PENN WV4 .....52 C4
Bevan Cl BILS/COS WV14 .....54 B2
RUSH/SHEL WS4 .....29 E1
Bevan Rd BRLYHL DY5 .....118 C2
TPTN/OCK DY4 .....85 H2
Bevan Wy SMTHWK B66 .....106 B1
Beverley Cl CSCFLD/WYGN B72 .....77 G4
Beverley Court Rd
RIDG/WDGT B32 .....140 B1
Beverley Crs
ETTPK/GDPK/PENN WV4 .....52 D4
Beverley Cft ERDW/GRVHL B23 .....92 B5
Beverley Dr KGSWFD DY6 .....99 G2
Beverley Gv
LGN/SDN/BHAMAIR B26 .....147 H2
Beverley Rd HHTH/SAND B71 .....71 H2
RBRY B45 .....188 A1
Beverston Rd
DUNHL/THL/PER WV6 .....35 E1
TPTN/OCK DY4 .....69 H1
Bevington Rd AST/WIT B6 .....109 F1
Bevin Rd WSLW WS2 .....40 C2
Bewdley Dr WOLV WV1 .....38 B3
Bewdley Rd BVILLE B30 .....160 B2
Bewdley Vls WSNGN B18 * 107 F5
Bewlay Cl BRLYHL DY5 .....118 D5
Bewley Rd SHHTH WV12 .....40 B1
Bewlys Av BFLD/HDSWWD B20 .....89 G2
Bexhill Gv EDG B15 .....126 C3
Bexley Gv HHTH/SAND B71 .....72 A4
Bexley Rd KGSTG B44 .....75 H3
Bhylls Crs BDMR/CCFT WV3 .....50 C1
Bhylls La BDMR/CCFT WV3 .....50 B1
Bibbey's Gn WOLVN WV10 .....13 F3
Bibsworth Av MOS/BIL B13 .....162 B2
Bibury Rd HLGN/YWD B28 .....162 C3
Bicester Sq CVALE B35 .....94 D2
Bickenhill La
CHWD/FDBR/MGN B37 .....132 C5
Bickenhill Park Rd
HIA/OLT B92 .....163 H1
Bickenhill Pkwy
CHWD/FDBR/MGN B37 .....149 H1
Bickenhill Rd
CHWD/FDBR/MGN B37 .....132 B5
Bickford Rd AST/WIT B6 .....91 G5
WOLVN WV10 .....23 H5
Bickington Rd RIDG/WDGT B32 .....157 H1
Bickley Av FOAKS/STRLY B74 .....32 C5
SPARK B11 * 145 E1
Bickley Gv
LGN/SDN/BHAMAIR B26 .....147 H2
Bickley Rd BILS/COS WV14 .....54 C2
RUSH/SHEL WS4 .....29 E3
Bicknell Cft
ALE/KHTH/YWD B14 .....178 A3
Bickton Cl ERDE/BCHGN B24 .....77 G5
Biddings La BILS/COS WV14 .....68 B1
Biddlestone Pl DARL/WED WS10 .....54 B2
Biddleston Gv DSYBK/YTR WS5 .....58 A5
Bideford Dr SLYOAK B29 .....159 E1
Bideford Rd SMTHWK B66 .....106 D4
Bidford Cl SHLY B90 .....180 D3
Bidford Rd NFLD/LBR B31 .....175 E2
Bierton Rd YDLY B25 .....129 G4
Biggin Cl CVALE B35 .....94 C3
DUNHL/THL/PER WV6 .....20 C5
The Big Peg WSNGN B18 * 2 C2
Bigwood Dr MGN/WHC B75 .....63 G2
RIDG/WDGT B32 .....157 G1
Bilberry Crs WALM/CURD B76 .....63 E5
Bilberry Dr RBRY B45 .....188 A2
Bilberry Rd
ALE/KHTH/YWD B14 .....160 C4
Bilboe Rd BILS/COS WV14 .....54 B5
Bilbrook Ct CDSL WV8 .....10 D4
Bilbrook Gv CDSL WV8 .....10 D4
SLYOAK B29 .....141 F5
Bilbrook Rd CDSL WV8 .....10 C3
Bilhay La WBROM B70 .....87 E1
Bilhay St WBROM B70 .....87 F1
Billau Rd BILS/COS WV14 .....68 D1
Billesley La MOS/BIL B13 .....161 G2
Billingham Cl SOLH B91 .....181 H5
Billingsley Rd
LGN/SDN/BHAMAIR B26 .....130 C4
Bills La SHLY B90 .....179 H5
Billsmore Gn HIA/OLT B92 .....165 E3
Bills St DARL/WED WS10 .....55 G2
Billy Buns La WMBN WV5 .....65 E3
Billy Wright Cl
ETTPK/GDPK/PENN WV4 .....50 D2
Bilport La DARL/WED WS10 .....70 D3
Bilston La WLNHL WV13 .....39 H5
Bilston Rd BKHL/PFLD WV2 .....37 H5
TPTN/OCK DY4 .....69 H1
WLNHL WV13 .....54 C1
WOLV WV1 .....7 H5
Bilston St DARL/WED WS10 .....55 F2
SEDG DY3 .....67 F3
WLNHL WV13 .....39 G4
Bilston Street Island WOLV WV1 .....7 H5
Bilton Grange Rd
LGN/SDN/BHAMAIR B26 .....130 B5
Binbrook Rd SHHTH WV12 .....40 B1
Bincomb Av
LGN/SDN/BHAMAIR B26 .....147 H1
Binfield St TPTN/OCK DY4 .....85 G2
Bingley Av WASH/WDE B8 .....111 F5
Bingley St BDMR/CCFT WV3 .....36 C5
Binley Cl
LGN/SDN/BHAMAIR B26 .....146 D1
SHLY B90 .....180 A5
Binstead Rd KGSTG B44 .....75 G1
Binswood Rd RMSLY B62 .....123 E5
Binton Cft MOS/BIL B13 .....161 F2
Binton Rd SHLY B90 .....179 H4
Birbeck Pl BRLYHL DY5 .....100 D3
Birchall St BHTH/HG B12 .....127 F3
Birch Av BRLYHL DY5 .....120 A2
BRWNH WS8 .....9 E4
NFLD/LBR B31 .....174 C4
Birch Cl BVILLE B30 .....159 F4
WALM/CURD B76 .....78 B1
Birch Coppice BRLYHL DY5 .....120 A3
WMBN WV5 .....64 C5
Birchcoppice Gdns
SHHTH WV12 .....40 C1
Birch Crs OLDBY B69 .....85 H5
Birch Cft ALDR WS9 .....30 C2
CHWD/FDBR/MGN B37 .....132 C3
ERDE/BCHGN B24 .....93 H1
Birchcroft SMTHWK B66 * 107 E4
Birch Croft Rd MGN/WHC B75 .....62 D1
Birchdale BILS/COS WV14 .....53 H1
Birchdale Av ERDW/GRVHL B23 .....92 C3
Birchdale Rd ERDW/GRVHL B23 .....92 B1
Birch Dr FOAKS/STRLY B74 .....32 B5
MGN/WHC B75 .....65 F1
RMSLY B62 .....122 C3
Birches Av CDSL WV8 .....21 G1
Birches Barn Av
BDMR/CCFT WV3 .....51 F1
Birches Barn Rd
BDMR/CCFT WV3 .....36 B5
Birches Cl MOS/BIL B13 .....161 F1
Birches Green Rd
ERDE/BCHGN B24 .....93 F4
Birches Park Rd CDSL WV8 .....10 C5
Birches Ri WLNHL WV13 .....39 F4
Birches Rd CDSL WV8 .....10 D5
Birchfield Av
DUNHL/THL/PER WV6 .....21 F4
Birchfield Cl HALE B63 .....138 A5
Birchfield Crs HAG/WOL DY9 .....136 D4
Birchfield Gdns AST/WIT B6 * 108 D1
Birchfield La OLDBY B69 .....104 C5
Birchfield Rd HAG/WOL DY9 .....136 D4
PBAR/PBCH B42 .....90 D3
Birchfields Rd SHHTH WV12 .....25 G5
Birchfield Wy DSYBK/YTR WS5 .....57 H4
Birchgate HAG/WOL DY9 .....136 D3
Birchglade BDMR/CCFT WV3 .....35 H4
Birch Gv LGLYGN/QTN B68 .....123 H5
Birch Hill Av WMBN WV5 .....80 D1
Birch Hollow EDG B15 .....142 D1
Birchill Pl WMBN WV5 .....80 D1
Birchills St WSLW WS2 .....4 A2
Birch La ALDR WS9 .....30 D1
LGLYGN/QTN B68 .....123 H5
RUSH/SHEL WS4 .....29 E1
Birchley Park Av OLDBY B69 .....104 C3
Birchley Ri HIA/OLT B92 .....147 F2
Birchmoor Cl HLGN/YWD B28 .....163 F3
Birchover Rd WSLW WS2 .....41 E1
Birch Rd AST/WIT B6 .....91 G4
LGLYGN/QTN B68 .....123 H5
RBRY B45 .....187 G2
SEDG DY3 .....67 H2
WNSFLD WV11 .....25 F1
Birch Rd East AST/WIT B6 .....91 G3
Birch St LGLYGN/QTN B68 .....105 G3
TPTN/OCK DY4 .....85 F1
WOLV WV1 .....6 E4
WSLW WS2 .....4 B1
Birch Ter DUDS DY2 .....102 C5
Birch Tree Gdns ALDR WS9 .....30 B5
Birchtree Gdns BRLYHL DY5 .....120 A3
Birch Tree Gv SOLH B91 .....181 E1
Birchtree Hollow SHHTH WV12 .....26 B5
Birchtrees ERDE/BCHGN B24 .....93 H2
Birchtrees Cft
LGN/SDN/BHAMAIR B26 .....146 D2
Birchtrees Dr STETCH B33 .....131 F1
Birch Wk LGLYGN/QTN B68 .....123 H5
Birchwood Cl WNSFLD WV11 .....15 E4
Birchwood Crs BHTH/HG B12 .....144 C3
Birchwood Rd BHTH/HG B12 .....144 C3
ETTPK/GDPK/PENN WV4 .....51 G3
Birchwoods RIDG/WDGT B32 .....140 B5
Birchy Cl SHLY B90 .....193 H2
Birchy Leasowes La SHLY B90 .....193 G3
Birdbrook Rd KGSTG B44 .....75 E3
Bird End HHTH/SAND B71 .....72 B3
Birdie Cl HWK/WKHTH B38 .....176 B4
Birdlip Gv RIDG/WDGT B32 .....140 C1
Birds Meadow BRLYHL DY5 .....100 D2
Bird St SEDG DY3 .....83 E3
Birdwell Cft MOS/BIL B13 .....161 F4
Birkdale Av SLYOAK B29 .....159 H1
Birkdale Cl STRBR DY8 .....152 B1
WOLV WV1 .....38 A3
Birkdale Dr OLDBY B69 .....103 G2
Birkdale Gv SLYOAK B29 .....160 A2
Birkdale Rd BLOX/PEL WS3 .....16 C4
Birkenshaw Rd KGSTG B44 .....75 E3
Birley Gv HALE B63 .....154 C2
Birmingham New Rd
BILS/COS WV14 .....68 B2
DUDN DY1 .....68 C5
ETTPK/GDPK/PENN WV4 .....52 C4
Birmingham Rd ALDR WS9 .....30 A5
BKHL/PFLD WV2 .....37 F5
BLKHTH/ROWR B65 .....122 A2
BRGRVW B61 .....187 E4
CBROM B36 .....112 C1
CHWD/FDBR/MGN B37 .....114 B4
CSCFLD/WYGN B72 .....77 F3
CSHL/WTROR B46 .....95 H4
DSYBK/YTR WS5 .....58 A1
DUDN DY1 .....85 E4
GTB/HAM B43 .....73 G2
HAG/WOL DY9 .....153 F4
HALE B63 .....138 D4
KIDD DY10 .....168 C3
LICHS WS14 .....33 E1
OLDBY B69 .....105 F2
RCOVN/BALC/EX CV7 .....151 F4
WBROM B70 .....88 A5
WSL WS1 .....5 G6
Birmingham St
DARL/WED WS10 .....55 F2
DUDS DY2 .....84 D5
HALE B63 .....138 D4
OLDBY B69 .....105 E1
STRBR DY8 .....135 H2
WLNHL WV13 .....39 H3
WSL WS1 .....5 F5
Birnham Cl TPTN/OCK DY4 .....84 D1
Bisell Wy BRLYHL DY5 .....136 B1
Bishbury Cl EDG B15 .....125 G4
Bishop Asbury Crs
GTB/HAM B43 .....72 D3
Bishop Cl RBRY B45 .....173 G4
Bishop Rd DARL/WED WS10 .....71 G1
Bishops Cl DUDS DY2 .....103 E1
SMTHWK B66 .....107 E5
Bishop's Ct
CHWD/FDBR/MGN B37 .....133 E4
Bishops Ga NFLD/LBR B31 .....175 G3
Bishopsgate St EDG B15 .....2 B7
Bishops Meadow
MGN/WHC B75 .....48 A2
Bishops Rd SCFLD/BOLD B73 .....62 B5
Bishop St DIG/EDG B5 .....127 E4
Bishops Wk HALE B63 .....138 C1
Bishops Wy FOAKS/STRLY B74 .....32 D5
Bishopton Cl SHLY B90 .....180 C4
Bishopton Rd SMTHWKW B67 .....124 B3
Bishton Gv DUDS DY2 .....102 D5
Bissel Dr DARL/WED WS10 .....56 B5
Bissell Cl HLGN/YWD B28 .....162 D4
Bissell St DIG/EDG B5 .....127 E4
RIDG/WDGT B32 .....140 A1
Bissel St BILS/COS WV14 .....54 B3
Biton Cl HRBN B17 .....141 H2
Bittell Cl WOLVN WV10 .....13 E3
Bitterne Dr
DUNHL/THL/PER WV6 .....36 C1
Blackacre Rd DUDS DY2 .....102 D1
Blackberry Av BORD B9 .....129 E1
Blackberry Cl DUDN DY1 .....101 G1
Blackberry La ALDR WS9 .....19 H3
BLKHTH/ROWR B65 .....103 F4
FOAKS/STRLY B74 .....32 C5
HALE B63 .....138 C5
Blackbird Cft CBROM B36 .....114 A2
Blackbrook Cl DUDS DY2 .....120 A1
Blackbrook Rd DUDS DY2 .....102 A4
Blackbrook Wy WOLVN WV10 .....13 E3
Blackburn Av
DUNHL/THL/PER WV6 .....22 A3
Blackburne Rd HLGN/YWD B28 .....162 D4
Blackbushe Cl HRBN B17 .....124 B5
Blackcat Cl
CHWD/FDBR/MGN B37 .....132 A1
Black Country New Rd
BILS/COS WV14 .....54 C2
Black Country Route
BILS/COS WV14 .....54 B2
Blackdown Cl RBRY B45 .....174 A3
Blackdown Rd DOR/KN B93 .....197 F2
Blackfirs La
CHWD/FDBR/MGN B37 .....132 D5
Blackford Cl HALE B63 .....137 H5
Blackford Rd SHLY B90 .....194 C1
SPARK B11 .....145 E3
Blackford St WSNGN B18 .....107 G4
Blackhalve La WNSFLD WV11 .....24 B2
Blackham Dr SCFLD/BOLD B73 .....77 E4
Blackham Rd WNSFLD WV11 .....25 F2
Black Haynes Rd SLYOAK B29 .....158 C3
Blackhorse La BRLYHL DY5 .....119 G3
Black Lake HHTH/SAND B71 .....71 E5
Blackmoor Cft STETCH B33 .....131 F2
Blackrock Rd ERDW/GRVHL B23 .....75 H5
Blackroot Rd FOAKS/STRLY B74 .....62 A1
Blacksmiths La HOCK/TIA B94 .....198 A5
Blacksmith Wy WBROM B70 .....87 G4
Blackthorn Cl BVILLE B30 .....159 E5
Blackthorne Cl SOLH B91 .....181 E1
Blackthorne Rd
DSYBK/YTR WS5 .....57 F3
DUDN DY1 .....83 H2
SMTHWKW B67 .....105 H5
Blackthorn Rd BVILLE B30 .....159 E4
CBROM B36 .....113 E1
STRBR DY8 .....118 B3
Blackwater Cl BRLYHL DY5 .....100 C4
Blackwell Rd
CSCFLD/WYGN B72 .....77 H2
Blackwood Av WNSFLD WV11 .....24 B2
Blackwood Dr
FOAKS/STRLY B74 .....45 E5
Blackwood Rd
FOAKS/STRLY B74 .....45 E4
Blades Rd WBROM B70 .....86 B2
Blaenwern Dr HALE B63 .....120 B5
Blagdon Rd HALE B63 .....138 C1
Blair Gv CHWD/FDBR/MGN B37 .....132 D3
Blakedon Rd DARL/WED WS10 .....55 G5
Blakedown Rd HALE B63 .....138 B5
Blake Hall Cl BRLYHL DY5 .....118 D5
Blakeland Rd KGSTG B44 .....75 E5
Blakeland St BORD B9 .....128 D2
Blake La BORD B9 .....128 D2
Blakeley Av
DUNHL/THL/PER WV6 .....22 B3
Blakeley Hall Gdns OLDBY B69 .....105 F2
Blakeley Hall Rd OLDBY B69 .....105 F2
Blakeley Heath Dr WMBN WV5 .....81 E1
Blakeley Ri
DUNHL/THL/PER WV6 .....22 B3
Blakeley Wood Rd
TPTN/OCK DY4 .....70 A3
Blakemere Av YDLY B25 .....130 A4
Blakemore Cl RIDG/WDGT B32 .....141 F4
Blakemore Dr MGN/WHC B75 .....63 F2
Blakemore Rd ALDR WS9 .....19 H4
WBROM B70 .....87 E4
Blakenall Cl BLOX/PEL WS3 .....27 H1
Blakenall Heath BLOX/PEL WS3 .....27 H2
Blakenall La BLOX/PEL WS3 .....27 H2
Blakenall Rw BLOX/PEL WS3 .....27 H2
Blakeney Av HRBN B17 .....124 C5
STRBR DY8 .....134 D1
Blakeney Cl SEDG DY3 .....67 E3
Blakenhale Rd STETCH B33 .....130 D3
Blakenhall Gdns
BKHL/PFLD WV2 .....52 B1
Blake Pl BORD B9 .....128 D2
Blakesley Cl WALM/CURD B76 .....94 B1
Blakesley Ms YDLY B25 .....129 H4
Blakesley Rd YDLY B25 .....129 H3
Blake St FOAKS/STRLY B74 .....32 D4
Blakewood Cl BKDE/SHDE B34 .....113 E4
Blandford Av CBROM B36 .....95 G5
Blandford Dr STRBR DY8 .....118 A2
Blandford Rd RIDG/WDGT B32 .....141 E2
Blanefield CDSL WV8 .....22 A1
Blay Av WSLW WS2 .....41 F3
Blaydon Av MGN/WHC B75 .....48 A3
Blaydon Rd COVEN WV9 .....22 C1
Blaythorn Av HIA/OLT B92 .....147 G4
Blaze Hill Rd KGSWFD DY6 .....99 E1
Blaze Pk KGSWFD DY6 .....99 F1
Bleak Hill Rd ERDW/GRVHL B23 .....92 A1
Bleakhouse Rd
LGLYGN/QTN B68 .....123 G3
Bleak St SMTHWKW B67 .....106 B3
Blenheim Cl RUSH/SHEL WS4 .....29 F3
Blenheim Dr GTB/HAM B43 .....73 F3
Blenheim Rd KGSWFD DY6 .....100 C3
MOS/BIL B13 .....161 F1
SHHTH WV12 .....25 H4
SHLY B90 .....180 D3
Blenheim Wy CVALE B35 .....94 C4
DUDN DY1 .....83 G4
KGSTG B44 .....75 F3
Bletchley Rd ERDE/BCHGN B24 .....94 A2
Blewitt Cl CBROM B36 .....95 F4
Blewitt St BRLYHL DY5 .....101 E3
Blews St AST/WIT B6 .....109 E4
Blithe Cl STRBR DY8 .....118 C4
Blithfield Dr BRLYHL DY5 .....118 D5
Blithfield Gv ERDE/BCHGN B24 .....93 G1
Blithfield Rd BRWNH WS8 .....8 C2
Blockall DARL/WED WS10 .....55 F1
Bloomfield Cl WMBN WV5 .....64 B5
Bloomfield Dr SHHTH WV12 .....26 B1
Bloomfield Pk TPTN/OCK DY4 .....68 D5
Bloomfield Rd MOS/BIL B13 .....144 C4
TPTN/OCK DY4 .....69 E4
Bloomfield St North HALE B63 .....138 B2
Bloomfield St West HALE B63 .....138 B3
Bloomfield Ter TPTN/OCK DY4 .....68 D5
Bloomsbury Gv
ALE/KHTH/YWD B14 .....160 C3
Bloomsbury St BKHL/PFLD WV2 .....6 E6
VAUX/NECH B7 .....109 H4
Bloomsbury Wk
VAUX/NECH B7 * 109 H4
Blossom Av SLYOAK B29 * 142 D5
Blossomfield Cl
HWK/WKHTH B38 .....176 B5
KGSWFD DY6 .....100 A1
Blossomfield Rd SOLH B91 .....181 F3
Blossom Gv CBROM B36 .....111 H1
Blossom Hl ERDE/BCHGN B24 .....93 E2
Blossom Rd ERDE/BCHGN B24 .....93 G2
Blossom's Fold WOLV WV1 .....7 F4
Blossomville Wy ACGN B27 .....146 B3
Blowers Green Crs DUDS DY2 .....102 B2
Blower's Green Rd DUDS DY2 .....102 B2
Bloxcidge St LGLYGN/QTN B68 .....105 F4
Bloxwich La WSLW WS2 .....27 E4
Bloxwich Rd BLOX/PEL WS3 .....27 H3
Bloxwich Rd North
SHHTH WV12 .....26 B4
Bloxwich Rd South
WLNHL WV13 .....39 G2
Blucher St CBHAMW B1 .....2 E7
Blue Ball La HALE B63 .....137 G1
Bluebell Cl STRBR DY8 .....117 G2
Bluebell Crs WNSFLD WV11 .....24 D5
Bluebell Dr
CHWD/FDBR/MGN B37 .....132 D2
Bluebell Rd ALDR WS9 .....19 H4
CDYHTH B64 .....121 E1
DUDN DY1 .....84 B3
Bluebellwood Cl
WALM/CURD B76 .....63 G5
Blue Cedars STRBR DY8 .....134 C1
Blue Cft NFLD/LBR B31 .....175 E1
Blue Lake Rd DOR/KN B93 .....199 F1
Blue La East WSLW WS2 .....4 C1
Blue La West WSLW WS2 .....4 B2
Blue Rock Pl OLDBY B69 .....104 A3
Blundell Rd SPARK B11 .....145 F2
Blythefield Av GTB/HAM B43 .....73 E2
Blythe Gdns CDSL WV8 .....10 B3
Blythe Ga HOCK/TIA B94 .....195 G5
Blythe Gv KGSTG B44 .....60 B5
Blythe Rd CSHL/WTROR B46 .....115 H1
Blytheway SOLH B91 .....182 C2
Blythewood Cl DOR/KN B93 .....182 D4
Blythsford Rd HLGN/YWD B28 .....179 H1
Blythswood Rd SPARK B11 .....146 A3
Blyton Cl LDYWD/EDGR B16 .....107 H5
Board School Gdns SEDG DY3 .....67 G5
Boar Hound Cl WSNGN B18 * 108 A5
Boatman's La ALDR WS9 .....19 E5
Bobbington Wy DUDS DY2 .....102 D4
Bobs Coppice Wk BRLYHL DY5 .....119 H5
Bodenham Rd
LGLYGN/QTN B68 .....123 F4
NFLD/LBR B31 .....175 E3
Boden Rd HLGN/YWD B28 .....163 E3
Bodens La ALDR WS9 .....59 E1
Bodicote Gv MGN/WHC B75 .....48 A2
Bodington Rd MGN/WHC B75 .....47 F2
Bodmin Cl DSYBK/YTR WS5 .....58 B1
Bodmin Gv VAUX/NECH B7 .....109 H4
Bodmin Ri DSYBK/YTR WS5 .....58 B1
Bodmin Rd DUDS DY2 .....120 D2
Bognop Rd WNSFLD WV11 .....14 B3
Boldmere Cl SCFLD/BOLD B73 .....77 E4
Boldmere Dr SCFLD/BOLD B73 .....77 E3
Boldmere Gdns
SCFLD/BOLD B73 .....77 E3
Boldmere Ga SCFLD/BOLD B73 * 61 H5
Boldmere Rd SCFLD/BOLD B73 .....76 D2
Boldmere Ter SLYOAK B29 * 159 G1
Boleyn Rd RBRY B45 .....173 G4
Bolney Rd RIDG/WDGT B32 .....141 E2
Bolton Rd SMHTH B10 .....127 H3
WNSFLD WV11 .....24 C5

Bolton St BORD B9 127 H2
Bolton Wy BLOX/PEL WS3 16 B4
Bomers Fld RBRY B45 188 C1
Bond Dr CVALE B35 94 C4
Bondfield Rd MOS/BIL B13 161 H4
Bond Sq WSNGN B18 108 A5
Bond St BILS/COS WV14 68 A3
BKHL/PFLD WV2 7 F6
BLKHTH/ROWR B65 122 C1
BVILLE B30 160 A3
LOZ/NWT B19 2 E2
WBROM B70 87 G4
Bone Mill La WOLV WV1 37 E1
Bonfire Hl HAG/WOL DY9 186 A2
Bonham Gv YDLY B25 129 H3
Boningale Wy DOR/KN B93 196 B5
Bonner Dr WALM/CURD B76 94 B1
Bonner Gv ALDR WS9 29 H5
Bonnington Wy GTB/HAM B43 59 H4
Bonsall Rd ERDW/GRVHL B23 77 E5
Bonville Gdns WOLVN WV10 13 E3
Booth Cl BLOX/PEL WS3 27 H2
KGSWFD DY6 100 C3
Booth Rd DARL/WED WS10 71 G1
Booths Farm Rd
PBAR/PBCH B42 74 A4
Booth's La PBAR/PBCH B42 74 B2
Booth St BLOX/PEL WS3 27 G2
DARL/WED WS10 40 B5
HDSW B21 107 E2
Bordeaux Cl DUDN DY1 83 G3
Borden Cl CDSL WV8 22 B2
Bordesley Circ SMHTH B10 127 H3
Bordesley Cl BORD B9 129 E2
Bordesley Gn BORD B9 128 C2
Bordesley Gn East STETCH B33 130 A2
Bordesley Green Rd BORD B9 128 B2
Bordesley Park Rd SMHTH B10 127 H3
Bordesley St DIG/EDG B5 3 J5
Borneo St RUSH/SHEL WS4 42 B1
Borough Crs OLDBY B69 104 C4
STRBR DY8 135 E2
Borrowdale Cl BRLYHL DY5 118 D4
Borrowdale Gv NFLD/LBR B31 174 D2
Borrowdale Rd NFLD/LBR B31 174 C2
Borrow St WLNHL WV13 39 G2
Borwick Av WBROM B70 87 E3
Boscobel Av TPTN/OCK DY4 85 F2
Boscobel Cl DUDN DY1 83 H3
Boscobel Crs WOLV WV1 37 E1
Boscobel Rd GTB/HAM B43 73 F1
SHLY B90 194 D3
WSL WS1 5 K6
Boscombe Av SPARK B11 * 145 E1
Boscombe Rd SPARK B11 145 G3
Boston Gv KGSTG B44 75 H3
Bosty La ALDR WS9 29 F5
Boswell Cl DARL/WED WS10 55 F3
DARL/WED WS10 70 A2
Boswell Rd BILS/COS WV14 54 B1
FOAKS/STRLY B74 62 C2
KGSTG B44 75 F5
Bosworth Cl SEDG DY3 67 H5
Bosworth Dr
CHWD/FDBR/MGN B37 131 H2
Bosworth Rd
LGN/SDN/BHAMAIR B26 147 E3
Botany Dr SEDG DY3 83 F1
Botany Rd DSYBK/YTR WS5 57 F3
Botany Wk
LDYWD/EDGR B16 * 126 A2
Botha Rd BORD B9 128 C1
Botteley Rd WBROM B70 71 E5
Bottetourt Rd HRBN B17 141 G4
Botteville Rd ACGN B27 146 C5
Bott La HAG/WOL DY9 136 B1
WSL WS1 5 G4
Boughton Rd YDLY B25 129 G5
The Boulevard BRLYHL DY5 119 G2
SCFLD/BOLD B73 77 F3
Boultbee Rd CSCFLD/WYGN B72 77 G4
Boulton Middleway
WSNGN B18 108 B4
Boulton Retreat HDSW B21 * 107 G1
Boulton Rd HDSW B21 107 G2
SOLH B91 165 E3
WBROM B70 87 H5
Boulton Sq WBROM B70 87 H5
Boulton Wk ERDW/GRVHL B23 91 H2
Boundary Av
BLKHTH/ROWR B65 122 C2
Boundary Crs SEDG DY3 83 E3
Boundary Dr MOS/BIL B13 143 H5
Boundary Hl SEDG DY3 83 E2
Boundary La KINVER DY7 116 C3
Boundary Pl HDSW B21 88 D5
Boundary Rd ALDR WS9 19 F4
FOAKS/STRLY B74 60 B1
WLNHL WV13 38 C4
Boundary Wy
DUNHL/THL/PER WV6 34 D3
ETTPK/GDPK/PENN WV4 50 C2
Bourlay Cl RBRY B45 173 G3
Bournbrook Rd SLYOAK B29 142 D4
Bourne Av RMSLY B62 139 H3
TPTN/OCK DY4 70 A4
Bournebrook Cl DUDS DY2 102 C4
Bournebrook Crs RMSLY B62 140 A3
Bourne Cl MOS/BIL B13 162 A4
SOLH B91 165 G4
Bourne Gn RIDG/WDGT B32 141 E1
Bourne Hill Cl DUDS DY2 103 E5
Bourne Rd AST/WIT B6 109 H2
Bournes Cl HALE B63 138 B4
Bournes Crs HALE B63 138 A3
Bournes Hl HALE B63 138 A3
Bourne St BILS/COS WV14 68 A4
DUDS DY2 84 D5
Bourne V ALDR WS9 44 D2
Bourne Way Gdns SLYOAK B29 160 A2
Bourn Mill Dr AST/WIT B6 109 E3
Bournville La BVILLE B30 159 F3
Bourton Cl DSYBK/YTR WS5 57 G5
Bourton Cft HIA/OLT B92 164 B2
Bourton Rd HIA/OLT B92 164 B2
Bovey Cft WALM/CURD B76 78 C4
Bovingdon Rd CVALE B35 94 C3
Bowater Av STETCH B33 129 H3
Bowater St WBROM B70 87 G3
Bowbrook Av SHLY B90 195 G3
Bowcroft Gv ERDE/BCHGN B24 77 G5
Bowden Rd SMTHWKW B67 106 A3
Bowdler Rd BKHL/PFLD WV2 37 F5
Bowen Av
ETTPK/GDPK/PENN WV4 53 E5
Bowen-Cooke Av CDSL WV8 20 C4
Bowen St
ETTPK/GDPK/PENN WV4 52 C3
Bowercourt Cl SOLH B91 181 H4
Bower La BRLYHL DY5 119 H4
Bowes Rd RBRY B45 187 G1
Bowker St WLNHL WV13 38 C3
Bowlas Av MGN/WHC B75 47 F5
Bowling Green Cl
DARL/WED WS10 55 F1
ERDW/GRVHL B23 76 C4
Bowling Green La
BFLD/HDSWWD B20 108 A1
Bowling Green Rd BORD B9 * 128 A3
DUDS DY2 120 D1
STRBR DY8 135 E2
Bowman Rd PBAR/PBCH B42 74 B2
Bowman's Ri WOLV WV1 38 A2
Bowood Crs NFLD/LBR B31 175 G3
Bowood Dr
DUNHL/THL/PER WV6 21 H5
Bowood End WALM/CURD B76 62 D5
Bowshot Cl CBROM B36 95 F5
Bowstoke Rd GTB/HAM B43 73 E3
Bow St BILS/COS WV14 54 A2
CBHAMW B1 126 D3
WLNHL WV13 39 G4
Bowyer Rd WASH/WDE B8 110 B5
Bowyer St BORD B9 127 G3
Boxhill Cl AST/WIT B6 109 F3
Box Rd CHWD/FDBR/MGN B37 132 C4
Box St WSL WS1 5 G5
Box Trees Rd HOCK/TIA B94 198 A2
Boyd Gv ACGN B27 146 B5
Boydon Cl BKHL/PFLD WV2 53 E2
Boyleston Rd HLGN/YWD B28 163 E4
Boyne Rd
LGN/SDN/BHAMAIR B26 130 D5
Boyton Gv KGSTG B44 60 B5
Brabazon Gv CVALE B35 94 B3
Brabham Crs FOAKS/STRLY B74 60 B2
Bracadale Av ERDE/BCHGN B24 93 E2
Bracebridge Rd
ERDE/BCHGN B24 92 D5
FOAKS/STRLY B74 47 E5
Bracebridge St AST/WIT B6 109 E3
Braceby Av MOS/BIL B13 162 A3
Brace St WSL WS1 4 D7
Brackenbury Rd KGSTG B44 75 H3
Bracken Cl CDSL WV8 22 A1
Bracken Cft
CHWD/FDBR/MGN B37 132 C1
Brackendale Dr
DSYBK/YTR WS5 57 H5
Brackendale Wy
HAG/WOL DY9 136 B3
Bracken Dr MGN/WHC B75 63 G3
Brackenfield Rd HALE B63 138 A4
KGSTG B44 74 C1
Brackenfield Vw BRLYHL DY5 101 F1
Bracken Park Gdns
STRBR DY8 118 B2
Bracken Rd ERDE/BCHGN B24 93 G4
Bracken Wy FOAKS/STRLY B74 45 F5
HWK/WKHTH B38 190 B1
Bracken Wd DSYBK/YTR WS5 58 B3
Brackenwood Dr
WNSFLD WV11 25 F5
Brackley Av
BFLD/HDSWWD B20 90 C5
Brackleys Wy HIA/OLT B92 147 F5
Bradburne Wy VAUX/NECH B7 109 G4
Bradburn Rd WNSFLD WV11 24 B2
Bradbury Cl BRWNH WS8 19 F2
Bradbury Rd HIA/OLT B92 164 B2
Braden Rd
ETTPK/GDPK/PENN WV4 50 D4
Brades Cl HALE B63 120 B5
Brades Ri OLDBY B69 104 B1
Brades Rd OLDBY B69 104 C1
Bradewell Rd CBROM B36 95 F5
Bradfield Rd PBAR/PBCH B42 74 D4
Bradford Cl GTB/HAM B43 73 H4
Bradford La HAG/WOL DY9 184 B3
WSL WS1 4 D5
Bradford Rd BRWNH WS8 9 E4
CBROM B36 112 C2
DUDS DY2 101 H3
Bradford St DIG/EDG B5 3 H7
WSL WS1 4 D5
Bradgate Cl SHHTH WV12 26 A4
Bradgate Dr FOAKS/STRLY B74 32 C5
Bradley La BILS/COS WV14 54 B5
Bradleymore Rd BRLYHL DY5 119 E1
Bradley Rd BKDE/SHDE B34 113 F3
BKHL/PFLD WV2 52 C1
STRBR DY8 135 F1
Bradleys Cl CDYHTH B64 121 E5
Bradley's La BILS/COS WV14 69 E3
Bradley St BILS/COS WV14 54 B4
BRLYHL DY5 100 D2
TPTN/OCK DY4 85 F4
Bradmore Cl SOLH B91 181 G5
Bradmore Gv SLYOAK B29 158 C2
Bradmore Rd BDMR/CCFT WV3 36 B5
Bradnock Cl MOS/BIL B13 162 A3
Bradshaw Av DARL/WED WS10 54 D3
HWK/WKHTH B38 176 B4
Bradshaw Cl TPTN/OCK DY4 85 G3
Bradshawe Cl
ALE/KHTH/YWD B14 179 F2
Bradshaw St WOLV WV1 * 7 H4
Bradstock Rd BVILLE B30 177 G1
Bradwell Cft MGN/WHC B75 48 A2
Braemar Av STRBR DY8 117 G3
Braemar Cl SEDG DY3 67 E2
SHHTH WV12 25 G4
Braemar Dr ERDW/GRVHL B23 91 H1
Braemar Rd HIA/OLT B92 164 A1
SCFLD/BOLD B73 76 D1
Braeside Cft
CHWD/FDBR/MGN B37 132 D2
Braeside Wy BLOX/PEL WS3 17 H4
Bragg Rd BFLD/HDSWWD B20 90 D4
Braggs Farm La SHLY B90 194 A4
Braid Cl HWK/WKHTH B38 176 B4
Brailes Cl HIA/OLT B92 165 G3
Brailes Dr WALM/CURD B76 63 F5
Brailes Gv BORD B9 129 F3
Brailsford Cl WNSFLD WV11 25 E2
Brailsford Dr SMTHWK B66 106 C4
Braithwaite Cl KGSWFD DY6 99 H3
Braithwaite Rd SPARK B11 127 G5
Brake La STRBR DY8 152 A4
Bramah Wy TPTN/OCK DY4 70 A5
Bramber Dr WMBN WV5 64 D5
Bramber Wy STRBR DY8 135 F5
Bramble Cl AST/WIT B6 109 E2
BRWNH WS8 19 E2
CDYHTH B64 103 F5
CSHL/WTROR B46 115 G2
NFLD/LBR B31 158 B5
SHHTH WV12 26 A3
Bramble Dell BORD B9 129 E1
Bramble Dr
LGN/SDN/BHAMAIR B26 147 G1
Bramble Gn DUDN DY1 83 H1
Brambleside STRBR DY8 118 B3
The Brambles HAG/WOL DY9 136 B4
WALM/CURD B76 78 C3
Bramblewood WMBN WV5 65 E4
Bramblewood Dr
BDMR/CCFT WV3 36 A5
Bramblewoods
BKDE/SHDE B34 113 E4
Brambling Wk EDG B15 126 C5
Bramcote Dr HIA/OLT B92 165 E3
Bramcote Ri FOAKS/STRLY B74 62 C1
Bramcote Rd RIDG/WDGT B32 140 C2
Bramerton Cl WNSFLD WV11 24 A4
Bramford Dr DUDN DY1 68 B5
Bramley Cl DSYBK/YTR WS5 43 F5
GTB/HAM B43 59 H5
Bramley Cft SHLY B90 180 C3
Bramley Dr
BFLD/HDSWWD B20 90 B3
HLYWD B47 192 D2
Bramley Mews Ct ACGN B27 146 C3
Bramley Rd ACGN B27 146 C2
DSYBK/YTR WS5 57 H4
Brampton Av HLGN/YWD B28 163 E4
Brampton Crs HIA/OLT B92 163 F4
Bramshall Dr DOR/KN B93 196 C5
Bramshaw Cl
ALE/KHTH/YWD B14 178 B3
Bramstead Av
DUNHL/THL/PER WV6 35 F3
Branchal Rd ALDR WS9 30 C1
Branch Rd HWK/WKHTH B38 176 B5
Brandhall La LGLYGN/QTN B68 123 F3
Brandhall Rd LGLYGN/QTN B68 123 F3
Brandon Cl FOAKS/STRLY B74 45 F2
SEDG DY3 67 G4
WBROM B70 87 E4
Brandon Gv NFLD/LBR B31 189 F1
Brandon Pk BDMR/CCFT WV3 51 E1
Brandon Pl BKDE/SHDE B34 113 F2
Brandon Rd HLGN/YWD B28 145 G5
RMSLY B62 122 C3
SOLH B91 165 E3
Brandon Wy BRLYHL DY5 119 G4
WBROM B70 87 E4
Brandwood Gv
ALE/KHTH/YWD B14 160 D5
Brandwood Park Rd
ALE/KHTH/YWD B14 177 G1
Brandwood Rd
ALE/KHTH/YWD B14 160 D5
Branfield Cl BILS/COS WV14 68 A2
Branksome Av HDSW B21 107 H1
Branscombe Cl
ALE/KHTH/YWD B14 160 D5
Bransdale Cl
DUNHL/THL/PER WV6 22 C5
Bransdale Rd BRWNH WS8 9 E5
Bransford Ri SOLH B91 166 B5
Brantford Rd YDLY B25 129 G4
Branthill Cft SOLH B91 181 H4
Brantley Av BDMR/CCFT WV3 35 G4
Brantley Rd AST/WIT B6 91 G4
Branton Hill La ALDR WS9 30 C5
Brasshouse La SMTHWK B66 106 B3
Brassie Cl HWK/WKHTH B38 176 B4
Brassington Av
SCFLD/BOLD B73 62 B3
Bratch Cl DUDS DY2 120 C1
Bratch Common Rd
WMBN WV5 64 C4
Bratch Hollow WMBN WV5 65 E3
Bratch La WMBN WV5 65 E3
Bratch Pk WMBN WV5 64 C3
Bratt St WBROM B70 87 G2
Braunston Cl WALM/CURD B76 78 C1
Brayford Av BRLYHL DY5 118 D5
Braymoor Rd STETCH B33 131 G3
Brays Rd
LGN/SDN/BHAMAIR B26 147 G1
Bray St WLNHL WV13 39 H3
Bream Cl
CHWD/FDBR/MGN B37 132 C2
WOLV WV1 38 B1
Breamore Crs DUDN DY1 83 H3
Brean Av
LGN/SDN/BHAMAIR B26 147 F2
Brearley Cl LOZ/NWT B19 108 D4
Brearley St HDSW B21 107 F1
LOZ/NWT B19 108 D4
Brecknock Rd HHTH/SAND B71 71 E5
Brecon Dr STRBR DY8 135 H1
Brecon Rd BFLD/HDSWWD B20 108 B1
Bredon Av HAG/WOL DY9 136 A2
Bredon Ct HALE B63 138 C4
Bredon Cft WSNGN B18 108 A4
Bredon Rd OLDBY B69 104 B4
STRBR DY8 135 G1
Breech Cl FOAKS/STRLY B74 60 A1
Breedon Rd BVILLE B30 160 A5
Breedon Ter WSNGN B18 * 108 A4
Breedon Wy RUSH/SHEL WS4 29 E1
Breen Rydding Dr
BILS/COS WV14 68 B2
Brelades Cl DUDN DY1 83 G3
Brendan Cl CSHL/WTROR B46 115 G4
Brennand Rd LGLYGN/QTN B68 123 F3
Brentford Rd
ALE/KHTH/YWD B14 161 F5
SOLH B91 181 E2
Brentmill Cl WOLVN WV10 13 F3
Brentnall Dr MGN/WHC B75 47 F2
Brenton Rd
ETTPK/GDPK/PENN WV4 51 F4
Brent Rd BVILLE B30 160 C2
Brentwood Cl SOLH B91 181 E2
Brentwood Gv KGSTG B44 75 E3
Brenwood Cl KGSWFD DY6 99 F2
Brereton Cl DUDS DY2 85 E5
Brereton Rd SHHTH WV12 26 A3
Bretby Gv ERDW/GRVHL B23 77 E5
Bretshall Cl SHLY B90 195 F3
Brett Dr RIDG/WDGT B32 157 G2
Brettell La STRBR DY8 118 B4
Brettell St DUDS DY2 102 B2
Bretton Rd ACGN B27 146 D5
Brett St HHTH/SAND B71 87 F1
Brevitt Rd BKHL/PFLD WV2 52 B2
Brewers Dr BLOX/PEL WS3 28 C1
Brewer St WSLW WS2 42 A1
Brewery St AST/WIT B6 109 E4
DUDS DY2 85 E5
HDSW B21 107 F1
SMTHWKW B67 106 B3
TPTN/OCK DY4 85 F2
Brewins Wy BRLYHL DY5 101 H5
Breydon Gv WLNHL WV13 39 F5
Brian Rd SMTHWKW B67 106 A3
Briar Av FOAKS/STRLY B74 45 G4
Briarbeck RUSH/SHEL WS4 29 E2
Briar Cl ERDE/BCHGN B24 93 E2
Briarfield Rd SPARK B11 146 A4
Briars Cl BRLYHL DY5 101 E5
The Briars ERDW/GRVHL B23 76 B5
Briar Wood Cl BKHL/PFLD WV2 53 E1
Briarwood Cl SHLY B90 194 D4
Brickbridge La WMBN WV5 80 C1
Brickfield Rd YDLY B25 146 B1
Brickheath Rd WOLV WV1 38 A2
Brickhill Dr
CHWD/FDBR/MGN B37 132 A2
Brickhouse La WBROM B70 70 D5
Brickhouse La South
TPTN/OCK DY4 70 B5
Brickhouse Rd
BLKHTH/ROWR B65 103 G5
Bricklin St BRWNH WS8 9 F5
Brick Kiln La HLYWD B47 192 B4
KGSTG B44 75 E4
SEDG DY3 82 C3
SOLH B91 181 F5
Brick Kiln St BRLYHL DY5 101 G4
BRLYHL DY5 120 A4
TPTN/OCK DY4 69 E5
Brickkiln St WLNHL WV13 39 F4
Brick St SEDG DY3 67 F3
Brickyard Rd ALDR WS9 29 H1
The Bridal Pth HLGN/YWD B28 163 F5
Briddsland Rd STETCH B33 131 G2
Bridge Av TPTN/OCK DY4 70 A4
Bridgeburn Rd NFLD/LBR B31 158 A2
Bridge Cl SPARK B11 144 D4
Bridge Cft BHTH/HG B12 144 A1
Bridgeford Rd
BKDE/SHDE B34 112 D3
Bridgelands Wy
BFLD/HDSWWD B20 90 D5
Bridgeman Cft CBROM B36 113 E2
Bridgeman St WSLW WS2 4 C4
Bridgemary Cl WOLVN WV10 13 F3
Bridge Meadow Dr
DOR/KN B93 196 D3
Bridgend Cft BRLYHL DY5 100 D3
Bridge Piece NFLD/LBR B31 175 H3
Bridge Rd RUSH/SHEL WS4 28 D1
TPTN/OCK DY4 70 A4
WASH/WDE B8 128 C1
Bridge St BILS/COS WV14 54 A3
BILS/COS WV14 68 C3
BRWNH WS8 19 E1
CBHAMW B1 2 D7
DARL/WED WS10 70 D1
HALE B63 120 C5
OLDBY B69 105 E1
STRBR DY8 118 A3
WBROM B70 87 F2
WLNHL WV13 39 F4
WOLVN WV10 23 G5
WSL WS1 4 E3
Bridge St North SMTHWK B66 106 D3
Bridge St South SMTHWK B66 106 D3
Bridge St West LOZ/NWT B19 108 D3
The Bridge WSL WS1 4 D4
Bridge Vw CSHL/WTROR B46 * 115 F2
Bridge Wk ACGN B27 * 146 D4
Bridgewater Av OLDBY B69 105 E5
Bridgewater Crs DUDS DY2 85 E5
Bridgewater Dr
BILS/COS WV14 68 C1
Bridge Wy BRWNH WS8 19 E1
Bridgnorth Av WMBN WV5 80 D2
Bridgnorth Gv SHHTH WV12 25 H4
Bridgnorth Rd
DUNHL/THL/PER WV6 35 G3
KINVER DY7 134 C1
SEDG DY3 80 A1
SEDG DY3 81 E3
STRBR DY8 135 E1
Bridgwater Cl ALDR WS9 19 F3
Bridle Gv HHTH/SAND B71 72 B3
Bridle La FOAKS/STRLY B74 59 H2
Bridle Md HWK/WKHTH B38 176 B5
Bridle Rd STRBR DY8 134 D1
Bridlewood FOAKS/STRLY B74 45 F5
Brierley Hill Rd STRBR DY8 118 A2
Brierley La BILS/COS WV14 69 E1
Brier Road Rd HALE B63 139 E4
Briery Cl CDYHTH B64 121 F5
Briery Rd HALE B63 138 A4
Brigfield Crs MOS/BIL B13 161 H5
Brigfield Rd MOS/BIL B13 161 H5
Brighton Cl WSLW WS2 4 B1
Brighton Pl BDMR/CCFT WV3 6 B4
Brighton Rd BHTH/HG B12 144 B2
Bright Rd LGLYGN/QTN B68 105 F4
Brightstone Cl WOLVN WV10 13 F3
Brightstone Rd RBRY B45 174 A3
Bright St DARL/WED WS10 55 F3
STRBR DY8 134 D2
WOLV WV1 6 D1
Brightwell Crs DOR/KN B93 196 C5
Brimfield Pl
DUNHL/THL/PER WV6 * 36 B1
Brindle Cl
LGN/SDN/BHAMAIR B26 147 E2
Brindlefields Wy TPTN/OCK DY4 85 G4
Brindle Rd DSYBK/YTR WS5 58 A4
Brindley Av WNSFLD WV11 25 G1
Brindley Cl STRBR DY8 118 A3
WMBN WV5 64 B5
WSLW WS2 26 D5
Brindley Ct LGLYGN/QTN B68 * 123 F5
TPTN/OCK DY4 85 E1
Brindley Dr CBHAMW B1 2 C5
Brindley Pl CBHAMW B1 2 B6
Brindley Rd HHTH/SAND B71 71 E3
Brindley Wy SMTHWK B66 * 107 E4
Brineton Gv SLYOAK B29 158 C1
Brineton St WSLW WS2 4 A6
Bringewood Gv
RIDG/WDGT B32 157 F2
Brinklow Cft BKDE/SHDE B34 113 F2
Brinklow Rd SLYOAK B29 141 F5
Brinley Wy KGSWFD DY6 99 G3
Brinsford Rd WOLVN WV10 12 C4
Brinsley Cl SOLH B91 181 H3
Brinsley Rd
LGN/SDN/BHAMAIR B26 130 D4
Brisbane Rd SMTHWKW B67 106 A3
Briseley Cl BRLYHL DY5 119 E4
Bristam Cl OLDBY B69 104 C3
Bristnall Hall La
LGLYGN/QTN B68 123 G1
Bristnall Hall Rd
LGLYGN/QTN B68 123 G2
Bristol Rd DIG/EDG B5 143 F4
DUDS DY2 120 D2
ERDW/GRVHL B23 92 C3
SLYOAK B29 159 F2
Bristol Rd South
NFLD/LBR B31 158 C5
RBRY B45 188 A1
Bristol St BDMR/CCFT WV3 6 C7
BILS/COS WV14 53 H3
DIG/EDG B5 126 D4
Briston Cl BRLYHL DY5 119 E4
Britannia Gdns
BLKHTH/ROWR B65 122 A1
Britannia Pk DARL/WED WS10 * 55 F5
Britannia Rd BILS/COS WV14 54 B5
BLKHTH/ROWR B65 122 A1
Britannia St OLDBY B69 86 A4
Britannic Gdns MOS/BIL B13 143 H5
Britford Cl ALE/KHTH/YWD B14 178 B2
Brittan Cl BKDE/SHDE B34 113 G3
Brittania Wy WSL WS1 56 D3
Britton Dr CSCFLD/WYGN B72 77 G3
Britwell Rd SCFLD/BOLD B73 77 E1
Brixfield Wy SHLY B90 194 A3
Brixham Rd LDYWD/EDGR B16 107 F5
Broad Acres NFLD/LBR B31 158 A4
Broad Cft TPTN/OCK DY4 70 A5
Broadfern Rd DOR/KN B93 183 F5
Broadfield Cl HHTH/SAND B71 72 B3
KGSWFD DY6 99 H4
Broadfields HAG/WOL DY9 152 C4
Broadfields Rd
ERDW/GRVHL B23 77 F4
Broadfield Wk LDYWD/EDGR B16 2 A7
Broadheath Dr RUSH/SHEL WS4 29 F2
Broadhidley Dr
RIDG/WDGT B32 157 F1
Broadlands WOLVN WV10 12 D2
Broadlands Dr BRLYHL DY5 101 G4
Broad La ALE/KHTH/YWD B14 177 H2
BDMR/CCFT WV3 36 A5
BLOX/PEL WS3 27 F2
RUSH/SHEL WS4 29 E1
WNSFLD WV11 15 H2
Broad Lane Gdns
BLOX/PEL WS3 16 C5
Broad La North SHHTH WV12 25 H4
Broad Lanes BILS/COS WV14 53 G4
Broad La South SHHTH WV12 25 G4
Broad Meadow ALDR WS9 30 B2
Broadmeadow Cl BVILLE B30 177 F2
Broadmeadow Gn
BILS/COS WV14 53 G1

Broad Meadow La BVILLE B30 ..177 F2
Broadmeadows Rd
SHHTH WV12 ......26 C2
Broadmoor Av
LGLYGN/QTN B68 ......123 H2
Broadmoor Cl BILS/COS WV14....53 G4
Broadmoor Rd BILS/COS WV14....53 G4
Broad Oaks WALM/CURD B76 ....78 C3
Broad Oaks Rd SOLH B91 ......164 B5
Broad Rd ACGN B27 ......146 B4
Broadstone Av BLOX/PEL WS3 ....27 H3
HALE B63 ......137 F3
Broadstone Cl
ETTPK/GDPK/PENN WV4 ......52 B3
Broadstone Rd
LGN/SDN/BHAMAIR B26 ......130 B2
Broad St BILS/COS WV14 ......53 G2
BILS/COS WV14 ......68 C3
BRLYHL DY5 ......101 E3
EDG B15 ......2 B7
KGSWFD DY6 ......99 H4
OLDBY B69 ......105 E4
WOLV WV1 ......7 G3
Broad Street Jct WOLV WV1 ......7 H3
Broadwaters Av
DARL/WED WS10 ......55 E4
Broadwaters Rd
DARL/WED WS10 ......55 E4
Broad Wy RUSH/SHEL WS4 ......18 C5
Broadway BDMR/CCFT WV3 ......35 G4
CDSL WV8 ......10 A4
LGLYGN/QTN B68 ......123 G3
SHLY B90 ......180 B1
WOLVN WV10 ......13 E5
WSL WS1 ......57 G2
Broadway Av BORD B9 ......129 E2
HALE B63 ......138 C5
Broadway Cft
LGLYGN/QTN B68 ......123 G3
LGN/SDN/BHAMAIR B26 ......147 G1
Broadway North WSL WS1 ......5 J2
Broadway Plaza
LDYWD/EDGR B16 ......126 A3
The Broadway
BFLD/HDSWWD B20 ......90 D4
DUDN DY1 ......84 A3
DUDN DY1 ......84 C4
HHTH/SAND B71 ......71 E4
STRBR DY8 ......134 D5
WMBN WV5 ......81 E1
Broadway West WSL WS1 ......56 D2
Broadwell Rd HIA/OLT B92 ......147 G5
OLDBY B69 ......105 E1
Broadyates Gv YDLY B25 ......146 C1
Broadyates Rd YDLY B25 ......146 C1
Brobury Cft SHLY B90 ......180 D1
Brockeridge Cl SHHTH WV12 ......26 A1
Brockhall Gv
CHWD/FDBR/MGN B37 ......113 H4
Brockhill La ALVE B48 ......191 F5
Brockhurst Crs DSYBK/YTR WS5 ..57 F4
Brockhurst Dr
DUNHL/THL/PER WV6 ......36 C1
HLGN/YWD B28 ......163 E5
Brockhurst La SHLY B90 ......194 B3
Brockhurst Pl DSYBK/YTR WS5 ....57 F3
Brockhurst Rd CBROM B36 ......111 G3
MGN/WHC B75 ......47 H4
Brockhurst St DSYBK/YTR WS5 ....57 E2
Brockley Cl BRLYHL DY5 ......119 F1
Brockley Gv MOS/BIL B13 ......160 C1
Brockley Pl VAUX/NECH B7 ......110 A2
Brockmoor Cl HAG/WOL DY9 ......136 A5
Brock Rd TPTN/OCK DY4 ......85 H2
Brockwell Gv KGSTG B44 ......60 A4
Brockwell Rd KGSTG B44 ......60 A4
Brockworth Rd
ALE/KHTH/YWD B14 ......177 G3
Brocton Cl BILS/COS WV14 ......53 E5
Brogden Cl HHTH/SAND B71 ......72 B3
Bromfield Cl AST/WIT B6 ......109 E2
Bromfield Ct
DUNHL/THL/PER WV6 * 35 F2
Bromfield Crs DARL/WED WS10 ..56 C5
Bromford Cl ERDW/GRVHL B23 ......92 C1
Bromford Crs ERDE/BCHGN B24 ..93 E4
Bromford Dl
DUNHL/THL/PER WV6 * 36 B2
Bromford Dell NFLD/LBR B31 ......176 A1
Bromford Dr CBROM B36 ......111 G1
Bromford Hl
BFLD/HDSWWD B20 ......90 C3
Bromford La ERDE/BCHGN B24 ..93 E5
OLDBY B69 ......105 E1
WASH/WDE B8 ......111 F2
WBROM B70 ......87 F5
Bromford Ri BDMR/CCFT WV3 ......36 D5
Bromford Rd CBROM B36 ......111 F2
DUDS DY2 ......102 A3
WBROM B70 ......87 E5
Bromley BRLYHL DY5 ......100 D4
Bromley Gdns CDSL WV8 ......10 C3
Bromley La KGSWFD DY6 ......100 A5
Bromley Pl
ETTPK/GDPK/PENN WV4 ......51 G3
Bromley St BKHL/PFLD WV2 ......52 A1
BORD B9 ......127 G3
HAG/WOL DY9 ......136 D1
Brompton Dr BRLYHL DY5 ......118 D5
Brompton Lawns
DUNHL/THL/PER WV6 ......35 E2
Brompton Pool Rd
HLGN/YWD B28 ......179 G2
Brompton Rd KGSTG B44 ......60 A4
Bromsgrove Rd HAG/WOL DY9 ..170 C2
RMSLY B62 ......155 H1
RMSLY B62 ......172 C2
Bromsgrove St DIG/EDG B5 ......126 D3
Bromwall Rd MOS/BIL B13 ......161 H4
Bromwich Dr MGN/WHC B75 ......62 C1
Bromwich La HAG/WOL DY9 ......152 D3
Bromwynd Cl BKHL/PFLD WV2 ..51 H2
Bromyard Av WALM/CURD B76 ..78 C3
Bromyard Rd SPARK B11 ......145 G4
Bronte Cl SHLY B90 ......180 D4
Bronte Farm Rd SHLY B90 ......180 D4
Bronte Rd BKHL/PFLD WV2 ......52 D2
Bronwen Rd BILS/COS WV14 ......68 C4
Bronwen Vis DARL/WED WS10 * ..55 F2
Brookbank Av
BKDE/SHDE B34 ......113 F3
Brookbank Gdns SEDG DY3 ......82 D4
Brookbank Rd SEDG DY3 ......82 D4
Brook Cl ALDR WS9 ......19 G4
LGN/SDN/BHAMAIR B26 ......147 H2
SHLY B90 ......179 H4
STETCH B33 ......112 A5
Brook Crs HAG/WOL DY9 ......136 D4
HAG/WOL DY9 ......152 D5
KGSWFD DY6 ......99 G2
Brook Cft
CHWD/FDBR/MGN B37 ......132 B5
LGN/SDN/BHAMAIR B26 ......130 D5
Brookdale SEDG DY3 ......83 E3
Brookdale Cl RBRY B45 ......173 H4
Brookdale Dr
ETTPK/GDPK/PENN WV4 ......50 D2
Brook Dr RIDG/WDGT B32 ......157 H1
Brookend Dr RBRY B45 ......187 H1
Brookes Cl OLDBY B69 ......103 H1
Brooke St DUDS DY2 ......102 C1
Brookfield Cl ALDR WS9 ......30 A1
Brookfield Rd ALDR WS9 ......30 A1
CDSL WV8 ......10 D4
WSNGN B18 ......107 H4
Brookfields Rd
LGLYGN/QTN B68 ......105 G5
Brookfield Wy HIA/OLT B92 ......163 H3
TPTN/OCK DY4 ......69 G5
Brook Gv CDSL WV8 ......10 D4
Brookhill Cl SHHTH WV12 ......26 A1
Brook Hill Rd WASH/WDE B8 ......111 E5
Brook Holloway HAG/WOL DY9 ..136 C4
Brook House Cl WOLVN WV10 ......13 H1
Brookhouse La WOLVN WV10 ......13 F1
Brook House La WOLVN WV10 ......13 G1
Brookhouse Rd
DSYBK/YTR WS5 ......57 H1
Brookhus Farm Rd
WALM/CURD B76 ......78 C3
Brooking Cl GTB/HAM B43 ......59 H4
Brookland Gv ALDR WS9 ......19 F5
Brookland Rd ALDR WS9 ......19 F4
HAG/WOL DY9 ......152 C5
Brooklands STRBR DY8 ......118 B3
Brooklands Cl HLGN/YWD B28 ..162 D1
Brooklands Dr
ALE/KHTH/YWD B14 ......161 E5
Brooklands Gv ALDR WS9 ......19 F5
Brooklands Pde WOLV WV1 ......38 B3
Brooklands Rd HLGN/YWD B28 ..162 D1
The Brooklands SEDG DY3 ......80 C5
Brooklands Wy
CHWD/FDBR/MGN B37 ......132 B4
Brook La ALDR WS9 ......19 G4
ALE/KHTH/YWD B14 ......161 F2
CDYHTH B64 ......121 E2
HIA/OLT B92 ......163 H2
RIDG/WDGT B32 ......141 F2
Brooklea Gv HWK/WKHTH B38 ..177 E4
Brooklyn Av AST/WIT B6 ......109 F2
Brooklyn Gv BILS/COS WV14 ......68 D3
KGSWFD DY6 ......99 F1
Brookmans Av
RIDG/WDGT B32 ......140 D3
Brookmeadow Ct
HLGN/YWD B28 ......162 B4
Brook Meadow Rd
BKDE/SHDE B34 ......112 C3
RUSH/SHEL WS4 ......29 F2
Brook Mdw CDSL WV8 ......10 D2
Brook Rd EDG B15 ......125 G5
LGLYGN/QTN B68 ......123 E2
RBRY B45 ......187 G1
STRBR DY8 ......135 H4
WLNHL WV13 ......39 E4
WMBN WV5 ......64 D5
Brooksbank Dr CDYHTH B64 ......103 F5
Brooksby Gv DOR/KN B93 ......199 E1
Brooks Cft CVALE B35 ......94 C4
Brookside DARL/WED WS10 ......56 B5
GTB/HAM B43 ......73 F5
NFLD/LBR B31 ......158 B5
SEDG DY3 ......83 F4
Brookside Av MOS/BIL B13 ......161 H3
Brookside Cl ERDW/GRVHL B23 ..76 A4
HALE B63 ......137 H4
WMBN WV5 ......64 B5
Brookside Wy KGSWFD DY6 ......99 F2
KIDD DY10 ......168 B3
Brooks Rd CSCFLD/WYGN B72 ......77 G2
Brook St BILS/COS WV14 ......54 A3
BRLYHL DY5 ......120 A4
CBHAMNW B3 ......2 D3
HAG/WOL DY9 ......136 D2
KGSWFD DY6 ......81 F5
SEDG DY3 ......68 A4
SEDG DY3 ......83 E3
SMTHWK B66 ......106 D3
STRBR DY8 ......118 B3
STRBR DY8 ......135 E2
TPTN/OCK DY4 ......69 E5
WBROM B70 ......87 F2
WSLW WS2 ......4 B4
Brook Ter BILS/COS WV14 ......54 A3
Brookthorpe Dr SHHTH WV12 ......40 A1
Brookvale Gv HIA/OLT B92 ......163 H1
Brookvale Ms SLYOAK B29 ......143 F5
Brookvale Park Rd
ERDW/GRVHL B23 ......91 H1
Brookvale Rd AST/WIT B6 ......91 G3
HIA/OLT B92 ......163 H1
Brookview SMTHWKW B67 * 124 B1
Brook View Cl LOZ/NWT B19 ......108 C3
Brook Wk RIDG/WDGT B32 ......140 D5
Brookwillow Rd HALE B63 ......137 H5
Brookwood Av
HLGN/YWD B28 ......162 B5
Broomcroft Rd
CHWD/FDBR/MGN B37 ......113 H4
Broomdene Av
BKDE/SHDE B34 ......112 C2
Broom Dr ALE/KHTH/YWD B14 ..178 A1
Broome Av GTB/HAM B43 ......73 E4
Broome Cl HALE B63 ......138 C4
Broome Gdns MGN/WHC B75 ......62 C3
Broomehill Cl BRLYHL DY5 ......119 E5
Broome La HAG/WOL DY9 ......169 E2
Broome Rd WOLVN WV10 ......23 F3
Broomfield SMTHWKW B67 ......106 B4
Broomfield Rd DARL/WED WS10 ..56 C5
ERDW/GRVHL B23 ......92 B4
Broomfields Cl SOLH B91 ......165 F5
Broomhall Av WNSFLD WV11 ......24 D4
Broom Hall Crs ACGN B27 ......163 F3
Broom Hall Gv ACGN B27 ......163 G3
Broomhill Cl GTB/HAM B43 ......73 F3
Broomhill La GTB/HAM B43 ......73 E3
Broomhill Rd ERDW/GRVHL B23 ..75 H4
Broomhurst EDG B15 ......125 G4
Broomie Cl MGN/WHC B75 ......62 D4
Broom La SHLY B90 ......194 A2
Broomlea Cl FOAKS/STRLY B74 ....45 E5
Broom Rd DSYBK/YTR WS5 ......57 H5
DUDN DY1 ......84 A2
Broomy Cl STETCH B33 ......112 C4
Broseley Av NFLD/LBR B31 ......175 G5
Broseley Brook Cl BORD B9 ......128 A3
Brosil Av BFLD/HDSWWD B20 ......89 G3
Brougham St LOZ/NWT B19 ......108 B2
Brough Cl
ETTPK/GDPK/PENN WV4 ......52 D5
VAUX/NECH B7 ......109 H3
Broughton Ct
DUNHL/THL/PER WV6 ......35 E2
Broughton Crs NFLD/LBR B31 ......174 D5
Broughton Rd BDMR/CCFT WV3 ..35 G4
BFLD/HDSWWD B20 ......108 A1
HAG/WOL DY9 ......136 B4
Brownfield Rd
BKDE/SHDE B34 ......113 E3
Brownhills Rd BRWNH WS8 ......19 F2
Browning Cl SHHTH WV12 ......26 C3
Browning Crs WOLVN WV10 ......12 C5
Browning Gv
DUNHL/THL/PER WV6 ......34 C1
Browning Rd SEDG DY3 ......82 C2
Brownley Rd SHLY B90 ......195 E1
Brown Lion St TPTN/OCK DY4 ......69 E4
Brown Rd DARL/WED WS10 ......55 E1
Brown's Coppice Av SOLH B91 ..163 H5
Browns Dr SCFLD/BOLD B73 ......76 D3
Brownsea Cl RBRY B45 ......173 G4
Brownsea Dr CBHAMW B1 ......2 E7
Browns Gn BFLD/HDSWWD B20 ..89 H3
Brownshore La WNSFLD WV11 ......15 E4
Browns La DOR/KN B93 ......196 C2
Brownsover Cl CBROM B36 ......94 D5
Brown St BKHL/PFLD WV2 ......52 B1
Brownswall Rd SEDG DY3 ......66 D4
Broxwood Pk
DUNHL/THL/PER WV6 ......35 F2
Brueton Av SOLH B91 ......182 B2
Brueton Dr ERDE/BCHGN B24 ......93 E3
Brueton Rd BILS/COS WV14 ......54 C1
Bruford Rd BDMR/CCFT WV3 ......36 C5
Brunel Cl BHTH/HG B12 ......144 C2
Brunel Ct BILS/COS WV14 ......69 E3
Brunel Dr TPTN/OCK DY4 ......69 E2
Brunel Gv CDSL WV8 ......20 C4
Brunel Rd OLDBY B69 ......104 B3
Brunel St CBHAM B2 ......2 E6
Brunel Wk DARL/WED WS10 * 55 H2
Brunel Wy BKHL/PFLD WV2 ......53 E1
Brunslow Cl WLNHL WV13 ......40 A4
WOLVN WV10 ......23 E1
Brunswick Ga STRBR DY8 ......152 C1
Brunswick Park Rd
DARL/WED WS10 ......56 A5
Brunswick Rd BHTH/HG B12 ......144 C2
HDSW B21 ......89 H5
Brunswick St CBHAMW B1 ......2 B6
WSLW WS2 ......56 C1
Brunswick Ter
DARL/WED WS10 ......55 H5
Brunton Rd SMHTH B10 ......128 D5
Brushfield Rd PBAR/PBCH B42 ..74 D3
Brutus Dr CSHL/WTROR B46 ......97 E5
Bryan Av
ETTPK/GDPK/PENN WV4 ......50 D4
Bryan Rd WSLW WS2 ......56 C2
Bryanston Ct SOLH B91 * 164 B3
Bryanston Rd SOLH B91 ......164 B4
Bryant St WSNGN B18 ......107 G4
Bryce Rd BRLYHL DY5 ......100 D4
Brylan Cft KGSTG B44 ......75 F5
Bryn Arden Rd
LGN/SDN/BHAMAIR B26 ......147 E2
Bryndale Av
ALE/KHTH/YWD B14 ......160 C5
Brynmawr Rd
ETTPK/GDPK/PENN WV4 ......52 D5
Brynside Cl BVILLE B30 ......177 H3
Bryony Gdns DARL/WED WS10 ....55 F1
Bryony Rd SLYOAK B29 ......158 D3
Buchanan Cl RUSH/SHEL WS4 ......42 C2
Buchanan Rd RUSH/SHEL WS4 ......5 J1
Buchanan Vw RUSH/SHEL WS4 ....42 C2
Buckbury Cl HAG/WOL DY9 ......153 F1
Buckbury Cft SHLY B90 ......195 H2
Buckingham Cl
DARL/WED WS10 ......56 C4
Buckingham Dr SHHTH WV12 ......25 H3
Buckingham Gv KGSWFD DY6 ......99 G2
Buckingham Ms
SCFLD/BOLD B73 ......77 E1
Buckingham Ri DUDN DY1 ......83 G4
Buckingham Rd
BLKHTH/ROWR B65 ......104 B5
CBROM B36 ......113 H2
ETTPK/GDPK/PENN WV4 ......51 G4
Buckingham St LOZ/NWT B19 ......2 E1
Buckland End
BKDE/SHDE B34 ......112 C3
Bucklands End La
BKDE/SHDE B34 ......112 B3
Buckle Cl WSL WS1 ......4 E7
Buckley Rd
ETTPK/GDPK/PENN WV4 ......50 D3
Buckminster Dr DOR/KN B93 ....196 C4
Bucknall Rd WNSFLD WV11 ......25 G1
Bucknell Cl SOLH B91 ......165 E5
Buckridge Cl HWK/WKHTH B38 ..190 B1
Buckridge La SHLY B90 ......194 A3
Buckton Cl MGN/WHC B75 ......48 A3
Budbrook Gv BKDE/SHDE B34 ..113 G3
Budden Rd TPTN/OCK DY4 ......68 D4
Bude Rd DSYBK/YTR WS5 ......58 B1
Buffery Rd DUDS DY2 ......102 D2
Bufferys Cl SOLH B91 ......181 H5
Buildwas Cl BLOX/PEL WS3 ......16 B5
Bulford Cl ALE/KHTH/YWD B14 ..178 B3
Bulger Rd BILS/COS WV14 ......53 G1
Bullace Cft EDG B15 ......142 B4
Buller St
ETTPK/GDPK/PENN WV4 ......52 C3
Bullfields Cl
BLKHTH/ROWR B65 ......103 F4
Bullfinch Cl DUDN DY1 ......101 G1
Bullivents Cl DOR/KN B93 ......196 D3
Bull La BILS/COS WV14 ......54 D5
WBROM B70 ......87 E3
WMBN WV5 ......65 F4
Bullmeadow La WMBN WV5 ......65 E4
Bullock's Rw WSL WS1 ......5 F4
Bullock St VAUX/NECH B7 ......109 G4
WBROM B70 ......105 H1
Bullows Rd BRWNH WS8 ......18 C1
Bull Ring HALE B63 ......138 D4
Bull's La WALM/CURD B76 ......79 E1
Bull St BRLYHL DY5 ......118 D3
CBHAM B2 ......3 G4
DARL/WED WS10 ......55 G2
DUDN DY1 ......102 A1
HRBN B17 ......142 B1
SEDG DY3 ......83 E4
WBROM B70 ......87 H4
Bulrush Cl BRWNH WS8 ......9 E5
Bulwell Cl AST/WIT B6 ......109 G2
Bumblehole Mdw WMBN WV5 ......64 D4
Bunbury Gdns NFLD/LBR B31 ......176 A1
Bunbury Rd NFLD/LBR B31 ......176 A1
Bundle Hl HALE B63 ......138 C4
The Bungalows WBROM B70 * 70 D5
Bunker's Hill La BILS/COS WV14 ..39 E5
Bunn's La DUDS DY2 ......85 F5
Burbage Cl WOLVN WV10 ......23 G4
Burbidge Rd BORD B9 ......128 B1
Burbury St LOZ/NWT B19 ......108 C3
Burbury St South
LOZ/NWT B19 * 108 C3
Burcot Av WOLV WV1 ......38 A3
Burcote Rd ERDE/BCHGN B24 ......93 H3
Burdock Cl DSYBK/YTR WS5 ......57 G5
Burdock Rd SLYOAK B29 ......158 C4
Burdons Cl STETCH B33 ......112 C4
Bure Gv WLNHL WV13 ......40 B4
Burfield Rd HALE B63 ......137 G1
Burford Cl DSYBK/YTR WS5 ......57 G4
HIA/OLT B92 ......147 G4
Burford Rd HLYWD B47 ......192 B2
KGSTG B44 ......75 F4
Burgess Cft HIA/OLT B92 ......165 H3
Burghley Dr HHTH/SAND B71 ......72 B1
Burghley Wk BRLYHL DY5 ......118 D4
Burgh Wy WSLW WS2 ......41 E1
Burhill Wy
CHWD/FDBR/MGN B37 ......114 B5
Burke Av MOS/BIL B13 ......162 B1
Burkitt Dr TPTN/OCK DY4 ......70 A3
Burland Av
DUNHL/THL/PER WV6 ......22 A3
Burleigh Cl SHHTH WV12 ......25 H4
Burleigh Rd BDMR/CCFT WV3 ......51 G1
Burleigh St WSL WS1 ......5 G5
Burleton Rd STETCH B33 ......131 G2
Burley Cl SHLY B90 ......179 H3
Burlington Rd SMHTH B10 ......128 D3
WBROM B70 ......87 H5
Burlington St AST/WIT B6 ......109 E3
Burlish Av HIA/OLT B92 ......164 B1
Burman Cl SHLY B90 ......180 A3
Burman Dr CSHL/WTROR B46 ......115 F4
Burman Rd SHLY B90 ......179 H3
Burmese Wy
BLKHTH/ROWR B65 ......103 F3
Burnaston Crs SHLY B90 ......196 A1
Burnaston Rd HLGN/YWD B28 ..162 C2
Burnbank Gv ERDE/BCHGN B24 ..93 F2
Burn Cl SMTHWKW B67 ......106 C5
Burncross Wy WOLVN WV10 ......23 H4
Burnell Gdns BDMR/CCFT WV3 ....36 A5
Burnel Rd SLYOAK B29 ......141 G5
Burnett Rd FOAKS/STRLY B74 ......45 H3
Burney La WASH/WDE B8 ......111 G5
Burnfields Cl ALDR WS9 ......30 A3
Burnham Av WOLVN WV10 ......23 E2
YDLY B25 ......146 C1
Burnham Cl KGSWFD DY6 ......100 B5
Burnham Meadow
HLGN/YWD B28 ......163 E4
Burnham Rd KGSTG B44 ......75 E4
Burnhill Gv SLYOAK B29 ......158 C2
Burnlea Gv NFLD/LBR B31 ......176 A4
Burnsall Cl
CHWD/FDBR/MGN B37 ......131 H2
COVEN WV9 ......12 A4
Burns Av TPTN/OCK DY4 ......69 G4
WOLVN WV10 ......12 D5
Burns Cl STRBR DY8 ......118 C4
Burns Gv SEDG DY3 ......82 C2
Burnside Gdns DSYBK/YTR WS5 ..58 B2
Burnside Wy NFLD/LBR B31 ......189 F1
Burns Pl DARL/WED WS10 ......54 C3
Burns Rd DARL/WED WS10 ......54 C3
Burnthurst Crs SOLH B91 ......195 G1
Burnt Oak Dr STRBR DY8 ......135 G2
Burnt Tree TPTN/OCK DY4 ......85 F4
Burrington Rd
RIDG/WDGT B32 ......157 E2
Burrowes St WSLW WS2 ......4 C1
Burrow Hill Cl CBROM B36 ......113 E1
Burrows Rd KGSWFD DY6 ......100 B5
Burrows St WSLW WS2 ......4 B1
Burslem Cl BLOX/PEL WS3 ......16 C3
Bursnips Rd WNSFLD WV11 ......15 G3
Burton Av RUSH/SHEL WS4 ......28 D3
Burton Crs WOLVN WV10 ......7 J2
Burton Farm Rd
RUSH/SHEL WS4 ......42 D2
Burton Rd DUDN DY1 ......83 H2
WOLVN WV10 ......7 K1
Burton Wood Dr
BFLD/HDSWWD B20 ......90 D4
Buryfield Rd SOLH B91 ......164 C4
Bury Hill Rd OLDBY B69 ......104 B2
Bush Av SMTHWK B66 ......107 E4
Bushbury Cft
CHWD/FDBR/MGN B37 ......132 C1
Bushbury La WOLVN WV10 ......13 F5
Bushbury Rd STETCH B33 ......112 C4
WOLVN WV10 ......24 A4
Bushell Dr SOLH B91 ......182 B1
Bushey Cl FOAKS/STRLY B74 ......45 F3
Bushey Fields Rd DUDN DY1 ......101 G2
Bush Gv BLOX/PEL WS3 ......18 A5
HDSW B21 ......89 E5
Bushley Cft SOLH B91 ......181 H5
Bushman Wy BKDE/SHDE B34 ..113 G4
Bushmore Rd HLGN/YWD B28 ......163 E4
Bush Rd DUDS DY2 ......120 C2
TPTN/OCK DY4 ......85 E2
Bush St DARL/WED WS10 ......55 F1
Bushway Cl BRLYHL DY5 ......118 C2
Bushwood Dr DOR/KN B93 ......197 E5
Bushwood Rd SLYOAK B29 ......158 D1
Bustleholme Av
HHTH/SAND B71 ......72 B2
Bustleholme Crs
HHTH/SAND B71 ......72 A2
Bustleholme La
HHTH/SAND B71 ......72 B1
Butchers La HALE B63 ......120 C5
Butchers Rd HIA/OLT B92 ......167 G4
Butcroft Gdns DARL/WED WS10 ..55 G2
Bute Cl RBRY B45 ......173 G4
SHHTH WV12 ......25 H4
Butler Rd HIA/OLT B92 ......147 F4
Butlers Cl BFLD/HDSWWD B20 ......90 A3
ERDW/GRVHL B23 ......76 B2
Butlers La FOAKS/STRLY B74 ......46 D2
Butlers Prec WSL WS1 ......4 D3
Butler's Rd BFLD/HDSWWD B20 ..90 A3
Butler St WBROM B70 ......87 E2
Butlin St VAUX/NECH B7 ......110 A2
Buttercup Cl DSYBK/YTR WS5 ......57 G5
Butterfield Cl
DUNHL/THL/PER WV6 ......34 B2
Butterfield Rd BRLYHL DY5 ......100 D2
Buttermere Cl BRLYHL DY5 ......118 D5
DUNHL/THL/PER WV6 ......21 H2
Buttermere Ct
DUNHL/THL/PER WV6 ......34 D1
Buttermere Dr
RIDG/WDGT B32 ......141 F4
WNSFLD WV11 ......15 E5
Buttermere Gv SHHTH WV12 ......25 H1
Butterworth Cl BILS/COS WV14 ..68 A2
Buttery Rd SMTHWKW B67 ......106 A3
Buttons Farm Rd
ETTPK/GDPK/PENN WV4 ......50 D5
Buttress Wy SMTHWK B66 ......106 C3
Butts Rd
ETTPK/GDPK/PENN WV4 ......51 F4
RUSH/SHEL WS4 ......42 B2
Butts St RUSH/SHEL WS4 ......42 B2
The Butts RUSH/SHEL WS4 ......42 B2
Buxton Cl BLOX/PEL WS3 ......17 E4
Buxton Rd BLOX/PEL WS3 ......17 E4
DUDS DY2 ......102 A3
ERDW/GRVHL B23 ......75 H5
SCFLD/BOLD B73 ......77 E2
Byfield Cl STETCH B33 ......131 G3
Byfleet Cl
ETTPK/GDPK/PENN WV4 ......53 E5
Byford Wy
CHWD/FDBR/MGN B37 ......132 B4
Byland Wy BLOX/PEL WS3 ......16 B5
Byrchen Moor Gdns
BRLYHL DY5 ......100 D2
Byrne Rd BKHL/PFLD WV2 ......52 B1
Byron Av AST/WIT B6 ......91 H3
Byron Cl SMHTH B10 * 128 B5
Byron Crs DUDN DY1 ......84 B1
Byron Cft FOAKS/STRLY B74 ......32 D4
SEDG DY3 ......82 C2
Byron Rd SHHTH WV12 ......26 C3
SMHTH B10 ......128 B5
WOLVN WV10 ......24 A1
Byron St BRLYHL DY5 ......101 F2
HHTH/SAND B71 ......87 F1
Byways BLOX/PEL WS3 ......17 E4

C

Caban Cl NFLD/LBR B31 158 A5
Cable Dr WSLW WS2 41 G1
Cable St BKHL/PFLD WV2 37 G5
Cabot Gv DUNHL/THL/PER WV6 34 C1
Cadbury Dr CVALE B35 94 B5
Cadbury Rd MOS/BIL B13 144 D3
Cadbury Wy HRBN B17 141 H2
Caddick Crs HHTH/SAND B71 71 H4
Caddick Rd PBAR/PBCH B42 74 B2
Caddick St BILS/COS WV14 68 A3
Cadet Dr SHLY B90 180 A2
Cadgwith Gdns BILS/COS WV14 69 G1
Cadine Gdns MOS/BIL B13 160 C1
Cadle Rd WOLVN WV10 23 F3
Cadman Crs WOLVN WV10 24 A4
Cadnam Cl HRBN B17 142 A4
WLNHL WV13 39 H5
Caernarvon Cl SHHTH WV12 26 A3
Caernarvon Wy DUDN DY1 83 G4
Caesar Wy CSHL/WTROR B46 97 E5
Cairn Dr WSLW WS2 40 D3
Cairns St WSLW WS2 4 A1
Caister Dr WLNHL WV13 39 F5
Cakemore Rd RMSLY B62 122 C2
Cala Dr EDG B15 126 B5
Calcot Dr DUNHL/THL/PER WV6 22 A3
Calcutt Wy SHLY B90 194 A2
Caldecote Gv BORD B9 129 G3
Caldeford Av SHLY B90 195 G1
Calder Av WSL WS1 5 H3
Calder Dr WALM/CURD B76 78 C3
Calderfields Cl RUSH/SHEL WS4 42 C2
Calder Gv BFLD/HDSWWD B20 89 H4
Calder Ri DUDN DY1 67 H5
Caldmore Gn WSL WS1 4 E7
Caldmore Rd WSL WS1 4 E5
Caldwell Gv SOLH B91 165 E5
Caldwell Rd BORD B9 129 F1
Caldwell St HHTH/SAND B71 71 H3
Caledonia BRLYHL DY5 119 F5
Caledonian Cl GTB/HAM B43 58 A5
Caledonia Rd BKHL/PFLD WV2 37 G5
Caledonia St BILS/COS WV14 54 A2
Caledon Pl WSLW WS2 56 C1
Caledon St WSLW WS2 56 C1
Calewood Rd BRLYHL DY5 119 F5
California Rd OLDBY B69 85 G5
California Wy RIDG/WDGT B32 141 F4
Callcott Dr BRLYHL DY5 119 F5
Callear Rd DARL/WED WS10 70 B2
Calley Cl TPTN/OCK DY4 85 F3
Callowbridge Rd RBRY B45 187 H1
Callowbrook La RBRY B45 187 H1
Calshot Rd PBAR/PBCH B42 74 A3
Calstock Rd SHHTH WV12 40 B1
Calthorpe Cl DSYBK/YTR WS5 58 C2
Calthorpe Man EDG B15 * 126 B3
Calthorpe Rd
BFLD/HDSWWD B20 90 C4
DSYBK/YTR WS5 58 B2
EDG B15 126 A4
Calver Crs WNSFLD WV11 25 F5
Calver Gv KGSTG B44 59 H5
Calverley Rd HWK/WKHTH B38 176 B4
Calverton Gv GTB/HAM B43 73 G3
Calves Cft WLNHL WV13 39 G2
Calvin Cl WMBN WV5 80 D1
WOLVN WV10 12 D4
Camberley Crs
ETTPK/GDPK/PENN WV4 67 G1
Camberley Dr
ETTPK/GDPK/PENN WV4 51 G4
Camberley Gv
ERDW/GRVHL B23 76 C5
Camberley Rd KGSWFD DY6 100 C5
Camborne Cl AST/WIT B6 109 E2
Camborne Rd DSYBK/YTR WS5 58 B1
Cambourne Rd
BLKHTH/ROWR B65 122 A1
Cambrai Dr HLGN/YWD B28 162 C2
Cambria Cl SHLY B90 193 G1
Cambridge Av SCFLD/BOLD B73 77 F3
SOLH B91 181 E2
Cambridge Cl ALDR WS9 30 A2
Cambridge Crs EDG B15 126 C5
Cambridge Dr
CHWD/FDBR/MGN B37 131 H3
Cambridge Rd DUDS DY2 102 A2
MOS/BIL B13 161 F1
SMTHWK B66 106 C2
Cambridge St CBHAMW B1 2 D5
WBROM B70 87 F4
WOLVN WV10 37 F1
WSL WS1 57 E1
Cambridge Wy ACGN B27 146 D3
Camden Cl CBROM B36 112 C1
DSYBK/YTR WS5 * 57 G4
Camden Dr CBHAMW B1 2 B3
Camden St ALDR WS9 19 E3
CBHAMW B1 2 B3
WSL WS1 4 C7
WSNGN B18 108 A5
Camden Wy KGSWFD DY6 81 H5
Camellia Gdns COVEN WV9 11 H4
Camelot Wy SMTHTH B10 128 A4
Cameo Dr STRBR DY8 118 B4
Cameron Rd RUSH/SHEL WS4 5 J1
Camford Gv
ALE/KHTH/YWD B14 178 B2
Cam Gdns BRLYHL DY5 100 D2
Camino Rd RIDG/WDGT B32 141 F4
Camomile Cl DSYBK/YTR WS5 57 G5
Campbell Cl RUSH/SHEL WS4 42 C2
Campbell Pl DARL/WED WS10 55 F2
Campbells Gn
LGN/SDN/BHAMAIR B26 147 H2
Campbell St BRLYHL DY5 101 E5
Campden Gn HIA/OLT B92 147 G4
Camp Hl BHTH/HG B12 127 G4
Camp Hill Circ BHTH/HG B12 127 G4
Camphill La DARL/WED WS10 70 D1
Campion Cl DSYBK/YTR WS5 57 G5
WMBN WV5 64 C5
Campion Gv HALE B63 137 H4
Campion Wy SHLY B90 194 A3
Camp La HDSW B21 88 D4
HWK/WKHTH B38 176 D2
Camplea Cft
CHWD/FDBR/MGN B37 132 A2
Camplin Crs
BFLD/HDSWWD B20 89 G1
Camp Rd MGN/WHC B75 33 H4
Camp St BORD B9 128 A3
DARL/WED WS10 70 D1
WOLV WV1 7 F1
Campville Crs HHTH/SAND B71 72 A2
Campville Gv
CHWD/FDBR/MGN B37 113 H4
Camp Wood Cl SLYOAK B29 159 G2
Camrose Cft BHTH/HG B12 144 A1
BKDE/SHDE B34 112 D3
Camrose Gdns COVEN WV9 12 A4
Canal La ERDE/BCHGN B24 93 E5
Canal Side BVILLE B30 * 177 E3
DUDS DY2 103 E5
Canalside Cl BLOX/PEL WS3 28 A1
HHTH/SAND B71 72 A1
Canal St BRLYHL DY5 101 G4
OLDBY B69 104 D2
STRBR DY8 135 F1
Canary Gv LOZ/NWT B19 108 C1
Canberra Rd DSYBK/YTR WS5 58 A3
Canberra Wy BHTH/HG B12 * 127 F4
Canford Cl BHTH/HG B12 127 F5
Canford Crs CDSL WV8 10 A4
Canning Cl DSYBK/YTR WS5 58 B2
Canning Gdns WSNGN B18 107 G5
Canning Rd DSYBK/YTR WS5 58 B2
Cannock Rd SHHTH WV12 26 A3
WOLVN WV10 37 F1
Cannon Dr BILS/COS WV14 68 C1
Cannon Hill Gv BHTH/HG B12 * 144 A2
Cannon Hill Pl BHTH/HG B12 * 144 A2
Cannon Hill Rd BHTH/HG B12 143 H2
Cannon Rd WMBN WV5 65 E5
Cannon St CBHAM B2 3 G5
WLNHL WV13 39 H3
WSLW WS2 42 A1
Cannon St North WSLW WS2 42 A1
Canterbury Av WLNHL WV13 40 B3
Canterbury Cl
BLKHTH/ROWR B65 104 C5
BLOX/PEL WS3 18 A2
HHTH/SAND B71 72 A3
Canterbury Dr
CHWD/FDBR/MGN B37 132 A5
DUNHL/THL/PER WV6 34 B1
Canterbury Rd
BFLD/HDSWWD B20 90 D5
ETTPK/GDPK/PENN WV4 50 D3
HHTH/SAND B71 71 H3
Cantlow Rd MOS/BIL B13 161 G4
Canton La WALM/CURD B76 97 G1
Canute Cl WSL WS1 57 F1
Canvey Cl RBRY B45 173 G4
Canwell Av
CHWD/FDBR/MGN B37 113 H4
Canwell Gdns BILS/COS WV14 53 F4
Canwell Ga MGN/WHC B75 48 A1
Capcroft Rd MOS/BIL B13 161 H4
Cape Hl SMTHWK B66 106 D5
Capener Rd GTB/HAM B43 74 A1
Capern Gv RIDG/WDGT B32 141 F2
Cape St WBROM B70 86 C2
WSNGN B18 107 F5
Capethorn Rd SMTHWK B66 124 C1
Capilano Rd ERDW/GRVHL B23 76 A4
Capponfield Cl BILS/COS WV14 53 F5
Capstone Av WOLVN WV10 22 D2
WSNGN B18 108 A5
Captain's Cl BDMR/CCFT WV3 35 H3
Carcroft Rd YDLY B25 129 G4
Cardale St BLKHTH/ROWR B65 122 B2
Carden Cl WBROM B70 86 D2
Carder Crs BILS/COS WV14 53 H4
Carder Dr BRLYHL DY5 119 E2
Cardiff St BDMR/CCFT WV3 6 C7
Cardigan Cl HHTH/SAND B71 71 G4
Cardigan Dr SHHTH WV12 25 H4
Cardigan St CBHAMNE B4 3 K3
Cardington Av PBAR/PBCH B42 74 B2
Cardoness Pl DUDN DY1 83 H4
Careless Gn HAG/WOL DY9 136 D3
Carhampton Rd MGN/WHC B75 63 G2
Carillon Gdns
BLKHTH/ROWR B65 122 A1
Carisbrooke Av
CHWD/FDBR/MGN B37 132 C2
Carisbrooke Cl DARL/WED WS10 72 A1
Carisbrooke Ct
DUNHL/THL/PER WV6 35 E2
Carisbrooke Crs
DARL/WED WS10 57 E5
Carisbrooke Dr RMSLY B62 139 F4
Carisbrooke Gdns WOLVN WV10 13 E4
Carisbrooke Rd
DUNHL/THL/PER WV6 35 E2
HRBN B17 124 D3
WOLVN WV10 13 E4
Carless Av HRBN B17 124 D5
Carless St WSL WS1 4 E7
Carlisle St WSNGN B18 107 G4
Carl St WSLW WS2 27 H5
Carlton Av BILS/COS WV14 54 B1
FOAKS/STRLY B74 45 F3
HAG/WOL DY9 136 C4
HDSW B21 89 G5
WNSFLD WV11 24 A3
Carlton Cl DUDN DY1 68 C5
MGN/WHC B75 62 D1
Carlton Cft FOAKS/STRLY B74 45 G3
Carlton Ms CBROM B36 113 E1
Carlton Rd BDMR/CCFT WV3 51 G1
BORD B9 128 B3
SMTHWK B66 106 C1
Carlyle Gv WOLVN WV10 24 A2
Carlyle Rd BLKHTH/ROWR B65 122 A2
LDYWD/EDGR B16 125 G3
LOZ/NWT B19 108 C1
WOLVN WV10 23 H2
Carmel Gv RIDG/WDGT B32 157 F1
Carmodale Av PBAR/PBCH B42 74 B5
Carnegie Av TPTN/OCK DY4 85 G2
Carnegie Dr DARL/WED WS10 56 A5
Carnegie Rd
BLKHTH/ROWR B65 121 H2
Carnford Rd
LGN/SDN/BHAMAIR B26 147 H1
Carnforth Cl KGSWFD DY6 99 F2
Carnoustie Cl BLOX/PEL WS3 16 C4
MGN/WHC B75 47 H5
Carnwath Rd SCFLD/BOLD B73 76 C1
Carol Crs HALE B63 138 B2
WNSFLD WV11 25 E4
Carol Gdns STRBR DY8 118 B4
Caroline Rd MOS/BIL B13 144 B3
Caroline St CBHAMW B1 2 D2
DUDS DY2 85 E5
WBROM B70 87 F4
Carpenter Gld HALE B63 137 H2
Carpenter Rd EDG B15 126 B5
Carpenters Ct BHTH/HG B12 * 127 F4
Carpenter's Rd LOZ/NWT B19 108 C2
Carrick Cl BLOX/PEL WS3 18 A2
Carriers Cl WSLW WS2 40 D4
Carriers Fold WMBN WV5 * 65 F4
Carrington Rd DARL/WED WS10 71 H1
Carrisbrooke Rd
DARL/WED WS10 71 H1
Carroway Head Hl
MGN/WHC B75 49 E1
Carrs La CBHAMNE B4 3 H5
Carshalton Gv BKHL/PFLD WV2 37 G5
Carshalton Rd KGSTG B44 75 G1
Cartbridge Crs BLOX/PEL WS3 28 C5
Cartbridge La RUSH/SHEL WS4 28 C5
Cartbridge La South
RUSH/SHEL WS4 28 C5
Carter Av CDSL WV8 10 D4
Carter Rd DUNHL/THL/PER WV6 22 D5
GTB/HAM B43 73 H1
Carters Cl WALM/CURD B76 63 F5
Carter's Gn WBROM B70 87 F2
Carters Hurst STETCH B33 130 D3
Carter's La RMSLY B62 139 H3
Cartland Rd BVILLE B30 160 B3
SPARK B11 128 A5
The Cartway
DUNHL/THL/PER WV6 34 B1
Cartwright Gdns OLDBY B69 86 A4
Cartwright Rd MGN/WHC B75 47 G2
Cartwright St BKHL/PFLD WV2 37 F5
Carver Ct TPTN/OCK DY4 * 69 G2
Carver Gdns STRBR DY8 135 E5
Carver St WSNGN B18 2 A2
Casern Vw MGN/WHC B75 63 G2
Casewell Rd KGSWFD DY6 99 G1
Casey Av ERDW/GRVHL B23 76 B3
Cash Joynson Av
DARL/WED WS10 40 A5
Caslon Crs STRBR DY8 134 D3
Caslon Rd HALE B63 137 G1
Cassandra Cl BRLYHL DY5 83 E5
Cassowary Rd
BFLD/HDSWWD B20 89 H3
Castello Dr CBROM B36 95 F5
The Castings BILS/COS WV14 68 D1
Castlebridge Rd WNSFLD WV11 25 G3
Castle Cl BRWNH WS8 9 F2
CDYHTH B64 121 H3
HIA/OLT B92 164 D1
Castle Crs CBROM B36 113 E1
Castle Cft LGLYGN/QTN B68 123 H4
Castlecroft Av BDMR/CCFT WV3 35 E5
Castlecroft Gdns
BDMR/CCFT WV3 35 F5
Castlecroft La BDMR/CCFT WV3 34 D5
Castlecroft Rd BDMR/CCFT WV3 34 D5
BILS/COS WV14 54 A1
Castle Dr CSHL/WTROR B46 115 F4
SHHTH WV12 25 H5
Castleford Gv SPARK B11 * 145 E3
Castleford Rd SPARK B11 145 E3
Castlefort Rd ALDR WS9 19 G4
Castlegate Dr DUDN DY1 85 E4
Castlegate Wy DUDN DY1 85 E4
Castle Grounds DUDN DY1 * 84 D4
Castle Gv STRBR DY8 135 H4
Castle Hts CDYHTH B64 * 121 H4
Castle Hl DUDN DY1 84 D4
Castlehills Dr CBROM B36 112 C1
Castle La HIA/OLT B92 164 C1
Castle Mill Rd DUDN DY1 84 C2
Castle Rd ALDR WS9 19 G5
BVILLE B30 176 D1
SLYOAK B29 141 G5
TPTN/OCK DY4 84 D2
Castle Rd East
LGLYGN/QTN B68 123 H4
Castle Rd West
LGLYGN/QTN B68 123 G4
Castle St BILS/COS WV14 68 C3
BRWNH WS8 9 F2
DARL/WED WS10 40 B5
DUDS DY2 84 D5
SEDG DY3 67 F3
TPTN/OCK DY4 85 E1
WBROM B70 71 E4
WOLV WV1 7 G4
Castleton Rd BLOX/PEL WS3 17 E4
PBAR/PBCH B42 74 D4
Castleton St DUDS DY2 102 C4
Castle Vw DUDN DY1 84 B4
Castle View Cl DARL/WED WS10 54 C4
Castle View Rd
DARL/WED WS10 54 C4
Caswell Rd SEDG DY3 67 E3
Cat And Kittens La
WOLVN WV10 13 E1
Cater Dr WALM/CURD B76 78 B1
Caterham Dr STRBR DY8 118 B1
Catesby Dr KGSWFD DY6 99 H1
Catesby Rd SHLY B90 180 B4
Cateswell Rd HLGN/YWD B28 145 H5
Cathcart Rd STRBR DY8 135 E2
Cathel Dr PBAR/PBCH B42 74 A4
Catherine De Barnes La
HIA/OLT B92 166 C4
Catherine Dr SCFLD/BOLD B73 62 A2
Catherine Rd BILS/COS WV14 68 A2
Catherines Cl SOLH B91 183 F1
Catherine St AST/WIT B6 109 G2
Catherton Cl TPTN/OCK DY4 70 A1
Catholic La SEDG DY3 67 E4
Catisfield Crs CDSL WV8 22 B1
Cat La BKDE/SHDE B34 112 D2
Caton Gv HLGN/YWD B28 163 E3
Cato St VAUX/NECH B7 109 H5
Cato St North VAUX/NECH B7 110 A4
Catshill Rd BRWNH WS8 9 G5
Cattell Dr MGN/WHC B75 63 H3
Cattell Rd BORD B9 128 A3
Cattells Gv VAUX/NECH B7 110 A3
Cattermole Gv GTB/HAM B43 59 G5
Cattock Hurst Dr
CSCFLD/WYGN B72 77 H4
Causeway BLKHTH/ROWR B65 122 A2
Causeway Green Rd
LGLYGN/QTN B68 123 E1
Causeway Rd BILS/COS WV14 68 D3
The Causeway YDLY B25 129 H5
Causey Farm Rd HALE B63 154 C2
Cavalier Circ WOLVN WV10 13 E3
Cavandale Av KGSTG B44 75 E2
Cavell Closet WSLW WS2 4 B3
Cavell Rd DUDS DY2 85 F5
Cavendish Cl HWK/WKHTH B38 177 F4
KGSWFD DY6 99 H5
Cavendish Dr HAG/WOL DY9 169 F1
Cavendish Gdns WSLW WS2 41 E1
Cavendish Rd
LDYWD/EDGR B16 125 F1
RMSLY B62 139 H3
WOLV WV1 38 B4
WSLW WS2 27 E5
Cavendish Wy ALDR WS9 30 B5
Caversham Rd KGSTG B44 75 G1
Cawdon Gv DOR/KN B93 198 C1
Cawdor Crs LDYWD/EDGR B16 125 H3
Caxton Gv KGSTG B44 76 A2
Caynham Rd RIDG/WDGT B32 157 F2
Cayton Gv ERDW/GRVHL B23 76 D5
Cecil Dr OLDBY B69 86 B4
Cecil Rd ERDE/BCHGN B24 92 D3
SLYOAK B29 160 C1
Cecil St CBHAMNE B4 3 G1
RUSH/SHEL WS4 42 B2
STRBR DY8 135 F2
Cedar Av BILS/COS WV14 68 A4
BRWNH WS8 9 G4
CBROM B36 113 E2
Cedar Bridge Cft
FOAKS/STRLY B74 47 E5
Cedar Cl BVILLE B30 159 F4
DSYBK/YTR WS5 57 H4
LGLYGN/QTN B68 123 G4
STRBR DY8 134 C5
Cedar Dr ERDE/BCHGN B24 93 G1
FOAKS/STRLY B74 45 E4
NFLD/LBR B31 189 H1
Cedar Gv BDMR/CCFT WV3 51 F1
CDSL WV8 10 D4
HAG/WOL DY9 152 C4
Cedarhurst RIDG/WDGT B32 141 G2
SOLH B91 182 A2
Cedar Park Rd SHHTH WV12 26 A1
Cedar Rd BVILLE B30 159 G4
DARL/WED WS10 71 E1
DUDN DY1 84 B3
TPTN/OCK DY4 84 D1
WLNHL WV13 39 E3
Cedars Av ACGN B27 146 C3
KGSWFD DY6 99 H5
WMBN WV5 81 E1
The Cedars
DUNHL/THL/PER WV6 * 21 H5
DUNHL/THL/PER WV6 * 36 B2
YDLY B25 130 A3
Cedar Wy NFLD/LBR B31 175 F4
WNSFLD WV11 24 C3
Cedarwood FOAKS/STRLY B74 47 F5
Cedarwood Cft
PBAR/PBCH B42 73 H3
Cedar Wood Rd SEDG DY3 83 E2
Celandine Cl STRBR DY8 99 G5
Celandine Rd DUDN DY1 84 A2
The Celandines WMBN WV5 64 C5
Celbury Wy GTB/HAM B43 73 F3
Celts Cl BLKHTH/ROWR B65 104 A5
Cemetery La WSNGN B18 108 B4
Cemetery Rd HAG/WOL DY9 136 B2
LGLYGN/QTN B68 105 G3
SMTHWKW B67 106 B5
WLNHL WV13 39 G2
WSLW WS2 40 D5
Cemetery St BILS/COS WV14 53 G1
Cemetery Wy BLOX/PEL WS3 * 27 F1
Centenary Cl NFLD/LBR B31 175 G4
Centenary Dr HDSW B21 89 G5
Centenary Sq CBHAMW B1 2 D5
Central Ar WOLV WV1 7 F4
Central Av BILS/COS WV14 54 A1
BLKHTH/ROWR B65 122 A2
CDYHTH B64 120 D5
HAG/WOL DY9 136 C4
NFLD/LBR B31 175 F5
TPTN/OCK DY4 69 F5
Central Cl BLOX/PEL WS3 27 E1
Central Dr BILS/COS WV14 68 D4
BLOX/PEL WS3 26 D2
SEDG DY3 83 F4
Central Gv ACGN B27 146 C5
Central Pk DUDS DY2 * 121 E1
Central Park Dr WSNGN B18 107 H4
Central Sq ERDE/BCHGN B24 * 93 E2
Central Wy BRLYHL DY5 119 H1
Centre La HALE B63 138 D4
The Centreway
ALE/KHTH/YWD B14 179 F1
Centurion Cl CSHL/WTROR B46 97 E5
Century Pk BORD B9 128 A2
Century Rd OLDBY B69 105 E1
Ceolmund Crs
CHWD/FDBR/MGN B37 132 B1
Chaceley Gv
ERDW/GRVHL B23 * 76 B4
Chadbury Cft SOLH B91 181 H5
Chadbury Rd HALE B63 139 E4
Chaddersley Cl RBRY B45 173 H5
Chaddesley Cl OLDBY B69 104 B4
Chaddesley Dr HAG/WOL DY9 152 D1
Chaddesley Rd HALE B63 138 B5
HWK/WKHTH B38 176 B3
Chadley Cl SOLH B91 164 C4
Chad Rd BILS/COS WV14 68 B4
EDG B15 125 H4
Chadshunt Cl CBROM B36 95 F4
Chadsmoor Ter
VAUX/NECH B7 109 H3
Chadstone Cl SHLY B90 195 H2
Chad Valley Cl HRBN B17 142 B1
Chadwell Dr HIA/OLT B92 163 F4
Chadwell Gdns CDSL WV8 10 B3
Chadwich La HAG/WOL DY9 186 A2
Chadwick Av RBRY B45 188 B2
Chadwick Cl
ETTPK/GDPK/PENN WV4 50 C2
Chadwick Ct GTB/HAM B43 * 73 G3
Chadwick Rd MGN/WHC B75 63 F3
Chadworth Av DOR/KN B93 196 C4
Chaffcombe Rd
LGN/SDN/BHAMAIR B26 148 A1
Chaffinch Cl SEDG DY3 67 E1
Chaffinch Dr CBROM B36 114 B2
Chaffinch Rd HAG/WOL DY9 136 A4
Chainmakers Cl BILS/COS WV14 53 G5
Chain Wk LOZ/NWT B19 108 D1
Chalcot Gv BFLD/HDSWWD B20 89 G1
Chaldon Cl COVEN WV9 12 A5
Chale Gv ALE/KHTH/YWD B14 178 C2
Chalfont Pl HAG/WOL DY9 136 C5
Chalford Rd ERDW/GRVHL B23 76 A3
Chalford Wy SHLY B90 180 C5
Chalgrove Av
HWK/WKHTH B38 176 C4
Chalgrove Crs SOLH B91 181 H4
Challenge Wy WOLVN WV10 23 G5
Challenor Av WLNHL WV13 38 D3
Chalybeate Cl RBRY B45 173 H4
Chamberlain Cl OLDBY B69 86 B4
Chamberlain Ct MOS/BIL B13 161 E1
WSNGN B18 2 C1
Chamberlain Crs SHLY B90 180 A3
Chamberlain Rd MOS/BIL B13 161 F4
Chamberlain's La
ETTPK/GDPK/PENN WV4 51 E5
Chamberlain Sq CBHAMNW B3 2 E5
Chamberlain Wk
CSHL/WTROR B46 * 115 F2
SMTHWK B66 * 106 C3
Chance Cft LGLYGN/QTN B68 123 F4
Chancellor's Cl EDG B15 125 G4
Chancel Wy RMSLY B62 139 E2
Chancery Wy BRLYHL DY5 119 H2
Chandler Dr
ETTPK/GDPK/PENN WV4 50 D5
Chandlers Cl COVEN WV9 22 C1
WSNGN B18 107 H4
Chandlers Keep BRWNH WS8 19 F1
Channon Dr BRLYHL DY5 119 F4
Chanston Av
ALE/KHTH/YWD B14 178 A1
Chanterelle Gdns
ETTPK/GDPK/PENN WV4 51 G4
Chantrey Crs BILS/COS WV14 54 B1
GTB/HAM B43 59 H4
Chantry Av BLOX/PEL WS3 27 H2
Chantry Cl HLYWD B47 192 C1
Chantry Dr RMSLY B62 139 H1
Chantry Heath Crs
DOR/KN B93 183 F5
Chantry Rd HDSW B21 107 H1
KINVER DY7 117 G5
MOS/BIL B13 144 A3
Chapel Ash WOLV WV1 6 C4
Chapel Ash Island WOLV WV1 6 D4
Chapel Av BRWNH WS8 9 E2
Chapel Cl CDYHTH B64 121 H4
WMBN WV5 80 D1
Chapel Dr BRWNH WS8 9 E2
HLYWD B47 192 B5
Chapelfield Ms RBRY B45 187 H2
STRBR DY8 135 G3
Chapelfield Rd RBRY B45 174 A5
Chapel Fields Rd HIA/OLT B92 147 F5
Chapel Gn WLNHL WV13 39 H3
Chapel House La HALE B63 137 G2
Chapelhouse Rd
CHWD/FDBR/MGN B37 131 H2
Chapel House St BHTH/HG B12 * 3 K7
Chapel La CDSL WV8 10 B4
GTB/HAM B43 58 D4
HAG/WOL DY9 185 H1
HOCK/TIA B94 199 G4
RMSLY B62 154 C4

SEDG DY3 ....80 A2
SLYOAK B29 ....142 C5
Chapel St *BILS/COS* WV14 ....54 B4
BKHL/PFLD WV2 ....52 B1
BLOX/PEL WS3 ....17 H4
BLOX/PEL WS3 ....27 H2
BRLYHL DY5 ....101 E2
BRLYHL DY5 ....119 F2
BRLYHL DY5 ....119 H3
BRWNH WS8 ....9 E2
CBHAMNE B4 ....3 J4
DARL/WED WS10 ....55 G5
DUDS DY2 ....102 D5
HAG/WOL DY9 ....136 C2
HAG/WOL DY9 ....152 C5
HALE B63 ....138 C4
HDSW B21 ....107 F2
KGSWFD DY6 ....99 F1
OLDBY B69 ....104 C2
STRBR DY8 ....117 H1
STRBR DY8 ....135 G3
TPTN/OCK DY4 ....85 E1
WBROM B70 ....87 F1
WMBN WV5 ....80 D1
Chapel Vw *SMTHWKW* B67 ....106 B5
Chapel Wk *BVILLE* B30 ....177 E2
SEDG DY3 ....83 E4
Chapelwood Gv
PBAR/PBCH B42 * 90 D1
Chapman Rd *SMHTH* B10 ....128 A4
Chapman's Hl *BRGRVW* B61 ....172 D5
Chapmans Pas *CBHAMW* B1 * 2 E7
Chapman St *WBROM* B70 ....87 F3
Chapter House *WBROM* B70 * 87 E1
Charfield Cl *BVILLE* B30 ....159 F3
Charingworth Rd *HIA/OLT* B92 ..148 A5
Charlbury Av
CHWD/FDBR/MGN B37 ....131 H2
Charlbury Crs
LGN/SDN/BHAMAIR B26 ....130 B4
Charlecote Cft *SHLY* B90 ....180 C5
Charlecote Dr *DUDN* DY1 ....83 G3
ERDW/GRVHL B23 ....76 C4
Charlecote Gdns
SCFLD/BOLD B73 ....77 E3
Charlecote Ri *WLNHL* WV13 ....39 F4
Charlecott Cl *MOS/BIL* B13 ....162 B3
Charlemont Av *HHTH/SAND* B71 ..72 B3
Charlemont Cl *DSYBK/YTR* WS5 ..58 A2
Charlemont Crs
HHTH/SAND B71 ....72 A3
Charlemont Gdns
DSYBK/YTR WS5 ....57 H2
Charlemont Rd *DSYBK/YTR* WS5 ..57 H2
HHTH/SAND B71 ....72 A3
Charles Av *BLKHTH/ROWR* B65 ..104 A5
ETTPK/GDPK/PENN WV4 ....51 H3
WNSFLD WV11 ....14 D3
Charles Cl *WASH/WDE* B8 ....110 B5
Charles Crs *BLOX/PEL* WS3 ....18 A2
Charlesdale Dr *ALDR* WS9 ....44 B1
Charles Dr *VAUX/NECH* B7 ....109 H3
Charles Edward Rd
LGN/SDN/BHAMAIR B26 ....146 D1
Charles Foster St
DARL/WED WS10 ....55 E2
Charles Henry St *DIG/EDG* B5 ....127 E4
Charles Holland St
WLNHL WV13 ....39 H3
Charles Rd *AST/WIT* B6 ....91 G5
BFLD/HDSWWD B20 ....90 C5
BRLYHL DY5 ....120 A3
HALE B63 ....138 B3
SMHTH B10 ....128 C4
SOLH B91 ....181 E3
STRBR DY8 ....135 E3
TPTN/OCK DY4 ....69 G4
Charles St *SMTHWK* B66 ....107 E2
WBROM B70 ....86 C1
WLNHL WV13 ....40 A2
WSLW WS2 ....4 B4
Charles Wk
BLKHTH/ROWR B65 ....104 A4
Charles Wesley Ct
BDMR/CCFT WV3 * 51 G1
Charlesworth Av *SHLY* B90 ....195 H2
Charleville Rd *LOZ/NWT* B19 ....108 B2
Charlotte Cl *TPTN/OCK* DY4 ....85 G4
Charlotte Rd *BVILLE* B30 ....160 A4
DARL/WED WS10 ....70 A2
EDG B15 ....126 C4
Charlotte St *CBHAMNW* B3 ....2 D4
DUDN DY1 ....102 B1
WSL WS1 ....5 H3
Charlton Dr *CDYHTH* B64 ....120 D5
Charlton Rd *KGSTG* B44 ....75 G4
Charlton St *BRLYHL* DY5 ....118 C1
DUDN DY1 ....84 B5
Charminster Av *YDLY* B25 ....129 H4
Charnley Dr *MGN/WHC* B75 ....48 A3
Charnwood Av *SEDG* DY3 ....67 F1
Charnwood Cl *BILS/COS* WV14 ....54 D5
BRLYHL DY5 ....118 D5
RBRY B45 ....174 B2
Charnwood Ct *HAG/WOL* DY9 ....136 C5
Charnwood Rd *DSYBK/YTR* WS5 ..57 G4
PBAR/PBCH B42 ....73 H4
Charter Crs *CDYHTH* B64 ....121 H4
Charterfield Dr *KGSWFD* DY6 ....81 H5
Charterhouse Dr *SOLH* B91 ....181 H4
Charter Rd *TPTN/OCK* DY4 ....70 A2
Charters Av *CDSL* WV8 ....21 F1
Charter St *BRLYHL* DY5 ....101 G4
Chartist Rd *WASH/WDE* B8 ....110 B3
Chartley Cl *DOR/KN* B93 ....196 C5
DUNHL/THL/PER WV6 ....34 D1
Chartley Rd *ERDW/GRVHL* B23 ....92 A5
HHTH/SAND B71 ....71 H5
The Chartway *BLOX/PEL* WS3 ....18 B3
Chartwell Cl *DUDN* DY1 ....68 B5
Chartwell Dr *FOAKS/STRLY* B74 ....46 B1
SHLY B90 ....194 D3
WMBN WV5 ....80 D1
WOLVN WV10 ....23 G1
Chase Gv *ERDE/BCHGN* B24 ....77 H5
The Chase Link *BRWNH* WS8 * 9 G3
Chasepool Rd *SEDG* DY3 ....98 A2
Chase Rd *BLOX/PEL* WS3 ....27 E2
BRWNH WS8 ....9 G3
SEDG DY3 ....82 D5
The Chase
DUNHL/THL/PER WV6 ....22 D4
WALM/CURD B76 ....77 H4
Chase Vw
ETTPK/GDPK/PENN WV4 ....67 G1
Chater Dr *WALM/CURD* B76 ....78 C2
Chaters Cl *TPTN/OCK* DY4 ....85 E1
Chatham Rd *NFLD/LBR* B31 ....175 G2
Chatsworth Av *GTB/HAM* B43 ....73 E2
Chatsworth Cl
CSCFLD/WYGN B72 ....77 H4
SHHTH WV12 ....25 H5
SHLY B90 ....194 D3
Chatsworth Crs
RUSH/SHEL WS4 ....29 F3
Chatsworth Ms *STRBR* DY8 * 117 G2
Chatsworth Rd *CDYHTH* B64 ....121 G5
Chattaway St *VAUX/NECH* B7 ....110 A2
Chattle Hl *CSHL/WTROR* B46 ....97 E4
Chattock Av *SOLH* B91 ....182 C1
Chattock Cl *CBROM* B36 ....112 A2
Chatwell Gv *SLYOAK* B29 ....141 H5
Chatwin Pl *BILS/COS* WV14 ....54 A5
Chatwin St *SMTHWK* B66 ....106 B2
Chatwins Whf *TPTN/OCK* DY4 ....85 F1
Chaucer Av *SEDG* DY3 ....82 C1
SHHTH WV12 ....26 C2
TPTN/OCK DY4 ....69 H3
Chaucer Cl *BILS/COS* WV14 ....68 D3
ERDW/GRVHL B23 ....91 H3
STRBR DY8 ....118 C4
Chaucer Gv *ACGN* B27 ....163 F1
Chaucer Rd *BLOX/PEL* WS3 ....28 A2
Chauson Gv *SOLH* B91 ....181 G5
Chavasse Rd *CSCFLD/WYGN* B72 ..62 C5
Chawn Hl *HAG/WOL* DY9 ....136 A4
Chawnhill Cl *HAG/WOL* DY9 ....136 A4
Chawn Park Dr *HAG/WOL* DY9 ..136 A4
Chaynes Gv *STETCH* B33 ....131 F2
Cheadle Dr *ERDW/GRVHL* B23 ....76 B3
Cheam Gdns
DUNHL/THL/PER WV6 ....22 A2
Cheapside *BHTH/HG* B12 ....127 F4
WLNHL WV13 ....39 G4
Cheatham St *VAUX/NECH* B7 ....110 A3
Checketts St *WSLW* WS2 ....4 A3
Checkley Cl *SHLY* B90 ....180 A1
Checkley Cft *WALM/CURD* B76 ....78 B3
Cheddar Rd *BHTH/HG* B12 ....144 A1
Chedworth Cl *SLYOAK* B29 ....158 D3
Cheedon Cl *DOR/KN* B93 ....198 C1
Chelford Crs *KGSWFD* DY6 ....118 C1
Chells Gv *MOS/BIL* B13 ....161 H5
Chelmar Cl *CBROM* B36 ....113 H1
Chelmar Dr *BRLYHL* DY5 ....100 C3
Chelmarsh Av *BDMR/CCFT* WV3 ..35 E4
Chelmorton Rd
PBAR/PBCH B42 ....74 C3
Chelmscote Rd *HIA/OLT* B92 ....164 B1
Chelmsley Av
CSHL/WTROR B46 ....115 F3
Chelmsley Cir
CHWD/FDBR/MGN B37 ....132 B2
Chelmsley Gv *STETCH* B33 ....131 G1
Chelmsley La
CHWD/FDBR/MGN B37 ....131 H4
Chelmsley Rd
CHWD/FDBR/MGN B37 ....132 A1
Chelsea Cl *RIDG/WDGT* B32 ....141 F3
Chelsea Dr *FOAKS/STRLY* B74 ....46 D1
Chelsea Wy *KGSWFD* DY6 ....99 G3
Chelston Dr
DUNHL/THL/PER WV6 ....36 A1
Chelston Rd *NFLD/LBR* B31 ....175 E3
Cheltenham Dr *CBROM* B36 ....111 H1
KGSWFD DY6 ....99 F3
Chelthorn Wy *SOLH* B91 ....182 A3
Cheltondale Rd *SOLH* B91 ....164 B5
Chelveston Crs *SOLH* B91 ....181 H4
Chelwood Gdns
ETTPK/GDPK/PENN WV4 ....53 F3
Chelworth Rd
HWK/WKHTH B38 ....177 F3
Chem Rd *BILS/COS* WV14 ....53 F3
Cheniston Rd *SHHTH* WV12 ....26 A4
Chepstow Cl
DUNHL/THL/PER WV6 ....34 D1
Chepstow Gv *RBRY* B45 ....188 B2
Chepstow Rd *BLOX/PEL* WS3 ....26 D1
WOLVN WV10 ....12 D2
Chepstow Vls *BHTH/HG* B12 * 144 D2
Chequerfield Dr
BDMR/CCFT WV3 ....51 G2
Chequers Av *WMBN* WV5 ....65 E2
Chequer St *BDMR/CCFT* WV3 ....51 G2
Cherhill Covert
ALE/KHTH/YWD B14 ....177 G3
Cherington Rd *SLYOAK* B29 ....160 A2
Cheriton Gv
DUNHL/THL/PER WV6 ....34 C2
Cherrington Gdns
DUNHL/THL/PER WV6 ....35 F3
HAG/WOL DY9 ....153 E2
Cherrington Wy *SOLH* B91 ....181 H4
Cherry Crs *ERDE/BCHGN* B24 ....92 D3
Cherry Dr *BORD* B9 ....127 H3
Cherry Gn *DUDN* DY1 ....83 H2
Cherry Gv *SMTHWK* B66 ....107 E4
STRBR DY8 ....135 E3
Cherry La *DARL/WED* WS10 ....71 E1
SCFLD/BOLD B73 ....77 E4
SEDG DY3 ....81 F3
Cherry Lea *BKDE/SHDE* B34 ....112 D3
Cherry Orch *CDYHTH* B64 ....121 F3
Cherry Orchard Av *HALE* B63 ....138 B2
Cherry Orchard Crs *HALE* B63 ....138 B2
Cherry Orchard Rd
BFLD/HDSWWD B20 ....89 H1
Cherry Rd *TPTN/OCK* DY4 ....69 F4
Cherry St *BDMR/CCFT* WV3 ....6 C5
CBHAM B2 ....3 G5
HALE B63 ....138 B2
STRBR DY8 ....135 E3
Cherry Tree Av *DSYBK/YTR* WS5 ..57 H4
Cherrytree Ct *HAG/WOL* DY9 ....136 C4
Cherry Tree Gdns *CDSL* WV8 ....10 D4
Cherry Tree La *CDSL* WV8 ....10 D4
HALE B63 ....154 D1
Cherry Tree Rd *KGSWFD* DY6 ....100 A1
Cherry Wk *HLYWD* B47 ....192 D3
Cherrywood Cl *BILS/COS* WV14 ....68 C2
Cherrywood Crs *SOLH* B91 ....182 A5
Cherrywood Gn *BILS/COS* WV14 ..38 D5
Cherrywood Rd *BORD* B9 ....128 B2
FOAKS/STRLY B74 ....44 D4
Cherrywood Wy
FOAKS/STRLY B74 ....46 B1
Chervil Cl *PBAR/PBCH* B42 ....74 C4
Chervil Ri *WOLVN* WV10 ....37 H2
Cherwell Dr *BRWNH* WS8 ....8 C2
CBROM B36 ....113 H1
Cherwell Gdns *AST/WIT* B6 * 108 D1
Cheshire Av *SHLY* B90 ....180 A2
Cheshire Cl *STRBR* DY8 ....117 H4
Cheshire Gv
DUNHL/THL/PER WV6 ....34 C1
Cheshire Rd *AST/WIT* B6 ....91 G4
SMTHWKW B67 ....106 C5
WSLW WS2 ....40 D3
Cheshunt Pl
ALE/KHTH/YWD B14 * 161 E2
Chessetts Gv *MOS/BIL* B13 ....161 G4
Chessetts Wood Rd
HOCK/TIA B94 ....199 G3
Chester Av
DUNHL/THL/PER WV6 ....22 B3
Chester Cl
CHWD/FDBR/MGN B37 ....132 A2
WLNHL WV13 ....40 B3
Chesterfield Cl *NFLD/LBR* B31 ....175 H3
Chesterfield Ct *ALDR* WS9 * 19 F3
Chester Gdns *SCFLD/BOLD* B73 ....76 C2
Chestergate *ERDE/BCHGN* B24 ....93 H2
Chester Pl *WSLW* WS2 ....41 F4
Chester Ri *LGLYGN/QTN* B68 ....123 G4
Chester Rd *ALDR* WS9 ....31 E1
BRWNH WS8 ....19 H2
CBROM B36 ....112 C1
CDYHTH B64 ....120 C4
CHWD/FDBR/MGN B37 ....114 B5
CSHL/WTROR B46 ....133 E3
CVALE B35 ....94 B3
FOAKS/STRLY B74 ....45 F3
HHTH/SAND B71 ....71 F2
RCOVN/BALC/EX CV7 ....150 D3
SCFLD/BOLD B73 ....76 B2
Chester Rd North *BRWNH* WS8 ....8 D3
FOAKS/STRLY B74 ....60 C2
Chester St *AST/WIT* B6 ....109 G3
DUNHL/THL/PER WV6 ....36 D1
Chesterton Av *BHTH/HG* B12 ....144 D2
Chesterton Cl *SOLH* B91 ....164 A5
Chesterton Rd *BHTH/HG* B12 ....144 C2
WOLVN WV10 ....24 A2
Chesterwood *ALDR* WS9 ....45 E3
HLYWD B47 ....192 C2
Chesterwood Gdns
BFLD/HDSWWD B20 ....90 D4
Chesterwood Rd *MOS/BIL* B13 ..161 F4
Chestnut Av *DUDN* DY1 ....84 C3
TPTN/OCK DY4 ....69 F4
Chestnut Cl *CDSL* WV8 ....10 B5
FOAKS/STRLY B74 ....45 G3
HIA/OLT B92 ....163 H2
STRBR DY8 ....134 C5
Chestnut Ct *CBROM* B36 ....113 G2
Chestnut Dr *CBROM* B36 ....112 C1
ERDE/BCHGN B24 ....93 G2
RBRY B45 ....188 C4
RUSH/SHEL WS4 ....28 D2
WMBN WV5 ....81 E1
Chestnut Gv *CSHL/WTROR* B46 ..115 G2
HRBN B17 ....142 B2
KGSWFD DY6 ....100 B3
Chestnut Pl *BLOX/PEL* WS3 ....27 H4
Chestnut Rd *BLOX/PEL* WS3 ....28 A4
DARL/WED WS10 ....71 E1
LGLYGN/QTN B68 ....123 G5
MOS/BIL B13 ....144 C3
Chestnuts Av
LGN/SDN/BHAMAIR B26 ....130 D5
Chestnut Wy *BDMR/CCFT* WV3 ....35 H5
Chestom Rd *BILS/COS* WV14 ....53 F3
Cheston Rd *VAUX/NECH* B7 ....109 G3
Cheswell Cl
DUNHL/THL/PER WV6 ....35 F3
Cheswick Cl *WLNHL* WV13 ....39 F5
Cheswick Wy *SHLY* B90 ....194 D5
Cheswood Dr *WALM/CURD* B76 ..78 D5
Chetland Cft *HIA/OLT* B92 ....165 H3
Chettle Rd *BILS/COS* WV14 ....54 B5
Chetton Gn *WOLVN* WV10 ....12 B4
Chetwood Cl
DUNHL/THL/PER WV6 ....22 C5
Chetwynd Cl *WSLW* WS2 ....40 A2
Chetwynd Rd *BKHL/PFLD* WV2 ....51 H2
WASH/WDE B8 ....111 F4
Cheveley Av *RBRY* B45 ....188 B1
Chevening Cl *SEDG* DY3 ....67 G4
Cheveridge Cl *SOLH* B91 ....181 G4
Cheverton Rd *NFLD/LBR* B31 ....175 E2
Cheviot Rd *BKHL/PFLD* WV2 ....52 D1
STRBR DY8 ....135 G1
Cheviot Wy *HALE* B63 ....137 H4
Cheylesmore Cl
SCFLD/BOLD B73 ....62 B4
Cheyne Gdns *HLGN/YWD* B28 ....179 G2
Cheyne Wk *BRLYHL* DY5 ....119 E5
Cheyney Cl
DUNHL/THL/PER WV6 ....22 C5
Chichester Av *DUDS* DY2 ....102 D4
Chichester Ct
SCFLD/BOLD B73 * 62 B3
Chichester Dr *RIDG/WDGT* B32 ..140 A2
Chichester Gv
CHWD/FDBR/MGN B37 ....132 B3
Chigwell Cl *CVALE* B35 ....94 C3
Chilcote Cl *HLGN/YWD* B28 ....179 H1
Childs Av *BILS/COS* WV14 ....68 A1
Chilgrove Gdns
DUNHL/THL/PER WV6 ....21 G5
Chilham Dr
CHWD/FDBR/MGN B37 ....132 C2
Chillinghome Rd *CBROM* B36 ....111 H1
Chillington Dr *CDSL* WV8 ....10 B3
DUDN DY1 ....83 H3
Chillington Flds *WOLV* WV1 ....38 A4
Chillington Pl *BILS/COS* WV14 ....53 G3
Chillington Rd *TPTN/OCK* DY4 ....70 A2
Chillington St *WOLV* WV1 ....37 H5
Chiltern Cl *HALE* B63 ....137 G5
SEDG DY3 ....83 F3
Chiltern Dr *WLNHL* WV13 ....38 D4
Chiltern Rd *STRBR* DY8 ....135 H1
Chilton Rd *ALE/KHTH/YWD* B14 ..179 F1
Chilwell Cl *SOLH* B91 ....181 H4
Chilwell Cft *LOZ/NWT* B19 ....109 E3
Chilworth Av *WNSFLD* WV11 ....25 F3
Chilworth Cl *AST/WIT* B6 ....109 F3
Chimes Cl *STETCH* B33 ....131 G3
Chimney Rd *TPTN/OCK* DY4 ....70 B4
Chingford Cl *STRBR* DY8 ....99 G5
Chingford Rd *KGSTG* B44 ....75 G3
Chinley Gv *KGSTG* B44 ....76 A2
Chinn Brook Rd *MOS/BIL* B13 ....161 H5
Chip Cl *HWK/WKHTH* B38 ....176 B3
Chipperfield Rd *CBROM* B36 ....112 A1
Chipstead Rd *ERDW/GRVHL* B23 ..76 B4
Chipstone Cl *SOLH* B91 ....182 A5
Chirbury Gv *NFLD/LBR* B31 ....175 H4
Chirton Gv
ALE/KHTH/YWD B14 ....160 D4
Chiseldon Cft
ALE/KHTH/YWD B14 ....178 C2
Chisholm Gv *ACGN* B27 ....163 G2
Chiswell Rd *WSNGN* B18 ....107 G5
Chivington Cl *SHLY* B90 ....195 H2
Chorley Av *BKDE/SHDE* B34 ....112 B2
Chorley Gdns *BILS/COS* WV14 ....53 F3
Christchurch Cl *EDG* B15 ....125 G4
Christ Church Gv *WSL* WS1 ....57 G1
Christine Cl *DARL/WED* WS10 ....70 A1
Christopher Rd *BKHL/PFLD* WV2 ..37 G5
RMSLY B62 ....139 G4
SLYOAK B29 ....142 A5
Chubb St *WOLV* WV1 ....7 H3
Chuckery Rd *WSL* WS1 ....5 H4
Chudleigh Gv *GTB/HAM* B43 ....73 F3
Chudleigh Rd *ERDW/GRVHL* B23 ..92 C2
Church Av
BFLD/HDSWWD B20 * 90 C5
HAG/WOL DY9 ....170 C3
MOS/BIL B13 * 144 B4
STRBR DY8 ....118 C5
Churchbridge *OLDBY* B69 ....104 D3
Church Cl
CHWD/FDBR/MGN B37 ....114 A3
HLYWD B47 ....192 B5
Church Cft *HALE* B63 ....138 C3
HRBN B17 ....141 H3
Church Cross Vw *BRLYHL* DY5 ....101 F1
Churchdale Rd *KGSTG* B44 ....59 H5
Church Dr *BVILLE* B30 ....160 B3
Churchfield Av *TPTN/OCK* DY4 ....69 F3
Churchfield Cl *VAUX/NECH* B7 ....110 A3
Churchfield Rd *WOLVN* WV10 ....22 D2
Churchfields Rd
DARL/WED WS10 ....55 H5
Churchfield St *DUDS* DY2 ....102 C1
Church Gdns *SMTHWKW* B67 * ..124 C1
WOLVN WV10 ....38 A1
Church Gn *BFLD/HDSWWD* B20 ....89 H4
BILS/COS WV14 ....38 C5
Church Gv
BFLD/HDSWWD B20 * 90 B5
MOS/BIL B13 ....162 A5
Church Hl *BRLYHL* DY5 ....119 F2
CDSL WV8 ....10 B2
CSHL/WTROR B46 ....115 G2
DARL/WED WS10 ....55 H5
ETTPK/GDPK/PENN WV4 ....51 E4
HAG/WOL DY9 ....184 B2
NFLD/LBR B31 ....175 G2
RIDG/WDGT B32 ....157 E5
WSL WS1 ....5 F4
Church Hill Cl *SOLH* B91 ....182 A3
Church Hill Rd
BFLD/HDSWWD B20 ....90 B5
DUNHL/THL/PER WV6 ....21 H4
SOLH B91 ....182 A3
Church Hill St *SMTHWKW* B67 ....106 B3
Churchill Cl *OLDBY* B69 ....86 A4
Churchill Dr
BLKHTH/ROWR B65 ....121 H2
STRBR DY8 ....118 C5
Churchill Gdns *SEDG* DY3 ....67 E4
Churchill La *KIDD* DY10 ....168 B3
Churchill Pl *STETCH* B33 ....130 D3
Churchill Rd *BORD* B9 ....128 D2
HALE B63 ....138 B5
MGN/WHC B75 ....63 G3
SCFLD/BOLD B73 ....76 A1
WSLW WS2 ....40 C2
Church La *AST/WIT* B6 ....109 G1
BFLD/HDSWWD B20 ....89 H4
BKHL/PFLD WV2 ....6 E6
CDSL WV8 ....10 B3
HALE B63 ....138 D3
HHTH/SAND B71 ....87 F1
HIA/OLT B92 ....166 D1
STETCH B33 ....130 B1
WALM/CURD B76 ....79 H2
Church Moat Wy
BLOX/PEL WS3 ....27 F2
Churchover Cl *WALM/CURD* B76 ..77 H5
Church Pl *BLOX/PEL* WS3 ....27 H2
Church Rd *AST/WIT* B6 ....109 G1
BDMR/CCFT WV3 ....51 E1
BILS/COS WV14 ....68 D2
BLKHTH/ROWR B65 ....122 A1
BLOX/PEL WS3 ....18 A4
BRWNH WS8 ....9 F5
CDSL WV8 ....10 B3
DUDS DY2 ....102 B4
DUNHL/THL/PER WV6 ....22 A5
DUNHL/THL/PER WV6 ....34 C1
DUNHL/THL/PER WV6 ....35 F2
EDG B15 ....126 A5
ERDE/BCHGN B24 ....93 E2
HAG/WOL DY9 ....136 C2
HAG/WOL DY9 ....184 B1
HALE B63 ....120 C5
LGN/SDN/BHAMAIR B26 ....130 A4
LGN/SDN/BHAMAIR B26 ....146 D1
LGN/SDN/BHAMAIR B26 ....148 A2
MOS/BIL B13 ....144 C4
NFLD/LBR B31 ....175 G2
PBAR/PBCH B42 ....90 D1
SCFLD/BOLD B73 ....62 B5
SCFLD/BOLD B73 ....76 D3
SEDG DY3 ....80 C4
SHHTH WV12 ....26 B4
SHLY B90 ....180 B3
SMTHWKW B67 ....106 B5
STETCH B33 ....130 B2
STRBR DY8 ....117 H2
STRBR DY8 ....135 H4
WMBN WV5 ....65 F4
WOLVN WV10 ....23 E1
YDLY B25 ....130 A4
Churchside Vw *ALDR* WS9 ....19 H5
Church Sq *OLDBY* B69 ....105 E2
Church St *BILS/COS* WV14 ....53 H3
BKHL/PFLD WV2 ....6 E6
BLOX/PEL WS3 ....27 G2
BRLYHL DY5 ....101 F2
BRLYHL DY5 ....119 E2
BRLYHL DY5 ....119 H3
BRWNH WS8 ....19 E2
CBHAMNW B3 ....3 F4
CDYHTH B64 ....121 E3
DARL/WED WS10 ....54 D4
DARL/WED WS10 ....55 F2
DUDS DY2 ....102 C1
HAG/WOL DY9 ....152 C5
LOZ/NWT B19 ....108 C2
OLDBY B69 ....105 E1
RMSLY B62 ....122 B3
SEDG DY3 ....83 F3
STRBR DY8 ....135 G2
TPTN/OCK DY4 ....85 G4
WBROM B70 ....87 G2
WLNHL WV13 ....39 H3
WOLVN WV10 ....38 A1
WSL WS1 ....5 F5
Church Ter *MGN/WHC* B75 * 47 G2
STETCH B33 * 130 A3
Church V *BFLD/HDSWWD* B20 ....90 B5
HHTH/SAND B71 ....71 H5
Church Vw *ALDR* WS9 ....19 F4
SPARK B11 ....145 E1
Church View Cl *BLOX/PEL* WS3 ....27 G2
Church View Dr *CDYHTH* B64 ....121 F3
Church Vls *HDSW* B21 * 89 G4
Church Wk *BDMR/CCFT* WV3 ....51 F1
DUNHL/THL/PER WV6 ....22 A5
WASH/WDE B8 ....111 E3
Churchward Cl *STRBR* DY8 ....135 H1
Churchward Gv *WMBN* WV5 ....65 E3
Church Wy *RUSH/SHEL* WS4 ....18 B5
Churchyard Rd *TPTN/OCK* DY4 ....85 H1
Churnet Gv
DUNHL/THL/PER WV6 ....34 D1
Churn Hill Rd *ALDR* WS9 ....44 A1
Churns Hill La *SEDG* DY3 ....81 F3
Churston Cl *BLOX/PEL* WS3 ....16 C4
Cider Av *BRLYHL* DY5 ....119 G4
Cinder Bank *DUDS* DY2 ....102 C3
Cinder Rd *SEDG* DY3 ....82 D5
Cinder Wy *DARL/WED* WS10 ....55 G5
Cinquefoil Leasow
TPTN/OCK DY4 ....70 A5
Circuit Cl *WLNHL* WV13 ....39 H2
Circular Rd *ACGN* B27 ....163 G1
Circus Av
CHWD/FDBR/MGN B37 ....132 C2
City Plaza *CBHAM* B2 * 3 G5
City Rd *LDYWD/EDGR* B16 ....125 E2
OLDBY B69 ....103 H2
City Vw *WASH/WDE* B8 ....110 B5
Civic Cl *CBHAMW* B1 ....2 C5
Claerwen Gv *NFLD/LBR* B31 ....158 A5
Claines Rd *HALE* B63 ....137 H2
NFLD/LBR B31 ....176 A1
Clandon Cl
ALE/KHTH/YWD B14 ....177 F3
Clanfield Av *WNSFLD* WV11 ....25 F2
Clapgate Gdns
ETTPK/GDPK/PENN WV4 ....53 E5
Clap Gate Gv *WMBN* WV5 ....64 C5
Clapgate La *RIDG/WDGT* B32 ....140 C5
Clap Gate Rd *WMBN* WV5 ....64 C4
Clapton Gv *KGSTG* B44 ....75 H2
Clare Av *WNSFLD* WV11 ....25 F1
Clare Crs
ETTPK/GDPK/PENN WV4 ....67 H1
Clare Dr *EDG* B15 ....125 H4
Clarel Av *WASH/WDE* B8 ....128 A1
Claremont Ms *BDMR/CCFT* WV3 ..51 G1
Claremont Pl *WSNGN* B18 * 108 A4

Claremont Rd BDMR/CCFT WV3 ..51 G1
SEDG DY3 ....67 G3
SMTHWK B66 ....106 D5
SPARK B11 ....127 H5
WSNGN B18 ....108 A3
Claremont St BILS/COS WV14 ....53 G2
CDYHTH B64 ....121 E3
Claremont Wy HALE B63 ....138 C4
Clarence Av HDSW B21 * 107 E1
Clarence Gdns
FOAKS/STRLY B74 ....46 D3
Clarence Rd BILS/COS WV14 ....54 A1
DUDS DY2 ....102 D3
ERDW/GRVHL B23 ....92 B3
FOAKS/STRLY B74 ....32 C5
HDSW B21 ....107 E1
HRBN B17 ....142 B1
MOS/BIL B13 ....161 G2
SPARK B11 ....145 E3
WOLV WV1 ....6 E3
Clarence St SEDG DY3 ....83 G1
WOLV WV1 ....6 E4
Clarenden Pl HRBN B17 ....142 A2
Clarendon Dr TPTN/OCK DY4 ....70 B3
Clarendon Pl BLOX/PEL WS3 ....17 H3
RMSLY B62 ....139 H1
Clarendon Rd
LDYWD/EDGR B16 ....125 G3
MGN/WHC B75 ....47 G2
RUSH/SHEL WS4 ....18 C5
SMTHWKW B67 ....106 B5
Clarendon St BDMR/CCFT WV3 ....6 B4
BLOX/PEL WS3 ....27 F1
Clare Rd BLOX/PEL WS3 ....28 B4
WOLVN WV10 ....23 G3
Clarewell Av SOLH B91 ....181 G4
Clarkes Gv TPTN/OCK DY4 ....70 A5
Clarke's La HHTH/SAND B71 ....71 G4
WLNHL WV13 ....40 A3
Clark Rd BDMR/CCFT WV3 ....36 B3
Clarkson Rd DARL/WED WS10 ....56 A5
Clark St LDYWD/EDGR B16 ....125 H2
STRBR DY8 ....135 E2
Clarry Dr FOAKS/STRLY B74 ....46 D5
Clary Gv DSYBK/YTR WS5 ....57 G5
Clatterbach La HAG/WOL DY9 ....171 E1
Claughton Rd DUDS DY2 ....84 D5
Claughton Rd North DUDS DY2 ..84 D5
Clausen Cl GTB/HAM B43 ....60 A4
Clavedon Cl NFLD/LBR B31 ....158 A3
Claverdon Cl BRWNH WS8 ....9 G4
SOLH B91 ....181 E1
Claverdon Dr FOAKS/STRLY B74 ..45 H1
GTB/HAM B43 ....73 F3
Claverdon Gdns ACGN B27 ....146 B2
Claverley Dr
ETTPK/GDPK/PENN WV4 ....50 D3
Claybrook St DIG/EDG B5 ....127 E3
Claycroft Ter DUDN DY1 ....68 B5
Claydon Gv
ALE/KHTH/YWD B14 ....178 C2
Claydon Rd KGSWFD DY6 ....81 G5
Clay Dr RIDG/WDGT B32 ....140 A2
Clayhanger La BRWNH WS8 ....18 D1
Clayhanger Rd BRWNH WS8 ....19 F1
Clay La
LGN/SDN/BHAMAIR B26 ....147 E3
OLDBY B69 ....105 E5
Claypit Cl WBROM B70 ....87 E3
Clay Pit La SHLY B90 ....194 A3
Claypit La WBROM B70 ....87 E3
Clayton Cl BKHL/PFLD WV2 ....52 A1
Clayton Dr CBROM B36 ....113 E1
Clayton Rd BILS/COS WV14 ....68 B4
WASH/WDE B8 ....110 B4
Clear Vw KGSWFD DY6 ....99 F3
Clearwell Gdns DUDN DY1 ....83 H3
Clee Hill Dr BDMR/CCFT WV3 ....34 D4
Clee Hill Rd SEDG DY3 ....83 E2
Clee Rd DUDS DY2 ....102 A2
LGLYGN/QTN B68 ....105 G5
NFLD/LBR B31 ....175 G5
STRBR DY8 ....135 G1
Cleeve Dr FOAKS/STRLY B74 ....32 D4
Cleeve Rd ALE/KHTH/YWD B14 ..179 E1
BLOX/PEL WS3 ....16 B4
Cleeve Wy BLOX/PEL WS3 ....16 B5
Clee View Meadow SEDG DY3 ....67 F1
Clee View Rd WMBN WV5 ....80 C1
Clematis Dr COVEN WV9 ....11 H4
Clement Pl BILS/COS WV14 * 53 H1
Clement Rd BILS/COS WV14 ....53 H1
RMSLY B62 ....122 B3
Clements Cl OLDBY B69 ....104 D5
Clements Rd YDLY B25 ....129 H4
Clement St CBHAMW B1 ....2 B4
WSLW WS2 ....4 B5
Clemson St WLNHL WV13 ....39 G3
Clent Dr HAG/WOL DY9 ....153 E4
Clent Hill Dr
BLKHTH/ROWR B65 ....103 G4
Clent Rd HDSW B21 ....89 F5
LGLYGN/QTN B68 ....105 G5
RBRY B45 ....173 G5
STRBR DY8 ....135 G1
Clent View Rd HALE B63 ....137 G3
RIDG/WDGT B32 ....157 E1
STRBR DY8 ....134 C5
Clent Vls BHTH/HG B12 * 144 D3
Clent Wy RIDG/WDGT B32 ....156 D2
Cleobury La HOCK/TIA B94 ....194 A5
Cleton St TPTN/OCK DY4 ....85 H3
Clevedon Av CBROM B36 ....95 G5
Clevedon Rd BHTH/HG B12 ....144 A1
Cleveland Cl WLNHL WV13 ....38 D4
WNSFLD WV11 ....25 F1
Cleveland Pas BKHL/PFLD WV2 ....7 G5
Cleveland Rd BKHL/PFLD WV2 ....7 H6
Cleveland St BKHL/PFLD WV2 ....7 F5
DUDN DY1 ....84 B5
STRBR DY8 ....135 E3
Cleves Dr RBRY B45 ....187 G1
Cleves Rd RBRY B45 ....173 G5
Clewley Dr COVEN WV9 ....12 A4
Clewley Gv RIDG/WDGT B32 ....140 B2
Clews Cl WSL WS1 ....57 E1
Clewshaw La
HWK/WKHTH B38 ....191 F4
Cley Cl DIG/EDG B5 ....143 H1
Cliffe Dr STETCH B33 ....130 D1
Clifford Rd DOR/KN B93 ....196 D4
SMTHWKW B67 ....124 B3
WBROM B70 ....87 E4
Clifford St DUDN DY1 ....102 B1
DUNHL/THL/PER WV6 ....6 A1
LOZ/NWT B19 ....108 D2
Clifford Wk LOZ/NWT B19 ....108 D2
Cliff Rock Rd RBRY B45 ....188 B1
Clift Av SHHTH WV12 ....26 B3
Clift Cl SHHTH WV12 ....26 A4
Clifton Av ALDR WS9 ....30 C2
BRWNH WS8 ....18 D1
Clifton Cl AST/WIT B6 ....109 F2
OLDBY B69 ....104 D5
Clifton Crs SHLY B90 ....181 F4
Clifton Gdns CDSL WV8 ....11 E4
Clifton Gn HLGN/YWD B28 ....163 E5
Clifton La HHTH/SAND B71 ....72 A3
Clifton Rd AST/WIT B6 ....109 F2
BHTH/HG B12 ....144 C2
CBROM B36 ....113 G1
DUNHL/THL/PER WV6 ....21 H5
RMSLY B62 ....122 B4
SCFLD/BOLD B73 ....62 A4
SMTHWKW B67 ....106 B5
Clifton St BDMR/CCFT WV3 ....6 C4
BILS/COS WV14 ....67 H2
CDYHTH B64 ....121 F3
STRBR DY8 ....135 F3
Clifton Ter ERDW/GRVHL B23 * ...92 D2
Clinic Dr HAG/WOL DY9 ....136 C2
Clinton Gv SHLY B90 ....180 D4
Clinton Rd BILS/COS WV14 ....54 C1
CSHL/WTROR B46 ....115 F3
SHLY B90 ....181 E5
Clinton St WSNGN B18 ....107 G4
Clipper Vw LDYWD/EDGR B16 ....125 G3
Clipston Rd WASH/WDE B8 ....110 D4
Clissold Cl BHTH/HG B12 ....127 E5
Clissold Pas WSNGN B18 ....108 A5
Clissold St WSNGN B18 ....108 A5
Clive Cl MGN/WHC B75 ....47 H3
Cliveden Av ALDR WS9 ....30 B1
PBAR/PBCH B42 ....90 C2
Cliveden Coppice
FOAKS/STRLY B74 ....46 D4
Clivedon Wy CDYHTH B64 ....121 G5
Cliveland St CBHAMNE B4 ....3 G1
Clive Rd RIDG/WDGT B32 ....123 H5
Clive St HHTH/SAND B71 ....87 G1
Clockfields Dr STRBR DY8 ....118 C3
Clock La HIA/OLT B92 ....149 H5
Clockmill Av BLOX/PEL WS3 ....17 G4
Clockmill Pl BLOX/PEL WS3 ....17 H4
Clockmill Rd BLOX/PEL WS3 ....17 G4
Clodeshall Rd WASH/WDE B8 ....110 C5
Cloister Dr RMSLY B62 ....139 F4
The Cloisters RUSH/SHEL WS4 ....5 F1
Clonmel Rd BVILLE B30 ....160 A4
Clopton Crs
CHWD/FDBR/MGN B37 ....114 C5
Clopton Rd STETCH B33 ....131 E4
The Close DARL/WED WS10 ....55 G5
HALE B63 ....137 H1
HIA/OLT B92 ....164 B2
HLYWD B47 ....192 C3
HRBN B17 ....124 B5
RMSLY B62 ....155 G3
SEDG DY3 ....80 C4
SEDG DY3 ....83 E2
SLYOAK B29 * 159 F2
Clothier Gdns WLNHL WV13 ....39 G2
Clothier St WLNHL WV13 ....39 G2
Cloudbridge Dr HIA/OLT B92 ....165 H3
Cloudsley Gv HIA/OLT B92 ....147 F4
Clover Av
CHWD/FDBR/MGN B37 ....132 D2
Cloverdale
DUNHL/THL/PER WV6 ....34 B1
Clover Dr RIDG/WDGT B32 ....140 C5
Clover Hl DSYBK/YTR WS5 ....43 G5
Clover La KGSWFD DY6 ....99 E2
Clover Lea Sq WASH/WDE B8 ....111 E3
Clover Ley WOLVN WV10 ....37 H2
Clover Piece TPTN/OCK DY4 ....70 A5
Clover Rd SLYOAK B29 ....158 C3
Club La WOLVN WV10 ....12 C1
Club Rw SEDG DY3 ....83 G1
Club Vw HWK/WKHTH B38 ....176 B3
Clunbury Cft BKDE/SHDE B34 ....112 D4
Clunbury Rd NFLD/LBR B31 ....175 G5
Clun Cl DUDS DY2 ....85 F5
Clun Rd NFLD/LBR B31 ....158 B4
Clyde Av RMSLY B62 ....122 C4
Clyde Ms BRLYHL DY5 ....100 D3
Clyde Rd DOR/KN B93 ....199 E1
Clydesdale
LGN/SDN/BHAMAIR B26 ....147 G2
Clydesdale Rd RIDG/WDGT B32 ..140 B1
Clyde St BHTH/HG B12 ....127 G3
CDYHTH B64 ....121 E3
Coalbourne Gdns HALE B63 ....137 G2
Coalbourn La STRBR DY8 ....118 B5
Coalheath La RUSH/SHEL WS4 ....29 E2
Coal Pool La BLOX/PEL WS3 ....28 B3
Coalport Rd WOLV WV1 ....38 A4
Coalway Av BDMR/CCFT WV3 ....51 G2
LGN/SDN/BHAMAIR B26 ....148 A3
Coalway Gdns BDMR/CCFT WV3 ..50 D2
Coalway Rd BDMR/CCFT WV3 ....50 D2
BLOX/PEL WS3 ....27 E2
The Cobbles CSCFLD/WYGN B72 ..77 G4
Cobble Wk WSNGN B18 * 108 A4
Cobden Cl DARL/WED WS10 ....55 H2
TPTN/OCK DY4 ....69 F3
Cobden Gdns BHTH/HG B12 ....144 A2
Cobden St DARL/WED WS10 ....55 H2
STRBR DY8 ....134 D1
WSL WS1 ....56 D1
Cobham Cl CVALE B35 ....94 B3
Cobham Court Ms
HAG/WOL DY9 ....153 F4
Cobham Rd BORD B9 ....128 B2
DARL/WED WS10 ....72 A1
HALE B63 ....138 D3
STRBR DY8 ....135 G5
Cob La NFLD/LBR B31 ....159 E3
Cobs Fld BVILLE B30 ....159 E4
Coburg Cft TPTN/OCK DY4 ....70 A5
Coburn Dr MGN/WHC B75 ....47 H3
Cochrane Cl HAG/WOL DY9 ....153 E2
TPTN/OCK DY4 * 70 A5
Cochrane Rd BRLYHL DY5 ....101 H4
Cock Hill La RBRY B45 ....173 H5
Cocksheds La RMSLY B62 ....122 A4
Cockshut Hl
LGN/SDN/BHAMAIR B26 ....130 C4
Cockshutt La BKHL/PFLD WV2 * ..52 B1
Cockshutts La BKHL/PFLD WV2 ....52 B1
Cocksmead Cft
ALE/KHTH/YWD B14 ....160 D5
Cockthorpe Cl HRBN B17 ....124 B5
Cocton Cl DUNHL/THL/PER WV6 ..20 C5
Codsall Gdns CDSL WV8 ....10 A3
Codsall Rd CDSL WV8 ....21 G1
CDYHTH B64 ....121 E4
DUNHL/THL/PER WV6 ....22 A3
Cofield Rd SCFLD/BOLD B73 ....76 D2
Cofton Ct RBRY B45 ....188 D1
Cofton Gv NFLD/LBR B31 ....189 E2
Cofton Lake Rd RBRY B45 ....188 C5
Cofton Rd NFLD/LBR B31 ....189 H1
Cokeland Pl CDYHTH B64 ....120 D4
Colaton Cl WOLVN WV10 ....37 G1
Colbourne Rd TPTN/OCK DY4 ....85 G2
Colbrand Gv EDG B15 ....126 D4
Coldbath Rd MOS/BIL B13 ....161 H2
Coldridge Cl COVEN WV9 ....22 B1
Coldstream Dr STRBR DY8 ....118 A1
Coldstream Rd
WALM/CURD B76 ....78 A3
Cole Bank Rd HLGN/YWD B28 ....162 C2
Colebourne Rd MOS/BIL B13 ....162 B4
Colebridge Crs
CSHL/WTROR B46 ....115 F1
Colebrook Cft SHLY B90 ....179 H3
Colebrook Rd SHLY B90 ....179 G3
SPARK B11 ....145 F2
Cole Ct CHWD/FDBR/MGN B37 ..132 B2
Coleford Cl STRBR DY8 ....117 G2
Coleford Dr
CHWD/FDBR/MGN B37 ....132 A2
Cole Gn SHLY B90 ....179 G3
Cole Hall La BKDE/SHDE B34 ....112 C3
Colehurst Cft SHLY B90 ....195 F2
Coleman Rd DARL/WED WS10 ....56 A3
Coleman St
DUNHL/THL/PER WV6 ....36 C1
Colemeadow Rd
CSHL/WTROR B46 ....115 F2
MOS/BIL B13 ....161 H5
Colenso Rd SMTHWK B66 ....107 E5
Coleraine Rd PBAR/PBCH B42 ....74 A5
Coleridge Cl BLOX/PEL WS3 * 18 A2
SHHTH WV12 ....26 C3
Coleridge Dr
DUNHL/THL/PER WV6 ....34 C1
Coleridge Pas CBHAMNE B4 ....3 H3
Coleridge Ri SEDG DY3 ....82 C2
Coleridge Rd GTB/HAM B43 ....73 G4
Colesbourne Av
ALE/KHTH/YWD B14 ....177 G3
Colesbourne Rd HIA/OLT B92 ....147 H4
Coleshill Heath Rd
CHWD/FDBR/MGN B37 ....149 G1
Coleshill Rd BKDE/SHDE B34 ....112 B2
CHWD/FDBR/MGN B37 ....132 A5
CSHL/WTROR B46 ....96 C4
MGN/WHC B75 ....62 D3
WALM/CURD B76 ....96 B1
Coleshill St CBHAMNE B4 ....3 J3
MGN/WHC B75 ....62 C3
Coleside Av MOS/BIL B13 ....162 B3
Coles La CSCFLD/WYGN B72 ....62 C5
HHTH/SAND B71 ....71 E4
The Colesleys
CSHL/WTROR B46 ....115 G3
Cole St DUDS DY2 ....103 E5
Cole Valley Rd HLGN/YWD B28 ..162 B4
Coleview Crs STETCH B33 ....131 G1
Coleville Rd WALM/CURD B76 ....78 D5
Coleys La NFLD/LBR B31 ....175 G3
Colgreave Av MOS/BIL B13 ....145 F5
Colindale Rd KGSTG B44 ....60 C5
Colleen Av BVILLE B30 ....177 F2
College Cl DARL/WED WS10 ....71 E1
College Dr BFLD/HDSWWD B20 ....89 H4
College Farm Dr
ERDW/GRVHL B23 ....76 B3
College Gv
BFLD/HDSWWD B20 * 108 B2
College Hl SCFLD/BOLD B73 ....62 B4
College Rd BFLD/HDSWWD B20 ..89 G4
DUNHL/THL/PER WV6 ....35 H1
KGSTG B44 ....91 E1
MOS/BIL B13 ....145 E5
RMSLY B62 ....140 A1
SCFLD/BOLD B73 ....76 B2
STRBR DY8 ....135 G3
WASH/WDE B8 ....128 C1
College St WSNGN B18 ....108 A5
College Vw
DUNHL/THL/PER WV6 ....35 H2
Collet Rd CDSL WV8 ....20 C5
Collets Brook MGN/WHC B75 ....48 C3
Collett Cl STRBR DY8 ....135 G1
Colletts Gv
CHWD/FDBR/MGN B37 ....113 H5
Colley Av WOLVN WV10 ....23 H2
Colley Ga HALE B63 ....137 G1
Colley La HALE B63 ....137 G1
Colley Orch HALE B63 ....137 G1
Colley St WBROM B70 ....87 H2
Collier Cl BRWNH WS8 ....8 C5
Colliers Cl SHHTH WV12 ....25 H4
Colliery Dr BLOX/PEL WS3 ....16 B4
Colliery Rd HHTH/SAND B71 ....88 C5
WOLV WV1 ....37 H3
Collindale Ct KGSWFD DY6 ....81 H5
Collingbourne Av CBROM B36 ..111 H2
Collingdon Av
LGN/SDN/BHAMAIR B26 ....148 A1
Colling Wk
CHWD/FDBR/MGN B37 ....114 A4
Collingwood Dr GTB/HAM B43 ....59 H5
Collingwood Rd WOLVN WV10 ....13 E5
Collins Cl RIDG/WDGT B32 ....140 A2
Collins Rd BRWNH WS8 ....19 G2
DARL/WED WS10 ....56 B5
Collins St WBROM B70 ....86 C3
WSL WS1 ....57 E1
Collis St STRBR DY8 ....118 C4
Collister Cl SHLY B90 ....163 F5
Collumbine Cl DSYBK/YTR WS5 ....57 F5
Colly Cft
CHWD/FDBR/MGN B37 ....113 G4
Collycroft Pl ACGN B27 ....146 B2
Colman Av WNSFLD WV11 ....25 F4
Colman Crs LGLYGN/QTN B68 ....123 G2
Colman Hl HALE B63 ....137 H2
Colman Hill Av HALE B63 ....137 H1
Colmore Av
ALE/KHTH/YWD B14 ....160 D3
Colmore Circus Queensway
CBHAMNE B4 ....3 G3
Colmore Crs MOS/BIL B13 ....161 H1
Colmore Dr MGN/WHC B75 ....63 G3
Colmore Flats LOZ/NWT B19 * 3 F1
Colmore Rd
ALE/KHTH/YWD B14 ....160 D3
Colmore Rw CBHAMNW B3 ....3 F4
Coln Cl NFLD/LBR B31 ....158 B4
Colonial Rd BORD B9 ....128 D2
Colshaw Rd STRBR DY8 ....135 E3
Colston Rd ERDE/BCHGN B24 ....93 F3
Colt Cl FOAKS/STRLY B74 ....60 A1
Coltham Rd SHHTH WV12 ....26 B4
Coltishall Cft CVALE B35 ....94 B4
Coltsfoot Cl WNSFLD WV11 ....25 E5
Columbia Cl DIG/EDG B5 ....143 H1
Colville Cl TPTN/OCK DY4 ....70 B3
Colville Rd BHTH/HG B12 ....144 D2
Colville Wk BHTH/HG B12 ....144 D2
Colwall Rd SEDG DY3 ....83 F2
Colwall Wk ACGN B27 ....146 D3
Colworth Rd NFLD/LBR B31 ....175 E1
Colyns Gv STETCH B33 ....112 B4
Comber Cft MOS/BIL B13 ....162 B2
Comber Dr BRLYHL DY5 ....100 D3
Comberford Ct
DARL/WED WS10 * 56 A5
Comberford Dr
DARL/WED WS10 ....56 D4
Comberton Rd
LGN/SDN/BHAMAIR B26 ....130 D5
Combine Cl MGN/WHC B75 ....47 H2
Comet Rd
LGN/SDN/BHAMAIR B26 ....149 G3
Commercial Rd WOLV WV1 ....7 K5
WSLW WS2 ....27 E3
Commercial St CBHAMW B1 ....2 D7
Commonfield Cft
WASH/WDE B8 ....110 B4
Common La
LGN/SDN/BHAMAIR B26 ....147 G2
WASH/WDE B8 ....110 D3
Common Rd WMBN WV5 ....80 D2
Commonside BLOX/PEL WS3 ....18 A5
BRLYHL DY5 ....101 E3
Common Side BRWNH WS8 ....19 G2
Communication Rw EDG B15 ....126 C3
Compton Cl SOLH B91 ....180 D1
Compton Cft
CHWD/FDBR/MGN B37 ....132 D3
Compton Dr DUDS DY2 ....103 F1
FOAKS/STRLY B74 ....60 A1
KGSWFD DY6 ....99 H4
Compton Gv HALE B63 ....137 G3
KGSWFD DY6 ....99 H4
Compton Hill Dr
BDMR/CCFT WV3 ....35 H3
Compton Rd BDMR/CCFT WV3 ....36 B3
CDYHTH B64 ....120 C3
ERDE/BCHGN B24 ....92 C5
HAG/WOL DY9 ....153 F1
RMSLY B62 ....139 H2
Compton Rd West
BDMR/CCFT WV3 ....35 H3
Comsey Rd GTB/HAM B43 ....59 F5
Comwall Cl BLOX/PEL WS3 ....27 G3
Conchar Cl CSCFLD/WYGN B72 ....77 G1
Conchar Rd CSCFLD/WYGN B72 ....77 G1
Concorde Rd
LGN/SDN/BHAMAIR B26 ....149 G3
Condover Cl WSLW WS2 ....40 B2
Condover Rd NFLD/LBR B31 ....175 H5
Coneyford Rd BKDE/SHDE B34 ..113 E3
Coney Gn STRBR DY8 ....135 H2
Coney Green Dr NFLD/LBR B31 ..175 F5
Coneygree Rd TPTN/OCK DY4 ....85 G3
Conifer Cl BRLYHL DY5 ....119 E4
Conifer Ct MOS/BIL B13 ....144 A5
Conifer Dr HDSW B21 ....107 G2
NFLD/LBR B31 ....175 H2
Conifer Paddock RMSLY B62 ....122 C4
Conifer Rd FOAKS/STRLY B74 ....45 E5
Conington Gv HRBN B17 ....141 G2
Coniston Av HIA/OLT B92 ....147 F3
Coniston Cl HLGN/YWD B28 ....162 D3
Coniston Crs GTB/HAM B43 ....73 H4
Coniston Dr KGSWFD DY6 ....99 F2
Coniston Rd
DUNHL/THL/PER WV6 ....21 H2
ERDW/GRVHL B23 ....92 B1
FOAKS/STRLY B74 ....45 F2
Connaught Av DARL/WED WS10 ..56 C5
Connaught Cl DSYBK/YTR WS5 ....58 A1
Connaught Dr WMBN WV5 ....65 E2
Connaught Rd BILS/COS WV14 ....54 B1
WOLV WV1 ....6 B3
Connops Wy HAG/WOL DY9 ....136 C2
Connor Rd HHTH/SAND B71 ....72 A3
Conolly Dr RBRY B45 ....174 B4
Conrad Cl BHTH/HG B12 ....127 G5
Consort Crs BRLYHL DY5 ....101 E3
Consort Dr DARL/WED WS10 ....40 A5
Consort Rd BVILLE B30 ....177 E2
Constable Cl GTB/HAM B43 ....59 G5
The Constables
LGLYGN/QTN B68 ....123 F2
Constance Av WBROM B70 ....87 H5
Constance Rd DIG/EDG B5 ....143 H2
Constantine La
CSHL/WTROR B46 ....97 F5
Constantine Wy BILS/COS WV14 ..69 G1
Constitution Hl DUDS DY2 ....102 D1
LOZ/NWT B19 ....2 E1
Containerbase
PBAR/PBCH B42 * 91 F1
Convent Cl BKHL/PFLD WV2 ....7 G6
Conway Av HHTH/SAND B71 ....71 F2
LGLYGN/QTN B68 ....123 F2
RIDG/WDGT B32 ....140 B1
Conway Cl DUDN DY1 ....68 C5
KGSWFD DY6 ....100 B5
SHLY B90 ....180 D4
Conway Crs SHHTH WV12 ....26 A3
Conway Gv GTB/HAM B43 ....73 F4
Conway Rd
CHWD/FDBR/MGN B37 ....132 A1
DUNHL/THL/PER WV6 ....34 D2
SHLY B90 ....180 D4
SPARK B11 ....145 E1
Conwy Cl WSLW WS2 ....41 E1
Conybere St BHTH/HG B12 ....127 F5
Conyworth Cl ACGN B27 ....146 D3
Cook Av DUDS DY2 ....102 D2
Cook Cl DOR/KN B93 ....197 G2
DUNHL/THL/PER WV6 ....34 C1
Cookes Cft NFLD/LBR B31 ....176 A3
Cookesley Cl GTB/HAM B43 ....59 H4
Cooke St BKHL/PFLD WV2 ....52 A1
Cookley Cl HALE B63 ....138 B5
Cooknell Dr STRBR DY8 ....118 A2
Cook Rd BLOX/PEL WS3 ....17 F5
Cooksey La KGSTG B44 ....60 B4
Cooksey Rd SMHTH B10 ....127 H4
Cooks La STETCH B33 ....131 G1
Cook St DARL/WED WS10 ....55 H2
VAUX/NECH B7 ....110 A2
Coombe Cft COVEN WV9 * 12 A4
Coombe Hl CDYHTH B64 ....121 H4
Coombe Pk FOAKS/STRLY B74 ....61 H1
Coombe Rd BFLD/HDSWWD B20 ..91 E5
SHLY B90 ....180 C3
Coombes La NFLD/LBR B31 ....189 F2
Coombs Rd RMSLY B62 ....138 D1
Cooper Av BRLYHL DY5 ....118 C2
Cooper Cl WBROM B70 ....88 A4
Cooper's Bank Rd BRLYHL DY5 ....83 E5
Coopers La SMTHWK B66 ....106 C4
Coopers Rd BFLD/HDSWWD B20 ..90 A3
Cooper St WBROM B70 ....87 H3
WOLV WV1 ....37 H5
Copeley Hl AST/WIT B6 ....92 A5
Copes Crs WOLVN WV10 ....24 A4
Cope St BLOX/PEL WS3 ....27 G4
DARL/WED WS10 ....55 G2
WSNGN B18 ....126 A1
Cophall St TPTN/OCK DY4 ....86 B1
Cophams Cl HIA/OLT B92 ....148 A5
Coplow Cottages
LDYWD/EDGR B16 * 125 H1
Coplow St LDYWD/EDGR B16 ....125 H1
Coplow Ter LDYWD/EDGR B16 ..125 H1
Copnor Gv
LGN/SDN/BHAMAIR B26 ....147 E1
Coppenhall Gv STETCH B33 ....130 C1
Copperbeech Cl
RIDG/WDGT B32 ....141 F2
Copperbeech Dr
BHTH/HG B12 * 144 C2
Copper Beech Dr KGSWFD DY6 ....81 H5
WMBN WV5 ....65 F5
Copper Beech Gdns
BFLD/HDSWWD B20 ....89 H4
Coppice Av HAG/WOL DY9 ....136 D4
Coppice Cl ERDE/BCHGN B24 ....92 D3
RBRY B45 ....187 H1
SEDG DY3 ....67 E4
SHLY B90 ....194 C4
SOLH B91 * 164 C3
WNSFLD WV11 ....25 G1
Coppice Crs BRWNH WS8 ....8 D5
Coppice Dr ACGN B27 ....146 B5
Coppice Farm Wy
SHHTH WV12 ....25 H1
Coppice Hollow
RIDG/WDGT B32 ....157 F1
Coppice La ALDR WS9 ....29 H1
BRLYHL DY5 ....119 H3
BRWNH WS8 ....8 D4
DUNHL/THL/PER WV6 ....21 F4
POL/KGSB/FAZ B78 ....49 E3
SHHTH WV12 ....26 A4
Coppice Ri BRLYHL DY5 ....120 A2
Coppice Rd ALDR WS9 ....19 F3
BDMR/CCFT WV3 ....35 H5
BILS/COS WV14 ....68 A3
CDYHTH B64 ....121 E5

HIA/OLT B92 165 G3
MOS/BIL B13 144 C4
Coppice Side BRWNH WS8 8 D4
Coppice St TPTN/OCK DY4 69 E5
WBROM B70 87 E2
The Coppice
BFLD/HDSWWD B20 90 A4
NFLD/LBR B31 174 C3
SHHTH WV12 26 A4
STRBR DY8 152 B5
TPTN/OCK DY4 70 A2
Coppice View Rd
SCFLD/BOLD B73 60 C4
Coppice Wk SHLY B90 194 C4
Copplestone Cl
BKDE/SHDE B34 112 D3
Coppy Hall Gv ALDR WS9 30 B1
Copse Cl NFLD/LBR B31 175 G3
Copse Crs BLOX/PEL WS3 18 A3
Copse Rd DUDS DY2 120 B1
The Copse FOAKS/STRLY B74 46 D4
Copstone Dr DOR/KN B93 196 D5
Copston Gv SLYOAK B29 158 D2
Copthall Rd HDSW B21 89 E4
Copt Heath Cft DOR/KN B93 183 F5
Copt Heath Dr DOR/KN B93 197 E1
Copthorne Rd BDMR/CCFT WV3 51 G1
KGSTG B44 60 A5
Coralin Cl
CHWD/FDBR/MGN B37 132 B2
Corbett Crs STRBR DY8 118 C5
Corbett Rd BRLYHL DY5 119 G3
HLYWD B47 192 C1
Corbetts Cl HIA/OLT B92 167 H3
Corbett St SMTHWK B66 106 D5
Corbridge Av KGSTG B44 75 F2
Corbridge Rd SCFLD/BOLD B73 76 D1
Corbyn Rd BORD B9 129 F1
DUDN DY1 101 H1
Corbyns Cl BRLYHL DY5 100 D2
Corbyns Hall La BRLYHL DY5 100 D2
Corbyns Hall Rd BRLYHL DY5 100 D2
Cordley St WBROM B70 87 F2
Corfe Cl DUNHL/THL/PER WV6 34 D2
RIDG/WDGT B32 141 F2
Corfe Dr OLDBY B69 103 G1
Corfe Rd BILS/COS WV14 68 A3
Corfton Dr
DUNHL/THL/PER WV6 35 G2
Coriander Cl NFLD/LBR B31 174 B4
Corinne Cl RBRY B45 188 A2
Corinne Cft
CHWD/FDBR/MGN B37 114 A5
Corisande Rd SLYOAK B29 142 A5
Corley Av NFLD/LBR B31 175 H2
Corley Cl SHLY B90 179 G4
Cornbrook Rd SLYOAK B29 158 B4
Cornbury Gv SHLY B90 180 D1
Corncrake Cl CSCFLD/WYGN B72 77 H1
Corncrake Dr CBROM B36 114 A1
Corncrake Rd DUDN DY1 83 G3
Cornel Cl
CHWD/FDBR/MGN B37 132 C4
Cornerway HWK/WKHTH B38 190 D1
Cornfield CDSL WV8 11 H5
Cornfield Cl KGSWFD DY6 99 E1
Cornfield Cft
CHWD/FDBR/MGN B37 132 D1
WALM/CURD B76 63 F5
Cornfield Rd
BLKHTH/ROWR B65 103 F5
NFLD/LBR B31 175 H1
WALM/CURD B76 78 B2
Cornflower Crs DUDS DY2 103 F1
Cornflower Rd BRWNH WS8 18 D1
Corngreaves Rd CDYHTH B64 120 D4
The Corngreaves
BKDE/SHDE B34 113 E3
Corngreaves Wk CDYHTH B64 121 E5
Corn Hl DSYBK/YTR WS5 43 G5
WOLV WV1 7 H4
Cornhill Gv BVILLE B30 160 C4
Corn Mill Cl RIDG/WDGT B32 158 A1
WALM/CURD B76 78 B2
Cornmill Cl WSL WS1 56 D1
Cornmill Gv
DUNHL/THL/PER WV6 34 B2
Cornovian Cl
DUNHL/THL/PER WV6 20 C5
Corns Gv WMBN WV5 80 D1
Cornwall Av LGLYGN/QTN B68 123 F4
Cornwall Cl ALDR WS9 30 A1
DARL/WED WS10 56 D5
KGSWFD DY6 99 H1
Cornwall Ga SHHTH WV12 25 H5
Cornwallis Rd WBROM B70 87 E5
Cornwall Pl WSLW WS2 40 C2
Cornwall Rd
BFLD/HDSWWD B20 89 H4
DSYBK/YTR WS5 57 H1
DUNHL/THL/PER WV6 35 G1
RBRY B45 173 G3
SMTHWK B66 * 106 D2
STRBR DY8 117 H4
Cornwall St CBHAMNW B3 2 E4
Cornwell Cl TPTN/OCK DY4 85 G1
Cornyx La SOLH B91 165 F4
Coronation Av WLNHL WV13 40 B3
Coronation Rd ALDR WS9 19 F4
BILS/COS WV14 53 G2
DARL/WED WS10 56 C5
GTB/HAM B43 58 C4
RUSH/SHEL WS4 18 B5
SLYOAK B29 142 D5
TPTN/OCK DY4 69 H3
WASH/WDE B8 110 D3
WNSFLD WV11 24 A5
Corporation Rd DUDS DY2 85 F5
Corporation St CBHAM B2 3 C5
CBHAMNE B4 3 H2
DARL/WED WS10 71 E1
WOLV WV1 6 E4
WSL WS1 4 D7
Corporation St West WSLW WS2 4 B6
Corrie Cft
LGN/SDN/BHAMAIR B26 130 D5
RIDG/WDGT B32 157 F3
Corrin Gv KGSWFD DY6 99 G1
Corron Hl HALE B63 * 138 D3
Corser St DUDN DY1 83 H4
STRBR DY8 135 G4
WOLV WV1 37 H4
Corsican Cl SHHTH WV12 26 C3
Corvedale Rd SLYOAK B29 158 C4
Corve Gdns
DUNHL/THL/PER WV6 22 A5
Corve Vw SEDG DY3 * 67 E2
Corville Gdns
LGN/SDN/BHAMAIR B26 147 H3
Corville Rd RMSLY B62 139 H1
Corwen Cft NFLD/LBR B31 158 A4
Cory Cft TPTN/OCK DY4 85 G1
Coseley Rd BILS/COS WV14 53 G4
Cosford Crs CVALE B35 94 C3
Cosford Dr DUDS DY2 103 E4
Cossington Rd
ERDW/GRVHL B23 76 B4
Costock Cl
CHWD/FDBR/MGN B37 132 B4
Cotford Rd
ALE/KHTH/YWD B14 178 C3
Cotheridge Cl SHLY B90 196 A2
Cot La STRBR DY8 99 H5
Cotleigh Gv KGSTG B44 59 H5
Cotman Cl GTB/HAM B43 59 G5
Coton Gv SHLY B90 179 G3
Coton La ERDW/GRVHL B23 92 D2
Coton Rd
ETTPK/GDPK/PENN WV4 51 H3
Cotsdale Rd
ETTPK/GDPK/PENN WV4 51 E5
Cotsford SOLH B91 * 181 G2
Cotswold Cl ALDR WS9 30 C1
OLDBY B69 104 C4
RBRY B45 174 A4
Cotswold Ct BKHL/PFLD WV2 51 G2
Cotswold Cft HALE B63 137 G5
Cotswold Gv SHHTH WV12 25 H1
Cotswold Rd BKHL/PFLD WV2 52 D1
STRBR DY8 135 H1
Cottage Cl WNSFLD WV11 24 C4
Cottage Gdns RBRY B45 187 H2
Cottage La WALM/CURD B76 79 F5
WOLVN WV10 12 D4
Cottage Ms ALDR WS9 45 E1
Cottage St BRLYHL DY5 119 F1
KGSWFD DY6 99 H2
Cottage Vw CDSL WV8 10 D3
Cotteridge Rd BVILLE B30 177 E1
Cotterills Av WASH/WDE B8 111 F5
Cotterills La WASH/WDE B8 111 G5
Cotterills Rd TPTN/OCK DY4 69 H4
Cottesbrook Rd ACGN B27 146 C3
Cottesfield Cl WASH/WDE B8 111 F5
Cottesmore Cl HHTH/SAND B71 72 B3
Cottle Cl WSLW WS2 40 D2
Cotton La MOS/BIL B13 144 C5
Cottrell St HHTH/SAND B71 87 H2
Cottsmeadow Dr
WASH/WDE B8 111 G5
Cotwall End Rd SEDG DY3 82 D2
Cotysmore Rd MGN/WHC B75 62 D1
Couchman Rd WASH/WDE B8 110 C5
Coulter Gv
DUNHL/THL/PER WV6 34 B1
Counterfield Dr
BLKHTH/ROWR B65 103 F4
Countess Dr RUSH/SHEL WS4 29 F3
Countess St WSL WS1 56 D1
County Cl BVILLE B30 160 C4
RIDG/WDGT B32 140 C4
County Park Av RMSLY B62 139 E4
Court Crs KGSWFD DY6 99 G4
Courtenay Gdns GTB/HAM B43 73 G1
Courtenay Rd KGSTG B44 75 E4
Court Farm Rd
ERDW/GRVHL B23 76 C5
Courtland Rd KGSWFD DY6 100 A1
Courtlands Cl DIG/EDG B5 143 G1
The Courtlands
DUNHL/THL/PER WV6 36 A1
Court La ERDW/GRVHL B23 76 C3
Court Oak Gv RIDG/WDGT B32 141 F1
Court Oak Rd RIDG/WDGT B32 141 F1
Court Pas DUDN DY1 * 84 C5
Court Rd BHTH/HG B12 144 A1
DUNHL/THL/PER WV6 36 B1
ETTPK/GDPK/PENN WV4 53 E4
SPARK B11 145 E3
Court St CDYHTH B64 121 E3
Court Wy WSLW WS2 4 C2
Courtway Av
ALE/KHTH/YWD B14 178 D4
The Courtyard
CSHL/WTROR B46 * 97 F4
Cousins St BKHL/PFLD WV2 52 B1
Coveley Gv WSNGN B18 108 A4
Coven Cl BLOX/PEL WS3 18 A2
Coven Gv SLYOAK B29 141 H5
Coven St WOLVN WV10 37 F1
Coventry Rd CSHL/WTROR B46 133 G1
HIA/OLT B92 150 D4
LGN/SDN/BHAMAIR B26 147 E1
LGN/SDN/BHAMAIR B26 148 B3
SMHTH B10 127 H3
SMHTH B10 128 C5
Coventry St DIG/EDG B5 3 J6
STRBR DY8 135 G2
WOLV WV1 38 A3
Cover Cft WALM/CURD B76 78 C2
Coverdale Rd HIA/OLT B92 147 G3
Covers La KINVER DY7 116 C3
The Covert CDSL WV8 22 A1
Cowles Cft YDLY B25 130 A3
Cowley Cl CBROM B36 95 H5
Cowley Dr ACGN B27 146 D3
DUDN DY1 83 H4
Cowley Rd SPARK B11 145 G2
Cowper Cl SHHTH WV12 26 C3
Cowslip Cl HWK/WKHTH B38 176 D5
SLYOAK B29 158 C3
Coxcroft Av BRLYHL DY5 119 H4
Coxmoor Cl BLOX/PEL WS3 * 16 B4
Cox Rd BILS/COS WV14 69 E2
Cox's La CDYHTH B64 121 F2
Cox St CBHAMNW B3 2 E2
Coxwell Av WOLVN WV10 23 E5
Coxwell Gdns
LDYWD/EDGR B16 125 H2
Coyne Cl TPTN/OCK DY4 84 D1
Coyne Rd WBROM B70 87 F4
Crabbe St HAG/WOL DY9 136 D2
Crab La SHHTH WV12 26 B1
Crabmill Cl DOR/KN B93 197 G1
Crab Mill Cl HWK/WKHTH B38 190 C1
Crabmill La HWK/WKHTH B38 177 G5
Crabourne Rd DUDS DY2 120 B2
Crabtree Cl HHTH/SAND B71 72 B3
NFLD/LBR B31 176 A3
Crabtree Dr
CHWD/FDBR/MGN B37 131 H1
Crabtree Rd WSL WS1 5 J3
WSNGN B18 108 A4
Crackley Wy DUDS DY2 102 A3
Craddock Rd SMTHWKW B67 106 A3
Craddock St
DUNHL/THL/PER WV6 36 C1
Cradley Cft HDSW B21 89 F3
Cradley Flds HALE B63 137 H2
Cradley Forge HALE B63 120 A4
Cradley Park Rd DUDS DY2 120 C2
Cradley Rd CDYHTH B64 120 C4
DUDS DY2 120 D1
Cradock Rd WASH/WDE B8 110 C4
Craig Cft
CHWD/FDBR/MGN B37 132 D2
Crail Gv GTB/HAM B43 59 F5
Cramlington Rd
PBAR/PBCH B42 74 A3
Cramnore Cl TPTN/OCK DY4 69 G3
Cramp Hl DARL/WED WS10 55 F2
Cranbourne Av
ETTPK/GDPK/PENN WV4 52 C5
Cranbourne Cl RBRY B45 174 B3
Cranbourne Gv KGSTG B44 75 G3
Cranbourne Pl
HHTH/SAND B71 * 87 H2
Cranbourne Rd KGSTG B44 75 F2
STRBR DY8 135 G3
Cranbrook Gv
DUNHL/THL/PER WV6 34 D2
Cranbrook Rd HDSW B21 89 E5
Cranby St WASH/WDE B8 110 A4
Craneberry Rd STETCH B33 131 G1
Crane Hollow WMBN WV5 * 80 C1
Cranehouse Rd KGSTG B44 75 G1
Cranemoor Cl VAUX/NECH B7 * 110 A3
Crane Rd BILS/COS WV14 54 B5
Cranesbill Rd SLYOAK B29 158 C4
Cranes Park Rd
LGN/SDN/BHAMAIR B26 148 A2
Crane Ter DUNHL/THL/PER WV6 22 A5
Cranfield Gv
LGN/SDN/BHAMAIR B26 130 B4
Cranfield Pl DSYBK/YTR WS5 57 F4
Cranford Gv SOLH B91 * 182 A4
Cranford Rd BDMR/CCFT WV3 35 G5
Cranford St SMTHWK B66 107 E4
Cranford Wy SMTHWK B66 107 E4
Cranham Dr KGSWFD DY6 99 H4
Cranhill Cl HIA/OLT B92 164 D1
Crankhall La DARL/WED WS10 56 C5
Cranleigh Cl ALDR WS9 30 B5
SHHTH WV12 26 A1
Cranleigh Pl KGSTG B44 91 E1
Cranley Dr CDSL WV8 10 B3
Cranmer Av SHHTH WV12 26 B3
Cranmere Av
DUNHL/THL/PER WV6 21 E4
Cranmere Ct
DUNHL/THL/PER WV6 * 21 E4
Cranmer Gv FOAKS/STRLY B74 32 D4
Cranmoor Crs HALE B63 138 C2
Cranmore Av HDSW B21 107 F2
SHLY B90 181 E5
Cranmore Bvd SHLY B90 180 D5
Cranmore Dr SHLY B90 181 E4
Cranmore Rd BDMR/CCFT WV3 36 B2
CBROM B36 95 G5
SHLY B90 180 D5
Cransley Gv SOLH B91 181 G4
Crantock Cl SHHTH WV12 26 A1
Crantock Rd PBAR/PBCH B42 90 C2
Cranwell Gn WMBN WV5 80 D1
Cranwell Gv ERDE/BCHGN B24 93 H3
Cranwell Wy CVALE B35 94 C3
Crathorne Av WOLVN WV10 23 E1
Craufurd Ct STRBR DY8 135 G4
Craven St BKHL/PFLD WV2 52 D2
Crawford Av DARL/WED WS10 55 E1
ETTPK/GDPK/PENN WV4 52 D5
SMTHWKW B67 106 A4
Crawford Rd BDMR/CCFT WV3 6 A4
WALM/CURD B76 78 B3
Crawford St WASH/WDE B8 110 A4
Crawshaws Rd CBROM B36 95 E5
Crayford Rd KGSTG B44 75 G2
Craythorne Av
BFLD/HDSWWD B20 89 G1
Crecy Cl WALM/CURD B76 63 E4
Credenda Rd WBROM B70 87 E5
Credon Gv EDG B15 142 D2
Cregoe St EDG B15 126 C3
Cremore Av WASH/WDE B8 110 C4
Cremorne Rd MGN/WHC B75 47 F3
Cremorne Wk MGN/WHC B75 * 47 F3
Crendon Rd
BLKHTH/ROWR B65 103 G3
Crescent Ar SOLH B91 * 182 A1
Crescent Av BRLYHL DY5 119 E2
The Crescent Grange Rd
HAG/WOL DY9 * 136 A3
Crescent Rd DARL/WED WS10 55 F2
DUDS DY2 102 B4
WLNHL WV13 40 A3
Crescent Studios
WSNGN B18 * 108 B3
The Crescent BILS/COS WV14 53 H2
BLKHTH/ROWR B65 121 H2
CDYHTH B64 121 G5
CHWD/FDBR/MGN B37 133 E4
DARL/WED WS10 56 A4
DUDN DY1 85 E2
DUNHL/THL/PER WV6 35 F2
GTB/HAM B43 74 A2
HAG/WOL DY9 152 B5
HIA/OLT B92 167 H3
SHLY B90 180 A1
SOLH B91 181 H1
WLNHL WV13 40 A4
WSL WS1 5 J5
WSNGN B18 108 B3
Cressage Av NFLD/LBR B31 175 G4
Cressett Av BRLYHL DY5 100 D5
Cressett La BRLYHL DY5 101 E5
Cressington Dr
FOAKS/STRLY B74 47 E4
Cresswell Crs BLOX/PEL WS3 16 B5
Cresswell Gv ERDE/BCHGN B24 93 H2
The Crest NFLD/LBR B31 189 H2
Crest Vw ALE/KHTH/YWD B14 178 D1
FOAKS/STRLY B74 45 F4
Crestwood Dr KGSTG B44 75 E4
Crestwood Gln
DUNHL/THL/PER WV6 22 A3
Creswell Rd HLGN/YWD B28 163 F3
Creswick Gv RBRY B45 188 C1
Crew Rd DARL/WED WS10 56 A4
Creynolds Cl SHLY B90 194 D4
Creynolds La SHLY B90 195 F3
Cricket Cl DSYBK/YTR WS5 57 H1
Cricketers Meadow
CDYHTH B64 121 F5
Cricket Meadow SEDG DY3 83 G1
WOLVN WV10 12 D3
Crick La BFLD/HDSWWD B20 108 A1
Cricklewood Dr RMSLY B62 139 F4
Crimmond Ri HALE B63 138 A2
Crimscote Cl SHLY B90 195 F2
Cripps Rd WSLW WS2 40 C2
Crocketts Av HDSW B21 * 107 F2
Crockett's La SMTHWK B66 106 C4
Crocketts Rd HDSW B21 107 F2
Crockett St DUDN DY1 84 A4
Crockford Dr MGN/WHC B75 47 E2
Crockford Rd HHTH/SAND B71 71 G2
Crocus Crs COVEN WV9 12 A4
Croft Cl YDLY B25 130 A4
Croft Ct CBROM B36 * 112 D1
Croft Crs BRWNH WS8 8 D5
Croft Down Rd HIA/OLT B92 148 B3
Croftdown Rd HRBN B17 141 F1
Crofters Cl STRBR DY8 135 H3
Crofters Ct EDG B15 142 C1
Croft La WOLVN WV10 23 H3
Croftleigh Gdns SOLH B91 * 181 E3
Croft Rd
LGN/SDN/BHAMAIR B26 130 A4
The Crofts WALM/CURD B76 78 C4
Croft St WLNHL WV13 39 G3
WSLW WS2 41 H2
The Croft DSYBK/YTR WS5 43 F5
DUDS DY2 101 H3
KIDD DY10 168 C3
NFLD/LBR B31 175 H2
SEDG DY3 67 G2
WLNHL WV13 39 G3
WMBN WV5 80 B1
The Croftway
BFLD/HDSWWD B20 73 G5
Croftwood Rd HAG/WOL DY9 136 B3
Cromdale Dr HALE B63 137 H4
Cromer Gdns
DUNHL/THL/PER WV6 22 B5
Crome Rd GTB/HAM B43 59 H5
Cromer Rd BHTH/HG B12 144 B2
Crompton Av
BFLD/HDSWWD B20 * 90 C5
Crompton Cl WSLW WS2 27 E5
Crompton Ct CDSL WV8 10 D3
Crompton Rd
BFLD/HDSWWD B20 90 C5
RBRY B45 173 F4
TPTN/OCK DY4 85 G2
VAUX/NECH B7 110 A1
Cromwell Cl
BLKHTH/ROWR B65 103 F4
WSLW WS2 40 C1
Cromwell Dr DUDS DY2 103 F1
Cromwell La RIDG/WDGT B32 157 H2
Cromwell Rd WOLVN WV10 13 E4
Cromwell St DUDS DY2 103 E1
VAUX/NECH B7 109 H4
Crondal Pl EDG B15 126 B5
Cronehills Linkway
WBROM B70 87 H3
Cronehills St WBROM B70 87 H2
Crookham Cl HRBN B17 124 B5
Crookhay La HHTH/SAND B71 71 E3
Crook La ALDR WS9 59 E2
Croome Cl SPARK B11 144 D4
Cropredy Rd NFLD/LBR B31 175 G5
Cropthorne Dr HLYWD B47 192 D1
Cropthorne Rd SHLY B90 180 D1
Crosbie Rd HRBN B17 141 H1
Crosby Cl CBHAMW B1 2 A4
DUNHL/THL/PER WV6 22 B5
Cross Cl CDYHTH B64 121 F2
Cross Farm Rd HRBN B17 142 B3
Cross Farms La RBRY B45 173 H4
Crossfield Rd STETCH B33 130 C1
Crossgate Rd DUDS DY2 101 H3
Crosskey Cl STETCH B33 131 G2
Crossland Crs
DUNHL/THL/PER WV6 22 B4
Cross La GTB/HAM B43 73 G2
SEDG DY3 67 F3
Crossley St DUDS DY2 102 D5
Cross Pl SEDG DY3 67 G2
Cross St BILS/COS WV14 69 F1
BLKHTH/ROWR B65 122 A3
BLOX/PEL WS3 28 C1
DARL/WED WS10 55 G5
DUDN DY1 84 C5
HALE B63 138 C4
HDSW B21 107 E1
KGSWFD DY6 99 F1
LGLYGN/QTN B68 105 E5
STRBR DY8 117 H1
STRBR DY8 135 E2
WLNHL WV13 39 G4
WOLV WV1 37 H4
Cross St North WOLV WV1 37 F1
Cross St South BKHL/PFLD WV2 52 A1
Cross Walks Rd HAG/WOL DY9 136 C2
Crossway La KGSTG B44 75 F5
Crosswells Rd
LGLYGN/QTN B68 105 F4
Crowberry Cl BRWNH WS8 18 D1
Crowesbridge Ms
BILS/COS WV14 68 B3
Crowhurst Rd NFLD/LBR B31 189 E1
Crowland Av
DUNHL/THL/PER WV6 34 C1
Crowle Dr HAG/WOL DY9 136 A2
Crown Cl BLKHTH/ROWR B65 104 B5
SEDG DY3 67 F2
Crown Ct DARL/WED WS10 40 A5
Crown La FOAKS/STRLY B74 46 C3
STRBR DY8 135 F1
Crownmeadow Dr
TPTN/OCK DY4 70 B4
Crown Rd BORD B9 128 B2
BVILLE B30 177 E1
Crown St WOLV WV1 23 F5
Crown Wk TPTN/OCK DY4 85 G4
Crows Nest Cl WALM/CURD B76 63 F5
Crowther Gdns HALE B63 120 C5
Crowther Gv
DUNHL/THL/PER WV6 36 B1
Crowther Rd
DUNHL/THL/PER WV6 22 B5
ERDW/GRVHL B23 92 B1
Crowther St WOLVN WV10 37 G1
Croxall Wy SMTHWK B66 106 D4
Croxdene Av BLOX/PEL WS3 26 D1
Croxley Gdns WLNHL WV13 39 F5
Croxstalls Av BLOX/PEL WS3 27 E2
Croxstalls Cl BLOX/PEL WS3 27 E1
Croxstalls Pl BLOX/PEL WS3 27 E2
Croxstalls Rd BLOX/PEL WS3 27 E1
Croxton Gv STETCH B33 112 C5
Croyde Av PBAR/PBCH B42 74 A3
Croydon Rd ERDE/BCHGN B24 93 E5
SLYOAK B29 142 D4
Croy Dr CVALE B35 94 D2
The Crucible BILS/COS WV14 68 C1
Crusader Cl OLDBY B69 104 C4
Crychan Cl RBRY B45 174 B3
Cryersoak Cl SHLY B90 195 G1
Crystal Av STRBR DY8 118 B3
Crystal Dr SMTHWK B66 105 G1
Cubley Rd HLGN/YWD B28 162 C1
Cuckoo Rd VAUX/NECH B7 110 B1
Cuin Dr SMTHWK B66 107 E4
Cuin Rd SMTHWK B66 107 E4
Culey Gv STETCH B33 131 F2
Culford Dr RIDG/WDGT B32 157 G2
Culham Cl ACGN B27 146 D5
Cullwick St WOLV WV1 53 E1
Culmington Gv NFLD/LBR B31 175 F5
Culmington Rd NFLD/LBR B31 175 F5
Culmore Cl SHHTH WV12 40 B1
Culmore Rd RMSLY B62 122 C3
Culverhouse Dr STRBR DY8 118 C3
Culverley Crs DOR/KN B93 196 D2
Culwell St WOLVN WV10 7 H2
Cumberford Av STETCH B33 131 G3
Cumberland Av DIG/EDG B5 127 E5
Cumberland Cl KGSWFD DY6 100 A5
Cumberland Rd BILS/COS WV14 53 H1
HHTH/SAND B71 71 H5
LGLYGN/QTN B68 123 F4
WLNHL WV13 40 B3
Cumberland St CBHAMW B1 2 B6
Cumbrian Cft HALE B63 137 H5
Cumbria Wy WASH/WDE B8 110 B3
Cunningham Rd
DUNHL/THL/PER WV6 34 C1
WSLW WS2 40 C3
Cupfields Av TPTN/OCK DY4 70 A3
Cupfields Crs TPTN/OCK DY4 70 A4
Curbar Rd PBAR/PBCH B42 74 C5
Curdale Rd RIDG/WDGT B32 157 F2
Curdworth La WALM/CURD B76 79 H2
Curlews Cl ERDW/GRVHL B23 76 A3
Curral Rd BLKHTH/ROWR B65 121 H1
Curtin Dr DARL/WED WS10 54 D4
Curtis Cl SMTHWK B66 107 E5
Curzon Circ CBHAMNE B4 127 G1
Curzon St BKHL/PFLD WV2 52 B1
CBHAMNE B4 3 K4
Cuthbert Rd WSNGN B18 107 G5
Cutlers Rough Cl
NFLD/LBR B31 158 B5
Cutler St SMTHWK B66 106 D4
Cutsdean Cl NFLD/LBR B31 158 B4
Cutshill Cl CBROM B36 113 E1
The Cutting RUSH/SHEL WS4 42 B1
Cutworth Cl WALM/CURD B76 63 G5

Cygnet Dr BRWNH WS8 9 E5
Cygnet Gv ERDW/GRVHL B23 75 G5
Cygnet La BRLYHL DY5 101 E2
Cygnet Rd WBROM B70 87 E1
Cygnus Wy WBROM B70 86 D1
Cypress Av SEDG DY3 83 F1
Cypress Gdns KGSWFD DY6 99 G5
Cypress Gv NFLD/LBR B31 175 E4
Cypress Rd DSYBK/YTR WS5 58 A4
DUDS DY2 85 F5
Cypress Sq ACGN B27 146 C2
Cypress Wy NFLD/LBR B31 175 F5
Cyprus Cl SLYOAK B29 158 C3
Cyprus St BKHL/PFLD WV2 51 H2
OLDBY B69 105 E1
Cyril Gv SMHTH B10 * 128 A4
Cyril Rd SMHTH B10 128 A4

D

Dacer Cl BVILLE B30 160 B5
Dace Rd WOLV WV1 38 B1
Dadford Vw BRLYHL DY5 118 D2
Dad's La MOS/BIL B13 160 C1
Daffodil Cl SEDG DY3 67 G4
Daffodil Pl DSYBK/YTR WS5 43 F5
Daffodil Rd DSYBK/YTR WS5 43 F5
Daffodil Wy NFLD/LBR B31 175 E5
Dagger La HHTH/SAND B71 88 A1
Dagnall Rd ACGN B27 146 D4
Dahlia Cl WOLV WV1 38 C4
Daimler Cl CBROM B36 95 H5
Daimler Rd
ALE/KHTH/YWD B14 179 F2
Dainton Gv RIDG/WDGT B32 157 G1
Dairy Cl TPTN/OCK DY4 85 H1
Dairy Ct LGLYGN/QTN B68 123 H5
Daisy Bank Cl BLOX/PEL WS3 18 B5
Daisy Bank Crs DSYBK/YTR WS5 43 F5
Daisy Dr ERDW/GRVHL B23 91 G1
Daisy Farm Rd
ALE/KHTH/YWD B14 178 D3
Daisy Meadow TPTN/OCK DY4 70 A5
Daisy Rd LDYWD/EDGR B16 125 H2
Daisy St BILS/COS WV14 69 E1
DUNHL/THL/PER WV6 36 C1
Daisy Wk COVEN WV9 12 A4
Dalbeg Cl CDSL WV8 22 A2
Dalbury Rd HLGN/YWD B28 162 C5
Dalby Rd BLOX/PEL WS3 28 B4
Dale Cl GTB/HAM B43 73 F2
SMTHWKW B67 124 C1
TPTN/OCK DY4 86 B1
Dalecote Av HIA/OLT B92 165 G2
Dale End CBHAMNE B4 3 H5
DARL/WED WS10 55 F2
Dale Rd RMSLY B62 122 D4
SLYOAK B29 142 C4
STRBR DY8 135 F5
Dales Cl DUNHL/THL/PER WV6 22 D4
Dalesman Cl KGSWFD DY6 99 F2
Dale St BDMR/CCFT WV3 6 D6
BILS/COS WV14 54 B3
DARL/WED WS10 55 G5
SMTHWK B66 124 C1
WSL WS1 57 E1
Daleswood Pk RMSLY B62 * 172 B3
Dale Ter OLDBY B69 104 A1
Daleview Rd
ALE/KHTH/YWD B14 179 E2
Dalewood Cft
LGN/SDN/BHAMAIR B26 147 F1
Dalewood Rd
CHWD/FDBR/MGN B37 113 H4
Daley Cl CBHAMW B1 2 A4
Daley Rd BILS/COS WV14 69 F1
Dalkeith Rd SCFLD/BOLD B73 76 C1
Dalkeith St WSLW WS2 4 A1
Dallas Rd ERDW/GRVHL B23 92 A2
Dallimore Cl HIA/OLT B92 147 F4
Dalloway Cl DIG/EDG B5 143 H1
Dalston Cl DUDS DY2 102 D3
Dalston Rd ACGN B27 146 C3
Dalton Ct WMBN WV5 64 C4
Dalton Rd WSLW WS2 41 E2
Dalton St BDMR/CCFT WV3 36 D5
CBHAMNE B4 3 H4
Dalton Wy CBHAM B2 3 G4
Dalvine Rd DUDS DY2 120 B2
Dalwood Cl BILS/COS WV14 68 B4
Damar Cft ALE/KHTH/YWD B14 177 H1
Damien Cl SMTHWKW B67 106 B4
Damson Cl SHHTH WV12 25 G4
Damson La SOLH B91 165 G5
Damson Pkwy HIA/OLT B92 148 D4
Damson Whf TPTN/OCK DY4 85 G3
Danbury Cl WALM/CURD B76 78 C1
Danbury Rd SHLY B90 180 B2
Danby Gv ERDE/BCHGN B24 93 F4
Dando Rd DUDS DY2 102 D1
Dandy Bank Rd KGSWFD DY6 100 C1
Dandy's Wk WSL WS1 5 F6
Dane Gv MOS/BIL B13 160 D2
Danesbury Crs KGSTG B44 75 G3
Danes Cl WNSFLD WV11 14 D3
Danescourt Rd
DUNHL/THL/PER WV6 21 G4
Daneswood Dr ALDR WS9 19 F4
Dane Ter BLKHTH/ROWR B65 104 A4
Daneways Cl FOAKS/STRLY B74 45 G5
Danford Cl STRBR DY8 135 G3
Danford Gdns SMHTH B10 128 A4
Danford La SOLH B91 181 E2
Danford Rd HLYWD B47 192 B2
Danford Wy GTB/HAM B43 73 F3
Dangerfield La
DARL/WED WS10 55 E3
Daniels La ALDR WS9 44 C1
Daniels Rd BORD B9 129 E2
Danks St TPTN/OCK DY4 85 G4
Danzey Green Rd CBROM B36 94 D5
Danzey Gv BVILLE B30 177 G2
Darby Cl BILS/COS WV14 68 A1
Darby End Rd
BLKHTH/ROWR B65 103 E5
Darby Rd DARL/WED WS10 56 B5
LGLYGN/QTN B68 105 G4
Darbys Hill Rd OLDBY B69 103 H2
Darby St BLKHTH/ROWR B65 122 A3
Darell Cft WALM/CURD B76 63 E5
Daren Cl CBROM B36 113 H1
Dare Rd ERDW/GRVHL B23 92 C2
Darfield Wk BHTH/HG B12 * 127 F4
Darkhouse La BILS/COS WV14 68 C1
Dark La HAG/WOL DY9 184 C1
HWK/WKHTH B38 191 H1
RMSLY B62 172 B1
Darlaston La BILS/COS WV14 54 C1
Darlaston Rd DARL/WED WS10 55 F3
WSLW WS2 41 E5
Darley Av BKDE/SHDE B34 112 B3
Darleydale Av KGSTG B44 75 E2
Darley Dr DUNHL/THL/PER WV6 22 D5
Darley Green Rd DOR/KN B93 199 F2
Darley Wy FOAKS/STRLY B74 60 B1
Darlington St DARL/WED WS10 55 F3
WOLV WV1 6 E4
Darlington Yd WOLV WV1 * 6 E4
Darnel Cft SMHTH B10 127 H3
Darnel Hurst Rd MGN/WHC B75 47 G2
Darnford Cl CSCFLD/WYGN B72 77 H4
HLGN/YWD B28 163 E5
Darnick Rd SCFLD/BOLD B73 61 F5
Darnley Rd LDYWD/EDGR B16 125 H2
Darris Rd SLYOAK B29 160 A2
Dartford Rd BLOX/PEL WS3 26 D1
Dartmoor Cl RBRY B45 174 A3
Dartmouth Av BLOX/PEL WS3 28 A5
STRBR DY8 117 H1
WLNHL WV13 39 F3
Dartmouth Circ AST/WIT B6 109 F4
Dartmouth Cl BLOX/PEL WS3 28 A5
Dartmouth Crs BILS/COS WV14 54 C1
Dartmouth Dr ALDR WS9 29 H5
Dartmouth Middleway
VAUX/NECH B7 3 K1
Dartmouth Pl BLOX/PEL WS3 28 A4
Dartmouth Rd SLYOAK B29 142 D5
SMTHWK B66 106 B1
Dartmouth St BKHL/PFLD WV2 7 H7
WBROM B70 87 F3
Dart St BORD B9 127 H3
Darvel Rd SHHTH WV12 40 B1
Darwall St WSL WS1 4 E3
Darwin Ct
DUNHL/THL/PER WV6 34 C1
Darwin Pl WSLW WS2 27 F4
Darwin Rd WSLW WS2 27 F4
Darwin St BHTH/HG B12 127 F4
Dassett Gv BORD B9 129 G2
Dassett Rd DOR/KN B93 196 D4
Dauntsey Covert
ALE/KHTH/YWD B14 177 H3
Davena Dr SLYOAK B29 141 E5
Davena Gv BILS/COS WV14 53 H5
Davenport Dr CVALE B35 95 E3
Davenport Rd
DUNHL/THL/PER WV6 21 F5
WNSFLD WV11 25 E4
Daventry Gv RIDG/WDGT B32 140 C1
Davey Rd BFLD/HDSWWD B20 91 E5
WBROM B70 87 E2
David Peacock Cl TPTN/OCK DY4 85 G1
David Rd BFLD/HDSWWD B20 90 B4
TPTN/OCK DY4 69 G4
The Davids NFLD/LBR B31 159 E4
Davies Av BILS/COS WV14 53 H5
Davis Av TPTN/OCK DY4 85 E2
Davis Gv
LGN/SDN/BHAMAIR B26 146 D1
Davison Rd SMTHWKW B67 124 B1
Davis Rd SHHTH WV12 26 B2
Davy Rd WSLW WS2 27 E5
Dawberry Cl
ALE/KHTH/YWD B14 160 D5
Dawberry Fields Rd
ALE/KHTH/YWD B14 160 C5
Dawberry Rd
ALE/KHTH/YWD B14 160 C5
Daw End RUSH/SHEL WS4 29 E4
Daw End La RUSH/SHEL WS4 28 D4
Dawes Av WBROM B70 87 G5
Dawley Brook Rd KGSWFD DY6 99 H2
Dawley Crs
CHWD/FDBR/MGN B37 132 B3
Dawley Rd KGSWFD DY6 99 G1
Dawlish Rd DUDN DY1 84 C1
SLYOAK B29 142 D5
SMTHWK B66 106 D4
Dawn Dr DARL/WED WS10 70 A1
Dawney Dr MGN/WHC B75 47 E1
Dawn Rd NFLD/LBR B31 158 A4
Dawson Av BILS/COS WV14 67 H1
Dawson Rd HDSW B21 107 G1
Dawson Sq BILS/COS WV14 * 53 G3
Dawson St BLOX/PEL WS3 27 H2
SMTHWK B66 124 C1
Day Av WNSFLD WV11 25 E3
Dayhouse Bank RMSLY B62 172 D4
Daylesford Rd HIA/OLT B92 147 G4
Day St WSLW WS2 4 D1
Deakin Av BRWNH WS8 9 F3
Deakin Rd ERDE/BCHGN B24 92 D3
MGN/WHC B75 63 E1
Deakins Rd YDLY B25 129 F5
Deal Dr DUDS DY2 85 F5
Deal Gv NFLD/LBR B31 175 G1
Deanbrook Cl SHLY B90 195 G2
Dean Cl CSCFLD/WYGN B72 77 F4
KGSTG B44 75 H3
STRBR DY8 135 H1
Dean Ct CDSL WV8 20 C5
Deanery Rw WOLV WV1 7 F2
Dean Rd ERDW/GRVHL B23 92 D1
RUSH/SHEL WS4 29 E3
WMBN WV5 80 D1
Deansfield Rd WOLV WV1 38 A3
Deans Pl BLOX/PEL WS3 28 B4
Dean's Rd WOLV WV1 38 A2
Dean St DIG/EDG B5 3 H7
SEDG DY3 67 F3
Dearman Rd SPARK B11 127 H5
Dearmont Rd NFLD/LBR B31 189 E1
Dearne Ct SEDG DY3 68 A5
Debden Cl DOR/KN B93 198 C1
Debenham Crs YDLY B25 129 H3
Debenham Rd YDLY B25 129 H3
Deblen Dr LDYWD/EDGR B16 125 F3
Deborah Cl
ETTPK/GDPK/PENN WV4 52 A2
Dee Gv HWK/WKHTH B38 176 C5
Deelands Rd RBRY B45 173 H5
Deeley Cl CDYHTH B64 121 E5
EDG B15 126 C5
Deeley Dr TPTN/OCK DY4 70 A5
Deeley Pl BLOX/PEL WS3 27 F2
Deeley St BLOX/PEL WS3 * 27 F2
BRLYHL DY5 * 119 G3
Deepdale Av
LGN/SDN/BHAMAIR B26 147 H3
Deepdale La DUDN DY1 83 G3
Deepdales WMBN WV5 64 C5
Deeplow Cl
CSCFLD/WYGN B72 * 62 C4
Deepmoor Rd STETCH B33 130 B1
Deepmore Av WSLW WS2 41 F3
Deepwood Cl RUSH/SHEL WS4 28 D2
Deer Cl BLOX/PEL WS3 27 G1
Deerhurst Rd
BFLD/HDSWWD B20 89 H1
Dee Rd BLOX/PEL WS3 28 A1
Deer Park Wy SOLH B91 182 A4
Defford Av RUSH/SHEL WS4 29 E1
Defford Dr LGLYGN/QTN B68 105 F5
De Havilland Dr CVALE B35 94 C4
Deighton Rd DSYBK/YTR WS5 57 H4
Delamere Cl CBROM B36 95 F5
Delamere Dr GTB/HAM B43 58 A5
Delamere Rd HLGN/YWD B28 162 D3
SHHTH WV12 26 A3
Delancey Keep MGN/WHC B75 63 G3
Delhurst Av
ETTPK/GDPK/PENN WV4 52 C5
Delhurst Rd KGSTG B44 74 D2
Delia Dr RIDG/WDGT B32 157 H2
Dell Farm Cl DOR/KN B93 197 F2
Dellows Cl HWK/WKHTH B38 190 B1
Dell Rd BRLYHL DY5 100 D4
BVILLE B30 160 A5
The Dell HIA/OLT B92 164 C1
LDYWD/EDGR B16 * 125 H2
NFLD/LBR B31 157 H4
STRBR DY8 135 E1
Delmore Wy WALM/CURD B76 78 D5
Delph Dr BRLYHL DY5 119 G5
Delphinium Cl BORD B9 128 D1
Delph La BRLYHL DY5 119 F4
Delph Rd BRLYHL DY5 119 F3
Delrene Rd HLGN/YWD B28 179 H2
Delves Crs DSYBK/YTR WS5 57 G3
Delves Green Rd
DSYBK/YTR WS5 57 G2
Delves Rd WSL WS1 57 F1
Delville Rd DARL/WED WS10 55 H5
De Marnham Cl WBROM B70 88 A5
De Moram Gv HIA/OLT B92 165 H3
Demuth Wy OLDBY B69 104 D4
Denaby Gv
ALE/KHTH/YWD B14 179 F1
Denbigh Cl DUDN DY1 83 H4
Denbigh Crs HHTH/SAND B71 71 F5
Denbigh Dr DARL/WED WS10 56 D4
HHTH/SAND B71 71 F5
Denbigh Rd TPTN/OCK DY4 86 A2
Denbigh St BORD B9 128 B2
Denby Cl VAUX/NECH B7 109 H4
Denby Cft SHLY B90 195 H2
Dencer Cl RBRY B45 173 H5
Dencil Cl HALE B63 137 H2
Dene Av KGSWFD DY6 99 G5
Dene Court Rd HIA/OLT B92 164 B1
Denegate Cl WALM/CURD B76 78 D5
Dene Hollow MOS/BIL B13 162 A4
Dene Rd STRBR DY8 135 F4
Denewood Av
BFLD/HDSWWD B20 90 A4
Denford Gv
ALE/KHTH/YWD B14 160 D5
Denham Gdns
BDMR/CCFT WV3 35 F5
Denham Rd ACGN B27 146 B2
Denholme Gv
ALE/KHTH/YWD B14 178 C2
Denholm Rd SCFLD/BOLD B73 61 F5
Denise Dr BILS/COS WV14 68 B3
CHWD/FDBR/MGN B37 113 H5
HRBN B17 142 A3
Denleigh Rd KGSWFD DY6 100 B5
Denmark Cl
DUNHL/THL/PER WV6 36 C1
Denmead Dr WNSFLD WV11 25 F2
Denmore Gdns WOLV WV1 38 B3
Dennis Hall Rd STRBR DY8 118 C4
Dennis Rd BHTH/HG B12 144 D3
Dennis St STRBR DY8 118 B4
Denshaw Rd
ALE/KHTH/YWD B14 160 D4
Denton Cft DOR/KN B93 196 B5
Denton Gv GTB/HAM B43 73 F4
STETCH B33 129 H2
Denton Rd HAG/WOL DY9 137 E3
Denver Rd
ALE/KHTH/YWD B14 178 C3
Denville Cl BILS/COS WV14 54 A1
Denville Crs BORD B9 129 F1
Depwo Gv RIDG/WDGT B32 157 F2
Derby Av DUNHL/THL/PER WV6 22 A3
Derby Dr
CHWD/FDBR/MGN B37 132 B2
Derby St DIG/EDG B5 127 G2
WSLW WS2 41 H1
Dereham Cl WASH/WDE B8 110 A5
Dereham Wk BILS/COS WV14 69 E1
Dereton Cl DUDN DY1 101 G2
Derron Av
LGN/SDN/BHAMAIR B26 147 E2
Derry Cl HRBN B17 141 G4
Derrydown Cl ERDW/GRVHL B23 92 C3
Derrydown Rd PBAR/PBCH B42 90 B1
Derry St BKHL/PFLD WV2 37 F5
BRLYHL DY5 119 E2
Derwent Cl BRLYHL DY5 100 D3
FOAKS/STRLY B74 45 F3
WLNHL WV13 40 A3
Derwent Gv BVILLE B30 160 C1
Derwent Rd BVILLE B30 160 C2
DUNHL/THL/PER WV6 21 H2
Desford Av PBAR/PBCH B42 74 C4
Dettonford Rd
RIDG/WDGT B32 157 F2
Devereux Cl CBROM B36 113 E1
Devereux Rd MGN/WHC B75 47 G4
WBROM B70 88 A5
Devey Dr TPTN/OCK DY4 70 B5
Devine Cft TPTN/OCK DY4 85 G1
Devitts Cl SHLY B90 195 F1
Devon Crs ALDR WS9 30 A1
DUDS DY2 101 H2
HHTH/SAND B71 71 G5
Devon Rd DARL/WED WS10 56 C4
RBRY B45 173 H4
SMTHWKW B67 124 A5
STRBR DY8 117 H5
WLNHL WV13 40 B4
WOLV WV1 6 D1
Devonshire Av WSNGN B18 107 H3
Devonshire Dr HHTH/SAND B71 88 A3
Devonshire Rd
BFLD/HDSWWD B20 89 H4
SMTHWKW B67 106 A3
Devonshire St WSNGN B18 107 H3
Devon St VAUX/NECH B7 110 A5
Devoran Cl
DUNHL/THL/PER WV6 36 D1
Dewberry Dr DSYBK/YTR WS5 57 G5
Dewberry Rd STRBR DY8 118 B3
Dewhurst Cft STETCH B33 130 D1
Dewsbury Cl STRBR DY8 118 A1
Dewsbury Dr
ETTPK/GDPK/PENN WV4 51 G5
Dewsbury Gv PBAR/PBCH B42 90 C1
Deykin Av AST/WIT B6 91 G4
D'Eyncourt Rd WNSFLD WV11 24 A3
Dial Cl ALE/KHTH/YWD B14 178 A3
Dial La STRBR DY8 118 A4
WBROM B70 70 D5
Diamond Park Dr STRBR DY8 118 A3
Diana Cl ALDR WS9 19 H4
Diane Cl TPTN/OCK DY4 69 H1
Dibble Cl SHHTH WV12 26 B5
Dibble Rd SMTHWKW B67 106 B3
Dibdale Rd DUDN DY1 83 H3
Dibdale St DUDN DY1 83 H4
Dice Pleck NFLD/LBR B31 176 A3
Dickens Cl SEDG DY3 82 D1
Dickens Gv
ALE/KHTH/YWD B14 178 C2
Dickens Heath Rd SHLY B90 193 G4
Dickens Rd BILS/COS WV14 68 D1
WOLVN WV10 24 A2
Dickinson Av WOLVN WV10 23 H3
Dickinson Dr WALM/CURD B76 63 E4
WSLW WS2 56 C2
Dickinson Rd WMBN WV5 81 E2
Dick Sheppard Av
TPTN/OCK DY4 69 H3
Diddington Av HLGN/YWD B28 163 E5
Didgley Gv
CHWD/FDBR/MGN B37 114 A4
Digbeth DIG/EDG B5 3 H6
WSL WS1 4 E4
Digby Crs CSHL/WTROR B46 96 B3
Digby Dr
CHWD/FDBR/MGN B37 149 F1
Digby Rd CSHL/WTROR B46 115 F3
KGSWFD DY6 99 H1
SCFLD/BOLD B73 62 A5
Dilke Rd ALDR WS9 29 H5
Dilloways La WLNHL WV13 39 E4
Dimmingsdale Bank
RIDG/WDGT B32 140 C3
Dimminsdale WLNHL WV13 39 G4
Dimmocks Av BILS/COS WV14 68 D3
Dimmock St
ETTPK/GDPK/PENN WV4 52 C3
Dimsdale Gv NFLD/LBR B31 175 E2
Dimsdale Rd NFLD/LBR B31 174 D2
Dingle Av CDYHTH B64 121 E4
Dingle Cl BVILLE B30 159 F3
DUDS DY2 103 E2
Dingle Hollow OLDBY B69 104 B1
Dingle La SOLH B91 181 F3
WLNHL WV13 39 G1
Dingle Md ALE/KHTH/YWD B14 177 G1
Dingle Rd BRWNH WS8 19 E2
DUDS DY2 103 E2
HAG/WOL DY9 135 H5
KGSWFD DY6 100 C5
WMBN WV5 80 D1
Dingle St OLDBY B69 104 B1
The Dingle BDMR/CCFT WV3 35 H4
OLDBY B69 104 B1
SHLY B90 194 D3
SLYOAK B29 142 C5
Dingle Vw SEDG DY3 67 E4
Dingley Rd DARL/WED WS10 56 A3
Dinham Gdns DUDN DY1 83 G3
Dinmore Av NFLD/LBR B31 175 H1
Dippons Dr
DUNHL/THL/PER WV6 35 E3
Dippons Mill Cl
DUNHL/THL/PER WV6 35 E2
Dirtyfoot La
ETTPK/GDPK/PENN WV4 50 A3
Discovery Cl TPTN/OCK DY4 86 A1
The Ditch WSL WS1 5 F4
Ditton Gv NFLD/LBR B31 189 F2
Dixon Cl CVALE B35 94 C4
TPTN/OCK DY4 70 A5
Dixon Rd SMHTH B10 127 H4
Dixon's Green Rd DUDS DY2 103 E1
Dixon St BKHL/PFLD WV2 52 C2
Dobbins Oak Rd HAG/WOL DY9 153 F1
Dobbs Mill Cl SLYOAK B29 143 F5
Dobbs St BKHL/PFLD WV2 7 F7
Dockar Rd NFLD/LBR B31 175 E3
Dock La DUDN DY1 84 B5
Dock Meadow Dr
ETTPK/GDPK/PENN WV4 53 E4
Dock Rd STRBR DY8 118 B2
The Dock HAG/WOL DY9 136 D2
Doctors Hl HAG/WOL DY9 136 A4
Doctors La KGSWFD DY6 98 D4
Doctor's Piece WLNHL WV13 39 H3
Doddington Gv
RIDG/WDGT B32 157 F2
Dodford Cl RBRY B45 187 H1
Doe Bank La ALDR WS9 59 H2
Doe Bank Rd TPTN/OCK DY4 70 A2
Dogge Lane Cft ACGN B27 146 B5
Dogkennel La LGLYGN/QTN B68 105 G4
Dog Kennel La HALE B63 138 D4
SHLY B90 194 C1
WSL WS1 5 G3
Dogpool La BVILLE B30 160 B1
Doidge Rd ERDW/GRVHL B23 92 B3
Dollery Dr DIG/EDG B5 143 G2
Dollis Gv KGSTG B44 60 B5
Dollman St VAUX/NECH B7 127 H1
Dolman Rd AST/WIT B6 109 E1
Dolobran Rd SPARK B11 127 H5
Dolphin Cl BLOX/PEL WS3 28 B1
Dolphin La ACGN B27 163 G1
Dolphin Rd SPARK B11 145 F2
Dolton Wy TPTN/OCK DY4 69 E5
Dominic Cl BVILLE B30 176 B1
Doncaster Wy CBROM B36 111 G1
Don Cl EDG B15 125 F4
Donegal Rd FOAKS/STRLY B74 60 C3
Donibristle Cft CVALE B35 94 C2
Dooley Cl WLNHL WV13 39 E3
Doran Cl HALE B63 154 D1
Doranda Wy HHTH/SAND B71 88 B5
Dora Rd HDSW B21 107 G2
SMHTH B10 128 C5
WBROM B70 87 G5
Dora St WSLW WS2 56 B1
Dorchester Cl SHHTH WV12 26 A2
Dorchester Ct SOLH B91 181 G1
Dorchester Dr HRBN B17 141 H3
Dorchester Rd HAG/WOL DY9 136 B5
SHHTH WV12 26 A2
SOLH B91 181 G1
Dordale Cl NFLD/LBR B31 174 C4
Dordale Rd HAG/WOL DY9 184 B5
Dordon Cl SHLY B90 179 G4
Doreen Gv ERDE/BCHGN B24 93 F4
Doris Rd BORD B9 128 B3
CSHL/WTROR B46 115 F1
SPARK B11 144 D3
Dorking Gv EDG B15 126 C3
Dorlcote Rd WASH/WDE B8 111 E5
Dormie Cl HWK/WKHTH B38 176 B4
Dormington Rd KGSTG B44 60 B5
Dormston Cl SOLH B91 182 A5
Dormston Dr SEDG DY3 67 F3
SLYOAK B29 141 F5
Dormy Dr NFLD/LBR B31 189 G1
Dorncliffe Av STETCH B33 131 F5
Dornie Dr HWK/WKHTH B38 176 D4
Dornton Rd BVILLE B30 160 C2
Dorothy Rd SMTHWKW B67 124 C1
SPARK B11 146 B2
Dorothy St WSL WS1 56 D1
Dorridge Cft DOR/KN B93 198 D1
Dorridge Rd DOR/KN B93 199 E1
Dorrington Gn PBAR/PBCH B42 90 A1
Dorrington Rd PBAR/PBCH B42 90 A1
Dorset Cl RBRY B45 173 H3
Dorset Dr ALDR WS9 30 A1
Dorset Pl BLOX/PEL WS3 27 G3
Dorset Rd HRBN B17 124 D1
STRBR DY8 117 H5
WASH/WDE B8 110 A3
Dorset Tower WSNGN B18 * 2 A2
Dorsett Rd DARL/WED WS10 55 E2
DARL/WED WS10 71 H1
Dorsett Road Ter
DARL/WED WS10 55 E2
Dorsheath Gdns
ERDW/GRVHL B23 92 D2
Dorsington Rd ACGN B27 163 H1
Dorstone Covert
ALE/KHTH/YWD B14 177 G3
Dorville Cl HWK/WKHTH B38 176 B5
Douay Rd ERDE/BCHGN B24 77 F5
Double Rw DUDS DY2 103 E5
Doughty St TPTN/OCK DY4 86 A1
Douglas Av CBROM B36 111 H3
LGLYGN/QTN B68 105 H4
Douglas Davies Cl SHHTH WV12 40 A1
Douglas Pl WOLVN WV10 23 E4
Douglas Rd ACGN B27 146 B3
BILS/COS WV14 68 D3
CSCFLD/WYGN B72 62 C5

HDSW B21 ... 107 G1
HLYWD B47 ... 192 C1
LGLYGN/QTN B68 ... 105 H5
RMSLY B62 ... 122 C3
Douglass Rd DUDS DY2 ... 102 D1
Doulton Cl RIDG/WDGT B32 ... 141 F4
Doulton Dr SMTHWK B66 ... 106 C3
Doulton Rd
BLKHTH/ROWR B65 ... 103 G5
Dovebridge Cl WALM/CURD B76 ... 63 F4
Dove Cl DARL/WED WS10 ... 56 B4
WSL WS1 ... 5 H5
YDLY B25 ... 130 A4
Dovecote Cl
DUNHL/THL/PER WV6 ... 35 G1
SOLH B91 ... 164 D2
TPTN/OCK DY4 ... 86 A1
The Dovecotes MGN/WHC B75 ... 47 F2
Dovedale Av BLOX/PEL WS3 ... 18 A2
SHHTH WV12 ... 39 G1
SHLY B90 ... 180 B4
Dovedale Ct
ETTPK/GDPK/PENN WV4 ... 67 H1
Dovedale Dr HLGN/YWD B28 ... 162 D4
Dovedale Rd ERDW/GRVHL B23 ... 76 A5
ETTPK/GDPK/PENN WV4 ... 52 C5
KGSWFD DY6 ... 100 A1
Dove Dr STRBR DY8 ... 118 C4
Dove Gdns HWK/WKHTH B38 ... 177 F3
Dove House La HIA/OLT B92 ... 164 B3
Dovehouse Pool Rd
AST/WIT B6 ... 109 E1
Dover Cl RIDG/WDGT B32 ... 157 E3
Dovercourt Rd
LGN/SDN/BHAMAIR B26 ... 148 A2
Doverdale Cl HALE B63 ... 137 H2
Dove Rdg STRBR DY8 ... 118 C5
Doveridge Cl SOLH B91 ... 164 A4
Doveridge Pl WSL WS1 ... 5 F7
Doveridge Rd HLGN/YWD B28 ... 162 C5
Doversley Rd
ALE/KHTH/YWD B14 ... 160 C5
Dover St BILS/COS WV14 ... 53 H2
WSNGN B18 ... 107 H3
Dove Wy CBROM B36 ... 113 H1
Dovey Dr WALM/CURD B76 ... 78 C4
Dovey Rd MOS/BIL B13 ... 145 F5
OLDBY B69 ... 104 B1
Dovey Tower VAUX/NECH B7 * ... 109 G5
Dowar Rd RBRY B45 ... 188 C1
Dowells Gdns STRBR DY8 ... 117 H1
The Doweries RBRY B45 ... 173 H5
Dower Rd MGN/WHC B75 ... 47 G5
Dowles Cl SLYOAK B29 ... 158 D4
Downcroft Av
HWK/WKHTH B38 ... 176 C3
Downend Cl WOLVN WV10 ... 13 F3
Downes Ct TPTN/OCK DY4 ... 85 E1
Downey Cl SPARK B11 ... 127 H5
Downfield Cl BLOX/PEL WS3 * ... 16 C3
Downfield Dr SEDG DY3 ... 67 G5
Downham Cl DSYBK/YTR WS5 ... 43 G4
Downham Pl BDMR/CCFT WV3 ... 36 B5
Downie Rd CDSL WV8 ... 11 E4
Downing Cl
BLKHTH/ROWR B65 ... 122 A3
DOR/KN B93 ... 197 E4
WNSFLD WV11 ... 25 G3
Downing St HALE B63 ... 138 C2
SMTHWK B66 ... 107 E2
Downland Cl HWK/WKHTH B38 ... 176 D4
Downsfield Rd
LGN/SDN/BHAMAIR B26 ... 130 D5
Downside Rd ERDE/BCHGN B24 ... 92 C5
Downs Rd WLNHL WV13 ... 40 A5
The Downs FOAKS/STRLY B74 ... 45 E3
WOLVN WV10 ... 23 E4
Downton Crs STETCH B33 ... 131 G1
Dowty Wy COVEN WV9 ... 12 A4
Drake Cl BLOX/PEL WS3 ... 27 F1
Drake Rd BLOX/PEL WS3 ... 27 G1
ERDW/GRVHL B23 ... 92 A3
SMTHWK B66 ... 105 H2
Drakes Cross Pde HLYWD B47 ... 192 C3
Drakes Hill Cl KINVER DY7 ... 134 C3
Drake St HHTH/SAND B71 ... 87 G1
Drancy Av SHHTH WV12 ... 26 B4
Drawbridge Rd SHLY B90 ... 179 G5
Draycote Cl HIA/OLT B92 ... 165 F3
Draycott Av ERDW/GRVHL B23 ... 92 B1
Draycott Cl
ETTPK/GDPK/PENN WV4 ... 50 C3
Draycott Dr NFLD/LBR B31 ... 158 A3
Draycott Rd SMTHWK B66 ... 106 A2
Drayman Cl WSL WS1 ... 5 F7
Drayton Cl MGN/WHC B75 ... 47 F2
Drayton Rd
ALE/KHTH/YWD B14 ... 161 E2
HAG/WOL DY9 ... 184 B2
SHLY B90 ... 181 E5
SMTHWK B66 ... 124 C3
Drayton St BKHL/PFLD WV2 ... 37 E5
WSLW WS2 ... 41 G3
Dreadnought Rd BRLYHL DY5 ... 100 D2
The Dreel EDG B15 ... 125 G5
Dreghorn Rd CBROM B36 ... 112 A1
Drem Cft CVALE B35 ... 94 C4
Dresden Cl
ETTPK/GDPK/PENN WV4 ... 53 E4
Drew Crs HAG/WOL DY9 ... 136 B4
Drew Rd HAG/WOL DY9 ... 136 B4
Drews Holloway HALE B63 ... 137 H2
Drews Holloway South
HALE B63 ... 137 H2
Drews La WASH/WDE B8 ... 111 E3
Drews Meadow Cl
ALE/KHTH/YWD B14 ... 177 G3
Driffold SCFLD/BOLD B73 ... 62 B5
Driftwood Cl HWK/WKHTH B38 ... 190 B1
Drive Flds
ETTPK/GDPK/PENN WV4 ... 50 B2
The Drive ALVE B48 ... 189 H5
BFLD/HDSWWD B20 ... 90 A4
BLOX/PEL WS3 ... 17 G5
BRLYHL DY5 ... 101 E4
CDSL WV8 ... 10 B4
CSHL/WTROR B46 * ... 115 G3
DUNHL/THL/PER WV6 * ... 21 G5
ERDW/GRVHL B23 ... 92 C4
HALE B63 ... 137 H2
HALE B63 ... 138 C4
RUSH/SHEL WS4 ... 29 E1
The Droveway COVEN WV9 ... 11 H5
Druid Park Rd SHHTH WV12 ... 26 A1
Druids Av ALDR WS9 ... 30 C2
BLKHTH/ROWR B65 ... 104 B5
Druids La ALE/KHTH/YWD B14 ... 177 G4
Druids Wk ALDR WS9 ... 19 G4
Drummond Cl WNSFLD WV11 ... 15 E5
Drummond Gv GTB/HAM B43 ... 59 G5
Drummond Rd BORD B9 ... 128 D2
HAG/WOL DY9 ... 136 D3
Drummond St WOLV WV1 ... 6 E2
Drummond Wy
CHWD/FDBR/MGN B37 ... 132 C2
Drury La CDSL WV8 ... 10 B3
SOLH B91 ... 182 A2
STRBR DY8 ... 135 G2
Drybrook Cl HWK/WKHTH B38 ... 176 C5
Dryden Cl SHHTH WV12 ... 26 C2
TPTN/OCK DY4 ... 69 G4
Dryden Gv ACGN B27 ... 146 B5
Dryden Pl BLOX/PEL WS3 ... 28 A3
Dryden Rd BLOX/PEL WS3 ... 28 A3
WOLVN WV10 ... 23 H1
Drylea Gv CBROM B36 ... 112 B1
Dubarry Av KGSWFD DY6 ... 99 G2
Duchess Pde WBROM B70 * ... 87 H3
Duchess Rd LDYWD/EDGR B16 ... 126 A3
WSL WS1 ... 56 D3
Duckhouse Rd WNSFLD WV11 ... 24 D3
Duck La CDSL WV8 ... 10 D5
Duddeston Dr WASH/WDE B8 ... 110 B5
Duddeston Mill Rd
VAUX/NECH B7 ... 109 H5
Dudding Rd
ETTPK/GDPK/PENN WV4 ... 52 B3
Dudhill Rd CDYHTH B64 ... 121 G1
Dudley Cl BLKHTH/ROWR B65 ... 103 F3
Dudley Crs WNSFLD WV11 ... 25 E4
Dudley Park Rd ACGN B27 ... 146 C4
Dudley Port TPTN/OCK DY4 ... 85 G3
Dudley Rd BKHL/PFLD WV2 ... 52 B1
BLKHTH/ROWR B65 ... 103 G4
BRLYHL DY5 ... 101 F5
HAG/WOL DY9 ... 136 C1
HALE B63 ... 138 D1
KGSWFD DY6 ... 99 G1
KGSWFD DY6 ... 100 B2
OLDBY B69 ... 104 C1
RMSLY B62 ... 138 D2
SEDG DY3 ... 67 F4
SEDG DY3 ... 81 G3
TPTN/OCK DY4 ... 84 D1
WSNGN B18 ... 107 F5
Dudley Rd East OLDBY B69 ... 86 A4
Dudley Rd West OLDBY B69 ... 85 H4
Dudley Rw DUDS DY2 ... 84 D5
Dudley Southern By-Pass
DUDS DY2 ... 102 A2
Dudley St BILS/COS WV14 ... 53 H4
DARL/WED WS10 ... 70 C1
DIG/EDG B5 ... 3 G6
SEDG DY3 ... 67 F3
WBROM B70 ... 86 D1
WOLV WV1 ... 7 F4
WSL WS1 ... 4 E5
Dudley Wk
ETTPK/GDPK/PENN WV4 ... 52 A3
Dudley Wood Av DUDS DY2 ... 120 C2
Dudley Wood Rd DUDS DY2 ... 120 C3
Dudmaston Wy DUDN DY1 ... 83 G3
Dudnill Gv RIDG/WDGT B32 ... 157 E2
Duffield Cl CDSL WV8 ... 22 B1
Dufton Rd RIDG/WDGT B32 ... 141 E2
Dugdale Crs MGN/WHC B75 ... 47 G2
Dugdale St WSNGN B18 ... 107 F5
Dukes Rd BVILLE B30 ... 176 D2
Duke St BDMR/CCFT WV3 ... 51 G1
BLKHTH/ROWR B65 ... 121 H2
CSCFLD/WYGN B72 ... 62 B4
SEDG DY3 ... 83 F1
STRBR DY8 ... 135 G2
WBROM B70 ... 87 F2
WNSFLD WV11 ... 24 D5
WOLV WV1 ... 7 J5
Dulvern Gv
ALE/KHTH/YWD B14 ... 160 D5
Dulverton Rd AST/WIT B6 ... 91 G5
Dulwich Gv KGSTG B44 ... 75 H3
Dulwich Rd KGSTG B44 ... 75 G3
Dumbleberry Av SEDG DY3 ... 67 E4
Dumblederry La ALDR WS9 ... 29 G2
Dunard Rd SHLY B90 ... 179 H2
Dunbar Gv GTB/HAM B43 ... 59 F4
Duncalfe Dr MGN/WHC B75 ... 47 F2
Duncan Edwards Cl DUDN DY1 ... 102 A1
Duncan St BKHL/PFLD WV2 ... 52 A1
Dunchurch Crs
SCFLD/BOLD B73 ... 61 E5
Dunchurch Dr NFLD/LBR B31 ... 158 A3
Duncombe Gn
CSHL/WTROR B46 ... 115 F2
Duncombe Gv HRBN B17 ... 124 B5
Duncombe St STRBR DY8 ... 134 D1
Duncroft Rd
LGN/SDN/BHAMAIR B26 ... 130 B4
Duncumb Rd MGN/WHC B75 ... 63 G3
Dundas Av OLDBY B69 ... 103 F1
Dunedin Rd KGSTG B44 ... 60 A5
Dunkirk Av WBROM B70 ... 86 C2
Dunkley St WOLV WV1 ... 6 E2
Dunley Cft SHLY B90 ... 195 F2
Dunlin Cl ERDW/GRVHL B23 ... 92 A4
KGSWFD DY6 ... 100 C3
Dunlop Wy ERDE/BCHGN B24 ... 94 A5
Dunnerdale Rd BRWNH WS8 ... 18 D1
Dunnigan Rd RIDG/WDGT B32 ... 141 F4
Dunns Bank BRLYHL DY5 ... 119 H5
Dunsfold Cl BILS/COS WV14 ... 53 E5
Dunsfold Cft AST/WIT B6 ... 109 F3
Dunsford Cl BRLYHL DY5 ... 118 D5
Dunsford Rd SMTHWK B66 ... 124 C2
Dunsink Rd AST/WIT B6 ... 91 F5
Dunslade Crs BRLYHL DY5 ... 119 H4
Dunslade Rd ERDW/GRVHL B23 ... 76 C4
Dunsley Dr STRBR DY8 ... 118 A1
Dunsley Gv
ETTPK/GDPK/PENN WV4 ... 51 G4
Dunsmore Dr BRLYHL DY5 ... 119 H4
Dunsmore Gv SOLH B91 ... 164 B3
Dunsmore Rd HLGN/YWD B28 ... 162 C1
Dunstall Av
DUNHL/THL/PER WV6 ... 23 E5
Dunstall Gv SLYOAK B29 ... 158 B2
Dunstall Hl
DUNHL/THL/PER WV6 ... 23 E5
Dunstall La
DUNHL/THL/PER WV6 ... 22 D5
Dunstall Rd
DUNHL/THL/PER WV6 ... 36 D1
HALE B63 ... 137 H4
Dunstan Cft SHLY B90 ... 180 C5
Dunster Cl BVILLE B30 ... 177 F1
Dunster Gv
DUNHL/THL/PER WV6 ... 34 D2
Dunster Rd
CHWD/FDBR/MGN B37 ... 132 C1
Dunston Cl KGSWFD DY6 ... 99 H2
Dunton Cl MGN/WHC B75 ... 47 E1
Dunton Hall Rd SHLY B90 ... 180 A5
Dunton Rd
CHWD/FDBR/MGN B37 ... 113 H5
Dunvegan Rd ERDE/BCHGN B24 ... 93 E2
Durant Cl RBRY B45 ... 173 F4
Durban Rd SMTHWK B66 ... 107 E5
D'Urberville Rd BKHL/PFLD WV2 ... 52 D2
Durham Av WLNHL WV13 ... 40 A2
Durham Cft
CHWD/FDBR/MGN B37 ... 132 A2
Durham Dr HHTH/SAND B71 ... 71 H4
Durham Pl WSLW WS2 ... 41 F4
Durham Rd
BLKHTH/ROWR B65 ... 104 C5
DARL/WED WS10 ... 56 D4
DUDS DY2 ... 120 D2
SPARK B11 ... 144 D3
STRBR DY8 ... 117 H4
WSLW WS2 ... 41 F5
Durley Dean Rd SLYOAK B29 ... 142 A5
Durley Dr SCFLD/BOLD B73 ... 61 E5
Durley Rd YDLY B25 ... 146 C2
Durlston Gv HLGN/YWD B28 ... 163 E2
Durnford Cft
ALE/KHTH/YWD B14 ... 178 A4
Dursley Cl HIA/OLT B92 ... 164 D2
SHHTH WV12 ... 40 B1
Dutton's La MGN/WHC B75 ... 48 A1
Duxford Rd PBAR/PBCH B42 ... 74 B3
Dwellings La RIDG/WDGT B32 ... 140 B2
Dyas Av PBAR/PBCH B42 ... 74 A4
Dyas Rd HLYWD B47 ... 192 C1
KGSTG B44 ... 74 D3
Dyce Cl CVALE B35 ... 94 C2
Dymoke St BHTH/HG B12 ... 127 F4
Dynes Wk SMTHWKW B67 ... 106 C4
Dyott Rd MOS/BIL B13 ... 161 G1
Dyson Cl WSLW WS2 ... 40 D2
Dysons Gdns WASH/WDE B8 ... 110 C4

E

Eachelhurst Rd
ERDE/BCHGN B24 ... 94 A2
Eachus Rd BILS/COS WV14 ... 68 D3
Eachway RBRY B45 ... 187 H2
Eachway La RBRY B45 ... 188 A2
Eagle Cl BLKHTH/ROWR B65 ... 103 F5
DUDN DY1 ... 83 H5
Eagle Ct BDMR/CCFT WV3 * ... 51 G1
Eagle Cft ALE/KHTH/YWD B14 ... 178 A3
Eagle Gdns ERDE/BCHGN B24 ... 93 E4
Eagle Gv CBROM B36 ... 114 A1
Eagle La TPTN/OCK DY4 ... 70 B5
Eagle St BDMR/CCFT WV3 ... 51 G1
BKHL/PFLD WV2 ... 7 K7
TPTN/OCK DY4 ... 70 A5
Ealing Gv KGSTG B44 ... 75 G2
Earlsbury Gdns
BFLD/HDSWWD B20 ... 90 D5
Earls Court Rd HRBN B17 ... 141 G1
Earls Ferry Gdns
RIDG/WDGT B32 ... 157 F3
Earlsmead Rd HDSW B21 ... 107 E1
Earls Rd RUSH/SHEL WS4 ... 29 E3
Earlston Wy GTB/HAM B43 ... 73 F3
Earl St BILS/COS WV14 ... 53 H3
BILS/COS WV14 ... 68 D3
KGSWFD DY6 ... 99 H5
WBROM B70 ... 87 F2
WSL WS1 ... 56 D1
Earls Wy HALE B63 ... 138 D3
Earlswood Ct
BFLD/HDSWWD B20 ... 90 A4
Earlswood Crs COVEN WV9 ... 12 A4
Earlswood Dr MGN/WHC B75 ... 62 C1
Earlswood Rd DOR/KN B93 ... 198 B1
KGSWFD DY6 ... 100 A2
Easby Wy BLOX/PEL WS3 ... 16 B5
WASH/WDE B8 ... 110 C4
Easenhall Cl DOR/KN B93 ... 197 E4
Easmore Cl
ALE/KHTH/YWD B14 ... 177 H3
East Av OLDBY B69 ... 104 A2
WNSFLD WV11 ... 24 C4
Eastbourne Av
BKDE/SHDE B34 ... 111 H3
Eastbourne St RUSH/SHEL WS4 ... 42 B2
Eastbrook Cl WALM/CURD B76 ... 62 D4
Eastbury Dr HIA/OLT B92 ... 147 G5
East Car Park Rd
BHAMNEC B40 ... 150 B3
Eastcote Cl SHLY B90 ... 180 D2
Eastcote La HIA/OLT B92 ... 167 G5
Eastcote Rd ACGN B27 ... 163 E1
WOLVN WV10 ... 23 H5
East Croft Rd
ETTPK/GDPK/PENN WV4 ... 50 C4
Eastdean Cl ERDW/GRVHL B23 ... 76 A5
East Dr DIG/EDG B5 ... 143 G3
Eastern Av BRLYHL DY5 ... 118 D2
Eastern Cl DARL/WED WS10 ... 55 E5
Eastern Rd SCFLD/BOLD B73 ... 77 F2
SLYOAK B29 ... 143 F4
Easterton Cft
ALE/KHTH/YWD B14 ... 178 A3
East Farm Cft SMHTH B10 ... 128 B4
Eastfield Cl ALDR WS9 ... 30 A4
Eastfield Dr HIA/OLT B92 ... 165 G2
Eastfield Gv WOLV WV1 ... 37 H3
Eastfield Retreat WOLV WV1 ... 37 H3
Eastfield Rd BORD B9 ... 129 G2
TPTN/OCK DY4 ... 69 G3
WOLV WV1 ... 37 H3
East Ga LDYWD/EDGR B16 ... 125 G1
East Gn
ETTPK/GDPK/PENN WV4 ... 50 D2
Eastham Rd MOS/BIL B13 ... 162 A4
East Holme BORD B9 ... 128 A2
Easthope Rd STETCH B33 ... 112 C5
Eastlake Cl GTB/HAM B43 ... 59 H5
Eastlands Rd MOS/BIL B13 ... 161 G1
Eastleigh SEDG DY3 ... 66 D3
Eastleigh Cft WALM/CURD B76 ... 78 C4
Eastleigh Dr RMSLY B62 ... 172 C1
Eastleigh Gv YDLY B25 ... 129 H4
East Meadway STETCH B33 ... 131 F1
East Ms KGSTG B44 ... 74 D1
Eastmoor Cl FOAKS/STRLY B74 ... 45 H3
Eastney Crs CDSL WV8 ... 22 A2
Easton Gdns WNSFLD WV11 ... 25 F5
Easton Gv ACGN B27 ... 163 G1
HLYWD B47 ... 192 D1
East Park Wy WOLV WV1 ... 38 A4
East Pathway HRBN B17 ... 142 A1
East Ri MGN/WHC B75 ... 62 D2
East Rd TPTN/OCK DY4 ... 69 H3
WOLVN WV10 ... 13 G1
East St BRLYHL DY5 ... 120 A4
DUDS DY2 ... 103 E1
SEDG DY3 ... 83 E3
WOLV WV1 ... 7 J5
WSL WS1 ... 57 F1
East View Rd WALM/CURD B76 ... 62 D5
Eastville NFLD/LBR B31 ... 175 H2
Eastward Gln CDSL WV8 ... 21 G1
East Wy BHAMNEC B40 ... 150 B4
Eastway HRBN B17 ... 142 A1
Eastwood Rd BHTH/HG B12 ... 143 H2
GTB/HAM B43 ... 73 G3
Eatesbrook Rd STETCH B33 ... 131 E1
Eathorpe Cl BKDE/SHDE B34 ... 113 F3
Eaton Av WBROM B70 ... 87 E2
Eaton Ct FOAKS/STRLY B74 ... 62 B1
Eaton Crs SEDG DY3 ... 82 D3
Eaton Pl KGSWFD DY6 ... 100 A4
Eaton Ri SHHTH WV12 ... 25 H4
Eaton Wd ERDE/BCHGN B24 ... 93 H3
Eaton Wood Dr
LGN/SDN/BHAMAIR B26 ... 146 D2
Eaves Court Dr SEDG DY3 ... 67 E1
Eaves Green Gdns ACGN B27 ... 146 B2
Ebenezer St BILS/COS WV14 ... 68 B3
WBROM B70 ... 70 D5
Ebley Rd BFLD/HDSWWD B20 ... 90 A2
Ebmore Dr
ALE/KHTH/YWD B14 ... 177 H3
Ebrington Av HIA/OLT B92 ... 147 H4
Ebrington Cl
ALE/KHTH/YWD B14 ... 177 H1
Ebrington Rd HHTH/SAND B71 ... 71 H5
Ebrook Rd CSCFLD/WYGN B72 ... 62 C4
Ebury Rd BVILLE B30 ... 177 F1
Eccleshall Av WOLVN WV10 ... 23 E2
Ecclestone Rd WNSFLD WV11 ... 25 G2
Echo Wy
ETTPK/GDPK/PENN WV4 ... 53 E4
Eckersall Rd HWK/WKHTH B38 ... 176 C2
Edale Cl
ETTPK/GDPK/PENN WV4 ... 52 C5
KGSWFD DY6 ... 99 F2
Edale Rd PBAR/PBCH B42 ... 74 C4
Eddish Rd STETCH B33 ... 112 D5
Edelweiss Cl DSYBK/YTR WS5 ... 57 H5
Edenbridge Rd
HLGN/YWD B28 ... 163 F2
Edenbridge Vw DUDN DY1 ... 83 G3
Eden Cl NFLD/LBR B31 ... 175 E5
OLDBY B69 ... 86 B4
Edendale Rd
LGN/SDN/BHAMAIR B26 ... 147 H1
Eden Gv
CHWD/FDBR/MGN B37 ... 132 D3
HHTH/SAND B71 ... 87 G1
Edenhall Rd RIDG/WDGT B32 ... 140 B1
Edenhurst Rd NFLD/LBR B31 ... 189 F2
Eden Pl CBHAMNW B3 ... 2 E5
Eden Rd HIA/OLT B92 ... 148 B4
Edensor Cl WOLVN WV10 ... 37 G1
Edgbaston Park Rd EDG B15 ... 143 E2
Edgbaston Rd BHTH/HG B12 ... 144 A3
DIG/EDG B5 ... 143 G2
SMTHWK B66 ... 124 D1
Edgbaston Rd East
BHTH/HG B12 * ... 144 A2
Edgbaston St DIG/EDG B5 ... 3 G6
Edgcombe Rd HLGN/YWD B28 ... 162 D1
Edge Hill Av WOLVN WV10 ... 24 A1
Edge Hill Dr
DUNHL/THL/PER WV6 ... 34 C2
SEDG DY3 ... 67 E1
Edge Hill Rd FOAKS/STRLY B74 ... 46 C1
Edgehill Rd NFLD/LBR B31 ... 175 G4
Edgemond Av
ERDE/BCHGN B24 ... 94 B2
Edge St BILS/COS WV14 ... 68 C3
Edgewood Cl CDYHTH B64 ... 121 F4
Edgewood Rd
HWK/WKHTH B38 ... 190 C1
RBRY B45 ... 188 B1
Edgeworth Cl SHHTH WV12 ... 40 A1
Edgware Rd ERDW/GRVHL B23 ... 92 F2
Edinburgh Av WSLW WS2 ... 40 C2
Edinburgh Ct ERDE/BCHGN B24 ... 93 H2
Edinburgh Crs STRBR DY8 ... 117 G3
Edinburgh Dr RUSH/SHEL WS4 ... 29 F3
SHHTH WV12 ... 25 H4
Edinburgh La WSLW WS2 * ... 41 E1
Edinburgh Rd BILS/COS WV14 ... 54 B5
DSYBK/YTR WS5 ... 42 D5
DUDS DY2 ... 102 D3
LGLYGN/QTN B68 ... 123 F4
Edison Gv RIDG/WDGT B32 ... 140 D2
Edison Rd WALM/CURD B76 ... 97 G3
WSLW WS2 ... 27 E5
Edith Rd SMTHWK B66 ... 124 D1
Edith St WBROM B70 ... 87 F3
Edmonds Cl STETCH B33 ... 130 D2
Edmonds Rd LGLYGN/QTN B68 ... 123 G2
Edmonton Av KGSTG B44 ... 75 H2
Edmoor Cl SHHTH WV12 ... 26 A4
Edmund Rd SEDG DY3 ... 67 G5
WASH/WDE B8 ... 110 B5
Edmund St CBHAMNW B3 ... 3 F4
Ednam Cl HHTH/SAND B71 ... 72 B3
Ednam Gv WMBN WV5 ... 65 E2
Ednam Rd DUDN DY1 ... 84 C4
ETTPK/GDPK/PENN WV4 ... 52 A2
Edsome Wy CBROM B36 ... 112 B1
Edstone Cl DOR/KN B93 ... 196 D5
Edstone Ms CBROM B36 ... 112 B1
Edward Av ALDR WS9 ... 30 A3
Edward Cl BILS/COS WV14 ... 54 A5
Edward Fisher Dr
TPTN/OCK DY4 ... 85 G1
Edward Rd
ALE/KHTH/YWD B14 ... 178 B4
CSHL/WTROR B46 ... 96 C3
DIG/EDG B5 ... 143 H1
DUNHL/THL/PER WV6 ... 20 C5
HALE B63 ... 138 B3
LGLYGN/QTN B68 ... 123 G4
SMTHWKW B67 ... 106 B5
TPTN/OCK DY4 ... 69 G4
Edwards Rd DUDS DY2 ... 102 C5
ERDE/BCHGN B24 ... 93 E1
MGN/WHC B75 ... 47 H2
Edward St CBHAMW B1 ... 2 B5
DARL/WED WS10 ... 55 G2
DUDN DY1 ... 84 B5
ETTPK/GDPK/PENN WV4 ... 52 D2
LGLYGN/QTN B68 ... 105 E5
WBROM B70 ... 87 G3
WSLW WS2 ... 41 F2
Edwin Phillips Dr
HHTH/SAND B71 ... 71 F3
Edwin Rd BVILLE B30 ... 160 B3
Eel St OLDBY B69 ... 104 D2
Effingham Rd MOS/BIL B13 ... 162 A4
Egbert Cl AST/WIT B6 ... 109 H1
Egelwin Cl
DUNHL/THL/PER WV6 ... 20 C5
Egerton Rd ERDE/BCHGN B24 ... 93 H3
FOAKS/STRLY B74 ... 45 F4
WOLVN WV10 ... 13 E4
Egghill La RIDG/WDGT B32 ... 174 A1
Eggington Rd STRBR DY8 ... 117 H5
Egginton Rd HLGN/YWD B28 ... 162 C5
Egmont Gdns WNSFLD WV11 ... 25 F5
Eileen Gdns
CHWD/FDBR/MGN B37 ... 114 A5
Eileen Rd SPARK B11 ... 144 D4
Elan Cl SEDG DY3 ... 83 F3
Elan Rd NFLD/LBR B31 ... 174 C3
SEDG DY3 ... 67 E3
Elbow St CDYHTH B64 ... 121 F3
Elbury Cft DOR/KN B93 ... 196 D3
Elcock Dr PBAR/PBCH B42 ... 90 D1
Eldalade Wy DARL/WED WS10 ... 71 G2
Elderberry Cl STRBR DY8 ... 134 C4
Elderfield Rd BVILLE B30 ... 177 F2
Elder Gv WMBN WV5 ... 64 D5
Eldersfield Gv SOLH B91 ... 195 H1
Elder Wy ERDW/GRVHL B23 ... 92 B4
Eldon Dr WALM/CURD B76 ... 78 A4
Eldon Rd LDYWD/EDGR B16 ... 125 H3
RIDG/WDGT B32 ... 140 A4
Eldon St DARL/WED WS10 ... 55 F1
WSL WS1 ... 5 G5
Eldridge Cl COVEN WV9 ... 11 H5
Eleanor Rd BILS/COS WV14 ... 53 H2
Electric Av AST/WIT B6 ... 91 H5
Elford Cl ALE/KHTH/YWD B14 ... 161 E5
Elford Gv BILS/COS WV14 ... 53 G4
CHWD/FDBR/MGN B37 ... 132 B3
Elford Rd HHTH/SAND B71 ... 72 A2
HRBN B17 ... 141 H4
Elgar Crs BRLYHL DY5 ... 101 F2
Elgin Cl SEDG DY3 ... 67 G2
STRBR DY8 ... 118 C5
Elgin Ct DUNHL/THL/PER WV6 ... 34 C1
Elgin Gv YDLY B25 ... 129 G5
Elgin Rd BLOX/PEL WS3 ... 16 C3
Eliot Cft BILS/COS WV14 ... 68 D1
Eliot St VAUX/NECH B7 ... 110 A1

Elizabeth Av BILS/COS WV14 54 B5
DARL/WED WS10 56 C5
ETTPK/GDPK/PENN WV4 51 H3
Elizabeth Crs LGLYGN/QTN B68 123 H2
Elizabeth Gv DUDS DY2 103 F2
SHLY B90 180 C3
Elizabeth Ms OLDBY B69 85 G4
Elizabeth Rd DSYBK/YTR WS5 57 H1
HALE B63 138 B4
MOS/BIL B13 143 G5
SCFLD/BOLD B73 76 A2
STETCH B33 129 H1
TPTN/OCK DY4 86 B2
Elizabeth Wk TPTN/OCK DY4 69 G2
Elkington Cft SHLY B90 195 F3
Elkington St AST/WIT B6 109 E4
Elkstone Cl HIA/OLT B92 147 H4
Elkstone Covert
ALE/KHTH/YWD B14 177 G3
Ellards Dr WNSFLD WV11 25 F5
Ellen St WSNGN B18 2 A1
Ellenvale Cl BILS/COS WV14 68 A3
Ellerby Gv ERDE/BCHGN B24 94 A2
Ellerside Gv NFLD/LBR B31 175 F3
Ellerslie Cl BRLYHL DY5 119 F4
Ellerslie Rd MOS/BIL B13 162 A3
Ellerton Rd KGSTG B44 75 H2
Ellerton Wk WOLVN WV10 23 H5
Ellesboro' Rd HRBN B17 124 D4
Ellesmere Rd WASH/WDE B8 110 B5
Ellice Dr CBROM B36 114 B2
Elliot Gdns RBRY B45 188 B3
Elliott Rd SLYOAK B29 142 C5
Elliotts La CDSL WV8 10 C4
Elliott's Rd TPTN/OCK DY4 85 E1
Ellis Av BRLYHL DY5 118 C2
Ellison St WBROM B70 87 G5
Ellis St CBHAMW B1 2 E7
Elliston Av KGSTG B44 75 E3
Ellowes Rd SEDG DY3 83 E2
Elm Av BHTH/HG B12 144 C2
BILS/COS WV14 53 H2
DARL/WED WS10 55 H4
WNSFLD WV11 24 B2
Elmay Rd
LGN/SDN/BHAMAIR B26 130 C5
Elm Bank MOS/BIL B13 144 C4
Elmbank Gv
BFLD/HDSWWD B20 89 G1
Elmbank Rd DSYBK/YTR WS5 58 A4
Elmbridge Cl HALE B63 137 H2
Elmbridge Dr SHLY B90 195 H2
Elmbridge Rd KGSTG B44 75 E5
Elmbridge Wy SEDG DY3 67 G5
Elm Cl SEDG DY3 82 D4
STRBR DY8 134 C5
Elm Cft LGLYGN/QTN B68 123 G5
Elmcroft Av RIDG/WDGT B32 157 E1
Elmcroft Gdns WOLVN WV10 13 E4
Elmcroft Rd
LGN/SDN/BHAMAIR B26 130 B5
Elmdale RMSLY B62 123 E5
Elmdale Crs NFLD/LBR B31 175 E1
Elmdale Dr ALDR WS9 30 C2
Elmdale Gv NFLD/LBR B31 175 E1
Elmdale Rd BILS/COS WV14 68 A4
Elm Dale Rd
ETTPK/GDPK/PENN WV4 51 G3
Elmdon Cl HIA/OLT B92 148 B5
WOLVN WV10 22 C1
Elmdon Coppice HIA/OLT B92 165 H3
Elmdon La
CHWD/FDBR/MGN B37 131 H5
LGN/SDN/BHAMAIR B26 149 E4
Elmdon Park Rd HIA/OLT B92 148 B5
Elmdon Rd ACGN B27 146 C3
CHWD/FDBR/MGN B37 149 E1
SLYOAK B29 143 E5
WOLVN WV10 22 C1
Elm Dr GTB/HAM B43 73 F2
KIDD DY10 168 B3
RMSLY B62 122 C3
Elm Farm Av
CHWD/FDBR/MGN B37 131 H5
Elm Farm Rd BKHL/PFLD WV2 52 B1
Elmfield Av ERDE/BCHGN B24 94 A2
Elmfield Crs MOS/BIL B13 144 B5
Elmfield Rd CBROM B36 113 G2
Elmfield Vw DUDN DY1 84 A3
Elm Gn DUDN DY1 84 A1
Elm Gv CDSL WV8 10 C4
CHWD/FDBR/MGN B37 113 H3
Elmhurst Av
BLKHTH/ROWR B65 122 A1
Elmhurst Dr KGSWFD DY6 100 B5
Elmhurst Rd HDSW B21 89 G5
Elmley Cl BILS/COS WV14 68 B4
Elmley Gv BVILLE B30 177 F2
DUNHL/THL/PER WV6 34 D2
Elm Ldg HIA/OLT B92 * 167 G3
Elmore Cl
CHWD/FDBR/MGN B37 114 A5
Elmore Green Cl BLOX/PEL WS3 27 F2
Elmore Green Rd
BLOX/PEL WS3 27 E1
Elmore Rd STETCH B33 130 C1
Elmore Rw BLOX/PEL WS3 27 F1
Elm Rd BLOX/PEL WS3 27 H4
BVILLE B30 159 H2
DUDN DY1 84 C3
KGSWFD DY6 100 A3
WALM/CURD B76 78 B1
Elms Cl SOLH B91 165 F5
Elmsdale DUNHL/THL/PER WV6 34 D3
Elms Rd CSCFLD/WYGN B72 62 B5
Elmstead Av STETCH B33 131 F5
Elmstead Cl DSYBK/YTR WS5 43 G4
Elmstead Wd DSYBK/YTR WS5 43 G5
The Elms LDYWD/EDGR B16 * 125 H1
Elm St BDMR/CCFT WV3 6 A5
WLNHL WV13 39 H3
Elm Ter OLDBY B69 85 G5
Elm Tree Cl WMBN WV5 80 D1
Elm Tree Gv HALE B63 137 H1
Elm Tree Ri HIA/OLT B92 167 G4
Elm Tree Rd BVILLE B30 160 A4
HRBN B17 141 G1
Elmtree Rd FOAKS/STRLY B74 44 D5
Elm Tree Wy CDYHTH B64 * 121 F3
Elmwood Av WNSFLD WV11 15 E4
Elmwood Gdns
BFLD/HDSWWD B20 90 B4
Elmwood Gv HLYWD B47 192 C2
Elmwood Ri SEDG DY3 66 D2
Elmwood Rd ERDE/BCHGN B24 93 G4
FOAKS/STRLY B74 60 C2
STRBR DY8 117 G1
Elmwoods RIDG/WDGT B32 140 B5
Elphinstone End
CSCFLD/WYGN B72 77 G5
Elsma Rd LGLYGN/QTN B68 123 G4
Elston Hall La WOLVN WV10 23 G1
Elston Hall Ter WOLVN WV10 * 23 G1
Elstree Rd ERDW/GRVHL B23 92 B1
Elswick Gv KGSTG B44 75 H3
Elswick Pl KGSTG B44 75 H2
Elsworth Gv YDLY B25 146 C1
Eltham Gv KGSTG B44 75 H2
Elton Cl WOLVN WV10 13 E3
Elton Cft DOR/KN B93 196 D4
Elton Gv ACGN B27 146 A5
Eltonia Cft
LGN/SDN/BHAMAIR B26 147 H1
Elva Cft CBROM B36 95 H5
Elvetham Rd EDG B15 126 C4
Elviron Dr
DUNHL/THL/PER WV6 21 F5
Elwells Cl
ETTPK/GDPK/PENN WV4 53 E5
Elwell St DARL/WED WS10 56 B5
WBROM B70 86 C1
Elwyn Rd SCFLD/BOLD B73 62 A5
Ely Cl BLKHTH/ROWR B65 104 C5
CHWD/FDBR/MGN B37 132 B2
Ely Crs HHTH/SAND B71 71 F5
Ely Gv RIDG/WDGT B32 141 F3
Ely Pl WSLW WS2 41 F4
Ely Rd WSLW WS2 41 F4
Emay Cl WBROM B70 70 D3
The Embankment BRLYHL DY5 119 G2
Embassy Dr OLDBY B69 104 C1
Embassy Rd OLDBY B69 104 C1
Embleton Gv BKDE/SHDE B34 112 C3
Emerson Cl SEDG DY3 82 C2
Emerson Gv WOLVN WV10 23 H2
Emerson Rd HRBN B17 142 A1
WOLVN WV10 23 H1
Emery Cl ERDW/GRVHL B23 92 B5
WSL WS1 5 F6
Emery St WSL WS1 5 G6
Emily Gdns LDYWD/EDGR B16 125 H1
Emily Rd
LGN/SDN/BHAMAIR B26 146 D1
Emily St BHTH/HG B12 127 F5
WBROM B70 87 F4
Emmanuel Rd SCFLD/BOLD B73 77 F4
Emmeline St BORD B9 127 H3
Empire Cl ALDR WS9 29 H2
Empress Wy DARL/WED WS10 40 B5
Emscote Dr SCFLD/BOLD B73 77 F4
Emscote Gn SOLH B91 181 E3
Emscote Rd AST/WIT B6 91 F5
Emsworth Crs COVEN WV9 12 A5
Emsworth Gv
ALE/KHTH/YWD B14 160 D4
Enderby Cl DOR/KN B93 196 D4
Enderby Dr
ETTPK/GDPK/PENN WV4 51 F4
Enderby Rd ERDW/GRVHL B23 76 A4
Enderley Cl BLOX/PEL WS3 * 16 D4
Enderley Dr BLOX/PEL WS3 16 D4
Enderly Gv WSNGN B18 107 G5
End Hall Rd
DUNHL/THL/PER WV6 35 E2
Endhill Rd KGSTG B44 60 C5
Endicott Rd AST/WIT B6 91 F5
Endmoor Gv ERDW/GRVHL B23 76 B5
Endsleigh Gv HLGN/YWD B28 163 E2
Endwood Court Rd
BFLD/HDSWWD B20 90 A4
Endwood Dr FOAKS/STRLY B74 46 A1
SOLH B91 181 F3
Enfield Cl ERDW/GRVHL B23 76 D5
Enfield Rd BLKHTH/ROWR B65 122 B1
EDG B15 126 B4
Enford Cl BKDE/SHDE B34 113 F3
Engine La BRLYHL DY5 101 H5
BRWNH WS8 8 C4
DARL/WED WS10 54 C4
HAG/WOL DY9 136 B2
Engine St OLDBY B69 105 E3
SMTHWK B66 106 D3
Englestede Cl
BFLD/HDSWWD B20 89 H3
Englewood Dr HLGN/YWD B28 163 E2
Ennerdale Cl BRWNH WS8 9 E5
Ennerdale Dr
DUNHL/THL/PER WV6 34 D1
HALE B63 137 H5
Ennerdale Rd
DUNHL/THL/PER WV6 21 H2
GTB/HAM B43 73 G4
Ennersdale Bungalows
CSHL/WTROR B46 97 F5
Ennersdale Cl CSHL/WTROR B46 97 F5
Ennersdale Rd
CSHL/WTROR B46 97 F5
Ensall Dr STRBR DY8 118 A3
Ensbury Cl SHHTH WV12 40 B1
Ensdale Rw WLNHL WV13 39 G4
Ensdon Gv KGSTG B44 75 H2
Ensford Cl FOAKS/STRLY B74 46 C1
Enstone Rd DUDN DY1 101 H1
ERDW/GRVHL B23 77 E5
Enterprise Dr
FOAKS/STRLY B74 * 60 A1
HAG/WOL DY9 136 D1
Enterprise Gv BLOX/PEL WS3 18 B2
Enterprise Wy CBHAMNE B4 3 J1
Enville Cl BLOX/PEL WS3 16 C4
CHWD/FDBR/MGN B37 132 B3
Enville Gv SPARK B11 145 F2
Enville Pl STRBR DY8 * 135 F2
Enville Rd
ETTPK/GDPK/PENN WV4 50 C3
KGSWFD DY6 99 F1
SEDG DY3 83 F2
Enville St STRBR DY8 135 F2
Epping Cl BLOX/PEL WS3 28 B4
RBRY B45 174 B3
Epping Gv KGSTG B44 75 G4
Epsom Cl DUNHL/THL/PER WV6 34 D1
Epsom Gv KGSTG B44 75 H3
Epwell Gv KGSTG B44 75 F5
Epwell Rd KGSTG B44 75 F5
Equipoint YDLY B25 * 146 D1
Erasmus Rd SPARK B11 127 G5
Ercall Cl ERDW/GRVHL B23 75 G5
Erdington Hall Rd
ERDE/BCHGN B24 92 D4
Erdington Rd ALDR WS9 44 C3
Erica Cl SLYOAK B29 158 C2
Erica Rd DSYBK/YTR WS5 57 H5
Ermington Crs CBROM B36 112 A2
Ermington Rd
ETTPK/GDPK/PENN WV4 52 B3
Ernest Clarke Cl SHHTH WV12 40 A1
Ernest Ct HWK/WKHTH B38 177 E4
Ernest Rd BHTH/HG B12 144 D3
DUDS DY2 85 F5
SMTHWKW B67 106 A3
Ernest St CBHAMW B1 126 D3
Ernsford Cl DOR/KN B93 198 D1
Erskine St VAUX/NECH B7 127 H1
Esher Rd HHTH/SAND B71 71 H5
KGSTG B44 60 B4
Eskdale Cl WOLV WV1 38 A3
Eskdale Wk BRLYHL DY5 118 D4
Esme Rd SPARK B11 144 D3
Esmond Cl BVILLE B30 159 F5
Essendon Rd WASH/WDE B8 111 F5
Essex Av DARL/WED WS10 56 C4
HHTH/SAND B71 71 G4
KGSWFD DY6 99 F4
Essex Gdns STRBR DY8 117 H5
Essex Rd DUDS DY2 101 H3
MGN/WHC B75 47 H4
Essex St DIG/EDG B5 127 E3
WSLW WS2 27 H5
Essington Cl STRBR DY8 118 A4
Essington Rd SHHTH WV12 25 H1
Essington St LDYWD/EDGR B16 2 B7
Essington Wy WOLV WV1 38 B4
Este Rd
LGN/SDN/BHAMAIR B26 130 C4
Estone Wk AST/WIT B6 109 F2
Estria Rd EDG B15 126 B5
Ethelfleda Ter DARL/WED WS10 55 H5
Ethelred Cl FOAKS/STRLY B74 47 E2
Ethel Rd HRBN B17 142 B2
Ethel St CBHAM B2 3 F5
LGLYGN/QTN B68 105 E5
SMTHWKW B67 124 B2
Etheridge Rd BILS/COS WV14 53 H1
Eton Cl SEDG DY3 67 H4
Eton Dr STRBR DY8 135 G4
Eton Rd BHTH/HG B12 144 D3
Eton Wk HAG/WOL DY9 152 C4
Etruria Wy BILS/COS WV14 54 A1
Etta Gv KGSTG B44 60 A4
Ettingshall Park Farm La
ETTPK/GDPK/PENN WV4 52 B4
Ettingshall Rd BILS/COS WV14 68 A2
BKHL/PFLD WV2 53 E1
Ettington Cl DOR/KN B93 198 B1
Ettington Rd AST/WIT B6 109 E1
Ettymore Cl SEDG DY3 67 F3
Ettymore Rd SEDG DY3 67 F3
Ettymore Rd West SEDG DY3 67 E3
Etwall Rd HLGN/YWD B28 162 C5
Euan Cl HRBN B17 125 E4
Europa Av WBROM B70 88 B4
Evans Cl TPTN/OCK DY4 84 C1
Evans Pl BILS/COS WV14 54 A1
Evans St BILS/COS WV14 67 H2
DUNHL/THL/PER WV6 36 D1
WLNHL WV13 38 D4
Eva Rd LGLYGN/QTN B68 123 G2
WSNGN B18 107 G3
Eve La DUDN DY1 83 H1
Evelyn Cft SCFLD/BOLD B73 77 E3
Evelyn Rd SPARK B11 145 E3
Evenlode Gv WLNHL WV13 40 B4
Evenlode Rd HIA/OLT B92 147 G4
Everest Cl SMTHWK B66 106 A1
Everest Rd BFLD/HDSWWD B20 90 A3
WSLW WS2 40 D2
Evergreen Cl BILS/COS WV14 68 B3
Everitt Dr DOR/KN B93 197 E2
Eversley Dl ERDE/BCHGN B24 93 E4
Eversley Gv SEDG DY3 67 E1
WNSFLD WV11 24 C4
Eversley Rd BORD B9 128 B3
Evers St BRLYHL DY5 120 A4
Everton Rd WASH/WDE B8 111 G5
Eves Cft RIDG/WDGT B32 157 G1
Evesham Crs BLOX/PEL WS3 16 B4
Evesham Ri DUDS DY2 120 D1
Eveson Rd STRBR DY8 134 D5
Evington Pl YDLY B25 * 129 E5
Ewart Rd WSLW WS2 40 C2
Ewell Rd ERDE/BCHGN B24 93 F2
Ewhurst Av SLYOAK B29 159 H1
Ewhurst Cl WLNHL WV13 39 F5
Exbury Cl COVEN WV9 11 H5
Excelsior Gv BLOX/PEL WS3 18 B2
Exchange St BRLYHL DY5 101 F5
The Exchange BLOX/PEL WS3 * 27 F1
Exe Cft NFLD/LBR B31 175 H5
Exeter Dr
CHWD/FDBR/MGN B37 131 H4
Exeter Pas CBHAMW B1 126 D3
Exeter Pl WSLW WS2 41 F4
Exeter Rd DUDS DY2 120 D2
SLYOAK B29 142 D5
SMTHWK B66 106 D4
Exeter St CBHAMW B1 2 E7
Exford Cl BRLYHL DY5 118 D5
Exhall Cl SOLH B91 181 E3
Exhibition Wy BHAMNEC B40 149 H3
Exmoor Gn WNSFLD WV11 24 C3
The Expressway WBROM B70 87 G2
Exton Cl WNSFLD WV11 25 F2
Exton Gdns SMTHWK B66 * 107 F3
Exton Wy WASH/WDE B8 110 B4
Eyland Gv WSL WS1 5 F3
Eymore Cl SLYOAK B29 158 D4
Eyre St WSNGN B18 126 A1
Eyston Av TPTN/OCK DY4 70 B3
Eyton Cft BHTH/HG B12 127 F5
Ezekiel La SHHTH WV12 26 A4

F

Fabian Cl RBRY B45 173 H3
Fabian Crs SHLY B90 180 B4
Facet Rd HWK/WKHTH B38 177 E3
Factory Rd TPTN/OCK DY4 69 E5
WSNGN B18 107 H3
Factory St DARL/WED WS10 55 E2
Fairbourne Av
BLKHTH/ROWR B65 104 C5
KGSTG B44 75 E1
Fairburn Crs BLOX/PEL WS3 18 B2
Faircroft Av WALM/CURD B76 78 B5
Faircroft Rd CBROM B36 95 F5
Fairfax Rd MGN/WHC B75 63 F4
NFLD/LBR B31 175 G5
WOLVN WV10 12 D4
Fairfield Dr BLOX/PEL WS3 18 B3
CDSL WV8 10 A4
RMSLY B62 122 C3
Fairfield Gv RMSLY B62 122 C3
Fairfield Mt WSL WS1 5 F7
Fairfield Ri STRBR DY8 134 C2
Fairfield Rd
ALE/KHTH/YWD B14 161 E2
DUDS DY2 102 D2
HALE B63 138 C5
RMSLY B62 122 C3
STRBR DY8 118 B2
Fairford Gdns STRBR DY8 118 A1
Fairford Rd KGSTG B44 75 F5
Fairgreen Gdns BRLYHL DY5 101 E4
Fairgreen Wy FOAKS/STRLY B74 45 G4
SLYOAK B29 159 H1
Fairground Wy WSL WS1 4 C6
Fairhaven Cft RMSLY B62 122 C3
Fairhills SEDG DY3 67 F3
Fairhill Wy SPARK B11 127 H5
Fairholme Rd CBROM B36 111 F2
Fairlawn EDG B15 * 126 A5
Fairlawn Cl SHHTH WV12 26 A1
Fairlawn Dr KGSWFD DY6 99 H5
Fairlawns
LGN/SDN/BHAMAIR B26 130 B3
WALM/CURD B76 78 C3
Fairlie Crs HWK/WKHTH B38 176 B4
Fairmead Ri HWK/WKHTH B38 176 C4
Fairmile Rd HALE B63 138 B1
Fairoak Dr
DUNHL/THL/PER WV6 35 E2
Fairview Av PBAR/PBCH B42 74 B5
Fairview Cl WNSFLD WV11 24 B3
Fairview Crs KGSWFD DY6 100 B3
WNSFLD WV11 24 B3
Fairview Gv WNSFLD WV11 24 B3
Fairview Ms
CSHL/WTROR B46 * 115 F2
Fairview Rd DUDN DY1 84 A4
ETTPK/GDPK/PENN WV4 50 C4
WNSFLD WV11 24 B3
Fairway NFLD/LBR B31 175 E3
RUSH/SHEL WS4 29 F1
Fairway Av OLDBY B69 103 G1
Fairway Dr RBRY B45 187 H2
Fairway Gn BILS/COS WV14 53 G1
Fairway Rd LGLYGN/QTN B68 122 D3
Fairways Av STRBR DY8 135 E5
Fairways Cl STRBR DY8 135 E5
The Fairway HWK/WKHTH B38 176 B3
Fairyfield Av GTB/HAM B43 73 F2
Fakenham Cft HRBN B17 124 B5
Falcon Crs BILS/COS WV14 67 H1
Falcondale Rd SHHTH WV12 26 A1
Falconhurst Rd SLYOAK B29 142 A5
Falcon Lodge Crs
MGN/WHC B75 63 G3
Falcon Pl OLDBY B69 104 A2
Falcon Ri STRBR DY8 134 C1
Falcon Rd LGLYGN/QTN B68 122 D2
The Falcons MGN/WHC B75 63 H3
Falcon Wy DUDN DY1 83 H5
Falfield Cl OLDBY B69 104 A3
Falfield Gv NFLD/LBR B31 189 E1
Falkland Cft BVILLE B30 160 B4
Falklands Cl SEDG DY3 80 C4
Falkland Wy CBROM B36 114 B4
Falkwood Gv DOR/KN B93 196 D2
Fallindale Rd
LGN/SDN/BHAMAIR B26 147 H1
Fallings Heath Cl
DARL/WED WS10 55 H1
Fallowfield CDSL WV8 11 G5
DUNHL/THL/PER WV6 34 B1
Fallow Fld FOAKS/STRLY B74 45 H2
Fallowfield Av HLGN/YWD B28 162 D5
Fallow Field Rd
BLKHTH/ROWR B65 121 G1
Fallowfield Rd DSYBK/YTR WS5 43 G5
HALE B63 137 H4
HIA/OLT B92 148 A5
Fallows Rd SPARK B11 145 E1
Fallow Wk RIDG/WDGT B32 140 A5
Falmouth Rd BKDE/SHDE B34 112 A4
DSYBK/YTR WS5 58 B1
Falstaff Av HLYWD B47 192 C2
Falstaff Cl WALM/CURD B76 78 C4
Falstaff Rd SHLY B90 180 C3
Falstone Rd SCFLD/BOLD B73 76 B1
Fancott Rd NFLD/LBR B31 158 C5
Fancourt Av
ETTPK/GDPK/PENN WV4 50 D3
Fane Rd WNSFLD WV11 25 G1
Fanshawe Rd ACGN B27 163 G1
Faraday Av RIDG/WDGT B32 140 D2
WALM/CURD B76 97 E1
Faraday Rd WSLW WS2 27 F4
Faraday Whf VAUX/NECH B7 * 3 K1
Farbrook Wy SHHTH WV12 25 H4
Farcroft Av HDSW B21 89 F5
Farcroft Gv HDSW B21 89 F5
Farcroft Rd HDSW B21 89 F5
Fardon Wy ERDW/GRVHL B23 76 B3
Fareham Crs
ETTPK/GDPK/PENN WV4 50 C2
Farfield Cl NFLD/LBR B31 175 H3
Far Highfield WALM/CURD B76 62 D4
Far Hill Cl HHTH/SAND B71 72 B3
Farlands Dr STRBR DY8 135 G4
Farlands Gv GTB/HAM B43 73 H4
Farlands Rd STRBR DY8 135 G4
Farleigh Dr BDMR/CCFT WV3 35 E5
Farleigh Rd
DUNHL/THL/PER WV6 35 E2
Farley Centre WBROM B70 * 87 H4
Farley La HAG/WOL DY9 172 A5
Farley Rd ERDW/GRVHL B23 91 H2
Farley St TPTN/OCK DY4 86 B1
Farlow Cft
CHWD/FDBR/MGN B37 131 H5
Farlow Rd NFLD/LBR B31 176 A2
Farmacre BORD B9 127 H2
Farm Av LGLYGN/QTN B68 123 E1
Farmbridge Cl WSLW WS2 40 B2
Farmbridge Rd WSLW WS2 40 B3
Farmbrook Av WOLVN WV10 12 D4
Farm Cl CDSL WV8 10 D5
HIA/OLT B92 148 A5
SEDG DY3 66 D4
STETCH B33 130 B1
Farmcote Rd STETCH B33 112 C5
Farm Cft LOZ/NWT B19 108 C3
Farmcroft Rd HAG/WOL DY9 136 C5
Farmdale Gv RBRY B45 188 A2
Farmer Rd SMTHH B10 129 E5
Farmers Cl WALM/CURD B76 63 E4
Farmers Ct HALE B63 138 B3
Farmers Fold WOLV WV1 7 F4
Farmers Wk HDSW B21 107 F2
Farmer Wy TPTN/OCK DY4 69 H2
Farmhouse Rd SHHTH WV12 26 B5
Farm House Wy GTB/HAM B43 58 C4
Farmhouse Wy SHLY B90 195 H2
Farmoor Gv BKDE/SHDE B34 113 G3
Farmoor Wy WOLVN WV10 13 E3
Farm Rd BDMR/CCFT WV3 35 G5
BLKHTH/ROWR B65 103 G5
BRLYHL DY5 119 G3
LGLYGN/QTN B68 123 E1
SMTHWKW B67 124 A1
SPARK B11 144 D1
TPTN/OCK DY4 69 H4
Farmside Cl HAG/WOL DY9 137 E4
Farmside Gn COVEN WV9 11 H5
Farmstead Cl WSL WS1 57 E3
Farmstead Rd HIA/OLT B92 148 A5
Farm St LOZ/NWT B19 108 C3
WBROM B70 87 G5
WSLW WS2 42 A1
Farnborough Ct MGN/WHC B75 47 G3
Farnborough Dr SHLY B90 195 F2
Farnborough Rd CVALE B35 94 C4
Farnbury Cft HWK/WKHTH B38 177 F3
Farncote Dr FOAKS/STRLY B74 46 D2
Farndale Av
DUNHL/THL/PER WV6 22 C5
Farndale Cl BRLYHL DY5 135 H1
Farndon Av
CHWD/FDBR/MGN B37 132 B5
Farndon Rd WASH/WDE B8 110 D4
Farnham Cl GTB/HAM B43 73 H3
Farnham Rd HDSW B21 89 F4
Farnhurst Rd CBROM B36 111 F2
Farnol Rd
LGN/SDN/BHAMAIR B26 130 B4
Farnworth Gv CBROM B36 95 G5
Farquhar Rd EDG B15 142 D1
MOS/BIL B13 144 B4
Farquhar Rd East EDG B15 142 D1
Farren Rd NFLD/LBR B31 174 D4
Farrier Cl WALM/CURD B76 78 B3
Farrier Rd GTB/HAM B43 59 H5
Farriers Ml BLOX/PEL WS3 17 G3
The Farriers
LGN/SDN/BHAMAIR B26 147 H2
Farrier Wy KGSWFD DY6 99 E2
Farringdon St WSLW WS2 4 B2
Farrington Rd
ERDW/GRVHL B23 91 H1
ETTPK/GDPK/PENN WV4 67 G1
Farrow Rd KGSTG B44 60 A5
Farthing La CSCFLD/WYGN B72 62 B4
Farthing Pools Cl
CSCFLD/WYGN B72 62 C4

Farthings La DUDS DY2 102 A2
The Farthings HRBN B17 142 B1
Farvale Rd WALM/CURD B76 79 E5
Far Vw ALDR WS9 19 H5
Farway Gdns CDSL WV8 10 B5
Far Wood Rd NFLD/LBR B31 158 A2
Fashoda Rd SLYOAK B29 160 B1
Fastlea Rd RIDG/WDGT B32 157 H1
Fastmoor Ov STETCH B33 131 G3
Fast Pits Rd YDLY B25 129 F4
Fatherless Barn Crs HALE B63 137 G3
Faulkland Crs WOLV WV1 7 G2
Faulkner Cl STRBR DY8 135 F3
Faulkner Rd HIA/OLT B92 164 D1
Faulkners Farm Dr
ERDW/GRVHL B23 75 H5
Faulknor Dr BRLYHL DY5 100 D2
Faversham Cl CDSL WV8 22 A2
WSLW WS2 40 B2
Fawdry Cl SCFLD/BOLD B73 62 B3
Fawdry St DIG/EDG B5 127 G2
SMTHWK B66 107 E4
WOLV WV1 6 D1
Fawley Cl WLNHL WV13 39 F5
Fawley Gv ALE/KHTH/YWD B14 160 B5
Fazeley St DIG/EDG B5 3 K5
Fearon Pl SMTHWK B66 * 106 C3
Featherstone Cl SHLY B90 180 D3
Featherstone Crs SHLY B90 180 D4
Featherstone Rd
ALE/KHTH/YWD B14 161 E4
Featherston Rd
FOAKS/STRLY B74 45 G3
Felashill Rd SEDG DY3 80 B3
Felbrigg Cl BRLYHL DY5 119 F4
The Feldings ERDE/BCHGN B24 93 G2
Feldon La RMSLY B62 122 C5
Felgate Cl SHLY B90 195 G2
Fellbrook Cl STETCH B33 112 B5
Fell Gv HDSW B21 89 E5
Fellmeadow Rd STETCH B33 130 C2
Fellmeadow Wy SEDG DY3 67 G5
Fellows Av KGSWFD DY6 99 G1
Fellows La HRBN B17 141 G1
Fellows Rd BILS/COS WV14 53 H1
Fellows St BKHL/PFLD WV2 37 E5
Felsted Wy VAUX/NECH B7 109 G5
Felstone Rd KGSTG B44 75 E2
Feltham Cl STETCH B33 131 G3
Felton Cft STETCH B33 130 C1
Felton Gv SOLH B91 181 H4
Fenbourne Cl RUSH/SHEL WS4 29 E2
Fenchurch Cl WSLW WS2 41 H1
Fencote Av
CHWD/FDBR/MGN B37 114 A5
Fenmere Cl
ETTPK/GDPK/PENN WV4 52 B3
Fennel Cft BKDE/SHDE B34 112 D2
Fennel Rd BRLYHL DY5 119 E5
Fennis Cl DOR/KN B93 196 D5
Fenn Ri SHHTH WV12 25 H4
STRBR DY8 117 G1
Fens Crs BRLYHL DY5 101 E4
Fens Pool Av BRLYHL DY5 101 F4
The Fensway BKDE/SHDE B34 112 C4
Fenter Cl MOS/BIL B13 144 B3
Fentham Cl HIA/OLT B92 167 H4
Fentham Ct HIA/OLT B92 164 B1
Fentham Gn HIA/OLT B92 167 G3
Fentham Rd AST/WIT B6 108 D1
ERDW/GRVHL B23 92 B3
HIA/OLT B92 167 G3
Fenton Rd ACGN B27 146 B2
HLYWD B47 192 C1
Fenton St BRLYHL DY5 119 F1
SMTHWK B66 106 A2
Fenton Wy ACGN B27 146 B3
Fereday Rd ALDR WS9 19 H4
Fereday's Cft SEDG DY3 67 F4
Fereday St TPTN/OCK DY4 69 F3
Ferguson Dr TPTN/OCK DY4 69 H5
Ferguson Rd LGLYGN/QTN B68 105 H4
Ferguson St WNSFLD WV11 25 G1
Fern Av TPTN/OCK DY4 69 F4
Fernbank Cl HALE B63 137 H5
Fernbank Crs DSYBK/YTR WS5 58 A4
Fernbank Rd WASH/WDE B8 111 E5
Ferncliffe Rd HRBN B17 141 H3
Fern Cl BILS/COS WV14 68 B3
RUSH/SHEL WS4 29 E1
Ferndale Av GTB/HAM B43 73 H4
Ferndale Cl HAG/WOL DY9 152 C5
Ferndale Ct CSHL/WTROR B46 115 G4
Ferndale Crs BHTH/HG B12 127 G4
Ferndale Ms CSHL/WTROR B46 115 G4
Ferndale Pk HAG/WOL DY9 153 E2
Ferndale Rd CSHL/WTROR B46 115 G4
FOAKS/STRLY B74 45 F5
HLGN/YWD B28 162 D2
LGLYGN/QTN B68 123 E2
WNSFLD WV11 15 F4
Ferndene Rd SPARK B11 145 H4
Ferndown Av SEDG DY3 67 E4
Ferndown Cl BLOX/PEL WS3 16 D3
LGN/SDN/BHAMAIR B26 130 C3
Ferndown Gdns
WNSFLD WV11 25 F5
Ferndown Rd SOLH B91 164 D4
Fernhill Gv KGSTG B44 60 B5
Fernhill Rd HIA/OLT B92 147 E5
Fernhurst Dr BRLYHL DY5 100 D2
Fernhurst Rd WASH/WDE B8 129 E1
Fernleigh Gdns STRBR DY8 117 G1
Fernleigh Rd RUSH/SHEL WS4 42 D2
Fernley Rd SPARK B11 145 E3
Fern Leys BDMR/CCFT WV3 35 H4
Fern Rd BDMR/CCFT WV3 6 D7
DUDN DY1 84 C2
ERDE/BCHGN B24 93 E2
Fernside Gdns SPARK B11 144 D4
Fern Vls DARL/WED WS10 * 55 G2
Fernwood Cl SCFLD/BOLD B73 76 C2
Fernwood Cft
ALE/KHTH/YWD B14 161 E4
TPTN/OCK DY4 85 F2
Fernwood Rd SCFLD/BOLD B73 76 C3
Fernwoods RIDG/WDGT B32 140 B5
Ferrers Cl MGN/WHC B75 47 H3
Ferrie Gv BRWNH WS8 9 E4
Ferris Gv ACGN B27 163 E1
Festival Av DARL/WED WS10 55 E4
Festival Wy
DUNHL/THL/PER WV6 22 D5
Ffernfail Ct ERDW/GRVHL B23 92 C1
Fibbersley WLNHL WV13 39 F1
Fibbersley Bank WLNHL WV13 39 F1
Fiddlers Gn HIA/OLT B92 167 G3
Field Av NFLD/LBR B31 158 B5
Field Cl BLOX/PEL WS3 18 B5
BLOX/PEL WS3 27 G2
LGN/SDN/BHAMAIR B26 147 G1
STRBR DY8 118 C2
Field Cottage Dr STRBR DY8 135 H4
Fieldfare Cl
BLKHTH/ROWR B65 103 F5
Fieldfare Cft CBROM B36 114 A1
Fieldfare Rd HAG/WOL DY9 136 B3
Field Head Pl
DUNHL/THL/PER WV6 35 F1
Fieldhead Rd SPARK B11 146 A4
Fieldhouse La RMSLY B62 172 A1
Fieldhouse Rd
ETTPK/GDPK/PENN WV4 52 C4
YDLY B25 129 G4
Field La HAG/WOL DY9 170 A1
RIDG/WDGT B32 157 E2
RUSH/SHEL WS4 18 B5
SOLH B91 166 A5
STRBR DY8 135 G4
Field Ms DUDS DY2 121 E2
Fieldon Cl SHLY B90 180 C2
Field Rd BLOX/PEL WS3 27 G1
DUDS DY2 85 E5
TPTN/OCK DY4 69 F3
The Fields CDSL WV8 10 D3
Field St BILS/COS WV14 54 A5
WLNHL WV13 39 G3
WOLVN WV10 7 J1
Fieldview Cl BILS/COS WV14 68 D1
Field View Dr
BLKHTH/ROWR B65 122 D2
Field Wk ALDR WS9 30 B3
Field Wy HOCK/TIA B94 198 A5
Fieldways Cl HLYWD B47 192 C1
Fifield Gv STETCH B33 130 B1
Fifth Av BORD B9 128 D2
WOLVN WV10 23 F3
Filey Rd WOLVN WV10 12 B5
Fillingham Cl
CHWD/FDBR/MGN B37 132 D3
Filton Cft CVALE B35 94 C2
Fimbrell Cl STRBR DY8 118 C4
Finbury Cl HIA/OLT B92 164 B1
Finchall Cft HIA/OLT B92 165 G3
Fincham Cl COVEN WV9 12 A4
Finch Cl BLKHTH/ROWR B65 103 F5
Finchdene Gv BDMR/CCFT WV3 35 H4
Finch Dr FOAKS/STRLY B74 60 C3
Finches End BKDE/SHDE B34 113 E4
Finchfield Cl STRBR DY8 134 C3
Finchfield Gdns
BDMR/CCFT WV3 36 A4
Finchfield Hl BDMR/CCFT WV3 35 H3
Finchfield La BDMR/CCFT WV3 35 G5
Finchfield Rd BDMR/CCFT WV3 36 A4
Finchfield Rd West
BDMR/CCFT WV3 35 G4
Finchley Av LOZ/NWT B19 * 108 C1
Finchley Cl SEDG DY3 83 F4
Finchley Rd KGSTG B44 75 H1
Finchmead Rd STETCH B33 131 G2
Finchpath Rd WBROM B70 71 E5
Finch Rd LOZ/NWT B19 108 C1
Findlay Rd
ALE/KHTH/YWD B14 161 E1
Findon Rd WASH/WDE B8 111 F3
Finger Post Dr BLOX/PEL WS3 18 A2
Finlarigg Dr EDG B15 142 D1
Finmere Rd HLGN/YWD B28 162 D2
Finmere Wy SHLY B90 180 D3
Finnemore Rd BORD B9 129 E2
Finney Well Cl BILS/COS WV14 53 F5
Finsbury Dr BRLYHL DY5 119 E5
Finsbury Gv ERDW/GRVHL B23 76 B5
Finstall Cl CSCFLD/WYGN B72 77 G2
VAUX/NECH B7 109 G5
Finwood Cl HIA/OLT B92 165 G2
Fir Av BHTH/HG B12 144 C2
Firbank Cl BVILLE B30 159 G3
Firbank Wy BLOX/PEL WS3 17 H5
Firbarn Cl WALM/CURD B76 62 D5
Firbeck Gv KGSTG B44 75 G2
Firbeck Rd KGSTG B44 75 G2
Fircroft BILS/COS WV14 54 C5
Fir Cft BRLYHL DY5 119 E4
Fircroft NFLD/LBR B31 158 B2
SOLH B91 164 B4
Firecrest Cl ERDW/GRVHL B23 75 H4
Fir Gv ALE/KHTH/YWD B14 161 F5
BDMR/CCFT WV3 6 A6
STRBR DY8 134 C1
Firhill Cft ALE/KHTH/YWD B14 177 H3
Firmstone St STRBR DY8 118 A5
Firsbrook Cl
DUNHL/THL/PER WV6 22 C5
Firs Cl SMTHWKW B67 106 C4
Firs Dr SHLY B90 180 A4
Firs Farm Dr CBROM B36 112 B2
Firsholm Cl SCFLD/BOLD B73 77 E4
Firs Rd KGSWFD DY6 100 A3
Firs St DUDS DY2 84 D5
First Av BORD B9 128 C3
BRWNH WS8 9 G4
KGSWFD DY6 100 C1
SLYOAK B29 143 F4
WALM/CURD B76 94 C1
WOLVN WV10 23 G4
First Exhibition Av
BHAMNEC B40 149 H3
The Firs SPARK B11 145 E1
First Meadow Piece
RIDG/WDGT B32 141 E3
Fir St SEDG DY3 66 B4
Firsvale Rd WNSFLD WV11 25 F5
Firsway DUNHL/THL/PER WV6 35 E4
Firswood Rd STETCH B33 131 E3
Firth Dr ALE/KHTH/YWD B14 161 H5
RMSLY B62 122 C4
Firth Park Crs RMSLY B62 122 C4
Fir Tree Cl KGSTG B44 75 E4
Fir Tree Dr DSYBK/YTR WS5 57 H4
SEDG DY3 67 G4
Fir Tree Gv SCFLD/BOLD B73 76 D2
Fir Tree Rd BDMR/CCFT WV3 50 D1
Firtree Rd ERDE/BCHGN B24 93 F4
Fisher Rd BLOX/PEL WS3 16 B5
OLDBY B69 105 G2
Fishers Dr SHLY B90 193 H3
Fisher St BDMR/CCFT WV3 6 C7
BRLYHL DY5 118 D1
DUDS DY2 84 D5
TPTN/OCK DY4 85 G3
TPTN/OCK DY4 86 B1
WLNHL WV13 40 A3
Fishley Cl BLOX/PEL WS3 17 E3
Fishley La BLOX/PEL WS3 17 E3
Fishpool Cl CBROM B36 111 G1
Fishpool La
RCOVN/BALC/EX CV7 150 D1
Fistral Gdns BDMR/CCFT WV3 51 F1
Fitters Mill Cl DIG/EDG B5 * 144 A1
Fitton Av KGSWFD DY6 100 C4
Fitzgerald Pl BRLYHL DY5 135 H1
Fitzguy Cl WBROM B70 88 A5
Fitzmaurice Rd WNSFLD WV11 25 F3
Fitz Roy Av HRBN B17 124 B5
Fitzroy Rd NFLD/LBR B31 174 C2
Five Broadway
LDYWD/EDGR B16 * 126 B3
Five Fields Rd SHHTH WV12 25 G5
Five Oaks Rd WLNHL WV13 39 E5
Five Ways LDYWD/EDGR B16 126 B3
Flackwell Rd ERDW/GRVHL B23 76 C4
Fladbury Cl DUDS DY2 120 D1
Fladbury Crs SLYOAK B29 142 B5
Fladbury Gdns
BFLD/HDSWWD B20 * 108 C1
Fladbury Pl LOZ/NWT B19 * 108 C2
Flamborough Cl
BKDE/SHDE B34 112 C2
Flamborough Wy
BILS/COS WV14 68 B4
Flanders Dr KGSWFD DY6 99 H1
Flash La WMBN WV5 64 C1
Flash Rd OLDBY B69 105 E2
Flatlea NFLD/LBR B31 175 F1
The Flatts DARL/WED WS10 55 G1
Flavell Av BILS/COS WV14 68 D2
Flavell Cl RIDG/WDGT B32 157 F1
Flavells La SEDG DY3 82 D4
YDLY B25 129 G4
Flavell St DUDN DY1 68 B5
Flax Cl HLYWD B47 192 C3
Flax Gdns HWK/WKHTH B38 176 D5
Flaxhall St WSLW WS2 41 F5
Flaxley Rd STETCH B33 130 B1
Flaxton Gv STETCH B33 112 C5
Flecknoe Cl CBROM B36 95 E5
Fledburgh Dr WALM/CURD B76 62 D5
Fleet St CBHAMNW B3 2 D4
Fleetwood Gv
LGN/SDN/BHAMAIR B26 130 C3
Fleming Pl WSLW WS2 27 E4
Fleming Rd RIDG/WDGT B32 140 D2
WSLW WS2 27 E4
Flemmynge Cl CDSL WV8 10 A3
Fletcher Gv DOR/KN B93 197 F4
Fletcher Rd SHHTH WV12 26 B1
Fletcher's La WLNHL WV13 40 A3
Fletcher St HAG/WOL DY9 136 D2
Fletton Gv
ALE/KHTH/YWD B14 178 C2
Flinkford Cl DSYBK/YTR WS5 58 A2
Flint Green Rd ACGN B27 146 B4
Flintham Cl ACGN B27 147 E4
The Flintway STETCH B33 112 A5
Floodgate St DIG/EDG B5 3 K7
Flood St DUDS DY2 84 D5
Flora Rd YDLY B25 129 F5
Florence Av
ETTPK/GDPK/PENN WV4 52 D4
SPARK B11 144 D2
Florence Gv HHTH/SAND B71 72 A2
Florence Rd ACGN B27 146 D3
ALE/KHTH/YWD B14 161 F2
CDSL WV8 11 E4
ERDW/GRVHL B23 77 F4
HDSW B21 107 F1
OLDBY B69 104 B2
SMTHWK B66 106 D5
TPTN/OCK DY4 69 G4
WBROM B70 88 A5
Florence St CBHAMW B1 126 D3
WSL WS1 5 H5
Florence Vls SPARK B11 * 128 A5
Florian Gv DARL/WED WS10 55 G1
Florida Wy KGSWFD DY6 100 C4
Flowerdale Cl BILS/COS WV14 68 B3
Floyds La RUSH/SHEL WS4 29 E4
Floyer Rd SMTHH B10 128 C3
Flyford Cft SLYOAK B29 141 F5
Foden Rd PBAR/PBCH B42 74 A3
Foinavon Cl
BLKHTH/ROWR B65 103 F3
Fold St WOLV WV1 6 E5
The Fold DARL/WED WS10 55 F2
ETTPK/GDPK/PENN WV4 51 F4
Foldyard Cl WALM/CURD B76 78 C3
Foley Av DUNHL/THL/PER WV6 35 F2
Foley Church Cl
FOAKS/STRLY B74 45 G3
Foley Dr DUNHL/THL/PER WV6 35 G2
Foley Gv WMBN WV5 80 C1
Foley Rd HAG/WOL DY9 135 H5
WASH/WDE B8 111 F3
Foley Rd East FOAKS/STRLY B74 45 F4
Foley Rd West
FOAKS/STRLY B74 44 D4
Foley St DARL/WED WS10 56 A5
Foley Wood Cl
FOAKS/STRLY B74 45 E4
Foliot Flds YDLY B25 129 H4
Folkes Rd HAG/WOL DY9 137 E1
Folkestone Cft CBROM B36 112 A1
Folliott Rd STETCH B33 130 C1
Follyhouse Cl WSL WS1 57 F1
Follyhouse La WSL WS1 5 F7
Fontley Cl
LGN/SDN/BHAMAIR B26 130 C3
Fontwell Rd WOLVN WV10 12 D3
Footherley La LICHS WS14 32 D1
Fordbridge Rd
CHWD/FDBR/MGN B37 113 H5
Ford Brook La BLOX/PEL WS3 28 D1
Forder Gv ALE/KHTH/YWD B14 178 C3
Forde Way Gdns
HWK/WKHTH B38 190 B1
Fordfield Rd STETCH B33 113 E5
Fordham Gv COVEN WV9 12 A4
Fordhouse La BVILLE B30 160 B4
Fordhouse Rd WOLVN WV10 23 F1
Fordraught La RMSLY B62 172 D4
The Fordrift
CHWD/FDBR/MGN B37 149 E2
Fordrough YDLY B25 128 D5
Fordrough Av BORD B9 128 C1
Fordrough La BORD B9 128 C1
The Fordrough
FOAKS/STRLY B74 47 E4
NFLD/LBR B31 175 H5
SHLY B90 193 E1
Fords Rd SHLY B90 193 G1
Ford St SMTHWKW B67 106 B3
WSLW WS2 56 C1
WSNGN B18 108 B4
Fordwater Rd
FOAKS/STRLY B74 60 B2
Foredraft Cl RIDG/WDGT B32 140 C5
Foredraft St HALE B63 137 H2
Foredrove La HIA/OLT B92 165 G4
Forest Av BLOX/PEL WS3 27 H3
Forest Cl FOAKS/STRLY B74 60 A1
SMTHWK B66 106 A2
Forest Ct DOR/KN B93 196 D5
Forest Dl RBRY B45 188 B2
Forest Dr CDYHTH B64 121 E2
HRBN B17 142 B1
Forest Ga SHHTH WV12 26 B2
Forest Hill Rd
LGN/SDN/BHAMAIR B26 148 A2
Forest La BLOX/PEL WS3 28 A5
Forest Pk WALM/CURD B76 63 E4
Forest Pl BLOX/PEL WS3 28 A4
Fore St CBHAM B2 3 G5
Forest Rd DOR/KN B93 197 E5
DUDN DY1 84 C2
LGLYGN/QTN B68 123 G5
MOS/BIL B13 144 C4
YDLY B25 146 C1
Forest Wy HLYWD B47 192 D2
Forge Cl CDSL WV8 22 A1
Forge Cft WALM/CURD B76 78 D5
Forge La ALDR WS9 31 F4
CDYHTH B64 120 B4
FOAKS/STRLY B74 32 A4
HAG/WOL DY9 184 B1
HHTH/SAND B71 72 C5
KGSWFD DY6 99 E1
KIDD DY10 168 B4
LICHS WS14 31 H2
RMSLY B62 139 E2
WALM/CURD B76 78 D5
Forge Leys WMBN WV5 64 C5
Forge Rd BLOX/PEL WS3 17 H2
DARL/WED WS10 54 D2
SHHTH WV12 40 A1
STRBR DY8 135 F1
Forge St DARL/WED WS10 55 G4
The Forge HALE B63 120 A4
Forge Valley Wy WMBN WV5 64 C5
Forge Wy OLDBY B69 104 C3
Formans Rd SPARK B11 145 G4
Formby Av
DUNHL/THL/PER WV6 34 B1
Formby Wy BLOX/PEL WS3 16 C4
Forrell Gv NFLD/LBR B31 189 H1
Forrest Av WNSFLD WV11 15 E3
Forrester St WSLW WS2 4 A3
Forrester Street Prec WSLW WS2 4 A3
Forster St SMTHWKW B67 106 A2
VAUX/NECH B7 127 G1
Forsythia Cl NFLD/LBR B31 158 B2
Forsythia Gv CDSL WV8 10 C4
Fort Crs ALDR WS9 19 G4
Forth Dr
CHWD/FDBR/MGN B37 114 B5
Forth Gv HWK/WKHTH B38 176 C5
Forth Wy RMSLY B62 122 C4
Fortnum Cl STETCH B33 131 E2
Forton Cl DUNHL/THL/PER WV6 35 F3
Fort Pkwy ERDE/BCHGN B24 94 B4
ERDE/BCHGN B24 111 F1
Fosbrooke Rd SMTHH B10 129 E4
Fosseway Dr ERDW/GRVHL B23 76 C3
Fossil Dr RBRY B45 188 A1
Foster Av BILS/COS WV14 68 B2
Foster Gdns WSNGN B18 * 107 H3
Foster Gn DUNHL/THL/PER WV6 34 C2
Foster Pl STRBR DY8 135 E1
Foster Rd WOLVN WV10 23 G4
Foster St BLOX/PEL WS3 27 H2
DARL/WED WS10 55 F1
Foster St East STRBR DY8 135 G2
Foster Wy DIG/EDG B5 143 G2
Fotherley Brook Rd ALDR WS9 31 F5
Foundry La BLOX/PEL WS3 17 G4
SMTHWK B66 106 D2
Foundry Rd KGSWFD DY6 99 F1
WSNGN B18 107 F4
Foundry St BILS/COS WV14 68 C2
KGSWFD DY6 99 F1
TPTN/OCK DY4 69 E3
Fountain Arcade Chambers
DUDN DY1 * 84 C5
Fountain Cl NFLD/LBR B31 189 E2
Fountain Ct CBHAMNE B4 * 3 G3
Fountain La BILS/COS WV14 68 D3
OLDBY B69 86 D5
Fountain Rd HRBN B17 124 D5
Fountains Rd BLOX/PEL WS3 16 A5
Fountains Wy BLOX/PEL WS3 16 A5
Four Acres RIDG/WDGT B32 140 C3
Four Ashes Rd DOR/KN B93 196 B5
Four Crosses Rd
RUSH/SHEL WS4 29 E1
Fourlands Av
CSCFLD/WYGN B72 77 H4
Fourlands Rd NFLD/LBR B31 158 A4
Four Oaks Common Rd
FOAKS/STRLY B74 46 C2
Four Oaks Rd FOAKS/STRLY B74 46 D3
Four Stones Cl SOLH B91 181 G4
Four Stones Gv DIG/EDG B5 143 H1
Fourth Av BORD B9 128 D2
BRWNH WS8 9 G4
SLYOAK B29 143 G4
WOLVN WV10 23 F4
Four Winds Rd DUDS DY2 103 E2
Fowey Cl WALM/CURD B76 78 C4
Fowey Rd BKDE/SHDE B34 112 B3
Fowgay Dr SOLH B91 181 F4
Fowler Cl CDSL WV8 20 C4
SMTHWK B66 106 C1
Fowler Rd MGN/WHC B75 63 G3
Fowler St BKHL/PFLD WV2 52 A2
VAUX/NECH B7 109 H4
Fowlmere Rd PBAR/PBCH B42 74 B3
Foxbury Dr DOR/KN B93 197 E5
Foxcote Av HDSW B21 107 G2
Foxcote Cl SHLY B90 180 D5
Foxcote Dr SHLY B90 180 D5
Foxcote La HAG/WOL DY9 137 F4
Fox Covert STRBR DY8 135 E2
Fox Crs SPARK B11 * 145 F3
Foxdale Dr BRLYHL DY5 118 D1
Foxdale Gv STETCH B33 131 E2
Foxes Meadow BVILLE B30 176 D1
WALM/CURD B76 78 C3
Foxes Rdg CDYHTH B64 121 E4
Foxfield Dr STRBR DY8 135 G4
Fox Foot Dr BRLYHL DY5 101 E5
Foxford Cl CBROM B36 95 F5
CSCFLD/WYGN B72 77 G4
Foxglove Cl BLOX/PEL WS3 18 A2
WNSFLD WV11 25 E5
Foxglove Crs
CHWD/FDBR/MGN B37 131 G1
Foxglove Rd DUDN DY1 83 H2
Foxglove Wy ERDW/GRVHL B23 75 H4
HDSW B21 107 F2
Fox Green Crs ACGN B27 146 A5
Fox Gv ACGN B27 146 A5
Fox Hl SLYOAK B29 159 E2
Fox Hill Cl SLYOAK B29 159 E2
Fox Hill Rd MGN/WHC B75 48 B3
Foxhills Pk DUDS DY2 102 C5
Foxhills Rd
ETTPK/GDPK/PENN WV4 50 C5
STRBR DY8 117 H3
Foxhollies Dr HALE B63 138 A3
Fox Hollies Rd ACGN B27 146 B4
WALM/CURD B76 78 B3
Fox Hollow
DUNHL/THL/PER WV6 35 G3
Foxhope Cl HWK/WKHTH B38 177 F4
Foxhunt Rd HALE B63 138 A5
Foxland Av RBRY B45 188 C1
Foxland Cl
CHWD/FDBR/MGN B37 132 D2
SHLY B90 194 D4
Foxlands Av
ETTPK/GDPK/PENN WV4 50 D5
Foxlands Crs
ETTPK/GDPK/PENN WV4 50 C5
Foxlands Dr
CSCFLD/WYGN B72 77 H4
ETTPK/GDPK/PENN WV4 50 C5
SEDG DY3 83 F1
Foxlea Rd HALE B63 154 D1
Foxley Dr SOLH B91 166 B5
Foxmeadow Cl SEDG DY3 67 G4
Foxoak St CDYHTH B64 120 C3
Fox's La WOLV WV1 23 F5
Fox St CBHAMNE B4 3 J4
DUDN DY1 68 C5
Foxton Rd WASH/WDE B8 110 D4
Fox Wk ALDR WS9 19 H4
Foxwell Gv BORD B9 129 F2
Foxwell Rd BORD B9 129 F2
Foxwood Av GTB/HAM B43 59 F5
Foxwood Gv
CHWD/FDBR/MGN B37 113 H4
Foxwood Rd
CHWD/FDBR/MGN B37 113 H4
Foxyards Cl TPTN/OCK DY4 * 84 D1
Foxyards Rd TPTN/OCK DY4 84 D1
Foyle Rd HWK/WKHTH B38 176 D4
Fozdar Crs BILS/COS WV14 68 A2
Fradley Cl BVILLE B30 176 B1
Framefield Dr SOLH B91 165 G4

Framlingham Gv
DUNHL/THL/PER WV6 ....35 E2
Frampton Cl BVILLE B30 ....159 F3
CHWD/FDBR/MGN B37 ....132 D1
Frampton Wy GTB/HAM B43 ....59 H4
Frances Dr BLOX/PEL WS3 ....16 D5
Frances Rd BVILLE B30 ....160 A5
ERDW/GRVHL B23 ....92 B3
LOZ/NWT B19 ....108 C1
Franchise Gdns
DARL/WED WS10 ....55 H2
Franchise St DARL/WED WS10 ....55 G3
PBAR/PBCH B42 ....91 E4
Francis Cl FOAKS/STRLY B74 ....45 F5
KGSWFD DY6 ....99 H1
Francis Rd ACGN B27 ....146 D2
LDYWD/EDGR B16 ....126 A3
SMTHWKW B67 ....105 H4
STETCH B33 ....129 H1
STRBR DY8 ....134 C2
YDLY B25 ....146 A1
Francis St VAUX/NECH B7 ....109 G5
WBROM B70 ....87 H5
WOLV WV1 ....37 E1
Francis Wk NFLD/LBR B31 ....189 G1
Francis Ward Cl
HHTH/SAND B71 ....71 E3
Frankburn Rd
FOAKS/STRLY B74 ....45 E5
Frankfort St LOZ/NWT B19 ....108 D3
Frankholmes Dr SHLY B90 ....195 G2
Frankley Av RMSLY B62 ....139 H2
Frankley Beeches Rd
NFLD/LBR B31 ....174 D2
Frankley Gn RMSLY B62 ....156 B5
Frankley Green La
RIDG/WDGT B32 ....156 D5
Frankley Hill La
RIDG/WDGT B32 ....173 H1
Frankley La NFLD/LBR B31 ....157 G4
Frankley Lodge Rd
NFLD/LBR B31 ....174 D1
Frankley Rd LGLYGN/QTN B68 ....123 E4
Frankley Ter HRBN B17 * 141 H2
Franklin Rd BVILLE B30 ....159 H5
Franklin St WSNGN B18 ....107 G4
Franklin Wy BVILLE B30 ....159 H3
Franklyn Cl
DUNHL/THL/PER WV6 ....20 C5
Frank Rd SMTHWKW B67 ....106 A3
Frank St BHTH/HG B12 ....127 F5
Franks Wy STETCH B33 ....130 A2
Frank Tommey Cl
BLKHTH/ROWR B65 * 122 A3
Frankton Cl HIA/OLT B92 ....147 H5
Frankton Gv BORD B9 ....129 F2
Fraser Rd SPARK B11 ....145 E2
Fraser St BILS/COS WV14 ....54 A2
Frayne Av KGSWFD DY6 ....99 G2
Freasley Cl SHLY B90 ....180 D2
Freasley Rd BKDE/SHDE B34 ....113 F4
Freda Ri OLDBY B69 ....104 B1
Freda Rd WBROM B70 ....87 H5
Fredas Gv HRBN B17 ....141 G3
Frederick Rd AST/WIT B6 ....109 E1
EDG B15 ....126 B4
ERDW/GRVHL B23 ....92 B4
LGLYGN/QTN B68 ....123 H5
SCFLD/BOLD B73 ....77 E1
SLYOAK B29 ....142 B5
SPARK B11 ....145 E3
STETCH B33 ....129 G1
WNSFLD WV11 ....24 C5
Fredericks Cl STRBR DY8 ....135 E3
Frederick St BKHL/PFLD WV2 ....7 F7
CBHAMW B1 ....2 C2
WBROM B70 ....87 G2
WSLW WS2 ....4 B4
Frederick William St
WLNHL WV13 ....39 H3
Fred Smith Cl DARL/WED WS10 ....56 B3
Freeland Gv KGSWFD DY6 ....100 B5
Freeman Dr MGN/WHC B75 ....63 F4
Freeman Pl BILS/COS WV14 ....39 E5
Freeman Rd DARL/WED WS10 ....56 C5
VAUX/NECH B7 ....109 H4
Freeman St DIG/EDG B5 ....3 H5
WOLVN WV10 ....37 H3
Freer Rd AST/WIT B6 ....108 D1
Freer St WSL WS1 ....4 E5
Freeth Rd BRWNH WS8 ....9 G3
Freeth St LDYWD/EDGR B16 ....126 A2
OLDBY B69 ....104 D1
Freezeland St BILS/COS WV14 ....53 F2
Fremont Dr DUDN DY1 ....83 G3
French Rd DUDS DY2 ....85 E5
Frensham Cl
CHWD/FDBR/MGN B37 ....132 C2
Frensham Wy HRBN B17 ....142 A1
Frenshaw Gv KGSTG B44 ....75 F3
Freshwater Dr BRLYHL DY5 ....118 D3
Friardale Cl DARL/WED WS10 ....56 D5
Friar Park Rd DARL/WED WS10 ....56 C5
Friars Cl STRBR DY8 ....117 G1
Friars Gorse KINVER DY7 ....117 G5
Friar St DARL/WED WS10 ....56 B5
Friary Av SHLY B90 ....195 G2
Friary Crs RUSH/SHEL WS4 ....29 E4
Friary Dr FOAKS/STRLY B74 ....46 D2
Friary Gdns HDSW B21 ....89 F4
Friary Rd HDSW B21 ....89 G4
Friday La HIA/OLT B92 ....183 H1
Friesland Dr WOLV WV1 ....38 B2
Friezeland Rd WSLW WS2 ....41 F3
Friezland La BRWNH WS8 ....19 G2
Friezland Wy BRWNH WS8 ....19 G2
Frinton Gv HDSW B21 ....107 E2
Frisby Rd RIDG/WDGT B32 ....141 E2
Friston Av LDYWD/EDGR B16 ....2 A7
Frodesley Rd
LGN/SDN/BHAMAIR B26 ....130 D4
Froggatt Rd BILS/COS WV14 ....53 H1
Froggatts Ride
WALM/CURD B76 ....63 F5
Frogmill Rd NFLD/LBR B31 ....174 B3
Frome Cl DUDN DY1 ....83 F4
Frome Dr WNSFLD WV11 ....24 C5
Frome Wy ALE/KHTH/YWD B14 ..160 C4
Frost St BKHL/PFLD WV2 ....53 E2
Froxmere Cl SOLH B91 ....181 H5
Froyle Cl DUNHL/THL/PER WV6 ....21 G5
Froysell St WLNHL WV13 ....39 H3
Fryer Rd NFLD/LBR B31 ....189 H1
Fryers Cl BLOX/PEL WS3 ....27 F3
Fryers Rd WSLW WS2 ....27 E4
Fryer St WOLV WV1 ....7 G3
Fuchsia Dr COVEN WV9 ....11 H4
Fugelmere Cl HRBN B17 ....124 B5
Fulbrook Gv SLYOAK B29 ....158 B2
Fulbrook Rd DUDN DY1 ....84 A5
Fulford Dr WALM/CURD B76 ....94 D1
Fulford Gv
LGN/SDN/BHAMAIR B26 ....148 A1
Fulford Hall Rd HOCK/TIA B94 ....193 F5
Fulham Rd SPARK B11 ....144 D2
Fullbrook Cl SHLY B90 ....195 G3
Fullbrook Rd DSYBK/YTR WS5 ....57 E3
Fullelove Rd BRWNH WS8 ....19 G1
Fullerton Cl CDSL WV8 ....22 A1
Fullwood Crs DUDS DY2 ....101 G3
Fullwoods End BILS/COS WV14 ....68 C3
Fulmer Wk WSNGN B18 * 126 A1
Fulwell Gv KGSTG B44 ....75 G3
Fulwell Ms
CHWD/FDBR/MGN B37 ....132 B4
Fulwood Av RMSLY B62 ....122 D4
Furber Pl KGSWFD DY6 ....100 B3
Furlong La HALE B63 ....137 G1
Furlong Meadow
NFLD/LBR B31 ....176 A3
Furlongs Rd SEDG DY3 ....67 F5
The Furlongs STRBR DY8 ....135 H4
WNSFLD WV11 ....24 B5
The Furlong DARL/WED WS10 ....55 G3
Furlong Wk SEDG DY3 ....83 F2
Furnace Cl WMBN WV5 ....80 C1
Furnace Hl HALE B63 ....138 D1
Furnace La HALE B63 ....138 D2
Furnace Pde TPTN/OCK DY4 ....69 E5
Furnace Rd DUDS DY2 ....102 C1
Furness Cl BLOX/PEL WS3 ....16 B4
Furst St BRWNH WS8 ....9 G4
Furzebank Wy SHHTH WV12 ....40 C1
Furze Wy DSYBK/YTR WS5 ....43 F5

G

The Gables ERDE/BCHGN B24 ....93 H2
Gaddesby Rd
ALE/KHTH/YWD B14 ....161 F2
Gadds Dr BLKHTH/ROWR B65 ....104 B5
Gadsby Av WNSFLD WV11 ....25 G3
Gads Gn DUDS DY2 ....102 D4
Gads Green Crs DUDS DY2 ....103 E3
Gads La DUDN DY1 ....84 C5
WBROM B70 ....87 E3
Gadwall Cft ERDW/GRVHL B23 ....91 H3
Gail Cl ALDR WS9 ....19 H3
Gailey Cft KGSTG B44 ....60 A5
Gailey Pk WOLVN WV10 * 12 C1
Gail Pk BDMR/CCFT WV3 ....50 D1
Gainford Cl COVEN WV9 ....22 B1
Gainford Rd KGSTG B44 ....76 A2
Gainsborough Crs
DOR/KN B93 ....197 E2
GTB/HAM B43 ....59 H4
Gainsborough Dr
DUNHL/THL/PER WV6 ....34 D1
Gainsborough Hl STRBR DY8 ....135 G4
Gainsborough Pl DUDN DY1 ....83 G4
Gainsborough Rd
PBAR/PBCH B42 ....74 B5
Gainsford Dr RMSLY B62 ....138 D1
Gairloch Rd SHHTH WV12 ....25 H1
Gaitskell Ter OLDBY B69 ....86 B4
Gaitswell Wy SMTHWK B66 ....106 B2
Galahad Wy DARL/WED WS10 ....71 E1
Galbraith Cl BILS/COS WV14 ....68 D3
Galena Wy AST/WIT B6 ....109 E3
Gale Wk BLKHTH/ROWR B65 ....103 F4
Gallery Sq WSL WS1 ....4 D3
Galloway Av BKDE/SHDE B34 ....112 B3
Galton Cl ERDE/BCHGN B24 ....94 B2
TPTN/OCK DY4 ....70 A5
Galton Dr DUDS DY2 ....102 B3
Galton Rd SMTHWK B67 ....124 B3
Galtons La HAG/WOL DY9 ....185 E1
Gamesfield Gn
BDMR/CCFT WV3 ....36 B4
Gammage St DUDS DY2 ....102 B1
Gandy Rd SHHTH WV12 ....25 G4
Gannahs Farm Cl
WALM/CURD B76 ....63 F5
Gannow Green La RBRY B45 ....173 E4
Gannow Manor Crs RBRY B45 ....173 G4
Gannow Manor Gdns
RBRY B45 ....173 H4
Gannow Rd RBRY B45 ....187 G1
Gannow Wk RBRY B45 ....187 G1
Ganton Rd BLOX/PEL WS3 ....16 C3
Garden Cl DOR/KN B93 ....196 D2
RBRY B45 ....174 A3
WASH/WDE B8 ....111 E4
Garden Crs BLOX/PEL WS3 ....17 H4
Garden Cft ALDR WS9 ....30 B3
Gardeners Wy WMBN WV5 ....80 D2
Garden Gv BFLD/HDSWWD B20 ....73 G5
The Gardens ERDW/GRVHL B23 ..92 C3
Garden St WSLW WS2 ....4 D1
Garden Wk BILS/COS WV14 ....54 B2
SEDG DY3 ....83 E4
Garfield Rd
LGN/SDN/BHAMAIR B26 ....130 D4
Garland Crs RMSLY B62 ....122 C4
The Garlands WNSFLD WV11 ....24 C3
Garland St BORD B9 ....128 A1
Garland Wy NFLD/LBR B31 ....175 H1
Garman Cl GTB/HAM B43 ....73 G1
Garner Cl BILS/COS WV14 ....53 H5
Garnet Av GTB/HAM B43 ....59 F5
Garnett Dr MGN/WHC B75 ....63 E2
Garrard Gdns SCFLD/BOLD B73 ....62 B3
Garrat St BRLYHL DY5 ....101 G4
Garratt Cl LGLYGN/QTN B68 ....105 G5
Garratt's La CDYHTH B64 ....121 F2
Garratt St HHTH/SAND B71 ....87 F1
Garratts Wk
ALE/KHTH/YWD B14 ....178 A4
Garret Cl KGSWFD DY6 ....81 H5
Garretts Green La
LGN/SDN/BHAMAIR B26 ....130 C5
Garrick Cl DUDN DY1 ....83 H3
Garrick St WOLV WV1 ....7 G5
Garrington St DARL/WED WS10 ..55 E1
Garrison Circ BORD B9 ....127 G2
Garrison La BORD B9 ....127 H2
Garrison St BORD B9 ....127 H2
The Garth ALE/KHTH/YWD B14 ..179 F1
Garway Gv YDLY B25 ....146 B1
Garwood Rd
LGN/SDN/BHAMAIR B26 ....130 B2
Gas St CBHAMW B1 ....2 C6
Gatacre St SEDG DY3 ....83 F3
Gatcombe Cl WOLVN WV10 ....13 F3
Gatcombe Rd DUDN DY1 ....83 G4
Gate Cl WMBN WV5 ....81 E1
Gatehouse Fold DUDS DY2 * 84 D5
Gate La HOCK/TIA B94 ....196 A5
SCFLD/BOLD B73 ....76 D1
Gateley Rd LGLYGN/QTN B68 ....123 H5
Gate St SEDG DY3 ....67 G4
TPTN/OCK DY4 ....85 G4
WASH/WDE B8 ....110 B4
Gatis St DUNHL/THL/PER WV6 ....22 C5
Gatwick Rd CVALE B35 ....94 D2
Gauden Rd HAG/WOL DY9 ....153 F1
Gavin Wy PBAR/PBCH B42 ....91 F2
Gawne La DUDS DY2 ....103 E5
Gaydon Cl
DUNHL/THL/PER WV6 ....20 C5
Gaydon Gv SLYOAK B29 ....141 G5
Gaydon Pl SCFLD/BOLD B73 ....62 B4
Gaydon Rd ALDR WS9 ....44 A1
HIA/OLT B92 ....148 B4
Gayfield Av BRLYHL DY5 ....119 F3
Gay Hill La HWK/WKHTH B38 ....177 F5
Gayhurst Dr YDLY B25 ....130 A4
Gayle Gv ACGN B27 ....163 G2
Gayton Rd HHTH/SAND B71 ....71 H5
Gaywood Cft EDG B15 ....126 C4
Geach St LOZ/NWT B19 ....108 D3
Gedney Cl ALE/KHTH/YWD B14 ..179 E2
Geeson Cl CVALE B35 ....94 D2
Gee St LOZ/NWT B19 ....108 D3
Gem Vls SPARK B11 * 128 A5
Geneva Rd TPTN/OCK DY4 ....84 D2
Genge Av
ETTPK/GDPK/PENN WV4 ....52 C4
Genners La RIDG/WDGT B32 ....157 G2
Genthorn Cl
ETTPK/GDPK/PENN WV4 ....52 D4
Gentian Cl NFLD/LBR B31 ....158 B4
Geoffrey Cl WALM/CURD B76 ....78 D4
Geoffrey Pl SPARK B11 * 145 E4
Geoffrey Rd SHLY B90 ....179 H2
SPARK B11 ....145 E4
George Arthur Rd
WASH/WDE B8 ....110 B5
George Av BLKHTH/ROWR B65 ..122 B2
George Bird Cl SMTHWK B66 * 106 C3
George Cl DUDS DY2 ....103 E1
George Frederick Rd
SCFLD/BOLD B73 ....60 C4
George Henry Rd
TPTN/OCK DY4 ....70 C4
George Rd BILS/COS WV14 ....68 D2
CSHL/WTROR B46 ....96 C3
EDG B15 ....126 B4
ERDW/GRVHL B23 ....92 A3
GTB/HAM B43 ....73 H1
HALE B63 ....138 B3
LGLYGN/QTN B68 ....123 G2
SCFLD/BOLD B73 ....76 B2
SLYOAK B29 ....142 C5
SOLH B91 ....182 A2
YDLY B25 ....146 A1
George Rose Gdns
DARL/WED WS10 ....54 D2
George St BHTH/HG B12 ....144 B2
BKHL/PFLD WV2 ....7 F6
CBHAMNW B3 ....2 C4
DUDN DY1 ....68 B5
HDSW B21 ....107 E1
LOZ/NWT B19 ....108 B2
STRBR DY8 ....118 B3
WBROM B70 ....87 H4
WLNHL WV13 ....39 G1
WSL WS1 ....4 E5
George St West WSNGN B18 ....108 A5
Georgina Av BILS/COS WV14 ....53 H5
Geraldine Rd YDLY B25 ....129 F5
Gerald Rd STRBR DY8 ....118 A5
Geranium Gv BORD B9 ....128 D1
Geranium Rd DUDS DY2 ....103 F1
Gerardsfield Rd STETCH B33 ....131 F1
Germander Dr DSYBK/YTR WS5 ..57 G5
Gerrard Cl LOZ/NWT B19 ....108 D2
Gerrard Rd WLNHL WV13 ....39 E4
Gerrard St LOZ/NWT B19 ....108 C3
Gervase Dr DUDN DY1 ....84 C3
Geston Rd DUDN DY1 ....101 H1
Gibbet La KINVER DY7 ....134 A3
Gibbins Rd SLYOAK B29 ....159 E1
Gibbons Gv
DUNHL/THL/PER WV6 ....36 A1
Gibbons Hill Rd SEDG DY3 ....67 F1
Gibbons La BRLYHL DY5 ....100 C2
Gibbons Rd
DUNHL/THL/PER WV6 ....36 B1
MGN/WHC B75 ....47 F2
Gibbs Hill Rd NFLD/LBR B31 ....189 H1
Gibbs Rd HAG/WOL DY9 ....137 E2
Gibbs St DUNHL/THL/PER WV6 ....36 C1
Gibb St BORD B9 ....3 K7
Gibson Dr BFLD/HDSWWD B20 ....90 B5
Gibson Rd BFLD/HDSWWD B20 ..108 B1
DUNHL/THL/PER WV6 ....34 C2
Gideon Cl
LGN/SDN/BHAMAIR B26 ....146 D1
Gideons Cl SEDG DY3 ....83 F1
Giffard Rd WOLV WV1 ....53 F1
WOLVN WV10 ....13 E4
Giggetty La WMBN WV5 ....64 C5
Gigmill Wy STRBR DY8 ....135 E3
Gilbanks Rd STRBR DY8 ....117 H5
Gilberry Cl DOR/KN B93 ....197 E3
Gilbert Av OLDBY B69 ....103 H2
Gilbert Cl WNSFLD WV11 ....25 G3
Gilbert La WMBN WV5 ....65 F4
Gilbert Rd SMTHWK B66 ....106 D5
Gilbertstone Av
LGN/SDN/BHAMAIR B26 ....147 E2
Gilbert St TPTN/OCK DY4 ....85 F4
Gilbeys Cl STRBR DY8 ....118 A3
Gilby Rd LDYWD/EDGR B16 ....126 A3
Gilchrist Dr EDG B15 ....125 G4
Gildas Av HWK/WKHTH B38 ....177 E4
Giles Cl HIA/OLT B92 ....165 H3
STETCH B33 ....130 A1
Giles Rd LGLYGN/QTN B68 ....105 F4
Gilldown Pl EDG B15 ....126 B5
Gillespie Cft AST/WIT B6 ....109 F2
Gillhurst Rd HRBN B17 ....124 D5
Gilling Gv BKDE/SHDE B34 ....112 C3
Gillingham Cl DARL/WED WS10 ....56 D4
Gillity Av DSYBK/YTR WS5 ....42 D5
Gillity Cl DSYBK/YTR WS5 ....42 D5
Gilliver Rd SHLY B90 ....180 B3
Gillman Cl
LGN/SDN/BHAMAIR B26 ....148 B3
Gillott Cl SOLH B91 ....182 C2
Gillott Rd LDYWD/EDGR B16 ....125 F2
Gillows Cft SHLY B90 ....195 G1
Gillscroft Rd STETCH B33 ....130 C1
Gill St DUDS DY2 ....121 E1
WBROM B70 ....87 G5
Gilmorton Cl HRBN B17 ....124 D5
SOLH B91 ....182 A4
Gilpin Cl CBROM B36 ....111 G3
Gilpin Crs BLOX/PEL WS3 ....18 A3
Gilson Dr CSHL/WTROR B46 ....114 D1
Gilson Rd CSHL/WTROR B46 ....96 D5
CSHL/WTROR B46 ....115 E1
Gilson St TPTN/OCK DY4 ....70 A3
Gilson Wy
CHWD/FDBR/MGN B37 ....114 A4
Gilwell Rd BKDE/SHDE B34 ....113 G3
Gimble Wk HRBN B17 ....124 B4
Gipsy La ERDW/GRVHL B23 ....91 H1
WLNHL WV13 ....39 H4
Gisborn Cl SMHTH B10 * 127 H4
Gladeside Cl RUSH/SHEL WS4 ....29 E2
The Glades ALDR WS9 ....30 B3
The Glade CDSL WV8 ....22 A1
FOAKS/STRLY B74 ....45 E4
HAG/WOL DY9 ....136 C2
LGN/SDN/BHAMAIR B26 ....148 B3
Gladstone Dr OLDBY B69 ....86 A3
Gladstone Gv KGSWFD DY6 ....99 H1
Gladstone Rd DOR/KN B93 ....199 E1
ERDW/GRVHL B23 ....92 B3
LGN/SDN/BHAMAIR B26 ....146 D1
SPARK B11 ....144 D1
STRBR DY8 ....134 D1
Gladstone St AST/WIT B6 ....109 G1
DARL/WED WS10 ....55 G2
HHTH/SAND B71 ....87 G1
WSLW WS2 ....41 H1
Gladys Rd SMTHWKW B67 ....124 B2
YDLY B25 ....129 F5
Gladys Ter SMTHWKW B67 * 124 C2
Glaisdale Gdns
DUNHL/THL/PER WV6 ....22 C5
Glaisdale Rd HLGN/YWD B28 ....163 E2
Glaisedale Gv WLNHL WV13 ....40 A3
Glaisher Dr WOLVN WV10 ....23 E4
Glamis Rd SHHTH WV12 ....25 H3
Glanville Dr MGN/WHC B75 ....47 E1
Glasbury Cft HWK/WKHTH B38 ..190 C1
Glascote Cl SHLY B90 ....180 A2
Glascote Gv BKDE/SHDE B34 ....113 E3
Glasshouse Hl STRBR DY8 ....135 H4
Glastonbury Crs BLOX/PEL WS3 ..16 A5
Glastonbury Rd
ALE/KHTH/YWD B14 ....162 A5
HHTH/SAND B71 ....71 H3
Glastonbury Wy BLOX/PEL WS3 ..26 C1
Glaston Dr SOLH B91 ....181 G5
Gleads Cft RIDG/WDGT B32 ....140 A4
Gleave Rd SLYOAK B29 ....159 G1
Glebe Dr SCFLD/BOLD B73 ....76 D3
Glebe Farm Rd STETCH B33 ....112 C4
Glebefields Rd TPTN/OCK DY4 ....69 G3
Glebeland Cl LDYWD/EDGR B16 ....2 A7
Glebe La STRBR DY8 ....135 E3
Glebe Pl DARL/WED WS10 ....54 D2
Glebe Rd SOLH B91 ....165 F5
WLNHL WV13 ....39 F5
Glebe St WSL WS1 ....4 D6
The Glebe HAG/WOL DY9 ....184 C2
Glenavon Rd
ALE/KHTH/YWD B14 ....178 C2
Glen Cl RUSH/SHEL WS4 ....42 C2
Glencoe Rd SMTHWK B66 ....107 E5
Glen Ct BDMR/CCFT WV3 ....36 A3
Glencroft Rd HIA/OLT B92 ....148 B4
Glendale Cl BDMR/CCFT WV3 ....35 G5
HALE B63 ....138 D3
Glendale Dr STETCH B33 ....130 B1
WMBN WV5 ....65 E5
Glendene Crs
HWK/WKHTH B38 ....190 A1
Glen Devon Cl RBRY B45 ....174 A3
Glendon Rd ERDW/GRVHL B23 ....76 B5
Glendon Wy DOR/KN B93 ....196 C5
Glendower Rd ALDR WS9 ....30 B1
PBAR/PBCH B42 ....90 C1
Gleneagles Dr GTB/HAM B43 ....58 C4
MGN/WHC B75 ....62 C1
OLDBY B69 ....103 G2
Gleneagles Rd BLOX/PEL WS3 ....16 B4
DUNHL/THL/PER WV6 ....20 B5
LGN/SDN/BHAMAIR B26 ....130 C4
Glenelg Dr STRBR DY8 ....135 H5
Glenelg Ms DSYBK/YTR WS5 ....58 B3
Glenfern Rd BILS/COS WV14 ....68 A3
Glenfield CDSL WV8 ....11 G5
Glenfield Cl SOLH B91 ....182 A5
WALM/CURD B76 ....63 E5
Glenfield Gv SLYOAK B29 ....160 A1
Glengarry Cl RIDG/WDGT B32 ....157 F3
Glengarry Gdns
BDMR/CCFT WV3 ....36 B4
Glenhill Dr HWK/WKHTH B38 ....177 E5
Glenhurst Cl WSLW WS2 ....40 B2
Glenmead Rd KGSTG B44 ....74 D3
Glenmore Cl BDMR/CCFT WV3 ....51 E1
Glenmore Dr HWK/WKHTH B38 ..176 B4
Glen Park Rd SEDG DY3 ....83 F4
Glenpark Rd WASH/WDE B8 ....110 C4
Glen Ri MOS/BIL B13 ....162 A4
Glen Rd SEDG DY3 ....67 G5
STRBR DY8 ....135 F4
Glenroyde HWK/WKHTH B38 ....190 C1
Glen Side RIDG/WDGT B32 ....140 D5
Glenside Av HIA/OLT B92 ....147 H4
Glenthorne Rd
ERDE/BCHGN B24 ....93 E4
Glenthorne Wy
ERDE/BCHGN B24 ....93 E4
Glentworth Dr
WALM/CURD B76 ....78 C1
Glentworth Gdns
DUNHL/THL/PER WV6 ....22 D5
Glenville Dr ERDW/GRVHL B23 ....92 C1
Glenwood Cl BRLYHL DY5 ....119 F4
Glenwood Dr SHLY B90 ....194 D4
Glenwood Rd
HWK/WKHTH B38 ....176 B5
Globe St DARL/WED WS10 ....70 D2
Gloucester Pl WLNHL WV13 ....40 B3
Gloucester Rd DARL/WED WS10 ..56 C5
DSYBK/YTR WS5 ....42 D5
DUDS DY2 ....120 D2
Gloucester St DIG/EDG B5 ....3 G7
DUNHL/THL/PER WV6 ....36 D1
Gloucester Wy
CHWD/FDBR/MGN B37 ....132 A3
Glover Cl HLGN/YWD B28 ....162 D4
Glover Rd MGN/WHC B75 ....63 F3
Glovers Cft
CHWD/FDBR/MGN B37 ....131 H1
Glovers Field Dr
VAUX/NECH B7 ....110 A2
Glovers Rd SMHTH B10 ....128 A4
Glover St BORD B9 ....127 G2
WBROM B70 ....87 H5
Glyme Dr DUNHL/THL/PER WV6 ..22 A5
Glyn Av BILS/COS WV14 ....54 D5
Glyn Dr BILS/COS WV14 ....54 D5
Glyn Farm Rd RIDG/WDGT B32 ..140 C2
Glynn Crs HALE B63 ....120 B5
Glynne Av KGSWFD DY6 ....99 H5
Glyn Rd RIDG/WDGT B32 ....140 D1
Glynside Av RIDG/WDGT B32 ....140 C2
Goffs Cl RIDG/WDGT B32 ....141 F4
Goldborough Cl BILS/COS WV14 ..53 H5
Goldcrest Cl DUDS DY2 ....120 D2
Goldcrest Cft CBROM B36 ....114 A1
Goldencrest Dr OLDBY B69 ....104 C1
Golden Cft BFLD/HDSWWD B20 ..89 H5
Golden End Dr DOR/KN B93 ....197 H2
Golden Hillock Rd DUDS DY2 ....120 C1
SPARK B11 ....145 F2
Goldfinch Cl SLYOAK B29 ....159 F2
Goldfinch Rd HAG/WOL DY9 * 136 A4
Goldicroft Rd DARL/WED WS10 ....56 A4
Goldieslie Cl SCFLD/BOLD B73 ....77 F1
Goldieslie Rd SCFLD/BOLD B73 ....77 F1
Golds Hill Gdns HDSW B21 ....107 H2
Golds Hill Rd HDSW B21 ....107 H1
Golds Hill Wy TPTN/OCK DY4 ....70 B4
Goldsmith Rd
ALE/KHTH/YWD B14 ....161 F2
BLOX/PEL WS3 ....28 A2
Goldstar Wy STETCH B33 ....131 E2
Goldthorn Av
ETTPK/GDPK/PENN WV4 ....51 H3
Goldthorn Crs
ETTPK/GDPK/PENN WV4 ....51 G2
Goldthorne Av
LGN/SDN/BHAMAIR B26 ....148 A3
Goldthorne Wk BRLYHL DY5 ....119 F4
Goldthorn Hl
ETTPK/GDPK/PENN WV4 ....51 H2
Goldthorn Rd
ETTPK/GDPK/PENN WV4 ....51 H2
Golf La BILS/COS WV14 ....53 H1
Golson Cl MGN/WHC B75 ....63 E2
Gomeldon Av
ALE/KHTH/YWD B14 ....178 B2
Gomer St WLNHL WV13 ....39 G3
Gomer St West WLNHL WV13 ....39 G3
Gooch Cl STRBR DY8 ....135 G1
Gooch St DIG/EDG B5 ....127 E4

Gooch St North DIG/EDG B5 ......127 E3
Goodall Gv GTB/HAM B43..............60 A3
Goodall St WSL WS1 ....5 F4
Goodby Rd MOS/BIL B13 ....143 H4
Goode Av WSNGN B18 ....108 A4
Goode Cl LGLYGN/QTN B68..........105 G5
Goodeve Wk MGN/WHC B75 ....63 H3
Goodison Gdns
ERDE/BCHGN B24 ....93 F1
Goodman Cl HLGN/YWD B28 ....162 D4
Goodman St CBHAMW B1 ....2 A4
Goodrest Av RMSLY B62..............140 A1
Goodrest Cft
ALE/KHTH/YWD B14 ....179 E1
Goodrest La HWK/WKHTH B38 ..190 D2
Goodrich Av
DUNHL/THL/PER WV6 ....35 E2
Goodrich Covert
ALE/KHTH/YWD B14 ....177 G3
Goodrick Wy VAUX/NECH B7 * ..109 H3
Goodway Ct CBHAMNE B4 ....3 G2
Goodway Rd HIA/OLT B92 ....148 C4
KGSTG B44 ....75 E3
Goodwood Cl CBROM B36 ....111 H1
Goodwood Dr
FOAKS/STRLY B74 ....60 B2
Goodwyn Av LGLYGN/QTN B68 ..123 H5
Goodyear Av WOLVN WV10 ....23 G3
Goodyear Rd SMTHWKW B67 ......123 H2
Goosemoor La
ERDW/GRVHL B23 ....76 D4
Gopsal St CBHAMNE B4 ....127 G1
Gorcott La SHLY B90 ....194 A3
Gordon Av
ETTPK/GDPK/PENN WV4 ....52 D5
HHTH/SAND B71 ....71 G3
LOZ/NWT B19.............................108 D2
Gordon Cl OLDBY B69 ....86 B4
Gordon Crs BRLYHL DY5 ....101 G4
Gordon Dr TPTN/OCK DY4 ....86 A1
Gordon Pl BILS/COS WV14 ....53 G3
Gordon Rd HRBN B17 ....142 B1
LOZ/NWT B19..............................108 C1
Gordon St BKHL/PFLD WV2 ....7 H7
BORD B9 * 127 H2
DARL/WED WS10...........................55 F2
Gorey Cl SHHTH WV12...................25 H2
Gorge Rd SEDG DY3.......................67 G3
Gorleston Gv
ALE/KHTH/YWD B14 ....178 D3
Gorleston Rd
ALE/KHTH/YWD B14 ....178 D3
Gorsebrook Rd
DUNHL/THL/PER WV6 ....22 D5
Gorse Cl
CHWD/FDBR/MGN B37.............131 H2
SLYOAK B29 ....158 C2
Gorse Farm Rd GTB/HAM B43.......73 G3
Gorsefield Rd BKDE/SHDE B34 ..113 E4
Gorse Green La HAG/WOL DY9 ..171 F5
Gorsemoor Wy WNSFLD WV11 .....15 F4
Gorse Rd DUDN DY1 ....84 A2
WNSFLD WV11 ....25 G2
Gorsey La CSHL/WTROR B46 ....97 E4
HLYWD B47 ....192 C4
Gorsey Wy ALDR WS9 ....29 G5
Gorsly Piece RIDG/WDGT B32 ....140 C3
Gorstie Cft GTB/HAM B43..............73 G3
Gorsty Av BRLYHL DY5 ....101 E5
Gorsty Cl HHTH/SAND B71 ....72 B3
Gorsty Hayes CDSL WV8.................10 B4
Gorsty Hill Rd RMSLY B62 ....121 H4
Gorsymead Gv NFLD/LBR B31.....174 C3
Gorsy Rd RIDG/WDGT B32 ....140 D3
Gorway Cl WSL WS1 ....57 F1
Gorway Gdns WSL WS1...................57 G1
Gorway Rd WSL WS1.......................57 G1
Goscote Cl BLOX/PEL WS3 ....28 B3
Goscote La BLOX/PEL WS3............17 G5
Goscote Lodge Crs
BLOX/PEL WS3............................28 C3
Goscote Pl BLOX/PEL WS3 ....28 C3
Goscote Rd BLOX/PEL WS3 ....28 B1
Gosford St BHTH/HG B12..............144 B1
Gospel End Rd SEDG DY3...............66 D3
Gospel End St SEDG DY3 ....67 F4
Gospel Farm Rd ACGN B27...........163 F2
Gospel La ACGN B27 ....163 G3
Gospel Oak Rd TPTN/OCK DY4......69 H2
Gosport Cl WOLV WV1....................53 F1
Goss Cft SLYOAK B29...................159 F1
Gossey La STETCH B33 ....131 E2
The Goss BRLYHL DY5 ....119 F3
Gotham Rd
LGN/SDN/BHAMAIR B26............147 E1
Gothersley La KINVER DY7 ....116 B2
Goths Cl BLKHTH/ROWR B65 ......104 A5
Gough Av WNSFLD WV11 ....24 B2
Gough Rd BILS/COS WV14 ....68 C2
EDG B15 ....126 C5
SPARK B11 ....145 F2
Gough St CBHAMW B1 ....2 E7
WLNHL WV13 ....40 A3
WOLV WV1 ....7 J4
Gould Firm La ALDR WS9 ....31 E4
Gowan Rd WASH/WDE B8 ....110 C5
Gower Av KGSWFD DY6 ....100 B5
Gower Rd RMSLY B62 ....139 G1
SEDG DY3 ....66 D2
Gower St BKHL/PFLD WV2 ....7 J7
LOZ/NWT B19.............................108 D2
WLNHL WV13 ....39 G3
WSLW WS2 ....56 B1
Gozzard St BILS/COS WV14 ....54 A3
Gracemere Crs HLGN/YWD B28..179 G1
Grace Rd OLDBY B69....................104 A1
SPARK B11 ....145 E1
TPTN/OCK DY4.............................69 G4
Gracewell Rd MOS/BIL B13 ....162 B1
Grafton Dr WLNHL WV13 ....38 D4
Grafton Gdns SEDG DY3................82 D3
Grafton Gv LOZ/NWT B19 * 108 C2
Grafton Pl BILS/COS WV14 ....54 A1
Grafton Rd HDSW B21 ....89 F5
HHTH/SAND B71 ....87 H2
LGLYGN/QTN B68.......................122 D2
SHLY B90 ....179 E3
SPARK B11 ....127 H5
Graham Cl TPTN/OCK DY4 ....69 H2
Graham Crs RBRY B45 ....187 H1
Graham Rd HHTH/SAND B71 ....87 H2
RMSLY B62 ....122 A4
STRBR DY8 ....99 H5
WASH/WDE B8...........................128 D1
YDLY B25 ....146 C1
Graham St CBHAMW B1 ....2 C3
LOZ/NWT B19.............................108 C2
Grainger Cl TPTN/OCK DY4............70 B5
Grainger's La CDYHTH B64...........120 C4
Grainger St DUDS DY2 ....102 D2
Graiseley Ct BDMR/CCFT WV3 ....6 D6
Graiseley Hl BKHL/PFLD WV2.........36 D5
Graiseley La WNSFLD WV11 ....24 C5
Graiseley Rw BKHL/PFLD WV2.......37 E5
Graiseley St BDMR/CCFT WV3 ....6 D6
Graith Cl ALE/KHTH/YWD B14 ....179 G2
Grammar School La HALE B63 ..138 C3
Grampian Rd STRBR DY8 ....135 G1
Granary Cl KGSWFD DY6 ....99 E1
Granary La WALM/CURD B76.........63 F5
Granary Rd CDSL WV8...................22 A1
The Granary ALDR WS9..................30 B4
Granbourne Rd SHHTH WV12 ......40 B1
Granby Av STETCH B33 ....131 E3
Granby Cl HIA/OLT B92 ....164 A3
Grandborough Dr SOLH B91 .....181 G4
Grand Cl SMTHWK B66 ....124 D1
Grand Junction Wy WSL WS1 .....56 D3
Grand Union Canal Wk
CBHAMNE B4 ....3 F2
DOR/KN B93...............................197 H3
SOLH B91 ....183 F2
SPARK B11 ....128 A5
YDLY B25 ....146 A1
Grandys Cft
CHWD/FDBR/MGN B37............131 H2
Grange Av ALDR WS9 ....30 A1
MGN/WHC B75 ....47 G2
WASH/WDE B8 * 111 F3
Grange Ct BDMR/CCFT WV3 * 6 D6
HAG/WOL DY9 * 136 A4
WSLW WS2 * 40 B3
Grange Crs HALE B63 ....138 D4
RBRY B45 ....173 G5
RUSH/SHEL WS4 ....28 D2
Grange Farm Dr
HWK/WKHTH B38 ....176 B5
Grangefield Cl CDSL WV8 ....22 B1
Grange Hl RMSLY B62 ....139 E5
Grange Hill Rd
HWK/WKHTH B38 ....176 C4
Grange La HAG/WOL DY9 ....136 B3
KGSWFD DY6 ....100 B5
MGN/WHC B75 ....47 G2
Grange Ri HWK/WKHTH B38 ......190 D1
Grange Rd
ALE/KHTH/YWD B14 ....160 D2
AST/WIT B6 ....109 E1
BILS/COS WV14 ....68 B4
BKHL/PFLD WV2 ....51 H2
BORD B9 ....128 B4
CDYHTH B64..............................121 G3
DOR/KN B93...............................198 C2
DUDN DY1 ....84 B5
DUNHL/THL/PER WV6 ....21 G5
ERDE/BCHGN B24 ....93 F1
HAG/WOL DY9 ....136 A3
HALE B63 ....138 D4
HIA/OLT B92 ....164 A3
SLYOAK B29 ....142 D4
SMTHWK B66 ....124 C1
WBROM B70..................................87 F3
Grange St DUDN DY1 ....84 B5
WSL WS1......................................57 F1
The Grange WMBN WV5..................65 E4
Grangewood Ct HIA/OLT B92 * ..164 A3
Granshaw Cl
HWK/WKHTH B38 ....176 D4
Grant Cl HHTH/SAND B71 ....87 G1
KGSWFD DY6 ....99 H1
Grantham Cl BRLYHL DY5...........118 D5
Grantham Rd SMTHWK B66.........124 D1
SPARK B11 ....144 D1
Grantley Crs KGSWFD DY6 ....99 G2
Grantley Dr
CHWD/FDBR/MGN B37............132 A2
Granton Cl
ALE/KHTH/YWD B14 ....160 D5
Granton Rd
ALE/KHTH/YWD B14 ....160 D5
Grantown Gv GTWY WS6 ....16 C3
Grant St BLOX/PEL WS3 ....27 F2
EDG B15 ....126 D4
Granville Cl BKHL/PFLD WV2 ....7 H7
Granville Dr KGSWFD DY6...........100 B5
Granville Rd CDYHTH B64............121 H4
DOR/KN B93...............................199 E1
Granville Sq EDG B15 ....2 C7
Granville St BKHL/PFLD WV2 ....7 H7
CBHAMW B1 ....2 D7
WLNHL WV13 ....39 G2
Grasdene Gv HRBN B17 ....142 A3
Grasmere Av
DUNHL/THL/PER WV6 ....34 D1
FOAKS/STRLY B74 ....45 G2
Grasmere Cl
DUNHL/THL/PER WV6 ....21 H2
GTB/HAM B43 ....73 H4
KGSWFD DY6 ....99 F2
WNSFLD WV11 ....24 C3
Grasmere Rd HDSW B21..............107 H2
Grassington Dr
CHWD/FDBR/MGN B37............131 H3
Grassmere Dr STRBR DY8............135 F4
Grassmoor Rd
HWK/WKHTH B38 ....176 C3
Grassy La WOLVN WV10 ....24 B1
Graston Cl LDYWD/EDGR B16 .....126 A2
Grattidge Rd HIA/OLT B92 ....146 D5
Gravel Bank RIDG/WDGT B32 ....140 D5
Gravel Hl WMBN WV5 ....65 F5
Gravelly Hl ERDE/BCHGN B24 ......92 C4
Gravelly Hl North
ERDE/BCHGN B24 ....92 C3
Gravelly La ERDW/GRVHL B23 ......92 D1
Grayfield Av MOS/BIL B13 ....144 B4
Grayland Cl ACGN B27 ....146 B5
Grayling Cl DARL/WED WS10 ....54 D5
Grayling Rd BRLYHL DY5 ....136 A1
Grayling Wk
CHWD/FDBR/MGN B37............132 C2
WOLV WV1 ....38 B1
Grayshott Cl ERDW/GRVHL B23....92 C1
Grays Rd HRBN B17 ....142 B1
Gray St BORD B9 ....127 H2
Grayswood Park Rd
RIDG/WDGT B32 ....140 C1
Grayswood Rd NFLD/LBR B31....189 F1
Grazebrook Cft
RIDG/WDGT B32 ....157 H2
Grazebrook Rd DUDS DY2 ....102 C2
Grazewood Cl SHHTH WV12...........25 H3
Greadier St SHHTH WV12 ....26 A5
Great Arthur St SMTHWK B66 ....106 B2
Great Barr St BORD B9 ....127 G2
Great Brickkiln St
BDMR/CCFT WV3............................6 C6
Great Br TPTN/OCK DY4 ....86 B1
Great Bridge Rd BILS/COS WV14..54 C4
Great Bridge St WBROM B70.........86 C1
Great Brook St VAUX/NECH B7 ..109 G5
Great Charles St BRWNH WS8 ....9 F4
Great Charles St Queensway
CBHAMNW B3 ....2 E4
Great Colmore St EDG B15 ....126 D4
Great Cornbow HALE B63 ....138 D4
Great Croft St DARL/WED WS10 ..55 F2
Great Farley Dr NFLD/LBR B31 ..174 C4
Great Francis St
VAUX/NECH B7 ....109 H5
Great Hampton Rw
LOZ/NWT B19................................2 D1
Great Hampton St WOLV WV1.........6 D1
Great King St LOZ/NWT B19.........108 C4
Great Lister St VAUX/NECH B7 ....3 K1
Greatrey Ct HHTH/SAND B71..........71 F3
Great Stone Rd NFLD/LBR B31 ..175 G2
Great Tindal St
LDYWD/EDGR B16.......................126 A2
Great Western Ar CBHAMNW B3 ..3 G4
Great Western Cl WSNGN B18 ....107 G3
Great Western Dr CDYHTH B64..121 G3
Great Western St
DARL/WED WS10...........................70 C1
WOLV WV1 ....7 G2
Great Western Wy
TPTN/OCK DY4 ....70 B5
Great Wood Rd BORD B9 ....128 A3
Greaves Av DSYBK/YTR WS5 ....43 E5
Greaves Cl DSYBK/YTR WS5 ....43 E5
Greaves Crs SHHTH WV12..............26 A2
Greaves Rd DUDS DY2 ....102 D4
Greaves Sq HWK/WKHTH B38 ....177 F4
The Greaves WALM/CURD B76 ......79 H5
Grebe Cl ERDW/GRVHL B23 ....91 H3
Greenacre Dr CDSL WV8................10 D5
Greenacre Rd TPTN/OCK DY4 ....69 G2
Green Acres ACGN B27 ....146 B5
WMBN WV5 ....80 D1
Greenacres
DUNHL/THL/PER WV6 ....21 F5
SEDG DY3 ....66 D2
WALM/CURD B76 ....78 C3
Greenacres Av WOLVN WV10.........24 B1
Greenacres Cl FOAKS/STRLY B74..45 E3
Green Acres Rd
HWK/WKHTH B38 ....176 B5
Greenaleigh Rd
ALE/KHTH/YWD B14 ....179 F2
Green Av HLGN/YWD B28 ....162 C1
Greenaway Cl GTB/HAM B43.........59 G5
Green Bank Av HLGN/YWD B28...162 C1
Greenbank Gdns STRBR DY8 ......118 A2
Green Barns La LICHS WS14..........33 G1
Greenbush Dr HALE B63..............138 C2
Green Cl HLYWD B47 ....192 C5
Green Ct HLGN/YWD B28 ....162 D2
Green Cft BORD B9 ....129 E1
Greencroft BILS/COS WV14 ....53 H2
KGSWFD DY6 ....99 H5
Green Dr RIDG/WDGT B32 ....157 G1
WOLVN WV10...............................23 E3
Greenend Rd MOS/BIL B13 ....144 B5
Greenfels Ri DUDS DY2...............103 F1
Greenfield Av CDYHTH B64 ....120 B3
STRBR DY8 ....135 F2
Greenfield Crs EDG B15 ....126 A4
Greenfield Cft BILS/COS WV14 .....53 H5
Greenfield La WOLVN WV10...........12 D2
Greenfield Rd GTB/HAM B43.........73 E4
HRBN B17 ....142 A2
SMTHWKW B67 ....106 A5
Greenfields ALDR WS9 ....30 A3
Greenfields Rd KGSWFD DY6 ......100 A4
RUSH/SHEL WS4 ....18 D5
WMBN WV5 ....81 E1
Greenfield Vw SEDG DY3 ....66 D4
Greenfinch Rd CBROM B36 ....114 A2
HAG/WOL DY9 ....136 B4
Greenford Rd
ALE/KHTH/YWD B14 ....178 D2
Green Gables HLYWD B47 ....192 C1
MGN/WHC B75 * 62 B1
Green Gables Dr HLYWD B47 * ..192 C1
Greenhill WMBN WV5 ....65 F5
Greenhill Cl SHHTH WV12 ....25 H5
Greenhill Dr SLYOAK B29 ....159 E1
Greenhill Gdns GTB/HAM B43 ......73 F1
RMSLY B62 ....139 F1
WMBN WV5 ....81 F1
Greenhill Rd CSCFLD/WYGN B72 ..77 F3
HDSW B21 ....89 F4
MOS/BIL B13 ....161 F1
RMSLY B62 ....122 B5
SEDG DY3 ....83 G1
Greenhill Vls WSL WS1 * 5 F7
Greenhill Wy ALDR WS9 ....30 B1
Green Hill Wy SHLY B90 ....163 F5
Greenholm Rd KGSTG B44 ....75 E4
Greening Dr EDG B15 ....126 B5
Greenland Cl KGSWFD DY6...........100 A1
Greenland Ri HIA/OLT B92 ....165 F3
Greenland Rd SLYOAK B29 ....160 B1
Greenlands WMBN WV5 ....64 D4
Greenlands Rd
CHWD/FDBR/MGN B37............132 C2
Green La ALDR WS9.......................31 E5
BLOX/PEL WS3.............................18 A3
BLOX/PEL WS3.............................27 G3
BNTWD WS7 ....9 G2
BORD B9.....................................128 A3
CBROM B36 ....113 G1
CSHL/WTROR B46 ....115 G4
DUDN DY1 ....83 H1
DUNHL/THL/PER WV6 ....22 A3
GTB/HAM B43 ....73 F4
HAG/WOL DY9 ....136 B2
HDSW B21 ....107 E1
HWK/WKHTH B38 ....176 C5
KGSWFD DY6 ....99 H2
RIDG/WDGT B32 ....140 C1
RMSLY B62 ....122 B3
RUSH/SHEL WS4 ....18 D4
SHLY B90 ....179 G4
WSLW WS2 ....4 C2
Green Lanes BILS/COS WV14 ....53 G1
SCFLD/BOLD B73 ....77 F4
Greenleas Gdns HALE B63 ....139 E4
Green Leigh ERDW/GRVHL B23 ....76 D3
Greenleighs SEDG DY3 ....52 B5
Greenly Rd
ETTPK/GDPK/PENN WV4 ....52 B3
Green Meadow HAG/WOL DY9 ..152 D2
WNSFLD WV11.............................24 D5
Green Meadow Cl WMBN WV5 ....64 C5
Green Meadow Rd
SHHTH WV12 ....25 H3
SLYOAK B29 ....158 B3
Greenoak Crs BVILLE B30 ....160 C2
SEDG DY3 ....68 A4
Green Oak Rd CDSL WV8 ....10 D5
Green Park Av BILS/COS WV14 .....38 B5
Green Park Dr BILS/COS WV14 .....38 C5
Green Park Rd DUDS DY2..............85 F5
NFLD/LBR B31 ....175 E3
Greenridge Rd
BFLD/HDSWWD B20 ....89 G1
Green Rd DUDS DY2 ....102 D2
MOS/BIL B13 ....162 B1
Green Rock La BLOX/PEL WS3......27 H1
Greenroyde HAG/WOL DY9 ....152 D1
Greensand Dr BILS/COS WV14 .....68 C1
Greensforge La KINVER DY7 ....116 B4
Greenside HRBN B17...................142 A2
Greenside Rd ERDE/BCHGN B24 ..93 G1
Greenside Wy DSYBK/YTR WS5 ....57 G4
Greensill Av TPTN/OCK DY4 ....69 F3
Greenslade Cft NFLD/LBR B31.....175 G3
Greenslade Rd DSYBK/YTR WS5 ..58 A1
SEDG DY3 ....66 D1
SHLY B90 ....179 E3
Greensleeves FOAKS/STRLY B74 ..46 D3
Greenstead Rd MOS/BIL B13......162 B1
The Greens
DUNHL/THL/PER WV6 * 34 C2
Green St BHTH/HG B12 ....127 F3
BILS/COS WV14 ....68 C3
OLDBY B69 ....105 E2
SMTHWKW B67 ....106 B4
STRBR DY8 ....135 F2
WBROM B70...............................106 A1
WSLW WS2 ....41 G2
Greensway WNSFLD WV11..............24 B2
The Green ALDR WS9.....................30 C4
BLOX/PEL WS3.............................27 F1
CBROM B36 ....112 D2
CSCFLD/WYGN B72 ....77 H2
DARL/WED WS10..........................40 B5
HWK/WKHTH B38 ....176 D3
LGLYGN/QTN B68.......................123 F2
RIDG/WDGT B32 ....140 A1
SOLH B91 ....165 F5
Greenvale NFLD/LBR B31............158 B5
Greenvale Av
LGN/SDN/BHAMAIR B26...........148 B1
Green Wk HRBN B17 ....124 B5
Greenway ALDR WS9 ....19 H5
BFLD/HDSWWD B20 ....73 H5
SEDG DY3 ....67 G2
Greenway Av STRBR DY8............118 A3
Greenway Dr SCFLD/BOLD B73 ....61 E5
Greenway Gdns
HWK/WKHTH B38 ....190 C1
SEDG DY3 ....67 G2
Greenway Rd BILS/COS WV14 ......54 A4
Greenways HALE B63 ....137 G2
NFLD/LBR B31 ....158 B2
STRBR DY8 ....117 G3
Greenway St BORD B9 ....128 A3
The Greenway
CHWD/FDBR/MGN B37............149 E1
HAG/WOL DY9 ....152 B5
SCFLD/BOLD B73 ....60 D5
Greenwood YDLY B25..................179 E5
Greenwood Av ACGN B27 ....146 A5
BLKHTH/ROWR B65....................122 B2
LGLYGN/QTN B68.......................105 F4
Greenwood Cl
ALE/KHTH/YWD B14 ....161 E5
Greenwood Pk ALDR WS9 ....30 C1
Greenwood Pl KGSTG B44 ....75 H2
Greenwood Rd ALDR WS9 ....19 H5
HHTH/SAND B71 ....71 F3
WOLVN WV10...............................23 E3
The Greenwoods STRBR DY8......135 E2
Greethurst Dr MOS/BIL B13........145 E5
Greets Green Rd WBROM B70......86 C2
Greetville Cl STETCH B33 ....112 C4
Gregory Av SLYOAK B29 ....158 C2
Gregory Cl DARL/WED WS10 ....70 D1
Gregory Dr DUDN DY1 ....84 A4
Gregory Rd STRBR DY8...............134 C2
Grendon Dr SCFLD/BOLD B73 ......61 F5
Grendon Gdns BDMR/CCFT WV3..50 D2
Grendon Rd
ALE/KHTH/YWD B14 ....178 C2
HIA/OLT B92...............................164 A2
Grenfell Dr EDG B15 ....125 H4
Grenfell Rd BLOX/PEL WS3...........17 F4
Grenville Cl WSLW WS2 ....40 B2
Grenville Dr ERDW/GRVHL B23 ....91 H3
SMTHWK B66 ....105 H1
Grenville Pl WBROM B70 ....86 C3
Grenville Rd DUDN DY1 ....83 G5
SHLY B90 ....180 B3
Gresham Rd HLGN/YWD B28 ....162 D4
LGLYGN/QTN B68.......................105 F3
Gresley Cl MGN/WHC B75..............47 E1
Gressel La STETCH B33 ....131 E1
Grestone Av
BFLD/HDSWWD B20 ....89 G3
Greswolde Dr ERDE/BCHGN B24..93 F2
Greswolde Park Rd ACGN B27.....146 B4
Greswolde Rd SOLH B91.............164 A4
SPARK B11 ....145 E4
Greswold Gdns STETCH B33........112 C4
Greswold St HHTH/SAND B71 ....87 G1
Gretton Crs ALDR WS9 ....29 H5
Gretton Rd ALDR WS9...................29 H5
ERDW/GRVHL B23........................76 B4
Greville Dr EDG B15....................143 G1
Grevis Cl MOS/BIL B13 ....144 B3
Grevis Rd STETCH B33.................130 A3
Greyfort Crs HIA/OLT B92............164 B1
Greyfriars Cl DUDN DY1 ....83 G3
HIA/OLT B92...............................163 H3
Greyhound La STRBR DY8 ....134 D5
Greyhurst Cft SOLH B91..............181 H5
Grey Mill Cl SHLY B90 ....195 F2
Greystoke Av CBROM B36 ....111 H2
Greystoke Dr KGSWFD DY6 ....99 H3
Greystone Pas DUDN DY1 ....84 B5
Greystone St DUDS DY2 ....84 C5
Grey Tree Crs DOR/KN B93 ....196 C5
Grice St WBROM B70...................105 G1
Griffin Gdns HRBN B17 ....142 B3
Griffin Rd ERDW/GRVHL B23 ....92 A1
Griffins Brook Cl BVILLE B30 .....159 F4
Griffins Brook La BVILLE B30.....159 E4
Griffin St DUDS DY2....................102 C5
WBROM B70..................................87 H3
WOLV WV1 ....37 H4
Griffiths Dr WMBN WV5 ....81 E1
WNSFLD WV11 ....25 F2
Griffiths Rd DUDN DY1 ....68 A5
HHTH/SAND B71 ....71 G2
SHHTH WV12 ....26 B2
Grigg Gv NFLD/LBR B31 ....175 E4
Grimley Rd NFLD/LBR B31 ....176 B3
Grimpits La HWK/WKHTH B38 ....191 E1
Grimshaw Rd HLGN/YWD B28 ....163 E1
Grimstock Hl
CSHL/WTROR B46 * 97 E5
Grimstone St WOLVN WV10 ....7 H2
Grindleford Rd PBAR/PBCH B42 ..74 D4
Gristhorpe Rd SLYOAK B29..........160 A2
Grizedale Cl RBRY B45 ....174 B3
Grocott Rd DARL/WED WS10 ....54 D4
Grosmont Av BHTH/HG B12.........144 C1
Grosvenor Av
BFLD/HDSWWD B20 ....90 C4
FOAKS/STRLY B74 ....45 F4
Grosvenor Cl MGN/WHC B75 ....47 G4
WOLVN WV10...............................12 D5
Grosvenor Crs WOLVN WV10 ....12 D5
Grosvenor Pk
ETTPK/GDPK/PENN WV4 ....51 F3
Grosvenor Rd AST/WIT B6 ....109 H1
BFLD/HDSWWD B20 ....90 C4
ETTPK/GDPK/PENN WV4 ....52 C5
HRBN B17 ....141 G1
LGLYGN/QTN B68.......................105 E5
SEDG DY3 ....83 F4
SOLH B91 ....181 F4
WOLVN WV10...............................12 D5
Grosvenor Sq HLGN/YWD B28....162 C5
Grosvenor St CBHAMNE B4 ....3 J4
WOLVN WV10...............................37 H2
Grosvenor St West
LDYWD/EDGR B16..........................2 A7
Grosvenor Wy BRLYHL DY5 ....119 F5
Grotto La DUNHL/THL/PER WV6 ..22 A5
Groucutt St BILS/COS WV14.........68 C3
Grounds Dr FOAKS/STRLY B74 .....46 D2
Grounds Rd FOAKS/STRLY B74 .....46 D2
Grout St WBROM B70 ....86 C2
Grove Av HALE B63 ....138 B4
HDSW B21 * 107 H1
MOS/BIL B13 ....144 C5
SLYOAK B29 * 159 G1
SOLH B91 ....165 E5
Grove Cottage Rd BORD B9 ......128 B2
Grove Ct PBAR/PBCH B42 * 73 H5
Grove Crs BLOX/PEL WS3 ....17 H4
BRLYHL DY5 ....101 E4
Grove Farm Dr MGN/WHC B75 ....63 F3
Grove Gdns HDSW B21 ....89 H4
Grove Hl DSYBK/YTR WS5..............43 G5

Grove Hill Rd HDSW B21 89 H5
Grove House WSL WS1 * 5 F5
Groveland Rd TPTN/OCK DY4 85 G3
Grovelands Crs WOLVN WV10 12 D4
Grove La BFLD/HDSWWD B20 89 H4
DUNHL/THL/PER WV6 35 F3
HDSW B21 107 H1
HRBN B17 142 A3
SMTHWK B66 107 E4
WALM/CURD B76 79 H1
Groveley La NFLD/LBR B31 189 F2
RBRY B45 188 C4
Grove Ms NFLD/LBR B31 175 H5
Grove Pk KGSWFD DY6 99 G1
Grove Rd ALE/KHTH/YWD B14 160 D3
DOR/KN B93 197 F5
HAG/WOL DY9 136 D3
LGLYGN/QTN B68 123 H3
SOLH B91 165 E5
SPARK B11 145 E4
Groveside Wy BLOX/PEL WS3 18 A2
Grove St BKHL/PFLD WV2 37 F5
DUDS DY2 103 E1
WOLVN WV10 37 H2
WSNGN B18 107 F5
Grove Ter WSL WS1 5 F5
The Grove BLKHTH/ROWR B65 122 A2
BRLYHL DY5 119 E3
CSHL/WTROR B46 115 F5
DSYBK/YTR WS5 57 H5
ETTPK/GDPK/PENN WV4 52 C3
FOAKS/STRLY B74 32 B5
GTB/HAM B43 58 C4
HIA/OLT B92 167 G2
LDYWD/EDGR B16 * 125 H2
NFLD/LBR B31 175 H5
RBRY B45 188 D4
WASH/WDE B8 110 A5
WNSFLD WV11 24 B4
Grove Vale Av GTB/HAM B43 73 E2
Grove Wy FOAKS/STRLY B74 60 B1
Grovewood Dr
HWK/WKHTH B38 176 C4
Guardian Ct NFLD/LBR B31 174 D2
SOLH B91 182 B2
Guardians Wy NFLD/LBR B31 158 A2
Guernsey Dr CBROM B36 114 B3
Guest Av WNSFLD WV11 24 C2
Guest Gv LOZ/NWT B19 108 C3
Guild Av BLOX/PEL WS3 27 H3
Guild Cl LDYWD/EDGR B16 126 A2
Guild Cft LOZ/NWT B19 108 D3
Guildford Cft
CHWD/FDBR/MGN B37 131 H4
Guildford Dr LOZ/NWT B19 108 D3
Guildford St LOZ/NWT B19 108 D2
Guiting Rd SLYOAK B29 158 C3
Gullane Cl HWK/WKHTH B38 176 B4
Gullswood Cl
ALE/KHTH/YWD B14 177 H3
Gumbleberrys Cl
WASH/WDE B8 111 G5
Gunmakers Wk LOZ/NWT B19 108 D2
Gunner Gv MGN/WHC B75 63 G2
Gunner La RBRY B45 187 F1
Gunns Wy HIA/OLT B92 163 H3
Guns La WBROM B70 87 F2
Gunstock Cl FOAKS/STRLY B74 60 A1
Gunstone La CDSL WV8 10 B2
Gunter Rd ERDE/BCHGN B24 94 A3
Gurnard Cl SHHTH WV12 25 H1
Gurney Pl WSLW WS2 27 E5
Gurney Rd WSLW WS2 27 E5
Guthrie Cl LOZ/NWT B19 108 D3
Guthrum Cl
DUNHL/THL/PER WV6 20 D5
ERDW/GRVHL B23 76 C3
The Gutter HAG/WOL DY9 186 A1
Guy Av WOLVN WV10 23 G4
Guys Cliffe Av WALM/CURD B76 78 B2
Guy's La SEDG DY3 82 D4
Gwalia Gv ERDW/GRVHL B23 * 92 D2
Gwendoline Wy ALDR WS9 19 H3
Gypsy La CSHL/WTROR B46 96 D4

H

Habberley Rd
BLKHTH/ROWR B65 122 B2
Habberly Cft SOLH B91 181 H4
Hackett Cl BILS/COS WV14 67 H2
Hackett Dr SMTHWK B66 105 H2
Hackett Rd BLKHTH/ROWR B65 122 C1
Hackett St TPTN/OCK DY4 70 A4
Hackford Rd
ETTPK/GDPK/PENN WV4 52 D4
Hackman's Gate La
HAG/WOL DY9 169 G5
Hack St BORD B9 127 G3
Hackwood Rd DARL/WED WS10 71 F1
Hadcroft Gra HAG/WOL DY9 136 B3
Hadcroft Rd HAG/WOL DY9 136 A3
Haddock Rd BILS/COS WV14 53 G1
Haddon Crs SHHTH WV12 26 A3
Haddon Cft HALE B63 154 C1
Haddon Rd PBAR/PBCH B42 74 D4
Haden Circ BHTH/HG B12 127 F5
Haden Cl CDYHTH B64 121 F5
STRBR DY8 117 H2
Haden Crs WNSFLD WV11 25 F4
Haden Cross Dr CDYHTH B64 121 G5
Hadendale CDYHTH B64 121 G5
Haden Hl BDMR/CCFT WV3 6 A4
Haden Hill Rd CDYHTH B64 121 G5
HALE B63 138 C1
Haden Park Rd CDYHTH B64 121 E5
Haden Rd CDYHTH B64 121 E2
TPTN/OCK DY4 69 G2
Haden St BHTH/HG B12 144 B1
Haden Wy BHTH/HG B12 144 B1
Hadfield Cl ERDE/BCHGN B24 94 A3
Hadfield Cft LOZ/NWT B19 108 C4
Hadfield Wy
CHWD/FDBR/MGN B37 114 A5
Hadland Rd STETCH B33 130 D3
Hadleigh Cft WALM/CURD B76 78 C5
Hadley Cl DUDS DY2 103 E5
HLYWD B47 192 C3
Hadley Cft SMTHWK B66 106 C2
Hadley Pl BILS/COS WV14 53 G1
Hadley Rd BILS/COS WV14 53 G1
WSLW WS2 26 D4
Hadley St LGLYGN/QTN B68 105 E5
Hadlow Cft STETCH B33 131 F5
Hadrian Dr CSHL/WTROR B46 97 E5
Hadyn Gv
LGN/SDN/BHAMAIR B26 147 H1
Hadzor Rd LGLYGN/QTN B68 123 H4
Hafren Cl RBRY B45 174 B3
Hafton Gv BORD B9 * 128 B3
Haggar St BKHL/PFLD WV2 52 A2
Hagley Cswy HAG/WOL DY9 153 H3
Hagley Cl HAG/WOL DY9 153 E4
Hagley Park Dr RBRY B45 188 A2
Hagley Rd HAG/WOL DY9 153 E2
HALE B63 138 A5
HALE B63 138 D4
HALE B63 155 E1
HRBN B17 125 E3
LDYWD/EDGR B16 125 H4
STRBR DY8 135 H4
Hagley Rd West HRBN B17 124 C3
RIDG/WDGT B32 140 A1
RMSLY B62 139 H1
Hagley View Rd DUDS DY2 102 C1
Hagley Vls BHTH/HG B12 * 144 D3
Hagley Wood La
HAG/WOL DY9 154 B4
Haig Cl MGN/WHC B75 62 C1
Haig Rd DUDS DY2 85 F5
Haig St HHTH/SAND B71 71 G5
Hailes Park Cl BKHL/PFLD WV2 52 B2
Hailsham Rd ERDW/GRVHL B23 92 D1
Hailstone Cl
BLKHTH/ROWR B65 103 G3
Haines Cl TPTN/OCK DY4 85 H2
Haines St WBROM B70 87 H4
Hainfield Dr SOLH B91 165 G5
Hainge Rd OLDBY B69 86 A4
Hainult Cl STRBR DY8 99 H5
Halberton St WSNGN B18 107 F5
Haldon Gv NFLD/LBR B31 189 E1
Hale Ct WSL WS1 * 5 J6
Halecroft Av WNSFLD WV11 24 D5
Hale Gv ERDE/BCHGN B24 93 H2
Hales Crs SMTHWKW B67 106 A5
Halescroft Sq NFLD/LBR B31 158 A4
Hales Gdns ERDW/GRVHL B23 76 A3
Hales La SMTHWKW B67 106 A5
Halesmere Wy HALE B63 * 139 E4
Halesowen Rd CDYHTH B64 121 F4
DUDS DY2 102 C4
RMSLY B62 139 G1
Halesowen St OLDBY B69 104 D2
RMSLY B62 122 A4
Hales Rd DARL/WED WS10 56 A4
HALE B63 138 C3
Hales Wy OLDBY B69 104 D2
Halesworth Rd COVEN WV9 11 H5
Halewood Gv HLGN/YWD B28 163 E3
Haley St SHHTH WV12 26 A5
Halfcot Av HAG/WOL DY9 136 A4
Halford Crs BLOX/PEL WS3 28 B5
Halford Rd SOLH B91 164 A4
Halford's La SMTHWK B66 106 C2
Halfshire La KIDD DY10 168 B4
Halfway Cl KGSTG B44 75 E5
Halifax Gv WSNGN B18 * 107 G5
Halifax Rd SHLY B90 180 B2
Haliscombe Gv AST/WIT B6 * 109 E1
Halladale HWK/WKHTH B38 176 D4
Hallam Cl HHTH/SAND B71 88 A2
Hallam Crs WOLVN WV10 23 G4
Hallam Dr HHTH/SAND B71 87 H1
Hallam St BHTH/HG B12 144 A2
HHTH/SAND B71 87 H2
Hallbridge Cl BLOX/PEL WS3 17 H5
Hallbridge Wy OLDBY B69 85 H4
Hallchurch Rd DUDS DY2 101 H2
Hall Crs HHTH/SAND B71 71 G5
Hallcroft Cl CSCFLD/WYGN B72 77 G4
Hallcroft Wy ALDR WS9 30 C5
DOR/KN B93 197 E2
Hall Dale Cl HLGN/YWD B28 162 D5
Hall Dr CHWD/FDBR/MGN B37 132 A5
HAG/WOL DY9 153 F4
Hall End DARL/WED WS10 55 H5
Hallens Dr DARL/WED WS10 55 F5
Hallet Dr BDMR/CCFT WV3 6 D6
Hallewell Rd
LDYWD/EDGR B16 125 F2
Hall Green Rd HHTH/SAND B71 71 H2
Hallgreen St BILS/COS WV14 54 A5
Hall Gv BILS/COS WV14 68 C2
Hall Hays Rd BKDE/SHDE B34 113 G2
Hall La ALDR WS9 19 E5
BILS/COS WV14 67 H2
BLOX/PEL WS3 17 H4
HAG/WOL DY9 153 F4
TPTN/OCK DY4 69 H3
Hall Meadow HAG/WOL DY9 153 F3
Hallmoor Rd STETCH B33 130 D1
Hallot Cl ERDW/GRVHL B23 76 B3
Halloughton Rd
FOAKS/STRLY B74 62 A1
Hall Park St BILS/COS WV14 53 F2
Hall Rd BFLD/HDSWWD B20 108 A2
CBROM B36 112 C1
SMTHWKW B67 106 A5
WASH/WDE B8 110 B5
Hallstead Rd MOS/BIL B13 161 H5
Hall St BILS/COS WV14 54 A3
CDYHTH B64 121 F2
DARL/WED WS10 54 D1
DUDS DY2 84 D5
LGLYGN/QTN B68 105 F4
SEDG DY3 67 F3
STRBR DY8 135 G4
TPTN/OCK DY4 85 E1
WBROM B70 87 G4
WLNHL WV13 39 H4
WNSFLD WV11 24 C5
WSLW WS2 41 H2
WSNGN B18 2 D1
Hall St East DARL/WED WS10 55 E1
Hall St South WBROM B70 105 H1
Hall Wk CSHL/WTROR B46 115 F5
Halsbury Gv KGSTG B44 75 H3
Halstead Gv SOLH B91 181 G5
Halswelle Gv GTB/HAM B43 60 A4
Halton Rd SCFLD/BOLD B73 61 F5
Halton St DUDS DY2 102 C4
Hamar Wy
CHWD/FDBR/MGN B37 132 A3
Hamberley Ct WSNGN B18 107 F5
Hamble Cl BRLYHL DY5 100 C3
Hambledon Cl COVEN WV9 12 A5
Hamble Gv
DUNHL/THL/PER WV6 34 C1
Hamble Rd
ETTPK/GDPK/PENN WV4 50 C2
PBAR/PBCH B42 73 H2
Hambleton Rd HALE B63 137 H5
Hambletts Rd WBROM B70 87 E3
Hambrook Cl
DUNHL/THL/PER WV6 22 C5
Hambury Dr
ALE/KHTH/YWD B14 160 D3
Hamilton Av HRBN B17 124 C4
RMSLY B62 139 E4
STRBR DY8 134 D1
Hamilton Cl SEDG DY3 67 E3
STRBR DY8 117 G2
Hamilton Dr OLDBY B69 86 A4
SLYOAK B29 159 E2
STRBR DY8 117 G2
Hamilton Gdns WOLVN WV10 13 F4
Hamilton Rd HDSW B21 107 F1
SMTHWKW B67 124 A2
TPTN/OCK DY4 70 A5
Hamilton St BLOX/PEL WS3 27 G1
Ham La HAG/WOL DY9 136 A5
KGSWFD DY6 82 A5
Hamlet Gdns HLGN/YWD B28 162 D2
Hamlet Rd HLGN/YWD B28 162 D3
Hammer Bank HALE B63 120 A4
Hammersley Cl HALE B63 120 C5
Hammond Av WOLVN WV10 23 G2
Hammond Dr ERDW/GRVHL B23 92 D1
Hammond Wy STRBR DY8 118 C5
Hampden Cl BRLYHL DY5 120 A4
Hampden Retreat
BHTH/HG B12 144 A1
Hampshire Dr EDG B15 125 G4
Hampshire Rd HHTH/SAND B71 71 E2
Hampson Cl SPARK B11 144 D1
Hampstead Cl WNSFLD WV11 24 C4
Hampstead Gld HALE B63 139 E4
Hampton Cl SCFLD/BOLD B73 76 A1
Hampton Ct WNSFLD WV11 * 13 H3
Hampton Court Rd HRBN B17 141 F1
Hampton Dr FOAKS/STRLY B74 47 F5
Hampton Gdns HAG/WOL DY9 136 A4
Hampton Gv BLOX/PEL WS3 17 H3
Hampton La SOLH B91 166 B5
Hampton Rd AST/WIT B6 108 D1
DOR/KN B93 197 G1
ERDW/GRVHL B23 92 B2
WOLVN WV10 22 D1
Hampton St BILS/COS WV14 68 B3
DUDS DY2 102 B4
LOZ/NWT B19 2 E1
Hams La WALM/CURD B76 97 F1
Hams Rd WASH/WDE B8 110 B5
Hamstead Hall Av
BFLD/HDSWWD B20 89 G1
Hamstead Hall Rd
BFLD/HDSWWD B20 89 G2
Hamstead Hl
BFLD/HDSWWD B20 89 H2
Hamstead Rd
BFLD/HDSWWD B20 90 B5
GTB/HAM B43 73 F4
Hamstead Ter DARL/WED WS10 71 E1
Hanam Cl MGN/WHC B75 63 F2
Hanbury Cl HALE B63 * 138 B5
Hanbury Crs BDMR/CCFT WV3 51 E2
Hanbury Cft ACGN B27 147 E4
Hanbury Hl STRBR DY8 135 G3
Hanbury Rd BRWNH WS8 9 E2
DOR/KN B93 196 D5
WBROM B70 87 E3
Hanch Pl WSL WS1 5 G6
Hancock Rd WASH/WDE B8 110 D5
Hancox St LGLYGN/QTN B68 123 F2
Handley Gv NFLD/LBR B31 174 C3
Handley St DARL/WED WS10 56 A4
Handsworth Cl HDSW B21 107 F2
Handsworth Dr GTB/HAM B43 59 E5
Handsworth New Rd
WSNGN B18 107 G4
Handsworth Wood Rd
BFLD/HDSWWD B20 89 H3
Hanging La NFLD/LBR B31 175 E4
Hangleton Dr SPARK B11 145 F1
Hanley Cl HALE B63 138 A3
Hanley St LOZ/NWT B19 3 F1
Hannafore Rd
LDYWD/EDGR B16 125 F1
Hannah Rd BILS/COS WV14 54 C5
Hanney Hay Rd BNTWD WS7 9 H1
Hannon Rd
ALE/KHTH/YWD B14 161 E5
Hanover Cl AST/WIT B6 109 E2
Hanover Ct
DUNHL/THL/PER WV6 35 G1
WSLW WS2 40 C4
Hanover Dr VAUX/NECH B7 110 D1
Hanover Rd
BLKHTH/ROWR B65 104 A5
Hansell Dr DOR/KN B93 198 C1
Hansom Rd RIDG/WDGT B32 140 C2
Hanson Gv HIA/OLT B92 147 F2
Hanson's Bridge Rd
ERDE/BCHGN B24 94 B1
Hanwell Cl WALM/CURD B76 78 D4
Hanwood Cl BHTH/HG B12 127 F4
Harald Cl DUNHL/THL/PER WV6 20 C5
Harbeck Av KGSTG B44 75 F3
Harberrow Cl HAG/WOL DY9 152 C4
Harbet Dr BHAMNEC B40 150 A3
Harbinger Rd HWK/WKHTH B38 177 F3
Harborne La SLYOAK B29 142 B5
Harborne Park Rd HRBN B17 142 A3
Harborne Rd EDG B15 142 C1
SMTHWKW B67 123 H3
Harborough Dr ALDR WS9 30 A5
CBROM B36 95 F5
Harborough Wk HAG/WOL DY9 135 H5
Harbours Hl HAG/WOL DY9 186 A2
Harbury Cl WALM/CURD B76 78 D5
Harbury Rd BHTH/HG B12 143 H2
Harby Cl
CHWD/FDBR/MGN B37 132 B4
Harcourt Dr DUDN DY1 83 F4
FOAKS/STRLY B74 46 C1
Harcourt Rd CDYHTH B64 121 F4
DARL/WED WS10 55 H4
ERDW/GRVHL B23 76 C5
Harden Cl BLOX/PEL WS3 28 A3
Harden Gv BLOX/PEL WS3 28 A3
Harden Manor Ct HALE B63 * 139 E4
Harden Rd BLOX/PEL WS3 27 H3
Harden V HALE B63 * 138 A2
Harding St BILS/COS WV14 68 D2
Hardon Rd
ETTPK/GDPK/PENN WV4 52 D3
Hardware St WBROM B70 87 H2
Hardwick Dr CDYHTH B64 121 G5
Hardwicke Wy HAG/WOL DY9 136 B2
Hardwick Rd FOAKS/STRLY B74 45 F3
LGN/SDN/BHAMAIR B26 147 E3
Hardwike Wk
ALE/KHTH/YWD B14 177 G3
Hardy Rd BLOX/PEL WS3 28 A2
DARL/WED WS10 56 A5
Hardy Sq BKHL/PFLD WV2 * 52 D2
Harebell Cl DSYBK/YTR WS5 57 G5
Harebell Crs DUDN DY1 84 A2
Harebell Gdns
HWK/WKHTH B38 176 D5
Hare Gv NFLD/LBR B31 174 D2
Hare St BILS/COS WV14 54 B3
Harewell Dr MGN/WHC B75 47 G4
Harewood Av DARL/WED WS10 56 C5
GTB/HAM B43 73 E1
Harewood Cl HLGN/YWD B28 162 C5
Harford St LOZ/NWT B19 2 D1
Hargate La HHTH/SAND B71 87 G2
Hargrave Cl CSHL/WTROR B46 96 B3
Hargrave Rd SHLY B90 179 F3
Hargreave Cl WALM/CURD B76 78 B4
Hargreaves St BKHL/PFLD WV2 53 E1
Harland Rd FOAKS/STRLY B74 47 E2
Harlech Cl OLDBY B69 85 G5
RIDG/WDGT B32 157 E4
Harlech Rd SHHTH WV12 26 A4
Harlech Wy DUDN DY1 83 H4
Harleston Rd KGSTG B44 75 F3
Harley Cl BRWNH WS8 19 G1
Harley Dr BILS/COS WV14 53 F4
Harlow Gv HLGN/YWD B28 163 E4
Harlstones Cl STRBR DY8 118 C5
Harlyn Cl BILS/COS WV14 69 G1
Harman Rd CSCFLD/WYGN B72 77 F4
Harmer St WSNGN B18 108 A4
Harmon Rd STRBR DY8 134 C2
Harnall Cl SHLY B90 195 E1
Harness Cl DSYBK/YTR WS5 57 E4
Harold Rd LDYWD/EDGR B16 125 H3
SMTHWKW B67 124 A1
Harold Ter LOZ/NWT B19 * 108 C1
Harper Av WNSFLD WV11 24 C3
Harper Rd BILS/COS WV14 53 H2
Harpers Rd HLYWD B47 178 C4
NFLD/LBR B31 175 G3
Harper St WLNHL WV13 39 G3
Harpur Cl RUSH/SHEL WS4 42 C1
Harpur Rd RUSH/SHEL WS4 42 C1
Harrier Rd ACGN B27 146 D5
Harriet Cl BRLYHL DY5 100 D4
Harringay Dr STRBR DY8 135 E4
Harringay Rd KGSTG B44 75 F1
Harris Dr PBAR/PBCH B42 74 A3
SMTHWK B66 124 D1
Harrison Cl BLOX/PEL WS3 27 G1
Harrison Rd ERDE/BCHGN B24 92 D2
FOAKS/STRLY B74 32 C5
RUSH/SHEL WS4 18 C5
STRBR DY8 118 C3
Harrison's Fold DUDS DY2 102 C4
Harrisons Gn EDG B15 142 C1
Harrisons Pleck MOS/BIL B13 144 B4
Harrison's Rd EDG B15 142 C1
Harrison St BLOX/PEL WS3 27 G1
Harrold Av BLKHTH/ROWR B65 122 C1
Harrold Rd BLKHTH/ROWR B65 122 C1
Harrold St TPTN/OCK DY4 70 A4
Harrold Ter LOZ/NWT B19 108 C1
Harrop Wy STRBR DY8 118 A4
Harrowby Dr TPTN/OCK DY4 85 G2
Harrowby Pl WLNHL WV13 40 A4
Harrowby Rd BILS/COS WV14 54 C4
WOLVN WV10 12 B4
Harrow Cl HAG/WOL DY9 152 C4
Harrowfield Rd STETCH B33 112 A5
Harrow Rd KGSWFD DY6 81 H5
SLYOAK B29 142 D4
Harrow St WOLV WV1 36 D1
Harry Perks St WLNHL WV13 39 G2
Hart Dr SCFLD/BOLD B73 77 E3
Hartfield Crs ACGN B27 163 E1
Hartford Cl HRBN B17 124 C5
Hartill Rd
ETTPK/GDPK/PENN WV4 50 D5
Hartill St WLNHL WV13 39 H5
Hartington Cl DOR/KN B93 196 C5
Hartington Rd LOZ/NWT B19 108 D1
Hartland Av BILS/COS WV14 68 A3
Hartland Rd HHTH/SAND B71 72 B4
NFLD/LBR B31 189 E2
TPTN/OCK DY4 84 D1
Hartland St BRLYHL DY5 101 F2
Hartlebury Cl DOR/KN B93 196 D5
Hartlebury Rd HALE B63 138 B5
OLDBY B69 104 B4
Hartledon Rd HRBN B17 141 H2
Hartle La HAG/WOL DY9 184 D2
Hartley Dr ALDR WS9 44 B1
Hartley Gv KGSTG B44 60 D5
Hartley Pl EDG B15 125 H4
Hartley Rd KGSTG B44 60 C5
Hartley St BDMR/CCFT WV3 6 A4
Harton Wy
ALE/KHTH/YWD B14 160 C5
Hartopp Rd FOAKS/STRLY B74 46 D4
WASH/WDE B8 110 C5
Hart Rd ERDE/BCHGN B24 93 E1
WNSFLD WV11 38 D1
Hartsbourne Dr RMSLY B62 139 F3
Harts Cl HRBN B17 142 B1
Harts Green Rd HRBN B17 141 G2
Hartshill Rd BKDE/SHDE B34 112 C3
HIA/OLT B92 146 D5
Hartshorn St BILS/COS WV14 53 H3
Hartside Cl HALE B63 137 G5
Harts Rd WASH/WDE B8 110 C4
Hart St WSL WS1 4 E6
Hartswell Dr MOS/BIL B13 161 F4
Hartwell Cl SOLH B91 181 H4
Hartwell Rd ERDE/BCHGN B24 93 F4
Harvard Cl DUDN DY1 83 H2
Harvard Rd HIA/OLT B92 147 H3
Harvest Cl BVILLE B30 160 B5
SEDG DY3 83 G1
Harvesters Cl FOAKS/STRLY B74 45 E3
Harvesters Rd SHHTH WV12 26 B5
Harvester Wy KGSWFD DY6 99 E1
Harvest Fields Wy
MGN/WHC B75 48 A2
Harvest Gdns
LGLYGN/QTN B68 105 E5
Harvest Rd BLKHTH/ROWR B65 103 G5
SMTHWKW B67 123 H1
Harvey Ct STETCH B33 * 131 F1
Harvey Dr MGN/WHC B75 47 G3
Harvey Rd
LGN/SDN/BHAMAIR B26 129 H5
WSLW WS2 27 F5
Harvills Hawthorn WBROM B70 70 D4
Harvine Wk STRBR DY8 135 E4
Harvington Dr SHLY B90 195 H2
Harvington Rd BILS/COS WV14 68 B2
HALE B63 138 B5
LGLYGN/QTN B68 123 E4
SLYOAK B29 158 C2
Harvington Wy
WALM/CURD B76 78 B3
Harwin Cl DUNHL/THL/PER WV6 22 B3
Harwood Gv SHLY B90 180 C5
Harwood St WBROM B70 87 F3
Hasbury Cl HALE B63 138 A5
Hasbury Rd RIDG/WDGT B32 157 E2
Haseley Rd HDSW B21 107 G2
SOLH B91 164 A4
Haselor Rd SCFLD/BOLD B73 76 C2
Haselour Rd
CHWD/FDBR/MGN B37 113 H4
Haskell St WSL WS1 57 F1
Haslucks Cl SHLY B90 193 G1
Haslucks Cft SHLY B90 180 A2
Haslucks Green Rd SHLY B90 179 G5
Hassop Rd PBAR/PBCH B42 74 D4
Hastings Ct DUDN DY1 83 G4
Hastings Rd ERDW/GRVHL B23 75 H4
Haswell Rd HALE B63 137 H4
Hatcham Rd KGSTG B44 76 A1
Hatchett St LOZ/NWT B19 109 E4
Hatchford Av HIA/OLT B92 148 A4
Hatchford Brook Rd
HIA/OLT B92 148 A4
Hatch Heath Cl WMBN WV5 64 D4
Hateley Dr
ETTPK/GDPK/PENN WV4 52 C4
Hatfield Cl ERDW/GRVHL B23 76 B4
Hatfield Rd HAG/WOL DY9 136 A3
LOZ/NWT B19 108 D1
Hathaway Cl WLNHL WV13 39 F5
Hathaway Ms STRBR DY8 * 117 G1
Hathaway Rd MGN/WHC B75 47 E1
SHLY B90 180 B4
Hatherden Dr WALM/CURD B76 78 C1
Hathersage Rd PBAR/PBCH B42 74 D4
Hatherton Gdns WOLVN WV10 13 E5
Hatherton Gv SLYOAK B29 158 B1
Hatherton Pl ALDR WS9 30 A3
Hatherton Rd BILS/COS WV14 54 B2
WSL WS1 4 E3
Hatherton St WSL WS1 4 E2
Hattersley Gv SPARK B11 146 A4
Hatton Crs WNSFLD WV11 24 A3
Hatton Gdns PBAR/PBCH B42 74 B4
Hatton Rd BDMR/CCFT WV3 * 36 B2
Hattons Gv CDSL WV8 10 D5
Hatton St BILS/COS WV14 54 A4

Haughton Rd
BFLD/HDSWWD B20 90 C5
Haunch La MOS/BIL B13 161 F4
Haunchwood Dr
WALM/CURD B76 78 B4
Havacre La BILS/COS WV14 68 C1
Havelock Cl BDMR/CCFT WV3 51 E1
Havelock Rd
BFLD/HDSWWD B20 90 C4
SPARK B11 145 G3
WASH/WDE B8 110 C4
Haven Cft GTB/HAM B43 73 F3
Haven Dr ACGN B27 146 B4
The Haven
ALE/KHTH/YWD B14 179 F1
BKHL/PFLD WV2 37 E5
STRBR DY8 117 H2
Haverford Dr RBRY B45 188 B2
Havergal Wk HALE B63 137 F3
Haverhill Cl BLOX/PEL WS3 16 C4
Hawbridge Cl SHLY B90 195 H2
Hawbush Rd BLOX/PEL WS3 28 A4
BRLYHL DY5 118 C2
Hawcroft Gv BKDE/SHDE B34 113 E3
Hawes Cl WSL WS1 57 F2
Hawes La BLKHTH/ROWR B65 103 H5
Hawes Rd WSL WS1 57 F2
Haweswater Dr KGSWFD DY6 99 H3
Hawfield Cl OLDBY B69 104 A2
Hawfield Gv CSCFLD/WYGN B72 77 G4
Hawfield Rd OLDBY B69 104 A2
Hawker Dr CVALE B35 94 B4
Hawkesbury Rd SHLY B90 179 H4
Hawkes Cl SLYOAK B29 160 A2
Hawkesford Cl CBROM B36 112 C1
FOAKS/STRLY B74 47 F4
Hawkesford Rd STETCH B33 131 F1
Hawkes La HHTH/SAND B71 71 E4
Hawkesley Crs NFLD/LBR B31 175 F4
Hawkesley Dr NFLD/LBR B31 175 F5
Hawkesley End
HWK/WKHTH B38 176 B5
Hawkesley Mill La
NFLD/LBR B31 175 F3
Hawkesley Rd DUDN DY1 101 H1
Hawkes St BORD B9 128 B3
Hawkestone Crs WBROM B70 70 D5
Hawkestone Rd SLYOAK B29 158 C3
Hawkeswell Cl HIA/OLT B92 164 A2
Hawkeswell Dr KGSWFD DY6 99 H1
Hawkeswell La
CSHL/WTROR B46 133 H1
Hawkesyard Rd
ERDE/BCHGN B24 92 C5
Hawkhurst Rd
ALE/KHTH/YWD B14 178 B3
Hawkinge Dr CVALE B35 94 C2
Hawkins Cl DIG/EDG B5 144 A1
Hawkins Cft TPTN/OCK DY4 85 G3
Hawkins St WBROM B70 71 E3
Hawkley Cl WOLV WV1 38 B3
Hawkley Rd WOLV WV1 38 B3
Hawkmoor Gdns
HWK/WKHTH B38 177 E5
Hawksford Crs WOLVN WV10 23 F3
Hawkshead Dr DOR/KN B93 196 D2
Hawksmoor Dr
DUNHL/THL/PER WV6 34 B2
Hawkstone Ct CDSL WV8 20 B5
Hawkswell Av WMBN WV5 81 E1
Hawkswell Dr WLNHL WV13 39 F5
Hawkswood Dr
DARL/WED WS10 54 D5
Hawkswood Gv
ALE/KHTH/YWD B14 178 D2
Hawley Cl RUSH/SHEL WS4 42 B1
Hawnby Gv WALM/CURD B76 78 C1
Hawne Cl HALE B63 138 A1
The Hawnelands HALE B63 138 B2
Hawne La HALE B63 138 A1
Hawskford Crs WOLVN WV10 23 F3
Hawthorn Brook Wy
ERDW/GRVHL B23 76 C3
Hawthorn Cl BORD B9 127 H3
ERDW/GRVHL B23 76 D4
Hawthorn Coppice
HAG/WOL DY9 152 C4
Hawthorn Cft
LGLYGN/QTN B68 123 H5
Hawthorne Dr HLYWD B47 192 D2
Hawthorne Gv SEDG DY3 83 F4
Hawthorne La CDSL WV8 20 D1
Hawthorne Rd BKHL/PFLD WV2 52 B2
BVILLE B30 159 F5
CBROM B36 113 G2
DUDN DY1 84 C2
EDG B15 125 G5
HALE B63 138 A5
SHHTH WV12 26 B3
WNSFLD WV11 15 E4
WNSFLD WV11 25 F5
Hawthorn Gv LOZ/NWT B19 * 108 C1
Hawthorn Pk
BFLD/HDSWWD B20 89 G3
Hawthorn Pl WSLW WS2 40 C2
Hawthorn Rd BRLYHL DY5 119 G4
CSCFLD/WYGN B72 77 G2
DARL/WED WS10 55 H4
DSYBK/YTR WS5 57 F3
FOAKS/STRLY B74 45 G4
KGSTG B44 75 G4
RUSH/SHEL WS4 28 D2
TPTN/OCK DY4 69 G3
WOLV WV1 38 B5
The Hawthorns MOS/BIL B13 * 144 B4
Hawthorn Ter DARL/WED WS10 55 H4
Haxby Av BKDE/SHDE B34 112 C3
The Haybarn WALM/CURD B76 78 C2
Haybridge Av STRBR DY8 152 B5
Haybrook Dr SPARK B11 145 H3
Haycock Pl DARL/WED WS10 55 E1
Haycroft Av WASH/WDE B8 110 C4
Haycroft Dr MGN/WHC B75 47 E1
Haydn Sanders Sq WSL WS1 4 D6
Haydock Cl CBROM B36 111 G1
DUNHL/THL/PER WV6 22 D5
Haydon Cl DOR/KN B93 198 D1
Haydon Cft STETCH B33 130 C1
Haye House Gv CBROM B36 112 A2
Hayes Crs LGLYGN/QTN B68 105 H4
Hayes Cft HWK/WKHTH B38 190 C1
WOLVN WV10 13 H5
Hayes Gv ERDE/BCHGN B24 77 H5
Hayes La HAG/WOL DY9 137 E1
Hayes Meadow
WALM/CURD B76 77 H4
Hayes Rd LGLYGN/QTN B68 105 H4
Hayes St WBROM B70 87 E2
The Hayes HAG/WOL DY9 137 E2
NFLD/LBR B31 190 A1
SHHTH WV12 25 H4
Hayfield Ct MOS/BIL B13 144 D5
Hayfield Rd MOS/BIL B13 144 D5
Hay Gn HAG/WOL DY9 136 B2
Hay Green La BVILLE B30 159 E4
Hay Hall Rd SPARK B11 145 H2
Hay Hl DSYBK/YTR WS5 43 G5
Hayland Rd ERDW/GRVHL B23 76 C5
Hay La SHLY B90 195 G2
Hayle Cl HWK/WKHTH B38 177 F3
Hayley Green Rd
RIDG/WDGT B32 157 F2
Hayley Park Rd HALE B63 154 C2
Hayling Cl RBRY B45 173 H4
Hayling Gv BKHL/PFLD WV2 51 H2
The Haylofts HALE B63 154 C1
Haynes La DSYBK/YTR WS5 57 H4
Hay Pk DIG/EDG B5 143 H1
Haypits Cl HHTH/SAND B71 72 A4
Hayrick Dr KGSWFD DY6 99 F2
Hay Rd YDLY B25 129 E5
Hayseech CDYHTH B64 121 G5
Hayseech Rd HALE B63 138 B1
The Hays Kent's Moat
LGN/SDN/BHAMAIR B26 130 C3
Haytor Av ALE/KHTH/YWD B14 160 D5
Haywain Cl COVEN WV9 * 11 H5
Hayward Rd MGN/WHC B75 62 C1
Haywards Cl BLOX/PEL WS3 17 H4
ERDW/GRVHL B23 92 C1
Hayward St BILS/COS WV14 68 B3
Haywharf Rd BRLYHL DY5 100 D4
Haywood Dr
DUNHL/THL/PER WV6 35 G1
RMSLY B62 122 A4
Haywood Rd STETCH B33 131 F2
Haywood's Farm
HHTH/SAND B71 72 B1
Hazel Av DARL/WED WS10 56 A4
SCFLD/BOLD B73 76 A2
Hazelbank HWK/WKHTH B38 176 C3
Hazelbeach Rd WASH/WDE B8 110 D4
Hazelbeech Rd WBROM B70 87 F4
Hazel Cft
CHWD/FDBR/MGN B37 132 B3
NFLD/LBR B31 175 G2
Hazeldene Gv AST/WIT B6 * 109 E1
Hazeldene Rd HALE B63 138 A5
STETCH B33 131 F5
Hazel Dr HLYWD B47 192 D2
Hazeley Cl HRBN B17 124 B5
Hazel Gdns ACGN B27 * 146 C3
CDSL WV8 10 C3
Hazel Gv BILS/COS WV14 54 A1
HOCK/TIA B94 198 A5
STRBR DY8 134 C4
WBROM B70 87 G5
WMBN WV5 65 E4
Hazelhurst Rd
ALE/KHTH/YWD B14 161 E3
CBROM B36 113 G2
Hazelmere Dr BDMR/CCFT WV3 35 E4
Hazelmere Rd HLGN/YWD B28 162 D2
Hazeloak Rd SHLY B90 180 A4
Hazel Rd BDMR/CCFT WV3 51 E1
DUDN DY1 84 C4
KGSWFD DY6 100 A4
RBRY B45 187 H2
TPTN/OCK DY4 70 A2
Hazelton Cl SOLH B91 181 H4
Hazeltree Cft ACGN B27 146 B5
Hazeltree Gv DOR/KN B93 196 C5
Hazelville Gv HLGN/YWD B28 163 E4
Hazelville Rd HLGN/YWD B28 163 E4
Hazelwell Crs BVILLE B30 160 B4
Hazelwell Dr
ALE/KHTH/YWD B14 160 D4
Hazelwell Fordrough
BVILLE B30 160 B3
Hazelwell La BVILLE B30 160 A3
Hazelwell Rd BVILLE B30 160 A4
Hazelwood Dr WNSFLD WV11 24 A5
Hazelwood Gv SHHTH WV12 26 B5
Hazelwood Rd ACGN B27 146 B5
DUDN DY1 83 H1
FOAKS/STRLY B74 44 D4
Hazlemere Dr FOAKS/STRLY B74 47 E4
Hazlitt Gv BVILLE B30 176 B1
Headingley Rd HDSW B21 89 G4
Headland Dr WASH/WDE B8 110 B4
Headland Rd BDMR/CCFT WV3 34 D4
The Headlands
FOAKS/STRLY B74 46 A2
Headley Cft HWK/WKHTH B38 176 B5
Headley Heath La
HWK/WKHTH B38 191 F1
Headley Ri SHLY B90 180 D3
Headway Rd WOLVN WV10 12 C4
Heale Cl HALE B63 120 A5
Heanor Cft AST/WIT B6 109 H1
Heantun Ri WOLV WV1 * 37 E1
Heantun Rw WNSFLD WV11 * 15 F5
Heartland Ms
BLKHTH/ROWR B65 121 H2
Heartlands Pkwy
VAUX/NECH B7 110 A4
Heartlands Pl WASH/WDE B8 110 C5
Heath Acres DARL/WED WS10 55 E4
Heath Bridge Cl BLOX/PEL WS3 28 C2
Heathbrook Av KGSWFD DY6 99 F2
Heathcliff Rd DUDS DY2 103 F2
SPARK B11 145 H3
Heath Cl BVILLE B30 159 F5
TPTN/OCK DY4 85 H1
Heathcote Av SOLH B91 181 E2
Heathcote Rd BVILLE B30 160 A5
Heath Cft NFLD/LBR B31 189 G1
Heath Croft Rd MGN/WHC B75 47 G4
Heath End Rd HAG/WOL DY9 185 G1
Heather Av DSYBK/YTR WS5 57 H4
Heather Cl CBROM B36 114 A1
WNSFLD WV11 25 E5
Heather Court Gdns
FOAKS/STRLY B74 47 E5
Heather Cft KGSTG B44 75 F2
Heather Dl MOS/BIL B13 143 G5
Heather Dr RBRY B45 187 H2
Heather Gv SHHTH WV12 40 C1
SOLH B91 165 G4
Heatherleigh Rd CBROM B36 113 H1
Heather Rd BLOX/PEL WS3 26 D2
DUDN DY1 84 C2
GTB/HAM B43 73 E3
SMHTH B10 128 D4
SMTHWKW B67 106 A4
Heath Farm Rd CDSL WV8 10 D5
STRBR DY8 135 E4
Heathfield Av
BFLD/HDSWWD B20 108 B1
Heathfield Cl CDYHTH B64 121 F2
DOR/KN B93 197 E3
Heathfield Dr BLOX/PEL WS3 16 D5
Heathfield Gdns STRBR DY8 135 F3
Heathfield La DARL/WED WS10 55 E2
Heathfield La West
DARL/WED WS10 54 D3
Heathfield Rd
ALE/KHTH/YWD B14 161 E2
FOAKS/STRLY B74 46 D2
HALE B63 138 A4
LOZ/NWT B19 108 B2
Heathfield Wy CDYHTH B64 121 F3
Heath Gdns SOLH B91 165 F4
Heath Gn DUDN DY1 83 H1
Heathgreen Cl
CHWD/FDBR/MGN B37 132 D1
Heath Green Gv WSNGN B18 * 107 G5
Heath Green Rd WSNGN B18 107 G5
Heath Gv CDSL WV8 10 D4
Heath Hill Rd
DUNHL/THL/PER WV6 34 C4
Heath House Dr WMBN WV5 80 B1
Heath House La CDSL WV8 20 C2
Heathland Av BKDE/SHDE B34 112 C2
Heathlands WMBN WV5 80 B1
Heathlands Cl KGSWFD DY6 100 A1
Heathlands Rd
SCFLD/BOLD B73 76 D1
The Heathlands
BLKHTH/ROWR B65 122 A3
STRBR DY8 135 H3
WMBN WV5 80 B1
Heath La HHTH/SAND B71 71 H4
STRBR DY8 135 G3
Heathleigh Rd
HWK/WKHTH B38 176 A5
Heathmere Av YDLY B25 129 H4
Heathmere Dr
CHWD/FDBR/MGN B37 131 H2
Heath Mill Cl SEDG DY3 80 B2
Heath Mill La BORD B9 127 G3
Heath Mill Rd SEDG DY3 80 B2
Heath Pk WOLVN WV10 * 12 C1
Heath Ri ALE/KHTH/YWD B14 178 C4
Heath Rd BVILLE B30 176 A1
DARL/WED WS10 40 C5
DUDS DY2 120 B2
HLYWD B47 192 C1
SHHTH WV12 26 B2
SOLH B91 165 F4
Heath Rd South NFLD/LBR B31 175 H1
Heathside Dr BLOX/PEL WS3 18 A3
HWK/WKHTH B38 177 F4
Heath St BLKHTH/ROWR B65 122 A3
STRBR DY8 135 F2
WSNGN B18 107 F4
Heath St South WSNGN B18 * 107 H5
Heath Wy BKDE/SHDE B34 112 B2
Heathy Farm Cl
RIDG/WDGT B32 157 F1
Heathy Ri RIDG/WDGT B32 140 A5
Heaton Cl WOLVN WV10 13 E2
Heaton Dr EDG B15 125 G4
Heaton Rd SOLH B91 164 B3
Heaton St WSNGN B18 108 B3
Hebden Gv HLGN/YWD B28 179 F2
SHHTH WV12 25 H1
Heddon Pl VAUX/NECH B7 * 127 G1
Hedera Cl DSYBK/YTR WS5 57 H5
Hedgefield Gv HALE B63 137 G3
Hedgerow Dr KGSWFD DY6 81 H5
The Hedgerows RMSLY B62 172 B1
The Hedges WMBN WV5 64 C5
Hedgetree Cft
CHWD/FDBR/MGN B37 132 C2
Hedgley Gv STETCH B33 112 C5
Hedingham Gv
CHWD/FDBR/MGN B37 132 D2
Hedley Cft CVALE B35 94 D2
Hednesford Rd BRWNH WS8 8 C2
Heeley Rd SLYOAK B29 142 D5
Hefford Dr SMTHWK B66 106 C3
Helena St CBHAMW B1 2 C4
Helenny Cl WNSFLD WV11 24 A5
Helford Cl TPTN/OCK DY4 84 D2
Hellaby Cl CSCFLD/WYGN B72 62 B4
Hellier Av TPTN/OCK DY4 85 H2
Hellier Dr WMBN WV5 64 C4
Hellier Rd WOLVN WV10 13 E5
Hellier St DUDS DY2 102 C1
Helming Dr WOLV WV1 38 B2
Helmsdale Wy SEDG DY3 68 A4
Helmsley Cl BRLYHL DY5 119 E4
Helmsley Rd WNSFLD WV11 24 C2
Helmswood Dr
CHWD/FDBR/MGN B37 132 C4
Helston Cl DSYBK/YTR WS5 58 B1
STRBR DY8 117 G2
Helstone Gv SPARK B11 146 A3
Helston Rd DSYBK/YTR WS5 58 A2
Hembs Crs GTB/HAM B43 73 E3
Hemlingford Cft
CHWD/FDBR/MGN B37 132 A5
Hemlingford Rd
CHWD/FDBR/MGN B37 113 G3
WALM/CURD B76 78 B4
Hemmings Cl STRBR DY8 135 E2
WOLVN WV10 7 K1
Hemmings St DARL/WED WS10 40 A5
Hemplands Rd STRBR DY8 135 F2
Hempole La TPTN/OCK DY4 70 B5
Hemyock Rd SLYOAK B29 158 D2
Henbury Rd ACGN B27 146 D4
Henderson Wk TPTN/OCK DY4 69 H3
Henderson Wy
BLKHTH/ROWR B65 122 A3
Hendon Cl SEDG DY3 83 F4
WOLVN WV10 23 G2
Hendon Rd SPARK B11 144 D2
Heneage Pl VAUX/NECH B7 * 109 G5
Heneage St VAUX/NECH B7 3 K1
Heneage St West VAUX/NECH B7 3 K2
Henfield Cl WNSFLD WV11 24 D4
Hengham Rd
LGN/SDN/BHAMAIR B26 130 C3
Henley Cl BLOX/PEL WS3 28 A1
SCFLD/BOLD B73 77 F3
TPTN/OCK DY4 86 B1
Henley Crs SOLH B91 164 D3
Henley Dr MGN/WHC B75 47 E2
Henley Rd WOLVN WV10 22 D1
Henley St SPARK B11 127 G5
Henley Vls BTH/HG B12 * 144 D2
Henlow Cl TPTN/OCK DY4 84 D1
Henlow Rd
ALE/KHTH/YWD B14 178 B3
The Hennalls CBROM B36 112 B2
Henn Dr TPTN/OCK DY4 69 E2
Henne Dr BILS/COS WV14 68 C2
Henn St TPTN/OCK DY4 69 G3
Henrietta St CBHAMNW B3 2 E2
LOZ/NWT B19 3 F2
Henry Rd YDLY B25 146 C1
Henry St WSLW WS2 4 B4
Hensborough SHLY B90 194 A3
Hensel Dr BDMR/CCFT WV3 35 G5
Henshaw Gv YDLY B25 129 G5
Henshaw Rd SMHTH B10 128 B4
Henstead St DIG/EDG B5 126 D4
Henwood Cl
DUNHL/THL/PER WV6 35 H2
Henwood La SOLH B91 183 F1
Henwood Rd
DUNHL/THL/PER WV6 35 H2
Hepburn Cl ALDR WS9 44 A1
Hepburn Edge
ERDE/BCHGN B24 93 F2
Hepworth Cl
DUNHL/THL/PER WV6 34 D1
Herbert Rd ALDR WS9 30 A1
HDSW B21 89 H5
SMHTH B10 128 A3
SMTHWKW B67 124 C3
SOLH B91 181 H2
Herberts Park Rd
DARL/WED WS10 54 D2
Herbert St BILS/COS WV14 53 F2
WBROM B70 87 H3
WOLV WV1 7 G2
Herbhill Cl
ETTPK/GDPK/PENN WV4 52 B4
Hereford Av BTH/HG B12 144 C1
Hereford Cl ALDR WS9 30 A2
RBRY B45 174 A3
Hereford Pl HHTH/SAND B71 71 F4
Hereford Rd DUDS DY2 121 E1
LGLYGN/QTN B68 123 F5
Hereford Sq WASH/WDE B8 110 A4
Hereford St WSLW WS2 42 A1
Hereward Ri RMSLY B62 138 D2
Heritage Cl LGLYGN/QTN B68 105 G5
Heritage Wy STETCH B33 131 F1
TPTN/OCK DY4 85 H1
Hermes Rd
LGN/SDN/BHAMAIR B26 149 G3
Hermitage Dr WALM/CURD B76 63 G4
Hermitage Rd EDG B15 125 E4
ERDW/GRVHL B23 92 B3
SOLH B91 165 E5
The Hermitage SOLH B91 165 E4
Hermit St SEDG DY3 83 F2
Hernall Cft
LGN/SDN/BHAMAIR B26 130 C5
Herne Cl WSNGN B18 108 A5
Hernefield Rd
BKDE/SHDE B34 112 C2
Hernehurst RIDG/WDGT B32 140 C1
Hern Rd BRLYHL DY5 136 A1
Heron Cl SHLY B90 194 D5
Herondale Rd
LGN/SDN/BHAMAIR B26 147 F1
STRBR DY8 134 C3
Heronfield Dr NFLD/LBR B31 189 F2
Heronfield Wy SOLH B91 165 G5
Heron Ml BLOX/PEL WS3 17 G4
Heron Rd LGLYGN/QTN B68 123 E2
The Heronry
DUNHL/THL/PER WV6 34 D3
Herons Wy SLYOAK B29 142 A4
Heronswood Dr BRLYHL DY5 119 F3
Heronswood Rd RBRY B45 188 B2
Heronville Dr WBROM B70 71 E4
Heronville Rd WBROM B70 71 E5
Heron Wy RBRY B45 187 G1
Herrick Rd WASH/WDE B8 110 C4
Herrick St BDMR/CCFT WV3 6 D5
Herringshaw Cft
WALM/CURD B76 63 E5
Hertford St BTH/HG B12 144 C2
Hertford Wy DOR/KN B93 197 F4
Hervey Gv ERDE/BCHGN B24 77 H5
Hesket Av LGLYGN/QTN B68 123 G3
Hesketh Crs ERDW/GRVHL B23 92 A1
Hessian Cl BILS/COS WV14 68 B1
Hestia Dr SLYOAK B29 159 G2
Heston Av PBAR/PBCH B42 74 A3
Hever Av KGSTG B44 75 G2
Hever Cl DUDN DY1 83 G4
Hewell Cl KGSWFD DY6 81 H5
NFLD/LBR B31 189 F1
Hewitson Gdns
SMTHWKW B67 * 124 B2
Hewitt St DARL/WED WS10 55 E2
Hexham Wy DUDN DY1 83 H4
Hexton Cl SHLY B90 179 F3
Heybarnes Rd SMHTH B10 129 E5
Heycott Gv HWK/WKHTH B38 177 G3
Heydon Rd BRLYHL DY5 100 D4
Heyford Gv SOLH B91 182 A5
Heyford Wy CVALE B35 94 C2
Heygate Wy ALDR WS9 30 B1
Heynesfield Rd STETCH B33 131 E1
Heythrop Gv MOS/BIL B13 162 B2
Hickman Av WOLV WV1 38 A5
Hickman Gdns
LDYWD/EDGR B16 125 H3
Hickman Rd BILS/COS WV14 53 G3
BRLYHL DY5 101 E5
SPARK B11 144 D1
TPTN/OCK DY4 69 F3
Hickman's Av DUDS DY2 121 E2
Hickmans Cl RMSLY B62 140 A1
Hickman St HAG/WOL DY9 136 A1
Hickmerelands La SEDG DY3 67 F3
Hickory Dr HRBN B17 124 D2
Hidcote Av WALM/CURD B76 78 C3
Hidcote Gv
CHWD/FDBR/MGN B37 132 A5
STETCH B33 131 E4
Hidson Rd ERDW/GRVHL B23 92 A2
Higgins Av BILS/COS WV14 68 D1
Higgins La RIDG/WDGT B32 140 C2
Higgins Wk SMTHWK B66 106 D3
Higgs Field Crs
BLKHTH/ROWR B65 121 H3
Higgs Rd WNSFLD WV11 25 G1
Higham's Cl
BLKHTH/ROWR B65 121 H1
Higham Wy WOLVN WV10 23 G4
High Arcal Dr SEDG DY3 67 H4
High Arcal Rd SEDG DY3 82 B2
High Av CDYHTH B64 121 F4
High Beeches GTB/HAM B43 73 F2
Highbridge Rd DUDS DY2 102 B5
SCFLD/BOLD B73 77 E2
High Brink Rd
CSHL/WTROR B46 115 F2
Highbrook Cl COVEN WV9 12 A5
High Brow HRBN B17 124 D5
High Bullen DARL/WED WS10 55 H5
Highbury Av
BLKHTH/ROWR B65 122 B1
HDSW B21 * 107 H1
Highbury Cl
BLKHTH/ROWR B65 122 B1
Highbury Rd
ALE/KHTH/YWD B14 160 D2
FOAKS/STRLY B74 46 A2
LGLYGN/QTN B68 105 F4
High Clere CDYHTH B64 121 G5
Highcrest Cl NFLD/LBR B31 189 G1
High Cft ALDR WS9 19 H5
GTB/HAM B43 73 E2
Highcroft BLOX/PEL WS3 * 18 B1
Highcroft Av STRBR DY8 117 F1
Highcroft Cl HIA/OLT B92 148 A5
Highcroft Dr FOAKS/STRLY B74 46 C2
Highcroft Rd ERDW/GRVHL B23 92 C3
Highdown Crs SHLY B90 195 G2
High Ercal Av BRLYHL DY5 119 E2
High Farm Rd HALE B63 138 B4
RMSLY B62 122 D4
Highfield Av BILS/COS WV14 54 A4
RUSH/SHEL WS4 29 E2
WOLVN WV10 13 G5
Highfield Cl HLGN/YWD B28 162 B5
Highfield Crs
BLKHTH/ROWR B65 121 H4
HALE B63 137 H2
WNSFLD WV11 24 B4
Highfield Dr ERDW/GRVHL B23 76 D4
Highfield La HAG/WOL DY9 171 E2
HALE B63 138 C4
RIDG/WDGT B32 140 C3
Highfield Rd
ALE/KHTH/YWD B14 162 B5
BLKHTH/ROWR B65 121 H3
BLOX/PEL WS3 18 A3
DUDS DY2 85 E5
EDG B15 126 A4
GTB/HAM B43 73 E4
HALE B63 137 H2
MOS/BIL B13 144 C4
SEDG DY3 67 F2
SMTHWKW B67 106 B4
STRBR DY8 118 C2
TPTN/OCK DY4 69 G4
WASH/WDE B8 110 C4
Highfield Rd North
BLOX/PEL WS3 17 H2

Highfields Ct
  ETTPK/GDPK/PENN WV4 * 50 D2
Highfields Dr BILS/COS WV14 ....55 H5
  WMBN WV5.....................81 E1
Highfields Rd BILS/COS WV14 ...53 H5
The Highfields
  DUNHL/THL/PER WV6 ....35 E3
Highfield Wy ALDR WS9 ....19 H5
Highgate FOAKS/STRLY B74 ......45 H4
  SEDG DY3 ....83 C1
Highgate Av
  ETTPK/GDPK/PENN WV4 ....50 D2
  WSL WS1.......................5 G7
Highgate CI BHTH/HG B12 ....127 F5
  WSL WS1......................57 F1
Highgate Dr WSL WS1............57 F1
Highgate Middleway
  BHTH/HG B12 ....127 F5
Highgate Rd BHTH/HG B12 ......127 G5
  DUDS DY2 ....101 H3
Highgate Sq BHTH/HG B12 * 127 F5
Highgate St BHTH/HG B12 ....127 F5
  CDYHTH B64 ....121 F2
Highgrove
  DUNHL/THL/PER WV6 ....35 G2
Highgrove CI SHHTH WV12 ....25 H4
Highgrove PI DUDN DY1 ....83 H4
High Haden Crs CDYHTH B64 ....121 G4
High Haden Rd CDYHTH B64 .....121 H4
High Heath CI BVILLE B30.......159 F5
High HI WNSFLD WV11 ....15 E5
High Holborn SEDG DY3 ....67 F4
High House Dr RBRY B45 ....187 H5
Highland Ms BILS/COS WV14 ......68 D2
Highland Rdg RMSLY B62 ....139 G2
High Land Rd ALDR WS9 ....19 H4
Highland Rd CDYHTH B64 ....121 E2
  DUDN DY1 ....84 A3
  ERDW/GRVHL B23 ....92 D1
  GTB/HAM B43 ....66 B1
Highlands Rd BDMR/CCFT WV3...35 H5
  SHLY B90 ....181 E5
The Highlands SHLY B90 * 181 E5
High Leasowes HALE B63 ....138 C3
High Meadow Rd
  HWK/WKHTH B38 ....177 E3
High Mdw
  DUNHL/THL/PER WV6 ....35 G3
  WMBN WV5 ....65 E5
Highmoor CI BILS/COS WV14 .....53 H5
  SHHTH WV12 ....25 H3
Highmoor Rd
  BLKHTH/ROWR B65 ....121 H1
Highmore Dr RIDG/WDGT B32 ....157 G2
High Oak BRLYHL DY5 ....101 E5
Highover Dr MGN/WHC B75 ....47 E1
Highpark Av STRBR DY8 ....134 D2
High Park CI SEDG DY3 ....67 F2
  SMTHWK B66 ....106 D4
High Park Crs SEDG DY3 ....67 F2
High Park Rd HALE B63 ....137 F2
High Park St VAUX/NECH B7 .....109 H3
High Rdg ALDR WS9 ....29 G5
High Ridge CI ALDR WS9 ....29 G5
  DARL/WED WS10 ....54 C4
High Rd SHHTH WV12 ....26 A5
High St ALDR WS9 ....19 F4
  ALDR WS9 ....30 B4
  ALE/KHTH/YWD B14 ....161 E2
  BILS/COS WV14 ....54 C4
  BLKHTH/ROWR B65 ....122 A3
  BLOX/PEL WS3 ....18 A4
  BLOX/PEL WS3 ....27 F1
  BRLYHL DY5 ....101 E2
  BRLYHL DY5 ....101 E5
  BRLYHL DY5 ....119 H3
  BRWNH WS8 ....9 E1
  CBHAM B2 ....3 G5
  CSHL/WTROR B46 ....115 F2
  DARL/WED WS10 ....54 C4
  DARL/WED WS10 ....55 E2
  DOR/KN B93 ....197 G2
  DUDS DY2 ....2 E5
  DUNHL/THL/PER WV6 ....35 H1
  ERDE/BCHGN B24 ....92 D2
  HAG/WOL DY9 ....136 C2
  HALE B63 ....138 D3
  HIA/OLT B92 ....167 G4
  HRBN B17 ....142 A2
  KGSWFD DY6 ....99 H3
  LOZ/NWT B19 ....109 E2
  RIDG/WDGT B32 ....140 A1
  SCFLD/BOLD B73 ....62 C2
  SEDG DY3 ....80 C4
  SEDG DY3 ....67 H4
  SHLY B90 ....179 E3
  SMTHWK B66 ....106 C4
  SOLH B91 ....182 A1
  STRBR DY8 ....118 A2
  STRBR DY8 ....118 B5
  STRBR DY8 ....135 G2
  TPTN/OCK DY4..................84 C2
  TPTN/OCK DY4..................85 E1
  WASH/WDE B8 ....110 B4
  WBROM B70 ....87 G2
  WBROM B70 ....87 H4
  WBROM B70 ....88 A4
  WMBN WV5 ....65 G5
  WNSFLD WV11 ....24 C5
  WSL WS1.......................5 F4
High St Bordesley BORD B9 ....127 G3
High St Deritend DIG/EDG B5 ...3 K7
Highters CI
  ALE/KHTH/YWD B14 ....178 D5
Highter's Heath La
  ALE/KHTH/YWD B14 ....178 C4
Highters Rd
  ALE/KHTH/YWD B14 ....178 C2

High Timbers RBRY B45 ....173 H4
High Tower VAUX/NECH B7 * 109 H4
Hightree CI RIDG/WDGT B32 ....157 F1
High Trees BFLD/HDSWWD B20 ..89 H3
High Trees Rd DOR/KN B93 .....197 F2
High Vw BILS/COS WV14 ....67 H2
Highview Dr KGSWFD DY6 ....100 B5
Highview St DUDS DY2 ....85 E5
Highwood Av HIA/OLT B92 ......164 C1
High Wood CI KGSWFD DY6 ......99 G3
Highwood Cft
  HWK/WKHTH B38 ....176 B4
Hiker CI
  CHWD/FDBR/MGN B37..........132 D2
Hilary Cft DUDN DY1 ....68 B5
Hilary Dr ALDR WS9 ....30 A5
  BDMR/CCFT WV3 ....50 D1
  WALM/CURD B76................63 G5
Hilary Gv NFLD/LBR B31 ....175 F1
Hilden Rd VAUX/NECH B7 ....109 G5
Hilderic Crs DUDN DY1 ....101 H2
Hilderstone Rd YDLY B25 ....146 C1
Hildicks Crs BLOX/PEL WS3 .....28 B5
Hildicks PI BLOX/PEL WS3 ....28 B5
Hillaire CI HWK/WKHTH B38 ....177 G4
Hillaries Rd ERDW/GRVHL B23 ..92 B4
Hillary Av DARL/WED WS10 ......55 G5
Hillary Crest SEDG DY3 * 83 G1
Hillary St WSLW WS2 ....56 C2
Hill Av
  ETTPK/GDPK/PENN WV4 ....50 D5
Hill Bank HAG/WOL DY9 ....136 C4
Hillbank OLDBY B69 ....104 B1
Hill Bank Dr STECH B33........111 H5
Hill Bank Rd HALE B63 ....137 E3
  STECH B33 ....111 H5
Hillborough Rd HIA/OLT B92 ....146 D5
Hillbrook Gv STECH B33........130 D1
Hillbury Dr SHHTH WV12 ....25 H2
Hill CI NFLD/LBR B31 ....175 H4
  SEDG DY3 ....67 G2
Hill Crest SEDG DY3 ....82 D2
Hill Crest Av BRLYHL DY5 .....119 E3
Hillcrest Av GTB/HAM B43 ....73 C1
  HALE B63 ....120 B5
  WOLVN WV10 ....23 C2
Hillcrest CI DUDS DY2 ....102 C4
Hillcrest Gdns SHHTH WV12 .....26 B5
Hill Crest Gv KGSTG B44 ....75 G4
Hill Crest Rd DUDS DY2 ....85 E3
  MOS/BIL B13 ....144 A5
Hillcrest Rd CSCFLD/WYGN B72 ..77 C3
  GTB/HAM B43 ....73 D1
  RMSLY B62 ....172 B1
Hill Croft Rd
  ALE/KHTH/YWD B14 ....160 C4
Hillcroft Rd KGSWFD DY6 ......100 A2
Hillcross Wk CBROM B36 ....112 B2
Hilldene Rd KGSWFD DY6 ....99 G5
Hilldrop Gv HRBN B17 ....142 B4
Hilleys Cft
  CHWD/FDBR/MGN B37..........131 H1
Hillfield Ms SOLH B91 ....91 H5
Hillfield Rd SOLH B91 ....181 H5
  SPARK B11 ....145 F4
Hillfields SMTHWKW B67 ....123 H1
Hillfields Rd BRLYHL DY5 ......118 D5
Hill Gv BFLD/HDSWWD B20 * 90 C1
Hill Hook Rd FOAKS/STRLY B74 ..32 C4
Hill House La STECH B33 ....130 B1
Hillhurst Gv CBROM B36 ....95 G5
Hilliards Cft PBAR/PBCH B42 ....74 A3
Hillingford Av GTB/HAM B43 .....59 H4
Hill La GTB/HAM B43 ....73 C1
  HAG/WOL DY9 ....170 C1
  MGN/WHC B75 ....48 D5
Hillman Dr DUDS DY2 ....103 E2
Hillman Gv CBROM B36 ....95 G5
Hillmeads Dr DUDS DY2 ....103 E2
Hillmeads Rd
  HWK/WKHTH B38 ....177 E4
Hillmorton Rd DOR/KN B93 ....197 E3
  FOAKS/STRLY B74 ....46 A4
Hillmount CI HLGN/YWD B28 ...145 G5
Hill Pk ALDR WS9 ....19 G5
Hill Pas CDYHTH B64 ....121 E2
Hill PI WNSFLD WV11 ....25 C1
Hill Rd HAG/WOL DY9 ....136 C2
  OLDBY B69 ....85 G4
  WMBN WV5 ....38 D4
Hill Side SEDG DY3 ....83 E2
Hillside BRWNH WS8 ....9 H5
  WMBN WV5 ....64 C4
Hillside Av BLKHTH/ROWR B65 .121 H4
  BRLYHL DY5 ....119 H1
  HALE B63 ....137 H1
Hillside CI RIDG/WDGT B32 ....157 E2
Hillside Crs BLOX/PEL WS3 ......17 H5
Hillside Cft HIA/OLT B92 ......148 C3
Hillside Dr
  CHWD/FDBR/MGN B37..........113 H5
  FOAKS/STRLY B74 ....60 B1
  PBAR/PBCH B42 ....74 A5
Hillside Gdns
  CHWD/FDBR/MGN B37 * 113 H5
  WOLV WV1 ....38 A2
Hillside Rd DUDN DY1 ....84 A2
  ERDW/GRVHL B23 ....92 B4
  FOAKS/STRLY B74 ....46 D1
  GTB/HAM B43 ....73 F1
Hillstone Gdns WOLVN WV10 ....23 H2
Hillstone Rd BKDE/SHDE B34 ...113 H4
Hill St BILS/COS WV14 ....54 A4
  BRLYHL DY5 ....119 F2
  BRLYHL DY5 ....120 A4
  CBHAM B2 ....2 E5
  DARL/WED WS10 ....55 G2
  DUDS DY2 ....2 B4
  HAG/WOL DY9 ....136 D2
  HALE B63 ....138 D3
  SEDG DY3 ....83 G1
  SMTHWK B66 ....106 C4

STRBR DY8 ....118 B4
  STRBR DY8 ....135 F3
  TPTN/OCK DY4..................85 F2
  WNSFLD WV11 ....14 D4
  WSL WS1.......................5 F5
The Hill RIDG/WDGT B32 ....140 D5
Hilltop HAG/WOL DY9 ....136 C4
Hill Top HHTH/SAND B71 ....71 E4
Hill Top Av RMSLY B62 ....122 C5
Hill Top CI KGSTG B44 ....75 E5
Hilltop Dr CBROM B36..........111 H2
Hilltop Rd DUDS DY2 ....103 E1
Hill Top Rd LCLYGN/QTN B68 ..123 G2
  NFLD/LBR B31 ....175 F2
Hill Top Wk ALDR WS9 ....30 C1
Hill Vw ALDR WS9 ....19 H5
Hillview CI HALE B63 ....138 A1
Hillview Rd RBRY B45 ....175 C5
Hill Village Rd MGN/WHC B75 ...47 E1
Hillville Gdns STRBR DY8 ......135 H4
Hill Wd BLOX/PEL WS3 ....17 H5
Hillwood Av SHLY B90 ....195 G2
Hillwood CI STRBR DY8 ....99 C5
Hillwood Common Rd
  MGN/WHC B75 ....33 F5
Hill Wood Rd MGN/WHC B75 .....33 G5
Hillwood Rd NFLD/LBR B31 ....158 A3
  RMSLY B62 ....122 A5
Hillyfields Rd ERDW/GRVHL B23 .92 A2
Hilly Rd BILS/COS WV14 ....69 E1
Hilsea CI COVEN WV9 ....11 H5
Hilston Av
  ETTPK/GDPK/PENN WV4 ....50 C4
  HALE B63 ....138 B3
Hilton Av HLGN/YWD B28 ....179 G1
Hilton CI BLOX/PEL WS3 ....26 D1
Hilton Crs WOLVN WV10 ....13 H2
Hilton Dr CSCFLD/WYGN B72 ....77 C3
Hilton La GT/WY WV6 ....54 A3
Hilton Rd
  ETTPK/GDPK/PENN WV4 ....52 D4
  OLDBY B69 ....104 A1
  SHHTH WV12 ....26 A2
  WOLV WV10 ....87 E3
Himbleton Cft SHLY B90 ....195 G2
Himley Av DUDN DY1 ....83 H4
Himley CI GTB/HAM B43 ....73 C1
  SHHTH WV12 ....25 G5
Himley Crs
  ETTPK/GDPK/PENN WV4 ....52 A3
Himley Gdns SEDG DY3 ....82 B2
Himley Gv RBRY B45 ....188 B2
Himley La SEDG DY3 ....80 D4
Himley Rd DUDN DY1 ....83 G4
  SEDG DY3 ....82 A3
Himley St DUDN DY1 ....84 A5
Himley Wd Rd DUDN DY1 ....83 G5
Hinchliffe Av BILS/COS WV14 ..68 B1
Hinckes Rd
  DUNHL/THL/PER WV6 ....21 F5
Hinckley Ct LCLYGN/QTN B68 * .123 F5
Hinckley St DIG/EDG B5 ....3 F5
Hincks St BRLYHL DY5 ....103 H4
Hindhead Rd
  ALE/KHTH/YWD B14 ....179 E1
Hindlip CI HALE B63 ....138 D5
Hindlow CI VAUX/NECH B7 .....109 H5
Hindon Gv ACGN B27 ....163 F3
Hindon Sq EDG B15 ....125 H4
Hingeston St WSNGN B18 ....2 A1
Hingley Cft FOAKS/STRLY B74 ...45 F2
Hingley Rd HALE B63 ....137 E1
Hingley St CDYHTH B64 ....120 D5
Hinksford Gdns DUDS DY2 ....80 C4
Hinksford La SEDG DY3 ....80 C5
Hinsford CI KGSWFD DY6 ......100 A1
Hinstock CI
  ETTPK/GDPK/PENN WV4 ....51 G4
Hinstock Rd
  BFLD/HDSWWD B20 ....89 H5
Hintlesham Av EDG B15........142 B2
Hinton Gv WNSFLD WV11 ....25 H2
Hintons Coppice DOR/KN B93 ..196 C2
Hipkins St TPTN/OCK DY4 ....69 E4
Hipsley La RMSLY B62 ....139 C3
Hipsley CI CBROM B36 ....95 G5
Hipsmoor CI
  CHWD/FDBR/MGN B37..........131 H1
Hirdemonsgas SHLY B90 ....193 H3
Histons Dr CDSL WV8 ....10 B5
Histons HI CDSL WV8 ....10 B5
Hitchcock CI SMTHWKW B67 ...105 H4
Hitches La EDG B15 ....126 B5
Hitherside SHLY B90 ....194 B2
Hoarstone STRBR DY8 ....152 B5
Hobacre CI RBRY B45 ....174 A5
Hobart Cft VAUX/NECH B7 .....109 G4
Hobart Dr DSYBK/YTR WS5 ......58 A2
Hobart Rd TPTN/OCK DY4 ....69 E2
Hobble End La CTWY WS6 ....16 C1
Hobgate CI WOLVN WV10 ....37 H1
Hobgate Rd WOLVN WV10 ....37 H1
Hob Green Rd HAG/WOL DY9 ...136 A5
Hobhouse CI GTB/HAM B43 ......73 H4
Hobley St WLNHL WV13 ....40 A3
Hobmoor Cft YDLY B25 ....129 H5
Hob Moor Rd
  LGN/SDN/BHAMAIR B26 ......129 H5
  SMHTH B10 ....129 E3
Hobnock Rd WNSFLD WV11 ....15 E5
Hobs Hole La ALDR WS9 ....30 D3
Hob's Meadow HIA/OLT B92 ....147 H5
Hob's Moat Rd HIA/OLT B92 ...147 H5
Hobson CI WSNGN B18 ....2 A1
Hobson Rd SLYOAK B29 ....160 B1
Hobs Rd DARL/WED WS10 ....56 A4
Hockley Brook La
  HAG/WOL DY9 ....184 C4
Hockley CI LOZ/NWT B19 ....108 D3
Hockley HI WSNGN B18..........108 B3

Hockley La DUDS DY2 ....120 B1
Hockley Pool CI WSNGN B18 ...108 B4
Hockley Rd BILS/COS WV14 .....68 A4
  ERDW/GRVHL B23 ....92 B2
Hockley St LOZ/NWT B19 ....108 C4
  WSNGN B18 ....89 F5
The Hill RIDG/WDGT B32 ....140 D5
Hodge Hill Av HAG/WOL DY9 ...136 D4
Hodge Hill Rd BKDE/SHDE B34 ..112 A4
Hodgetts CI SMTHWKW B67....125 H1
Hodgetts Dr HALE B63 ....154 C2
Hodgkins CI BRWNH WS8 ....19 C1
Hodnet CI CBROM B36 ....95 C5
Hodnet Dr BILS/COS WV14 ......53 F3
Hodnet Dr BRLYHL DY5 ....101 E3
Hodnet Gv DIG/EDG B5 ....127 E4
Hodson Av WLNHL WV13 ....40 A4
Hodson CI WNSFLD WV11 ....25 F4
Hoff Beck Court Ct BORD B9 * .127 H2
Hogarth CI GTB/HAM B43 ....59 G5
  WLNHL WV13 ....39 E3
Hoggs La NFLD/LBR B31 ....175 E1
Holbeache La KGSWFD DY6 ......81 H5
Holbeache Rd KGSWFD DY6 ......99 G1
  KINVER DY7 ....99 E5
Holbeach Rd STECH B33 ....130 D2
Holbeche Rd DOR/KN B93 ......197 E1
  MGN/WHC B75 ....63 H4
Holberg Gv WNSFLD WV11 ....25 F4
Holborn HI VAUX/NECH B7 .....109 H1
Holbury CI COVEN WV9 ....12 A5
Holcombe Rd SPARK B11 ....144 A4
Holcroft Rd HAG/WOL DY9 .....136 A5
  HALE B63 ....137 C2
  KGSWFD DY6 ....81 G5
Holcroft St TPTN/OCK DY4 ......85 E2
  WOLV WV1 ....38 E3
Holden CI ERDW/GRVHL B23 .....92 C4
Holden Crs BLOX/PEL WS3 ....28 A5
Holden Cft TPTN/OCK DY4 ....85 C3
Holden PI BLOX/PEL WS3 ....28 A5
Holden Rd DARL/WED WS10 .....71 E1
  ETTPK/GDPK/PENN WV4 ....50 D5
Holder Rd SPARK B11 ....145 E1
  YDLY B25 ....129 C5
Holders Gdns MOS/BIL B13 ....143 G5
Holders La MOS/BIL B13 ....143 G5
Holdford Rd AST/WIT B6 ....91 F4
Holdgate Rd SLYOAK B29 ......158 D3
Hole Farm Rd NFLD/LBR B31 ..159 E5
Hole Farm Wy
  HWK/WKHTH B38 ....190 D1
Hole La NFLD/LBR B31 ....159 E4
Holford Av WSLW WS2 ....56 D2
Holford Dr PBAR/PBCH B42 .....91 E2
Holford Wy AST/WIT B6 ....91 F4
Holifast Rd CSCFLD/WYGN B72 ..77 G3
Holland Av DOR/KN B93 ....183 F5
  LGLYGN/QTN B68 ....105 G3
Holland Rd BILS/COS WV14 .....54 A1
  CSCFLD/WYGN B72 ....62 B5
  GTB/HAM B43 ....59 F3
Holland Rd West AST/WIT B6 ..109 F3
Hollands PI BLOX/PEL WS3 ......27 H1
Hollands Rd BLOX/PEL WS3 .....27 H1
Holland St CBHAMNW B3 ....2 C4
  CSCFLD/WYGN B72 ....62 B4
  DUDN DY1 ....102 B1
  TPTN/OCK DY4 ....70 A4
Hollemeadow Av
  BLOX/PEL WS3 ....27 H3
Holliars Gv
  CHWD/FDBR/MGN B37..........113 H4
Holliday St ERDE/BCHGN B24 ....93 E2
  HDSW B21 ....107 H2
Holliday La NFLD/LBR B31 .....174 C5
Hollie Lucas Rd MOS/BIL B13 .161 F3
Hollies Cft DIG/EDG B5 ....143 G2
Hollies Dr DARL/WED WS10 .....55 H5
  RMSLY B62 * 139 G1
Hollies Ri CDYHTH B64 ....121 F4
Hollies Rd OLDBY B69 ....103 G1
Hollies St BRLYHL DY5 ....101 F2
The Hollies AST/WIT B6 ....109 H1
  BKHL/PFLD WV2 ....6 E7
  SMTHWK B66 ....107 E5
Hollin Brow DOR/KN B93 ......197 F5
Hollingberry La
  WALM/CURD B76................63 F5
Hollings Gv SOLH B91 ....181 H5
Hollington Rd WOLV WV1 ....38 B5
Hollington Wy SOLH B91 ......196 A1
Hollinwell CI BLOX/PEL WS3 ...16 C4
Hollister Dr RIDG/WDGT B32 ..141 F4
Holloway NFLD/LBR B31 ....158 A4
Holloway Bank
  DARL/WED WS10 ....70 D3
Holloway Circus Queensway
  CBHAMW B1 ....3 F7
Holloway Dr WMBN WV5 ....80 C1
Holloway Head EDG B15 ....126 D3
Holloway St SEDG DY3 ....83 F2
Holloway St West SEDG DY3 ....83 F1
The Holloway
  DUNHL/THL/PER WV6 ....35 F3
  SEDG DY3 ....80 B5
  STRBR DY8 ....118 B5
Hollow Cft NFLD/LBR B31 .....175 H2
Hollow Croft Rd SHHTH WV12 ..25 H3
The Hollow MOS/BIL B13 ......144 A3
Holly Av BHTH/HG B12 ....144 C2
  SLYOAK B29 ....160 B1
Hollybank Av WNSFLD WV11 ....15 E4
Hollybank CI BLOX/PEL WS3 ....27 E1
Hollybank Rd MOS/BIL B13 ....161 F3
Hollyberry Av SOLH B91 ......181 G5
Hollyberry Cft BKDE/SHDE B34 113 G3
Hollybrow SLYOAK B29 ....158 C3
Holly Bush Gv RIDG/WDGT B32 123 H5
Hollybush La
  ETTPK/GDPK/PENN WV4 ....50 D4

STRBR DY8 ....118 B5
  WALM/CURD B76................78 B1
Hollycot Gdns BHTH/HG B12 ...144 B3
Hollycroft Rd HDSW B21 ....89 F5
Hollydale Rd
  BLKHTH/ROWR B65 ....122 B1
  ERDE/BCHGN B24 ....93 G3
Holly Dell HWK/WKHTH B38 ....177 F3
Holly Dr ACGN B27 ....146 A1
  HLYWD B47 ....192 D1
Hollyfaste Rd STECH B33 ......130 D5
Hollyfield Av SOLH B91 ....181 E2
Hollyfield Ct MGN/WHC B75 ....63 E3
Hollyfield Crs MGN/WHC B75 ...63 E4
Hollyfield Dr MGN/WHC B75 ....63 E4
Hollyfield Rd MGN/WHC B75 ....63 E4
Holly Gv BDMR/CCFT WV3 ....51 F1
  BVILLE B30 ....159 H2
  LOZ/NWT B19 ....109 E3
  STRBR DY8 ....135 F2
Holly Hall Rd DUDS DY2 ....102 A3
Hollyhedge CI NFLD/LBR B31 ..157 H4
  WSLW WS2 ....4 A2
Hollyhedge La WSLW WS2 ....4 A1
Hollyhedge Rd HHTH/SAND B71 .71 F3
Hollyhill Rd RBRY B45 ....174 A3
Hollyhock Rd ACGN B27 ....162 D1
  DUDS DY2 ....102 C4
Hollyhurst CSHL/WTROR B46 ....96 C4
Hollyhurst Dr STRBR DY8 ......118 C1
Holly La
  LGN/SDN/BHAMAIR B26 ......147 E1
  SHLY B90 ....180 B5
Hollyhurst Rd SCFLD/BOLD B73 .60 D5
Holly La ALDR WS9 ....31 F2
  CHWD/FDBR/MGN B37..........131 H4
  ERDE/BCHGN B24 ....93 G3
  ERDE/BCHGN B24 ....92 D1
  MGN/WHC B75 ....63 E3
  SMTHWK B66 ....106 A2
  SMTHWKW B66 ....106 A2
Hollymoor NFLD/LBR B31 ......175 C3
Hollymount RMSLY B62 ....123 E5
Hollyoak Cft NFLD/LBR B31 ...175 H5
Hollyoake LGLYGN/QTN B68 ...104 D2
Hollyoake CI LGLYGN/QTN B68 123 E1
Hollyoak Rd FOAKS/STRLY B74 ..60 B2
Hollyoak St HHTH/SAND B71 ....87 H2
Holly Park Dr ERDE/BCHGN B24 93 F3
Holly PI AST/WIT B6 * 109 H1
  BVILLE B30 ....159 H2
  DARL/WED WS10 ....55 E3
  DUDN DY1 ....84 A3
  HDSW B21 ....72 A3
  HHTH/SAND B71 ....72 C4
  LDYWD/EDGR B16 ....125 E3
  LGLYGN/QTN B68 ....123 C4
Holly St DUDN DY1 ....101 G2
  SMTHWKW B67 ....106 E3
Hollywell Rd DOR/KN B93 .....197 E3
  LGN/SDN/BHAMAIR B26 ......147 H1
Hollywell St BILS/COS WV14 ....68 A2
Hollywood By-Pass
  HLYWD B47 ....192 A3
Hollywood Cft PBAR/PBCH B42 ..73 H3
Hollywood Gdns HLYWD B47 ...178 C5
Hollywood La HLYWD B47 ......178 C5
Holman Cl WLNHL WV13 ....39 E3
Holman Rd WLNHL WV13 ....39 E3
Holmbridge Gv RUSH/SHEL WS4 18 D5
Holme MI WOLVN WV10 ....12 D3
Holmes Dr RBRY B45 ....187 H2
Holmesfield Rd
  PBAR/PBCH B42 ....74 C4
Holmes Rd SHHTH WV12 ....26 B3
The Holmes WOLVN WV10 ....12 D4
Holme Wy RUSH/SHEL WS4 ......28 D3
Holmwood Rd BORD B9 ....128 B3
Holt Ct North VAUX/NECH B7 * ..3 K2
Holt Ct South VAUX/NECH B7 * ..3 K2
Holte Dr MGN/WHC B75 ....47 H3
Holte Rd AST/WIT B6 ....91 G5
  SPARK B11 ....145 F2
Holtes Wk AST/WIT B6 * 109 H2
Holt La RMSLY B62 ....171 H1
Holt Rd RMSLY B62 ....122 C3
Holtshill La WSL WS1............5 J1
Holy Cross Gn HAG/WOL DY9 ..170 C3
Holy Cross La HAG/WOL DY9 ..170 C5
Holyhead Rd CDSL WV8 ....20 B5
  DARL/WED WS10 ....55 E4
  HDSW B21 ....107 F1
Holyhead Wy HDSW B21 ....91 F5
Holyoak CI AST/WIT B6 ....91 H5
Holyrood Gv AST/WIT B6 * 109 E1
Holy Well CI LDYWD/EDGR B16 124 A2
Holywell La RBRY B45 ....187 F2
Homecroft Rd YDLY B25 ....130 A4
Homedene Rd NFLD/LBR B31 ..158 A3
Homefield Rd CDSL WV8 ....10 D4
Homelands PBAR/PBCH B42 .....74 B4
The Homelands WOLVN WV10 * ..12 C1
Homelea Rd YDLY B25 ....129 H3
Homemead Gv RBRY B45 ....187 H1
Homer Hill Rd HALE B63 ......120 B5
Homer Rd MGN/WHC B75 ....63 E3
  SOLH B91 ....181 H2
Homers Fold BILS/COS WV14 ...53 H3
Homer St BHTH/HG B12 ....144 B2
Homerton Rd KGSTG B44 ....75 H2
Homestead CI SEDG DY3 ....83 G1
Homestead Dr MGN/WHC B75 ....47 H5
Homestead Rd STECH B33 ......131 E3
Homewood CI WALM/CURD B76...63 E5
Honesty CI BRWNH WS8 ....8 D5

Honeswode Cl
BFLD/HDSWWD B20 ... 108 A1
Honeyborne Rd MGN/WHC B75 ... 62 D1
Honeybourne Cl HALE B63 ... 138 C4
Honeybourne Crs WMBN WV5 ... 80 D1
Honeybourne Rd HALE B63 ... 139 E4
STETCH B33 ... 131 E4
Honeybourne Wy WLNHL WV13 ... 40 A3
Honeycomb Wy
NFLD/LBR B31 ... 175 E2
Honeysuckle Av KGSWFD DY6 ... 100 A2
Honeysuckle Cl
RIDG/WDGT B32 ... 140 B2
Honeysuckle Dr
DSYBK/YTR WS5 ... 57 G5
Honeysuckle Gv ACGN B27 ... 146 C2
Honeytree Cl KGSWFD DY6 ... 118 B1
Honiley Dr SCFLD/BOLD B73 ... 76 A1
Honiley Rd STETCH B33 ... 130 C2
Honister Cl BRLYHL DY5 ... 119 H3
Honiton Cl NFLD/LBR B31 ... 175 E1
Honiton Crs NFLD/LBR B31 ... 175 E1
Honiton Wk SMTHWK B66 ... 106 D4
Honiton Wy ALDR WS9 ... 29 H5
Honnington Ct SLYOAK B29 * ... 158 B1
Honor Av
ETTPK/GDPK/PENN WV4 ... 52 A3
Hood Gv BVILLE B30 ... 176 B1
Hook Dr FOAKS/STRLY B74 ... 46 C1
Hooper St WSNGN B18 ... 107 H5
Hoosen Cl RMSLY B62 ... 140 A1
Hopedale Rd RIDG/WDGT B32 ... 140 C2
Hope Pl SLYOAK B29 * ... 142 D5
Hope Rd TPTN/OCK DY4 ... 70 A5
Hope St DIG/EDG B5 ... 126 D4
DUDS DY2 ... 102 C1
RMSLY B62 ... 122 B4
STRBR DY8 ... 117 H1
WBROM B70 ... 88 A4
WSL WS1 ... 4 E6
Hopkins Dr HHTH/SAND B71 ... 72 A4
Hopkins St TPTN/OCK DY4 ... 85 G4
Hopstone Gdns
ETTPK/GDPK/PENN WV4 ... 51 F3
Hopstone Rd SLYOAK B29 ... 158 C1
Hopton Cl
DUNHL/THL/PER WV6 ... 34 D2
TPTN/OCK DY4 ... 70 A1
Hopton Crs WNSFLD WV11 ... 25 E4
Hopton Gdns DUDN DY1 ... 84 A3
Hopton Gv MOS/BIL B13 ... 162 A5
Hopwas Gv
CHWD/FDBR/MGN B37 ... 113 H4
Hopwood Cl HALE B63 ... 138 C5
Hopwood Gv NFLD/LBR B31 ... 189 E2
Hopyard Cl SEDG DY3 ... 82 D3
Hopyard Gdns BILS/COS WV14 ... 53 F5
Hopyard La SEDG DY3 ... 82 D4
Hopyard Rd WSLW WS2 ... 40 C3
Horace Partridge Rd
DARL/WED WS10 ... 54 C3
Horace St BILS/COS WV14 ... 68 A3
Horatio Dr MOS/BIL B13 ... 144 B3
Hordern Cl
DUNHL/THL/PER WV6 ... 22 B5
Hordern Crs BRLYHL DY5 ... 119 F4
Hordern Gv
DUNHL/THL/PER WV6 ... 22 B5
Hordern Pk WOLVN WV10 * ... 12 C1
Hordern Rd
DUNHL/THL/PER WV6 ... 22 B5
Hornbeam Cl SLYOAK B29 ... 158 D3
Hornbeam Wk BDMR/CCFT WV3 ... 6 B5
Hornbrook Gv HIA/OLT B92 ... 163 G3
Hornby Gv
ALE/KHTH/YWD B14 ... 179 E1
Hornby Rd
ETTPK/GDPK/PENN WV4 ... 52 A4
Horne Wy BKDE/SHDE B34 ... 113 G4
Horning Dr BILS/COS WV14 ... 53 G5
Hornsey Gv KGSTG B44 ... 75 G1
Hornsey Rd KGSTG B44 ... 75 G1
Hornton Cl FOAKS/STRLY B74 ... 32 B5
Horrell Rd
LGN/SDN/BHAMAIR B26 ... 130 C5
LGN/SDN/BHAMAIR B26 ... 147 H1
SHLY B90 ... 179 H3
Horsecroft Dr HHTH/SAND B71 ... 72 C3
Horsehills Dr BDMR/CCFT WV3 ... 36 A3
Horselea Cft WASH/WDE B8 ... 111 G5
Horseley Flds WOLV WV1 ... 7 J4
Horseley Heath TPTN/OCK DY4 ... 85 H2
Horseley Rd TPTN/OCK DY4 ... 69 H5
Horseshoe Cl WSLW WS2 ... 56 B1
Horse Shoes La
LGN/SDN/BHAMAIR B26 ... 147 H2
The Horseshoe
LGLYGN/QTN B68 ... 123 G2
Horsfall Rd MGN/WHC B75 ... 63 G3
Horsham Av STRBR DY8 ... 117 G1
Horsley Rd FOAKS/STRLY B74 ... 45 H3
GTB/HAM B43 ... 59 H4
Horton Cl DARL/WED WS10 ... 55 F1
SEDG DY3 ... 67 E3
Horton Gv SHLY B90 ... 195 G3
Horton Pl DARL/WED WS10 ... 55 F1
Horton Sq BHTH/HG B12 ... 127 E5
Horton St DARL/WED WS10 ... 55 F1
TPTN/OCK DY4 ... 86 B1
WBROM B70 ... 87 G5
Hospital La BILS/COS WV14 ... 68 B4
Hospital St LOZ/NWT B19 ... 3 F1
WOLV WV1 ... 7 H6
WSLW WS2 ... 41 H1
Hossil La HAG/WOL DY9 ... 170 B4
Hothersall Dr SCFLD/BOLD B73 ... 76 D3
Hotspur Rd KGSTG B44 ... 75 F2
Hough Pl WSLW WS2 ... 56 B1
Hough Rd ALE/KHTH/YWD B14 ... 160 D4
WSLW WS2 ... 56 A1
Houghton Ct HLGN/YWD B28 ... 179 F1
Houghton St OLDBY B69 ... 104 D3
WBROM B70 ... 105 H1
Houldey Rd NFLD/LBR B31 ... 175 H4
Houliston Cl DARL/WED WS10 ... 56 B3
Houndsfield Cl HLYWD B47 ... 193 E2
Houndsfield Gv HLYWD B47 ... 192 C3
Houndsfield La HLYWD B47 ... 192 C3
The Houx STRBR DY8 ... 118 A4
Hove Rd ACGN B27 ... 163 F1
Howard Rd
ALE/KHTH/YWD B14 ... 160 D3
BFLD/HDSWWD B20 ... 90 B4
BILS/COS WV14 ... 54 B5
GTB/HAM B43 ... 73 E3
HIA/OLT B92 ... 147 E4
WNSFLD WV11 ... 25 F2
YDLY B25 ... 146 C1
Howard Rd East
ALE/KHTH/YWD B14 ... 161 E3
Howard St BKHL/PFLD WV2 ... 7 G7
LOZ/NWT B19 ... 2 E1
TPTN/OCK DY4 ... 85 H1
WBROM B70 ... 70 D4
Howarth Wy AST/WIT B6 ... 109 G2
Howden Pl STETCH B33 ... 112 C4
Howdle's La BRWNH WS8 ... 9 F2
Howe Crs SHHTH WV12 ... 26 A4
Howell Dr TPTN/OCK DY4 ... 85 G1
Howell Rd BKHL/PFLD WV2 ... 52 C1
Howes Cft CVALE B35 ... 94 C4
Howe St CBHAMNE B4 ... 3 K3
Howford Gv VAUX/NECH B7 ... 109 H5
Howland Cl COVEN WV9 ... 11 H5
Howley Av KGSTG B44 ... 75 E2
Howley Grange Rd RMSLY B62 ... 139 H3
Hoylake Cl BLOX/PEL WS3 ... 16 D4
Hoylake Dr OLDBY B69 ... 103 G2
Hoylake Rd
DUNHL/THL/PER WV6 ... 20 B5
Hoyland Wy BVILLE B30 ... 159 G2
Hubert Cft SLYOAK B29 ... 142 C5
Hubert Rd SLYOAK B29 ... 142 D5
Hubert St AST/WIT B6 ... 109 F4
The Hub SOLH B91 * ... 182 A2
Hucker Cl WSLW WS2 ... 56 A1
Hucker Rd WSLW WS2 ... 56 A1
Huddlestone Cl WOLVN WV10 ... 13 G1
Huddocks Vw BLOX/PEL WS3 ... 17 H2
Hudson Av CSHL/WTROR B46 ... 115 F3
Hudson Gv
DUNHL/THL/PER WV6 ... 20 C5
Hudson Rd BFLD/HDSWWD B20 ... 90 A2
TPTN/OCK DY4 ... 86 A2
Hudson's Dr BVILLE B30 ... 177 E1
Hudswell Dr BRLYHL DY5 ... 119 F4
Hughes Av BDMR/CCFT WV3 ... 36 B5
Hughes Pl BILS/COS WV14 ... 53 H1
Hughes Rd BILS/COS WV14 ... 53 H1
DARL/WED WS10 ... 54 C3
Hugh Rd SMTHH B10 ... 128 C3
SMTHWKW B67 ... 105 H4
Hugh Vls SMTHH B10 * ... 128 C3
Hulbert Dr DUDS DY2 ... 102 B3
Hulland Pl BRLYHL DY5 ... 119 E1
Hullbrook Rd MOS/BIL B13 ... 162 A5
Humber Av WALM/CURD B76 ... 78 C4
Humber Gdns HALE B63 ... 137 F2
Humber Gv CBROM B36 ... 95 H5
Humber Rd BDMR/CCFT WV3 ... 6 B5
Humberstone Rd
ERDE/BCHGN B24 ... 94 A2
Hume St SMTHWK B66 ... 106 D5
Humpage Rd BORD B9 ... 128 C2
Humphrey Middlemore Dr
HRBN B17 ... 142 B3
Humphrey St SEDG DY3 ... 83 F3
Humphries Crs BILS/COS WV14 ... 69 F1
Humphries Rd WOLVN WV10 ... 23 F3
Hundred Acre Rd
FOAKS/STRLY B74 ... 60 B1
Hungary Cl HAG/WOL DY9 ... 136 A2
Hungary Hl HAG/WOL DY9 ... 136 A2
Hungerfield Rd CBROM B36 ... 95 E5
Hungerford Rd STRBR DY8 ... 135 E5
Hunningham Gv SOLH B91 ... 181 H5
Hunnington Cl
RIDG/WDGT B32 ... 157 E1
Hunnington Crs HALE B63 ... 138 D5
Hunscote Cl SHLY B90 ... 179 H4
Hunslet Cl RIDG/WDGT B32 ... 141 F3
Hunslet Rd RIDG/WDGT B32 ... 141 F3
Hunstanton Av HRBN B17 ... 124 B4
Hunstanton Cl BRLYHL DY5 ... 119 E4
Hunter Crs BLOX/PEL WS3 ... 28 B4
Hunters Cl BILS/COS WV14 ... 54 C1
Hunter's Ride KINVER DY7 ... 117 F2
Hunters Rd LOZ/NWT B19 ... 108 B3
Hunter St DUNHL/THL/PER WV6 ... 36 C1
Hunters V LOZ/NWT B19 ... 108 C3
Huntingdon Gdns HALE B63 ... 120 C5
Huntingdon Rd
HHTH/SAND B71 ... 71 F4
Huntington Rd SHHTH WV12 ... 26 B3
Huntingtree Rd HALE B63 ... 138 A3
Huntlands Rd HALE B63 ... 138 A5
Huntley Dr SOLH B91 ... 181 H3
Huntly Rd LDYWD/EDGR B16 ... 126 A3
Hunton Hl ERDW/GRVHL B23 ... 92 B3
Hunton Rd ERDW/GRVHL B23 ... 92 C3
Hunt's La SHHTH WV12 ... 26 B4
Huntsman Cl BILS/COS WV14 ... 68 D1
Hunts Mill Dr BRLYHL DY5 ... 83 E5
Hunts Rd BVILLE B30 ... 160 A3
Hurdis Rd SHLY B90 ... 180 A3
Hurdlow Av WSNGN B18 ... 108 B4
Hurley Cl CSCFLD/WYGN B72 ... 77 G1
DSYBK/YTR WS5 ... 58 B2
Hurley Gv
CHWD/FDBR/MGN B37 ... 113 H4
Hurleys Fold DUDS DY2 ... 102 B4
Hurlingham Rd KGSTG B44 ... 75 G2
Hurricane Wy CVALE B35 ... 94 C4
Hursey Dr TPTN/OCK DY4 ... 85 G1
Hurstbourne Crs WOLV WV1 ... 38 B4
Hurst Cl CBROM B36 ... 113 G2
Hurstcroft Rd STETCH B33 ... 130 D1
Hurst Green Rd DOR/KN B93 ... 196 D4
RMSLY B62 ... 122 C4
WALM/CURD B76 ... 79 F5
Hurst La BKDE/SHDE B34 ... 113 F3
BRLYHL DY5 ... 119 H1
TPTN/OCK DY4 ... 84 D1
Hurst La North
BKDE/SHDE B34 ... 113 G2
Hurst Rd BILS/COS WV14 ... 67 H2
SMTHWKW B67 ... 123 H2
Hurst St DIG/EDG B5 ... 3 F7
The Hurst HLYWD B47 ... 192 C2
MOS/BIL B13 ... 162 A3
The Hurstway
ERDW/GRVHL B23 ... 76 A3
Hurstwood Rd KGSTG B44 ... 76 A3
Hussey Rd BRWNH WS8 ... 9 E4
Hutton Av WASH/WDE B8 ... 110 B4
Hutton Rd BFLD/HDSWWD B20 ... 90 B5
WASH/WDE B8 ... 110 B4
Huxbey Dr HIA/OLT B92 ... 165 H2
Huxley Cl COVEN WV9 ... 12 A4
Hyatt Sq BRLYHL DY5 ... 119 E5
Hyde Rd WNSFLD WV11 ... 24 D4
Hydes Rd DARL/WED WS10 ... 56 A5
HHTH/SAND B71 ... 71 G2
The Hyde HAG/WOL DY9 ... 136 B5
Hyett Wy TPTN/OCK DY4 ... 69 H1
Hylda Rd BFLD/HDSWWD B20 ... 90 B5
Hylstone Crs WNSFLD WV11 ... 24 D4
Hylton St WSNGN B18 ... 108 C4
Hyperion Dr
ETTPK/GDPK/PENN WV4 ... 51 G5
Hyperion Rd CBROM B36 ... 94 A5
KINVER DY7 ... 117 G4
Hyron Hall Rd ACGN B27 ... 146 C5
Hyssop Cl VAUX/NECH B7 ... 109 G4
Hytall Rd SHLY B90 ... 179 E3
Hythe Gv YDLY B25 ... 129 H4

I

Ibberton Rd
ALE/KHTH/YWD B14 ... 178 D2
Ibis Gdns KGSWFD DY6 ... 100 C3
Ibstock Dr STRBR DY8 ... 135 G3
Icknield Cl FOAKS/STRLY B74 ... 45 G4
Icknield Port Rd
LDYWD/EDGR B16 ... 125 G1
Icknield Sq LDYWD/EDGR B16 ... 126 A1
Icknield St HWK/WKHTH B38 ... 177 F5
WSNGN B18 ... 2 A2
Ida Rd WBROM B70 ... 87 H5
WSLW WS2 ... 41 G4
Idbury Rd KGSTG B44 ... 75 G4
Idmiston Cft
ALE/KHTH/YWD B14 ... 178 B3
Idonia Rd DUNHL/THL/PER WV6 ... 20 C5
Ilford Rd ERDW/GRVHL B23 ... 76 B5
Iliffe Wy HRBN B17 ... 142 B3
Ilkley Gv
CHWD/FDBR/MGN B37 ... 131 H2
Illey Cl NFLD/LBR B31 ... 174 B4
Illey La RMSLY B62 ... 156 A1
Illshaw COVEN WV9 ... 12 A4
Illshaw Heath Rd
HOCK/TIA B94 ... 194 D5
Ilmington Dr SCFLD/BOLD B73 ... 61 E5
Ilmington Rd SLYOAK B29 ... 158 B1
Ilsham Gv NFLD/LBR B31 ... 189 E2
Ilsley Rd ERDW/GRVHL B23 ... 92 C2
Imperial Ri CSHL/WTROR B46 ... 97 E4
Imperial Rd BORD B9 ... 128 C3
Impsley Cl CBROM B36 ... 112 D1
Ince Rd DARL/WED WS10 ... 55 E1
Incestre Dr GTB/HAM B43 ... 73 E2
Inchcape Av
BFLD/HDSWWD B20 ... 90 A3
Inchford Rd HIA/OLT B92 ... 165 G3
Inchlaggan Rd WOLVN WV10 ... 23 H4
Infantry Pl MGN/WHC B75 ... 63 G2
Ingatestone Dr STRBR DY8 ... 117 G1
Ingestre Cl BLOX/PEL WS3 ... 16 B4
Ingestre Dr GTB/HAM B43 ... 73 E2
Ingestre Rd HAG/WOL DY9 ... 136 D3
Inge St DIG/EDG B5 ... 126 D3
Ingestre Rd HLGN/YWD B28 ... 162 D3
WOLVN WV10 ... 23 E1
Ingham Wy HRBN B17 ... 124 B5
Ingleby Gdns
DUNHL/THL/PER WV6 ... 22 C5
Ingledew Cl WSLW WS2 ... 40 B2
Inglefield Rd STETCH B33 ... 130 B1
Inglemere Gv SLYOAK B29 ... 158 B3
Inglenook Dr
BFLD/HDSWWD B20 ... 90 B4
Ingleside Vls SPARK B11 * ... 145 E2
Ingleton Rd WASH/WDE B8 ... 111 E2
Inglewood Av BDMR/CCFT WV3 ... 36 B5
Inglewood Cl KGSWFD DY6 * ... 99 H4
Inglewood Gv
FOAKS/STRLY B74 ... 45 F4
Inglewood Rd SPARK B11 ... 145 E2
Ingoldsby Rd NFLD/LBR B31 ... 176 A2
Ingot Cl WSLW WS2 ... 27 F4
Ingram Gv ACGN B27 ... 146 A5
Ingram Pl BLOX/PEL WS3 ... 27 H1
Ingram Rd BLOX/PEL WS3 ... 27 H1
Inhedge St SEDG DY3 ... 83 G1
The Inhedge DUDN DY1 ... 84 C5
Inkberrow Rd HALE B63 ... 138 B5
Inkerman St VAUX/NECH B7 ... 109 H5
WOLVN WV10 ... 37 H2
Inland Rd ERDE/BCHGN B24 ... 93 F4
Innage Rd NFLD/LBR B31 ... 175 H1
The Innage HLYWD B47 ... 192 C3
Innsworth Dr CVALE B35 ... 94 C2
Inshaw Cl STETCH B33 ... 130 A1
Institute Rd
ALE/KHTH/YWD B14 ... 161 F2
Instone Rd HALE B63 ... 138 B4
Instow Cl SHHTH WV12 ... 25 H2
Insull Av ALE/KHTH/YWD B14 ... 178 D4
Intended St HALE B63 ... 120 C5
International Dr
LGN/SDN/BHAMAIR B26 ... 149 G3
International Sq
CHWD/FDBR/MGN B37 * ... 149 G1
Intown WSL WS1 ... 5 F3
Intown Rw WSL WS1 ... 5 F3
Inverclyde Rd
BFLD/HDSWWD B20 ... 90 A3
Inverness Rd NFLD/LBR B31 ... 175 F2
Inworth COVEN WV9 ... 12 B4
Ipsley Gv ERDW/GRVHL B23 ... 91 G1
Ipstones Av STETCH B33 ... 112 B5
Ipswich Crs PBAR/PBCH B42 ... 74 B4
Ireland Green Rd WBROM B70 ... 87 E3
Ireton Rd BFLD/HDSWWD B20 ... 90 A2
WOLVN WV10 ... 12 D4
Iris Cl DUDS DY2 ... 85 F5
SLYOAK B29 ... 158 D2
Iris Dr ALE/KHTH/YWD B14 ... 177 H1
Irnham Rd FOAKS/STRLY B74 ... 47 E3
Iron Bridge Wk HAG/WOL DY9 ... 152 D2
Iron La STETCH B33 ... 111 H5
Irvan Av WBROM B70 ... 86 D1
Irvine Cl BLOX/PEL WS3 ... 27 F3
Irvine Rd BLOX/PEL WS3 ... 27 F2
Irving Cl SEDG DY3 ... 82 C2
Irving Rd HIA/OLT B92 ... 148 C3
TPTN/OCK DY4 ... 69 G2
Irving St EDG B15 ... 126 D3
Irwin Av RBRY B45 ... 188 C2
Isaac Walton Pl WBROM B70 ... 70 C4
Isbourne Wy BORD B9 ... 127 H1
Isis Gv CBROM B36 ... 113 H1
WLNHL WV13 ... 40 A3
Island Rd HDSW B21 ... 89 E5
Islington HALE B63 ... 138 C3
Islington Rw EDG B15 ... 126 B3
Ismere Rd ERDE/BCHGN B24 ... 93 F4
Itchen Gv DUNHL/THL/PER WV6 ... 34 C2
Ithon Gv HWK/WKHTH B38 ... 176 C5
Ivanhoe Rd BKHL/PFLD WV2 ... 52 D2
GTB/HAM B43 ... 59 F5
Ivanhoe St DUDS DY2 ... 102 A2
Ivatt Cl RUSH/SHEL WS4 ... 28 D3
Iverley Rd HALE B63 ... 139 E4
Iverley Wk HAG/WOL DY9 ... 135 H5
Ivor Rd SPARK B11 ... 144 D3
Ivy Av BHTH/HG B12 ... 144 C2
Ivybridge Gv PBAR/PBCH B42 ... 90 C3
Ivy Cft COVEN WV9 ... 11 H4
Ivydale Av
LGN/SDN/BHAMAIR B26 ... 148 A2
Ivyfield Rd ERDW/GRVHL B23 ... 91 H1
Ivy Gv BRWNH WS8 ... 19 G3
WSNGN B18 ... 107 G5
Ivyhouse La BILS/COS WV14 ... 68 B3
Ivyhouse Rd HWK/WKHTH B38 ... 176 A5
Ivy House Rd OLDBY B69 ... 104 B3
Ivy La CBHAMNE B4 ... 127 G2
RMSLY B62 ... 154 D5
Ivy Lodge Cl
CHWD/FDBR/MGN B37 ... 132 A4
Ivy Rd BVILLE B30 ... 160 A4
DUDN DY1 ... 84 A2
HDSW B21 ... 108 A2
SCFLD/BOLD B73 ... 76 D2
TPTN/OCK DY4 ... 69 F4
Ivy Wy SHLY B90 ... 194 A2
Izons La WBROM B70 ... 87 E5
Izons Rd WBROM B70 ... 87 G3

J

Jacey Rd LDYWD/EDGR B16 ... 125 F2
SHLY B90 ... 180 B1
Jackdaw Cl SEDG DY3 ... 67 E1
Jackdaw Dr CBROM B36 ... 114 A1
Jack Hayward Wy WOLV WV1 ... 7 F1
Jack Holden Av BILS/COS WV14 ... 68 A1
Jackson Cl LGLYGN/QTN B68 ... 105 F4
SPARK B11 * ... 127 H5
TPTN/OCK DY4 ... 69 H2
WOLVN WV10 ... 13 G1
Jackson Dr SMTHWKW B67 ... 105 H4
Jackson Rd WASH/WDE B8 ... 110 D5
Jackson St
DUNHL/THL/PER WV6 ... 36 D1
HAG/WOL DY9 ... 136 C2
LGLYGN/QTN B68 ... 105 F5
Jackson Wk CVALE B35 ... 94 C4
Jackson Wy RIDG/WDGT B32 ... 140 A2
Jacmar Crs SMTHWKW B67 ... 106 A3
Jacobean La DOR/KN B93 ... 183 F4
Jacoby Pl EDG B15 ... 143 G2
Jaffray Crs ERDE/BCHGN B24 ... 92 D3
Jaffray Rd ERDE/BCHGN B24 ... 92 D3
Jakeman Rd BHTH/HG B12 ... 144 A2
James Bridge Cl WSLW WS2 * ... 56 B1
James Cl DARL/WED WS10 ... 55 H1
SMTHWKW B67 ... 106 C4
James Dee Cl BRLYHL DY5 ... 119 H3
James Eaton Cl
HHTH/SAND B71 ... 87 G1
Jameson Rd AST/WIT B6 ... 110 A1
Jameson St
DUNHL/THL/PER WV6 ... 36 D1
James Rd CSHL/WTROR B46 ... 115 F1
GTB/HAM B43 ... 73 G4
SPARK B11 ... 145 H1
James Samuel Pl
BHTH/HG B12 ... 127 F5
James Scott Rd HALE B63 ... 137 E1
James St BILS/COS WV14 ... 54 A2
CBHAMW B1 ... 2 D3
WLNHL WV13 ... 39 G3
James Turner St WSNGN B18 ... 107 G3
James Watt Dr
BFLD/HDSWWD B20 ... 108 B1
James Watt Queensway
CBHAMNE B4 ... 3 H3
James Watt St HHTH/SAND B71 ... 71 F3
Jane Lane Cl WSLW WS2 ... 40 D1
Janice Gv ALE/KHTH/YWD B14 ... 178 D1
Janine Av WNSFLD WV11 ... 25 E3
Jaques Cl CSHL/WTROR B46 ... 96 B4
Jardine Rd AST/WIT B6 ... 91 F5
Jarvis Crs OLDBY B69 ... 105 E5
Jarvis Rd ERDW/GRVHL B23 ... 76 D5
Jarvis Wy ERDE/BCHGN B24 ... 92 D5
VAUX/NECH B7 ... 110 C1
Jasmin Cft
ALE/KHTH/YWD B14 ... 178 A2
Jasmine Cl COVEN WV9 ... 11 H4
Jasmine Gv CDSL WV8 ... 10 D4
Jasmine Rd DUDS DY2 ... 85 F5
Jasmine Wy DARL/WED WS10 ... 55 F1
Jason Rd HAG/WOL DY9 ... 136 D3
Jayne Cl HHTH/SAND B71 ... 72 A2
WNSFLD WV11 ... 24 D3
Jay Rd KGSWFD DY6 ... 99 H1
Jays Av TPTN/OCK DY4 ... 85 H2
Jayshaw Av GTB/HAM B43 ... 73 G3
Jean Dr TPTN/OCK DY4 ... 70 B5
Jeavons Pl BILS/COS WV14 ... 53 G3
Jedburgh Av
DUNHL/THL/PER WV6 ... 34 C1
Jeddo St BKHL/PFLD WV2 ... 6 E7
Jeffcock Rd BDMR/CCFT WV3 ... 36 C5
Jefferson Cl HHTH/SAND B71 ... 71 F3
Jeffrey Av
ETTPK/GDPK/PENN WV4 ... 52 D2
Jeffrey Rd BLKHTH/ROWR B65 ... 122 C1
Jeffs Av BKHL/PFLD WV2 ... 37 F5
Jenkins Cl BILS/COS WV14 ... 53 G3
Jenkinson Rd DARL/WED WS10 ... 70 B2
Jenkins St SMHTH B10 ... 128 A4
Jenks Av WOLVN WV10 ... 23 G2
Jenks Rd WMBN WV5 ... 80 D1
Jennens Rd CBHAMNE B4 ... 3 K3
Jenner Cl WSLW WS2 ... 26 D4
Jenner Rd WSLW WS2 ... 26 D4
Jenner St BKHL/PFLD WV2 ... 7 J6
Jennings St CDYHTH B64 ... 121 F2
Jenny Cl BILS/COS WV14 ... 69 E2
Jenny Walkers La
DUNHL/THL/PER WV6 ... 34 B5
Jephcott Rd WASH/WDE B8 ... 129 E1
Jephson Dr
LGN/SDN/BHAMAIR B26 ... 130 B5
Jeremy Gv HIA/OLT B92 ... 147 H3
Jeremy Rd
ETTPK/GDPK/PENN WV4 ... 52 A3
Jerome Rd CSCFLD/WYGN B72 ... 62 D4
WSLW WS2 ... 41 F4
Jerrard Dr MGN/WHC B75 ... 62 C3
Jerrard Ms MGN/WHC B75 * ... 62 C3
Jerry's La ERDW/GRVHL B23 ... 76 B4
Jersey Cft CBROM B36 ... 114 B3
Jersey Rd WASH/WDE B8 ... 110 B5
Jervis Cl BRLYHL DY5 ... 101 E2
Jervis Crs FOAKS/STRLY B74 ... 46 B2
Jervis Pk FOAKS/STRLY B74 ... 46 A1
Jervis Ter HDSW B21 * ... 107 F1
Jervoise Dr NFLD/LBR B31 ... 158 D5
Jervoise La HHTH/SAND B71 ... 72 A2
Jervoise Rd SLYOAK B29 ... 158 B1
Jervoise St WBROM B70 ... 87 E2
Jesmond Gv ERDE/BCHGN B24 ... 93 H2
Jessel Rd WSLW WS2 ... 4 A2
Jessie Rd ALDR WS9 ... 30 A1
Jesson Cl WSL WS1 ... 57 G1
Jesson Rd MGN/WHC B75 ... 63 G3
SEDG DY3 ... 68 A5
WSL WS1 ... 5 G6
Jesson St WBROM B70 ... 88 A4
Jevons Rd SCFLD/BOLD B73 ... 61 E5
Jevon St BILS/COS WV14 ... 68 C3
Jew's La DUDN DY1 ... 83 G2
Jiggins La RIDG/WDGT B32 ... 157 G2
Jill Av GTB/HAM B43 ... 73 E2
Jillcot Rd HIA/OLT B92 ... 147 H4
Jinnah Cl BHTH/HG B12 ... 127 F4
Joan St BKHL/PFLD WV2 ... 52 C2
Jockey Fld SEDG DY3 ... 67 G5
Jockey La DARL/WED WS10 ... 56 A4
Jockey Rd SCFLD/BOLD B73 ... 76 B1
Joeys La CDSL WV8 ... 11 E4
John Bosco Cl HHTH/SAND B71 ... 71 F4
John Bright Cl TPTN/OCK DY4 ... 69 F3
John Bright St CBHAM B2 ... 3 F6
John Fletcher Cl
DARL/WED WS10 ... 56 B4
John Harper St WLNHL WV13 ... 39 H3
John Kempe Wy BHTH/HG B12 ... 127 G5
John Riley Dr SHHTH WV12 ... 26 A2
John Rd RMSLY B62 ... 139 H3
Johns Gv GTB/HAM B43 ... 73 E3
John's La OLDBY B69 ... 86 A4
TPTN/OCK DY4 ... 85 H2
Johnson Av WNSFLD WV11 ... 25 F3
Johnson Cl CBROM B36 ... 111 G3
DARL/WED WS10 ... 55 F3
SPARK B11 ... 145 E2
Johnson Dr CVALE B35 ... 94 B3
Johnson Pl BILS/COS WV14 ... 54 B1
Johnson Rd DARL/WED WS10 ... 55 F3
DARL/WED WS10 ... 71 G1
ERDW/GRVHL B23 ... 92 D1
SHHTH WV12 ... 26 B3
Johnsons Bridge Rd

Johnsons Gv LGLYGN/QTN B68 ...123 C4
Johnson St BILS/COS WV14 ...67 H2
BKHL/PFLD WV2 ...37 F5
VAUX/NECH B7 ...110 A3
Johnstone St LOZ/NWT B19 ...108 D1
Johnston St WBROM B70 ...87 H5
John St BKHL/PFLD WV2 ...53 E2
BLKHTH/ROWR B65 ...122 A3
BRLYHL DY5 ...101 F5
LOZ/NWT B19 ...108 B2
OLDBY B69 ...105 E2
STRBR DY8 ...118 B3
WBROM B70 ...86 D1
WLNHL WV13 ...39 G4
WSLW WS2 ...4 D1
John St North HHTH/SAND B71 ...87 F1
Joiners Cft HIA/OLT B92 ...165 G2
Joinings Bank
LGLYGN/QTN B68 ...105 F5
Jones Field Crs WOLV WV1 ...38 B3
Jones Rd SHHTH WV12 ...26 B1
WOLVN WV10 ...23 E4
Jones Wood Cl
WALM/CURD B76 ...78 B4
Jonquil Cl ERDW/GRVHL B23 ...76 A4
Jordan Cl MGN/WHC B75 ...47 F4
SMTHWK B66 ...106 D4
Jordan Leys TPTN/OCK DY4 ...85 H1
Jordan Pl BILS/COS WV14 ...54 A5
Jordan Rd MGN/WHC B75 ...47 F4
Jordan Wy ALDR WS9 ...30 B1
Joseph St OLDBY B69 ...104 D3
Josiah Houses BILS/COS WV14 * ...68 C3
Josiah Rd NFLD/LBR B31 ...174 D3
Jowett's La HHTH/SAND B71 ...71 F3
Joyberry Dr STRBR DY8 ...135 F4
Joynson St DARL/WED WS10 ...55 G3
Jubilee Av HHTH/SAND B71 ...71 F4
Jubilee Cl BLOX/PEL WS3 ...28 A4
Jubilee Gdns ERDW/GRVHL B23 ...75 H4
Jubilee Rd BILS/COS WV14 ...54 C4
RBRY B45 ...173 G3
TPTN/OCK DY4 ...69 G4
Jubilee St HHTH/SAND B71 ...71 H4
Judge Cl OLDBY B69 ...105 E2
Judge Rd BRLYHL DY5 ...119 H5
Julia Av ERDE/BCHGN B24 ...94 B2
Julia Gdns HHTH/SAND B71 ...72 B3
Julian Cl WOLV WV1 ...38 B3
Julian Rd WOLV WV1 ...38 B3
Julie Cft BILS/COS WV14 ...69 E2
Juliet Rd RMSLY B62 ...139 G3
Julius Dr CSHL/WTROR B46 ...97 F5
Junction Rd BKHL/PFLD WV2 ...53 F1
HDSW B21 ...107 E1
STRBR DY8 ...118 A4
STRBR DY8 ...135 H3
Junction St DUDS DY2 ...102 B1
OLDBY B69 ...86 C5
WSL WS1 ...56 D1
Junction St South OLDBY B69 ...105 E4
The Junction STRBR DY8 ...118 A4
June Cft
LGN/SDN/BHAMAIR B26 ...148 B2
Juniper Cl ACGN B27 ...146 B2
Juniper Dr DSYBK/YTR WS5 ...57 H4
WALM/CURD B76 ...78 C4
Juniper Ri HALE B63 ...137 G2
Jury Rd BRLYHL DY5 ...119 H5
Jutland Rd MOS/BIL B13 ...161 H3

K

Karen Wy BRLYHL DY5 ...119 F4
Katherine Rd SMTHWKW B67 ...124 B2
Kathleen Rd CSCFLD/WYGN B72 ...62 C4
YDLY B25 ...129 G5
Katie Rd SLYOAK B29 ...159 G1
Kayne Cl KGSWFD DY6 ...99 G2
Keanscott Dr LGLYGN/QTN B68 ...105 G5
Keasdon Gv WLNHL WV13 ...40 A2
Keating Gdns MGN/WHC B75 ...47 E1
Keats Av SMTHH B10 ...128 B5
Keats Cl FOAKS/STRLY B74 ...32 D4
SEDG DY3 ...82 C1
STRBR DY8 ...118 C4
Keats Dr BILS/COS WV14 ...68 D1
Keats Gv ACGN B27 ...163 F1
WOLVN WV10 ...24 A2
Keats Rd BLOX/PEL WS3 ...28 A3
SHHTH WV12 ...26 C3
WOLVN WV10 ...24 A1
Keble Gv
LGN/SDN/BHAMAIR B26 ...147 H1
WSL WS1 ...57 G1
Kedleston Cl BLOX/PEL WS3 * ...16 C4
Kedleston Rd HLGN/YWD B28 ...162 D4
Keel Dr MOS/BIL B13 ...162 B1
Keeley St BORD B9 ...127 H2
Keelinge St TPTN/OCK DY4 ...85 H1
Keen St SMTHWK B66 ...107 E5
Keepers Cl ALDR WS9 ...19 F4
CSHL/WTROR B46 ...115 G5
KGSWFD DY6 ...99 F1
Keepers Gate Cl MGN/WHC B75 ...62 C1
Keepers La CDSL WV8 ...21 E2
Keepers Rd FOAKS/STRLY B74 ...32 A5
Keer Ct BORD B9 * ...127 H1
Kegworth Rd ERDW/GRVHL B23 ...92 A5
Keir Pl STRBR DY8 ...118 A4
Keir Rd DARL/WED WS10 ...71 C1
Kelby Cl NFLD/LBR B31 ...175 E2
Kelby Rd NFLD/LBR B31 ...175 E1
Keldy Cl DUNHL/THL/PER WV6 ...22 B5
Kelfield Av HRBN B17 ...141 H3
Kelia Dr SMTHWKW B67 ...106 B3
Kellett Rd VAUX/NECH B7 ...109 G5
Kelling Cl BRLYHL DY5 * ...119 E4
Kellington Cl WASH/WDE B8 ...110 D5
Kelmarsh Dr SOLH B91 ...181 H4
Kelmscott Rd HRBN B17 ...124 D5
Kelsall Cl WOLV WV1 ...38 B3
Kelsall Cft CBHAMW B1 ...2 A4
Kelsey Cl VAUX/NECH B7 * ...109 H5
Kelso Gdns
DUNHL/THL/PER WV6 ...34 B1
Kelsull Cft
CHWD/FDBR/MGN B37 ...132 A2
Kelton Ct EDG B15 ...126 A5
Kelvedon Gv SOLH B91 ...182 A1
Kelverdale Gv
ALE/KHTH/YWD B14 ...177 G1
Kelverley Gv HHTH/SAND B71 ...72 C2
Kelvin Pl WSLW WS2 ...27 F4
Kelvin Rd NFLD/LBR B31 ...175 G4
WSLW WS2 ...27 E4
Kelvin Wy WBROM B70 ...87 G5
Kelway Av GTB/HAM B43 ...59 F5
Kelwood Dr HALE B63 ...138 B2
Kelynmead Rd STETCH B33 ...130 C2
Kemberton Cl BDMR/CCFT WV3 ...35 G4
Kemberton Rd
BDMR/CCFT WV3 ...35 G4
SLYOAK B29 ...141 G5
Kemble Cl SHHTH WV12 ...40 B1
Kemble Cft DIG/EDG B5 ...127 E5
Kemble Dr CVALE B35 ...94 C3
Kemelstowe Crs HALE B63 ...154 C2
Kemerton Wy SHLY B90 ...195 F3
Kempe Rd STETCH B33 ...112 C5
Kempsey Cl HALE B63 ...138 A3
HIA/OLT B92 ...147 F4
OLDBY B69 ...104 B5
Kempsey Covert
HWK/WKHTH B38 ...190 C1
Kempson Av CSCFLD/WYGN B72 ...77 G2
HHTH/SAND B71 ...87 F1
Kempson Rd CBROM B36 ...112 B1
Kempsons Gv BILS/COS WV14 ...53 F5
Kempthorne Av WOLVN WV10 ...23 G2
Kempthorne Gdns
BLOX/PEL WS3 ...16 C5
Kempthorne Rd BILS/COS WV14 ...54 B2
Kempton Park Rd CBROM B36 ...111 H1
Kempton Wy STRBR DY8 ...135 E4
Kemsey Dr BILS/COS WV14 ...54 B4
Kemshead Av NFLD/LBR B31 ...175 E5
Kemsley Rd
ALE/KHTH/YWD B14 ...178 B3
Kendal Av CSHL/WTROR B46 ...115 F2
RBRY B45 ...188 B1
Kendal Cl DUNHL/THL/PER WV6 ...22 B4
Kendal Ct ALDR WS9 * ...19 F3
Kendal Gv HIA/OLT B92 ...165 H2
Kendall Ri KGSWFD DY6 ...100 B4
Kendal Ri DUNHL/THL/PER WV6 ...22 B4
LGLYGN/QTN B68 ...123 F1
Kendal Rise Rd RBRY B45 ...188 B1
Kendal Rd SPARK B11 ...127 H5
Kendrick Av BKDE/SHDE B34 ...113 F5
Kendrick Cl HIA/OLT B92 ...165 H4
Kendrick Pl BILS/COS WV14 ...54 C4
Kendrick Rd BILS/COS WV14 ...54 C4
ERDE/BCHGN B24 ...94 B1
WOLVN WV10 ...23 G4
Kendricks Rd DARL/WED WS10 ...55 H1
Kendrick St DARL/WED WS10 ...56 A5
Kenelm Rd BILS/COS WV14 ...68 C2
LGLYGN/QTN B68 ...123 E1
SCFLD/BOLD B73 ...62 B4
SMTHH B10 ...128 C4
Kenelm's Ct RMSLY B62 ...155 G5
Kenilworth Cl
FOAKS/STRLY B74 ...47 E5
STRBR DY8 ...117 H2
TPTN/OCK DY4 ...84 D2
Kenilworth Ct DUDN DY1 ...101 H2
EDG B15 * ...125 H4
Kenilworth Crs
ETTPK/GDPK/PENN WV4 ...52 C4
WSLW WS2 ...41 E1
Kenilworth Rd
BFLD/HDSWWD B20 ...91 E5
DOR/KN B93 ...197 H2
DUNHL/THL/PER WV6 ...34 D1
LGLYGN/QTN B68 ...123 H4
RCOVN/BALC/EX CV7 ...151 E5
Kenley Gv BVILLE B30 ...177 E3
Kenley Wy SHLY B90 ...180 D1
Kenmare Wy WNSFLD WV11 ...38 C1
Kenmure Rd STETCH B33 ...131 E5
Kennedy Crs DARL/WED WS10 ...55 E1
SEDG DY3 ...83 F2
Kennedy Cft
LGN/SDN/BHAMAIR B26 ...130 C5
Kennedy Gv BVILLE B30 ...160 B4
Kennedy Rd WOLVN WV10 ...7 H2
Kennerley Rd
LGN/SDN/BHAMAIR B26 ...146 D1
Kennet Cl BRWNH WS8 ...8 C2
Kennet Gv CBROM B36 ...113 H1
Kenneth Gv ERDW/GRVHL B23 ...91 G1
Kennford Cl OLDBY B69 ...104 A3
Kennington Rd WOLVN WV10 ...23 H5
Kenrick Cft CVALE B35 ...94 B4
Kenrick Wy SMTHWK B66 ...106 B1
Kensington Av BTHH/HG B12 ...144 C3
Kensington Dr
FOAKS/STRLY B74 ...32 D5
Kensington Gdns STRBR DY8 ...117 G3
Kensington Rd SHHTH WV12 ...25 H3
SLYOAK B29 ...160 A1
Kensington St LOZ/NWT B19 ...108 D3
Kenswick Dr HALE B63 ...138 C5
Kent Av WSLW WS2 ...41 F2
Kent Cl ALDR WS9 ...30 B1
BLOX/PEL WS3 ...28 A5
HHTH/SAND B71 ...71 F4
Kentish Rd HDSW B21 ...107 E1
Kenton Av
DUNHL/THL/PER WV6 ...36 B1
Kent Pl DUDS DY2 ...102 A3
Kent Rd BKHL/PFLD WV2 ...52 C1
DARL/WED WS10 ...56 D4
RBRY B45 ...173 H4
RMSLY B62 ...139 G1
STRBR DY8 ...117 H4
Kent's Cl HIA/OLT B92 ...147 F4
Kent St DIG/EDG B5 ...127 E4
SEDG DY3 ...83 G1
WSLW WS2 ...28 A5
Kent St North WSNGN B18 ...107 H4
Kenward Cft HRBN B17 ...124 B5
Kenway HLYWD B47 ...192 C1
Kenwick Rd HRBN B17 ...141 H3
Kenwood Rd BORD B9 ...129 F2
Kenyon Cl STRBR DY8 ...135 G1
Kenyon St CBHAMNW B3 ...2 D2
Kerby Rd ERDW/GRVHL B23 ...92 A2
Keresley Cl SOLH B91 ...165 E5
Keresley Gv SLYOAK B29 ...141 F5
Kernthorpe Rd
ALE/KHTH/YWD B14 ...177 G1
Kerr Dr TPTN/OCK DY4 ...69 E3
Kerridge Cl COVEN WV9 ...12 A5
Kerry Cl BRLYHL DY5 ...101 E5
NFLD/LBR B31 ...158 B4
Kersley Gdns WNSFLD WV11 ...25 F4
Kerswell Dr SHLY B90 ...195 G3
Kesterton Rd FOAKS/STRLY B74 ...32 C5
Kesteven Cl EDG B15 ...143 F1
Kesteven Rd HHTH/SAND B71 ...71 G4
Keston Rd KGSTG B44 ...60 B4
Kestrel Av YDLY B25 ...129 F4
Kestrel Cl ERDW/GRVHL B23 ...76 B5
Kestrel Dr FOAKS/STRLY B74 ...32 D5
Kestrel Gv SHHTH WV12 ...26 A2
SLYOAK B29 ...159 F2
Kestrel Ri DUNHL/THL/PER WV6 ...22 B3
Kestrel Rd DUDN DY1 ...102 A1
HALE B63 ...120 B5
LGLYGN/QTN B68 ...122 D2
Keswick Dr KGSWFD DY6 ...99 H3
Keswick Gv FOAKS/STRLY B74 ...45 F3
Keswick Rd HIA/OLT B92 ...147 F3
Ketley Cft BTHH/HG B12 ...127 F5
Ketley Flds KGSWFD DY6 ...100 C4
Ketley Hill Rd DUDN DY1 ...101 H1
Ketley Rd KGSWFD DY6 ...100 B3
Kettlebrook Rd SHLY B90 ...195 H2
Kettlehouse Rd KGSTG B44 ...60 B5
Kettlesbank Rd SEDG DY3 * ...83 E4
Kettlewell Wy
CHWD/FDBR/MGN B37 ...131 H2
Ketton Gv STETCH B33 ...131 F5
Kew Cl CHWD/FDBR/MGN B37 ...131 H1
Kew Dr DUDN DY1 ...84 A4
Kew Gdns STETCH B33 ...129 H3
Kewstoke Cl SHHTH WV12 ...25 H1
Kewstoke Cft NFLD/LBR B31 ...158 A4
Kewstoke Rd SHHTH WV12 ...26 A1
Keyes Dr KGSWFD DY6 ...81 H5
Key Hl WSNGN B18 ...108 B4
Key Hill Circ WSNGN B18 ...108 B4
Key Hill Dr WSNGN B18 ...108 C4
Keynell Covert BVILLE B30 ...177 G3
Keynes Dr BILS/COS WV14 ...54 A2
Keys Crs HHTH/SAND B71 ...71 G5
Keyse Rd MGN/WHC B75 ...63 F1
Keyte Cl TPTN/OCK DY4 ...85 G1
The Keyway WLNHL WV13 ...39 G5
Keyworth Cl TPTN/OCK DY4 ...85 H1
Khyber Cl DARL/WED WS10 ...40 A5
Kidd Cft DARL/WED WS10 ...70 A1
Kidderminster Rd
HAG/WOL DY9 ...152 D5
KGSWFD DY6 ...99 F2
Kidderminster Rd South
KIDD DY10 ...169 E2
Kielder Cl DSYBK/YTR WS5 ...58 A5
Kielder Gdns HAG/WOL DY9 ...152 D1
Kier's Bridge Cl TPTN/OCK DY4 ...85 G3
Kilburn Dr KGSWFD DY6 ...82 A5
Kilburn Gv KGSTG B44 ...60 B5
Kilburn Pl DUDS DY2 ...102 D3
Kilburn Rd KGSTG B44 ...60 B5
Kilby Av LDYWD/EDGR B16 ...126 A2
Kilbys Gv BFLD/HDSWWD B20 ...89 H4
Kilcote Rd SHLY B90 ...179 E3
Kilmet Wk SMTHWK B67 * ...106 B4
Kilmore Cft CBROM B36 ...94 A5
Kilmorie Rd ACGN B27 ...146 C2
Kiln La SHLY B90 ...193 H4
YDLY B25 ...146 B1
Kilsby Gv SOLH B91 ...182 A5
Kilvert Rd DARL/WED WS10 ...71 F1
Kimberley Av WASH/WDE B8 ...110 C4
Kimberley Cl FOAKS/STRLY B74 ...45 G3
Kimberley Pl BILS/COS WV14 ...68 B4
Kimberley Rd HIA/OLT B92 ...147 G5
SMTHWK B66 ...106 C2
Kimberley St BDMR/CCFT WV3 ...6 B6
Kimble Gv ERDE/BCHGN B24 ...93 H3
Kimbley Ri HHTH/SAND B71 ...71 E4
Kimpton Cl
ALE/KHTH/YWD B14 ...178 A3
Kimsan Cft FOAKS/STRLY B74 ...60 C1
Kinchford Cl SOLH B91 ...181 H5
Kineton Cft RIDG/WDGT B32 ...157 H2
Kineton Green Rd HIA/OLT B92 ...163 H2
Kineton Ri SEDG DY3 ...67 E1
Kineton Rd RBRY B45 ...187 G1
SCFLD/BOLD B73 ...76 C2
Kinfare Dr
DUNHL/THL/PER WV6 ...35 F1
Kinfare Ri SEDG DY3 ...83 G2
King Charles Av WSLW WS2 ...40 C3
King Charles Cl KGSTG B44 ...75 H1
King Charles Rd RMSLY B62 ...139 H3
King Edmund St DUDN DY1 ...84 B4
King Edward Rd MOS/BIL B13 ...144 B4
King Edwards Cl
BFLD/HDSWWD B20 * ...108 B1
King Edwards Gdns
BFLD/HDSWWD B20 * ...108 B2
King Edward's Rd CBHAMW B1 ...2 B5
King Edward's Rw
BKHL/PFLD WV2 * ...37 E5
King Edward's Sq
SCFLD/BOLD B73 ...62 C3
King Edward St
DARL/WED WS10 ...55 F3
Kingfield Rd SHLY B90 ...179 E3
Kingfisher Cl
LGN/SDN/BHAMAIR B26 ...147 G1
SEDG DY3 ...67 E1
Kingfisher Dr CBROM B36 ...114 A1
STRBR DY8 ...134 C3
Kingfisher Gv SHHTH WV12 ...25 H2
Kingfisher Rd
ERDW/GRVHL B23 ...76 A4
Kingfisher Veiw STETCH B33 ...112 C4
Kingfisher Wy SLYOAK B29 ...159 F2
King George Crs
RUSH/SHEL WS4 ...28 D4
King George Pl RUSH/SHEL WS4 ...28 D4
King George Vi Av
DSYBK/YTR WS5 ...43 E5
Kingham Cl SEDG DY3 ...83 E4
Kingham Covert
ALE/KHTH/YWD B14 ...177 H3
King's Av OLDBY B69 ...85 H4
Kingsbridge Rd
RIDG/WDGT B32 ...157 H1
Kingsbridge Wk SMTHWK B66 ...106 D4
Kingsbrook Dr SOLH B91 ...181 H5
Kingsbury Av ERDE/BCHGN B24 ...93 H3
Kingsbury Cl RUSH/SHEL WS4 ...42 D1
WALM/CURD B76 ...95 F1
Kingsbury Rd ERDE/BCHGN B24 ...92 C4
TPTN/OCK DY4 ...69 G3
WALM/CURD B76 ...95 E1
Kingsclere Wk
ETTPK/GDPK/PENN WV4 ...50 C1
Kingscliff Rd SMTHH B10 ...129 E4
Kings Cl ALE/KHTH/YWD B14 ...160 C4
Kingscote Rd DOR/KN B93 ...198 C1
EDG B15 ...125 F5
King's Ct
CHWD/FDBR/MGN B37 ...133 E3
STRBR DY8 ...135 E2
Kings Cft CBROM B36 ...113 H2
LGN/SDN/BHAMAIR B26 ...147 G2
Kingscroft Cl FOAKS/STRLY B74 ...45 G5
Kingscroft Rd FOAKS/STRLY B74 ...60 C1
Kingsdene Av STRBR DY8 ...99 G5
Kingsdown Av PBAR/PBCH B42 ...73 H5
Kingsdown Rd NFLD/LBR B31 ...158 A1
Kingsfield Rd
ALE/KHTH/YWD B14 ...161 E2
Kingsford Cl CBROM B36 ...95 F5
Kingsford Nouveau
KGSWFD DY6 ...100 C4
Kings Gdn BVILLE B30 ...176 C1
Kings Green Av
HWK/WKHTH B38 ...176 D3
Kingshayes Rd ALDR WS9 ...19 H5
Kingshill Dr HWK/WKHTH B38 ...176 D3
King's Hill Fld DARL/WED WS10 ...55 G3
Kingshurst Rd NFLD/LBR B31 ...175 G2
SHLY B90 ...179 H4
Kingshurst Wy
CHWD/FDBR/MGN B37 ...113 H4
Kingsland Dr DOR/KN B93 ...196 C5
Kingsland Rd KGSTG B44 ...60 A4
WOLV WV1 ...6 C1
Kingslea Rd SOLH B91 ...181 E3
Kingsleigh Cft MGN/WHC B75 ...47 F3
Kingsleigh Dr CBROM B36 ...112 C1
Kingsleigh Rd
BFLD/HDSWWD B20 ...90 B4
Kingsley Av
DUNHL/THL/PER WV6 ...35 F1
Kingsley Ct YDLY B25 * ...130 A4
Kingsley Gdns CDSL WV8 ...10 A4
Kingsley Gv SEDG DY3 ...82 C1
Kingsley Rd BTHH/HG B12 ...144 C2
BVILLE B30 ...176 B1
KGSWFD DY6 ...99 G4
Kingsley St DUDS DY2 ...102 C4
WSLW WS2 ...56 B1
Kingslow Av
ETTPK/GDPK/PENN WV4 ...50 D2
King's Meadow HAG/WOL DY9 ...170 C3
Kingsmere Cl ERDE/BCHGN B24 ...92 C4
Kings Mill Cl DARL/WED WS10 ...55 G3
Kings Rd ALE/KHTH/YWD B14 ...160 C4
ERDW/GRVHL B23 ...92 A2
KGSTG B44 ...60 A5
RUSH/SHEL WS4 ...29 E4
SEDG DY3 ...67 G3
SPARK B11 ...146 A2
Kings Sq BILS/COS WV14 * ...68 A3
Kings Street Prec
DARL/WED WS10 ...55 F2
Kingstanding Rd KGSTG B44 ...75 F1
Kings Ter ALE/KHTH/YWD B14 ...160 C4
Kingsthorpe Rd
ALE/KHTH/YWD B14 ...178 C2
Kingston Rd BORD B9 ...127 H3
Kingston Rw CBHAMW B1 ...2 C5
Kingston Wy KGSWFD DY6 ...99 G2
King St ALDR WS9 ...19 F5
BILS/COS WV14 ...54 A5
BILS/COS WV14 ...68 A3
BRLYHL DY5 ...119 H4
CDYHTH B64 ...121 F3
DARL/WED WS10 ...70 C1
DUDS DY2 ...84 C5
HAG/WOL DY9 ...136 D3
HALE B63 ...138 C3
SMTHWK B66 ...106 D2
SPARK B11 ...144 C1
STRBR DY8 ...135 E1
WLNHL WV13 ...39 H3
WOLV WV1 ...7 F4
WSL WS1 ...56 D1
King Street Pas BRLYHL DY5 ...120 A4
DUDS DY2 ...84 D5
Kingsway LGLYGN/QTN B68 ...123 F5
STRBR DY8 ...117 H4
WNSFLD WV11 ...15 E3
WOLVN WV10 ...24 A4
Kingsway Av TPTN/OCK DY4 ...69 G3
Kingsway Dr HWK/WKHTH B38 ...176 D3
Kingsway North ALDR WS9 * ...29 G4
Kingsway Rd WOLVN WV10 ...24 A4
Kingsway South ALDR WS9 * ...29 G4
Kingsway Ter WNSFLD WV11 * ...15 E3
Kingswear Av
DUNHL/THL/PER WV6 ...34 D2
Kingswinford Rd BRLYHL DY5 ...101 G2
Kingswood Cl SHLY B90 ...180 D4
Kingswood Cft VAUX/NECH B7 ...110 A2
Kingswood Dr BVILLE B30 ...177 G2
FOAKS/STRLY B74 ...60 B4
Kingswood Gdns
BDMR/CCFT WV3 ...51 F2
Kingswood Rd MOS/BIL B13 ...144 C3
NFLD/LBR B31 ...189 F2
STRBR DY8 ...99 G5
Kingswood Ter YDLY B25 * ...129 F5
Kington Cl SHHTH WV12 ...25 H2
Kington Gdns
CHWD/FDBR/MGN B37 ...131 H2
Kington Wy STETCH B33 ...130 A3
King William St STRBR DY8 ...118 B4
Kiniths Crs HHTH/SAND B71 ...88 A2
Kiniths Wy HHTH/SAND B71 ...88 A2
RMSLY B62 ...122 C3
Kinlet Cl BDMR/CCFT WV3 ...35 E5
Kinlet Gv NFLD/LBR B31 ...176 A3
Kinloch Dr DUDN DY1 ...83 H3
Kinnerley St WSL WS1 ...5 H5
Kinnersley Crs OLDBY B69 ...104 B4
Kinnerton Crs SLYOAK B29 ...141 F5
Kinross Crs GTB/HAM B43 ...59 F4
Kinsey Gv ALE/KHTH/YWD B14 ...178 B1
Kinsham Dr SOLH B91 ...181 H5
Kintore Cft RIDG/WDGT B32 ...157 F3
Kintyre Cl RBRY B45 ...173 G4
Kinver Av SHHTH WV12 ...25 H5
Kinver Crs ALDR WS9 ...30 C1
Kinver Cft BTHH/HG B12 ...144 A1
WALM/CURD B76 ...78 B3
Kinver Dr
ETTPK/GDPK/PENN WV4 ...50 C3
HAG/WOL DY9 ...153 E3
Kinver Rd NFLD/LBR B31 ...176 B3
Kinver St STRBR DY8 ...117 H3
Kinwarton Cl
LGN/SDN/BHAMAIR B26 ...146 D1
Kipling Av BILS/COS WV14 ...68 B2
Kipling Cl TPTN/OCK DY4 ...69 G3
Kipling Rd NFLD/LBR B31 ...176 A1
SEDG DY3 ...82 C1
SHHTH WV12 ...26 C3
WOLVN WV10 ...12 D5
Kirby Cl BILS/COS WV14 ...54 A5
Kirby Dr DUDN DY1 ...83 G3
Kirby Rd WSNGN B18 ...107 G3
Kirkby Gn SCFLD/BOLD B73 ...62 A5
Kirkham Gdns BRLYHL DY5 ...101 E3
Kirkham Gv STETCH B33 ...112 B5
Kirkham Wy TPTN/OCK DY4 ...85 G1
Kirkside Gv BRWNH WS8 ...9 F5
Kirkstall BLOX/PEL WS3 ...16 B5
Kirkstall Crs BLOX/PEL WS3 ...16 B5
Kirkstone Ct BRLYHL DY5 ...118 D4
Kirkstone Crs GTB/HAM B43 ...73 H5
WMBN WV5 ...64 D5
Kirkstone Wy BRLYHL DY5 ...118 D4
Kirkwall Rd RIDG/WDGT B32 ...157 H1
Kirkwood Av ERDW/GRVHL B23 ...76 D4
Kirstead Gdns
DUNHL/THL/PER WV6 ...35 F2
Kirton Gv DUNHL/THL/PER WV6 ...35 G1
SOLH B91 ...181 G4
STETCH B33 ...112 C5
Kitchener Rd DUDS DY2 ...85 F5
SLYOAK B29 ...160 B1
Kitchener St SMTHWK B66 ...107 F3
Kitchen La WNSFLD WV11 ...15 E5
WNSFLD WV11 ...25 E2
Kitebrook Cl SHLY B90 ...195 G1
Kitsland Rd BKDE/SHDE B34 ...113 G3
Kitswell Gdns RIDG/WDGT B32 ...157 E2
Kittiwake Dr BRLYHL DY5 ...119 E5
Kittoe Rd FOAKS/STRLY B74 ...46 D2
Kitt's Green Rd STETCH B33 ...130 D1
Kitwell La RIDG/WDGT B32 ...157 E2
Kitwood Dr HIA/OLT B92 ...165 F3
Kixley La DOR/KN B93 ...197 G2
Knaresdale Cl BRLYHL DY5 ...119 E4
Knaves Castle Av BRWNH WS8 ...9 F2
Knebworth Cl KGSTG B44 ...75 E3
Knightcote Dr SOLH B91 ...181 H5
Knightley Rd SOLH B91 ...181 F3
Knightlow Rd HRBN B17 ...124 D4
Knighton Cl FOAKS/STRLY B74 ...46 D2
Knighton Dr FOAKS/STRLY B74 ...46 D3
Knighton Rd DUDS DY2 ...102 D5
FOAKS/STRLY B74 ...32 B5
NFLD/LBR B31 ...176 A1
Knights Av
DUNHL/THL/PER WV6 ...22 A4
Knightsbridge Cl
FOAKS/STRLY B74 ...46 D1
Knightsbridge La SHHTH WV12 ...25 H4
Knightsbridge Rd HIA/OLT B92 ...164 B1
Knights Cl ERDW/GRVHL B23 ...92 C4
Knights Ct
CHWD/FDBR/MGN B37 ...133 E4
Knights Crs
DUNHL/THL/PER WV6 ...22 A3

Knightsfield Cl SCFLD/BOLD B73....61 E5
Knights Hl ALDR WS9 .....44 B2
Knights Rd SPARK B11 ....146 A3
Knightstone Av WSNGN B18 ..108 A5
Knights Wood Cl
  HWK/WHC B75 ....62 D1
Knightwick Crs
  ERDW/GRVHL B23 ....92 A1
Knipersley Rd
  ERDW/GRVHL B23 ....77 E5
Knoll Cft ALDR WS9 ....30 C1
Knollcroft B16 * 126 A2
The Knoll KGSWFD DY6 ....100 A4
  RIDG/WDGT B32 ....157 C1
Knottsall La LGLYGN/QTN B68 ..123 F1
Knotts Farm Rd KGSWFD DY6 ..100 C5
Knowlands Rd SOLH B91 ....195 C1
Knowle Cl RBRY B45 ....145 F4
Knowle Hill Rd DUDS DY2 ..102 B5
Knowle Rd BLKHTH/ROWR B65 ..103 F5
  SPARK B11 ....145 F4
Knowles Dr FOAKS/STRLY B74 ..62 A1
Knowles Rd WOLV WV1 ......37 H4
Knowles St DARL/WED WS10 ..56 A5
Knowle Wood Rd DOR/KN B93 ..199 F1
Knox Rd BKHL/PFLD WV2 ....52 A2
Knutswood Cl MOS/BIL B13 * ..162 B3
Kohima Dr STRBR DY8 ....135 E2
Kossuth Rd BILS/COS WV14 ..68 A2
Kyle Cl WOLVN WV10 ....22 D1
Kyles Wy RIDG/WDGT B32 ..157 F5
Kynaston Crs CDSL WV8 .....10 D5
Kyngsford Rd STECH B33 ....131 F1
Kyotts Lake Rd SPARK B11 ..127 G5
Kyrwicks La BHTH/HG B12 ..127 G3
  SPARK B11 ....144 C1
Kyter La CBROM B36 ....112 D1

L

Laburnham Rd KGSWFD DY6 ..100 A3
Laburnum Av
  CHWD/FDBR/MGN B37 ..113 H3
  SMTHWKW B67 ....106 A5
Laburnum Cl BLOX/PEL WS3 ..17 H5
  CHWD/FDBR/MGN B37 ..113 H3
  HLYWD B47 ....192 C1
Laburnum Dr OLDBY B69 ....85 H4
Laburnum Gv WALM/CURD B76 ..65 G5
  WSLW WS2 ....40 C2
Laburnum Rd ALDR WS9 ....159 H5
  BVILLE B30 ....159 H5
  DARL/WED WS10 ....58 A5
  DSYBK/YTR WS5 ....57 G4
  DUDN DY1 ....84 B2
  ETTPK/GDPK/PENN WV4 ..52 C5
  TPTN/OCK DY4 ....69 F4
  WOLV WV1 ....38 B5
Laburnum St BDMR/CCFT WV3 ..6 B5
  STRBR DY8 ....118 A5
Laburnum Vls SPARK B11 * ..145 E2
Laburnum Wy NFLD/LBR B31 ..175 G4
Ladbroke Dr WALM/CURD B76 ..78 B1
Ladbroke Gv ACGN B27 ......163 G2
Ladbrook Gv SEDG DY3 ......82 C3
Ladbrook Rd SOLH B91 ......182 A2
Ladbury Gv DSYBK/YTR WS5 ..57 G4
Ladbury Rd DSYBK/YTR WS5 ..57 G4
Ladeler Gv STECH B33 ....131 F2
Ladies Wk SEDG DY3 ....67 F3
Lady Bank RIDG/WDGT B32 ..157 F3
Lady Bracknell Ms
  NFLD/LBR B31 ....176 A1
Lady Byron La DOR/KN B93 ..196 D1
Ladycroft LDYWD/EDGR B16 ..2 A6
Lady Grey's Wk STRBR DY8 ..134 D2
Ladymoor Rd BILS/COS WV14 ..68 C1
Ladypool Av SPARK B11 * 144 D1
Ladypool Pl RUSH/SHEL WS4 ..28 C5
Ladypool Rd BHTH/HG B12 ..143 G2
Ladysmith Rd HALE B63 .....137 G1
Ladywell Cl WMBN WV5 ......65 E3
Ladywell Wk DIG/EDG B5 ....3 G5
Ladywood Circ
  LDYWD/EDGR B16 ....126 A2
Ladywood Cl BRLYHL DY5 ...119 H2
Ladywood Middleway
  LDYWD/EDGR B16 ....126 A2
Ladywood Rd FOAKS/STRLY B74 ..47 E5
  LDYWD/EDGR B16 ....125 H3
Lake Av DSYBK/YTR WS5 ....57 H1
Lake Cl DSYBK/YTR WS5 ....58 A1
Lakedown Cl
  HWK/WKHTH B38 ....176 A4
Lakefield Cl HLGN/YWD B28 ..163 F3
Lakefield Rd WNSFLD WV11 ..25 E5
Lakehouse Ct
  HWK/WKHTH B38 ....176 B2
Lakehouse Rd
  ERDW/GRVHL B23 ....76 C2
Lakeside
  CHWD/FDBR/MGN B37 ..133 E4
  FOAKS/STRLY B74 ....31 H5
Lakeside Cl WLNHL WV13 ....39 E2
Lakeside Ct BRLYHL DY5 .....118 D4
Lakeside Dr SHLY B90 ....196 A3
Lakeside Rd WBROM B70 ....71 F5
Lake St SEDG DY3 ....83 F3
Lakewood Dr RBRY B45 .....174 B4
Lakey La HLGN/YWD B28 ....163 E2
Lambah Cl BILS/COS WV14 ..54 A1
Lamb Cl BKDE/SHDE B34 ...113 G4
Lamb Crs WMBN WV5 ....80 D1

Lambert Cl ERDW/GRVHL B23 ..92 B1
Lambert Ct KGSWFD DY6 ....99 H1
Lambert End WBROM B70 ...87 F3
Lambert Fold DUDS DY2 .....103 E1
Lambert Rd WOLVN WV10 ...23 H4
Lambert St WBROM B70 .....87 F3
Lambeth Cl
  CHWD/FDBR/MGN B37 ..114 B5
Lambeth Rd BILS/COS WV14 ..53 F1
  KGSTG B44 ....68 A3
Lambourne Qv STETCH B33 ..131 G2
Lambourne Wy BRLYHL DY5 ..118 D4
Lambourn Rd
  ERDW/GRVHL B23 ....92 B2
  WLNHL WV13 ....40 B4
Lambscote Cl SHLY B90 ......179 E5
Lammas Cl HIA/OLT B92 .....165 E1
Lammas Rd STRBR DY8 ......117 C1
Lammermoor Av
  GTB/HAM B43 ....58 D2
Lamont Av RIDG/WDGT B32 ..141 F4
Lamorna Cl BDMR/CCFT WV3 ..35 F5
Lanark Cft CVALE B35 ....94 B3
Lancaster Av ALDR WS9 .....30 B2
  WBROM B70 ....56 C5
  RBRY B45 ....146 A3
Lancaster Circus Queensway
  CBHAMNE B4 ....3 H2
Lancaster Dr CVALE B35 ....94 C4
Lancaster Gdns
  ETTPK/GDPK/PENN WV4 ..51 E5
Lancaster Pl BLOX/PEL WS3 ..17 E5
Lancaster Rd BRLYHL DY5 ..119 E2
Lancaster St CBHAMNE B4 ..3 H1
Lancelot Cl WASH/WDE B8 ..128 C1
Lanchester Rd
  HWK/WKHTH B38 ....177 E4
Lanchester Wy CBROM B36 ..95 H5
Lancot Cl RBRY B45 ....188 A2
Land La CHWD/FDBR/MGN B37 ..132 A5
Landor Rd DOR/KN B93 .....197 E2
Landor St WASH/WDE B8 ....127 H1
Landport Rd WOLV WV1 .....51 G3
Landrake Rd KGSWFD DY6 ..100 B3
Landsdown Pl WSNGN B18 ..108 A4
Landseer Gv GTB/HAM B43 ..59 H4
Landsgate STRBR DY8 ....152 C1
Landswood Cl KGSTG B44 ..75 C2
Landswood Rd
  LGLYGN/QTN B62 ....105 C5
Lane Av WSLW WS2 ....41 F2
Lane Cl WSLW WS2 ....41 F2
Lane Cft WALM/CURD B76 ...78 B1
Lane Green Av CDSL WV8 ...21 C1
Lane Green Rd CDSL WV8 ...21 H1
Lanes Cl WMBN WV5 ....78 C4
Lanesfield Dr
  ETTPK/GDPK/PENN WV4 ..53 E4
Laneside Av FOAKS/STRLY B74 ..46 D3
Laneside Gdns WSLW WS2 ..41 E3
Lane St BILS/COS WV14 .....54 A5
Langcomb Rd SHLY B90 .....180 A5
Langdale Cl CVALE B35 ......94 C4
Langdale Cft HDSW B21 .....107 G2
Langdale Dr BILS/COS WV14 ..54 A1
Langdale Gv GTB/HAM B43 ..73 H4
Langdon St WASH/WDE B8 ..128 C1
Langdon St BORD B9 ....128 B1
Langfield Rd DOR/KN B93 ..197 E1
Langford Av GTB/HAM B43 ..73 G3
Langford Cl STECH B33 ......111 F5
Langford Gv SOLH B91 ......182 A3
Langford Rd HRBN B17 .....142 C1
Langham Cl
  LGLYGN/QTN B62 ....150 C5
Langham Gn FOAKS/STRLY B74 ..45 F4
Langholm Dr SCFLD/BOLD B73 ..76 B2
Langland Dr SEDG DY3 ......67 E3
Langley Av BILS/COS WV14 ..54 C4
Langley Crs LGLYGN/QTN B68 ..105 F5
Langley Dr CVALE B35 ....94 C5
Langley Gdns BDMR/CCFT WV3 ..50 C5
Langley Green Rd OLDBY B69 ..105 E5
Langley Gv SMHTH B10 * ...128 B4
Langley Hall Dr MGN/WHC B75 ..63 H2
Langley Hall Rd HIA/OLT B92 ..163 G3
  MGN/WHC B75 ....63 H3
Langley Heath Dr
  WALM/CURD B76 ....80 C1
Langley High St OLDBY B69 ..105 E4
Langley Rd
  ETTPK/GDPK/PENN WV4 ..50 C1
  LGLYGN/QTN B68 ....105 F5
  SMHTH B10 ....128 B4
Langleys Rd SLYOAK B29 ...159 G1
Langmead Cl WSLW WS2 ....40 B2
Langsett Rd WOLVN WV10 ..37 C1
Langstone Rd
  ALE/KHTH/YWD B14 ......178 D3
  DUDN DY1 ....83 F4
Langton Cl CBROM B36 .....114 B3
Langton Pl BILS/COS WV14 ..54 D1
Langton Rd WASH/WDE B8 ..128 C4
Langtree Av SOLH B91 ....181 H4
Langwood Ct CBROM B36 ...112 C1
Langworth Av ACGN B27 ....146 C2
Lannacombe Rd
  NFLD/LBR B31 ....189 E2
Lansbury Av DARL/WED WS10 ..55 H1
Lansbury Gn CDYHTH B64 ..121 H4
Lansdale Av HIA/OLT B92 ..165 H3
Lansdowne Av CDSL WV8 ...10 A5
Lansdowne Rd BILS/COS WV14 ..54 B4
  DUDS DY2 ....103 F3
  ERDE/BCHGN B24 ....92 D3
  HALE B63 ....137 H5
  HDSW B21 ....108 A2
  RMSLY B62 ....122 D4
  WOLV WV1 ....37 H4
Lansdowne St WSNGN B18 ..108 H5
Lansdown Pl WSNGN B18 * ..108 A4
Lantern Rd DUDS DY2 ......120 C2
Lapal La RIDG/WDGT B32 ..140 A5
Lapal La North RMSLY B62 ..139 G4
Lapal La South RMSLY B62 ..139 G4
Lapley Cl WOLV WV1 ....38 B3
Lapper Av
  ETTPK/GDPK/PENN WV4 ..67 H1
Lapwing Cft ERDW/GRVHL B23 ..76 A4
Lapwing Dr HIA/OLT B92 ...167 H5
Lapwood Av KGSWFD DY6 ..100 C4
Lapworth Cl RBRY B45 ......188 A1
Lapworth Gv BHTH/HG B12 ..144 B1
Lara Cl HRBN B17 ....124 D4
Lara Gv TPTN/OCK DY4 .....85 C4
Larch Av HDSW B21 ....89 F4
Larch Cft
  CHWD/FDBR/MGN B37 ..132 B2
  OLDBY B69 ....85 H4
Larches La BDMR/CCFT WV3 ..6 A4
Larches St SPARK B11 ....144 C1
Larchfield Cl
  BFLD/HDSWWD B20 .....90 B3
Larch Gv SEDG DY3 ....67 G4
Larchmere Dr HLGN/YWD B28 ..162 D2
  WNSFLD WV11 ....15 E4
Larch Rd KGSWFD DY6 .....100 A2
Larchwood Crs
  FOAKS/STRLY B74 ....45 E5
Larchwood Gn DSYBK/YTR WS5 ..57 C4
Larchwood Rd DSYBK/YTR WS5 ..57 C4
Larcombe Dr
  ETTPK/GDPK/PENN WV4 ..52 B5
Large Av DARL/WED WS10 ..55 E4
Lark Cl ALE/KHTH/YWD B14 ..178 C5
Larkfield Av CBROM B36 ....112 D1
Larkhill Rd STRBR DY8 ......134 C3
Lark Meadow Dr
  CHWD/FDBR/MGN B37 ..131 G1
Larkspur Cft CBROM B36 ...111 H1
Larkspur Rd DUDS DY2 .....103 F1
Larkspur Wy BRWNH WS8 ..18 D1
Larkswood Dr
  ETTPK/GDPK/PENN WV4 ..66 C5
Larne Rd
  LGN/SDN/BHAMAIR B26 ..130 C5
Latches Cl DARL/WED WS10 ..55 G2
Latelow Rd STECH B33 ......130 C2
Latham Av GTB/HAM B43 ...73 G4
Latham Crs TPTN/OCK DY4 ..85 H1
Lath La SMTHWK B66 ....105 H1
Lathom Gv STECH B33 ......112 B4
Latimer Gdns EDG B15 .....126 D5
Latimer Pl WSNGN B18 .....107 G3
Latimer Rd HIA/OLT B92 ...165 G1
Latymer Cl WALM/CURD B76 ..78 C4
Lauder Cl SEDG DY3 ....67 E2
  WLNHL WV13 ....39 F4
Lauderdale Cl BRWNH WS8 ..9 E1
Lauderdale Gdns WOLVN WV10 ..13 E4
Laughton Cl NFLD/LBR B31 ..189 H1
Launceston Cl DSYBK/YTR WS5 ..58 B1
Launceston Rd DSYBK/YTR WS5 ..58 B1
The Launde
  ALE/KHTH/YWD B14 ......179 F2
Laundry Rd SMTHWK B66 ..106 D1
Laural Av SMTHWK B66 .....106 C1
Laureates Wk FOAKS/STRLY B74 ..47 E4
Laurel Av BHTH/HG B12 ....144 C2
Laurel Cl FOAKS/STRLY B74 ..45 E5
  SMTHWK B66 ....106 C1
Laurel Gdns HDSW B21 .....106 D1
  ACGN B27 ....146 B1
Laurel Dr BDMR/CCFT WV3 ..51 E2
  BILS/COS WV14 ....54 C4
  BVILLE B30 ....159 G4
Laurel La HALE B63 ....138 D4
Laurel Rd BVILLE B30 ....177 E1
  DSYBK/YTR WS5 ....57 H3
  DUDN DY1 ....84 A3
  HDSW B21 ....89 C4
  TPTN/OCK DY4 ....69 F4
The Laurels
  LGN/SDN/BHAMAIR B26 ..148 A2
  SMTHWK B66 ....107 E5
Laurence Gv
  DUNHL/THL/PER WV6 ...22 A3
Lauriston Cl DUDS DY2 .....83 H3
Lavender Cl COVEN WV9 ...11 H4
Lavender Gdns
  ERDW/GRVHL B23 ....75 H4
Lavender Gv BILS/COS WV14 ..54 D2
  BLOX/PEL WS3 ....18 C5
Lavender La STRBR DY8 ....134 C4
Lavender Rd DUDN DY1 ....84 C1
Lavendon Rd PBAR/PBCH B42 ..90 A1
Lavinia Rd RMSLY B62 ......138 C5
Law Cliff Rd PBAR/PBCH B42 ..74 B5
Law Cl OLDBY B69 ....86 B4
Lawden Rd SMHTH B10 .....127 G1
Lawford Cl VAUX/NECH B7 ..127 C1
Lawford Gv DIG/EDG B5 * ..127 E4
  SHLY B90 ....179 F3
Lawfred Av WNSFLD WV11 ..28 C1
Lawley Cl RUSH/SHEL WS4 ..28 D1
Lawley Middleway
  CBHAMNE B4 ....127 G1
Lawley Rd BILS/COS WV14 ..53 F2
Lawley St DUDN DY1 ....84 A5
  WBROM B70 ....86 B5
The Lawley HALE B63 ....154 C4
Lawn Av STRBR DY8 ....135 E5
Lawn La COVEN WV9 ....11 H2
Lawnoaks Cl BRWNH WS8 ..8 D2
Lawn Rd BKHL/PFLD WV2 ..52 C2

Lawnsdale Cl
  CSHL/WTROR B46 ....115 F3
Lansdown Rd BILS/COS WV14 ..119 H5
Lawnsfield Gv
  ERDW/GRVHL B23 ....76 B4
Lawnside Gn BILS/COS WV14 ..38 D5
Lawn St STRBR DY8 ....135 E3
Lawnswood KINVER DY7 ....78 A5
  WALM/CURD B76 ....78 C3
Lawnswood Av
  DUNHL/THL/PER WV6 ...22 A2
  ETTPK/GDPK/PENN WV4 ..52 C4
  SHLY B90 ....99 G5
  STRBR DY8 ....99 G5
Lawnswood Dr ALDR WS9 ..19 G4
  KINVER DY7 ....117 G2
Lawnswood Gv ALDR WS9 ..89 E5
Lawnswood Rd
  DUNHL/THL/PER WV6 ...22 A2
  DUDS DY2 ....120 C2
Lawnwood Rd DUDS DY2 ..120 C2
Lawrence Av WNSFLD WV11 ..25 F4
  WOLV WV1 ....38 A1
Lawrence Dr WALM/CURD B76 ..79 F5
Lawrence La HAG/WOL DY9 ..136 A1
  WLNHL WV13 ....39 G2
Lawrence Wk GTB/HAM B43 ..59 H4
Lawson Cl ALDR WS9 ....44 B3
Lawson St CBHAMNE B4 ....3 H2
Law St HHTH/SAND B71 ....87 G1
Lawton Cl OLDBY B69 ....104 A3
Laxey Rd LDYWD/EDGR B16 ..125 E1
Laxford Cl BHTH/HG B12 ...144 A1
Laxton Cl KGSWFD DY6 ....100 C4
Laxton Gv YDLY B25 ....129 H3
Lazy Hill HWK/WKHTH B38 ..177 F3
Lazy Hill Rd ALDR WS9 .....30 C1
Lea Av DARL/WED WS10 ....70 B2
Lea Bank Rd DUDS DY2 ....120 B1
Leabon Gv HRBN B17 ......142 A3
Leabrook
  LGN/SDN/BHAMAIR B26 ..130 B4
Leabrook Rd DARL/WED WS10 ..70 B2
Leabrook Rd North
  DARL/WED WS10 ....70 B2
Leach Green La RBRY B45 ..188 A1
Leach Heath La RBRY B45 ..187 H1
Leacliffe Wy FOAKS/STRLY B74 ..45 F2
Leacote Dr
  DUNHL/THL/PER WV6 ...35 G1
Leacroft SHHTH WV12 ......26 A3
Leacroft Av WOLVN WV10 ..23 G2
Leacroft Cl ALDR WS9 ......30 B1
Leacroft Gv HHTH/SAND B71 ..71 F3
Leacroft Rd KGSWFD DY6 ..100 A1
Lea Dr LGN/SDN/BHAMAIR B26 ..147 G1
Lea End La ALVE B48 ....190 A4
Leafield Crs STECH B33 ....113 G3
Leafield Gdns RMSLY B62 ..122 B4
Leafield Rd HIA/OLT B92 ...165 F1
Lea Ford Rd STECH B33 ....113 G5
Leaford Wy KGSWFD DY6 ..100 B4
Leafy Gld FOAKS/STRLY B74 ..45 G2
Lea Gdns BDMR/CCFT WV3 ..36 D5
Lea Green Av TPTN/OCK DY4 ..84 C1
Lea Green La HAG/WOL WV47 ..193 E2
Lea Hall Rd STECH B33 .....130 C2
Leahill Cft
  CHWD/FDBR/MGN B37 ..131 H2
Lea Hill Rd BFLD/HDSWWD B20 ..90 C4
Leaholme Gdns HAG/WOL DY9 ..135 H5
Leahouse Gdns
  LGLYGN/QTN B68 ....123 E1
Lea House Rd BVILLE B30 ..160 A3
Leahouse Rd LGLYGN/QTN B68 ..123 E1
Leahurst Crs HRBN B17 ....142 A3
Lea Manor Dr
  ETTPK/GDPK/PENN WV4 ..51 E5
Leam Crs HIA/OLT B92 ......165 F1
Leamington Rd BHTH/HG B12 ..144 D2
Leamore Cl WSLW WS2 .....27 E3
Leamore La WSLW WS2 .....26 D2
Leamount Dr KGSTG B44 ..76 A1
Leander Gdns
  ALE/KHTH/YWD B14 ......179 E5
Leander Rd HAG/WOL DY9 ..136 D3
Lea Rd BDMR/CCFT WV3 ...51 E3
  SPARK B11 ....145 F3
Leason La WOLVN WV10 ...23 H4
Leasow Dr EDG B15 ....142 B4
Leasowe Rd RBRY B45 .....173 H5
  TPTN/OCK DY4 ....85 E2
Leasowes Ct HALE B63 .....138 B5
Leasowes Dr BDMR/CCFT WV3 ..50 D2
Leasowes La RMSLY B62 ..139 E2
Leasowes Rd
  ALE/KHTH/YWD B14 ......161 F1
The Leasow ALDR WS9 .....29 G5
The Lea STECH B33 ....130 C1
Leatherhead Cl AST/WIT B6 ..109 F3
Lea Vale Rd STRBR DY8 ....135 E3
Leaverton Dr
  LGN/SDN/BHAMAIR B26 ..147 G2
Lea Wk ALDR WS9 ....29 G5
  SHHTH WV12 ....29 G5
Lea Village STECH B33 .....130 C1
Lea Wk RBRY B45 ....173 H5
Lea Yield Cl SLYOAK B29 ..160 A5
Lechlade Rd GTB/HAM B43 ..73 C3
Leckie Rd WSLW WS2 ....42 A1
Ledbury Cl RUSH/SHEL WS4 ..30 C1
  LDYWD/EDGR B16 ....126 A2
Ledbury Dr WOLV WV1 .....38 C4
Ledbury Wy WALM/CURD B76 ..79 F5
Ledsam Gv RIDG/WDGT B32 ..141 F1
Ledsam St LDYWD/EDGR B16 ..126 A2
Ledwell SHLY B90 ....194 D3

Lee Bank Middleway EDG B15 ..126 C4
Leebank Rd HALE B63 ....138 A5
Leech St TPTN/OCK DY4 ...86 A1
Lee Gv ERDE B15 * 126 C4
Lee Gdns SMTHWKW B67 ..106 A4
Lee Mt EDG B15 * 126 C4
Lee Rd CDYHTH B64 ....121 F4
  HLYWD B47 ....192 C1
Leeson Wk HRBN B17 ......142 B3
Lees Rd BILS/COS WV14 ...54 B5
Lees St WSNGN B18 ....107 H4
Lees Ter BILS/COS WV14 ..54 B5
Lee St WBROM B70 ....71 E3
Legge La BILS/COS WV14 ..68 C1
  CBHAMW B3 * 2 B5
Legge St AST/WIT B6 ....3 J1
  BKHL/PFLD WV2 ....52 C2
  WBROM B70 ....87 H3
Legion Rd RBRY B45 ....187 G1
Legs La WOLVN WV10 ....13 H4
Leicester Cl SMTHWKW B67 ..124 A3
Leicester Pl HHTH/SAND B71 ..71 G4
Leicester St
  DUNHL/THL/PER WV6 ...36 D1
  WSL WS1 ....4 E3
Leigham Dr HRBN B17 .....124 B5
Leigh Cl RUSH/SHEL WS4 ..42 C1
Leigh Rd MGN/WHC B75 ...63 H2
  WSL WS1 ....5 K5
  WASH/WDE B8 ....110 C3
Leighs Cl RUSH/SHEL WS4 ..29 E1
Leighs Rd RUSH/SHEL WS4 ..28 D1
Leighswood Av ALDR WS9 ..30 A3
Leighswood Gv ALDR WS9 ..30 A3
Leighswood Rd ALDR WS9 ..30 A3
Leighton Cl DUDN DY1 .....83 G4
  GTB/HAM B43 ....59 G5
Leighton Rd BDMR/CCFT WV3 ..51 F2
  BILS/COS WV14 ....54 A4
  MOS/BIL B13 ....144 B5
Leisure Av STECH B33 .....130 C2
Lelant Gv HRBN B17 ....141 G2
Lellow St HHTH/SAND B71 ..71 G3
Le More FOAKS/STRLY B74 ..47 E3
Lemox Rd WBROM B70 .....71 E3
Lench Cl RMSLY B62 ....122 A3
Lenchs Gn DIG/EDG B5 ....127 E5
Lench St CBHAMNE B4 .....3 C1
Lenchs Trust Houses
  RBRY B45 * 127 F5
Len Davies Rd SHHTH WV12 ..25 G3
Lennard Gdns SMTHWK B66 * ..107 F3
Lennox Gdns BDMR/CCFT WV3 ..6 A7
Lennox Gv SCFLD/BOLD B73 ..77 F4
Lennox St LOZ/NWT B19 ...108 D3
Lenton Cft
  LGN/SDN/BHAMAIR B26 ..130 A5
Lenwade Rd LGLYGN/QTN B68 ..123 H4
Leominster Rd SPARK B11 ..145 G4
Leonard Av LOZ/NWT B19 ..108 C1
Leonard Gv LOZ/NWT B19 ..108 C1
Leonard Rd LOZ/NWT B19 ..108 C2
  STRBR DY8 ....134 C2
Leopold Av BFLD/HDSWWD B20 ..89 G1
Leopold St BHTH/HG B12 ..127 F4
Lepid Gv SLYOAK B29 ......142 B5
Lerryn Cl KGSWFD DY6 ....100 B4
Lerwick Cl KGSWFD DY6 ..100 B4
Lesley Dr KGSWFD DY6 ...100 A5
Leslie Dr TPTN/OCK DY4 ..69 E2
Leslie Rd BFLD/HDSWWD B20 ..104 A1
  FOAKS/STRLY B74 ....45 H3
  LDYWD/EDGR B16 ....125 H2
  MGN/WHC B75 ....37 H1
Lesscroft Cl COVEN WV9 ...12 A4
Lester Gv ALDR WS9 ....3 E5
Lester St BILS/COS WV14 ..54 B5
Levante Gdns STECH B33 ..129 H2
Leve La WLNHL WV13 ......39 H4
Leven Cr WALM/CURD B76 ..78 D4
Leven Dr SHHTH WV12 .....25 H1
Levenwick Wy KGSWFD DY6 ..100 C4
The Leveretts HDSW B21 ..89 E3
Lever St BKHL/PFLD WV2 ...7 G7
Leverton Ri WOLVN WV10 ..23 E4
Leveson Cl DUDS DY2 ......103 E1
Leveson Dr TPTN/OCK DY4 ..69 E5
Leveson Rd WNSFLD WV11 ..25 F2
Leveson St WLNHL WV13 ..39 G5
Levington Cl
  DUNHL/THL/PER WV6 ...20 D5
Lewis Av WOLV WV1 ....38 B2
Lewis Cl SHHTH WV12 ......26 B5
Lewis Gv WNSFLD WV11 ...24 D4
Lewisham Rd SMTHWK B66 ..106 C2
  WOLVN WV10 ....13 H5
Lewisham St WBROM B70 ..87 H2
Lewis Rd BVILLE B30 ....160 C3
  HAG/WOL DY9 ....136 B2
  LGLYGN/QTN B68 ....123 F5
Lewis St BILS/COS WV14 ..54 A2
  TPTN/OCK DY4 ....54 A2
  WSLW WS2 ....86 B1
Lewthorn Ri
  ETTPK/GDPK/PENN WV4 ..52 B4
Lexington Gn BRLYHL DY5 ..119 E5
Leybourne Crs COVEN WV9 ..11 H5
Leybourne Gv ACGN B27 ..146 B1
Leybrook Rd RBRY B45 ....188 B1
Leyburn Cl SHHTH WV12 ...40 B1
Leyburn Rd LDYWD/EDGR B16 ..126 A3
Leycester Cl NFLD/LBR B31 ..189 G1
Leycroft Av STECH B33 .....131 F1
Ley Hill Farm Rd
  NFLD/LBR B31 ....158 A5
Ley Hill Rd MGN/WHC B75 ..62 C3
Leyland Cft MOS/BIL B13 ..162 B3
Leylan Cft MOS/BIL B13 ....162 B3
Leyland Av BDMR/CCFT WV3 ..36 B4
Leyman Cl ALE/KHTH/YWD B14 ..178 D3

Leyman Cl ALE/KHTH/YWD B14 179 E1
Ley Ri SEDG DY3 67 E2
Leys Cl HAG/WOL DY9 136 A5
Leys Crs BRLYHL DY5 118 D1
Leysdown Gv ACGN B27 163 G2
Leysdown Rd ACGN B27 163 G2
Leys Rd BRLYHL DY5 118 D1
The Leys DARL/WED WS10 55 E2
NFLD/LBR B31 158 D5
Leys Wood Cft
LGN/SDN/BHAMAIR B26 147 G1
Leyton Cl BRLYHL DY5 119 F4
Leyton Gv KGSTG B44 75 G2
Leyton Rd HDSW B21 107 H1
Libbards Ga SOLH B91 182 A5
Libbards Wy SOLH B91 181 H5
Library Wy RBRY B45 187 H1
Lich Av WNSFLD WV11 25 E3
Lichfield Rd ALDR WS9 19 G3
AST/WIT B6 109 G3
BLOX/PEL WS3 17 E5
BLOX/PEL WS3 18 B2
BRWNH WS8 9 F4
CSHL/WTROR B46 97 E5
FOAKS/STRLY B74 32 D5
MGN/WHC B75 33 E5
MGN/WHC B75 62 B1
RUSH/SHEL WS4 42 C1
WALM/CURD B76 96 D2
WNSFLD WV11 24 D5
Lichfield St BILS/COS WV14 54 A2
TPTN/OCK DY4 69 F3
WOLV WV1 7 F4
WSL WS1 5 F3
Lichwood Rd WNSFLD WV11 25 F3
Lickey Coppice RBRY B45 188 C4
Lickey Rd RBRY B45 188 C2
STRBR DY8 135 H1
Liddon Gv ACGN B27 163 G2
Liddon Rd ACGN B27 163 G2
Lifford Cl ALE/KHTH/YWD B14 177 F1
Lifford La BVILLE B30 160 A5
Lifton Cft KGSWFD DY6 100 B4
Lighthorne Av
LDYWD/EDGR B16 126 A1
Lighthorne Rd SOLH B91 164 D4
Lightning Wy NFLD/LBR B31 189 H1
Lightwood Cl DOR/KN B93 183 F5
Lightwood Rd DUDN DY1 84 A3
Lightwoods Hl SMTHWKW B67 124 A4
Lightwoods Rd HAG/WOL DY9 153 E1
SMTHWKW B67 124 B3
Lilac Av BHTH/HG B12 144 C2
DSYBK/YTR WS5 57 G4
FOAKS/STRLY B74 60 A1
KGSTG B44 75 E4
TPTN/OCK DY4 69 E4
Lilac Dr WMBN WV5 64 D5
Lilac Gv DARL/WED WS10 71 E1
WSLW WS2 40 C2
Lilac Rd DUDN DY1 84 B2
SHHTH WV12 26 C3
WOLV WV1 38 B5
Lilac Wy RMSLY B62 122 D4
Lilian Gv BILS/COS WV14 69 E2
Lilleshall Crs BKHL/PFLD WV2 52 B1
Lilleshall Rd
LGN/SDN/BHAMAIR B26 130 D5
Lilley La NFLD/LBR B31 175 H5
Lillington Gv BKDE/SHDE B34 113 F4
Lillington Rd SHLY B90 180 B5
Lilycroft La HWK/WKHTH B38 191 E1
Lily Rd LGN/SDN/BHAMAIR B26 146 D1
Lily St HHTH/SAND B71 87 G1
Limberlost Cl
BFLD/HDSWWD B20 90 A3
Limbrick Cl SHLY B90 179 H3
Limbury Gv HIA/OLT B92 * 165 H2
Lime Av SLYOAK B29 * 142 D5
WSLW WS2 40 C2
Lime Cl HLYWD B47 192 C3
TPTN/OCK DY4 85 E1
WBROM B70 87 E2
WSLW WS2 40 C2
Lime Ct SPARK B11 145 E3
Lime Gv BHTH/HG B12 144 B2
BILS/COS WV14 38 C5
CHWD/FDBR/MGN B37 132 B3
LGN/SDN/BHAMAIR B26 146 D1
LOZ/NWT B19 108 C1
RUSH/SHEL WS4 29 E4
SCFLD/BOLD B73 77 F4
SMTHWK B66 106 D5
Limehurst Av BDMR/CCFT WV3 35 G4
Limehurst Rd RUSH/SHEL WS4 29 E5
Lime Kiln Cl HWK/WKHTH B38 190 B1
Limekiln La
ALE/KHTH/YWD B14 178 C1
Lime La BLOX/PEL WS3 8 A3
Limepit La DUDN DY1 84 A3
Lime Rd BILS/COS WV14 67 H2
DARL/WED WS10 55 H4
Limes Av BLKHTH/ROWR B65 122 A2
BRLYHL DY5 101 E4
Limescroft Cl RUSH/SHEL WS4 28 D3
Limes Rd DUDN DY1 84 B3
DUNHL/THL/PER WV6 35 G1
The Limes ERDE/BCHGN B24 92 D3
LDYWD/EDGR B16 * 125 H1
SPARK B11 145 E1
WSL WS1 5 J3
Lime St BDMR/CCFT WV3 6 B7
BILS/COS WV14 68 A3
WSL WS1 5 G4
Limes Vw SEDG DY3 67 F4
Lime Tree Av
DUNHL/THL/PER WV6 35 E2
Lime Tree Gdns CDSL WV8 10 D4
Lime Tree Gv NFLD/LBR B31 176 A3
Lime Tree Rd ACGN B27 146 C2
CDSL WV8 10 D4
DSYBK/YTR WS5 57 G4
Limetree Rd FOAKS/STRLY B74 44 D4
Lime Tree Rd WASH/WDE B8 110 D3
Linchmere Rd HDSW B21 89 E4
Lincoln Av WLNHL WV13 40 B3
Lincoln Cl ACGN B27 147 E4
Lincoln Gn WOLVN WV10 12 D5
Lincoln Gv
CHWD/FDBR/MGN B37 132 A4
Lincoln Rd DUDS DY2 120 D1
HHTH/SAND B71 71 H2
HIA/OLT B92 146 D5
SMTHWKW B67 124 A2
WSL WS1 5 H3
Lincoln Rd North HIA/OLT B92 147 E4
Lincoln St BHTH/HG B12 144 A1
WOLVN WV10 7 K2
Lindale Av CBROM B36 111 G3
Lindale Crs BRLYHL DY5 135 H1
Lindale Dr WMBN WV5 64 D5
Linden Av GTB/HAM B43 73 F3
OLDBY B69 104 B1
RMSLY B62 122 C5
Linden Cl WSLW WS2 * 40 B3
Linden Dr STRBR DY8 135 G4
Linden La SHHTH WV12 26 C3
Linden Lea BDMR/CCFT WV3 35 H4
Linden Rd DUDN DY1 84 B3
SLYOAK B29 159 G2
SMTHWK B66 124 C2
Lindens Dr FOAKS/STRLY B74 60 B3
The Lindens
DUNHL/THL/PER WV6 36 A2
RIDG/WDGT B32 124 A5
Lindenwood SCFLD/BOLD B73 62 B2
Lindford Wy HWK/WKHTH B38 177 F3
Lindley Av TPTN/OCK DY4 85 F3
Lindon Cl BRWNH WS8 19 G1
Lindon Dr BRWNH WS8 19 F1
Lindon Rd BRWNH WS8 19 G1
Lindon Vw BRWNH WS8 19 G2
Lindrick Cl BLOX/PEL WS3 16 B4
Lindridge Dr WALM/CURD B76 79 E5
Lindridge Rd ERDW/GRVHL B23 92 A1
MGN/WHC B75 63 F1
SHLY B90 179 H4
Lindrosa Rd FOAKS/STRLY B74 45 F2
Lindsay Rd PBAR/PBCH B42 74 B2
Lindsey Av NFLD/LBR B31 176 A1
Lindsey Pl BRLYHL DY5 119 E1
Lindsey Rd HHTH/SAND B71 71 G4
Lindsworth Ap BVILLE B30 177 G2
Lindsworth Rd BVILLE B30 177 F2
Linfield Gdns SEDG DY3 67 E2
Linford Gv YDLY B25 129 H3
Linforth Dr FOAKS/STRLY B74 60 C1
Lingard Cl VAUX/NECH B7 109 H4
Lingard Rd MGN/WHC B75 63 F3
Lingfield Av KGSTG B44 75 E2
WOLVN WV10 12 D2
Lingfield Gdns
BKDE/SHDE B34 112 D3
Lingfield Gv
DUNHL/THL/PER WV6 34 D1
Lingfield Wy KGSWFD DY6 100 C4
Lingham Cl HIA/OLT B92 165 F3
Linhope Dr KGSWFD DY6 100 C4
Link Rd ALDR WS9 19 H4
LDYWD/EDGR B16 125 G1
WMBN WV5 65 E4
Links Av DUNHL/THL/PER WV6 21 H3
Links Dr RBRY B45 188 A2
SOLH B91 164 D4
STRBR DY8 135 E5
Links Rd
ETTPK/GDPK/PENN WV4 51 G5
HLYWD B47 178 C4
LGLYGN/QTN B68 123 F4
Links Side Wy ALDR WS9 30 C2
Links Vw FOAKS/STRLY B74 45 G4
RMSLY B62 139 F3
Linkswood Cl MOS/BIL B13 161 H1
The Link ACGN B27 162 D1
Linley Cl ALDR WS9 29 G5
Linley Dr WOLVN WV10 23 G1
Linley Gv ALE/KHTH/YWD B14 160 C4
SEDG DY3 82 D4
Linley Rd RUSH/SHEL WS4 29 F3
Linley Wood Rd ALDR WS9 29 G5
Linnet Cl RMSLY B62 138 D1
SLYOAK B29 159 G2
Linnet Gv SHHTH WV12 26 A2
Linpole Wk
ALE/KHTH/YWD B14 177 G3
Linsey Rd HIA/OLT B92 148 A5
Linslade Cl
ETTPK/GDPK/PENN WV4 52 B4
Linthouse La WNSFLD WV11 24 D2
Linton Av SOLH B91 181 G4
Linton Cl HALE B63 137 G2
Linton Cft BILS/COS WV14 53 H4
Linton Rd CDYHTH B64 121 F1
ETTPK/GDPK/PENN WV4 51 E3
GTB/HAM B43 59 G4
SPARK B11 146 A3
Linwood Rd DUDN DY1 84 B1
HDSW B21 107 G1
SOLH B91 163 H5
Lionel St CBHAMNW B3 2 E3
Lion Pas STRBR DY8 135 F2
Lion St STRBR DY8 135 F2
Liskeard Rd DSYBK/YTR WS5 58 B1
Lisko Cl STRBR DY8 118 C4
Lismore Cl RBRY B45 173 G4
Lismore Dr HRBN B17 141 G4
Lisson Gv KGSTG B44 60 B4
Listelow Cl CBROM B36 112 D1
Lister Cl TPTN/OCK DY4 85 G2
WSLW WS2 27 F5
Lister Rd DUDS DY2 102 C2
WSLW WS2 27 F5
Lister St VAUX/NECH B7 3 J1
WLNHL WV13 39 H4
Listowel Rd
ALE/KHTH/YWD B14 160 D4
Lisures Dr WALM/CURD B76 62 D4
Little Albert St WSL WS1 * 4 E2
Little Ann St DIG/EDG B5 3 K6
Little Aston Hall Dr
FOAKS/STRLY B74 31 G5
Little Aston La
FOAKS/STRLY B74 32 B4
Little Aston Park Rd
FOAKS/STRLY B74 45 G2
Little Aston Rd ALDR WS9 30 C4
Little Barr St BORD B9 127 G2
Little Bell Hall Cottages
HAG/WOL DY9 * 184 B2
Little Birches BDMR/CCFT WV3 36 B5
Little Brickiln St
BKHL/PFLD WV2 6 E6
Little Bromwich Rd BORD B9 129 F3
Little Broom St BHTH/HG B12 127 G4
Little Caldmore WSL WS1 4 E6
Little Checkhill La KINVER DY7 98 B5
Little Clothier St WLNHL WV13 39 G2
Little Clover Cl VAUX/NECH B7 110 A3
Little Cornbow HALE B63 138 D4
Littlecote Cft
ALE/KHTH/YWD B14 178 C2
Littlecote Dr ERDW/GRVHL B23 76 D4
Little Cottage St BRLYHL DY5 119 F1
Little Cft GTB/HAM B43 73 E2
Little Cross St DARL/WED WS10 55 E1
Little Edward St BORD B9 127 G2
Little Fields Wy OLDBY B69 104 D2
Little Francis Gv
VAUX/NECH B7 109 H4
Little Gorway WSL WS1 57 F1
Little Green La BORD B9 128 A3
Little Green Lanes
SCFLD/BOLD B73 77 F4
Little Hall Rd VAUX/NECH B7 109 H5
Little Hardwick Rd ALDR WS9 44 D3
Little Hay La LICHS WS14 33 F2
Little Heath Cft
BKDE/SHDE B34 112 D3
Little Hl DARL/WED WS10 55 H5
Little Hill Gv HWK/WKHTH B38 177 E4
Little Hill Wy RIDG/WDGT B32 140 D5
Little Johnson's La ALDR WS9 44 B4
Little John St BRLYHL DY5 101 F5
Little La HHTH/SAND B71 87 H1
SHHTH WV12 26 B3
Little Lawns Cl BRWNH WS8 19 F2
Little London WSL WS1 57 E1
Littlemead Av NFLD/LBR B31 176 A4
Little Meadow Cft
NFLD/LBR B31 158 B5
Littlemead Rd SHLY B90 179 G5
Little Moor Hl SMTHWKW B67 106 B4
Little Newport St WSL WS1 4 D4
Little Oaks Rd AST/WIT B6 109 E1
Littleover Av HLGN/YWD B28 162 D4
Little Pk RIDG/WDGT B32 140 B3
Little Park St WOLV WV1 * 7 H4
Little Pitts Cl ERDE/BCHGN B24 93 H1
Little Potter St BRLYHL DY5 119 F3
Little Pountney St
BKHL/PFLD WV2 * 7 F7
Little Shadwell St CBHAMNE B4 * 3 G2
Littleshaw Cft HLYWD B47 193 E4
Littleshaw La HLYWD B47 193 E4
Little's La WOLV WV1 7 G2
Little Station St WSL WS1 4 D3
Little St DUDS DY2 84 D5
Little Sutton La MGN/WHC B75 47 G4
Little Sutton Rd MGN/WHC B75 47 H3
Littleton Cl WALM/CURD B76 78 C1
Littleton Cft SOLH B91 182 A5
Littleton Rd SHHTH WV12 26 A3
Littleton St East WSL WS1 4 E2
Littleton St West WSLW WS2 4 D2
Littlewood Cl SOLH B91 181 H5
Little Wood St WLNHL WV13 39 G3
Littleworth Av DUDN DY1 68 B5
Littleworth Gv
WALM/CURD B76 63 F4
Liveridge Cl DOR/KN B93 196 D2
Liverpool Cft
CHWD/FDBR/MGN B37 131 H3
Liverpool St BORD B9 127 G2
Livery St CBHAMNW B3 2 E2
Livingstone Av
DUNHL/THL/PER WV6 20 C5
Livingstone Rd
ALE/KHTH/YWD B14 161 E4
BFLD/HDSWWD B20 90 C5
BILS/COS WV14 53 F3
BLOX/PEL WS3 17 G5
WBROM B70 87 F5
Lloyd Dr
ETTPK/GDPK/PENN WV4 65 G1
Lloyd Hl
ETTPK/GDPK/PENN WV4 * 50 C5
Lloyd Rd BFLD/HDSWWD B20 90 A2
DUNHL/THL/PER WV6 21 H5
Lloyd Sq EDG B15 * 125 G4
Lloyds Rd RMSLY B62 122 A5
Lloyd St DARL/WED WS10 55 G5
DUDS DY2 102 D1
DUNHL/THL/PER WV6 36 B1
HHTH/SAND B71 88 A2
SMHTH B10 128 B4
Locarno Rd TPTN/OCK DY4 69 F5
Lochalsh Gv WNSFLD WV11 25 H1
Lochranza Cft GTB/HAM B43 73 G1
Lock Dr STETCH B33 129 H1
Locke Pl VAUX/NECH B7 * 127 G1
Locket Cl WSLW WS2 40 D1
Lockfield Cl STRBR DY8 118 B2
Lockhart Dr MGN/WHC B75 47 G4
Locking Cft CVALE B35 94 D3
Lockington Cft RMSLY B62 139 H1
Lockley Cl WOLVN WV10 37 H1
Lockside ALDR WS9 29 H3
WMBN WV5 64 C4
Locksmith Cl WLNHL WV13 39 H3
Lock St WOLV WV1 7 H2
Locks Vw STRBR DY8 117 H3
Lockton Rd BVILLE B30 160 C2
Lockwood Rd NFLD/LBR B31 175 F1
Lode La SOLH B91 165 E3
Lodge Cl DSYBK/YTR WS5 58 B2
RMSLY B62 139 F4
Lodge Crs DUDS DY2 102 A5
HAG/WOL DY9 152 D5
Lodge Cft DOR/KN B93 197 F2
NFLD/LBR B31 158 A5
Lodge Dr
LGN/SDN/BHAMAIR B26 130 A4
Lodge Farm Cl
WALM/CURD B76 63 F5
Lodgefield Rd RMSLY B62 121 H5
Lodge Gv ALDR WS9 30 A5
Lodge Hill Rd SLYOAK B29 159 F1
Lodge La KGSWFD DY6 99 F3
Lodgepool Cl KGSTG B44 75 E5
Lodge Rd AST/WIT B6 109 E1
BILS/COS WV14 54 B4
DARL/WED WS10 55 F3
DOR/KN B93 197 F2
DSYBK/YTR WS5 58 B3
RUSH/SHEL WS4 28 D1
SMTHWKW B67 106 A2
WBROM B70 87 F3
WOLVN WV10 22 D2
WSNGN B18 107 G4
Lodge St OLDBY B69 105 E2
SHHTH WV12 26 A5
Loeless Rd STETCH B33 130 C1
Lofthouse Crs NFLD/LBR B31 175 F2
Lofthouse Gv NFLD/LBR B31 175 F2
Lofthouse Rd
BFLD/HDSWWD B20 89 G4
Loftus Cl NFLD/LBR B31 158 B2
Logan Cl WOLVN WV10 23 E4
Lomaine Dr BVILLE B30 176 C1
Lomas Dr NFLD/LBR B31 175 E2
Lomas St WOLV WV1 37 E1
Lombard Av DUDS DY2 120 D1
Lombard St BHTH/HG B12 127 F4
WBROM B70 87 G3
Lombard St West WBROM B70 * 87 G3
Lombardy Cft RMSLY B62 140 A1
Lombardy Gdns SHHTH WV12 26 C3
Lomond Cl BKDE/SHDE B34 113 G3
Lomond Rd SEDG DY3 67 E2
Londonderry Gv
SMTHWKW B67 106 B4
Londonderry La
SMTHWKW B67 106 B4
London Hts DUDN DY1 84 A4
London Rd BFLD/HDSWWD B20 91 E4
MGN/WHC B75 48 C1
London St SMTHWK B66 107 E4
Lones Rd HHTH/SAND B71 106 D1
Long Acre CDSL WV8 10 A5
VAUX/NECH B7 109 H3
Longacre WLNHL WV13 39 G5
Longacres WLNHL WV13 39 G5
Long Acre St WSLW WS2 4 C1
Longbank Rd OLDBY B69 104 A1
Longboat La STRBR DY8 118 A4
Longboat Quay DUDS DY2 102 D5
Longbow Rd SLYOAK B29 158 B3
Longbridge La NFLD/LBR B31 175 E5
NFLD/LBR B31 189 F1
Long Cl HAG/WOL DY9 169 G1
Long Close Wk CVALE B35 94 C3
Long Compton Dr
HAG/WOL DY9 152 C4
Longcroft Cl CVALE B35 94 C3
The Longcroft HALE B63 138 A3
RUSH/SHEL WS4 29 E3
Longdales Rd
HWK/WKHTH B38 190 B1
Longdon Av
ETTPK/GDPK/PENN WV4 52 B3
Longdon Cft DOR/KN B93 183 E5
Longdon Dr FOAKS/STRLY B74 46 C1
Longdon Rd DOR/KN B93 197 E2
Longfellow Rd BVILLE B30 176 B2
SEDG DY3 82 C1
Longfield Cl HLGN/YWD B28 162 D4
Longfield Rd HAG/WOL DY9 136 B2
NFLD/LBR B31 158 A3
Longford Cl DOR/KN B93 197 F5
RIDG/WDGT B32 157 E3
WMBN WV5 80 B1
Longford Gv KGSTG B44 60 C5
Longford Rd KGSTG B44 75 G1
WOLVN WV10 37 H1
Longham Cft RIDG/WDGT B32 141 F3
Longhurst Cft NFLD/LBR B31 189 G1
Long Hyde Rd SMTHWKW B67 124 B3
Long Innage HALE B63 137 F1
Long Knowle La WNSFLD WV11 24 B2
Longlake Av
DUNHL/THL/PER WV6 35 E2
Longlands Rd RMSLY B62 139 G4
The Longlands WMBN WV5 65 E5
Long La BLKHTH/ROWR B65 122 B3
WNSFLD WV11 15 H2
Long Leasow SELYOAK B29 158 D3
Longleat GTB/HAM B43 73 E2
Longleat Dr DUDN DY1 83 G4
SHLY B90 195 E3
Longleat Rd ALDR WS9 19 G5
Long Ley WOLVN WV10 37 H2
Longley Av WALM/CURD B76 95 F1
Longley Crs
LGN/SDN/BHAMAIR B26 147 E3
Long Leys Ct
CSHL/WTROR B46 * 96 B4
Long Leys Cft CSHL/WTROR B46 96 B4
Longmeadow Cl MGN/WHC B75 63 E3
Longmeadow Crs
BKDE/SHDE B34 113 G3
Long Meadow Dr SEDG DY3 66 D2
Longmeadow Gv
NFLD/LBR B31 189 G2
Longmeadow Rd
DSYBK/YTR WS5 43 G5
Long Mill Av WNSFLD WV11 24 B3
Long Ml North WNSFLD WV11 24 B3
Long Ml South WNSFLD WV11 24 B3
Longmoor Cl WNSFLD WV11 25 F5
Longmoor Rd HALE B63 138 A4
SCFLD/BOLD B73 60 D5
Longmore Av WSLW WS2 40 D4
Longmore Cl SCFLD/BOLD B73 60 C3
Longmore Rd SHLY B90 180 D4
Longmore St BHTH/HG B12 127 E5
DARL/WED WS10 55 H5
Long Mynd HALE B63 154 D1
Long Mynd Cl SHHTH WV12 * 25 H1
Long Mynd Rd NFLD/LBR B31 158 A4
Long Nuke Rd NFLD/LBR B31 158 A3
Long Saw Dr NFLD/LBR B31 174 D4
Longshaw Gv BKDE/SHDE B34 113 F3
Longstone Cl SHLY B90 195 H2
Longstone Rd PBAR/PBCH B42 74 C4
Long St SPARK B11 144 C1
WOLV WV1 7 G3
WSLW WS2 4 B5
Long Wd BVILLE B30 159 G5
Longwood La RUSH/SHEL WS4 43 G3
Longwood Ri SHHTH WV12 26 B5
Longwood Rd ALDR WS9 44 B3
RBRY B45 188 A1
Lonicera Cl DSYBK/YTR WS5 57 H5
Lonsdale Cl SHHTH WV12 25 H5
Lonsdale Rd BDMR/CCFT WV3 36 D5
BILS/COS WV14 54 B2
DSYBK/YTR WS5 58 A2
HRBN B17 141 H1
SMTHWK B66 105 H2
Lord's Dr WSLW WS2 4 E1
Lords La KINVER DY7 116 C3
Lordsmore Cl BILS/COS WV14 68 D2
Lord St BDMR/CCFT WV3 6 C5
BILS/COS WV14 54 A5
VAUX/NECH B7 3 K1
WSL WS1 56 D2
Lord St West BILS/COS WV14 54 A5
Lordswood Rd HRBN B17 124 C4
Lordswood Sq HRBN B17 * 124 D5
Lorimer Wy GTB/HAM B43 59 H3
Lorne St TPTN/OCK DY4 69 F3
Lorrainer Av STRBR DY8 118 C4
Lothians Rd BLOX/PEL WS3 18 A2
DUNHL/THL/PER WV6 21 H4
Lottie Rd SLYOAK B29 159 G1
Lotus Cft SMTHWKW B67 106 B5
Lotus Wy BLKHTH/ROWR B65 103 F5
Loughton Gv HALE B63 138 B3
Louisa St CBHAMW B1 2 C4
Louise Cft ALE/KHTH/YWD B14 178 A3
Louise Lorne Rd MOS/BIL B13 144 B3
Louise Rd HDSW B21 107 G2
Louise St SEDG DY3 82 D3
Lount Wk LOZ/NWT B19 109 E4
Lovat St WOLV WV1 6 D4
Lovatt Cl TPTN/OCK DY4 70 A2
Loveday St CBHAMNE B4 3 G2
Lovelace Av SOLH B91 182 B5
Love La DUNHL/THL/PER WV6 21 H4
HAG/WOL DY9 136 C2
HLYWD B47 192 A1
STRBR DY8 135 G4
VAUX/NECH B7 3 J1
WSL WS1 57 E1
Lovell Cl SLYOAK B29 158 C4
Loveridge Cl CDSL WV8 10 A4
Lovett Av OLDBY B69 104 B4
Low Av GTB/HAM B43 73 H1
Lowbridge Cl SHHTH WV12 26 A5
Lowbrook La SHLY B90 193 F4
Lowden Cft
LGN/SDN/BHAMAIR B26 147 E3
Lowe Av DARL/WED WS10 54 D1
Lowe Dr KGSWFD DY6 100 A5
SCFLD/BOLD B73 61 F5
Lower Beeches Rd
NFLD/LBR B31 174 C3
Lower Chapel St OLDBY B69 86 A4
Lower Church La
TPTN/OCK DY4 69 G5
Lower City Rd OLDBY B69 86 A5
Lowercroft Wy
FOAKS/STRLY B74 32 C4
Lower Dartmouth St
BORD B9 127 H2
Lower Darwin St
BHTH/HG B12 127 F4
Lower Derry St BRLYHL DY5 119 F2
Lower Essex St DIG/EDG B5 127 E3
Lower Forster St WSL WS1 5 F2
Lower Gn TPTN/OCK DY4 * 85 E1
Lower Ground Cl AST/WIT B6 * 91 F5
Lower Hall La WSL WS1 4 E4
Lower Hall St WSL WS1 4 E5
Lower High St CDYHTH B64 120 C4
DARL/WED WS10 70 D1
STRBR DY8 135 F1
Lower Higley Cl
RIDG/WDGT B32 141 E3
Lower Horseley Flds WOLV WV1 37 H3
Lower Lichfield St WLNHL WV13 39 H3
Lower Loveday St
LOZ/NWT B19 3 F1
Lower Moor SLYOAK B29 * 159 G2
Lower North St
RUSH/SHEL WS4 42 A2
The Lower Pde
CSCFLD/WYGN B72 62 C3
Lower Prestwood Rd
WNSFLD WV11 24 C3

Lower Queen St
CSCFLD/WYGN B72 62 C4
Lower Reddicroft
SCFLD/BOLD B73 62 C3
Lower Rushall St WSL WS1 5 F3
Lower Severn St CBHAMW B1 2 E6
Lowerstack Cft
CHWD/FDBR/MGN B37 131 H1
Lower St DUNHL/THL/PER WV6 22 A5
Lower Temple St CBHAM B2 3 F5
Lower Tower St LOZ/NWT B19 108 D4
Lower Trinity St BORD B9 127 G3
Lower Valley Rd BRLYHL DY5 118 C2
Lower Vauxhall WOLV WV1 6 A3
Lower Villiers St
BKHL/PFLD WV2 52 A1
Lower Walsall St WOLV WV1 37 H4
Lower White Rd
RIDG/WDGT B32 140 D2
Lowesmoor Rd
LGN/SDN/BHAMAIR B26 130 D5
Lowe St BHTH/HG B12 127 G4
DUNHL/THL/PER WV6 36 C1
Loweswater Dr SEDG DY3 83 F3
Lowfield Cl RIDG/WDGT B32 140 A4
Low Hill Crs WOLVN WV10 23 G2
Lowhill La RBRY B45 188 C2
Lowland Cl CDYHTH B64 121 F3
Lowlands Av
DUNHL/THL/PER WV6 22 A4
FOAKS/STRLY B74 45 E5
Lowndes Rd STRBR DY8 135 E1
Lowry Cl DUNHL/THL/PER WV6 34 D1
SMTHWKW B67 106 B3
WLNHL WV13 38 D3
Low Thatch HWK/WKHTH B38 190 C1
Low Town OLDBY B69 105 E2
Low Wood Rd
ERDW/GRVHL B23 92 C1
Loxdale Sidings BILS/COS WV14 54 B4
Loxdale St BILS/COS WV14 54 B4
DARL/WED WS10 70 D1
Loxley Av ALE/KHTH/YWD B14 179 E3
SHLY B90 179 H4
Loxley Cl NFLD/LBR B31 158 A2
Loxley Rd MGN/WHC B75 47 H2
SMTHWKW B67 124 B3
Loxton Cl FOAKS/STRLY B74 32 B5
Loynells Rd RBRY B45 188 A1
Loyns Cl
CHWD/FDBR/MGN B37 131 G1
Lozells Rd LOZ/NWT B19 108 B2
Lozells St LOZ/NWT B19 108 C2
Lozells Wood Cl LOZ/NWT B19 108 B2
Lucas Circ LOZ/NWT B19 108 C3
Luce Cl CVALE B35 94 D2
Luce Rd WOLVN WV10 23 G4
Lucknow Rd SHHTH WV12 25 H5
Luddington Rd HIA/OLT B92 165 G3
Ludford Cl MGN/WHC B75 63 E1
Ludford Rd RIDG/WDGT B32 157 E1
Ludgate Cl CSHL/WTROR B46 96 A3
OLDBY B69 103 H1
Ludgate Hl CBHAMNW B3 2 E3
Ludgate St DUDN DY1 * 84 B5
Ludlow Cl
CHWD/FDBR/MGN B37 132 C2
SHHTH WV12 25 H4
Ludlow La WSLW WS2 41 E1
Ludlow Rd WASH/WDE B8 128 D1
Ludlow Wy DUDN DY1 83 G4
Ludmer Wy BFLD/HDSWWD B20 90 C4
Ludstone Av
ETTPK/GDPK/PENN WV4 50 D3
Ludstone Rd SLYOAK B29 158 B1
Ludworth Av
CHWD/FDBR/MGN B37 132 B3
Lugtrout La SOLH B91 165 H4
Lulworth Cl HALE B63 137 G1
Lulworth Rd HLGN/YWD B28 163 E2
Lumley Gv
CHWD/FDBR/MGN B37 132 D2
Lumley Rd WSL WS1 5 J5
Lundy Vw CBROM B36 114 B3
Lunt Gv RIDG/WDGT B32 140 D2
Lunt Pl BILS/COS WV14 54 C2
Lunt Rd BILS/COS WV14 54 C1
Lupin Gv BORD B9 128 D1
DSYBK/YTR WS5 57 H4
Lupin Rd DUDS DY2 85 F5
Lusbridge Cl HALE B63 137 F3
Lutley Av HALE B63 138 A3
Lutley Cl BDMR/CCFT WV3 51 E1
Lutley Dr HAG/WOL DY9 136 A4
Lutley Gv RIDG/WDGT B32 157 F1
Lutley La HALE B63 137 G5
Lutley Mill Rd HALE B63 138 A3
Luton Rd SLYOAK B29 142 D4
Luttrell Rd FOAKS/STRLY B74 46 D5
Lyall Gdns RBRY B45 173 G4
Lyall Gv ACGN B27 146 A5
Lychgate Av HAG/WOL DY9 153 E1
Lydate Rd RMSLY B62 139 H3
Lydbrook Covert
HWK/WKHTH B38 176 C5
Lydbury Gv STETCH B33 112 C5
Lyd Cl WNSFLD WV11 24 B5
Lydd Cft CVALE B35 94 D2
Lyddington Dr RMSLY B62 121 H5
Lyde Gn HALE B63 120 C5
Lydford Gv ERDE/BCHGN B24 93 E4
Lydford Rd BLOX/PEL WS3 16 D5
Lydgate Rd KGSWFD DY6 100 B4
Lydget Gv ERDW/GRVHL B23 76 B4
Lydham Cl BILS/COS WV14 53 F4
ERDW/GRVHL B23 75 G5
Lydia Cft FOAKS/STRLY B74 32 C4
Lydian Cl DUNHL/THL/PER WV6 36 D1
Lydiate Ash Rd BRGRVW B61 187 E5
Lydiate Av NFLD/LBR B31 174 D4
Lydiates Cl SEDG DY3 66 D4
Lydney Cl SHHTH WV12 40 B1
Lydney Gv NFLD/LBR B31 175 F2
Lye Av RIDG/WDGT B32 140 A5
Lye By-Pass HAG/WOL DY9 136 C1
Lye Close La RIDG/WDGT B32 139 H5
Lyecroft Av
CHWD/FDBR/MGN B37 132 D2
Lye Cross Rd OLDBY B69 103 H2
Lygon Gv RIDG/WDGT B32 141 E3
Lymedene Rd PBAR/PBCH B42 90 B1
Lyme Green Rd STETCH B33 112 B5
Lymer Rd WOLVN WV10 23 E1
Lymington Rd WLNHL WV13 40 B3
Lymsey Cft STRBR DY8 117 G1
Lynbrook Cl DUDS DY2 102 D3
HLYWD B47 178 C5
Lyncourt Gv RIDG/WDGT B32 140 B1
Lyncroft Rd SPARK B11 145 H5
Lyndale Dr WNSFLD WV11 25 F5
Lyndale Rd DUDS DY2 103 E3
SEDG DY3 66 D1
Lyndhurst Dr STRBR DY8 118 B3
Lyndhurst Rd BDMR/CCFT WV3 51 G1
ERDE/BCHGN B24 92 D4
HHTH/SAND B71 72 A4
Lyndon HHTH/SAND B71 87 H1
Lyndon Cl BFLD/HDSWWD B20 90 B4
CBROM B36 113 E1
HALE B63 138 A2
SEDG DY3 67 G2
Lyndon Cft
CHWD/FDBR/MGN B37 132 B5
Lyndon Gv HHTH/SAND B71 87 H2
KGSWFD DY6 99 F1
Lyndon Rd HIA/OLT B92 147 F5
RBRY B45 187 G1
SCFLD/BOLD B73 62 B3
STETCH B33 130 A1
Lyndworth Rd BVILLE B30 160 C3
Lyneham Gdns
WALM/CURD B76 78 C5
Lyneham Wy CVALE B35 94 B3
Lynfield Cl HWK/WKHTH B38 190 D1
Lyng La WBROM B70 87 G4
Lynmouth Cl ALDR WS9 29 H5
Lynn Gv SLYOAK B29 142 A4
Lynton Av
DUNHL/THL/PER WV6 22 A3
HHTH/SAND B71 71 G4
SMTHWK B66 106 C3
Lynton Rd AST/WIT B6 109 G2
Lynval Rd BRLYHL DY5 119 H5
Lynwood Av KGSWFD DY6 99 F1
Lynwood Cl SHHTH WV12 26 C2
Lynwood Dr KIDD DY10 168 B3
Lynwood Wk HRBN B17 142 A3
Lyons Gv SPARK B11 145 E4
Lysander Rd RBRY B45 174 A3
Lysways St WSL WS1 5 F6
Lytham Cl STRBR DY8 135 G5
WALM/CURD B76 78 D5
Lytham Cft EDG B15 126 D3
Lytham Gv BLOX/PEL WS3 16 C3
Lytham Rd
DUNHL/THL/PER WV6 34 B1
Lythwood Dr BRLYHL DY5 119 E4
Lyttelton Rd
LDYWD/EDGR B16 125 F3
STETCH B33 129 H2
STRBR DY8 134 D2
Lyttleton Av RMSLY B62 122 C5
Lyttleton Cl DUDS DY2 102 C5
Lyttleton St WBROM B70 87 G4
Lytton Av
ETTPK/GDPK/PENN WV4 50 D4
Lytton Gv ACGN B27 163 F1
Lytton La RIDG/WDGT B32 141 F4

M

Maas Rd NFLD/LBR B31 175 G1
Macarthur Rd CDYHTH B64 120 C4
Macdonald Cl OLDBY B69 86 B4
Macdonald St DIG/EDG B5 127 E4
Mace St CDYHTH B64 121 E3
Machin Rd ERDW/GRVHL B23 92 D2
Mackadown La STETCH B33 131 F2
Mackay Rd BLOX/PEL WS3 17 F5
Mackenzie Rd SPARK B11 145 E5
Mackmillan Rd
BLKHTH/ROWR B65 122 A2
Macmillan Cl OLDBY B69 86 A4
Macrome Rd
DUNHL/THL/PER WV6 22 A2
Madam's Hill Rd SHLY B90 194 D1
Maddocks Hl
CSCFLD/WYGN B72 77 G1
Madehurst Rd
ERDW/GRVHL B23 76 C5
Madeira Av CDSL WV8 10 C5
Madeley Rd HAG/WOL DY9 186 A1
KGSWFD DY6 100 C5
SPARK B11 145 E2
Madin Rd TPTN/OCK DY4 85 E2
Madison Av CBROM B36 111 H3
WSLW WS2 41 F3
Madley Cl RBRY B45 173 G5
Madresfield Dr HALE B63 138 D5
Maer Cl BLKHTH/ROWR B65 122 A1
Mafeking Rd SMTHWK B66 106 C2
Mafeking Vls RMSLY B62 * 121 H5
Magdala St WSNGN B18 107 G4
Magdalen Cl DUDN DY1 84 A4
Magdalene Rd WSL WS1 57 G1
Magness Crs SHHTH WV12 26 A5
Magnolia Cl SLYOAK B29 158 C3
Magnolia Dr DSYBK/YTR WS5 57 F4
Magnolia Gv CDSL WV8 10 C4
Magnolia Wy STRBR DY8 118 B4
Magnum Cl FOAKS/STRLY B74 * 60 B1
Magpie Cl DUDS DY2 121 E1
Maidendale Rd KGSWFD DY6 99 F2
Maidensbridge Gdns
KGSWFD DY6 81 F5
Maidensbridge Rd KGSWFD DY6 81 F5
Maidstone Dr STRBR DY8 118 A1
Maidstone Rd
BFLD/HDSWWD B20 91 E5
Maidwell Dr SHLY B90 181 E5
Main Rd
LGN/SDN/BHAMAIR B26 148 D4
Mainstream Wy
VAUX/NECH B7 110 A5
Main St SPARK B11 127 G5
Main Ter BHTH/HG B12 * 127 G5
Mainwaring Dr MGN/WHC B75 48 A3
Maisonettes CDSL WV8 * 10 D4
The Maisonettes
ERDE/BCHGN B24 * 92 C4
Maitland Rd DUDN DY1 83 F5
WASH/WDE B8 110 D5
Majestic Wy
BLKHTH/ROWR B65 104 A5
Major St BKHL/PFLD WV2 52 C1
Majuba Rd LDYWD/EDGR B16 107 E5
Malcolm Av ERDE/BCHGN B24 93 G1
Malcolm Gv RBRY B45 188 A1
Malcolm Rd SHLY B90 180 B3
Malcolmson Cl EDG B15 125 H5
Malfield Dr ACGN B27 147 E4
Malins Rd
ETTPK/GDPK/PENN WV4 52 B3
HRBN B17 142 B2
Malkit Cl WSLW WS2 40 C1
Mallaby Cl SHLY B90 180 A5
Mallard Cl ACGN B27 146 C4
BLOX/PEL WS3 18 A1
BRLYHL DY5 119 E5
Mallard Dr ERDW/GRVHL B23 91 H3
OLDBY B69 122 D1
Mallender Dr DOR/KN B93 196 D1
Mallen Dr OLDBY B69 85 H5
Mallin St SMTHWK B66 105 H2
Mallory Crs BLOX/PEL WS3 17 F5
Mallory Ri MOS/BIL B13 162 A1
Mallory Rd
DUNHL/THL/PER WV6 34 C2
Mallow Cl DSYBK/YTR WS5 57 F5
Mallow Ct
DUNHL/THL/PER WV6 * 22 D5
Mallow Ri ERDW/GRVHL B23 75 H4
Mallows Cl DARL/WED WS10 * 55 F2
Malmesbury Rd SMHTH B10 145 G1
Malpas Dr RIDG/WDGT B32 157 G2
Malpass Gdns CDSL WV8 10 A3
Malpass Rd BRLYHL DY5 119 H5
Malpass Wk WOLVN WV10 38 A1
Malt Cl EDG B15 142 B1
Malthouse Cft AST/WIT B6 109 E1
Malthouse Dr DUDN DY1 84 A4
Malthouse Gdns LOZ/NWT B19 108 D2
Malthouse Gv YDLY B25 130 A3
Malthouse La
DUNHL/THL/PER WV6 21 H4
PBAR/PBCH B42 74 D3
WASH/WDE B8 110 C3
Malthouse Rd TPTN/OCK DY4 85 E1
Malthouse Rw
CHWD/FDBR/MGN B37 132 A4
The Maltings ALDR WS9 * 30 C4
WMBN WV5 * 65 E5
WOLV WV1 7 G1
Malt Mill La RMSLY B62 122 A4
Malton Gv MOS/BIL B13 161 H3
Malvern Av HAG/WOL DY9 136 A2
Malvern Cl HHTH/SAND B71 87 H1
SHHTH WV12 39 H1
Malvern Ct ACGN B27 * 146 C3
WOLVN WV10 23 F2
Malvern Crs DUDS DY2 101 H3
Malvern Dr ALDR WS9 30 C2
WALM/CURD B76 78 C3
WOLV WV1 38 B4
Malvern Hill Rd VAUX/NECH B7 110 A2
Malvern Park Av SOLH B91 182 B2
Malvern Rd ACGN B27 146 C3
LGLYGN/QTN B68 123 F4
Malvern St BHTH/HG B12 144 C2
Malvern View Rd SEDG DY3 83 F2
Mamble Rd STRBR DY8 135 E2
Mammoth Dr WOLVN WV10 23 H4
Manby Cl DUNHL/THL/PER WV6 36 C1
Manby Rd CVALE B35 94 C2
Manby St TPTN/OCK DY4 69 F3
Mancetter Rd SHLY B90 180 C2
Manchester St AST/WIT B6 109 E4
OLDBY B69 105 F2
Mancroft Cl KGSWFD DY6 99 F2
Mancroft Gdns
DUNHL/THL/PER WV6 21 G5
Mancroft Rd
DUNHL/THL/PER WV6 21 G5
Mandale Rd WOLVN WV10 23 H4
Manderley Cl SEDG DY3 67 E1
Manders Est WOLV WV1 * 37 H2
Mander St BDMR/CCFT WV3 6 D7
Manderville Gdns KGSWFD DY6 99 G3
Mandeville Gdns WSL WS1 5 G6
Maney Cnr CSCFLD/WYGN B72 62 B4
Maney Hill Rd
CSCFLD/WYGN B72 62 C5
Manfield Rd WLNHL WV13 38 C2
Manilla Rd SLYOAK B29 160 B1
Manitoba Cft
HWK/WKHTH B38 176 D5
Manley Cl WBROM B70 * 87 E3
Manlove St BDMR/CCFT WV3 6 B7
Manningford Rd
ALE/KHTH/YWD B14 178 B3
Manor Abbey Dr RMSLY B62 139 G4
Manor Abbey Rd RMSLY B62 139 G3
Manor Cl CDSL WV8 10 D4
ETTPK/GDPK/PENN WV4 51 F4
WLNHL WV13 39 F2
Manor Ct DOR/KN B93 * 198 D1
WSLW WS2 * 41 G4
Manor Dr SCFLD/BOLD B73 62 B4
SEDG DY3 80 C4
SEDG DY3 82 D3
SLYOAK B29 * 158 D3
Manor Farm Dr SHHTH WV12 26 B5
Manor Farm Rd SPARK B11 145 G3
Manorford Av HHTH/SAND B71 72 C2
Manor Gdns STETCH B33 129 H3
WMBN WV5 * 65 F4
Manor Gv NFLD/LBR B31 174 C4
Manor Hl SCFLD/BOLD B73 62 B4
Manor House Cl SLYOAK B29 158 B1
Manor House La
CSHL/WTROR B46 96 B3
LGN/SDN/BHAMAIR B26 147 E1
Manor House Pk CDSL WV8 10 D3
Manor House Rd
DARL/WED WS10 55 H4
Manor Houses RMSLY B62 * 139 H2
Manor La BRGRVW B61 187 E3
RMSLY B62 139 G3
STRBR DY8 134 D4
Manor Pk KGSWFD DY6 99 H3
NFLD/LBR B31 174 C3
Manor Park Rd CBROM B36 113 F2
Manor Rd AST/WIT B6 91 F5
DARL/WED WS10 71 H1
DOR/KN B93 196 D5
ETTPK/GDPK/PENN WV4 51 F4
ETTPK/GDPK/PENN WV4 53 E3
FOAKS/STRLY B74 45 G5
HLYWD B47 192 C5
LDYWD/EDGR B16 125 F3
SCFLD/BOLD B73 62 B3
SMTHWKW B67 105 H4
SOLH B91 164 D5
STETCH B33 130 A1
STRBR DY8 117 H2
TPTN/OCK DY4 85 F1
WOLVN WV10 23 E5
WSLW WS2 41 G3
Manor Rd North
LDYWD/EDGR B16 125 F3
Manor Road Prec WSLW WS2 41 G3
Manor St DUNHL/THL/PER WV6 21 G5
Manor Wy HALE B63 155 F1
RMSLY B62 139 E5
Mansard Cl BDMR/CCFT WV3 36 B5
WNSFLD WV11 24 B2
Mansell Cl HALE B63 120 B5
Mansell Rd TPTN/OCK DY4 69 G3
Mansel Rd SMHTH B10 128 C4
Mansfield Rd AST/WIT B6 108 D1
YDLY B25 146 C2
Mansion Cl DUDN DY1 84 A3
Mansion Crs SMTHWKW B67 106 A5
Mansion Dr TPTN/OCK DY4 86 A1
Manston Dr
DUNHL/THL/PER WV6 20 C5
Manston Rd
LGN/SDN/BHAMAIR B26 130 D5
Manton Cft DOR/KN B93 196 C5
Manway Cl BFLD/HDSWWD B20 89 H1
Manwoods Cl
BFLD/HDSWWD B20 90 B4
Maple Av DARL/WED WS10 56 C4
Maple Bank EDG B15 * 126 A5
Maplebeck Ct SOLH B91 * 165 E5
Maple Cl BILS/COS WV14 68 A4
HDSW B21 89 G5
STRBR DY8 134 D5
Maple Ct ALE/KHTH/YWD B14 161 F4
Mapledene Rd
LGN/SDN/BHAMAIR B26 148 B1
Maple Dr DSYBK/YTR WS5 57 H4
KGSTG B44 75 H3
RUSH/SHEL WS4 28 D2
SEDG DY3 82 D4
Maple Gn DUDN DY1 84 A1
Maple Gv BDMR/CCFT WV3 35 G3
BILS/COS WV14 54 B4
CHWD/FDBR/MGN B37 113 H3
KGSWFD DY6 100 A3
LOZ/NWT B19 108 C1
Maple Leaf Dr
CHWD/FDBR/MGN B37 132 B4
Maple Leaf Rd DARL/WED WS10 70 A2
Maple Ri LGLYGN/QTN B68 123 G2
Maple Rd BDMR/CCFT WV3 36 A5
BLOX/PEL WS3 17 H5
BVILLE B30 159 G2
CSCFLD/WYGN B72 62 C5
DUDN DY1 84 C3
RBRY B45 187 H2
RMSLY B62 122 B4
Maple St BLOX/PEL WS3 17 F5
Mapleton Gv HLGN/YWD B28 163 F3
Mapleton Rd HLGN/YWD B28 163 F4
Maple Tree La HALE B63 137 G1
Maple Wy NFLD/LBR B31 175 F5
Maplewood WALM/CURD B76 78 D4
Mapperley Gdns MOS/BIL B13 143 G4
Mappleborough Rd SHLY B90 179 G4
Marans Cft HWK/WKHTH B38 190 B1
Marbury Cl HWK/WKHTH B38 176 B3
Marbury Ms BRLYHL DY5 119 F3
Marchant Rd BDMR/CCFT WV3 36 B3
BILS/COS WV14 53 G1
March End Rd WNSFLD WV11 24 D5
Marchmont Rd BORD B9 129 E2
Marchmount Rd
CSCFLD/WYGN B72 77 G3
March Wy ALDR WS9 30 C1
Marcliff Crs SHLY B90 179 E3
Marcos Dr CBROM B36 95 H5
Marcot Rd HIA/OLT B92 147 F2
Marden Cl WLNHL WV13 39 F4
Marden Gv NFLD/LBR B31 189 G1
Mardon Rd
LGN/SDN/BHAMAIR B26 147 H2
Maree Gv WNSFLD WV11 25 H1
Marfield Cl WALM/CURD B76 78 C5
Margam Crs BLOX/PEL WS3 16 B5
Margam Ter BLOX/PEL WS3 16 B5
Margam Wy BLOX/PEL WS3 16 B5
Margaret Av HALE B63 138 B3
Margaret Cl BRLYHL DY5 119 G4
Margaret Dr STRBR DY8 135 H3
Margaret Gdns SMTHWKW B67 106 A4
Margaret Gv HRBN B17 125 E5
Margaret Rd DARL/WED WS10 55 E4
HRBN B17 142 A2
SCFLD/BOLD B73 76 B2
WSLW WS2 40 C2
Margaret St CBHAMNW B3 2 E4
WBROM B70 87 F4
Margaret V TPTN/OCK DY4 70 A2
Marholm Cl COVEN WV9 11 H5
Marian Cft
LGN/SDN/BHAMAIR B26 148 B2
Maria St WBROM B70 105 H1
Marie Dr ACGN B27 163 F2
Marigold Crs DUDN DY1 84 A2
Marine Crs STRBR DY8 118 A3
Marine Dr KGSTG B44 75 E5
Marine Gdns STRBR DY8 118 A3
Mariner Av LDYWD/EDGR B16 125 G3
Marion Cl BRLYHL DY5 119 H2
Marion Rd SMTHWKW B67 105 H3
Marion Wy HLGN/YWD B28 162 C3
Marita Cl DUDS DY2 121 E1
Marjoram Cl HWK/WKHTH B38 176 D5
Marjorie Av BVILLE B30 177 F2
Mark Av DARL/WED WS10 55 G5
Markby Rd WSNGN B18 107 G3
Market Hall BILS/COS WV14 * 53 H3
Market Pl
BLKHTH/ROWR B65 * 122 A3
BLOX/PEL WS3 27 F1
DARL/WED WS10 70 D1
TPTN/OCK DY4 86 B1
WLNHL WV13 39 G3
Market Sq CDYHTH B64 * 120 C4
Market St KGSWFD DY6 99 H3
OLDBY B69 105 E1
STRBR DY8 135 G2
WOLV WV1 7 G4
Market Wy HAG/WOL DY9 153 E4
Markfield Rd
LGN/SDN/BHAMAIR B26 130 D4
Markford Wk LOZ/NWT B19 108 D3
Markham Crs HIA/OLT B92 165 H1
Markham Cft COVEN WV9 12 A5
Markham Dr KGSWFD DY6 100 A5
Markham Rd SCFLD/BOLD B73 61 E5
Marklew Cl BRWNH WS8 19 G2
Marklin Av WOLVN WV10 23 F1
Mark Rd DARL/WED WS10 55 G5
Marksbury Cl
DUNHL/THL/PER WV6 22 C5
Marlbank Rd STRBR DY8 118 C3
Marlborough Cl
FOAKS/STRLY B74 32 C4
Marlborough Dr STRBR DY8 135 G4
Marlborough Gdns
DUNHL/THL/PER WV6 36 A1
STRBR DY8 117 G2
Marlborough Gv YDLY B25 129 H3
Marlborough Rd BORD B9 128 C3
CBROM B36 113 F1
SEDG DY3 67 H5
SMTHWK B66 124 C1
Marlborough St
BLOX/PEL WS3 27 F1
Marlbrook Cl HIA/OLT B92 148 A3
Marlbrook Dr
ETTPK/GDPK/PENN WV4 51 H2
Marlburn Wy WMBN WV5 64 C5
Marlcliff Gv MOS/BIL B13 161 G4
Marldon Rd
ALE/KHTH/YWD B14 160 D4
Marlene Cft
CHWD/FDBR/MGN B37 132 C3
Marley Rd KGSWFD DY6 100 C5
Marling Cft HIA/OLT B92 165 G3
Marlow Cl DUDS DY2 121 E1
Marlowe Dr SHHTH WV12 25 G3
Marlow Rd ERDW/GRVHL B23 92 A1
Marlow St BLKHTH/ROWR B65 121 H3
WSLW WS2 42 A1
Marlpit La MGN/WHC B75 47 H2
Marlpool Dr BLOX/PEL WS3 28 B1
Marl Rd DUDS DY2 102 B5
Marl Top HWK/WKHTH B38 176 D3
Marmion Dr GTB/HAM B43 73 H1
Marmion Gv DUDN DY1 102 A1
Marmion Wy WBROM B70 70 D5
Marnel Dr BDMR/CCFT WV3 35 H5
Marquis Dr CDYHTH B64 121 G5
Marriott Rd DUDS DY2 102 C5
SMTHWK B66 105 H2
Marroway St
LDYWD/EDGR B16 125 H1
Marrowfat La HDSW B21 107 H2
Mars Cl BILS/COS WV14 68 A2
Marsden Cl HIA/OLT B92 164 A1
Marshall Cl ALDR WS9 44 B1
Marshall Gv KGSTG B44 75 F4
Marshall Lake Rd SHLY B90 180 D5
Marshall Rd LGLYGN/QTN B68 123 G3
WLNHL WV13 38 D4
Marshall St CBHAMW B1 2 E7
SMTHWKW B67 105 H2
Marsham Court Rd SOLH B91 164 B3
Marsham Rd
ALE/KHTH/YWD B14 178 B2
Marshbrook Cl
ERDE/BCHGN B24 94 A2

Marshbrook Rd
ERDE/BCHGN B24 93 H2
Marsh Crs STRBR DY8 117 H1
Marsh End HWK/WKHTH B38 177 E5
Marshfield SHLY B90 194 A3
Marshfield Gdns
ERDE/BCHGN B24 92 C4
Marsh Hl ERDW/GRVHL B23 92 A2
Marshland Wy WSLW WS2 40 C4
Marsh La CSHL/WTROR B46 96 B3
ERDW/GRVHL B23 92 C1
HHTH/SAND B71 71 H3
SOLH B91 182 C2
WOLVN WV10 12 B5
WSLW WS2 4 C3
Marsh Lane Pde WOLVN WV10 12 C5
Marshmont Wy
ERDW/GRVHL B23 76 B3
Marsh St WSLW WS2 4 C3
The Marsh DARL/WED WS10 55 G5
Marshwood Cft
RIDG/WDGT B32 140 A4
Marsland Cl HRBN B17 125 E4
Marsland Rd HIA/OLT B92 164 A3
Marston Av DARL/WED WS10 55 E2
Marston Cl STRBR DY8 134 C3
Marston Cft
CHWD/FDBR/MGN B37 131 H4
Marston Dr
CHWD/FDBR/MGN B37 114 A4
Marston Gv GTB/HAM B43 73 E3
Marston Rd BKHL/PFLD WV2 52 A1
DUDN DY1 101 F1
SCFLD/BOLD B73 77 E4
SLYOAK B29 158 C2
Marston St WLNHL WV13 40 A3
Martham Dr
DUNHL/THL/PER WV6 35 F3
Martin Cl BILS/COS WV14 68 D4
LGN/SDN/BHAMAIR B26 146 D1
Martindale Wk BRLYHL DY5 135 H1
Martin Dr SHHTH WV12 26 A5
Martineau Pl CBHAM B2 * 3 G5
Martineau Sq CBHAM B2 3 G5
Martingale Cl DSYBK/YTR WS5 57 F4
Martin Hill St DUDS DY2 102 C1
Martin Ri
CHWD/FDBR/MGN B37 131 H4
Martin Rd BILS/COS WV14 54 B5
DSYBK/YTR WS5 43 E5
TPTN/OCK DY4 85 G1
Martin St
ETTPK/GDPK/PENN WV4 52 D2
Martlesham Sq CVALE B35 94 C2
Martley Cft RIDG/WDGT B32 141 E3
SOLH B91 181 H5
Martley Dr HAG/WOL DY9 136 A3
Martley Rd OLDBY B69 104 B3
RUSH/SHEL WS4 29 E1
Marton Cl VAUX/NECH B7 109 H3
Marwood Cft FOAKS/STRLY B74 45 G3
Mary Ann St CBHAMNW B3 2 E3
WOLV WV1 * 7 J5
Maryland Av BKDE/SHDE B34 112 A4
Maryland Dr NFLD/LBR B31 158 D5
Maryland Rd BRLYHL DY5 119 H5
Marylebone Cl STRBR DY8 118 C5
Mary Macarthur Dr
CDYHTH B64 120 C3
Mary Rd HDSW B21 107 G2
OLDBY B69 104 A1
STETCH B33 129 H1
WBROM B70 87 H5
Mary St BHTH/HG B12 144 A2
CBHAMNW B3 2 D2
WSLW WS2 41 H2
Mary Vale Rd BVILLE B30 159 G4
Marywell Cl RIDG/WDGT B32 157 F3
Masefield Av DUDN DY1 68 C4
Masefield Cl BILS/COS WV14 69 F1
Masefield Ri RMSLY B62 139 F4
Masefield Rd BLOX/PEL WS3 28 A2
SEDG DY3 82 C2
WOLVN WV10 24 A1
Masefield Sq NFLD/LBR B31 176 A1
Masham Cl STETCH B33 130 A2
Mashie Gdns HWK/WKHTH B38 176 B4
Maslen Pl HALE B63 138 D4
Maslin Dr BILS/COS WV14 68 A2
Mason Crs
ETTPK/GDPK/PENN WV4 51 E3
Masonleys Rd NFLD/LBR B31 174 D2
Mason Rd ERDE/BCHGN B24 93 E2
WSLW WS2 27 F5
Masons Cl HALE B63 137 H4
Masons Cottages
ERDE/BCHGN B24 * 93 F1
Mason St BILS/COS WV14 68 B4
BKHL/PFLD WV2 52 A1
WBROM B70 87 F2
Masons Wy HIA/OLT B92 147 E5
Massbrook Gv WOLVN WV10 23 H4
Massbrook Rd WOLVN WV10 23 H4
Masshouse La
HWK/WKHTH B38 176 D4
Masters La RMSLY B62 122 C3
Matchlock Cl FOAKS/STRLY B74 60 A1
Matfen Av SCFLD/BOLD B73 76 D1
Math Meadow
RIDG/WDGT B32 141 F2
Matlock Cl BLOX/PEL WS3 17 E4
DUDS DY2 120 D1
Matlock Rd BLOX/PEL WS3 17 E4
SPARK B11 145 H4
Matlock Vls BHTH/HG B12 * 144 D2
Matthews Cl
BLKHTH/ROWR B65 121 H3
Mattox Rd WNSFLD WV11 24 D4
Matty Rd LGLYGN/QTN B68 105 G5
Maud Rd CSHL/WTROR B46 96 D3
WBROM B70 87 G5
Maughan St BRLYHL DY5 120 A4
DUDN DY1 84 A5
Maurice Gv WOLVN WV10 24 A4
Maurice Rd
ALE/KHTH/YWD B14 161 E4
SMTHWKW B67 124 A2
Mavis Gdns LGLYGN/QTN B68 123 F4
Mavis Rd NFLD/LBR B31 175 E4
Maw St WSL WS1 57 F2
Maxholm Rd FOAKS/STRLY B74 45 E5
Max Rd RIDG/WDGT B32 140 D2
Maxstoke Cl BLOX/PEL WS3 16 C4
Maxstoke Cft SHLY B90 180 C5
Maxstoke La CSHL/WTROR B46 115 G3
Maxstoke Rd SCFLD/BOLD B73 76 C1
Maxstoke St BORD B9 127 H2
Maxted Rd ERDW/GRVHL B23 76 A3
Maxwell Av BFLD/HDSWWD B20 90 B5
Maxwell Rd BKHL/PFLD WV2 7 H7
Mayall Dr MGN/WHC B75 47 G1
May Av BHTH/HG B12 144 C2
Maybank BORD B9 128 D1
Maybank Pl PBAR/PBCH B42 75 E5
Maybank Rd DUDS DY2 120 C1
Mayberry Cl
ALE/KHTH/YWD B14 178 D3
Maybridge Dr SOLH B91 181 H5
Maybrook Rd BRWNH WS8 19 F2
WALM/CURD B76 94 C1
Maybury Cl CDSL WV8 10 A3
Maybush Gdns WOLVN WV10 23 E1
Maydene Cft BHTH/HG B12 144 B1
Mayfair HAG/WOL DY9 136 B5
Mayfair Cl DUDN DY1 84 A4
KGSTG B44 75 H4
Mayfair Dr KGSWFD DY6 99 G2
Mayfair Gdns BDMR/CCFT WV3 35 H3
TPTN/OCK DY4 85 G2
May Farm Cl HLYWD B47 192 B2
Mayfield Cl SOLH B91 182 A4
Mayfield Crs
BLKHTH/ROWR B65 121 G1
Mayfield Rd BVILLE B30 160 A4
DUDN DY1 84 B2
FOAKS/STRLY B74 45 F5
HALE B63 137 H5
LOZ/NWT B19 108 C1
MOS/BIL B13 144 C5
RMSLY B62 122 D3
SCFLD/BOLD B73 77 E1
SPARK B11 146 A3
WOLV WV1 38 B4
Mayfields Dr BRWNH WS8 8 B2
Mayflower Cl LOZ/NWT B19 108 D3
Mayflower Dr BRLYHL DY5 100 C2
Mayford Gv MOS/BIL B13 161 H4
Maygrove Rd KGSWFD DY6 99 G2
Mayhurst Cl HLYWD B47 193 E2
TPTN/OCK DY4 69 G3
Mayhurst Rd HLYWD B47 192 D1
Mayland Dr FOAKS/STRLY B74 60 B3
Mayland Rd LDYWD/EDGR B16 125 E2
May La ALE/KHTH/YWD B14 161 F5
HLYWD B47 192 C1
Maynard Av STRBR DY8 134 D4
Maypole Cl CDYHTH B64 120 B4
Maypole Ct WMBN WV5 65 E5
Maypole Dr STRBR DY8 135 E2
Maypole Flds HALE B63 120 A5
Maypole Gv
ALE/KHTH/YWD B14 178 D3
Maypole Hl HALE B63 120 A4
Maypole La
ALE/KHTH/YWD B14 178 C3
Maypole Rd LGLYGN/QTN B68 123 F3
Maypole St WMBN WV5 65 F4
May St BLOX/PEL WS3 27 H4
Mayswood Dr
DUNHL/THL/PER WV6 34 D4
Mayswood Gv RIDG/WDGT B32 140 D3
Mayswood Rd HIA/OLT B92 148 A5
Maythorn Av WALM/CURD B76 78 C5
Maythorn Gdns CDSL WV8 10 C3
DUNHL/THL/PER WV6 35 G1
Maythorn Gv SOLH B91 181 H5
Maytree Cl
CHWD/FDBR/MGN B37 132 A2
May Tree Gv
BFLD/HDSWWD B20 89 H3
Maywell Dr HIA/OLT B92 165 H2
Maywood Cl KGSWFD DY6 99 F3
McBean Rd
DUNHL/THL/PER WV6 36 B1
McDougall Rd DARL/WED WS10 56 C5
McGregor Cl AST/WIT B6 91 F5
McKean Rd OLDBY B69 87 E5
McKen Ct WBROM B70 * 87 G4
McLean Rd WOLVN WV10 12 C5
Meaburn Cl SLYOAK B29 158 C3
Mead Cl ALDR WS9 30 B4
Mead Crs BORD B9 129 F1
Meadfoot Av
ALE/KHTH/YWD B14 178 B2
Meadfoot Dr KGSWFD DY6 99 F2
The Meadlands WMBN WV5 64 C5
Meadow Av HHTH/SAND B71 72 B2
Meadowbrook Gdns CDSL WV8 10 D3
Meadowbrook Rd HALE B63 137 H4
Meadow Brook Rd
NFLD/LBR B31 158 B5
Meadow Cl FOAKS/STRLY B74 45 F4
HOCK/TIA B94 198 A5
HRBN B17 124 D3
RUSH/SHEL WS4 * 29 E2
Meadow Cft
DUNHL/THL/PER WV6 34 B2
HAG/WOL DY9 169 F1
HLYWD B47 192 C5
Meadow Dr HIA/OLT B92 167 G4
Meadowfield Rd RBRY B45 188 A1
Meadowfields Cl STRBR DY8 118 A2
Meadow Grange Dr
SHHTH WV12 25 H3
Meadow Gv HIA/OLT B92 163 H1
Meadowhill Dr STRBR DY8 118 A2
Meadow Hill Rd
HWK/WKHTH B38 176 C3
Meadowlands Dr
RUSH/SHEL WS4 29 E2
Meadow La BILS/COS WV14 68 B1
SHHTH WV12 25 G5
WMBN WV5 65 E3
WOLVN WV10 12 C1
Meadowpark Rd STRBR DY8 117 H4
Meadow Pleck La SHLY B90 193 H2
Meadow Ri BVILLE B30 159 F3
Meadow Rd ALDR WS9 44 A1
BDMR/CCFT WV3 35 G5
DUDN DY1 84 A2
HLYWD B47 192 C5
HRBN B17 124 D3
LGLYGN/QTN B68 123 F2
RIDG/WDGT B32 140 A1
RMSLY B62 122 A4
SMTHWKW B67 106 B5
Meadows Gv CDSL WV8 10 C3
Meadowside Cl GTB/HAM B43 73 G2
Meadowside Rd
FOAKS/STRLY B74 46 D1
The Meadows ALDR WS9 29 G5
HAG/WOL DY9 152 D3
Meadow St CDYHTH B64 121 F4
WOLV WV1 6 C4
WSL WS1 4 C6
Meadowsweet Av
HWK/WKHTH B38 176 D5
Meadowsweet Wy
KGSWFD DY6 100 C3
Meadow V CDSL WV8 21 F1
Meadow Vw MOS/BIL B13 162 A2
SEDG DY3 67 E2
Meadow View Whf
DUNHL/THL/PER WV6 * 36 A1
Meadow Wk
ALE/KHTH/YWD B14 178 A4
CDYHTH B64 120 D4
Meadow Wy CDSL WV8 10 A5
STRBR DY8 117 G2
Mead Ri EDG B15 142 D1
The Mead SEDG DY3 66 D3
Meadthorpe Rd KGSTG B44 74 D3
Meadvale Rd RBRY B45 188 B2
Meadway STETCH B33 130 B2
The Meadway
DUNHL/THL/PER WV6 21 E5
Mears Cl ERDW/GRVHL B23 76 B3
Mears Coppice BRLYHL DY5 136 C1
Mears Dr STETCH B33 111 H5
Mearse Cl WSNGN B18 108 A4
Mearse La HAG/WOL DY9 184 D2
Mease Cft BORD B9 127 H2
Measham Gv
LGN/SDN/BHAMAIR B26 147 E2
Measham Wy WNSFLD WV11 25 E3
Medcroft Av
BFLD/HDSWWD B20 89 G2
Medina Rd SPARK B11 145 G3
Medina Wy KGSWFD DY6 99 G3
Medley Rd SPARK B11 145 F2
Medlicott Rd SPARK B11 145 E2
Medway Cl BRLYHL DY5 100 C3
Medway Cft CBROM B36 113 H2
Medway Gv HWK/WKHTH B38 176 C5
Medway Rd BRWNH WS8 8 C2
Medwin Gv ERDW/GRVHL B23 76 B4
Meer End HWK/WKHTH B38 190 C1
Meerhill Av SHLY B90 195 F2
Meeting House La
NFLD/LBR B31 175 G1
Meeting La BRLYHL DY5 118 D3
Meeting St DARL/WED WS10 55 G5
DUDS DY2 102 C5
TPTN/OCK DY4 70 A5
Melbourne Av LOZ/NWT B19 108 C3
SMTHWK B66 106 D2
Melbourne Cl KGSWFD DY6 100 A5
WBROM B70 71 E3
Melbourne Gdns
DSYBK/YTR WS5 57 H2
Melbourne Rd HALE B63 138 D2
SMTHWK B66 106 C2
Melbourne St BKHL/PFLD WV2 7 G6
Melbury Cl BDMR/CCFT WV3 * 6 B6
Melbury Gv
ALE/KHTH/YWD B14 161 E5
Melchett Rd BVILLE B30 176 D2
Melcote Gv KGSTG B44 75 E3
Meldon Dr BILS/COS WV14 69 G1
Melford Cl SEDG DY3 67 E1
Melford Hall Rd SOLH B91 164 B3
Melfort Gv
ALE/KHTH/YWD B14 178 C2
Melksham Sq CVALE B35 94 C3
Mellis Gv ERDW/GRVHL B23 91 G1
Mellish Dr RUSH/SHEL WS4 42 D2
Mellish Rd RUSH/SHEL WS4 42 D2
Mellor Dr FOAKS/STRLY B74 46 C2
Mellors Cl HRBN B17 141 H4
Mellowdew Rd STRBR DY8 117 G1
Mell Sq SOLH B91 182 A1
Melplash Av SOLH B91 181 G1
Melrose Av BHTH/HG B12 144 C1
HHTH/SAND B71 71 H2
SCFLD/BOLD B73 76 C1
SPARK B11 145 E1
STRBR DY8 135 G5
Melrose Cl HWK/WKHTH B38 176 D4
Melrose Dr
DUNHL/THL/PER WV6 34 B1
Melrose Gv LOZ/NWT B19 108 B2
Melrose Rd BFLD/HDSWWD B20 91 E5
Melstock Cl TPTN/OCK DY4 84 D1
Melstock Rd
ALE/KHTH/YWD B14 160 D3
Melton Av HIA/OLT B92 147 G3
Melton Dr EDG B15 126 C5
Melton Rd ALE/KHTH/YWD B14 161 F2
Melverley Gv KGSTG B44 75 F4
Melverton Av WOLVN WV10 23 F2
Melville Hall
LDYWD/EDGR B16 * 125 F3
Melville Rd LDYWD/EDGR B16 125 F3
Melvina Rd VAUX/NECH B7 109 H5
Membury Rd WASH/WDE B8 110 B3
Memorial Cl WLNHL WV13 39 G3
Memory La DARL/WED WS10 40 B5
WNSFLD WV11 24 B5
Menai Cl SHHTH WV12 26 A4
Mendip Av WASH/WDE B8 110 C4
Mendip Cl BKHL/PFLD WV2 52 D2
SEDG DY3 83 F3
Mendip Rd HALE B63 154 D1
STRBR DY8 135 H1
WASH/WDE B8 110 C5
Menin Crs MOS/BIL B13 161 H3
Menin Rd MOS/BIL B13 161 H3
TPTN/OCK DY4 84 D1
Meon Gv DUNHL/THL/PER WV6 34 C1
STETCH B33 130 D4
Meon Ri HAG/WOL DY9 136 A4
Meon Wy WNSFLD WV11 25 F3
Meranti Cl SHHTH WV12 26 A2
Mercer Av CSHL/WTROR B46 96 A3
Mercer Gv WNSFLD WV11 24 D3
Merchants Wy ALDR WS9 30 A3
Mercia Dr ALE/KHTH/YWD B14 160 D4
DUNHL/THL/PER WV6 20 C5
Mere Av CVALE B35 94 C3
Mere Cl SHHTH WV12 25 G5
Merecote Rd HIA/OLT B92 163 H3
Meredith Pool Cl WSNGN B18 * 107 H3
Meredith Rd SEDG DY3 82 C1
WNSFLD WV11 24 C2
Meredith St CDYHTH B64 120 D3
Mere Dr MGN/WHC B75 47 F3
Mere Green Cl MGN/WHC B75 47 G3
Mere Green Rd MGN/WHC B75 47 G3
Mere Oak Rd
DUNHL/THL/PER WV6 20 C5
Mere Pool Rd MGN/WHC B75 47 H3
Mere Rd ERDW/GRVHL B23 92 B3
STRBR DY8 135 E1
Mereside Wy HIA/OLT B92 164 A2
Meres Rd HALE B63 137 G2
Merevale Rd HIA/OLT B92 147 H5
Mere Vw RUSH/SHEL WS4 29 E2
Meriden Av STRBR DY8 134 D1
Meriden Cl STRBR DY8 117 H5
Meriden Dr
CHWD/FDBR/MGN B37 114 A4
Meriden Ri HIA/OLT B92 148 B4
Meriden Rd WOLVN WV10 22 C2
Meriden St DIG/EDG B5 3 J6
Merino Av NFLD/LBR B31 175 G5
Merlin Cl CVALE B35 94 C3
DUDN DY1 101 H1
Merlin Gv
LGN/SDN/BHAMAIR B26 147 H2
Merrick Cl HALE B63 137 H5
Merrick Rd WNSFLD WV11 25 G4
Merridale Av BDMR/CCFT WV3 36 B3
Merridale Crs BDMR/CCFT WV3 6 A4
Merridale Gdns BDMR/CCFT WV3 6 A5
Merridale Gv BDMR/CCFT WV3 36 A4
Merridale La BDMR/CCFT WV3 6 A4
Merridale Rd BDMR/CCFT WV3 36 B4
Merridale St BDMR/CCFT WV3 6 D6
Merridale St West
BDMR/CCFT WV3 6 A7
Merrills Hall WLNHL WV13 39 E1
Merrill's Hall La WNSFLD WV11 39 E1
Merrington Cl SOLH B91 182 A5
Merrion's Cl GTB/HAM B43 58 C4
Merrishaw Rd NFLD/LBR B31 175 G5
Merritts Brook Cl SLYOAK B29 158 C5
Merritt's Brook La
NFLD/LBR B31 158 A5
Merritt's Hl NFLD/LBR B31 158 A4
Merrivale Rd RMSLY B62 122 D4
SMTHWK B66 124 C2
Merryfield Cl HIA/OLT B92 165 F3
Merryfield Gv HRBN B17 142 A3
Merryfield Rd DUDN DY1 83 F5
Merry Hl BRLYHL DY5 119 H3
Merryhill Dr WSNGN B18 107 H3
Mersey Gv HWK/WKHTH B38 176 C5
Mersey Rd BLOX/PEL WS3 28 A1
Merstal Dr HIA/OLT B92 165 H3
Merstone Cl BILS/COS WV14 53 G2
Merstowe Cl ACGN B27 146 B4
Merton Cl LGLYGN/QTN B68 123 F2
Merton Rd MOS/BIL B13 144 D4
Mervyn Pl BILS/COS WV14 54 B5
Mervyn Rd BILS/COS WV14 54 B5
HDSW B21 89 F5
Meryhurst Rd DARL/WED WS10 56 B4
Messenger La WBROM B70 87 H3
Messenger Rd SMTHWK B66 106 D3
Metchley Ct HRBN B17 142 B3
Metchley Cft SHLY B90 195 F2
Metchley Dr HRBN B17 142 A2
Metchley La EDG B15 142 B3
Metchley Park Rd EDG B15 142 B3
Metfield Cft HRBN B17 142 B3
KGSWFD DY6 100 B3
Metlin Gv STETCH B33 131 G1
Metric Wk SMTHWKW B67 106 C4
Metro Triangle
VAUX/NECH B7 * 110 B2
Metro Wy SMTHWK B66 107 E2
The Mews BLKHTH/ROWR B65 121 H2
Meyrick Rd WBROM B70 71 E5
Meyrick Wk LDYWD/EDGR B16 125 H3
Miall Park Rd SOLH B91 164 A5
Miall Rd HLGN/YWD B28 163 E2
Michael Dr EDG B15 126 C5
Michael Rd DARL/WED WS10 54 D1
SMTHWKW B67 106 A3
Michelle Cl MOS/BIL B13 161 G5
Micklehill Dr SHLY B90 180 B5
Mickle Meadow
CSHL/WTROR B46 96 B3
Mickleover Rd WASH/WDE B8 111 G4
Mickleton Av STETCH B33 131 E4
Mickleton Rd HIA/OLT B92 163 H2
Mickley Av WOLVN WV10 23 G5
Midacre WLNHL WV13 39 G4
Middle Acre Rd
RIDG/WDGT B32 141 E5
Middle Av WLNHL WV13 39 E5
Middle Bickenhill La
HIA/OLT B92 150 C3
Middle Crs BLOX/PEL WS3 28 B3
Middle Cross WOLV WV1 7 H5
Middle Dr RBRY B45 188 D4
Middlefield CDSL WV8 11 G5
Middlefield Av DOR/KN B93 197 F4
RMSLY B62 122 D4
Middlefield Cl RMSLY B62 122 D3
Middlefield Gdns RMSLY B62 122 D4
Middlefield La HAG/WOL DY9 152 D4
Middle Field Rd NFLD/LBR B31 176 A3
Middlefield Rd OLDBY B69 103 G1
Middle Gdns WLNHL WV13 39 H3
Middlehill Ri RIDG/WDGT B32 140 D5
Middle La HLYWD B47 192 B5
HWK/WKHTH B38 191 G1
Middle Leaford STETCH B33 112 C4
Middle Leasowe
RIDG/WDGT B32 140 C3
Middle Meadow Av
RIDG/WDGT B32 140 C2
Middlemist Gv GTB/HAM B43 73 H5
Middlemore La ALDR WS9 29 H4
Middlemore La West ALDR WS9 29 G4
Middlemore Rd NFLD/LBR B31 175 H3
SMTHWK B66 106 D2
Middle Park Cl SLYOAK B29 158 D2
Middlepark Rd DUDN DY1 101 G1
Middle Park Rd SLYOAK B29 158 D2
Middle Rd BRGRVW B61 186 B4
Middleton Cl DSYBK/YTR WS5 57 F3
Middleton Gdns BVILLE B30 176 B1
Middleton Gra NFLD/LBR B31 176 A1
Middleton Hall Rd BVILLE B30 176 C1
Middleton Rd
ALE/KHTH/YWD B14 161 E3
BRWNH WS8 9 G3
FOAKS/STRLY B74 45 G4
SHLY B90 180 A3
Middletree Rd HALE B63 120 C5
Middle Vauxhall WOLV WV1 6 B3
Middleway Av STRBR DY8 117 G1
Middleway Gn BILS/COS WV14 38 C5
Middleway Rd BILS/COS WV14 38 C5
Middleway Vw WSNGN B18 126 A1
Midford Gv EDG B15 126 C4
Midgley Dr FOAKS/STRLY B74 47 E3
Midhill Dr OLDBY B69 104 A3
Midhurst Gv
DUNHL/THL/PER WV6 21 G5
Midhurst Rd BVILLE B30 177 F2
Midland Cl HDSW B21 107 H2
Midland Dr CSCFLD/WYGN B72 62 C3
Midland Rd BVILLE B30 159 H5
DARL/WED WS10 40 A5
FOAKS/STRLY B74 62 A1
WSL WS1 4 D5
Midland St WASH/WDE B8 128 A1
Midpoint Pk WALM/CURD B76 * 95 E1
Midvale Dr
ALE/KHTH/YWD B14 177 H3
Milburn Rd KGSTG B44 60 C5
Milcote Dr SCFLD/BOLD B73 61 E5
WLNHL WV13 38 D4
Milcote Rd SLYOAK B29 158 C2
SMTHWKW B67 124 B2
SOLH B91 181 H1
Milcote Wy KGSWFD DY6 99 F2
Mildenhall Rd PBAR/PBCH B42 74 A2
Mildred Rd CDYHTH B64 121 E2
Mildred Wy OLDBY B69 104 A3
Milebrook Gv RIDG/WDGT B32 157 F2
Milebush Av CBROM B36 95 F5
Mile Flat KGSWFD DY6 98 D2
Miles Gv DUDS DY2 103 F2
Miles Meadow Cl SHHTH WV12 26 A2
Milestone Dr HAG/WOL DY9 169 G1
Milestone La HDSW B21 107 F1
Milestone Wy SHHTH WV12 25 H2
Milford Av BHTH/HG B12 144 C1
SHHTH WV12 25 G5
Milford Cl STRBR DY8 118 A1
Milford Copse HRBN B17 141 H2
Milford Ct LOZ/NWT B19 108 D4
Milford Cft BLKHTH/ROWR B65 103 F3
Milford Gv SHLY B90 196 A1
Milford Pl
ALE/KHTH/YWD B14 * 161 E2
Milford Rd BKHL/PFLD WV2 52 A1
HRBN B17 141 H2
Milholme Gn HIA/OLT B92 165 F3
Milking Bank DUDN DY1 83 G4
Milk St DIG/EDG B5 3 K7
Millard Rd BILS/COS WV14 68 B2
Mill Bank SEDG DY3 67 F3
Millbank Gv ERDW/GRVHL B23 75 H5
Millbank St WNSFLD WV11 25 F1
Millbrook Dr NFLD/LBR B31 175 E5
Millbrook Rd
ALE/KHTH/YWD B14 160 C4
Millbrook Wy BRLYHL DY5 118 D4
Mill Burn Wy BORD B9 127 H2
Mill Cl HLYWD B47 192 C1
KIDD DY10 168 B3
SEDG DY3 67 F5
Mill Cft BILS/COS WV14 54 A2
Millcroft Cl RIDG/WDGT B32 141 E5
Millcroft Rd FOAKS/STRLY B74 45 G5

Millcroft Rd FOAKS/STRLY B74 ....45 G5
Milldale Crs WOLVN WV10 ....12 D4
Milldale Rd WOLVN WV10 ....12 D3
Mill Dr SMTHWK B66 ....106 D4
Millenium Pk WBROM B70 ....87 E1
Millennium Cl BLOX/PEL WS3 ....18 A3
Millennium Gdns CDYHTH B64 ..121 F2
Millennium Pk WBROM B70 * 87 E1
Millennium Wy CDSL WV8 ....10 D3
Miller Crs BILS/COS WV14 ....68 A2
Millers Cl WSLW WS2 ....40 D4
Millersdale Dr HHTH/SAND B71 ....72 B1
Millers Green Dr KGSWFD DY6 ....99 E1
Miller St AST/WIT B6 ....109 E4
Millers V WMBN WV5 ....80 B1
Millers Wk BLOX/PEL WS3 ....17 G4
Mill Farm Rd HRBN B17 ....142 A4
Millfield NFLD/LBR B31 * 175 G1
Millfield Av BLOX/PEL WS3 ....17 F5
RUSH/SHEL WS4 ....28 D1
Millfield Rd BFLD/HDSWWD B20 ..89 H1
BRWNH WS8 ....9 G5
Millfields STETCH B33 ....131 G1
Millfields Rd BKHL/PFLD WV2 ....53 E3
HHTH/SAND B71 ....71 F2
Millfields Wy WMBN WV5 ....80 B1
Millfield Vw HALE B63 ....138 A3
Millford Cl HLGN/YWD B28 ....163 E5
Mill Gdns SMTHWKW B67 * 124 B2
Mill Gn WOLVN WV10 ....12 D3
Mill Gv CDSL WV8 ....11 E4
Millhaven Av BVILLE B30 ....160 B4
Mill Hl SMTHWKW B67 ....124 B1
Millhouse Rd YDLY B25 ....129 G4
Millichip Rd WLNHL WV13 ....39 E4
Millington Rd CBROM B36 ....112 A1
TPTN/OCK DY4 ....69 F2
WOLVN WV10 ....23 G4
Millison Gv SOLH B91 ....195 G1
Mill La ALDR WS9 ....31 G4
BRGRVW B61 ....186 B5
CDSL WV8 ....10 B2
DIG/EDG B5 ....3 J7
DOR/KN B93 ....196 C4
DUNHL/THL/PER WV6 ....35 E3
KIDD DY10 ....168 B3
NFLD/LBR B31 ....175 F3
OLDBY B69 ....105 E5
RIDG/WDGT B32 ....141 E5
RMSLY B62 ....139 E3
RUSH/SHEL WS4 ....42 B1
SHHTH WV12 ....26 A5
SOLH B91 ....182 A1
WMBN WV5 ....65 F4
WNSFLD WV11 ....24 B3
Mill Lane Ar SOLH B91 * 182 A2
Millmead Rd SLYOAK B29 ....141 E5
Mill Pl BLOX/PEL WS3 ....42 A1
Mill Pool Cl HAG/WOL DY9 ....169 G1
WMBN WV5 ....80 B1
Millpool Gdns
ALE/KHTH/YWD B14 ....178 B2
Millpool Hl Alcester Rd South
ALE/KHTH/YWD B14 ....178 B1
Mill Pool La DOR/KN B93 ....199 E3
Millpool Wy SMTHWKW B67 ....106 C5
Mill Race La STRBR DY8 ....135 G1
Mill Rd BRWNH WS8 ....9 G5
CDYHTH B64 ....121 E5
RUSH/SHEL WS4 ....28 D1
Mills Av WALM/CURD B76 ....63 E4
Mills Cl WNSFLD WV11 ....24 B2
Mills Crs BKHL/PFLD WV2 ....37 G5
Millside HLGN/YWD B28 ....179 G2
WMBN WV5 * 80 C1
Mills Rd BKHL/PFLD WV2 ....37 G5
Millstone Cl WALM/CURD B76 ....78 B2
Mill St AST/WIT B6 ....109 F4
BILS/COS WV14 ....53 G3
BRLYHL DY5 ....119 F2
CDYHTH B64 ....120 C5
CSCFLD/WYGN B72 ....62 C3
DARL/WED WS10 ....55 E2
STRBR DY8 ....118 A2
TPTN/OCK DY4 ....86 B1
WBROM B70 ....87 G2
WLNHL WV13 ....40 A3
WSLW WS2 ....42 A2
Millthorpe Cl WASH/WDE B8 ....110 D4
Mill Vw STETCH B33 ....113 E5
Millwalk Dr COVEN WV9 ....12 A4
The Mill Wk NFLD/LBR B31 ....175 F4
Millward St BORD B9 ....128 A3
WBROM B70 ....87 E3
Millwright Cl TPTN/OCK DY4 ....85 H1
Milner Rd SLYOAK B29 ....160 A1
Milner Wy MOS/BIL B13 ....162 B2
Milsom Gv BKDE/SHDE B34 ....113 F3
Milstead Rd
LGN/SDN/BHAMAIR B26 ....130 C3
Milston Cl ALE/KHTH/YWD B14 ..178 A4
Milton Av BHTH/HG B12 ....144 C1
Milton Cl DOR/KN B93 ....196 D4
SHHTH WV12 ....26 C3
STRBR DY8 ....118 C5
WSL WS1 ....56 C2
Milton Ct DUNHL/THL/PER WV6 ..34 C1
Milton Crs SEDG DY3 ....82 C1
YDLY B25 ....129 H5
Milton Dr HAG/WOL DY9 ....153 F3
Milton Gv HDSW B21 * 107 E1
Milton Pl WSL WS1 ....56 D2
Milton Rd BILS/COS WV14 ....68 D4
DOR/KN B93 ....196 D4
SMTHWKW B67 ....105 H4
WOLVN WV10 ....24 A5
Milton St BRLYHL DY5 ....101 F2
HHTH/SAND B71 ....87 F1
LOZ/NWT B19 ....109 E3
WSL WS1 ....56 D2
Milverton Cl HALE B63 ....138 C1
WALM/CURD B76 ....78 B4
Milverton Rd DOR/KN B93 ....197 G3
ERDW/GRVHL B23 ....92 C1
Mimosa Cl SLYOAK B29 ....158 D2
Mimosa Wk KGSWFD DY6 ....100 A1
Mincing La BLKHTH/ROWR B65 ..122 A1
Mindelsohn Wy EDG B15 ....142 B3
Minden Gv SLYOAK B29 ....158 D1
Minehead Rd DUDN DY1 ....101 F1
WOLVN WV10 ....12 B5
Miner St WSLW WS2 ....41 G2
Minerva Cl SHHTH WV12 ....40 C1
Minewood Cl BLOX/PEL WS3 ....16 B4
Minith Rd BILS/COS WV14 ....68 D3
Miniva Dr WALM/CURD B76 ....78 C1
Minivet Dr BHTH/HG B12 ....144 A1
Minley Av HRBN B17 ....124 B5
The Minories CBHAMNW B3 ....3 G4
DUDS DY2 ....84 D5
Minstead Rd ERDE/BCHGN B24 ....92 B5
Minster Cl BLKHTH/ROWR B65 ....122 C1
DOR/KN B93 ....183 F5
Minster Ct MOS/BIL B13 * 144 C3
Minster Dr SMHTH B10 ....128 A5
Minsterley Cl BDMR/CCFT WV3 ....36 A5
The Minster BDMR/CCFT WV3 ....51 F1
Mintern Rd YDLY B25 ....129 G3
Minton Cl WOLV WV1 ....38 A4
Minton Rd RIDG/WDGT B32 ....141 F3
Minworth Rd CSHL/WTROR B46 ..96 B3
Miranda Cl RBRY B45 ....174 A3
Mirfield Cl COVEN WV9 ....12 A4
Mirfield Rd SOLH B91 ....164 C4
STETCH B33 ....130 D2
Mission Cl CDYHTH B64 ....121 G3
Mission Dr TPTN/OCK DY4 ....85 G2
Mistletoe Dr DSYBK/YTR WS5 ....57 G5
Mitcham Gv KGSTG B44 ....75 H2
Mitcheldean Covert
ALE/KHTH/YWD B14 ....177 H3
Mitchell Av BILS/COS WV14 ....68 B2
Mitchel Rd KGSWFD DY6 ....100 B5
Mitford Dr HIA/OLT B92 ....165 F3
Mitre Cl SHHTH WV12 ....26 B3
WNSFLD WV11 ....15 E4
Mitre Fold WOLV WV1 ....6 E3
Mitre Rd HAG/WOL DY9 ....136 C2
Mitten Av RBRY B45 ....173 H4
Mitton Rd BFLD/HDSWWD B20 ....89 G4
Moat Brook Av CDSL WV8 ....10 A3
Moat Coppice RIDG/WDGT B32 ..157 E1
Moat Cft
CHWD/FDBR/MGN B37 ....132 A2
WALM/CURD B76 ....78 D4
Moat Dr RMSLY B62 ....122 D3
Moat Farm Dr RIDG/WDGT B32 ..157 E1
Moat Farm Wy BLOX/PEL WS3 ....18 A2
Moatfield Ter DARL/WED WS10 ....56 A5
Moat Green Av WNSFLD WV11 ....25 E3
Moat House La East
WNSFLD WV11 ....24 D3
Moathouse La West
WNSFLD WV11 ....24 D3
Moat House Rd WASH/WDE B8 ..111 E5
Moat La DIG/EDG B5 ....3 H6
LGN/SDN/BHAMAIR B26 ....130 A5
SOLH B91 ....165 E4
Moat Mdw RIDG/WDGT B32 ....141 E3
Moat Rd LGLYGN/QTN B68 ....123 F1
TPTN/OCK DY4 ....69 G4
WSLW WS2 ....41 G3
Moatside Cl BLOX/PEL WS3 ....18 A2
Moat St WLNHL WV13 ....39 G3
Mobberley Rd BILS/COS WV14 ....68 A2
Mob La RUSH/SHEL WS4 ....18 C5
Mockley Wood Rd
DOR/KN B93 ....197 F1
Modbury Av RIDG/WDGT B32 ....157 H1
Moden Cl SEDG DY3 ....83 F1
Moden Hl SEDG DY3 ....67 E5
Mogul La HALE B63 ....120 A5
Moillett St WSNGN B18 ....107 F5
Moilliett Ct SMTHWK B66 ....107 E3
Moira Crs ALE/KHTH/YWD B14 ..179 E1
Moises Hall Rd WMBN WV5 ....65 F5
Moland St AST/WIT B6 ....3 H1
Mole St SPARK B11 ....144 D1
Molineux St WOLV WV1 ....7 F2
Mollington Crs SHLY B90 ....180 C2
Molyneux Rd DUDS DY2 ....121 E2
Monarch Dr TPTN/OCK DY4 ....70 A5
Monarch's Wy
BLKHTH/ROWR B65 ....103 F5
COVEN WV9 ....11 G2
HAG/WOL DY9 ....136 A4
KGSWFD DY6 ....98 C3
OLDBY B69 ....86 A4
WNSFLD WV11 ....14 B4
WSLW WS2 ....41 E2
Monarch Wy DUDS DY2 ....102 B5
Mona Rd ERDW/GRVHL B23 ....92 D1
Monastery Dr SOLH B91 ....164 A4
Monckton Rd
LGLYGN/QTN B68 ....123 E5
Moncrieffe Cl DUDS DY2 ....103 E1
Moncrieffe St WSL WS1 ....5 H5
Money La BRGRVW B61 ....186 C2
Monica Rd SMHTH B10 ....128 D4
Monins Av TPTN/OCK DY4 ....85 G3
Monk Cl TPTN/OCK DY4 ....85 H3
Monk Rd WASH/WDE B8 ....111 F4
Monks Cl WMBN WV5 ....64 C5
Monkseaton Rd
CSCFLD/WYGN B72 ....77 F1
Monksfield Av GTB/HAM B43 ....73 F2
Monkshood Ms
ERDW/GRVHL B23 ....75 H3
Monkshood Retreat
HWK/WKHTH B38 ....176 D5
Monks Kirby Rd
WALM/CURD B76 ....63 F5
Monkspath SHLY B90 ....195 G2
WALM/CURD B76 ....78 B3
Monkspath Cl SHLY B90 ....194 D1
Monkspath Hall Rd SHLY B90 ....195 F2
SOLH B91 ....181 H5
Monksway HWK/WKHTH B38 ....177 F3
Monkswell Cl BRLYHL DY5 ....119 F3
SMHTH B10 ....128 B5
Monkswood Rd NFLD/LBR B31 ..176 A3
Monkton Rd SLYOAK B29 ....141 G4
Monmer Cl WLNHL WV13 ....39 H2
Monmer La WLNHL WV13 ....39 H2
Monmore Rd WOLV WV1 ....38 A5
Monmouth Dr HHTH/SAND B71 ..71 F4
SCFLD/BOLD B73 ....61 E4
SCFLD/BOLD B73 ....61 H5
Monmouth Rd
RIDG/WDGT B32 ....157 H2
SMTHWKW B67 ....124 A4
WSLW WS2 ....40 C2
Monsal Av WOLVN WV10 ....37 G1
Monsaldale Cl BRWNH WS8 ....18 D1
Monsal Rd PBAR/PBCH B42 ....74 C4
Mons Rd DUDS DY2 ....85 E5
Montague Rd ERDE/BCHGN B24 ..93 E5
HDSW B21 ....107 H1
LDYWD/EDGR B16 ....125 G3
SMTHWK B66 ....124 D1
Montague St AST/WIT B6 ....109 H1
CBHAMNE B4 ....127 G1
Montana Av PBAR/PBCH B42 ....90 A1
Monteagle Dr KGSWFD DY6 ....81 H5
Montford Gv SEDG DY3 * 67 F4
Montfort Rd CSHL/WTROR B46 ..115 F4
WSLW WS2 ....56 B2
Montgomery Crs BRLYHL DY5 ....119 H5
Montgomery Cft SPARK B11 ....128 A5
Montgomery Rd WSLW WS2 ....40 C3
Montgomery St SPARK B11 ....127 H5
Montgomery Wy
WASH/WDE B8 ....111 E5
Montpelier Rd
ERDE/BCHGN B24 ....93 E5
Montpellier Gdns DUDN DY1 ....83 G4
Montpellier St BHTH/HG B12 ....144 C1
Montrose Dr CVALE B35 ....94 C3
DUDN DY1 ....102 A1
Montsford Cl DOR/KN B93 ....196 D2
Monument Av HAG/WOL DY9 ....136 C3
Monument La HAG/WOL DY9 ....153 F3
RBRY B45 ....187 H4
SEDG DY3 ....67 G2
Monument Rd
LDYWD/EDGR B16 ....125 H3
Monway Ter DARL/WED WS10 ....55 G5
Monwood Gv SOLH B91 ....181 F3
Monyhull Hall Rd BVILLE B30 ....177 F2
Moodyscroft Rd STETCH B33 ....131 E1
Moorcroft Dr DARL/WED WS10 ....70 A1
Moorcroft Pl VAUX/NECH B7 * ..109 G5
Moorcroft Rd MOS/BIL B13 ....143 H4
Moordown Av HIA/OLT B92 ....147 G5
Moore Cl DUNHL/THL/PER WV6 ..34 D1
FOAKS/STRLY B74 ....32 D4
Moore Crs LGLYGN/QTN B68 ....123 G1
Moorend Av
CHWD/FDBR/MGN B37 ....132 A3
Moor End La ERDE/BCHGN B24 ....93 E2
Moore Rd SHHTH WV12 ....26 B2
Moore's Rw DIG/EDG B5 ....3 K7
Moore St WOLV WV1 ....37 H4
Moorfield Av DOR/KN B93 ....196 D2
Moorfield Dr HALE B63 ....138 C2
SCFLD/BOLD B73 ....76 D3
Moorfield Rd BKDE/SHDE B34 ....112 C3
BKHL/PFLD WV2 ....51 H1
Moorfoot Av HALE B63 ....154 C1
Moor Green La MOS/BIL B13 ....160 C1
Moor Hall Dr HAG/WOL DY9 ....171 E4
MGN/WHC B75 ....48 A4
Moorhills Cft SHLY B90 ....180 B5
The Moorings BRLYHL DY5 ....101 H5
COVEN WV9 * 11 H5
OLDBY B69 ....104 C1
Moorland Av WOLVN WV10 ....23 E4
Moorland Rd BLOX/PEL WS3 ....27 E2
LDYWD/EDGR B16 ....125 F3
Moorlands Dr SHLY B90 ....180 C3
Moorlands Rd HHTH/SAND B71 ....71 G2
The Moorlands
FOAKS/STRLY B74 ....46 D5
Moor La AST/WIT B6 ....75 F5
AST/WIT B6 ....91 G2
BLKHTH/ROWR B65 ....121 G1
LICHS WS14 ....32 C1
Moor Leasow NFLD/LBR B31 ....176 A3
Moor Meadow Rd
MGN/WHC B75 ....62 D1
Moor Pk BLOX/PEL WS3 ....16 D4
DUNHL/THL/PER WV6 ....20 B5
Moorpark Rd NFLD/LBR B31 ....175 G4
Moor Pool Av HRBN B17 ....142 A1
Moors Cft RIDG/WDGT B32 ....157 F1
Moorside Gdns WSLW WS2 ....41 F2
Moorside Rd
ALE/KHTH/YWD B14 ....179 E1
Moors La NFLD/LBR B31 ....158 A2
Moors Mill La TPTN/OCK DY4 ....70 A4
Moorsom St AST/WIT B6 ....109 E4
The Moors CBROM B36 ....112 B1
Moor St BRLYHL DY5 ....118 C1
CBHAMNE B4 ....3 H5
DARL/WED WS10 ....71 F1
WBROM B70 ....87 G4
Moor St South BKHL/PFLD WV2 ..52 A1
The Moor WALM/CURD B76 ....78 C3
Moorville Wk SPARK B11 ....127 G5
Morar Cl CVALE B35 ....94 D2
Moray Cl RMSLY B62 ....122 C4
Morcom Rd SPARK B11 ....145 G2
Morcroft BILS/COS WV14 ....54 C5
Mordaunt Dr MGN/WHC B75 ....47 H3
Morden Rd STETCH B33 ....129 H1
Moreland Cft WALM/CURD B76 ....78 D5
The Morelands NFLD/LBR B31 ....175 H4
Morestead Av
LGN/SDN/BHAMAIR B26 ....148 A2
Moreton Av
ETTPK/GDPK/PENN WV4 ....52 C4
GTB/HAM B43 ....74 C1
Moreton Cl RIDG/WDGT B32 ....141 F2
TPTN/OCK DY4 ....69 H1
Moreton Rd SHLY B90 ....180 C3
WOLVN WV10 ....23 F1
Moreton St CBHAMW B1 ....2 A2
Morford Rd ALDR WS9 ....30 A3
Morgan Cl OLDBY B69 ....104 B1
WLNHL WV13 ....39 H1
Morgan Gv CBROM B36 ....95 H5
Morgrove Av DOR/KN B93 ....196 D2
Morjon Dr GTB/HAM B43 ....73 H1
Morland Rd GTB/HAM B43 ....59 G4
Morley Gv
DUNHL/THL/PER WV6 ....37 E1
Morley Rd WASH/WDE B8 ....111 F3
Morlich Ri BRLYHL DY5 ....118 D4
Morning Pines STRBR DY8 ....135 E3
Morningside SCFLD/BOLD B73 ....62 B2
Mornington Rd SMTHWK B66 ....106 D2
Morris Av WSLW WS2 ....40 C3
Morris Cl ACGN B27 ....146 D3
Morris Cft CBROM B36 ....95 G5
Morris Field Cft
HLGN/YWD B28 ....179 G1
Morrison Av WOLVN WV10 ....23 F2
Morrison Rd TPTN/OCK DY4 ....86 A2
Morris Rd WASH/WDE B8 ....111 F3
Morris St WBROM B70 ....87 G5
Mortimers Cl
ALE/KHTH/YWD B14 ....178 D4
Morton Rd BRLYHL DY5 ....119 F5
Morvale Gdns HAG/WOL DY9 ....136 C2
Morvale St HAG/WOL DY9 ....136 C2
Morven Rd SCFLD/BOLD B73 ....76 D1
Morville Cl DOR/KN B93 ....196 B5
Morville Cft
ETTPK/GDPK/PENN WV4 ....53 F4
Morville Rd DUDS DY2 ....102 D5
Morville St LDYWD/EDGR B16 ....2 A7
Mosborough Crs LOZ/NWT B19 ..108 C4
Mosedale Dr WNSFLD WV11 ....25 F5
Moseley Ct WNSFLD WV11 ....14 D4
Moseley Dr
CHWD/FDBR/MGN B37 ....131 H4
Moseley Old Hall La
WOLVN WV10 ....13 G2
Moseley Rd BHTH/HG B12 ....144 B1
WLNHL WV13 ....38 D4
WOLVN WV10 ....13 G2
Moseley St DIG/EDG B5 ....127 F3
DUNHL/THL/PER WV6 ....37 E1
TPTN/OCK DY4 ....70 A4
Moss Cl ALDR WS9 ....30 A5
RUSH/SHEL WS4 ....42 C2
Mossdale Wy SEDG DY3 ....67 G4
Moss Dr CSCFLD/WYGN B72 ....62 C5
Mossfield Rd
ALE/KHTH/YWD B14 ....161 E3
Moss Gdns BILS/COS WV14 ....53 F5
Moss Gv ALE/KHTH/YWD B14 ....160 D4
KGSWFD DY6 ....99 H2
Moss House Cl EDG B15 ....126 B3
Mossley Cl BLOX/PEL WS3 ....26 D1
Mossley La BLOX/PEL WS3 ....16 B5
Mossvale Cl CDYHTH B64 ....121 E3
Mossvale Gv WASH/WDE B8 ....110 D4
Moss Wy FOAKS/STRLY B74 ....60 B1
Mostyn Crs HHTH/SAND B71 ....71 E4
Mostyn Rd HDSW B21 ....107 H1
LDYWD/EDGR B16 ....125 H3
Mostyn St WOLV WV1 ....36 D1
Mott Cl TPTN/OCK DY4 * 70 A3
Mottram Cl WBROM B70 ....87 E4
Mottrams Cl CSCFLD/WYGN B72 ..77 G1
Mott St LOZ/NWT B19 ....2 E1
Mott's Wy CSHL/WTROR B46 ....115 G3
Moundsley Gv
ALE/KHTH/YWD B14 ....178 C2
Mountain Ash Dr
HAG/WOL DY9 ....136 A5
Mountain Ash Rd BRWNH WS8 ....19 E2
Mount Av BRLYHL DY5 ....101 E5
Mountbatten Cl WBROM B70 ....88 B4
Mountbatten Rd WSLW WS2 ....40 D3
Mount Cl MOS/BIL B13 ....144 B3
SEDG DY3 ....83 E4
WMBN WV5 ....65 E4
Mount Cottages
ETTPK/GDPK/PENN WV4 * 51 F5
Mount Ct
DUNHL/THL/PER WV6 * 35 F2
Mount Dr WMBN WV5 ....65 E4
Mountfield Cl
ALE/KHTH/YWD B14 ....178 C3
Mountford Cl
BLKHTH/ROWR B65 ....122 A1
Mountford Crs ALDR WS9 ....30 B2
Mountford Dr MGN/WHC B75 ....47 G5
Mountford La BILS/COS WV14 ....53 H1
Mountford Rd SHLY B90 ....179 F4
Mountford St SPARK B11 ....145 F2
Mount Gdns CDSL WV8 ....10 B3
Mountjoy Crs HIA/OLT B92 ....148 A4
Mount La HAG/WOL DY9 ....170 C1
SEDG DY3 ....83 E4
Mount Pleasant
ALE/KHTH/YWD B14 ....161 E1
BILS/COS WV14 ....54 A2
BKHL/PFLD WV2 * 52 D1
BRLYHL DY5 ....119 G3
ETTPK/GDPK/PENN WV4 * 51 F5
KGSWFD DY6 ....99 G5
LGLYGN/QTN B68 * 105 F5
SMHTH B10 ....127 H3
Mount Pleasant Av HDSW B21 ....89 G5
WMBN WV5 ....64 D4
Mount Pleasant St
BILS/COS WV14 ....68 B3
WBROM B70 ....87 G4
Mountrath St WSL WS1 ....4 D5
Mount Rd BLKHTH/ROWR B65 ....122 C1
BLOX/PEL WS3 ....18 A3
DUNHL/THL/PER WV6 ....35 E3
ETTPK/GDPK/PENN WV4 ....51 G4
ETTPK/GDPK/PENN WV4 ....67 H1
HDSW B21 ....107 F2
OLDBY B69 ....104 A1
STRBR DY8 ....117 H3
STRBR DY8 ....135 H2
WLNHL WV13 ....39 E5
WMBN WV5 ....65 E4
Mounts Rd DARL/WED WS10 ....70 D1
Mount St HALE B63 ....138 C5
STRBR DY8 ....135 G2
TPTN/OCK DY4 ....70 A5
VAUX/NECH B7 ....110 A3
WSL WS1 ....4 D6
Mounts Wy VAUX/NECH B7 ....110 A2
The Mount CDYHTH B64 ....121 G3
ERDW/GRVHL B23 ....92 B5
WALM/CURD B76 ....96 C1
Mount Vw MGN/WHC B75 ....63 E4
Mountwood Covert
DUNHL/THL/PER WV6 ....35 F2
Mousehall Farm Rd
BRLYHL DY5 ....119 F5
Mouse Hl BLOX/PEL WS3 ....17 H4
Mousesweet Cl DUDS DY2 ....103 E5
Mousesweet La DUDS DY2 ....121 E1
Mousesweet Wk CDYHTH B64 ....120 B4
Mowbray Cl RBRY B45 ....174 A3
Mowbray St DIG/EDG B5 ....127 E4
Mowe Cft
CHWD/FDBR/MGN B37 ....132 A5
Moxhull Cl SHHTH WV12 ....26 A1
Moxhull Dr WALM/CURD B76 ....78 A3
Moxhull Gdns SHHTH WV12 ....26 A1
Moxhull Rd
CHWD/FDBR/MGN B37 ....114 A4
Moxley Rd DARL/WED WS10 ....54 D4
Moyle Dr HALE B63 ....120 B5
Moyses Cft SMTHWK B66 ....106 C1
Muchall Rd
ETTPK/GDPK/PENN WV4 ....51 G3
Mucklow Hl RMSLY B62 ....139 F2
Muirfield Cl BLOX/PEL WS3 ....16 C4
Muirfield Crs OLDBY B69 ....103 G2
Muirfield Gdns
HWK/WKHTH B38 ....176 B4
Muirville Cl STRBR DY8 ....117 H1
Mulberry Dr MOS/BIL B13 ....161 H1
Mulberry Gn DUDN DY1 ....83 H1
Mulberry Pl BLOX/PEL WS3 ....26 D1
Mulberry Rd BLOX/PEL WS3 ....26 D1
NFLD/LBR B31 ....159 E5
Mull Cl RBRY B45 ....173 G4
Mull Cft CBROM B36 ....114 A2
Mullensgrove Rd
CHWD/FDBR/MGN B37 ....114 A4
Mullett Rd WNSFLD WV11 ....24 B3
Mullett St BRLYHL DY5 ....100 D4
Mulliners Cl
CHWD/FDBR/MGN B37 * 132 D2
Mullion Cft HWK/WKHTH B38 ....176 C4
Mulroy Rd FOAKS/STRLY B74 ....62 B2
Mulwych Rd STETCH B33 ....131 G1
Munches La HAG/WOL DY9 ....171 G5
Munslow Gv NFLD/LBR B31 ....175 F5
Muntz Crs HOCK/TIA B94 ....198 A5
Muntz St SMHTH B10 ....128 B4
Murcroft Rd HAG/WOL DY9 ....153 F1
Murdoch Rd BILS/COS WV14 ....54 B2
Murdock Gv HDSW B21 ....107 G2
Murdock Rd SMTHWK B66 ....107 F3
Murdock Wy WSLW WS2 ....26 D5
Murray Ct SCFLD/BOLD B73 ....62 A5
Murrell Cl DIG/EDG B5 ....126 D5
Musborough Cl CBROM B36 ....95 E5
Muscott Gv HRBN B17 ....141 G2
Muscovy Rd ERDW/GRVHL B23 ....92 A3
Musgrave Cl WALM/CURD B76 ....63 E5
Musgrave Rd WSNGN B18 ....107 H4
Mushroom Hall Rd
LGLYGN/QTN B68 ....105 G4
Musk La SEDG DY3 ....82 D3
Musk La West SEDG DY3 ....82 D3
Muswell Cl SOLH B91 ....165 F5
Muxloe Cl BLOX/PEL WS3 ....16 C4
Myatt Av ALDR WS9 ....29 H5
BKHL/PFLD WV2 ....52 C2
Myatt Cl BKHL/PFLD WV2 ....52 C2
Myddleton St WSNGN B18 ....108 A5
Myles Ct BRLYHL DY5 ....101 F5
Mynors Crs HLYWD B47 ....192 C3
Myring Dr MGN/WHC B75 ....63 F3
Myrtle Av ALE/KHTH/YWD B14 ..178 B3
BHTH/HG B12 ....144 C2
Myrtle Cl SHHTH WV12 ....26 C3
Myrtle Gv BDMR/CCFT WV3 ....51 E2
LOZ/NWT B19 * 108 C1
Myrtle Pl SLYOAK B29 * 143 F5
Myrtle Rd DUDN DY1 ....84 A3
Myrtle St BKHL/PFLD WV2 ....52 D2
Myrtle Ter TPTN/OCK DY4 ....69 H1
Myton Dr SHLY B90 ....179 F3
Mytton Cl DUDS DY2 ....85 E5
Mytton Gv TPTN/OCK DY4 ....85 E1
Mytton Rd BVILLE B30 ....159 E5
CSHL/WTROR B46 ....95 H3
Myvod Rd DARL/WED WS10 ....56 A3

N

Naden Rd LOZ/NWT B19 ...108 B3
Nadin Rd SCFLD/BOLD B73 ...77 E3
Naesby Rd
DUNHL/THL/PER WV6 ...34 D2
Nafford Gv
ALE/KHTH/YWD B14 ...178 B3
Nagersfield Rd BRLYHL DY5 ...118 C1
Nailers Cl RIDG/WDGT B32 ...139 H5
Nailors Fold BILS/COS WV14 ...68 C1
Nailors Rw WMBN WV5 * ...80 D1
Nailstone Crs ACGN B27 ...163 G2
Nailsworth Rd DOR/KN B93 ...198 B1
Nairn Cl HLGN/YWD B28 ...162 D5
Nairn Rd BLOX/PEL WS3 ...16 C3
Nally Dr BILS/COS WV14 ...68 A1
Nanaimo Wy KGSWFD DY6 ...100 C5
Nansen Rd SPARK B11 ...145 E4
WASH/WDE B8 ...110 C4
Nantmel Gv RIDG/WDGT B32 ...157 G2
Naomi Wy ALDR WS9 ...19 H3
Napier Dr TPTN/OCK DY4 ...70 A5
Napier Rd BKHL/PFLD WV2 ...52 B1
WSLW WS2 ...27 E5
Napton Gv SLYOAK B29 ...141 F5
Narraway Gv TPTN/OCK DY4 ...70 B3
Narrowboat Wy DUDS DY2 ...102 A4
Narrow La BRWNH WS8 ...9 F4
RMSLY B62 ...122 C5
WSLW WS2 ...56 B1
Naseby Dr HALE B63 ...137 H5
Naseby Rd SOLH B91 ...164 D4
WASH/WDE B8 ...110 D4
Nash Av DUNHL/THL/PER WV6 ...34 C2
Nash Cl BLKHTH/ROWR B65 ...122 A3
Nash Cft
CHWD/FDBR/MGN B37 ...132 B4
Nash La HAG/WOL DY9 ...184 B1
Nash Sq PBAR/PBCH B42 ...90 D2
Nash Wk SMTHWK B66 * ...107 E4
Nately Gv SLYOAK B29 ...141 H4
Nathan Cl MGN/WHC B75 ...47 G5
Naunton Cl SLYOAK B29 ...158 C3
Naunton Rd WSLW WS2 ...41 E2
Navenby Cl
ALE/KHTH/YWD B14 ...179 E2
Navigation Dr BRLYHL DY5 ...102 A5
Navigation La DARL/WED WS10 ..72 B1
Navigation St CBHAMW B1 ...2 E6
WOLV WV1 ...7 J6
WSLW WS2 ...4 C3
Navigation Wy WBROM B70 ...86 D4
WSNGN B18 ...107 H4
Nayland Cft HLGN/YWD B28 ...163 E5
Naylors Gv SEDG DY3 ...83 G2
Neachells Ct WLNHL WV13 ...39 E4
Neachells La WLNHL WV13 ...38 D2
WNSFLD WV11 ...24 D5
Neachless Av WMBN WV5 ...81 E1
Neachley Gv STETCH B33 ...112 B5
Neale St WSLW WS2 ...4 A2
Nearhill Rd HWK/WKHTH B38 ...176 A5
Near Lands Cl RIDG/WDGT B32 ..140 B3
Nearmoor Rd BKDE/SHDE B34 ..113 F4
Neasden Gv KGSTG B44 ...75 H3
Neath Rd BLOX/PEL WS3 ...16 B5
Neath Wy BLOX/PEL WS3 ...16 B5
SEDG DY3 ...68 A5
Nebsworth Cl SHLY B90 ...163 H5
Nechells Park Rd
VAUX/NECH B7 ...110 A2
Nechells Pkwy VAUX/NECH B7 ..109 G5
Nechells Pl VAUX/NECH B7 ...109 H3
Needham St VAUX/NECH B7 ...110 A2
Needhill Cl DOR/KN B93 ...196 D2
Needless Aly CBHAM B2 * ...3 G5
Needwood Cl BKHL/PFLD WV2 ...51 H2
Needwood Dr
ETTPK/GDPK/PENN WV4 ...52 D4
Needwood Gv HHTH/SAND B71 ..72 A2
Nelson Av BILS/COS WV14 ...53 G1
Nelson Rd AST/WIT B6 ...91 F5
DUDN DY1 ...84 B5
Nelson St CBHAMW B1 ...2 B4
HHTH/SAND B71 ...87 G1
OLDBY B69 ...105 F3
WLNHL WV13 ...39 H2
Nene Cl STRBR DY8 ...135 G3
Nene Wy CBROM B36 ...113 H1
Neptune St TPTN/OCK DY4 ...84 D1
Nesbit Gv BORD B9 ...129 F1
Nesfield Cl HWK/WKHTH B38 ...176 A4
Nesfield Gv HIA/OLT B92 ...167 H3
Nesscliffe Gv
ERDW/GRVHL B23 ...76 B4
Nest Common BLOX/PEL WS3 ...17 H2
Neston Gv STETCH B33 ...129 H2
Netheravon Cl
ALE/KHTH/YWD B14 ...177 H4
Netherby Rd SEDG DY3 ...67 E3
Nethercote Gdns SHLY B90 ...179 G2
Netherdale Cl
CSCFLD/WYGN B72 ...77 G4
Netherdale Rd
ALE/KHTH/YWD B14 ...178 C4
Netherend Cl HALE B63 ...120 A5
Netherend La HALE B63 ...120 B5
Netherend Sq HALE B63 ...120 A5
Netherfield Gdns ACGN B27 ...146 B4
Nethergate SEDG DY3 ...83 H1
Netherstone Gv
FOAKS/STRLY B74 ...32 D5
Netherton Gv STETCH B33 ...131 E1
Netherwood Cl SOLH B91 ...164 A4
Nethy Dr DUNHL/THL/PER WV6 ..21 F5
Netley Gv SPARK B11 ...145 H4
Netley Rd BLOX/PEL WS3 ...16 A5
Netley Wy BLOX/PEL WS3 ...16 A5
Nevada Wy
CHWD/FDBR/MGN B37 ...132 C3
Neve Av WOLVN WV10 ...23 H1
Neville Av
ETTPK/GDPK/PENN WV4 ...52 B2
Neville Rd CBROM B36 ...95 G5
ERDW/GRVHL B23 ...92 A3
SHLY B90 ...179 H4
Nevin Gv PBAR/PBCH B42 ...90 C1
Nevis Ct BDMR/CCFT WV3 ...36 A3
Nevis Gv SHHTH WV12 ...25 H1
Nevison Gv GTB/HAM B43 ...59 F4
Newark Cft
LGN/SDN/BHAMAIR B26 ...147 H1
Newark Rd DUDS DY2 ...120 D2
SHHTH WV12 ...26 A3
Newbank Gv BORD B9 ...129 E1
New Bartholomew St
DIG/EDG B5 ...3 J5
New Birmingham Rd
OLDBY B69 ...85 G5
Newbold Cl DOR/KN B93 ...196 D3
Newbold Cft VAUX/NECH B7 ...109 H4
Newbolds Rd WOLVN WV10 ...24 A4
Newbolt Rd BILS/COS WV14 ...54 A2
Newbolt St DSYBK/YTR WS5 ...57 E3
New Bond St BORD B9 ...127 H3
DUDS DY2 ...102 D1
Newborough Gv
HLGN/YWD B28 ...179 H1
Newborough Rd
HLGN/YWD B28 ...179 H1
Newbridge Av
DUNHL/THL/PER WV6 ...36 A2
Newbridge Crs
DUNHL/THL/PER WV6 ...36 A1
Newbridge Gdns
DUNHL/THL/PER WV6 ...36 A1
Newbridge Ms
DUNHL/THL/PER WV6 * ...36 B1
Newbridge Rd BORD B9 ...129 F4
KGSWFD DY6 ...99 G1
Newbridge St
DUNHL/THL/PER WV6 ...36 B1
Newburn Cft RIDG/WDGT B32 ...140 B2
Newbury Cl RMSLY B62 ...139 F4
Newbury La OLDBY B69 ...104 B3
Newbury Rd STRBR DY8 ...117 G2
WOLVN WV10 ...12 C5
Newby Gv
CHWD/FDBR/MGN B37 ...114 B5
New Canal St DIG/EDG B5 ...3 J6
Newcastle Cft CVALE B35 ...95 E3
New Church Rd
SCFLD/BOLD B73 ...77 E3
New College Cl WSL WS1 ...57 G1
Newcombe Rd HDSW B21 ...89 F4
Newcomen Dr TPTN/OCK DY4 ...85 F3
Newcott Cl COVEN WV9 ...11 H5
New Coventry Rd
LGN/SDN/BHAMAIR B26 ...147 F2
New Cft LOZ/NWT B19 ...109 E2
Newcroft Gv
LGN/SDN/BHAMAIR B26 ...130 A5
New Cross Av WNSFLD WV11 ...38 B1
New Cross St DARL/WED WS10 ...55 F3
TPTN/OCK DY4 ...85 E1
Newdigate Rd MGN/WHC B75 ...63 G4
New Dudley Rd KGSWFD DY6 ...99 G1
Newells Dr TPTN/OCK DY4 ...70 B4
Newells Rd
LGN/SDN/BHAMAIR B26 ...130 C4
New England RMSLY B62 ...122 C5
New England Cl OLDBY B69 ...86 C5
Newent Cl SHHTH WV12 ...40 B1
Newent Rd NFLD/LBR B31 ...176 A1
Newey Cl RBRY B45 ...188 A2
Newey Rd HLGN/YWD B28 ...162 D4
WNSFLD WV11 ...25 G2
Newey St DUDN DY1 ...84 A4
New Farm Rd HAG/WOL DY9 ...136 A2
Newfield Cl SOLH B91 ...165 F4
WSLW WS2 ...27 G5
Newfield Crs HALE B63 ...138 C2
Newfield Dr KGSWFD DY6 ...100 A5
Newfield Gdns HAG/WOL DY9 ...169 G1
Newfield La HALE B63 ...138 C2
Newfield Pl HAG/WOL DY9 ...169 G1
Newfield Rd HAG/WOL DY9 ...169 G1
OLDBY B69 ...104 D1
New Forest Rd BLOX/PEL WS3 ...28 A4
New Gas St WBROM B70 ...71 E5
Newhall Ct CBHAMNW B3 * ...2 C3
New Hall Dr WALM/CURD B76 ...62 D4
Newhall Farm Cl
WALM/CURD B76 ...62 D4
Newhall Hl CBHAMW B1 ...2 C3
New Hall Pl DARL/WED WS10 * ...56 A5
Newhall Rd
BLKHTH/ROWR B65 ...122 A1
Newhall St CBHAMNW B3 ...2 E4
TPTN/OCK DY4 ...69 E3
WBROM B70 ...87 G4
New Hall St WLNHL WV13 ...39 G3
Newhall St WSL WS1 ...4 E6
New Hampton Rd East
WOLV WV1 ...6 C1
New Hampton Rd West
DUNHL/THL/PER WV6 ...36 C1
Newhaven Cl VAUX/NECH B7 ...109 G5
Newhay Cft LOZ/NWT B19 ...108 C2
New Heath Cl WNSFLD WV11 ...24 B5
New Henry St
LGLYGN/QTN B68 ...105 E5
Newhope Cl EDG B15 ...126 D4
New Hope Rd SMTHWK B66 ...107 E5
Newhouse Farm Cl
WALM/CURD B76 * ...63 F5
Newick Av FOAKS/STRLY B74 ...45 H2
Newick Gv
ALE/KHTH/YWD B14 * ...160 C5
Newick St DUDS DY2 ...102 C5
Newington Rd
CHWD/FDBR/MGN B37 ...132 B4
New Inn Rd LOZ/NWT B19 ...90 D5
New Inns Cl HDSW B21 ...107 F1
New Inns La RBRY B45 ...173 G4
New John St AST/WIT B6 ...109 E4
RMSLY B62 ...122 A3
New John St West
LOZ/NWT B19 ...108 B3
New King St DUDS DY2 * ...84 C5
Newland Cl RUSH/SHEL WS4 ...18 C5
Newland Gdns CDYHTH B64 ...121 E4
Newland Gv DUDS DY2 ...101 H2
Newland Rd SMHTH B10 ...128 D3
Newlands Cl WLNHL WV13 ...39 G4
Newlands Dr RMSLY B62 ...122 C5
Newlands La
CHWD/FDBR/MGN B37 ...149 E1
Newlands Rd BVILLE B30 ...160 B3
DOR/KN B93 ...196 C4
Newlands Wk
LGLYGN/QTN B68 * ...105 F5
New Landywood La
WNSFLD WV11 ...16 A1
Newlyn Rd CDYHTH B64 ...120 D3
NFLD/LBR B31 ...175 F2
Newman Av
ETTPK/GDPK/PENN WV4 ...52 D4
Newman College Cl
RIDG/WDGT B32 * ...157 G2
Newman Pl BILS/COS WV14 ...54 B1
Newman Rd ERDE/BCHGN B24 ...92 D2
TPTN/OCK DY4 ...70 A2
WOLVN WV10 ...24 A1
Newmans Cl SMTHWK B66 * ...107 E5
Newman Wy RBRY B45 ...188 A1
Newmarket Cl
DUNHL/THL/PER WV6 ...22 C5
New Market St CBHAMNW B3 * ...2 E4
Newmarket Wy CBROM B36 ...111 F2
Newmarsh Rd WALM/CURD B76 ..78 C5
New Meadow Cl
NFLD/LBR B31 ...175 H3
New Meeting St OLDBY B69 ...105 E1
New Mills St WSL WS1 ...56 D1
New Mill St DUDS DY2 ...84 D5
Newmore Gdns
DSYBK/YTR WS5 ...58 A2
New Moseley Rd
BHTH/HG B12 ...127 G4
Newnham Gv ERDW/GRVHL B23 ..76 C5
Newnham Ri SHLY B90 ...180 D2
Newnham Rd LDYWD/EDGR B16 125 E2
New Pool Rd CDYHTH B64 ...120 B4
Newport Rd BHTH/HG B12 ...144 C3
CBROM B36 ...112 B1
Newport St WOLVN WV10 ...37 G1
WSL WS1 ...4 D4
Newquay Cl DSYBK/YTR WS5 ...58 C1
Newquay Rd DSYBK/YTR WS5 ...58 B1
New Rd ALDR WS9 ...30 A5
BRWNH WS8 ...9 F5
CSHL/WTROR B46 ...96 B3
DUDS DY2 ...102 C2
DUNHL/THL/PER WV6 ...36 A1
HALE B63 ...138 D3
HLYWD B47 ...178 B5
RBRY B45 ...187 G1
SOLH B91 ...182 A2
STRBR DY8 ...135 G2
TPTN/OCK DY4 ...70 B5
WLNHL WV13 ...39 G4
WNSFLD WV11 ...24 B2
New Rowley Rd DUDS DY2 ...103 E2
New Spring St WSNGN B18 ...108 A5
New Spring St North
WSNGN B18 ...108 A4
Newstead Rd KGSTG B44 ...60 C5
New St BDMR/CCFT WV3 ...50 D2
BKHL/PFLD WV2 ...53 E2
BLOX/PEL WS3 ...27 F1
BRLYHL DY5 ...120 A4
CBHAM B2 ...3 F5
CBROM B36 ...112 D1
DARL/WED WS10 ...55 F2
DARL/WED WS10 ...70 D2
DUDN DY1 ...84 C5
ERDW/GRVHL B23 ...92 D1
ETTPK/GDPK/PENN WV4 ...52 C3
KGSWFD DY6 ...99 G1
KGSWFD DY6 ...99 H5
RBRY B45 ...174 A3
RUSH/SHEL WS4 ...28 D3
RUSH/SHEL WS4 ...29 F1
SEDG DY3 ...83 E3
SMTHWK B66 ...106 D3
STRBR DY8 ...117 H2
STRBR DY8 ...135 G2
TPTN/OCK DY4 ...85 E1
WBROM B70 ...71 E4
WBROM B70 ...87 H3
WLNHL WV13 ...39 E4
WNSFLD WV11 ...15 E4
WSL WS1 ...5 F5
New St North HHTH/SAND B71 ...87 H3
New Summer St LOZ/NWT B19 ...3 F1
New Swan La WBROM B70 ...87 E1
Newton Cl GTB/HAM B43 ...73 E3
Newton Gdns GTB/HAM B43 ...72 D3
Newton Gv SLYOAK B29 * ...142 D5
Newton Manor Cl
GTB/HAM B43 ...73 F3
Newton Pl WSLW WS2 ...27 F4
WSNGN B18 ...107 H2
Newton Rd DOR/KN B93 ...197 F1
GTB/HAM B43 ...73 E3
HHTH/SAND B71 ...72 B5
SPARK B11 ...144 D2
WSLW WS2 ...27 F5
Newton Sq GTB/HAM B43 ...73 G2
Newton St CBHAMNE B4 ...3 H3
HHTH/SAND B71 ...72 A4
New Town BRLYHL DY5 ...100 D5
DUDS DY2 ...120 D3
Newtown Dr LOZ/NWT B19 ...108 C3
Newtown La CDYHTH B64 ...120 D3
HAG/WOL DY9 ...171 H5
RBRY B45 ...173 E4
Newtown Middleway
AST/WIT B6 ...109 E4
New Town Rw LOZ/NWT B19 ...109 E4
Newtown St CDYHTH B64 ...120 D2
New Village DUDS DY2 ...120 G3
New Vis WNSFLD WV11 * ...24 A5
New Wood Cl KINVER DY7 ...117 G4
New Wood Gv ALDR WS9 ...19 E4
New Wood La KIDD DY10 ...168 A5
Niall Cl EDG B15 ...125 H4
Nicholas Rd FOAKS/STRLY B74 ...45 E5
Nicholds Cl BILS/COS WV14 ...68 B2
Nicholls Fold WNSFLD WV11 ...24 D5
Nicholls Rd TPTN/OCK DY4 ...69 E2
Nicholls St WBROM B70 ...87 H4
Nichols Cl HIA/OLT B92 ...165 H3
Nigel Av NFLD/LBR B31 ...158 C5
Nigel Rd DUDN DY1 ...83 H4
WASH/WDE B8 ...110 C3
Nightingale Av CBROM B36 ...114 A1
Nightingale Cl
ERDW/GRVHL B23 ...76 A4
Nightingale Crs BRLYHL DY5 ...119 F5
SHHTH WV12 ...25 H2
Nightingale Dr TPTN/OCK DY4 ...86 A1
Nightingale Pl BILS/COS WV14 ...53 H1
Nightingale Wk EDG B15 ...126 C5
Nightjar Gv ERDW/GRVHL B23 ...76 A5
Nighwood Dr FOAKS/STRLY B74 ..60 B1
Nijon Cl HDSW B21 ...89 E5
Nimmings Cl NFLD/LBR B31 ...189 F2
Nimmings Rd RMSLY B62 ...122 B3
Nineacres Dr
CHWD/FDBR/MGN B37 ...132 A2
Nine Elms La WOLVN WV10 ...37 G1
Nine Leasowes SMTHWK B66 ...106 A2
Nine Locks Rdg BRLYHL DY5 ...119 F2
Nineveh Av HDSW B21 ...107 H2
Nineveh Rd HDSW B21 ...107 G2
Ninfield Rd ACGN B27 ...146 A3
Nith Pl DUDN DY1 ...84 B4
Nocke Rd WNSFLD WV11 ...25 F1
Nock St TPTN/OCK DY4 * ...70 A4
Noddy Pk ALDR WS9 ...30 B3
Noddy Park Rd ALDR WS9 ...30 B3
Noel Av BHTH/HG B12 ...144 C1
Noele Gordon Gdns WSL WS1 * ...4 D7
Noel Rd LDYWD/EDGR B16 ...125 H3
Nolton Cl GTB/HAM B43 ...73 F3
Nooklands Cft STETCH B33 ...130 C2
The Nook BRLYHL DY5 ...100 D4
Noose Crs WLNHL WV13 ...39 E3
Noose La WLNHL WV13 ...39 F2
Nora Rd SPARK B11 ...145 E4
Norbiton Rd KGSTG B44 ...75 G3
Norbreck Cl GTB/HAM B43 ...73 F3
Norbury Av BLOX/PEL WS3 ...17 H4
Norbury Crs
ETTPK/GDPK/PENN WV4 ...52 D4
Norbury Dr BRLYHL DY5 ...119 F3
Norbury Gv HIA/OLT B92 ...147 G4
Norbury Rd BILS/COS WV14 ...54 B2
KGSTG B44 ...60 B5
WBROM B70 ...70 D4
WOLVN WV10 ...23 H4
Norcombe Gv SHLY B90 ...195 G3
Nordley Rd WNSFLD WV11 ...24 C5
Norfolk Av HHTH/SAND B71 ...71 H4
Norfolk Cl BVILLE B30 ...160 B4
Norfolk Crs ALDR WS9 ...30 B2
Norfolk Dr DARL/WED WS10 ...56 D4
Norfolk Gdns MGN/WHC B75 ...47 F5
Norfolk New Rd WSLW WS2 ...41 E1
Norfolk Pl WSLW WS2 ...27 H5
Norfolk Rd BDMR/CCFT WV3 ...36 C5
DUDS DY2 ...102 A2
EDG B15 ...125 F4
ERDW/GRVHL B23 ...92 D1
LGLYGN/QTN B68 ...123 F5
MGN/WHC B75 ...62 C1
RBRY B45 ...173 H4
STRBR DY8 ...117 H4
Norfolk Tower WSNGN B18 * ...108 B4
Norgrave Rd HIA/OLT B92 ...148 A5
Norlan Dr ALE/KHTH/YWD B14 ..178 B2
Norland Rd ACGN B27 ...163 G1
Norley Gv MOS/BIL B13 ...162 A3
Norman Av RIDG/WDGT B32 ...124 A5
Normandy Rd
BFLD/HDSWWD B20 ...90 D5
Norman Rd DSYBK/YTR WS5 ...43 E5
NFLD/LBR B31 ...175 H2
SMTHWKW B67 ...123 H3
Norman St DUDS DY2 ...102 D1
WSNGN B18 ...107 G4
Norman Ter
BLKHTH/ROWR B65 ...104 A5
Normanton Av
LGN/SDN/BHAMAIR B26 ...148 B2
Norrington Gv NFLD/LBR B31 ...174 C2
Norrington Rd NFLD/LBR B31 ...174 C2
Norris Dr STETCH B33 ...130 A1
Norris Rd AST/WIT B6 ...91 F5
Norris Wy MGN/WHC B75 ...62 D3
Northampton St WSNGN B18 ...2 C1
Northam Wk
DUNHL/THL/PER WV6 ...36 D1
Northanger Rd ACGN B27 ...146 B5
North Av BHAMNEC B40 ...150 B2
WNSFLD WV11 ...24 C4
Northbrook Rd SHLY B90 ...163 G5
Northbrook St
LDYWD/EDGR B16 ...107 H5
Northcote Rd STETCH B33 ...111 H5
Northcote St WSLW WS2 ...41 H1
Northcott Rd BILS/COS WV14 ...54 A4
DUDS DY2 ...102 D5
Northdown Rd SOLH B91 ...181 F4
North Dr BFLD/HDSWWD B20 ...108 B1
DIG/EDG B5 ...143 G2
MGN/WHC B75 ...62 C2
Northfield Gv BDMR/CCFT WV3 ..50 C1
Northfield Rd BVILLE B30 ...176 B1
DUDS DY2 ...102 D4
HRBN B17 ...141 G4
Northfields Wy BRWNH WS8 ...8 D5
Northgate ALDR WS9 ...30 A1
CDYHTH B64 ...120 D4
North Ga HRBN B17 ...125 E5
Northgate Wy ALDR WS9 ...30 A2
North Gn
ETTPK/GDPK/PENN WV4 ...50 D2
North Holme BORD B9 ...128 A2
Northland Rd SHLY B90 ...181 E4
Northlands Rd MOS/BIL B13 ...161 G1
Northleach Av
ALE/KHTH/YWD B14 ...177 H3
Northleigh Rd WASH/WDE B8 ...111 E3
Northolt Dr CVALE B35 ...94 C2
Northolt Gv PBAR/PBCH B42 ...73 H2
North Ov SEDG DY3 ...83 G1
Northover Cl COVEN WV9 ...12 A5
North Park Rd
ERDW/GRVHL B23 ...91 H3
North Pathway HRBN B17 ...124 D5
North Rd BFLD/HDSWWD B20 ...91 E4
HRBN B17 ...142 B1
SLYOAK B29 ...142 C4
TPTN/OCK DY4 ...69 H3
WOLV WV1 ...37 E1
North Roundhay STETCH B33 ...112 C5
Northside Dr FOAKS/STRLY B74 ..45 F5
North Springfield SEDG DY3 ...67 G2
North St BRLYHL DY5 ...119 E2
DARL/WED WS10 ...55 H5
DUDS DY2 ...84 D5
SMTHWKW B67 ...106 B4
WOLV WV1 ...7 F3
WSLW WS2 ...42 A1
Northumberland St
VAUX/NECH B7 ...127 G1
North View Dr BRLYHL DY5 ...101 G4
North Warwick St BORD B9 * ...128 B3
Northway BHAMNEC B40 ...150 B2
SEDG DY3 ...67 E3
North Western Ar CBHAM B2 ...3 G4
North Western Rd
SMTHWK B66 ...106 B3
North Western Ter
WSNGN B18 ...107 H2
Northwick Crs SOLH B91 ...181 H4
Northwood Park Cl
WOLVN WV10 ...13 E4
Northwood Park Rd
WOLVN WV10 ...13 E5
North Wood St CBHAMW B1 ...2 C3
Northwood St CBHAMW B1 ...2 D2
Northwood Wy STRBR DY8 ...118 D4
North Worcestershire Pth
HAG/WOL DY9 ...152 D4
HAG/WOL DY9 ...171 G1
RBRY B45 ...188 A4
Northycote La WOLVN WV10 ...13 F3
Norton Cl
ETTPK/GDPK/PENN WV4 ...50 C5
SMTHWK B66 ...107 E4
Norton Crs BILS/COS WV14 ...68 D2
BORD B9 ...129 F1
DUDS DY2 ...121 E1
Norton Ga HWK/WKHTH B38 ...176 C4
Norton Green La
DOR/KN B93 ...199 F1
Norton La SHLY B90 ...193 F4
Norton Rd BLOX/PEL WS3 ...18 A2
CSHL/WTROR B46 ...115 F1
Norton St WSNGN B18 ...107 H4
Norton Ter BVILLE B30 * ...160 A4
Norton Vw
ALE/KHTH/YWD B14 ...160 D4
Nortune Cl HWK/WKHTH B38 ...176 B3
Norwich Cft
CHWD/FDBR/MGN B37 ...131 H3
Norwich Dr HRBN B17 ...124 B4
Norwich Rd DUDS DY2 ...120 D2
WSLW WS2 ...41 F4
Norwood Av CDYHTH B64 ...121 E5
Norwood Gv LOZ/NWT B19 ...108 B2
Norwood Rd BORD B9 ...128 C2
BRLYHL DY5 ...119 E1
Nottingham Dr SHHTH WV12 ...26 A3
Nottingham Wy BRLYHL DY5 ...119 H2
Nova Ct PBAR/PBCH B42 ...74 B2
Nova Scotia St CBHAMNE B4 ...3 J4
Nowell St DARL/WED WS10 ...55 G3
Nugent Cl AST/WIT B6 ...109 E2
Nugent Gv SHLY B90 ...194 D5
Nursery Av ALDR WS9 ...30 B5
BHTH/HG B12 ...144 B2
Nursery Cl BVILLE B30 ...159 H5
HAG/WOL DY9 ...152 C5
Nursery Dr WMBN WV5 ...80 D2
Nursery Gdns CDSL WV8 ...10 B3
SHLY B90 * ...179 G5
STRBR DY8 ...118 B3
Nursery La FOAKS/STRLY B74 ...47 E3
Nursery Rd BLOX/PEL WS3 ...27 F2
BVILLE B30 ...159 G5
EDG B15 ...125 F5
LOZ/NWT B19 ...108 B3
Nursery View Cl ALDR WS9 ...45 E3
Nursery Wk
DUNHL/THL/PER WV6 ...21 H5
Nutbush Dr NFLD/LBR B31 ...157 H4
Nutfield Wk RIDG/WDGT B32 ...141 F2
Nutgrove Cl
ALE/KHTH/YWD B14 ...161 F3
Nuthatch Dr BRLYHL DY5 ...119 E5
Nuthurst MGN/WHC B75 ...63 G4

Nuthurst Gv
ALE/KHTH/YWD B14 178 B3
DOR/KN B93 197 E4
Nuthurst Rd NFLD/LBR B31 189 F2
Nutley Dr TPTN/OCK DY4 70 B3
Nutmeg Gv WSL WS1 5 J3
Nuttall Gv HDSW B21 107 E2

O

Oak Av BHTH/HG B12 144 C2
WBROM B70 87 F3
WSLW WS2 40 C2
Oak Bank WSNGN B18 108 A3
Oak Barn Rd RMSLY B62 122 B4
Oak Cl HRBN B17 141 G1
TPTN/OCK DY4 69 G2
Oak Ct HALE B63 138 B5
Oak Crs BLOX/PEL WS3 27 H4
OLDBY B69 85 H5
Oak Cft CHWD/FDBR/MGN B37 131 G1
Oakcroft Rd MOS/BIL B13 161 H3
Oakdale Cl BRLYHL DY5 100 C2
LGLYGN/QTN B68 123 E2
Oakdale Rd CBROM B36 112 A1
LGLYGN/QTN B68 122 D2
Oak Dr ERDW/GRVHL B23 76 A4
Oaken Covert CDSL WV8 10 A5
Oaken Dr CDSL WV8 10 A4
SHHTH WV12 26 C3
SOLH B91 164 B5
Oaken Gv CDSL WV8 10 A5
Oakenhayes Crs BRWNH WS8 9 F3
WALM/CURD B76 95 E1
Oakenhayes Dr BRWNH WS8 9 F3
Oaken Lanes CDSL WV8 10 A5
Oaken Pk CDSL WV8 10 C5
Oakenshaw Rd SHLY B90 180 D4
Oakeswell St DARL/WED WS10 56 A5
Oakeywell St DUDS DY2 84 D5
Oak Farm Cl WALM/CURD B76 78 C4
Oak Farm Rd BVILLE B30 159 G5
Oakfield Av BHTH/HG B12 144 C2
DUDN DY1 68 B5
KGSWFD DY6 100 A4
SPARK B11 145 E1
Oakfield Cl SMTHWK B66 107 E3
STRBR DY8 118 B3
Oakfield Dr BLOX/PEL WS3 18 A2
RBRY B45 188 D4
Oakfield Rd BHTH/HG B12 144 A3
CDSL WV8 10 D5
ERDE/BCHGN B24 92 D3
HAG/WOL DY9 136 D5
SLYOAK B29 143 E4
SMTHWK B66 107 E4
STRBR DY8 118 C3
Oakfields Wy SOLH B91 166 B5
Oak Gn DUDN DY1 84 A1
DUNHL/THL/PER WV6 35 F2
Oak Gv NFLD/LBR B31 175 E4
WNSFLD WV11 24 B3
Oakhall Dr DOR/KN B93 196 D4
Oakham Av DUDS DY2 103 E2
Oakham Crs DUDS DY2 103 E2
Oakham Dr DUDS DY2 103 F1
Oakham Rd DUDS DY2 103 E2
HRBN B17 124 D5
Oak Hl BDMR/CCFT WV3 35 G5
Oakhill Cl HRBN B17 124 D4
Oakhill Crs ACGN B27 163 F2
Oakhill Dr BRLYHL DY5 118 D5
Oak Hill Dr EDG B15 125 G5
Oakhurst Rd ACGN B27 163 F1
CSCFLD/WYGN B72 77 F3
Oakland Cl SOLH B91 182 C1
Oakland Dr SEDG DY3 82 D4
Oakland Rd BLOX/PEL WS3 28 A3
HDSW B21 107 G1
MOS/BIL B13 144 C4
Oaklands NFLD/LBR B31 175 F1
RMSLY B62 140 A3
WALM/CURD B76 96 B1
Oaklands Av HRBN B17 141 G2
Oaklands Cft WALM/CURD B76 78 D4
Oaklands Dr
BFLD/HDSWWD B20 89 H4
Oaklands Gn BILS/COS WV14 38 C5
Oaklands Rd BDMR/CCFT WV3 36 D5
FOAKS/STRLY B74 47 F5
The Oaklands
BDMR/CCFT WV3 * 36 D5
CHWD/FDBR/MGN B37 132 A5
Oaklands Wy BLOX/PEL WS3 18 B4
NFLD/LBR B31 174 C4
Oak La KGSWFD DY6 82 A5
WBROM B70 87 F3
Oaklea Dr CDYHTH B64 121 F2
Oakleaf Cl RIDG/WDGT B32 140 C5
Oak Leaf Dr MOS/BIL B13 144 C4
Oak Leasow RIDG/WDGT B32 140 B3
Oakleigh NFLD/LBR B31 176 A3
Oakleigh Dr CDSL WV8 10 C4
SEDG DY3 67 E4
Oak Leigh Rd STRBR DY8 135 G5
Oakleighs STRBR DY8 117 G3
Oakley Av ALDR WS9 30 A5
TPTN/OCK DY4 69 G5
Oakley Gv
ETTPK/GDPK/PENN WV4 50 D3
Oakley Rd BVILLE B30 160 B5
ETTPK/GDPK/PENN WV4 50 D3
SMTHH B10 128 A5
Oak Leys BDMR/CCFT WV3 35 G4
Oakley Wood Dr SOLH B91 182 C1
Oakmeadow Cl
LGN/SDN/BHAMAIR B26 146 D2
STETCH B33 131 F2
Oakmeadow Wy
ERDE/BCHGN B24 93 H3
Oakmount Cl BLOX/PEL WS3 17 H4
Oakmount Rd
FOAKS/STRLY B74 60 C1
Oak Park Rd STRBR DY8 118 B3
Oakridge Cl SHHTH WV12 40 A1
Oakridge Dr SHHTH WV12 40 A1
Oak Ri CSHL/WTROR B46 115 F4
Oak Rd ALDR WS9 19 G4
BLOX/PEL WS3 17 H2
DUDN DY1 84 C3
LGLYGN/QTN B68 123 G5
RUSH/SHEL WS4 29 E2
TPTN/OCK DY4 69 E5
WBROM B70 87 F4
WLNHL WV13 39 E3
Oaks Crs BDMR/CCFT WV3 6 B5
Oaks Dr BDMR/CCFT WV3 6 B4
WMBN WV5 81 E1
Oakslade Dr HIA/OLT B92 165 G2
The Oaks BDMR/CCFT WV3 * 6 B4
BKDE/SHDE B34 112 D2
BLOX/PEL WS3 27 E1
HWK/WKHTH B38 190 D2
SMTHWKW B67 * 106 B4
Oak St BDMR/CCFT WV3 6 B5
BILS/COS WV14 68 B4
BRLYHL DY5 119 H3
CDYHTH B64 120 D3
DUDS DY2 103 E5
KGSWFD DY6 99 G4
Oakthorpe Dr
CHWD/FDBR/MGN B37 113 H4
Oakthorpe Gdns OLDBY B69 85 G4
Oak Tree Cl DOR/KN B93 196 C4
Oak Tree Crs RMSLY B62 139 H1
Oak Tree Gdns STRBR DY8 118 C3
Oak Tree La HLYWD B47 192 D2
SLYOAK B29 159 G1
Oaktree Rd DARL/WED WS10 56 B5
Oak Tree Rd WASH/WDE B8 110 B3
The Oak Wk NFLD/LBR B31 175 G4
Oak Wy WALM/CURD B76 78 B1
Oakwood Cl ALDR WS9 19 E3
WNSFLD WV11 15 F4
Oakwood Crs DUDS DY2 101 H3
Oakwood Cft SOLH B91 182 A4
Oakwood Dr
ALE/KHTH/YWD B14 177 H1
FOAKS/STRLY B74 45 E5
Oakwood Rd BLOX/PEL WS3 28 A3
HLYWD B47 192 C2
SCFLD/BOLD B73 76 C2
SMTHWKW B67 106 B5
SPARK B11 145 E4
Oakwood St WBROM B70 87 F1
Oasthouse Cl KGSWFD DY6 99 E2
Oaston Rd CBROM B36 113 F1
Oatlands Wk
ALE/KHTH/YWD B14 177 G3
Oatlands Wy
DUNHL/THL/PER WV6 34 B2
Oatmill Cl DARL/WED WS10 * 55 G3
Oban Rd HIA/OLT B92 164 B1
Oberon Cl RBRY B45 174 A3
Oberon Dr SHLY B90 180 A4
Occupation Rd BRWNH WS8 19 G3
Occupation St DUDN DY1 84 A4
Ocean Dr DARL/WED WS10 70 B2
Ockam Cft NFLD/LBR B31 176 A3
Ocker Hill Rd TPTN/OCK DY4 69 H2
O'connor Dr TPTN/OCK DY4 70 A2
Oddingley Rd NFLD/LBR B31 176 A3
Odell Crs BLOX/PEL WS3 27 G3
Odell Pl DIG/EDG B5 143 G2
Odell Rd BLOX/PEL WS3 27 F3
Odensil Gn HIA/OLT B92 147 H5
Odnall La HAG/WOL DY9 170 C1
Offa's Dr DUNHL/THL/PER WV6 20 C5
Offenham Covert
HWK/WKHTH B38 176 C5
Offini Cl WBROM B70 88 B4
Offmoor Rd RIDG/WDGT B32 157 F2
Ogbury Cl
ALE/KHTH/YWD B14 177 G3
Ogley Crs BRWNH WS8 9 G5
Ogley Dr MGN/WHC B75 63 G3
Ogley Hay Rd BNTWD WS7 9 G2
Ogley Rd BRWNH WS8 9 G5
O'Keeffe Cl SPARK B11 144 D1
Okehampton Dr
HHTH/SAND B71 71 G5
Okement Dr WNSFLD WV11 24 B5
Old Abbey Gdns HRBN B17 142 B3
Old Acre Cl WALM/CURD B76 77 H5
Old Acre Dr HDSW B21 107 G2
Oldacre Rd LGLYGN/QTN B68 123 E5
Old Bank Rd NFLD/LBR B31 175 H3
Old Barn Rd BVILLE B30 159 E3
STRBR DY8 118 C3
Old Beeches ERDW/GRVHL B23 76 A3
Old Bell Rd ERDW/GRVHL B23 77 F5
Oldberrow Cl SHLY B90 195 G2
Old Birchills WSLW WS2 41 G2
Old Bridge St LOZ/NWT B19 108 B3
Old Bridge Wk
BLKHTH/ROWR B65 103 F4
Old Bromford La CBROM B36 111 F3
Old Brookside STETCH B33 130 A2
Oldbury Ring Wy OLDBY B69 104 D2
Oldbury Rd
BLKHTH/ROWR B65 122 B2
SMTHWK B66 105 G2
WBROM B70 86 D3
Oldbury St DARL/WED WS10 56 B5
Old Bush St BRLYHL DY5 119 G1
Old Camp Hl SPARK B11 127 G4
Old Castle Gv BRWNH WS8 9 F2
Old Chapel Rd SMTHWKW B67 124 B1
Old Church Gn STETCH B33 130 A2
Old Church Rd
CSHL/WTROR B46 96 B3
HRBN B17 141 H2
Old Croft La CBROM B36 112 D2
Old Cross St TPTN/OCK DY4 85 E1
Old Crown Cl RIDG/WDGT B32 157 F1
Old Damson La HIA/OLT B92 148 D5
Old Dickens Heath Rd
SHLY B90 194 A3
Old End La BILS/COS WV14 68 C4
Old Fallings Crs WOLVN WV10 23 H4
Old Fallings La WOLVN WV10 23 H2
Old Farm Dr CDSL WV8 10 C3
Old Farm Gv
ALE/KHTH/YWD B14 162 A5
Old Farm Meadow
BDMR/CCFT WV3 35 G5
Old Farm Rd STETCH B33 112 A5
Oldfield Dr STRBR DY8 135 G4
Oldfield Rd BHTH/HG B12 144 C1
BILS/COS WV14 68 A3
Oldfields CDYHTH B64 120 D4
HAG/WOL DY9 152 D4
Old Fordrove WALM/CURD B76 62 D5
Old Forest Wy
BKDE/SHDE B34 112 D3
Old Grange Rd SPARK B11 145 E3
Old Grove Gdns HAG/WOL DY9 136 B4
Old Hall Cl STRBR DY8 118 C5
Old Hall La ALDR WS9 59 F3
Old Hall St WOLV WV1 7 G5
Old Ham La HAG/WOL DY9 136 A5
Old Hampton La WNSFLD WV11 14 A5
Old Hawne La HALE B63 138 C2
Old Heath Crs WOLV WV1 38 A4
Old Heath Rd WOLV WV1 38 A3
Old Hl DUNHL/THL/PER WV6 21 H5
Old Hobicus La
LGLYGN/QTN B68 105 F4
Old Horns Crs PBAR/PBCH B42 74 C1
Oldhouse Farm Cl
HLGN/YWD B28 162 D4
Old House La RMSLY B62 172 D4
Oldington Gv SOLH B91 181 G5
Old Kingsbury Rd
WALM/CURD B76 95 E1
Oldknow Rd SMHTH B10 145 G1
Old Landywood La
WNSFLD WV11 15 G1
Old La BLOX/PEL WS3 27 G3
DUNHL/THL/PER WV6 34 D3
Old Level Wy DUDS DY2 102 D5
Old Lime Gdns
HWK/WKHTH B38 176 C5
Old Lindens Cl
FOAKS/STRLY B74 60 A1
Old Lode La HIA/OLT B92 147 H5
The Old Mnr
DUNHL/THL/PER WV6 * 21 H5
Old Masters Cl WSL WS1 5 H4
Old Meadow Rd NFLD/LBR B31 189 H1
Old Meeting Rd BILS/COS WV14 68 C3
Old Meeting St HHTH/SAND B71 87 F1
Old Mill Cl SHLY B90 179 F3
Old Mill Gdns RUSH/SHEL WS4 18 C5
Old Mill Gv
BFLD/HDSWWD B20 * 90 C4
Old Mill Rd CSHL/WTROR B46 115 F2
Old Moat Dr NFLD/LBR B31 175 H2
Old Moat Wy WASH/WDE B8 111 F3
Oldnall Cl HAG/WOL DY9 136 D3
Oldnall Rd HAG/WOL DY9 137 E3
Old Oak Cl ALDR WS9 30 B2
Old Oak Rd HWK/WKHTH B38 177 E3
Old Oscott Hl KGSTG B44 75 E2
Old Oscott La KGSTG B44 75 E3
Old Pk SLYOAK B29 158 C5
Old Park La OLDBY B69 105 E4
Old Park Rd DARL/WED WS10 55 G2
DUDN DY1 83 H2
Old Park Wk LOZ/NWT B19 109 E2
Old Pleck Rd WSLW WS2 41 G4
Old Port Cl TPTN/OCK DY4 * 85 H4
Old Portway HWK/WKHTH B38 190 C1
Old Postway LOZ/NWT B19 108 D2
Old Quarry Cl RBRY B45 173 H5
Old Quarry Dr SEDG DY3 83 F1
Old Rectory Gdns ALDR WS9 30 C4
Old School Cl WLNHL WV13 39 G3
Old School Dr
BLKHTH/ROWR B65 121 H1
Old Scott Cl STETCH B33 131 E2
Old Smithy Pl WSNGN B18 108 A4
Old Snow Hl CBHAMW B3 3 F2
Old Sq CBHAMNE B4 3 G4
Old Stables Wk VAUX/NECH B7 110 A2
Old Station Rd HIA/OLT B92 150 B5
STETCH B33 111 H5
Old Stone Cl RBRY B45 173 H4
Old Stowheath La
WLNHL WV13 * 38 C4
Old Tokengate HRBN B17 142 B1
Old Town Cl HWK/WKHTH B38 176 D3
Old Town La BLOX/PEL WS3 17 H4
Old Vicarage Cl BLOX/PEL WS3 18 A5
Old Walsall Rd GTB/HAM B43 73 H3
Old Warwick Ct HIA/OLT B92 164 A1
Old Warwick Rd HIA/OLT B92 164 A1
Oldway Dr SOLH B91 182 C3
Old Well Cl RUSH/SHEL WS4 28 D3
Old Wharf Rd STRBR DY8 135 F1
Olga Dr TPTN/OCK DY4 69 H2
Olinthus Av WNSFLD WV11 25 E3
Olive Av
ETTPK/GDPK/PENN WV4 52 C3
Olive Dr RMSLY B62 122 A4
Olive Hill Rd RMSLY B62 122 B4
Olive La RMSLY B62 122 A4
Olive Pl ALE/KHTH/YWD B14 * 161 E3
Oliver Cl DUDS DY2 103 E1
Oliver Ct BLKHTH/ROWR B65 121 H2
Oliver Crs BILS/COS WV14 69 E1
Oliver Rd ERDW/GRVHL B23 76 D5
SMTHWK B66 125 E1
Oliver St VAUX/NECH B7 109 G4
Ollerton Rd
LGN/SDN/BHAMAIR B26 130 B5
Ollison Dr FOAKS/STRLY B74 45 F3
Olliver Cl RIDG/WDGT B32 139 H5
Olorenshaw Rd
LGN/SDN/BHAMAIR B26 148 B2
Olton Bvd East ACGN B27 146 C5
Olton Bvd West SPARK B11 145 H4
Olton Cft ACGN B27 146 D4
Olton Mere HIA/OLT B92 * 146 D5
Olton Rd SHLY B90 163 F5
Olton Whf HIA/OLT B92 147 E5
Olympus Dr TPTN/OCK DY4 70 B5
Ombersley Cl OLDBY B69 104 B4
Ombersley Rd BHTH/HG B12 144 C1
HALE B63 138 B5
Onibury Rd HDSW B21 89 F5
Onslow Crs HIA/OLT B92 164 C1
Onslow Rd SPARK B11 146 A3
Ontario Cl HWK/WKHTH B38 177 E5
Oozells Sq CBHAMW B1 2 B6
Oozells St CBHAMW B1 2 C6
Open Field Cl NFLD/LBR B31 175 H3
Openfield Cft CSHL/WTROR B46 96 C4
The Orangery HAG/WOL DY9 153 F3
Orchard Av SOLH B91 165 F5
Orchard Cl BLKHTH/ROWR B65 121 G1
CSHL/WTROR B46 115 F2
HAG/WOL DY9 169 H1
HALE B63 137 G1
HDSW B21 89 H5
RUSH/SHEL WS4 * 29 E5
WLNHL WV13 39 H4
Orchard Ct BDMR/CCFT WV3 50 B1
KGSWFD DY6 99 H3
Orchard Dr NFLD/LBR B31 189 F1
Orchard Gv ALDR WS9 44 B1
ETTPK/GDPK/PENN WV4 51 G4
FOAKS/STRLY B74 46 D2
SEDG DY3 82 D3
Orchard La CDSL WV8 10 D4
HAG/WOL DY9 136 C1
Orchard Meadow Wk
CVALE B35 94 D3
Orchard Ri
LGN/SDN/BHAMAIR B26 130 B5
Orchard Rd DSYBK/YTR WS5 57 H5
DUDS DY2 120 C2
ERDE/BCHGN B24 93 E1
HOCK/TIA B94 198 A5
WLNHL WV13 39 H4
WNSFLD WV11 24 C3
The Orchards FOAKS/STRLY B74 47 E4
HLYWD B47 192 C1
SHLY B90 194 D4
Orchard St BRLYHL DY5 101 F5
OLDBY B69 85 F4
Orchards Wy BHTH/HG B12 144 A1
The Orchard BILS/COS WV14 54 A3
BLOX/PEL WS3 17 F5
CHWD/FDBR/MGN B37 131 H4
DUNHL/THL/PER WV6 22 A4
Orchard Wy ACGN B27 146 B3
GTB/HAM B43 73 H2
HLYWD B47 178 C5
Orcheston Wk
ALE/KHTH/YWD B14 177 H4
Orchid Cl SMTHWK B66 105 H2
Orchid Dr LOZ/NWT B19 108 D3
Oregon Cl KGSWFD DY6 100 B3
Oregon Dr SHHTH WV12 26 C3
Orford Gv HDSW B21 107 E2
Oriel Cl DUDN DY1 83 G4
Oriel Dr WOLVN WV10 12 D4
Oriel Vls SPARK B11 * 145 E2
Orion Cl WASH/WDE B8 111 F5
Orkney Av BKDE/SHDE B34 112 B3
Orkney Cft CBROM B36 114 B2
Orlando Cl WSL WS1 4 E6
Ormande Cl HALE B63 120 B5
Orme Cl STRBR DY8 118 C4
Ormes La DUNHL/THL/PER WV6 35 G2
Ormond Pl BILS/COS WV14 54 A2
Ormond Rd RBRY B45 173 G4
Ormsby Gv ACGN B27 163 F3
Ormscliffe Rd RBRY B45 188 B2
Orphanage Rd
CSCFLD/WYGN B72 77 G4
ERDE/BCHGN B24 93 F1
Orpington Rd KGSTG B44 60 A5
Orpwood Rd STETCH B33 130 C2
Orton Av WALM/CURD B76 78 B5
Orton Cl CSHL/WTROR B46 96 A3
Orton Gv
ETTPK/GDPK/PENN WV4 50 D4
Orton Wy CVALE B35 94 C4
Orwell Cl STRBR DY8 134 D3
WNSFLD WV11 25 F5
Orwell Dr HHTH/SAND B71 71 H5
NFLD/LBR B31 175 H5
Orwell Pas DIG/EDG B5 3 H6
Orwell Rd WSL WS1 5 K6
Osberton Dr DUDN DY1 83 H4
Osborne Cl AST/WIT B6 109 G2
BRLYHL DY5 119 H4
Osborne Dr DARL/WED WS10 40 B5
Osborne Gv LOZ/NWT B19 * 108 C2
Osborne Rd ERDW/GRVHL B23 92 D1
ETTPK/GDPK/PENN WV4 51 F3
HDSW B21 107 H1
WBROM B70 87 G3
Osborn Rd SPARK B11 145 E1
Osbourne Cft SHLY B90 194 D3
Oscott Rd PBAR/PBCH B42 91 E3
Oscott School La KGSTG B44 75 E1
Osier Gv ERDW/GRVHL B23 75 H5
Osier Pl WOLV WV1 37 H3
Osier St WOLV WV1 37 H3
Osler St LDYWD/EDGR B16 125 H2
Osmaston Rd HRBN B17 141 G4
STRBR DY8 135 E5
Osmington Gv HALE B63 137 H1
Osprey Dr DUDN DY1 83 H5
Osprey Rd ERDW/GRVHL B23 76 A5
HIA/OLT B92 146 D5
Ostler Cl KGSWFD DY6 99 F2
Oswin Pl BLOX/PEL WS3 28 B5
Oswin Rd BLOX/PEL WS3 28 B5
Otley Gv BORD B9 129 G1
Otter Cft BKDE/SHDE B34 113 F4
Otterstone Cl SEDG DY3 67 E1
Oughton Rd BHTH/HG B12 127 G5
Oundle Rd KGSTG B44 75 F4
Ounsdale Crs WMBN WV5 65 E4
Ounsdale Dr DUDS DY2 102 C5
Ounsdale Rd WMBN WV5 64 D4
Ounty John La STRBR DY8 152 C2
Outmore Rd STETCH B33 130 D3
Out Wood Dr NFLD/LBR B31 174 D4
Oval Rd ERDE/BCHGN B24 92 C5
TPTN/OCK DY4 69 F5
The Oval DARL/WED WS10 55 H4
DUDN DY1 101 G1
SMTHWKW B67 123 H2
Overbrook Cl SEDG DY3 83 E4
Over Brunton Cl
NFLD/LBR B31 175 H3
Overbury Cl NFLD/LBR B31 176 A2
RMSLY B62 138 D5
Overbury Rd NFLD/LBR B31 176 A1
Overdale Av WALM/CURD B76 94 B1
Overdale Cl SHHTH WV12 40 A2
Overdale Dr WSLW WS2 40 A2
Overdale Rd RIDG/WDGT B32 141 E2
Overend Rd HALE B63 137 H1
Overend St WBROM B70 87 H3
Overfield Dr BILS/COS WV14 53 E5
Overfield Rd DUDN DY1 101 G1
RIDG/WDGT B32 158 A1
Over Green Dr
CHWD/FDBR/MGN B37 113 H4
Overlea Av ACGN B27 146 B4
Over Mill Dr SLYOAK B29 143 F5
Overmoor Cl LOZ/NWT B19 108 C2
Over Pool Rd WASH/WDE B8 111 E3
Overseal Rd WNSFLD WV11 25 E2
Overslade Rd SOLH B91 181 F3
Oversley Rd WALM/CURD B76 78 C5
Overstrand COVEN WV9 11 H3
Overton Cl HLGN/YWD B28 163 E4
Overton Dr CSHL/WTROR B46 96 C3
Overton Gv ACGN B27 163 G2
Overton Pl HHTH/SAND B71 71 H5
VAUX/NECH B7 * 109 G5
Overton Rd ACGN B27 163 F2
Overwood Cft WASH/WDE B8 128 C1
Owen Pl BILS/COS WV14 53 H2
Owen Rd BDMR/CCFT WV3 6 B7
BILS/COS WV14 53 H1
WLNHL WV13 39 H4
Owens Cft HWK/WKHTH B38 177 E4
Owen St DARL/WED WS10 55 F1
DUDS DY2 103 E1
TPTN/OCK DY4 85 E1
Owens Wy CDYHTH B64 121 G3
Ownall Rd BKDE/SHDE B34 113 E3
Oxbarn Av BDMR/CCFT WV3 51 E1
Oxenton Cft HALE B63 137 H5
Oxford Cl WASH/WDE B8 111 F4
Oxford Dr ACGN B27 146 D3
STRBR DY8 135 F3
Oxford Rd ACGN B27 146 C4
ERDW/GRVHL B23 92 D2
MOS/BIL B13 144 C5
SMTHWK B66 106 C1
WBROM B70 87 F3
Oxford St BILS/COS WV14 54 A3
BVILLE B30 160 A3
DARL/WED WS10 71 F1
DIG/EDG B5 3 J7
DUDN DY1 84 B5
WOLV WV1 7 H5
WSLW WS2 56 C1
Oxhill Rd HDSW B21 89 F4
SHLY B90 179 E3
Ox Leasow RIDG/WDGT B32 140 C5
Oxley Av WOLVN WV10 23 E4
Oxley Cl DUDS DY2 120 B2
Oxley Gv SLYOAK B29 158 C2
Oxley La WOLV WV1 7 F1
Oxley Links Rd WOLVN WV10 22 D2
Oxley Moor Rd COVEN WV9 22 C2
Ox Leys Rd MGN/WHC B75 63 H4
Oxley St WOLV WV1 37 E1
Oxlip Cl DSYBK/YTR WS5 57 G5
Oxpiece Dr CBROM B36 111 H1
Oxstall Cl WALM/CURD B76 95 F1
Ox St SEDG DY3 83 F1
Oxted Cl WNSFLD WV11 25 F5
Oxted Cft ERDW/GRVHL B23 92 C3
Oxwood La RMSLY B62 173 F1
Oxygen St VAUX/NECH B7 3 J1

P

Pace Crs BILS/COS WV14 69 F1
Pacific Av DARL/WED WS10 70 B2
Packenham Dr
WALM/CURD B76 78 B3
Packhorse La
HWK/WKHTH B38 191 H2
Packington Av
BKDE/SHDE B34 113 E4
Packington La
CSHL/WTROR B46 115 G5
Packmores SHLY B90 194 A3

Packwood Cl
BFLD/HDSWWD B20 90 A4
DOR/KN B93 196 C4
WLNHL WV13 39 F5
Packwood Cottages
DOR/KN B93 * 198 D2
Packwood Ct SLYOAK B29 158 B1
Packwood Dr GTB/HAM B43 73 F2
Packwood Rd HOCK/TIA B94 199 E5
LGN/SDN/BHAMAIR B26 130 D4
OLDBY B69 85 G5
Padarn Cl SEDG DY3 67 E2
Padbury COVEN WV9 12 B4
Paddington Rd HDSW B21 89 E5
Paddock Dr DOR/KN B93 199 E1
LGN/SDN/BHAMAIR B26 130 C5
Paddock La ALDR WS9 30 A5
WSL WS1 5 G4
Paddocks Gn WSNGN B18 108 A4
Paddocks Rd HLYWD B47 192 B2
The Paddock BILS/COS WV14 68 D2
CDSL WV8 10 C5
DUNHL/THL/PER WV6 34 B1
HAG/WOL DY9 152 D2
SEDG DY3 83 G1
WMBN WV5 64 C5
Paddock Vw
DUNHL/THL/PER WV6 22 D5
Padgate Cl CVALE B35 94 D3
Padstow Rd ERDE/BCHGN B24 93 H2
Paganal Dr WBROM B70 88 A5
Paganel Dr DUDN DY1 84 C3
Paganel Rd SLYOAK B29 141 G5
Pages Cl MGN/WHC B75 62 C3
Pages La GTB/HAM B43 73 G2
Paget Cl BILS/COS WV14 * 68 B3
Paget Rd DUNHL/THL/PER WV6 36 B2
ERDE/BCHGN B24 93 H3
Paget St WOLV WV1 6 D1
Pagham Cl COVEN WV9 11 H5
Pagnell Gv MOS/BIL B13 162 A4
Paignton Rd L
DYWD/EDGR B16 125 F1
Pailton Gv SLYOAK B29 158 C1
Pailton Rd SHLY B90 163 F5
Painswick Cl DSYBK/YTR WS5 57 H5
Painswick Rd HLGN/YWD B28 162 C3
Paint Cup Rw DUDS DY2 120 C2
Painters Cft BILS/COS WV14 69 E2
Pakefield Rd BVILLE B30 177 F2
Pakenham Cl WALM/CURD B76 78 B3
Pakenham Rd EDG B15 126 C5
Pakfield Wk AST/WIT B6 * 91 F5
Palace Cl BLKHTH/ROWR B65 104 B5
Palace Dr SMTHWK B66 105 G1
Palace Rd BORD B9 128 C3
Palefield Rd SHLY B90 195 F2
Pale La HRBN B17 124 B4
Pale St SEDG DY3 83 G1
Palethorpe Rd TPTN/OCK DY4 69 G3
Palfrey Rd STRBR DY8 134 D2
Palmcourt Av HLGN/YWD B28 162 C3
Palm Cft BRLYHL DY5 119 E4
Palmer Cl WNSFLD WV11 25 F1
Palmers Cl CDSL WV8 11 E5
SHLY B90 163 F5
Palmers Gv CBROM B36 112 A1
Palmerston Dr OLDBY B69 106 B4
Palmerston Rd SPARK B11 144 D1
Palmer St BORD B9 127 G2
Palmers Wy CDSL WV8 21 G1
Palmvale Cft
LGN/SDN/BHAMAIR B26 147 G1
Palomino Pl LDYWD/EDGR B16 125 H2
Pamela Rd NFLD/LBR B31 175 G3
Pan Cft CBROM B36 111 G2
Panjab Gdns SMTHWKW B67 * 106 B3
Pannel Cft LOZ/NWT B19 108 D3
Panther Cft BKDE/SHDE B34 113 F4
Paper Mill End
PBAR/PBCH B42 74 D5
Papyrus Wy CBROM B36 94 B5
The Parade BRWNH WS8 9 E3
CDYHTH B64 121 E4
DUDN DY1 84 B4
KGSWFD DY6 99 F2
WNSFLD WV11 * 24 A2
Paradise DUDS DY2 102 D1
Paradise Circus Queensway
CBHAMNW B3 2 D5
Paradise Gv BLOX/PEL WS3 17 H4
Paradise La BLOX/PEL WS3 17 H4
HLGN/YWD B28 162 C4
Paradise Pl CBHAMNW B3 * 2 E5
Paradise St CBHAM B2 2 E5
WBROM B70 87 H3
Pardington Cl HIA/OLT B92 165 G2
Pargeter Rd SMTHWKW B67 124 B2
Pargeter St STRBR DY8 135 F3
WSLW WS2 41 G3
Par Gn NFLD/LBR B31 176 A4
Parish Gdns HAG/WOL DY9 152 D1
Park Ap ERDW/GRVHL B23 92 A4
Park Av BLKHTH/ROWR B65 122 A1
BVILLE B30 160 A5
CSHL/WTROR B46 115 F3
ETTPK/GDPK/PENN WV4 52 A3
LGLYGN/QTN B68 123 F1
SMTHWKW B67 * 106 B5
SOLH B91 182 B2
TPTN/OCK DY4 85 E1
WLNHL WV13 39 F3
WMBN WV5 80 D1
WOLV WV1 6 D3
WSNGN B18 108 A2
Park Cl BILS/COS WV14 68 B4
BRWNH WS8 9 F4
ERDE/BCHGN B24 93 H1
HIA/OLT B92 148 B5
OLDBY B69 104 A2
Park Crs HHTH/SAND B71 87 H2
WOLV WV1 6 D3
Park Cft HLYWD B47 192 C3
Parkdale Av DARL/WED WS10 56 A4
Parkdale Cl ERDE/BCHGN B24 92 D4
Park Dale Ct WOLV WV1 6 A2
Parkdale Dr NFLD/LBR B31 189 G1
Park Dl East WOLV WV1 6 A2
Parkdale Rd
LGN/SDN/BHAMAIR B26 148 A1
Park Dl West WOLV WV1 6 A2
Park Dr
ETTPK/GDPK/PENN WV4 52 A3
FOAKS/STRLY B74 46 A1
FOAKS/STRLY B74 46 D3
Park Edge HRBN B17 125 E5
Park End Dr RIDG/WDGT B32 157 H1
Parker Rd WNSFLD WV11 25 F1
Parker St BLOX/PEL WS3 27 E1
LDYWD/EDGR B16 125 H3
Parkes Av CDSL WV8 10 D5
Parkes Crs WNSFLD WV11 15 E3
Parkes Hall Rd DUDN DY1 84 A1
Parkes La SEDG DY3 68 A4
TPTN/OCK DY4 69 F3
Parkes St BRLYHL DY5 119 F1
SMTHWKW B67 106 B5
WLNHL WV13 39 H4
Parkeston Crs KGSTG B44 75 H2
Park Farm Rd GTB/HAM B43 59 F5
Parkfield RIDG/WDGT B32 139 H5
Parkfield Chalet Land
BKHL/PFLD WV2 * 52 B2
Parkfield Cl EDG B15 126 C5
RMSLY B62 140 A2
Parkfield Colliery
ETTPK/GDPK/PENN WV4 52 D3
Parkfield Crs BKHL/PFLD WV2 52 C2
Parkfield Dr CBROM B36 95 E5
Parkfield Gv BKHL/PFLD WV2 52 C2
Parkfield Rd CSHL/WTROR B46 115 F2
DUDS DY2 102 D3
ETTPK/GDPK/PENN WV4 52 C2
LGLYGN/QTN B68 123 E1
STRBR DY8 135 H2
WASH/WDE B8 128 C1
Park Gv CSHL/WTROR B46 96 C3
SMHTH B10 * 128 B4
Park Hall Cl DSYBK/YTR WS5 58 A2
Park Hall Crs CBROM B36 112 D1
Parkhall Cft CBROM B36 113 E2
Park Hall Rd DSYBK/YTR WS5 58 A2
ETTPK/GDPK/PENN WV4 52 B4
Park Head Crs DUDS DY2 * 102 B1
Parkhead Locks DUDS DY2 * 102 A3
Park Head Rd DUDS DY2 102 B1
Park Hl BLKHTH/ROWR B65 121 H3
DARL/WED WS10 56 C4
MOS/BIL B13 144 A3
Park Hill Dr BFLD/HDSWWD B20 89 H2
Park Hill Rd HRBN B17 142 A1
SMTHWKW B67 106 B4
Parkhill Rd WALM/CURD B76 78 B5
Park Hill St DUDS DY2 103 E1
Parkhouse Av WNSFLD WV11 24 B4
Parkhouse Dr
ERDW/GRVHL B23 91 G1
Parkhouse Gdns SEDG DY3 83 E2
Parklands Dr FOAKS/STRLY B74 46 D5
Parklands Gdns WSL WS1 5 J7
Parklands Rd BILS/COS WV14 53 H5
DARL/WED WS10 55 G3
WOLV WV1 38 A4
The Parklands BDMR/CCFT WV3 35 H3
ERDW/GRVHL B23 76 B5
HAG/WOL DY9 136 B4
Park La AST/WIT B6 109 E2
CVALE B35 94 D1
DARL/WED WS10 55 H2
HALE B63 137 E1
HHTH/SAND B71 88 D2
KGSWFD DY6 100 A2
OLDBY B69 105 E3
WOLVN WV10 23 G5
Park La East TPTN/OCK DY4 85 H2
Park La West TPTN/OCK DY4 85 E2
Park Lime Dr RUSH/SHEL WS4 42 D1
Park Meadow Av
BILS/COS WV14 38 C5
Park Ms SLYOAK B29 * 158 D1
Park Pl VAUX/NECH B7 110 A2
Park Retreat SMTHWK B66 106 D5
Park Rdg FOAKS/STRLY B74 62 A1
Park Ridge Dr HALE B63 137 F1
Park Ri BDMR/CCFT WV3 36 A3
Park Rd AST/WIT B6 109 G2
BILS/COS WV14 53 G3
BLOX/PEL WS3 27 F1
BRLYHL DY5 119 H4
CSHL/WTROR B46 115 F3
DARL/WED WS10 54 D2
DSYBK/YTR WS5 58 B3
DUDN DY1 68 B5
DUDS DY2 102 C3
ERDW/GRVHL B23 92 A4
HAG/WOL DY9 152 D5
HALE B63 137 F1
MOS/BIL B13 144 B3
OLDBY B69 104 A1
RUSH/SHEL WS4 29 E5
SCFLD/BOLD B73 62 B3
SEDG DY3 82 D2
SMTHWKW B67 124 B3
SPARK B11 145 E4
STRBR DY8 134 D2
WLNHL WV13 39 F2
WSNGN B18 107 H2
Park Rd East WOLV WV1 6 C1
Park Rd South WSNGN B18 108 B4
Park Rd West STRBR DY8 134 C2
WOLV WV1 6 B2
Parkside RIDG/WDGT B32 157 G1
Parkside Av WLNHL WV13 39 E3
Parkside Cl DARL/WED WS10 56 B5
Parkside Rd
BFLD/HDSWWD B20 89 G1
HALE B63 137 H2
Parkside Wy FOAKS/STRLY B74 45 G4
NFLD/LBR B31 174 C4
Park Sq CHWD/FDBR/MGN B37 132 D4
Parkstone Cl RUSH/SHEL WS4 29 E1
Park St AST/WIT B6 109 G2
BLKHTH/ROWR B65 122 B3
CDYHTH B64 120 D2
DARL/WED WS10 55 E3
DARL/WED WS10 55 H5
DIG/EDG B5 3 J5
HAG/WOL DY9 136 D2
KGSWFD DY6 99 H3
OLDBY B69 104 D3
STRBR DY8 118 B4
STRBR DY8 135 G3
TPTN/OCK DY4 85 G1
WBROM B70 87 H3
WSL WS1 4 D3
Park St South BKHL/PFLD WV2 52 A2
Park Ter DARL/WED WS10 54 D2
HDSW B21 107 G1
Park Vw DARL/WED WS10 55 E2
HOCK/TIA B94 198 A5
SCFLD/BOLD B73 62 A2
Parkview Ct KGSWFD DY6 99 F1
Parkview Crs WSLW WS2 41 E1
Parkview Dr WASH/WDE B8 111 E3
Parkview Rd BILS/COS WV14 38 C5
Park View Rd
FOAKS/STRLY B74 46 B2
HAG/WOL DY9 136 D3
NFLD/LBR B31 175 F2
Park Vls BORD B9 * 127 H2
Parkville Av HRBN B17 141 H4
Park Wk BRLYHL DY5 119 H4
Park Wy RBRY B45 174 B5
WNSFLD WV11 25 G1
Parkway WASH/WDE B8 111 E4
Parkway Rd DUDN DY1 84 A4
The Parkway CDSL WV8 20 B4
RUSH/SHEL WS4 29 E2
Parkwood Cl BRWNH WS8 19 G2
Parkwood Cft PBAR/PBCH B42 74 B2
Parkwood Dr SCFLD/BOLD B73 76 A1
Parkyn St BKHL/PFLD WV2 37 G5
Parliament St AST/WIT B6 109 F3
SMHTH B10 128 A4
WBROM B70 87 H5
Parlows End HWK/WKHTH B38 190 B1
Parry Rd WNSFLD WV11 25 G2
Parsonage Dr HALE B63 120 A5
RBRY B45 188 D4
Parsonage St HHTH/SAND B71 71 H5
OLDBY B69 105 F3
Parson's Hl BVILLE B30 177 F3
LGLYGN/QTN B68 123 F3
Parsons St DUDN DY1 84 C5
Partons Rd
ALE/KHTH/YWD B14 160 D4
Partridge Av DARL/WED WS10 54 D2
Partridge Cl
CHWD/FDBR/MGN B37 132 C1
Partridge Ml BLOX/PEL WS3 17 G4
Partridge Rd
LGN/SDN/BHAMAIR B26 130 C3
STRBR DY8 134 C5
Passey Rd MOS/BIL B13 145 F5
Passfield Rd STETCH B33 130 B1
The Pastures
DUNHL/THL/PER WV6 34 B1
Pasture Vw BLOX/PEL WS3 28 B1
Patent Dr DARL/WED WS10 70 A1
Paternoster Rw DIG/EDG B5 * 3 H5
WOLV WV1 6 E3
Paterson Pl BRWNH WS8 19 H2
Pathlow Crs SHLY B90 180 A4
Paton Gv MOS/BIL B13 144 B5
Patricia Av
ALE/KHTH/YWD B14 179 E1
ETTPK/GDPK/PENN WV4 52 A3
Patricia Crs DUDN DY1 68 B5
Patricia Dr TPTN/OCK DY4 85 G4
Patrick Gregory Rd
WNSFLD WV11 25 F3
Patrick Rd
LGN/SDN/BHAMAIR B26 130 A5
Patriot Cl WSL WS1 56 D3
Patshull Av WOLVN WV10 12 C4
Patshull Cl GTB/HAM B43 73 F2
Patshull Gv WOLVN WV10 12 B4
Patshull Pl LOZ/NWT B19 * 108 C2
Patterdale Rd
ERDW/GRVHL B23 92 B2
Patterdale Wy BRLYHL DY5 118 D4
Patterton Dr WALM/CURD B76 78 B3
Pattingham Rd
DUNHL/THL/PER WV6 34 A3
Pattison Gdns
ERDW/GRVHL B23 92 B4
Pattison St DSYBK/YTR WS5 57 E3
Paul Byrne Ct
BFLD/HDSWWD B20 90 B5
Paul Pursehouse Rd
BILS/COS WV14 53 H5
Pauls Coppice BRWNH WS8 19 F2
Paul St BILS/COS WV14 68 A2
BKHL/PFLD WV2 6 E7
DARL/WED WS10 71 E1
Paul V TPTN/OCK DY4 85 H1
Pavenham Dr DIG/EDG B5 143 G3
Pavilion Av SMTHWKW B67 124 A1
Pavilion Dr PBAR/PBCH B42 91 F3
Pavilion End KINVER DY7 116 C3
Pavilion Gdns DUDS DY2 120 C2
Pavilion Rd PBAR/PBCH B42 91 F3
The Pavilions CBHAMNE B4 * 3 H5
CHWD/FDBR/MGN B37 132 D4
Pavillion Cl ALDR WS9 30 B2
Paxford Wy NFLD/LBR B31 158 B4
Paxton Av
DUNHL/THL/PER WV6 34 C2
Paxton Rd HAG/WOL DY9 137 E3
WSNGN B18 108 A4
Payne St BLKHTH/ROWR B65 122 A3
Payton Cl OLDBY B69 86 C5
Payton Rd HDSW B21 107 F1
Peach Av DARL/WED WS10 55 E2
Peachley Cl HALE B63 138 D5
Peach Ley Rd SLYOAK B29 158 B3
Peach Rd SHHTH WV12 25 G4
Peacock Av WNSFLD WV11 25 G3
Peacock Cl TPTN/OCK DY4 85 H2
Peacock Rd DARL/WED WS10 54 D1
MOS/BIL B13 161 F4
Peacocks Est CDYHTH B64 * 120 C3
Peak Cft CBROM B36 111 H1
Peak Dr SEDG DY3 83 F3
Peake Crs BRWNH WS8 19 F2
Peake Dr TPTN/OCK DY4 85 H2
Peake Rd BRWNH WS8 19 F2
Peak House Rd GTB/HAM B43 58 C5
Peakman Cl RBRY B45 188 A2
Peak Rd STRBR DY8 135 H1
Peal St WSL WS1 5 F4
Pearce Cl DUDN DY1 101 G1
Pearl Gv ACGN B27 146 B4
Pearman Rd RBRY B45 173 F4
SMTHWK B66 124 C1
Pearmans Cft HLYWD B47 192 C2
Pearsall Dr OLDBY B69 104 C1
Pearson St BKHL/PFLD WV2 37 E5
BRLYHL DY5 119 F1
CDYHTH B64 121 E3
HAG/WOL DY9 136 D3
WBROM B70 87 F2
Pear Tree Av TPTN/OCK DY4 85 F1
Peartree Av WLNHL WV13 39 H4
Pear Tree Cl GTB/HAM B43 72 D2
SHLY B90 179 F3
STETCH B33 129 H2
Pear Tree Ct
BLKHTH/ROWR B65 122 B1
Pear Tree Crs SHLY B90 179 E2
Pear Tree Dr
BLKHTH/ROWR B65 122 B1
GTB/HAM B43 73 E2
Peartree Dr STRBR DY8 135 G5
Pear Tree Gv SHLY B90 179 F3
Pear Tree La BILS/COS WV14 68 D3
BRWNH WS8 8 C2
WNSFLD WV11 24 B1
Peartree La CDYHTH B64 121 E3
DUDS DY2 101 H4
Pear Tree Rd BKDE/SHDE B34 113 E3
GTB/HAM B43 72 D2
SMTHWKW B67 106 A5
Peascroft La BILS/COS WV14 54 A2
Peasefield Cl HDSW B21 107 E1
Pebble Cl STRBR DY8 135 H2
Pebble Mill Rd DIG/EDG B5 143 F3
Pebworth Av SHLY B90 195 H2
Pebworth Cl SLYOAK B29 143 F4
Pebworth Gv DUDN DY1 84 A3
STETCH B33 131 E4
Peckham Rd KGSTG B44 75 G1
Peckover Cl
BLKHTH/ROWR B65 121 H3
Peddimore La WALM/CURD B76 79 F5
Pedmore Court Rd STRBR DY8 152 D1
Pedmore Gv KGSTG B44 75 F1
Pedmore Hall La
HAG/WOL DY9 153 E2
Pedmore La HAG/WOL DY9 153 E1
Pedmore Rd BRLYHL DY5 101 H5
HAG/WOL DY9 136 B2
Peel Cl DARL/WED WS10 40 B5
HIA/OLT B92 167 H4
WLNHL WV13 39 G4
Peel St BDMR/CCFT WV3 6 E5
DUDS DY2 103 E1
HHTH/SAND B71 87 G1
TPTN/OCK DY4 85 G2
WLNHL WV13 39 G4
WSNGN B18 107 G4
Peel Wk HRBN B17 124 B5
Peel Wy OLDBY B69 86 A4
Pegasus Wk SLYOAK B29 159 F1
Peglee Wk
ALE/KHTH/YWD B14 177 G3
Pelham Dr DUDN DY1 84 A4
Pelham Rd WASH/WDE B8 111 F5
Pelham St BDMR/CCFT WV3 6 B6
Pelsall La BLOX/PEL WS3 17 F4
RUSH/SHEL WS4 28 D3
Pelsall Rd BRWNH WS8 8 D5
Pemberly Rd ACGN B27 163 E1
Pemberton Cl SMTHWK B66 124 D1
Pemberton Crs
DARL/WED WS10 56 C4
Pemberton Rd BILS/COS WV14 68 D2
WBROM B70 71 E5
Pemberton St WSNGN B18 2 B2
Pembridge Cl BRLYHL DY5 119 H3
RIDG/WDGT B32 157 E3
Pembridge Rd DOR/KN B93 196 C5
Pembroke Av BKHL/PFLD WV2 53 E1
Pembroke Cl SHHTH WV12 25 H4
Pembroke Cft HLGN/YWD B28 163 E5
Pembroke Gdns STRBR DY8 117 G2
Pembroke Rd BHTH/HG B12 144 C3
HHTH/SAND B71 71 E5
Pembroke Wy HHTH/SAND B71 71 F4
HLGN/YWD B28 163 E5
Pembury Cl FOAKS/STRLY B74 60 B2
Pembury Cft KGSTG B44 75 G2
Pencombe Dr
ETTPK/GDPK/PENN WV4 52 B3
Pencroft Rd BKDE/SHDE B34 112 D2
Penda Gv DUNHL/THL/PER WV6 20 D5
Pendeen Rd
ALE/KHTH/YWD B14 179 E1
Pendeford Av
DUNHL/THL/PER WV6 22 A2
Pendeford Cl
DUNHL/THL/PER WV6 22 A2
Pendeford Hall La COVEN WV9 11 F2
Pendeford La COVEN WV9 12 A3
Pendeford Mill La CDSL WV8 11 E4
Pendennis Cl BVILLE B30 159 F5
Pendennis Dr OLDBY B69 103 G1
Penderell Cl WOLVN WV10 13 G1
Penderel St BLOX/PEL WS3 27 G1
Pendigo Wy BHAMNEC B40 150 B4
Pendinas Dr CDSL WV8 10 D4
Pendleton Gv ACGN B27 163 F2
Pendragon Rd PBAR/PBCH B42 90 C2
Pendrell Cl
CHWD/FDBR/MGN B37 132 A1
Pendrell Ct CDSL WV8 * 10 C4
Pendrill Rd WOLVN WV10 13 F4
Penfields Rd STRBR DY8 135 G1
Penge Gv KGSTG B44 60 A5
Penhallow Dr
ETTPK/GDPK/PENN WV4 52 C3
Penhurst Av
BFLD/HDSWWD B20 90 D5
Penkridge Cl WSLW WS2 41 H1
Penkridge Gv STETCH B33 112 B5
Penkridge St WSLW WS2 41 H2
Penk Ri DUNHL/THL/PER WV6 35 F1
Penleigh Gdns WMBN WV5 64 D4
Penley Gv WASH/WDE B8 111 F3
Pennant Gv SLYOAK B29 141 G5
Pennant Rd
BLKHTH/ROWR B65 121 H1
CDYHTH B64 120 D3
Pennard Gv RIDG/WDGT B32 141 F3
Penn Cl BLOX/PEL WS3 27 G1
Penn Common Rd
ETTPK/GDPK/PENN WV4 66 A2
Penncricket La
BLKHTH/ROWR B65 122 C1
Penn Croft La
ETTPK/GDPK/PENN WV4 66 C2
Pennhouse Av
ETTPK/GDPK/PENN WV4 51 F3
Pennine Dr SEDG DY3 83 F3
Pennine Wy SHHTH WV12 40 B1
STRBR DY8 135 G1
WASH/WDE B8 110 A4
Pennington Cl WBROM B70 87 E4
Penn Rd BKHL/PFLD WV2 6 E7
BLKHTH/ROWR B65 122 C1
ETTPK/GDPK/PENN WV4 51 E4
SEDG DY3 66 B2
Penn Road Island
BDMR/CCFT WV3 6 E6
Penns Lake Rd
WALM/CURD B76 78 A4
Penns La CSCFLD/WYGN B72 77 H4
CSHL/WTROR B46 115 F2
Penn St BDMR/CCFT WV3 6 D7
CBHAMNE B4 127 G1
CDYHTH B64 121 F4
Penns Wood Cl SEDG DY3 67 E1
Penns Wood Dr
WALM/CURD B76 78 B4
Pennwood La
ETTPK/GDPK/PENN WV4 51 F5
Pennyacre Rd
ALE/KHTH/YWD B14 177 H3
Pennyfield Cft STETCH B33 130 A1
Pennyhill La HHTH/SAND B71 72 A4
Pennyroyal Cl DSYBK/YTR WS5 57 G5
Penny Royal Cl SEDG DY3 83 F4
Penrice Dr DUDS DY2 85 F5
Penrith Cl BRLYHL DY5 118 D4
Penrith Cft RIDG/WDGT B32 157 H2
Penrith Gv
CHWD/FDBR/MGN B37 132 C2
Penryn Cl DSYBK/YTR WS5 58 B1
Penryn Rd DSYBK/YTR WS5 58 B1
Pensarn Vls DARL/WED WS10 * 55 E2
Pensby Cl MOS/BIL B13 162 A2
Pensford Rd NFLD/LBR B31 176 A2
Pensham Cft SHLY B90 195 G2
Penshaw Cl COVEN WV9 12 A5
Penshaw Gv MOS/BIL B13 162 B1
Pensnett Rd BRLYHL DY5 101 E5
DUDN DY1 101 G2
Penstock Dr OLDBY B69 104 D5
Pentland Cft BHTH/HG B12 127 F5
Pentlands Gdns
BDMR/CCFT WV3 36 A3
Pentos Dr SPARK B11 145 F3
Pentridge Cl WALM/CURD B76 94 B1
Penzer St KGSWFD DY6 99 H2
Peolsford Rd BLOX/PEL WS3 18 A3
Peplins Wy BVILLE B30 177 F2
Peplow Rd STETCH B33 112 C5
Pepperbox Dr TPTN/OCK DY4 85 G1
Pepper Hl STRBR DY8 135 G3
Pepperwood Cl BRGRVW B61 185 H5
Pepper Wood Dr
NFLD/LBR B31 174 C4
Perch Av
CHWD/FDBR/MGN B37 132 A1
Perch Cl WOLV WV1 38 B1
Perch Rd WSLW WS2 41 E1
Percival Rd LDYWD/EDGR B16 125 E3
Percy Rd SPARK B11 145 F4
Peregrine Cl DUDN DY1 83 H5
Pereira Rd HRBN B17 125 E5
Perimeter Rd BHAMNEC B40 149 H3
Perivale Gv BILS/COS WV14 68 D3
Perivale Wy STRBR DY8 118 C4
Periwinkle Cl BRWNH WS8 18 D1
Perkins Cl DUDN DY1 68 C5
Perks Rd WNSFLD WV11 25 G1
Perott Dr MGN/WHC B75 47 H3
Perrins Gv WASH/WDE B8 111 E3
Perrins La HAG/WOL DY9 136 D3
Perrins Ri HAG/WOL DY9 136 D3

Perrott Gdns STRBR DY8 ...118 D3
Perrott St WSNGN B18 ...107 F3
Perry Av PBAR/PBCH B42 ...90 C2
Perry Barr Locks
PBAR/PBCH B42 * ...74 B5
Perry Cl DUDS DY2 ...102 D1
Perry Common Rd
ERDW/GRVHL B23 ...75 H5
Perry Ct LGLYGN/QTN B68 ...123 F5
Perryford Dr SOLH B91 ...181 H5
Perry Hall Dr SHHTH WV12 ...25 H5
Perry Hall Rd WNSFLD WV11 ...25 F4
Perry Hill Crs LGLYGN/QTN B68 ..123 F5
Perry Hill La
LGLYGN/QTN B68 * ...123 F5
Perry Hill Rd LGLYGN/QTN B68 ..123 G5
Perry Park Crs
PBAR/PBCH B42 ...74 B5
Perry Park Rd CDYHTH B64 ...121 H3
Perry St BILS/COS WV14 ...54 A5
DARL/WED WS10 ...40 B5
DARL/WED WS10 ...70 D2
SMTHWK B66 ...106 C2
TPTN/OCK DY4 ...85 G2
Perry Villa Dr PBAR/PBCH B42 ...90 D1
Perry Wk ERDW/GRVHL B23 ...75 H5
Perrywell Rd PBAR/PBCH B42 ...91 G2
Perry Wood Rd
PBAR/PBCH B42 ...74 A3
Persehouse St WSL WS1 ...5 G3
Pershore Cl BLOX/PEL WS3 ...16 B5
Pershore Rd BLOX/PEL WS3 ...16 B5
BVILLE B30 ...176 D1
DIG/EDG B5 ...143 H1
HALE B63 ...138 C5
Pershore Rd South BVILLE B30 ..176 D2
Pershore St DIG/EDG B5 ...3 G7
Pershore Wy BLOX/PEL WS3 ...16 B5
Perth Rd SHHTH WV12 ...25 H4
Perton Brook V
DUNHL/THL/PER WV6 ...34 D3
Perton Gv
DUNHL/THL/PER WV6 ...34 D3
SLYOAK B29 ...158 C1
Perton Rd
DUNHL/THL/PER WV6 ...34 D3
Petchells Cl BRLYHL DY5 ...100 D4
Peter Av BILS/COS WV14 ...69 F1
Peterbrook Ri SHLY B90 ...179 F4
Peterbrook Rd SHLY B90 ...179 F4
Peterdale Dr
ETTPK/GDPK/PENN WV4 ...51 F5
Peters Av NFLD/LBR B31 ...175 F3
Petersfield Ct
HLGN/YWD B28 * ...162 D2
Petersfield Dr
BLKHTH/ROWR B65 ...122 C1
Petersfield Rd HLGN/YWD B28 ..162 C3
Petersham Pl EDG B15 ...142 C1
Petersham Rd KGSTG B44 ...76 A2
Peter's Hill Rd BRLYHL DY5 ...119 E5
Petershouse Dr
FOAKS/STRLY B74 ...32 D5
Peters St WBROM B70 ...71 E4
Petford St CDYHTH B64 ...121 E3
Petitt Cl ALE/KHTH/YWD B14 ...178 A4
Pettyfield Cl
LGN/SDN/BHAMAIR B26 ...147 G1
Pettyfields Cl DOR/KN B93 ...197 E3
Petworth Cl WLNHL WV13 ...39 F5
Petworth Gv
LGN/SDN/BHAMAIR B26 ...147 E1
Pevensey Cl DUDS DY2 ...103 F1
Peverell Dr HLGN/YWD B28 ...162 D3
Peveril Gv WALM/CURD B76 ...63 E4
Peveril Rd
DUNHL/THL/PER WV6 ...34 D1
ETTPK/GDPK/PENN WV4 ...52 C5
Pevril Wy GTB/HAM B43 ...73 H1
Pheasant Cft CBROM B36 ...114 A1
Pheasant Rd SMTHWKW B67 ...123 H2
Pheasant St BRLYHL DY5 ...119 E1
Philip Rd HALE B63 ...138 B4
TPTN/OCK DY4 ...86 B1
Philip Sidney Rd SPARK B11 ...144 D4
Philip St BILS/COS WV14 ...68 D2
Philip Victor Rd
BFLD/HDSWWD B20 ...89 H5
Phillimore Rd WASH/WDE B8 ...110 B4
Phillip Rd WSLW WS2 ...56 C2
Phillips Av WNSFLD WV11 ...25 F1
Phillips St AST/WIT B6 ...109 E3
Phipson Rd SPARK B11 ...144 D4
Phoenix Gn EDG B15 ...125 G5
Phoenix Pk
BLKHTH/ROWR B65 ...122 B3
Phoenix Ri DARL/WED WS10 ...55 F4
ERDW/GRVHL B23 ...75 H4
Phoenix Rd TPTN/OCK DY4 ...69 F5
WLNHL WV13 ...38 D2
Phoenix St BKHL/PFLD WV2 ...52 B2
WBROM B70 ...86 D1
Piccadilly Ar CBHAM B2 ...3 F5
Piccadilly Cl
CHWD/FDBR/MGN B37 ...132 C3
Pickenham Rd
ALE/KHTH/YWD B14 ...178 C4
Pickering Cft RIDG/WDGT B32 ...157 G1
Pickering Rd WNSFLD WV11 ...24 D5
Pickersleigh Cl HALE B63 ...138 C4
Pickford St DIG/EDG B5 ...3 K6
Pickrell Rd BILS/COS WV14 ...68 B2
Pickwick Gv MOS/BIL B13 ...145 E5
Pickwick Pl BILS/COS WV14 ...54 A4
Picton Cft
CHWD/FDBR/MGN B37 ...132 D3
Picton Gv MOS/BIL B13 ...161 H5
Picturedrome Wy
DARL/WED WS10 ...55 F2
Piddock Rd SMTHWK B66 ...106 C4
Pierce Av HIA/OLT B92 ...147 E4
Piercy St WBROM B70 ...87 E3
Piers Rd WSNGN B18 ...108 A2
Piggots Cft
CHWD/FDBR/MGN B37 ...131 H1
Pike Cl BFLD/HDSWWD B20 ...89 H5
Pike Dr CHWD/FDBR/MGN B37 ..132 C1
Pikehelve St TPTN/OCK DY4 ...70 C4
Pikehorne Cft CBROM B36 ...95 F4
Pike Rd WSLW WS2 ...41 E1
The Pikes RBRY B45 ...173 H5
Pilkington Av
CSCFLD/WYGN B72 ...62 B5
Pilson Cl CBROM B36 ...112 B1
Pimbury Rd SHHTH WV12 ...26 B3
Pimlico Ct SEDG DY3 ...83 F3
Pimpernel Dr DSYBK/YTR WS5 ...57 G5
Pinbury Cft
CHWD/FDBR/MGN B37 ...132 B4
Pinchers Cl HAG/WOL DY9 ...184 C1
Pineapple Cl
ALE/KHTH/YWD B14 ...160 C4
Pineapple Gv BVILLE B30 ...160 C2
Pineapple Rd BVILLE B30 ...160 C3
Pine Av DARL/WED WS10 ...55 H3
SMTHWK B66 ...106 A2
Pine Cl BDMR/CCFT WV3 ...6 A5
KGSWFD DY6 ...99 H4
SOLH B91 ...181 F3
Pine Gn DUDN DY1 ...84 A1
Pine Gv ALE/KHTH/YWD B14 ...161 G5
Pinehurst Dr HWK/WKHTH B38 ..176 D2
Pine Leigh FOAKS/STRLY B74 ...47 F4
Pineneedle Cft SHHTH WV12 ...40 C1
Pine Rd DUDN DY1 ...84 C1
OLDBY B69 ...103 G1
The Pines BDMR/CCFT WV3 ...35 H4
RBRY B45 ...174 A4
SHLY B90 ...194 D3
WSL WS1 ...5 F6
Pine St BLOX/PEL WS3 ...27 G1
Pinetree Dr FOAKS/STRLY B74 ...44 D4
Pineview NFLD/LBR B31 ...175 F3
Pine Wk CDSL WV8 ...10 B5
HAG/WOL DY9 ...136 B4
NFLD/LBR B31 ...175 H2
Pinewall Av HWK/WKHTH B38 ...176 D4
Pineways FOAKS/STRLY B74 ...46 A2
STRBR DY8 ...117 G2
Pineways Dr
DUNHL/THL/PER WV6 ...36 A2
The Pineways OLDBY B69 ...104 A4
Pinewood Cl BDMR/CCFT WV3 ...35 E5
BRWNH WS8 ...9 E2
DSYBK/YTR WS5 ...57 H4
KGSTG B44 ...75 E4
RBRY B45 ...173 F5
SHHTH WV12 ...26 B3
WMBN WV5 ...65 E5
Pinewood Dr RIDG/WDGT B32 ...157 E2
Pinewood Gv SOLH B91 ...181 F3
Pine Woods RIDG/WDGT B32 ...140 A5
Pinewoods RMSLY B62 ...123 E5
SLYOAK B29 ...158 B2
Pinewoods Av HAG/WOL DY9 ...169 F1
Pinewoods Cl HAG/WOL DY9 ...169 F1
Pinfold BLOX/PEL WS3 ...27 G2
Pinfold Ct DARL/WED WS10 ...55 E3
Pinfold Crs
ETTPK/GDPK/PENN WV4 ...50 D2
Pinfold Gdns WNSFLD WV11 ...24 D5
Pinfold Gv BDMR/CCFT WV3 ...50 D2
Pinfold La ALDR WS9 ...59 F1
ETTPK/GDPK/PENN WV4 ...51 E3
Pinfold Rd SOLH B91 ...165 G5
Pinfold St BILS/COS WV14 ...53 H3
CBHAM B2 ...3 F5
DARL/WED WS10 ...55 E3
OLDBY B69 ...105 E1
Pingle Cl HHTH/SAND B71 ...72 B2
Pinkney Pl LGLYGN/QTN B68 ...123 G1
Pinley Gv GTB/HAM B43 ...59 F5
Pinley Wy SOLH B91 ...181 G5
Pinner Gv RIDG/WDGT B32 ...141 E3
Pinson Rd WLNHL WV13 ...39 F4
Pintail Dr ERDW/GRVHL B23 ...92 A4
Pinto Cl LDYWD/EDGR B16 ...125 H2
Pinza Cft CBROM B36 ...111 H1
Pioli Pl WSLW WS2 * ...27 H5
Piper Cl DUNHL/THL/PER WV6 ...34 D1
Piper Pl STRBR DY8 ...118 B4
Piper Rd BDMR/CCFT WV3 ...35 F5
Pipers Gn HLGN/YWD B28 ...162 D5
Piper's Rw WOLV WV1 ...7 H4
Pipes Meadow BILS/COS WV14 ...54 A3
Pippin Av HALE B63 ...120 B5
Pirbright Cl BILS/COS WV14 ...54 A5
Pirrey Cl BILS/COS WV14 ...68 D2
Pitcairn Cl BVILLE B30 ...160 B4
Pitcairn Dr RMSLY B62 ...138 D1
Pitcairn Rd SMTHWKW B67 ...123 H3
Pitclose Rd NFLD/LBR B31 ...175 H4
Pitfield Rd STETCH B33 ...131 F3
Pitfield Rw DUDN DY1 ...84 B5
Pitfields Cl LGLYGN/QTN B68 ...123 E4
Pitfields Rd LGLYGN/QTN B68 ...123 E4
Pitfield St DUDN DY1 * ...84 B5
Pithall Rd BKDE/SHDE B34 ...113 F4
Pit Leasow Cl BVILLE B30 ...160 B2
Pitman Rd RIDG/WDGT B32 ...140 C2
Pitmaston Rd HLGN/YWD B28 ...163 E4
Pitsford St WSNGN B18 ...2 B1
Pitt La HIA/OLT B92 ...149 H5
Pitts Farm Rd
ERDE/BCHGN B24 ...93 G1
Pitt St VAUX/NECH B7 ...127 G1
Pixall Dr EDG B15 ...126 B5
Pixhall Wk CVALE B35 ...94 D3
Plainview Cl FOAKS/STRLY B74 ...45 E3
Plaistow Av CBROM B36 ...111 G2
Plane Gv
CHWD/FDBR/MGN B37 ...132 B3
Planetary Rd WLNHL WV13 ...38 C2
Plane Tree Rd DSYBK/YTR WS5 ...57 H4
Planetree Rd FOAKS/STRLY B74 ..44 D5
Planet Rd BRLYHL DY5 ...101 F5
Plank La CSHL/WTROR B46 ...96 A4
Planks La WMBN WV5 ...64 D5
Plantation Dr MGN/WHC B75 ...63 F2
Plantation La SEDG DY3 ...81 F2
Plantation Rd DSYBK/YTR WS5 ...57 G4
The Plantation BRLYHL DY5 ...100 D2
Plants Brook Rd
WALM/CURD B76 ...78 B5
Plants Cl SCFLD/BOLD B73 ...76 B2
Plants Gv ERDE/BCHGN B24 ...77 H5
Plants Hollow BRLYHL DY5 ...119 F3
Plant St CDYHTH B64 ...120 D3
STRBR DY8 ...118 A2
Plant Wy BLOX/PEL WS3 ...17 H3
Plascom Rd WOLV WV1 ...38 A4
Platts Crs STRBR DY8 ...118 A4
Platts Dr STRBR DY8 ...118 B4
Platts Rd STRBR DY8 ...118 A4
Platt St DARL/WED WS10 ...55 F3
Playdon Gv
ALE/KHTH/YWD B14 ...178 C2
Pleasant Cl KGSWFD DY6 ...99 G5
Pleasant Md ALDR WS9 ...29 G5
Pleasant St WBROM B70 ...71 E3
WBROM B70 ...87 G5
Pleasant Vw SEDG DY3 ...83 F4
Pleck Rd WSLW WS2 ...41 G5
Plestowes Cl SHLY B90 ...163 F5
Plimsoll Gv RIDG/WDGT B32 ...140 C2
Plough & Harrow Rd
LDYWD/EDGR B16 ...125 H3
Plough Av RIDG/WDGT B32 ...140 C5
Ploughmans Pl MGN/WHC B75 ...47 H1
Ploughmans Wk KGSWFD DY6 ...99 E2
Ploverdale Crs KGSWFD DY6 ...100 C3
Plowden Rd STETCH B33 ...112 B5
Plume St VAUX/NECH B7 ...109 H2
Plumstead Rd KGSTG B44 ...75 G3
Plym Cl WNSFLD WV11 ...24 C5
Plymouth Cl NFLD/LBR B31 ...189 G1
Plymouth Rd BVILLE B30 ...160 B3
Pocklington Pl
NFLD/LBR B31 * ...159 E4
Pointon Cl BILS/COS WV14 ...68 A1
Polden Cl HALE B63 ...154 C1
Polesworth Gv
BKDE/SHDE B34 ...112 D3
Pollard Rd ACGN B27 ...163 G1
The Pollards ERDW/GRVHL B23 ...76 C3
Polo Flds HAG/WOL DY9 ...152 D1
Pomeroy Rd GTB/HAM B43 ...59 H4
RIDG/WDGT B32 ...157 G1
Pommel Cl DSYBK/YTR WS5 ...57 F4
Pond Crs BKHL/PFLD WV2 ...52 C1
Pond Gv BKHL/PFLD WV2 ...52 C1
Pond La BKHL/PFLD WV2 ...37 F5
Poole Crs BILS/COS WV14 ...68 D1
BRWNH WS8 ...8 C2
HRBN B17 ...142 A4
Poolehouse Rd GTB/HAM B43 ...58 C5
Pool End Cl DOR/KN B93 ...196 D2
Pooles La SHHTH WV12 ...26 C3
Poole St STRBR DY8 ...135 E3
Pool Farm Rd ACGN B27 ...163 G1
Poolfield Dr SOLH B91 ...181 F2
Pool Furlong HAG/WOL DY9 ...170 C4
Pool Gn ALDR WS9 ...30 A5
Pool Hall Crs BDMR/CCFT WV3 ...34 D5
Pool Hall Rd BDMR/CCFT WV3 ...34 D5
Pool Hayes La SHHTH WV12 ...25 G5
Pool House Rd WMBN WV5 ...64 B5
Pool La OLDBY B69 ...104 D5
Pool Meadow WALM/CURD B76 ..78 C3
Pool Meadow Cl MOS/BIL B13 ..162 A1
SOLH B91 ...182 D4
Pool Rd BRWNH WS8 ...9 E2
HALE B63 ...138 D4
SMTHWK B66 ...106 D4
WNSFLD WV11 ...25 G4
Pool St AST/WIT B6 ...109 F3
BKHL/PFLD WV2 ...6 E6
DUDN DY1 ...84 C4
WSL WS1 ...5 G5
Pool Vw RUSH/SHEL WS4 ...29 F3
Pope Rd WOLVN WV10 ...24 A2
Popes La HWK/WKHTH B38 ...176 B2
OLDBY B69 ...105 F3
Pope St CBHAMW B1 ...2 A2
SMTHWK B66 ...106 D2
Poplar Ar SOLH B91 * ...182 A1
Poplar Av ALE/KHTH/YWD B14 ..161 E2
BHTH/HG B12 ...144 C3
BRWNH WS8 ...9 G4
CHWD/FDBR/MGN B37 ...132 C4
DSYBK/YTR WS5 ...57 G4
ERDW/GRVHL B23 * ...92 D2
HRBN B17 ...124 D2
LOZ/NWT B19 * ...108 C1
MGN/WHC B75 ...63 F1
OLDBY B69 ...103 H1
OLDBY B69 ...105 E4
TPTN/OCK DY4 ...84 D1
WBROM B70 ...88 A4
WNSFLD WV11 ...24 B3
WSLW WS2 ...40 B1
Poplar Cl OLDBY B69 ...86 A5
WMBN WV5 ...65 F5
WSLW WS2 ...40 C1
Poplar Crs DUDN DY1 ...84 B3
STRBR DY8 ...135 E4
Poplar Dr AST/WIT B6 ...91 F1
WASH/WDE B8 ...110 B3
Poplar Gn DUDN DY1 ...68 A5
Poplar Gv LOZ/NWT B19 * ...108 C1
SMTHWK B66 * ...124 D1
Poplar La RMSLY B62 ...172 C2
Poplar Ri FOAKS/STRLY B74 ...32 B5
OLDBY B69 ...104 A1
Poplar Rd ALE/KHTH/YWD B14 ..161 E2
BDMR/CCFT WV3 ...51 G2
BILS/COS WV14 ...54 B1
BRWNH WS8 ...9 G4
DARL/WED WS10 ...56 A2
DOR/KN B93 ...196 D5
KGSWFD DY6 ...100 A4
OLDBY B69 ...105 E1
SMTHWK B66 ...124 C3
SOLH B91 ...182 A1
SPARK B11 ...144 D2
STRBR DY8 ...135 E4
Poplars Dr CBROM B36 ...112 D1
CDSL WV8 ...10 B5
The Poplars
LDYWD/EDGR B16 * ...125 H1
SPARK B11 ...145 E1
STRBR DY8 ...118 B2
Poplar St BKHL/PFLD WV2 ...52 B2
SMTHWK B66 ...107 E4
Poplarwoods RIDG/WDGT B32 ..140 B5
Poppy Dr DSYBK/YTR WS5 ...57 F5
Poppy Gv WASH/WDE B8 ...110 D5
Poppy La ERDE/BCHGN B24 ...93 G1
Poppymead ERDW/GRVHL B23 ...75 H3
Porchester Cl ALDR WS9 ...19 G5
Porchester Dr LOZ/NWT B19 ...108 D3
Porchester St LOZ/NWT B19 ...108 D3
Porlock Crs NFLD/LBR B31 ...174 D2
Porlock Rd STRBR DY8 ...135 G1
Portal Rd WSLW WS2 ...40 D3
Portchester Dr WNSFLD WV11 ...24 D5
Porter Cl CSCFLD/WYGN B72 ...77 F4
Porters Cft HRBN B17 ...124 C4
Porters Fld DUDS DY2 ...84 D5
Portersfield Rd CDYHTH B64 ...120 C4
Portershill Dr SHLY B90 ...180 C5
Porter St DUDS DY2 ...84 D5
Porter St South DUDS DY2 ...84 D5
Porters Wy BORD B9 ...128 C2
Portfield Dr TPTN/OCK DY4 ...85 G3
Portfield Gv ERDW/GRVHL B23 ...77 E5
Porthkerry Gv SEDG DY3 ...66 D4
Port Hope Rd SPARK B11 ...127 G5
Porthouse Gv BILS/COS WV14 * ..53 F5
Portia Av SHLY B90 ...180 B3
Portland Av ALDR WS9 ...30 B5
Portland Crs HAG/WOL DY9 ...152 D1
Portland Dr HAG/WOL DY9 ...152 D1
Portland Pl BILS/COS WV14 ...68 B4
Portland Rd ALDR WS9 ...30 B4
LDYWD/EDGR B16 ...125 E2
Portland St AST/WIT B6 ...109 G2
WSLW WS2 ...4 D1
Portland Ter WSNGN B18 ...108 A4
Port La CDSL WV8 ...10 D1
Portman Rd
ALE/KHTH/YWD B14 ...161 F3
Portobello Cl WLNHL WV13 ...38 D4
Portobello Rd WBROM B70 ...70 D3
Portrush Av NFLD/LBR B31 ...176 A4
Portrush Rd
DUNHL/THL/PER WV6 ...34 B1
Portsdown Cl WOLVN WV10 ...23 H3
Portsdown Rd HALE B63 ...154 D1
Portsea St BLOX/PEL WS3 ...27 G4
Portswood Cl COVEN WV9 ...22 B1
Portway Cl KGSWFD DY6 ...100 A4
SOLH B91 ...181 E4
Portway Hl OLDBY B69 ...103 H3
Portway Rd BILS/COS WV14 ...54 A1
BLKHTH/ROWR B65 ...103 H5
DARL/WED WS10 ...70 C1
OLDBY B69 ...104 D2
The Portway KGSWFD DY6 ...100 A4
Posey Cl HDSW B21 ...89 E3
Poston Cft
ALE/KHTH/YWD B14 ...177 H1
Potter Cl ERDW/GRVHL B23 ...76 B3
Potters La AST/WIT B6 ...109 E2
DARL/WED WS10 ...70 C1
Potterton Wy SMTHWK B66 ...106 B1
Pottery Rd LGLYGN/QTN B68 ...123 G3
SMTHWK B66 ...106 C2
Pouk Hill Cl WSLW WS2 ...41 E2
Poultney St WBROM B70 ...70 D4
Poulton Cl MOS/BIL B13 ...144 C5
Pound Cl LGLYGN/QTN B68 ...122 D1
Pound La CSHL/WTROR B46 ...115 G5
RIDG/WDGT B32 ...173 H2
Poundley Cl CBROM B36 ...113 E1
Pound Rd ALE/KHTH/YWD B14 ..178 A4
DARL/WED WS10 ...56 A5
LGLYGN/QTN B68 ...122 D1
Pountney St BKHL/PFLD WV2 ...7 F7
Powell Av RIDG/WDGT B32 ...140 A1
Powell Pl BILS/COS WV14 ...54 A5
TPTN/OCK DY4 ...86 A1
Powell St CBHAMW B1 ...2 B3
HALE B63 ...138 D4
WOLVN WV10 ...37 H1
Power Crs LDYWD/EDGR B16 * ..126 A3
Powick Pl LOZ/NWT B19 * ...108 C2
Powick Rd ERDW/GRVHL B23 ...92 B5
Powis Av TPTN/OCK DY4 ...69 H4
Powke La BLKHTH/ROWR B65 ...121 G2
Powlers Cl HAG/WOL DY9 ...136 C5
Powlett St BKHL/PFLD WV2 ...7 G6
Poxon Rd ALDR WS9 ...19 G4
The Poynings
DUNHL/THL/PER WV6 ...21 G5
The Precinct SHHTH WV12 * ...25 H5
Premier Ct BVILLE B30 ...177 G2
Premier St VAUX/NECH B7 ...110 B1
Premier Wy SCFLD/BOLD B73 ...76 B1
Prescot Rd HAG/WOL DY9 ...136 A4
Prestbury Rd AST/WIT B6 ...109 E1
Presthope Rd SLYOAK B29 ...158 D3
Preston Av WALM/CURD B76 ...63 E5
Preston Rd
LGN/SDN/BHAMAIR B26 ...146 D1
WSNGN B18 ...107 G3
Prestons Rw BILS/COS WV14 ...53 E5
Prestwick Cl MGN/WHC B75 ...62 C1
Prestwick Rd CVALE B35 ...94 D2
KGSWFD DY6 ...99 G3
Prestwood Av WNSFLD WV11 ...24 D2
Prestwood Dr KINVER DY7 ...116 D4
Prestwood Rd SLYOAK B29 ...158 D2
WNSFLD WV11 ...24 A5
Prestwood Rd West
WNSFLD WV11 ...24 B4
Pretoria Rd BORD B9 ...128 C1
Priam Gv BLOX/PEL WS3 ...18 B2
Price Crs BILS/COS WV14 ...53 H1
Price Rd DARL/WED WS10 ...56 C5
HAG/WOL DY9 ...137 E1
Prices Rd SEDG DY3 ...83 E3
Price St BILS/COS WV14 ...54 B3
CBHAMNE B4 ...3 G2
DUDS DY2 ...103 E1
SMTHWK B66 ...106 D4
WBROM B70 ...87 G3
Priestfield Cl KGSTG B44 ...74 D1
Priestfield St BILS/COS WV14 ...53 F2
Priestland Rd BKDE/SHDE B34 ..112 D2
Priestley Cl BFLD/HDSWWD B20 ..90 A5
HALE B63 ...137 F1
Priestley Rd SPARK B11 ...127 G5
WSLW WS2 ...27 E5
Priest St CDYHTH B64 ...121 F3
Primley Av CBROM B36 ...111 H2
WSLW WS2 ...41 F5
Primley Cl WSLW WS2 ...41 F3
Primrose Av SPARK B11 ...145 E2
TPTN/OCK DY4 ...70 A3
WOLVN WV10 ...12 D4
Primrose Bank
LGLYGN/QTN B68 ...105 F5
Primrose Cl BLOX/PEL WS3 ...18 A2
CDYHTH B64 ...120 B4
Primrose Crs DUDN DY1 ...84 C2
Primrose Cft HLGN/YWD B28 ...162 D5
Primrose Gdns CDSL WV8 ...10 C4
HWK/WKHTH B38 ...176 D5
Primrose Hl HWK/WKHTH B38 ...176 D4
SMTHWKW B67 ...105 H5
STRBR DY8 ...118 A2
Primrose La HLGN/YWD B28 ...162 D5
WOLVN WV10 ...23 H2
Primrose Pk BRLYHL DY5 ...101 E2
Primrose Rd DUDS DY2 ...102 C5
The Primroses DSYBK/YTR WS5 ...57 H4
Primrose Woods
RIDG/WDGT B32 ...140 B5
Primsland Cl SOLH B91 ...196 A1
Prince Albert St BORD B9 ...128 B3
Prince Andrew Crs RBRY B45 ...173 G3
Prince Charles Cl RBRY B45 ...173 G3
Prince Charles Rd
BILS/COS WV14 ...54 B5
Prince Edward Dr RBRY B45 ...173 G3
Prince George Rd
DARL/WED WS10 ...56 A3
Prince of Wales La SHLY B90 ...179 E3
Princep Cl GTB/HAM B43 ...59 H4
Prince Philip Cl RBRY B45 ...173 G3
Prince Rd BVILLE B30 ...176 D2
Prince's Av WSL WS1 ...5 J3
Princes Dr CDSL WV8 ...10 C4
Princes Gdns CDSL WV8 ...10 B4
Princes Ga SOLH B91 ...181 H1
Prince's Rd OLDBY B69 ...85 G4
STRBR DY8 ...134 D5
Princess Alice Dr
SCFLD/BOLD B73 ...76 B1
Princess Aly WOLV WV1 ...7 G4
Princess Anne Rd
BILS/COS WV14 ...54 B5
WSLW WS2 ...40 D2
Princess Crs HALE B63 ...138 A1
Princess Gv HHTH/SAND B71 ...71 H4
Princess Pde WBROM B70 * ...87 H3
Princess Rd DIG/EDG B5 ...144 A1
LGLYGN/QTN B68 ...123 H2
Princess Sq BILS/COS WV14 ...54 B5
Princess St WOLV WV1 ...7 G4
Prince's St CBHAMNE B4 ...3 K3
Princess Wy DARL/WED WS10 ...40 A5
Prince St ALDR WS9 ...19 F5
CDYHTH B64 ...120 D3
DUDS DY2 ...102 C3
WSLW WS2 ...41 G5
Prince's Wy SOLH B91 ...181 H2
Princethorpe Cl
BKDE/SHDE B34 ...113 F2
SHLY B90 ...180 A3
Princethorpe Rd SLYOAK B29 ...158 D1
Princeton Gdns COVEN WV9 ...11 H5
Prince William Cl
ERDW/GRVHL B23 ...92 B4
Princip St CBHAMNE B4 ...3 G2
Printing House St CBHAMNE B4 ...3 G3
Priors Ml SEDG DY3 ...67 G5
Priors Wy ERDW/GRVHL B23 ...76 A3
Priory Av SLYOAK B29 ...143 F5
Priory Chambers DUDN DY1 * ...84 C5
Priory Cl CSHL/WTROR B46 * ...115 G4
DUDN DY1 ...84 B4
SMTHWK B66 ...107 E5
WBROM B70 ...88 B4
Priory Dr LGLYGN/QTN B68 ...105 G4
Priory Field Cl BILS/COS WV14 ...67 H2
Priorygate Wy BORD B9 ...128 C1
Priory La SEDG DY3 ...67 F4
The Priory Queensway
CBHAMNE B4 ...3 H4
Priory Rd ALE/KHTH/YWD B14 ..160 C3
ALE/KHTH/YWD B14 ...179 F1
AST/WIT B6 ...109 H1
DUDN DY1 ...84 C4
EDG B15 ...143 F1
RMSLY B62 ...139 G3
STRBR DY8 ...135 H4
Priory Sq CBHAMNE B4 ...3 H5
Priory St DUDN DY1 ...84 C5

The Priory SEDG DY3 67 F3
Priory Wk CBHAMNE B4 3 H4
CSCFLD/WYGN B72 77 G4
Pritchard Av WNSFLD WV11 25 E4
Pritchard Cl SMTHWK B66 106 D4
Pritchard St BRLYHL DY5 118 D1
DARL/WED WS10 55 H5
Pritchatts Rd EDG B15 142 D2
Pritchett Av
ETTPK/GDPK/PENN WV4 52 D5
Pritchett Rd NFLD/LBR B31 189 H1
Pritchett St AST/WIT B6 109 E4
Private Wy RBRY B45 188 C4
Privet Cl KGSTG B44 60 A5
Probert Rd WOLVN WV10 22 D1
Proctor St VAUX/NECH B7 109 G4
Proffitt Cl WSLW WS2 42 A1
Proffitt St WSLW WS2 42 A1
Prole St WOLVN WV10 37 G1
The Promenade BRLYHL DY5 119 F2
Prospect Gdns STRBR DY8 135 G3
Prospect Hl STRBR DY8 135 G3
Prospect La SOLH B91 163 H5
Prospect Pl BHTH/HG B12 * 144 B2
Prospect Rd MOS/BIL B13 161 F1
RMSLY B62 139 E2
SEDG DY3 82 D4
Prospect Rw DUDS DY2 102 D2
STRBR DY8 135 G4
Prospect St BILS/COS WV14 54 A2
TPTN/OCK DY4 70 A3
Prosper Meadow KGSWFD DY6 100 A2
Prospero Cl RBRY B45 174 A3
Prosser St BILS/COS WV14 53 H3
WOLVN WV10 23 G5
Prossers Wk CSHL/WTROR B46 115 F2
Proud's La BILS/COS WV14 38 D5
Provence Cl WOLVN WV10 37 H1
Providence Cl BLOX/PEL WS3 27 G3
Providence Dr HAG/WOL DY9 136 C1
Providence La BLOX/PEL WS3 27 G3
Providence Rw BILS/COS WV14 68 B3
Providence St CDYHTH B64 120 D3
HAG/WOL DY9 136 C1
TPTN/OCK DY4 86 A1
Providence Ter
DARL/WED WS10 * 55 G2
Pruden Av
ETTPK/GDPK/PENN WV4 52 D5
Pryor Rd LGLYGN/QTN B68 123 G1
Pudsey Dr MGN/WHC B75 47 G2
Pugh Crs WSLW WS2 40 C3
Pugh Rd AST/WIT B6 109 G2
BILS/COS WV14 54 A5
ETTPK/GDPK/PENN WV4 67 H1
Pugin Cl DUNHL/THL/PER WV6 34 B2
Pugin Gdns ERDW/GRVHL B23 76 B3
Pump St BKHL/PFLD WV2 53 E1
Puppy Gn TPTN/OCK DY4 85 H1
Purbeck Cl HALE B63 154 D1
Purbeck Cft RIDG/WDGT B32 141 F2
Purbrook Rd WOLV WV1 38 A5
Purcell Rd WOLVN WV10 23 F2
Purdy Rd BILS/COS WV14 69 E2
Purefoy Rd MOS/BIL B13 162 A5
Purley Gv ERDW/GRVHL B23 91 G1
Purnells Wy DOR/KN B93 197 E3
Purslet Rd WOLV WV1 38 A3
Purslow Gv NFLD/LBR B31 175 G4
Putney Av BFLD/HDSWWD B20 90 C5
Putney La RMSLY B62 172 D3
Putney Rd BFLD/HDSWWD B20 90 C5
Pype Hayes Cl
ERDE/BCHGN B24 93 H2
Pype Hayes Rd
ERDE/BCHGN B24 93 H2
Pytman Dr WALM/CURD B76 78 C4

Q

The Quadrangle BVILLE B30 * 159 H4
The Quadrant SEDG DY3 67 F2
Quadrille Lawns COVEN WV9 11 H5
Quail Gn DUNHL/THL/PER WV6 34 D3
Qualcast Rd WOLVN WV10 37 H3
Quantock Cl BRWNH WS8 19 G2
HALE B63 137 H5
RBRY B45 174 B3
Quantock Rd STRBR DY8 135 H1
Quantry La HAG/WOL DY9 186 A1
Quarrington Gv
ALE/KHTH/YWD B14 178 C2
Quarry Brow SEDG DY3 83 G1
Quarry Hl HALE B63 138 B5
Quarry House Cl RBRY B45 173 H4
Quarry La HALE B63 138 B5
NFLD/LBR B31 175 F2
Quarry Park Rd STRBR DY8 152 A1
Quarry Ri OLDBY B69 103 H1
Quarry Rd DUDS DY2 120 B2
SLYOAK B29 158 B1
Quarry Wk RBRY B45 188 A1
Quasar Centre WSL WS1 4 D3
Quayle Gv STRBR DY8 117 H1
Quayside Cl OLDBY B69 104 C1
Quayside Dr WSLW WS2 4 A6
Queen Eleanors Dr
DOR/KN B93 183 F5
Queen Elizabeth Av WSLW WS2 40 D3
Queen Elizabeth Rd RBRY B45 173 G3
Queen Mary St WSL WS1 56 D2
Queens Ar WOLV WV1 7 F4
Queens Av
ALE/KHTH/YWD B14 * 161 E2
OLDBY B69 85 H5
SHLY B90 180 B3
WSNGN B18 * 107 H3
Queensbridge Rd
MOS/BIL B13 143 H5
Queens Cl ERDE/BCHGN B24 92 D4
SMTHWKW B67 106 C4
Queens Ct SOLH B91 * 182 C1
Queens Crs BILS/COS WV14 68 A2
STRBR DY8 118 C5
Queen's Cross DUDS DY2 102 B1
Queens Dr BLKHTH/ROWR B65 104 B5
BVILLE B30 177 E1
DIG/EDG B5 3 F6
Queens Gdns BILS/COS WV14 53 H1
CDSL WV8 10 B4
DUDS DY2 102 B5
Queens Head Rd HDSW B21 107 G2
Queens Hl HAG/WOL DY9 184 B1
Queens Hospital Cl EDG B15 126 C3
Queen's Lea SHHTH WV12 26 A5
Queens Md SMTHWKW B67 * 106 C4
Queen's Park Rd HRBN B17 141 F1
Queen Sq WOLV WV1 7 F4
Queen's Ride MOS/BIL B13 143 G3
Queens Rd AST/WIT B6 109 G1
DSYBK/YTR WS5 57 H2
ERDW/GRVHL B23 92 A3
LGLYGN/QTN B68 105 H4
LGN/SDN/BHAMAIR B26 130 B3
RUSH/SHEL WS4 29 E3
SEDG DY3 67 G3
STRBR DY8 135 F1
Queens Tower
VAUX/NECH B7 * 109 H4
Queen St ALDR WS9 19 F5
BHTH/HG B12 144 D2
BILS/COS WV14 54 A3
BRLYHL DY5 101 F3
BRLYHL DY5 120 A4
CDYHTH B64 120 D3
CSCFLD/WYGN B72 62 B4
DARL/WED WS10 40 B5
DARL/WED WS10 54 D4
DARL/WED WS10 55 G5
HALE B63 138 C3
KGSWFD DY6 99 H2
OLDBY B69 105 E1
STRBR DY8 117 H1
STRBR DY8 135 F1
TPTN/OCK DY4 69 F3
WBROM B70 87 H3
WOLV WV1 7 G4
WSLW WS2 4 B5
Queensway CBHAMNE B4 3 H5
FOAKS/STRLY B74 45 G5
HAG/WOL DY9 136 C5
HALE B63 138 D4
LGLYGN/QTN B68 123 F3
Queensway Cl
LGLYGN/QTN B68 123 F4
Queenswood Rd
MGN/WHC B75 47 F4
MOS/BIL B13 144 C3
Quenby Dr DUDN DY1 84 A3
Quendale WMBN WV5 64 C5
Quentin Dr DUDN DY1 101 H1
Queslade Cl GTB/HAM B43 73 H2
Queslett Rd GTB/HAM B43 74 B1
KGSTG B44 59 H5
KGSTG B44 60 A5
Queslett Rd East
FOAKS/STRLY B74 60 B3
Quicksand La ALDR WS9 43 H1
Quigley Av BORD B9 127 H2
Quillets Rd STRBR DY8 117 G1
Quilter Cl BILS/COS WV14 68 A3
WSLW WS2 40 D2
Quilter Rd ERDE/BCHGN B24 93 F4
Quincey Dr ERDE/BCHGN B24 93 G3
Quincy Ri BRLYHL DY5 119 E5
Quinton Cl HIA/OLT B92 148 B3
Quinton Expy RIDG/WDGT B32 140 B1
Quinton La RIDG/WDGT B32 140 D1
Quinton Rd HRBN B17 141 H4
Quinton Rd West
RIDG/WDGT B32 140 B2
Quorn Crs STRBR DY8 117 G1
Quorn Gv ERDE/BCHGN B24 93 F4

R

Rabone La SMTHWK B66 106 D3
Raby Cl OLDBY B69 103 F1
Raby St BKHL/PFLD WV2 7 H7
Racecourse La STRBR DY8 152 A1
Racecourse Rd
DUNHL/THL/PER WV6 22 C5
Rachael Gdns DARL/WED WS10 56 C4
Rachel Cl TPTN/OCK DY4 70 A2
Rachel Gdns SLYOAK B29 142 B5
Radbourn Dr
FOAKS/STRLY B74 62 C2
Radbourne Dr HALE B63 120 A5
Radbourne Rd SHLY B90 180 D2
Radcliffe Dr RMSLY B62 139 G1
Raddens Rd RMSLY B62 139 H4
Raddington Dr HIA/OLT B92 163 H2
Raddlebarn Farm Dr
SLYOAK B29 159 H1
Raddlebarn Rd SLYOAK B29 159 H1
Radford Cl DSYBK/YTR WS5 57 G5
Radford Dr RUSH/SHEL WS4 18 C5
Radford Ri SOLH B91 165 G5
Radford Rd SLYOAK B29 158 C3
Radley Gv SLYOAK B29 141 G5
Radley Rd HAG/WOL DY9 136 D3
RUSH/SHEL WS4 29 E4
The Radleys STETCH B33 131 F5
Radlow Crs
CHWD/FDBR/MGN B37 132 B4
Radnor Cl RBRY B45 174 B3
Radnor Cft DSYBK/YTR WS5 58 A5
Radnor Gn HHTH/SAND B71 71 G4
Radnor Rd
BFLD/HDSWWD B20 108 B1
LGLYGN/QTN B68 123 F5
SEDG DY3 67 E3
Radnor St WSNGN B18 108 A3
Radstock Av CBROM B36 111 G2
Radstock Rd SHHTH WV12 26 A1
Radway Rd SHLY B90 195 E1
Raeburn Rd GTB/HAM B43 59 G4
Raford Rd ERDW/GRVHL B23 76 B5
Ragees Rd STRBR DY8 118 B1
Raglan Av
DUNHL/THL/PER WV6 34 D2
SMTHWK B66 107 E5
Raglan Cl FOAKS/STRLY B74 45 F2
SEDG DY3 66 D4
Raglan Rd DIG/EDG B5 143 H1
HDSW B21 107 E1
SMTHWK B66 107 E5
Raglan St BDMR/CCFT WV3 6 D4
BRLYHL DY5 101 E5
Raglan Wy
CHWD/FDBR/MGN B37 132 D2
Ragley Cl BLOX/PEL WS3 27 E1
DOR/KN B93 197 F1
Ragley Dr GTB/HAM B43 73 F1
LGN/SDN/BHAMAIR B26 148 A1
WLNHL WV13 39 F5
Ragnall Av STETCH B33 131 F5
Railswood Dr BLOX/PEL WS3 18 A4
Railway Dr BILS/COS WV14 54 A3
WOLV WV1 7 H3
Railway La WLNHL WV13 39 G4
Railway Rd BFLD/HDSWWD B20 91 F4
SCFLD/BOLD B73 62 B3
Railwayside Cl SMTHWK B66 106 A2
Railway St BILS/COS WV14 54 A3
TPTN/OCK DY4 86 A1
WBROM B70 87 F2
WOLV WV1 7 H3
Railway Ter DARL/WED WS10 70 D1
PBAR/PBCH B42 * 73 H5
VAUX/NECH B7 109 H2
Railwharf Sidings DUDS DY2 102 D5
Rainbow St BILS/COS WV14 53 H5
BKHL/PFLD WV2 37 E5
Rainham Cl TPTN/OCK DY4 84 D1
Rainsbrook Dr SHLY B90 195 F2
Rake Wy EDG B15 2 B7
Raleigh Cl HDSW B21 88 D5
Raleigh Cft GTB/HAM B43 58 C5
Raleigh Rd BILS/COS WV14 54 B5
BORD B9 128 B2
Raleigh St HHTH/SAND B71 87 G2
WSLW WS2 41 G3
Ralph Rd SHLY B90 180 D1
WASH/WDE B8 110 B5
Ralphs Meadow
RIDG/WDGT B32 140 D5
Ralston Cl BLOX/PEL WS3 16 C3
Ramp Rd
CHWD/FDBR/MGN B37 149 G2
Ramsay Cl HHTH/SAND B71 72 B3
Ramsay Rd LGLYGN/QTN B68 123 G3
TPTN/OCK DY4 69 E4
WSLW WS2 27 E5
Ramsden Cl SLYOAK B29 158 D3
Ramsey Cl RBRY B45 173 G4
Ramsey Rd VAUX/NECH B7 110 A2
Randall Cl KGSWFD DY6 100 B5
Randle Dr MGN/WHC B75 47 G2
Randle Rd HAG/WOL DY9 136 A3
Randwick Gv KGSTG B44 74 D2
Ranelagh Rd BKHL/PFLD WV2 52 A2
Rangeways Rd KGSWFD DY6 118 B1
Rangoon Rd HIA/OLT B92 148 C3
Ranleigh Av KGSWFD DY6 100 B5
Rann Cl LDYWD/EDGR B16 126 A3
Rannoch Cl BRLYHL DY5 118 D4
Ranscombe Dr SEDG DY3 83 E4
Ransom Rd ERDW/GRVHL B23 92 A2
Ranworth Ri
ETTPK/GDPK/PENN WV4 52 B4
Ratcliffe Cl SEDG DY3 67 H4
Ratcliffe Rd SOLH B91 165 E3
WNSFLD WV11 25 G4
Ratcliff Wk OLDBY B69 * 104 D2
Ratcliff Wy TPTN/OCK DY4 70 A5
Rathbone Cl BILS/COS WV14 53 H3
DIG/EDG B5 127 E5
Rathbone Rd SMTHWKW B67 124 B2
Rathlin Cl COVEN WV9 12 A4
Rathlin Cft CBROM B36 114 B4
Rathmore Cl STRBR DY8 135 E5
Rathwell Cl COVEN WV9 12 A5
Rattle Cft STETCH B33 130 A1
Ravenall Cl BKDE/SHDE B34 112 D2
Raven Crs WNSFLD WV11 25 F2
Ravenfield Cl WASH/WDE B8 110 D4
Ravenhayes La
RIDG/WDGT B32 157 E4
Raven Hays Rd NFLD/LBR B31 174 C3
Ravenhill Dr CDSL WV8 10 C4
Ravenhurst Dr GTB/HAM B43 58 C5
Ravenhurst Ms
ERDW/GRVHL B23 92 C3
Ravenhurst Rd HRBN B17 125 E5
Ravenhurst St BHTH/HG B12 127 G4
Raven Rd DSYBK/YTR WS5 57 H2
Ravensbourne Gv WLNHL WV13 40 A3
Ravenscroft STRBR DY8 134 C1
Ravenscroft Rd HIA/OLT B92 164 C2
SHHTH WV12 25 H5
Ravensdale Cl DSYBK/YTR WS5 57 H1
Ravensdale Gdns
DSYBK/YTR WS5 57 H2
Ravensdale Rd SMHTH B10 128 D5
Ravenshaw La SOLH B91 183 E1
Ravenshaw Rd
LDYWD/EDGR B16 125 E2
Ravenshaw Wy SOLH B91 183 E3
Ravenshill Rd
ALE/KHTH/YWD B14 179 E1
Ravensholme
DUNHL/THL/PER WV6 34 D3
Ravensitch Wk BRLYHL DY5 119 G3
Ravenswood EDG B15 125 G4
Ravenswood Cl
FOAKS/STRLY B74 47 F5
Ravenswood Dr SOLH B91 181 E4
Ravenswood Hl
CSHL/WTROR B46 115 F2
Rawdon Gv KGSTG B44 75 H3
Rawlings Rd SMTHWKW B67 124 C2
Rawlins Cft CVALE B35 94 D3
Rawlins St LDYWD/EDGR B16 126 A3
Raybolds Bridge Rd WSLW WS2 41 G1
Raybolds Bridge St WSLW WS2 41 G1
Raybon Cft RBRY B45 * 188 A2
Raybould's Fold DUDS DY2 102 C4
Rayford Dr HHTH/SAND B71 72 B1
Ray Hall La GTB/HAM B43 72 D3
Rayleigh Rd BDMR/CCFT WV3 36 C5
Raymond Av PBAR/PBCH B42 74 B5
Raymond Cl WSLW WS2 27 H5
Raymond Gdns WNSFLD WV11 25 E5
Raymond Rd WASH/WDE B8 110 C5
Raymont Gv GTB/HAM B43 59 F4
Rayners Cft
LGN/SDN/BHAMAIR B26 130 B2
Raynor Rd WOLVN WV10 23 H4
Rea Av RBRY B45 173 G5
Reabrook Rd NFLD/LBR B31 175 F5
Rea Cl NFLD/LBR B31 189 G1
Readers Wk GTB/HAM B43 73 H2
Rea Fordway RBRY B45 173 H4
Reansway Sq
DUNHL/THL/PER WV6 36 C1
Reapers Cl SHHTH WV12 26 B5
Reaside Crs
ALE/KHTH/YWD B14 160 B5
Reaside Cft BHTH/HG B12 * 144 A1
Reaside Dr RBRY B45 174 B5
Rea St DIG/EDG B5 127 F3
Rea St South DIG/EDG B5 127 E4
Rea Ter DIG/EDG B5 3 K6
Rea Valley Dr NFLD/LBR B31 175 H3
Reaview Dr SLYOAK B29 143 F5
Reaymer Cl WSLW WS2 27 F3
Reay Nadin Dr SCFLD/BOLD B73 60 D4
Rebecca Dr SLYOAK B29 142 C5
Rebecca Gdns
ETTPK/GDPK/PENN WV4 51 F4
Recreation St DUDS DY2 102 D4
Rectory Av DARL/WED WS10 55 F2
Rectory Cl STRBR DY8 135 H4
Rectory Gdns SOLH B91 182 B2
STRBR DY8 135 H4
Rectory Gv WSNGN B18 107 G3
Rectory La CBROM B36 112 C1
Rectory Park Av MGN/WHC B75 63 E4
Rectory Park Cl MGN/WHC B75 63 E4
Rectory Park Rd
LGN/SDN/BHAMAIR B26 148 A2
Rectory Rd MGN/WHC B75 62 C3
NFLD/LBR B31 175 H2
SOLH B91 182 A2
STRBR DY8 135 H4
Rectory St STRBR DY8 117 H1
Redacre Rd SCFLD/BOLD B73 76 D1
Redacres DUNHL/THL/PER WV6 22 A4
Redbank Av ERDW/GRVHL B23 92 A3
Redbourn Rd BLOX/PEL WS3 16 C3
Red Brick Cl CDYHTH B64 * 120 D5
Redbrook Covert
HWK/WKHTH B38 190 C1
Red Brook Rd WSLW WS2 27 E5
Redbrooks Cl SOLH B91 181 G4
Redburn Dr
ALE/KHTH/YWD B14 177 H3
Redcar Cft CBROM B36 111 G1
Redcar Rd WOLVN WV10 12 D3
Redcliffe Dr WMBN WV5 65 F5
Redcotts Cl WOLVN WV10 24 A3
Redcroft Dr ERDE/BCHGN B24 93 G1
Redcroft Rd DUDS DY2 103 E3
Reddal Hill Rd CDYHTH B64 121 E3
Reddicap Heath Rd
MGN/WHC B75 63 F4
Reddicap Hl WALM/CURD B76 62 D4
Reddicroft SCFLD/BOLD B73 62 C3
Reddings La HLGN/YWD B28 145 G5
Reddings Rd MOS/BIL B13 143 H5
The Reddings HLYWD B47 192 C3
Redditch Rd ALVE B48 189 H5
HWK/WKHTH B38 176 C4
Redfern Cl HIA/OLT B92 164 D1
Redfern Park Wy SPARK B11 146 A2
Redfern Rd SPARK B11 146 A2
Redfly La BRLYHL DY5 101 E3
Redford Cl MOS/BIL B13 144 D5
Redgate Cl HWK/WKHTH B38 176 B3
Redhall Rd LGLYGN/QTN B68 124 A5
SEDG DY3 83 E4
Red Hl STRBR DY8 135 H3
Redhill Av WMBN WV5 65 E5
Redhill Cl STRBR DY8 135 H3
Red Hill Gv HWK/WKHTH B38 190 D1
Redhill La BRGRVW B61 187 E3
Red Hill Pl RMSLY B62 155 G3
Redhill Rd HWK/WKHTH B38 190 B1
NFLD/LBR B31 175 H5
YDLY B25 146 A1
Red Hill St WOLV WV1 7 F1
Red House Av
DARL/WED WS10 56 B5
Redhouse Cl DOR/KN B93 196 C3
Red House La ALDR WS9 29 G5
Red House Park Rd
GTB/HAM B43 73 G1
Redhouse Rd
DUNHL/THL/PER WV6 21 F5
Red House Rd STETCH B33 130 A1
Redhouse St WSL WS1 57 E1
Redhurst Dr WOLVN WV10 12 B4
Redlake Dr HAG/WOL DY9 152 D2
Redlake Rd STRBR DY8 152 D1
Redlands Cl SOLH B91 165 F5
Redlands Rd SOLH B91 165 E5
Redlands Wy FOAKS/STRLY B74 45 G4
Red La SEDG DY3 66 D3
WNSFLD WV11 15 G5
Red Leasowes Rd HALE B63 138 B4
Redliff Av CBROM B36 95 F5
Red Lion Cl OLDBY B69 85 G5
Red Lion St WOLV WV1 6 E3
Redmead Cl NFLD/LBR B31 176 A1
Redmoor Gdns
ETTPK/GDPK/PENN WV4 51 G3
Redmoor Wy WALM/CURD B76 79 F5
Rednal Hill La RBRY B45 188 A2
Rednall Dr MGN/WHC B75 47 G2
Rednal Mill Dr RBRY B45 188 C1
Rednal Rd HWK/WKHTH B38 176 A5
Redpine Crest SHHTH WV12 40 B1
Red River Rd WSLW WS2 27 E5
Red Rock Dr CDSL WV8 10 B5
Redruth Cl DSYBK/YTR WS5 58 B1
KGSWFD DY6 99 H1
Redruth Rd DSYBK/YTR WS5 58 B1
Redstone Dr WNSFLD WV11 25 F5
Redstone Farm Rd
HLGN/YWD B28 163 F4
Redthorn Gv STETCH B33 129 H1
Redvers Rd BORD B9 128 C3
Redwing Gv ERDW/GRVHL B23 75 H4
Redwood Av DUDN DY1 83 H1
Redwood Cl BVILLE B30 176 C1
FOAKS/STRLY B74 45 F3
Redwood Cft
ALE/KHTH/YWD B14 161 E3
Redwood Dr OLDBY B69 85 H4
Redwood Gdns ACGN B27 * 146 B2
Redwood Rd BILS/COS WV14 68 D1
BVILLE B30 176 C1
DSYBK/YTR WS5 57 H4
Redwood Wy SHHTH WV12 25 H2
Reedham Gdns
ETTPK/GDPK/PENN WV4 50 D2
Reedly Rd SHHTH WV12 26 A1
Reedmace Cl HWK/WKHTH B38 176 D5
Reedswood Cl WSLW WS2 41 G2
Reedswood Gdns WSLW WS2 41 G2
Reedswood La WSLW WS2 41 G2
Reedswood Wy WSLW WS2 41 E1
Rees Dr WMBN WV5 65 F4
Reeves Gdns CDSL WV8 10 C3
Reeves Rd ALE/KHTH/YWD B14 160 C4
Reeves St BLOX/PEL WS3 27 F2
Reform St HHTH/SAND B71 87 H3
Regal Cft CBROM B36 111 F1
Regal Dr WSLW WS2 4 A7
Regan Av SHLY B90 180 A4
Regan Crs ERDW/GRVHL B23 76 C5
Regan Dr OLDBY B69 104 B1
Regency Cl BORD B9 128 B3
Regency Dr HWK/WKHTH B38 176 C3
Regency Gdns
ALE/KHTH/YWD B14 179 E2
Regency Wk FOAKS/STRLY B74 32 B5
Regent Av OLDBY B69 85 G5
Regent Cl DIG/EDG B5 143 H1
HALE B63 138 C3
KGSWFD DY6 99 G3
OLDBY B69 103 G1
Regent Ct SMTHWK B66 106 C4
Regent Dr OLDBY B69 85 G5
Regent Pde CBHAMW B1 2 C2
Regent Park Rd SMHTH B10 128 A4
Regent Pl CBHAMW B1 2 C2
OLDBY B69 85 H4
Regent Rd
ETTPK/GDPK/PENN WV4 51 E3
HDSW B21 107 F1
HRBN B17 142 A1
OLDBY B69 85 G5
Regents Ct BKHL/PFLD WV2 * 7 F6
Regent St BILS/COS WV14 53 H2
BVILLE B30 160 A3
CBHAMW B1 2 C2
CDYHTH B64 121 F2
DUDN DY1 68 C5
SMTHWK B66 106 C3
TPTN/OCK DY4 69 E3
WLNHL WV13 39 G2
Regina Av KGSTG B44 74 D3
Regina Cl RBRY B45 173 G4
Regina Crs
DUNHL/THL/PER WV6 35 F1
Regina Dr PBAR/PBCH B42 90 D3
RUSH/SHEL WS4 42 C1
Reginald Rd SMTHWKW B67 124 B2
WASH/WDE B8 110 B5
Regis Beeches
DUNHL/THL/PER WV6 * 21 G5
Regis Gdns BLKHTH/ROWR B65 122 A3
Regis Heath Rd
BLKHTH/ROWR B65 122 B2
Regis Rd BLKHTH/ROWR B65 122 A2
DUNHL/THL/PER WV6 21 F5
Reid Av SHHTH WV12 26 B4
Reid Rd LGLYGN/QTN B68 123 G3
Reigate Av WASH/WDE B8 111 G5
Relko Dr CBROM B36 111 G2
Remembrance Rd
DARL/WED WS10 56 C5
Remington Pl WSLW WS2 27 G5
Remington Rd WSLW WS2 27 F4
Renfrew Cl STRBR DY8 117 G1
Renfrew Sq CVALE B35 94 D2

Rennie Gv RIDG/WDGT B32 140 D2
Rennison Dr WMBN WV5 65 E5
Renown Cl BRLYHL DY5 100 D2
Renton Gv WOLVN WV10 22 C1
Renton Rd WOLVN WV10 22 C1
Repington Wy MGN/WHC B75 63 H3
Repton Av
DUNHL/THL/PER WV6 34 B2
Repton Gv BORD B9 129 F1
Repton Rd BORD B9 129 F1
Reservoir Cl WSLW WS2 41 F5
Reservoir Pas DARL/WED WS10 55 H5
Reservoir Pl WSLW WS2 41 F5
Reservoir Retreat
LDYWD/EDGR B16 125 H3
Reservoir Rd
BLKHTH/ROWR B65 122 B1
ERDW/GRVHL B23 92 B2
HIA/OLT B92 164 B2
LDYWD/EDGR B16 125 H2
LGLYGN/QTN B68 105 G5
RBRY B45 188 C5
SLYOAK B29 142 A4
Reservoir St WSLW WS2 41 F5
Retallack Cl SMTHWK B66 106 D1
Retford Dr WALM/CURD B76 63 E4
Retford Gv YDLY B25 146 C1
Retreat Gdns SEDG DY3 67 G4
The Retreat CDYHTH B64 121 E5
Revesby Wk VAUX/NECH B7 109 G5
Revival St BLOX/PEL WS3 27 F1
Reynards Cl SEDG DY3 68 A4
Reynolds Cl SEDG DY3 80 C4
Reynolds Gv
DUNHL/THL/PER WV6 20 D5
Reynolds Rd HDSW B21 107 G2
Reynoldstown Rd CBROM B36 111 G1
Reynolds Wk WNSFLD WV11 25 G2
Rhayader Rd NFLD/LBR B31 158 A5
Rhodes Cl SEDG DY3 82 C2
Rhone Cl SPARK B11 145 E4
Rhoose Cft CVALE B35 94 D4
Rhys Thomas Cl SHHTH WV12 40 B1
Ribbesford Av WOLVN WV10 22 D2
Ribbesford Cl HALE B63 137 H2
Ribbesford Crs BILS/COS WV14 68 D2
Ribblesdale Rd BVILLE B30 160 A3
Richard Pl DSYBK/YTR WS5 43 E5
Richard Rd DSYBK/YTR WS5 43 E5
Richards Cl NFLD/LBR B31 189 F2
OLDBY B69 104 C5
Richardson Dr STRBR DY8 118 A4
Richards Rd TPTN/OCK DY4 69 F2
Richards St DARL/WED WS10 55 F1
Richard St VAUX/NECH B7 109 F4
WBROM B70 87 F3
Richard St South WBROM B70 87 G4
Richard St West WBROM B70 87 F4
Richard Williams Rd
DARL/WED WS10 71 F1
Richborough Dr DUDN DY1 83 G3
Riches St DUNHL/THL/PER WV6 36 B2
Richford Gv STETCH B33 131 F2
Richmond Aston Dr
TPTN/OCK DY4 85 G1
Richmond Av BDMR/CCFT WV3 36 B4
BHTH/HG B12 * 144 B2
Richmond Cl
BFLD/HDSWWD B20 90 A4
Richmond Cft PBAR/PBCH B42 73 H5
Richmond Dr BDMR/CCFT WV3 36 A4
DUNHL/THL/PER WV6 34 D2
Richmond Gdns WMBN WV5 81 E1
Richmond Gv STRBR DY8 118 A4
Richmond Hl LGLYGN/QTN B68 105 G4
Richmond Hill Gdns EDG B15 142 C1
Richmond Hill Rd EDG B15 142 C1
Richmond Pk KGSWFD DY6 99 G1
Richmond Pl
ALE/KHTH/YWD B14 161 F2
Richmond Rd BDMR/CCFT WV3 36 A4
DUDS DY2 102 B1
HIA/OLT B92 147 E5
HLYWD B47 193 E1
RBRY B45 187 G1
SCFLD/BOLD B73 62 B2
SEDG DY3 67 G4
SMTHWK B66 124 C2
WSNGN B18 108 B3
YDLY B25 129 H2
Richmond St HALE B63 138 C3
WBROM B70 70 D5
WSL WS1 5 G5
Richmond St South
WBROM B70 86 C1
Richmond Wy
CHWD/FDBR/MGN B37 132 C1
Rickard Cl DOR/KN B93 196 C3
Rickman Dr EDG B15 126 D4
Rickyard Cl SLYOAK B29 158 C4
YDLY B25 129 H3
Rickyard Piece
RIDG/WDGT B32 141 E3
Riddfield Rd CBROM B36 112 A1
Ridding La DARL/WED WS10 70 D1
Riddings Crs BLOX/PEL WS3 17 H3
The Riddings HAG/WOL DY9 136 B5
STETCH B33 112 A5
WALM/CURD B76 78 D3
WOLVN WV10 24 A3
Ridgacre La RIDG/WDGT B32 140 C2
Ridgacre Rd HHTH/SAND B71 71 F5
RIDG/WDGT B32 140 B1
Ridgacre Rd West
RIDG/WDGT B32 140 A1
Ridge Cl MOS/BIL B13 162 A4
WSLW WS2 40 B2
Ridgefield Rd RMSLY B62 122 A4
Ridge Gv HAG/WOL DY9 136 A2
Ridge La WNSFLD WV11 24 D3
Ridgemount Dr
HWK/WKHTH B38 190 B1
Ridge Rd KGSWFD DY6 99 G4
Ridge St STRBR DY8 134 C1
Ridgewater Cl RBRY B45 188 B2
Ridge Wy ALDR WS9 44 B1
Ridgeway HRBN B17 124 D2
SEDG DY3 67 F4
Ridgeway Av RMSLY B62 140 A1
Ridgeway Ct WSLW WS2 40 D4
Ridgeway Dr
ETTPK/GDPK/PENN WV4 51 F5
Ridgeway Rd STRBR DY8 118 B2
TPTN/OCK DY4 69 G3
The Ridgeway
ERDW/GRVHL B23 75 G5
Ridgewood BKDE/SHDE B34 112 D3
Ridgewood Av STRBR DY8 134 C1
Ridgewood Cl WSL WS1 5 F6
Ridgewood Dr MGN/WHC B75 47 F4
Ridgewood Gdns KGSTG B44 75 F4
Ridgmont Cft RIDG/WDGT B32 141 E2
Riding Cl HHTH/SAND B71 72 B4
Riding Wy SHHTH WV12 26 B4
Ridley St CBHAMW B1 126 C3
Ridpool Rd STETCH B33 130 D1
Rifle St BILS/COS WV14 68 A3
Rigby St DARL/WED WS10 70 D2
Riland Rd MGN/WHC B75 62 D3
Riley Crs BDMR/CCFT WV3 51 G2
Riley Dr CBROM B36 96 A5
Riley Rd ALE/KHTH/YWD B14 179 F2
Riley St WLNHL WV13 39 H3
Rilstone Rd RIDG/WDGT B32 141 F2
Rindleford Av
ETTPK/GDPK/PENN WV4 50 C2
Ringhills Rd CDSL WV8 10 D5
Ringinglow Rd KGSTG B44 74 C1
Ringmere Av CBROM B36 112 D1
Ring Road St Andrews
WOLV WV1 6 D4
Ring Road St Davids WOLV WV1 7 H3
Ring Road St Georges
BKHL/PFLD WV2 7 G6
Ring Road St Johns
BKHL/PFLD WV2 6 E6
Ring Road St Marks
BDMR/CCFT WV3 6 D5
Ring Road St Patricks
WOLV WV1 7 G2
Ring Road St Peters WOLV WV1 6 E3
Ringswood Rd HIA/OLT B92 147 E3
The Ring YDLY B25 129 G4
Ringwood Av ALDR WS9 30 B5
Ringwood Dr RBRY B45 174 A4
Ringwood Rd WOLVN WV10 23 F1
Ripley Cl DUDS DY2 103 F1
Ripley Gv ERDW/GRVHL B23 91 H1
Ripon Dr HHTH/SAND B71 71 H2
Ripon Rd ALE/KHTH/YWD B14 179 E1
WOLVN WV10 23 E3
WSLW WS2 41 F3
Rippingille Rd GTB/HAM B43 59 G4
Ripple Rd BVILLE B30 160 B3
Rischale Wy RUSH/SHEL WS4 29 E2
Rise Av RBRY B45 188 A1
Riseley Crs DIG/EDG B5 143 H1
The Rise ALVE B48 189 H4
CHWD/FDBR/MGN B37 132 A5
KGSWFD DY6 100 A4
PBAR/PBCH B42 74 A3
Rising Brook
DUNHL/THL/PER WV6 35 F1
Rissington Av SLYOAK B29 160 A2
Ritchie Cl MOS/BIL B13 161 G1
Rivendell Gdns
DUNHL/THL/PER WV6 21 F5
Riverbank Rd WLNHL WV13 40 B3
River Brook Dr BVILLE B30 160 B3
River Lee Rd SPARK B11 * 145 G2
Rivermead Pk BKDE/SHDE B34 112 C4
Riversdale Rd
ALE/KHTH/YWD B14 179 F2
Riverside Ct HWK/WKHTH B38 176 B2
Riverside Crs HLGN/YWD B28 179 F1
Riverside Dr SOLH B91 182 C3
STETCH B33 111 H5
Riverside Gdns CDSL WV8 10 D2
Riversleigh Dr STRBR DY8 118 A4
River St DIG/EDG B5 127 G2
Riverway DARL/WED WS10 71 F1
Rivington Cl STRBR DY8 135 E3
Rivington Crs KGSTG B44 76 A2
Roach Cl BRLYHL DY5 101 F4
CHWD/FDBR/MGN B37 132 C1
Roach Crs WNSFLD WV11 * 25 F2
Roach Pool Cft
LDYWD/EDGR B16 125 E2
Road Eastwood DUDS DY2 103 E3
Robert Av ERDW/GRVHL B23 76 C5
Robert Rd BFLD/HDSWWD B20 90 B5
TPTN/OCK DY4 69 F5
Roberts Cl ALDR WS9 19 F5
Roberts Green Rd SEDG DY3 83 G2
Roberts La HAG/WOL DY9 152 D2
Robertson Knoll CBROM B36 112 B1
Robertsons Gdns
VAUX/NECH B7 110 A2
Roberts Rd ACGN B27 146 C4
BLOX/PEL WS3 28 B5
DARL/WED WS10 57 E5
Robert St SEDG DY3 83 G2
Robert Wynd BILS/COS WV14 67 H2
Robeson Cl TPTN/OCK DY4 84 D1
Robin Cl CBROM B36 114 A1
KGSWFD DY6 100 C3
Robin Gv WNSFLD WV11 24 C3
Robin Hood Crs
HLGN/YWD B28 162 C3
Robin Hood Cft
HLGN/YWD B28 162 D5
Robin Hood La HLGN/YWD B28 162 C3
Robin Hood Rd BRLYHL DY5 119 H2
Robin Rd ERDW/GRVHL B23 92 C2
Robin's Cl STRBR DY8 135 G4
Robinsfield Dr NFLD/LBR B31 189 G1
Robinson's Wy
WALM/CURD B76 95 F1
Robottom Cl WSLW WS2 27 F4
Rocester Av WNSFLD WV11 25 E3
Rochdale Wk SMHTH B10 128 A5
Roche Rd BLOX/PEL WS3 26 D1
Rochester Cft WSLW WS2 41 E1
Rochester Rd NFLD/LBR B31 175 G1
Roche Wy BLOX/PEL WS3 26 D1
Rochford Cl HALE B63 138 B5
RBRY B45 187 G1
WALM/CURD B76 78 C3
WSLW WS2 56 C1
Rochford Ct SHLY B90 195 G2
Rochford Gv
ETTPK/GDPK/PENN WV4 50 D3
Rock Av RBRY B45 188 C1
Rocket Pool Dr BILS/COS WV14 69 G1
Rockford Rd PBAR/PBCH B42 74 A4
Rock Gv HIA/OLT B92 147 E4
Rockingham Cl BLOX/PEL WS3 * 27 F1
DOR/KN B93 198 B1
SEDG DY3 82 D3
Rockingham Dr
DUNHL/THL/PER WV6 34 C2
Rockingham Gdns
FOAKS/STRLY B74 62 B2
Rockingham Hall Gdns
HAG/WOL DY9 153 F3
Rockingham Rd YDLY B25 129 H4
Rockland Dr STETCH B33 112 A5
Rockland Gdns WLNHL WV13 39 F5
Rocklands Dr MGN/WHC B75 47 F5
Rockley Gv RBRY B45 188 B1
Rockley Rd
BLKHTH/ROWR B65 103 G3
Rockmead Av KGSTG B44 75 F1
Rockmoor Cl STETCH B33 131 G1
Rock Rd BILS/COS WV14 67 H3
HIA/OLT B92 147 E4
Rock St SEDG DY3 83 G1
The Rock DUNHL/THL/PER WV6 21 H5
Rockville Rd WASH/WDE B8 111 E5
Rockwood Rd ACGN B27 146 B3
Rocky La AST/WIT B6 109 G3
PBAR/PBCH B42 73 H5
Rodborough Rd DOR/KN B93 198 C1
LGN/SDN/BHAMAIR B26 147 H1
Rodbourne Rd HRBN B17 142 A4
Roddis Cl ERDW/GRVHL B23 76 B3
Roderick Dr WNSFLD WV11 24 D3
Roderick Rd SPARK B11 145 E2
Rodlington Av KGSTG B44 75 F2
Rodman Cl EDG B15 125 F4
Rodney Cl HIA/OLT B92 * 164 D1
LDYWD/EDGR B16 126 A2
Rodney Rd HIA/OLT B92 164 D1
Rodway Cl BRLYHL DY5 119 F5
ETTPK/GDPK/PENN WV4 52 B5
LOZ/NWT B19 108 D2
Rodwell Gv KGSTG B44 75 F3
Roebuck Cl BKDE/SHDE B34 113 G5
Roebuck Gld SHHTH WV12 40 C1
Roebuck La WBROM B70 88 A5
Roebuck Pl BLOX/PEL WS3 28 A4
Roebuck Rd BLOX/PEL WS3 28 A4
Roebuck St WBROM B70 88 B5
Roedean Cl KGSTG B44 75 H4
Roford Ct SEDG DY3 83 G1
Rogerfield Rd
ERDW/GRVHL B23 77 E5
Rogers Cl WNSFLD WV11 25 G1
Rogers Rd WASH/WDE B8 111 F4
Rokeby Cl WALM/CURD B76 63 E4
Rokeby Rd GTB/HAM B43 73 H1
Rokewood Cl KGSWFD DY6 81 H5
Roland Gdns LOZ/NWT B19 108 C1
Roland Gv LOZ/NWT B19 108 C1
Rolan Dr SHLY B90 179 G5
Roland Rd LOZ/NWT B19 108 C1
Roland Ter LOZ/NWT B19 108 C1
Rolfe St SMTHWK B66 106 C3
Rollason Rd DUDS DY2 102 D1
ERDE/BCHGN B24 93 E3
Rollesby Dr WLNHL WV13 39 F5
Rolling Mill Cl DIG/EDG B5 * 127 E5
Rollingmill St WSLW WS2 4 A5
Rollswood Dr SOLH B91 181 F1
Roman Cl BRWNH WS8 9 E2
Roman La FOAKS/STRLY B74 45 H2
Roman Pk FOAKS/STRLY B74 45 H1
Roman Rd FOAKS/STRLY B74 32 A5
Roman Rod (Sandy La)
STRBR DY8 134 C3
Roman Wy BLKHTH/ROWR B65 122 A1
CSHL/WTROR B46 97 E4
EDG B15 142 B4
Romany Rd RBRY B45 173 F4
Romany Wy STRBR DY8 134 C4
Roma Rd SPARK B11 145 G2
Romford Cl
LGN/SDN/BHAMAIR B26 147 H1
Romilly Av BFLD/HDSWWD B20 90 B4
Romilly Cl STRBR DY8 135 E1
WALM/CURD B76 63 G4
Romney Cl HLGN/YWD B28 162 D3
Romney Wy GTB/HAM B43 59 H4
Romsey Gv WOLVN WV10 12 C4
Romsey Rd WOLVN WV10 12 C4
Romsey Wy BLOX/PEL WS3 16 B4
Romsley Cl RBRY B45 173 G5
RMSLY B62 138 D5
RUSH/SHEL WS4 18 C5
Romsley Rd HAG/WOL DY9 136 A2
LGLYGN/QTN B68 123 F2
RIDG/WDGT B32 157 F2
Romulus Cl BFLD/HDSWWD B20 90 B3
Ronald Gv CBROM B36 95 F5
Ronald Pl BORD B9 128 C2
Ronald Rd BORD B9 128 B2
Ron Davis Cl SMTHWK B66 * 106 D4
Rood End Rd LGLYGN/QTN B68 105 G3
Rooker Av BKHL/PFLD WV2 52 C2
Rooker Crs BKHL/PFLD WV2 52 D2
Rookery Av BRLYHL DY5 118 C2
ETTPK/GDPK/PENN WV4 53 E5
Rookery La BKHL/PFLD WV2 51 G2
Rookery Pk BRLYHL DY5 100 D4
Rookery Ri WMBN WV5 65 F5
Rookery Rd
ETTPK/GDPK/PENN WV4 53 E5
HDSW B21 89 G5
SLYOAK B29 142 D5
WMBN WV5 65 F5
Rookery St WNSFLD WV11 24 C5
The Rookery RIDG/WDGT B32 140 A5
Rooks Meadow HAG/WOL DY9 152 D4
Rookwood Dr
DUNHL/THL/PER WV6 34 D4
Rooth St DARL/WED WS10 56 B4
Roper Wy SEDG DY3 67 H5
Rosafield Av RMSLY B62 139 H1
Rosalind Av DUDN DY1 68 B5
Rosalind Gv WNSFLD WV11 25 G5
Rosamond St WSL WS1 56 D1
Rosary Rd ERDW/GRVHL B23 92 B4
Rosary Vls SPARK B11 * 145 E2
Rose Av KGSWFD DY6 100 B4
LGLYGN/QTN B68 123 G5
Rose Bank Dr BLOX/PEL WS3 * 42 A1
Rosebay Av HWK/WKHTH B38 176 D5
Rosebery Rd SMTHWK B66 107 E5
Rosebery St BDMR/CCFT WV3 6 C6
WSNGN B18 108 A5
Rosebury Gv WMBN WV5 64 C5
Rose Cl SMTHWK B66 107 E4
Rose Cottages SLYOAK B29 * 142 D5
Rosecroft Rd
LGN/SDN/BHAMAIR B26 148 A1
Rosedale Av ERDW/GRVHL B23 92 C3
SMTHWK B66 107 E4
Rosedale Gv YDLY B25 129 G4
Rosedale Pl WLNHL WV13 39 G5
Rosedene Dr
BFLD/HDSWWD B20 89 H4
Rose Dr BRWNH WS8 19 E2
Rosefield Cft AST/WIT B6 109 F2
Rosefield Rd SMTHWKW B67 106 C5
Rosehall Cl SOLH B91 181 F4
Rose Hl BRLYHL DY5 120 A3
RBRY B45 188 A4
WLNHL WV13 39 G4
Rose Hill Cl CBROM B36 112 D1
Rose Hill Gdns WLNHL WV13 39 G4
Rose Hill Rd HDSW B21 108 A2
Rosehip Cl DSYBK/YTR WS5 57 G5
Roseland Av DUDS DY2 85 F5
Roseland Wy EDG B15 126 B3
Roseleigh Rd RBRY B45 188 B2
Rosemary Av BILS/COS WV14 54 B2
ETTPK/GDPK/PENN WV4 52 A2
Rosemary Cl BRWNH WS8 18 D1
Rosemary Crs DUDN DY1 67 H5
ETTPK/GDPK/PENN WV4 52 A3
Rosemary Crs West
ETTPK/GDPK/PENN WV4 51 H3
Rosemary Dr FOAKS/STRLY B74 46 A2
Rosemary Hill Rd
FOAKS/STRLY B74 46 A3
Rosemary La STRBR DY8 134 D4
Rosemary Nook
FOAKS/STRLY B74 32 B5
Rosemary Rd HALE B63 137 H5
STETCH B33 130 B2
TPTN/OCK DY4 85 G1
Rosemoor Dr BRLYHL DY5 118 D5
Rose Rd CSHL/WTROR B46 115 F1
HRBN B17 142 B1
Rose St BILS/COS WV14 69 F1
Rose Vls YDLY B25 * 129 E5
Roseville Gdns CDSL WV8 10 B3
Roseville Prec BILS/COS WV14 * 68 C3
Rosewood Dr
ERDW/GRVHL B23 92 B4
SHHTH WV12 25 H2
Rosewood Gdns WNSFLD WV11 15 F4
Rosewood Rd DUDN DY1 84 B1
Roshven Rd BHTH/HG B12 144 C3
Roslin Gv LOZ/NWT B19 108 C2
Roslyn Cl SMTHWK B66 106 C3
Ross BLKHTH/ROWR B65 121 H2
Ross Cl BDMR/CCFT WV3 36 A3
Ross Dr KGSWFD DY6 99 G2
Rosse Ct HIA/OLT B92 165 H2
Rossendale Cl HALE B63 137 H1
Ross Hts BLKHTH/ROWR B65 121 H1
Rosslyn Rd WALM/CURD B76 78 B5
Ross Rd BLOX/PEL WS3 28 B4
Rostrevor Rd SMHTH B10 128 D3
Rotherby Gv
CHWD/FDBR/MGN B37 132 B5
Rotherfield Rd
LGN/SDN/BHAMAIR B26 130 D4
Rothesay Cft RIDG/WDGT B32 157 F3
Rothesay Dr STRBR DY8 117 G1
Rothesay Wy SHHTH WV12 25 H4
Rothwell Dr SHLY B90 163 H5
Rotton Park Rd
LDYWD/EDGR B16 125 F2
Rotton Park St
LDYWD/EDGR B16 125 H1
Rough Hay Pl DARL/WED WS10 55 E1
Rough Hay Rd DARL/WED WS10 55 E1
Rough Hill Dr
BLKHTH/ROWR B65 103 F3
Rough Hills Rd BKHL/PFLD WV2 52 D2
Roughlea Av CBROM B36 112 B2
Roughley Dr MGN/WHC B75 47 G3
Roughley Farm Rd
MGN/WHC B75 48 A2
Rough Rd KGSTG B44 60 C5
Rouncil Cl HIA/OLT B92 165 F3
The Roundabout
NFLD/LBR B31 174 D4
Round Cl SHLY B90 193 H2
Round Cft WLNHL WV13 39 F3
Round Hl SEDG DY3 67 F1
Round Hill Av HAG/WOL DY9 153 E1
Roundhill Cl WALM/CURD B76 63 E4
Roundhills Rd RMSLY B62 122 D4
Roundhill Ter RMSLY B62 122 C3
Roundhill Wy BRWNH WS8 9 G2
Round House Rd SEDG DY3 83 G2
Roundlea Cl SHHTH WV12 25 H3
Roundlea Rd NFLD/LBR B31 158 A3
Round Rd ERDE/BCHGN B24 93 F4
Round Saw Cft RBRY B45 173 H5
Rounds Green Rd OLDBY B69 104 C2
Rounds Hill Rd BILS/COS WV14 68 D3
Rounds Rd BILS/COS WV14 53 H5
Round St DUDS DY2 102 C3
Roundway Down
DUNHL/THL/PER WV6 34 C2
Rounton Cl FOAKS/STRLY B74 46 B1
Rousay Cl RBRY B45 173 H4
Rousdon Gv GTB/HAM B43 73 F3
Rover Dr ACGN B27 146 D3
CBROM B36 95 H5
Rowallan Rd MGN/WHC B75 47 H3
Rowan Cl HLYWD B47 192 D3
WALM/CURD B76 78 B1
Rowan Ct BVILLE B30 177 E3
Rowan Crs BDMR/CCFT WV3 51 E1
BILS/COS WV14 68 B2
Rowan Dr HLGN/YWD B28 163 E5
WNSFLD WV11 15 F4
Rowan Ri KGSWFD DY6 100 A3
Rowan Rd CSCFLD/WYGN B72 77 G1
DSYBK/YTR WS5 57 F4
SEDG DY3 67 H2
Rowantrees RBRY B45 188 B3
Rowan Wy
CHWD/FDBR/MGN B37 132 C3
NFLD/LBR B31 175 F4
Roway La OLDBY B69 86 C5
Rowbrook Cl SHLY B90 179 G5
Rowchester Ct CBHAMNE B4 * 3 G3
Rowcroft Covert
ALE/KHTH/YWD B14 177 G2
Rowdale Rd PBAR/PBCH B42 74 C4
Rowden Dr ERDW/GRVHL B23 77 E5
SOLH B91 181 E3
Rowena Gdns SEDG DY3 67 E1
Rowheath Rd BVILLE B30 176 D1
Rowington Av
BLKHTH/ROWR B65 122 B1
Rowington Rd
BKDE/SHDE B34 113 G3
Rowington Ter YDLY B25 * 129 F5
Rowland Gdns WSLW WS2 41 G2
Rowland Hill Dr
TPTN/OCK DY4 * 86 A2
Rowlands Av WOLV WV1 38 B3
WSLW WS2 40 C2
Rowlands Cl WSLW WS2 40 C1
Rowlands Crs SOLH B91 164 D2
Rowlands Rd
LGN/SDN/BHAMAIR B26 130 A5
Rowland St WSLW WS2 41 G2
Rowley Gv STETCH B33 131 F1
Rowley Hall Av
BLKHTH/ROWR B65 122 A1
Rowley Hill Vw CDYHTH B64 121 F4
Rowley Pl RUSH/SHEL WS4 28 D3
Rowley St WSL WS1 5 G3
Rowley Vw BILS/COS WV14 54 C5
WBROM B70 87 F3
Rowley Village
BLKHTH/ROWR B65 122 A1
Rowney Cft HLGN/YWD B28 179 G1
Rowood Dr HIA/OLT B92 165 E3
Rowthorn Cl FOAKS/STRLY B74 60 C1
Rowthorn Dr SHLY B90 195 G2
Rowton Av
DUNHL/THL/PER WV6 34 C2
Rowton Dr FOAKS/STRLY B74 60 B3
Roxall Cl KIDD DY10 168 C3
Roxburgh Gv GTB/HAM B43 59 G4
Roxburgh Rd SCFLD/BOLD B73 62 A5
Roxby Gdns
DUNHL/THL/PER WV6 22 C5
Royal Cl BLKHTH/ROWR B65 104 A4
BRLYHL DY5 119 E4
Royal Mail St CBHAMW B1 2 E6
Royal Oak Rd
BLKHTH/ROWR B65 103 F4
RMSLY B62 139 H3
Royal Rd MGN/WHC B75 62 C3
Royal Scot Gv WSL WS1 56 D3
Royal Star Cl STETCH B33 131 E2
Royal Wy TPTN/OCK DY4 85 G4
Roydon Rd ACGN B27 163 G2
Roylesden Crs SCFLD/BOLD B73 76 A1
Royston Cha FOAKS/STRLY B74 45 G2
Royston Cft BHTH/HG B12 144 B1
Royston Wy SEDG DY3 67 E3
Rubens Cl SEDG DY3 83 F1
Rubery Farm Gv RBRY B45 173 H5
Rubery Field Cl RBRY B45 174 A4
Rubery La RBRY B45 173 H4
Rubery La South RBRY B45 173 H5
Rubery St DARL/WED WS10 40 B5
Ruckley Av LOZ/NWT B19 * 108 C2
Ruckley Rd SLYOAK B29 158 C2
Rudd Gdns WOLV WV1 38 B1
Ruddington Wy LOZ/NWT B19 109 E4
Rudge Av WOLV WV1 38 B2
Rudge Cl SHHTH WV12 40 A1
Rudge Cft STETCH B33 112 C5
Rudge Wk WSNGN B18 * 126 A1
Rudgewick Cft AST/WIT B6 109 F3
Rudyard Cl WOLVN WV10 13 E3
Rudyard Gv STETCH B33 130 D1
Rudyngfield Dr STETCH B33 130 B1

Rufford Cl ERDW/GRVHL B23 76 B3
Rufford Rd HAG/WOL DY9 136 A3
Rufford St HAG/WOL DY9 136 B1
Rufford Wy ALDR WS9 29 G3
Rugby Rd STRBR DY8 117 H5
Rugby St WOLV WV1 6 C1
Rugeley Av SHHTH WV12 26 B2
Rugeley Cl TPTN/OCK DY4 85 E1
Ruislip Cl CVALE B35 94 C2
Ruiton St SEDG DY3 83 F2
Rumbow HALE B63 138 D3
Rumbow La RMSLY B62 171 H1
Rumbush La SHLY B90 193 H4
Runcorn Cl
CHWD/FDBR/MGN B37 114 C5
Runcorn Rd BHTH/HG B12 144 B2
Runnymede Rd SPARK B11 145 G4
Rupert St BDMR/CCFT WV3 6 A3
VAUX/NECH B7 109 G4
Rushall Cl RUSH/SHEL WS4 42 D1
STRBR DY8 118 A4
Rushall Manor Cl
RUSH/SHEL WS4 42 D1
Rushall Manor Rd
RUSH/SHEL WS4 42 D1
Rushall Rd WOLVN WV10 13 E5
Rushbrook Cl BRWNH WS8 19 E1
HIA/OLT B92 147 E5
Rushbrooke Cl MOS/BIL B13 144 B3
Rushbrooke Dr
SCFLD/BOLD B73 61 E4
Rushbrook Gv
ALE/KHTH/YWD B14 177 G2
Rushbury Cl BILS/COS WV14 53 F3
SHLY B90 180 D1
Rushden Cft KGSTG B44 75 F2
Rushes Ml BLOX/PEL WS3 17 G4
Rushey La SPARK B11 146 A2
Rushford Av WMBN WV5 65 E5
Rushford Cl SHLY B90 195 G1
Rush Gn RIDG/WDGT B32 141 E5
Rushleigh Rd SHLY B90 179 G5
Rushmead Gv RBRY B45 188 A1
Rushmere Rd TPTN/OCK DY4 69 G3
Rushmoor Cl FOAKS/STRLY B74 62 B2
Rushwater Cl WMBN WV5 64 C5
Rushwick Gv SHLY B90 195 G2
Rushwood Cl RUSH/SHEL WS4 42 C2
Rushy Piece RIDG/WDGT B32 140 D4
Ruskin Av BLKHTH/ROWR B65 122 B2
ETTPK/GDPK/PENN WV4 67 H1
SEDG DY3 82 C1
Ruskin Cl AST/WIT B6 109 F2
Ruskin Gv ACGN B27 146 B5
Ruskin Hall Gv AST/WIT B6 109 F2
Ruskin Rd WOLVN WV10 23 H2
Ruskin St HHTH/SAND B71 87 G1
Russell Bank Rd
FOAKS/STRLY B74 46 C1
Russell Cl OLDBY B69 86 B4
TPTN/OCK DY4 70 A2
WNSFLD WV11 25 F1
Russell Rd BILS/COS WV14 54 B1
HLGN/YWD B28 145 G5
MOS/BIL B13 143 H4
Russell's Hall Rd DUDN DY1 83 G5
The Russells MOS/BIL B13 143 H4
Russell St BDMR/CCFT WV3 6 D6
DARL/WED WS10 70 D1
DUDN DY1 84 B5
WLNHL WV13 39 H3
Russett Cl DSYBK/YTR WS5 43 F5
Russett Wy BRLYHL DY5 100 C2
Russet Wy NFLD/LBR B31 158 A4
Ruston St LDYWD/EDGR B16 126 A3
Ruthall Cl SLYOAK B29 159 E3
Ruth Cl DARL/WED WS10 70 A1
Rutherford Rd
ERDW/GRVHL B23 76 C4
WSLW WS2 27 E4
Rutland Av
ETTPK/GDPK/PENN WV4 50 D4
Rutland Crs ALDR WS9 30 B1
BILS/COS WV14 53 H1
Rutland Dr
LGN/SDN/BHAMAIR B26 130 A5
Rutland Pl STRBR DY8 117 H4
Rutland Rd DARL/WED WS10 56 C4
HHTH/SAND B71 71 G4
SMTHWK B66 124 C3
Rutland St BLOX/PEL WS3 28 A5
Rutland Ter WSNGN B18 * 108 A4
Rutley Gv RIDG/WDGT B32 141 F3
Rutters Meadow RIDG/WDGT B32 140 B3
Rutter St WSL WS1 57 E1
Ryan Av WNSFLD WV11 25 G3
Ryan Pl DUDS DY2 102 C3
Rycroft Gv STETCH B33 131 E2
Rydal Cl FOAKS/STRLY B74 45 F3
WNSFLD WV11 24 C3
Rydal Dr DUNHL/THL/PER WV6 34 D1
Rydding La HHTH/SAND B71 71 G3
Rydding Sq HHTH/SAND B71 71 F3
Ryde Gv ACGN B27 163 E1
Ryde Park Rd RBRY B45 188 C2
Ryders Green Rd WBROM B70 86 D2
Ryders Hayes La BLOX/PEL WS3 18 A3
Ryder St CBHAMNE B4 * 3 H3
STRBR DY8 117 H2
WBROM B70 86 D1
Ryebank Cl BVILLE B30 159 E5
Ryeclose Cft
CHWD/FDBR/MGN B37 132 D1
Rye Cft ACGN B27 146 C2
HAG/WOL DY9 136 C5
HLYWD B47 192 C3
Ryecroft Av
ETTPK/GDPK/PENN WV4 51 H3
Ryecroft Cl SEDG DY3 67 E3
Ryecroft Pk WSLW WS2 42 A2
Ryecroft Pl BLOX/PEL WS3 28 B4
Ryecroft St WSLW WS2 42 A2
Ryefield CDSL WV8 22 A1
Ryefield Cl HAG/WOL DY9 169 G1
SOLH B91 164 A5
Rye Grass Wk CVALE B35 94 D3
Rye Gv SPARK B11 145 H3
Ryknild Cl FOAKS/STRLY B74 32 C4
Ryland Cl HALE B63 138 A5
TPTN/OCK DY4 85 H1
Ryland Rd EDG B15 126 C5
ERDE/BCHGN B24 92 D5
SPARK B11 145 F3
Rylands Dr
ETTPK/GDPK/PENN WV4 51 G4
Ryland St LDYWD/EDGR B16 2 A7
Ryle St BLOX/PEL WS3 17 F5
Rymond Rd BKDE/SHDE B34 112 A3
Ryton Cl SCFLD/BOLD B73 62 B3
WNSFLD WV11 24 A5
Ryton Gv BKDE/SHDE B34 113 F2

S

Sabell Rd SMTHWKW B67 106 B3
Sabrina Rd
DUNHL/THL/PER WV6 34 C4
Saddlers Cl HALE B63 137 F2
Saddlers Ms SOLH B91 182 A4
The Saddlestones
DUNHL/THL/PER WV6 34 B1
Saddleworth Rd GTWY WS6 16 C3
Sadler Rd BRWNH WS8 9 G4
MGN/WHC B75 63 F1
Sadlers Ct WSLW WS2 56 B1
Sadlers Ml BRWNH WS8 * 9 G5
Sadlers Wk LDYWD/EDGR B16 126 A3
Saffron Gdns
ETTPK/GDPK/PENN WV4 51 G4
Sage Cft NFLD/LBR B31 158 B5
St Agatha's Rd WASH/WDE B8 111 F4
St Agnes Cl MOS/BIL B13 144 D5
St Agnes Rd MOS/BIL B13 144 D5
St Aidans Wk SMHTH B10 * 128 A4
St Albans Cl SMTHWKW B67 * 106 A3
WNSFLD WV11 25 G2
St Albans Rd MOS/BIL B13 144 C3
SMTHWKW B67 106 A3
St Alphege Cl SOLH B91 * 182 A2
St Ambrose Cl RMSLY B62 122 A4
St Andrews Av BLOX/PEL WS3 18 A2
St Andrews Cl
DUNHL/THL/PER WV6 36 C1
HRBN B17 141 G4
SEDG DY3 82 C3
STRBR DY8 135 F5
St Andrews Dr
DUNHL/THL/PER WV6 20 B5
OLDBY B69 103 H2
St Andrew's Rd BORD B9 127 H2
MGN/WHC B75 62 C1
St Andrew's St BORD B9 127 H2
DUDS DY2 102 C4
St Annes Cl BFLD/HDSWWD B20 89 H2
St Anne's Ct MOS/BIL B13 144 A3
St Annes Gv DOR/KN B93 197 E2
St Anne's Rd CDYHTH B64 120 C3
WLNHL WV13 39 H2
WOLVN WV10 22 D1
St Annes Wy KGSTG B44 75 G4
St Anthonys Dr BLOX/PEL WS3 18 B2
St Athan Cft CVALE B35 94 D3
St Augustine's Rd
LDYWD/EDGR B16 125 F3
St Augustus Cl HHTH/SAND B71 88 B3
St Austell Rd DSYBK/YTR WS5 58 B1
St Bartholomew Ter
DARL/WED WS10 55 H5
St Benedict's Cl WBROM B70 88 B4
St Benedicts Rd SMHTH B10 128 D4
WMBN WV5 65 E4
St Bernards Rd
CSCFLD/WYGN B72 77 G1
SOLH B91 163 H5
St Blaise Av CSHL/WTROR B46 96 B4
St Blaise Rd MGN/WHC B75 47 H2
St Brades Cl OLDBY B69 104 A2
St Brides Cl SEDG DY3 67 E3
WMBN WV5 64 D5
Saintbury Dr SOLH B91 196 A1
St Caroline Cl WBROM B70 88 B3
St Catharines Cl WSL WS1 57 G1
St Catherines Cl DUDS DY2 * 85 G5
MGN/WHC B75 63 F1
St Catherine's Crs
ETTPK/GDPK/PENN WV4 51 F4
St Chad's Circus Queensway
CBHAMNW B3 3 F3
St Chad's Cl SEDG DY3 82 D3
St Chads Queensway
CBHAMNE B4 3 G2
St Chad's Rd BILS/COS WV14 54 B1
MGN/WHC B75 63 E3
RBRY B45 187 H1
WOLVN WV10 23 H2
St Christopher Cl WBROM B70 88 A4
St Christophers
BFLD/HDSWWD B20 89 H2
St Clement's Av BLOX/PEL WS3 27 G3
St Clement's La
HHTH/SAND B71 87 H2
St Clements Rd
VAUX/NECH B7 110 A3
St Columbas Dr RBRY B45 188 D1
St Cuthbert's Cl WBROM B70 88 B4
St Davids Cl BLOX/PEL WS3 18 B2
WBROM B70 88 B4
St Davids Dr RIDG/WDGT B32 140 B2
St Davids Gv
BFLD/HDSWWD B20 89 H2
St Davids Pl BLOX/PEL WS3 17 F5
St Denis Rd SLYOAK B29 158 C4
St Dominic's Rd
ERDE/BCHGN B24 92 C5
St Edburghs Rd STETCH B33 130 A3
St Edmund's Cl
DUNHL/THL/PER WV6 * 36 B2
WBROM B70 88 B4
St Edward's Rd SLYOAK B29 142 D5
St Eleanor Cl WBROM B70 88 B3
St Francis Av SOLH B91 164 A4
St Francis Cl BLOX/PEL WS3 18 B2
St George Dr SMTHWK B66 * 106 C2
St Georges Av
ERDW/GRVHL B23 93 E1
St Georges Cl EDG B15 126 A5
MGN/WHC B75 63 F2
St Georges Ct FOAKS/STRLY B74 32 C5
St Georges Pde BKHL/PFLD WV2 7 G5
St Georges Pl WBROM B70 87 G2
St Georges Rd DUDS DY2 102 D3
SHLY B90 180 D5
STRBR DY8 134 D5
St George's St DARL/WED WS10 55 F1
LOZ/NWT B19 2 E1
St Gerards Rd SOLH B91 181 E3
St Giles Av BLKHTH/ROWR B65 103 H5
St Giles Cl BLKHTH/ROWR B65 103 H5
St Giles Crs WOLV WV1 38 A3
St Giles Rd STETCH B33 131 F2
WLNHL WV13 39 H4
WOLV WV1 38 A3
St Giles Rw STRBR DY8 * 135 G1
St Giles St DUDS DY2 102 C4
St Helens Av TPTN/OCK DY4 86 A1
St Helen's Rd SOLH B91 164 C4
St Heliers Rd NFLD/LBR B31 175 E1
St Ives Rd DSYBK/YTR WS5 58 B1
St James Av
BLKHTH/ROWR B65 103 G5
St James Cl BLOX/PEL WS3 * 18 B2
WBROM B70 88 B4
St James Pl SHLY B90 180 B3
VAUX/NECH B7 127 G1
St James Rd EDG B15 126 B4
HDSW B21 107 F1
MGN/WHC B75 47 G3
OLDBY B69 104 B1
St James's Rd DUDN DY1 84 B4
St James's Ter DUDN DY1 84 A4
St James St DARL/WED WS10 70 C1
SEDG DY3 83 F3
WOLV WV1 7 J5
St James Wk BRWNH WS8 9 F5
St John Cl MGN/WHC B75 47 H1
St Johns Av
BLKHTH/ROWR B65 103 H5
St John's Cl ALDR WS9 19 F4
DOR/KN B93 197 F2
SEDG DY3 80 B4
WBROM B70 88 B4
St Johns Ct NFLD/LBR B31 175 H4
St Johns Gv
CHWD/FDBR/MGN B37 131 H1
St Johns Rd BLOX/PEL WS3 18 B2
BRWNH WS8 19 G2
DARL/WED WS10 55 E3
DUDS DY2 102 D1
HALE B63 138 A3
HRBN B17 142 B1
LGLYGN/QTN B68 105 G4
SPARK B11 145 E2
STRBR DY8 135 G1
TPTN/OCK DY4 69 F4
WNSFLD WV11 15 E4
WSLW WS2 41 F5
St John's Sq BKHL/PFLD WV2 7 F6
St John's St DUDS DY2 102 C4
St Johns Wk PBAR/PBCH B42 90 D2
St Johns Wd RBRY B45 188 B3
St Josephs Av NFLD/LBR B31 158 D5
St Josephs Cl BLOX/PEL WS3 18 A3
St Josephs Rd WASH/WDE B8 111 F4
St Joseph St DUDS DY2 84 D5
St Judes Cl
ALE/KHTH/YWD B14 178 B3
MGN/WHC B75 63 F2
St Jude's Pas DIG/EDG B5 * 3 F7
St Jude's Rd
DUNHL/THL/PER WV6 36 B2
St Jude's Rd West
DUNHL/THL/PER WV6 36 B2
St Katherine's Rd
LGLYGN/QTN B68 123 G2
St Kenelms Av HALE B63 154 D1
St Kenelm's Cl WBROM B70 88 B4
St Kenelm's Rd RMSLY B62 154 D5
St Kilda's Rd WASH/WDE B8 * 110 C4
St Laurence Rd NFLD/LBR B31 158 C5
St Lawrence Cl DOR/KN B93 197 F3
St Lawrence Wy
DARL/WED WS10 55 F2
St Leonards Cl
CHWD/FDBR/MGN B37 132 A5
St Loye's Cl RMSLY B62 122 B5
St Lukes Cl BLKHTH/ROWR B65 103 H5
St Luke's Rd DARL/WED WS10 56 B5
DIG/EDG B5 127 E5
St Lukes St CDYHTH B64 120 D3
St Margaret's FOAKS/STRLY B74 46 A2
St Margarets Av
WASH/WDE B8 111 F3
St Margarets Dr HALE B63 138 B5
St Margarets Rd BLOX/PEL WS3 18 A3
GTB/HAM B43 73 H1
HIA/OLT B92 164 A1
WASH/WDE B8 111 E3
St Marks Crs CBHAMW B1 126 A1
St Mark's Rd BDMR/CCFT WV3 6 C5
BLOX/PEL WS3 18 A3
BRWNH WS8 19 G2
DUDS DY2 85 F5
HAG/WOL DY9 136 B2
SMTHWKW B67 123 H1
TPTN/OCK DY4 69 G3
St Mark's St BDMR/CCFT WV3 6 D5
CBHAMW B1 2 A3
St Martin's Cl BKHL/PFLD WV2 52 C2
WBROM B70 88 B4
St Martin's Dr TPTN/OCK DY4 85 G1
St Martins Rd MGN/WHC B75 63 F3
St Martin's St EDG B15 126 B3
St Martin's Ter BILS/COS WV14 54 A5
St Marys Cl ACGN B27 146 B4
BILS/COS WV14 67 H3
ERDE/BCHGN B24 93 H2
St Marys Ct WLNHL WV13 * 39 G3
St Mary's La STRBR DY8 135 H4
St Mary's Rd DARL/WED WS10 55 H5
HRBN B17 142 A2
St Mary's Rw CBHAMNE B4 3 G3
MOS/BIL B13 144 B4
St Mary's Wy ALDR WS9 30 A5
St Matthews Cl BLOX/PEL WS3 * 18 B2
WSL WS1 5 F5
St Matthews Rd
LGLYGN/QTN B68 123 E2
SMTHWK B66 107 E4
St Matthew St WOLV WV1 37 H4
St Mawes Rd
DUNHL/THL/PER WV6 34 D2
St Mawgen Cl CVALE B35 95 E2
St Michael's Cl BLOX/PEL WS3 17 H5
St Michael's Ct
DUNHL/THL/PER WV6 22 A5
St Michael's Crs OLDBY B69 104 D5
St Michael's Gv DUDS DY2 85 F5
St Michael's Rd
SCFLD/BOLD B73 76 D3
SEDG DY3 82 B1
WSNGN B18 108 A2
St Michael St WBROM B70 87 G3
WSL WS1 4 E7
St Michaels Wy TPTN/OCK DY4 85 G3
St Nicholas Cl BLOX/PEL WS3 18 A3
St Nicolas Gdns
HWK/WKHTH B38 176 D3
St Oswalds Rd SMHTH B10 128 C4
St Patricks Cl
ALE/KHTH/YWD B14 161 E4
St Paul's Av BHTH/HG B12 144 C2
St Pauls Crs BLOX/PEL WS3 18 B2
CSHL/WTROR B46 115 G2
WBROM B70 70 C4
St Pauls Dr RMSLY B62 122 B3
TPTN/OCK DY4 85 H2
St Paul's Rd BHTH/HG B12 144 B1
DARL/WED WS10 56 B3
DUDS DY2 102 D4
SMTHWK B66 105 H2
St Paul's Sq CBHAMNW B3 2 E2
St Paul's St WSL WS1 4 E3
St Peters Cl CSCFLD/WYGN B72 62 B5
CSHL/WTROR B46 96 B4
HLGN/YWD B28 162 B4
TPTN/OCK DY4 86 B2
St Peters Ct BLOX/PEL WS3 27 F1
St Peters Cft SCFLD/BOLD B73 * 62 B5
St Peters Dr BLOX/PEL WS3 18 A3
St Peters La HIA/OLT B92 166 D2
St Peter's Rd
BFLD/HDSWWD B20 90 C5
DUDS DY2 102 D3
HAG/WOL DY9 153 E1
HRBN B17 141 H2
St Peters Sq WOLV WV1 7 F3
St Peters Ter WSLW WS2 42 A1
St Philips Av BDMR/CCFT WV3 51 G1
St Philips Pl CBHAMNW B3 3 G4
St Phillips Av BDMR/CCFT WV3 51 F1
St Phillip's Gv BDMR/CCFT WV3 51 F1
St Quentin St WSLW WS2 41 G5
St Saviour's Cl BKHL/PFLD WV2 52 D2
St Saviour's Rd WASH/WDE B8 110 B5
St Silas' Sq LOZ/NWT B19 108 B2
St Simons Cl MGN/WHC B75 63 F2
St Stephen's Av WLNHL WV13 39 F3
St Stephens Gdns
WLNHL WV13 * 39 G4
St Stephens Rd
HHTH/SAND B71 106 D1
SLYOAK B29 160 B2
St Stephens St AST/WIT B6 109 E3
St Thomas' Cl ALDR WS9 30 B1
BLOX/PEL WS3 28 A4
MGN/WHC B75 63 F3
St Thomas' Rd
ERDW/GRVHL B23 92 B4
St Thomas St DUDS DY2 102 C4
St Valentines Cl WBROM B70 88 B4
St Vincent Crs WBROM B70 70 D5
St Vincent St LDYWD/EDGR B16 2 A5
St Vincent St West
LDYWD/EDGR B16 126 A2
Saladin Av OLDBY B69 104 C4
Salcombe Av
LGN/SDN/BHAMAIR B26 148 A2
Salcombe Dr BRLYHL DY5 119 E4
Salcombe Gv BILS/COS WV14 68 D2
Salcombe Rd SMTHWK B66 106 D4
Salem St TPTN/OCK DY4 86 B1
Salford St AST/WIT B6 110 A1
Salisbury Chambers
MOS/BIL B13 * 144 B3
Salisbury Cl DUDN DY1 83 H3
MOS/BIL B13 144 A4
Salisbury Dr CSHL/WTROR B46 96 C3
Salisbury Gv CSCFLD/WYGN B72 77 G4
Salisbury Rd LOZ/NWT B19 108 D1
MOS/BIL B13 144 A4
SMTHWK B66 106 D5
WASH/WDE B8 110 C4
WBROM B70 88 A5
Salisbury St BDMR/CCFT WV3 6 C6
DARL/WED WS10 55 G1
Sallow Gv BRWNH WS8 9 F3
Sally Ward Dr ALDR WS9 19 G3
Salop Cl HHTH/SAND B71 71 F4
Salop Dr LGLYGN/QTN B68 123 G2
Salop Rd LGLYGN/QTN B68 123 G1
Salop St BHTH/HG B12 127 F4
BILS/COS WV14 54 A4
BKHL/PFLD WV2 6 E5
DUDN DY1 84 A4
OLDBY B69 86 C5
Salstar Cl AST/WIT B6 109 E1
Saltash Gv YDLY B25 129 G3
Saltbrook Rd HAG/WOL DY9 120 A5
Salter Rd TPTN/OCK DY4 69 F4
Salter's La HHTH/SAND B71 88 A2
Salter's Rd ALDR WS9 19 G4
Salters V WBROM B70 88 A5
Saltley Cottages
ERDE/BCHGN B24 * 92 D5
Saltley Rd VAUX/NECH B7 109 H4
Saltley Viad VAUX/NECH B7 110 A4
Saltney Cl ERDE/BCHGN B24 93 H1
Saltwells La DUDS DY2 120 A2
Saltwells Rd DUDS DY2 120 B2
Salwarpe Gv SLYOAK B29 141 F5
Sambourn Cl SOLH B91 165 G4
Sambourne Dr
BKDE/SHDE B34 113 F2
Sambrook Rd WOLVN WV10 24 A4
Sampson Cl HDSW B21 89 E5
OLDBY B69 104 A2
Sampson Rd SPARK B11 127 H5
Sampson Rd North SPARK B11 127 G4
Sampson St DARL/WED WS10 56 B5
Sams La WBROM B70 87 G4
Samuels Rd RIDG/WDGT B32 140 A2
Samuel St BLOX/PEL WS3 27 F1
Sanda Cft CBROM B36 114 B3
Sandals Cl NFLD/LBR B31 174 D4
Sandal Ri SOLH B91 182 C2
Sandals Ri RMSLY B62 139 F4
Sandalwood Cl SHHTH WV12 25 H2
Sand Bank BLOX/PEL WS3 27 F1
Sandbarn Cl SHLY B90 195 F2
Sandbeds Rd SHHTH WV12 40 A1
Sandbourne Rd
WASH/WDE B8 111 E5
Sanderling Ri BRLYHL DY5 100 C3
Sanders Cl DUDS DY2 103 E2
Sandfield Cl SHLY B90 180 A5
Sandfield Gv SEDG DY3 82 D4
Sandfield Rd HHTH/SAND B71 72 A2
STRBR DY8 118 B2
Sandfields Av SMHTH B10 127 H4
Sandfields Rd
LGLYGN/QTN B68 123 G2
Sandford Av
BLKHTH/ROWR B65 122 A1
Sandford Ri
DUNHL/THL/PER WV6 22 A4
Sandford Rd DUDN DY1 83 G5
MOS/BIL B13 144 C4
Sandgate Rd HLGN/YWD B28 179 H1
TPTN/OCK DY4 69 G3
Sandhills Crs SOLH B91 181 H5
Sandhill St BLOX/PEL WS3 27 E1
Sandhurst Av CBROM B36 111 H3
HAG/WOL DY9 136 B5
Sandhurst Dr
ETTPK/GDPK/PENN WV4 51 G4
Sandhurst Gv STRBR DY8 118 A1
Sandhurst Rd
FOAKS/STRLY B74 32 D5
KGSWFD DY6 100 C5
MOS/BIL B13 144 A5
Sandland Cl BILS/COS WV14 54 B2
Sandland Rd SHHTH WV12 26 A2
Sandmartin Cl DUDS DY2 120 C2
Sandmere Gv
ALE/KHTH/YWD B14 179 F2
Sandmere Ri WOLVN WV10 23 G1
Sandmere Rd
ALE/KHTH/YWD B14 179 F2
Sandon Gv ERDE/BCHGN B24 93 E2
Sandon Rd HAG/WOL DY9 136 D3
HRBN B17 124 C3
WOLVN WV10 12 B5
Sandown Dr
DUNHL/THL/PER WV6 34 D1
Sandown Rd CBROM B36 111 H1
Sandpiper Cl HAG/WOL DY9 136 D2
Sandpiper Gdns
HWK/WKHTH B38 190 D1
Sandpiper Wy
ERDW/GRVHL B23 76 A5
Sandpit SLYOAK B29 * 159 G2
Sand Pits Pde CBHAMW B1 2 B4
Sandra Cl ALDR WS9 30 B5
Sandringham Av SHHTH WV12 25 H4
Sandringham Dr ALDR WS9 30 B1
BLKHTH/ROWR B65 104 A5
Sandringham Pl STRBR DY8 117 H3
Sandringham Rd
ETTPK/GDPK/PENN WV4 51 G4
PBAR/PBCH B42 74 B5
RMSLY B62 121 H5
STRBR DY8 117 G3
WMBN WV5 64 D5
Sandringham Wy BRLYHL DY5 119 E4
Sandstone Av RBRY B45 174 A5
Sandstone Cl SEDG DY3 83 F2
Sand St WBROM B70 86 C2
Sandway Gdns WASH/WDE B8 110 B3
Sandway Gv MOS/BIL B13 162 A3
Sandwell Av DARL/WED WS10 54 D3
Sandwell Pl SHHTH WV12 26 B3
Sandwell Rd HDSW B21 89 F5
WBROM B70 87 G2
WOLVN WV10 22 D1

Sandwell Rd North
HHTH/SAND B71 87 H2
Sandwell St WSL WS1 5 F6
Sandwell Wk WSL WS1 5 F7
Sandwood Dr KGSTG B44 75 F3
Sandyacre Wy STRBR DY8 135 H2
Sandy Crs WNSFLD WV11 25 G2
Sandy Cft CSCFLD/WYGN B72 62 C5
MOS/BIL B13 162 A3
Sandyfields Rd SEDG DY3 82 B1
Sandy Gv BRWNH WS8 9 F3
Sandy Hill Ri SHLY B90 180 A1
Sandy Hill Rd SHLY B90 180 A1
Sandy Hollow
DUNHL/THL/PER WV6 35 G3
Sandy La AST/WIT B6 109 G2
BRGRVW B61 186 B3
CDSL WV8 10 B3
DARL/WED WS10 57 F5
DUNHL/THL/PER WV6 22 A4
KIDD DY10 168 B5
PBAR/PBCH B42 74 D3
WOLVN WV10 23 G1
Sandy Mt WMBN WV5 65 F4
Sandy Mount Rd WSL WS1 5 G7
Sandys Gv TPTN/OCK DY4 85 E1
Sandy Wy EDG B15 2 B7
Sangwin Rd TPTN/OCK DY4 68 C4
Sansome Ri SHLY B90 179 H3
Sansome Rd SHLY B90 179 H3
Sanstone Cl BLOX/PEL WS3 17 E4
Sanstone Rd BLOX/PEL WS3 16 D4
Santolina Dr DSYBK/YTR WS5 57 G5
Sant Rd NFLD/LBR B31 189 H1
The Saplings WALM/CURD B76 78 C3
Saracen Dr MGN/WHC B75 63 F2
Sara Cl FOAKS/STRLY B74 47 E2
Sarah Cl BILS/COS WV14 69 E2
Sarah Gdns DSYBK/YTR WS5 57 F4
Sarah St BORD B9 127 H2
Saredon Cl BLOX/PEL WS3 28 C1
Sarehole Rd HLGN/YWD B28 162 B3
Sargent Cl GTB/HAM B43 59 H4
Sark Dr CBROM B36 114 B3
Saunton Wy SLYOAK B29 159 E1
Saveker Dr WALM/CURD B76 63 E4
Savernake Cl RBRY B45 174 A3
Saville Cl RBRY B45 188 B1
Savoy Cl RIDG/WDGT B32 141 F2
Saw Mill Cl RUSH/SHEL WS4 4 E1
Saxelby Cl
ALE/KHTH/YWD B14 178 A3
Saxoncourt
DUNHL/THL/PER WV6 21 G5
Saxondale Av
LGN/SDN/BHAMAIR B26 147 F1
Saxon Dr BLKHTH/ROWR B65 104 A5
Saxonfields
DUNHL/THL/PER WV6 21 G5
Saxons Wy
ALE/KHTH/YWD B14 178 C3
Saxon Wy
CHWD/FDBR/MGN B37 131 H1
Saxon Wood Cl NFLD/LBR B31 175 G1
Saxon Wood Rd SHLY B90 194 D3
Saxton Dr FOAKS/STRLY B74 32 D4
Scafell Dr BILS/COS WV14 54 B1
ERDW/GRVHL B23 92 A1
Scafell Rd STRBR DY8 135 H1
Scampton Cl
DUNHL/THL/PER WV6 20 C5
Scarborough Cl WSLW WS2 41 F5
Scarborough Rd WSLW WS2 41 E5
Scarecrow La MGN/WHC B75 48 A1
Scarsdale Rd PBAR/PBCH B42 74 D3
Schofield Av HHTH/SAND B71 71 F3
Schofield Rd
CHWD/FDBR/MGN B37 113 H4
Scholars Ga STETCH B33 130 D2
Schoolacre Ri FOAKS/STRLY B74 45 E4
Schoolacre Rd
BKDE/SHDE B34 112 D3
School Av BRWNH WS8 9 F4
School Cl BDMR/CCFT WV3 50 B1
CDSL WV8 10 C3
CHWD/FDBR/MGN B37 114 A3
OLDBY B69 104 A2
WMBN WV5 64 A2
School Cottages WOLVN WV10 * 12 B5
School Dr BILS/COS WV14 * 68 C2
BILS/COS WV14 69 G1
HLYWD B47 192 C5
STRBR DY8 118 B4
The School Dr DUDS DY2 102 D2
Schoolgate Cl RUSH/SHEL WS4 29 F1
WASH/WDE B8 111 E3
School Gn BILS/COS WV14 38 C5
Schoolhouse Cl
HWK/WKHTH B38 177 F3
School La BKDE/SHDE B34 112 D2
BLOX/PEL WS3 17 H3
BRLYHL DY5 100 D5
HAG/WOL DY9 153 F4
HALE B63 138 B5
SOLH B91 182 B1
STETCH B33 130 B3
WOLVN WV10 12 D5
School Rd ALE/KHTH/YWD B14 161 F1
ALE/KHTH/YWD B14 178 D1
BRLYHL DY5 120 A2
DARL/WED WS10 71 H1
DUNHL/THL/PER WV6 35 E1
HLGN/YWD B28 162 D2
RBRY B45 187 G2
SEDG DY3 81 F3
SHLY B90 180 B3
WMBN WV5 64 A2
WMBN WV5 65 F4
WNSFLD WV11 24 B4
School St BRLYHL DY5 101 F2
CDYHTH B64 120 D3
DARL/WED WS10 55 E2
DARL/WED WS10 55 F3
DUDN DY1 84 B5
RUSH/SHEL WS4 29 F1
SEDG DY3 67 G3
STRBR DY8 135 F1
WLNHL WV13 39 F3
WOLV WV1 6 E5
School St West BILS/COS WV14 68 C3
School Ter SLYOAK B29 * 142 D5
School Wk BILS/COS WV14 38 C5
Scorers Cl HIA/OLT B92 163 F4
The Scotchings CBROM B36 112 A1
Scotland La RIDG/WDGT B32 157 G3
Scotland St CBHAMW B1 2 C4
Scott Av DARL/WED WS10 71 F1
ETTPK/GDPK/PENN WV4 51 E4
Scott Gv HIA/OLT B92 147 E4
Scott Rd DSYBK/YTR WS5 58 B2
GTB/HAM B43 73 H1
HIA/OLT B92 147 E5
Scott's Green Cl DUDN DY1 101 H1
Scott's Rd STRBR DY8 135 F1
Scott St TPTN/OCK DY4 86 A1
Scotwell Cl BLKHTH/ROWR B65 121 H1
Scout Cl STETCH B33 131 E2
Scribbans Cl SMTHWK B66 106 D5
Scribers La HLGN/YWD B28 179 G1
Sculthorpe Rd KIDD DY10 168 B3
Seacroft Av STETCH B33 130 A3
Seafield Cl KGSWFD DY6 100 A5
Seaforth Gv SHHTH WV12 25 H1
Seagar St HHTH/SAND B71 87 H2
Seager's La BRLYHL DY5 119 F2
Seagull Bay Dr BILS/COS WV14 68 D2
Seal Cl WALM/CURD B76 63 E5
Seals Gn HWK/WKHTH B38 190 B1
Seaton Cl WNSFLD WV11 25 F5
Seaton Gv MOS/BIL B13 160 D1
Seaton Pl STRBR DY8 117 G2
Second Av BORD B9 128 C3
BRWNH WS8 9 G4
KGSWFD DY6 100 C2
SLYOAK B29 143 F4
WOLVN WV10 23 H4
Second Exhibition Av
BHAMNEC B40 149 H3
Sedge Av HWK/WKHTH B38 176 D2
Sedgeberrow Covert
HWK/WKHTH B38 176 C5
Sedgeberrow Rd HALE B63 138 C5
Sedgebourne Cl
NFLD/LBR B31 174 C4
Sedgefield Cl DUDN DY1 83 G3
Sedgefield Gv
DUNHL/THL/PER WV6 34 D1
Sedgeford Cl BRLYHL DY5 119 F4
Sedgehill Av HRBN B17 141 H3
Sedgemere Gv RUSH/SHEL WS4 29 E2
Sedgemere Rd
LGN/SDN/BHAMAIR B26 130 B3
Sedgley Gv BFLD/HDSWWD B20 89 G2
Sedgley Hall Av SEDG DY3 67 E3
Sedgley Rd
ETTPK/GDPK/PENN WV4 66 B1
Sedgley Rd East TPTN/OCK DY4 85 G2
Sedgley Rd West
TPTN/OCK DY4 68 C5
Sedgley St BKHL/PFLD WV2 52 A1
Seedhouse Ct CDYHTH B64 121 G4
Seeds La BRWNH WS8 9 F4
Seeleys Rd SPARK B11 145 F3
Sefton Dr BLKHTH/ROWR B65 103 F3
Sefton Gv DARL/WED WS10 70 A1
Sefton Rd LDYWD/EDGR B16 125 H3
Segbourne Rd RBRY B45 173 G5
Segundo Cl DSYBK/YTR WS5 57 E4
Segundo Rd DSYBK/YTR WS5 57 F4
Selborne Cl WSL WS1 * 5 H4
Selborne Gv MOS/BIL B13 162 A5
Selborne Rd
BFLD/HDSWWD B20 90 A4
DUDS DY2 102 D2
Selborne St WSL WS1 5 H4
Selbourne Crs WOLV WV1 38 B4
Selby Cl
LGN/SDN/BHAMAIR B26 130 B3
Selby Gv MOS/BIL B13 162 A5
Selby Wy BLOX/PEL WS3 16 A5
Selcombe Wy
HWK/WKHTH B38 190 D1
Selcroft Av RIDG/WDGT B32 141 F2
Selecta Av KGSTG B44 74 D1
Selkirk Cl HHTH/SAND B71 71 G5
Selly Av SLYOAK B29 143 E5
Selly Cl SLYOAK B29 143 F5
Selly Hall Cft BVILLE B30 159 H4
Selly Hill Rd SLYOAK B29 142 D5
Selly Oak Rd BVILLE B30 159 G3
Selly Park Rd SLYOAK B29 143 E5
Selly Whf SLYOAK B29 159 G1
Sellywick Dr SLYOAK B29 143 F5
Selly Wick Rd SLYOAK B29 143 E5
Sellywood Rd BVILLE B30 159 G3
Selma Gv ALE/KHTH/YWD B14 162 B5
Selmans Hl BLOX/PEL WS3 17 E4
Selmans Pde BLOX/PEL WS3 * 17 E5
Selsdon Cl HLYWD B47 193 E3
Selsdon Rd BLOX/PEL WS3 16 B4
Selsey Av HRBN B17 124 D1
Selsey Rd HRBN B17 124 D1
Selston Rd AST/WIT B6 109 E2
Selvey Av GTB/HAM B43 59 F5
Selworthy Rd CBROM B36 113 H2
Selwyn Cl BKHL/PFLD WV2 52 A1
Selwyn Rd BILS/COS WV14 54 B2
LDYWD/EDGR B16 125 F1
Selwyn Wk FOAKS/STRLY B74 46 A1
Senneleys Park Rd
NFLD/LBR B31 158 A2
Sennen Cl WLNHL WV13 39 F4
Sensall Rd HAG/WOL DY9 136 D4
Sentry Wy MGN/WHC B75 63 G2
Serpentine Rd AST/WIT B6 91 G5
HRBN B17 142 A2
SLYOAK B29 143 E4
Settle Av BKDE/SHDE B34 112 B3
Settle Cft
CHWD/FDBR/MGN B37 131 H3
Setton Dr SEDG DY3 67 G4
Seven Acres ALDR WS9 30 B5
Seven Acres Rd NFLD/LBR B31 176 A4
RMSLY B62 140 A2
Sevendwellings Vw
BRLYHL DY5 119 E3
Seven Star Rd SOLH B91 164 C5
Seven Stars Rd OLDBY B69 105 E3
Severn Cl CBROM B36 113 H2
SHHTH WV12 25 G3
TPTN/OCK DY4 85 F1
Severn Dr BRLYHL DY5 100 D2
DUNHL/THL/PER WV6 34 C1
Severne Gv ACGN B27 163 G1
Severne Rd ACGN B27 163 G2
Severn Gv LOZ/NWT B19 * 108 C2
SPARK B11 * 145 E1
Severn Rd BLOX/PEL WS3 27 H2
BRWNH WS8 8 C2
HALE B63 137 F2
STRBR DY8 135 F4
Severn St CBHAMW B1 2 E7
Sevington Cl SOLH B91 182 A5
Seymour Cl SLYOAK B29 143 F5
Seymour Gdns
FOAKS/STRLY B74 46 C3
Seymour Rd HAG/WOL DY9 136 D2
OLDBY B69 105 G2
TPTN/OCK DY4 70 A2
Shackleton Dr
DUNHL/THL/PER WV6 20 B5
Shackleton Rd BLOX/PEL WS3 17 F5
Shadowbrook La HIA/OLT B92 166 D3
Shadwell Dr SEDG DY3 83 F4
Shadwell St CBHAMNE B4 3 G2
Shady La KGSTG B44 74 D1
Shadymoor Dr BRLYHL DY5 119 E4
Shaftesbury Av HAG/WOL DY9 136 A4
Shaftesbury Rd
DARL/WED WS10 71 F1
Shaftesbury Sq
HHTH/SAND B71 87 G1
Shaftesbury St
HHTH/SAND B71 87 G2
Shaftmoor La HLGN/YWD B28 145 G5
Shaftsbury Av HALE B63 120 B5
Shaftsbury Cl BILS/COS WV14 54 B1
Shaftsbury Rd
LGN/SDN/BHAMAIR B26 148 A2
Shahjalal Rd WASH/WDE B8 110 B4
Shakespeare Cl BILS/COS WV14 68 D1
Shakespeare Crs BLOX/PEL WS3 28 A2
Shakespeare Dr SHLY B90 180 B4
Shakespeare Pl BLOX/PEL WS3 28 A3
Shakespeare Rd AST/WIT B6 91 H3
SEDG DY3 82 C2
SHLY B90 180 D4
SMTHWKW B67 105 H5
TPTN/OCK DY4 69 G3
Shakespeare St SPARK B11 145 E2
WOLV WV1 7 J5
Shaldon Wk SMTHWK B66 106 D4
The Shales WMBN WV5 * 80 C1
Shale St BILS/COS WV14 53 G3
Shalford Rd HIA/OLT B92 147 E3
Shallcross La SEDG DY3 83 F3
Shalnecote Gv
ALE/KHTH/YWD B14 160 C5
Shambles DARL/WED WS10 70 D1
Shandon Cl RIDG/WDGT B32 141 F4
Shannon Dr BRWNH WS8 8 C2
Shannon Rd HWK/WKHTH B38 176 D5
Shapinsay Dr RBRY B45 173 H4
Shard End Crs BKDE/SHDE B34 113 E4
Shardlow Rd WNSFLD WV11 25 E2
The Shardway
BKDE/SHDE B34 113 E4
Sharesacre St WLNHL WV13 39 H2
Sharington Cl DUDS DY2 103 E1
Sharman Rd WOLVN WV10 23 G4
Sharmans Cross Rd SOLH B91 181 E1
Sharon Cl
ETTPK/GDPK/PENN WV4 52 C3
Sharps Cl RBRY B45 188 A1
Sharrat Fld MGN/WHC B75 47 H3
Sharrocks St WOLV WV1 7 J6
Shawberry Av CVALE B35 94 C3
Shawberry Rd
CHWD/FDBR/MGN B37 * 113 H4
Shawbrook Gv
ALE/KHTH/YWD B14 178 C2
Shawbury Gv BHTH/HG B12 127 F4
DUNHL/THL/PER WV6 20 C5
Shawbury Rd WOLVN WV10 23 H5
Shaw Dr STETCH B33 130 A2
Shawfield HLYWD B47 192 C3
Shaw Hellier Av BRLYHL DY5 119 G2
Shaw Hill Rd WASH/WDE B8 111 E5
Shawhurst Cft HLYWD B47 192 C1
Shawhurst La HLYWD B47 192 C2
Shaw La
DUNHL/THL/PER WV6 35 F2
Shawley Cft ACGN B27 147 E3
Shaw Rd BILS/COS WV14 68 B2
BKHL/PFLD WV2 52 A2
DUDS DY2 102 B2
TPTN/OCK DY4 86 A2
WOLVN WV10 23 F4
Shawsdale Rd CBROM B36 112 B2
Shaw's Pas DIG/EDG B5 3 J5
Shaw St WBROM B70 70 C3
WSLW WS2 4 D2
Shayler Gv BKHL/PFLD WV2 52 B1
Sheaf La
LGN/SDN/BHAMAIR B26 147 H3
Shearwater Cl RBRY B45 187 H2
Shearwater Wk
ERDW/GRVHL B23 75 H5
Sheaves Cl
ETTPK/GDPK/PENN WV4 53 E5
Shedden St DUDS DY2 102 D1
Sheddington Rd
ERDW/GRVHL B23 76 B4
Sheen Rd KGSTG B44 60 A4
Sheepclose Dr
CHWD/FDBR/MGN B37 132 A1
Sheepcote St LDYWD/EDGR B16 2 A5
Sheepfold Cl
BLKHTH/ROWR B65 103 G5
Sheepmoor Cl HRBN B17 124 B4
Sheepwash La TPTN/OCK DY4 86 B1
Sheerwater Dr BRLYHL DY5 119 E5
Sheffield Rd SCFLD/BOLD B73 77 E4
Sheffield St BRLYHL DY5 120 A3
Shefford Rd AST/WIT B6 109 F4
Sheila Av WNSFLD WV11 25 E3
Shelah Rd HALE B63 138 C1
Shelbourne Cl OLDBY B69 86 B4
Sheldon Av DARL/WED WS10 56 A4
Sheldon Cl BILS/COS WV14 53 H5
Sheldon Dr NFLD/LBR B31 174 D4
Sheldonfield Rd
LGN/SDN/BHAMAIR B26 148 B3
Sheldon Gv
LGN/SDN/BHAMAIR B26 147 H2
Sheldon Hall Av STETCH B33 131 F1
Sheldon Heath Rd STETCH B33 130 C2
Sheldon Rd HHTH/SAND B71 72 A3
WOLVN WV10 22 C1
Shelfield Cl HOCK/TIA B94 198 A5
Shelfield Rd
ALE/KHTH/YWD B14 177 G2
Shelley Av TPTN/OCK DY4 69 G3
Shelley Cl SEDG DY3 82 C1
STRBR DY8 118 C4
Shelley Dr AST/WIT B6 91 H3
FOAKS/STRLY B74 32 D4
Shelley Rd SHHTH WV12 26 C3
WOLVN WV10 12 D5
Shelly Cl
CHWD/FDBR/MGN B37 131 H2
Shelly Crs SHLY B90 195 H2
Shelly Cft STETCH B33 130 C1
Shelly La SHLY B90 195 H2
Shelsley Av OLDBY B69 104 B4
Shelsley Dr MOS/BIL B13 161 H1
Shelsley Wy SOLH B91 181 H4
Shelton Cl DARL/WED WS10 56 C3
Shelton La HALE B63 138 A2
Shelwick Gv DOR/KN B93 196 D4
Shenley Av DUDN DY1 68 B5
Shenley Fields Dr
NFLD/LBR B31 158 A2
Shenley Fields Rd SLYOAK B29 158 C3
Shenley Gdns SLYOAK B29 158 C3
Shenley Hl NFLD/LBR B31 158 A4
Shenley La SLYOAK B29 158 C4
Shenstone Av RMSLY B62 139 G3
STRBR DY8 134 D5
Shenstone Cl FOAKS/STRLY B74 32 C4
Shenstone Ct BDMR/CCFT WV3 51 G2
Shenstone Dr ALDR WS9 30 A2
Shenstone Rd
ALE/KHTH/YWD B14 178 C4
GTB/HAM B43 73 G3
LDYWD/EDGR B16 125 E1
Shenstone Valley Rd
RMSLY B62 139 H1
Shenton Wk
CHWD/FDBR/MGN B37 113 H4
Shepheard Rd
LGN/SDN/BHAMAIR B26 148 B2
Shepherd Dr SHHTH WV12 25 H5
Shepherds Brook Rd
HAG/WOL DY9 136 B2
Shepherds Fold
BLKHTH/ROWR B65 121 H2
Shepherds Gdns EDG B15 126 B3
Shepherds Green Rd
ERDE/BCHGN B24 92 D4
Shepherds Pool Rd
MGN/WHC B75 48 A3
Shepherds Standing
BKDE/SHDE B34 * 112 D3
Shepherds Wy
ERDW/GRVHL B23 76 A3
Shepley Rd RBRY B45 188 B2
Sheppey Dr CBROM B36 114 B4
Shepwell Gn WLNHL WV13 40 A4
Sherard Cft CBROM B36 114 B3
Sheraton Cl ALDR WS9 30 B4
Sheraton Gra STRBR DY8 135 F5
Sherborne Cl BLOX/PEL WS3 27 G3
CSHL/WTROR B46 115 G5
Sherborne Gdns CDSL WV8 10 C4
Sherborne Gv CBHAMW B1 126 A1
Sherborne Rd WOLVN WV10 23 F1
Sherborne St
LDYWD/EDGR B16 2 A6
Sherbourne Dr ACGN B27 146 C3
Sherbourne Rd ACGN B27 146 B3
BHTH/HG B12 127 E5
CDYHTH B64 121 G4
STRBR DY8 135 H3
Sherdmore Cft SHLY B90 195 F2
Sheridan Cl WSLW WS2 56 B1
Sheridan Gdns SEDG DY3 82 B1
Sheridan St HHTH/SAND B71 87 H2
WSLW WS2 56 B1
Sheridan Wk CVALE B35 * 94 C3
Sheriff Dr BRLYHL DY5 119 H2
Sherifoot La MGN/WHC B75 47 F2
Sheringham EDG B15 125 G4
Sheringham Rd BVILLE B30 177 F2
Sherington Dr
ETTPK/GDPK/PENN WV4 52 B3
Sherlock Cl SHHTH WV12 26 B5
Sherlock St DIG/EDG B5 127 E4
Sherrans Dell
ETTPK/GDPK/PENN WV4 52 B5
Sherratt Cl WALM/CURD B76 78 B3
Sherringham Dr SHHTH WV12 26 A1
Sherron Gdns BHTH/HG B12 144 B2
Sherston Covert BVILLE B30 177 G3
Shervale Cl
ETTPK/GDPK/PENN WV4 51 G2
Sherwin Av BILS/COS WV14 68 A1
Sherwood Av TPTN/OCK DY4 85 F2
Sherwood Cl HIA/OLT B92 164 B2
HLGN/YWD B28 162 D5
Sherwood Dr BRLYHL DY5 119 H3
Sherwood Ms HLGN/YWD B28 162 C4
Sherwood Rd HLGN/YWD B28 162 C3
SMTHWKW B67 124 C3
STRBR DY8 118 A5
Sherwood St WOLV WV1 6 E1
Sherwood Wk RUSH/SHEL WS4 29 F3
Shetland Cl
DUNHL/THL/PER WV6 22 D4
LDYWD/EDGR B16 125 H2
Shetland Dr SMTHWK B66 105 H2
Shidas La OLDBY B69 104 C2
Shifrall Wy MGN/WHC B75 63 F1
Shillcock Gv LOZ/NWT B19 109 E4
Shilton Cl SHLY B90 195 F2
Shilton Gv SLYOAK B29 158 B2
Shinwell Crs OLDBY B69 86 B4
Shipbourne Cl RIDG/WDGT B32 141 F2
Shipley Flds ERDE/BCHGN B24 93 E3
Shipley Gv SLYOAK B29 158 C2
Shipston Rd NFLD/LBR B31 175 H4
Shipton Cl DUDN DY1 83 G3
Shipton Rd CSCFLD/WYGN B72 62 C5
Shipway Rd YDLY B25 129 E5
Shire Brook Cl AST/WIT B6 109 E1
Shire Cl LDYWD/EDGR B16 125 H2
LGLYGN/QTN B68 123 F2
Shireland Brook Gdns
WSNGN B18 * 107 F5
Shireland Cl
BFLD/HDSWWD B20 89 G3
Shireland Rd SMTHWK B66 106 D5
Shire Rdg ALDR WS9 19 G3
Shirestone Rd STETCH B33 131 G2
Shireview Gdns
BLOX/PEL WS3 * 18 B3
Shireview Rd BLOX/PEL WS3 18 B3
Shirland Rd
CHWD/FDBR/MGN B37 132 A3
Shirley Dr CSCFLD/WYGN B72 62 C4
Shirley Park Rd SHLY B90 180 B3
Shirley Rd BVILLE B30 160 A5
DUDS DY2 103 E1
HLGN/YWD B28 163 E2
LGLYGN/QTN B68 105 G3
Shirral Gv
CHWD/FDBR/MGN B37 113 H4
Shirrall Dr POL/KGSB/FAZ B78 49 F1
Sholing Cl CDSL WV8 22 B1
Shooters Cl DIG/EDG B5 126 D5
Shooters Hl CSCFLD/WYGN B72 77 H1
Shop La CDSL WV8 20 B1
Shopton Rd BKDE/SHDE B34 112 C2
Shoreham Cl WLNHL WV13 38 D4
Short Acre St WSLW WS2 4 C1
Shorters Av
ALE/KHTH/YWD B14 178 D1
Short Heath Rd
ERDW/GRVHL B23 76 C5
Shortland Cl DOR/KN B93 197 E2
Shortlands Cl BVILLE B30 177 E3
Shortlands La BLOX/PEL WS3 17 H3
Short Rd SMTHWKW B67 123 H1
WOLVN WV10 23 G1
Short St BILS/COS WV14 53 H2
BLKHTH/ROWR B65 122 A3
BRWNH WS8 9 F5
DARL/WED WS10 55 G5
DARL/WED WS10 55 H1
DUDN DY1 84 A4
HALE B63 138 B3
SHHTH WV12 26 A5
STRBR DY8 135 F2
WOLV WV1 7 G3
WSLW WS2 4 B4
Shorwell Pl BRLYHL DY5 119 E3
Shottery Gv WALM/CURD B76 78 B2
Shottery Rd SHLY B90 180 B4
Shotteswell Rd SHLY B90 194 B1
Showell Circ WOLVN WV10 23 G3
Showell Green La SPARK B11 144 D4
Showell La
ETTPK/GDPK/PENN WV4 50 A5
Showell Rd WOLVN WV10 23 F3
Showells Gdns VAUX/NECH B7 110 A2
Shrawley Cl HALE B63 138 C5
RBRY B45 187 H1
Shrawley Rd NFLD/LBR B31 176 A3
Shrewley Crs STETCH B33 131 G3
Shrewsbury Cl BLOX/PEL WS3 26 D1
Shrewton Av
ALE/KHTH/YWD B14 177 H3
Shrubbery Av TPTN/OCK DY4 84 D1
Shrubbery Cl WALM/CURD B76 77 H5
The Shrubbery DUDN DY1 84 B4
LDYWD/EDGR B16 * 125 H1
Shrublands Av
LGLYGN/QTN B68 123 F5
Shrub La ERDE/BCHGN B24 93 E2
Shugborough Dr DUDN DY1 83 G4
Shustoke La DSYBK/YTR WS5 57 H4
Shustoke Rd BKDE/SHDE B34 113 E3
SOLH B91 165 F5
Shutlock La MOS/BIL B13 160 D1
Shut Mill La RMSLY B62 171 H4
Shyltons Cft LDYWD/EDGR B16 126 A2
Sibdon Gv NFLD/LBR B31 175 G5
Sidaway Cl OLDBY B69 104 A3
Sidaway St CDYHTH B64 121 E3
Sidbury Gv DOR/KN B93 196 C5

Sidcup Cl BILS/COS WV14 53 F5
Sidcup Rd KGSTG B44 75 G2
Siddons Rd BILS/COS WV14 68 D1
Siddons Wy HHTH/SAND B71 71 E4
Sidenhill Cl SHLY B90 180 B5
Sidlaw Cl HALE B63 137 H5
WOLVN WV10 22 D4
Sidney St BKHL/PFLD WV2 6 E7
Sidwick Crs BKHL/PFLD WV2 53 F2
Sigmund Cl WOLV WV1 38 B2
Signal Gv BLOX/PEL WS3 27 E1
Signal Hayes Rd
WALM/CURD B76 78 C2
Silesbourne Cl CBROM B36 * 95 E5
Silhill Hall Rd SOLH B91 164 C5
Silva Av KGSWFD DY6 100 B5
Silver Birch Cl WASH/WDE B8 110 B3
Silver Birch Coppice
FOAKS/STRLY B74 32 B5
Silver Birch Dr HLYWD B47 192 D2
Silver Birch Rd BKHL/PFLD WV2 52 B1
CHWD/FDBR/MGN B37 113 H3
ERDE/BCHGN B24 77 F5
FOAKS/STRLY B74 45 F4
Silverbirch Rd SOLH B91 182 C2
Silvercroft Av HDSW B21 89 E2
Silverdale Dr WOLVN WV10 37 G1
Silverdale Gdns STRBR DY8 117 G1
Silverdale Rd ERDE/BCHGN B24 93 H2
Silverfield Cl
ALE/KHTH/YWD B14 161 E2
Silver Innage HALE B63 120 C5
Silverlands Av
LGLYGN/QTN B68 123 F1
Silverlands Cl HLGN/YWD B28 162 D1
Silvermead Ct HLYWD B47 192 A3
Silvermead Rd SCFLD/BOLD B73 77 E2
Silvermere Rd
LGN/SDN/BHAMAIR B26 148 B1
Silver's Cl BLOX/PEL WS3 17 H2
Silverstone Cl WSLW WS2 40 B2
Silverstone Dr
FOAKS/STRLY B74 60 B2
Silver St ALE/KHTH/YWD B14 161 E2
BRLYHL DY5 118 D2
BRWNH WS8 9 E5
HLYWD B47 192 A3
Silverthorne Av TPTN/OCK DY4 84 D1
Silverthorne La CDYHTH B64 120 B3
Silverton Crs MOS/BIL B13 162 B1
Silverton Hts SMTHWKW B67 * 106 B3
Silverton Rd SMTHWKW B67 106 A3
Silverton Wy WNSFLD WV11 25 F5
Silvertrees Rd TPTN/OCK DY4 85 F1
Silvester Rd BILS/COS WV14 54 A2
Silvester Wy STRBR DY8 118 D4
Silvington Cl SLYOAK B29 159 E3
Simcox Gdns RIDG/WDGT B32 140 D5
Simcox Rd DARL/WED WS10 55 H3
Simeon Bissell Cl TPTN/OCK DY4 85 G1
Simeon's Wk BRLYHL DY5 119 H5
Simmonds Cl BLOX/PEL WS3 17 F4
Simmonds Pl DARL/WED WS10 55 H1
Simmonds Rd BLOX/PEL WS3 17 F4
Simmonds Wy BRWNH WS8 19 G2
Simmons Dr RIDG/WDGT B32 140 D3
Simmons Leasow
RIDG/WDGT B32 140 D5
Simmons Rd WNSFLD WV11 25 H1
Simms La DUDS DY2 102 C4
HLYWD B47 192 C3
Simon Cl HHTH/SAND B71 72 A2
Simon Rd HLYWD B47 192 C1
Simpkins Cl ALDR WS9 19 G4
Simpson Gv WOLVN WV10 23 G4
Simpson Rd CSCFLD/WYGN B72 77 G2
WOLVN WV10 23 G4
WSLW WS2 27 F5
Simpson St OLDBY B69 105 E2
Singer Cft CBROM B36 95 H5
Sir Alfreds Wy WALM/CURD B76 63 E5
Sir Harrys Rd DIG/EDG B5 143 G1
Sir Hilton's Rd NFLD/LBR B31 189 H1
Sir John's Rd SLYOAK B29 143 G4
Sir Richards Dr HRBN B17 124 B5
Sisefield Rd HWK/WKHTH B38 177 E4
Siskin Dr BHTH/HG B12 144 A1
Siskin Rd HAG/WOL DY9 136 A4
Sister Dora Buildings WSL WS1 * 4 E4
Sister Dora Gdns WSL WS1 4 D5
Siviter's Cl BLKHTH/ROWR B65 121 H1
Siviter's La BLKHTH/ROWR B65 121 H1
Siviter St HALE B63 138 D3
Six Acres RIDG/WDGT B32 140 C3
Skelcher Rd SHLY B90 180 A1
Skemp Cl BILS/COS WV14 53 H4
Sketchley Cl SMTHWK B66 106 C3
Skidmore Av BDMR/CCFT WV3 36 B5
Skidmore Dr WBROM B70 87 E3
Skidmore Rd BILS/COS WV14 68 D1
Skinner La DIG/EDG B5 127 E3
Skinner St WOLV WV1 6 E4
Skip La DSYBK/YTR WS5 58 C3
Skipton Gn
DUNHL/THL/PER WV6 22 C5
Skipton Rd LDYWD/EDGR B16 126 A3
Skomer Cl RBRY B45 173 G4
Skye Cl CBROM B36 114 B3
Skye Wk CDYHTH B64 121 E3
Skylark Cl BRLYHL DY5 83 E5
ERDW/GRVHL B23 76 A4
Slack La HDSW B21 89 G4
Slacky La BLOX/PEL WS3 28 B1
Sladefield Rd WASH/WDE B8 111 E4
Slade Gdns CDSL WV8 10 C3
Slade Gv DOR/KN B93 196 D2
Slade Hl DUNHL/THL/PER WV6 * 36 B2
Slade La HLGN/YWD B28 179 G2
MGN/WHC B75 48 C2
Slade Lanker BKDE/SHDE B34 112 C4
Sladepool Farm Rd
ALE/KHTH/YWD B14 178 B2
Slade Rd ERDW/GRVHL B23 92 B4
HALE B63 137 G1
MGN/WHC B75 48 A2
WOLVN WV10 12 C4
Slaithwaite Rd HHTH/SAND B71 87 H2
Slaney Ct WSLW WS2 56 C1
Slaney Rd WSLW WS2 56 B2
Slatch House Rd
SMTHWKW B67 124 A2
Slateley Crs SHLY B90 195 F2
Slater Rd DOR/KN B93 196 C4
Slater's La WSLW WS2 56 B1
Slaters Pl WSLW WS2 56 C1
Slater St BILS/COS WV14 54 A5
DARL/WED WS10 55 F2
TPTN/OCK DY4 85 G2
WLNHL WV13 40 A2
Sleaford Gv HLGN/YWD B28 163 E3
Sleaford Rd HLGN/YWD B28 163 E3
Sledmore Rd DUDS DY2 102 D2
The Slieve BFLD/HDSWWD B20 90 A3
Slim Av BILS/COS WV14 54 A5
Slimbridge Cl SHLY B90 195 G2
Slim Rd WSLW WS2 40 C3
Slims Ga HALE B63 138 C3
Slingfield Rd NFLD/LBR B31 176 A4
The Sling DUDS DY2 102 C3
Sloane St CBHAMW B1 2 C4
Smallbrook La WMBN WV5 65 F4
Smallbrook Queensway
DIG/EDG B5 3 F7
Small Cl SMTHWKW B67 105 H4
Smalldale Rd PBAR/PBCH B42 74 D4
Small Heath Br SPARK B11 127 H5
Small Heath Hwy SMHTH B10 127 H4
YDLY B25 145 H1
Smallshire Cl WNSFLD WV11 25 F5
Smallshire Wy STRBR DY8 117 H4
Small St HHTH/SAND B71 87 F1
WSL WS1 4 D6
Smallwood Cl ERDE/BCHGN B24 93 H3
WALM/CURD B76 63 E5
Smallwood Rd CDSL WV8 11 G5
Smarts Av LICHS WS14 33 E3
Smeaton Gdns WSNGN B18 107 G5
Smeed Gv ERDE/BCHGN B24 93 F3
Smestow La SEDG DY3 80 A2
Smestow St WOLVN WV10 37 F1
Smirrells Rd HLGN/YWD B28 162 C5
Smith Av DARL/WED WS10 55 F4
Smith Cl BILS/COS WV14 68 A2
SMTHWKW B67 123 H1
Smithfield Rd BLOX/PEL WS3 27 H1
Smithmoor Crs HHTH/SAND B71 72 B3
Smith Pl TPTN/OCK DY4 85 H2
Smith Rd DARL/WED WS10 70 D2
WSLW WS2 56 C2
Smiths Cl RIDG/WDGT B32 157 F1
Smiths La DOR/KN B93 196 C2
Smith St BILS/COS WV14 53 H3
DUDS DY2 102 D2
LOZ/NWT B19 108 C4
Smiths Wy CSHL/WTROR B46 96 A3
Smithy Dr BLOX/PEL WS3 18 A3
Smithy La BRLYHL DY5 100 D1
The Smithy
LGN/SDN/BHAMAIR B26 147 H1
Smout Crs BILS/COS WV14 67 H1
Snapdragon Dr DSYBK/YTR WS5 57 F5
Snape Rd WNSFLD WV11 25 G1
Sneyd Hall Cl BLOX/PEL WS3 * 27 E2
Sneyd Hall Rd BLOX/PEL WS3 26 D1
Sneyd La WNSFLD WV11 26 A1
Snowberry Dr BRLYHL DY5 83 E5
Snowberry Gdns ACGN B27 * 146 C2
Snowdon Gv HALE B63 154 D1
Snowdon Ri SEDG DY3 67 F5
Snowdon Rd STRBR DY8 135 H1
Snowdon Wy SHHTH WV12 25 H1
WOLVN WV10 22 D4
Snowdrop Cl BRWNH WS8 18 D1
Snowford Cl SHLY B90 179 H4
Snow Hl BKHL/PFLD WV2 7 G5
Snow Hill Jct BKHL/PFLD WV2 7 G6
Snow Hill Queensway
CBHAMNE B4 3 F3
Snows Drive Hl SHLY B90 194 D3
Snowshill Gdns DUDN DY1 83 H2
Soberton Cl WNSFLD WV11 25 F3
Soho Av WSNGN B18 108 A2
Soho Cl SMTHWK B66 107 E3
Soho Hl WSNGN B18 108 A2
Soho Pool Wy WSNGN B18 108 A3
Soho Rd HDSW B21 107 G1
Soho Wy SMTHWK B66 106 D3
Solari Cl TPTN/OCK DY4 70 A3
Solent Cl COVEN WV9 11 H5
Solihull By-Pass SOLH B91 165 F5
Solihull La HLGN/YWD B28 163 E4
Solihull Pkwy
CHWD/FDBR/MGN B37 133 E5
Solihull Rd HIA/OLT B92 166 D4
SHLY B90 180 C2
SPARK B11 145 F4
Solihull Wy CBROM B36 94 D5
HIA/OLT B92 165 E1
Solly Gv TPTN/OCK DY4 70 B4
Solva Cl WOLV WV1 38 B4
Solway Cl DARL/WED WS10 56 C4
Somerby Dr SOLH B91 181 G5
Somercotes Rd
PBAR/PBCH B42 74 D3
Somerdale Rd NFLD/LBR B31 176 A1
Somerfield Cl RUSH/SHEL WS4 29 E1
Somerfield Rd BLOX/PEL WS3 27 F2
Somerford Gdns WOLVN WV10 13 E5
Somerford Pl WLNHL WV13 39 F4
Somerford Rd SLYOAK B29 158 B2
Somerford Wy BILS/COS WV14 68 B3
Somerland Rd
B26 130 C3
Somerset Crs DARL/WED WS10 56 D4
Somerset Dr NFLD/LBR B31 189 F1
STRBR DY8 117 H5
Somerset Rd
BFLD/HDSWWD B20 89 H4
EDG B15 142 C1
ERDW/GRVHL B23 76 C5
HHTH/SAND B71 71 H5
RUSH/SHEL WS4 42 C1
WLNHL WV13 40 B3
Somers Rd RMSLY B62 139 E2
WSLW WS2 56 A1
Somerton Dr
CHWD/FDBR/MGN B37 132 B5
ERDW/GRVHL B23 77 E5
Somerville Rd SCFLD/BOLD B73 62 A4
SMHTH B10 128 C4
Somery Rd DUDN DY1 84 C3
SLYOAK B29 141 G5
Sommerfield Rd
RIDG/WDGT B32 140 D4
Sommerville Dr
SCFLD/BOLD B73 62 A4
Sonning Dr COVEN WV9 11 H5
Sopwith Cft CVALE B35 94 C4
Sorrel Cl OLDBY B69 85 H4
Sorrel Dr ACGN B27 146 B5
DSYBK/YTR WS5 57 G5
Sorrel Gv ERDE/BCHGN B24 93 H3
Sorrell Dr ACGN B27 * 146 B5
Southacre Av DIG/EDG B5 127 E4
Southall Crs BILS/COS WV14 68 C2
Southall Rd WNSFLD WV11 25 G2
Southall's La DUDN DY1 84 B5
Southam Cl HLGN/YWD B28 162 C2
Southam Dr SCFLD/BOLD B73 77 F2
Southampton St WOLV WV1 7 G2
Southam Rd HLGN/YWD B28 162 C2
South Av STRBR DY8 135 F3
WNSFLD WV11 24 C5
South Bank Rd CDYHTH B64 121 F4
Southbank Vw KGSWFD DY6 100 A5
Southbourne Av
BKDE/SHDE B34 111 H3
WSLW WS2 41 F4
Southbourne Cl SLYOAK B29 143 E5
Southbourne Rd WOLVN WV10 12 C4
South Car Park Rd
BHAMNEC B40 150 B4
Southcote Gv
HWK/WKHTH B38 176 B4
Southcott Av BRLYHL DY5 119 F4
South Crs WOLVN WV10 14 A1
South Dene SMTHWKW B67 * 106 B4
Southdown Av WSNGN B18 108 A3
South Dr CSHL/WTROR B46 115 E3
DIG/EDG B5 143 G3
MGN/WHC B75 62 C2
Southern Cl KGSWFD DY6 118 B1
Southerndown Rd SEDG DY3 66 D3
Southern Rd WASH/WDE B8 111 G4
Southern Wy DARL/WED WS10 55 E5
Southey Cl SHHTH WV12 26 C2
SOLH B91 181 H5
Southfield Av CBROM B36 112 D1
LDYWD/EDGR B16 125 F1
Southfield Cl ALDR WS9 30 A5
Southfield Dr HLGN/YWD B28 163 E5
Southfield Gv
BDMR/CCFT WV3 50 C1
Southfield Rd
LDYWD/EDGR B16 125 E1
WNSFLD WV11 25 F5
Southfields Cl
CSHL/WTROR B46 115 G4
Southfields Rd SOLH B91 181 F4
South Gdns HAG/WOL DY9 169 G1
Southgate CDYHTH B64 120 D4
WOLV WV1 6 D3
Southgate Rd KGSTG B44 75 E1
South Gn
ETTPK/GDPK/PENN WV4 50 D3
South Gv ERDW/GRVHL B23 92 D1
LOZ/NWT B19 108 B1
South Holme BORD B9 128 A3
Southlands Rd MOS/BIL B13 161 G1
Southminster Dr
ALE/KHTH/YWD B14 161 E4
South Ov SEDG DY3 83 G1
South Pde CSCFLD/WYGN B72 62 C3
South Park Ms BRLYHL DY5 119 E2
South Range SPARK B11 144 D1
South Rd ALE/KHTH/YWD B14 161 E2
ERDW/GRVHL B23 92 D2
HAG/WOL DY9 169 G1
NFLD/LBR B31 175 F3
SMTHWKW B67 106 B4
SPARK B11 127 H5
STRBR DY8 135 F3
TPTN/OCK DY4 69 H3
WSNGN B18 108 A3
South Road Av WSNGN B18 108 A3
South Roundhay STETCH B33 130 C1
South St BRLYHL DY5 119 E2
HRBN B17 142 B1
WLNHL WV13 39 E4
WOLVN WV10 23 E4
WSL WS1 4 C7
South Street Gdns WSL WS1 4 C7
South Tower VAUX/NECH B7 * 109 H5
South Vw GTB/HAM B43 73 G4
South View Cl CDSL WV8 10 D5
WOLVN WV10 13 H1
South View Rd SEDG DY3 66 D3
Southville Bungalows
ALE/KHTH/YWD B14 * 178 D1
South Wy BHAMNEC B40 150 B4
Southway Ct KGSWFD DY6 100 B5
Southwick Pl BILS/COS WV14 53 H1
Southwick Rd RMSLY B62 122 B4
Southwold Av BVILLE B30 177 G2
Southwood Av
BKDE/SHDE B34 112 C2
Southwood Cl KGSWFD DY6 100 A4
Southwood Covert
ALE/KHTH/YWD B14 177 G3
Sovereign Dr DUDN DY1 83 F4
Sovereign Hts NFLD/LBR B31 174 C4
Sovereign Rd BVILLE B30 176 D1
Sovereign Wk WSL WS1 5 G3
Sovereign Wy MOS/BIL B13 144 B3
Sowerby March
ERDE/BCHGN B24 93 H2
Sowers Cl SHHTH WV12 26 B5
Sowers Ct MGN/WHC B75 47 H1
Sowers Gdns SHHTH WV12 26 B5
Spa Gv BVILLE B30 160 C2
Spark St SPARK B11 144 C1
Sparrey Dr SLYOAK B29 160 A2
Sparrow Cl DARL/WED WS10 56 B3
Speakers Cl OLDBY B69 103 H2
Speed Rd TPTN/OCK DY4 69 E5
Speedwell Cl ALDR WS9 29 H5
WNSFLD WV11 25 E5
Speedwell Gdns BRLYHL DY5 135 H1
Speedwell Rd DIG/EDG B5 143 H1
YDLY B25 146 A1
Spencer Av BILS/COS WV14 68 C3
Spencer Cl HHTH/SAND B71 72 B3
OLDBY B69 103 H1
SEDG DY3 82 C2
Spencer St WSNGN B18 2 C1
Spenser Av
DUNHL/THL/PER WV6 34 C1
Spernall Gv SLYOAK B29 158 C1
Spey Cl DIG/EDG B5 143 H1
Spiceland Rd NFLD/LBR B31 158 B4
Spiers Cl DOR/KN B93 197 E2
Spies Cl RMSLY B62 139 H1
Spies La RMSLY B62 139 H2
Spills Meadow SEDG DY3 83 G1
Spilsbury Cft SOLH B91 181 G5
Spindle La SHLY B90 194 A2
Spinners End Dr CDYHTH B64 120 D3
Spinney Cl BLOX/PEL WS3 18 A5
NFLD/LBR B31 175 G2
STRBR DY8 117 F1
Spinney Dr SHLY B90 194 D4
The Spinney BDMR/CCFT WV3 35 H4
BFLD/HDSWWD B20 89 G2
FOAKS/STRLY B74 31 H4
HLYWD B47 192 D4
SEDG DY3 83 E4
SOLH B91 182 A5
Spiral Cl RMSLY B62 122 C4
Spiral Gn ERDE/BCHGN B24 93 G2
Spitfire Rd ERDE/BCHGN B24 93 G4
Spitfire Wy CVALE B35 94 C4
Spondon Gv BKDE/SHDE B34 113 E4
Spondon Rd WNSFLD WV11 25 E2
Spon La WBROM B70 87 H5
Spon La South SMTHWK B66 105 H1
Spoon Dr HWK/WKHTH B38 176 B3
Spooner Cft DIG/EDG B5 127 E4
Spooners Cl HIA/OLT B92 165 H3
Spouthouse La GTB/HAM B43 73 G4
Spout La WSL WS1 4 E7
Spreadbury Cl HRBN B17 124 B4
Sprig Cft CBROM B36 111 G1
Spring Av BLKHTH/ROWR B65 122 A2
Springavon Cft HRBN B17 141 H1
Springbank BORD B9 128 D1
Springbank Rd EDG B15 126 C5
Springbrook Cl CBROM B36 95 F5
Spring Cl HAG/WOL DY9 169 F1
RUSH/SHEL WS4 18 C5
SOLH B91 181 F2
Spring Coppice Dr
DOR/KN B93 197 E5
Spring Ct WSL WS1 5 J7
Spring Crs CDYHTH B64 121 F5
Springcroft Rd SPARK B11 145 H5
Springfield ERDW/GRVHL B23 92 B3
Springfield Av BHTH/HG B12 144 C1
HAG/WOL DY9 136 C3
SEDG DY3 67 G2
Springfield Cl
BLKHTH/ROWR B65 103 G4
Springfield Ct
HLGN/YWD B28 * 162 D2
Springfield Crs DUDS DY2 103 F1
HIA/OLT B92 148 A4
WALM/CURD B76 63 G4
WBROM B70 88 A5
Springfield Dr
ALE/KHTH/YWD B14 * 161 E1
Springfield Gv SEDG DY3 67 F2
Springfield La
BLKHTH/ROWR B65 103 F4
WOLVN WV10 12 D3
Springfield Rd
ALE/KHTH/YWD B14 161 F2
BILS/COS WV14 54 A1
CBROM B36 113 F1
MOS/BIL B13 162 B1
RMSLY B62 122 B5
WALM/CURD B76 78 B1
WOLVN WV10 37 G1
Springfields CSHL/WTROR B46 115 F4
RUSH/SHEL WS4 28 D3
Springfields Rd BRLYHL DY5 118 D2
LGLYGN/QTN B68 105 G5
Springfield St WSNGN B18 126 A1
Springfield Ter
BLKHTH/ROWR B65 103 F4
Spring Gdns DUDS DY2 102 D1
HDSW B21 * 107 H2
Spring Gv LOZ/NWT B19 * 108 B3
Spring Grove Gdns
WSNGN B18 107 H3
Spring Head DARL/WED WS10 70 D1
Spring Hl ERDE/BCHGN B24 92 D3
WSNGN B18 108 A5
Springhill Av
ETTPK/GDPK/PENN WV4 50 C5
Spring Hill Circ CBHAMW B1 2 A3
Springhill Cl RUSH/SHEL WS4 29 F1
SHHTH WV12 26 B3
Springhill Gv
ETTPK/GDPK/PENN WV4 50 C4
Spring Hill La
ETTPK/GDPK/PENN WV4 50 A4
Springhill Pk
ETTPK/GDPK/PENN WV4 50 B5
Spring Hill Pas WSNGN B18 126 A1
Springhill Rd BRWNH WS8 9 G5
WNSFLD WV11 24 D2
WSL WS1 5 G5
Spring La ERDE/BCHGN B24 93 E3
RMSLY B62 171 H1
RUSH/SHEL WS4 18 C5
SHHTH WV12 39 H1
Spring Meadow CDYHTH B64 121 F3
HALE B63 138 B5
TPTN/OCK DY4 70 A5
Springmeadow Gv
LOZ/NWT B19 108 D3
Spring Meadow Rd DUDS DY2 120 C2
Spring Meadows Cl CDSL WV8 10 D3
Spring Parklands DUDN DY1 102 A1
Spring Rd DUDS DY2 102 D3
EDG B15 126 D5
ETTPK/GDPK/PENN WV4 53 E3
RUSH/SHEL WS4 29 F1
SMTHWK B66 105 H1
SPARK B11 145 H4
Springslade RIDG/WDGT B32 141 F2
Springslade Dr
ERDE/BCHGN B24 93 H3
The Springs CDYHTH B64 121 G3
Spring St EDG B15 126 D4
HAG/WOL DY9 136 C3
HALE B63 137 G1
TPTN/OCK DY4 70 A3
TPTN/OCK DY4 85 G1
Springthorpe Gn
ERDE/BCHGN B24 93 G2
Springthorpe Rd
ERDE/BCHGN B24 93 H3
Springvale Av BILS/COS WV14 53 F4
DSYBK/YTR WS5 58 A1
Spring Vale Cl BILS/COS WV14 68 A2
Spring Vale Rd
BLKHTH/ROWR B65 * 103 G4
Springvale St WLNHL WV13 39 H2
Springvale Wy BILS/COS WV14 53 G4
Spring Wk HALE B63 154 D1
OLDBY B69 105 E4
WSLW WS2 41 F2
Sproat Av DARL/WED WS10 55 E3
Spruce Gv ERDE/BCHGN B24 93 F4
Spruce Rd DSYBK/YTR WS5 57 H5
Spruce Wy BDMR/CCFT WV3 35 H4
Spur Tree Av BDMR/CCFT WV3 35 E4
Squadron Cl CVALE B35 95 E2
Square Cl RIDG/WDGT B32 140 C4
The Square BKHL/PFLD WV2 37 F5
HRBN B17 141 H1
SHHTH WV12 * 26 B2
SOLH B91 182 A2
TPTN/OCK DY4 70 B4
Squires Ct BRLYHL DY5 119 E3
Squires Cft WALM/CURD B76 78 C2
Squirrel Hollow
WALM/CURD B76 78 C1
Squirrels Hollow
LGLYGN/QTN B68 123 H5
Squirrel Wk
ETTPK/GDPK/PENN WV4 51 G4
FOAKS/STRLY B74 32 A5
Stable Ct SEDG DY3 67 G5
Stable Cft HHTH/SAND B71 72 B4
Stableford Cl RIDG/WDGT B32 141 F4
The Stables SLYOAK B29 143 E5
Stacey Cl CDYHTH B64 121 E3
Stacey Grange Gdns
RBRY B45 * 188 A2
Stackhouse Cl ALDR WS9 19 G3
Stackhouse Dr BLOX/PEL WS3 18 A3
Stadium Cl WLNHL WV13 39 H2
Stafford Cl BLOX/PEL WS3 17 E5
Stafford Dr HHTH/SAND B71 71 F4
Stafford La CDSL WV8 20 B1
Stafford Rd DARL/WED WS10 54 D2
GTWY WS6 16 C2
HDSW B21 107 H1
WOLVN WV10 23 E2
Staffordshire Pool Cl
AST/WIT B6 * 91 F5
Staffordshire Wy CDSL WV8 10 B2
Stafford St BILS/COS WV14 53 H3
CBHAMNE B4 3 H3
DARL/WED WS10 70 C1
DUDN DY1 84 B5
WLNHL WV13 39 G3
WOLV WV1 7 G3
WSLW WS2 4 D2
Stafford Street Jct WOLV WV1 7 F2
Stafford Wy GTB/HAM B43 73 G4
Stag Crs BLOX/PEL WS3 28 A4
Stag Hill Rd BLOX/PEL WS3 28 A3
Stag Wk WALM/CURD B76 77 H4
Stainsby Av LOZ/NWT B19 108 C4
Stainsby Cft SHLY B90 195 H3
Stakenbridge La KIDD DY10 168 C1
Stalling's La KGSWFD DY6 99 H1
Stambermill Cl HAG/WOL DY9 136 B2
Stamford Cft SOLH B91 181 H3
Stamford Gv
BFLD/HDSWWD B20 90 C4
Stamford Rd
BFLD/HDSWWD B20 90 C5
BRLYHL DY5 136 A1
STRBR DY8 135 H2
Stamford St STRBR DY8 118 B5
Stanbrook Rd SHLY B90 195 G3
Stanbury Av DARL/WED WS10 54 D2

Stanbury Rd
ALE/KHTH/YWD B14 ....178 D1
Stancroft Gv
LGN/SDN/BHAMAIR B26 ....130 C4
Standard Wy VAUX/NECH B7 ....110 D1
Standbridge Wy TPTN/OCK DY4 ..85 G1
Standhills Rd KGSWFD DY6 ....100 B4
Standlake Av CBROM B36 ....111 H2
Stanfield Rd GTB/HAM B43 ....59 H3
RIDG/WDGT B32 ....124 A5
Stanford Av PBAR/PBCH B42 ....74 A4
Stanford Gv HALE B63 ....154 C1
Stanford Rd BKHL/PFLD WV2 ....52 A1
BLKHTH/ROWR B65 ....121 H1
Stanhoe Cl BRLYHL DY5 ....119 F4
Stanhope Rd SMTHWKW B67 ....124 B1
Stanhope St BDMR/CCFT WV3 ....6 D5
BHTH/HG B12 ....127 F5
DUDS DY2 ....103 E5
Stanhope Wy GTB/HAM B43 ....59 H4
Stanhurst Wy HHTH/SAND B71 ....72 C1
Stanier Cl RUSH/SHEL WS4 ....28 D3
Stanier Gv BFLD/HDSWWD B20 ....90 B4
Staniforth St AST/WIT B6 ....3 H1
Stanley Av MGN/WHC B75 ....63 F4
RIDG/WDGT B32 ....124 A5
SHLY B90 ....180 B1
Stanley Cl HLGN/YWD B28 ....163 E5
WNSFLD WV11 ....25 F2
Stanley Ct
DUNHL/THL/PER WV6 ....34 C1
Stanley Dr SEDG DY3 ....80 C4
Stanley Pl BILS/COS WV14 ....53 F3
MOS/BIL B13 * 144 B4
RUSH/SHEL WS4 ....28 D4
Stanley Rd
ALE/KHTH/YWD B14 ....160 D3
DARL/WED WS10 ....55 F3
HHTH/SAND B71 ....72 A4
LGLYGN/QTN B68 ....123 G5
RUSH/SHEL WS4 ....28 D4
STRBR DY8 ....135 F4
VAUX/NECH B7 ....110 A2
WOLVN WV10 ....23 F1
Stanley St BLOX/PEL WS3 ....27 G2
Stanmore Gv RIDG/WDGT B32 ....140 A4
Stanmore Rd
LDYWD/EDGR B16 ....125 E3
Stanton Av DUDN DY1 ....67 H5
Stanton Gv
LGN/SDN/BHAMAIR B26 ....130 B4
SHLY B90 ....180 A1
TPTN/OCK DY4 ....85 G1
Stanton Rd GTB/HAM B43 ....73 F3
SHLY B90 ....180 A1
WOLV WV1 ....37 H3
Stanville Rd
LGN/SDN/BHAMAIR B26 ....148 A1
Stanway Gdns HHTH/SAND B71 ..71 H5
Stanway Gv KGSTG B44 ....60 B5
Stanway Rd HHTH/SAND B71 ....71 H5
SHLY B90 ....180 D1
Stanwell Gv ERDW/GRVHL B23 ....76 C5
Stanwick Av STETCH B33 ....131 G1
Stapenhall Rd SHLY B90 ....195 G3
Stapleford Cft
ALE/KHTH/YWD B14 ....177 G3
Stapleford Gv STRBR DY8 ....118 A2
Staple Hall Rd NFLD/LBR B31 ....175 H3
Staplehurst Rd
HLGN/YWD B28 ....162 D2
Staple Lodge Rd
NFLD/LBR B31 ....175 H4
Stapleton Cl WALM/CURD B76 ....78 D5
Stapleton Dr C
HWD/FDBR/MGN B37 ....132 A1
Stapleton Rd ALDR WS9 ....29 H5
Stapylton Av HRBN B17 ....141 H2
Starbank Rd SMHTH B10 ....129 E4
Starbold Crs DOR/KN B93 ....197 F3
Star Cl TPTN/OCK DY4 ....86 A1
WSLW WS2 ....40 D1
Starcross Rd ACGN B27 ....146 C5
Star Hl EDG B15 ....126 B4
Starkey Cft
CHWD/FDBR/MGN B37 ....132 C2
Starkie Dr LGLYGN/QTN B68 ....105 G5
Starley Wy
CHWD/FDBR/MGN B37 ....149 G1
Star St BDMR/CCFT WV3 ....36 A5
HAG/WOL DY9 ....136 D2
Statham Dr LDYWD/EDGR B16 ..125 E2
Station Ap DOR/KN B93 ....196 D5
FOAKS/STRLY B74 ....32 D4
SCFLD/BOLD B73 ....62 B2
SOLH B91 ....181 G1
Station Av LDYWD/EDGR B16 ....125 E3
Station Buildings
DUNHL/THL/PER WV6 * 36 A1
Station Cl BLOX/PEL WS3 ....27 F2
CDSL WV8 ....10 A4
Station Dr BRLYHL DY5 ....118 D3
FOAKS/STRLY B74 ....47 F5
HAG/WOL DY9 ....152 C5
HIA/OLT B92 ....164 A1
KIDD DY10 ....168 B3
TPTN/OCK DY4 ....85 H2
Station Link Rd
CHWD/FDBR/MGN B37 ....149 H3
Station Pl BLOX/PEL WS3 ....27 F2
Station Rd ACGN B27 ....146 C4
ALDR WS9 ....30 A5
ALE/KHTH/YWD B14 ....160 D2
AST/WIT B6 ....91 F5
BILS/COS WV14 ....54 A3
BLKHTH/ROWR B65 ....122 B2
BLOX/PEL WS3 ....18 A4
BRLYHL DY5 ....101 E5
BVILLE B30 ....159 G5
CDSL WV8 ....10 A4
CDYHTH B64 ....121 F4
CHWD/FDBR/MGN B37 ....132 A4
CSHL/WTROR B46 ....97 F5
DOR/KN B93 ....197 E5
ERDW/GRVHL B23 ....92 D1
HAG/WOL DY9 ....136 C1
HAG/WOL DY9 ....152 C4
HDSW B21 ....107 E1
HIA/OLT B92 ....167 G3
HLYWD B47 ....192 C5
HRBN B17 ....142 A1
HWK/WKHTH B38 ....176 D1
NFLD/LBR B31 ....175 G3
OLDBY B69 ....105 E4
RUSH/SHEL WS4 ....28 C4
SCFLD/BOLD B73 ....77 E2
SOLH B91 ....181 H1
STETCH B33 ....129 H1
WMBN WV5 ....65 E3
WOLVN WV10 ....37 H1
Station St BLOX/PEL WS3 ....27 F2
CDYHTH B64 ....120 C4
DARL/WED WS10 ....55 G2
DIG/EDG B5 ....3 F7
SCFLD/BOLD B73 ....62 B3
TPTN/OCK DY4 ....85 H1
WSL WS1 ....4 D3
Staunton Rd BLOX/PEL WS3 ....16 C4
Staveley Rd
ALE/KHTH/YWD B14 ....160 D4
WOLV WV1 ....37 E1
Stead Cl TPTN/OCK DY4 ....69 H2
WSLW WS2 ....27 G5
Steadman Cft TPTN/OCK DY4 * 70 B3
Stechford La WASH/WDE B8 ....111 G4
Stechford Rd BKDE/SHDE B34 ..111 H4
Steel Bright Rd SMTHWK B66 ....107 E3
Steel Dr WOLVN WV10 ....23 F2
Steel Gv YDLY B25 ....129 G5
Steelhouse La
BKHL/PFLD WV2 ....7 J7
CBHAMNE B4 ....3 H3
Steelpark Rd RMSLY B62 ....121 H5
Steel Rd NFLD/LBR B31 ....175 F3
Steene Gv NFLD/LBR B31 ....174 C2
The Steeples STRBR DY8 ....135 H4
Steepwood Cft BVILLE B30 ....176 B1
Stella Cft
CHWD/FDBR/MGN B37 ....132 C2
Stella Gv GTB/HAM B43 ....73 E3
Stella Rd TPTN/OCK DY4 ....69 F5
Stenbury Cl WOLVN WV10 ....13 F3
Stencills Dr RUSH/SHEL WS4 ....42 D2
Stencills Rd RUSH/SHEL WS4 ....42 D1
Stennels Av RMSLY B62 ....139 G3
Stennels Crs RMSLY B62 ....139 G3
Stephens Cl WNSFLD WV11 ....25 F2
Stephenson Av WSLW WS2 ....27 E4
Stephenson Dr
CHWD/FDBR/MGN B37 ....132 B2
DUNHL/THL/PER WV6 ....20 C5
Stephenson Sq WSLW WS2 ....27 F5
Stephenson St BDMR/CCFT WV3 ..6 D5
CBHAM B2 ....3 F6
Stephens Rd MGN/WHC B75 ....63 G4
Stepping Stone Cl WSLW WS2 ....40 D1
Stepping Stones STRBR DY8 ....135 H2
Steppingstone St DUDN DY1 ....84 B5
Sterling Pk BRLYHL DY5 * 101 H5
Sterndale Rd PBAR/PBCH B42 ....74 C5
Steven Dr BILS/COS WV14 ....69 E2
Stevens Av RIDG/WDGT B32 ....140 D5
Stevens Ga BKHL/PFLD WV2 ....37 E5
Stevens Rd HAG/WOL DY9 ....136 B5
Steward St WSNGN B18 ....126 A1
Stewart Rd ALDR WS9 ....19 G4
KGSWFD DY6 ....99 H5
Stewarts Rd RMSLY B62 ....122 B5
Stewart St BKHL/PFLD WV2 ....7 F7
Stewkins STRBR DY8 ....118 A4
Steyning Rd
LGN/SDN/BHAMAIR B26 ....147 E2
Stickley La SEDG DY3 ....83 E2
Stilehouse Crs
BLKHTH/ROWR B65 ....122 A2
Stilthouse Gv RBRY B45 ....188 A1
Stirling Crs SHHTH WV12 ....25 H5
Stirling Rd BILS/COS WV14 ....54 B5
DUDS DY2 ....103 E3
LDYWD/EDGR B16 ....125 H3
SCFLD/BOLD B73 ....76 B1
SHLY B90 ....181 E5
Stirrup Cl DSYBK/YTR WS5 ....57 F4
Stockbridge Cl
DUNHL/THL/PER WV6 ....34 D3
Stockdale Pl EDG B15 ....125 F4
Stock Exchange Buildings
CBHAMNW B3 * 2 E4
Stockfield Rd ACGN B27 ....146 B3
Stockhill Dr RBRY B45 ....187 H2
Stocking St HAG/WOL DY9 ....136 D2
Stockland Rd ERDW/GRVHL B23 ..92 A2
Stockley Crs SHLY B90 ....180 D2
Stockmans Cl
HWK/WKHTH B38 ....176 C5
Stockton Cl DOR/KN B93 ....197 F4
WALM/CURD B76 ....95 E1
WSLW WS2 ....41 H1
Stockton Gv STETCH B33 ....131 F3
Stockwell Av BRLYHL DY5 ....119 F4
Stockwell End
DUNHL/THL/PER WV6 ....21 H4
Stockwell Ri HIA/OLT B92 ....165 F3
Stockwell Rd
DUNHL/THL/PER WV6 ....21 H5
HDSW B21 ....89 G4
Stokes Av TPTN/OCK DY4 ....69 G3
Stokesay Av DUNHL/THL/PER WV634 D2
Stokesay Cl OLDBY B69 ....103 G1
Stokesay Gv NFLD/LBR B31 ....175 F5
Stokesay Ri DUDN DY1 ....83 G3
Stokes St BLOX/PEL WS3 ....27 F2
Stoke Wy EDG B15 ....2 C7
Stom Rd BILS/COS WV14 ....53 F3
Stoneacre Cl BDMR/CCFT WV3 ....35 E4
Stone Av MGN/WHC B75 ....63 G3
Stonebow Av SOLH B91 ....181 H5
Stonebridge Crs
CHWD/FDBR/MGN B37 ....113 H5
Stonebridge Rd
CSHL/WTROR B46 ....115 F2
CSHL/WTROR B46 ....115 F4
Stonebrook Wy
RIDG/WDGT B32 ....141 F5
Stonechat Dr ERDW/GRVHL B23 ..92 A4
Stone Cl HWK/WKHTH B38 ....176 D3
Stonecroft Av RBRY B45 ....188 A1
Stonecrop Cl BRWNH WS8 ....18 D1
HWK/WKHTH B38 ....176 D5
Stonedown Cl
ETTPK/GDPK/PENN WV4 ....53 E5
Stonefield Dr BRLYHL DY5 ....100 C2
Stonefield Rd BILS/COS WV14 * ..53 H3
Stoneford Rd SHLY B90 ....180 A1
Stonehaven Gv
HLGN/YWD B28 ....163 F2
Stonehenge Cft
ALE/KHTH/YWD B14 ....177 H4
Stonehill Cft SHLY B90 ....195 F2
Stonehouse Av WLNHL WV13 ....39 F2
Stonehouse Crs
DARL/WED WS10 ....71 F1
Stonehouse Dr
FOAKS/STRLY B74 ....45 H1
Stonehouse Hl SLYOAK B29 ....141 G5
Stonehouse La
RIDG/WDGT B32 ....140 D5
Stonehouse Rd
SCFLD/BOLD B73 ....61 H5
Stonehurst Rd GTB/HAM B43 ....59 G5
Stonelea ALDR WS9 ....30 B5
Stonelea Cl HHTH/SAND B71 ....72 A3
Stoneleigh Cl FOAKS/STRLY B74 ..46 D5
Stoneleigh Gdns CDSL WV8 ....10 B3
Stoneleigh Rd
BFLD/HDSWWD B20 ....91 E5
SOLH B91 ....163 H5
Stoneleigh Wy SEDG DY3 ....67 F5
Stone Rd EDG B15 ....126 D5
Stonerwood Av
HLGN/YWD B28 ....162 C3
Stones Gn ERDW/GRVHL B23 ....76 D5
Stone St DUDN DY1 ....84 C5
OLDBY B69 ....105 E2
Stoneton Gv SLYOAK B29 ....158 C2
Stone Upper Cl
WALM/CURD B76 * 63 E4
Stone Yd DIG/EDG B5 ....3 K7
Stoney Brook Leys WMBN WV5 ..80 C1
Stoney Cl HIA/OLT B92 ....165 G3
Stoneyford Gv
ALE/KHTH/YWD B14 ....178 D1
Stoneyhurst Rd
ERDE/BCHGN B24 ....92 D5
Stoney La BHTH/HG B12 ....144 D2
BLOX/PEL WS3 ....17 F4
DUDS DY2 ....120 C1
HAG/WOL DY9 ....169 E2
HHTH/SAND B71 ....87 H2
RIDG/WDGT B32 ....140 B1
STETCH B33 ....130 A3
Stoneymoor Dr CBROM B36 ....95 F5
Stoneythorpe Cl SOLH B91 ....181 H4
Stonnal Gv ERDW/GRVHL B23 ....77 E5
Stonnall Ga ALDR WS9 ....30 B2
Stonnall Rd ALDR WS9 ....30 C2
Stonor Park Rd SOLH B91 ....164 B4
Stonor Rd HLGN/YWD B28 ....180 A1
Stony La SMTHWKW B67 ....106 A4
Stony St SMTHWKW B67 ....106 B3
Stornoway Rd CVALE B35 ....94 D2
Storrs Cl BORD B9 ....128 A3
Storrs Pl BORD B9 ....128 B3
The Storrs Wy RIDG/WDGT B32 ..157 F3
Stot Fold Rd
ALE/KHTH/YWD B14 ....178 B3
Stourbridge Rd BRGRVW B61 ....185 H5
BRLYHL DY5 ....101 G4
DUDS DY2 ....102 A1
ETTPK/GDPK/PENN WV4 ....50 C5
HAG/WOL DY9 ....153 E3
HALE B63 ....138 B3
SEDG DY3 ....81 G2
WMBN WV5 ....65 G2
Stour Cl HALE B63 ....138 A1
Stourdale Rd CDYHTH B64 ....120 C5
Stourdell Rd HALE B63 ....138 A1
Stour Hl BRLYHL DY5 ....120 A5
Stourmore Cl SHHTH WV12 ....26 B4
Stour St WBROM B70 ....86 C3
WSNGN B18 ....126 A1
Stourton Cl DOR/KN B93 ....197 F1
WALM/CURD B76 ....63 F4
Stourton Dr
ETTPK/GDPK/PENN WV4 ....50 C3
Stourton Rd RIDG/WDGT B32 ....140 B2
Stour Vale Rd HAG/WOL DY9 ....136 D1
Stour Valley Cl BRLYHL DY5 ....119 F5
Stow Dr BRLYHL DY5 ....135 H1
Stowell Rd KGSTG B44 ....75 F4
Stowe St BLOX/PEL WS3 ....27 G3
Stow Gv CBROM B36 ....112 A2
Stow Heath La WOLV WV1 ....53 F1
Stow Heath Pl WOLV WV1 ....53 F1
Stowmans Cl BILS/COS WV14 ....53 F5
Straight Rd SHHTH WV12 ....26 A4
Straits Gn SEDG DY3 ....82 D2
Straits Rd SEDG DY3 ....82 D3
The Straits SEDG DY3 ....82 C2
Stratford Cl DUDN DY1 ....83 G4
Stratford Dr ALDR WS9 ....30 C2
Stratford Pl BHTH/HG B12 ....127 G4
Stratford Rd HLGN/YWD B28 ....145 G5
HOCK/TIA B94 ....195 H5
SHLY B90 ....180 B1
SPARK B11 ....144 D1
Stratford St SPARK B11 ....145 E2
Stratford St North SPARK B11 ..127 G4
Strathdene Rd SLYOAK B29 ....142 A5
Strathern Dr BILS/COS WV14 ....68 A2
Strathmore Crs WMBN WV5 ....65 E2
Strathmore Rd TPTN/OCK DY4 ....69 G3
Stratton St WOLVN WV10 ....37 G1
Strawberry Cl OLDBY B69 ....104 A2
Strawberry La WLNHL WV13 ....38 C2
Stream Meadow
RUSH/SHEL WS4 ....29 E1
Stream Pk KGSWFD DY6 ....99 H5
Stream Rd KGSWFD DY6 ....99 H5
KGSWFD DY6 ....100 A5
Streamside Wy HIA/OLT B92 ....148 B3
RUSH/SHEL WS4 ....29 F2
Streatham Gv KGSTG B44 ....75 G1
Streather Rd MGN/WHC B75 ....47 G4
Streetly Crs FOAKS/STRLY B74 ....46 B2
Streetly Dr FOAKS/STRLY B74 ....46 B2
Streetly La FOAKS/STRLY B74 ....46 C3
Streetly Rd ERDW/GRVHL B23 ....76 B5
Streetly Wd FOAKS/STRLY B74 ....45 G3
Streetsbrook Rd SHLY B90 ....163 F5
SOLH B91 ....164 A5
Streets Corner Gdns ALDR WS9 ..19 G3
Strensham Hl MOS/BIL B13 ....144 A3
Strensham Rd MOS/BIL B13 ....144 A3
Stretton Gdns CDSL WV8 ....10 B3
Stretton Gv LOZ/NWT B19 * 108 C2
SPARK B11 ....145 E1
WASH/WDE B8 ....111 F3
Stretton Pl BILS/COS WV14 ....68 A2
DUDS DY2 ....102 D5
Stretton Rd SHHTH WV12 ....26 A2
SHLY B90 ....180 B5
Stringer Cl MGN/WHC B75 ....47 E1
Stringes Cl WLNHL WV13 ....39 H2
Stringes La WLNHL WV13 ....39 H3
Strode Rd BKHL/PFLD WV2 ....52 A2
Stronsay Cl RBRY B45 ....173 H4
Stroud Av SHHTH WV12 ....26 A5
Stroud Cl SHHTH WV12 ....40 A1
Stroud Rd SHLY B90 ....179 H3
Strutt Cl EDG B15 ....125 F4
Stuart Crs DUDS DY2 ....85 E5
Stuart Rd BLKHTH/ROWR B65 ....104 A5
RMSLY B62 ....139 H2
Stuart's Dr STETCH B33 ....129 H3
Stuarts Gn HAG/WOL DY9 ....152 D2
Stuarts Rd STETCH B33 ....129 H2
Stuart St BLOX/PEL WS3 ....27 F2
VAUX/NECH B7 ....110 A2
Stuarts Wy RIDG/WDGT B32 ....157 F3
Stubbers Green Rd ALDR WS9 ....29 F2
Stubbington Cl WLNHL WV13 ....38 D4
Stubbs Rd BDMR/CCFT WV3 ....51 G1
Stubby La WNSFLD WV11 ....25 G4
Studley Dr WOLVN WV10 ....23 G5
Studland Rd HLGN/YWD B28 ....163 E2
Stud La STETCH B33 ....130 B1
Studley Cft HIA/OLT B92 ....148 A4
Studley Dr BRLYHL DY5 ....119 E4
Studley Ga STRBR DY8 ....134 D2
Studley Rd BDMR/CCFT WV3 ....35 G5
Studley St BHTH/HG B12 ....144 C1
Sturman Dr
BLKHTH/ROWR B65 ....121 H3
Suckling Green La CDSL WV8 ....10 B5
Sudbury Cl WNSFLD WV11 ....25 E2
Sudbury Gv KGSTG B44 ....75 H1
Sudeley Cl CBROM B36 ....94 D5
Sudeley Gdns SEDG DY3 ....83 F4
Suffield Gv ERDW/GRVHL B23 ....91 G1
Suffolk Cl LGLYGN/QTN B68 ....105 F5
WNSFLD WV11 ....24 C4
Suffolk Dr BRLYHL DY5 ....119 E5
Suffolk Gv ALDR WS9 ....30 B2
Suffolk Pl CBHAMW B1 * 3 F7
WSLW WS2 ....27 H5
Suffolk Rd DARL/WED WS10 ....56 C5
DUDS DY2 ....102 A2
Suffolk St Queensway
CBHAMW B1 ....2 E6
Suffrage St SMTHWK B66 ....106 D4
Sugden Gv DIG/EDG B5 ....127 E4
Sulgrave Cl DUDN DY1 ....84 A3
Sumburgh Cft CVALE B35 ....94 C3
Summercourt Dr KGSWFD DY6 ....99 G4
Summercourt Sq KGSWFD DY6 ....99 G4
Summer Cft LOZ/NWT B19 ....108 D3
Summer Dr SEDG DY3 ....83 E3
Summerfield Av KGSWFD DY6 ....99 G2
WBROM B70 ....87 G2
Summerfield Crs
LDYWD/EDGR B16 ....125 G1
Summerfield Dr SLYOAK B29 ....158 C3
Summerfield Gv WSNGN B18 * ..107 G5
Summerfield Rd DUDS DY2 ....102 D2
HAG/WOL DY9 ....170 C3
HIA/OLT B92 ....164 C1
LDYWD/EDGR B16 ....125 G1
WOLV WV1 ....6 C4
Summerfields Av RMSLY B62 ....122 D4
Summergate SEDG DY3 ....83 F3
Summer Hl HALE B63 ....138 D4
KGSWFD DY6 ....99 G3
Summerhill Rd BILS/COS WV14 ....68 D2
Summer Hill Rd CBHAMW B1 ....2 A3
Summer Hill St CBHAMW B1 ....2 B4
Summer Hill Ter CBHAMW B1 ....2 B4
Summerhouse Rd
BILS/COS WV14 ....68 A2
Summer La LOZ/NWT B19 ....3 F1
RUSH/SHEL WS4 ....18 B5
SEDG DY3 ....83 E3
WALM/CURD B76 ....79 F5
Summerlee Rd
ERDE/BCHGN B24 ....93 F4
Summer Rd ACGN B27 ....146 A5
BLKHTH/ROWR B65 ....122 B1
DUDN DY1 ....84 A2
EDG B15 ....126 C5
ERDW/GRVHL B23 ....92 D1
Summer Rw BKHL/PFLD WV2 ....7 F5
CBHAMNW B3 ....2 D4
Summer St HAG/WOL DY9 ....136 C2
HHTH/SAND B71 ....87 H2
KGSWFD DY6 ....99 H3
STRBR DY8 ....135 F2
WLNHL WV13 ....39 F3
Summerton Rd OLDBY B69 ....104 B1
Summervale Cl HAG/WOL DY9 ....152 C5
Summervale Rd HAG/WOL DY9 ..152 C5
Summerville Ter HRBN B17 * 142 A2
Summit Crs SMTHWK B66 ....106 A1
Summit Gdns HALE B63 ....138 B4
Summit Pl SEDG DY3 ....82 D4
The Summit HAG/WOL DY9 ....136 B3
Sumner Rd CSHL/WTROR B46 ....115 G3
Sunbeam Cl CBROM B36 ....95 H5
Sunbeam St BKHL/PFLD WV2 ....52 A1
Sunbeam Wy STETCH B33 ....131 E2
Sunbury Cl BILS/COS WV14 ....68 D2
Sunbury Rd HALE B63 ....138 B3
NFLD/LBR B31 ....175 E5
Suncroft RIDG/WDGT B32 ....140 C2
Sundbury Ri NFLD/LBR B31 ....158 D5
Sunderland Dr STRBR DY8 ....118 C4
Sunderton Rd
ALE/KHTH/YWD B14 ....178 A1
Sundew Cft CBROM B36 ....111 H1
Sundial La GTB/HAM B43 ....73 H2
Sundour Crs WNSFLD WV11 ....24 B1
Sundridge Rd KGSTG B44 ....60 A4
Sunleigh Gv ACGN B27 ....147 E3
Sunningdale RMSLY B62 ....139 G3
Sunningdale Av
DUNHL/THL/PER WV6 ....20 B5
Sunningdale Cl
BFLD/HDSWWD B20 ....89 G2
SCFLD/BOLD B73 ....77 E1
STRBR DY8 ....135 F5
Sunningdale Dr OLDBY B69 ....103 G2
Sunningdale Rd SEDG DY3 ....66 D2
SPARK B11 ....146 A4
Sunningdale Wy
BLOX/PEL WS3 ....16 C4
Sunny Av BHTH/HG B12 ....144 C2
Sunnybank Av KGSTG B44 ....75 H4
Sunnybank Cl
ALDR WS9 ....45 E3
Sunny Bank Rd
LGLYGN/QTN B68 ....123 G5
Sunnybank Rd
SCFLD/BOLD B73 ....77 E3
SEDG DY3 ....83 G1
Sunnydene WASH/WDE B8 ....111 E4
Sunny Hill Cl WMBN WV5 ....65 F5
Sunnymead Rd
LGN/SDN/BHAMAIR B26 ....147 F1
Sunnymead Wy
FOAKS/STRLY B74 ....60 B1
Sunnymede Rd KGSWFD DY6 ....100 C5
Sunnyside ALDR WS9 ....19 F5
OLDBY B69 ....103 H2
Sunnyside Av ERDW/GRVHL B23 ..92 C3
Sunridge Av LOZ/NWT B19 ....108 D3
WMBN WV5 ....65 E4
Sunset Pl
ETTPK/GDPK/PENN WV4 ....52 D5
Sun St BRLYHL DY5 ....119 H3
WOLVN WV10 ....7 J2
WSL WS1 ....56 D1
Surfeit Hl CDYHTH B64 ....121 E4
Surfeit Hill Rd CDYHTH B64 ....120 D4
Surrey Crs HHTH/SAND B71 ....71 E3
Surrey Dr BDMR/CCFT WV3 ....36 A4
STRBR DY8 ....100 A5
Surrey Rd DUDS DY2 ....102 A2
KGSTG B44 ....60 A4
Surrey Wk ALDR WS9 ....30 A2
Sussex Av ALDR WS9 ....30 A2
DARL/WED WS10 ....56 D4
HHTH/SAND B71 ....71 G5
Sussex Dr BDMR/CCFT WV3 ....36 A4
Sutherland Av SHLY B90 ....180 C2
WOLV WV1 ....37 H5
Sutherland Cl GTB/HAM B43 ....59 H4
Sutherland Dr MOS/BIL B13 ....144 B3
WMBN WV5 ....65 E3
Sutherland Gv
DUNHL/THL/PER WV6 ....34 D1
Sutherland Pl BKHL/PFLD WV2 ....7 H6
Sutherland Rd CDYHTH B64 ....121 E4
ETTPK/GDPK/PENN WV4 ....51 H3
Sutherland St AST/WIT B6 ....109 H1
Sutton Ap WASH/WDE B8 ....111 E5
Sutton Ct
ETTPK/GDPK/PENN WV4 ....67 G1
MGN/WHC B75 ....62 B1
Sutton Crs WBROM B70 ....87 E3
Sutton New Rd
ERDW/GRVHL B23 ....92 D2
Sutton Oak Rd SCFLD/BOLD B73 ..60 C4
Sutton Rd ALDR WS9 ....43 H4
DARL/WED WS10 ....54 C3
ERDE/BCHGN B24 ....93 E1
WSL WS1 ....5 H6
Sutton's Dr GTB/HAM B43 ....58 D4
Sutton St AST/WIT B6 ....109 F3
EDG B15 ....126 D3
STRBR DY8 ....118 A3
Swains Gv KGSTG B44 ....60 B4
Swale Gv HWK/WKHTH B38 ....176 D5
WLNHL WV13 ....40 B3
Swale Rd WALM/CURD B76 ....78 C2
Swallow Av CBROM B36 ....114 A1
Swallow Cl BHTH/HG B12 ....144 D2
DARL/WED WS10 ....56 B4
DUDS DY2 ....120 D2
Swallow Ct WOLVN WV10 ....23 F3
Swallowdale ALDR WS9 ....19 G3

DUNHL/THL/PER WV6 ....34 D3
Swallowfall Av STRBR DY8 ....134 C3
Swallowfields Rd SEDG DY3 ....52 A5
Swallows Cl BLOX/PEL WS3 ....18 A2
Swallows' Meadow SHLY B90 ....180 D5
Swallow St CBHAM B2 ....2 E6
WBROM B70 ....87 E2
Swanage Rd SMHTH B10 ....128 B4
Swan Av SMTHWK B66 ....106 A2
Swan Bank
ETTPK/GDPK/PENN WV4 ....51 F4
Swan Cl KIDD DY10 ....168 B4
Swan Copse YDLY B25 ....146 C2
Swancote Dr
ETTPK/GDPK/PENN WV4 ....50 C3
Swancote Rd DUDN DY1 ....102 A1
STETCH B33 ....112 B4
Swan Ctyd
LGN/SDN/BHAMAIR B26 * 146 D1
Swan Crs OLDBY B69 ....104 D5
Swancroft Rd TPTN/OCK DY4 ....69 F3
Swan Dr BRWNH WS8 ....9 E5
Swanfield Rd STRBR DY8 ....118 C3
Swan Gdns ERDW/GRVHL B23 ....92 D2
Swan La BRGRVW B61 ....185 H5
STRBR DY8 ....118 C2
WBROM B70 ....87 E1
Swanley Cl RIDG/WDGT B32 ....140 A4
Swanmore Cl BDMR/CCFT WV3 ....51 E1
Swann Rd BILS/COS WV14 ....68 A1
Swan Pool Gv RUSH/SHEL WS4 ....29 F1
Swansbrook Gdns
HWK/WKHTH B38 ....177 G3
Swanshurst La MOS/BIL B13 ....162 A2
Swan St BRLYHL DY5 ....101 E3
DUDS DY2 ....102 C3
STRBR DY8 ....135 E2
WOLV WV1 ....37 H3
Swanswell Rd ACGN B27 ....163 H2
Swanswood Gv
CHWD/FDBR/MGN B37 * 132 C1
Swarthmore Rd SLYOAK B29 ....158 D3
Sweetbriar La SHHTH WV12 ....26 B5
Sweetbriar Rd BKHL/PFLD WV2 ....53 E1
Sweetbrier Dr STRBR DY8 ....118 A3
Sweetman Pl
DUNHL/THL/PER WV6 ....6 B1
Sweetman St
DUNHL/THL/PER WV6 ....36 C1
Sweetmoor Cl CBROM B36 ....113 E1
Sweetpool La HAG/WOL DY9 ....152 B5
Swift Cl CBROM B36 ....114 A1
Swinbrook Gv KGSTG B44 ....75 E2
Swinbrook Wy SHLY B90 ....180 D1
Swincross Rd STRBR DY8 ....135 H4
Swindell Rd HAG/WOL DY9 ....153 E1
Swindon Rd HRBN B17 ....124 D1
KGSWFD DY6 ....98 D1
Swinford Gv DOR/KN B93 ....196 C5
Swinford Leys WMBN WV5 ....80 B1
Swinford Rd SLYOAK B29 ....141 G4
STRBR DY8 ....135 G5
WOLVN WV10 ....23 G5
Swin Forge Wy SEDG DY3 ....80 C4
Swiss Dr STRBR DY8 ....118 B2
Swynnerton Dr WNSFLD WV11 ....14 D3
Sycamore Av BHTH/HG B12 ....144 C2
Sycamore Cl ERDE/BCHGN B24 ....92 D3
RUSH/SHEL WS4 ....28 D2
STRBR DY8 ....134 D5
WALM/CURD B76 ....78 B1
Sycamore Crs
CHWD/FDBR/MGN B37 ....132 A4
ERDE/BCHGN B24 ....92 D3
Sycamore Dr BDMR/CCFT WV3 ....35 H4
HLYWD B47 ....192 D3
Sycamore Gn DUDN DY1 ....83 H1
Sycamore Paddock
STRBR DY8 ....118 C3
Sycamore Pl BILS/COS WV14 ....54 C5
Sycamore Rd AST/WIT B6 ....109 G1
BVILLE B30 ....159 H3
DARL/WED WS10 ....71 E1
DSYBK/YTR WS5 ....57 F3
ERDW/GRVHL B23 ....76 D4
GTB/HAM B43 ....58 C5
HDSW B21 ....107 F1
KGSWFD DY6 ....100 A3
OLDBY B69 ....105 E5
RUSH/SHEL WS4 ....28 D2
SMTHWK B66 ....124 D1
TPTN/OCK DY4 ....69 F4
The Sycamores WOLVN WV10 ....23 H2
Sycamore Ter
ALE/KHTH/YWD B14 * 160 C3
Sycamore Wy ACGN B27 ....146 C3
Sydenham Rd SMTHWK B66 ....106 C2
SPARK B11 ....145 E1
WOLV WV1 ....38 B3
Sydney Cl WBROM B70 ....71 E4
Sydney Rd BORD B9 ....128 A2
CDYHTH B64 ....120 B3
SMTHWKW B67 ....124 A2
Sylvan Av NFLD/LBR B31 ....175 F2
Sylvan Gn RMSLY B62 ....139 F2
Sylvia Av NFLD/LBR B31 ....175 H5
Symphony Ct CBHAMW B1 ....2 B6
Sytch La WMBN WV5 ....81 E1

T

Tack Farm Rd STRBR DY8 ....117 H3
Tackford Cl CBROM B36 ....95 E5
Tackley Cl SHLY B90 ....180 B5
Tadmore Cl BILS/COS WV14 ....53 G3
Tadworth Cl WOLV WV1 ....38 A3
Tait Cft HIA/OLT B92 ....165 H2
Talaton Cl COVEN WV9 ....12 A5
Talbot Av FOAKS/STRLY B74 ....45 H2
Talbot Cl ERDW/GRVHL B23 ....76 B3
WSLW WS2 ....27 G4
Talbot Pl BILS/COS WV14 ....53 G2
Talbot Rd BKHL/PFLD WV2 ....52 A2
DUDS DY2 ....102 B5
SMTHWK B66 ....124 C1
Talbots La BRLYHL DY5 ....119 G3
Talbot St BRLYHL DY5 ....119 F1
HAG/WOL DY9 ....136 D2
HALE B63 ....137 G1
STRBR DY8 ....135 G2
WSNGN B18 ....107 H3
Talbot Wy SMHTH B10 ....128 D5
Talford St AST/WIT B6 ....109 E3
Talfourd St BORD B9 ....128 B3
Talgarth Covert
HWK/WKHTH B38 ....190 C1
Talke Rd DSYBK/YTR WS5 ....57 F5
Talladale RIDG/WDGT B32 ....157 F3
Tallington Rd
LGN/SDN/BHAMAIR B26 ....131 E5
Tall Trees Cl FOAKS/STRLY B74 ....46 B1
SHHTH WV12 ....26 B4
Tall Trees Dr HAG/WOL DY9 ....136 B5
Talton Cl SHLY B90 ....195 G3
Tamar Cl BRWNH WS8 ....8 C2
Tamar Dr CBROM B36 ....113 H1
SEDG DY3 ....67 H5
WALM/CURD B76 ....78 D4
Tamar Gv DUNHL/THL/PER WV6 ....34 C1
WLNHL WV13 ....40 A3
Tamarisk Cl SLYOAK B29 ....158 D2
Tamar Ri STRBR DY8 ....118 C4
Tame Av DARL/WED WS10 ....56 C4
Tame Br DSYBK/YTR WS5 ....57 F4
Tame Cl WSL WS1 ....57 E2
Tame Crs HHTH/SAND B71 ....71 G5
Tame Dr BLOX/PEL WS3 ....28 C1
Tame Ri LGLYGN/QTN B68 ....123 F4
Tame Rd AST/WIT B6 ....91 G4
LGLYGN/QTN B68 ....123 E4
TPTN/OCK DY4 ....86 A1
Tamerton Rd RIDG/WDGT B32 ....157 H1
Tameside Dr CVALE B35 ....94 C5
PBAR/PBCH B42 ....91 F2
Tame St BILS/COS WV14 ....54 B3
WBROM B70 ....70 D3
WSL WS1 ....57 E2
Tame St East WSL WS1 ....57 F2
Tamworth Cl BRWNH WS8 ....9 F2
Tamworth Rd FOAKS/STRLY B74 ....62 C1
MGN/WHC B75 ....48 D3
Tanacetum Dr DSYBK/YTR WS5 ....57 G5
Tandy Dr ALE/KHTH/YWD B14 ....178 B2
Tanfield Cl
DUNHL/THL/PER WV6 ....35 F2
Tanfield Rd DUDS DY2 ....102 B2
STETCH B33 ....130 B1
Tanford Rd HIA/OLT B92 ....148 A4
Tanglewood Cl
BKDE/SHDE B34 ....113 E4
RIDG/WDGT B32 ....140 B3
Tanglewood Gv SEDG DY3 ....67 E1
Tangmere Cl
DUNHL/THL/PER WV6 ....20 C5
Tangmere Dr CVALE B35 ....94 C3
Tanhouse Av GTB/HAM B43 ....73 E4
Tanhouse Farm Rd
HIA/OLT B92 ....148 A5
Tanhouse La HALE B63 ....137 G2
Tanners Cl MGN/WHC B75 ....63 E1
Tannery Cl WSLW WS2 ....4 C1
Tansey Green Rd BRLYHL DY5 ....100 D1
Tansley Cl DOR/KN B93 ....196 D4
Tansley Gv KGSTG B44 ....75 F2
Tansley Hill Av DUDS DY2 ....103 F1
Tansley Hill Rd DUDS DY2 ....103 E1
Tansley Rd KGSTG B44 ....75 F3
Tansley Vw BKHL/PFLD WV2 ....52 B1
Tantany La HHTH/SAND B71 ....87 G2
Tantarra St WSL WS1 ....5 G4
Tanwood Cl SOLH B91 ....181 H5
Tanworth Gv BHTH/HG B12 ....144 B1
Tanworth La SHLY B90 ....194 B2
Tanyards ACGN B27 ....146 D4
Tapestries Av WBROM B70 ....87 E2
Tapton Cl BLOX/PEL WS3 ....17 E4
Tarmac Rd
ETTPK/GDPK/PENN WV4 ....53 F3
Tarragon Gdns NFLD/LBR B31 ....174 C3
Tarrant Gv RIDG/WDGT B32 ....141 F2
Tarrington Covert
HWK/WKHTH B38 ....176 C5
Tarry Hollow Rd BRLYHL DY5 ....100 D1
Tarry Rd WASH/WDE B8 ....110 C5
Tarvin Ms BRLYHL DY5 ....119 F3
Taryn Dr DARL/WED WS10 ....55 F1
Tasker St WBROM B70 ....86 C2
WSL WS1 ....4 C6
Tasman Gv
DUNHL/THL/PER WV6 ....20 C5
Tat Bank Rd OLDBY B69 ....105 F3
Taunton Av WOLVN WV10 ....12 D3
Taunton Cl NFLD/LBR B31 ....174 C2
Taunton Rd BHTH/HG B12 ....144 C3
Taverners Cl SHHTH WV12 ....26 A1
Taverner's Gn
BFLD/HDSWWD B20 ....89 H3
Tavistock Rd ACGN B27 ....163 G3
Taw Cl CBROM B36 ....113 H2
Tay Cft CHWD/FDBR/MGN B37 ....114 C5
Tay Gv HWK/WKHTH B38 ....176 D5
RMSLY B62 ....122 C4
Taylor Av BLOX/PEL WS3 ....27 H2
Taylor Rd ALE/KHTH/YWD B14 ....161 F5
DUDS DY2 ....121 E2
ETTPK/GDPK/PENN WV4 ....52 D3
Taylor's La HHTH/SAND B71 ....87 H2
OLDBY B69 ....104 C2
SMTHWKW B67 ....106 B4
Taylors Orch ERDW/GRVHL B23 ....91 H2
Taylor St WNSFLD WV11 ....24 C5
Taylor Wy OLDBY B69 ....103 H1
Tay Rd RBRY B45 ....174 B4
Taysfield Rd NFLD/LBR B31 ....158 A4
Taywood Dr SMHTH B10 ....128 A5
Tealby Gv SLYOAK B29 ....160 A1
Teal Dr ERDW/GRVHL B23 ....91 H3
Teal Gv DARL/WED WS10 ....54 D5
Teall Rd WASH/WDE B8 ....110 C4
Tean Cl SPARK B11 ....146 A4
Teasdale Wy HAG/WOL DY9 ....136 B3
Teasel Rd WNSFLD WV11 ....25 E5
Teazel Av BVILLE B30 ....159 F4
Tebworth Cl COVEN WV9 ....11 H5
Tedbury Crs ERDW/GRVHL B23 ....76 C5
Tedder Rd WSLW WS2 ....40 D3
Teddesley Gv STETCH B33 ....113 E5
Teddesley St RUSH/SHEL WS4 ....5 F1
Teddington Gv PBAR/PBCH B42 ....90 C3
Tedstone Rd RIDG/WDGT B32 ....141 E2
Teesdale Av BKDE/SHDE B34 ....112 B3
Teesdale Cl WOLV WV1 ....38 A3
Tees Gv HWK/WKHTH B38 ....176 D5
Teignmouth Rd SLYOAK B29 ....142 D5
Telford Cl HHTH/SAND B71 ....71 E3
SMTHWKW B67 ....123 H3
WSLW WS2 ....27 E5
Telford Gdns BDMR/CCFT WV3 ....50 D1
Telford Rd WSLW WS2 ....27 E5
Telford Wy SMTHWK B66 ....106 B2
Teme Gv WLNHL WV13 ....40 B3
Teme Rd HALE B63 ....137 F2
STRBR DY8 ....135 F4
Tempest St BKHL/PFLD WV2 ....7 G5
The Templars OLDBY B69 ....104 C4
Templars Wk WLNHL WV13 ....39 G3
Temple Av HLGN/YWD B28 ....163 E4
Temple Bar WLNHL WV13 ....39 G2
Templefield Gdns BORD B9 ....128 A3
Templefield Sq EDG B15 ....126 B5
Templefield St BORD B9 ....128 A3
Temple Meadows Rd
HHTH/SAND B71 ....88 A1
Templemore Dr GTB/HAM B43 ....73 G4
Temple Pas CBHAM B2 ....3 F5
Temple Rd DOR/KN B93 ....197 E5
WLNHL WV13 ....39 G2
Temple Rw CBHAM B2 ....3 G5
Temple Rw West CBHAMNW B3 ....3 F4
Temple Sq WLNHL WV13 ....39 G2
Temple St BILS/COS WV14 ....54 A3
BKHL/PFLD WV2 ....7 F5
CBHAM B2 ....3 F5
SEDG DY3 ....83 F3
WBROM B70 ....87 G2
Templeton Cl DOR/KN B93 ....197 E5
Templeton Rd KGSTG B44 ....75 E1
Temple Wy CSHL/WTROR B46 ....97 F5
OLDBY B69 ....86 A4
Tenacre La SEDG DY3 ....83 G1
Ten Acres End BVILLE B30 ....160 B2
Ten Ashes La RBRY B45 ....188 C4
Tenbury Cl ALDR WS9 ....30 C2
WSLW WS2 ....40 B2
Tenbury Ct
ETTPK/GDPK/PENN WV4 ....50 D3
Tenbury Gdns
ETTPK/GDPK/PENN WV4 ....50 D4
Tenbury Rd
ALE/KHTH/YWD B14 ....160 D4
Tenby Rd MOS/BIL B13 ....145 F5
Tenby St CBHAMW B1 ....2 B2
Tenby St North CBHAMW B1 ....2 B2
Tenlands Rd HALE B63 ....138 B4
Tennal Dr RIDG/WDGT B32 ....141 E1
Tennal Gv RIDG/WDGT B32 ....141 F1
Tennal La RIDG/WDGT B32 ....141 E2
Tennal Rd RIDG/WDGT B32 ....141 E1
Tennant St EDG B15 ....126 B3
Tennis Ct BVILLE B30 ....176 B1
Tennis Cts EDG B15 * 143 E2
Tennyson Av FOAKS/STRLY B74 ....32 D4
Tennyson Rd BLOX/PEL WS3 ....28 A2
SEDG DY3 ....82 C1
SHHTH WV12 ....26 C2
SMHTH B10 ....128 C5
WOLVN WV10 ....24 A1
Tennyson St BRLYHL DY5 ....101 F3
Tenter Ct HALE B63 ....138 D3
Tenter Dr HALE B63 ....139 E4
Tenterfields HALE B63 ....138 D3
Tern Cl ETTPK/GDPK/PENN WV4 ....52 B5
Tern Gv HWK/WKHTH B38 ....176 C5
Terrace Rd LOZ/NWT B19 ....108 A2
Terrace St BLKHTH/ROWR B65 ....121 H3
BRLYHL DY5 ....101 C4
DARL/WED WS10 ....55 H5
The Terrace BDMR/CCFT WV3 ....35 G4
CDYHTH B64 ....121 E4
Terrence Vls DARL/WED WS10 * 55 F1
Terry Dr WALM/CURD B76 ....78 B2
Terrys La ERDE/BCHGN B24 ....93 G3
Terry St DUDS DY2 ....84 D5
Tessall La NFLD/LBR B31 ....174 D3
NFLD/LBR B31 ....175 E4
Tetbury Gv NFLD/LBR B31 ....174 D2
Tetley Av RUSH/SHEL WS4 ....42 C1
Tetley Rd SPARK B11 ....145 G4
Tetnall St DUDS DY2 ....102 D1
Tettenhall Rd
DUNHL/THL/PER WV6 ....36 B2
Teviot Gdns BRLYHL DY5 ....100 C3
Teviot Gv HWK/WKHTH B38 ....176 D5
Tewkesbury Dr DUDS DY2 ....120 D1
Tewkesbury Rd
BFLD/HDSWWD B20 ....91 E5
BLOX/PEL WS3 ....16 A5
Tew Park Rd HDSW B21 ....107 G2
Thackeray Rd BVILLE B30 ....159 F5
Thames Cl BRLYHL DY5 ....100 D2
Thames Ct SCFLD/BOLD B73 * 62 B3
Thames Rd BLOX/PEL WS3 ....27 H2
Thanet Cl KGSWFD DY6 ....99 G3
Thanet Gv PBAR/PBCH B42 ....90 C2
The Thatchers RMSLY B62 ....122 C4
Thatchway Gdns
HWK/WKHTH B38 ....190 C1
Thaxted Rd STETCH B33 ....131 G1
Theatre Ap DIG/EDG B5 ....3 G7
Thelbridge Rd NFLD/LBR B31 ....189 E2
Thelma Rd TPTN/OCK DY4 ....69 E5
Thelma St WSL WS1 ....56 D1
Thelsford Wy HIA/OLT B92 ....165 F2
Theodore Cl HRBN B17 ....142 B3
OLDBY B69 ....86 C5
The Pavilions
CSHL/WTROR B46 ....132 D4
Theresa Rd SPARK B11 ....127 H5
Thetford Cl TPTN/OCK DY4 ....84 D1
Thetford Gdns WNSFLD WV11 ....24 D4
Thetford Rd PBAR/PBCH B42 ....74 B4
Thetford Wy DSYBK/YTR WS5 ....58 A5
Thickett Cl WSLW WS2 ....41 F5
Thicknall Dr HAG/WOL DY9 ....135 H5
Thicknall La HAG/WOL DY9 ....169 H2
Thicknall Ri HAG/WOL DY9 ....169 G1
Thimble End Rd
WALM/CURD B76 ....78 C1
Thimble Mill La AST/WIT B6 ....109 H2
Thimblemill Rd SMTHWKW B67 ....105 H5
Third Av BORD B9 ....128 D2
BRWNH WS8 ....9 G3
KGSWFD DY6 ....100 B1
SLYOAK B29 ....143 G4
WOLVN WV10 ....23 H3
Third Exhibition Av
BHAMNEC B40 ....149 H2
Third Rd BRGRVW B61 ....186 B4
Thirlmere Cl
DUNHL/THL/PER WV6 ....21 H2
Thirlmere Dr MOS/BIL B13 ....162 A2
WNSFLD WV11 ....15 E5
Thirlmere Gv
DUNHL/THL/PER WV6 ....34 D1
Thirlmere Wk BRLYHL DY5 ....118 D5
Thirsk Cft CBROM B36 ....111 G1
Thirston Cl WNSFLD WV11 ....25 G5
Thistle Cl SEDG DY3 ....67 H5
Thistle Cft WNSFLD WV11 ....24 D5
Thistle Down Cl
FOAKS/STRLY B74 ....45 G3
Thistledown Rd
BKDE/SHDE B34 ....113 E2
Thistle Gn HWK/WKHTH B38 ....190 C1
Thistlegreen Cl
BLKHTH/ROWR B65 ....103 F4
Thistlegreen Rd DUDS DY2 ....103 E5
Thistle La RIDG/WDGT B32 ....157 F2
Thomas Crs SMTHWK B66 ....107 E4
Thomas Guy Rd WBROM B70 ....70 C4
Thomas Mason Cl
WNSFLD WV11 ....24 D3
Thomas St AST/WIT B6 ....109 F3
BKHL/PFLD WV2 ....7 F7
SMTHWK B66 ....106 D4
WBROM B70 ....87 H4
WSLW WS2 ....4 B2
Thompson Av BKHL/PFLD WV2 ....52 B1
Thompson Cl DUDS DY2 ....120 B2
WLNHL WV13 ....39 G2
Thompson Dr VAUX/NECH B7 ....110 D1
Thompson Gdns
SMTHWKW B67 ....106 B5
Thompson Rd
LGLYGN/QTN B68 ....105 F5
SMTHWKW B67 ....106 B5
Thompson St BILS/COS WV14 ....53 H3
WLNHL WV13 ....39 G2
Thomson Av NFLD/LBR B31 ....176 A4
Thoresby Cft DUDN DY1 ....83 H3
Thornberry Dr DUDN DY1 ....101 F1
Thornberry Wk VAUX/NECH B7 ....110 A3
Thornbridge Av
PBAR/PBCH B42 ....74 C4
Thornbridge Gv ALDR WS9 ....19 F4
Thornbury Ct
DUNHL/THL/PER WV6 ....35 E2
Thornbury Rd
BFLD/HDSWWD B20 ....90 D4
Thornby Av SOLH B91 ....164 D5
Thornby Rd ERDW/GRVHL B23 ....76 A3
Thorncliffe Rd KGSTG B44 ....75 E1
Thorn Cl DARL/WED WS10 ....55 H4
Thorncroft Wy DSYBK/YTR WS5 ....57 H4
Thorne Av WOLVN WV10 ....23 G3
Thorne Rd WLNHL WV13 ....39 G1
Thorne St BKHL/PFLD WV2 ....53 E1
Thorneycroft La WOLVN WV10 ....24 A5
Thorneycroft Rd
BILS/COS WV14 ....54 C5
Thorney Rd FOAKS/STRLY B74 ....45 F4
Thornfield Cft SEDG DY3 ....67 G4
Thornfield Rd ACGN B27 ....146 C5
Thorngrove Av SOLH B91 ....182 A5
Thornham Wy
ALE/KHTH/YWD B14 ....177 H4
Thornhill Gv HDSW B21 ....107 H1
Thornhill Pk FOAKS/STRLY B74 ....45 G5
Thornhill Rd BRLYHL DY5 ....119 G3
DUDN DY1 ....84 C2
FOAKS/STRLY B74 ....45 G5
HALE B63 ....138 A4
HDSW B21 ....107 H1
SOLH B91 ....165 E3
SPARK B11 ....145 F4
Thornhurst Av
RIDG/WDGT B32 ....124 A5
Thornleigh SEDG DY3 ....83 F1
Thornley Cl MOS/BIL B13 ....161 G1
WNSFLD WV11 ....25 F1
Thornley Gv WALM/CURD B76 ....79 E5
Thornley Rd WNSFLD WV11 ....25 F1
Thornley St WOLV WV1 ....7 G2
Thorn Rd BVILLE B30 ....159 G3
Thorns Av BRLYHL DY5 ....119 G3
Thornsett Gv HIA/OLT B92 ....163 F4
Thorns Rd BRLYHL DY5 ....119 G4
Thornthwaite Cl RBRY B45 ....174 B3
Thornton Cl OLDBY B69 ....86 A4
Thornton Dr BRLYHL DY5 * 119 G3
Thornton Rd SHLY B90 ....195 F2
WASH/WDE B8 ....111 F4
WOLV WV1 ....38 B4
Thornwood Cl
LGLYGN/QTN B68 ....105 G4
Thornyfield Cl SHLY B90 ....180 C2
Thornyfield Rd SHLY B90 ....180 C2
Thorpe Cl MGN/WHC B75 ....62 C1
Thorpe Ct SOLH B91 ....164 B4
Thorpe Rd WSL WS1 ....57 E1
Thorp St DIG/EDG B5 ....3 F7
Three Acres La SHLY B90 ....193 H2
Three Broadway
LDYWD/EDGR B16 * 126 B3
Three Corner Cl SHLY B90 ....179 G5
Three Oaks Rd HLYWD B47 ....192 D4
Three Shires Oak Rd
SMTHWKW B67 ....124 B2
Three Tuns La WOLVN WV10 ....12 C5
Threshers Dr SHHTH WV12 ....26 B4
Throne Cl BLKHTH/ROWR B65 ....104 A4
Throne Crs BLKHTH/ROWR B65 ....104 B5
Throne Rd BLKHTH/ROWR B65 ....104 A4
Throstles Cl GTB/HAM B43 ....73 G4
Thrush Rd LGLYGN/QTN B68 ....122 D2
Thruxton Cl
ALE/KHTH/YWD B14 ....178 B2
Thurcroft Cl WASH/WDE B8 ....110 D5
Thuree Rd SMTHWKW B67 ....123 H2
Thurleigh Cl HAG/WOL DY9 ....135 H5
Thurlestone Rd NFLD/LBR B31 ....189 E1
Thurloe Crs RBRY B45 ....173 G4
Thurlston Av HIA/OLT B92 ....147 F3
Thurlstone Dr
ETTPK/GDPK/PENN WV4 ....51 F4
Thurlstone Rd BLOX/PEL WS3 ....16 D4
Thursfield Rd HHTH/SAND B71 ....72 A4
TPTN/OCK DY4 ....69 G5
Thurston Av OLDBY B69 ....104 D3
Thynne St WBROM B70 ....88 A4
Tibbats Cl RIDG/WDGT B32 ....140 C4
Tibberton Cl BDMR/CCFT WV3 ....50 D1
HALE B63 ....139 E4
SOLH B91 ....181 G5
Tibbets La HRBN B17 ....141 G3
Tibbington Rd TPTN/OCK DY4 ....69 F4
Tibbington Ter TPTN/OCK DY4 ....69 E4
Tiberius Cl CSHL/WTROR B46 ....97 F5
Tibland Rd ACGN B27 ....163 H1
Tiddington Cl CBROM B36 ....94 D5
Tideswell Rd PBAR/PBCH B42 ....74 C5
Tidworth Cft
ALE/KHTH/YWD B14 ....178 C2
Tierney Dr TPTN/OCK DY4 ....70 A5
Tiffany La COVEN WV9 ....11 H5
Tiffield Rd YDLY B25 ....146 C2
Tigley Av RIDG/WDGT B32 ....157 H1
Tilbury Cl BDMR/CCFT WV3 ....35 E5
Tilbury Gv MOS/BIL B13 ....160 D1
Tildasley St WBROM B70 ....87 F1
Tildesley Dr SHHTH WV12 ....25 H5
Tile Cross Rd STETCH B33 ....131 G3
Tiled House La BRLYHL DY5 ....100 D3
Tile Gv CHWD/FDBR/MGN B37 ....114 A4
Tilehouse Green La
DOR/KN B93 ....196 D1
Tilehouse La SHLY B90 ....193 G3
Tilesford Cl SHLY B90 ....195 G3
Tiller Gv MGN/WHC B75 ....47 H1
Tilley St DARL/WED WS10 ....55 G2
Tillyard Cft SLYOAK B29 ....159 E1
Tilshead Cl
ALE/KHTH/YWD B14 ....178 A2
Tilsley Gv ERDW/GRVHL B23 ....91 H1
Tilston Dr BRLYHL DY5 ....119 F3
Tilton Rd BORD B9 ....128 A3
Timberdine Cl HALE B63 ....137 H1
Timberlake Cl SHLY B90 ....195 H2
Timberley La BKDE/SHDE B34 ....113 E3
Timbers Wy ERDE/BCHGN B24 ....94 B2
SPARK B11 ....144 C1
Timbertree Crs CDYHTH B64 ....121 E5
Timbertree Rd CDYHTH B64 ....121 E5
Times Square Av BRLYHL DY5 ....119 H2
Timmins Cl SOLH B91 ....165 G5
Timmis Cl BILS/COS WV14 ....53 F5
Timmis Rd HAG/WOL DY9 ....136 A1
Timothy Rd OLDBY B69 ....104 A2
Tinacre Hl
DUNHL/THL/PER WV6 ....34 C3
Tinchbourne St DUDN DY1 * 84 C5
Tindal St BHTH/HG B12 ....144 B2
Tinkers Farm Gv
NFLD/LBR B31 ....175 E2
Tinkers Farm Rd
NFLD/LBR B31 ....175 E1
Tinmeadow Crs RBRY B45 ....188 C1
Tinsley St TPTN/OCK DY4 ....86 C1
Tintagel Cl
DUNHL/THL/PER WV6 ....34 D2
Tintagel Dr DUDN DY1 ....83 G4
Tintagel Wy ALDR WS9 ....29 F3
Tintern Cl FOAKS/STRLY B74 ....60 C1
Tintern Ct
DUNHL/THL/PER WV6 ....34 C1
Tintern Crs BLOX/PEL WS3 ....16 B5
Tintern Rd BFLD/HDSWWD B20 ....91 E5
Tintern Vls BTH/HG B12 * 144 D2
Tintern Wy BLOX/PEL WS3 ....16 B5
Tipperary Cl CBROM B36 ....112 A1
Tipps Stone Cl TPTN/OCK DY4 ....85 E2
Tipton Rd OLDBY B69 ....86 A4
SEDG DY3 ....67 G4
TPTN/OCK DY4 ....85 E2
Tirley Rd STETCH B33 ....112 C5

Titania Cl RBRY B45 174 A2
Titchfield Cl WOLVN WV10 * 13 E3
Titford Cl OLDBY B69 104 D5
Titford La OLDBY B69 104 C5
Titford Rd OLDBY B69 104 D5
Tithe Cft WOLVN WV10 37 H2
Tithe Rd WNSFLD WV11 24 D4
Titterstone Rd NFLD/LBR B31 175 G5
Tiverton Cl KGSWFD DY6 118 C1
Tiverton Dr HHTH/SAND B71 71 G5
Tiverton Gv SMTHWKW B67 * 106 B3
Tiverton Rd SLYOAK B29 142 D5
SMTHWK B66 106 D4
Tividale Rd OLDBY B69 85 G4
Tividale St TPTN/OCK DY4 85 G3
Tixall Rd HLGN/YWD B28 162 C5
Toberland BLOX/PEL WS3 * 27 F3
Toll End Rd TPTN/OCK DY4 70 A3
Tollgate Cl NFLD/LBR B31 175 F5
Tollgate Dr
BFLD/HDSWWD B20 108 A2
Toll House Rd RBRY B45 188 C1
Tollhouse Wy SMTHWK B66 106 B2
WMBN WV5 64 C4
Tolworth Gdns BKHL/PFLD WV2 52 C1
Tolworth Hall Rd
ERDE/BCHGN B24 93 F3
Tomey Rd SPARK B11 145 F2
Tomlan Rd NFLD/LBR B31 190 A1
Tomlinson Rd CBROM B36 95 F5
Tompstone Rd HHTH/SAND B71 72 B3
Tonadine Cl WNSFLD WV11 25 G1
Tonbridge Rd ERDE/BCHGN B24 93 E5
Tong St WSL WS1 5 J4
Top Croft Rd ERDW/GRVHL B23 76 D4
Topfield Wk
ALE/KHTH/YWD B14 177 H3
Topland Gv NFLD/LBR B31 174 C3
Top Rd BRGRVW B61 186 C4
Topsham Cft
ALE/KHTH/YWD B14 160 D5
Topsham Rd SMTHWKW B67 106 A3
Torfield CDSL WV8 11 G5
Toronto Gdns RIDG/WDGT B32 141 E1
Torre Av NFLD/LBR B31 175 E3
Torrey Gv WASH/WDE B8 111 G5
Torridge Dr WNSFLD WV11 24 C5
Torridon Cft MOS/BIL B13 143 H4
Torridon Rd SHHTH WV12 25 H1
Torvale Rd
DUNHL/THL/PER WV6 35 E3
Tor Wy BLOX/PEL WS3 17 H4
Totnes Gv SLYOAK B29 * 142 D5
Totnes Rd SMTHWKW B67 106 B3
Tottenham Crs KGSTG B44 75 H1
Touchwood Hall Cl SOLH B91 182 A1
Towcester Cft CBROM B36 111 H1
Tower Cft
CHWD/FDBR/MGN B37 114 B5
Tower Hl PBAR/PBCH B42 74 A5
Tower Ri OLDBY B69 104 A2
Tower Rd AST/WIT B6 109 F2
MGN/WHC B75 47 F2
OLDBY B69 104 A2
Tower St DUDN DY1 84 C5
LOZ/NWT B19 108 D4
SEDG DY3 67 F2
WOLV WV1 7 G4
WSL WS1 4 E3
Townend Sq WSL WS1 * 4 D3
Townend St WSLW WS2 4 D3
Townfold BLOX/PEL WS3 18 A3
Townley Gdns AST/WIT B6 91 E5
Townsend Av SEDG DY3 67 F3
Townsend Dr WALM/CURD B76 78 B4
Townsend Wy CBHAMW B1 2 B4
Townshend Gv
CHWD/FDBR/MGN B37 113 H5
Townson Rd WNSFLD WV11 25 F2
Townwell Fold WOLV WV1 * 6 E4
Towpath Cl BORD B9 127 H2
Towyn Rd MOS/BIL B13 162 B1
Toys La HALE B63 137 G2
Tozer St TPTN/OCK DY4 69 F4
Traceys Meadow RBRY B45 188 A1
Trafalgar Ct OLDBY B69 85 H5
Trafalgar Gv YDLY B25 * 146 A1
Trafalgar Rd ERDE/BCHGN B24 92 D3
HDSW B21 107 G1
MOS/BIL B13 144 B4
OLDBY B69 85 H5
SMTHWK B66 106 D5
Trajan Hl CSHL/WTROR B46 97 E5
Tram Wy SMTHWK B66 105 G2
Tramway Cl BILS/COS WV14 54 B1
DARL/WED WS10 55 G1
Tranter Rd WASH/WDE B8 111 E4
Tranwell Cl COVEN WV9 11 H5
Traquain Dr DUDN DY1 84 A3
Treaford La WASH/WDE B8 111 F5
Tredington Cl SLYOAK B29 158 C3
Tree Acre Gv HALE B63 137 G3
Treeford Cl SOLH B91 181 F4
Trees Rd WSL WS1 57 F2
Treeton Cft STETCH B33 130 C2
Treetops Dr SHHTH WV12 26 C5
Trefoil Cl SLYOAK B29 158 C3
Tregarron Rd HALE B63 137 G2
Tregea Ri GTB/HAM B43 73 E4
Trehern Cl DOR/KN B93 197 E3
Trehernes Dr HAG/WOL DY9 152 D1
Trehurst Av PBAR/PBCH B42 74 C4
Trejon Rd CDYHTH B64 121 E4
Tremaine Gdns WOLVN WV10 37 F1
Tremont St WOLVN WV10 7 K2
Trenchard Cl MGN/WHC B75 63 F3
Trent Cl DUNHL/THL/PER WV6 34 C1
STRBR DY8 135 G3
Trent Dr CBROM B36 113 H1
Trentham Av SHHTH WV12 25 G5
Trentham Gv
LGN/SDN/BHAMAIR B26 147 E2
Trentham Ri BKHL/PFLD WV2 52 D1
Trent Pl BLOX/PEL WS3 27 H2
Trent Rd BLOX/PEL WS3 28 C1
Trent St DIG/EDG B5 3 K6
Trenville Av BHTH/HG B12 144 D2
Tresco Cl RBRY B45 173 G4
Trescott Rd NFLD/LBR B31 174 D2
Tresham Rd KGSTG B44 75 E2
KGSWFD DY6 99 H1
Trevanie Av RIDG/WDGT B32 140 C1
Trevorne Cl BHTH/HG B12 144 B1
Trevor Rd BLOX/PEL WS3 17 H3
Trevor St VAUX/NECH B7 110 A3
Trevor St West VAUX/NECH B7 110 A2
Trevose Cl BLOX/PEL WS3 * 16 B4
Trevose Retreat BHTH/HG B12 144 B2
Trewman Cl WALM/CURD B76 78 B3
Treyamon Rd DSYBK/YTR WS5 58 B1
Treynham Cl WLNHL WV13 38 C4
The Triangle WSNGN B18 * 107 H3
Trickley Dr MGN/WHC B75 * 63 F2
Trident Cl ERDW/GRVHL B23 77 E4
WALM/CURD B76 78 B4
Trident Ct
CHWD/FDBR/MGN B37 133 E4
Trident Dr DARL/WED WS10 55 F5
LGLYGN/QTN B68 105 F4
Trident Rd
LGN/SDN/BHAMAIR B26 149 G3
Trigo Cft CBROM B36 112 A1
Trimpley Cl DOR/KN B93 196 C5
Trimpley Gdns
ETTPK/GDPK/PENN WV4 51 E5
Trimpley Rd RIDG/WDGT B32 157 F2
Trinder Rd SMTHWKW B67 123 H3
Trindle Rd DUDN DY1 84 D4
Tring Ct DUNHL/THL/PER WV6 36 B1
Trinity Cl HIA/OLT B92 164 D1
STRBR DY8 117 H2
Trinity Gv DARL/WED WS10 56 A5
Trinity Hl CSCFLD/WYGN B72 62 C3
Trinity Pk BHAMNEC B40 * 149 H4
Trinity Pl CSCFLD/WYGN B72 * 62 C3
Trinity Rd AST/WIT B6 91 E5
BILS/COS WV14 54 B3
DUDN DY1 84 C5
MGN/WHC B75 47 F4
SHHTH WV12 26 B4
STRBR DY8 118 C4
Trinity Rd North WBROM B70 87 H4
Trinity Rd South WBROM B70 87 H5
Trinity St BRLYHL DY5 119 F1
CDYHTH B64 121 E3
OLDBY B69 105 E4
SMTHWKW B67 106 C3
WBROM B70 87 H5
Trinity Ter SPARK B11 127 G4
Trinity Wy WBROM B70 87 H5
Trippleton Av RIDG/WDGT B32 157 F3
Tristram Av NFLD/LBR B31 175 H4
Trittiford Rd MOS/BIL B13 162 A4
Tromans Cl CDYHTH B64 121 E5
Troon Cl BLOX/PEL WS3 16 C4
MGN/WHC B75 47 H5
Troon Ct DUNHL/THL/PER WV6 20 B5
Troon Pl STRBR DY8 117 G1
Trotter's La HHTH/SAND B71 71 E4
Trouse La DARL/WED WS10 55 G5
Troutbeck Dr BRLYHL DY5 118 D4
Troy Gv ALE/KHTH/YWD B14 177 H1
Truda St WSL WS1 56 D1
Truemans Heath La
HLYWD B47 192 D1
Truro Cl BLKHTH/ROWR B65 104 C5
Truro Rd DSYBK/YTR WS5 58 B1
Trustin Crs HIA/OLT B92 165 G2
Tryon Pl BILS/COS WV14 54 A2
Trysull Av
LGN/SDN/BHAMAIR B26 148 A3
Trysull Gdns BDMR/CCFT WV3 50 D1
Trysull Rd BDMR/CCFT WV3 50 D1
WMBN WV5 64 C2
Trysull Wy DUDS DY2 102 C5
Tudbury Rd NFLD/LBR B31 174 D1
Tudman Cl WALM/CURD B76 78 C4
Tudor Cl HLYWD B47 178 C4
MOS/BIL B13 161 F4
SCFLD/BOLD B73 76 B1
Tudor Ct TPTN/OCK DY4 85 G2
WNSFLD WV11 14 D4
Tudor Crs BKHL/PFLD WV2 51 H2
Tudor Cft
CHWD/FDBR/MGN B37 131 H3
Tudor Gdns ERDW/GRVHL B23 92 C3
STRBR DY8 135 E2
Tudor Gv FOAKS/STRLY B74 45 G5
Tudor Hl SCFLD/BOLD B73 62 A2
Tudor Pl SEDG DY3 67 G5
Tudor Rd BLKHTH/ROWR B65 104 A4
DARL/WED WS10 54 D4
LGLYGN/QTN B68 105 G5
MOS/BIL B13 144 B4
SCFLD/BOLD B73 62 B3
SEDG DY3 67 G5
WOLVN WV10 38 A1
Tudors Cl SMHTH B10 * 128 A4
Tudor St TPTN/OCK DY4 85 G2
WSNGN B18 107 F5
Tudor Ter DUDS DY2 85 E5
HRBN B17 * 142 A1
Tudor V SEDG DY3 67 G5
Tufnell Gv WASH/WDE B8 111 E2
Tugford Rd NFLD/LBR B31 159 E5
Tulyar Cl CBROM B36 111 G1
Tunnel La ALE/KHTH/YWD B14 177 G1
Tunnel Rd WBROM B70 71 E5
Tunnel St BILS/COS WV14 68 C3
Tunstall Rd KGSWFD DY6 100 C4
Turchill Dr WALM/CURD B76 78 C3
Turfpits La ERDW/GRVHL B23 76 B5
Turf Pitts La MGN/WHC B75 48 B2
Turley St DUDN DY1 68 A5
Turls Hill Rd SEDG DY3 67 G3
Turls St SEDG DY3 67 G4
Turnberry Gv CDSL WV8 20 B5
Turnberry Rd BLOX/PEL WS3 16 D3
PBAR/PBCH B42 74 B3
Turner Av
ETTPK/GDPK/PENN WV4 67 H1
Turner Dr BRLYHL DY5 119 F5
Turner Gv DUNHL/THL/PER WV6 35 E1
Turners Cft HHTH/SAND B71 72 C3
Turner's Gv SEDG DY3 83 E2
Turner's Hl BLKHTH/ROWR B65 103 H3
Turner's Hill Rd SEDG DY3 83 E2
Turner's La BRLYHL DY5 119 E4
Turner St DUDN DY1 102 B1
SEDG DY3 83 F3
SPARK B11 144 C1
TPTN/OCK DY4 69 F4
WBROM B70 87 E2
Turney Rd STRBR DY8 135 F1
Turnham Gn
DUNHL/THL/PER WV6 34 C2
Turnhouse Rd CVALE B35 94 D2
Turnley Rd BKDE/SHDE B34 113 E3
Turnpike Cl SPARK B11 144 C1
Turnpike Dr CSHL/WTROR B46 96 C3
Turton Cl BLOX/PEL WS3 16 C3
Turton Rd TPTN/OCK DY4 69 F2
WBROM B70 87 F4
Turtons Cft BILS/COS WV14 53 F5
Turves Gn NFLD/LBR B31 175 F5
Turville Rd BFLD/HDSWWD B20 90 C5
Tustin Gv ACGN B27 163 G2
Tutbury Av
DUNHL/THL/PER WV6 34 D2
Tuxford Cl WOLVN WV10 37 G1
Tweeds Well RIDG/WDGT B32 157 F3
Twickenham Ct STRBR DY8 117 G5
Twickenham Rd KGSTG B44 75 H2
Two Gates HALE B63 137 F2
Two Gates La HALE B63 137 G2
Two Locks BRLYHL DY5 101 H5
Two Woods La BRLYHL DY5 119 G3
Twycross Gv CBROM B36 111 H2
Twydale Av OLDBY B69 85 H5
Twyford Cl ALDR WS9 30 B5
Twyford Gv WNSFLD WV11 25 F3
Twyford Rd WASH/WDE B8 111 G4
Twyning Rd BVILLE B30 160 B3
LDYWD/EDGR B16 107 F5
Tyber Dr BFLD/HDSWWD B20 90 B3
Tyberry Cl SHLY B90 180 A4
Tyburn Gv ERDE/BCHGN B24 93 H3
Tyburn Rd ERDE/BCHGN B24 92 B5
WOLV WV1 38 C4
Tyburn Sq ERDE/BCHGN B24 93 H3
Tyebeams BKDE/SHDE B34 113 E4
Tye Gdns HAG/WOL DY9 152 D1
Tyler Ct ERDE/BCHGN B24 92 D3
Tyler Gdns WLNHL WV13 39 H4
Tyler Gv PBAR/PBCH B42 74 A2
Tyler Rd WLNHL WV13 39 G5
Tylers Gn HWK/WKHTH B38 177 F4
Tylers Gv SHLY B90 195 F2
Tylney Cl DIG/EDG B5 126 D5
Tyndale Crs GTB/HAM B43 59 G5
Tyndall Wk RIDG/WDGT B32 140 A5
Tyne Cl BRWNH WS8 8 C2
CHWD/FDBR/MGN B37 114 B5
Tynedale Crs
ETTPK/GDPK/PENN WV4 52 C5
Tynedale Rd SPARK B11 145 H4
Tyne Gv YDLY B25 129 H4
Tyne Pl BRLYHL DY5 119 H2
Tyning Cl COVEN WV9 12 A5
Tyninghame Av
DUNHL/THL/PER WV6 21 H4
Tynings La ALDR WS9 30 A5
Tyrley Cl DUNHL/THL/PER WV6 35 F3
Tyrol Cl STRBR DY8 134 D1
Tyseley Hill Rd SPARK B11 146 A3
Tyseley La SPARK B11 146 A3
Tysoe Cl HOCK/TIA B94 198 A5
Tysoe Dr MGN/WHC B75 63 F4
Tysoe Rd KGSTG B44 75 F4
Tythebarn Dr KGSWFD DY6 99 E2
Tythebarn La SHLY B90 193 H2
Tyzack Cl BRLYHL DY5 119 E2

U

Udall Rd BILS/COS WV14 53 H5
Uffculme Rd BVILLE B30 160 D2
Uffmoor Est HALE B63 138 A5
Uffmoor La RMSLY B62 154 D4
Ufton Cl SHLY B90 181 E2
Ufton Crs SHLY B90 180 D2
Ullenhall Rd DOR/KN B93 197 E2
WALM/CURD B76 78 B3
Ullenwood HDSW B21 107 F2
Ulleries Rd HIA/OLT B92 147 G5
Ullrik Gn ERDE/BCHGN B24 92 D4
Ullswater Cl RIDG/WDGT B32 141 F5
Ullswater Gdns KGSWFD DY6 99 H3
Ullswater Ri BRLYHL DY5 101 F4
Ullswater Rd SHHTH WV12 25 H1
Ulster Dr KGSWFD DY6 100 A5
Ulverley Crs HIA/OLT B92 164 B2
Ulverley Green Rd
HIA/OLT B92 164 B2
Ulwine Dr NFLD/LBR B31 175 G1
Umberslade Rd SLYOAK B29 160 A2
Underhill La WOLVN WV10 13 G4
Underhill Rd TPTN/OCK DY4 70 A5
WASH/WDE B8 128 D1
Underhill St OLDBY B69 105 E4
Underley Cl KGSWFD DY6 99 F2
The Underpass BHAMNEC B40 150 A3
Underwood Cl EDG B15 142 B4
ERDW/GRVHL B23 92 A2
Underwood Rd
BFLD/HDSWWD B20 89 G1
Unett St LOZ/NWT B19 108 C4
SMTHWK B66 107 E5
Unett Wk LOZ/NWT B19 108 C4
Union La WMBN WV5 64 B2
Union Mill St WOLV WV1 7 J4
Union Rd AST/WIT B6 109 H1
OLDBY B69 86 C4
SHLY B90 180 C3
SOLH B91 182 A1
Union Rw HDSW B21 107 H1
Union St BILS/COS WV14 53 G3
BLKHTH/ROWR B65 122 A3
CBHAM B2 3 G5
DARL/WED WS10 70 D1
DUDS DY2 84 C5
HAG/WOL DY9 136 C2
STRBR DY8 135 G3
TPTN/OCK DY4 69 F2
TPTN/OCK DY4 85 F1
WBROM B70 105 H1
WLNHL WV13 39 G3
WOLV WV1 7 H4
WSL WS1 5 G3
Unity Cl DARL/WED WS10 55 E4
Unity Pl OLDBY B69 * 105 E1
SLYOAK B29 * 142 D5
Unketts Rd SMTHWKW B67 124 A1
Unwin Crs STRBR DY8 135 E2
Upavon Cl CVALE B35 94 C2
Upland Rd SLYOAK B29 143 E5
Uplands HALE B63 137 H5
Uplands Av BDMR/CCFT WV3 35 H5
BLKHTH/ROWR B65 122 B1
WLNHL WV13 38 D4
Uplands Cl DUDS DY2 103 E2
Uplands Dr BDMR/CCFT WV3 36 A5
SEDG DY3 67 F3
Uplands Gv WLNHL WV13 38 C4
Uplands Rd DUDS DY2 103 F2
HDSW B21 89 F4
WLNHL WV13 38 C4
The Uplands SMTHWKW B67 106 B5
Upper Ashley St RMSLY B62 122 A3
Upper Balsall Heath Rd
BHTH/HG B12 144 B1
Upper Brook St WSLW WS2 4 B4
Upper Chapel St OLDBY B69 85 H4
Upper Church La
TPTN/OCK DY4 69 F4
Upper Clifton Rd
SCFLD/BOLD B73 62 B3
Upper Cl RIDG/WDGT B32 140 D4
Upper Coneybere St
BHTH/HG B12 127 F5
Upper Dean St DIG/EDG B5 3 G7
Upper Ettingshall Rd
BILS/COS WV14 68 A3
Upper Forster St
RUSH/SHEL WS4 5 F1
Upper Gough St CBHAMW B1 126 D3
Upper Gn DUNHL/THL/PER WV6 21 H5
Upper Green La WSLW WS2 41 G1
Upper Grosvenor Rd
BFLD/HDSWWD B20 90 B4
Upper Hall La WSL WS1 4 E5
Upper Highgate St
BHTH/HG B12 127 F5
Upper High St CDYHTH B64 120 D3
DARL/WED WS10 55 H5
Upper Holland Rd
CSCFLD/WYGN B72 62 C4
Upper Lichfield St WLNHL WV13 39 G3
Upper Marshall St CBHAMW B1 2 E7
Upper Meadow Rd
RIDG/WDGT B32 140 C2
Upper Navigation St
WSLW WS2 4 C3
Upper Rushall St WSL WS1 5 F4
Upper Russell St
DARL/WED WS10 70 D1
Upper St Mary's Rd
SMTHWKW B67 124 B3
Upper Short St WSLW WS2 4 B4
Upper Sneyd Rd WNSFLD WV11 15 F5
Upper St DUNHL/THL/PER WV6 21 H5
Upper Sutton St AST/WIT B6 109 F2
Upper Thomas St AST/WIT B6 109 F3
Upper Trinity St BORD B9 127 G3
Upper Vauxhall WOLV WV1 6 B3
Upper Villiers St
ETTPK/GDPK/PENN WV4 51 H2
Upper William St CBHAMW B1 2 C7
Upper Zoar St BDMR/CCFT WV3 6 C7
Upton Gdns BILS/COS WV14 53 G3
Upton Gv YDLY B25 129 G3
Upton Rd STETCH B33 129 G2
Upton St DUDS DY2 102 C4
Upwey Av SOLH B91 181 G1
Usk Wy CBROM B36 113 H1
Uttoxeter Cl
DUNHL/THL/PER WV6 22 D5
Uxbridge Cl SEDG DY3 83 F4
Uxbridge St LOZ/NWT B19 108 D4

V

Valbourne Rd
ALE/KHTH/YWD B14 177 G1
Vale Av ALDR WS9 44 D3
Vale Cl RIDG/WDGT B32 141 F4
Vale Ct CDYHTH B64 * 120 D5
Valencia Cft CVALE B35 94 D2
Valentine Cl FOAKS/STRLY B74 60 B1
Valentine Rd
ALE/KHTH/YWD B14 161 E1
LGLYGN/QTN B68 123 G2
Valepits Rd STETCH B33 131 E3
Valerie Gv GTB/HAM B43 73 E3
Vale Rd DUDS DY2 103 E5
Vale Rw SEDG DY3 83 F1
Vales Cl WALM/CURD B76 78 A4
Vale St BKHL/PFLD WV2 53 E2
HHTH/SAND B71 72 A5
SEDG DY3 83 F1
STRBR DY8 118 B4
The Vale SPARK B11 144 D5
Vale Vw ALDR WS9 44 B2
Valley Farm Rd RBRY B45 187 H2
Valley La HOCK/TIA B94 199 H4
Valley Rd BLOX/PEL WS3 27 H2
CDYHTH B64 121 E5
FOAKS/STRLY B74 60 B1
GTB/HAM B43 73 E4
HAG/WOL DY9 136 D2
HIA/OLT B92 148 A3
RMSLY B62 122 D4
SEDG DY3 67 G5
SMTHWKW B67 124 B1
WOLVN WV10 23 H5
Valley Side BLOX/PEL WS3 17 H5
Valley Vw BRWNH WS8 9 G5
Vallian Cft CBROM B36 112 B2
Vanborough Wk DUDN DY1 84 A4
Vanbrugh Ct
DUNHL/THL/PER WV6 34 C2
Van Diemans Rd WMBN WV5 80 C1
Vanguard Cl CBROM B36 112 A1
Vanguard Rd
LGN/SDN/BHAMAIR B26 149 G3
Vann Cl SMHTH B10 128 A4
Vantage Point WBROM B70 * 87 G4
Varden Cft DIG/EDG B5 126 D5
Vardon Wy HWK/WKHTH B38 176 B4
Varley Rd ERDE/BCHGN B24 93 H2
Varley V ERDE/BCHGN B24 93 H2
Varlins Wy HWK/WKHTH B38 190 B2
Varney Av WBROM B70 87 H4
Vaughan Cl FOAKS/STRLY B74 32 D4
Vaughan Gdns CDSL WV8 10 B3
Vaughan Rd WLNHL WV13 38 D4
Vaughton Dr MGN/WHC B75 63 E2
Vaughton St BHTH/HG B12 127 F4
Vaughton St South
DIG/EDG B5 127 E5
Vauxhall Av WOLV WV1 6 B3
Vauxhall Crs CBROM B36 95 H5
Vauxhall Gdns DUDS DY2 103 E2
Vauxhall Gv VAUX/NECH B7 127 H1
Vauxhall Pl VAUX/NECH B7 * 127 G1
Vauxhall Rd STRBR DY8 135 G2
VAUX/NECH B7 127 G1
Vauxhall St DUDN DY1 102 B1
Velsheda Rd SHLY B90 180 A3
Venetia Rd BORD B9 128 A2
Venning Gv GTB/HAM B43 73 F4
Ventnor Av CBROM B36 111 H2
LOZ/NWT B19 108 C2
Ventnor Cl LGLYGN/QTN B68 123 G5
Ventnor Rd HIA/OLT B92 148 A4
Venture Wy VAUX/NECH B7 3 K1
Vera Rd
LGN/SDN/BHAMAIR B26 130 A5
Verbena Gdns VAUX/NECH B7 109 G4
Verbena Rd NFLD/LBR B31 158 B5
Vercourt FOAKS/STRLY B74 45 H2
Vere St DIG/EDG B5 126 D4
Verity Wk STRBR DY8 118 A3
Verney Av STETCH B33 131 F5
Vernier Av KGSWFD DY6 100 C4
Vernolds Cft DIG/EDG B5 * 127 E4
Vernon Av BFLD/HDSWWD B20 89 H2
BRWNH WS8 9 G5
TPTN/OCK DY4 85 E2
Vernon Cl FOAKS/STRLY B74 32 C5
RMSLY B62 122 A4
WLNHL WV13 39 E4
WNSFLD WV11 14 D3
Vernon Ct LDYWD/EDGR B16 125 G3
LGLYGN/QTN B68 * 123 F5
Vernon Rd BILS/COS WV14 54 B2
LDYWD/EDGR B16 125 F3
LGLYGN/QTN B68 105 G3
RMSLY B62 122 A4
Vernon St WBROM B70 86 G3
Vernon Wy BLOX/PEL WS3 26 C1
Veronica Av
ETTPK/GDPK/PENN WV4 52 C3
Veronica Cl SLYOAK B29 158 B4
Veronica Rd KGSWFD DY6 100 C3
Verstone Cft NFLD/LBR B31 175 G3
Verstone Rd SHLY B90 180 C1
Verwood Cl WLNHL WV13 38 D4
Vesey Cl CSHL/WTROR B46 96 B4
FOAKS/STRLY B74 46 D3
Vesey Rd SCFLD/BOLD B73 77 F2
Vesey St CBHAMNE B4 3 G2
Vestry Cl CDYHTH B64 121 F3
Vestry Ct STRBR DY8 135 E1
Viaduct Dr
DUNHL/THL/PER WV6 22 D4
Viaduct St VAUX/NECH B7 127 G1
Vibart Rd
LGN/SDN/BHAMAIR B26 130 B4
Vicarage Cl BRLYHL DY5 119 E5
BRWNH WS8 9 G4
BVILLE B30 160 B3
PBAR/PBCH B42 74 D4
TPTN/OCK DY4 85 E1
Vicarage Gdns RMSLY B62 122 B3
WALM/CURD B76 78 B4
Vicarage La BRLYHL DY5 101 F1
CSHL/WTROR B46 96 B4
Vicarage Pl WSL WS1 4 D5
Vicarage Prospect DUDN DY1 84 B5

Vicarage Rd
ALE/KHTH/YWD B14 160 C3
AST/WIT B6 109 G2
BILS/COS WV14 68 C4
BKHL/PFLD WV2 7 H7
BLOX/PEL WS3 18 A5
BRWNH WS8 9 F5
DARL/WED WS10 55 H5
EDG B15 125 H4
ETTPK/GDPK/PENN WV4 51 E5
HAG/WOL DY9 136 D2
HHTH/SAND B71 71 H5
HOCK/TIA B94 194 C5
HOCK/TIA B94 198 C4
HRBN B17 141 H2
LGLYGN/QTN B68 105 F5
RMSLY B62 122 A4
SEDG DY3 83 G1
SMTHWKW B67 106 B4
STETCH B33 130 A3
STRBR DY8 117 H5
WNSFLD WV11 24 B4
WSNGN B18 108 A2
Vicarage Rd West DUDN DY1 68 C5
Vicarage St LGLYGN/QTN B68 105 F4
Vicarage Ter WSLW WS2 41 G5
Vicarage Wk WSL WS1 4 D5
Vicar St DARL/WED WS10 56 A5
DUDS DY2 102 C1
SEDG DY3 67 F3
Vicars Wk HAG/WOL DY9 136 C5
Viceroy Cl EDG B15 143 G1
KGSWFD DY6 100 C4
Victor Cl BKHL/PFLD WV2 53 F2
Victoria Ar WOLV WV1 7 F4
Victoria Av BLOX/PEL WS3 27 G1
RMSLY B62 139 H1
SMHTH B10 * 128 B5
SMTHWK B66 106 C4
Victoria Gdns CDYHTH B64 * 121 F2
Victoria Gv WMBN WV5 65 E3
Victoria Ms OLDBY B69 122 D1
RUSH/SHEL WS4 42 C2
Victoria Park Rd SMTHWK B66 106 D4
Victoria Pas WOLV WV1 7 F4
Victoria Pl DARL/WED WS10 * 40 B5
Victoria Rd ACGN B27 146 C5
AST/WIT B6 109 E2
BDMR/CCFT WV3 51 E1
BLOX/PEL WS3 18 A4
BRLYHL DY5 120 A3
BVILLE B30 160 A3
CDYHTH B64 121 F2
CSCFLD/WYGN B72 62 C3
DARL/WED WS10 55 F2
DUNHL/THL/PER WV6 22 A5
ERDW/GRVHL B23 92 B3
HDSW B21 107 G2
HRBN B17 141 H2
LGLYGN/QTN B68 105 G3
RMSLY B62 122 B4
SEDG DY3 67 G3
STETCH B33 129 H1
TPTN/OCK DY4 85 F1
WNSFLD WV11 24 B4
WOLVN WV10 23 H5
Victoria Sq CBHAMNW B3 2 E5
Victoria St BORD B9 128 B2
BRLYHL DY5 101 E2
BRLYHL DY5 119 F1
DARL/WED WS10 70 C1
HALE B63 138 C3
KGSWFD DY6 81 F5
STRBR DY8 135 G2
WBROM B70 86 D1
WBROM B70 87 G3
WLNHL WV13 39 G2
WOLV WV1 7 F5
Victoria Ter RUSH/SHEL WS4 42 B2
Victor Rd HIA/OLT B92 148 C4
WSNGN B18 107 G3
Victor St BLOX/PEL WS3 28 C1
WSL WS1 57 E1
Victory Av DARL/WED WS10 55 E4
Victory La WSLW WS2 41 E1
Victory Ri HHTH/SAND B71 87 H1
View Dr DUDS DY2 103 E1
Viewfield Crs SEDG DY3 67 F4
Viewlands Dr
DUNHL/THL/PER WV6 35 E3
View Point OLDBY B69 103 H1
Vigo Cl ALDR WS9 19 F5
Vigo Pl ALDR WS9 30 A3
Vigo Rd ALDR WS9 19 F5
Vigo Ter ALDR WS9 19 F4
Viking Ri BLKHTH/ROWR B65 104 A5
Village Rd AST/WIT B6 91 G5
The Village KGSWFD DY6 100 A2
Village Wy BILS/COS WV14 53 F3
Villa Rd LOZ/NWT B19 108 B2
Villa St LOZ/NWT B19 108 C3
STRBR DY8 118 C4
Villa Wk LOZ/NWT B19 108 C3
Villette Gv
ALE/KHTH/YWD B14 179 E1
Villiers Av BILS/COS WV14 53 H2
Villiers St WLNHL WV13 39 G3
WSL WS1 57 E1
WSNGN B18 107 G4
Vimy Rd DARL/WED WS10 56 A4
MOS/BIL B13 161 H2
Vincent Cl BHTH/HG B12 144 B1
Vincent Dr EDG B15 142 B4
Vincent Pde BHTH/HG B12 144 B1
Vincent Rd MGN/WHC B75 63 E1
Vincent St BHTH/HG B12 144 B2
WSL WS1 57 F1
Vince St SMTHWK B66 124 C1
Vinculum Wy WLNHL WV13 39 H5
Vine Av BHTH/HG B12 144 C2
Vine Crs HHTH/SAND B71 71 H5
Vine Gdns CDYHTH B64 121 F2
Vine La HAG/WOL DY9 170 D2
HALE B63 138 D4
STRBR DY8 * 118 A3
The Vineries ACGN B27 147 E3
Vine St AST/WIT B6 109 H2
BRLYHL DY5 101 G4
STRBR DY8 118 A3
Vineyard Rd NFLD/LBR B31 158 B5
Vinnall Gv RIDG/WDGT B32 157 F2
Vintage Cl BKDE/SHDE B34 112 C4
Vinyard Cl WSNGN B18 107 H2
Violet Cft TPTN/OCK DY4 69 H2
Violet La HAG/WOL DY9 170 C1
Virginia Dr
ETTPK/GDPK/PENN WV4 51 F4
Viscount Cl CVALE B35 94 C4
Vista Gn HWK/WKHTH B38 177 F4
The Vista SEDG DY3 67 F2
Vittoria St CBHAMW B1 2 C2
SMTHWK B66 107 F3
Vivian Cl HRBN B17 142 A2
Vivian Rd HRBN B17 142 A2
Vixen Cl WALM/CURD B76 77 H4
Vulcan Rd BILS/COS WV14 54 B3
SOLH B91 165 E4
Vyrnwy Gv HWK/WKHTH B38 176 C5
Vyse St AST/WIT B6 109 H1
WSNGN B18 2 C1

W

Waddell Cl BILS/COS WV14 67 H2
Waddens Brook La
WNSFLD WV11 25 E5
Waddington Av GTB/HAM B43 73 G2
Wadesmill Lawns WOLVN WV10 13 E3
Wadham Cl OLDBY B69 104 A3
Wadhurst Rd HRBN B17 124 D2
Wadleys Rd SOLH B91 164 B4
Waen Cl TPTN/OCK DY4 69 H3
Waggon St CDYHTH B64 121 F2
Waggon Wk HWK/WKHTH B38 176 A5
Wagoners Cl WASH/WDE B8 110 D3
Wagon La HIA/OLT B92 147 F3
Wagstaff Cl BILS/COS WV14 68 D3
Wainwright Cl KGSWFD DY6 99 E2
Wainwright St AST/WIT B6 109 G2
Waite Rd WLNHL WV13 39 E5
Wakefield Cl SCFLD/BOLD B73 77 E1
Wakefield Ct MOS/BIL B13 * 144 D5
Wakefield Gv CSHL/WTROR B46 96 B3
Wakeford Rd NFLD/LBR B31 176 A4
Wake Green Pk MOS/BIL B13 144 D5
Wake Green Rd MOS/BIL B13 144 C5
TPTN/OCK DY4 69 G2
Wakelam Gdns GTB/HAM B43 73 F2
Wakeley Hl
ETTPK/GDPK/PENN WV4 51 G5
Wakelin Rd SHLY B90 194 B1
Wakeman Ct WNSFLD WV11 14 D4
Wakeman Dr OLDBY B69 103 H1
Wakeman Gv STETCH B33 131 F5
Wakes Cl WLNHL WV13 39 H4
Wakes Rd DARL/WED WS10 71 E1
Walcot Cl MGN/WHC B75 47 F2
Walcot Dr GTB/HAM B43 73 G5
Walcot Gdns BILS/COS WV14 53 F3
Walcot Gn DOR/KN B93 199 E1
Waldale Cl SHHTH WV12 26 A1
Walden Gdns
ETTPK/GDPK/PENN WV4 51 E2
Walden Rd SPARK B11 146 A4
Waldeve Gv HIA/OLT B92 165 H2
Waldley Gv ERDE/BCHGN B24 93 G3
Waldron Av BRLYHL DY5 118 D2
Waldron Cl DARL/WED WS10 55 H2
Waldrons Moor
ALE/KHTH/YWD B14 160 C5
Walford Av BDMR/CCFT WV3 36 B5
Walford Dr HIA/OLT B92 148 B4
Walford Rd SPARK B11 145 E1
Walford St OLDBY B69 85 F4
Walhouse Cl WSL WS1 5 G3
Walhouse Rd WSL WS1 5 G3
Walker Av BRLYHL DY5 119 F5
HAG/WOL DY9 136 B4
OLDBY B69 104 A2
WOLVN WV10 23 G2
Walker Dr VAUX/NECH B7 110 C1
Walker Pl BLOX/PEL WS3 28 A2
Walker Rd BLOX/PEL WS3 27 H2
Walkers Fold SHHTH WV12 26 B4
Walkers Heath Rd
HWK/WKHTH B38 177 F4
Walker St DUDS DY2 102 C5
TPTN/OCK DY4 70 A4
Walkers Wy CSHL/WTROR B46 115 G3
Walk La WMBN WV5 65 E5
The Walk SEDG DY3 67 F2
Wallace Cl OLDBY B69 104 B3
Wallace Ri CDYHTH B64 121 E5
Wallace Rd BILS/COS WV14 54 C5
BRWNH WS8 9 E4
OLDBY B69 104 B3
SLYOAK B29 143 F5
Wall Av CSHL/WTROR B46 115 F4
Wallbank Rd WASH/WDE B8 111 E3
Wallbrook St BILS/COS WV14 68 D3
Wall Cft ALDR WS9 30 B3
Wall Dr FOAKS/STRLY B74 46 D1
Wall End Cl WSLW WS2 27 E3
Wallface HHTH/SAND B71 71 E4
Walling Cft BILS/COS WV14 53 F5
Wallington Cl BLOX/PEL WS3 16 D5
Wallington Heath
BLOX/PEL WS3 16 D5
Wallows La WSL WS1 56 C2
Wallows Pl BRLYHL DY5 101 E4
Wallows Rd BRLYHL DY5 101 E5
Wallows Wd SEDG DY3 82 C2
Wall St WOLV WV1 38 A3
Wall Well HALE B63 138 B4
Wall Well La HALE B63 138 B4
Walmead Cft HRBN B17 124 B5
Walmer Gv ERDW/GRVHL B23 91 H1
Walmer Meadow ALDR WS9 30 B3
The Walmers ALDR WS9 30 B3
Walmer Wy
CHWD/FDBR/MGN B37 132 C1
Walmesley Wy NFLD/LBR B31 175 E2
Walmley Ash Rd
WALM/CURD B76 78 B4
Walmley Cl HALE B63 120 B5
WALM/CURD B76 78 B3
Walmley Rd MGN/WHC B75 63 E4
Walnut Av CDSL WV8 10 D4
Walnut Cl
CHWD/FDBR/MGN B37 132 B3
HAG/WOL DY9 152 D1
Walnut Dr BDMR/CCFT WV3 35 H4
SMTHWK B66 106 D4
Walnut La DARL/WED WS10 71 E1
Walnut Rd DSYBK/YTR WS5 57 G5
Walnut Wy NFLD/LBR B31 175 F5
Walpole St DUNHL/THL/PER WV6 6 B1
Walpole Wk WBROM B70 87 H5
Walsall Rd ALDR WS9 19 E5
ALDR WS9 43 H1
BLOX/PEL WS3 18 A5
DARL/WED WS10 55 G2
DSYBK/YTR WS5 57 F4
FOAKS/STRLY B74 32 A4
HHTH/SAND B71 72 A1
PBAR/PBCH B42 74 A3
WLNHL WV13 39 H3
Walsall St BILS/COS WV14 53 H3
DARL/WED WS10 55 F2
DARL/WED WS10 55 H5
WBROM B70 87 H3
WLNHL WV13 39 H4
WOLV WV1 7 J5
Walsall Wood Rd ALDR WS9 19 G5
Walsgrave Dr HIA/OLT B92 165 F3
Walsham Cft BKDE/SHDE B34 113 E4
Walsh Dr WALM/CURD B76 63 F4
Walsh Gv ERDW/GRVHL B23 76 B3
Walsingham St WSL WS1 5 H5
Walstead Rd DSYBK/YTR WS5 57 F3
Walstead Rd West
DSYBK/YTR WS5 57 E3
Waltdene Cl GTB/HAM B43 73 G1
Walter Cobb Dr SCFLD/BOLD B73 77 E2
Walter Rd BILS/COS WV14 54 A5
SMTHWKW B67 106 A3
Walters Cl NFLD/LBR B31 189 F2
Walters Rd LGLYGN/QTN B68 123 E5
Walters Rw DUDN DY1 84 A5
Walter St BLOX/PEL WS3 28 C1
VAUX/NECH B7 109 H3
WBROM B70 87 H4
Waltham Gv KGSTG B44 75 H1
Walthamstow Ct BRLYHL DY5 119 F3
Walton Av BLKHTH/ROWR B65 121 H4
Walton Cl BLKHTH/ROWR B65 103 G5
HALE B63 138 B5
Walton Crs
ETTPK/GDPK/PENN WV4 52 C3
Walton Cft SOLH B91 181 H4
Walton Dr HAG/WOL DY9 136 A2
Walton Gdns CDSL WV8 10 B3
Walton Gv BVILLE B30 177 F3
Walton Heath BLOX/PEL WS3 16 B4
Walton Pool La HAG/WOL DY9 170 D3
Walton Ri HAG/WOL DY9 171 E2
Walton Rd ALDR WS9 30 A1
DARL/WED WS10 71 G1
ETTPK/GDPK/PENN WV4 52 D3
LGLYGN/QTN B68 123 G3
STRBR DY8 135 G1
Walton St TPTN/OCK DY4 85 F1
Wanderers Av BKHL/PFLD WV2 52 A2
Wanderer Wk
ERDE/BCHGN B24 94 A5
Wandle Gv SPARK B11 146 A4
Wandsworth Rd KGSTG B44 60 A5
Wannerton Rd KIDD DY10 168 B4
Wansbeck Gv
HWK/WKHTH B38 176 C5
Wansbeck Wk SEDG DY3 67 H5
Wanstead Gv KGSTG B44 75 G2
Wantage Rd CSHL/WTROR B46 97 E5
Ward Cl WASH/WDE B8 111 E4
Warden Av SCFLD/BOLD B73 76 D3
Ward End Cl WASH/WDE B8 110 D3
Ward End Hall Gv
WASH/WDE B8 111 E3
Ward End Park Rd
WASH/WDE B8 110 D4
Wardend Rd WASH/WDE B8 111 E3
Warden Rd SCFLD/BOLD B73 76 D3
Ward Gv
ETTPK/GDPK/PENN WV4 52 D5
Wardle Cl MGN/WHC B75 47 E1
Wardlow Cl
ETTPK/GDPK/PENN WV4 51 H2
Wardlow Rd VAUX/NECH B7 109 G4
Wardour Dr
CHWD/FDBR/MGN B37 132 C2
Wardour Gv KGSTG B44 76 A3
Ward Rd CDSL WV8 10 B4
ETTPK/GDPK/PENN WV4 52 B3
Ward St BILS/COS WV14 68 B3
BKHL/PFLD WV2 53 F2
LOZ/NWT B19 3 G1
WLNHL WV13 39 H2
WOLV WV1 7 J4
WSL WS1 5 G2
Wareham Rd RBRY B45 174 B3
Wareing Dr ERDW/GRVHL B23 76 B3
Warewell Cl WSL WS1 5 F3
Warewell St WSL WS1 5 F4
Waring Cl TPTN/OCK DY4 69 E3
Waring Rd TPTN/OCK DY4 69 G3
The Warings WMBN WV5 80 D2
War La HRBN B17 141 H2
Warley Cft LGLYGN/QTN B68 123 H4
Warley Hall Rd
LGLYGN/QTN B68 123 H3
Warley Rd LGLYGN/QTN B68 105 G4
Warmington Dr
SCFLD/BOLD B73 62 B4
Warmington Rd HLYWD B47 192 C2
LGN/SDN/BHAMAIR B26 148 A2
Warmley Cl
DUNHL/THL/PER WV6 22 D5
SOLH B91 165 F5
Warner Dr BRLYHL DY5 119 F3
Warner Pl BLOX/PEL WS3 28 B4
Warner Rd BLOX/PEL WS3 28 C4
CDSL WV8 10 B4
DARL/WED WS10 71 G1
Warner St BHTH/HG B12 127 G4
Warners Wk SMHTH B10 128 A4
Warple Rd RIDG/WDGT B32 140 C2
Warren Av WOLVN WV10 23 H5
Warren Cl TPTN/OCK DY4 69 F4
Warren Dr BLKHTH/ROWR B65 103 F4
DOR/KN B93 197 E5
SEDG DY3 67 E1
Warren Farm Rd KGSTG B44 75 F3
Warren Gdns KGSWFD DY6 99 G3
Warren Gv WASH/WDE B8 * 110 C3
Warren Hill Rd KGSTG B44 75 G4
Warren House Wk
WALM/CURD B76 78 B2
Warren La RBRY B45 188 B5
Warren Pl BRWNH WS8 9 G5
Warren Rd BVILLE B30 160 A3
KGSTG B44 75 G5
WASH/WDE B8 110 C3
Warrens Cft DSYBK/YTR WS5 58 B3
Warrens End HWK/WKHTH B38 176 D5
Warrens Hall Rd DUDS DY2 103 E2
Warrington Cl
WALM/CURD B76 78 C2
Warrington Dr
ERDW/GRVHL B23 76 B4
Warsash Cl WOLV WV1 38 B5
Warstock La
ALE/KHTH/YWD B14 178 C1
Warstock Rd
ALE/KHTH/YWD B14 178 C1
Warston Av RIDG/WDGT B32 140 D4
Warstone Dr HHTH/SAND B71 88 A2
Warstone La CBHAMW B1 2 C2
Warstone Ms WSNGN B18 * 2 C2
Warstone Pde East WSNGN B18 2 B1
Warstones Crs
ETTPK/GDPK/PENN WV4 50 D3
Warstones Dr
ETTPK/GDPK/PENN WV4 50 C3
Warstones Gdns
ETTPK/GDPK/PENN WV4 50 C2
Warstones Rd
ETTPK/GDPK/PENN WV4 50 D4
Warstone Ter HDSW B21 107 G1
Wartell Bank KGSWFD DY6 99 H2
Warwards La SLYOAK B29 160 A1
Warwell La
LGN/SDN/BHAMAIR B26 146 D1
Warwick Av DARL/WED WS10 56 C5
DUNHL/THL/PER WV6 34 D2
WLNHL WV13 40 B3
Warwick Cl LGLYGN/QTN B68 123 F2
WBROM B70 70 C4
Warwick Crest EDG B15 * 126 B5
Warwick Dr CDSL WV8 10 A4
Warwick Gdns OLDBY B69 86 A4
Warwick Gra SOLH B91 164 B3
Warwick Gv HIA/OLT B92 163 H1
Warwick Pas CBHAM B2 3 G5
Warwick Rd ACGN B27 146 A3
DOR/KN B93 197 F1
DUDS DY2 121 E1
LGLYGN/QTN B68 123 H5
SCFLD/BOLD B73 76 A1
SOLH B91 164 B3
SOLH B91 182 B2
SPARK B11 145 E2
STRBR DY8 117 H3
Warwick St BHTH/HG B12 127 G3
BILS/COS WV14 54 A3
RUSH/SHEL WS4 5 F1
WOLV WV1 7 J5
Warwick Wy ALDR WS9 30 A1
Wasdale Dr KGSWFD DY6 100 A3
Wasdale Rd BRWNH WS8 * 18 D1
NFLD/LBR B31 175 F1
Waseley Rd RBRY B45 173 G5
Washbrook Rd WASH/WDE B8 111 E3
Washford Gv YDLY B25 129 F4
Washington Dr
BFLD/HDSWWD B20 90 B3
Washington St CBHAMW B1 2 D7
DUDS DY2 120 D1
Washington Whf CBHAMW B1 2 D7
Wash La YDLY B25 129 G4
Washwood Heath Rd
WASH/WDE B8 111 G4
Wasperton Cl CBROM B36 112 D1
Wassell Ct HALE B63 138 A5
Wassell Grove Rd
HAG/WOL DY9 153 H1
Wassell Rd BILS/COS WV14 53 H1
HAG/WOL DY9 136 C5
HALE B63 138 A5
Wast Hill Gv HWK/WKHTH B38 190 D1
Wasthill La HWK/WKHTH B38 190 B3
Wastwater Ct
DUNHL/THL/PER WV6 34 D1
Watchbury Cl CBROM B36 95 E5
Watchman Av BRLYHL DY5 119 H5
Water Dl BDMR/CCFT WV3 36 A3
Waterdale SHLY B90 194 D3
WMBN WV5 80 C1
Waterfall Cl SMTHWK B66 106 A2
Waterfall La CDYHTH B64 121 G3
Waterfall Rd BRLYHL DY5 119 E5
Waterfield Cl TPTN/OCK DY4 84 C1
Waterford Pl STETCH B33 131 E1
Waterford Rd KGSWFD DY6 99 H2
Waterfront East BRLYHL DY5 101 G5
The Waterfront BRLYHL DY5 * 101 G5
Waterfront Wy BRLYHL DY5 101 G5
WSLW WS2 4 B3
Waterfront West BRLYHL DY5 119 G1
Waterglade La WLNHL WV13 39 G4
Waterhaynes Cl RBRY B45 188 A2
Waterhead Cl WOLVN WV10 13 G5
Waterhead Dr WOLVN WV10 13 H5
Water La HHTH/SAND B71 72 B4
Waterlinks Bvd AST/WIT B6 109 G2
Waterloo Av
CHWD/FDBR/MGN B37 114 B5
Waterloo Rd
ALE/KHTH/YWD B14 161 E2
SMTHWK B66 124 C1
WOLV WV1 6 E1
YDLY B25 146 B1
Waterloo St CBHAM B2 3 F5
DUDN DY1 102 A1
TPTN/OCK DY4 85 F1
Waterloo St East
TPTN/OCK DY4 85 F1
Watermead Gra BRWNH WS8 9 E5
Watermeadow Dr
RUSH/SHEL WS4 29 F1
Watermere RUSH/SHEL WS4 29 F2
Water Mill Cl SLYOAK B29 142 B4
Watermill Cl WOLVN WV10 12 D4
Water Mill Crs WALM/CURD B76 78 B2
Water Orton La
WALM/CURD B76 95 F1
Water Orton Rd CBROM B36 113 E1
Water Rd SEDG DY3 83 E4
Waters Dr FOAKS/STRLY B74 46 B2
The Waters Edge CBHAMW B1 2 B6
Waterside Cl BORD B9 127 H2
ERDE/BCHGN B24 94 C2
Waterside Dr WSNGN B18 107 H4
Waterside Pk TPTN/OCK DY4 * 70 B4
Waterside Vw BRLYHL DY5 118 D3
WSNGN B18 108 A4
Waterside Wy BRWNH WS8 8 C2
Water Side Wy COVEN WV9 12 A5
Waterson Cft
CHWD/FDBR/MGN B37 132 D1
Water St CBHAMNW B3 2 E3
KGSWFD DY6 99 H2
WBROM B70 87 H4
WOLVN WV10 7 H1
Waters Vw BLOX/PEL WS3 18 B2
Waterward Cl HRBN B17 142 A2
Waterways Dr OLDBY B69 86 C5
Waterways Gdns STRBR DY8 118 A3
Waterworks Dr NFLD/LBR B31 157 H5
Waterworks Rd
LDYWD/EDGR B16 125 H3
Waterworks St AST/WIT B6 109 H1
Watery La CDSL WV8 10 C2
RIDG/WDGT B32 140 A4
SHLY B90 194 C4
SMTHWKW B67 106 C4
STRBR DY8 118 A2
TPTN/OCK DY4 85 F1
WLNHL WV13 39 E2
WSL WS1 4 D7
Watery La Middleway
BORD B9 127 H2
Watford Gap Rd
MGN/WHC B75 33 E3
Watford Rd BVILLE B30 159 H5
Wathan Av BILS/COS WV14 67 H1
Watkins Gdns NFLD/LBR B31 175 H2
Watkins Rd SHHTH WV12 26 A5
Watland Gn BKDE/SHDE B34 112 C4
Watling St BRWNH WS8 9 H3
Watney Gv KGSTG B44 76 A3
Watson Cl CSCFLD/WYGN B72 77 F1
Watson Rd BILS/COS WV14 67 H1
DARL/WED WS10 54 C3
VAUX/NECH B7 110 C1
WOLVN WV10 12 B5
Watsons Cl DUDS DY2 103 E1
Watson's Green Flds
DUDS DY2 103 F1
Watson's Green Rd DUDS DY2 85 E5
Wattisham Sq CVALE B35 94 C2
Wattis Rd SMTHWKW B67 124 C2
Wattle Rd WBROM B70 87 E3
Watton Cl BILS/COS WV14 68 A2
Watton Gn CVALE B35 94 C4
Watton La CSHL/WTROR B46 96 C4
Watton St WBROM B70 87 G4
Watt Rd ERDW/GRVHL B23 92 C2
TPTN/OCK DY4 69 H3
Watts Cl TPTN/OCK DY4 84 C1
Watt's Rd SMHTH B10 128 B4
Watt St SMTHWK B66 106 D3
Wattville Av HDSW B21 * 107 E1
Wattville Rd HDSW B21 107 E1
Watwood Rd SHLY B90 179 H2
Waugh Cl
CHWD/FDBR/MGN B37 132 B2
Waugh Dr HALE B63 154 D2
Wavell Rd BRLYHL DY5 119 H5
WASH/WDE B8 110 C4
WSLW WS2 40 C3
Waveney Av
DUNHL/THL/PER WV6 34 C1
Waveney Cft CBROM B36 113 H1
Waverhill Rd HDSW B21 107 H2
Waverley Av GTB/HAM B43 59 F4

Waverley Crs
ETTPK/GDPK/PENN WV4 ... 51 H2
ETTPK/GDPK/PENN WV4 ... 52 D5
RMSLY B62 ... 172 B1
Waverley Gdns *WMBN* WV5 ... 65 F4
Waverley Gv *SOLH* B91 ... 181 E2
Waverley Rd *BLOX/PEL* WS3 ... 16 B5
DARL/WED WS10 ... 55 F2
SMHTH B10 ... 128 B5
Waverley St *DUDS* DY2 ... 102 A1
Waxland Rd *HALE* B63 ... 138 D5
Wayfield Cl *SHLY* B90 ... 180 C2
Wayfield Rd *SHLY* B90 ... 180 C2
Wayford Dr *CSCFLD/WYGN* B72 ... 77 H4
Wayford Gld *WLNHL* WV13 ... 39 F5
Waynecroft Rd *GTB/HAM* B43 ... 73 G1
Wayside
CHWD/FDBR/MGN B37 ... 132 A4
Wayside Acres *CDSL* WV8 ... 10 B5
Wayside Dr *FOAKS/STRLY* B74 ... 46 A2
Wayside Gdns *SHHTH* WV12 ... 26 C5
Wayside Wk *WSLW* WS2 ... 41 E2
Waystone La *HAG/WOL* DY9 ... 184 B5
Wealden Hatch *WOLVN* WV10 ... 13 E3
Wealdstone Dr *SEDG* DY3 ... 83 F4
Weaman St *CBHAMNE* B4 ... 3 G3
Weatheroak Rd *SPARK* B11 ... 145 E2
Weatheroaks *ALDR* WS9 ... 19 H3
Weather Oaks *HRBN* B17 ... 141 H2
Weatheroaks *RMSLY* B62 ... 123 E5
Weaver Av
LGN/SDN/BHAMAIR B26 ... 147 H1
WALM/CURD B76 ... 78 C2
Weaver Cl *BRLYHL* DY5 ... 100 D3
Weaver Gv *WLNHL* WV13 ... 40 B3
Weavers Ri *DUDS* DY2 ... 120 D1
Webb Av *DUNHL/THL/PER* WV6 ... 20 C5
Webbcroft Rd *STETCH* B33 ... 112 A5
Webb La *HLGN/YWD* B28 ... 162 C4
Webb Rd *TPTN/OCK* DY4 ... 70 A4
Webb St *BILS/COS* WV14 ... 68 C1
WLNHL WV13 ... 39 F3
Webley Ri *WOLVN* WV10 ... 13 F3
Webster Cl *CSCFLD/WYGN* B72 ... 77 F4
SPARK B11 ... 144 D1
Webster Rd *WLNHL* WV13 ... 39 G2
WSLW WS2 ... 27 H5
Webster Wy *WALM/CURD* B76 ... 78 D4
Weddell Wynd *BILS/COS* WV14 ... 69 E2
Wedgbury Wy *BRLYHL* DY5 ... 118 D3
Wedge St *WSL* WS1 ... 5 G3
Wedgewood Av *WBROM* B70 ... 70 D4
Wedgewood Dr
BFLD/HDSWWD B20 ... 90 B4
Wedgewood Pl *WBROM* B70 ... 70 D4
Wedgewood Rd
RIDG/WDGT B32 ... 140 C2
Wedgwood Cl *WMBN* WV5 ... 64 D4
WOLV WV1 ... 38 A4
Wednesbury Oak Rd
TPTN/OCK DY4 ... 69 G2
Wednesbury One
DARL/WED WS10 * ... 55 F5
Wednesbury Rd *WSLW* WS2 ... 56 C1
Wednesfield Rd *WLNHL* WV13 ... 39 G2
WOLVN WV10 ... 7 K2
Wednesfield Wy *WNSFLD* WV11 ... 25 E5
WOLV WV1 ... 38 A1
Weeford Dell *MGN/WHC* B75 ... 48 A2
Weeford Dr
BFLD/HDSWWD B20 ... 89 H2
Weeford Rd *MGN/WHC* B75 ... 48 A4
Weirbrook Cl *SLYOAK* B29 ... 158 D3
Welbeck Av *WOLVN* WV10 ... 23 F3
Welbeck Cl *RMSLY* B62 ... 139 G2
Welbeck Dr *RUSH/SHEL* WS4 ... 29 F3
Welbeck Gv *ERDW/GRVHL* B23 ... 91 H1
Welbury Gdns
DUNHL/THL/PER WV6 ... 22 B5
Welby Rd *HLGN/YWD* B28 ... 162 D1
Welches Cl *NFLD/LBR* B31 ... 158 D5
Welcombe Dr *WALM/CURD* B76 ... 78 A3
Welcombe Gv *SOLH* B91 ... 181 F2
Welford Av
LGN/SDN/BHAMAIR B26 ... 130 B4
Welford Gv *FOAKS/STRLY* B74 ... 46 D2
Welford Rd
BFLD/HDSWWD B20 ... 108 A1
SCFLD/BOLD B73 ... 76 C2
SHLY B90 ... 180 C1
Welham Cft *SHLY* B90 ... 195 G2
Welland Cl *CSHL/WTROR* B46 ... 96 B4
Welland Dr *STRBR* DY8 ... 118 C4
Welland Gv *ERDE/BCHGN* B24 ... 93 G3
WLNHL WV13 ... 40 A3
Welland Rd *HALE* B63 ... 138 C5
Welland Wy *WALM/CURD* B76 ... 78 C4
Well Cl *CBROM* B36 * ... 112 A1
Wellcroft Rd *BKDE/SHDE* B34 ... 112 C2
Wellcroft St *DARL/WED* WS10 ... 55 H5
Wellesbourne Cl
BDMR/CCFT WV3 ... 35 F5
Wellesbourne Dr
BILS/COS WV14 ... 68 B4
Wellesbourne Rd
BFLD/HDSWWD B20 ... 90 B5
Wellesley Dr *TPTN/OCK* DY4 ... 85 F1
Wellesley Gdns *MOS/BIL* B13 ... 162 B1
Wellesley Rd *LGLYGN/QTN* B68 ... 105 F3
Wellfield Gdns *DUDS* DY2 ... 103 E3
Wellfield Rd *ALDR* WS9 ... 30 B2
HLGN/YWD B28 ... 163 F4
Wellhead La *PBAR/PBCH* B42 ... 91 E4
Wellington Av *BDMR/CCFT* WV3 ... 51 F1
Wellington Cl *KGSWFD* DY6 ... 100 A5
Wellington Gv *SOLH* B91 ... 164 B4
Wellington Pl *WLNHL* WV13 ... 39 F2
Wellington Rd
BFLD/HDSWWD B20 ... 90 B4
BILS/COS WV14 ... 53 G2
DSYBK/YTR WS5 ... 58 A2
DUDN DY1 ... 84 B5
EDG B15 ... 143 G1
SMTHWKW B67 ... 124 C1
TPTN/OCK DY4 ... 85 G1
Wellington St *CDYHTH* B64 ... 121 F2
HHTH/SAND B71 ... 87 G2
OLDBY B69 ... 105 F2
WSLW WS2 ... 56 B1
WSNGN B18 ... 107 F4
Wellington St South
WBROM B70 ... 87 G2
Wellington Ter *LOZ/NWT* B19 * ... 108 B2
WLNHL WV13 * ... 39 G2
Wellington Wy *CVALE* B35 ... 94 D4
Well La *BLOX/PEL* WS3 ... 27 H3
DIG/EDG B5 ... 3 H6
WNSFLD WV11 ... 38 C1
Wellman Cft *SLYOAK* B29 ... 159 F1
Wellman's Rd *WLNHL* WV13 ... 40 A4
Well Meadow *RBRY* B45 ... 188 A2
Well Pl *BLOX/PEL* WS3 ... 28 A2
Wells Av *DARL/WED* WS10 ... 54 D2
Wells Cl *DUNHL/THL/PER* WV6 ... 34 B1
HHTH/SAND B71 ... 71 H3
TPTN/OCK DY4 ... 69 G2
Wellsford Av *HIA/OLT* B92 ... 147 G3
Wells Green Rd *HIA/OLT* B92 ... 147 G3
Wells Rd *BILS/COS* WV14 ... 54 A5
BLKHTH/ROWR B65 ... 122 C1
BRLYHL DY5 ... 118 D1
ETTPK/GDPK/PENN WV4 ... 51 F3
LGN/SDN/BHAMAIR B26 ... 148 A3
Well St *DARL/WED* WS10 ... 55 G2
LOZ/NWT B19 ... 108 C4
Welney Gdns *COVEN* WV9 ... 12 A4
Welsby Av *GTB/HAM* B43 ... 73 G4
Welsh House Farm Rd
RIDG/WDGT B32 ... 141 F3
Welshmans Hl *SCFLD/BOLD* B73 ... 75 H1
Welton Cl *WALM/CURD* B76 ... 78 C1
Welwyndale Rd
CSCFLD/WYGN B72 ... 77 G5
Wembley Gv *YDLY* B25 ... 129 G4
Wem Gdns *WNSFLD* WV11 ... 24 D4
Wendell Crest *WOLVN* WV10 ... 13 F4
Wendover Rd
BLKHTH/ROWR B65 ... 103 G3
ERDW/GRVHL B23 ... 76 A4
ETTPK/GDPK/PENN WV4 ... 67 G1
Wendron Gv
ALE/KHTH/YWD B14 ... 177 H1
Wenlock Av *BDMR/CCFT* WV3 ... 36 A5
Wenlock Cl *HALE* B63 ... 137 H5
SEDG DY3 ... 67 E4
Wenlock Gdns *BLOX/PEL* WS3 ... 28 A5
Wenlock Rd
BFLD/HDSWWD B20 ... 91 E5
STRBR DY8 ... 135 H1
Wenman St *BHTH/HG* B12 ... 144 B1
Wensley Cft *HIA/OLT* B92 ... 163 F4
Wensleydale Rd
PBAR/PBCH B42 ... 74 B5
Wensley Rd
LGN/SDN/BHAMAIR B26 ... 147 F1
Wentbridge Rd *WLNHL* WV13 ... 38 C4
Wentworth Av *CBROM* B36 ... 112 D1
Wentworth Dr *OLDBY* B69 ... 103 G2
Wentworth Ga *HRBN* B17 ... 141 H1
Wentworth Gv
DUNHL/THL/PER WV6 ... 20 B5
Wentworth Park Av
HRBN B17 ... 141 H1
Wentworth Ri *RMSLY* B62 ... 139 F4
Wentworth Rd *BLOX/PEL* WS3 ... 16 B3
FOAKS/STRLY B74 ... 47 E5
HIA/OLT B92 ... 147 F4
HRBN B17 ... 141 H1
STRBR DY8 ... 117 H5
WOLVN WV10 ... 13 F5
Wentworth Wy
RIDG/WDGT B32 ... 141 F4
Wenyon Cl *TPTN/OCK* DY4 ... 85 H2
Weoley Av *SLYOAK* B29 ... 142 A5
Weoley Castle Rd *SLYOAK* B29 ... 158 C1
Weoley Hl *SLYOAK* B29 ... 159 E2
Weoley Park Rd *SLYOAK* B29 ... 158 D1
Wergs Dr *DUNHL/THL/PER* WV6 ... 21 E3
Wergs Gdns *CDSL* WV8 * ... 20 D1
Wergs Hall Rd *CDSL* WV8 ... 20 D1
Wergs Rd *DUNHL/THL/PER* WV6 ... 21 E4
Werneth Gv *BLOX/PEL* WS3 ... 16 C3
Wesley Av *CDSL* WV8 ... 10 D5
HALE B63 ... 120 B5
Wesley Cl *CDYHTH* B64 ... 121 F3
Wesley Gv *DARL/WED* WS10 ... 55 G5
Wesley Pl *TPTN/OCK* DY4 ... 70 A4
Wesley Rd *BRLYHL* DY5 ... 100 D4
CDSL WV8 ... 10 D5
ERDW/GRVHL B23 ... 92 D1
Wesley's Fold *DARL/WED* WS10 ... 55 F2
Wesley St *BILS/COS* WV14 ... 69 E1
BKHL/PFLD WV2 ... 53 E2
OLDBY B69 ... 105 E1
WBROM B70 ... 87 F3
Wessex Cl *BRWNH* WS8 ... 9 F5
Wessex Rd *BKHL/PFLD* WV2 ... 52 D2
Wesson Gdns *HALE* B63 ... 138 C4
Wesson Rd *DARL/WED* WS10 ... 55 E1
West Acre *WLNHL* WV13 ... 39 F4
Westacre Crs *BDMR/CCFT* WV3 ... 35 F5
Westacre Dr *BRLYHL* DY5 ... 119 H4
Westacre Gdns *STETCH* B33 ... 130 B2
West Av *BFLD/HDSWWD* B20 ... 89 H2
CBROM B36 ... 113 F1
OLDBY B69 ... 103 H1
WNSFLD WV11 ... 24 C4
Westbook Wy *WMBN* WV5 ... 80 D1
West Bvd *RIDG/WDGT* B32 ... 141 E1
Westbourne Av
BKDE/SHDE B34 ... 112 A3
Westbourne Crs *EDG* B15 ... 126 A4
Westbourne Gdns *EDG* B15 ... 126 A5
Westbourne Gv *HDSW* B21 * ... 107 H2
Westbourne Rd
DARL/WED WS10 ... 55 H1
EDG B15 ... 125 H4
ETTPK/GDPK/PENN WV4 ... 51 G3
HDSW B21 ... 89 F5
HIA/OLT B92 ... 164 B3
RMSLY B62 ... 139 G1
RUSH/SHEL WS4 ... 42 B1
WBROM B70 ... 87 F5
Westbourne St *RUSH/SHEL* WS4 ... 42 B2
West Bromwich Ringway
WBROM B70 ... 87 G3
West Bromwich Rd
DSYBK/YTR WS5 ... 57 F4
West Bromwich St *OLDBY* B69 ... 86 D5
WSL WS1 ... 4 E7
Westbrook Av *ALDR* WS9 ... 29 H5
Westbury Av *DARL/WED* WS10 ... 55 H2
Westbury Rd *DARL/WED* WS10 ... 55 H2
HRBN B17 ... 124 D1
Westbury St *WOLV* WV1 ... 7 G3
Westcliff Pl *NFLD/LBR* B31 ... 175 F1
Westcombe Gv
RIDG/WDGT B32 ... 157 E1
West Coppice Rd *BRWNH* WS8 ... 8 C4
Westcote Av *NFLD/LBR* B31 ... 174 C3
Westcote Cl *HIA/OLT* B92 ... 147 G5
Westcott Cl *STRBR* DY8 ... 118 B1
Westcott Rd
LGN/SDN/BHAMAIR B26 ... 130 C4
Westcroft Av *WOLVN* WV10 ... 24 A1
Westcroft Gv *NFLD/LBR* B31 ... 176 A2
Westcroft Rd *CDSL* WV8 ... 20 D4
SEDG DY3 ... 66 D1
Westcroft Wy
ALE/KHTH/YWD B14 ... 178 D4
Westdean Cl *RMSLY* B62 ... 139 E3
West Dr *BFLD/HDSWWD* B20 ... 108 B1
DIG/EDG B5 ... 143 G3
West End Av *SMTHWK* B66 ... 105 H2
Westerdale Cl *SEDG* DY3 ... 68 A4
Westerham Cl *DOR/KN* B93 ... 196 D2
Westeria Cl *CBROM* B36 ... 113 E1
Westering Pkwy *WOLVN* WV10 ... 13 E3
Westerings *BFLD/HDSWWD* B20 ... 90 C4
Western Av *BRLYHL* DY5 ... 118 D2
RMSLY B62 ... 139 G3
SEDG DY3 ... 66 D3
WSLW WS2 ... 40 B2
Western Cl *WSLW* WS2 ... 40 B2
Western Rd *CDYHTH* B64 ... 120 D4
ERDE/BCHGN B24 ... 93 E3
HAG/WOL DY9 ... 169 H1
OLDBY B69 ... 105 F4
SCFLD/BOLD B73 ... 77 E2
STRBR DY8 ... 135 F3
WSNGN B18 ... 107 H5
Western Wy *DARL/WED* WS10 ... 55 E5
Westfield Av
ALE/KHTH/YWD B14 ... 178 D3
Westfield Cl *DOR/KN* B93 ... 198 C1
Westfield Dr *ALDR* WS9 ... 30 A4
WMBN WV5 ... 64 D4
Westfield Gra
ALE/KHTH/YWD B14 ... 161 E1
Westfield Gv *BDMR/CCFT* WV3 ... 35 G5
Westfield Mnr *MGN/WHC* B75 ... 47 E1
Westfield Rd *ACGN* B27 ... 146 B4
ALE/KHTH/YWD B14 ... 160 D2
BILS/COS WV14 ... 53 F1
BRLYHL DY5 ... 119 H4
DUDS DY2 ... 102 D2
EDG B15 ... 125 F4
RMSLY B62 ... 122 C3
SEDG DY3 ... 67 F2
SMTHWKW B67 ... 106 B4
WLNHL WV13 ... 39 E5
Westford Gv *HLGN/YWD* B28 ... 179 G2
Westgate *ALDR* WS9 ... 29 G3
West Ga *LDYWD/EDGR* B16 ... 125 G1
Westgate Cl *SEDG* DY3 ... 67 G4
West Gn
ETTPK/GDPK/PENN WV4 ... 50 C3
West Green Cl *EDG* B15 ... 126 B4
Westgrove Av *SHLY* B90 ... 195 F2
Westhaven Dr *NFLD/LBR* B31 ... 158 A3
Westhaven Rd
FOAKS/STRLY B74 ... 62 C2
Westhay Rd *HLGN/YWD* B28 ... 163 F3
West Heath Rd *NFLD/LBR* B31 ... 175 H4
WSNGN B18 ... 107 F5
Westhill *BDMR/CCFT* WV3 ... 35 G3
Westhill Cl *HIA/OLT* B92 ... 164 A2
Westhill Rd *HWK/WKHTH* B38 ... 176 D2
West Holme *BORD* B9 ... 128 A2
Westholme Cft *BVILLE* B30 ... 159 G3
Westhouse Gv
ALE/KHTH/YWD B14 ... 177 H1
Westland Av *BDMR/CCFT* WV3 ... 36 B3
Westland Cl *ERDW/GRVHL* B23 ... 92 D1
Westland Gdns
BDMR/CCFT WV3 ... 36 B3
STRBR DY8 ... 118 B5
Westland Rd *BDMR/CCFT* WV3 ... 36 B3
Westlands Rd *MOS/BIL* B13 ... 161 G1
WALM/CURD B76 ... 78 B5
Westleigh Rd *WMBN* WV5 ... 80 D1
Westley Cl *HLGN/YWD* B28 ... 163 F4
Westley Rd *ACGN* B27 ... 146 B4
Westley St *BORD* B9 ... 127 G2
DUDN DY1 ... 102 B1
Westmead Crs
ERDE/BCHGN B24 ... 93 G2
West Mead Dr
ALE/KHTH/YWD B14 ... 161 E4
Westmead Dr
LGLYGN/QTN B68 ... 105 F5
West Ms *KGSTG* B44 ... 74 D1
West Midlands Freeport
LGN/SDN/BHAMAIR B26 * ... 148 D4
West Mill Cft
HWK/WKHTH B38 ... 190 C1
Westminster Av
ETTPK/GDPK/PENN WV4 ... 51 H3
Westminster Cl *DUDN* DY1 ... 84 A4
Westminster Dr
ALE/KHTH/YWD B14 ... 160 D4
Westminster Rd
BFLD/HDSWWD B20 ... 90 C4
HHTH/SAND B71 ... 71 H2
RUSH/SHEL WS4 ... 28 D3
SLYOAK B29 ... 160 A1
STRBR DY8 ... 117 G2
Westmore Wy *DARL/WED* WS10 ... 56 D3
Westmorland Rd
HHTH/SAND B71 ... 71 G5
Weston Av *LOZ/NWT* B19 * ... 108 C2
OLDBY B69 ... 85 H5
SPARK B11 ... 145 E1
Weston Cl *DOR/KN* B93 ... 199 E1
WSL WS1 ... 57 E2
Weston Crs *ALDR* WS9 ... 44 B1
Weston Dr *BILS/COS* WV14 ... 53 G4
DARL/WED WS10 ... 70 A1
Weston La *SPARK* B11 ... 145 G3
Weston Rd *LOZ/NWT* B19 ... 108 B2
SMTHWKW B67 ... 124 B2
Weston St *WSL* WS1 ... 57 E2
Weston Ter *LOZ/NWT* B19 * ... 108 D1
Westover Rd
BFLD/HDSWWD B20 ... 89 G2
West Park Av *NFLD/LBR* B31 ... 175 E3
West Park Rd *SMTHWKW* B67 ... 105 H2
West Pathway *HRBN* B17 ... 142 A1
Westport Crs *WNSFLD* WV11 ... 25 F5
Westray Cl *RBRY* B45 ... 173 G4
Westridge *SEDG* DY3 ... 67 E3
Westridge Rd *MOS/BIL* B13 ... 162 A4
West Ri *MGN/WHC* B75 ... 62 C2
West Rd *GTB/HAM* B43 ... 73 G4
HALE B63 ... 137 F1
TPTN/OCK DY4 ... 69 H3
West Rd South *HALE* B63 ... 137 F1
Westside Dr *RIDG/WDGT* B32 ... 157 H1
West St *BLKHTH/ROWR* B65 ... 122 A3
BLOX/PEL WS3 ... 27 G3
BRLYHL DY5 ... 119 H4
DUDN DY1 ... 84 B4
DUNHL/THL/PER WV6 ... 23 E5
STRBR DY8 ... 135 F2
VAUX/NECH B7 * ... 3 K2
Westthorpe Gv *LOZ/NWT* B19 ... 108 C4
West Vw *WASH/WDE* B8 ... 111 G5
West View Dr *KGSWFD* DY6 ... 100 A4
West View Rd *MGN/WHC* B75 ... 63 E2
Westville Rd *WSLW* WS2 ... 41 E2
Westward Cl *KGSTG* B44 ... 75 F3
West Wy *RUSH/SHEL* WS4 ... 18 B5
Westwood Av *SPARK* B11 ... 145 G3
STRBR DY8 ... 134 D4
Westwood Dr *RBRY* B45 ... 174 B4
Westwood Gv *SOLH* B91 ... 181 F2
Westwood Rd *AST/WIT* B6 ... 91 G4
SCFLD/BOLD B73 ... 60 C4
Westwood St *BRLYHL* DY5 ... 118 C3
Westwood Vw
ERDE/BCHGN B24 ... 93 G3
Wetherby Cl *WOLVN* WV10 ... 12 D3
Wetherby Rd *ACGN* B27 ... 146 C5
BLOX/PEL WS3 ... 16 C3
Wetherfield Rd *SPARK* B11 ... 146 A4
Wexford Cl *DUDN* DY1 ... 83 H4
Weybourne Rd *KGSTG* B44 ... 75 E1
Weycroft Rd *ERDW/GRVHL* B23 ... 75 H4
Weyhill Cl *COVEN* WV9 ... 11 G5
Weymoor Rd *HRBN* B17 ... 141 G4
Weymouth Dr
FOAKS/STRLY B74 ... 46 D1
Wharf Ap *ALDR* WS9 ... 29 H3
Wharfdale Rd *SPARK* B11 ... 146 A2
Wharfedale Cl *KGSWFD* DY6 ... 99 F2
Wharfedale St *DARL/WED* WS10 ... 70 D1
Wharf La *SOLH* B91 ... 165 F4
WSNGN B18 ... 108 A4
Wharf Rd *BVILLE* B30 ... 177 E3
YDLY B25 ... 146 B2
Wharfside *OLDBY* B69 ... 104 D2
Wharfside St *CBHAMW* B1 ... 2 D7
Wharf St *AST/WIT* B6 ... 109 G2
WOLV WV1 ... 7 J5
WSLW WS2 ... 4 A5
WSNGN B18 ... 108 A3
Whar Hall Rd *HIA/OLT* B92 ... 165 G2
Wharton Av *HIA/OLT* B92 ... 165 G3
Wharton St *VAUX/NECH* B7 ... 110 B1
Whatcote Gn *HIA/OLT* B92 ... 165 F2
Whateley Av *BLOX/PEL* WS3 ... 28 B4
Whateley Crs *CBROM* B36 ... 113 F1
Whateley Gn *FOAKS/STRLY* B74 ... 47 E5
Whateley Hall Cl
DOR/KN B93 * ... 197 G1
Whateley Hall Rd *DOR/KN* B93 ... 197 F1
Whateley Pl *BLOX/PEL* WS3 * ... 28 B4
Whateley Rd *BLOX/PEL* WS3 ... 28 B4
HDSW B21 ... 107 G1
Wheatcroft Cl *MGN/WHC* B75 ... 48 A2
RMSLY B62 ... 122 D4
Wheatcroft Dr
CHWD/FDBR/MGN B37 ... 132 C3
Wheatcroft Gv *DUDS* DY2 ... 85 F5
Wheatcroft Rd *STETCH* B33 ... 130 B2
Wheaten Cl C
HWD/FDBR/MGN B37 ... 132 D1
Wheatfield Cl *CBROM* B36 ... 114 A2
Wheatfield Vw *NFLD/LBR* B31 ... 157 H5
Wheat Hl *DSYBK/YTR* WS5 ... 43 G5
Wheathill Cl
ETTPK/GDPK/PENN WV4 ... 51 E5
Wheatlands Cft *STETCH* B33 ... 131 G1
The Wheatlands
DUNHL/THL/PER WV6 ... 34 B2
Wheatley Cl *HIA/OLT* B92 ... 165 G2
LGLYGN/QTN B68 ... 123 G4
MGN/WHC B75 ... 47 G2
Wheatley Rd *LGLYGN/QTN* B68 ... 123 G4
Wheatley St *BKHL/PFLD* WV2 ... 52 C2
WBROM B70 ... 87 E2
Wheatmill Cl *KIDD* DY10 ... 168 B3
Wheatmoor Ri *MGN/WHC* B75 ... 63 E2
Wheatmoor Rd *MGN/WHC* B75 ... 63 F1
Wheaton Cl *WOLVN* WV10 ... 23 E3
Wheaton V *BFLD/HDSWWD* B20 ... 89 G3
Wheatridge Cl *KGSWFD* DY6 ... 99 E2
Wheats Av *HRBN* B17 ... 141 H4
Wheatsheaf Rd *CDSL* WV8 ... 22 A1
LDYWD/EDGR B16 ... 125 F2
OLDBY B69 ... 103 G1
Wheatstone Cl *SEDG* DY3 ... 67 G5
Wheatstone Gv *STETCH* B33 ... 112 B4
Wheel Av *CDSL* WV8 ... 10 B4
Wheeler Cl *CDSL* WV8 ... 10 A3
Wheeler Rd *WNSFLD* WV11 ... 24 C2
Wheeler's Fold *WOLV* WV1 ... 7 G4
Wheelers La *MOS/BIL* B13 ... 161 F3
Wheeler St *LOZ/NWT* B19 ... 108 D3
STRBR DY8 ... 135 F2
Wheeley Moor Rd
CHWD/FDBR/MGN B37 ... 114 A4
Wheeley Rd *HIA/OLT* B92 ... 165 F3
Wheeley's La *EDG* B15 ... 126 C4
Wheeley's Rd *EDG* B15 ... 126 B5
Wheelock Cl *FOAKS/STRLY* B74 ... 60 B1
Wheelwright Rd
ERDE/BCHGN B24 ... 92 C4
Wheldrake Av *BKDE/SHDE* B34 ... 113 E4
Whernside Dr
DUNHL/THL/PER WV6 ... 22 C5
Wherretts Well La *SOLH* B91 ... 165 G5
Whetstone Cl *EDG* B15 * ... 142 D2
Whetstone Gn *WOLVN* WV10 * ... 23 F1
Whetstone Gv *WOLVN* WV10 ... 23 F2
Whetstone La *ALDR* WS9 ... 30 B5
Whetstone Rd *WOLVN* WV10 ... 23 F2
Whettybridge Rd *RBRY* B45 ... 187 G2
Whetty La *RBRY* B45 ... 187 G1
Whichford Cl *WALM/CURD* B76 ... 77 H5
Whichford Gv *BORD* B9 ... 129 F2
While Rd *CSCFLD/WYGN* B72 ... 62 B4
Whilmot Cl *WOLVN* WV10 ... 13 H1
Whinberry Ri *BRLYHL* DY5 ... 83 E5
Whisley Brook La
HLGN/YWD B28 ... 145 H5
Whiston Av *WNSFLD* WV11 ... 25 G3
Whiston Gv *SLYOAK* B29 ... 158 D2
Whitacre Rd *BORD* B9 ... 128 C1
DOR/KN B93 ... 197 F1
Whitbourne Cl *BHTH/HG* B12 ... 144 D2
Whitburn Av *PBAR/PBCH* B42 ... 90 A1
Whitburn Cl *COVEN* WV9 ... 12 A5
Whitby Cl *BLOX/PEL* WS3 ... 16 B4
Whitby Rd *BHTH/HG* B12 ... 144 C3
Whitcot Gv *NFLD/LBR* B31 * ... 175 F5
Whitebeam Cl *BRWNH* WS8 ... 19 E1
SEDG DY3 ... 83 E2
Whitebeam Cft
HWK/WKHTH B38 ... 176 C5
White Beam Rd
CHWD/FDBR/MGN B37 ... 132 C4
White City Rd *BRLYHL* DY5 ... 120 A3
White Cl *HAG/WOL* DY9 ... 136 A5
Whitecrest *GTB/HAM* B43 ... 73 H1
Whitecroft Rd
LGN/SDN/BHAMAIR B26 ... 148 B2
White Falcon Ct *SOLH* B91 ... 181 F3
White Farm Rd
FOAKS/STRLY B74 ... 46 C1
White Field Av *HRBN* B17 ... 141 G1
Whitefield Cl *CDSL* WV8 ... 10 D5
Whitefields Crs *SOLH* B91 ... 181 H3
Whitefields Ga *SOLH* B91 ... 181 G4
Whitefields Rd *SOLH* B91 ... 181 G4
Whitefriars Dr *HALE* B63 ... 138 C3
Whitegates Rd *BILS/COS* WV14 ... 68 D1
Whitehall Dr *DUDN* DY1 ... 84 A4
HALE B63 ... 138 D3
Whitehall Rd *BORD* B9 ... 128 B3
CDYHTH B64 ... 120 C3
ETTPK/GDPK/PENN WV4 ... 51 H4
HALE B63 ... 138 D3
HDSW B21 ... 108 A2
KGSWFD DY6 ... 99 G3
STRBR DY8 ... 135 H5
TPTN/OCK DY4 ... 86 B1
WSL WS1 ... 57 E1
Whitehead Dr *WALM/CURD* B76 ... 79 F5
Whitehead Rd *AST/WIT* B6 ... 109 E2
Whitehill La *SLYOAK* B29 ... 158 C5
White Hollies *BLOX/PEL* WS3 ... 17 G3
White Horse Rd *BRWNH* WS8 ... 9 E2
Whitehouse Av
BDMR/CCFT WV3 ... 35 G5
DARL/WED WS10 ... 54 D1
DARL/WED WS10 ... 55 H5
White House Av *WNSFLD* WV11 ... 25 F3
White House Cl *SOLH* B91 ... 181 F2
Whitehouse Common Rd
MGN/WHC B75 ... 63 E1
Whitehouse Crs *MGN/WHC* B75 ... 48 A5
WNSFLD WV11 ... 25 F1
Whitehouse Dr *SMTHWK* B66 ... 106 C2
White House Gn *SOLH* B91 ... 181 F2
Whitehouse Pl *RBRY* B45 ... 187 H2
White Houses La *WOLVN* WV10 ... 13 G1
Whitehouse St *AST/WIT* B6 ... 109 F3
BILS/COS WV14 ... 68 C3
TPTN/OCK DY4 ... 85 G4
WSLW WS2 ... 41 H2
Whitehouse Wy *ALDR* WS9 ... 43 H1
White House Wy *SOLH* B91 ... 181 G2
Whitemoor Dr *SOLH* B91 ... 195 G1
White Oak Dr *BDMR/CCFT* WV3 ... 35 G4
KGSWFD DY6 ... 99 G3
White Rd *RIDG/WDGT* B32 ... 140 D1
SMTHWKW B67 ... 106 B3
SPARK B11 ... 128 A5
White Rw *WMBN* WV5 ... 64 A2

White's Dr SEDG DY3 67 G3
Whiteslade Cl DOR/KN B93 197 E1
Whitesmith Cl SEDG DY3 67 F3
White's Rd HHTH/SAND B71 71 G5
Whitestone Rd HALE B63 138 C1
White St BHTH/HG B12 144 C2
WSL WS1 4 D6
Whites Wd WMBN WV5 81 E1
Whitethorn Crs
FOAKS/STRLY B74 44 D4
Whitethorn Rd STRBR DY8 118 C3
Whitewood Gld SHHTH WV12 40 C1
Whitfield Gv EDG B15 126 D4
Whitford Dr SHLY B90 195 H1
Whitgreave Av WOLVN WV10 23 G2
Whitgreave Ct WOLVN WV10 * 13 H1
Whitgreave St WBROM B70 86 C3
Whitland Cl RBRY B45 188 B2
Whitland Dr
ALE/KHTH/YWD B14 178 B2
Whitley Cl
DUNHL/THL/PER WV6 35 F3
Whitley Court Rd
RIDG/WDGT B32 140 C1
Whitley Dr FOAKS/STRLY B74 45 G5
Whitley St DARL/WED WS10 55 G5
Whitlock Gv
ALE/KHTH/YWD B14 178 C2
Whitminster Av
ERDE/BCHGN B24 93 F3
Whitminster Cl SHHTH WV12 40 A1
Whitmore Hl WOLV WV1 6 E3
Whitmore Rd SMHTH B10 128 A4
STRBR DY8 134 D2
Whitmore St WOLV WV1 7 G3
WSL WS1 56 D1
WSNGN B18 108 B4
Whitney Av STRBR DY8 134 D1
Whittaker St BKHL/PFLD WV2 52 C1
Whittall St CBHAMNE B4 3 G3
Whittimere St WSL WS1 5 F3
Whittingham Gv
WNSFLD WV11 25 F4
Whittingham Rd HALE B63 138 C2
Whittington Cl
ALE/KHTH/YWD B14 161 E5
HHTH/SAND B71 72 B3
Whittington Gv STETCH B33 130 B2
Whittington Ov STETCH B33 130 C2
Whittington Rd STRBR DY8 134 D4
Whittle Cft CVALE B35 94 B3
Whittleford Gv CBROM B36 95 E5
Whitton St DARL/WED WS10 55 G2
Whitwell Cl SHLY B90 195 G2
Whitworth Cl DARL/WED WS10 55 G1
Whitworth Dr HHTH/SAND B71 72 A2
Whyley St OLDBY B69 105 E4
WBROM B70 87 E2
Whyley Wk OLDBY B69 105 E4
Whynot St HALE B63 137 F2
Wibert Cl SLYOAK B29 160 A1
Wichnor Rd HIA/OLT B92 147 F2
Wicket La KINVER DY7 116 C3
Wickham Gdns WNSFLD WV11 24 A4
Wicklow Cl HALE B63 154 D1
Wideacre Dr KGSTG B44 75 E4
Wide Acres RBRY B45 173 H4
Widney Av ALDR WS9 30 B1
SLYOAK B29 142 A5
Widney Cl DOR/KN B93 196 D3
Widney La SOLH B91 181 E4
Widney Manor Rd SOLH B91 182 A3
Widney Rd DOR/KN B93 196 C3
Wiggins Cft WALM/CURD B76 63 F5
Wiggins Hill Rd
WALM/CURD B76 79 H3
Wigginsmill Rd
DARL/WED WS10 70 B2
Wiggin St LDYWD/EDGR B16 125 H1
Wight Cft CBROM B36 114 B3
Wightwick Bank
DUNHL/THL/PER WV6 34 D3
Wightwick Cl BLOX/PEL WS3 27 F1
Wightwick Gv
DUNHL/THL/PER WV6 35 E3
Wightwick Hall Rd
DUNHL/THL/PER WV6 34 C4
Wigmore Gv KGSTG B44 75 H3
Wigmore La HHTH/SAND B71 72 C3
Wigorn La HAG/WOL DY9 152 D2
Wigorn Rd SMTHWKW B67 124 B3
Wilberforce Wy HIA/OLT B92 165 G3
Wilbraham Rd WSLW WS2 41 G4
Wilcote Gv ACGN B27 163 G2
Wildacres STRBR DY8 134 C1
Wilday Cl TPTN/OCK DY4 85 G1
Wilde Cl ALE/KHTH/YWD B14 177 H1
Wilden Cl NFLD/LBR B31 174 C2
Wilderness La GTB/HAM B43 58 B5
Wildfell Rd ACGN B27 146 D5
Wildmoor Rd SHLY B90 163 F5
Wildtree Av WOLVN WV10 13 G5
Wiley Av DARL/WED WS10 55 E2
Wiley Av South
DARL/WED WS10 55 E3
Wilford Gv SOLH B91 181 H3
WALM/CURD B76 78 D5
Wilford Rd HHTH/SAND B71 71 H5
Wilkes Av WSLW WS2 40 D3
Wilkes Cl BLOX/PEL WS3 17 G4
Wilkes Cft SEDG DY3 67 F4
Wilkes Rd CDSL WV8 10 B4
Wilkes St HHTH/SAND B71 72 A4
WLNHL WV13 39 G4
Wilkin Rd BRWNH WS8 8 C2
Wilkinson Av BILS/COS WV14 54 A5
Wilkinson Cl SCFLD/BOLD B73 77 F1
Wilkinson Cft CBROM B36 111 G3
Wilkinson Rd DARL/WED WS10 54 C3
Wilkins Rd BILS/COS WV14 53 H1
Willard Rd YDLY B25 146 C1
Willaston Rd STETCH B33 131 F5
Willclare Rd
LGN/SDN/BHAMAIR B26 147 G1
Willcock Rd BKHL/PFLD WV2 52 C1
Willenhall La WSLW WS2 26 D3
Willenhall Rd BILS/COS WV14 54 B2
DARL/WED WS10 40 B5
WOLV WV1 38 B4
Willenhall St DARL/WED WS10 55 E2
Willerby Fold WOLVN WV10 13 F3
Willersey Rd MOS/BIL B13 162 B2
Willes Rd WSNGN B18 107 G3
Willett Rd HHTH/SAND B71 72 A3
Willetts Dr HALE B63 137 F3
Willetts Rd NFLD/LBR B31 175 G4
Willetts Wy CDYHTH B64 121 F2
Willey Gv ERDE/BCHGN B24 93 F4
William Booth La CBHAMNE B4 3 F2
William Cook Rd
WASH/WDE B8 111 F4
William Edward St
BHTH/HG B12 * 127 F4
William Green Rd
DARL/WED WS10 56 C5
William Harper Rd
WLNHL WV13 39 H4
William Henry St
VAUX/NECH B7 109 G3
William Ker Rd TPTN/OCK DY4 86 A1
William Rd SMTHWKW B67 123 H1
Williams Cl SHHTH WV12 26 A5
Williamson St BDMR/CCFT WV3 6 D7
William St BRLYHL DY5 119 E1
EDG B15 126 C3
RUSH/SHEL WS4 42 B2
WBROM B70 86 C1
William St North LOZ/NWT B19 3 F1
William St West SMTHWK B66 106 D2
William Wiggin Av
BLOX/PEL WS3 16 D5
Willingsworth Rd
DARL/WED WS10 70 A2
Willingworth Cl
ETTPK/GDPK/PENN WV4 53 E5
Willis Pearson Av
BILS/COS WV14 69 F1
Willmore Gv HWK/WKHTH B38 176 D5
Willmore Rd
BFLD/HDSWWD B20 90 D4
Willmott Cl MGN/WHC B75 47 H2
Willmott Rd MGN/WHC B75 47 H2
Willoughby Dr SOLH B91 181 H4
Willoughby Gv SLYOAK B29 158 C1
Willow Av DARL/WED WS10 55 H4
HRBN B17 124 C2
WNSFLD WV11 24 B2
Willow Bank BDMR/CCFT WV3 35 G4
Willow Bank Rd DOR/KN B93 196 D2
Willow Cl CDYHTH B64 121 E3
HAG/WOL DY9 152 B5
Willow Coppice
RIDG/WDGT B32 157 G1
Willow Ct SMTHWK B66 105 H1
Willowdale Gra
DUNHL/THL/PER WV6 22 A5
Willow Dr CDSL WV8 10 D4
HDSW B21 89 E5
OLDBY B69 104 A2
SHLY B90 194 D4
Willow End HAG/WOL DY9 136 B4
Willow Gdns
LDYWD/EDGR B16 107 H5
Willow Gv WNSFLD WV11 15 F4
Willow Hts CDYHTH B64 121 G4
Willowherb Cl DSYBK/YTR WS5 57 G5
Willowherb Wy SHLY B90 194 A3
Willow Ms SLYOAK B29 158 D1
Willow Park Dr STRBR DY8 135 G5
Willow Ri BRLYHL DY5 119 E3
Willow Rd BDMR/CCFT WV3 35 H5
BVILLE B30 159 H2
DUDN DY1 84 A2
GTB/HAM B43 73 H2
SOLH B91 181 E3
Willowsbrook Rd RMSLY B62 122 D4
Willows Crs BHTH/HG B12 143 H2
Willowside RUSH/SHEL WS4 29 E2
Willows Rd BHTH/HG B12 144 A2
RUSH/SHEL WS4 29 E2
WSL WS1 5 J4
The Willows ACGN B27 146 B5
HLYWD B47 192 C2
WALM/CURD B76 78 B1
WMBN WV5 80 D1
Willow Wy
CHWD/FDBR/MGN B37 132 B2
Wills Av HHTH/SAND B71 71 F4
Willsbridge Covert
ALE/KHTH/YWD B14 177 G2
Willson Cft
ALE/KHTH/YWD B14 179 F2
Wills St LOZ/NWT B19 108 C2
Wills Wy SMTHWK B66 107 E5
Wilmcote Cl BHTH/HG B12 144 A1
Wilmcote Dr MGN/WHC B75 47 F2
Wilmcote Rd SOLH B91 164 B4
Wilmington Rd
RIDG/WDGT B32 140 B1
Wilmore La HLYWD B47 192 A4
Wilmot Av CSHL/WTROR B46 115 F3
Wilmot Dr ERDW/GRVHL B23 77 E5
TPTN/OCK DY4 69 E5
Wilmot Gdns DUDN DY1 84 A4
Wilnecote Gv PBAR/PBCH B42 90 C2
Wilner's Vw BLOX/PEL WS3 17 H2
Wilsford Cl
ALE/KHTH/YWD B14 177 H4
RUSH/SHEL WS4 29 E2
Wilson Dr MGN/WHC B75 63 G3
Wilson Rd BILS/COS WV14 68 C4
BRLYHL DY5 101 E5
LGLYGN/QTN B68 123 H4
LOZ/NWT B19 90 D5
SMTHWK B66 124 D1
Wilsons Rd DOR/KN B93 197 G2
Wilson St TPTN/OCK DY4 85 G1
Wilton Cl SEDG DY3 67 G4
Wilton Rd BFLD/HDSWWD B20 90 B5
ERDW/GRVHL B23 92 D1
SPARK B11 144 D2
Wilton St LOZ/NWT B19 108 D1
Wiltshire Cl WSLW WS2 41 H1
Wiltshire Dr HALE B63 120 B5
Wiltshire Wy HHTH/SAND B71 71 G4
Wimbledon Dr STRBR DY8 135 H5
Wimborne Rd WOLVN WV10 24 A4
Wimbourne Rd
LDYWD/EDGR B16 125 F1
WALM/CURD B76 63 G4
Wimperis Wy GTB/HAM B43 59 G4
Wimpole Gv KGSTG B44 75 H4
Wimshurst Meadow
WOLVN WV10 13 F3
Wincanton Cft CBROM B36 111 G1
Winceby Rd
DUNHL/THL/PER WV6 34 D2
Winchcombe Cl DUDN DY1 83 G3
HIA/OLT B92 147 H5
Winchcombe Rd HIA/OLT B92 147 H5
Winchester Cl
BLKHTH/ROWR B65 104 C5
HAG/WOL DY9 152 C3
Winchester Dr
CHWD/FDBR/MGN B37 132 A2
STRBR DY8 135 G4
Winchester Gdns
NFLD/LBR B31 175 G2
Winchester Gv HDSW B21 * 89 E5
Winchester Ms ALDR WS9 44 B1
Winchester Ri DUDN DY1 84 A4
Winchester Rd
BFLD/HDSWWD B20 90 D5
HHTH/SAND B71 71 F3
WOLVN WV10 12 C5
Winchfield Dr HRBN B17 124 B5
Wincote Dr
DUNHL/THL/PER WV6 35 G1
Wincrest Wy BKDE/SHDE B34 113 E4
Windermere Dr
FOAKS/STRLY B74 45 F2
KGSWFD DY6 99 H3
Windermere Rd
DUNHL/THL/PER WV6 21 H2
HDSW B21 89 G4
MOS/BIL B13 161 H1
Winding Ml North
BRLYHL DY5 * 119 G5
Winding Ml South
BRLYHL DY5 * 119 G5
Windlass Cft NFLD/LBR B31 158 B5
Windleaves Rd CBROM B36 113 G2
Windmill Av CSHL/WTROR B46 115 F2
RBRY B45 173 G5
Windmill Bank WMBN WV5 65 E4
Windmill Cl NFLD/LBR B31 159 E5
Windmill Cottages
PBAR/PBCH B42 * 90 A1
Windmill Crs BDMR/CCFT WV3 35 E4
SMTHWK B66 107 E4
Windmill End DUDS DY2 103 E4
Windmill Gv KGSWFD DY6 99 E1
Windmill Hl HALE B63 137 H2
NFLD/LBR B31 158 D5
Windmill La BDMR/CCFT WV3 35 E4
DOR/KN B93 198 D2
SMTHWK B66 106 D5
Windmill Prec SMTHWK B66 106 D4
Windmill Rd SHLY B90 179 G3
Windmill St CBHAMW B1 126 D3
DARL/WED WS10 55 H5
DUDN DY1 84 A4
SEDG DY3 83 F1
WSL WS1 4 E6
Windmill Vw BILS/COS WV14 68 B4
Windridge Crs HIA/OLT B92 165 H2
The Windrow
DUNHL/THL/PER WV6 34 B1
Windrush Gv SLYOAK B29 160 A2
Windrush Rd HLYWD B47 192 D1
Windsor Av
ETTPK/GDPK/PENN WV4 51 E2
LGLYGN/QTN B68 123 E1
Windsor Cl BLKHTH/ROWR B65 104 A5
HALE B63 138 B4
NFLD/LBR B31 189 G2
RBRY B45 174 A3
Windsor Ct SEDG DY3 82 D5
Windsor Crs DUDS DY2 102 D3
Windsor Dr ERDE/BCHGN B24 93 G1
HIA/OLT B92 147 H5
Windsor Gdns
BDMR/CCFT WV3 50 A1
CDSL WV8 10 B4
Windsor Ga SHHTH WV12 40 A1
Windsor Gv RUSH/SHEL WS4 18 C5
STRBR DY8 118 A3
Windsor Pl ERDW/GRVHL B23 92 C3
VAUX/NECH B7 * 127 G1
Windsor Rd
BLKHTH/ROWR B65 104 A4
BVILLE B30 160 B5
CBROM B36 113 H2
ETTPK/GDPK/PENN WV4 52 D3
HALE B63 138 B3
HHTH/SAND B71 71 F3
LGLYGN/QTN B68 123 E1
SCFLD/BOLD B73 76 B2
STRBR DY8 134 D4
TPTN/OCK DY4 69 G3
WMBN WV5 64 D5
Windsor St BILS/COS WV14 53 G2
VAUX/NECH B7 109 G5
WSL WS1 57 E1
Windsor St South
VAUX/NECH B7 109 G5
Windsor Ter
LDYWD/EDGR B16 * 125 H3
Windsor Vw RIDG/WDGT B32 157 F3
Windsor Wk DARL/WED WS10 40 B5
Windsor Wy RUSH/SHEL WS4 29 F3
Winds Point HAG/WOL DY9 152 C4
Windward Wy CBROM B36 113 H2
Windyridge Rd
WALM/CURD B76 78 B5
Winford Av KGSWFD DY6 100 A5
Wingate Cl BVILLE B30 176 D1
Wingate Rd WSLW WS2 40 C3
Wing Cl WSLW WS2 40 D1
Wingfield Cl
CHWD/FDBR/MGN B37 131 H1
Wingfield Rd
CSHL/WTROR B46 115 F4
PBAR/PBCH B42 74 C4
Wingfoot Av WOLVN WV10 23 F2
Winkle St WBROM B70 87 F2
Winleigh Rd
BFLD/HDSWWD B20 89 H4
Winnall Cl BILS/COS WV14 68 D1
Winnie Rd SLYOAK B29 159 G1
Winnington Rd WASH/WDE B8 111 E2
Winnipeg Rd HWK/WKHTH B38 177 E5
Winrush Cl SEDG DY3 83 F3
Winsford Cl HALE B63 138 C1
WALM/CURD B76 63 E5
Winsham Gv HDSW B21 107 F1
Winslow Dr
DUNHL/THL/PER WV6 36 A1
Winson Green Rd WSNGN B18 107 G4
Winson St WSNGN B18 107 F5
Winstanley Rd STETCH B33 129 H2
Winster Av DOR/KN B93 196 C4
Winster Gv KGSTG B44 74 D1
Winster Rd GTB/HAM B43 73 F3
WOLV WV1 38 B4
Winston Dr
BFLD/HDSWWD B20 90 B5
RMSLY B62 172 C1
Winston Rd SEDG DY3 80 C4
Winterbourne Cft
ALE/KHTH/YWD B14 177 G3
Winterbourne Rd SOLH B91 181 F1
Winterley Gdns SEDG DY3 67 G5
Winterley La RUSH/SHEL WS4 29 E3
Winterton Rd KGSTG B44 60 C5
Winthorpe Dr SOLH B91 182 A5
Wintney Cl HRBN B17 124 C5
Winton Gv WALM/CURD B76 78 C5
Winwood Heath Rd
RMSLY B62 172 A3
Winwood Rd
BLKHTH/ROWR B65 122 C1
Winwoods Gv RIDG/WDGT B32 157 E2
Wiremill Cl KGSTG B44 75 E5
Wirral Rd NFLD/LBR B31 158 B4
Wiseacre Cft SHLY B90 179 G3
Wiseman Gv ERDW/GRVHL B23 76 B2
Wisemore WSL WS1 4 D2
Wishaw Cl SHLY B90 179 G3
Wishaw Gv
CHWD/FDBR/MGN B37 113 H4
Wishaw La WALM/CURD B76 79 G4
Wisley Wy RIDG/WDGT B32 141 F2
Wistaria Cl NFLD/LBR B31 158 C4
Wisteria Dr DSYBK/YTR WS5 57 F4
Wisteria Gv KGSTG B44 75 E1
Wistmans Cl DUDN DY1 83 F5
Wistwood Hayes
WOLVN WV10 13 F3
Witham Cft SOLH B91 182 A4
Withdean Cl SPARK B11 145 F2
Witherford Cl SLYOAK B29 159 E2
Witherford Cft SHLY B90 180 D3
Witherford Wy SLYOAK B29 159 E1
Withern Wy SEDG DY3 83 E3
Withers Rd CDSL WV8 10 D4
Withers Wy HHTH/SAND B71 87 H2
Withington Covert
ALE/KHTH/YWD B14 177 H3
Withington Gv DOR/KN B93 196 C4
Withybrook Rd SHLY B90 180 B5
Withy Gv
CHWD/FDBR/MGN B37 113 G4
Withy Hill Rd MGN/WHC B75 48 D5
Withymere La WMBN WV5 65 G3
Withymoor Rd DUDS DY2 103 E5
STRBR DY8 118 C5
Withy Rd BILS/COS WV14 53 G5
Withywood Cl SHHTH WV12 25 H1
Witley Av HALE B63 138 A3
SOLH B91 182 A3
Witley Crs OLDBY B69 104 C4
Witley Farm Cl SOLH B91 182 A3
Witley Rd NFLD/LBR B31 176 B3
Witney Dr
CHWD/FDBR/MGN B37 131 H2
Witney Gv WOLVN WV10 12 B4
Witton Bank RMSLY B62 * 139 H1
Witton La AST/WIT B6 91 F5
HHTH/SAND B71 71 E3
Witton Lodge Rd
ERDW/GRVHL B23 75 H4
Witton Rd AST/WIT B6 109 E1
ETTPK/GDPK/PENN WV4 51 G2
Witton St BORD B9 127 H2
STRBR DY8 135 E3
Wixford Gv SHLY B90 180 D3
Wobaston Rd CDSL WV8 11 F4
Woburn Av SHHTH WV12 25 H4
Woburn Crs GTB/HAM B43 73 F2
Woburn Dr BRLYHL DY5 118 D4
CDYHTH B64 121 G5
Woburn Gv ACGN B27 163 G1
Wodehouse Cl WMBN WV5 80 C1
Wodehouse La SEDG DY3 66 A3
Woden Av WNSFLD WV11 24 C4
Woden Cl WMBN WV5 64 D4
Woden Crs WNSFLD WV11 24 C4
Woden Rd WOLVN WV10 37 H1
Woden Rd East
DARL/WED WS10 56 B3
Woden Rd North
DARL/WED WS10 55 G3
Woden Rd South
DARL/WED WS10 70 D2
Woden Rd West
DARL/WED WS10 55 F4
Wold Wk MOS/BIL B13 161 H4
Wolfsbane Dr DSYBK/YTR WS5 57 G5
Wolfson Dr EDG B15 142 B3
Wollaston Ct STRBR DY8 134 C1
Wollaston Crs WNSFLD WV11 24 D4
Wollaston Rd KINVER DY7 117 G5
STRBR DY8 118 A5
Wollerton Gv MGN/WHC B75 63 F2
Wollescote Rd HAG/WOL DY9 136 B4
Wollscote Dr SOLH B91 181 H3
Wolmer Rd WNSFLD WV11 14 D5
Wolseley Av ACGN B27 146 D3
Wolseley Bank WOLVN WV10 23 H3
Wolseley Cl CBROM B36 96 A5
WOLVN WV10 23 H3
Wolseley Dr WASH/WDE B8 111 E2
Wolseley Ga WOLVN WV10 23 H3
Wolseley Rd BILS/COS WV14 53 F1
WBROM B70 70 D5
Wolseley St BORD B9 127 H2
Wolston Cl SHLY B90 163 F5
Wolverhampton Rd
BLOX/PEL WS3 17 G4
BLOX/PEL WS3 27 F1
CDSL WV8 10 B4
KGSWFD DY6 99 G1
KINVER DY7 116 D5
LGLYGN/QTN B68 123 E1
SEDG DY3 52 B5
SEDG DY3 81 G4
WNSFLD WV11 14 D4
WOLVN WV10 37 H2
WSLW WS2 41 E3
Wolverhampton Rd East
ETTPK/GDPK/PENN WV4 52 C4
Wolverhampton Rd South
LGLYGN/QTN B68 124 A5
Wolverhampton Rd West
WSLW WS2 40 D3
Wolverhampton St
BILS/COS WV14 53 G2
DARL/WED WS10 54 D2
DUDN DY1 84 B5
WLNHL WV13 39 F4
WSLW WS2 4 C3
Wolverley Av
ETTPK/GDPK/PENN WV4 50 D3
STRBR DY8 134 C1
Wolverley Crs OLDBY B69 104 B4
Wolverley Rd HALE B63 * 138 B5
HIA/OLT B92 148 B5
RIDG/WDGT B32 157 F2
Wolverson Cl SHHTH WV12 40 A1
Wolverson Rd ALDR WS9 19 G3
Wolverton Rd
CHWD/FDBR/MGN B37 132 B5
DUDS DY2 85 E5
RBRY B45 188 C2
Wombourne Cl SEDG DY3 67 E3
Wombourne Pk WMBN WV5 80 D2
Wombourne Rd SEDG DY3 80 D3
Wombrook Dl WMBN WV5 64 B5
Woodacre Rd ERDE/BCHGN B24 93 G2
Woodall Rd AST/WIT B6 91 F5
Woodall St BLOX/PEL WS3 27 G2
CDYHTH B64 120 C3
Woodard Rd TPTN/OCK DY4 70 A4
Wood Av SEDG DY3 83 E2
WNSFLD WV11 24 C4
Wood Bank Rd
BDMR/CCFT WV3 35 E5
Woodbank Rd SEDG DY3 67 E4
Woodberry Dr WALM/CURD B76 78 C1
Woodberry Wk ACGN B27 146 D4
Woodbine Av SMHTH B10 * 128 B4
Woodbine Cft
LGN/SDN/BHAMAIR B26 147 G1
Woodbourne EDG B15 125 F4
Woodbourne Rd HRBN B17 124 D4
SMTHWKW B67 124 A2
Woodbridge Cl BLOX/PEL WS3 16 C4
RUSH/SHEL WS4 29 F1
Woodbridge Rd MOS/BIL B13 144 B4
Woodbrooke Rd BVILLE B30 159 F3
Woodburn Rd SMTHWK B66 107 F2
Woodbury Cl BRLYHL DY5 119 G3
RMSLY B62 122 D4
Woodbury Gv SOLH B91 181 H5
Woodbury Rd RMSLY B62 123 E4
Woodchester HAG/WOL DY9 169 H1
Woodchester Rd DOR/KN B93 198 C1
Woodchurch Gra
SCFLD/BOLD B73 76 D3
Wood Cl CSHL/WTROR B46 115 F2
Woodclose Rd
CHWD/FDBR/MGN B37 131 H1
Woodcock Cl NFLD/LBR B31 174 C4
Woodcock La ACGN B27 146 D4
NFLD/LBR B31 158 A2
Woodcock La North ACGN B27 146 D3
Woodcock St VAUX/NECH B7 3 K2
Woodcombe Cl BRLYHL DY5 118 D5
Wood Common Gra
BLOX/PEL WS3 17 G3
Woodcote Dr DOR/KN B93 199 F1
WASH/WDE B8 110 D4
Woodcote Pl LOZ/NWT B19 * 108 C2
Woodcote Rd
DUNHL/THL/PER WV6 35 G1
ERDE/BCHGN B24 93 H1
Woodcote Wy
FOAKS/STRLY B74 60 B2
WSNGN B18 108 A5

Wood Ct BFLD/HDSWWD B20 ...90 A4
Wood Cft HLYWD B47 ...192 D2
Woodcroft Av
BFLD/HDSWWD B20 ...89 G3
TPTN/OCK DY4 ...84 C1
Woodcroft Cl CDYHTH B64 ...121 F4
Woodcross La BILS/COS WV14 ...68 A1
Woodcross St BILS/COS WV14 ...67 H1
Woodend BFLD/HDSWWD B20 ...73 G5
Wood End La ERDE/BCHGN B24 ..92 D3
Woodend Pl
DUNHL/THL/PER WV6 ...35 F1
Wood End Rd DSYBK/YTR WS5 ...43 F5
ERDE/BCHGN B24 ...92 D3
WNSFLD WV11 ...24 C2
Woodfall Av BVILLE B30 ...159 H5
Woodfield HAG/WOL DY9 ...184 B1
Woodfield Av BRLYHL DY5 ...100 D2
CDYHTH B64 ...120 D4
ETTPK/GDPK/PENN WV4 ...51 F2
HAG/WOL DY9 ...136 D5
OLDBY B69 ...105 E5
Woodfield Cl DSYBK/YTR WS5 ...58 C3
MGN/WHC B75 ...47 F5
Woodfield Crs BHTH/HG B12 ...144 C1
Woodfield Hts
DUNHL/THL/PER WV6 ...35 H1
Woodfield La RMSLY B62 ...171 H5
Woodfield Rd
ALE/KHTH/YWD B14 ...161 F2
BHTH/HG B12 ...144 C1
SEDG DY3 ...83 E2
SOLH B91 ...164 D4
Woodfold Cft ALDR WS9 ...30 B3
Woodford Av CBROM B36 ...112 C1
Woodford Cl COVEN WV9 ...11 H5
Woodford Green Rd
HLGN/YWD B28 ...163 E2
Woodford La WMBN WV5 ...64 B3
Woodfort Rd GTB/HAM B43 ...73 G4
Woodgate Dr RIDG/WDGT B32 ..157 E1
Woodgate Gdns
RIDG/WDGT B32 ...140 A5
Woodgate La RIDG/WDGT B32 ..140 A5
Woodgate Wy HAG/WOL DY9 ...184 C1
Woodglade Cft
HWK/WKHTH B38 ...176 C3
Woodgreen Cft
LGLYGN/QTN B68 ...123 G5
Wood Green Rd
DARL/WED WS10 ...55 H5
WSNGN B18 ...107 F5
Woodgreen Rd
LGLYGN/QTN B68 ...123 G5
Woodhall Cl TPTN/OCK DY4 ...69 G3
Woodhall Cft HIA/OLT B92 ...147 F4
Woodhall Rd
ETTPK/GDPK/PENN WV4 ...51 E4
Woodham Cl RBRY B45 ...173 G4
Woodhaven RUSH/SHEL WS4 ...29 F1
Wood Hayes Rd WOLVN WV10 ...13 H5
Woodhill Cl WMBN WV5 ...64 D5
Wood Hill Dr WMBN WV5 ...64 D5
Woodhouse Fold
WNSFLD WV11 ...24 D5
Woodhouse Orch
HAG/WOL DY9 ...184 C1
Woodhouse Rd
DUNHL/THL/PER WV6 ...35 F2
RIDG/WDGT B32 ...141 E1
Woodhouse Rd North
DUNHL/THL/PER WV6 ...35 F1
Woodhouse Wy CDYHTH B64 ...120 C3
Woodhurst Rd MOS/BIL B13 ...144 C3
Wooding Crs TPTN/OCK DY4 ...69 H2
Woodington Rd MGN/WHC B75 ..63 G3
Woodland Av BRLYHL DY5 ...120 A3
DUDN DY1 ...84 C3
DUNHL/THL/PER WV6 ...35 F2
STRBR DY8 ...152 B5
Woodland Centre
SHHTH WV12 * ...26 C3
Woodland Cl HAG/WOL DY9 ...153 F1
SHHTH WV12 ...26 B4
Woodland Cottages
ETTPK/GDPK/PENN WV4 * ...51 F4
Woodland Ct LICHS WS14 ...33 E3
Woodland Crs
BDMR/CCFT WV3 ...50 D1
Woodland Dr SMTHWK B66 ...106 A2
Woodland Gv GTB/HAM B43 ...58 C5
SEDG DY3 ...82 D3
Woodland Ri CDYHTH B64 ...121 F4
SCFLD/BOLD B73 ...62 B4
Woodland Rd
BDMR/CCFT WV3 ...50 D1
HDSW B21 ...107 E1
NFLD/LBR B31 ...175 H2
RMSLY B62 ...122 B4
Woodlands Av
CSHL/WTROR B46 ...96 B4
DSYBK/YTR WS5 ...58 C3
Woodlands Cottages
ETTPK/GDPK/PENN WV4 ...51 F4
Woodlands Crs BLOX/PEL WS3 ...17 H2
Woodlands Farm Rd
ERDE/BCHGN B24 ...94 B2
Woodlands La SHLY B90 ...180 B5
Woodlands Paddock
ETTPK/GDPK/PENN WV4 ...51 E4
Woodlands Park Rd
BVILLE B30 ...159 E5
Woodlands Rd RBRY B45 ...187 F1
SPARK B11 ...145 E4
WASH/WDE B8 ...110 D5
WMBN WV5 ...81 E1
Woodlands St SMTHWK B66 ...107 E4
The Woodlands CDYHTH B64 ...121 G5
MGN/WHC B75 ...63 G2
STRBR DY8 ...135 G5
Woodlands Wy
CHWD/FDBR/MGN B37 ...132 D1
Wood La ALDR WS9 ...31 G2
BFLD/HDSWWD B20 ...90 B4
BLOX/PEL WS3 ...17 H2
BRGRVW B61 ...185 G5
CHWD/FDBR/MGN B37 ...132 A4
ERDE/BCHGN B24 ...93 F5
FOAKS/STRLY B74 ...45 E4
HRBN B17 ...141 G1
RIDG/WDGT B32 ...157 E1
SHHTH WV12 ...26 C3
WBROM B70 ...87 E3
WOLVN WV10 ...12 D5
Wood Lane Cl SHHTH WV12 * ...26 C3
Woodlawn Gv KGSWFD DY6 ...99 H4
Woodlea Dr ERDE/BCHGN B24 ...92 D4
SOLH B91 ...164 A5
Wood Leasow RIDG/WDGT B32 ..140 D5
Woodleaves HLYWD B47 ...178 B5
Woodleigh Av HRBN B17 ...142 B3
Woodleigh Cl HALE B63 ...138 C1
Woodleigh Rd
CSCFLD/WYGN B72 ...77 F2
The Woodleys
ALE/KHTH/YWD B14 ...178 D1
Woodloes Rd SHLY B90 ...194 B1
Woodman Cl DARL/WED WS10 ...56 B4
HALE B63 ...139 E4
Woodman La HAG/WOL DY9 ...170 B1
Woodman Rd
ALE/KHTH/YWD B14 ...178 C4
HALE B63 ...139 E4
Woodmeadow Rd BVILLE B30 ...177 E2
Woodnorton Dr MOS/BIL B13 ...144 A5
Woodnorton Rd
BLKHTH/ROWR B65 ...122 D2
Woodpecker Gv CBROM B36 ...114 A2
Woodperry Av SOLH B91 ...182 A4
Woodridge AST/WIT B6 ...91 E5
Woodridge Av
RIDG/WDGT B32 ...140 B3
Woodridge Rd HALE B63 ...138 C2
Wood Rd DUNHL/THL/PER WV6 ..35 F2
SEDG DY3 ...83 E3
WMBN WV5 ...65 F4
Woodrough Dr MOS/BIL B13 ...144 B5
Woodrow Crs DOR/KN B93 ...197 E3
Woodruff Wy DSYBK/YTR WS5 ...57 F4
Woodrush Dr HLYWD B47 ...192 C3
Woods Bank Ter
DARL/WED WS10 ...55 E3
Woods Crs BRLYHL DY5 ...120 A3
Woodsetton Cl DUDN DY1 ...68 B5
Woodshires Rd HIA/OLT B92 ...164 A3
Woodside
CHWD/FDBR/MGN B37 ...113 G5
FOAKS/STRLY B74 ...46 C3
Wood Side WNSFLD WV11 ...25 G2
Woodside Cl DSYBK/YTR WS5 ...58 B3
Woodside Crs DOR/KN B93 ...197 E4
Woodside Dr
FOAKS/STRLY B74 ...32 A5
Woodside Gv CDSL WV8 ...10 D4
Woodside Rd DSYBK/YTR WS5 ...58 C2
DUDS DY2 ...101 H3
SLYOAK B29 ...160 A1
Woodside Wy ALDR WS9 ...30 B5
RIDG/WDGT B32 ...157 E2
SHHTH WV12 ...26 C3
SOLH B91 ...164 A5
Woods La BRLYHL DY5 ...119 F5
CDYHTH B64 ...120 C4
Woodsome Gv
ERDW/GRVHL B23 ...76 A4
Woodsorrel Rd DUDN DY1 ...83 H2
The Woods MOS/BIL B13 ...161 F1
Woodstile BKDE/SHDE B34 ...112 D3
Woodstile Cl MGN/WHC B75 ...47 H2
Woodstock Cl DSYBK/YTR WS5 ...57 G5
DUDN DY1 ...102 A1
STRBR DY8 ...117 G3
Woodstock Crs DOR/KN B93 ...196 D5
Woodstock Dr
FOAKS/STRLY B74 ...46 B1
STRBR DY8 ...117 G2
Woodstock Rd HDSW B21 ...107 H1
MOS/BIL B13 ...144 C3
WOLV WV1 ...38 B4
Woodston Gv SOLH B91 ...182 A5
Wood St BILS/COS WV14 ...53 H3
DARL/WED WS10 ...55 H2
DUDS DY2 ...101 H3
ETTPK/GDPK/PENN WV4 ...53 E5
HAG/WOL DY9 ...136 D2
STRBR DY8 ...117 H5
TPTN/OCK DY4 ...69 E5
WLNHL WV13 ...39 G3
WOLVN WV10 ...23 G5
Woodthorne Cl SEDG DY3 ...83 F4
Woodthorne Rd
DUNHL/THL/PER WV6 ...21 E4
Woodthorne Rd South
DUNHL/THL/PER WV6 ...21 E5
Woodthorpe Dr
HAG/WOL DY9 ...136 B4
Woodthorpe Gdns
ALE/KHTH/YWD B14 ...161 E5
Woodthorpe Rd
ALE/KHTH/YWD B14 ...160 D5
Woodvale Dr HLGN/YWD B28 ...179 G1
Woodvale Rd HLGN/YWD B28 ...179 G1
RIDG/WDGT B32 ...157 E1
Woodview Dr EDG B15 ...126 C5
Woodville Gdns SEDG DY3 ...67 H2
Woodville Rd
ALE/KHTH/YWD B14 ...161 F1
HRBN B17 ...141 G1
Woodward Pl HAG/WOL DY9 ...136 A3
Woodwards Cl WSLW WS2 ...41 F5
Woodwards Pl WSLW WS2 ...41 F5
Woodwards Rd WSLW WS2 ...41 F5
Woodward St HHTH/SAND B71 ...87 H2
Woodway ERDE/BCHGN B24 ...93 F1
Woodwells Rd
WASH/WDE B8 ...111 E4
Woolacombe Lodge Rd
SLYOAK B29 ...142 A5
Woolmore Rd
ERDW/GRVHL B23 ...92 A2
Woolpack Cl
BLKHTH/ROWR B65 ...103 G5
Wooton Gv KGSTG B44 ...76 A3
Wootton Av WNSFLD WV11 ...24 D3
Wootton Rd BDMR/CCFT WV3 ...50 C1
NFLD/LBR B31 ...189 G1
Worcester Bar CBHAMW B1 * ...2 C6
Worcester Cl HAG/WOL DY9 ...152 C5
MGN/WHC B75 ...47 H2
Worcester Ct BDMR/CCFT WV3 ...51 G2
Worcester Gn HHTH/SAND B71 ...71 G4
Worcester Gv
DUNHL/THL/PER WV6 ...34 B1
Worcester La HAG/WOL DY9 ...152 D2
MGN/WHC B75 ...47 H2
STRBR DY8 ...135 H5
Worcester Ri SLYOAK B29 ...160 B1
Worcester Rd DUDS DY2 ...121 E1
HAG/WOL DY9 ...152 C5
LGLYGN/QTN B68 ...123 E4
WLNHL WV13 ...40 B3
Worcester St BKHL/PFLD WV2 ...6 E6
STRBR DY8 ...135 G3
Worcester Wk CBHAM B2 * ...3 G6
Word Hl HRBN B17 ...124 B5
Wordsworth Av
ETTPK/GDPK/PENN WV4 ...52 C4
Wordsworth Cl TPTN/OCK DY4 ...69 F3
Wordsworth Ct
DUNHL/THL/PER WV6 ...34 C1
Wordsworth Rd BLOX/PEL WS3 ..28 A2
SEDG DY3 ...82 D1
SHHTH WV12 ...26 C3
SMHTH B10 ...128 B5
WOLVN WV10 ...24 A2
Wordsworth St HHTH/SAND B71 ..87 G1
Worfield Cl RUSH/SHEL WS4 ...42 C1
Worfield Gdns BDMR/CCFT WV3 ..51 F2
World's End Av
RIDG/WDGT B32 ...140 D1
World's End La
RIDG/WDGT B32 ...140 D2
Worlds End Rd
BFLD/HDSWWD B20 ...90 A3
Worleys Wharf Av
DARL/WED WS10 ...72 A1
Worsey Dr TPTN/OCK DY4 ...70 B5
Worthen Gv NFLD/LBR B31 ...175 G5
The Worthings BVILLE B30 ...160 B4
Worthy Down WNSFLD WV11 ...25 F5
Wortley Av WOLVN WV10 * ...23 G4
Worton Rd HAG/WOL DY9 ...136 C5
Wragby Cl COVEN WV9 ...12 B4
Wrekin Cl HALE B63 ...154 C1
Wrekin Dr BDMR/CCFT WV3 ...36 A5
DUNHL/THL/PER WV6 ...21 E5
HAG/WOL DY9 ...136 B3
Wrekin Gv SHHTH WV12 ...25 H1
Wrekin La
DUNHL/THL/PER WV6 ...21 E5
Wrekin Rd KGSTG B44 ...75 F5
SCFLD/BOLD B73 ...77 E2
Wrekin Vw BRWNH WS8 ...19 G2
Wrekin View Rd SEDG DY3 ...67 E3
Wren Av DUNHL/THL/PER WV6 ...34 B2
Wrens Av KGSWFD DY6 ...100 C5
TPTN/OCK DY4 ...84 C1
Wrens Hill Rd DUDN DY1 ...84 B1
Wren's Nest Cl SHLY B90 ...194 A3
Wrens Nest Rd DUDN DY1 ...84 A2
Wrens Park Av
WALM/CURD B76 ...78 A4
Wren St DUDN DY1 ...68 B5
DUDS DY2 ...102 B4
Wrentham St DIG/EDG B5 ...127 E4
Wretham Rd LOZ/NWT B19 ...108 B3
Wrexham Av WSLW WS2 ...40 D4
Wright Av WNSFLD WV11 ...24 D3
Wrighton Cl SHHTH WV12 ...26 A2
Wrighton Dr SEDG DY3 ...83 E5
Wright Rd WASH/WDE B8 ...110 C4
Wright's La CDYHTH B64 ...121 F2
Wright St BILS/COS WV14 ...54 A4
HALE B63 ...138 D3
SMHTH B10 ...128 B4
WOLVN WV10 * ...37 F1
Wrottesley Park Rd CDSL WV8 ...20 B4
Wrottesley Rd
DUNHL/THL/PER WV6 ...21 F5
GTB/HAM B43 ...73 F2
Wrottesley Rd West
DUNHL/THL/PER WV6 ...20 D4
Wrottesley St DIG/EDG B5 ...3 G7
Wroxall Cl BRLYHL DY5 ...118 D4
Wroxall Gv MOS/BIL B13 ...161 G4
Wroxall Rd SOLH B91 ...164 A4
Wroxham Gln WLNHL WV13 ...39 F5
Wroxton Rd YDLY B25 ...130 A4
Wulfruna Gdns
BDMR/CCFT WV3 ...36 B4
Wulfruna St WOLV WV1 ...7 F3
Wulfrun Sq WOLV WV1 ...7 G5
Wulfrun Wy WOLV WV1 ...7 F5
Wyatt Cl DIG/EDG B5 ...143 G2
Wyatt Rd MGN/WHC B75 ...63 H2
Wychall Dr WOLVN WV10 ...13 E3
Wychall La HWK/WKHTH B38 ...176 B3
Wychall Park Gv
HWK/WKHTH B38 ...176 B3
Wychall Rd NFLD/LBR B31 ...175 H2
Wychbold Cl SHHTH WV12 ...26 B1
Wychbold Ct HAG/WOL DY9 ...153 E2
Wychbold Crs STETCH B33 ...131 E1
Wychbury WALM/CURD B76 ...78 C2
Wychbury Ct HALE B63 ...138 C4
Wychbury Dr HAG/WOL DY9 ...153 E3
Wychbury Rd BDMR/CCFT WV3 ..50 C1
BRLYHL DY5 ...119 G4
HAG/WOL DY9 ...153 G1
RIDG/WDGT B32 ...157 E2
Wyche Av ALE/KHTH/YWD B14 ..177 H1
Wychelm Farm Rd
ALE/KHTH/YWD B14 ...178 C4
Wych Elm Rd BRWNH WS8 ...18 D2
Wychnor Gv HHTH/SAND B71 ...72 A1
Wychwood Av DOR/KN B93 ...183 F5
Wychwood Crs
LGN/SDN/BHAMAIR B26 ...147 G1
Wyckham Cl HRBN B17 ...141 G3
Wyckham Rd CBROM B36 ...113 H2
Wycome Rd HLGN/YWD B28 ...162 D4
Wye Cliff Rd
BFLD/HDSWWD B20 ...108 B1
Wye Cl DUNHL/THL/PER WV6 ...34 D1
WALM/CURD B76 ...78 C4
Wyemanton Cl GTB/HAM B43 ...73 E2
Wye Rd BLOX/PEL WS3 ...28 A1
Wykeham Gv
DUNHL/THL/PER WV6 ...34 B2
Wyken Cl DOR/KN B93 ...198 C1
Wyld Cl HHTH/SAND B71 ...71 E3
Wylde Crs BLKHTH/ROWR B65 ...104 A5
Wylde Green Rd
CSCFLD/WYGN B72 ...77 G2
Wymering Av WNSFLD WV11 ...25 F3
Wynall La HAG/WOL DY9 ...136 D3
Wynall La South HAG/WOL DY9 137 E4
Wynbrook Gv SHLY B90 ...195 G2
Wynchcombe Av
ETTPK/GDPK/PENN WV4 ...50 D4
Wyndcliff Rd BORD B9 ...128 B3
Wyndham Gdns BVILLE B30 ...176 B1
Wyndham Rd
LDYWD/EDGR B16 ...125 H3
Wyndhurst Rd STETCH B33 ...112 A5
Wyndley Dr SCFLD/BOLD B73 ...62 B4
Wyndley La SCFLD/BOLD B73 ...62 A4
Wyndmill Crs HHTH/SAND B71 ...72 B2
Wynds Covert
ALE/KHTH/YWD B14 ...177 H3
Wyndshiels CSHL/WTROR B46 ...115 G3
Wynds Point NFLD/LBR B31 ...158 D5
The Wynd SEDG DY3 ...67 F2
Wynfield Gdns
ALE/KHTH/YWD B14 ...161 E5
Wynford Rd ACGN B27 ...146 C2
Wyn-Griffith Dr TPTN/OCK DY4 ...85 G3
Wynne Crs
ETTPK/GDPK/PENN WV4 ...50 C5
Wynn Rd
ETTPK/GDPK/PENN WV4 ...51 F2
Wynn St EDG B15 ...126 D4
Wynstead Covert
ALE/KHTH/YWD B14 ...177 G3
Wyntor La HHTH/SAND B71 ...71 F3
Wyre Cl ALDR WS9 ...19 F3
Wyre Rd STRBR DY8 ...118 A5
Wyrley Cl BRWNH WS8 ...9 F1
SHHTH WV12 ...26 A3
Wyrley Rd AST/WIT B6 ...91 G3
MGN/WHC B75 ...47 H4
WNSFLD WV11 ...25 G4
Wyrley St WOLVN WV10 ...37 H3
Wyrley Wy ERDW/GRVHL B23 ...75 G5
Wythall Green Wy HLYWD B47 ..192 A5
Wythall Rd HALE B63 ...138 C5
Wythwood Cl HAG/WOL DY9 ...153 F1
Wythwood Gv HLYWD B47 ...193 E2
TPTN/OCK DY4 ...69 G3
Wythwood Rd HLYWD B47 ...192 D2
Wyton Av LGLYGN/QTN B68 ...123 G2
Wyvern Cl FOAKS/STRLY B74 ...62 B1
LGLYGN/QTN B68 ...105 F5
SHHTH WV12 ...25 G3
Wyvern Gv SLYOAK B29 ...142 A5
Wyvern Rd FOAKS/STRLY B74 ...62 B1
Wyvis Cl BDMR/CCFT WV3 ...36 A3

Y

Yale Dr WNSFLD WV11 ...25 E5
Yardley Cl LGLYGN/QTN B68 ...123 F3
Yardley Fields Rd STETCH B33 ..129 H2
Yardley Green Rd BORD B9 ...128 D3
Yardley Rd ACGN B27 ...146 C3
Yardley St BRLYHL DY5 ...136 A1
DARL/WED WS10 ...55 E1
Yardley Wood Rd
ALE/KHTH/YWD B14 ...178 D1
MOS/BIL B13 ...144 D5
Yare Gv WLNHL WV13 ...40 B4
Yarnborough Hl STRBR DY8 ...135 G5
Yarnbury Cl
ALE/KHTH/YWD B14 ...178 A4
Yarn Cl HLYWD B47 ...192 C3
Yarner Cl DUDN DY1 ...83 G5
Yarnfield Rd SPARK B11 ...146 A4
Yarningale Rd
ALE/KHTH/YWD B14 ...160 C5
Yarrow Cl BLOX/PEL WS3 ...18 A2
WNSFLD WV11 ...25 F5
Yarrow Dr HWK/WKHTH B38 ...176 D5
Yarwell Cl WOLVN WV10 ...37 F1
Yateley Av PBAR/PBCH B42 ...74 A4
Yateley Crs PBAR/PBCH B42 ...74 A4
Yateley Rd EDG B15 ...125 G5
Yatesbury Av CVALE B35 ...94 B3
Yates Cft FOAKS/STRLY B74 ...32 D4
Yates La RMSLY B62 ...122 C2
Yeadon Gdns BDMR/CCFT WV3 ...35 H5
Yeames Cl GTB/HAM B43 ...59 G3
Yelverton Cl BLOX/PEL WS3 ...16 D3
Yelverton Dr EDG B15 ...125 G5
Yeman Rd LGLYGN/QTN B68 ...123 H1
Yemscroft Flats
RUSH/SHEL WS4 * ...28 C4
Yenton Gv CSCFLD/WYGN B72 ...77 G5
Yeomanry Cl MGN/WHC B75 ...63 G2
Yeomans Wy MGN/WHC B75 ...63 F2
Yerbury Gv ERDW/GRVHL B23 ...91 G1
Yew Croft Av HRBN B17 ...141 G1
Yewdale HRBN B17 ...142 A3
Yewhurst Rd SOLH B91 ...180 D1
Yew St BDMR/CCFT WV3 ...6 B5
Yew Tree Av HAG/WOL DY9 ...170 B5
Yew Tree Gdns CDSL WV8 ...10 C3
Yew Tree Hills DUDS DY2 ...120 C1
Yew Tree La BILS/COS WV14 ...68 D2
DARL/WED WS10 ...71 E1
DUNHL/THL/PER WV6 ...20 D4
LGN/SDN/BHAMAIR B26 ...130 A5
RMSLY B62 ...173 G2
SOLH B91 ...165 G5
Yewtree La
BLKHTH/ROWR B65 ...121 H2
Yew Tree Pl RMSLY B62 ...155 F5
Yew Tree Ri WALM/CURD B76 ...63 F5
Yew Tree Rd AST/WIT B6 ...91 G5
CBROM B36 ...113 G1
DSYBK/YTR WS5 ...57 G3
DUDS DY2 ...102 C5
EDG B15 ...126 C4
HALE B63 ...138 A4
MOS/BIL B13 ...143 H5
RUSH/SHEL WS4 ...28 D1
SMTHWKW B67 ...106 A5
Yewtree Rd FOAKS/STRLY B74 ...44 D5
SCFLD/BOLD B73 ...77 E4
Yew Tree Vls SCFLD/BOLD B73 * ..77 E4
Yockleton Rd STETCH B33 ...131 E1
York Av BDMR/CCFT WV3 ...36 A4
WLNHL WV13 ...40 B3
WSLW WS2 ...41 F3
Yorkbrooke Dr
LGN/SDN/BHAMAIR B26 ...147 H2
York Cl BVILLE B30 ...160 A4
TPTN/OCK DY4 ...84 D2
York Crs BDMR/CCFT WV3 ...35 H4
DARL/WED WS10 ...55 F2
STRBR DY8 ...117 H5
WBROM B70 ...71 E5
Yorkdale Cl SEDG DY3 ...83 F3
York Dr ERDE/BCHGN B24 ...111 F1
Yorke Av BRLYHL DY5 ...118 C3
York Gdns BDMR/CCFT WV3 ...36 A4
Yorklea Cl
CHWD/FDBR/MGN B37 ...131 H2
Yorklea Cft
CHWD/FDBR/MGN B37 ...131 H2
Yorkminster Dr
CHWD/FDBR/MGN B37 ...132 C1
York Rd ALE/KHTH/YWD B14 ...161 E2
BDMR/CCFT WV3 ...35 F5
BLKHTH/ROWR B65 ...122 C1
DUDS DY2 ...121 E1
ERDW/GRVHL B23 ...92 D2
HDSW B21 ...107 H1
HLGN/YWD B28 ...162 D1
LDYWD/EDGR B16 ...125 F3
RUSH/SHEL WS4 ...29 F3
York St HRBN B17 ...142 B1
WOLV WV1 ...7 J5
Yorks Wood Dr
CHWD/FDBR/MGN B37 ...113 G4
York Ter WSNGN B18 ...108 C4
Young St WBROM B70 ...87 E3
Yoxall Gv STETCH B33 ...130 C1
Yoxall Rd SHLY B90 ...180 D3

Z

Zions Cl CDYHTH B64 ...121 F3
Zoar St BDMR/CCFT WV3 ...6 C6
SEDG DY3 ...83 E3
Zouche Cl STRBR DY8 ...118 A4

The 3b Business Village *HDSW* B21 107 F2
Abberley Industrial Centre *SMTHWK* B66 107 F4
Abbey CP School *BLOX/PEL* WS3 16 A4
Abbey Infant School *SMTHWKW* B67 124 A2
Abbey Junior School *SMTHWKW* B67 124 A3
Abbey Tutorial College *CBHAMNW* B3 2 E3
Ace Business Park *STETCH* B33 131 E2
Acocks Green J & I School *ACGN* B27 146 B4
Acupoint Magneto Clinic *SMHTH* B10 128 C5
Adderley Primary School *WASH/WDE* B8 128 B1
Adderley Trading Estate *WASH/WDE* B8 110 A5
Albert Bradbeer Infant School *NFLD/LBR* B31 189 F1
Albert Bradbeer Junior School *NFLD/LBR* B31 189 F1
Albert Pritchard Infant School *DARL/WED* WS10 56 A3
Albion Business Park *SMTHWK* B66 106 A1
Albion Industrial Estate *WBROM* B70 87 E4
Albion Junior School *HHTH/SAND* B71 106 C1
Albion Road Junior School *WLNHL* WV13 39 H3
Alcott Hall Primary School *CHWD/FDBR/MGN* B37 132 B3
Alderbrook School *SOLH* B91 181 F3
Alder Coppice Primary School *SEDG* DY3 67 E2
Aldersley High School *CDSL* WV8 22 A1
Aldersley Leisure Village *DUNHL/THL/PER* WV6 22 B4
Aldersley Stadium *DUNHL/THL/PER* WV6 22 B4
Aldridge & Brownhills Magistrates Court *ALDR* WS9 30 B4
Aldridge School *ALDR* WS9 30 A5
Alexander Industrial Park *BILS/COS* WV14 53 G4
Alexandra High School & Sixth Form Centre *TPTN/OCK* DY4 69 H5
Alexandra Industrial Estate *TPTN/OCK* DY4 69 F5
Alexandra Medical Centre *HALE* B63 138 B2
Alexandra Theatre *DIG/EDG* B5 3 F6
Al-Furqan Community College *SPARK* B11 145 H3
Al-Furqan Primary School *SPARK* B11 145 H3
Al Hijrah School *BORD* B9 128 C2
Al Huda Girls School *WASH/WDE* B8 110 B4
Allens Croft Primary School *ALE/KHTH/YWD* B14 160 B5
Allens Rough JMI School *SHHTH* WV12 26 A1
All Saints CE J & I School *HHTH/SAND* B71 71 G5
All Saints Industrial Estate *WSNGN* B18 108 A4
Alma Industrial Estate *DARL/WED* WS10 55 E2
Alston Primary School *BORD* B9 129 E1
Alumrock Medical Centre *WASH/WDE* B8 110 C5
Alumwell Community School *WSLW* WS2 41 E4
Alumwell Infant School *WSLW* WS2 41 F3
Alumwell Junior School *WSLW* WS2 41 E3
Amblecote Primary School *STRBR* DY8 118 B4
AMC Cinema *LDYWD/EDGR* B16 126 A3
Amptronik Trading Estate *SEDG* DY3 80 B2
Anchor Brook Industrial Park *ALDR* WS9 30 B4
Anderton Park Primary School *BHTH/HG* B12 144 C3
Anglesey Primary School *LOZ/NWT* B19 108 C2
Anglo African Industrial Park *OLDBY* B69 86 C4
Anita Myatt Health Centre *ETTPK/GDPK/PENN* WV4 50 D4
Annie Lennard Infant School *SMTHWKW* B67 124 A1
Arboretum *RUSH/SHEL* WS4 5 J2
Arcadian Shopping Centre *DIG/EDG* B5 3 G7
Archbishop Grimshaw RC School *CHWD/FDBR/MGN* B37 131 H1
Archbishop Ilsey Catholic Technology College & 6th Form Centre *ACGN* B27 146 C4
Arden Hotel & Leisure Club *HIA/OLT* B92 149 G5
Arden Industrial Estate *WASH/WDE* B8 111 F2
Arden Primary School *SPARK* B11 145 E2
Arden School *DOR/KN* B93 197 F3
Armoury Trading Estate *SPARK* B11 145 F1
Arran Medical Centre *CBROM* B36 114 A2
Arrow Industrial Estate *SHHTH* WV12 25 H3
Arthur Terry School *FOAKS/STRLY* B74 47 E3
Ashbourne Centre *ERDW/GRVHL* B23 92 C3
Ashford Industrial Estate *BKHL/PFLD* WV2 52 D1
Ashfurlong Health Centre *MGN/WHC* B75 48 A5
Ashmore Park Clinic *WNSFLD* WV11 25 G2
Ashmores Industrial Estate *DUDN* DY1 84 D3
Ashtree Medical Centre *BVILLE* B30 160 A4
Ashwood Park Primary School *STRBR* DY8 117 H3
Aston Cross Business Park *AST/WIT* B6 109 G3
Aston Expressway Industrial Estate *AST/WIT* B6 109 E4
Aston Hall *AST/WIT* B6 109 F1
Aston Health Centre *AST/WIT* B6 91 E5
Aston Manor Cricket & Lucas Sports Club *PBAR/PBCH* B42 90 D1
Aston Manor School *AST/WIT* B6 109 F3
Aston Newtown Pool & Fitness Centre *LOZ/NWT* B19 109 E2
Aston Science Park *VAUX/NECH* B7 3 K1
Aston Tower Primary School *AST/WIT* B6 109 F2
Aston University *CBHAMNE* B4 3 J2
Aston University (Institute of Art & Design) *CBHAMNE* B4 3 J1
Aston Villa FC (Villa Park) *AST/WIT* B6 91 F5
Aston Wood Golf Club *LICHS* WS14 32 C4
Astoria Hotel *LDYWD/EDGR* B16 125 F3
Atlas Trading Estate *BILS/COS* WV14 69 F1
Atlas Trading Estate *SPARK* B11 145 F2
A1 Trading Estate *SMTHWK* B66 106 C2
SMTHWKW B67 124 C3
Attock Community Sports & Cricket Club *MOS/BIL* B13 162 A1
Attwood Business Centre *HAG/WOL* DY9 136 D2
Audley J & I School *STETCH* B33 112 C5
Autobase Industrial Estate *TPTN/OCK* DY4 85 H3
Avery Dell Industrial Estate *BVILLE* B30 159 H4
Axcess 10 Business Park *WSLW* WS2 40 C4
Baba Balak Nah Temple *WSL* WS1 4 D6
Baggeridge Country Park *SEDG* DY3 66 A5
Bagley Industrial Park *DUDS* DY2 102 D5
Balliol Business Park *COVEN* WV9 11 G4
Banners Gate Infant School *SCFLD/BOLD* B73 60 D4
Banners Gate Junior School *SCFLD/BOLD* B73 60 C4
Bantock House Museum *BDMR/CCFT* WV3 36 A4
Barber Institute of Fine Arts *EDG* B15 142 D3
Barford Primary School *LDYWD/EDGR* B16 125 G1
Barnfield Trading Estate *TPTN/OCK* DY4 69 E4
Baron Business Centre *HAG/WOL* DY9 136 C2
Barons Court Industrial Estate *ALDR* WS9 19 E5
Barons Court Trading Estate *ALDR* WS9 19 E5
The Barr Beacon School *ALDR* WS9 59 F3
Bartley Green FC *RIDG/WDGT* B32 157 G1
Bartley Green Health Centre *RIDG/WDGT* B32 157 F1
Bartley Green Technology College *RIDG/WDGT* B32 157 G1
Barton Industrial Estate *BILS/COS* WV14 54 A1
Baskerville Special School *HRBN* B17 141 G1
Bath Walk Industrial Estate *BHTH/HG* B12 144 A2
Baverstock GM School *ALE/KHTH/YWD* B14 178 A3
Bayer Hall Clinic *BILS/COS* WV14 68 C3
Beacon CP School *SHHTH* WV12 26 B2
Beacon Hill Cemetery *ETTPK/GDPK/PENN* WV4 67 G1
Beaconside Primary School *RBRY* B45 187 G2
Beacon Trading Estate *ALDR* WS9 29 H4
Bean Road Industrial Estate *TPTN/OCK* DY4 68 C5
Bearwood Medical Centre *SMTHWKW* B67 124 B2
Bearwood Primary School *SMTHWK* B66 124 C2
Bearwood Shopping Centre *SMTHWK* B66 124 C3
Beaufort Special School *CBROM* B36 111 H4
Beauty Bank Primary School *STRBR* DY8 135 F1
Beechdale CP School *WSLW* WS2 27 G5
Beeches Hospital *WOLV* WV1 6 A2
The Beeches Infant School *RBRY* B45 174 B3
Beeches Pool & Fitness Centre *PBAR/PBCH* B42 74 B4
Belbroughton CE First School *HAG/WOL* DY9 184 C2
Belfont Trading Estate *RMSLY* B62 139 E3
Bell Barn Shopping Centre *EDG* B15 126 C4
Belle Vue Medical Centre *EDG* B15 126 D5
Belle Vue Primary School *STRBR* DY8 117 G1
Bellfield J & I School *NFLD/LBR* B31 175 F1
Bells Farm Primary School *ALE/KHTH/YWD* B14 177 G3
The Bell Shopping Centre *NFLD/LBR* B31 175 G1
Bennetts Well Primary School *CHWD/FDBR/MGN* B37 131 H1
Benson Community School *WSNGN* B18 107 H3
Benson Industrial Estate *WSNGN* B18 107 H3
Bentley Bridge Business Park *WNSFLD* WV11 24 C5
Bentley Drive Primary School *WSLW* WS2 41 F2
Bentley Heath CE Primary School *DOR/KN* B93 196 D3
Bentley Lane Industrial Park *WSLW* WS2 41 F2
Bentley Mill Industrial Estate *WSLW* WS2 40 D3
Bentley West Primary School *WSLW* WS2 40 C2
Bescot Hotel *WSLW* WS2 56 B2
Bescot Industrial Estate *DARL/WED* WS10 55 F5
Bevan Industrial Estate *BRLYHL* DY5 118 C1
Beverley Hotel *RUSH/SHEL* WS4 42 C1
Bhylls Acre Primary School *BDMR/CCFT* WV3 50 B1
Bickenhill Trading Estate *CHWD/FDBR/MGN* B37 149 H2
Bickford Road Industrial Estate *AST/WIT* B6 91 G5
Bilbrook CE Middle School *CDSL* WV8 10 D3
Bilbrook Medical Centre *CDSL* WV8 10 D4
Billesley Primary School *MOS/BIL* B13 162 A4
Bilston Central Industrial Estate *BILS/COS* WV14 54 A3
Bilston CE Primary School *BILS/COS* WV14 53 F2
Bilston Health Centre *BILS/COS* WV14 53 H2
Bilston Industrial Estate *BILS/COS* WV14 54 C4
Bilston Key Industrial Estate *BILS/COS* WV14 54 C3
Bilston Leisure Centre *BILS/COS* WV14 53 H2
Bilston Public Library & Art Gallery *BILS/COS* WV14 54 A2
Bilston Town FC *BILS/COS* WV14 54 B2
Bilton Industrial Estate *HWK/WKHTH* B38 176 C5
Bingley Primary School *BDMR/CCFT* WV3 36 C5
Birches First School *CDSL* WV8 21 F1
Birches Green J & I School *ERDE/BCHGN* B24 93 F3
Birchfield Independent Girls School *AST/WIT* B6 109 E1
Birchfield Primary School *AST/WIT* B6 90 D5
Birchills CE School *WSLW* WS2 4 B2
Birchills Health Centre *WSLW* WS2 4 A1
Birchley Industrial Estate *OLDBY* B69 104 C4
Birch Road East Industrial Estate *AST/WIT* B6 91 H4
Birmingham Alexander Stadium *PBAR/PBCH* B42 74 C5
The Birmingham & Midland Hospital for Woman *SPARK* B11 145 E4
Birmingham Area Civil Service Sports Club *HIA/OLT* B92 149 E5
Birmingham Botanical Gardens & Glasshouses *EDG* B15 125 H5
Birmingham Business Centre *WBROM* B70 88 B4
Birmingham Business Park *CSHL/WTROR* B46 133 E4
Birmingham City FC (St Andrews Stadium) *BORD* B9 127 H3
Birmingham Community College *CBHAMNW* B3 3 F4
CSCFLD/WYGN B72 62 C3
Birmingham Conservatoire (UCE) *CBHAMNW* B3 2 D5
The Birmingham Crematorium *PBAR/PBCH* B42 90 C1
Birmingham Crown Court *CBHAMNE* B4 3 G3
Birmingham Heartlands Hospital *BORD* B9 129 F2
Birmingham International Airport *LGN/SDN/BHAMAIR* B26 149 E2
Birmingham Marriott Hotel *EDG* B15 126 B4
The Birmingham Mint *WSNGN* B18 2 B1
The Birmingham Nuffield Hospital *EDG* B15 142 D2
Birmingham One Industrial Estate *CBHAMW* B1 2 B4
Birmingham Repertory Theatre *CBHAMW* B1 2 D5
Birmingham Wheels Adventure Park *BORD* B9 128 A2
Birmingham Womens Hospital *EDG* B15 142 B2
Birmingham (Yardley) Crematorium *LGN/SDN/BHAMAIR* B26 146 D2
Bishop Ashbury's Cottage *GTB/HAM* B43 72 D2
The Bishop Challoner RC School *ALE/KHTH/YWD* B14 161 E2
Bishop Milner RC Secondary School *DUDN* DY1 84 A3
Bishop Veseys Grammar School *FOAKS/STRLY* B74 62 C2
Bishop Walsh Catholic School *WALM/CURD* B76 77 H1
Bishop Wilson CE Primary School *CHWD/FDBR/MGN* B37 132 C1
Bi-tec Industrial Park *WOLV* WV1 37 H4
Blackbrook Valley Industrial Estate *DUDS* DY2 102 A3
Blackbrook Valley Industrial Park *DUDS* DY2 102 A4
Black Country Living Museum *DUDN* DY1 84 D2
Blackheath Primary School *BLKHTH/ROWR* B65 121 H3
Blackheath Trading Estate *BLKHTH/ROWR* B65 122 C2
Black Lake Industrial Estate *WBROM* B70 71 E5
Blackwood School *ALDR* WS9 44 D3
Blakedown CE First School *KIDD* DY10 168 C4
Blakeley Heath Primary School *WMBN* WV5 81 E1
Blakenall FC *BLOX/PEL* WS3 27 G3
Blakenall Heath Junior School *BLOX/PEL* WS3 27 G2
Blakenhale Infant School *STETCH* B33 130 D3
Blakenhale Junior School *STETCH* B33 130 D3
Blakenhall Industrial Estate *BKHL/PFLD* WV2 51 H1
Blakesley Hall & Museum *YDLY* B25 129 H3
Blakesley Hall Primary School *YDLY* B25 129 H3
Blanford Mere Primary School *KGSWFD* DY6 100 A2
Bleakhouse Clinic *LGLYGN/QTN* B68 123 G3
Bleakhouse Junior School *LGLYGN/QTN* B68 123 G3
Blossomfield Infant School *SHLY* B90 180 D2
Blowers Green Primary School *DUDS* DY2 102 B1
Bloxwich Business Park *WSLW* WS2 27 F3
Bloxwich CE Primary School *BLOX/PEL* WS3 27 F1
Bloxwich Golf Club *BLOX/PEL* WS3 16 D3
Bloxwich Hospital *BLOX/PEL* WS3 27 F2
Bloxwich Lane Industrial Estate *WSLW* WS2 41 E2
Bloxwich Leisure Centre *BLOX/PEL* WS3 27 G2
Blue Coat CE Comprehensive School *WSL* WS1 5 F5
Blue Coat CE Infant School *WSL* WS1 5 F6
Blue Coat CE Junior School *WSL* WS1 5 G5
The Blue Coat School *EDG* B15 142 C1
Blythe Business Park *HOCK/TIA* B94 195 F5
Blythe Special School *CSHL/WTROR* B46 115 G5
BMI Priory Hospital *EDG* B15 143 F2
Boating Lakes *WOLV* WV1 6 C2
Boddis Industrial Park *CDYHTH* B64 121 G2
Boldmere Clinic *SCFLD/BOLD* B73 76 D2
Boldmere Golf Club *SCFLD/BOLD* B73 61 G5
Boldmere J & I School *SCFLD/BOLD* B73 76 D2
Boldmere St Michaels FC *SCFLD/BOLD* B73 76 D3
Bordesley Green Girls School *WASH/WDE* B8 128 C1
Bordesley Green Primary School *BORD* B9 129 E2
Bordesley Green Trading Estate *WASH/WDE* B8 128 B1
Borough Cemetery *DUDS* DY2 102 B1
Bosworth Wood Primary School *CBROM* B36 95 H5
Boulton Industrial Centre *WSNGN* B18 108 B4
The Boundary Hotel *WSL* WS1 57 H1
Boundary Industrial Estate *WOLVN* WV10 12 C2
Bourneville Infant School *BVILLE* B30 159 G3
Bourneville Junior School *BVILLE* B30 159 G3
Bournville College of FE *NFLD/LBR* B31 159 E3
Bournville School of Art & Craft *BVILLE* B30 159 G3
Bournville School & Sixth Form Centre *NFLD/LBR* B31 159 E4
Bowling Alley *BRLYHL* DY5 119 F2
Bowling Alley *LDYWD/EDGR* B16 126 A3
Brackendale Shopping Centre *SHHTH* WV12 40 B1
Bradford Street Clinic *WSL* WS1 4 D5
Braidwood School for Deaf Children *ERDW/GRVHL* B23 75 H5
Bramford Primary School *DUDN* DY1 68 A5
Brandhall Clinic *LGLYGN/QTN* B68 123 F4
Brandhall Golf Club *LGLYGN/QTN* B68 123 E2
Brandhall Primary School *LGLYGN/QTN* B68 123 F3
Brandon Way Industrial Estate *WBROM* B70 86 D3
Brandwood End Cemetery *ALE/KHTH/YWD* B14 161 E5
Brasshouse Infant School *SMTHWK* B66 106 B2
Brays Special School *LGN/SDN/BHAMAIR* B26 147 G1
Breener Industrial Estate *STRBR* DY8 118 D3
Brickhouse J & I School *BLKHTH/ROWR* B65 121 G1
Bridge Industrial Estate *HIA/OLT* B92 165 E2
Bridge Special School *ERDW/GRVHL* B23 92 C2
Bridge Street Industrial Estate *DARL/WED* WS10 70 D2
The Bridge Trading Estate *SMTHWK* B66 106 D2
The Brierley Hill Health Centre *BRLYHL* DY5 119 F1
Brierley Hill Primary School *BRLYHL* DY5 119 G2
The Brierley Trading Estate *BRLYHL* DY5 119 E1
Brierly Hill Leisure Centre *BRLYHL* DY5 119 G2
The Brier Special School *BRLYHL* DY5 119 G1
Brindley Place *CBHAMW* B1 2 C6
Brineton Industrial Estate *WSLW* WS2 4 A6

Bristnall Hall High School LGLYGN/QTN B68 123 H1
Britannia High School BLKHTH/ROWR B65 122 B2
Broadcott Industrial Estate CDYHTH B64 121 G3
Broadmeadow J & I School BVILLE B30 177 F3
Broad Street Gallery WOLV WV1 7 G3
Broadwalk Retail Park WSL WS1 56 D2
Broadway Medical Centre DSYBK/YTR WS5 57 F2
Broadway Plaza LDYWD/EDGR B16 126 A3
Broadway School BFLD/HDSWWD B20 91 E4
Broadwell Industrial Park OLDBY B69 87 E5
Broadwyn Trading Estate CDYHTH B64 121 G3
Brockmoor Industrial Estate KGSWFD DY6 118 C1
Brockmoor Primary School BRLYHL DY5 119 E1
Bromford J & I School CBROM B36 111 H2
Bromford Road Industrial Estate OLDBY B69 87 E5
Bromley Hills Primary School KGSWFD DY6 100 B5
Bromley Primary School BRLYHL DY5 100 D4
Brookfields Primary School WSNGN B18 2 A1
Brooklands Hospital CHWD/FDBR/MGN B37 132 B4
The Brook Primary School STRBR DY8 118 B3
Brookside Industrial Estate DARL/WED WS10 56 B5
Brook Street Business Centre TPTN/OCK DY4 69 E5
Brookvale Primary School ERDW/GRVHL B23 91 H2
Brookvale Trading Estate AST/WIT B6 91 G3
Brownhills Business Park BRWNH WS8 19 F2
Brownhills Clinic BRWNH WS8 9 F5
Brownhills Comprehensive School BRWNH WS8 9 F3
Brownhills West JMI School BRWNH WS8 8 C2
Browning Street Industrioal Estate LDYWD/EDGR B16 2 A6
Brownmead Primary School BKDE/SHDE B34 112 D3
Brunswick Park Trading Estate DARL/WED WS10 56 B4
Brymill Industrial Estate TPTN/OCK DY4 69 E4
BSA Business Park SPARK B11 145 F1
BT Tower CBHAMNW B3 2 E3
Bullring Shopping Centre DIG/EDG B5 3 H6
Bull Ring Trading Estate BORD B9 3 K7
Bull Street Trading Estate BRLYHL DY5 118 D3
The Burlington Hotel CBHAM B2 3 F5
Burman Infant School SHLY B90 180 A3
Burnt Tree Industrial Estate TPTN/OCK DY4 85 H4
Burnt Tree J & I School OLDBY B69 85 G4
Burton Industrial Estate CDYHTH B64 121 E4
Bushbury Baths WOLVN WV10 23 G1
Bushbury Health Centre WOLVN WV10 13 E5
Bushbury Hill J & I School WOLVN WV10 23 H1
Busill Jones JMI School BLOX/PEL WS3 26 D2
Butts JMI School RUSH/SHEL WS4 5 F1
Cadbury College HWK/WKHTH B38 176 D4
Cadbury World BVILLE B30 159 H3
Calderfields Golf Club & Academy RUSH/SHEL WS4 43 E3
Caldmore JMI School WSL WS1 4 E7
Caldmore Medical Centre WSL WS1 4 E7
Calthorpe Special School BHTH/HG B12 127 G4
Cambrian Wharf CBHAMW B1 2 C5
Cambridge Tutorial College SMHTH B10 128 B4
Campanile Hotel AST/WIT B6 109 F4
Camp Hill Old Edwardians RFC SHLY B90 180 B2
Camping & Caravanning Club Site RMSLY B62 172 A1
Canal Side Industrial Estate BRLYHL DY5 118 D3
Canal View Industrial Estate BRLYHL DY5 118 C3
Canning Wharf CBHAMNW B3 2 D4
Cannon Business Park BILS/COS WV14 68 C2
Canterbury Cross Primary NC School BFLD/HDSWWD B20 90 D4
Cape Hill Medical Centre SMTHWK B66 107 E5
Cape Primary School SMTHWK B66 107 E5
Cardinal Wiseman Catholic School KGSTG B44 75 F1
Carlton Business Centre VAUX/NECH B7 110 A4
Carlyle Business Park WBROM B70 86 D1
Carters Green Medical Centre WBROM B70 87 G2
Caslon Primary School HALE B63 137 F3
Castle Bromwich Business Park CVALE B35 94 B5
Castle Bromwich CC CBROM B36 113 E1
Castle Bromwich Hall Gardens CBROM B36 112 C1
Castle Bromwich Infant School CBROM B36 113 G1
Castle Bromwich Junior School CBROM B36 113 F2
Castlecroft J & I School BDMR/CCFT WV3 35 F4
Castle High School DUDN DY1 84 B4
The Castle Pool & Adventure Play Centre CVALE B35 94 D4
Castle Special School BLOX/PEL WS3 27 F3
Castle Vale Health Centre CVALE B35 94 B3
Castle Vale Industrial Estate WALM/CURD B76 94 C1
Castle Vale School CVALE B35 94 D3
Castle Vale Shopping Centre CVALE B35 94 B3
Castle View Industrial Estate TPTN/OCK DY4 85 F3
Causeway Green Primary School LGLYGN/QTN B68 122 D1
Central Business Park STETCH B33 131 F3
Central Clinic DUDS DY2 84 D5
Central Hall CBHAMNE B4 3 H3
Central Industrial Estate BKHL/PFLD WV2 52 D1
Central Park Industrial Estate BRLYHL DY5 119 H1
Central Park Industrial Estate DUDS DY2 102 C5
Central Park Industrial Estate DUDS DY2 121 E1
Central Trading Estate KGSWFD DY6 82 B5
Centre Link Industrial Estate VAUX/NECH B7 109 H3
Century Industrial Estate KGSTG B44 60 A5
Chad Vale Primary School EDG B15 125 F5
Chamber of Commerce WSL WS1 5 G2
Chamber of Commerce & Industry BDMR/CCFT WV3 6 A3
Chancel Industrial Estate DARL/WED WS10 55 F3
Chancel Industrial Estate KGSWFD DY6 81 H5
Chancel Industrial Estate WLNHL WV13 39 H3
Chancel Industrial Estate WOLV WV1 37 H4
Chancel Way Industrial Estate PBAR/PBCH B42 91 F1
Chandos Primary School DIG/EDG B5 127 E5
Chapel Fields Junior School HIA/OLT B92 147 F4
Chapel Street Industrial Estate DUDS DY2 102 D5
Charlemont Primary School HHTH/SAND B71 72 A3
Charles Street Industrial Estate TPTN/OCK DY4 86 C1
Charnwood Business Park BILS/COS WV14 53 G3
Charterfield Shopping Centre KGSWFD DY6 99 H1
Chasewater Light Railway CNCK/NC WS11 8 C1
Chase Watersports Centre BRWNH WS8 8 C1
Cheapside Industrial Estate BHTH/HG B12 127 F3
Chelmsley Wood Industrial Estate CHWD/FDBR/MGN B37 114 A4
Chelmsley Wood Shopping Centre CHWD/FDBR/MGN B37 132 B2
Chelsea Trading Estate AST/WIT B6 109 G3
Cherry Oak Special School SLYOAK B29 142 B5
Cherry Orchard Primary School BFLD/HDSWWD B20 90 A3
Cherry Trees Special School WMBN WV5 64 D5
Cherrywood Industrial Estate WASH/WDE B8 128 B1
Cheston Industrial Estate AST/WIT B6 109 H2
Cheswick Green Primary School SHLY B90 195 E3
Chilcote Primary School HLGN/YWD B28 179 H1
Chillington Works Industrial Estate WOLV WV1 37 H4
Chinese Quarter DIG/EDG B5 3 G7
The Chiropody Surgery YDLY B25 129 H3
Chivenor Primary School CVALE B35 94 C4
Christ Church CE Infant School DUNHL/THL/PER WV6 36 D1
Christ Church CE Junior School DUNHL/THL/PER WV6 35 G1
Christ Church CE Primary School BLOX/PEL WS3 27 H3
Christ Church CE Primary School OLDBY B69 105 E1
Christ Church CE Primary School SPARK B11 127 H5
Christ Church Infant School DUNHL/THL/PER WV6 35 E2
Christ Church Primary School BILS/COS WV14 68 D2
Christ the King RC Primary School KGSTG B44 75 G2
Chuckery Primary School WSL WS1 5 H4
Churchbridge Industrial Estate OLDBY B69 104 D3
Churchfield Industrial Estate DUDS DY2 102 C1
Churchill & Blakedown Golf Club KIDD DY10 168 A3
Churchill Precinct DUDS DY2 84 D5
Church Lane Health Centre STETCH B33 130 B1
Church Lane Industrial Estate HHTH/SAND B71 71 G5
Church of Ascension CE Primary School KGSWFD DY6 99 F1
Cineworld SOLH B91 182 A2
City College East Birmingham STETCH B33 130 D4
City Estate CDYHTH B64 120 D4
City Hospital NHS Trust WSNGN B18 107 H5
City Plaza Shopping Centre CBHAM B2 3 F5
City Road Primary School LDYWD/EDGR B16 125 F1
The City Technology College CHWD/FDBR/MGN B37 114 A5
City Trading Estate LDYWD/EDGR B16 125 H1
Claregate Primary School DUNHL/THL/PER WV6 22 B3
Clarkes Industrial Estate SCFLD/BOLD B73 77 E2
Clearwater Industrial Estate BKHL/PFLD WV2 52 D1
Clent Hills HAG/WOL DY9 154 A5
Clent Parochial First School HAG/WOL DY9 170 D3
Cleton Street Business Park TPTN/OCK DY4 85 H3
Clifton Infant School BHTH/HG B12 144 C2
Clifton Junior School BHTH/HG B12 144 C2
Clifton Road Industrial Estate BHTH/HG B12 144 B2
Clothier Street Primary School WLNHL WV13 39 G2
Cmt Industrial Estate OLDBY B69 105 E1
Coach House Evening Preparatory School SCFLD/BOLD B73 76 D1
Coalpool Clinic BLOX/PEL WS3 28 B4
Cobham Business Centre WASH/WDE B8 128 B1
Cockshut Hill Technology College LGN/SDN/BHAMAIR B26 130 C4
Cocks Moors Woods Leisure Centre ALE/KHTH/YWD B14 178 B1
Codsall Clinic CDSL WV8 10 C4
Codsall High School CDSL WV8 10 C4
Codsall Middle School CDSL WV8 10 B4
Cofton Medical Centre NFLD/LBR B31 189 G1
Cofton Primary School NFLD/LBR B31 189 G2
Coldland Colts FC SOLH B91 165 H4
Colebourne Primary School BKDE/SHDE B34 112 A4
Coleshill CE Primary School CSHL/WTROR B46 115 F3
Coleshill Clinic CSHL/WTROR B46 115 G3
Coleshill Heath Primary School CHWD/FDBR/MGN B37 132 C3
Coleshill Industrial Estate CSHL/WTROR B46 97 F4
Coleshill Leisure Centre CSHL/WTROR B46 115 F3
Coleshill School CSHL/WTROR B46 133 G1
Coleshill Town FC CSHL/WTROR B46 133 G1
The College High School ERDW/GRVHL B23 75 G5
College of Adult Education WOLV WV1 7 G5
College of Continuing Education BLOX/PEL WS3 27 H4
Colley Lane Health Clinic HALE B63 137 G1
Colley Lane Primary School HALE B63 137 F1
Collingwood Primary School WOLVN WV10 13 E5
Colmers Farm J & I School RBRY B45 174 B5
Colmers Farm Secondary School RBRY B45 174 B5
Colmore J & I School ALE/KHTH/YWD B14 160 D3
Colonial Industrial Park CDYHTH B64 120 D5
Colton Hills School ETTPK/GDPK/PENN WV4 51 H4
Combined Courts WOLV WV1 7 H4
Comfort Inn LDYWD/EDGR B16 125 F3
Community Leisure Centre TPTN/OCK DY4 68 D5
Coneygre Industrial Estate TPTN/OCK DY4 85 F3
Connect Business Park WASH/WDE B8 128 A2
Conway Primary School SPARK B11 144 D1
Cookley Wharf Industrial Estate BRLYHL DY5 118 C1
Cooper & Jordan CE J & I School ALDR WS9 30 C4
Copperfield House Hotel SLYOAK B29 143 E4
Coppice High Community School WNSFLD WV11 25 G3
Coppice Junior School HIA/OLT B92 165 G3
Coppice Primary School HLYWD B47 192 C2
Coppice Primary School MGN/WHC B75 47 G4
Coppice Side Industrial Estate BRWNH WS8 8 D5
Copt Heath Golf Club DOR/KN B93 183 E5
Copthorne Hotel BRLYHL DY5 101 G5
Copthorne Hotel CBHAMNW B3 2 D5
Corbett Hospital STRBR DY8 118 C5
Corbett Industrial Estate DUDS DY2 102 C3
Corbett Infant School SMTHWK B66 106 D4
Corngreaves Hall Golf Club CDYHTH B64 121 F4
Corngreaves J & I School CDYHTH B64 120 D3
Corngreaves Trading Estate CDYHTH B64 120 D5
Cornwall Industrial Estate SMTHWK B66 107 E2
Cornwall Industrial Estate WASH/WDE B8 110 A5
Cornwall Road Industrial Estate SMTHWK B66 107 E2
Corpus Christi RC Primary School STETCH B33 129 H2
WNSFLD WV11 25 G2
Coseley Medical Centre BILS/COS WV14 68 C3
The Coseley School BILS/COS WV14 68 B2
Coseley Swimming Pool & Supachute BILS/COS WV14 68 C3
Cotteridge Primary School BVILLE B30 160 A5
Cottesbrooke Infant School ACGN B27 146 D3
Cottesbrooke Junior School ACGN B27 146 C3
Cotwall End Primary School SEDG DY3 67 E4
County Bridge Primary School WSLW WS2 40 C4
Courtfarm Primary School ERDW/GRVHL B23 76 C5
c/PLEX (Under Development) WBROM B70 87 H3
Crabtree Clinic CHWD/FDBR/MGN B37 131 H2
Cradley CE Primary School HALE B63 120 C5
Cradley Heath Community Recreation Centre DUDS DY2 121 E2
Cradley High School HALE B63 137 F1
Cradley Town FC HALE B63 137 G3
Craig Croft Child Health Clinic CHWD/FDBR/MGN B37 132 C2
Craig Croft Medical Centre CHWD/FDBR/MGN B37 132 C2
Cranmore Industrial Estate SHLY B90 181 E5
Cranmore Infant School SOLH B91 181 E4
Crescent Industrial Park DUDS DY2 102 B2
Crescent Theatre LDYWD/EDGR B16 2 B6
Crescent Works Industrial Park DARL/WED WS10 40 B4
Crestwood Park Primary School KGSWFD DY6 100 C4
The Crestwood Secondary School KGSWFD DY6 100 B4
Crocketts Lane Primary School SMTHWK B66 106 C4
Croft Foundry Industrial Estate WLNHL WV13 39 G3
Croft Industrial Estate CHWD/FDBR/MGN B37 132 B2
Croft Industrial Estate CHWD/FDBR/MGN B37 132 D2
Croft Street JMI School WSLW WS2 41 H1
Cromwell Primary School VAUX/NECH B7 109 G3
Cronehill Primary School WBROM B70 87 G2
Cronehills Health Centre WBROM B70 87 G3
Crossings Industrial Estate BLOX/PEL WS3 27 E2
Cross Quays Business Park OLDBY B69 86 A4
Cross Street Health Centre DUDN DY1 84 C5
Crossways Shopping Centre WOLVN WV10 38 A2
Crowne Plaza Hotel CBHAMW B1 2 D6
Crown Wharf Shopping Centre WSLW WS2 4 C2
Crown Wharf Shopping Park WSLW WS2 41 G1
Crystal Leisure Centre STRBR DY8 135 F2
Culwell Industrial Park WOLVN WV10 7 J2
Culwell Trading Estate WOLVN WV10 37 H1
Dadsford Bridge Industrial Estate STRBR DY8 118 A2
Dame Elizabeth Cadbury School BVILLE B30 159 G3
Dame Ellen Pinsent School HRBN B17 124 D2
Damson Wood Infant School HIA/OLT B92 165 F3
Danesmore Park Primary School WNSFLD WV11 25 F1
Darlaston Central Trading Estate DARL/WED WS10 55 G1
Darlaston Clinic DARL/WED WS10 55 F2
Darlaston Community School DARL/WED WS10 54 D2
Darlaston FC DARL/WED WS10 55 F2
Darlaston Road Industrial Estate DARL/WED WS10 55 F3
Dartmouth Golf Club HHTH/SAND B71 72 A5
Dartmouth High School GTB/HAM B43 58 B5
David Lloyd Birmingham KGSTG B44 60 A5
Daw End School RUSH/SHEL WS4 28 D4
Dawley Brook Primary School KGSWFD DY6 99 G2
Dawley Trading Estate KGSWFD DY6 99 H1
Daylesford Infant School HIA/OLT B92 147 G4
Days Inn CBHAMW B1 2 D7
Deanery CE Primary School WALM/CURD B76 78 B3
Deansfield High School WOLV WV1 38 C3
Deeleys Industrial Estate WSLW WS2 27 F4
Deepdale Industrial Estate DUDN DY1 83 G3
The Dell Stadium BRLYHL DY5 100 D4

Delph Road Industrial Park *BRLYHL* DY5 119 F3
Delta Trading Estate *BKHL/PFLD* WV2 37 H5
Delves J & I School *DSYBK/YTR* WS5 57 G3
Dental Health Centre *KGSTG* B44 75 F1
Dental Hospital *CBHAMNE* B4 3 G2
Department of Art (UCE) *CBHAMNW* B3 2 E4
Devonshire J & I School *SMTHWKW* B67 106 A4
Deykin Avenue J & I School *AST/WIT* B6 91 G4
D'Eyncourt Primary School *WNSFLD* WV11 24 B3
Diana Princess of Wales Hospital (for Children) *CBHAMNE* B4 3 G3
Dickens Heath Primary School *SHLY* B90 193 H2
Digbeth Coach Station *DIG/EDG* B5 3 J7
Dingle Primary School *KGSWFD* DY6 100 C5
Dock Lane Industrial Estate *DUDN* DY1 84 B5
Dock Meadow Drive Industrial Estate *ETTPK/GDPK/PENN* WV4 53 E4
Doranda Way Industrial Park *HHTH/SAND* B71 88 B5
Dormston Secondary School *SEDG* DY3 67 G3
Dormston Trading Estate *DUDN* DY1 83 H2
Dorothy Pattison Hospital *WSLW* WS2 41 F4
Dorothy Purcell Junior School *BILS/COS* WV14 54 D5
Dorridge Cricket Club *DOR/KN* B93 198 C2
Dorridge J & I School *DOR/KN* B93 197 E5
Dorrington Primary School *PBAR/PBCH* B42 74 A5
Doulton Trading Estate *BLKHTH/ROWR* B65 103 F5
Dovecote J & I School *CDSL* WV8 22 A1
The Dovecote Surgery *LGLYGN/QTN* B68 123 H5
Downing Close Health Clinic *DOR/KN* B93 197 E4
Dreamwell Industrial Estate *YDLY* B25 145 H1
Driffold Gallery *SCFLD/BOLD* B73 62 B5
Droicon Industrial Estate *BLKHTH/ROWR* B65 103 H4
Druids Heath Golf Club *ALDR* WS9 30 C2
Duddeston Mill Trading Estate *WASH/WDE* B8 110 A5
Dudley Central Trading Estate *DUDS* DY2 102 B1
Dudley College *DUDN* DY1 84 B4
Dudley College (Mons Hill Campus) *DUDN* DY1 84 B2
Dudley County Court *BRLYHL* DY5 101 G5
Dudley Golf Club *BLKHTH/ROWR* B65 103 G3
Dudley Kingswinford RFC *KGSWFD* DY6 99 E2
Dudley Leisure Centre *DUDN* DY1 84 B5
Dudley Museum & Art Gallery *DUDN* DY1 84 C5
Dudley Town Hall *DUDN* DY1 84 C5
Dudley Water Sports Centre *DUDS* DY2 120 B1
Dudley Wood Primary School *DUDS* DY2 120 C2
Dudley Zoo & Castle *DUDN* DY1 84 D4
Dunstall Hill Industrial Estate *DUNHL/THL/PER* WV6 23 E5
Dunstall Hill Primary School *DUNHL/THL/PER* WV6 37 E1
Dunton Trading Estate *VAUX/NECH* B7 110 B2
Durberville Road Industrial Estate *BKHL/PFLD* WV2 52 D1
Eagle Industrial Estate *TPTN/OCK* DY4 70 B4
Eagle Trading Estate *HALE* B63 138 C3
Earls High School *HALE* B63 138 D3
Earlswood School *ERDW/GRVHL* B23 92 C4
Eastbourne House School *ACGN* B27 146 C3
Eastfield Primary School *WOLV* WV1 37 H3
East Park J & I School *WOLV* WV1 38 B5
East Park Trading Estate *WOLV* WV1 37 H5
Eaton Wood Medical Centre *ERDE/BCHGN* B24 93 H3
Ebrook Adult Training Centre *CSCFLD/WYGN* B72 62 D5
Eclipse Industrial Estate *TPTN/OCK* DY4 85 E1
Eclipse Trading Estate *TPTN/OCK* DY4 85 E1
Edgar Stammers J & I School *BLOX/PEL* WS3 28 B3
Edgbaston Golf Club *EDG* B15 143 F1
Edgbaston Health Clinic *EDG* B15 142 C2
Edgbaston Health Clinic *SOLH* B91 164 B4
Edgbaston High School for Girls & Prep Department *EDG* B15 125 H5
Edgbaston Shopping Centre *LDYWD/EDGR* B16 126 A4
Edgewood Road Clinic *RBRY* B45 188 B2
Edward Street Hospital *WBROM* B70 87 G3
Electra Park Industrial Estate *AST/WIT* B6 91 H5
Electric Cinema *DIG/EDG* B5 3 F6
The Ellowes Hall School *SEDG* DY3 83 E1
Elmdon Trading Estate *CHWD/FDBR/MGN* B37 149 G1
Elmore Green JMI School *BLOX/PEL* WS3 27 E1
Elms Farm Primary School *LGN/SDN/BHAMAIR* B26 131 E5
Elms Health Centre *HALE* B63 137 F1
Elm Street Infant School *WLNHL* WV13 40 A2
Elm Terrace Clinic *OLDBY* B69 85 H5
Elston Hall Primary School *WOLVN* WV10 12 D5
Ely House Hotel *BDMR/CCFT* WV3 6 B4
Embassy Industrial Estate *HAG/WOL* DY9 136 D2
Empire Industrial Park *ALDR* WS9 29 H1
English Martyrs RC Primary School *SPARK* B11 145 E3
Erdington Hall Primary School *ERDE/BCHGN* B24 92 D4
Erdington Industrial Park *ERDE/BCHGN* B24 94 B2
Erdington Medical Centre *ERDE/BCHGN* B24 92 C4
Erdington Pool & Turkish Suite *ERDW/GRVHL* B23 93 E2
Essington Light Industrial Estate *WNSFLD* WV11 14 D3
Ettingshall Primary School *BILS/COS* WV14 53 F1
Euro Business Park *OLDBY* B69 86 C5
European Business Park *OLDBY* B69 104 C2
Eversfield Preparatory School *SOLH* B91 182 A1
Express by Holiday Inn
CSHL/WTROR B46 133 F5
CVALE B35 94 C5
GTB/HAM B43 58 C4
HLGN/YWD B28 163 E4
OLDBY B69 104 C3
Expressway Industrial Estate *AST/WIT* B6 109 E3
Eye Infirmary *BDMR/CCFT* WV3 6 B4
Fairfax School *MGN/WHC* B75 63 F3
Fairfield First School *BRGRVW* B61 185 H5
Fairfield Villa FC *BRGRVW* B61 185 H5
Fairhaven Primary School *STRBR* DY8 117 H1
The Fairlawns at Aldridge Hotel *ALDR* WS9 31 E4
Fairway Primary School *HWK/WKHTH* B38 176 B3
Falcon Lodge Clinic *MGN/WHC* B75 63 G3
Fallings Park Industrial Estate *WOLVN* WV10 23 H5
Fallings Park Primary School *WOLVN* WV10 24 A3
Fazeley Industrial Estate *DIG/EDG* B5 3 K5
Featherstone Primary School *ERDW/GRVHL* B23 92 C2
Feldon Lane Clinic *RMSLY* B62 122 C5
Fernbank Medical Centre *WASH/WDE* B8 111 E5
Ferndale Primary School *GTB/HAM* B43 73 G3
Field Road Industrial Estate *BLOX/PEL* WS3 27 G2
Firs Primary School *CBROM* B36 112 A1
Fir Tree Primary School *DSYBK/YTR* WS5 57 G4
Five Ways Shopping Centre *LDYWD/EDGR* B16 126 B3
Flemings Hotel *HIA/OLT* B92 164 A1
The Foot Clinic *CBHAMNW* B3 2 E4
Fordbridge Infant School *CHWD/FDBR/MGN* B37 114 B4
Fordhouse Road Industrial Estate *WOLVN* WV10 23 E2
Fordhouses Cricket Club *WOLVN* WV10 12 D3
Forest Hotel *DOR/KN* B93 198 D1
Forest Oak School *CBROM* B36 95 G5
Forge Trading Estate *RMSLY* B62 139 E2
Formans Trading Estate *SPARK* B11 145 F4
Fort Industrial Park *ERDE/BCHGN* B24 94 B5
The Fort Shopping Park *ERDE/BCHGN* B24 93 G5
Foundry Primary School *WSNGN* B18 107 F3
Fountain Court Hotel *LDYWD/EDGR* B16 125 E3
Four Dwellings High School *RIDG/WDGT* B32 140 B2
Four Dwellings Infant School *RIDG/WDGT* B32 140 B2
Four Dwellings Junior School *RIDG/WDGT* B32 140 B2
Four Oaks J & I School *FOAKS/STRLY* B74 46 C1
Four Oaks Medical Centre *MGN/WHC* B75 47 F3
Four Oaks Saints Cricket Club *FOAKS/STRLY* B74 32 C5
Four Seasons Art Gallery *ERDE/BCHGN* B24 93 E1
Fox & Goose Shopping Centre *WASH/WDE* B8 111 G4
The Fox Hollies Leisure Centre *ACGN* B27 163 E1
Fox Hollies Special School *ACGN* B27 163 E1
Fox Hotel International *BKHL/PFLD* WV2 6 E6
Foxmill Estate *SPARK* B11 145 F5
Foxyards Primary School *TPTN/OCK* DY4 84 C1
Frank F Harrison Comprehensive School *WSLW* WS2 26 D3
Frankley Community High School *RBRY* B45 173 H3
Frankley Health Centre *RBRY* B45 174 A4
Frankley Industrial Park *RBRY* B45 174 B4
Friar Park Clinic *DARL/WED* WS10 56 D5
Frogmill Junior School *RBRY* B45 174 B3
Gainsborough Trading Estate *STRBR* DY8 135 H3
Gannow Middle School *RBRY* B45 187 F1
Garretts Green Trading Estate *STETCH* B33 131 E3
Gas Street Basin *CBHAMW* B1 2 C6
Gatehouse Trading Estate *BRWNH* WS8 9 G3
Gate Medical Centre *WASH/WDE* B8 110 B3
Gay Hill Golf Club *HLYWD* B47 178 C5
George Auden School *NFLD/LBR* B31 158 B5
George Betts Primary School *SMTHWK* B66 105 G2
George Dixon Lower School *HRBN* B17 125 E3
George Dixon School & 6th Form *HRBN* B17 125 E2
George Fentham J & I School *HIA/OLT* B92 167 G4
George Salter High School *WBROM* B70 87 E2
Gibbons Industrial Park *KGSWFD* DY6 100 C2
The Giffard RC Primary School *DUNHL/THL/PER* WV6 22 B5
Gig Mill Primary School *STRBR* DY8 135 E4
Gilbertstone Primary School *LGN/SDN/BHAMAIR* B26 146 D2
G K Davies Industrial Estate *HAG/WOL* DY9 137 E1
Glebefields Health Centre *TPTN/OCK* DY4 69 G3
Glebe Fields Primary School *TPTN/OCK* DY4 69 G2
Glenmead J & I School *PBAR/PBCH* B42 74 D3
Glynne Primary School *KGSWFD* DY6 99 G5
Golden Hillock School *SPARK* B11 145 F1
Goldtel Industrial Estate *ETTPK/GDPK/PENN* WV4 53 E3
Goldthorne Medical Centre *ETTPK/GDPK/PENN* WV4 52 A2
Goldthorn Park Primary School *ETTPK/GDPK/PENN* WV4 52 B3
Good Hope Hospital *MGN/WHC* B75 62 D2
Gornal Wood Crematorium *SEDG* DY3 82 D5
Goscote Hospital *BLOX/PEL* WS3 28 B2
Goscote Industrial Estate *BLOX/PEL* WS3 28 A1
Gossey Lane J & I School *STETCH* B33 131 E2
Gracechurch Shopping Centre *SCFLD/BOLD* B73 62 B3
Grace Mary Primary School *OLDBY* B69 104 A2
Graiseley Primary School *BKHL/PFLD* WV2 37 E5
Granby Business Park *STETCH* B33 131 F3
Grand Theatre *WOLV* WV1 7 G3
The Grange Arts & Media Centre *WSL* WS1 4 E2
The Grange Playhouse *WSL* WS1 42 D4
The Grange School *HAG/WOL* DY9 136 B3
Gravel Hill Surgery *WMBN* WV5 65 F5
Gravelly Industrial Park *VAUX/NECH* B7 110 C1
Grazebrook Industrial Estate *DUDS* DY2 102 A3
Grazebrook Industrial Park *DUDS* DY2 102 B3
Great Barr Business Park *PBAR/PBCH* B42 90 A1
Great Barr Golf Club *GTB/HAM* B43 58 D4
Great Barr Hotel & Conference Centre *GTB/HAM* B43 72 D2
Great Barr School *KGSTG* B44 74 D2
Great Bridge Industrial Estate *TPTN/OCK* DY4 70 A4
Great Bridge Primary School *TPTN/OCK* DY4 70 A5
Great Western Industrial Estate *WSNGN* B18 107 G3
Green Acres Primary School *BILS/COS* WV14 54 B2
Greenfield Primary School *RUSH/SHEL* WS4 29 E2
Greenfield Primary School *STRBR* DY8 135 F2
Greenfield Surgery *STRBR* DY8 135 F2
Greenholm J & I School *KGSTG* B44 75 E4
Green Lane Industrial Estate *BORD* B9 128 C2
Green Meadow Primary School *SLYOAK* B29 158 B3
Green Rock J & I School *BLOX/PEL* WS3 28 A1
Greet Primary School *SPARK* B11 145 F3
Greets Green Road Industrial Estate *WBROM* B70 86 D2
Gregston Industrial Estate *OLDBY* B69 105 F1
Grendon Primary School *ALE/KHTH/YWD* B14 178 C2
Grestone Primary School *BFLD/HDSWWD* B20 89 G2
Greswold Primary School *SOLH* B91 164 D4
Griffin Business Park *CHWD/FDBR/MGN* B37 132 C1
Griffin Industrial Estate *OLDBY* B69 122 D1
Griffins Brook Medical Centre *SLYOAK* B29 159 E3
Grimstock Country House Hotel *CSHL/WTROR* B46 97 E5
Grosvenor Shopping Centre *NFLD/LBR* B31 175 G1
Grove Medical Centre *BKHL/PFLD* WV2 37 G5
Grove Primary School *BKHL/PFLD* WV2 52 C1
Grove School *HDSW* B21 107 H1
Grove Vale Primary School *GTB/HAM* B43 73 F2
Guardian Angels RC Primary School *BKDE/SHDE* B34 113 F3
Guest Hospital *DUDN* DY1 85 E3
Gun Barrel Industrial Centre *CDYHTH* B64 121 F5
Guns Village Primary School *WBROM* B70 87 E3
Gunter Primary School *ERDE/BCHGN* B24 94 A2
Gupta Trading Estate *OLDBY* B69 86 D5
Guy Motors Industrial Park *WOLVN* WV10 23 G5
GWS Industrial Estate *DARL/WED* WS10 70 B2
GWS Trading Estate *TPTN/OCK* DY4 70 B2
Haden Hill Leisure Centre *CDYHTH* B64 121 F4
Hadley Stadium *SMTHWK* B66 124 C1
Hagley First & Middle School *HAG/WOL* DY9 152 D5
Hagley Golf & Country Club *HAG/WOL* DY9 154 A2
Hagley Hall *HAG/WOL* DY9 153 G4
Hagley RC High School *STRBR* DY8 152 B4
Halas Industrial Estate *HALE* B63 138 D2
Halcyon Gallery *CBHAM* B2 3 F6
Halesbury Special School *RMSLY* B62 122 C4
Halesowen CC *HALE* B63 138 D5
Halesowen CE Primary School *HALE* B63 138 C3
Halesowen College *HALE* B63 138 D2
Halesowen FC (The Grove Recreation Ground) *HALE* B63 138 C2
Halesowen Golf Club *RMSLY* B62 139 F2
Halesowen Harriers FC *HALE* B63 137 F2
Halesowen Health Centre *HALE* B63 138 D4
Halesowen Industrial Park *RMSLY* B62 138 D1
Halesowen Leisure Centre *HALE* B63 138 D4
Halesowen Magistrates Court *HALE* B63 138 D4
Hale Trading Estate *TPTN/OCK* DY4 85 H1
Hallfield School *EDG* B15 126 A5
Hall Green J & I School
HHTH/SAND B71 71 G2
HLGN/YWD B28 162 C3
Hall Green Little Theatre *ACGN* B27 146 A5
Hall Green Secondary School *HLGN/YWD* B28 162 C2
Hall Green Stadium *HLGN/YWD* B28 162 D1
Hallmoor Special School *STETCH* B33 130 D1
Hall of Memory *CBHAMW* B1 2 D5
Hamd House School *SMHTH* B10 128 C4
Ham Dingle Primary School *HAG/WOL* DY9 136 A5
Hamilton Special School *HDSW* B21 107 F1
Hams Hall International Freight Terminal *CSHL/WTROR* B46 97 G3
Hams Hall National Distribution Park *WALM/CURD* B76 97 H2
Hamstead Hall School *BFLD/HDSWWD* B20 73 G5
Hamstead J & I School *GTB/HAM* B43 73 F4
Handsworth Boys Grammar School *HDSW* B21 107 G1
Handsworth Cemetery *HDSW* B21 88 D4
Handsworth Golf Club *BFLD/HDSWWD* B20 89 F2
Handsworth Leisure Centre *BFLD/HDSWWD* B20 107 H1
Handsworth Rugby Club *DSYBK/YTR* WS5 58 B4
Handsworth Technical College *HDSW* B21 108 A2
Handsworth Wood Girls School & Sixth Form Centre *BFLD/HDSWWD* B20 89 H4
Harborne Church Farm Golf Club *HRBN* B17 141 H3
Harborne Golf Club *RIDG/WDGT* B32 141 G2
Harborne Hill School *EDG* B15 142 C1
Harborne Pool & Fitness Centre *HRBN* B17 141 H2
Harborne Primary School *HRBN* B17 142 A1
Harden Primary School *BLOX/PEL* WS3 28 A3
Hargate Primary School *HHTH/SAND* B71 87 G2
The Harper Bell School *BHTH/HG* B12 127 G4
Harry Mitchell Leisure Centre *SMTHWKW* B67 106 B4
Harvey Road Health Centre *LGN/SDN/BHAMAIR* B26 130 A5
Harvey Works Industrial Estate *HALE* B63 138 B1
Harvills Hawthorn Primary School *WBROM* B70 70 D4
Hasbury CE Primary School *HALE* B63 138 B5
Haslucks Green Junior School *SHLY* B90 180 A2
Hastingwood Industrial Park *ERDE/BCHGN* B24 93 F5
Hatchford Brook Golf Club *LGN/SDN/BHAMAIR* B26 148 C3
Hatchford Brook Primary School *HIA/OLT* B92 148 A4
Hatchford Gm Primary School *CHWD/FDBR/MGN* B37 131 H2
Hateley Heath Primary School *HHTH/SAND* B71 71 F4
Hatherton Lane Primary School *WSLW* WS2 26 D4
Hawbush Primary School *BRLYHL* DY5 118 D2

Hawkesley Church
Primary School
HWK/WKHTH B38 ....190 C1
Hawkesley Health Centre
HWK/WKHTH B38 ....190 C1
Hawksmill Industrial Estate
BORD B9 ....128 A3
Hawthorne Primary School
KGSTG B44 ....75 G4
Hawthorns Business Centre
SMTHWK B66 ....106 C1
Hawthorns Industrial Estate
HDSW B21 ....106 D1
Haybridge High School
STRBR DY8 ....152 B4
The Hayes Trading Estate
HAG/WOL DY9 ....137 E1
Hayley Green Hospital
HALE B63 ....154 D2
Hayward Industrial Park
ALDR WS9 ....30 A3
Hazel Oak School
SHLY B90 ....180 A3
The Heartlands High School
VAUX/NECH B7 ....109 G5
Heath Clinic
SOLH B91 ....165 F5
Heathfield Foundation
Technology College
CDYHTH B64 ....121 F2
Heathfield Primary School
BFLD/HDSWWD B20 ....108 C1
Heathlands Primary (NC) School
BKDE/SHDE B34 ....112 B2
Heath Lane Cemetery
HHTH/SAND B71 ....71 H4
Heath Lane Hospital
HHTH/SAND B71 ....71 H4
Heath Lodge Hotel
CHWD/FDBR/MGN B37 ....132 D4
Heath Mount Primary School
BHTH/HG B12 ....144 A1
Heath Park High School
WOLVN WV10 ....24 A5
Heath Street Industrial Estate
SMTHWK B66 ....107 F4
Heath Town Leisure Centre
WOLVN WV10 ....38 A1
Hebrew Congregation
CBHAMW B1 ....2 E7
The High Arcal
Secondary School
SEDG DY3 ....67 H5
Highclare St Paul's School
FOAKS/STRLY B74 ....62 B1
Highclare the Abbey School
ERDW/GRVHL B23 ....93 E1
Highclare Woodfield School
CSCFLD/WYGN B72 ....77 G2
Highcroft Hospital
ERDW/GRVHL B23 ....92 B3
Highfield Primary School
WASH/WDE B8 ....110 C4
Highfields Primary School
BILS/COS WV14 ....68 C1
BLKHTH/ROWR B65 ....122 A4
Highfields School
ETTPK/GDPK/PENN WV4 ....50 B3
Highgate Business Centre
BHTH/HG B12 ....144 D1
Highgate Medical Centre
BHTH/HG B12 ....127 F5
Highgate Primary School
DUDS DY2 ....101 H3
Highgate Retail Park
BHTH/HG B12 ....127 F5
Highgate Trading Estate
BHTH/HG B12 ....127 G5
Highgate United FC
SHLY B90 ....193 G2
High Meadow Infant School
CSHL/WTROR B46 ....115 F1
Highters Heath J & I School
ALE/KHTH/YWD B14 ....178 D2
Hillary Primary School
WSLW WS2 ....56 C1
Hill Avenue Primary School
ETTPK/GDPK/PENN WV4 ....52 D5
Hillcrest Business Park
DUDS DY2 ....102 C2
Hillcrest Industrial Estate
CDYHTH B64 ....120 D4
Hillcrest School
& 6th Form Centre
RIDG/WDGT B32 ....141 E4
Hillcrest School
& Community College
DUDS DY2 ....102 B4
Hillmeads Health Centre
HWK/WKHTH B38 ....177 E4
Hillstone Primary School
BKDE/SHDE B34 ....113 F4
Hill Top Industrial Estate
WBROM B70 ....70 D3
Hilltop Medical Centre
LGLYGN/QTN B68 ....123 G2
Hilltop Public Golf Course
BFLD/HDSWWD B20 ....89 E2
Hill West J & I School
FOAKS/STRLY B74 ....46 D1
Hilton Cross Business Park
WOLVN WV10 ....13 H1
Hilton Main Industrial Estate
WNSFLD WV11 ....14 A2
Hilton Trading Estate
ETTPK/GDPK/PENN WV4 ....52 D4
Himley Country Hotel
SEDG DY3 ....81 F3
Himley Hall
SEDG DY3 ....81 H3
Himley Hall Golf Centre
SEDG DY3 ....82 A2
Himley Hall & Park
SEDG DY3 ....81 H2
Himley House Hotel
SEDG DY3 ....81 G3
Hingley Industrial Park
DUDS DY2 ....120 C3
Hippodrome Theatre
DIG/EDG B5 ....3 G7
Hive Industrial Centre
WSNGN B18 ....108 A2
HM Prison
WSNGN B18 ....107 G4
Hob Green Primary School
HAG/WOL DY9 ....136 C5
Hobmoor Primary School
YDLY B25 ....129 H4
Hobs Moat Medical Centre
HIA/OLT B92 ....147 G5
Hockley Brook
Trading Estate
WSNGN B18 ....108 A3
Hockley Heath Pavilion
(Sports Centre)
HOCK/TIA B94 ....198 A5
Hockley Hill Industrial Estate
WSNGN B18 ....108 B4
Hodge Hill Girls School
CBROM B36 ....111 G2
Hodge Hill School
CBROM B36 ....111 G2
The Holborn Shopping Centre
SEDG DY3 ....67 G4
Holiday Inn
GTB/HAM B43 ....58 D5
LGN/SDN/BHAMAIR B26 ....149 E4
Holland House Infant School
CSCFLD/WYGN B72 ....62 C4
Holland Industrial Park
DARL/WED WS10 ....40 B5
Holliday Wharf
CBHAMW B1 ....2 D7
The Hollies Clinic
LGLYGN/QTN B68 ....105 F5
Hollies Industrial Estate
BDMR/CCFT WV3 ....6 D7
Holloway Bank Trading Estate
DARL/WED WS10 ....70 D2
Holly Bush Medical Centre
RIDG/WDGT B32 ....123 H5
Hollyfield Primary School
MGN/WHC B75 ....63 F4
Holly Hall Clinic
DUDN DY1 ....101 H2
Holly Hall (GM) School
DUDN DY1 ....101 H1
Hollyhedge Primary School
HHTH/SAND B71 ....72 A3
Holly Hill Infant School
RBRY B45 ....173 H3
Holly Lane Cemetery
SMTHWKW B67 ....105 H4
Holly Lodge High School
SMTHWKW B67 ....105 H2
Holly Park Industrial Estate
ERDE/BCHGN B24 ....93 G4
Hollywood Primary School
ALE/KHTH/YWD B14 ....178 C4
Holte School
LOZ/NWT B19 ....108 D2
Holt Farm Primary School
RMSLY B62 ....122 C3
Holy Child School
EDG B15 ....143 F1
Holy Family RC Primary School
SMHTH B10 ....128 C5
Holyhead Primary School
DARL/WED WS10 ....55 F5
Holyhead School
HDSW B21 ....107 F1
Holy Name RC Primary School
GTB/HAM B43 ....73 G2
Holy Rosary RC Primary School
WOLV WV1 ....38 A4
Holy Souls RC Primary School
ACGN B27 ....146 C4
Holy Trinity
Catholic Primary School
BILS/COS WV14 ....54 A3
Holy Trinity CE Primary School
BFLD/HDSWWD B20 ....90 C4
Holy Trinity CE Primary School
BRWNH WS8 ....18 D1
Holy Trinity CE Primary School
WBROM B70 ....87 H5
Holy Trinity RC School
SMHTH B10 ....128 A4
Horrell Road Health Centre
LGN/SDN/BHAMAIR B26 ....130 C5
Horse Shoe Associated FC
SHLY B90 ....193 H2
Hotel Clarine
LDYWD/EDGR B16 ....125 G3
Hotel Du Vin
CBHAMNW B3 ....3 F4
Hotel Ibis
DIG/EDG B5 ....3 G7
EDG B15 ....126 D3
SMHTH B10 ....127 H3
Howard Street Industrial Estate
WBROM B70 ....70 D4
Howley Grange Primary School
RMSLY B62 ....140 A2
HRS Business Park
STETCH B33 ....130 D3
HRS Industrial Estate
STETCH B33 ....131 E3
Hudson Industrial Estate
BKHL/PFLD WV2 ....52 D1
Hulbert Industrial Estate
DUDS DY2 ....102 B3
Huntingtree Primary School
HALE B63 ....138 A3
Hurst Business Park
BRLYHL DY5 ....101 H5
Hurstgreen Primary School
RMSLY B62 ....122 C4
Hurst Hill Primary School
BILS/COS WV14 ....68 A3
Hydesville Tower School
RUSH/SHEL WS4 ....5 H2
Ikon Gallery
CBHAMW B1 ....2 C6
IMAX Cinema
DIG/EDG B5 ....3 K4
Imex Business Park
BKHL/PFLD WV2 ....52 A1
BORD B9 ....128 B2
SPARK B11 ....145 H1
STETCH B33 ....111 H4
TPTN/OCK DY4 ....85 G3
Imex Industrial Estate
WSNGN B18 ....108 A5
Indian High Commission
WSNGN B18 ....2 C1
Industrial Kingston Estate
BORD B9 ....127 G3
Industrial Weston Estate
SPARK B11 ....145 G3
Infant Welfare Clinic
GTB/HAM B43 ....73 F1
Inkeeper's Hotel
DOR/KN B93 ....197 H5
Innisfree House School
HLYWD B47 ....193 E4
Innkeeper's Lodge Hotel
KGSWFD DY6 ....99 G3
LGN/SDN/BHAMAIR B26 ....147 H3
RIDG/WDGT B32 ....123 G5
SCFLD/BOLD B73 ....60 C3
International Convention Centre
CBHAMW B1 ....2 C5
International School
& Community College
STETCH B33 ....131 F1
Izons Lane Industrial Estate
WBROM B70 ....86 D5
Jack o'Watton Business Park
CSHL/WTROR B46 ....96 D3
Jack o'Watton Industrial Estate
CSHL/WTROR B46 ....96 D3
James Watt Industrial Park
SMTHWK B66 ....107 E3
James Watt J & I School
HDSW B21 ....107 G2
Jane Lane Special School
WSLW WS2 ....40 D2
Janet Shaw Clinic
CHWD/FDBR/MGN B37 ....132 B4
JAS Industrial Park
OLDBY B69 ....104 C5
Jerome Retail Park
WSL WS1 ....4 C5
Jervoise J & I School
SLYOAK B29 ....158 C1
Jessons CE First
& Middle School
DUDN DY1 ....84 A5
Jewellery Quarter
WSNGN B18 ....2 C1
The Jewellery Quarter
Discovery Centre
WSNGN B18 ....108 B4
Jewish Cemetery
AST/WIT B6 ....91 G1
JFK Memorial
CBHAMNE B4 ....3 F3
John Black Day Hospital
CHWD/FDBR/MGN B37 ....132 B4
John Willmott School
WALM/CURD B76 ....63 F4
Joseph Chamberlain
Sixth Form College
BHTH/HG B12 ....127 F5
Joseph Leckie
Comprehensive School
WSL WS1 ....57 E3
Joseph Turner Primary School
TPTN/OCK DY4 ....69 H4
Josiah Mason College
ERDW/GRVHL B23 ....92 A2
Jubilee Business Park
HAG/WOL DY9 ....136 D2
Jubilee Park Primary School
TPTN/OCK DY4 ....69 H3
Junction 2 Industrial Estate
OLDBY B69 ....104 D3
Junction 6 Industrial Park
AST/WIT B6 ....91 H4
Junction Industrial Estate
SMTHWK B66 ....106 B1
Jury's Inn
CBHAMW B1 ....2 C6
Karis Medical Centre
LDYWD/EDGR B16 ....125 H3
Kates Hill Primary School
DUDS DY2 ....103 E1
Kelvin Way Trading Estate
WBROM B70 ....87 F5
Kent Close Primary School
HHTH/SAND B71 ....71 G4
Key Business Park
ERDE/BCHGN B24 ....93 H3
Key Industrial Park
WLNHL WV13 ....38 D2
Keyway Retail Park
WLNHL WV13 ....39 H5
Khalsa Industrial Estate
SMTHWK B66 ....107 F5
Kineton Green Infant School
HIA/OLT B92 ....163 H1
King Charles Primary School
WSLW WS2 ....40 D3
King David Primary School
MOS/BIL B13 ....144 B5
King Edwards School (Boys)
EDG B15 ....143 E3
King Edwards VI Aston School
AST/WIT B6 ....109 F1
King Edwards VI
Handsworth School
HDSW B21 ....108 A2
King Edward VI
Camp Hill School for Boys
ALE/KHTH/YWD B14 ....160 D3
King Edward VI
Camp Hill School for Girls
ALE/KHTH/YWD B14 ....160 D2
King Edward VI College
STRBR DY8 ....135 G1
King Edward VI
Five Ways School
RIDG/WDGT B32 ....157 G2
King Edward VI
Girls High School
EDG B15 ....143 E3
Kingfisher Industrial Estate
WBROM B70 ....86 C2
Kingfisher Primary School
CBROM B36 ....114 A1
King George V
Primary School
HHTH/SAND B71 ....88 A3
Kingsbury Business Park
WALM/CURD B76 ....79 G5
Kingsbury School
ERDE/BCHGN B24 ....92 D4
Kings Business Park
KGSTG B44 ....59 H5
The Kings CE School
DUNHL/THL/PER WV6 ....21 F5
Kings Cinema
WBROM B70 ....87 H3
Kings Heath Boys School
MOS/BIL B13 ....161 G4
Kings Heath CC
ALE/KHTH/YWD B14 ....161 E4
Kings Heath J & I School
ALE/KHTH/YWD B14 ....161 E1
Kings Hill Business Park
DARL/WED WS10 ....55 G4
Kings Hill Clinic
DARL/WED WS10 ....55 G3
Kings Hill JMI School
DARL/WED WS10 ....55 G3
Kingshurst City
Technology College
CHWD/FDBR/MGN B37 ....132 B1
Kingshurst Clinic
CHWD/FDBR/MGN B37 ....114 A4
Kingshurst J & I School
CHWD/FDBR/MGN B37 ....114 A3
Kingsland Primary School
KGSTG B44 ....60 B4
Kingsley Preparatory School
DOR/KN B93 ....196 D4
Kings Norton Boys School
BVILLE B30 ....176 C1
Kings Norton Business Centre
BVILLE B30 ....176 D1
Kings Norton Girls School
BVILLE B30 ....159 G5
Kings Norton High School
HWK/WKHTH B38 ....176 D5
Kings Norton Primary School
BVILLE B30 ....177 E2
Kingsrise Community
Primary School
KGSTG B44 ....75 H1
Kings Road Industrial Estate
YDLY B25 ....145 H1
Kingstanding Leisure Centre
KGSTG B44 ....75 H3
Kingstanding Special School
KGSTG B44 ....75 E2
Kingsthorne Primary School
KGSTG B44 ....75 G2
The Kingswinford
Secondary School
KGSWFD DY6 ....99 H2
Kingswood School
SHLY B90 ....180 B3
Kitwell J & I School
RIDG/WDGT B32 ....157 E3
Klaxon Industrial Estate
SPARK B11 ....145 H3
Knowle CE Primary School
DOR/KN B93 ....197 G1
Knowle & Dorridge
Cricket Club
DOR/KN B93 ....197 E4
Knowle FC
DOR/KN B93 ....197 G1
Knowle Village Cricket Club
DOR/KN B93 ....197 G1
Krishna Temple
BKHL/PFLD WV2 ....51 H1
Ladypool Primary School
SPARK B11 ....144 D1
Ladywood Arts
& Leisure Centre
LDYWD/EDGR B16 ....126 A2
Ladywood Middleway
Health Centre
CBHAMW B1 ....126 A1
Lakeside JMI School
WLNHL WV13 ....39 E2
Lakeside Medical Centre
DUNHL/THL/PER WV6 ....34 C1
Lakey Lane Primary School
HLGN/YWD B28 ....163 E2
Lanchester School
CBROM B36 ....95 G5
Lane Green First School
CDSL WV8 ....10 D4
The Lane Medical Centre
BHTH/HG B12 ....144 D2
Lanesfield Primary School
ETTPK/GDPK/PENN WV4 ....53 E5
The Lanes Shopping Centre
SCFLD/BOLD B73 ....77 F4
Langley High School
LGLYGN/QTN B68 ....105 F5
Langley Primary School
HIA/OLT B92 ....163 H4
OLDBY B69 ....104 D4
Langley School
HIA/OLT B92 ....163 H3
Langley Special School
MGN/WHC B75 ....63 G2
Langley Swimming Centre
LGLYGN/QTN B68 ....105 F5
Lansdowne Health Centre
WSNGN B18 ....107 H5
Lapal Primary School
RMSLY B62 ....139 H3
Lasercare Clinics
EDG B15 ....126 B4
Laurie Pike Health Centre
AST/WIT B6 ....108 D1
Leamore Industrial Estate
WSLW WS2 ....27 E3
Leamore Primary School
BLOX/PEL WS3 ....27 G3
Lea Road Medical Practice
BDMR/CCFT WV3 ....36 C5
Leasowes Community College
RMSLY B62 ....139 G1
Leaverstock Industrial Estate
STETCH B33 ....131 E3
Lee Bank Business Centre
CBHAMW B1 ....2 E7
Legg Brothers Industrial Estate
ETTPK/GDPK/PENN WV4 ....52 D3
Leigh JI (NC) School
WASH/WDE B8 ....110 C3
Leighswood Junior School
ALDR WS9 ....30 B3
Leighswood School
ALDR WS9 ....30 A2
Lemar Industrial Estate
BVILLE B30 ....160 C1
Lennon Indoor Market
KGSTG B44 ....60 C5
Leona Industrial Estate
RMSLY B62 ....122 B3
Leviss Industrial Estate
STETCH B33 ....111 H5
Lewisham Industrial Estate
SMTHWK B66 ....106 C2
Leyhill Health Centre
NFLD/LBR B31 ....158 A4
Ley Hill Primary School
NFLD/LBR B31 ....157 H5
Leys Industrial Estate
BRLYHL DY5 ....118 C1
Lickey Hills Country Park
RBRY B45 ....188 A4
Lickey Hills Golf Club
RBRY B45 ....188 A4
Lifford Trading Estate
BVILLE B30 ....177 E1
Light Hall School
SHLY B90 ....180 B4
Light House Cinema
WOLV WV1 ....7 G3
Lightwoods Primary School
LGLYGN/QTN B68 ....123 H4
Linden Road Instruction
Swimming Pool
BVILLE B30 ....159 H3
Lindens Primary School
FOAKS/STRLY B74 ....60 B2
Lindley Lodge Industrial Estate
ALDR WS9 ....29 G4
Lindsworth North School
ERDW/GRVHL B23 ....77 E5
Lindsworth School
BVILLE B30 ....177 G2
Link One Industrial Park
WBROM B70 ....70 C5
Linkwood Industrial Estate
STRBR DY8 ....135 F1
Lion Industrial Park
ALDR WS9 ....30 A1
Little Aston CP School
FOAKS/STRLY B74 ....32 A4
Little Aston Golf Club
FOAKS/STRLY B74 ....45 H1
Little London JMI School
WLNHL WV13 ....39 G3
Little Sutton Primary School
MGN/WHC B75 ....47 H2
Living Museum
DUDN DY1 ....84 D3
Locarno Primary School
TPTN/OCK DY4 ....69 F5
The Lock Museum
WLNHL WV13 ....39 F4
Lode Heath School
SOLH B91 ....165 E4
Lodge Farm Primary School
WSLW WS2 ....40 C1
Lodge Forge Trading Estate
CDYHTH B64 ....120 C5
Lodge Hill Cemetery
SLYOAK B29 ....158 D1
Lodge Hill Crematorium
SLYOAK B29 ....141 H5
Lodge Primary School
WBROM B70 ....87 F3
Long Acre Trading Estate
VAUX/NECH B7 ....109 H2
Long Knowle Primary School
WNSFLD WV11 ....24 C2
Long Lane Medical Centre
RMSLY B62 ....122 B3
Long Lane Trading Estate
RMSLY B62 ....122 B3

Longmoor Special School SCFLD/BOLD B73 60 D4
Longwill Special School NFLD/LBR B31 158 C5
Lordswood Boys School HRBN B17 124 C4
Lordswood Girls School HRBN B17 124 D4
Lordswood Medical Practice HRBN B17 141 H1
Lower Farm JMI School BLOX/PEL WS3 17 E3
Lower Gornal Health Centre SEDG DY3 82 D4
Low Hill Medical Centre WOLVN WV10 23 G3
Loxdale Industrial Estate BILS/COS WV14 54 A4
Loxdale Primary School BILS/COS WV14 54 B4
Lozells Primary School LOZ/NWT B19 108 D2
Lugman Medical Centre WSL WS1 56 D1
Lutley Primary School HALE B63 154 D1
Lye Business Centre HAG/WOL DY9 119 H5
Lye CC HAG/WOL DY9 136 B2
Lye Town FC HAG/WOL DY9 136 B2
Lye Valley Industrial Estate HAG/WOL DY9 136 D1
Lyndon Green J & I School LGN/SDN/BHAMAIR B26 147 F1
Lyndon School HIA/OLT B92 147 G4
Lyng Primary School WBROM B70 87 G5
Magistrates Court (Victoria Law Courts) CBHAMNE B4 3 G3
Magreal Industrial Estate LDYWD/EDGR B16 125 H1
Maidensbridge Primary School KGSWFD DY6 81 F5
The Mailbox CBHAMW B1 2 E6
Mainstream Forty Seven Industrial Park VAUX/NECH B7 110 A4
Mainstream Industrial Park VAUX/NECH B7 110 A5
Malt Mill Lane Trading Estate RMSLY B62 122 B4
Mander Shopping Centre WOLV WV1 7 F4
Manders Industrial Estate WOLVN WV10 37 H2
Maney Hill Primary School CSCFLD/WYGN B72 77 H1
Manor Farm Community School RUSH/SHEL WS4 28 D4
The Manor General Hospital WSLW WS2 41 G4
Manor High School (Foundation) DARL/WED WS10 56 D5
Manor Industrial Estate WSLW WS2 4 A4
Manor Park Primary School AST/WIT B6 109 G1
Manor Primary School BILS/COS WV14 68 B1
FOAKS/STRLY B74 45 G4
Manor Way Primary School HALE B63 139 E4
Mansfield Green Primary School AST/WIT B6 109 E2
Maple Business Park VAUX/NECH B7 109 H3
Mapledene J & I School LGN/SDN/BHAMAIR B26 148 C1
Maple Leaf Industrial Estate WSLW WS2 41 F2
Marlborough J & I School SMHTH B10 128 C3
Marlow Estate BLKHTH/ROWR B65 121 H3
Marshalls Industrial Estate BKHL/PFLD WV2 52 A1
Marsh Hill Primary School ERDW/GRVHL B23 91 H2
Marston Green Clinic CHWD/FDBR/MGN B37 132 A5
Marston Green Infant School CHWD/FDBR/MGN B37 131 H5
Marston Green Junior School CHWD/FDBR/MGN B37 132 A5
Marston Road Industrial Estate BKHL/PFLD WV2 52 A1
Mary Elliot Special School WSLW WS2 42 A1
Maryvale Catholic Primary School KGSTG B44 75 E1
Maryvale Institute KGSTG B44 75 F1
Maternity Welfare Clinic BDMR/CCFT WV3 50 D2
Matthew Boulton College of Further & Higher Education DIG/EDG B5 126 D4
Matthew Boulton Community Primary School HDSW B21 107 G2
Maybrook Industrial Estate BRWNH WS8 19 F2
The Mayfair Centre DIG/EDG B5 3 G6
Mayfield Preparatory School WSL WS1 5 H6
Mayfield Special School BFLD/HDSWWD B20 108 C1
Maypole Health Centre ALE/KHTH/YWD B14 178 B2
Meadow Green Primary School HLYWD B47 192 C5
Meadows Primary School NFLD/LBR B31 175 E3
Meadow View JMI School GTB/HAM B43 59 H3
Meadwood Industrial Estate BILS/COS WV14 54 A3
Media Centre WOLV WV1 7 G3
Meeting Lane Industrial Estate BRLYHL DY5 118 D3
Memorial Clock WSNGN B18 2 B2
Menzies Baron's Court Hotel ALDR WS9 19 E5
Menzies High School HHTH/SAND B71 71 G3
Merridale Primary School BDMR/CCFT WV3 6 A6
Mere Green Combined School MGN/WHC B75 47 F3
Merry Hill Shopping Centre BRLYHL DY5 119 H2
Merstone School CHWD/FDBR/MGN B37 132 A3
Mesty Croft Primary School DARL/WED WS10 56 A5
Metalloys Industrial Estate WALM/CURD B76 94 D1
Middlemore Business Park ALDR WS9 29 G4
Middlemore Industrial Estate HDSW B21 88 D5
Middleton Trading Estate WLNHL WV13 39 E3
Middleway Industrial Estate BHTH/HG B12 127 F5
Midland House Dawley Trading Estate KGSWFD DY6 99 H1
Midland Institute CBHAMNW B3 2 E4
Midlands Arts Centre Cinema BHTH/HG B12 143 H3
Milking Bank Primary School DUDN DY1 83 G4
Millard Industrial Estate WBROM B70 87 E4
Millbuck Industrial Estate WOLVN WV10 23 F3
Millennium Point CBHAMNE B4 3 K4
Millfield CP School BRWNH WS8 9 G5
Millfield Special School HHTH/SAND B71 71 H3
Mill Lodge Primary School SHLY B90 179 G3
Minworth Industrial Park WALM/CURD B76 78 D5
Minworth J & I School WALM/CURD B76 95 F1
Moat Farm J & I School LGLYGN/QTN B68 123 G1
Mobarak Health Centre BHTH/HG B12 144 A2
Monarch Industrial Estate SPARK B11 146 A2
Monkspath Business Park SHLY B90 181 E5
Monkspath Primary School SHLY B90 195 H2
Monmer Close Industrial Estate WLNHL WV13 39 H2
Monmore Business Park BKHL/PFLD WV2 52 D1
Monmore Green Greyhound Stadium WOLV WV1 38 A5
Monmore Park Industrial Estate BKHL/PFLD WV2 52 D1
Montgomery Primary School SPARK B11 128 A5
Montgomery Street Business Centre SPARK B11 128 A5
Monway Industrial Estate DARL/WED WS10 55 F5
The Moore Group Business Centre WSL WS1 4 E7
Moor Green FC HLGN/YWD B28 162 C3
Moor Green J & I School MOS/BIL B13 160 C1
Moor Green Sports Centre MOS/BIL B13 143 G5
Moor Hall Golf Club MGN/WHC B75 47 H4
Moor Hall Hotel MGN/WHC B75 47 H4
Moor Hall Primary School MGN/WHC B75 47 H3
Moorlands Primary School HHTH/SAND B71 71 F3
Moor Lane Trading Estate AST/WIT B6 91 F2
Moor Street Industrial Estate BRLYHL DY5 119 E2
Moreton Community School WOLVN WV10 23 H1
Moseley CC HIA/OLT B92 163 G5
Moseley CE Primary School MOS/BIL B13 144 B5
Moseley Golf Club MOS/BIL B13 161 G2
Moseley Hall Hospital MOS/BIL B13 144 A4
Moseley Park School & Technology College BILS/COS WV14 39 E5
Moseley School MOS/BIL B13 145 E5
Mossley Clinic BLOX/PEL WS3 26 D1
Mossley Primary School BLOX/PEL WS3 16 B5
Mount Pleasant Primary School BRLYHL DY5 119 G3
Mount Street Business Centre VAUX/NECH B7 110 A3
Mount Street Business Park VAUX/NECH B7 110 B2
Moxley Industrial Centre DARL/WED WS10 55 E4
Moxley Infant School DARL/WED WS10 54 D4
Moxley Medical Centre DARL/WED WS10 55 E2
Mucklow Hill Industrial Estate RMSLY B62 139 E2
Mucklow Hill Trading Estate RMSLY B62 139 E2
Municipal Art Gallery WOLV WV1 7 F3
Munrow Sports Centre EDG B15 142 D3
Museum & Art Gallery CBHAMNW B3 2 E5
Nansen J & I School WASH/WDE B8 110 D4
National Exhibition Centre BHAMNEC B40 150 A2
National Indoor Arena CBHAMW B1 2 B5
National Institute of Conductive Education MOS/BIL B13 143 H3
National Motorcycle Museum HIA/OLT B92 150 C5
National Sea Life Centre CBHAMW B1 2 B5
The Natural Health Centre HWK/WKHTH B38 176 D3
Nature Centre HHTH/SAND B71 73 E5
Nature Park WALM/CURD B76 94 C1
Nature Reserve SEDG DY3 81 E3
Neachells Lane Industrial Estate WLNHL WV13 38 D1
Nechells Primary School VAUX/NECH B7 110 A1
Nelson Mandela Primary School BHTH/HG B12 144 C2
Nelson Primary School CBHAMW B1 2 A4
Neptune Industrial Estate WLNHL WV13 39 H5
Netherbrook Primary School DUDS DY2 120 D2
Netherton Business Park DUDS DY2 120 D1
Netherton CC DUDS DY2 102 B5
Netherton CE Primary School DUDS DY2 102 B4
Network Park Industrial Estate VAUX/NECH B7 110 A5
The New Art Gallery Walsall WSLW WS2 4 C3
Newbridge Preparatory School DUNHL/THL/PER WV6 36 A1
New Cross Hospital WNSFLD WV11 24 B5
New Cross Industrial Estate WLNHL WV13 38 C2
WOLV WV1 38 A2
Newfield Park Primary School HALE B63 138 C2
New Hall Hotel WALM/CURD B76 78 A1
New Hall J & I School MGN/WHC B75 63 H3
Newhampton Arts Centrel WOLV WV1 6 D2
New Invention CP School SHHTH WV12 26 A3
Newman College of Higher Education RIDG/WDGT B32 157 G2
New Oscott J & I School SCFLD/BOLD B73 61 E5
Newshire Industrial Estate SPARK B11 145 F1
Newton Industrial Estate BORD B9 128 B2
Newtown Health Centre LOZ/NWT B19 108 D3
Newtown Primary School WBROM B70 86 B3
Newtown Shopping Centre LOZ/NWT B19 109 E3
Ninestiles School ACGN B27 163 F1
Nonsuch Primary School RIDG/WDGT B32 140 D5
Norfolk House School EDG B15 125 F4
Norman Green Sports Centre & Athletics Track SOLH B91 181 G2
North Birmingham College PBAR/PBCH B42 75 E4
Northbrook Health Centre SHLY B90 163 G5
Northfield Manor Primary School SLYOAK B29 158 C3
Northfield Pool & Fitness Centre NFLD/LBR B31 175 F2
Northfield Road Primary School DUDS DY2 102 D4
Northicote Secondary School WOLVN WV10 13 E4
Northmoor Industrial Estate BRLYHL DY5 119 F1
Northside Business Centre WSNGN B18 107 G4
North Solihull Sports Centre & Track CHWD/FDBR/MGN B37 132 A1
North Walsall Primary School WSLW WS2 42 A1
North Worcestershire Golf Club NFLD/LBR B31 174 D2
Norwood Hotel NFLD/LBR B31 175 H1
Novotel CBHAMW B1 2 B6
LGN/SDN/BHAMAIR B26 149 G3
WOLV WV1 7 H4
Oak Cottage Primary School SOLH B91 164 A4
Oakdale Trading Estate KGSWFD DY6 81 H5
KGSWFD DY6 100 A1
Oakeswell Health Centre DARL/WED WS10 56 A5
Oakham Primary School OLDBY B69 103 H2
Oak House Museum WBROM B70 87 F4
The Oak Industrial Park KGSWFD DY6 82 A5
Oaklands Primary School ACGN B27 146 C5
Oakleigh Trading Estate BILS/COS WV14 68 B1
Oak Meadow Primary School WNSFLD WV11 25 G3
The Oaks Primary School ALE/KHTH/YWD B14 177 H3
Oakstreet Industrial Estate CDYHTH B64 120 D3
Oak Street Trading Estate BRLYHL DY5 119 H3
Oakwood Special School ALDR WS9 19 G4
Ocker Hill J & I School TPTN/OCK DY4 70 A3
Odeon Cinema CBHAM B2 3 G6
CSCFLD/WYGN B72 62 B5
Ogley Hay Infant School BRWNH WS8 9 F4
Oldbury Business Centre LGLYGN/QTN B68 123 E2
Oldbury Green Retail Park OLDBY B69 104 D1
Oldbury Health Centre OLDBY B69 105 E1
Oldbury Leisure Centre OLDBY B69 104 C3
Oldbury Road Industrial Estate SMTHWK B66 105 H2
WBROM B70 86 D4
Oldbury United FC BLKHTH/ROWR B65 122 C1
Old Bush Trading Estate BRLYHL DY5 101 F4
BRLYHL DY5 119 E3
BRLYHL DY5 119 G1
Old Church CE Primary School DARL/WED WS10 55 E2
Old Edwardians Sports Club HIA/OLT B92 163 G5
Oldfield Trading Estate CDYHTH B64 120 D4
Old Forge Trading Estate HAG/WOL DY9 136 C1
Old Halesonians RFC HAG/WOL DY9 153 H2
Old Hall Industrial Estate BLOX/PEL WS3 27 G2
Oldhall Special School WSLW WS2 26 C5
Old Hill CC CDYHTH B64 121 F4
Old Hill Primary School CDYHTH B64 121 F3
Oldknow Junior School SMHTH B10 128 C5
Old Limberlost Sports Club BFLD/HDSWWD B20 90 A3
Old Park Industrial Estate DARL/WED WS10 55 G4
Old Park Primary School DARL/WED WS10 55 G3
Old Park Special School DUDN DY1 101 H1
Old Rep Theatre DIG/EDG B5 3 F7
The Old Square Shopping Centre WSL WS1 4 E4
Oldswinford CE Primary School STRBR DY8 135 G4
Old Swinford Hospital School STRBR DY8 135 G3
Olive Hill Primary School RMSLY B62 122 B5
Olton Golf Club SOLH B91 164 C3
One Stop Retail Park PBAR/PBCH B42 90 D3
Oratory RC Primary School LDYWD/EDGR B16 125 H2
Orchard Lane Clinic HAG/WOL DY9 136 C1
The Orchard School SMTHWK B66 106 A2
SMTHWKW B67 106 B4
Orthodontists Surgery ACGN B27 146 A4
Osborne Primary School ERDW/GRVHL B23 93 E1
Oundsale High School WMBN WV5 64 D4
Ounsdale Sports Centre WMBN WV5 64 D4
Our Lady of Compassion RC Primary School HIA/OLT B92 163 H3
Our Lady of Fatima RC Primary School HRBN B17 124 B5
Our Lady of Lourdes RC Primary School MOS/BIL B13 162 B5
Our Lady of the Wayside RC Prim School SHLY B90 180 C5
Our Lady & St Chad RC Secondary School WOLVN WV10 23 H2
Our Lady & St Kenelm RC Primary School HALE B63 138 B4
Our Lady & St Rose of Lima RC Primary School SLYOAK B29 158 D1
Our Ladys RC Primary School STETCH B33 131 F2
The Oval Primary School STETCH B33 130 B2
Owen Road Industrial Estate WLNHL WV13 40 A4
Owen Road Trading Estate WLNHL WV13 40 A4
Oxbarn Social & Sports Club BDMR/CCFT WV3 51 F1
Oxford Street Industrial Park BILS/COS WV14 54 B3
Oxley Park Golf Club WOLVN WV10 23 E3
Paddys Wide Water Industrial Estate BRLYHL DY5 101 E4
Paganel J & I School SLYOAK B29 141 G5
Paget Primary School ERDE/BCHGN B24 93 G2
Palfrey Girls School WSL WS1 4 D4
Palfrey Infant School WSL WS1 56 D1
Palfrey Junior School WSL WS1 56 D1
Pallasades Shopping Centre CBHAM B2 3 F6
Palmers Cross Primary School DUNHL/THL/PER WV6 21 H2
Paper Mill End Industrial Estate PBAR/PBCH B42 74 D5
Parkbrook Industrial Estate HAG/WOL DY9 136 D2
Park Clinic ERDW/GRVHL B23 93 E1
Parkfield Clinic BKHL/PFLD WV2 52 B2
Parkfield High School ETTPK/GDPK/PENN WV4 52 C3
Parkfield Primary School ETTPK/GDPK/PENN WV4 52 C3
WASH/WDE B8 128 C1
Park Hall Hotel & Conference Centre ETTPK/GDPK/PENN WV4 52 A4
Park Hall Infant School DSYBK/YTR WS5 58 A1
Park Hall Junior School DSYBK/YTR WS5 58 A1
Park Hall School CBROM B36 95 G5
Park Hill Primary School DARL/WED WS10 56 C4
Park Hill Primary School MOS/BIL B13 144 B3
Park Lane Industrial Estate HHTH/SAND B71 88 C5
Park Lane Trading Estate OLDBY B69 105 E2
Park Lane Trading Estate WOLVN WV10 23 G5
Park Medical Centre SMHTH B10 128 C5
Parkrose Industrial Estate SMTHWK B66 106 D1
WOLV WV1 37 H4
Park Trading Estate WSNGN B18 108 A3
Park View School WASH/WDE B8 110 C4
Parkway Industrial Centre VAUX/NECH B7 109 G5

Pavilions Shopping Centre CBHAMNE B4 3 H5
PDH Industrial Estate DARL/WED WS10 55 E4
PDH Industrial Estate WLNHL WV13 38 D2
Peartree Industrial Park DUDS DY2 102 A3
Pedmore CE Primary School HAG/WOL DY9 152 D1
Pedmore Road Industrial Estate BRLYHL DY5 101 H5
Pegasus Primary School CVALE B35 94 D3
Pelsall Clinic BLOX/PEL WS3 18 A3
Pelsall Village School BLOX/PEL WS3 17 H3
Pendeford Business Park COVEN WV9 11 H4
Pendeford Health Centre COVEN WV9 12 A5
Pendeford High School WOLVN WV10 12 B5
Pendene Complimentary Medical Centre WOLV WV1 6 C3
Penderford Mill Nature Reserve COVEN WV9 11 G3
Pennfields Health Centre BDMR/CCFT WV3 6 C7
Penn Fields School BDMR/CCFT WV3 51 F1
Penn Golf Club ETTPK/GDPK/PENN WV4 66 C1
Penn Hall Special School ETTPK/GDPK/PENN WV4 51 E4
Penn Hospital ETTPK/GDPK/PENN WV4 51 E4
Penn Industrial Estate DUDS DY2 120 C3
Penn Manor Medical Centre ETTPK/GDPK/PENN WV4 51 F4
Penn Road Retail Park BKHL/PFLD WV2 36 D5
Penns Primary School CSCFLD/WYGN B72 77 G5
Pens Meadow Special School STRBR DY8 118 A1
The Pensnett School of Technology BRLYHL DY5 100 C3
Pensnett Trading Estate KGSWFD DY6 100 B1
The Pensnett Trading Estate KGSWFD DY6 82 C5
Percy Business Park OLDBY B69 104 D2
Percy Shurmer Primary School DIG/EDG B5 127 E5
Perry Barr Greyhound Stadium PBAR/PBCH B42 90 D3
Perry Beeches J & I School PBAR/PBCH B42 74 C3
Perry Common Primary School ERDW/GRVHL B23 75 H4
Perryfields High School LGLYGN/QTN B68 123 E4
Perryfields Primary School LGLYGN/QTN B68 123 E5
Perry Hall Primary School WNSFLD WV11 25 F4
Perry Street Industrial Estate BILS/COS WV14 54 A5
Personal & Child Health Centre BVILLE B30 160 A4
Perton Clinic DUNHL/THL/PER WV6 34 C1
Perton First School DUNHL/THL/PER WV6 20 C5
Perton Middle School DUNHL/THL/PER WV6 35 E1
Perton Park Golf Club DUNHL/THL/PER WV6 34 A2
Peterbrook Primary School SHLY B90 179 F3
Peters Hill Primary School BRLYHL DY5 119 E5
Pheasey Clinic GTB/HAM B43 59 G5
Pheasey Park Farm Primary School GTB/HAM B43 59 G4
Phillips Street Industrial Estate AST/WIT B6 109 E3
Phoenix Business Park VAUX/NECH B7 109 G3
Phoenix Industrial Estate BILS/COS WV14 54 B4
Phoenix International Industrial Estate WBROM B70 86 D1
Phoenix Road Industrial Estate WLNHL WV13 38 D2
Phoenix Works Industrial Estate DARL/WED WS10 40 C5
Piccadilly Cinema SPARK B11 144 D2
The Picture House STRBR DY8 135 G3
WASH/WDE B8 111 E4
WLNHL WV13 38 D1
Pines Special School CBROM B36 112 B1
Pinfold Industrial Estate BLOX/PEL WS3 27 G2
Pinfold Street Primary School DARL/WED WS10 55 E3
Planetary Industrial Estate WLNHL WV13 38 C1
Planet Ice Arena DIG/EDG B5 3 H7
Plantsbrook School CSCFLD/WYGN B72 62 C4
Pleck Business Park WSLW WS2 4 A4
Pleck Industrial Estate WSLW WS2 41 G5
Plough & Harrow Hotel LDYWD/EDGR B16 126 A3
Pool Hayes Comprehensive School SHHTH WV12 25 H5
Pool Hayes Primary School SHHTH WV12 25 H4
Poplar Road Clinic ALE/KHTH/YWD B14 161 F1
Poplar Trading Estate AST/WIT B6 91 F1
Portersfield Industrial Estate CDYHTH B64 120 C4
Portland Hotel LDYWD/EDGR B16 125 E3
Portway Road Industrial Estate OLDBY B69 104 C3
Posthouse Hotel DIG/EDG B5 3 F7
Powke Lane Industrial Estate BLKHTH/ROWR B65 121 G2
Premier Business Centre HAG/WOL DY9 136 D2
Premier Business Park WSLW WS2 4 B5
Premier Lodge LDYWD/EDGR B16 2 B7
MGN/WHC B75 63 F1
RBRY B45 174 B5
Premier Partnership Industrial Estate KGSWFD DY6 100 C5
Premier Trading Estate VAUX/NECH B7 109 F4
Priestley Smith Special School ERDW/GRVHL B23 75 H5
Primrose Hill Primary School HWK/WKHTH B38 176 D5
Primrose Hill Trading Estate DUDS DY2 102 D5
Primrose Lane Health Centre WOLVN WV10 24 A2
Prince Albert Primary School AST/WIT B6 109 E1
Princes End Industrial Park BILS/COS WV14 69 E2
Princes End Primary School TPTN/OCK DY4 69 E4
Princethorpe J & I School SLYOAK B29 158 C2
Priory Clinic DUDN DY1 84 B3
Priory Courts CBHAMNW B3 3 G4
Priory Green Junior & Infants School COVEN WV9 12 A5
Priory House Industrial Estate WSNGN B18 108 B4
Priory Junior Mixed & Infants School BLOX/PEL WS3 27 F3
Priory New Way Industrial Estate AST/WIT B6 109 E4
Priory Primary School DUDN DY1 84 B3
The Priory Primary School DARL/WED WS10 71 H1
Prospect Trading Estate CBHAMW B1 2 C4
Providence Industrial Estate HAG/WOL DY9 136 C1
Pype Hayes Golf Club WALM/CURD B76 78 A5
Qualcast Road Industrial Estate WOLV WV1 37 H3
Quality Hotel BDMR/CCFT WV3 36 D5
FOAKS/STRLY B74 62 C2
WSLW WS2 40 D3
Quarry Bank Primary School BRLYHL DY5 120 A3
Queen Alexandra College HRBN B17 141 G1
Queen Elizabeth Hospital EDG B15 142 C2
Queen Elizabeth Law Courts CBHAMNE B4 3 H4
Queen Elizabeth Psychiatric Hospital EDG B15 142 C3
Queen Marys Grammar School WSL WS1 5 J6
Queen Marys High School RUSH/SHEL WS4 5 G1
Queensbridge School MOS/BIL B13 144 A5
Queensbury Special School ERDE/BCHGN B24 92 D3
Queens College EDG B15 142 D2
Queens Court Trading Estate WBROM B70 86 D3
Queensway Trading Estate DIG/EDG B5 3 J4
Queen Victoria Primary School SEDG DY3 67 F3
Quinton Business Park RIDG/WDGT B32 140 A2
Quinton CE Primary School RIDG/WDGT B32 140 A1
Racecourse Road Industrial Estate DUNHL/THL/PER WV6 22 C5
Raddlebarn J & I School SLYOAK B29 159 H1
Radleys Primary School RUSH/SHEL WS4 29 E3
Radway Industrial Estate SHLY B90 195 E1
Rainbow Business Park WLNHL WV13 39 H2
Rake Gate Infant School WOLVN WV10 22 D1
Rake Gate Junior School WOLVN WV10 22 D1
Raleigh Industrial Estate HDSW B21 88 D5
Rathvilly School NFLD/LBR B31 175 H2
Rea Business Park VAUX/NECH B7 109 H5
Reaside Clinic RBRY B45 174 A4
Reaside Junior School RBRY B45 173 G4
Reddal Hill Primary School CDYHTH B64 121 E3
Reddicap Trading Estate MGN/WHC B75 62 D4
Red Hall Primary School SEDG DY3 83 E3
Redhill J & I School YDLY B25 129 E5
Redhill Secondary School STRBR DY8 135 H2
Red Hill Street Clinic WOLV WV1 37 E1
Redhouse Industrial Estate ALDR WS9 29 F4
ALDR WS9 30 A4
Redhouse JMI School ALDR WS9 29 G5
Rednal Hill J & I School RBRY B45 188 B1
Red Rooster Industrial Estate ALDR WS9 29 G4
Redwood Business Park SMTHWK B66 105 G2
Reedswood Retail Park WSLW WS2 41 F1
Reflex Industrial Park WLNHL WV13 39 F2
Regency Hotel SHLY B90 195 E1
Regents Park Primary School SMHTH B10 128 A4
Regent Special School OLDBY B69 85 G5
Regis Medical Centre BLKHTH/ROWR B65 122 A3
Reliance Trading Estate BILS/COS WV14 53 F3
Renaissance Solihull Hotel SOLH B91 181 H1
Retail Market Hall BDMR/CCFT WV3 6 E5
Retail Market Shops BKHL/PFLD WV2 6 E5
Reynalds Cross School HIA/OLT B92 163 H3
The Ridge Primary School STRBR DY8 134 C2
Ridgewood High School KINVER DY7 134 C1
Ridpool Primary School STETCH B33 130 D1
Riland Industrial Estate MGN/WHC B75 62 C3
River Brook Medical Centre BVILLE B30 160 B2
RMW Business Centre HAG/WOL DY9 136 D2
Robert Clinic BVILLE B30 159 G5
Roberts Primary School SEDG DY3 83 G2
Robin Hood Cemetery SHLY B90 163 F5
Robin Hood Golf Club HIA/OLT B92 163 G4
Robin Hood Primary School HLGN/YWD B28 163 F4
Robins Business Park TPTN/OCK DY4 70 C4
Rocky Lane Trading Estate VAUX/NECH B7 109 G3
Rollingmill Business Park WSLW WS2 4 A5
Romney House Industrial Estate BILS/COS WV14 54 D1
Rood End Primary School LGLYGN/QTN B68 105 G3
Rookery Primary School HDSW B21 89 G5
Rosary RC Primary School WASH/WDE B8 128 C1
Rosedale CE Infant School SHHTH WV12 26 B5
Rosewood Special School DUDN DY1 83 G5
Rosslyn School HLGN/YWD B28 163 E5
Rotton Park Medical Centre LDYWD/EDGR B16 125 F1
Rotunda CBHAM B2 3 G6
Rough Hay Primary School DARL/WED WS10 55 E1
Roughwood (Nature Reserve) SHHTH WV12 26 C4
Rounds Green Primary School OLDBY B69 104 C1
Rovex Business Park SPARK B11 145 H2
Rowley Hall Primary School BLKHTH/ROWR B65 104 A5
Rowley Regis Cemetery and Crematorium BLKHTH/ROWR B65 121 G2
Rowley Regis College BLKHTH/ROWR B65 121 H1
Rowley Regis Hospital BLKHTH/ROWR B65 121 H1
Royal Birmingham Society of Arts CBHAMNW B3 2 D2
Royal Brierley Trading Estate BRLYHL DY5 119 E1
Royal Mail Depot WOLVN WV10 7 K3
Royal Orthopaedic Hospital NFLD/LBR B31 158 D5
Royal Theatre CDYHTH B64 120 D3
The Royal Wolverhampton Junior School BDMR/CCFT WV3 51 G1
The Royal Wolverhampton School BDMR/CCFT WV3 51 H1
Rubery Clinic RBRY B45 187 G1
Ruckleigh School SOLH B91 182 A1
Rufford Primary School HAG/WOL DY9 136 A2
Rushall JM School & Education Development Centre RUSH/SHEL WS4 28 C1
Russell Medical Centre DARL/WED WS10 70 D1
Russells Hall Hospital BRLYHL DY5 101 F2
Russells Hall Primary School DUDN DY1 83 G5
Ryders Green Primary School WBROM B70 87 E2
Ryders Hayes JMI School BLOX/PEL WS3 18 A2
Sacred Heart RC Primary School BFLD/HDSWWD B20 90 D5
TPTN/OCK DY4 85 F2
Saddlers Shopping Centre WSL WS1 4 D4
Sai Medical Centre WSLW WS2 4 A3
St Albans CE Primary School WNSFLD WV11 25 H2
St Albans CE School BHTH/HG B12 127 F5
St Albans RC Primary School ALE/KHTH/YWD B14 178 B1
St Alphege CE Infant School SOLH B91 182 A2
St Alphege CE Junior School SOLH B91 182 A3
St Ambrose Barlow RC Primary School HLGN/YWD B28 163 E4
St Andrews CE Infant School DUNHL/THL/PER WV6 36 B1
St Andrews Industrial Estate BORD B9 128 A2
St Andrews Primary School BORD B9 127 H2
St Andrews RC Primary School HIA/OLT B92 147 G5
St Annes Industrial Estate WLNHL WV13 39 H2
St Anne's RC JMI School FOAKS/STRLY B74 45 E5
St Annes RC Primary School BHTH/HG B12 127 G4
CHWD/FDBR/MGN B37 132 A2
St Anthonys RC Primary School CHWD/FDBR/MGN B37 114 A4
WOLVN WV10 12 D4
St Augustines Catholic Primary School HDSW B21 89 F4
St Augustines Primary School SOLH B91 181 G3
St Barnabas CE Primary School ERDE/BCHGN B24 93 F3
St Bartholomews CE Primary School ETTPK/GDPK/PENN WV4 51 E5
St Benedict Biscop CE Primary School WMBN WV5 65 E4
St Benedicts Infant School SMHTH B10 128 D5
St Bernadettes RC JMI School BRWNH WS8 9 F4
St Bernadettes RC Primary School SMHTH B10 129 F4
WMBN WV5 64 D5
St Bernards RC Primary School MOS/BIL B13 162 A1
St Brigids RC Primary School NFLD/LBR B31 175 F2
St Catherine of Siena RC Primary School EDG B15 126 D4
St Chads Industrial Estate LOZ/NWT B19 109 E4
St Chad's RC Cathedral CBHAMNE B4 3 F2
St Chads RC Primary School LOZ/NWT B19 108 D4
SEDG DY3 67 F4
St Christophers RC Primary School CDSL WV8 10 C4
St Clares Primary School BFLD/HDSWWD B20 90 B5
St Clements CE Primary School VAUX/NECH B7 109 H2
St Columbas RC Primary School RBRY B45 188 D1
St Cuthberts RC Primary School WASH/WDE B8 111 G5
St Dunstans RC Primary School ALE/KHTH/YWD B14 161 E2
St Edmund Campion Lower School ERDE/BCHGN B24 77 G5
St Edmund Campion RC School ERDE/BCHGN B24 77 F5
St Edmund & John CE Primary School DUDS DY2 85 E5
St Edmunds Catholic School DUNHL/THL/PER WV6 35 H2
St Edmunds RC Primary School WSNGN B18 108 A5
St Edwards RC Primary School CSHL/WTROR B46 115 G4
CSHL/WTROR B46 133 G1
SLYOAK B29 160 B1
St Francis CE Primary School BVILLE B30 159 F4
St Francis of Assisi RC School ALDR WS9 30 C5
St Francis RC Primary School LOZ/NWT B19 108 B3
RUSH/SHEL WS4 29 E1
St Francis Xavier RC Primary School OLDBY B69 105 E1
St George & St Teresa RC Primary School DOR/KN B93 197 E4
St Georges CE Primary School LDYWD/EDGR B16 125 H3
St Georges School Edgbaston EDG B15 126 B4
St Georges Sixth Form & CE Primary School LOZ/NWT B19 108 D4
St Gerards Orthopaedic Hospital CSHL/WTROR B46 115 G4
St Gerards RC Primary School CVALE B35 94 D2
St Giles CE Primary School WLNHL WV13 39 H3
St Gregorys RC Primary School SMTHWKW B67 124 B2
St Huberts RC Primary School LGLYGN/QTN B68 123 G3
St James CE Junior School SHLY B90 180 B3
St James CE Primary School HDSW B21 89 F5
OLDBY B69 104 B4
STRBR DY8 117 H5
St James Medical Centre HDSW B21 107 F1
St James Primary School BRWNH WS8 9 F4
St James RC Primary School RBRY B45 188 A1
St John Bosco RC Primary School HHTH/SAND B71 71 F4
St John Fishers RC Primary School NFLD/LBR B31 189 H1
St John & St Monica RC Primary School MOS/BIL B13 144 A3
St Johns CE JMI School ALDR WS9 19 F4
St Johns CE Primary School DARL/WED WS10 70 D1
LDYWD/EDGR B16 126 A2
SEDG DY3 80 C4
SPARK B11 145 E3
WNSFLD WV11 15 E3
St Johns Retail Park BKHL/PFLD WV2 7 F6
St John the Baptist RC Primary School CBROM B36 114 A2
St John Wall RC School HDSW B21 89 F4
St Josephs Catholic Primary School DARL/WED WS10 55 E1
St Josephs Catholic Primary School MGN/WHC B75 62 C1
St Josephs Catholic Primary School STRBR DY8 135 F5
St Josephs RC Primary School BVILLE B30 159 G5
St Josephs RC Primary School DUDS DY2 85 E5
St Josephs RC Primary School VAUX/NECH B7 109 H3
St Judes CE Primary School BDMR/CCFT WV3 36 B2
St Judes RC Primary School ALE/KHTH/YWD B14 178 B3

St Kenelms CE First School *RMSLY* B62 172 C1
St Laurence CE J & I School *NFLD/LBR* B31 175 H1
St Lukes CE Aided Primary School *BKHL/PFLD* WV2 51 H1
St Margaret Mary RC Primary School *ERDW/GRVHL* B23 76 A5
St Margarets CE Primary School *GTB/HAM* B43 58 C4
HIA/OLT B92 147 F5
St Margarets Hospital *DSYBK/YTR* WS5 43 G5
St Marks CE Primary School *BRLYHL* DY5 101 E2
St Marks RC Primary School *PBAR/PBCH* B42 73 H4
St Martin de Porres RC Primary School *MOS/BIL* B13 144 C4
St Martins CE Primary School *BILS/COS* WV14 69 G1
St Martins CE Primary School *TPTN/OCK* DY4 85 H1
St Martins Industrial Estate *OLDBY* B69 105 E3
St Martins Market *DIG/EDG* B5 3 H7
St Martins School *SOLH* B91 182 B2
St Mary & Johns RC Primary School *BKHL/PFLD* WV2 37 F5
St Mary Magdalene CE Primary School *HHTH/SAND* B71 71 H5
St Mary of the Angels RC JMI School *ALDR* WS9 30 B5
St Mary's Abbey (Remains) *RMSLY* B62 139 F5
St Mary & St John RC Primary School *ERDE/BCHGN* B24 92 C3
St Mary & St Margarets CE Primary School *CBROM* B36 112 D1
St Marys CE Primary School *BFLD/HDSWWS* B20 90 B5
KGSWFD DY6 99 H2
SLYOAK B29 159 F1
St Marys RC Primary School *BRLYHL* DY5 119 G2
DARL/WED WS10 55 H4
HRBN B17 142 A2
WOLVN WV10 24 A3
St Marys the Mount RC School *WSL* WS1 5 H7
St Matthews CE Primary School *SMTHWK* B66 106 D4
VAUX/NECH B7 109 G5
St Michaels CE High School *OLDBY* B69 104 B4
St Michaels CE Primary School *BLOX/PEL* WS3 17 H5
HDSW B21 108 A2
RIDG/WDGT B32 157 G2
St Michaels RC Primary School *BDMR/CCFT* WV3 50 D1
St Nicholas CE Vc First School *CDSL* WV8 10 B3
St Nicholas RC JMI School *SCFLD/BOLD* B73 76 D1
St Patricks Catholic Primary School *CHWD/FDBR/MGN* B37 132 C2
WSLW WS2 4 C1
St Patricks RC Primary School *WNSFLD* WV11 24 C5
WSNGN B18 107 H5
St Pauls CE Primary School *TPTN/OCK* DY4 69 F5
St Pauls RC Primary School *HWK/WKHTH* B38 177 E4
St Pauls School *BHTH/HG* B12 144 C2
St Pauls School for Girls *LDYWD/EDGR* B16 125 G3
St Peter & Paul RC Primary School *ERDE/BCHGN* B24 93 G3
St Peters CE Infant School *HRBN* B17 141 H3
St Peters CE Junior School *HRBN* B17 142 A3
St Peters C JMI School *BLOX/PEL* WS3 16 D5
St Peters Collegiate Secondary School *DUNHL/THL/PER* WV6 36 A2
St Peters RC Primary School *RIDG/WDGT* B32 157 G1
St Peters RC School *SOLH* B91 181 H3
St Philips Cathedral *CBHAMNW* B3 3 F4
St Philips RC Primary School *SMTHWK* B66 106 D3
St Philips RC Sixth Form College *LDYWD/EDGR* B16 125 H4
St Saviours CE Primary School *WASH/WDE* B8 110 B4
St Stephens CE Primary School *WOLVN* WV10 37 G1
St Teresas RC Primary School *BFLD/HDSWWD* B20 90 A4
ETTPK/GDPK/PENN WV4 52 C3
St Thomas Aquinas RC School *HWK/WKHTH* B38 176 B2
St Thomas CE Primary School *EDG* B15 126 D3
St Thomas CE Primary School *WNSFLD* WV11 24 D3
St Thomas More Catholic School *WLNHL* WV13 39 H5
St Thomas More RC Primary School *LGN/SDN/BHAMAIR* B26 147 H2
St Thomas of Canterbury RC JMI School *BLOX/PEL* WS3 28 B4
St Vincents RC Primary School *VAUX/NECH* B7 127 H1
St Wilfrids RC Primary School *CBROM* B36 112 B1
Salafi Independent School *SMTHH* B10 128 B4
Salford Trading Estate *AST/WIT* B6 110 A1
Salisbury Place Industrial Estate *BDMR/CCFT* WV3 6 C6
Salisbury Primary School *DARL/WED* WS10 55 G1
Saltbrook Trading Estate *HALE* B63 120 A5
Saltley Business Park *WASH/WDE* B8 110 B3
Saltley Health Centre *WASH/WDE* B8 110 C4
Saltley Industrial Centre *WASH/WDE* B8 128 A1
Saltley Leisure Centre *BORD* B9 129 E1
Saltley School *BORD* B9 129 E1
Saltley Trading Estate *WASH/WDE* B8 110 A4
Sandown First School *DUNHL/THL/PER* WV6 34 D1
Sandwell Borough FC *OLDBY* B69 104 C2
Sandwell Business Development Centre *OLDBY* B69 105 G2
Sandwell Business Park *SMTHWK* B66 105 G1
Sandwell Business & Technology Centre *LGLYGN/QTN* B68 122 D2
Sandwell College *DARL/WED* WS10 71 E2
Sandwell College of Further & Higher Education *WBROM* B70 87 G3
Sandwell District General Hospital *HHTH/SAND* B71 87 H1
Sandwell Park Golf Club *HHTH/SAND* B71 88 B4
Sandwell Park Industrial Estate *HHTH/SAND* B71 88 B5
Sandwell Valley *HHTH/SAND* B71 72 C5
Sandyhill Industrial Estate *SHLY* B90 180 A1
Sapcote Business Centre *SMTHH* B10 145 G1
Sapcote Industrial Estate *CDYHTH* B64 121 F1
Sapcote Trading Centre *AST/WIT* B6 91 G3
CDYHTH B64 121 F1
SMTHH B10 145 G1
Sarehole Mill *MOS/BIL* B13 162 B2
Sarephed Medical Centre *SMTHWKW* B67 106 C4
Sargent Turner Trading Estate *HAG/WOL* DY9 136 D1
Satellite Industrial Park *WLNHL* WV13 38 C1
School of Jewellery (UCE) *CBHAMW* B1 2 C2
Scott Arms Shopping Centre *GTB/HAM* B43 73 G2
Sears Retail Park *SHLY* B90 180 C4
Sedgley Golf Centre *SEDG* DY3 66 D5
Selly Manor Museum *BVILLE* B30 159 H2
Selly Oak Health Centre *SLYOAK* B29 159 G1
Selly Oak Hospital *SLYOAK* B29 159 H1
Selly Oak Industrial Estate *SLYOAK* B29 159 G1
Selly Oak School *SLYOAK* B29 159 G2
Selly Park Technology College for Girls *SLYOAK* B29 160 B1
Severne Primary School *ACGN* B27 163 G2
Shaftmoor Industrial Estate *HLGN/YWD* B28 145 H5
Sharmans Cross Junior School *SOLH* B91 181 E1
Shaw Hill Primary School *WASH/WDE* B8 110 C5
Shaw Park Business Village *WOLVN* WV10 23 F4
The Sheila Godfrey Clinic *DOR/KN* B93 196 D5
Sheldon CC *YDLY* B25 129 H4
Sheldon Country Park *LGN/SDN/BHAMAIR* B26 148 C1
Sheldon Heath Community School *STETCH* B33 131 E4
Shelfield Clinic *RUSH/SHEL* WS4 29 E2
Shelfield Sports & Community College *RUSH/SHEL* WS4 18 C5
Shell Corner Trading Estate *RMSLY* B62 122 B4
Shelter Waterside Industrial Estate *ETTPK/GDPK/PENN* WV4 53 E3
Shenley Court School *NFLD/LBR* B31 158 B3
Shenley Lane Community Association Sports Centre *SLYOAK* B29 158 C4
Shenstone Trading Estate *HALE* B63 139 E3
Sherborne Wharf *LDYWD/EDGR* B16 2 A6
Sheriden House Hotel *BFLD/HDSWWD* B20 89 H3
Shireland Hall Primary School *SMTHWK* B66 125 E1
Shireland Language College *SMTHWK* B66 124 D1
Shire Oak School *BRWNH* WS8 19 G2
Shirestone Primary School *STETCH* B33 131 F2
Shirley Clinic *SHLY* B90 180 B2
Shirley Heath Junior School *SHLY* B90 180 C4
Shirley Park Sports Club & Golf Club *SHLY* B90 195 G4
Shirley Road Health Clinic *ACGN* B27 163 F1
Short Heath Clinic *SHHTH* WV12 26 B4
Short Heath Primary School *ERDW/GRVHL* B23 76 B5
Shorth Heath Junior School *SHHTH* WV12 26 B5
Showcase Cinema *DUDN* DY1 85 E3
ERDE/BCHGN B24 93 H4
WSLW WS2 40 D4
Showell Road Industrial Estate *WOLVN* WV10 23 F4
The Shrubbery School *WALM/CURD* B76 78 B4
Silhill FC *SOLH* B91 181 E1
Silver End Business Park *BRLYHL* DY5 118 D4
Sladefield Infant School *WASH/WDE* B8 111 E4
Slade Primary School *ERDW/GRVHL* B23 92 A4
Sledmere Primary School *DUDS* DY2 102 D3
Small Heath Business Park *SMTHH* B10 128 D5
Small Heath Lower School *SMTHH* B10 128 B5
Small Heath Trading Estate *SPARK* B11 145 F1
Small Heath Upper School & Sixth Form Centre *SMTHH* B10 128 B4
Smestow Bridge Industrial Estate *WMBN* WV5 64 A5
Smestow Secondary School *BDMR/CCFT* WV3 35 F4
Smethwick Medical Centre *SMTHWK* B66 106 C3
Smethwick Swimming Centre *SMTHWKW* B67 124 B2
Smith's Wood School *CBROM* B36 114 A3
Sneyd Community School *BLOX/PEL* WS3 16 A5
Snow Hill Clinic *BKHL/PFLD* WV2 7 G5
Soho Health Centre *HDSW* B21 107 H2
Soho House *WSNGN* B18 108 A2
Solihull College *SOLH* B91 181 G2
Solihull Hospital *SOLH* B91 182 B1
Solihull Ice Rink *HIA/OLT* B92 147 H4
Solihull Magistrates Court *SOLH* B91 182 A2
Solihull Retail Park *SHLY* B90 180 D4
Solihull School *SOLH* B91 182 B1
Solihull Sixth Form College *SOLH* B91 182 B3
Somerville Primary School *SMTHH* B10 128 B4
South Birmingham College *HLGN/YWD* B28 162 C2
South Birmingham Mental Health NHS Trust *BVILLE* B30 177 H2
Southside Business Centre *BHTH/HG* B12 144 C2
South Staffordshire Golf Club *DUNHL/THL/PER* WV6 21 G4
Sovereign Trading Estate *STRBR* DY8 135 E2
Sparkbrook Health Centre *SPARK* B11 127 H5
Sparkhill Pool & Fitness Centre *SPARK* B11 145 E3
Spartan Industrial Centre *WBROM* B70 70 C5
Speedwell Trading Estate *YDLY* B25 146 A1
Spines Clinic *WMBN* WV5 64 D5
Spinners End Industrial Estate *CDYHTH* B64 120 D3
Spon Lane Industrial Estate *SMTHWK* B66 105 H1
Spon Lane Trading Estate *WBROM* B70 87 G4
Springdale J & I School *ETTPK/GDPK/PENN* WV4 50 C3
Springfield Infant School *MOS/BIL* B13 145 F5
Springfield Junior School *BLKHTH/ROWR* B65 103 G5
SPARK B11 145 F5
Springfield Primary School *BLKHTH/ROWR* B65 103 G4
Spring Hill Industrial Estate *WSNGN* B18 107 H5
Spring Lane Industrial Estate *SHHTH* WV12 40 A1
Spring Road Industrial Estate *ETTPK/GDPK/PENN* WV4 53 E4
Springvale Business Park *BILS/COS* WV14 53 F4
Springvale Industrial Park *BILS/COS* WV14 53 F4
Spring Vale Primary School *ETTPK/GDPK/PENN* WV4 52 C4
Stafford Road Sports Club *BLOX/PEL* WS3 16 D5
Stag Industrial Estate *BILS/COS* WV14 54 C4
Stambermill Industrial Estate *BRLYHL* DY5 136 A1
Stanhope Road Clinic *SMTHWKW* B67 124 B1
Stanville Primary School *LGN/SDN/BHAMAIR* B26 130 D5
Starbank Primary School *SMTHH* B10 129 F4
Star City *VAUX/NECH* B7 110 B1
Starcrest Industrial Estate *BRLYHL* DY5 119 G3
Start Point Trading Estate *SPARK* B11 145 F3
Station Road Industrial Estate *BLKHTH/ROWR* B65 122 B2
CSHL/WTROR B46 97 F4
CSHL/WTROR B46 97 F5
CSHL/WTROR B46 115 G1
Stechford Cascades *STETCH* B33 130 A1
Stechford Health Centre *STETCH* B33 130 A2
Stechford Primary School *STETCH* B33 129 H2
Stechford Retail Park *STETCH* B33 112 A5
Stechford Trading Estate *STETCH* B33 112 A5
Steetley Industrial Estate *TPTN/OCK* DY4 68 C4
Stephens Industrial Estate *SPARK* B11 145 H3
Stevens Dental Health Centre *STRBR* DY8 135 F3
Stirchley Primary School *BVILLE* B30 160 A4
Stirchley Trading Estate *BVILLE* B30 160 B3
Stock Exchange *CBHAMNW* B3 2 E4
Stockland Clinic *ERDW/GRVHL* B23 92 B2
Stockland Green Health Centre *ERDW/GRVHL* B23 92 B2
Stockland Green School *ERDW/GRVHL* B23 92 A2
Stone Cross Clinic *HHTH/SAND* B71 72 A2
Stourbridge CC *STRBR* DY8 118 B5
Stourbridge Clinic *STRBR* DY8 135 H3
Stourbridge College of Technology & Art *STRBR* DY8 135 G3
Stourbridge Crematorium *STRBR* DY8 134 D3
Stourbridge FC *STRBR* DY8 135 F1
Stourbridge Golf Club *STRBR* DY8 152 C1
Stourbridge Industrial Estate *STRBR* DY8 135 G1
Stourbridge RC *KINVER* DY7 134 B1
Stourvale Industrial Estate *HAG/WOL* DY9 136 D1
Stourvale Trading Estate *HALE* B63 137 H1
Stowheath Industrial Estate & New Enterprise Centre *WOLV* WV1 38 A5
Stow Heath J & I School *WLNHL* WV13 38 D4
Stowlawn Primary School *BILS/COS* WV14 38 C5
Straits Primary School *SEDG* DY3 82 D1
Stratford Road School Clinic *SPARK* B11 145 F5
The Streetley School *FOAKS/STRLY* B74 60 C2
Streetly Cemetery *ALDR* WS9 44 D3
Streetly Clinic *FOAKS/STRLY* B74 45 E5
Streetly Hockey & Cricket Club *FOAKS/STRLY* B74 45 G4
Streetly Methodist Recreation Centre *FOAKS/STRLY* B74 45 F3
Streetsbrook Infant School *SHLY* B90 180 C1
Stuart Bathurst RC High School *DARL/WED* WS10 56 B3
Stuart Crystal *STRBR* DY8 118 A3
Summerfield Hospital *WSNGN* B18 107 H5
Summerfield Primary School *WSNGN* B18 107 G5
Summer Hill Industrial Park *CBHAMW* B1 2 A3
The Summerhill Secondary School *KGSWFD* DY6 99 F4
Sundridge Primary School *KGSTG* B44 60 A4
Sunfield School *HAG/WOL* DY9 170 C1
Sunrise Business Park *STRBR* DY8 118 A5
Sunshine Infant School *BLOX/PEL* WS3 27 G2
Superintendent Public Baths *SLYOAK* B29 159 H1
Sutton Arts Theatre *CSCFLD/WYGN* B72 62 C4
Sutton Coldfield College *FOAKS/STRLY* B74 62 C2
Sutton Coldfield Crematorium *MGN/WHC* B75 48 C3
Sutton Coldfield Girls School *SCFLD/BOLD* B73 62 B5
Sutton Coldfield Golf Club *FOAKS/STRLY* B74 45 H4
Sutton Coldfield Hospital *SCFLD/BOLD* B73 62 B4
Sutton Coldfield Magistrates Court *FOAKS/STRLY* B74 62 B2
Sutton Coldfield Town FC *CSCFLD/WYGN* B72 62 C5
Sutton Coldfield Town Hall *SCFLD/BOLD* B73 62 B2
The Sutton Special School *DUDN* DY1 101 H1
Sutton Town Sports Club *CSCFLD/WYGN* B72 62 C4
Sutton United FC *MGN/WHC* B75 63 E3
The Swallows Industrial Estate *SHLY* B90 180 D5
Swallows Rise Business Park *BRLYHL* DY5 119 G1
Swan Lane Industrial Estate *WBROM* B70 87 E1
Swan Medical Centre *YDLY* B25 129 H5
Swanpool Medical Centre *TPTN/OCK* DY4 69 G3
Swanshurst Girls School *MOS/BIL* B13 161 H3
Sycamore Green Primary School *DUDN* DY1 83 H1
Sycamore House Medical Centre *WSL* WS1 5 J7
Sycamore Industrial & Trading Estate *HDSW* B21 107 F2
Symphony Hall *CBHAMW* B1 2 C5
Talbots Lane Trading Estate *BRLYHL* DY5 119 G3
Tamar Medical Centre *DUNHL/THL/PER* WV6 34 C1
Tamebridge Industrial Estate *PBAR/PBCH* B42 91 E2
Tame Road Industrial Estate *AST/WIT* B6 91 H5
Tame Valley Primary School *ERDE/BCHGN* B24 111 H1
Tandon Medical Centre *SEDG* DY3 83 G1
Tansey Green Trading Estate *BRLYHL* DY5 100 D1
Telsen Industrial Centre *AST/WIT* B6 109 F3
Temple Meadow Primary School *CDYHTH* B64 121 F3
Tenterfields Primary School *HALE* B63 139 E3
Tettenhall College *DUNHL/THL/PER* WV6 35 H1
Tettenhall Wood Special School *DUNHL/THL/PER* WV6 35 F2
Thinktank Museum *DIG/EDG* B5 3 K4
Thornleigh Trading Estate *DUDS* DY2 102 A2
Thorns Community College *BRLYHL* DY5 119 F4
Thorns Primary School *BRLYHL* DY5 119 G5

Thornton Junior School
WASH/WDE B8 ....111 F4
Three Crowns Special School
DSYBK/YTR WS5 ....43 H4
Tidbury Green Primary School
SHLY B90 ....193 G4
Tile Cross Trading Estate
STETCH B33 ....131 F3
Timberley Primary School
BKDE/SHDE B34 ....113 F3
Timbertree Primary School
CDYHTH B64 ....121 E5
Tindal Primary School
BHTH/HG B12 ....144 B2
Tipper Trading Estate
HAG/WOL DY9 ....137 E2
Tipton Green Junior School
TPTN/OCK DY4 ....85 F2
Tipton Sports Academy
TPTN/OCK DY4 ....69 H2
Tiverton J & I School
SLYOAK B29 ....142 D5
Tividale Business Park
TPTN/OCK DY4 ....85 H3
Tividale Comprehensive School
OLDBY B69 ....86 A5
Tividale FC
OLDBY B69 ....85 H5
Tividale Hall Primary School
OLDBY B69 ....85 G5
Tividale Medical Centre
OLDBY B69 ....104 B1
Tividale Primary School
OLDBY B69 ....85 H4
Tollgate Shopping Precinct
SMTHWKW B67 ....106 B3
Topcliffe Primary School
CVALE B35 ....94 C3
Touchwood Shopping Centre
SOLH B91 ....182 A1
Tower Hill Health Centre
PBAR/PBCH B42 ....74 A5
Tower Works Industrial Estate
BDMR/CCFT WV3 ....6 A6
Town Gate Retail Park
DUDN DY1 ....85 F4
Town Junior School
CSCFLD/WYGN B72 ....62 C4
Town Wharf Business Park
WSLW WS2 ....4 B3
T P Riley Community School
BLOX/PEL WS3 ....17 E5
Tractor Spares Industrial Estate
WLNHL WV13 ....38 D3
Trading Estate Parkview
HWK/WKHTH B38 ....176 D2
Travel Inn
CBHAMW B1 ....2 D6
HAG/WOL DY9 ....153 H3
KGSWFD DY6 ....100 B2
SHLY B90 ....180 B2
SHLY B90 ....195 F3
VAUX/NECH B7 ....109 F4
WBROM B70 ....86 D1
WOLVN WV10 ....12 D2
WSLW WS2 ....40 C4
Travelodge
BRLYHL DY5 ....101 G5
CBHAMW B1 ....2 C7
LGN/SDN/BHAMAIR B26 ....147 E1
OLDBY B69 ....104 B2
RIDG/WDGT B32 ....156 D3
SCFLD/BOLD B73 ....76 D2
Trescott Primary School
NFLD/LBR B31 ....174 D2
Trevor Street Industrial Estate
VAUX/NECH B7 ....110 A3
Trident Retail Park
BORD B9 ....127 G2
Trident Shopping Centre
DUDN DY1 ....84 C5
Trinity Business Park
HIA/OLT B92 ....149 H4
Trinity CE Primary School
WOLVN WV10 ....37 H1
Tromans Industrial Estate
DUDS DY2 ....120 D1
Truck Stop Business Park
SPARK B11 ....146 B1
Tudor Grange School
SOLH B91 ....181 G3
Tudor Grange Sports Centre & Pool
SOLH B91 ....181 H2
Tudor Industrial Estate
SPARK B11 ....146 B2
Turves Green Boys School
NFLD/LBR B31 ....175 G5
Turves Green Girls School
NFLD/LBR B31 ....175 G4
Turves Green Primary School
NFLD/LBR B31 ....175 G4
Twickenham Primary School
KGSTG B44 ....76 A2
Two Woods Industrial Estate
BRLYHL DY5 ....119 G3
Two Woods Trading Estate
BRLYHL DY5 ....119 H3
Tyburn Industrial Estate
ERDE/BCHGN B24 ....93 H4
Tyseley Industrial Estate
SPARK B11 ....145 G2
Tyseley Locomotive Works Visitor Centre
SPARK B11 ....145 H2
UCI Cinema
BRLYHL DY5 ....119 G2
SHLY B90 ....195 E1
Uffculme Clinic
MOS/BIL B13 ....144 A5
Uffculme Special School
MOS/BIL B13 ....161 E1
UGC Cinema
DIG/EDG B5 ....3 G7
Ulverley Primary School
HIA/OLT B92 ....164 D2
Underhill J & I School
WOLVN WV10 ....24 B1
Underhill Primary School
WOLVN WV10 ....24 B1
Union Business Park
WSLW WS2 ....4 C4
Unisant Trading Estate
CDYHTH B64 ....121 F2
University of Birmingham
EDG B15 ....142 D4
EDG B15 ....143 E2
University of Central England
PBAR/PBCH B42 ....90 D3
University of Wolverhampton
DUNHL/THL/PER WV6 ....35 H3
WOLV WV1 ....7 F2
University of Wolverhampton Wulfrun Campus
DUNHL/THL/PER WV6 ....36 A2
Uplands Cemetery
SMTHWKW B67 ....124 A1
Uplands Junior School
BDMR/CCFT WV3 ....35 H5
Uplands Manor Primary School
SMTHWKW B67 ....124 A1
USAM Trading Estate
WOLVN WV10 ....12 D5
Valley Infant School
HIA/OLT B92 ....148 B4
Valley Park Campus
DUNHL/THL/PER WV6 ....22 B5
Vaughan Trading Estate
TPTN/OCK DY4 ....85 H3
Vauxhall Trading Estate
VAUX/NECH B7 ....109 H5
Vector Industrial Park
HHTH/SAND B71 ....71 G5
Venkat Medical Centre
STETCH B33 ....131 G1
Vernon Trading Estate
RMSLY B62 ....122 A4
Victoria Health Centre
SMTHWK B66 ....106 D5
Victoria Infant School
TPTN/OCK DY4 ....85 E1
Victoria Park Primary School
SMTHWK B66 ....106 D4
Victoria School
NFLD/LBR B31 ....158 C5
Villiers Primary School
BILS/COS WV14 ....53 H1
Villiers Trading Estate
BKHL/PFLD WV2 ....52 A1
VIVA! Health & Leisure Club
SOLH B91 ....196 A1
Vulcan House Industrial Estate
SOLH B91 ....165 E4
Vulcan Industrial Estate
WSLW WS2 ....27 G4
Wake Green FC
SHLY B90 ....179 G5
Wallbrook Primary School
BILS/COS WV14 ....69 E3
The Wallows Industrial Estate
BRLYHL DY5 ....101 F4
Walmley CC
WALM/CURD B76 ....78 A4
Walmley Golf Club
CSCFLD/WYGN B72 ....77 G3
Walmley Junior School
WALM/CURD B76 ....78 C4
Walsall Business Park
ALDR WS9 ....30 B5
ALDR WS9 ....43 G1
Walsall College of Arts & Technology
WSL WS1 ....4 D2
Walsall Cricket Club
WSL WS1 ....57 G1
Walsall FC (Bescot Stadium)
WSL WS1 ....56 D3
Walsall Gala Baths
WSL WS1 ....4 E3
Walsall Golf Club
DSYBK/YTR WS5 ....57 H2
Walsall Leather Museum
WSLW WS2 ....4 D1
Walsall Museum & Library
WSL WS1 ....5 F3
Walsall RFC
WSL WS1 ....57 F2
Walsall Wood Primary School
ALDR WS9 ....19 F3
Ward Arms Hotel
DUDN DY1 ....85 F4
Ward End Medical Centre
WASH/WDE B8 ....111 F4
Ward End Primary School
WASH/WDE B8 ....111 F3
Warley High School
LGLYGN/QTN B68 ....123 E2
Warley Infant School
LGLYGN/QTN B68 ....123 G2
Warley Magistrates Court
OLDBY B69 ....105 E2
Warley Woods Golf Club
SMTHWKW B67 ....124 A4
Warren Farm Primary School
KGSTG B44 ....75 H3
Warstones Primary School
ETTPK/GDPK/PENN WV4 ....51 E2
Wartell Bank Industrial Estate
KGSWFD DY6 ....99 H1
Warwick Road Trading Estate
SPARK B11 ....145 F3
Warwickshire CCC (Edgbaston)
DIG/EDG B5 ....143 H2
Waseley Hills Country Park
BRGRVW B61 ....173 E5
Waseley Hills High School
RBRY B45 ....187 F1
Washington Street Industrial Estate
DUDS DY2 ....120 D1
Washwood Heath Technology College
WASH/WDE B8 ....111 G4
Waterfall Lane Trading Estate
CDYHTH B64 ....121 G3
Waterfront Business Park
BRLYHL DY5 ....101 F5
Waterloo Industrial Estate
CBROM B36 ....114 B4
Waterloo Road Jamia Mosque
DUNHL/THL/PER WV6 ....37 E1
Watermill Primary School
SLYOAK B29 ....142 B4
Water Orton CC
CSHL/WTROR B46 ....96 B3
Water Orton Primary School
CSHL/WTROR B46 ....96 B4
Waterside Industrial Estate
BKHL/PFLD WV2 ....53 E2
BLKHTH/ROWR B65 ....103 F5
Watling Street Business Park
BLOX/PEL WS3 ....8 A2
Watling Street JMI School
BRWNH WS8 ....9 E3
Wattville Primary School
HDSW B21 ....106 D1
Wattville Road Industrial Estate
SMTHWK B66 ....106 D2
Waverley School
SMHTH B10 ....129 E4
Webnor Industrial Estate
BKHL/PFLD WV2 ....53 E2
Wednesbury Art Gallery
DARL/WED WS10 ....70 D1
Wednesbury Chiropody Surgery
DARL/WED WS10 ....55 H5
Wednesbury Cricket Club
DARL/WED WS10 ....56 A4
Wednesbury Leisure Centre
DARL/WED WS10 ....55 G5
Wednesbury Medical Centre
DARL/WED WS10 ....70 C1
Wednesbury Oak Primary School
TPTN/OCK DY4 ....69 F2
Wednesbury RFC
DARL/WED WS10 ....70 D2
Wednesbury Town Hall
DARL/WED WS10 ....70 D1
Wednesbury Trading Estate
DARL/WED WS10 ....55 G4
Wednesfield FC
WNSFLD WV11 ....24 C4
Wednesfield High School
WNSFLD WV11 ....25 E5
Wednesfield Village Primary School
WNSFLD WV11 ....24 D5
Wednesfield Way Industrial Estate
WNSFLD WV11 ....38 D1
Welford Primary School
BFLD/HDSWWD B20 ....108 B1
Wellington Industrial Estate
TPTN/OCK DY4 ....68 C4
Welsh House Farm Primary School
RIDG/WDGT B32 ....141 F3
Welsh RFC
HIA/OLT B92 ....149 G5
Weoley Castle Health Centre
SLYOAK B29 ....158 C1
Weoley Castle Ruins & Museum
SLYOAK B29 ....141 G5
Wergs Golf Club
CDSL WV8 ....21 E3
Westacre Infant School
BDMR/CCFT WV3 ....35 H4
West Bromwich Albion FC (The Hawthorns)
HHTH/SAND B71 ....88 C5
West Bromwich Dartmouth Cricket Club
HHTH/SAND B71 ....88 B5
West Bromwich Magistrates Court
WBROM B70 ....87 G3
West Croft Special School & Sports College
WOLVN WV10 ....13 H5
West Cross Shopping Centre
SMTHWK B66 ....105 H2
Western Business Park
RMSLY B62 ....121 H5
WSNGN B18 ....107 G3
Westfield Primary School
WMBN WV5 ....65 E4
Westgate Trading Estate
ALDR WS9 ....29 G4
West Heath Hospital
HWK/WKHTH B38 ....176 A5
West Heath J & I School
NFLD/LBR B31 ....176 A4
West House School
EDG B15 ....126 C4
The Westley Hotel
ACGN B27 ....146 B4
Westmead Hotel
ALVE B48 ....189 H4
West Midlands Hospital
HALE B63 ....137 H2
Westminster Industrial Estate
DUDS DY2 ....120 D2
Westminster Primary School
BFLD/HDSWWD B20 ....90 C5
Westminster School
TPTN/OCK DY4 ....69 G5
West Park Hospital
WOLV WV1 ....6 C3
West Park Primary School
WOLV WV1 ....6 C1
Westwood Business Park
AST/WIT B6 ....91 H4
Wharton Street Industrial Estate
VAUX/NECH B7 ....110 B1
Wheelers Lane J & I School
ALE/KHTH/YWD B14 ....161 F3
Wheelers Lane Technology College
ALE/KHTH/YWD B14 ....161 F3
Wheeler Street Shopping Centre
LOZ/NWT B19 ....108 C3
Whetstone Field Primary School
ALDR WS9 ....44 B1
Whitecrest Primary School
GTB/HAM B43 ....74 A1
Whitehall Industrial Park
TPTN/OCK DY4 ....86 C1
Whitehall Infant School
WSL WS1 ....57 E1
Whitehall Junior School
WSL WS1 ....57 F1
Whiteheath Clinic
OLDBY B69 ....104 B4
Whitehouse Common Primary School
MGN/WHC B75 ....62 D1
Whitesmore School
CHWD/FDBR/MGN B37 ....131 H3
Whitgreave J & I School
WOLVN WV10 ....23 G2
Whitmore Medical Centre
WOLV WV1 ....6 E1
Whitmore Reans Health Centre
DUNHL/THL/PER WV6 ....36 C1
Whitworth Industrial Park
BORD B9 ....128 A2
Wholesale Markets
DIG/EDG B5 ....3 H7
Widney Junior School
SOLH B91 ....181 F4
Wightwick Hall Special School
DUNHL/THL/PER WV6 ....34 C3
Wilkes Green J & I School
HDSW B21 ....89 G5
Wilkinson Primary School
BILS/COS WV14 ....54 B5
Willenhall Industrial Estate
WLNHL WV13 ....40 A2
Willenhall Lane Industrial Estate
BLOX/PEL WS3 ....27 E2
Willenhall Leisure Centre
WLNHL WV13 ....39 H4
Willenhall Town FC
WLNHL WV13 ....39 F2
Willenhall Trading Estate
WLNHL WV13 ....39 F4
William Cowper Primary School
LOZ/NWT B19 ....109 E3
William Hanke Industrial Estate
BRLYHL DY5 ....119 G3
Willingsworth High School
TPTN/OCK DY4 ....69 H1
Wilson Stuart Special School
ERDW/GRVHL B23 ....76 A5
Windmill Hill (Look out)
RBRY B45 ....173 E5
Windmill Works Industrial Park
DUDS DY2 ....102 B2
Windsor High School
HALE B63 ....138 B3
Windsor Industrial Estate
VAUX/NECH B7 ....109 G4
Windward Way Industrial Estate
CBROM B36 ....113 H1
Windy Arbor Primary School
CHWD/FDBR/MGN B37 ....132 D1
Winster Grove Industrial Centre
KGSTG B44 ....74 D1
Winster Grove Industrial Estate
KGSTG B44 ....75 E1
Withymoor Primary School
BRLYHL DY5 ....119 F3
Withy Road Industrial Estate
BILS/COS WV14 ....53 G5
Witton Industrial Estate
AST/WIT B6 ....91 G4
Witton Park Industrial Estate
AST/WIT B6 ....91 G5
Woden Primary School
WOLVN WV10 ....37 G1
Wodensborough Community Technology College
DARL/WED WS10 ....71 F1
Wodensfield Primary School
WNSFLD WV11 ....24 B4
Wollescote Business Park
HAG/WOL DY9 ....136 D2
Wollescote Primary School
HAG/WOL DY9 ....136 D3
Wolverhampton CC
DUNHL/THL/PER WV6 ....21 G4
Wolverhampton Central Baths
WOLV WV1 ....6 D3
Wolverhampton College (Bilston Campus)
WOLV WV1 ....53 F1
Wolverhampton Girls High School
DUNHL/THL/PER WV6 ....36 B2
Wolverhampton Grammar School
BDMR/CCFT WV3 ....36 B3
Wolverhampton Healthcare NHS Trust
WNSFLD WV11 ....38 B1
The Wolverhampton Nuffiled Hospital
DUNHL/THL/PER WV6 ....35 G1
Wolverhampton Racecourse
DUNHL/THL/PER WV6 ....22 C4
Wolverhampton University
WOLVN WV10 ....23 E4
Wolverhampton Wanderers FC (Molineux Stadium)
WOLV WV1 ....6 E1
Wombourne Cricket Tennis & Bowling Club
WMBN WV5 ....65 E4
Wombrook Business Centre
WMBN WV5 ....64 C4
Wombrook Industrial Estate
WMBN WV5 ....64 C5
Woodbourne Priory Hospital
HRBN B17 ....125 E3
Woodcock Hill Primary School
NFLD/LBR B31 ....158 A3
Woodcock Sports Centre
CBHAMNE B4 ....3 K2
Woodcross Clinic
BILS/COS WV14 ....68 A1
Wood End Primary School
WNSFLD WV11 ....24 C3
Woodfield J&ischool
BDMR/CCFT WV3 ....51 F2
Woodgate Business Park
RIDG/WDGT B32 ....140 B5
Woodgate Primary School
RIDG/WDGT B32 ....157 F1
Woodgate Valley
RIDG/WDGT B32 ....140-C3
Woodgate Valley Health Centre
RIDG/WDGT B32 ....140 C5
Wood Green High School College of Sport
DARL/WED WS10 ....56 B3
Wood Green Junior School
DARL/WED WS10 ....55 H4
Woodhouse J & I School
RIDG/WDGT B32 ....141 E1
Woodlands Cemetery
CSHL/WTROR B46 ....114 C4
Woodlands Infant School
SHLY B90 ....180 B5
Woodlands Primary School
SHHTH WV12 ....26 B4
The Woodrush High School
HLYWD B47 ....192 C2
Woodrush RFC
HWK/WKHTH B38 ....191 F4
The Woodsbank Industrial Estate
DARL/WED WS10 ....55 F4
The Woodsbank Trading Estate
DARL/WED WS10 ....55 F4
The Woodsetton Special School
SEDG DY3 ....67 H4
Woodside Industrial Estate
BRLYHL DY5 ....101 H4
Woodstock Girls School
BHTH/HG B12 ....144 C3
Woodthorpe Primary School
ALE/KHTH/YWD B14 ....161 E5
Woodview Primary School
EDG B15 ....126 C4
Worcester Street Surgery
STRBR DY8 ....135 G2
Wordsley Green Health Centre
STRBR DY8 ....117 H2
Wordsley Green Shopping Centre
STRBR DY8 ....117 H2
Wordsley Hospital
STRBR DY8 ....118 A1
Works Trading Estate
SMTHWK B66 ....106 C2
Worlds End J & I School
RIDG/WDGT B32 ....141 E2
The Worsley School
STRBR DY8 ....118 B1
Wren's Nest National Nature Reserve
DUDN DY1 ....84 B2
Wrens Nest Primary School
DUDN DY1 ....84 A2
Wrottesley Hall
CDSL WV8 ....20 A2
Wulfrun Shopping Centre
WOLV WV1 ....7 F5
Wulfrun Trading Estate
DUNHL/THL/PER WV6 ....23 E5
Wychall Farm Primary School
NFLD/LBR B31 ....176 A3
Wylde Green Primary School
SCFLD/BOLD B73 ....77 F4

Wyndcliffe Primary School
BORD B9 ....128 B3
Wyndley Leisure Centre
SCFLD/BOLD B73 ....62 A3
Wyndley Swimming Baths
SCFLD/BOLD B73 ....62 A4
Wynford Industrial Trading Est
YDLY B25 ....146 C2
Wynford Road Industrial Est
ACGN B27 ....146 C2

Wythall Health Centre
HLYWD B47 ....192 C1
Yardley Cemetery
LGN/SDN/BHAMAIR B26 ....146 D2
Yardley Green Health Centre
BORD B9 ....128 D3
Yardley Green Medical Centre
SMHTH B10 ....128 A4
Yardley J & I School
LGN/SDN/BHAMAIR B26 ....129 H5

Yardley Medical Centre
YDLY B25 ....129 F5
Yardleys School
SPARK B11 ....145 G4
Yardleys Secondary School
SPARK B11 ....145 H3
Yardley Wood Health Centre
ALE/KHTH/YWD B14 ....162 A5
Yardley Wood Primary School
ALE/KHTH/YWD B14 ....179 F1

Yarnfield Primary School
SPARK B11 ....146 A4
Yenton Infant School
ERDE/BCHGN B24 ....77 F5
Yenton Junior School
ERDE/BCHGN B24 ....93 F1
Yew Tree Community Junior School
AST/WIT B6 ....91 G5
Yew Tree Primary School
DSYBK/YTR WS5 ....57 H4

Yew Tree Primary School
SOLH B91 ....165 G5
York Mead Primary School
HLGN/YWD B28 ....145 G5
Yorks Wood Primary School
CHWD/FDBR/MGN B37 ....113 H4
Zip Theatre
WOLV WV1 ....6 D1

Acknowledgements

The Post Office is a registered trademark of Post Office Ltd. in the UK and other countries.

Schools address data provided by Education Direct.

Petrol station information supplied by Johnsons

One-way street data provided by © Tele Atlas N.V.   Tele Atlas

Garden centre information provided by:

Garden Centre Association  Britains best garden centres

Wyevale Garden Centres